Wycliffe Biographical Dictionary of the Church

Wycliffe Biographical Dictionary of the Church

by

Elgin Moyer
revised and enlarged by
Earle E. Cairns

MOODY PRESS
CHICAGO

ISBN: 0-8024-9693-8

Moyer, Elgin Sylvester, 1890-
Wycliffe biographical dictionary of the Church.
Bibliography: p.
Includes index.
1. Christian biography. I. Cairns, Earle Edwin, 1910- . II. Title.
BR1700.2.M66 1981 270'.092'2 [B] 81-22578
ISBN 0-8024-9693-8 AACR2

Printed in the United States of America

Preface

People from diverse places and periods constitute the dynamic force in the history of the church. For example, John of Damascus set forth the theology of the Eastern or Orthodox churches; Thomas Aquinas set forth that of the Roman Catholic Church, and John Calvin that of the Reformed churches. Without Martin Luther, Protestantism in Germany might never have developed as it did.

With that in mind, we add to this revision of the *Wycliffe Biographical Dictionary of the Church* over three hundred biographies. Thus this volume contains brief biographies of over two thousand men and women of all races, from all parts of the world, who have made major contributions to the cause of Christ. Included are biographies of leaders in the Roman Catholic, Eastern, and Protestant churches. Also noted are black leaders in Africa and of the United States and evangelicals, whose names are omitted from most dictionaries of church history. Theological or denominational biases have been excluded as criteria for inclusion in this volume.

Biographies are arranged in alphabetical order, both in the book and in the chronological index. The chronological index summarizes the main developments in the history of the church in each era and then lists in alphabetical order those who made contributions to or influenced the church.

Identifying letters in the index, found after the dates of the person's life, indicate the main area in which that person made a significant contribution. That enables one to trace the history of hymnology, missions, theology, and several other topics through the various eras by biographical studies. In the case of theology one can readily identify the theologians of each era, their main contributions, and the progress of doctrine. No other dictionary includes as many entries in the field of missions.

Following is a key to abbreviations used in the chronological index:

- A painter, sculptor, or architect
- B scholar who contributed to biblical studies in archaeology; historical, higher and lower, or textual criticism; concordances; lexicons
- C author of major commentaries on the Bible
- CF church fathers to A.D. 590
- CH writer of church histories
- E ecumenical leader
- H composer of hymns or other church music
- He heretic
- M missionary or associated in some way with missions
- Mo leading monastic figure
- My leading mystic
- P philosopher with an impact on Christianity
- Po pope
- R those linked with revivalism or major evangelistic thrusts
- S engaged in social reform, either theologian or activist
- T theologian

The reviser has consulted biographical or topical dictionaries of church history, general or national church histories such as those of Latourette or Ahlstrom, biographies or autobiographies of persons included in this work, and primary materials when available to insure as much accuracy as possible. Those who wish to pursue more detailed study of any figure in this book could well consult the following works:

Barker, William P. *Who's Who in Church History*. Old Tappan, N.J.: Revell, 1969.

Bender, Harold S., and Smith, C. Henry, eds. *The Mennonite Encyclopedia*. 4 vols. Scottdale, Pa.: Mennonite Publishing House, 1955–1959.

Blom, Eric, ed. *Grove's Dictionary of Music and Musicians*. 10 vols. London: Macmillan, 1954–1956.

Bodensieck, Julian, ed. *The Encyclopedia of the Lutheran Church*. 3 vols. Minneapolis: Augsburg, 1965.

Bowden, Henry W. *Dictionary of American Religious Biography*. Westport, Conn.: Greenwood, 1977.

Brauer, Jerald C., ed. *The Westminster Dictionary of Church History*. Philadelphia: Westminster, 1971.
Cross, Frank L., and Livingstone, E. A., eds. *The Oxford Dictionary of the Christian Church*. New York: Oxford, 1974.
Deen, Edith. *Great Women of the Christian Faith*. New York: Harper, 1959.
Dollar, George W. *A History of Fundamentalism*. Greenville, S.C.: Bob Jones U., 1973. See pp. 299–375 for short biographies of many evangelicals.
Douglas, J. D. *The New International Dictionary of the Christian Church*. 2d ed. Grand Rapids: Zondervan, 1978.
Julian, John. *A Dictionary of Hymnology*. 2 vols. 2d ed. rev. New York: Dover, 1909.
New Catholic Encyclopedia. New York: McGraw-Hill, 1967.
Thomson, Ronald W. *Who's Who of Hymn Writers*. London: Epworth, 1967.
Wallace, W. Stewart. *The Macmillan Dictionary of Canadian Biography*. 3d ed., rev. and enlarged. Toronto: Macmillan, 1963.
Webster's Biographical Dictionary. Springfield, Mass.: Merriam, 1976.

Other helpful multivolume sets are *Americana Encyclopedia, Contemporary Authors, Dictionary of American Biography, Dictionary of National Biography* (Great Britain), *Encyclopedia Britannica, National Cyclopedia of American Biography, New York Times Obituaries Index 1858–1968, Obituaries from the Times 1961–1975* (Great Britain), *Who Was Who in America, Who's Who in America, Who's Who* (Great Britain), *International Who's Who*.

The author and reviser hope that contact with these significant Christians will help develop a kinship of spirit and dispel our provincialism of denomination or theology. These people often had feet of clay but were devoted to Christ and served as David did their own generations (Acts 13:36), often at the cost of their lives (Acts 15:26). The heritage they have left enriches our lives and should inspire us to serve Christ as well in our day as they did in theirs.

KEY TO PRONUNCIATION

â as in âir
ā as in māte
ă as in căt
ä as in äre

ē as in tēe
ĕ as in mĕt
ẽ as in hẽr
ê as in thêre

ī as in mīte
ĭ as in ĭt

ō as in nōte
ŏ as in hŏt
ô as in nôr
ȯ as in sȯft
ö as in Böhm (Boehm)

ū as in mūle
ŭ as in ŭp
û as in bûrn
ü as in Müller (Mueller)

o͝o as in bo͝ok
o͞o as in to͞ot

Chronological Index and Outline of Church History

Ancient Church History 5 B.C.–A.D. 590

During this era the early or apostolic church developed into the Old Catholic Imperial church, and the outlines of what became the Roman Catholic church emerged in the Mediterranean basin in the political and cultural environment of the Roman Empire.

FROM APOSTOLIC TO OLD CATHOLIC CHURCH 5 B.C.–A.D. 313

The church began with Christ as its foundation and the Holy Spirit as its founder in a Jewish environment. It broke the bands of Judaism with the declaration of salvation by faith alone for all and soon spread throughout the Roman Empire.

The church met the external struggle for survival because of persecution by the Roman state with martyrdom and the apologists, such as Justin Martyr, who upheld the power of miracles, prophecy of Christ, and the purity of Christians and Christianity. It met the internal challenge of heresy by the writings of the polemicists, such as Irenaeus, who defended the faith against the Gnostics in his book *Against Heresy*. The development of a canon of Scripture and the creation of rules of faith or basic creeds, such as those of Tertullian and Irenaeus, also strengthened the church from within.

The developing ecclesiastical consitution of the church enhanced the power of the bishop in a threefold order of deacon, elder, and bishop in apostolic succession first fully set forth by the apostolic Father Ignatius. Eusebius in his *Ecclesiastical History* records these centuries of struggle for survival.

Africanus, Sextus Julius	c. 160–c.240	CH
Alexander of Jerusalem	?–251	
Ammonius, Saccas	c. 174–242	
Anacletus	first century	
Antoninus Pius	86–161	
Apollinaris	second century	CF
Aristides, Marcianus	late first/early second century	C, CF
Aristotle	384–322 B.C.	P
Arnobius	d. c. 327	
Artemon	d. c. 260	He
Augustus Caesar	63 B.C.–A.D. 14	
Bar Cocheba (Bar Kokba)	70–135	
Bardesanes	154–223	
Basilides	early second century	He
Beryllus of Bostra	third century	He
Calixtus I	d. c. 222	Po
Carpocrates	early second century	He
Cecilia	d. c. 177	
Celsus	second century	
Cerinthus	late first century	He
Clemens, Titus Flavius (Clement of Alexandria)	c. 150–c. 215	CF
Clement I (of Rome)	c. 30–c. 100	
Constantine the Great	c. 280–337	
Cyprian, Thascius Caecilius	c. 200–258	CF
Decius, Gaius Messius	d. 251	
Demetrius of Alexandria	d. 231	
Diocletian, Gaius Valerius	245–313	
Dionysius the Areopagite	first century	
Dionysius of Corinth	d. c. 195	
Domitian, Titus Flavius	51–96	
Domitilla	late first century	
Fabianus (Fabian)	d. 250	
Felicitas	d. 203	
Galerius	d. 311	
George, Saint	d. c. 303	
Gregory the Illuminator	c. 240–c. 332	M
Gregory Thaumaturgus	c. 213–270	
Hadrian, Publius Aelius	76–138	
Hegesippus	second century	CH
Helena	c. 250–c.330	
Heraclas	c. 170–248	
Hermas	second century	CF
Hippolytus	c. 170–c. 236	CF
Hosius of Cordova	c. 257–c. 357	CF
Ignatius	d. 117	CF
Irenaeus	late second century	CF
Josephus, Flavius	c. 37–c.100	
Justin Martyr	c. 100–165	CF
Lactantius, Lucius Caecilius Firmianus	c. 240–320	CH
Leonides	d. 202	
Lucian of Samosata	c. 125–190	
Marcion	d. c. 160	He

Marcus Aurelius	121–180	
Maximilla	d. 179	He
Melitus of Lycopolis	d. 325	
Melito	d. 190	CF
Miltiades	second century	CF
Minucius Felix Marcus	second or third century	CF
Montanus	second century	
Nero, Claudius Caesar	37–68	
Novatian	third century	
Novatus	d. after 251	
Origen	c. 185–c. 254	CF, B
Pantaenus	c. 190	
Papias	60–130	
Philo Judaeus	c. 20 B.C.–A.D. 50	
Plato	427–347 B.C.	P
Pliny the Younger	62–113	
Plotinus	c. 205–270	P
Polycarp	c. 69–c. 155/160	CF
Polycrates	c. 125–c. 195	
Porphory	c. 234–c. 305	P
Pothinus	c. 87–177	M
Praxeas	c. 200	He
Priscilla	second century	
Quadratus	second century	CF
Sabellius	d. after 260	He
Saturninus	second century	He
Sebastian	late third or early fourth century	
Simon Magus	first century	
Tacitus, Cornelius	c. 55–117	CH
Tatian	second century	CF
Tertullian, Quintus Septimius Florus	c. 160–c. 220	CF
Theodotus	second century	He
Theophilus of Antioch	second century	CF
Tiberius, Claudius Nero Caesar	42 B.C.–A.D. 37	
Trajan	52–117	
Valentinus	second century	He
Zeno of Cyprus	d. 264 B.C.	P

TRIUMPH OF THE OLD CATHOLIC IMPERIAL CHURCH 313–590

The Old Catholic Church faced the external problem of church-state relations in its union with the state after 380. In the East the emperor dominated the patriarch, but in the West the papacy more often controlled other rulers. The challenge of winning the heretical Arian Goth and pagan Frank and Anglo-Saxon invaders of the empire was the task of missionary monks. The internal challenge of the Arian, Christological, and Pelagian heresies led the church to define its faith at councils with the Nicene Creed and the statement of Christ as the God-Man at Chalcedon in 451.

In all of this the bishop of Rome, supported by the new monastic movement of Anthony, Pachomius, and Benedict, emerged as supreme bishop. Later church Fathers, such as Augustine in his *City of God*, formulated a Christian philosophy of history. Jerome gave the church a new Bible—the Latin Vulgate used for centuries by the Roman Catholic church.

Aetius	d. c. 367	He
Alaric	c. 370–410	
Alexander of Alexandria	d. 328	CF
Alypius	d. after 430	
Ambrose	c. 340–397	CF
Anthony	c. 251–356	Mo
Anthusa	c. 330–c. 374	
Apollinarius	c. 300–c. 390	He
Arius	c. 250–c. 336	He
Asaph	d. c. 600	M
Athanasius	c. 296–373	CF
Attila	d. 453	
Augustine, Archbishop of Canterbury	d. c. 604	
Augustine, Aurelius	354–430	CF
Baradeus, Jacobus	c. 490–578	
Basil the Great	c. 329–379	CF
Benedict of Nursia	c. 480–c. 543	Mo
Boethius, Ancius	c. 480–524	P
Brigid	c. 455–523	
Caecilian	d. 345	
Caesarius of Arles	c. 470–542	
Cassianus, Johnnes	c. 360–c. 435	
Cassiodorus, Flavius Magnus Aurelius	c. 477–c. 570	Mo
Celestius	early fifth century	He
Chrysostom, John	c. 347–407	CF
Clotilda	c. 475–c. 545	
Clovis	c. 466–511	
Columba	c. 521–597	M
Columban	c. 543–615	M
Commodianus	c. 200–c. 275	
Cyril of Alexandria	376–444	CF
Cyril of Jerusalem	c. 315–c. 386	CF
Damasus I	c. 305–384	Po
David	c. 520–589	
Didymus	c. 313–398	
Diodorus	d. c. 392	
Dionysisus Exiguus	d. c. 527	
Dioscorus	d. c. 454	
Donatus	d. 355	
Ephraim the Syrian	c. 300–373	
Epiphanius	c. 315–403	CF

Ethelbert	560–616	
Eunomius	d. c. 395	He
Eusebius of Caeserea	c. 263–c. 339	CH
Eusebius of Nicomedia	d. 342	He
Eustathius of Sebaste	c. 300–c. 377	
Eutyches	c. 378–454	He
Fridolin	probably sixth century	
Frumentius	c. 300–c. 380	M
Gelasius I	d. 496	Po
Gregory (I) the Great	540–604	Po
Gregory of Nazianzus	c. 330–c. 390	CF
Gregory of Nyssa	c. 330–c. 394	CF
Gregory of Tours	c. 538–594	M, CH
Hilarion	c. 291–371	Mo
Hilary of Poitiers	c. 315–368	
Hypatia	c. 375–415	
Ibas of Edessa	d. 457	
Jerome	c. 345–420	CF
John of Antioch	d. 441	
Jovian	c. 332–364	
Jovinian	d. 405	Mo
Julian the Apostate	c. 331–363	
Justinian I	483–565	
Kentigern	c. 518–603	
Leander of Seville	c. 550–c. 600	
Leo I, the Great	d. 461	Po
Macarius	d. c. 390	Mo
Macedonius	d. c. 362	He
Marcella	325–410	
Marcellus of Ancyra	d. c. 374	
Martin of Tours	c. 335–c. 400	M
Melitus of Antioch	d. 381	
Mercator, Marius	early fifth century	
Monica	c. 331–387	
Nectarius	d. 397	
Nestorius	d. 451	He
Ninian	c. 360–c. 432	M
Orosius, Paulus	c. 385–after 417	CH
Pachomius	c. 290–c. 346	Mo
Patrick	c. 389–c. 461	M
Pelagius	early fifth century	He
Philaster	d. c. 397	
Philostorgius	c. 368–c. 430	CH
Priscillan	d. 385	
Procopius	c. 490–562	CH
Prosper of Aquitaine	c. 390–c. 463	
Prudentius	348–c. 410	H
Recared I	d. 601	
Rufinus Tyrannius	c. 345–410	CH
Severus Sulpicius	c. 360–c. 420	CH
Simeon Stylites	c. 390–459	Mo
Socrates Scholasticus	380–450	CH
Sozomen, Salaminius Hermias	c. 375–c. 477	CH
Theodora	c. 500–c. 548	
Theodore of Mopsuestia	c. 350–428	
Theodoret of Cyrrhus	c. 390–c. 458	CH
Theodoric the Great	c. 455–526	
Theodosius I	c. 346–395	
Theophilus of Alexandria	d. 412	
Tyconius	d. 400	
Ulfilas	c. 311–c. 381	M
Valentinian III	419–455	
Valerian	193–c. 269	
Vigilantus	c. 370–c. 406	

Medieval Church History 590–1517

The church in this era faced the impact of the disintegration of the old Roman Empire. The Eastern or Orthodox church in the Asiatic segment of the empire came under control of the emperor and in 1054 finally split from the Western church. The African segment as well as part of the Asiatic segment came under Muslim control. In the European segment the dual institutions of the Holy Roman Empire and the Roman Catholic church fought for control.

Latin-Teutonic Christianity 590–1054

Much of the Asiatic and all of the African parts of the old Roman Empire were taken over by the Muslims until they were checked in the West by Charles Martel at Tours and in the East by Leo III. The Eastern church emerged from the Schism of 1054, wedded to the theology of the ecumenical councils set forth in the theology of John of Damascus.

The more dynamic Western church developed into a uniform, universal, corporate, hierarchical, sacramental system with a monopoly on salvation. The Anglo-Saxons, through Augustine and later the Franks, became Christian. The Franks warmly supported the papacy, giving it what later became the Vatican state by the Donation of Pepin in 754 and 756. Gregory I, influenced by Augustine, provided Medieval popular theology, but stressed the ideas of purgatory and the mass as a sacrifice to Christ. The Donation of Constantine and the Pseudo-Isidorian Decretals reinforced the right of the pope to be supreme over church and state.

Adalbert	c. 956–997	M
Aelfric	c. 995–c. 1020	
Alcuin	735–804	
Alfred the Great	849–899	
Alopen	seventh century	M
Andrew of Crete	c. 660–740	
Anskar	801–865	M
Avicenna, Ibn Sina	980–1037	P
Bede	c. 673–735	CH
Benedict IX	c. 1012–c. 1055	Po
Berengar of Tours	c. 1000–1088	T
Boniface	680–755	M
Boris	d. 907	
Bruno or Berno	d. 927	
Caedmon	Fl. c. 670	H
Canute the Great	c. 994–1035	
Cerularius, Michael	d. c. 1059	
Charlemagne	c. 742–814	
Charles Martel	688–741	
Colman	d. 676	
Cuthbert	d. c. 687	Mo
Cynewulf	Fl. from 750	
Cyril	c. 826–869	M
Dunstan	d. 988	M
Edward the Confessor	c. 1003–1066	
Einhard	c. 770–840	CH
Erigena, Johannes Scotus	c. 810–c. 877	T
Felix of Urgel	d. 818	T
Finan	d. 661	M
Gall	c. 550–c. 640	M
Germanus of Constantinople	c. 634–c. 733	
Gottschalk	c. 805–868	T
Gregory of Utrecht	c. 701–776	
Haakon the Good	c. 914–961	
Henry III	1017–1056	
Hilda	614–680	Mo
Hincmar of Rheims	c. 806–882	T
Humbert	d. 1061	
Irene	c. 752–803	
Isidore of Seville	c. 560–636	
John of Damascus	c. 675–749	T
Kilian	d. 689	M
Leo III	d. 816	Po
Leo IX	1002–1054	Po
Leo III, the Isaurian	c. 680–740	
Liudger, Saint	c. 744–809	M
Louis I (the Pious)	778–840	
Maximus Confessor I	c. 580–662	
Methodius	d. 885	M
Mohammed	c. 570–632	
Nicholas I	c. 800–868	Po
Nicholas II	c. 980–1061	Po
Odo of Cluny	879–942	Mo
Olaf II, Haraldson	c. 995–1030	
Olaf I, Tryggvesson	c. 969–1000	
Olga	d. 969	
Oswald	c. 605–642	
Otto I, the Great	912–973	
Paulinus of York	c. 584–644	
Pepin III	c. 714–768	
Photius	c. 820–891	
Rabanus Maurus	c. 776–c. 856	T
Radbertus, Paschasius	c. 785–c. 865	T
Ratramnus	d. c. 868	T
Sturm of Fulda	710–779	M
Theodore of Studium	759–826	
Theodore of Tarsus	c. 602–690	M
Theodulf of Orleans	c. 750–821	
Timothy I	728–823	
Vladimir I	956–1015	
Wenceslaus	c. 907–929	
Wilfrid	634–709	
William I, the Pious	d. 918	
Willibrord	658–739	M

THE TRIUMPH OF ROMAN CATHOLICISM 1054–1305

The Roman Catholic church, under such able leaders as Gregory VII and Innocent III, was supreme in its own organization and over the state. It even sponsored a Christian holy war against the Muslims to recover the holy places in Palestine in various crusades from 1095 to 1191. The new monastic orders, such as the Cistercian monks and the mendicant Franciscans and Dominicans, supported reform in the church. The scholastics, such as Anselm, Abelard, and particularly Thomas Aquinas, built theological systems that integrated the Bible and Aristotelian philosophy which was brought to western Europe by the Arabs of Spain. Artistic effort reached its highest expression and was unified in the soaring Gothic cathedrals.

Abelard	1079–1142	T
Adam of St. Victor	c. 1110–1180	H
Adrian IV	c. 1110–1159	Po
Ailred	c. 1109–1167	
Albertus Magnus	c. 1200–1280	T
Alexander II	d. 1073	Po

Alexander III	d. 1181	Po
Alexander of Hales	c. 1185–1245	T
Alexius Comnenus	1048–1118	
Anselm	1033–1109	T
Anthony of Padua	1195–1231	
Aquinas, Thomas	c. 1225–1274	T
Arnold of Brescia	c. 1100–1155	
Averroes	1126–1198	P
Avicenna, Ibn Sina	980–1037	P
Bacon, Roger	1214–1294	
Baldwin I	1058–1118	
Becket, Thomas à	c. 1118–1170	
Bernard of Clairvaux	c. 1090–1153	My, H
Bernard of Cluny	c. 1146	H
Berthold von Regensburg	1210–1272	
Bonaventura	c. 1217–1274	T
Boniface VIII	c. 1234–1303	Po
Callixtus II	d. 1124	Po
Celestine V	c. 1215–1296	Po
Clara Sciffi	c. 1194–1253	
Dante Aligheri	1265–1321	
Dominic de Guzman	1170–1221	
Duns Scotus	c. 1266–1308	T
Eadmer	c. 1055–c. 1130	CH
Eckhart, Meister	c. 1260–c. 1327	My
Eugenius IV	1383–1447	Po
Euthymus Zigabenus	c. 1100	
Francis of Assisi	1182–1226	Mo, My
Frederick I, Barbarossa	c. 1122–1190	
Frederick II, the Magnificent	1194–1250	
Godfrey of Bouillion	c. 1060–1100	
Gratian	twelfth century	
Gregory VII	c. 1023–c. 1085	Po
Gregory IX	c. 1145–1241	Po
Grosseteste, Robert	c. 1175–1253	T
Hélöise	c. 1098–1164	
Henry II	1133–1189	
Henry IV	1050–1106	
Henry of Lausanne	d. c. 1145	
Hildegard	1098–1179	Mo
Hugo of St. Victor	c. 1096–1141	My, T
Innocent III	1161–1216	
Joachim of Fiore	c. 1135–1202	My
John (Lackland)	c. 1167–1216	
John of Paris	c. 1250–1306	
Lanfranc	c. 1005–1089	
Langton, Stephen	d. 1228	
Louis IX	c. 1214–1270	
Lull, Raymond	c. 1235–1315	
Maimonides	c. 1135–1204	
Ockham, Williams	1300–1349	
Otto of Bamberg	c. 1060–1139	M
Otto of Freising	c. 1110/1115–1158	CH
Peter of Bruys	d. c. 1140	
Peter Damian	1000–1072	
Peter of Blois	c. 1130–c. 1200	
Peter the Hermit	c. 1050–1115	Mo
Peter Lombard	1095–c. 1159	T
Peter the Venerable	c. 1092–1156	Mo
Philip II, Augustus	1165–1223	
Philip IV, the Fair	1268–1314	
Prester John	twelfth century	
Richard I	1157–1199	
Richard of St. Victor	d. 1173	My, T
Robert de Molesme	c. 1027–1111	Mo
Roscellinus	c. 1050–c. 1125	T
Sorbon, Robert de	1201–1274	
Suger	c. 1081–1151	A
Urban II	1042–1099	Po
Waldo, Peter	d. c. 1217	
Walter the Penniless	d. 1097	
William I, Conqueror	1027–1087	
William of Champeaux	c. 1070–1121	T
William of Tyre	c. 1130–c. 1185	CH

REFORMERS BEFORE LUTHER 1305–1517

Almost as soon as the hierarchical sacramental system of the Roman Catholic church reached completion by 1305, it began to decline and face corruption, the Great Schism, and the Babylonian Captivity. Externally, the middle class and nation-state rulers opposed corruption. Internally, mystics such as Meister Eckhart; reformers such as Wycliffe, Hus, and Savonarola; reforming councils seeking to make the papacy a constitutional instead of an absolute monarchy; and biblical humanists such as Reuchlin and Erasmus sought to reform the institutional church. They had only relative success, and Luther was to launch the fifth and major wave of reform. A national Russian Orthodox church emerged in Russia by 1589.

Agricola, Rudolphus	c. 1444–1485	
Ailly, Pierre de	1350–1420	T
Alexander VI	c. 1431–1503	Po
Angelico, Fra	1378–1455	A
Bartolommeo, De Pagholo Del Fattorino, Fra.	1475–1517	A
Benedict XIII	c. 1328–1423	Po
Bernardino of Siena	1380–1444	

Bessarion, Johannes	c. 1403–1472	
Biel, Gabriel	1410–1495	T
Borgia, Cesare	1475–1507	
Botticelli, Alessandro	c. 1444–1510	A
Briçonnet, William	1472–1534	
Bridget of Sweden	1303–1373	My
Bude, Guillaume	1468–1540	
Capistrano, Giovanni de	1385–1456	
Catherine of Genoa	1447–1510	My
Catherine of Siena	1347–1380	My
Caxton, William	c. 1422–1491	
Chaucer, Geoffrey	c. 1340–1400	
Chelcicky, Peter	c. 1390–1460	
Chrysoloras Manuel	c. 1355–1415	
Clement V	1264–1314	Po
Clement VII	1342–1394	Po
Colet, John	c. 1467–1519	
Columbus, Christopher	c. 1446–1506	
Correggio, Antonio	1494–1534	A
Cosimo de Medici	1389–1464	
Courtenay, William	c. 1341–1396	
Durer, Albrecht	1471–1528	A
Erasmus, Desiderius	c. 1466–1536	B
Ferdinand V	1452–1516	
Ficino, Marsilio	1433–1499	
Florentius, Radewijns	1350–1400	
Gansfort, Wessel Harmenus	c. 1420–1489	T
Gerson, Jean Chevalier de	1363–1429	
Giotto, di Bondone	c. 1266–1337	A
Goch, Johann von	c. 1400–1475	
Gregory XI	c. 1329–1378	Po
Gregory XII	c. 1326–1417	Po
Grocyn, William	c. 1446–1519	
Groot, Gerard	1340–1384	
Gutenberg, Johann	c. 1398–1468	
Henry the Navigator	1394–1460	
Hus, John	c. 1373–1415	
Hutten, Ulrich von	1488–1523	
Ignatius of Loyola (Inigo Lopez de Recalde)	1491–1556	
Isabella of Castile	1451–1504	
Jimenes de Cisneros, Franzisco, see Ximenes		
Jerome of Prague	c. 1370–1416	
Joan of Arc	1412–1431	My
John XXIII	c. 1370–1419	Po
John of Gaunt	1340–1399	
John of Jandun	d. 1328	
John of Montecorvino	c. 1247–1330	M
John of Wessel	c. 1400–1481	
Jordanus	fourteenth century	M
Juliana of Norwich	c. 1342–c. 1413	My
Julius II	1443–1513	Po

Kempe, Margery	c. 1373–1433	My
Kempis, Thomas á	c. 1380–1471	My
Lefèvre d'Étaples, Jacques	c. 1455–1536	
Leo X	1475–1521	Po
Leonardo da Vinci	1452–1519	A
Linacre, Thomas	c. 1460–1524	
Lippi, Fra Filippo	c. 1406–1469	A
Lorenzo II, de Medici	1449–1492	
Machiavelli, Niccolo	1469–1527	P
Marsilius of Padua	c. 1275–1342	P
Michelangelo	1475–1504	
Nicholas V	1397–1455	Po
Nicholas of Cusa	c. 1401–1464	
Nicholas of Hereford	d. c. 1420	B
Ockham, William of	c. 1280 or 1300–1349	T
Oldcastle, John	c. 1378–1417	
Petrarch	1304–1374	
Pfefferkorn, Johannes	1469–1524	
Pico della Mirandola, Giovanni	1463–1494	
Pirckheimer, Willibald	1470–1530	
Purvey, John	c. 1353–1428	
Radewijns, Florentius	1350–1400	
Raphael, Santi	1483–1520	A
Reuchlin, Johannes	1455–1522	B
Rolle of Hampole, Richard	c. 1295–1349	My
Ruysbroeck, Jan Van	1293–1381	
del Sarto, Andrea	1486–1531	A
Savonarola, Girolamo	1452–1498	
Sickingen, Franz von	1481–1523	
Sigismund	1368–1437	
Suso, Heinrich	c. 1300–1366	My
Tauler, Johann	c. 1300–1361	My
Tetzel, Johann	c. 1465–1519	
Torquemada, Tomas de	1388–1468	
Urban V	1310–1370	Po
Urban VI	1318–1389	Po
Valla, Lorenzo	c. 1406–1457	
Wesel, John	c. 1400–c. 1481	
Wessel, John	c. 1420–1489	
Wycliffe, John	c. 1329–1384	B
Ximenes	1436–1517	
Zizka, Jan	c. 1360–1424	

Modern Church History 1517–Present

The Reformation brought Protestant creeds and freed churches to oppose the medieval, universal, institutional church. Christianity became a global religion with revivalistic forces of renewal and great Roman Catholic and Protestant missionary effort. Secular and materialistic forces such as materialism, biblical criticism, and Marxism rose to threaten its existence.

Protestant and Roman Catholic Reformation 1517–1648

Between 1517 and 1648 national Anglican, Lutheran (Germany and Scandinavia), and Reformed (Holland, Switzerland and Scotland) Protestant state churches and free Anabaptist churches emerged to oppose the universal Roman Catholic church.

Roman Catholicism, supported by Spain, the Inquisition, the Index and the Jesuits, held Protestant gains only to Holland after 1563. It was reformed internally, through the new monastic orders and the council of Trent. A sixteenth-century aggressive missionary effort in Central and South America, Indochina, the Philippines, and Japan made Roman Catholicism a global religion.

Our modern nation-state system and the balance of power in international relations developed after the Thirty Years' religious war.

Agricola, Johann	c. 1494–1566	
Agricola, Michael	c. 1510–1557	
Ainsworth, Henry	1571–1622	
Albert of Brandenburg	1490–1545	
Allen, William	1532–1594	
Alva, Fernando Alvarez de Toledo	1508–1582	
Ammann, Jacob	c. 1644–c. 1711	
Ames, William	1576–1633	T
Amsdorf, Nicolaus von	1483–1565	
Andrae, Jacob	1528–1590	T
Andrae, Johann Valentine	1586–1654	
Andrewes, Lancelot	1555–1626	
Angela de Merici	1474–1540	Mo
Arminius, Jacob	1560–1609	T
Arndt, Johann	1555–1621	
Askew, Anne	c. 1521–1546	
Bacon, Francis	1561–1626	P
Baronius, Caesar	1538–1607	CH
Barrow, Henry	c. 1550–1593	
Beaton, David	1494–1546	
Bellarmino, Robert Francesco Romolo	1542–1621	T
Beza, Theodore	1519–1605	
Biddle, John	1615–1662	
Blaurock, Georg	c. 1492–1529	
Boehme, Jacob	1574–1624	
Bora, Katherine von	1499–1552	
Borromeo, Charles	1538–1584	Mo
Bossuet, Jacques	1627–1704	
Bourgeois, Louis	c. 1510–c. 1561	H
Bradford, William	1590–1657	
Brebeuf, Jean de	1593–1649	M
Brenz, Johann	1499–1570	
Brewster, William	c. 1563–1644	
Browne, Robert	c. 1550–1633	
Brucioli, Antonio	c. 1500–c. 1554	
Bruno, Philipp Giordano	1548–1600	
Bucer, Martin	1491–1551	
Buchanan, George	1507–1582	
Bugenhagen, Johann	1485–1558	
Bullinger, Johann Heinrich	1504–1575	
Cajetan, St. Gaetano da Thiene	1480–1547	Mo
Calixtus, George	1586–1656	T
Calvert, George	c. 1580–1632	
Calvin, John	1509–1564	T
Campanella, Tommaso	1568–1639	
Campeggio, Lorenzo	c. 1472–1539	
Canisius, Peter	1521–1597	T
Capito, Wolfgang Fabricius	1478–1541	
Carlstadt, Andreas Bodenstein	c. 1480–1541	
Cartwright, Thomas	1535–1603	
Carver, John	1575–1621	
Castellio, Sebastian	1515–1563	
Catherine de Medici	1519–1589	
Champlain, Samuel de	c. 1570–1635	
Charles I	1600–1649	
Charles II	1630–1685	
Charles V	1500–1558	
Chemnitz, Martin	1522–1586	
Chillingworth, William	1602–1644	
Christian III	1503–1559	
Clement VIII	1536–1605	Po
Coligny, Gaspard de	1519–1572	
Contarini, Gasparo	1483–1542	
Coornhert, Dirck Volkertszoon	1552–1590	T
Cop, Nicholas	early sixteenth century	
Copernicus, Nicolaus	1473–1543	
Cotton, John	1584–1652	CH, T
Coverdale, Miles	1488–1568	B
Cranmer, Thomas	1489–1556	
Crashaw, Richard	c. 1613–1649	
Cromwell, Oliver	1599–1658	
Cromwell, Thomas	c. 1485–1540	
Cruger, Johann	1598–1662	H

Davenport, John	1597–1670	
Denck, Johannes	1495–1527	
De Nobili, Robert	1577–1656	M
Descartes, Rene	1596–1650	P
Donne, John	1573–1631	
Dunster, Henry	1609–1659	
Eck, Johann Maier	1486–1543	
Edward VI	1537–1553	
Einarsen, Gisser	sixteenth century	
Elizabeth I	1533–1603	
Endecott (or Endicott) John	c. 1589–1665	
Episcopius, Simon	1583–1643	T
Estienne, Robert	1503–1559	
Farel, Guillaume	1489–1565	
Fisher, John	1459–1535	
Flacius, Matthias Illyricus	1520–1575	CH
Foxe, John	1516–1587	CH
Francis de Sales	1567–1622	My
Franck, Sebastian	1499–c. 1542	
Frederick III, the Pious	1515–1576	
Frederick III, the Wise	1463–1525	
Frith, John	1503–1533	
Froben, John	c. 1460–1527	
Froment, Antoine	1509–1584	
Fuller, Thomas	1608–1661	
Galilei, Galileo	1564–1642	
George of Brandenberg	1484–1543	
Gerhard, Johann	1582–1637	
Gomar, Francis	1563–1641	T
Goodwin, Thomas	1600–1680	
Grebel, Conrad	c. 1498–1526	
Greenwood, John	d. 1593	
Gregory XIII	1502–1585	Po
Grotius, Hugo	1583–1645	T
Gustavus Adolphus	1594–1632	
Gustavus Vasa	1496–1560	
Hall, Joseph	1574–1656	
Hamilton, Patrick	c. 1504–1528	
Harvard, John	1607–1638	
Helwys, Thomas	c. 1550–c. 1616	
Henderson, Alexander	c. 1583–1646	
Henry IV of Navarre	1553–1610	
Henry VIII	1491–1547	
Herbert, Edward	1583–1648	
Herbert, George	1593–1633	
Herrick, Robert	1591–1674	
Heurnius, Justus	c. 1585–1656	
Higginson, Francis	c. 1587–1630	
Hobbes, Thomas	1588–1679	P
Hoffman, Melchior	c. 1500–c. 1543	
Hooker, Richard	c. 1553–1600	T
Hooker, Thomas	1586–1647	
Hooper, John	c. 1495–1555	
Hübmaier, Balthasar	c. 1480–1528	
Hunt, Robert	c. 1568–1608	
Hutchinson, Anne	1591–1643	
Hutter, Jacob	d. 1536	
Ignatius of Loyola	1491–1556	Mo
Jacob, Henry	1563–1624	
James I	1566–1625	
Jansen, Cornelius Otto	1585–1638	T
Jewel, John	1522–1571	
Jogues, Isaac	1607–1646	M
John of Avila	1500–1569	My
John of the Cross	1542–1591	My
John of Leyden	c. 1509–1536	
John the Constant	1468–1532	
Jonas, Justus	1493–1555	
Jud, Leo	1482–1542	
Knox, John	c. 1514–1572	
Lambert, Francois	1486–1530	
Las Casas, Bartolomé de	1474–1566	M
Lasco, Johannes à	1499–1560	
Latimer, Hugh	c. 1485–1555	
Laud, William	1573–1645	
Lilburne, John	c. 1614–1657	
Locke, John	1632–1704	
Louis XIII	1601–1643	
Lucar, Cyril	1572–1638	
Luther, Katherina	1499–1552	
Luther, Martin	1483–1546	T
Major, George	1502–1574	T
Manz, Felix	1498–1527	
Margaret of Navarre	1492–1549	
Marot, Clemens	c. 1497–1544	
Mary Stuart	1542–1587	
Mary Tudor	1516–1558	
Mather, Richard	1596–1669	
Matthys, Jan	d. 1534	
Maurice of Saxony	1521–1553	
Melanchthon, Philipp	1497–1560	T
Melville, Andrew	1545–1622	
Menno Simons	1496–1559	T
Michaelangelo Buonarotti	1475–1564	A
Miltitz, Karl von	1490–1529	
More, Sir Thomas	1478–1535	
Münzer, Thomas	c. 1490–1525	
Murton, John	d. 1625	
Myconius, Friedrich	1491–1546	
Myconius, Oswald	1488–1522	
Neri, Philip	1515–1595	
Nobili, Robert de	1577–1656	M
Ochino, Bernardino	1487–1564	
Oecolampadius, Johannes	1482–1531	
Oldenbarneveldt, Jan van	1547–1619	
Olevianus, Kaspar	1536–1587	
Olivétan, Pierre Robert	c. 1506–1538	
Osiander, Andreas	1498–1552	T
Palestrina, Giovanni Pierluigi	c. 1525–1594	H
Palladius, Peter	1504–1560	
Parker, Matthew	1504–1575	
Pascal, Blaise	1623–1662	
Paul III	1468–1549	Po

Paul IV	1476–1559	Po
Petri, Olaus	1493–1552	
Philip II	1527–1598	
Philip of Hesse	1504–1567	
Philips, Obbe	c. 1500–c. 1568	
Pole, Reginald	1500–1558	
Prynne, William	1600–1669	
Ramus, Peter	1515–1572	P
Reublin, Wilhelm	c. 1480–c. 1529	
Ricci, Matteo	1552–1610	M
Richelieu, Arman Jean de Plessis	1585–1642	
Ridley, Nicholas	c. 1500–1555	
Robinson, John	c. 1576–1625	
Rubens, Peter Paul	1577–1640	A
Sadoleto, Jacopo	1477–1547	
Samson, Bernhardino	sixteenth century	
Scaliger, Joseph Justus	1540–1609	CH
Schall, Johann Adam	1591–1666	M
Schwenkfeld, Caspar von Ossig	1489–1561	My
Servetus, Miguel	1511–1553	He
Smyth, John	d. 1612	
Southwell, Robert	c. 1561–1595	
Sozzini, Fausto Paulo	1539–1604	He
Spalatin, Georg	1484–1545	
Staupitz, Johann von	c. 1469–1524	
Stillingfleet, Edward	1635–1699	
Sturm, Jakob	1498–1553	
Sturm, Johannes	1507–1589	
Suarez, Francisco	1548–1617	T
Tasso, Torquato	1544–1595	
Tausen, Hans	1494–1561	
Teresa of Avila	1515–1582	My
Titian	1477–1576	P
Travers, Walter	c. 1548–1636	
Tyndale, William	c. 1494–1536	B
Urban VIII	1568–1644	Po
Ursinus, Zacharias	1534–1583	
Ussher, James	1581–1656	B
Valdés, Juan de	c. 1500–1541	
Vane, Henry	1613–1662	
Vermigli, Pietro	1500–1562	
Villegaignon, Nicolas Durand de	1510–1571	
Vincent de Paul	c. 1580–1660	Mo
Viret, Pierre	1511–1571	
Voetius, Gisbert	1588–1676	T
Vossius, Gerhardus Johnannes	1577–1649	T
Whitgift, John	c. 1530–1604	
William I (the Silent)	1533–1584	
Williams, Roger	c. 1603–c. 1683	
Winslow, Edward	1595–1655	
Winthrop, John	1588–1649	CH
Wishart, George	c. 1513–1546	
Wolsey, Thomas	c. 1474–1530	
Xavier, Francis	1506–1552	M
Zwilling, Gabriel	c. 1487–1558	Mo
Zwingli, Ulrich	1484–1531	T

CHRISTIAN EXPANSION, DENOMINATIONALISM, RATIONALISM, AND REVIVALS 1648–1789

The Reformation churches in this era spread to South Africa, New Zealand, Australia, and North America as settlers moved from Britain and Holland to the new imperial possessions. Deism, an intellectual religion, spread from England to the Continent and the colonies. Its greatest impact was in the upper class, but it was checked by the Pietism of Spener in the Lutheran churches in Europe and by the Methodism of the Wesleys and Whitefield in England. Denominations began to replace state churches, especially in North America.

Addison, Joseph	1672–1719	H
Aitken, Robert	1734–1802	
Alacoque, Marguerite Marie	1647–1690	
Alleine, Joseph	1634–1668	
Alline, Henry	1748–1784	R
Anne (of England)	1665–1714	
Arnauld, Antoine	1612–1694	
Arnold, Gottfried	1666–1714	
Asbury, Francis	1745–1816	R
Astruc, Jean	1684–1766	B
Avvakum	c. 1620–c. 1682	
Bach, John Sebastian	1685–1750	H
Backus, Issac	1724–1806	
Barclay, Robert	1648–1690	T
Barrow, Isaac	1630–1677	
Bartoli, Daniello	1608–1685	CH
Baxter, Richard	1615–1691	My
Beissel, Johann Konrad	1690–1768	
Bellamy, Joseph	1719–1790	
Benezet, Anthony	1713–1784	S
Bengel, Johann Albrecht	1687–1752	
Berkeley, George	1685–1753	P
Beveridge, William	1637–1708	
Blair, James	c. 1655–1743	
Boardman, Richard	1738–1782	
Boehm, Martin	1725–1812	
Böhler, Peter	1712–1775	R
Borrow, George Henry	1803–1881	
Boston, Thomas	1677–1732	T
Bourdaloue, Louis	1632–1704	
Brainerd, David	1718–1747	M
Bramwell, William	1759–1818	
Bray, Thomas	1656–1730	M
Bridaine, Jacques	1701–1767	

Brother Lawrence (See Herman, Nicholas)	1611–1691	My
Browne, Sir Thomas	1605–1682	
Bunyan, John	1628–1688	
Burnet, Gilbert	1643–1715	
Butler, Joseph	1692–1752	P
Calamy, Edmund	1600–1666	
Cameron, Richard	c. 1648–1680	
Campanius, John	1601–1683	
Canstein, Karl Hildebrand Frieher von	1667–1719	
Carroll, John	1735–1815	
Cavalier, Jean	1681–1740	
Charnock, Stephen	1628–1680	T
Clarke, John	1609–1676	
Claude, Jean	1619–1687	
Clement XI	1649–1721	Po
Clement XIV	1705–1774	Po
Coeccius, Johannes	1603–1669	T
Collins, Anthony	1676–1729	
Comenius, Johann Amos	1592–1671	
Compton, Henry	1632–1713	
Cook, Captain James	1728–1779	
Court, Antoine	1696–1760	
Cruden, Alexander	c. 1699–1770	B
Cudworth, Ralph	1617–1688	
Davenport, James	1716–1751	R
David, Christian	1691–1751	
Davies, Samuel	1723–1761	R
Dickinson, Jonathan	1688–1747	
Diderot, Denis	1713–1784	
Dober, Leonard John	1706–1766	M
Dock, Christopher	1698–1771	
Doddridge, Philip	1702–1751	H
Dositheos	1641–1707	
Durie, John	1596–1680	E
Dwight, Timothy	1752–1817	R
Dyer, Mary	d. 1660	
Edwards, Jonathan	1703–1758	R, T
Edwards, Jonathan (the younger)	1745–1801	T
Egede, Hans	1686–1758	M
Eliot, John	1604–1690	M
Embury, Philip	1728–1773	R
Engle, Jacob	1753–1832	
Ernest, Johann August	1707–1781	
Erskine, Ebenezer	1680–1754	
Fell, Margaret (Fox)	1614–1702	
Fenelon, Francoise de Salignac de la Mothe	1651–1715	My
Fichte, Johann Gottlieb	1762–1814	P
Flavel, John	c. 1630–1691	
Fléchiee, Valentin Esprit	1632–1710	
Fleetwood, William	1656–1723	
Fletcher, John William	1729–1785	
Fox, George	1624–1691	My
Francke, August Herrmann	1663–1727	R
Franklin, Benjamin	1706–1790	
Frederick IV	1671–1730	
Freeman, James	1759–1835	
Frelinghuysen Theodore Jacob	1691–c. 1748	R
Fuller, Andrew	1754–1815	
Garnier, Jean	1612–1681	
Gerhard, Paul	c. 1607–1676	
Gibbon, Edward	1737–1794	CH
Gillespie, Thomas	1708–1774	
Griesbach, Johann Jacob	1745–1812	B
Grigg, Joseph	1720–1768	H
Grimshaw, William	1708–1763	R
Gruber, Eberhard Ludwig	1665–1728	
Guyon, Jeanne Marie Bouvier	1648–1717	My
Handel, George Frederick	1685–1759	H
Harris, Howell	1714–1773	R
Haweis, Thomas	1734–1820	R
Haydn, Franz Josef	1732–1809	H
Heck, Barbara Ruckle	1734–1804	M
Henry, Matthew	1662–1714	C
Herman, Nicholas (Brother Lawrence)	c. 1611–1691	My
Hervey, James	1714–1758	
Hochmann, Ernst Christoph	1670–1721	
Hopkins, Samuel	1721–1803	T
Howard, John	c. 1726–1790	S
Howe, John	1630–1706	
Hume, David	1711–1776	P
Huntingdon, Countess of (Selina Hastings)	1707–1791	R
Inglis, Charles	1734–1816	
Jablonski, Daniel Ernst	1660–1741	
James II	1633–1701	
Jarratt, Devereux	1733–1801	R
Jefferson, Thomas	1743–1826	
Johnson, Richard	1753–1827	
Jones, Griffith	1683–1761	R
Kant, Immanuel	1724–1804	P
Keith, George	c. 1639–1716	
Ken, Thomas	1637–1711	H
Klopstock, Friedrich Gottlieb	1724–1803	
Law, William	1686–1761	My
Laval, Montmorency Francois Xavier	1623–1708	
Leclerc, Jean	1657–1736	
Lee, Ann	1736–1784	My
Liebnitz, Gottfried Wilhelm	1646–1716	P
Leighton, Robert	1611–1684	
Lessing, Gotthold Ephraim	1729–1781	

Liguori, Alphonsus	1696–1787	T
Lindsey, Theophilus	1723–1808	
Louis XIV	1638–1715	
Louis XVI	1754–1793	
Lyttleton, George	1709–1773	
Mabillon, Jean	1632–1707	CH
McGready, James	c. 1758–1817	R
Mack, Alexander	1679–1735	
MacCaulay, Zachary	1768–1838	
Manning, James	1735–1791	
Marquette, Jacques	1637–1675	
Marshall, Daniel	1768–1837	R
Martyn, Henry	1781–1812	M
Massillon, Jean Baptiste	1663–1742	
Mather, Cotton	1663–1728	CH
Mather, Increase	1639–1723	
Mayhew, Experience	1673–1758	M
Mayhew, Jonathan	1720–1766	
Milner, Isaac	1750–1820	
Milner, Joseph	1744–1797	CH
Milton, John	1608–1674	T
Molinos, Miguel de	1640–1697	My
More, Hannah	1745–1833	S
Morris, Samuel	c. 1700–c. 1770	R
Mosheim, Johann Lorenz von	1694–1755	CH
Mountain, Jacob	1749–1825	M
Mozart, Johann Chrysostom Wolfgang	1756–1791	H
Mühlenberg, Henry Melchior	1711–1787	M
Murillo, Bartolome Esteban	1617–1682	A
Murray, John	1741–1815	
Napoleon I	1769–1821	
Neal, Daniel	1678–1743	CH
Neander, Joachim Neumann	1650–1680	CH
Newton, Sir Isaac	1642–1727	
Nikon	1605–1681	
Nitschmann, David	1696–1772	M
Oates, Titus	1649–1705	
Oberlin, Jean Frederic	1740–1826	S
Occom, Samson	1723–1792	M
O'Kelly, James	c. 1757–1826	
Otterbein, Philip William	1726–1813	
Owen, John	1616–1683	T
Paine, Thomas	1737–1809	
Paley, William	1743–1805	T
Pastorius, Francis Daniel	1651–c. 1720	
Pearson, John	1613–1686	
Penn, William	1644–1718	
Pennington, Isaac	1616–1679	My
Peter the Great	1672–1725	
Pilmoor, Joseph	1739–1825	
Plutschau, Heinrich	c. 1677–1747	M
Priestley, Joseph	1733–1804	
Provoost, Samuel	1742–1815	
Purcell, Henry	1659–1695	H
Quesnel, Pasquier	1634–1719	
Rabaut, Paul	1718–1794	
Raikes, Robert	1735–1811	
Randall, Benjamin	1749–1808	
Rankin, Thomas	1738–1810	M
Reimarus, Hermann Samuel	1694–1768	B
Reinhard, Franz Volkmar	1752–1812	
Rembrandt, Harmenszoon Van Rijn	1606–1669	A
Rock, Johann Frederick	1678–1749	
Romaine, William	1714–1795	
Rousseau, Jean Jacques	1712–1778	
Rowland, Daniel	c. 1713–1790	R
Rutherford, Samuel	c. 1600–1661	T
Saurin, Jacques	1677–1730	
Schiller, Johann Christoph Friedrich	1759–1805	P
Schlatter, Michael	1716–1790	
Schmidt, Georg	1709–1785	M
Schwartz, Christian Frederick	1726–1798	M
Scott, Thomas	1747–1821	C
Scougal, Henry	1650–1678	
Seabury, Samuel	1729–1796	
Sergeant, John	1710–1749	M
Sharp, Granville	1735–1813	S
South, Robert	1634–1716	
Sower (Saur), Christopher	1693–1758	
Spangenberg, August Gottlieb	1704–1792	M, T
Spener, Philipp Jacob	1635–1705	R
Spinoza, Baruch	1632–1677	P
Strachan, John	1778–1867	
Stearns, Shubal	1706–1771	R
Stiles, Ezra	1727–1795	
Stoddard, Solomon	1643–1729	
Strawbridge, Robert	d. 1781	M
Swedenborg, Emmanuel	1688–1772	My
Swift, Jonathan	1667–1745	
Tate, Nahum	1652–1715	
Taylor, Jeremy	1613–1667	
Tennent, Gilbert	1703–1764	R
Tennent, William	1673–1746	R
Tennison, Thomas	1636–1715	
Tersteegen, Gerhard	1697–1769	H, My
Thornton, Henry	1760–1815	S
Toplady, Augustus Montague	1740–1778	H
Traherne, Thomas	c. 1637–1674	
Trapp, John	1601–1669	
Vasey, Thomas	1731–1826	M
Venn, Sir Henry	1725–1797	
Verbiest, Ferdinand	1623–1688	
Voltaire, Jean Francois Marie Arouet	1694–1778	
Warburton, William	1698–1779	

Name	Dates	
Washington, George	1732–1799	
Watts, Isaac	1674–1748	H
Webb, Thomas	1724–1796	
Weltz, Baron Justinian Ernst von	1621–1688	M
Wesley, Charles	1708–1788	H, R
Wesley, John	1703–1791	R
Wesley Sr., Samuel	1662–1735	
Wesley, Susannah	1669–1742	
West, Gilbert	1703–1756	
Wheelock, Eleazar	1711–1779	
Whitby, Daniel	1638–1726	
Whitefield, George	1714–1770	R
William III	1650–1702	
Witherspoon, John	1723–1794	
Woolman, John	1720–1772	S
Wren, Christopher	1632–1723	A
Yale, Elihu	1649–1721	
Zeisberger, David	1721–1808	M
Ziegenbalg, Bartholomaeus	1682–1719	M
Zinzendorf, Nikolaus Ludwig	1700–1760	M

ROMAN CATHOLICISM, REVIVALS, REFORM, MISSIONS, AND LIBERALISM 1789–1914

From 1789 to 1914 Catholicism recovered from losses incurred in the French Revolution early in the era, but in the process became a more closed society to liberal external forces. Recurring Protestant revivals brought a surge of Protestant global missions abroad and domestic social reform, which benefitted black slaves and white workers. It had, however, to face the challenge of romanticism, biblical criticism, evolution, and Marxism.

Name	Dates	
Abbott, Lyman	1835–1922	
Abeel, David	1804–1846	M
Abel, Charles William	1863–1930	M
Addams, Jane	1860–1935	
Adeney, Walter F.	1849–1920	
Adler, Felix	1851–1933	P
Afrikaner	d. c. 1820	
Aggrey, James Emman	1875–1927	M
Aglipay, Cruz Y Labayan Gregorio	1860–1940	
Agnew, Eliza	1807–1883	
Albright, Jacob	1759–1808	
Alexander I	1777–1825	
Alexander Archibald	1772–1851	T
Alexander, Cecil F.	c. 1823–1895	H
Alexander, Charles H.	1867–1920	H
Alford, Henry	1810–1871	B
Allen, Ethan	c. 1738–1789	
Allen, Horace Fenton	1858–1932	M
Allen, Richard	1760–1831	
Anderson, Robert	1841–1918	B
Anderson, Rufus	1796–1880	M
Andrews, Charles Freer	1871–1940	
Angus, Joseph	1816–1902	B
Anthony, Susan Brownell	1820–1906	
Arnold, Thomas	1795–1842	
Arnot, Frederick Stanley	1858–1914	M
Arthur, William	1819–1901	M
Babcock, Malthie Davenport	1858–1901	H
Bacon, Leonard	1802–1881	H
Baedeker, Frederich Wilhelm	1823–1906	
Bahaullah	1817–1892	
Baird, Robert	1798–1863	CH
Ballou, Hosea	1771–1852	He
Baring-Gould, Sabine	1834–1924	
Barnardo, Thomas John	1845–1905	S
Banks, Albert	1855–1913	
Barnby, Joseph	1838–1896	H
Barnes, Albert	1798–1870	C
Barton, Clara	1821–1912	S
Barton, William Eleazer	1861–1930	
Bashford, James Whitford	1849–1919	
Bauer, Bruno	1809–1882	
Baur, Ferdinand Christian	1792–1860	B
Bavinck, Herman	1854–1921	T
Beach, Harlan Page	1854–1933	M
Beecher, Henry Ward	1813–1887	
Beecher, Lyman	1775–1863	
Beecher, Willis Judson	1838–1912	
Beet, Joseph Agar	1840–1924	
Beethoven, Ludwig Van	1770–1827	H
Benson, Edward White	1829–1896	
Bernadette	1844–1879	My
Bernard, Thomas Dehany	1815–1904	
Bersier, Eugene Arthur Francois	1831–1889	
Besant, Annie	1847–1933	He
Bigg, Charles	1840–1908	
Bickersteth, Edward	1786–1850	
Bilderdijk, Willem	1756–1831	
Bilhorn, Peter Philip	1862–1936	H
Bingham, Hiram Sr.	1789–1869	M
Bingham, Hiram Jr.	1831–1908	M
Binney, Thomas	1798–1874	
Birks, Thomas Rawson	1810–1883	
Birney, James Gillespie	1792–1857	S
Bismarck, Otto Von	1815–1898	

Name	Dates	
Black, John	1818–1882	
Black, William	1760–1834	
Blackstone, William Eugene	1841–1935	
Blaikie, William Gardon	1820–1899	
Blanchard, Charles	1848–1925	
Blanchard, Jonathan	1811–1892	
Blavatsky, Helena Petrovna	1831–1891	He
Bliss, Daniel	1823–1916	M
Bliss, Philip Paul	1838–1876	H
Blumhard, Christian Gottlieb	1779–1838	M
Blumhardt, Johann Christoph	1805–1880	
Boardman, George Dana, Sr.	1801–1831	M
Boardman, George Dana, Jr.	1828–1903	M
Bogue, David	1750–1825	
Bompas, William Carpenter	1834–1906	M
Bonar, Andrew Alexander	1810–1892	
Bonar, Horatius	1808–1889	H
Booth, Ballington	c. 1857–1940	
Booth, Catherine Mumford	1829–1890	
Booth, William	1829–1912	
Borden, William W.	1887–1913	M
Bounds, Edward McKendree	1835–1913	
Bourne, Hugh	1772–1852	
Bowen, George	1816–1888	M
Bowne, Borden Parker	1847–1910	P
Bowring, Sir John	1792–1872	H
Bradbury, William Bachelder	1816–1868	H
Brahms, Johannes	1833–1897	H
Bray, William	1794–1868	M
Bridgman, Elijah Coleman	1801–1861	M
Briggs, Charles Augustus	1841–1913	B
Broadus, John Albert	1827–1895	
Brookes, James Hall	1830–1897	
Brooks, Philips	1835–1893	H
Brown, David	1803–1897	
Brown, John	1800–1859	S
Brown, Samuel Robbins	1810–1880	M
Brown, William Adams	1865–1943	
Browning, Elizabeth Barrett	1806–1861	
Browning, Robert	1812–1889	
Bruce, Alexander Balmain	1831–1899	
Brumbaugh, Martin Grove	1862–1930	
Bryant, William Cullen	1794–1878	
Buchanan, Claudius	1776–1815	M
Buck, Dudley	1839–1909	H
Bunting, Jabez	1779–1858	R
Burns, William Chalmers	1815–1868	M
Burrell, David James	1844–1926	
Bury, John Bagnell	1861–1927	
Bush, George	1796–1859	
Bushnell, Horace	1802–1876	
Butler, Josephine	1828–1907	S
Butler, William	1818–1899	M
Buxton, Thomas Fowell	1786–1845	S
Byrennios, Philotheos	1833–1914	B
Cabrini, Frances Xavier	1850–1917	
Caird, John	1820–1898	
Cairns, John	1818–1892	T
Calvert, James	1813–1892	M
Campbell, Alexander	1788–1866	
Candlish, Robert Smith	1806–1873	C
Carey, William	1761–1834	M
Carlile, Wilson	1847–1942	
Carlyle, Thomas	1795–1881	
Carman, Albert	1833–1917	
Carroll, Benajah Harvey	1843–1914	
Cartwright, Peter	1785–1872	R
Cary, Alice	1820–1871	H
Cary, Phoebe	1824–1871	H
Caswall, Edward	1814–1878	H
Chalmers, James	1841–1901	M
Chalmers, Thomas	1780–1847	R
Chamberlain, Jacob	1835–1908	M
Chambers, Oswald	1874–1917	
Channing, William Ellery	1780–1842	
Chapman, Wilbur	1859–1918	R
Charles, Elizabeth Rundle	1828–1896	
Charles, Thomas	1775–1814	
Chateaubriand, Francois Auguste Rene	1768–1848	
Chauncy, Charles	1705–1787	
Cheney, Charles Edward	1836–1916	
Cheyne, Thomas Kelly	1841–1915	
Chiniquy, Charles Paschal Telesphore	1809–1899	
Christlieb, Theodor	1833–1889	T
Church, Richard William	1815–1890	
Clark, Francis Edward	1851–1927	
Clarke, Adam	c. 1762–1832	C
Clarke, George R.	1827–1892	
Clarke, James Freeman	1810–1888	
Clarke, Sarah Dunn	1835–1917	
Clarke, William Newton	1841–1912	T
Clarkson, Thomas	1760–1846	S
Clough, John Everett	1836–1910	M
Coan, Titus	1801–1882	M
Coillard, Francois	1834–1904	M
Coke, Thomas	1747–1814	M

Name	Dates	
Colenso, John William	1814–1883	B
Coleridge, Samuel Taylor	1772–1834	
Comba, Emilio	1839–1904	
Comber, Thomas James	1852–1887	M
Comte, Isidore Auguste Marie Francois Xavier	1798–1857	
Conwell, Russell Herman	1843–1925	
Conybeare, William John	1815–1857	
Cook, David Caleb	1850–1927	
Cooper, Anthony Ashley	1801–1855	
Cowman, Charles Elmer	1864–1924	M
Cowper, William	1731–1800	H
Crawford, Daniel	1870–1926	M
Cremer, August Herrmann	1834–1903	B
Crosby, Fanny	1820–1915	H
Crowther, Samuel Adjai	c. 1816–1891	
Cumming, John	1807–1881	
Cummins, George David	1822–1876	
Cunningham, William	1805–1861	T
Dabney, Robert	1820–1898	T
Da Costa, Izaak	1798–1860	
Dale, Robert William	1829–1895	T
Damien, Joseph De Veuster	1840–1889	M
Darby, John Nelson	1800–1882	
Darwin, Charles	1809–1882	
D'Aubigne, Jean Henri Merle	1794–1872	CH
Davidson, Randall Thomas	1848–1930	B
Delitzsch, Franz Julius	1813–1890	C
Denney, James	1856–1917	T
De Rossi, Giovanni Battista	1822–1894	
Dix, Dorothea Lynde	1802–1887	S
Dixon, Amzi Clarence	1854–1925	
Doane, George Washington	1799–1859	H
Doane, William Howard	1832–1916	H
Dods, Marcus	1834–1909	B
Döllinger, Johann Joseph Ignaz	1799–1890	
Dorner, Isaak August	1809–1884	T
Dostoevsky, Fyodor Michael	1821–1881	
Douglas, Frederick	1817–1895	
Dow, John Alexander	1847–1907	
Dow, Lorenzo	1777–1834	
Driver, Samuel Rolles	1846–1914	B

Name	Dates	
Drummond, Henry	1786–1860	
Drummond, Henry	1851–1897	
Duchesne, Louis Marie Olivier	1843–1922	CH
Duff, Alexander	1806–1878	M
Duffield, George	1818–1888	H
Duncan, John	1796–1870	
Eadie, John	1810–1876	B
Ebrard, Johannes Heinrich	1818–1888	T
Eddy, Mary Baker	1821–1910	He
Edersheim, Alfred	1825–1899	B
Edwards, Lewis	1809–1897	
Eichhorn, Johann Gottfried	1752–1857	
Ellicott, Charles John	1819–1905	B
Eliott, Charlotte	1789–1871	H
Ellis, William	1794–1872	M
Emerson, Ralph Waldo	1803–1882	
Emmons, Nathaniel	1745–1840	
Eucken, Rudolf Christoph	1846–1926	P
Evans, Christmas	1766–1838	
Excell, Edwin Othello	1851–1921	H
Exell, Joseph Samuel	1849–c. 1909	H
Faber, Frederick William	1814–1863	H
Fairbairn, Andrew Martin	1838–1912	T
Fairbairn, Patrick	1805–1874	
Farrar, Frederic William	1831–1903	
Fausset, Andrew Robert	1821–1910	C
Fawcett, John	1740–1817	
Fillmore, Charles	1854–1948	He
Findlay, George Gillanders	1849–1919	
Finney, Charles Grandison	1792–1875	R
Fisher, George Park	1827–1909	CH
Fisk, Pliny	1792–1825	M
Fisk, Wilbur	1792–1839	
Fiske, Fidelia	1816–1864	M
Fliedner, Theodor	1800–1864	
Flint, Robert	1838–1910	T
Forsyth, Peter Taylor	1848–1921	T
Foster, John	1770–1843	
Fox, Margaret	1833–1893	He
Franck, Caesar Auguste	1822–1890	H
Franson, Fredrik	1852–1908	
Frazer, Sir James George	1854–1941	
Freeman, Thomas B.	1809–1890	M
Froude, Richard Hurell	1803–1836	
Fry, Elizabeth Gurney	1780–1845	S
Fuller, Richard	1804–1876	
Gamewell, Francis Dunlap	1857–1950	M

Name	Dates	
Gapon, Georgi Apollonovich	c. 1870–1906	
Gardiner, Allen Francis	1794–1851	M
Garrettson, Freeborn	1752–1827	
Garrison, William Lloyd	1805–1879	
Gasquet, Francis Aidan	1846–1929	CH
Gaussen, Francois Samuel	1790–1863	B
Geddie, John	1815–1872	M
Geikie, John Cunningham	1824–1906	B
Gesenius, Heinrich Friedrich Wilhelm	1786–1842	B
Gibbons, James	1834–1921	
Gilmour, James	1843–1891	M
Girdlestone, Robert Baker	1836–1923	B
Gladden, Washington	1836–1918	S
Gladstone, William Ewart	1809–1898	
Gloag, Paton James	1823–1906	C
Gobat, Samuel	1799–1879	M
Godet, Frederic Louis	1812–1900	C
Goforth, Jonathan	1859–1936	M
Goodell, William	1792–1867	M
Gordon, Charles George	1833–1885	
Gordon, Samuel Dickey	1859–1936	
Gore, Charles	1853–1932	C
Gossner, Johannes Evangelista	1773–1858	M
Goulburn, Edward Meyrick	1818–1897	H
Gounod, Charles	1818–1893	
Graf, Karl Heinrich	1815–1869	B
Grant, Charles	1746–1823	
Grant, George Monro	1835–1902	
Green, Samuel Gosnell	1822–1905	B
Grellet, Stephen	1733–1855	M
Grenfell, George	1849–1906	M
Griffith, John	1831–1912	M
Grimke Sarah Moore Angelina	1792–1873	S
Groves, Anthony Norris	1795–1853	
Grubb, William Barbrooke	1865–1930	
Gruber, Franz Xavier	1787–1863	H
Grundtvig, Nikolai Frederik Severin	1783–1872	S
Guinness, Henry Grattan	1835–1910	M
Guizot, Francois Pierre Guillaume	1787–1874	
Gunkel, Hermann	1862–1932	B
Gunsaulus, Frank Wakeley	1856–1921	
Guthrie, Thomas	1803–1873	
Gutzlaff, Karl Friedrich August	1803–1851	M
Haeckel, Ernst Heinrich	1834–1919	P
Hagenbach, Karl Rudolph	1801–1874	T
Haldane, James	1768–1851	R
Haldane, Robert	1764–1842	R
Hale, Edward Everett	1822–1909	
Hall, Gordon	1784–1826	M
Hall, Robert	1764–1831	
Hamlin, Cyrus	1811–1900	M
Hannington, James M.	1847–1885	
Harms, Claus	1778–1855	
Harnack, Karl Gustav Adolph von	1851–1930	T, CH
Harper, William	1856–1906	
Hase, Karl August von	1800–1890	CH
Hastings, Horace Lorenzo	1831–1899	
Hastings, James	1852–1922	B
Hastings, Thomas H.	1784–1872	H
Hauge, Hans Nielsen	1771–1824	R
Havergal, Frances Ridley	1836–1879	H
Heber, Reginald	1783–1826	H, M
Hecker, Isaac Thomas	1819–1888	Mo
Hefele, Karl Joseph von	1809–1893	CH
Hegel, George Wilhelm Friedrich	1770–1831	P
Hengstengberg, Ernst Wilhelm	1822–1869	T
Hepburn, James Curtis	1815–1911	M
Herder, Johann Gottfried van	1744–1803	P
Herron, George D.	1862–1925	
Herzog, Johann Jokob	1805–1882	T
Hicks, Elias	1748–1830	
Hill, Rowland	1744–1833	R
Hillis, Newell Dwight	1858–1929	
Hodge, Archibald Alexander	1823–1886	T
Hodge, Charles	1797–1878	T
Hoffman, Elisha A.	1839–1929	H
Hoffmann, Johann Michael Ferdinand Heinrich	1824–1902	A
Horne, Charles Silvester	1865–1914	
Horne, Thomas Hartwell	1780–1862	B
Horner, Ralph	1853–1921	
Hort, Fenton John Anthony	1828–1892	B
How, William Walsham	1823–1897	H

Name	Dates	
Howe, Julia Ward	1819–1910	H
Howson, John Saul	1816–1885	
Hügel, Baron Friedrich von	1852–1925	
Hughes, John Joseph	1797–1864	
Hunt, John	1812–1848	M
Hunt, William Holman	1827–1910	A
Huntington, William Reed	1838–1909	
Hurlbut, Jessee Lyman	1843–1930	
Hurst, John Fletcher	1834–1903	CH
Huxley, Thomas Henry	1825–1895	
Hyde, John	1865–1912	M
Ingersoll, Robert Green	1833–1899	
Ireland, John	1838–1918	
Ireland, John	1761–1842	
Irving, Edward	1792–1834	
Iverach, James	1839–1922	T
Jackson, Samuel Macaulay	1851–1912	CH
Jackson, Sheldon	1834–1909	M
Jacobs, Charles Michael	1875–1938	CH
James, William	1842–1910	P
Jamieson, Robert	1802–1880	
Jasper, John	1812–1901	
Jefferson, Charles Edward	1860–1937	
Jessup, Henry	1832–1910	
Johnson, Gisle	1822–1894	R
Johnson, Herrick	1832–1913	
Jones, Abner	1772–c. 1841	
Jones, David	1796–1841	
Jones, Samuel Porter	1847–1906	R
Jowett, Benjamin	1817–1893	B
Jowett, John Henry	1864–1923	
Judson, Adoniram	1788–1850	M
Julicher, Gustav Adolf	1857–1938	B
Kahn, Ida	1872–1932	M
Kanamori, Tsurin Paul	c. 1856–c. 1928	R
Keble, John	1792–1866	
Keil, Johann Karl Friedrich	1807–1888	C
Keith-Falconer, Ion Grant Neville	1856–1887	M
Kellogg, Samuel Henry	1839–1899	M
Kelly, William	1821–1906	
Kelvin, William Thomson	1824–1907	
Kenrick, Francis Patrick	1796–1863	
Key, Francis Scott	1779–1843	H
Khama	c. 1828–1923	
Kierkegaard, Soren Aaby	1813–1855	T
King, Henry Churchill	1858–1934	
King, Jonas	1792–1869	M
Kingsley, Charles	1819–1875	S

Name	Dates	
Kirkpatrick, William James	1838–1921	M
Kittel, Rudolf	1853–1929	B
Kitto, John	1804–1854	B
Knudsen, Albert Cornelius	1873–1953	T
Knibb, William	1803–1845	M
Krapf, Johann Ludwig	1810–1881	M
Krüdener, Barbara Juliana	1764–1824	My
Krummacher, Friedrich Wilhelm	1796–1868	
Kurtz, Johann Heinrich	1809–1890	CH
Kuyper, Abraham	1837–1920	T
Lacordaire, Jean Baptiste Henri	1802–1861	Mo
Lachmann, Karl	1793–1851	B
Lamennais, Hugues Félicite Robert de	1782–1854	
Lange, Johann Peter	1802–1884	
Lanphier, Jeremiah C.	1809–?	R
Lathbury, Mary Artemisia	c. 1841–1913	H
Latourette, Kenneth Scott	1884–1968	CH
Laubach, Frank Charles	1884–1970	M
Lawrance, Uriah Marion	1850–1924	
Laws, Robert	1851–1934	M
Lea, Henry Charles	1825–1909	CH
Lee, Jason	1803–1845	M
Lee, Jesse	1758–1816	
Legge, James	1815–1897	M
Leo XIII	1810–1903	Po
Liddell, Henry George	1811–1898	B
Liddon, Henry Parry	1829–1890	
Lightfoot, Joseph Barber	1828–1889	B
Lincoln, Abraham	1809–1865	
Lincoln, William	1825–1888	
Lindsay, Thomas Martin	1843–1914	CH
Lisle, George	c. 1750–c. 1845	
Liszt, Franz	1811–1886	
Livingstone, David	1813–1873	
Lock, Walter	1846–1933	
Löhe, Johann Konrad Wilhelm	1808–1872	T
Loisy, Alfred Firmin	1857–1940	
Longfellow, Samuel	1819–1892	
Losee, William R.	1764–?	
Lotze, Rudolph Hermann	1817–1881	
Lovejoy, Elijah Parish	1802–1837	
Lowry, Robert H.	1826–1899	
Luthardt, Christoph Ernst	1823–1902	T
Lutkin, Peter Christian	1857–1931	H
Lyon, Mary	1797–1849	
Lyte, Henry Francis	1793–1847	H

McAll, Robert Whitaker	1821–1893	M
McCabe, Charles Cardwell	1836–1906	
McGiffert, Arthur Cushman	1861–1933	T
McGranahan, James	1840–1907	H
Machen, John Gresham	1881–1937	T
Machray, Robert	1831–1904	
MacKay, Alexander Murdoch	1849–1890	M
MacKay, George Leslie	1844–1901	M
McKendree, William	1757–1835	
MacKenzie, John	1835–1899	M
MacKenzie, John Kenneth	1850–1888	M
Mackintosh, Charles Henry	1820–1906	C
MacLaren, Alexander	1826–1910	C
MacLeod, Norman	1812–1872	
Mahan, Asa	1800–1889	T
Maitland, Samuel Roffey	1792–1866	CH
Makemie, Francis	1658–1708	
Malan, Cesar Henri Abraham	1787–1864	R
Manning, Henry Edward	1808–1892	
Marsden, Samuel	1764–1838	M
Marshman, Joshua	1768–1837	M
Martensen, Hans Lassen	1808–1884	T
Martin, William Alexander Parsons	1827–1916	M
Martineau, James	1805–1900	
Marx, Karl	1818–1883	P
Mason, C. H.	d. after 1907	
Mason, Lowell	1792–1872	H
Mateer, Calvin	1836–1908	M
Matheson, George	1842–1906	H
Maurice, John Frederick	1805–1872	
Max Müller, Friedrich	1823–1900	B
Mears, Henrietta Cornelia	1890–1963	
Medhurst, Walter Henry	1796–1857	M
Mendelssohn, Bartholdy Jakob Ludwig Felix	1809–1847	H
Mercier, Désiré Joseph	1851–1926	
Merle D'Aubigne, Jean Henri	1794–1872	CH
Meyer, Frederick Brotherton	1847–1929	
Meyer, Heinrich August Wilhelm	1800–1873	
Migne, Jacques Paul	1800–1875	CH
Miley, John	1813–1895	T
Miller, James Russell	1840–1912	
Miller, Lewis	1829–1899	
Miller, William	1782–1849	
Milligan, George	1860–1934	
Milligan, William	1821–1893	
Mills, Benjamin Fay	1857–1916	R
Mills, Samuel John	1783–1818	
Milman, Henry Hart	1791–1868	CH
Milne, William	1785–1822	M
Mirza, Ali Mohammed	1819–1850	
Moffat, Robert	1795–1883	M
Möhler, Johan Adam	1796–1838	CH
Mohr, Joseph	1792–1848	H
Mommsen, Theodor	1817–1903	
Monier-Williams, Sir Monier	1819–1899	
Monod, Adolphe Theodore	1802–1856	R
Monod, Frederic Joel Jean Gerard	1794–1863	R
Montgomery, James	1771–1854	H
Moody, Dwight Lyman	1837–1899	R
Moorehead, William Gallogly	1836–1914	B
Moorehouse, Henry	1840–1880	R
Morison, James	1816–1893	
Morrison, Robert	1782–1834	M
Moule, Handley Carr Glyn	1841–1920	C
Moulton, James Hope	1863–1917	B
Moulton, Richard Green	1849–1924	B
Moulton, William Fiddian	1835–1898	B
Mozley, James Bowling	1813–1878	
Mühlenberg, William August	1796–1877	
Müller, George	1805–1898	S
Müller, Julius	1801–1878	T
Mullins, Edgar Young	1860–1928	
Murray, Andrew	1828–1917	R
Mynster, Jakob Pier	1775–1854	T
Nation, Cary Amelia	1846–1911	S
Neale, John Mason	1818–1866	H
Neander, Johann August Wilhelm	1789–1850	CH
Neesima, Joseph Hardy	1843–1890	
Nestle, Eberhard	1851–1913	B
Nettleton, Asahel	1783–1844	R
Nevin, John William	1803–1886	T
Nevius, John Livingston	1829–1893	M
Newberry, Thomas	1811–1901	B
Newell, Samuel	1785–1821	M
Newman, John Henry	1801–1890	
Newton, Benjamin Wills	1807–1899	
Newton, John	1725–1807	H
Nicolai, Ivan	c. 1835–1912	M
Nicoll, William Robertson	1851–1923	

Nielsen, Fredrik Kristian 1846–1907 CH
Nitobe, Inanzo 1862–1933
Nommensen, Ludwig Enger 1834–1918 M
Nott, Samuel, Jr. 1788–1869 M
Noyes, John Humphrey 1811–1886

Oastler, Richard 1789–1861 S
Obookiah, Henry 1792–1818
O'Connell, Daniel 1775–1847 S
Oehler, Gustav Friedrich von 1812–1872 T
Olshausen, Hermann 1796–1839 B
Oosterzee, Jan Jakob van 1817–1882
Orr, James 1844–1913 T

Palmer, Ray 1808–1877
Parker, Daniel 1781–1834
Parker, Joseph 1830–1902
Parker, Peter 1804–1888 M
Parker, Theodore 1810–1860
Parsons, Levi 1792–1822 M
Passavant, William Alfred 1821–1894 S
Paton, John 1824–1907
Patteson, John Coleridge 1827–1871 M
Patton, Francis Landey 1843–1932 T
Peake, Arthur Samuel 1865–1929 C
Peck, John Mason 1789–1858 M
Peloubet, Francis Nathan 1831–1920
Pentecost, George Frederick 1842–1920
Perkins, Justin 1805–1869 M
Perowne, Edward Henry 1826–1906
Perowne, John James 1823–1904
Petrie, William Matthew Flinders 1853–1942 B
Phelps, Austin 1820–1890
Philip, John 1775–1851 M
Phillips, Wendell 1811–1884
Pierson, Arthur Tappan 1837–1911
Pierson, Delavan Leonard 1867–1938
Pilkington, George Lawrence 1865–1897 M
Pius IX 1792–1878 Po
Pius X 1835–1914 Po
Plummer, Alfred 1841–1926 CH
Plumptre, Edward Hayes 1821–1891 CH
Pollard, Samuel 1864–1915 M
Pond, Enoch 1791–1882
Pott, Francis Lister Hawks 1864–1947 M
Pratt, Waldo 1857–1939
Prentiss, Elizabeth Payson 1818–1878
Pressence, Edmond DeHault de 1824–1891
Pressly, John Taylor 1795–1870
Punshon, William Morley 1824–1881
Purves, George Tybout 1852–1901 B
Pusey, Edward Bouverie 1800–1882

Quimby, Phineas Parkhurst 1802–1866

Rader, Paul 1879–1938
Rainy, Robert 1826–1906 CH
Ramabai, Pandita Sarasvati 1858–1922 R, S
Ramsay, Sir William Mitchell 1857–1939 B
Ranke, Leopold von 1795–1886
Rapp, Johann Georg 1757–1847
Rasputin, Grigori Yefimovich c. 1871–1916 Mo
Rauschenbusch, Walter 1861–1918 S, T
Rawlinson, George 1812–1902 B
Rebmann, Johannes c. 1819–1876 M
Reed, Mary 1854–1943 M
Renan, Joseph Ernest 1823–1892 B
Reuss, Edward Guillame Eugene 1804–1891 B
Rice, Luther 1783–1836 M
Richard, Timothy 1845–1919 M
Richter, Julius 1862–1940 CH
Riggs, Elias 1810–1901 M
Ritschl, Albrecht Benjamin 1822–1889 T
Roberts, Benjamin Titus 1823–1893
Roberts, Evans John 1875–1951 B
Robertson, Archibald Thomas 1863–1934 B
Robertson, Frederick William 1816–1853
Robinson, Charles Seymour 1829–1899 H
Robinson, Edward 1794–1863
Robinson, George Livingstone 1864–1958
Root, George Frederick 1820–1895 H
Rosenius, Karl Olof 1816–1868 R
Rosetti, Gabriel Charles Dante 1828–1882 A
Routh, Martin Joseph 1755–1854
Rowntree, Joseph 1801–1859 S
Royce, Josiah 1855–1916 P
Ruskin, John 1819–1900 A, S
Russell, Charles Taze 1852–1916 He
Rutherford, Joseph Franklin 1869–1942 He
Ryerson, Adolphus Egerton 1803–1882
Ryle, John Charles 1816–1900 C

Sabatier, Charles Paul Marie	1858–1928	CH
Sabatier, Louis August	1839–1901	T
Saker, Alfred	1814–1880	M
Sanctis, Luigi de	1808–1869	
Sanday, William	1843–1920	
Sanders, Frank Wright	1861–1933	
Saint, Nathanael, see Elliott, James	1923–1956	
Sankey, Ira David	1840–1908	H
Saphir, Aaron Adolph	1831–1891	
Sayce, Archibald Henry	1845–1933	B
Schaff, David	1852–1929	CH
Schaff, Philip	1819–1893	CH, E
Schauffler, Adolf Frederick	1845–1919	
Schauffler, Albert Henry	1837–1905	M
Schechter, Solomon	1847–1915	
Schelling, Friedrich Wilhelm Joseph von	1775–1854	P
Schereschewsky, Samuel Isaac Joseph	1831–1906	M
Schleiermacher, Friedrich Daniel Ernst	1768–1834	T, P
Schmucker, Samuel Simon	1799–1873	E
Schopenhauer, Arthur	1788–1860	P
Schubert, Franz Peter	1797–1828	H
Schuman, Robert Alexander	1810–1856	H
Schurer, Emil	1844–1910	B
Scofield, Cyrus Ingerson	1843–1921	B
Scott, George	1804–1874	
Scott, Walter, Sir	1771–1832	
Scott, Walter	1796–1861	
Scudder, John	1793–1855	M
Seiss, Joseph Augustus	1823–1904	C
Selwyn, George Augustus	1809–1878	M
Seton, Elizabeth Ann	1774–1821	Mo
Seymour, William ?	late nineteenth, early twentieth centuries	
Shaftesbury, Seventh Earl of	1801–1885	S
Shaw, Barnabas	c. 1793–1857	M
Shaw, William	1798–1872	M
Shedd, William Greenough Thayer	1820–1894	T
Sheldon, Charles Monroe	1857–1946	S
Sheldon, Henry Clay	1845–1928	CH, T
Shembe, Isaiah	c. 1870–1935	
Shore, John	1751–1834	
Simeon, Charles	1759–1836	
Simpson, Albert Benjamin	1843–1919	
Simpson, Matthew	1811–1884	
Slessor, Mary	1848–1915	M
Smith, Arthur Henderson	1845–1932	M
Smith, Eli	1801–1857	M
Smith, Elias	1769–1846	
Smith, George	1840–1876	
Smith, George Adam	1856–1942	B
Smith, Hannah Whitall	1832–1911	
Smith, Harry Boynton	1815–1877	
Smith, Henry Preserved	1847–1927	
Smith, John Taylor	1860–1907	
Smith, Joseph	1805–1844	
Smith, Joseph, Jr.	1832–1914	
Smith, Rodney (Gipsy)	1861–1947	R
Smith, Samuel Francis	1808–1895	H
Smith, William	1813–1893	
Smith, William Robertson	1846–1894	B
Sohm, Rudolph	1841–1917	CH
Speer, Robert Elliott	1867–1947	M, E
Spellman, Francis Joseph	1889–1967	
Sprague, William Buell	1795–1876	
Spurgeon, Charles Haddon	1834–1892	R
Stainer, Sir John	1840–1901	H
Stalker, James	1848–1927	
Stanley, Arthur Penrhyn	1815–1881	
Stanley, Henry Morton	1841–1904	
Stebbins, George Coles	1846–1945	
Stephen, James	1789–1859	S
Stewart, Lyman	1840–1923	
Stewart, James	1831–1905	M
Stone, Barton	1772–1844	
Stowe, Harriet Beecher Elizabeth	1811–1896	S
Strachan, John	1778–1867	
Strauss, David Friedrich	1808–1874	T
Streeter, Bernard Hillman	1874–1937	B
Strong, Augustus Hopkins	1836–1921	T
Strong, James	1822–1894	
Strong, Josiah	1847–1916	E
Stuart, Moses	1780–1852	C
Studd, Charles T.	1862–1931	M
Sullivan, Sir Arthur Seymour	1842–1900	H
Swain, Clara A.	1834–1910	M
Swete, Henry Barclay	1835–1917	B
Swing, David	1830–1894	
Tait, Archibald Campbell	1811–1882	

Name	Dates	
Talmage, Thomas DeWitt	1832–1902	
Tappan, Arthur	1786–1865	S
Tappan, Lewis	1788–1873	S
Taylor, Graham	1851–1938	S
Taylor, James Hudson	1832–1905	M
Taylor, Nathaniel William	1786–1858	
Taylor, William	1821–1902	M
Taylor, William Mackergo	1829–1895	
Tchaikovsky, Peter Ilich	1840–1893	H
Tennyson, Alfred	1809–1892	
Terry, Milton Spenser	1840–1914	C
Thayer, Joseph Henry	1828–1901	B
Thoburn, Isabella	1840–1901	M
Thoburn, James Mills	1836–1922	M
Tholuck, Friedrich August Gottreu	1799–1877	T
Thomas, John	1805–1871	
Thomas, Norman	1884–1968	
Thompson, Francis	1859–1907	
Thomson, James	d. c. 1850	
Thomson, William McClure	1806–1894	
Thornwell, James Henry	1812–1862	
Thorvaldsen, Albert Bertel	1770–1844	A
Tischendorf, Lobegott Friedrich Konstantin von	1815–1874	B
Tissot, James Joseph Jacques	1836–1902	A
Tolstoi, Lyov Nikolayeich	1828–1910	
Towner, Daniel Brink	1850–1919	H
Townsend, Luther Tracy	1838–1922	
Toy, Crawford Howell	1836–1919	B
Tregelles, Samuel Prideaux	1813–1875	B
Trench, Richard Chenevix	1807–1886	B
Troeltsch, Ernst	1865–1923	S
Trotter, Isabel Licias	1853–1928	M
Trumbull, David	1819–1889	M
Trumbull, Henry Clay	1830–1903	
Truth, Sojourner Isabella	c. 1797–1883	
Tucker, Alfred Robert	1849–1914	M
Tulloch, John	1823–1886	T
Tyrrell, George H.	1861–1909	
Ullmann, Karl	1796–1865	T
Underwood, Horace Grant	1859–1916	M
Upham, Thomas Cogswell	1799–1872	A
Vanderkemp, Johannes Theodores	1747–1811	M
Van Raalte, Albertus Christian	1811–1876	
Varley, Henry	1835–1912	R
Vaughan, Charles John	1816–1897	
Vedder, Henry Clay	1853–1935	
Venn, Henry	1796–1873	
Venn, John	1759–1813	
Verbeck, Guido Herman Fridolin	1830–1898	M
Veregin, Peter	d. 1924	
Vilatte, Joseph Rene	1854–1929	
Vincent, John Heyl	1832–1920	
Vincent, Marvin Richardson	1834–1922	
Vinet, Alexandre	1797–1847	R
Von Hugel, Friedrich	1852–1925	
Vos, Geerhardus	1862–1949	T
Wace, Henry	1836–1924	CH
Wagner, Charles	1852–1918	
Waldenstrom, Paul Peter	1838–1917	
Walker, Thomas	1859–1912	M
Walker, Williston	1860–1922	CH
Wallace, Lewis	1827–1905	
Wallin, Johan Olof	1779–1839	H
Walther, Carl Ferdinand Wilhelm	1811–1887	
Walton, William Spencer	1850–1906	M
Wanamaker, John	1838–1922	S
Ward, William	1769–1823	M
Ware, Henry	1764–1845	
Warfield, Benjamin Breckenridge	1851–1921	T
Warneck, Gustav Adolf	1834–1910	CH
Warner, Daniel Sidney	1842–1925	
Washington, Booker Taliaferro	c. 1856–1915	
Watson, John	1850–1907	
Wayland, Francis	1796–1865	
Webb-Peploe, Hanmer William	1837–1923	
Weidner, Revere Franklin	1851–1915	T
Weiss, Carl Philipp Bernhard	1827–1918	B
Weiss, John	1863–1914	
Weld, Theodore Dwight	1803–1895	S
Wellhausen, Julius	1844–1918	B
Westcott, Brooke Foss	1825–1901	B
Weston, Agnes	1840–1918	S
Whatcoat, Richard	1736–1806	
Whateley, Richard	1787–1863	
White, Alma	1862–1946	
White, Ellen Gould	1827–1915	
White, John	1866–1933	M
White, William	1748–1836	

Name	Dates	
Whitman, Marcus	1802–1847	M
Whittier, John Greenleaf	1807–1892	H
Whittle, Daniel Webster	1840–1901	R
Whyte, Alexander	1837–1921	
Wichern, Johan Heinrich	1803–1881	R, S
Wilberforce, William	1759–1833	S
Wilder, Robert Parmalee	1863–1938	M, E
Wilkes, A. Paget	1871–1934	M
Willard, Frances Elizabeth Caroline	1839–1898	S
Williams, George	1821–1905	S
Williams, John	1796–1839	M
Williams, Samuel	1812–1884	M
Wilson, John	1804–1875	M
Winebrenner, John	1797–1860	
Winer, Johann George Benedict	1789–1858	B
Wise, Isaac Meyer	1819–1900	
Woodsworth, James	d. 1917	
Wordsworth, Christopher	1807–1885	
Wordsworth, William	1770–1850	
Wright, Charles Hamilton Henry	1836–1909	
Young, Andrew	1869–1922	M
Young, Brigham	1801–1877	
Young, Egerton Ryerson	1840–1909	
Young, Robert	1822–1888	B
Zahn, Theodor	1838–1933	C, B

CHURCH-STATE TENSION, ECUMENICALISM AND THEOLOGICAL DISSOLUTION, 1914–PRESENT

Between 1914 and the present, the church faced increasing problems with the growth of the warfare-welfare secular totalitarian states of the left and right, and even democratic states. Ecumenical fusion by nondenominational and interdenominational agencies, organic reunion, and national and international confederations replaced the fission of the reformation. Theological liberalism by 1930 gave way to neo-orthodoxy, and it, in turn, about 1950, to radical theologies. But during this time, the evangelical cause had a remarkable resurgence.

Name	Dates	
Aberhart, William	1878–1943	
Albright, William Foxwell	1891–1971	B
Allis, Oswald Thompson	1880–1973	B
Althaus, Paul	1888–1966	
Argue, Andrew Harry	1865–1959	R
Arndt, William Frederick	1880–1957	
Asch, Sholem	1880–1957	
Athearn, Walter Scott	1872–1934	
Aulén, Gustav	1879–1978	T
Aylward, Gladys	1902–1970	M
Azariah, Vedanayakum Samuel	1874–1945	M
Baillie, John	1886–1960	T
Baker, George	c. 1885–1965	He
Balfour, Arthur James	1848–1930	
Ballard, Guy Warren	1878–1939	He
Barnhouse, Donald Grey	1895–1960	C
Barth, Karl	1886–1968	T
Barton, George Aaron	1859–1942	B
Bauer, Walter	1877–1960	
Bea, Augustin	1881–1968	E
Begbie, Harold	1871–1929	
Bell, George Kennedy Allen	1883–1958	E
Bell, L. Nelson	1894–1973	
Bender, Carl J.	1869–1935	M
Benson, Clarence Herbert	1879–1954	
Benson, Louis Fitzgerald	1855–1930	H
Berdyaev, Nicolai Aleksandrovich	1874–1948	T
Berggraev, Eivind	1884–1959	
Bergson, Henri Louis	1859–1941	P
Berkhof, Louis	1873–1957	T
Biederwolf, William Edward	1867–1939	
Bingham, Rowland Victor	1872–1942	M
Black, Hugh	1868–1953	
Blackwood, Andrew Watterson	1882–1966	
Boegner, Marc	1881–1967	E
Bonhoeffer, Dietrich	1906–1945	T
Booth, Evangeline Cory	1865–1950	
Booth, Maud Ballington	1865–1948	
Boreham, Frank William	1871–1959	
Boville, Robert G.	late nineteenth—early twentieth centuries	
Breasted, Henry James	1865–1935	B
Brent, Charles Henry	1862–1929	E
Brightman, Edgar Sheffield	1884–1953	P
Brown, Charles Reynolds	1862–1950	
Brown, John Elward	1879–1957	
Brunner, Emil	1889–1966	T

Bryan, William Jennings	1860–1925	
Buber, Martin	1878–1965	P
Buchman, Frank Nathan Daniel	1878–1961	
Bulgakov, Sergius Nikolaevich	1871–1944	T
Bultmann, Rudolf	1884–1976	B, T
Burton, Ernest DeWitt	1856–1925	B
Buswell, James Oliver, Jr.	1895–1975	
Cadbury, Henry Joel	1883–1974	B
Cadman, Samuel Parkes	1864–1936	
Camus, Albert	1913–1960	
Carmichael, Amy Wilson	1867–1951	M
Carnell, Edward John	1919–1967	T
Carver, George Washington	c. 1864–1943	
Carver, William Owen	1868–1954	
Case, Shirley Jackson	1872–1947	CH
Cavert, Samuel McCrea	1888–1976	E
Chafer, Lewis Sperry	1871–1952	T
Charles, Robert Henry	1855–1931	B
Cheng, Ching Yi	1881–1940	
Chiang Kai-Shek	1887–1975	
Chisholm, Thomas	1866–1960	H
Clark, Glenn	1882–1956	
Coffin, Henry Sloan	1877–1954	
Coughlin, Charles Edward	1891–1979	
Culbertson, William	1905–1971	
Daniel-Rops (Petiot) Henri	1901–1965	CH
Darrow, Clarence	1857–1938	
Deissmann, Gustav Adolf	1866–1937	B
Dewey, John	1859–1952	P
Dibelius, Martin	1883–1947	T
Dibelius, Otto	1880–1967	T
Diffendorfer, Ralph	1879–1951	
Dodd, Charles Harold	1884–1973	
Dooyewerd, Herman	1894–1977	T
Douglas, Lloyd Cassell	1877–1951	
Douglass, Harlan Paul	1871–1953	
Eddy, Sherwood	1871–1963	
Edman, Victor Raymond	1900–1967	
Eliot, Thomas Stearns	1888–1965	
Elliott, Harrison Sackett	1882–1951	
Elliott, James	1927–1956	M
Erdman, Charles Rosenbury	1866–1960	
Evans, William	1870–1950	
Faulhaber, Michael von	1869–1952	
Feng, Yu-Hsiang	1882–1948	
Fitzwater, Perry Braxton	1871–1957	T
Flanagan, Edward	1886–1948	S
Fosdick, Harry Emerson	1878–1969	
Freud, Sigmund	1856–1939	
Fuller, Charles E.	1887–1968	R
Gabriel, Charles Hutchinson	1856–1932	H
Gaebelein, Arno Clemens	1861–1945	
Gairdner, William Henry Temple	1873–1928	M
Garvie, Alfred Ernest	1861–1945	
Gilson, Etienne Henri	1884–1978	P
Glegg, Alexander	1882–1975	R
Glover, Terrot Reaveley	1869–1943	B
Goodspeed, Edgar Johnson	1871–1962	B
Gordon, Adoniram Judson	1836–1895	M
Gordon, Charles William	1860–1937	
Grace, Charles Emmanuel	1881–1960	He
Gray, James Martin	1851–1935	
Grenfell, Wilfred Thomason	1866–1940	M
Hallesby, Ole Kristian	1879–1961	R
Hallock, Gerhard Benjamin Fleet	1856–1953	
Higginbotham, Sam	1874–1958	M
Hocking, William Ernest	1873–1966	P
Holmes, John Haynes	1879–1964	
Hone, William	1780–1842	
Horton, Douglas E.	1891–1968	
Houghton, William Henry	1887–1946	
Hromodka, Josef	1889–1969	T
Inge, William Ralph	1860–1954	My
Ironside, Henry Allan	1876–1951	C
Jackson, Frederick John Foakes	1855–1941	CH, B
Jaspers, Carl	1883–1969	P
John XXIII	1881–1963	Po
Jones, Stanley	1884–1973	M
Jones, Robert (Bob)	1883–1968	R
Jones, Rufus Matthew	1863–1948	My
Kagawa, Toyohiko	1888–1960	S

Kelly, Howard Atwood	1858–1943	
Kennedy, John Fitzgerald	1917–1963	
Kenyon, Frederick George	1863–1952	B
Kerr, Hugh Thompson	1871–1950	
Kidd, Beresford James	1864–1948	CH
Kimura, Henry Seimatsu	1875–1958	R
King, Martin Luther, Jr.	1929–1968	S
Kittel, Gerhard	1888–1948	B
Kraemer, Hendrik	1888–1965	M
Kyle, Melvin Grove	1858–1933	B
Lake, Kirsopp	1872–1946	B
Laws, Curtis Lee	1868–1946	
Lenski, Richard	1864–1936	C
LeTourneau, Robert Gilmour	1888–1969	
Lewis, Clive Staples	1898–1963	
Leitzmann, Hans	1875–1942	CH
Little, Paul	1928–1975	
McAuley, Jeremiah	1839–1884	
McCarrell, William	1896–1979	
Macartney, Clarence Edward	1879–1957	
McCheyne, Robert Murray	1813–1843	R
McClintock, John	1814–1870	T
McCloskey, John	1810–1885	
McCormick, Cyrus Hall	1809–1884	
McCosh, James	1811–1894	T, P
McCrie, Thomas	1772–1835	CH
McDowell, William Fraser	1858–1937	
McDonald, George	1824–1905	
Macintosh, Douglas Clyde	1877–1948	T
Mackintosh, Hugh Ross	1870–1936	T
McNicol, John	1869–1956	C
McPherson, Aimee Semple	1890–1944	R
Maier, Walter Arthur	1893–1950	
Manalo, Felix	1886–1963	
Maritain, Jacques	1882–1973	P
Marshall, Peter	1902–1949	
Matthews, Basil Joseph	1879–1951	
Matthews, Shailer	1863–1941	B
Milligan, George	1860–1934	B
Moffatt, James	1870–1944	B
Monroe, Harry	1853–1916	S
Montalembert, Charles Forbes Rene	1810–1870	
Montgomery, Helen Barett	1861–1934	B
Moore, George Foote	1851–1931	B
Morgan, George Campbell	1863–1945	
Morrison, Charles Clayton	1874–1966	
Moton, Robert Russa	1867–1940	
Mott, John Raleigh	1865–1955	M, E
Mundelien, George William	1872–1939	
Murray, John Courtney	1904–1967	T
Nee, Henry or Watchman	1903–1972	R
Neitzsche, Friedrich Wilhelm	1844–1900	P
Neve, Juergen Ludwig	1865–1943	T, CH
Newell, William Reed	1865–1956	
Newman, Albert Henry	1852–1933	CH
Niebuhr, Karl Paul Reinhold	1892–1971	T
Niebuhr, Richard Helmut	1894–1962	T
Nightingale, Florence	1820–1910	
Norris, J. Frank	1877–1952	
North, Frank Mason	1850–1935	E
Norton, Ralph	1868–1934	M
Oesterley, William Oscar Emil	1866–1950	B
Oldham, Joseph Houldsworth	1874–1969	E
Otto, Rudolf	1869–1937	P
Page, Kirby	1890–1957	
Parham, Charles Fox	1873–1929	
Paul VI	1897–1968	Po
Paul, Kanakarayan Tiruselvam	1876–1931	E
Pidgeon, George C.	1872–1971	E
Pierce, Robert Willard	1914–1978	R, S
Pike, James Alnert	1913–1969	
Pius XI	1857–1939	Po
Pius XII	1876–1958	Po
Price, Ira Maurice	1856–1939	B
Purdie, James Eustace	1880–1977	
Purnell, Benjamin	1861–1927	
Rayburn, James C., Jr.	1909–1970	
Rees, Thomas Bonner	1911–1970	R
Rice, John R.	1895–1980	
Riley, William Bell	1861–1947	
Robinson, Frank Bruce	1886–1948	He
Rodeheaver, Homer Alvan	1880–1955	H
Sangster, William Edwyn Robert	1900–1960	
Schweitzer, Albert	1875–1965	M, T
Scopes, John Thomas	c. 1900–1970	

Scroggie, William Graham	1877–c. 1959	C
Scudder, Ida	1870–1960	M
Seagrave, Gordon Stifler	1897–1965	M
Seeberg, Reinhold	1859–1935	T
Seymour, William J.	late nineteenth century, early twentieth century	
Sheen, Fulton	1895–1979	
Shields, Thomas Todhunter	1873–1955	
Shoemaker, Samuel Moor	1893–1963	
Singh, Sadhu Sundar	1889–1929	R
Smith, Edwin William	1876–1957	
Smith, Herbert Augustine	1874–1952	H
Smith, Wilbur Moorhead	1894–1977	B
Söderbloom, Lars Olaf Jonathan	1866–1931	E
Souter, Alexander	1873–1949	B
Stam, John and Betty	1907–1934	M
Stone, John Timothy	1868–1954	
Stone, Mary	1873–1954	M
Stonehouse, Ned Bernard	1902–1962	B
Strachan, Robert Kenneth	1910–1965	M
Straton, John Roach	1875–1929	
Sunday, William Ashley	1862–1935	R
Sung, John	1901–1944	R
Sweet, William Warren	1881–1959	CH
Teilhard de Chardin, Pierre	1881–1955	P
Temple, William	1881–1944	E
Thomas, Norman	1884–1968	S
Thomas, William Henry Griffith	1861–1924	
Tilila, Osmo Antera	1904–1972	
Tikhon, Belavin	1865–1925	
Tillich, Paul	1886–1965	P, T
Tingley, Katherine Augusta	1852–1929	He
Tomlinson, Ambrose Jessup	1865–1943	
Torrey, Charles Cutler	1863–1956	B
Torrey, Reuben Archer	1856–1928	R
Trotman, Dawson	1906–1956	
Truett, George Washington	1867–1944	
Trumbull, Charles Gallaudet	1872–1941	
Uchimura, Kanzo	1861–1930	
Uermura, Masakisa	1857–1925	
Unamuno, Miguel de	1864–1937	P
Underhill, Evelyn	1875–1941	My
Unger, Merrill F.	1909–1980	
Van Dusen, Henry Pitney	1897–1975	
Van Til, Cornelius	1895–1964	T
Voliva, Wilbur Glenn	1870–1942	
Wells, Amos Russell	1862–1933	
White, Wilbert Webster	1863–1944	B
Whitehead, Alfred North	1861–1947	P
Wilson, Robert Dick	1856–1930	B
Wilson, Walter Lewis	1881–1969	
Winrod, Gerald	1900–1957	
Wise, Stephen Samuel	1874–1949	
Wright, J. Elwin	1896–1966	E
Wright, George Frederick	1838–1921	
Young, Dinsdale Thomas	1861–1938	
Young, Edward Joseph	1907–1968	B
Zenos, Andreas Constantinides	1855–1942	CH
Zwemer, Samuel Marinus	1867–1952	M

A

ABBOTT, LYMAN (1835-1922), clergyman and editor, born at Roxbury, Massachusetts; educated at New York University, A.B. (1853); studied law and practiced at the bar from 1853 to 1859, then studied theology with uncle, John S. C. Abbott. Ordained 1860, became pastor of the Congregational Church in Terre Haute, Indiana. In 1865, made secretary of the American Union (Freedman's) Commission, at the same time pastor of the New England Church, New York City (1865-1869). Became associate editor, 1869, of *Harper's Magazine;* appointed by American Tract Society to editorship of *The Illustrated Christian Weekly* (1871-1876). Became associate editor, with Henry Ward Beecher, 1876, of the *Christian Union,* later becoming editor-in-chief. Name of the paper changed to *Outlook* in 1893. Succeeded Beecher from 1888 to 1889 as pastor of Plymouth Church, Brooklyn. In latter decades of his life became especially interested in social reform. Tried to reconcile evolution and biblical criticism with evangelical theology in his preaching and writing. Some of his many books are *Life and Literature of the Ancient Hebrews, Jesus of Nazareth, Life of Henry Ward Beecher, Christianity and Social Problems, Life and Letters of Paul,* and *Christ's Secret of Happiness.*

ABEEL (ȧ bēl′), **DAVID** (1804-1846), American missionary to China; born in New Brunswick, New Jersey, studied at Rutgers College, and Theological Seminary of the Dutch Reformed Church, N.J. Ordained in 1829; pastor in Athens, New York two years; went to Canton, China as American Seamen's Friend Society Chaplain in 1830. In 1831 transferred to American Board of Commissioners for Foreign Missions. Traveled extensively in Siam, Indonesia, and Malaya until forced home by ill health. Promoted missions in Europe and America from 1833 until 1838, when he returned to China. Inaugurated mission of Dutch Reformed Church at Amoy, 1842. Invalided home again, 1845. Addresses and appeals in London led to formation of Interdenominational Society for Promoting Female Education in the East 1834. Through his influence the Women's Union Missionary Society of America was formed after his death. Published *Journal of a Residence in China.* Is remembered as a saintly, self-sacrificing, vigorous missionary.

ABEL, CHARLES WILLIAM (1863-1930), apostle to the Papuans, born in London, England of high Puritan ancestry. Converted at age eleven during the Moody and Sankey campaign at Islington, London. Ambitious, went to New Zealand in 1881. Finally settled among the savage Maoris, determined to identify himself with them. Won their confidence and respect; led some of the young men to Christ. Returned to England in 1884, and entered Cheshunt college. Spent five years in college, the last one in medical training at the London Hospital. Offered himself to the London Missionary Society; was appointed to a newly opened field in New Guinea. In 1889 ordained and left for his field of labor, landing first in Australia. Left Sydney, 1890, to take up his rugged work among savage Papuans on and near the island of Kwato in southeastern New Guinea. Worked and traveled at times with veteran James Chalmers. Exhaustion from fever forced him to make a trip to Australia, 1892. Won confidence and hearts of the people by self-sacrificing deeds and by identifying with the people. Natives were taught the dignity of labor, independence, and industry and to substitute crafts, industries, and sports for inter-tribal warfare. Lived to see the major share of the responsibility of the Church in Papua placed upon the shoulders of Papuans.

ABELARD (ABAILARD), PETER (1079-1142), French philosopher and theologian, born in Nantes, northern France, educated in Paris. Studied under William of Champeaux and Anselm of Laon. An able teacher with a magnetic personality, he drew students from all over Europe to his lectures on philosophy and theology. Arnold of Brescia, who advocated separation of church and state and the end of priestly control in the church, was one of his most famous pupils. His arrogance and his love affair with Héloïse (c. 1113), niece of Fulbert the canon of Notre Dame led to the birth of a son, their marriage, his castration by Fulbert's servants, and her retirement to a convent in order not to further damage his career. In his *Sic et Non* (1122) he arranged contradictory statements from the church Fathers and the Bible for students to reconcile. A moderate realist, he believed that universal ideas existed in the mind of God, were embodied in things on earth, but were also subjective ideas in the mind of man. This challenged the teachings of early realists, such as Anselm. This liberalism incited the strong opposition of Bernard of

Clairvaux. He believed Christ's death demonstrated God's love but was not vicarious. Bernard claimed that Abelard had confounded the true faith with the teachings of pure philosophy. Abelard refused to retract his views and writings, and Bernard charged him with heresy and had him excommunicated at the council of Sens, two years before his death. Following this condemnation and humiliation, permitted to reside at the monastery of Cluny, he spent his last days writing *Confession* and *Apology.* Twenty-two years later Héloïse was buried beside him. We learn much of his life and trials from his autobiography, *Story of My Misfortunes.*

ABERHART (ā ber härt), **WILLIAM** (1878-1943), Canadian Baptist lay preacher, school teacher, radio Bible teacher, and politician. Born in Hibbard township, Ontario; educated at Chatham Business College, Hamilton Normal College, and Queens University (B.A., 1906). Taught school in Ontario until 1910 and at Crescent Heights High School in Calgary from 1910 until 1935, became its principal in 1915. Bible class began in 1914 in Westbourne Baptist Church which became the Calgary Prophetic Bible Institute in 1918. Began radio broadcasts in 1925. During the great depression adopted Social Credit system of C. H. Douglas and organized the Social Credit Party, which won the legislature with him as premier from 1935 until 1943. His evangelical religious and political ideas were continued after his death by his ablest pupil, Ernest C. Manning. See Manning, Ernest C.

ADALBERT (ăd′el bĕrt) **of PRAGUE** (c. 956-997), missionary martyr and bishop of Prague, born near Prague, the son of a nobleman, studied at Magdeburg, ordained priest in 981 and consecrated second bishop of Prague in 982. Stern, severe, energetic man, labored diligently, but with little success to convert Bohemians from paganism, to introduce to them the ordinances of the church of Rome and promote spiritual welfare in the church. After five years left his diocese to make pilgrimage to Jerusalem; then entered the monastery of St. Boniface in Rome, where lived a devoted ascetic life for a few years. Went to Hungary for brief time and baptized Prince Stephen. In 996, with the support of the Duke of Poland, went as a missionary to the Prussians. Killed by a pagan priest before achieving much success.

ADAM OF ST. VICTOR (c. 1110-1180). Famous medieval and liturgical hymn writer. Educated in Paris. About 1130 went to the Abbey of St. Victor, where he lived until his death. Composed over forty sequences that the fourth Lateran Council approved for use in the mass in 1215. Those sequences embodied biblical, theological, and legendary data in an allegorical system. Another monk, H. Spanke, composed the melodies for the sequences.

ADDAMS, JANE (1860-1935), American social settlement worker. Born at Cedarville, Illinois. Graduated from Rockford College; then spent one year in Women's Medical College, Philadelphia. When health came near the breaking point, went to Europe. Spent six years aimlessly wandering about, always haunted by conditions and needs of the poor. Pursuing postgraduate study in England, became interested in Toynbee Hall, a university settlement in east London. With Miss Ellen Gates Starr she secured the help of wealthy people, in 1888 began a settlement in Chicago in building that had been erected by a Mr. Hull in 1856. It was America's first settlement house, and she was identified with its activities the rest of her life. Interested in helping the poor; in her settlement did many things that the home, the church, and the school were not doing. Devoted much of her time to lecturing and writing on social problems and the cause of peace. For three years served as inspector of streets and alleys in her district. In 1909 was elected president of National Conference of Charities and Correction; in 1915 was elected president of the International Peace Congress which met at the Hague. In 1931 she and Nicholas Murray Butler were cowinners of the Nobel Peace Prize. Among writings: *Twenty Years at Hull House, The Second Twenty Years at Hull House, Democracy and Social Ethics, Newer Ideals of Peace, The Spirit of Youth and the City Streets.*

ADDISON, JOSEPH (1672-1719), English essayist and hymn writer, born in Milston, near Amesbury, Wiltshire, England, a son of the dean of Lichfield, educated at the Charter House, and at Queen's and Magdalen colleges, Oxford; made a fellow of Magdalen College, 1699-1711; planned to enter the church, but employment as a Whig writer altered his intent. For a short time was Secretary of State. Wrote for Richard Steele's *Tattler* and the *Spectator.* In those two papers and their successor, the *Guardian,* appeared his essays, later published under the title *Evidences of the Christian Religion*. Wrote several hymns including "The Spacious Firmament on High."

ADENEY (ăd′ĭ nĭ) **WALTER FREDERIC** (1849-1920), English clergyman, educator, and author, born at Ealing, Middlesex, England, educated at New College and University College, London. For seventeen years pastor of Congregational church at Acton; for two years lecturer in Bible and systematic theology at New College, London. From 1889 to 1903 professor of New Testament exegesis and church history at New College, part of that time lecturer on church history at Hackney College, London. After 1893, principal of Lancashire Independent College, Manchester. As a theologian accepted the results of biblical criticism and welcomed scientific and philosophic investigations and criticism of religion. His works include nine volumes of *The Pulpit Commentary* and two volumes of *The Expositor's Bible,* as well as *History of the Greek and Eastern Churches, From Christ to Constantine, From Constantine to Charles the Great*. Was also editor of the *Century Bible*.

ADLER, FELIX (1851-1933), founder of Society for Ethical Culture, born Alzey, Germany, son of a Jewish Rabbi who emigrated to America in 1857. Educated at Columbia College, University of Berlin, and University of Heidelberg, Ph.D. (1873); professor of Hebrew and Oriental literature at Cornell University, 1874-1876. Founded the Society for Ethical Culture in New York in 1876 and became lecturer. He founded the society as the new religion of humanity. The society tried to link the best moral teachings of the past from the earliest times to the present, to bring about the application of the ethical factor in all phases of life, and make men aware of the value of human personality. Gave regular Sunday discourses to the New York Society for Ethical Culture. Resumed educational work as professor of political and social ethics, Columbia University, from 1902 until 1921. Roosevelt exchange professor in the University of Berlin, 1908-1909. Took conspicuous part in agitation against child labor, white slavery, tenement congestion, and other evils; was active in promoting proper race relations, refugee work, and social settlements. One of the founders of the National Child Labor Committee, and its chairman from 1904 to 1921. Presided over the first Universal Race Congress in London, 1911. His major work was *Creed and Deed* (1877).

ADRIAN IV (Nicolas Breakspear) (c. 1110-1159), pope, 1154-1159. Only Englishman to sit on papal throne. Went to France as a boy; studied at Paris and Arles. Finally settled in the monastery of St. Rufus near Avignon. Became a priest, then in 1137, abbot. About 1149 was made cardinal bishop of Albana by the pope and sent as legate to Norway and Sweden. In 1154 became pope. Strove for universal domination of the papacy. In this confronted both mighty Emperor Frederick I (Barbarossa) and the reformer, Arnold of Brescia. Arnold's ethical opposition to the hierarchy aimed at reestablishing the ancient sovereignty of Rome and its independence of the papal see. Adrian IV agreed to crown Frederick if the latter would surrender Arnold. Emperor delivered up Arnold to be hanged and burned. Frederick then was crowned by the pope. War soon broke out between the two. There began a long and bitter contest between the popes and the house of Hohenstauffen. After Adrian's death the conflict with Frederick was left to Adrian's successor, Alexander III.

AELFRIC (ăl'frĭk) (c. 955-c. 1020), Anglo-Saxon abbot. Was educated in the Benedictine monastery at Winchester under Ethelwold. Monk in Cerne Abbas in Dorsetshire; abbot of Eynsham in Oxfordshire. Author of many homilies, a Latin grammar and glossary, a treatise on the Old and New Testaments, and a volume of lives of the saints. Translated parts of the Old Testament, denounced theory of the Immaculate Conception, and opposed doctrine of Transubstantiation. Wrote good Anglo-Saxon prose.

AETIUS (ā ē'shĭ ŭs) (d. c. 367), leader of extreme Arianism after Nicea. Called "the ungodly," born in Antioch and sold into slavery. When liberated, studied medicine and theology, and was ordained deacon about 350; banished in 360 but recalled to Constantinople by Julian and made bishop about 361. Became leader of radical Arians, teaching that the Son was of a different and inferior substance, even unlike the Father. Became known with his followers as an Anomoean, or Eunomian from Eunomius, a pupil and chief apologist. Held that the Son was created out of nothing, denied that Christ possessed any divine nature, held that the Holy Spirit was but a creature made by the Father and the Son before all other creatures.

AFRICANUS, SEXTUS JULIUS (c. 160-c. 240), Christian historian. Raised in Palestine, but traveled extensively through Asia Minor. Along with Clement and Origen one of the most learned of the Ante-Nicene fathers. Greatest writing was *History of the World,* which sought to make a complete synopsis of sacred and secular history from the time of creation, and to synchronize the two. Eusebius of Caesarea referred to this history and incorporated parts of it in his *Ecclesiastical History*. Only work now complete is a letter to Origen.

AFRIKANER (ăf rĭ kän'er) (died c. 1820), Hottentot chief in Namaqualand, South Africa. In reprisal for wrong done him, turned robber and outlaw and became terror to both colonists and native tribes; but won to Christ by some missionaries and baptized by Mr. Ebner, one of their number. After Robert Moffat arrived at Capetown in 1816, he decided to go to Namaqualand. He met Afrikaner in the chief's own kraal. He won the confidence of the converted outlaw.

AGGREY, JAMES EMMAN KWEGYIR (1875-1927), African educator, born in Fanti tribe at Anamabu, Ghana, West Africa; attended Richmond College, the Wesleyan Methodist school at Cape Coast. Became a Christian at age of eight and was baptized at fourteen. Led his father, mother, brothers, and sisters to Christ. Was an avid student, painstaking and industrious in his studies. Taught school (age 15-23), spending much time preaching the gospel in West Africa. In 1898 entered Livingstone College, Salisbury, North Carolina, earning his B.A. four years later at the top of his class. After graduating, taught at his alma mater for twenty years, holding two small pastorates. In 1904 was offered the presidency of the college; but declined, feeling his first call to be Africa. Attended Columbia University, and finally received M.A. degree from Columbia, and passed creditably preliminary examinations for a Ph.D. In 1920, as the only Negro member, went with Phelps-Stokes Commission to study educational affairs in Africa. After a time in America returned to Africa in 1924 to help establish Prince of Wales College at Achimota on the Gold Coast. Was to become member of the staff but died suddenly of meningitis in America while completing his Ph.D.

AGLIPAY CRUZ Y LABAYAN, GREGORIO (1860-1940), founder (in 1902) and supreme bishop until his death of the Philippine Independent Catholic Church. A Roman Catholic priest in Manila until in the anti-Spanish insurrection in 1898 he became military chaplain in the Revolutionary Army. His appointment as vicar-general by General Aguinaldo led to his excommunication from the Roman Catholic church.

AGNEW, ELIZA (1807-1883), missionary to Ceylon, born in New York City. At eight years decided to be a missionary. At thirty-two following the death of parents offered herself to the American Board. Early in 1840 began work as the first single woman missionary to Ceylon. Became head of Central Boarding School for girls, opened in 1824 at Uduville in the province of Jaffna. Remained as the head of this school for forty years. Never returned to her native land. During those forty years more than 1,000 pupils came under her care and teaching. More than half her pupils became Christians.

AGRICOLA (å grĭk'ō lå) **JOHANN** (c. 1494-1566), German Protestant reformer, born at Eisleben, Upper Saxony, Germany, studied at Leipzig and Wittenberg. Taught theology in Wittenberg for a while, was a close friend and ardent adherent of Luther, became a distinguished preacher at Frankfort, Eisleben, Wittenberg, and Leipzig. Was Luther's secretary at Leipzig Debate in 1519, was present at both diets of Spires (1526 and 1529), signed both the Augsburg Confession (1530), and the Schmalkald Articles (1537). When a new chair of theology was created at Wittenberg to which he aspired, but to which Melanchthon was appointed, his pride was offended and he fell out with Melanchthon. About this time began to promote a sort of antinomianism in controversy with both Luther and Melanchthon, urging that repentance must be produced by preaching of the gospel, and not of the law, while Luther maintained that both law and gospel should be preached. After growing estrangement from the Reformers, finally fled to Berlin in 1540 under protection of Elector of Brandenburg, and was made court preacher and general superintendent. Was commissioned by elector to help draw up the so-called Augsburg Interim; did much to have it adopted by all Protestant countries, thereby greatly widening the breach between himself and the Reformers. Wrote a number of theological treatises.

AGRICOLA, MICHAEL (c. 1510-1557), Finnish reformer; a learned Swede born in Finland. Studied theology under Martin Luther at the University of Wittenberg. One of the first to write in Finnish vernacular; published version of New Testament in Finnish (1548). In 1554 Gustavus Adolphus appointed him bishop of Abo, and sent him to preach to the Laplanders.

AGRICOLA, RUDOLPHUS (c. 1444-1485), Dutch Reformed humanist, born near Groningen, Holland. He studied at Erfurt, Louvain, and Cologne in Northern Europe, and in Pavia and Ferrara in Italy. Was a close friend of Reuchlin. During and after 1482 was lecturer on Greek and Roman literature at University of Heidelberg and at Worms. In his last two or three years turned his attention to theology, and studied Hebrew.

AIDAN (ā'dŭn) (d. 651), an Irish Celtic monk. About 630 entered the monastery at Iona, the famous island missionary center off the coast of Scotland. In 635 was ordained and sent as bishop to the island of Lindisfarne, near the northeast coast of England. Brought fellow workers to the island, and founded a school for English boys to train them for the church. Efforts to evangelize the community were well supported by friend, Oswald, king of Northumbria, who had earlier studied in Ireland.

AILLY, (å yē) **PIERRE d'** (1350-1420), French theologian and philosopher, bishop and cardinal, born in Campiegne, France, educated at the College of Navarre, becoming its rector in 1384. He became chancellor of the University of Paris, 1389, and almoner and confessor of Charles VI. Was then successively bishop of Le Puy and of Cambrai. Was a teacher and lifelong friend of John Gerson. Was made cardinal in 1411 or 1412, and later papal legate to Germany. Maintained that a general council was superior to the pope, and warmly advocated reform in the church, said the Christian church is founded on the living Christ, not on the erring Peter; on the Bible, not on canon law; existing evils could be cured by a general council. Induced emperor to call Council of Constance, 1414, and took a chief part in it. Departed from traditional practice by instituting method of voting by nations in order to forestall intrigue and the party influence of John XXIII. Though interested in reform and leader of the reform party in the Catholic church, agreed to sentences pronounced against reformers John Huss and Jerome of Prague. Writings were numerous, including guides to contemplation, meditation, and prayer. Luther received much help and inspiration from his writings, especially those which expressed doubts concerning doctrine of transubstantiation. Was a nominalist in philosophy.

AILRED (ăl′rĕd) or **AELRED** or **ETHELRED** (c. 1109-1167), English theologian, historical writer and abbot, born in Hexham, Northumberland, England, spent youth in court of David I, king of Scotland, as attendant to Prince Henry. Then entered abbey of Rievaulx in Yorkshire to become Cistercian monk. Became abbot of Revesby, Lincolnshire; then returned to Rievaulx as abbot in 1147, placing himself at head of Cistercian abbots of England. Did missionary work among Picts of Scotland; wrote historical and theological works. Historical works included lives of *Edward the Confessor, St. Ninian,* and *St. Margaret; Genealogy of the Kings of England.* Also left collection of sermons and other theological writings. Was canonized in 1191.

AINSWORTH, HENRY (1571-1622), English Puritan separatist and rabbinical and Hebraic scholar. Educated at Caius College, Cambridge. After flight to Netherlands served as teacher in Francis Johnson's English congregation. Wrote a confession of faith in 1604, a *Defence* of the Separatists, and the scholarly *Annotations* on the Pentateuch, Psalms and the Song of Solomon.

AITKEN, ROBERT (1734-1802), American printer, publisher, engraver, bookseller; born in Dalkeith, Scotland. Emigrated to Philadelphia in 1769 and opened a bookstore, adding a book bindery two years later. Printed numerous documents and state papers for Continental Congress and war reports and letters for General Washington. The Aitken Bible was the first complete English Bible printed in America (1782). Congress authorized and approved the printing of this Bible. He had prior to this, however, printed four editions of the New Testament.

ALACOQUE (ȧ lȧ kŏk′) **MARGUERITE MARIE** (1647-1690), founder of cult, "The Devotion to the Sacred Heart of Jesus," born at Lhautecour, France. As a child was deeply mystical. In 1671 entered convent of the Visitation at Paray-le-Monial, Burgundy, Central France, where she became novice mistress and assistant superior. Is said to be most notable saint of Order of Visitation or Visitandise, order for women. Sisters of the Visitation became active in deeds of mercy, especially nursing the sick; now devote themselves chiefly to education. Here she claimed to receive several revelations of "Sacred Heart" with command to establish "Devotion to the Sacred Heart of Jesus." Was canonized in 1920. Treatise *Le Devotion au Coeur de Jesus* describes visions.

ALARIC (ăl′ȧ rĭk) (c. 370-410), Visigothic chieftain, born on island in the Danube of one of the noblest Gothic families. Served as a general of the barbarian auxiliaries under Emperor Theodosius I. Theodosius, dying in 395, left the empire to his two sons. Alaric, disappointed in not receiving territory, decided to conquer a kingdom for himself. Was declared king of the Visigoths and marched through Greece conquering the land. Besieged Rome (408, 409, 410); following third siege entered and sacked the city. Alaric led his victorious troops southward to subjugate Sicily, and to found an empire in North Africa. The sacking of Rome with the consequent distress of the people was the occasion of Augustine's *City of God*. Like most of the Goths, Alaric belonged to the Arian branch of Christianity.

ALBERT (ALBRECHT) OF BRANDENBURG (1490-1545), archbishop and cardinal, born in Brandenburg, a prince in House of Hohenzollern. At age eighteen became canon of Mainz; at twenty-three, archbishop of Magdeburg and administrator of diocese of Halberstadt; at twenty-four archbishop and elector of Mainz, holding all three appointments at the same time. At twenty-five stood at head of German clergy; was chancellor of German Empire, and at twenty-eight was made cardinal. Borrowed large sums of money to obtain the archbishopric of Mainz. In 1514 obtained from pope privilege of preaching indulgences in Brandenburg and Saxony to pay his debt, half of the proceeds to be kept by himself. Appointed Johann Tetzel to sell indulgences. Dominican monk Tetzel's conduct paved way for proclamation of Luther's Ninety-five Theses and for the Reformation. Was a friend of Erasmus, following his advice that he have nothing to do with Luther if he cared for his own tranquility. Became, possibly under influence of Jesuits whom he introduced into Germany, violent opponent of Reformation. Took an interest in Council of Trent and appointed legates, but did not live to see its opening.

ALBERTUS MAGNUS (ALBERT THE GREAT), (c. 1200-1280), German philosopher and theologian. Born at Lauingen, Swabia, Southern Germany of a noble family, studied at University of Padua. In 1223 entered Dominican Order. Encyclopedic knowledge earned him the title "Universal Doctor." Preached and taught at Dominican abbey and school at Cologne. Also lectured at University of Paris. In about 1254 was elected provincial of his order in Germany. During his lifetime taught in many places and was a leader in the church. In 1260 was appointed bishop of Regensberg, resigned to continue teaching at Cologne. Chief contribution to the church was teaching and writing. Used voluminous comments of great Arabian scholars to aid him in interpretation of Aristotle. Sought to adapt doctrine of Aristotle to purposes of the church. Was great compiler and commentator rather than original theological genius. Chief theological work was his commentary on the *Sentences* of Peter the Lombard. His teachings were expressed more clearly and forcibly by Thomas Aquinas, his pupil; was canonized by Pope Pius XI in 1932.

ALBRIGHT, JACOB (1759-1808), founder of Evangelical Association of North America, born near Pottstown, Pennsylvania, confirmed a Lutheran. In 1792 joined the Methodists; in 1796 became a licensed Methodist exhorter and itinerant evangelist among Germans in eastern Pennsylvania. Organized a new denomination because Methodists did not wish to start a German church. In 1803 was ordained as presiding elder and chief pastor by General Assembly. Was elected first bishop at first conference, 1807. His Methodist influence and training stamped upon the new church the imprint of Methodistic ideas and ideals, in doctrine and organization. In 1816, his church became Evangelical Association in North America; in 1922 the United Evangelical Church; in 1946 part of Evangelical United Brethren Church; in 1968 part of United Methodist Church.

ALBRIGHT, WILLIAM FOXWELL (1891-1971), orientalist. Born in Coquimbo, Chile. Educated at Upper Iowa University and Johns Hopkins University (Ph.D., 1916). Director of American School of Oriental Research, Jerusalem, 1920-1929, 1933-1936. Professor of Semitic languages, Johns Hopkins, 1929-1958. Research Professor, Jewish Theological Seminary, 1957-1959. Director of archaeological expeditions, Palestine, 1922-1934 and director or member of other archaeological expeditions. President of Palestine Oriental Society in 1921-1922. Wrote over 800 articles or books on archaeological and biblical subjects, such as *The Excavation of Tell Beit Mersim* (1932-1943), *From the Stone Age to Christianity* (1940), *Archaeology of Palestine* (1949). His work helped to supplement, complement, and substantiate the historical accuracy of the Bible and discredit many erroneous ideas of the Bible developed by nineteenth century liberalism.

ALCUIN (al'kwin) or **FLACCUS ALBINUS (EALHWINE)** (c. 735-804), ecclesiastical and educational adviser to Charlemagne, born in northern England, related to Willibrord. Received education at famous cathedral school at York. In 766 succeeded Ethelbert as master of school. After a commission to Rome and his return to England accepted call from Charlemagne about 781 to become master of School of the Palace at Aachen. With the exception of two visits on political business to his native land, spent rest of his life on the Continent. Served Frankish king as head of court school and library which he established; also in many capacities of statecraft. Helped superintend grand reformatory schemes of Charlemagne, helped advance education in the empire, largely wrote Caroline Books on church life for the emperor; helped defend the church against heresy of Adoptionism and image worship. Was given control of several monasteries and income from them. In 796 was appointed by Charlemagne as abbot of St. Martin's of Tours. Under him the school of Tours became nursery of ecclesiastical and liberal education for the whole kingdom. When age and failing sight caused him to give up the management of schools, continued as counselor of the emperor until his own death in 804. Was loyal to the pope and the emperor. Was part of great Carolingian renaissance; contributed much to educational, religious, and cultural advancement of Europe. Purposed to elevate and educate clergy and monks, improve preaching, regulate life of the people, and advance faith among the heathen by instruction rather than force. Promoted classical learning, but not at expense of ecclesiastical. Was ardent student of church Fathers. Had many notable pupils, Rabanus Maurus being most famous. Writings include commentaries on books of the Bible (based upon the church Fathers), a work on the Trinity, biographies, poems and hymns, textbooks of grammar, orthography, and rhetoric.

ALEXANDER I (1777-1825), as Czar of Russia (1810-1825) held and practiced liberal democratic ideas in the Russian empire but was autocratic in Russia. Influenced by Juliania von Krüdener, a Russian-born Pietist, he persuaded the sovereigns of Europe to sign the Holy Alliance in 1815 which committed them to Christian principles in international relations.

ALEXANDER II (ANSELMO BACKGIUS) (d. 1073), pope (1061-1073), born of noble family at Baggio, near Milan, Italy. Ordained priest in 1155 and in 1057 appointed bishop of Lucca by Emperor Henry III of Germany. Served twice as papal legate to Milan; in 1061 through influence of Cardinal Hildebrand was elected pope. Was driven from Rome when imperial party elected Cadalus, bishop of Parma, as rival pope taking the name Honorius II. In 1064 Council of Mantua declared him legitimate pope and he was seated permanently in Rome. Honorius II was excommunicated, but contest continued until anti-pope's death, 1072. Reign under influence of Hildebrand and Peter Damiani carried out church reform according to Cluniac reform pattern, involving abrogation of simony and clerical marriage, and emancipation of church from secular control. Came into conflict with Henry IV, emperor of Germany, but soon died leaving contest to successor, Gregory VII. Favored William the Conqueror's invasion of England and Norman conquest of Italy.

ALEXANDER III (ROLANDO BANDINELLI) (d. 1181), pope (1159-1181), born in Siena, taught canon law at Bologna from about 1140. About 1150 was made cardinal. Anti-popé supported by Emperor Frederick I (Barbarossa); Alexander placed under imperial ban, spent time in exile. In 1176, when Frederick lost battle of Legnano, Frederick was forced to recognize Alexander and sign Peace of Venice, 1177. Gained a still greater triumph when he forced Henry II of England to do penance at grave of Thomas à Becket, and to withdraw offending articles of Constitutions of Clarendon. Pope excommunicated William the Lion of Scotland for opposing him. Crowning triumph in Alexander's success marked by Third Lateran Council, 1179. Cathari were excommunicated and Peter Waldo and companions, and Humiliati forbidden to preach; and above all, council passed canon which vested exclusive right of papal election in two-thirds vote of cardinals; conferred on pope alone right of canonization. When new anti-pope elected, Alexander again driven from Rome. Died in exile at Civata Castellana.

ALEXANDER VI (RODRIGO BORGIA or **BORJA)** (c. 1431-1503), pope (1492-1503), born at Xativa, near Valetia, Spain. Lived with uncle, Pope Calixtus III; thenceforth was destined for the church. Studied law for a time at University of Bologna. Early life flagrantly dissolute. Fond uncle made Rodrigo cardinal-deacon in 1456 and cardinal-bishop a little later; bestowed upon him many archbishoprics, bishoprics, abbacies, and other appointments. For several years had as mistress Vanozza dei Cattanei, who bore him at least five illegitimate children—Pedro Luis, Juan, Caesar, Lucretia, and Joffre. Rodrigo gave his children lucrative and prominent positions in both church and state. In 1492, after being cardinal and since 1456 vice-chancellor to pope upon death of Innocent VIII, succeeded in buying enough votes of cardinals in conclave to secure election to papacy. Took name of Alexander VI, and became notoriously corrupt pope. Bent every energy to make his son Caesar Borgia great, powerful, wealthy in ecclesiastical circles; failing in this, appropriated church funds to give his son power and position in political world. Alexander VI proved to be able and strong administrator and politician. Recovered territories of Papal States, apportioned new world between Spain and Portugal (1493-1494), condemned Savonarola to be burned as a heretic, and originated the Index Expurgatorius. Supported crusade against Moors in Spain in 1498. Called into being Jubilee celebration in 1500, which brought hundreds of thousands of pilgrims and great sums of money to Rome. To gain his ends, whether personal or ecclesiastical, employed weapons of the age—perjury, poison, and dagger. He subsidized Michaelangelo's creation of the Pietà. Was a true Machiavellian, was patron of the arts and sciences, a typical Renaissance pope.

ALEXANDER, ARCHIBALD (1772-1851), American Presbyterian educator and theologian. Born near Lexington, Virginia. Tutored by the Rev. William Graham, who had opened Liberty Hall Academy near Alexander home. Studied theology with Mr. Graham; was ordained in 1794. Spent several years as itinerant missionary in Virginia. Became president of Hampden Sidney College, 1796, and in 1806 pastor of Third Presbyterian Church (Pine Street), Philadelphia. In 1812 General Assembly established Princeton Theological Seminary. He became its first professor from 1812 to 1851. Over eighteen hundred candidates for Christian ministry studied under him. Through preaching and writing wielded beneficient influence upon church. Some writings were, *A Brief Outline of the Evidences of the Christian Religion* and *The Canon of the Old and New Testaments Ascertained*.

ALEXANDER, CECIL F. (c. 1823-1895), Irish hymn writer. Born in Dublin. Married William Alexander, a country rector, who became Archbishop of Armagh. She wrote about 400 hymns. Best known hymns are "Once in Royal David's City," "There is a Green Hill Far Away," "All Things Bright and Beautiful," and "Jesus Calls, O'er the Tumult."

ALEXANDER, CHARLES McCALLON (1867-1920), evangelistic gospel song leader and personal worker. Born on farm at Meadow, Tennessee of Christian parents; educated in Maryville Academy and College near parental home. Took advanced musical training at Washington College; became musical director for short time at Maryville College. Went to Bible Institute of Chicago in 1890, now Moody Bible Institute, to prepare for evangelistic work. Became associated with Dwight L. Moody, 1893, in revival services connected with World's Fair in Chicago. Was singing associate of Milan B. Williams in evangelistic campaigns in Middle West, chiefly Iowa, 1894-1901. Worked with R. A. Torrey in globe-girdling campaigns in Australia, Tasmania, New Zealand, India, England, Ireland, Scotland, Canada, and the United States, 1902-1906. In 1904 married Helen Cadbury of Birmingham, England, who made a world tour with him in 1906-1907. Made their home in Birmingham. From 1908 to close of his life was associated with J. Wilbur Chapman in campaigns to countries in Europe, Asia, and America. During World War I campaign carried them into army camps, where they did much effective evangelistic work. Supported Pocket Testament League started by Helen Cadbury. During Chapman-Alexander campaign in Philadelphia, 1908, League formally launched as worldwide Bible-reading movement. Was not a composer; left no permanent literature or musical compositions.

ALEXANDER OF ALEXANDRIA (d. 328), patriarch of Alexandria (c. 312-328). Was proponent of orthodoxy when Arian heresy broke out between him and Arius, an eloquent parish priest in an Alexandrian church. Controversy became so sharp that Alexander called synod in Alexandria which had Arius and friends condemned and excommunicated. Arius found refuge with friend and fellow student of Lucian School, powerful bishop, Eusebius of Nicomedia, and continued propagation of anti-trinitarian views. Meanwhile, with help of able young archdeacon and private secretary, Athanasius, Alexander promoted trinitarian view among clergymen. Controversy became so involved that Emperor Constantine intervened. Failing to effect reconciliation through mediation of Hosius, bishop of Cordova, Spain, Constantine called council of entire church at Nicea in 325, which became first Ecumenical Council. Traveling and other expenses of those representing churches at gathering paid out of state treasury. Athanasius assumed leadership in defense of orthodox trinitarian doctrine, at and following time of council. In 328, after death of Alexander, Athanasius succeeded him as bishop of Alexandria.

ALEXANDER OF HALES (hālz), (c. 1185-1245), English scholastic theologian. Called "Irrefragable Doctor." Born Hales, Gloucestershire, England; received early education at monastic school in native village and Oxford. At University of Paris attained master's degree in philosophy and theology. About 1220 joined faculty of theology in University of Paris, where became celebrated teacher; continued teaching until 1238; meanwhile (1236) had joined Franciscan Order. Was first to teach and popularize Christian theology in light of Aristotle's writings. Sought to harmonize Aristotle with Augustinianism. Held high regard for Augustine's writings; held Scripture as only final truth. Said in worldly things knowledge proceeds from rational conviction; in spiritual things faith precedes knowledge. Theology is therefore rather body of wisdom than a science; not so much knowledge drawn from study as knowledge drawn from experience. In this teaching, in definition of treasury of merit, in distinction between "attrition" and "contrition," in development of doctrine of penance, in defense of doctrine of purgatory, in teaching on transubstantiation, he had controlling influence over later schoolmen. Was a moderate realist. Chief work was *Summa Theologica,* completed by his pupils.

ALEXANDER OF JERUSALEM (d. 251), Bishop of Jerusalem. Early friend and fellow student with Origen under Clement of Alexandria in catechetical school. Became bishop of see in Asia Minor at beginning of third century; suffered imprisonment in persecution under Septimus Severus, 204-212. Here was visited in prison by old teacher, Clement. After release in 212, visited Jerusalem and was chosen coadjutor to aged bishop Narcissus. This is first case on record of translation of a bishop from one see to another; also of appointment of coadjutor bishop. On death of Narcissus, succeeded as sole bishop of Jerusalem. Fame rests on Christian library founded at Jerusalem, first of its kind; and upon boldness of support and defense of Origen against Bishop Demetrius of Alexandria, when Origen offended Bishop Demetrius by preaching in Caesarea at invitation of Bishop Alexander. Also helped ordain Origen as presbyter at Caesarea, act that led to Demetrius calling two synods in Alexandria to condemn and banish Origen. Was imprisoned again, this time under Decius; died in prison at Caesarea.

ALEXIUS I COMNENUS (Kŏm. nē̆ nŭs) (1048-1118), emperor of the Eastern Empire (1081-1118). Defended it from Eastern invaders. His appeal to the West for help was a factor in bringing about the First Crusade. The *Alexiad* (1148) by his daughter Anna describes in detail the account of his reign.

ALFORD, HENRY (1810-1871), biblical scholar and critic, born in London; studied at Trinity College, Cambridge. Was elected deacon, 1833, priest the next year. Became vicar of Wymeswold, Leicestershire, England, 1835, remaining there eighteen years. Became minister of Quebec Chapel in London, 1853; dean of Canterbury (1857-1871). Was an original member of New Testament Revision Committee. Great work was edition of *Greek New Testament,* made distinguished by introducing to English readers German learning of Olshausen, Stier, Meyer, and Tischendorf. His digest of German New Testament exegesis has permanent value. Editor of *Expositor's Greek Testament* and author of *How to Study the New Testament*. He edited the works of John Donne (1839), composed the hymns: "Ten Thousand Times Ten Thousand" and "Come Ye Thankful People Come". First editor of *Contemporary Review.*

ALFRED THE GREAT (849-899), king of West Saxons, born at Wantage, Berkshire, England. In youth was educated at Rome; resided for a time at French court of Charles the Bald. In 871 succeeded to throne of Wessex on death of brother Ethelred. Was first in war, first in peace of all Anglo-Saxon rulers. Instituted valuable military reforms, improved navy, earned title "Protector of the Poor" by concern for administration of justice. Conquered invading Danes by land and sea, delivering England from foreign rule. Was both churchman and patron of education, thus introducing new era of religious education. Conceived plan of general education for people; founded school in Oxford to which British and foreign scholars were invited to occupy influential positions, among them John Scotus Erigena and Asser. Enhanced own education by learning Latin in his thirties under Asser. Translated standard works from Latin to Anglo-Saxon; made collections of choice sentences from Bible and church Fathers. During reign, *Anglo-Saxon Chronicle* was being compiled—beginning of writing of English history. Loved justice, sought to treat all subjects with fairness and respect. Codified laws for them.

ALLEINE, JOSEPH (1634-1668), born at Devizes in Wiltshire. Studied at Lincoln College and Corpus Christi College, Oxford. Tutor and chaplain in Corpus Christi College. Ordained as Presbyterian minister in 1655 and became assistant at St. Mary Magdalene Church in Taunton until he was ejected in 1662. Imprisoned in 1663 for singing psalms and preaching to his family in his own home. About 70 thousand copies of his most important work, *An Alarm to the Unconverted* (1672) and its republication in 1675 as *Sure Guide to Heaven,* were sold.

ALLEN, ETHAN (c. 1738-1789), born at Litchfield, Connecticut. Revolutionary leader of the Green Mountain Boys of Vermont in the struggle to keep land grants disputed by New York in the 1770s. Captured Fort Ticonderoga in 1775 during the American Revolution. Became a deist and wrote *Reason the Only Oracle of Man* (1785) in which he rejected biblical special revelation and condemned "tyranny" of church leaders. Reason alone, he argued, through science would unlock the scientific and religious secrets of nature.

ALLEN, HORACE NEWTON (1858-1932), Presbyterian missionary surgeon and diplomat, born in Delaware, Ohio; graduated from Ohio Wesleyan University (1881). Studied medicine at Miami Medical College (1883), in Cincinnati, Ohio. Went as Presbyterian medical missionary to China. Went to Korea, 1884, as first Protestant missionary entering Korea after signing of treaty between Korea and United States in 1882. Medical skill in saving life of a relative of the queen Minyonik brought him high favor at court for himself and the mission. Was made court physician and established hospital under government control. When first Korean legation went to Washington, 1887, acted as interpreter and secretary; then returned in 1890 to Korea as United States secretary of legation. In 1897 was made United States minister there; served as minister until 1905. Wrote *Korean Tales, Korea: Fact and Fancy, Things Korean,* and *A Chronological Index of the Foreign Relation of Korea from the Beginning of the Christian Era to the Twentieth Century.*

ALLEN, RICHARD (1760-1831), first black Methodist bishop in America, born of slave parents, in Philadelphia. When seventeen was converted with other members of his family; joined Methodist church. Under preaching and spiritual influence of Freeborn Garretson, owner led to encourage Richard and his brother to purchase freedom. Ordained in 1784 and became itinerant preacher. In 1786 invited to preach in St. George's Methodist Church where held membership. Racial discrimination led to separation of races in congregation. In 1787 with Absolom Jones, another free black Methodist, organized Free African Society to help with economic needs of black members. In 1791 group decided to adopt church government. Some incorporated as African Episcopal Church of St. Thomas, with Jones as pastor. Allen held to Methodism and organized others into Bethel African Methodist Episcopal Church. Bishop Asbury preached dedicatory sermon in 1794. In 1799 Allen was ordained deacon, in 1816, elder. Until 1816 church was integral part of Methodist Episcopal church; but in that year Allen organized it with other independent black churches into separate denomination, African Methodist Episcopal church. Was chosen by new church as first bishop (1816-1831). Continued as pastor of original Bethel Church in Philadelphia as well as bishop of new church.

ALLEN, WILLIAM (1532-1594), Roman Catholic scholar, teacher and cardinal. Born in Rosall, Lancashire. Educated at Oriel College, Oxford. Principal of St. Mary's Hall in 1556. Left England and ordained in 1565. Founded college at Douai, France (1568) to train priests to win England back to the Roman Catholic faith. Inspired and supervised the production of the Douai version of the Bible from 1578. Cardinal in 1587. Supported the Spanish Armada and intrigues against Elizabeth.

ALLINE, HENRY (1748-1784), Canadian revivalist. Born in Newport, Rhode Island. Converted and called to preach in 1775. Leader of the Great Awakening in Nova Scotia, Canada. His followers were known as Newlights. His autobiographical *Two Mites Cast into the Offering of God for the Benefit of Mankind* (1781) was also a journal of that revival. Indirectly a force in the disintegration of Congregationalism and in the development of the Baptist church in that area.

ALLIS, OSWALD THOMPSON (1880-1973), Old Testament scholar and editor. Born in Wallingford, Pennsylvania. Educated at Princeton University, Princeton Theological Seminary and the University of Berlin (Ph.D., 1913). Professor at Princeton Theological Seminary (1918-1929) and Westminster Theological Seminary (1929-1936). Was for many years editor of *The Princeton Theological Review.* Author of *The First Five Books of Moses* and *The Unity of Isaiah* in which he upheld conservative theology.

ALOPEN (seventh century), first Christian Nestorian missionary to China. According to the Nestorian tablet discovered at Hsianfu in Shensi Province, China, in 1625, he went to China A.D. 635 when T'ai Tsung was emperor in the T'ang Dynasty. Established a church that existed with royal favor for about a century and a half. It seems great numbers adhered to the Christian faith. About 845 a great reaction seems to have set in against both Christianity and Buddhism. The blow severely checked the growth of Nestorian Christianity, though the faith did not die out at that time. Remnants of Nestorianism were there when, in the early part of the eleventh century, a call was made to the West for missionaries to be sent, and again in the thirteenth century when Kublai Khan called for one hundred missionaries, again when John of Monte Corvino reached Peking in 1291.

ALSTYNE, FRANCES JANE VAN. See **CROSBY, FANNY J.**

ALTHAUS, PAUL (1888-1966), Lutheran expositor, biblical critic and theologian. From 1914 he taught successively in Göttingen, Rostock, and Erlangen. Noted for his expositions of Paul's epistles, his study of the Synoptic problem, and his theological work, *Die Christliche Wahrheit: Lehrbuch der Dogmatik*. Concerned specially with justification by faith, the relation of the law and the gospel, and church-state relations.

ALVA, FERNANDO ALVAREZ DE TOLEDO, DUKE (1508-1582), Spanish general, born of noble Castilian family; trained from boyhood by grandfather, Frederick of Toledo, to be warrior and statesman. From age sixteen was on battlefield fighting wars in France, Italy, Africa, Hungary, Germany, Netherlands, Portugal. Served under Emperor Charles V and King Philip II of Spain. Like Philip, was deceitful, fanatical, cruel, merciless. Was one of ablest generals of the age; unwise in governing. Notoriety rests upon his cruel dealing with inhabitants of Netherlands. Sent by Philip into low countries with army to subdue people that revolted against Spain, and to exterminate heresy against church. Made triumphal entry into Brussels in 1567. In six years there were thousands sentenced to death by his court, called "Council of Blood." Oppressive taxes imposed, trade brought completely to standstill. With more oppression came more rebellion; people seized chief coast towns, attacked Spanish shipping, cut dikes. As reward for services to the faith, Pope Pius V presented him with consecrated hat and sword, distinction heretofore reserved for sovereigns. Was recalled, 1573. In 1580 given command of campaign against Portugal, which was successful, and helped temporarily make that country part of Spain.

ALYPIUS (å lĭp'ŭs) (died after 430), Bishop of Tagaste; born at Tagaste, Numidia, friend and pupil of Augustine. Went with Augustine to Rome to study law; obtained position there in imperial treasury, later accompanying Augustine to Milan. As followed Augustine into Manichaeism, so followed him into Christianity. Easter eve, 387, he, Augustine, and the latter's son Adeodatus baptized by Bishop Ambrose of Milan. Returned with Augustine to Africa, lived with him at Tagaste until 391 when Augustine ordained priest by people of Hippo; Alypius became abbot of monastery Augustine established at Hippo. Made a trip to the Holy Land where met Jerome; in 394 became bishop of Tagaste. Present at Council of Carthage (411) a Catholic representative in conference with Donatists.

AMBROSE (c. 340-397), Bishop of Milan, son of Roman of high rank, born in Gaul. At time of birth, father was prefect of one of four great prefectures of empire, one including Gaul, Britain, Spain. Father died early and family moved to Rome where Ambrose was educated for legal profession. Later was appointed civil governor over large territory, having headquarters at Milan. Made admirable magistrate; known as high-minded, conscientious, religious. When Auxentius, Arian bishop of Milan, died, strife between Catholic and Arian party threatened; Ambrose in consular authority went to church to maintain order. Some one cried, "Ambrose for bishop!" Crowd took up shout, "We will have Ambrose for bishop!" Though only catechist, not baptized, though long Christian at heart, was pressed to accept this popular election. Received baptism, summarily passed through intermediary offices; on eighth day was consecrated bishop of Milan. Had reluctantly accepted office; entered upon duties in humble but devoted spirit. Feeling deficiency of theological education, went to work studying the Bible and Greek theologians and preachers. Preached regularly on Sundays, often on other occasions. Had to begin to learn and teach at same time. Entered bishopric A.D. 374, for twenty-three years labored indefatigably as Bishop of Milan. Was orthodox in doctrine, was excellent orator and preacher. One secret of success in church was admission of people into all interests and cares. Though firm disciplinarian, was greatly beloved. When Theodosius massacred over seven thousand at Thessalonica in 390, Ambrose refused to give him communion until he repented. One significant result of preaching was conversion of Augustine; it fell to lot of Ambrose to baptize great bishop of Hippo. One difficult task was keeping peace between Catholics and Arians, at same time defending orthodox doctrine. As writer, left multitude of works, consisting largely of addresses and expositions; show competent learning and intellectual liveliness. The bishop of Milan noted, too, for composition of hymns, for particular style of music known as Ambrosian chant and for introducing congregational singing. See of Milan not dependent upon that of Rome, yet Ambrose showed respect to bishop of Rome, helping to develop unity of Catholic church.

AMMANN, JACOB (c. 1644-c. 1711), founder of Amish Mennonites. Mennonite minister from either Alsace or Switzerland; insisted on following strictly Eighteen Articles of Confession of Faith, adopted, 1632, by early Mennonites at Dortrecht, Holland. Special point of divergence was relative to "avoidance" or the "ban." Visited all Mennonite churches in Switzerland and Alsace, emphasizing doctrine and practice of "avoidance." Held this practice to be necessary. With about forty-five hundred followers severed relations with Mennonite church, 1693. Though attempts made about turn of century to effect reconciliation, efforts proved unsuccessful, the schism continued, to this day is perpetuated in Amish Mennonites. Little more known of Ammann's life.

AMES, WILLIAM (1576-1633), Puritan theologian and casuist. Born at Ipswich, Suffolk. Educated at Christ's College, Cambridge where he was influenced by William Perkins his tutor. Chaplain to English governor of Brill in Holland. Advised Calvinists at the Synod of Dort. Professor of theology from 1622 and rector (1626) of the University of Franeker until 1633. Attacked Arminianism and defended Calvinism in his 1623 *Medulla Theologiae* (English translation, *The Marrow of Sacred Divinity* [1642]) which greatly influenced later Puritanism. Set forth Reformed casuistry in *De Conscientia* (1632).

AMMONIUS SACCAS (am mō'ni us săk'kas) (c. 174-242), founder of Neo-Platonism. Purpose was to harmonize doctrines of Plato and Aristotle; hence his school called Eclectic or Neo-Platonic school. Among pupils were the Christian Origen, and the pagan Plotinus.

AMSDORF, NIKOLAUS VON (1483-1565), German Protestant theologian and reformer.

Educated at Wittenberg where he later taught theology. Ordained in 1524 as pastor and superintendent at Magdeburg. Lutheran bishop, 1542-1547. Founded the University of Jena. Superintendent at Eisenach from 1552. In the Lutheran controversy over good works he argued that they were useless and even harmful. Died at Jena.

ANACLETUS (an a klē'tus) or **CLETUS** (first century), third bishop (pope) of Rome, following Linus, preceding Clement, according to Roman Catholic tradition and list of popes. Was bishop about 79-92.

ANDERSON, SIR ROBERT (1841-1918), British barrister and writer, born in Dublin, Ireland in Christian home, converted at age nineteen. Was educated at Trinity College, Dublin, entered legal profession in Ireland, 1863; in 1868 became adviser on Irish affairs to Home Office in matters relating to political crime. Showed skill and tact in dealing with plots of Irish and American-Irish conspirators. Retired, 1877, called back to service, 1880. In 1888 was appointed head of Criminal Investigation Department. With all duties of state, found time to delve deeply into theology; wrote and preached with conviction and authority on theological subjects. Books show staunch respect and conviction for fundamental truths of the Bible. Spoke boldly and critically against critics. Over half a century was preacher of the gospel, in church and mission hall, to rich and poor, to learned and unlearned. Was frequent speaker at Mildmay Conferences; was associated with Evangelical Alliance, Prophecy Investigation Society, Lawyers' Prayer Union, Bible League, Alliance of Honor, various denominational organizations. A few of his many literary works are: *The Coming Prince, Daniel in the Critic's Den, The Silence of God, The Bible and Modern Criticism* and *Pseudo-Criticism: Or the Higher Criticism and Its Counterfeit.* Wrote words for beautiful hymn, "Safe in Jehovah's Keeping."

ANDERSON, RUFUS (1796-1880), American Congregational foreign missions secretary, born at North Yarmouth, Maine, graduated from Bowdoin College and Andover Theological Seminary. After acting as assistant for ten years, 1822-1832, became secretary of American Board of Commissioners for Foreign Missions, holding office until 1866. From 1866 to 1874 was member of Prudential Committee. Was lecturer on foreign missions in Andover Theological Seminary, 1867-1869. Officially visited the missions of board in Mediterranean area, India, Hawaiian Islands. Volume in which were published proceedings of deputation became authority in Europe as well as America. Dr. Robert E. Speer classed to Anderson as one of the two greatest foreign mission secretaries. Among writings were: *Observations on the Peloponnesus and Greek Islands, Foreign Missions: Their Relations and Claims, A Heathen Nation Evangelized,* and *The Hawaiian Islands.* Was strong advocate of training young churches to develop independence in administration, support, propagation as rapidly as possible. Was educational promoter in America. In 1837 helped found Mount Holyoke Female Seminary at South Hadley, Massachusetts; was for several years president of board of trustees of Bradford Academy, Massachusetts; member of board of trustees of Andover Theological Seminary.

ANDREAE (än drā'ĕ) **JACOB** (1528-1590), post-Reformation Lutheran theologian, born at Waiblingen, Württemberg, Germany, educated at Paedagogium at Stuttgart and at University of Tübingen. Upon leaving University, 1546, was made deacon in Stuttgart. Though pastoral life and activity chiefly in Stuttgart, where was highly esteemed as strong and eloquent preacher, labors and influence reached far outside this city. In 1561 became professor of theology at University of Tübingen; was active in sharing in doctrinal disputations of the time. With Martin Chemnitz was a chief architect of Formula of Concord. Formula of Concord completed and accepted, 1577; included in Book of Concord, 1580 of which he was the editor. Was noted debater and wise counselor among brethren. In later life traveled in Bohemia and Germany working for consolidation of Lutheran Reformation. Was author of more than 150 works, chiefly polemical writings against Calvinism.

ANDREAE JOHANN VALENTIN (1586-1654), German Lutheran theologian and satirist, born at Herrenberg, near Tübingen, Württemberg, Germany, studied at University of Tübingen. Became deacon, 1614. In 1619 wrote *Res Publicae Christianopolitana,* a description of a model state based on that at Geneva. During Thirty Years' War served local community as physician, minister, and gravedigger, when people were carried off in great numbers by slaughter and plague. In 1639 was called to Stuttgart to become court preacher. There helped reorganize church system and schools which had largely fallen into ruin during the war. In 1650 became general superintendent of Württemberg, which he had to give up due to failing health.

ANDREW OF CRETE (c. 660-740), Archbishop of Crete, born at Damascus. As young man entered monastery in Jerusalem, becoming known also as Andrew of

Jerusalem. Sent by Patriarch Theodore of Jerusalem to Sixth Ecumenical Council at Constantinople, 680, where was ordained deacon of St. Sophia. About 692 was made archbishop of Crete, which church he governed for many years. Was member of pseudo-synod of Constantinople, 712, which nullified council of 680 and restored Monothelite heresy; later renounced his error and returned to orthodoxy. This change and advocacy of image veneration, numbered him among saints. Besides sermons, homilies, and orations, wrote many hymns, some included in Greek Service Books. Among Greek hymn writers occupies a prominent place as inventor of so-called canons. His penitential canon, the "Great Canon" of 250 stanzas, is especially famous.

ANDREWES, LANCELOT (1555-1626), High Churchman and Anglican preacher, born at Barking, near London, in time of Mary Tudor ("Bloody Mary"). Received good education at Pembroke Hall, Cambridge, afterward becoming its master. Was ordained to priesthood in 1580 and became eloquent preacher. Was for a while prebendary of St. Paul's, became chaplain to Queen Elizabeth and dean of Westminster; then successively bishop of Chichester, Ely, Winchester. Was thoroughgoing High churchman, devoted to episcopacy and King James. Was one of first appointees to commission assigned to translating Authorized or King James version of the Bible, his part being first twelve books of the Old Testament. Was man of austere piety, rigorous in performance of private devotion, liberal in charities, one of the most learned men of his time. Though sermons are controversial in character, his prayers and meditations in his *Private Devotions* (1648) breathe spirit of mystical devotion.

ANDREWS (ăn'drōōz) **CHARLES FREER** (1871-1940), English clergyman and Indian resident for thirty-five years, born at Newcastle-on-Tyne, England, died at Calcutta, India. Educated at King Edward VI School, Birmingham, and Pembroke College, Cambridge. Father was minister in Catholic Apostolic church (Irvingite); went to India as Anglican clergyman in connection with Cambridge Mission, 1904. That same year joined Cambridge Brotherhood at Delhi. Associated many years with St. Stephens College at Delhi. Remained unmarried, was very close friend and admirer of Rabindranath Tagore and Mohandas Gandhi. Identified himself largely with India and its people, seeing in their religious quest, quest for God even outside pale of traditional Christian claims of the Gospel as way of salvation. Traveled widely, not only in India, but much of the world, seeking to be reconciler of races and champion of oppressed. Supported Gandhi in claims for Indian laborers in South Africa; represented Indians at Fiji, Kenya, and British Guiana in labor problems. Became outstanding authority on India, Indian labor, drink and opium problems of India. Was correspondent of *Manchester Guardian, Natal Advertiser, Toronto Star, Modern Review* in Calcutta. Some writings were *Renaissance in India, Mahatma Gandhi's Ideas, Mahatma Gandhi: His Own Story, Mahatma Gandhi at Work, Sadhu Sundar Singh, Christ and Prayer, The True India, The Drink and Opium Evil, Indian Independence*.

ANGELA de MERICI (ăn'jelȧ dā mā rē'chĕ) or **ANGELA of BRESCIA** (1474-1540), founder of Ursulines, born at Desenzano, near Verona, Italy. In youth became Franciscan tertiary. At twenty left convent and began teaching children elements of Christianity. Was called to Brescia to teach and there spent the rest of her life. In 1535 helped found order of the Ursuline nuns to teach little children, aid the poor, care for the sick. Was mother superior of order last five years of her life. Members not required to take vows nor live in convents. Died in 1540, canonized in 1807.

ANGELICO, FRA (da FIESOLE) (1378-1455), a celebrated Florentine painter, born near Castello di Vicchio in Tuscany. Was Dominican monk, devout Christian, most religious painter of Renaissance period. Was convicted that to picture Christ perfectly the painter himself must be Christlike. Accordingly, it is said he prefaced paintings with prayer. Commissioned by Nicholas V to decorate one chapel of Vatican. Painted "The Last Judgment," "The Coronation of the Virgin," "The Madonna of the Star."

ANGUS, JOSEPH (1816-1902), Baptist educator, born at Bolan, Northumberland, England. Studied at King's College, London, Stepney College, London, Edinburgh University. After graduating spent two years at New Park Street Church, Southwark, in pulpit filled by Charles Haddon Spurgeon sixteen years later. In 1842 secretary of Baptist Missionary Society. In 1849 called to presidency of Stepney College, now known as Regent's Park College, London, retiring in 1893. In 1865 was chosen president of Baptist Union, highest honor church could give him. In seventies became member of New Testament Revision Committee. Always remained interested in work of Baptist Missionary Society. Privileged to moderate both golden jubilee of missionary society in

1842 as secretary of the society, and centenary, in 1892, year before retiring from presidency of the college. Among his more important religious writings is *Bible Handbook of the English Tongue*.

ANNE (1665-1714), ruler of England, 1702-1714. Strongly supported the Anglican church. Provided before her death for the Protestant House of Hanover (now Windsor) peacefully to take over the English throne. During her reign (in 1717) Scotland was united with England.

ANSELM (ăn'sĕlm) (1033-1109), born in northern Italy. Father of Schoolmen, a great theologian of eleventh century. Father not a religious man, but his mother, Ermenburga, was pious, devout, Christian woman, rearing her son with studious care. After mother's early death, and a quarrel with his father, went to England and in 1060 entered a monastery in Bec, where Lanfranc was abbot. After Lanfranc became archbishop of Canterbury, Anselm became in 1063 abbot of Bec; in 1093 succeeded as archbishop of Canterbury. In this office stoutly maintained church's privileges against arrogance of the king; he was banished; later recalled. During banishment wrote famous treatise on incarnation and atonement of our Lord, *Cur Deus Homo (Why God Man),* in which he states that sin leaves man with a debt of sin through disobedience to God. Only Christ's death cancels that debt. This idea was in opposition to the patristic idea that Christ's death was a ransom to Satan. Is said to have been most original thinker in church following days of Augustine. Was realist; endeavored to prove ontologically existence of God in *Proslogion*. Our idea of God demands real existence of such a being. Put faith foremost in philosophy saying, "I believe that I may understand." Was a great man in whom mysticism combined with scholasticism, gentleness with strength of character, pious devotion with lofty speculation, prayer with logical analysis.

ANSKAR or ANSGAR (ans'gär) (801-865), missionary, "Apostle to the North." French Benedictine monk, born of Frankish parents near Amiens, in northwestern France, educated at famous monastery of Corbie. Accepted call from Christian king and queen of Denmark for a missionary. Established a mission and school for boys in Schleswig. Two years later the king became unpopular and had to flee; Ansgar spent two years in Sweden. Then a new king came to the throne of Denmark and recalled Ansgar. In 829 bishopric established at Hamburg for all northern country and Ansgar consecrated first bishop; later Bremen and Hamburg united and he was made archbishop in 831 over enlarged diocese. Using Bremen as base, continued to extend mission endeavor in Denmark and Sweden. Following appointment to archbishopric, made a trip to Rome to receive papal consecration, bestowal of pallium, papal commission as legate to the Swedes, Danes, Slavs, other races of the North. Amid vicissitudes and opposition, succeeded in breaking down opposition from kings of Denmark and Sweden and laid foundations for Christianity in those lands. Yet those countries were not won to Christianity until nearly 150 years later.

ANTHONY (ANTONIUS) (c. 251-356), the "founder of Christian monasticism," born at Coma in Upper Egypt of wealthy Coptic Christian parents. Education very limited. Sought to follow the Scriptures literally, especially as to personal life. After death of parents, when about eighteen, he became a hermit. First attempted to live the self-denying life in his own village, then moved to a sepulcher; then for twenty years lived in the ruins of an old castle on mountain, Der el Memum, on the east bank of the Nile. Lived in strict solitude there except for a trip down mountain twice a year to get food, which consisted of bread and salt with occasionally a few dates. He drank only water, slept on the ground or at best on a pallet of straw. His wardrobe consisted of a hair shirt, a sheepskin, and a girdle. Sought solitude in order to get away from society, even from monks who sought his words of counsel. In 311 during the persecution of Maximian, appeared in Alexandria to encourage the martyrs, hoping himself to gain the martyr's crown. Withdrew to more complete isolation near the Red Sea. About 335 at the urgent invitation of Athanasius, appeared at Alexandria to help defend the orthodox faith against Arianism. Then saying "As a fish out of water, so a monk out of solitude dies," he went back into solitude. About five years later, age 105, in the presence of two disciples who ministered to his wants during his last fifteen years, he died. According to instructions, his body secretly buried in the desert. Anthony had great influence upon the church for many centuries. Many of the church Fathers followed his ascetic zeal. Athanasius wrote his biography.

ANTHONY, SUSAN BROWNELL (1820-1906), American reformer, born at South Adams, Massachusetts of Quaker family. Received education chiefly at Friends Boarding School at West Philadelphia; taught school for fifteen years. Early became interested in temperance and anti-slavery, and co-education. In 1852 assisted in organizing the Woman's New York

State Temperance Society, first women's state temperance society in America. In 1856 became a leader in the anti-slavery movement, and in 1858 advocated the co-education of the sexes. After the Civil War devoted herself to black and woman suffrage movements and was elected president in 1869 of the American Woman Suffrage Association, which she helped organize. In 1868 founded, and for three years published *The Revolution,* a woman's rights paper. Was vice-president-at-large of the National Woman's Suffrage Association from the date of its origin in 1869 until 1892, when she became president. In Rochester, New York in 1872 for casting her vote in the presidential election, she was arrested and fined one hundred dollars, which she refused to pay. For almost forty years after the Civil War traveled in the United States and England, lecturing and promoting the cause of women's rights. In 1888 organized the International Council of Women.

ANTHONY or **ANTONY OF PADUA** (1195-1231), Franciscan monk and preacher, born at Lisbon, Portugal, baptized as Ferdinand. At fifteen joined the Augustinian Order, received a good education at the University of Coimbra. About 1220 joined the Conventuals of the new Franciscan Order, changed name to Anthony in honor of St. Anthony; became the most celebrated follower of St. Francis. Sailed to North Africa to preach to the Muslims, hoping there to become a martyr. After a long siege of illness became a preacher. Leaving Africa, and hearing of general council of his order that was going on at Assisi, went there, met St. Francis, founder and head of his order. Entered a hermitage where he learned humility and practiced asceticism. When with several others he came up in 1222 for ordination to the priesthood, he was called upon to preach before the brothers, he brilliantly demonstrated oratorical ability. With the consent of St. Francis he was made preacher of his order, and advancement came rapidly. Taught theology in Bologna, Toulouse, Montpellier, and Padua; took part in the leading questions and debates of the day. In 1229 made provincial of his order, but his office hindered his preaching; was released that he might give full attention to preaching. Finally had to give up preaching. Took up residence near Padua. Worked on putting his sermons in shape for publication. In 1232 canonized by Gregory IX. Regarded today as the patron saint of Padua and of Portugal.

ANTHUSA (ăn thū'za) (c. 330-c. 374), mother of John Chrysostom. Wife of a distinguished military officer, left a widow at twenty, soon after the birth of John. Young, good-looking, cultured, of excellent family and standing, and well-to-do, she attracted many suitors; but rejected all that she might devote herself to the rearing of her two children, John and older daughter. Gave her son the best educational training that could be obtained in Antioch under the pagan teacher, Libanius. John seems to have remained with his mother as long as she lived, leading an ascetic life at home, then to have entered a monastery in the mountains near Antioch after her death.

ANTONINUS PIUS, (originally **TITUS AURELIUS FULVUS BOIONIUS ARRIUS ANTONINUS),** (86-161), Roman Emperor (138-161), made a consul in 120 and adopted by Hadrian in 138. Reign relatively peaceful and happy, and he found favor with his subjects by reason of his wisdom and clemency. Engaged in war very little except in Britain, where he extended power of Rome and built a wall between the Firth of Forth (East) and the Clyde on West (140-142) as a defense against invasions from the north. During reign Marcion and the Gnostic schools flourished. Antoninus followed the policies of Trajan and Hadrian of forbidding mob violence, punishing Christians only after regular legal proceedings. Polycarp was martyred during his reign.

APOLLINARIS (second century), apologist, bishop of Hierapolis in Phrygia, about A.D. 175. Acquainted with heathen literature, used this knowledge in refutation of heresey, the chief heresy being Phrygian Montanism. Apollinaris also took a leading part in the Paschal controversy. His chief writing was *Apology* addressed to Emperor Marcus Aurelius. Only fragments of his writings have been preserved. It is thought that he died before the close of the second century.

APOLLINARIUS, (c. 310-c. 390), bishop of Laodicea in Syria, distinguished for piety, classical culture, a scholarly vindication of Christian truth, and a firm adhesion to Nicene orthodoxy. Wrote against Arianism, Manichaeism, and other heresies; and in defense of Christianity against Emperor Julian (the Apostate), and Porphyry, the Neo-Platonic opponent of Christianity. In zeal to maintain the true deity of Christ, he fell into the error of denying Christ's full humanity. Attributed to Christ a human body and a human soul, but *Logos* replaced the human spirit. Taught the deity of Christ but denied the completeness of His humanity. This error was the beginning of a prolonged Christological controversy, and in a sense prepared the way for Monophysitism. Apollinarianism itself, however, was condemned at the second ecumenical council at

Constantinople in 381. Imperial decrees also were issued against the heresy. During the fifth century some of Apollinaris' followers were absorbed in the Catholic church, while others merged with the Monophysites.

AQUINAS, THOMAS (ȧ kwī'nȧs) (c. 1225-1274), medieval religious philosopher and theologian. Was born near Naples. Received early education at the well-known Benedictine monastery of Monte Cassino. In youth went to the University of Naples where in 1244 he became a Dominican monk. This step greatly displeased his family; they forced him to remain at home for about two years. During this time read and absorbed the Bible, some works of Aristotle, and the *Sentences* of Peter the Lombard. After about two years, when his family relented and released him, he went to Paris and later to Cologne where he became the most outstanding pupil of the famous schoolman, Albertus Magnus. Spent several years in the University of Paris, received his doctorate. Upon the completion of scholastic preparation at once became deeply involved in the work of the church, was sent on successful commissions by the pope, and became a very popular preacher and lecturer. Paris, Bologna, Naples, Rome, and Cologne itself became scenes and centers of his arduous activities. By this time his friends were calling him *Doctor Angelicus.* His work bears witness to his industry, logical discernment, depth of thought, and Catholic orthodoxy. His two greatest works were *Summa Contra Gentile* (1261-1274) and his masterpiece *Summa Theologiae* (1265-1273). The former was an apology based on natural reason to train missionaries. In the latter he used the Aristotelian categories of reason to prove such doctrines as the existence of God and then faith in biblical revelation to establish such doctrines as the incarnation and the atonement. His theology became normative for Roman Catholics at the Council of Trent (1545-1563) and was declared relevant for modern times by Leo XIII in his *Aeterni Patris* in 1879. Aquinas held that prior reason was always to lead to subsequent faith.

ARGUE, ANDREW HARVEY (1865-1959), evangelist and one of the founders of Canadian Pentecostalism. Born in the family of a Methodist lay preacher in Ontario. Successful businessman in Winnipeg. Visited Chicago in 1907 where he spoke in tongues. Opened mission in Winnipeg and evangelized in Canada and the United States.

ARISTIDES, MARCIANUS (late first and early second centuries), Christian apologist. Eloquent Athenian philosopher, became a Christian in the early part of the second century, was a contemporary of the apologist Quadratus. Aristides continued to wear his philosopher's robe after becoming a Christian. His apology for the Christian faith was highly esteemed by the early church. Jerome says that this apology was filled with passages from the writings of the philosophers, and that Justin afterward made much use of it. The apology was long lost, but late in the nineteenth century was discovered. It compared Christian, Chaldean, Greek, Egyptian, and Jewish methods of worship in the first fourteen chapters to prove the superiority of the Christian form of worship, and in last three chapters gave a clear picture of early Christian customs and ethics.

ARISTOTLE (384 B.C.-322 B.C.), Greek thinker, teacher, scientist, and philosopher, born at Stagira in Thrace, son of a court physician to Amyntas, king of Macedonia, the grandfather of Alexander. In 367 became a pupil of Plato at the Academy, and remained with him until his death. King Philip of Macedonia, placed his son Alexander c. 343 under the teaching of Aristotle, a man of culture and encyclopedic knowledge. Plato the brilliant teacher, Aristotle the brilliant student held opinions that often were at variance with one another, but the men always respected each other. Aristotle opposed the Platonic doctrine of "ideas" and introduced "form" or "phenomenon," hence was more concrete, practical, and empirical in his philosophy. Emphasized the experimental and inductive. A research scholar, but more especially a teacher, disappointed in not having been appointed successor to Plato in the Academy. When fifty years old opened a school in the Lyceum at Athens, taught the last thirteen years of his life. Mornings taught advanced students, walking as he taught, hence the name Perepatetic School. In the afternoon delivered lectures to the general public. Aristotle's three chief topics of interest were God, the state, and man. He dealt with them respectively in his *Metaphysics,* his *Politics,* and his *Ethics.* His *Republic* portrayed his view of the ideal state. Another very important and infuential writing was his *Organon* or *Instrument of Correct Thinking*. Aristotle was introduced into the Latin Church by Boëthius and Cassiadorus, and gained wide influence in the Arabic and Jewish world when his works were translated into Arabic, Syriac, and Hebrew. Aristotle's philosophy thus made its impact upon the medieval church through the Italian Renaissance and through the scholastic teachings of Alexander of Hales, Albertus Magnus, Thomas Aquinas, and other schoolmen. By some schoolmen Aristotle was considered as of almost equal authority with the church Fathers. Today the recognized Thomistic theology of the Roman Catholic church is colored by the Aristotelian philosophy.

ARIUS (âr'ĭ ŭs) (c. 250-c. 336), born in North Africa. In early life was a pupil of Lucian of Antioch. A man of ascetic character, pure morals, decided convictions. Arius was a parish priest of Baucalis, the oldest and one of the most important churches of Alexandria, and began to disseminate the view that Jesus, though the Son of God, could not be coeternal with His Father; and that He must be regarded as external to the divine essence, and only a creature. Archbishop Alexander called conferences with about one hundred of his clergy; and finally at a council in 320 Arius was excommunicated. Though under the ban of the archbishop and of the Council, increased in power and influence among the clergy, even gaining partial support of Eusebius of Caesarea, and strong support of Eusebius of Nicomedia, in whose diocese he had taken up abode. When he later returned to Palestine, he was permitted by Eusebius of Caesarea and other bishops to hold religious assemblies in their dioceses. The emperor sent Hosius, Bishop of Cordova, Spain, to Egypt to put an end to the controversy. But the controversy continued to rage. The emperor summoned some bishops and other clergy from all parts of the empire to meet at Nicea in Bithynia in 325 to arrive at some agreement on the disputed doctrine. After much discussion a decision centering around the orthodox conviction of Athanasius was reached and signed by all but three of the bishops. Arius and two of his supporters, refusing to sign, were deposed from office and sentenced to banishment. Soon after the close of the council, the controversy was resumed. Arius's supporters were permitted to return to their churches, and Arius was later permitted to return from exile. The tide began to turn and orthodox bishops including Athanasius were exiled. The controversy broke forth in all its fury, and continued almost unabated until long after Constantine's death in 337. Arius, on the surface, had agreed to the Nicene statement and had signed it. He was about to be readmitted to communion when he died a sudden, tragic death in 336, the year before Constantine died. His death led to a temporary lull in the controversy. Constantine's sons accepted the Arian views and allowed a renewal of the controversy which raged until 381, when the question was officially settled by the church. The revised Nicene Creed which was adopted at the Council of Constantinople was based on the fourth century creed of the church at Jerusalem.

ARMINIUS, JACOB or **JAMES,** Dutch Jakob Hermanss or Harmensen (1560-1609), Dutch theologian, born at Oudewater, Holland. Jacob received early education at Utrecht and Marburg through the generosity of friends, later sent by the civic authorities of Amsterdam to Geneva and Basel where he studied under Theodor Beza. Studied at Leyden for six years. Traveled widely in Italy. Ordained and pastor from 1588 to 1603 in Amsterdam. Received doctor's degree from Leyden (1603) and then became professor of theology at the university. When the United Netherlands (Dutch Republic) was declared independent in 1609, Calvinism was declared the official state religion. But some of the ministers of Holland did not accept the full import of the Calvinistic doctrine of predestination and grace. Resulting discussion brought to the fore Jacob Arminius, young theologian of Leyden, who could not accept the ultrapredestination viewpoint of his colleague Francis Gomar. In attempt to modify Calvinism so that, as he thought, God might not be construed to be the author of sin nor man an automaton in the hands of God, he encountered strong opposition on the part of many ultra-predestinarians. Arminius was reluctant to give expression to any definitely anti-Calvinistic views. Arminius urged that the government call a national synod concerning this controversy and declared willingness to state clearly at this synod his views. In midst of the controversy he was stricken with illness and died in 1609. In 1610 his followers stated his doctrine in a five point remonstrance to the five main points of Calvinism as follows: (1) Before the foundation of the world God determined to save through Christ those who believe on Christ and persevere in the faith to the end; and to leave the unbelieving under condemnation. (2) Christ died for all and redemption is for all, but only those who believe will be saved. (3) Man is in a state of apostasy and sin, and has no saving grace of himself; it is needful that he be born again and renewed in Christ that he may rightly understand, think, will, and do what is truly good. (4) Without the grace of God man can do nothing; but this grace is not irresistible. (5) Those who have become partakers of Christ are given sufficient grace to win the victory over all sin, and all who are actively willing and ready to accept Christ's help will be kept by him from falling into the hands of Satan. The five points of Calvinism's counter remonstrance are: (1) Election is determined solely by the sovereign will of God. (2) Christ died for the elect only. (3) Man's whole nature is affected by the fall, and he is without any merit to attain salvation. (4) All the elect will be saved. God's grace is irresistible. (5) God's elect are eternally secure. At the Synod of Dort in 1618, Arminianism was condemned, and Arminians deposed, excluded from the communion, and some banished from the country. Arminius was one of the most learned men of his age and was popular as a preacher. His teachings were carried on by some High Church Anglicans, the Methodists, the Salvation Army, Nazarenes and holiness groups.

ARNAULD (är'nō), **ANTOINE** (1612-1694), French theologian. "The Great Arnauld," born in Paris, twentieth child of Antoine Arnauld, the lawyer (1560-1619), who was distinguished for his powerful and successful defense of the University of Paris against the Jesuits in 1594. His family formed the nucleus of the sect of Jansenists of whom the young Antoine became a leader and literary defender against the Jesuits. Young Arnauld studied at Calvi and Lisieux, first law, then turning to theology. In 1634 entered the Sorbonne, and in 1641 made a priest and a doctor of the Sorbonne. Became an ardent disciple of Descartes, and was first to teach Cartesianism in the Sorbonne. In 1643 published his *De la Frequente Communion,* a book with which he began life-long contest with the Jesuits. His outspoken letters against them in defense of the Jansenists finally caused his explusion from the Sorbonne in 1656, and a long retirement at the convent of Port Royal des Champs, near Paris. In defense of Arnauld, Pascal wrote his *Provincial Letters* against the Jesuits. Arnauld's continued controversies with the Jesuits led to a stormy persecution, which compelled him to leave France and to take refuge in the Netherlands and Belgium. Last sixteen years spent in incessant controversy with Jesuits, Calvinists, and other opponents.

ARNDT, JOHANN (1555-1621), German Lutheran theologian and mystic, born in a pastor's home at Edderitz, Anhalt, Germany. Studied at Helmstedt, Wittenberg, Strassburg, and Basel. Well prepared in piety and theological learning, became pastor at Badeborn in Anhalt (1583). Sermons and writings, however, not agreeing with the stated orthodox doctrines of the church, aroused opposition. Forced to move from one church to another, until in 1609 he received important post of general superintendent of the Lüneburg Church system at Celle, which position he held until death. Absorbed in the mysticism of the Middle Ages. Especially influenced by Bernard of Clairvaux, John Tauler, and Thomas à Kempis, asserted in his *Four Books Of True Christianity* (1606-1609) that the orthodox doctrine was insufficient, that the true Christian life consists in moral purification by right living and by mystical union of the soul with God. Though formally holding firmly to the doctrine of the Lutheran church, he was a precursor, if not the real founder of the Pietistic movement which found its culmination in Spener and Francke a century later. One of the great German mystics and a man of refined, gentle piety.

ARNDT, WILLIAM FREDERICK (1880-1957), Lutheran (Missouri Synod) theologian, born at Mayville, Wisconsin. Studied at Concordia College, St. Paul, Minn.; Concordia College, Milwaukee, Wisc.; Concordia Seminary, St. Louis, Mo.; University of Chicago; and Washington University, St. Louis, Mo. Ordained in the Lutheran ministry in 1903 and between 1903 and 1912 was pastor successively in Bluff City, Tenn., St. Joseph, Mo., and Brooklyn, N.Y. Taught Latin, Greek, and Hebrew at St. Paul's College, Concordia, Mo., professor of New Testament at Concordia Seminary in St. Louis, Mo., from 1921 until his death in 1957. Editor at different times of *Homiletical Magazine, Theological Monthly,* and *Concordia Theological Monthly;* and wrote *Does the Bible Contradict Itself?, Bible Difficulties, Christian Prayer, Fundamental Christian Beliefs, New Testament History, Life of St. Paul, From the Nile to the Waters of Damascus.* Arndt collaborated with F. W. Gingrich in the translation and adaptation of Bauer's *Lexicon of the Greek New Testament.* For many years a member of the foreign mission board of his church, and also a member of the committee on Lutheran union. Died in Cambridge, England while on leave from the seminary to help the Evangelical Lutheran Church in England establish a seminary in conjunction with Cambridge University.

ARNOBIUS (är nō'bi us), (d.c. 327), Christian apologist. Lived in the licentious city of Sicca, Numidia, North Africa. A teacher of rhetoric, having many pupils in his classes, one of whom was Lactantius, the church historian. After becoming a Christian became an ardent Latin apologist for Christianity, devotedly defending Christianity and refuting pagan error. He wrote *Disputationes Adversus Nationes* (or *Gentes*). Zeal for and defense of his new faith, however, were carried on in spite of his woeful ignorance of the Bible. Yet somehow he was quite familiar with the life of Christ, and exalted Him in his writings. He failed to come up to the standard of Catholic orthodoxy. More successful in his refutation of error than in the defense of truth.

ARNOLD, GOTTFRIED (1666-1714), Pietist, writer of mystic theology, and church historian, born at Annaberg, Saxony, father a school teacher. In 1685 he became a theological student at Wittenberg and a follower of Spener. In 1697 appointed professor of church history at Giessen, but the next year resigned and lived in retirement at Quedlinburg about six years. After successive pastorates at Werben and Berleberg, made court historian to Frederick I. In his chief book on church history he gave significant importance to so-called heretics in the church, holding that they often had more truth for the church at large than the orthodox church at any one time ever held. His writings had a marked influence on the Pietist Ernst Christof Hochmann, and on Alexander Mack the founder of the German Baptist Brethren. Arnold advocated such practices and beliefs as trine immersion, believers' baptism, feet-washing, the salutation of the kiss, non-resistance, and non-oath-taking. Some of his beautiful religious songs have found a place in evangelical hymnals.

ARNOLD, THOMAS (1795-1842), Master of Rugby, Broad church leader, father of Matthew Arnold, born at West Cowes, Isle of Wight. Educated at Warminster and Winchester schools and at Corpus Christi College, Oxford. Became fellow of Oriel College. Ordained deacon in 1818, and later became instructor of young men at Laleham. Ordained priest in 1828, and appointed headmaster of the school at Rugby, Warwickshire. During his fourteen years of administration of school, the intense religious character of his whole life and his severe and lofty estimation of duty gave the school a wide reputation for intellectual, moral, and religious discipline, and stamped itself upon the educational system of England. He laid the foundation for the English public school system. In 1841 made regius professor of modern history at Oxford, where he remained until his death the next year. His proper field, however, was education, especially in religion. A strong opponent to the Oxford Tractarian movement. Became the founder of the Broad church party. He held that the doors of the Anglican church should be opened so that all English Christians could find room in it; differences of doctrine, constitution, and ritual were minor matters and should be disregarded; the essential thing in Christianity is practical goodness, manifesting itself in individual and social life. Buried under the communion table in the chancel of Rugby Chapel. His principal works were *A History of Rome, Oxford Lectures on Modern History,* and Rugby Chapel sermons.

ARNOLD OF BRESCIA (c. 1100-1155), Italian religious and political reformer, born in Brescia in Lombardy and studied at Paris where he became a friend and pupil of Abelard by whom he was profoundy influenced, though the two men differed widely in many respects. Abelard tended to undermine the traditional orthodoxy of the church; Arnold attacked the morals of the clergy and the temporal power of the church. He advocated the separation of church and state and the abolition of the priestly government in the church. Bitterly opposed the worldiness in the church and high living of the clergy. Austere asceticism and powerful eloquence gained him great authority and popularity. But his effective preaching and his quarrel with the bishop of Brescia led to condemnation as a schismatic at the second Lateran Council and again at the council of Sens in 1140. Being expelled from Italy he went to France where he joined with Abelard against Bernard of Clairvaux. When the king expelled him from France he went to Switzerland and later to Bohemia. After a few years gained papal permission to go to Rome, where he gained a following and soon incited revolt. Began again to preach the doctrine of apostolic poverty, condemning the church and the clergy for their corruption and abuses. He was protected by the Roman senate and idolized by the people. Went beyond the ecclesiastical and entered the political sphere. His republican experiment failed and the people were forced by Pope Adrian IV into submission. Arnold was banished as a heretic from Rome in 1154. The next year by orders of Pope Adrian and of Emperor Frederick I, he was hanged, his body burned and ashes were thrown into the Tiber, lest admirers should worship his bones. In Italy his name is held in admiration by lovers of liberty.

ARNOT (är′nŏt), **FREDERICK STANLEY** (1858-1914), Plymouth Brethren missionary explorer to Central Africa, born in Glasgow, Scotland. Early influenced by David Livingstone and followed in Livingstone's footsteps as an explorer. At the age of twenty-three (1881) went to South Africa. From there proceeded to the upper Zambezi region, stopping en route for three months with Christian King Khama at Shoshong. This was the first of nine exploration journeys into Africa. In 1885 accepted an earnest appeal of Msidi, king of Gerenganze, for the white man to come to his country, in what is now a part of the Congo. This was the beginning of the Gerenganze Mission. In 1888, after seven years of pioneer traveling and exploring, started for the coast and home. At home he was made a fellow of the Royal Geographic Society, and received special awards from the society. While at home on this furlough married a young woman who became faithful companion for the rest of his life. Like Livingstone, a missionary explorer rather than a local missionary; yet out of his work of exploration there developed the Brethren's Christian Mission in Many Lands in the southern part of the Belgian Congo and in Northern Rhodesia. In 1910 Arnot aided the South African General Mission in getting started. Arnot belonged to no society and had no body of supporters when he left Scotland for Africa.

ARTEMON (är′te mun) or **ARTEMAS** (d.c. 260), adoptionist heretic. He declared the doctrine of the deity of Christ to be an innovation and a relapse into pagan polytheism. He was excommunicated probably by Bishop Zephyrinus, 202-217. The views of Artemon were later developed more fully by Paul of Samosata.

ARTHUR, WILLIAM (1819-1901), Wesleyan missionary and clergyman, born at Kells, County Antrim, Ireland. About sixteen began career as a local preacher, and admitted into the Irish Conference. Entered the Wesleyan Theological Institute (Hoxton College), London. In 1839 sent to India by the Wesleyan Missionary Society where he opened a new mission at Gutti, Mysore; but worked so strenuously that his health completely broke and he returned to England in 1841. Recovering, was stationed at Boulogne in 1846, in Paris in 1847-1848, preached in London 1849-1850, and was appointed one of the secretaries of the Wesleyan Missionary Society in 1851. From 1868 to 1871 became the first principal of the Belfast Methodist College and in 1871 made honorary secretary of the missionary society. In 1866 president of his Conference. Books included: *A Mission to Mysore; On the Difference between Physical and Moral Law; Religion without God and God without Religion*.

ASAPH (d.c. 600), a Welsh Celtic missionary and bishop. Became a pupil of Kentigern, while Kentigern was an exile in Wales from persecution in Scotland. Before Kentigern returned to Scotland about 570, he consecrated Asaph as a bishop to care for the monastery at Llanelwy, and to shepherd the people of Wales. Thus he became the first bishop of the Welsh see. Wrote *A Life of St. Kentigern*.

ASBURY, FRANCIS (1745-1816), first Methodist bishop ordained in America, born at Handsworth, near Birmingham, Staffordshire, England, of pious Methodist parents. Converted at age thirteen. Became a local preacher, appointed by John Wesley as an itinerant minister from 1766 to 1771. In 1771, at own request, sent as a missionary to America, and the next year was made Wesley's "general assistant in America." Superseded by Thomas Rankin the following year. On outbreak of the Revolutionary War, Rankin returned to England, while Asbury chose to remain in America, believing that America would become free and independent. Being a non-juror and consistently refusing to take the oath of allegiance, Asbury was misunderstood by the officials, and consequently suffered much persecution during the war. After the war the Methodists were organized into an independent church, as the Methodist Episcopal Church, Thomas Coke and Francis Asbury being chosen as joint Superintendents at the Christmas conference at Baltimore in 1784. Coke, who had been ordained by Wesley, had been commissioned by Wesley to ordain Asbury as joint superintendent. Much against John Wesley's wishes, Coke and Asbury were called bishops after 1787, a title that supplanted that of superintendent in America. From time of ordination to the day of his death, Asbury's whole life was devoted to the preaching of the gospel and to the superintendence of the churches. As preacher and administrator traveled nearly 300,000 miles altogether, over roadless swamps, pathless forests, untraveled wilderness. He ordained more than 4,000 preachers, and presided over no less than 224 annual conferences. In common with most early Methodist ministers (in America) Asbury never married; received an annual salary of sixty-four dollars. Generous almost to a fault. Early education was meager, yet in later life acquired some knowledge of Greek and Hebrew. In 1785 he laid the foundation for Cokesbury, the first Methodist college, and formed a plan for dividing the country into districts with an academy in each district. Coke was in England a part of each year, and after Wesley's death in 1791 he returned permanently to England to direct the work there. The brunt of the superintendence of the work in America fell upon Asbury. He may well be called the maker of Methodism in America. Methodists numbered over 200,000 at his death.

ASCH (äsh), **SHOLEM** (1880-1957), Yiddish novelist, born in Kutno, near Warsaw, Poland, educated in Hebrew and Yiddish schools and Rabbinical College at Yeshiva, Poland. Internationally known as a Yiddish novelist and playwright whose works have been translated into more than twenty languages. Many of his novels are based on biblical history, some on New Testament history and biography. Stressed common roots of Judaism and Christianity, and regretted the Jewish-Gentile divisions that exist in the world. Resident of many countries, notably France, Switzerland, Poland, and the United States. Due to the attack of extremist members of the Jewish community because of his apparent shift of views toward Christianity, he found his continued residence in the United States an intellectual impossibility, and so left in 1953 settling in Israel in 1956. Some of his writings are: *Tales of My People, The Nazarene, The Apostle, The Mother, Mary, Isaiah* and *Children of Abraham*. Wrote almost exclusively in Yiddish, his books translated into German, then into English and other languages.

ASKEW, ANNE (c. 1521-1546), English Protestant martyr, born at Stallingborough, Lincolnshire, England. Went to London, persecutors followed her. In 1545 arrested and tried for heresy, but was released. The next year (1546) rearrested, tried again, and condemned to death as a heretic. Charges were brought against her for interpreting the Scriptures contrary to the Roman Catholic faith, refusing to go to confession, opposing the Roman Catholic view of the eucharist. After the trial, tortured by the rack at the Tower to extort from her a confession of her heresy; remained firm. Taken to Smithfield, chained to a stake and burned with three men of like faith.

ASTRUC, JEAN (1684-1766). French doctor and formulator of early Pentateuchal criticism. Born in Languedoc into a Huguenot pastor's family which became Roman Catholic in 1685. Studied at Monpellier and taught medicine there and at Toulouse and Paris. Court physician to Louis XV. Argued in his *Conjectures on the Mémoires originaux dont il paraît que Moise s'est servi pour composer le livre de la Genèse* that Moses used earlier sources, a Yahweh and Elohim source based on the names of God, in writing the book of Genesis.

ATHANASIUS (ăth ȧ nā shĭ ŭs) (c.296-373), presbyter and bishop of Alexandria, defender of orthodoxy. A young arch-deacon under Bishop Alexander at the time of the rise of the Arian controversy about A.D. 320. At time of the first ecumenical council at Nicea (325) he was a young presbyter in the Alexandrian church. Came into his own as a celebrated leader and theologian, as chief defender of the trinitarian doctrine against the Arian heresy. The dying Bishop Alexander of Alexandria recommended him as his successor. About 328 Athanasius accordingly was raised to the highest ecclesiastical dignity of the East, not only as bishop of Alexandria, but also as metropolitan of all Egypt and Libya. Consecrated Frumentius as bishop of Ethiopia about 330. During his forty-six years as bishop he continued to be an indefatigable opponent of the Arian heresy. Four times banished from his church by Arian emperors and once by Julian the Apostate, because of strict adherence to the trinitarian doctrine, spending a total of twenty years in exile. Five times permitted to return to his church, and spent his last years peaceably but vigorously writing against heresy. The passion of his life was to vindicate the deity of Christ. Considered Arianism or anti-trinitarianism as the most dangerous enemy to the true faith. In his *Three Orations Against Arius* and in his *Of the Incarnation of the Word of God,* he attacked Arianism and stated Christ was consubstantial, co-eternal, and co-equal with God.

ATHEARN, WALTER SCOTT (1872-1934), American Disciples of Christ, leader in religious education, born at Marengo, Iowa. Studied at Drake University, State University of Iowa, and the University of Chicago. Principal of schools in Delta, Iowa, 1894-1899; taught pedagogy at Drake University, 1900-1904; dean of the Highland Park Normal College, 1906-1909; again professor of religious education at Drake University, 1909-1916; professor of religious education at Boston University, 1916-1929, where he was also dean of the School of Religious Education and Social Service, 1918-1929; and president of Butler University, 1931-1934. In 1934 elected president of Oklahoma City University. Dr. Athearn was active in promoting religious education, and wrote *The Church School, The City Institute of Religious Teachers, The Organization and Administration of the Church School, Religious Education and American Democracy, A National System of Education, Adventure in Religious Education,* and *The Minister and the Teacher.*

ATHENAGORAS (ăth ē năg′ō rŭs) (latter half of second century), Christian philosopher and apologist, born in Athens perhaps before the middle of the second century, professor at Athens. Before conversion to Christianity bent on writing against the Christians; but studying the Scriptures in order better to refute them, became convinced of their truth, and consequently, turned from being a persecutor to being an ardent teacher and defender of the Christian faith, the experience of the apostle Paul. Addressed an apology, *A Supplication for the Christians,* to the emperor Marcus Aurelius and Lucius Aurelius Commodus about 177. Refuted stock charges against the Christians and had an idea of God as a trinity. Another treatise under his name is *On the Resurrection of the Dead.*

ATTILA (d. 453), Hunnish chief from 433 whose Mongols briefly dominated Central Europe. They were checked at Châlons in Gaul in 451 and Italy where Pope Leo I convinced Attilla not to sack Rome and to go back beyond the Danube in 452. Known as the "Scourge of God" because of his ferocity.

AUGUSTINE, AURELIUS (354-430), Bishop of Hippo and great theologian. He was one of the greatest of the church Fathers, born at Tagaste, town of Numidia in North Africa. Father, Patricius, a member of the city council, seems to have been a man of fiery temper and dissolute habits, and remained a pagan until near the close of his life. Monica, one of the truly saintly mothers of the Christian world, saw her three children and her husband all become Christians before she died. Augustine did not yield until he was thirty-three. Augustine was sent to the best schools at home and in Carthage, where he prepared to teach rhetoric. In school days, joining a class of students who loathed good conduct, and spurning the Christian teaching of his mother, he went deep into sin. At eighteen he associated himself with a young woman whom he never married but with whom he lived for thirteen years. To them was born a boy whom he named Adeodatus (by God Given). He became a teacher of rhetoric at Carthage. From Carthage he went to Rome, and from Rome to Milan. Along with teaching he became interested in the study of philosophy and in the search for truth. After disappointment in his discovery of only partial truth in the *Hortensius* of Cicero, he turned to dualistic Manichaeism, which pagan system he followed for about a decade. Throwing off the shackles of Manichaeism turned to Academic Skepticism. Again sadly disappointed, yet drawing nearer to his goal, went to hear the logic and rhetoric of Bishop Ambrose as he preached in the church at Milan. Here he heard truth that was challenging but that was too deep and foreign for his comprehension. Took up the study of Platonism and Neo-Platonism and believed himself to be near goal of final truth. In this state of turmoil and search, again turned to the Christian Scriptures. One day in 386 he took up his Bible and read Romans 13:13, 14. He became a Christian. Bishop Ambrose had the joy of baptizing both Augustine and his son. Augustine with his friends and relatives then returned to Rome. On the way his overjoyed mother died. His son also died in youth. Augustine then went back to North Africa, and gave himself to prayer, study, and meditation in a monastery. His monasteries at Tagaste and Hippo became the theological seminaries where many priests and deacons and at least ten bishops were trained for the service of the church in North Africa. In 391 chosen by the people of Hippo to be a priest and a little later, when he had been a Christian five years, made associate bishop of Hippo, in 395 sole bishop of Hippo, which position he held until his death in 430. Became the chief bishop of North Africa and the leading genius of many of the church synods of North Africa, including the Synod of Carthage in 397. Augustine exerted a powerful influence as bishop, theologian, defender of the faith, preacher, and writer. His defense of the faith included preaching and writing against the Manichaeans, the Donatists, and the Pelagians. Chief of his writings were *The City of God; Confessions; Retractions; Soliloquia;* and the *Enchiridion*. Augustine was a Christian of the ages, and still enjoys, from both Protestant and Catholic, a profound respect. The whole church is greatly indebted to him. His writings came out of crises in his life. The *Confessions* describes the crisis of conversion. His writings on grace were opposed to the ideas of Pelagius concerning sin in man and how one receives grace. His writings against the Donatists who claimed to have a pure church asserted that the church was a mixture of true and professing Christians. *The City of God,* a magnificent Christian philosophy of history, grew out of the horror occasioned by the sack of Rome early in the fifth century. His main theological ideas were developed in his *Enchiridion ad Laurentium,* an early work on systematic theology. His *De Trinitate* is an able formulation of the doctrine of the Trinity. The Reformers put his writings second only to the Bible and the scholastic realists followed him in many of their ideas.

AUGUSTINE, ARCHBISHOP OF CANTERBURY (d.c. 604), missionary to England and prior of St. Andrews monastery in Rome. In A.D. 596 Pope Gregory I sent him and several companions as missionaries from Rome to England. They were kindly received by King Ethelbert and permitted to worship in the Church of St. Martin where the Christian queen Bertha worshiped. In 597 the king was baptized. Later many of his subjects likewise were baptized. Augustine then went to Arles, France (597), to be consecrated as first archbishop of Canterbury. Gregory then made Augustine metropolitan bishop of England, which made England independent of the French see. He was successful in winning Kent and Essex to the Roman church.

AUGUSTUS CAESAR (63 B.C.-14 A.D.), first Roman emperor, 27 B.C.-14 A.D. Grand nephew and adopted son and heir of Julius Caesar. Original name, Gaius Octavius. After the death of Julius received the name of Gaius Julius Caesar Octavianus. When imperator (emperor) in the year 27 B.C. the title

Augustus (revered or venerable) was conferred by the Roman Senate. Octavianus at the age of thirty-four became sole master of the Roman world. Augustus, patron of art, letters, and science, was the friend of Ovid, Horace, Vergil, and Livy. So beautified the city of Rome that he boasted that he found Rome a city of brick and left it a city of marble. Gave Rome a good administration, seeking to strengthen and stabilize rather than to enlarge the borders of the empire. Rome reached its greatest glory during his reign, which came to be known as the Augustan Age and the golden era of literature. By decree of the senate the Roman month Sextilis was renamed Augustus, (now August) in his honor. Three times during Augustus' reign of forty-one years were the gates of Janus closed, which meant Rome was at peace at these times. One of these occasions was significantly at the time that Christ, the Prince of Peace, was born in Bethlehem of Judea.

AULÉN, GUSTAV (1879-1978), Swedish theologian. Received doctorate in theology in 1915 at Uppsala. Professor at Lund from 1913 to 1933. Bishop of Strängnäs from 1933 until retirement in 1952. Opposed Germany in World War II. In his lectures in 1930 published as *Christus Victor,* he presented a modern version of the medieval "ransom to Satan" interpretation of Christ's death. Interested in ideas behind a doctrine rather than its form. Strongly supported the ecumenical movement.

AVVAKUM (1620-c. 1682), led Raskolniki or Old believers in Russia. Son of a priest. Ascetic after ordination. Twice deported to Siberia, martyred for opposing Patriarch Nikon's liturgical reforms such as making the sign of the cross with three fingers instead of two and a threefold instead of a twofold allelluia. Dispute created schism in the Russian Orthodox church between spiritual and liturgical reformers. Wrote a well-respected autobiography.

AVERROES (ȧ vĕr'ō ēz) (1126-1198), renowned Spanish-Arabian philosopher, jurist, and physician, born of an ancient noble family, at Cordova, Spain. Received education in philosophy and medicine. Regarded Aristotle as the greatest of all philosophers, and wrote many large volumes of commentaries on his writings and doctrines. A favorite of the calif of Cordova; but his philosophic ideas, and his insistence that the Koran be explained in the light of reason and not merely along traditional mystical lines, were judged contrary to orthodox Islam; brought suspicion and charge of heresy from his co-religionists. He was accordingly exiled to Fez, Morocco, where he lived in great poverty and amid much abuse. Wrote numerous works on medicine, law, grammar, and astronomy; but is chiefly noted for commentaries on the works of Aristotle. These commentaries had great influence upon the intellectual life of the Middle Ages, especially upon Maimonides, the great Jewish philosopher and theologian, upon the University of Padua, and upon Alexander of Hales and succeeding scholastic theologians.

AVICENNA (IBN SINA) (980-1037), Arab doctor and philosopher. Born in Bokhara, Persia. His *Canon* was the basic medical text in Europe until 1500. His *Book of Healing* summarized Aristotle's ideas and influenced medieval scholastic theologians greatly. Held to an hierarchy of emanations from God that relate man to God. He also reflects Neoplatonic ideas.

AYLWARD, GLADYS (1902-1970), born in London. A London parlormaid rejected as a missionary to China because of lack of education. Paid own way to China in 1932 via Siberia and Japan. With a colleague (Mrs. Jeannie Lawson) opened an inn for muleteers as a center to tell Bible stories. Led one hundred children to safety over mountains after 1940 Japanese invasion. After several years in England she opened an orphanage in Taiwan in 1953.

AZARIAH (ăz ȧ rī'ȧ), **VEDANAYAKUM SAMUEL** (1874-1945), bishop of Dornakal, India, born at Vellalanvilai in the Tinnevelly District, about fifty miles from the southern tip of India. Father was the village pastor. Family was from the low caste Nadars, but not outcastes. People came en masse into the Christian church from this caste, Azariah being a product of a mass movement. He received a good education, high school training at Megnanapuram, and college training at Tinnevelly and Madras. Following college became a Y.M.C.A. secretary for ten years. Met and formed a very close and helpful friendship with G. Sherwood Eddy, a Y.M.C.A. secretary from America. In 1903 took the lead in founding the India Missionary Society of Tinnevelly, and urged young Indian Christians to become missionaries. Soon decided that he must do what he was urging others to do; offered to go as a missionary among his people. Decided to go to the poor and ignorant of Dornakal. Azariah advocated that leadership and responsibility in the Indian church be given more rapidly to the Indian Christians. Ordained deacon in 1909, and in 1912, at the age of thirty-eight, consecrated a bishop. A small diocese at Dornakal with six clergy and about eight thousand Christians was created for him, the first Indian bishop of the Anglican church in India. In 1930 when the Anglican church in India became an independent church, Azariah found himself the bishop of a diocese as large as England with over 100,000 Christians. In 1939 it was a great day for the bishop and his church when the Cathedral of Dornakal was consecrated in the presence of bishops from all the five continents of the world. He served as bishop for 33 years, left a Christian community of more than four hundred thousand. A strong bishop, a man of faith, a good Bible student, a stern disciplinarian, and a devout and humble Christian. Insisted on his church's being an evangelistic and witnessing church. He had a wholesome and far-reaching influence on the entire Church of India. He promoted lay evangelism, self-supporting indigeneous churches, and protestant union. He honored native tunes and customs in worship.

B

BABCOCK, MALTBIE DAVENPORT (1858-1901), author of the hymn, "This Is My Father's World." American Presbyterian clergyman, born at Syracuse, New York, graduated from Syracuse University and Auburn Theological Seminary. Took high rank as a student, prominent in athletics and sports. Reached high attainments in music, wrote religious poetry, and possessed considerable craftsmanship ability. Ordained as soon as he completed seminary work. Between 1882 and 1899 a successful pastor, serving successively in the First Presbyterian Church, Lockport, New York; in the Brown Memorial Church, Baltimore, Maryland; and in the Brick Presbyterian Church, New York city. He died as the result of Mediterranean fever and melancholia at Naples, Italy. Writings were published posthumously, including *Three Whys and Their Answers, The Success of Defeat,* and *Letters from Egypt and Palestine*.

BACH (bäk), **JOHANN SEBASTIAN** (1685-1750), master organist and composer, born at Eisenach, Germany, youngest son of the family of noted musical ancestry. At a very early age young Bach gave evidence of special musical talent. From the age of fourteen he had to provide for his own education, which included Latin, Greek, logic, arithmetic, rhetoric, and theology. However, music was his chief interest. Bach married twice and was the father of twenty children, several of whom became celebrated musicians. In 1709 he was appointed court musician at Weimar in Thuringia. From that time on he was a noted musician and composer. He played before Frederick the Great at Potsdam. His hundreds of compositions were chiefly church music: oratorios, cantatas, masses, preludes, fugues, sonatas, etc. He wrote for organ, violin, orchestra, and the human voice. In his last years Bach became completely blind, but regained his eyesight a few days before he died in 1750. During his life he never received all the credit or praise due him for his masterly work in music composition. Bach was a zealous Lutheran who devoted most of his genius to the service of the church.

BACKUS (băk'us), **ISAAC** (1724-1806), American Separatist and Baptist minister, born at Norwich, Connecticut, converted in the Great Awakening in 1741. Separated from the Congregational church in 1746, and in 1748 was ordained and joined the Baptist church. He held that baptism must be accompanied by a profession of faith. He was a New Light or Separatist minister, 1748-1756. Organized the Baptist church, 1756, at Middleborough, Massachusetts, and was pastor from 1756 until his death. During long pastorate he was also an evangelist and home missionary of some note, making over nine hundred trips and covering over sixty-eight thousand miles, mostly on horseback. Backus was a champion of religious liberty in the tradition of Roger Williams, and became known for advocacy of the entire separation of church and state. In 1774 sent to Philadelphia as a representative of Baptist churches to enlist sympathy of the Continental Congress in behalf of the oppressed Baptists in the colonies. For many years a trustee of Brown University. Author of *A History of New England, with Particular Reference to the Denomination of Christians Called Baptists.*

BACON, FRANCIS (1561-1626), English statesman and philosopher, born at York House, in the Strand, London. Educated at Trinity College, Cambridge, and at Gray's Inn, admitted to the bar at twenty-one, and elected to Parliament where from 1584 to 1614 he had a long and conspicuous service. Courted royal favor and advancement in government was rapid, especially after the accession of James I. In 1603, was knighted, and became secretary general in 1607. In 1613, promoted to the attorney-generalship, in 1617, lord keeper of the Great Seal, lord chancellor in 1618 with the title of Baron Verulam, and created Viscount of St. Albans in 1621. After a brilliant career in public office, in 1621 Bacon was accused and convicted of bribery and corruption, deposed from office and heavily fined and imprisoned. He was soon released, but never restored to Parliament or court. Bacon thenceforth lived in retirement, devoting himself to literature and science. Perhaps his most important works were *Essays, Advancement of Learning, Novum Organum,* the utopian *New Atlantis*. Bacon's philosophy was a method rather than a system. He repudiated Aristotle and the schoolmen as inadequate and useless, and advocated the new inductive method of study; emphasized the practical or utilitarian aim of scientific knowledge. He separated science and philosophy from theology, and held that philosophy must be reduced to science. Modern science is based on his inductive method.

Bacon died of bronchitis resulting from a scientific experiment he had made.

BACON, LEONARD (1802-1881), American Congregational clergyman, born at Detroit, Michigan. Educated at Yale University and Andover Theological Seminary, ordained as an evangelist in 1824. From 1825 to 1866, pastor of the First Church in New Haven, Connecticut. Among his parishioners were Noah Webster, Eli Whitney, and members of the Yale University faculty. In 1866 he was made acting professor of revealed theology at Yale Divinity School until 1871, and lecturer on church polity and American church history until his death. Bacon was one of the founders and the editor for twenty years of *The New Englander*. He was one of the editors of the *Christian Spectator* for twelve years, also one of the founders, and from 1846 to 1881 an editor of *The Independent,* an anti-slavery organ; and was a leader in the anti-slavery movement. He also contributed to the missionary life and the missionary hymnody of the church. He made in 1823 the first collection of hymns for missionary meetings printed in America. A loyal Congregationalist, and Calvinist; but moderate in his theological views as an advocate of the Edwardean or New Haven Theology. Among his written works: *Slavery Discussed in Occasional Essays* and *The Genesis of the New England Churches*. He wrote the hymn, "O God Beneath Thy Guiding Hand." His son Leonard Woolsey Bacon (1830-1907) was also a Congregational clergyman, author, and hymnologist.

BACON, ROGER (1214-1294), born at Ilchester, Somersetshire. Studied at Oxford and Paris, later professor at Oxford. He joined the Franciscan Order about 1257. While teaching he did much writing along scientific, philosophical, and theological lines, sought to relate all these in a definite way to the Holy Scriptures. Said that all science has its source in revelation, especially in holy Scripture, advocated a wide comprehensive knowledge for the priests. A scientific scholar whose mind spanned the age ahead, but whose heart held him rooted in the scholastic age which he had so nearly outlived, and yet which kept him faithful to the church of his fathers. Naturally Bacon's writings did not always please the leaders of the church. He was an early exponent of the inductive method and must be reckoned among the most eminent scientists.

BAEDEKER (bā'de ker), **FRIEDRICH WILHELM** (1823-1906), pioneer evangelist and colporter to Russia, born at Witten, in Westphalia, Germany. Later moved to Weston-super-Mare, England. At sixteen left school to start in business and at twenty-one went into the army for two years. Studied in several universities and took his doctor's degree at Bonn. He was converted in 1866 under the preaching of Lord Radstock in one of the Brethren meetings. After ten years of Bible study and preaching at home, Dr. Baedeker began preaching tours on the Continent, first to Germany, then to Russia. During last thirty years, he made many trips to Russia, traveling through the empire, holding meetings, bringing encouragement to Stundists, Baptists, Mennonites, and other Protestant groups. Gave special attention to prisoners of whom there were great numbers in many parts of Russia. For eighteen years given official permits to visit prison camps all over the land. His tours to convict camps carried him across Russia and Siberia from Warsaw to Saghalien, and from the fortress prisons of Caucasia on the south to the most northerly desolations of Siberia, preaching everywhere and distributing Bibles.

BAHAULLAH (1817-1892), founder of Bahaism. Originally named Mirza Husayn Ali, born in Teheran, Persia, of old and noble Persian family. Became a follower of Babism, 1850. It had been founded by Mirza Ali Mohammed (1812-1850) of Shiraz. In the persecution of the Babists Mirza Husayn Ali was imprisoned in an underground dungeon, and finally exiled with a few of his followers to Baghdad in Mesopotamia. A few months later withdrew into the wilderness, spent two years in prayer and meditation, living the simple life of the dervish. Returned to Baghdad where he gained a large following, but was soon exiled, first to Constantinople, then to Adrianople, and finally confined for life in the desolate barracks of Akka (Acre), Palestine, a Turkish penal colony, where he died in 1892. There he instructed a large number of disciples. In 1863, declared to a few followers that he was the "manifestation" promised by the Bab, Mirza Ali Mohammed. Husayn took the name Bahaullah (Splendor of God), and became the virtual founder of Bahaism. For forty years under persecution and imprisonment inscribed this message of his new faith in *The Tablets of Bahaullah,* and his teaching became an established religion. It teaches that God can be known through His "Manifestation," that continues endlessly to reveal Himself to mankind; that Bahaism is the present-day religion which is to unite humanity under one religious faith and in one social order to promote the universal brotherhood of man, the unity of religion, and peace in the whole world. Bahaullah also wrote *Hidden Words, Seven Valleys,* and *The Book of Iqan*. When Bahaullah "ascended" in

1892, he left as his successor, his eldest surviving son, Abbas Effendi (1844-1921) to be known as Abdul Baha. The new leader was held in prison by the Turks at Acre from 1868 to 1908. He became the authoritative interpreter of his father's teachings. Major centers of Bahaism are temples in Wilmette, Illinois and Haifa, Israel.

BAILLIE, JOHN (1886-1960), Scottish Presbyterian theologian. From 1919 to 1934 taught in Auburn and Union Seminaries in the United States and in the University of Edinburgh from 1934 to 1956. Moderator of Scottish General Assembly in 1934 and a president of the World Council of Churches. Christian apologetic note in *Invitation to Pilgrimage*. Gave the Gifford Lectures which were published under the title *The Sense of the Presence of God*.

BAIRD, ROBERT (1798-1863), American church historian and prominent Presbyterian minister. Educated at Jefferson College and Princeton Theological Seminary. Ordained 1828. Founded and ran a grammar school at Princeton for five years. Promoted the American Bible Society and for five years the American Sunday School Union. From 1834 to 1843 in Europe promoted temperance and Protestant renewal. In 1846 a delegate to the Evangelical Alliance meeting. Wrote well and extensively on Christianity in America.

BAKER, GEORGE OR DIVINE, MAJOR J. OR FATHER DIVINE (c. 1885-1965), born in Georgia and known as George Baker. By 1907 made claims that he was God. In 1915 moved to Harlem, New York and organized Peace Mission Movement as a cooperative and an employment agency. Later moved his headquarters to Philadelphia. His group flourished in the Great Depression of 1929 to 1932. Made claim to godship. Promoted inter-racial cooperation in his group. Group became less significant following his death.

BALDWIN I (1058-1118), Latin king of Jerusalem. Accompanied his brother Godfrey of Bouillon on First Crusade. Left main army, went to Edessa; made count of Edessa (1098-1100). Upon death of Godfrey became first king of Jerusalem (1100-1118). Increased the Latin kingdom by taking Acre, Beirut, Sidon, and other cities. Died in Egypt (1118); succeeded by cousin, Baldwin II.

BALFOUR, ARTHUR JAMES (1848-1930), British statesman and philosopher, born at Whittingehame, near Edinburgh, Scotland, educated at Eton, and Trinity College, Cambridge. Entered Parliament as a conservative in 1874, in Parliament almost continuously until 1911, first from Hertford, then from Manchester, and finally from London. Prime minister, 1902-1905. Foreign secretary for the British Government, 1916-1919, came to the United States in 1917 to help promote cooperation between England and United States on the progress of the War. He spoke before the House of Representatives, first time that a British subject had ever addressed an American Congress. In 1919, elected chancellor of Cambridge University. Was a British delegate to the Peace Conference of Paris in 1919, and headed the British delegation to the Washington Conference for the Limitation of Armament, 1921-1922. In 1922, made the first Earl of Balfour. Throughout a long, full life, Lord Balfour retained his early interest in philosophy. Philosophical aim was the defense of Christian theism. Some of his works were *The Foundations of Belief, A Defense of Philosophic Doubt, Theism and Humanism, Theism and Thought,* and *Essays Speculative and Political*. Favored making Palestine the national home of the Jews, was the promoter of the Balfour Declaration.

BALLARD, GUY WARREN (1878-1939), born in Newton, Kansas. Cofounder of the I AM movement. Little known of his childhood. Before marriage he had been a fortuneteller, his wife, Edna (1886-1971) a musician. Became a medium and practiced spiritualism. 1930, claimed to be visited by Ascended Master, St. Germain, receiving from him a magic potion and revealed truth; traveled with him through space and time. He, wife and son Donald then started I AM movement, proclaiming St. Germain and Jesus chief Ascended Masters. After death in 1939, was proclaimed an Ascended Master. Movement with headquarters in Chicago is conglomeration of Hinduism, with its transmigration, Mazdaism, theosophy, divine science, Christian Science, New Theology, Rosicrucianism, spiritualism, metaphysics and Christianity. Ballard edited a magazine, *The Voice of I Am,* and wrote *Unveiled Mysteries* and *The Magic Presence*.

BALLOU, HOSEA (1771-1852), American Universalist Minister, one of the founders of the denomination, born at Richmond, New Hampshire. Early joined the Baptist church, but expelled because of accepting Universalist and Unitarian teachings. In 1794 ordained by Universalists at Philadelphia at time that the Philadelphia Declaration was adopted by a group of the New England Universalists. Soon after invited to a permanent charge at Dana, Massachusetts. From 1794 to 1852 held charges at Barnard, Vermont; Portsmouth, New Hampshire; and the Second Church in Boston. In 1819 founded and edited *Universalist Magazine,* later called

The Trumpet; edited the *Universalist Expositor,* later called the *Universalist Quarterly Review.* Gave the Universalists their first consistent and complete philosophy in *Treatise on the Atonement.* Rejected the doctrines of total depravity, endless punishment in hell, the trinity, and the miracles. He held that man is potentially good and capable of perfectibility, that the nature of the atonement was not a bloody sacrifice to appease the divine wrath, but the heroic sacrifice of Jesus who was not God, but a son of the universal God revealing God's love to men.

BANKS, LOUIS ALBERT (1855-1913), Methodist minister, born at Corvallis, Oregon in 1855. Educated at Philomath College, Oregon, and Boston University. Held pastorates in Oregon, Washington, Idaho, Ohio, New York, Massachusetts, Colorado, and Missouri. Was Prohibition candidate for governor of Massachusetts in 1893. After 1911 spent time as evangelist in union efforts. Last twenty years lecturer for Anti-Saloon League of America and for World Prohibition Movement. Typical of his scores of writings are: *Christ and His Friends, Paul and His Friends, The Great Portraits of the Bible, Heroic Personalities, Immortal Hymns and Their Story, Sermon Stories for Boys and Girls, The Problems of Youth, Wonderful Bible Conversions, Sermons for Reviving, The Great Themes of the Bible, The Winds of God, The Religious Life of Famous Americans.*

BARADAEUS (băr ȧ dē'ŭs) (or **ZANZALUS**), **JACOBUS** (about 490-578), Syrian Monophysite bishop, born at Tella, fifty-five miles east of Edessa. Entered the monastery of Phasilta, near Nisibis. A disciple of Severus of Antioch, the head of the Monophysites. Well educated and fluent in use of Greek, Arabic, and Syriac. After living fifteen years a monk in Constantinople, consecrated bishop of Edessa about 542. Devoted all his energies to the defense of Monophysitism. As a bishop for nearly forty years, traveled from Nisibis in Mesopotamia to Alexandria in Egypt, garbed in ragged horsecloth, organizing churches and ordaining bishops, priests, and deacons. He extended Monophysitism, strengthening and somewhat stabilizing it. The Jacobite wing of Monophysitism was named after Jacobus Baradaeus.

BARCLAY, ROBERT (1648-1690), a Quaker theologian, born at Gordonstown, near Aberdeen, Scotland. Went to Paris for education. While there, strongly inclined toward Roman Catholicism. In 1664 he was called home, and in 1667 followed his father into the Society of Friends. Preaching, he traveled throughout Great Britain, Holland, and Germany. Became the most prominent, indeed the only remarkable theologian of early Quaker faith. In 1673 wrote *A Catechism* and *Confession of Faith,* the nearest approach to a Quaker confession of faith ever written. In 1676 published chief work, a treatise upon which his fame rests: *An Apology for the True Christian Divinity.* This was a systematic presentation of the mystical spiritualism on which Quakerism is based. Through friendship with the Duke of York was granted East New Jersey and was made its governor in 1683.

BAR COCHEBA (bar kōk'e ba) or **BAR KOKBA, SIMON** (70-135), insurrectionist and false Messiah. A leader among the Jews, who, under the support and planning of Rabbi Akiba ben Joseph, led an insurrection against the Romans in the reign of Hadrian, A.D. 132-135. Leading an army of 400,000 Jews gathered from the various provinces, Bar Cocheba defeated the Romans and captured fortresses and hundreds of villages and hamlets. He had coins struck to celebrate his triumph; but his success was short-lived. When Jerusalem was attacked and razed, Bar Cocheba and his followers fled to Bether, a mountain fortress. In 135, Bether, the last stronghold, was taken after a siege of nearly a year, and Bar Cocheba was killed. After the rebellion the Christians were honored by the government for their neutrality in the rebellion.

BARDESANES (bär de sā'nēz) or **BARDAISAN** (154-222), Syrian Christian hymn writer, born in Edessa, Mesopotamia, first known missionary in the East after apostolic days. Was counselor to Agbar IX the ruler of Edessa, whom he may have led to Christ. When Edessa fell to Caracalla, emperor of Rome, and attempt was made to force Bardesanes to deny the faith, he witnessed a bold confession. He went to Armenia, continuing preaching and writing, held converse with men from India, later returned to Edessa. Though the first missionary we know of in this area, Bardesanes tells that Christianity had already spread into Parthia, Media, Persia, and Bactria. He wrote a book against the heresy of Marcion. His son Harmonius, like his father, was a composer of hymns. The hymns of father and son were used much in the Syrian church until they were superseded by the hymns of Ephraem the Syrian in the fourth century.

BARING-GOULD, SABINE (1834-1924), Church of England clergyman and author, born at Dix's Field, Exeter, England, educated at Clare College, Cambridge. For seven years assistant master at Hurst-Pierpoint College; traveled in Iceland and in various parts of Europe, priest in 1865. From

1864 to 1924 he was successively curate of Horbury, Yorkshire; vicar of Dalton, Thirsk, Yorkshire; rector of East Mersea, Colchester, Essex; and rector of Lew-Trenchard, North Devon (1881-1824). From 1854 on Baring-Gould wrote about one hundred books on travel, fiction, biography, history, folklore, mythology, and religion. Also theological writings: *The Origin and Development of Religious Belief, Lives of the Saints, The Church Revival, The Evangelical Revival, The Mystery of Suffering, The Seven Last Words, A Study of St. Paul, Conscience and Sin, The Nativity,* and *The Resurrection*. In hymnody he wrote *Church Songs* and *Songs of the West*. Among his choice hymns we have "Onward Christian Soldiers" and "Now the Day is Over."

BARNARDO, THOMAS JOHN (1845-1905), English philanthropist, founder of homes for waifs, born in Dublin, Ireland. Studied medicine at the London Hospital, and later at Paris and Edinburgh, with the purpose of becoming a medical missionary to China. Some medical work he did in the east end of London during the epidemic of cholera in 1865, while still in training, led him to change plans. The first of his institutions for the rescue of London's waifs was opened in 1870 in Stepney Causeway, London, which remained the headquarters of his institutions. The object of his institutions was to search for and rescue waifs and strays to feed, clothe, educate, and where possible, to give an industrial training suitable to each child. At his death, one hundred twelve district "homes" had been established, besides subsidiary branches in England and Canada; and nearly sixty thousand children had been rescued, trained, and placed out in life. Stress was made on the religious training of the children under his care. In 1899 his institutions and organizations were legally incorporated under the title, "The National Association for the Reclamation of Destitute Waif Children," but familiarly known as "Dr. Barnardo Homes." He founded the Young Helpers' League in 1891 and wrote much on the reclamation of destitute children. He helped twenty thousand to migrate to British Colonies.

BARNBY, SIR JOSEPH (1838-1896), English composer, conductor, and organist, born at York, England; sang in the choir at York Minster when seven, taught other boys at ten, entered Royal Academy of Music at sixteen. In 1863, organist of St. Andrews, Wells Street, London; later organist at St. Ann's, Soho; from 1871 until his death, conductor of the Royal Albert Hall Choral Society, as successor of its founder, Charles Gounod. He was precentor and director of music at Eton College 1875-1892, when he became principal of Guildhall School of Music, London. Distinguished chiefly as conductor and choirmaster, he was, nevertheless, famous both in England and the United States, for his several cantatas, forty-six anthems, organ and piano pieces, nearly two hundred fifty hymn tunes, some songs, the motet, "King All Glorious," and other church music. Author of the well-known song, "Sweet and Low." Edited five hymn books. Knighted in 1892 and a fellow of the Royal Academy of Music.

BARNES, ALBERT (1798-1870), American Presbyterian preacher and Bible expositor, born at Rome, New York, educated at Hamilton College, Clinton, New York and Princeton Theological Seminary. Became pastor of the Presbyterian church at Morristown, New Jersey in 1825 and pastor of the First Presbyterian Church in Philadelphia from 1830 to 1867. In 1835 brought to trial by the Second Presbytery of Philadelphia for his belief in unlimited atonement, but was acquitted. The case continued to stir the denomination and was one of the causes of the split in the Presbyterian church in the United States in 1837. A member of the New School party; he lived to rejoice in the reunion of 1870. Active advocate of total abstinence, the abolition of slavery, and the Sunday school cause. Wrote the widely used eleven-volume *Notes on the New Testament*, and *Notes on the Old Testament*.

BARNHOUSE, DONALD GREY (1895-1960), editor and pioneer radio preacher; born at Watsonville, California. Studied at Los Angeles Bible Institute, University of Chicago, Princeton University, Princeton Theological Seminary, University of Grenoble, France, University of Pennsylvania, Eastern Theological Seminary. Received Th.D. from Aix-en-Provence, France. In 1919 joined the Belgian Gospel Mission; in 1921 began pastoral work in small French Protestant churches; studied at the University of Grenoble; was director of Ecole Eglise Reformée de France (1921-1923); married in 1922. In 1927 returned to the U.S.A. and began thirty-three-year pastorate in the Tenth Presbyterian Church in Philadelphia and a thirty-three-year radio ministry. In 1940 released from church one-half of each year for worldwide touring and preaching. From 1928 until death, a noted radio preacher; other activities: Moderator of General Assembly of Presbyterian Church (1928); director of Stony Brook School for Boys; editor of *Revelation* (1931-1949), of *Eternity* (1950-1960); member of Victoria Institute; associate member of American Schools of Oriental Research. Before death completed eleven years of weekly broadcast on the Epistle to the Romans. Author of thirty books, among them: *God's Method for Holy Living, Life by the Son, Teaching the Word of Truth, Man's Ruin, God's Wrath, God's Remedy, God's River.*

BARONIUS (ba rō'ni us) **CAESAR** or **CESARE de BARONIO** (1538-1607), Roman Catholic church historian; born at Sora, Naples; educated at Veroli and Naples. Became member of Oratory under St. Philip Neri in Rome in 1557, superior in 1593. Was confessor to Pope Clement VIII, made cardinal (1596), librarian to the Vatican (1597). Twice failed election to the papacy because of Spanish opposition. Wrote first critical church history, which was, however, pro-Roman Catholic, weak on Eastern church: *Annales Ecclesiastici a Christo Nato ad Annum 1198,* written in reply to the Protestant *Magdeburg Centuries;* sought to demonstrate historical identity of Roman Catholic with primitive church.

BARROW, ISAAC (1630-1677), eminent English theologian and mathematician. Born in London, and educated at the Charterhouse, at Trinity College and St. Peter's College, Cambridge, and at the University of Oxford. His scope of education included Latin and Greek, botany, astronomy, anatomy, medicine, mathematics, and theology. In the latter he leaned toward Arminianism. In mathematics he was the teacher of the famous Isaac Newton. In 1655 he began a four-year period of travel and study in Europe and Asia Minor. Upon his return in 1659 he was ordained and was called to the Greek professorship at Cambridge, and in 1662 to the professorship of geometry at Gresham College. In 1663 he was chosen as the first member of the Royal Society after its incorporation, and soon after this was appointed the first Lucasian professor of mathematics, which position he held until 1669, when he resigned in favor of his most distinguished pupil, Isaac Newton, and devoted himself to preaching. In 1670, by royal mandate, he was made doctor of divinity, and was made chaplain to the king. In 1672 Charles II appointed him master of Trinity College, considering him the best scholar in England. In 1675 appointed him vice-chancellor of the university. Sermons are elaborate and exhaustive, ponderous in style and inordinately long. His theological works were four volumes of sermons, and *Treatise of the Pope's Supremacy*. Wrote books on mathematics in Latin. With the notable exception of Newton, considered the greatest mathematician of his time, particularly in geometry.

BARROW or BARROWE, HENRY (c. 1550-1593), English separatist, born at Shipdam, Norfolk, England. Educated at Clare Hall, Cambridge, admitted to the bar at Gray's Inn, 1576. After conversion became a strict Puritan. He and John Greenwood strongly influenced by the separatist views of Robert Browne; they unreservedly accepted separatism. Both imprisoned about 1586 for holding separatist meetings in London; kept in prison the rest of their lives. During imprisonment, Barrow was engaged in correspondence with Browne. In collaboration with Greenwood wrote several tracts and books in defense of separatism and congregational independency. Among these: *Creeds and Platforms of Congregationalism,* and *A Brief Discovery of the False Church*. Barrow and Greenwood were charged with devising and circulating seditious books, sentenced to death, and hanged at Tyburn in 1593. Barrow taught separatist and congregational views.

BARTH, KARL (1886-1968), Swiss theologian and founder of the dialectical or neo-orthodox school. Born in Basel. Educated in Berne, Berlin, Tübungen, and Marburg. Liberal pastor of two Swiss churches from 1909 to 1921. Horrors of World War I and his study of Kierkegaard, Calvin, and the Bible shattered his liberal optimism and led to the formulation of his crisis theology, first set forth in his Römerbrief in 1919. Professor at Göttingen, Münster, and Bonn from 1921 to 1935 and at Basel from 1935 to 1962. His ideas are set forth in The Barmen Declaration, which he mainly wrote in 1934 for the Confessional church against Nazism and in his multivolume *Church Dogmatics*. He pictures God as transcendent, sovereign, and outside history with basic discontinuity of sin separating man and God. Man can only relate to God in a spiritual crisis when the Holy Spirit uses the Bible to relate man to God through Christ. Universalism seems inherent in his system. He was opposed to natural revelation and clashed with Brunner on this point. Thus neo-orthodoxy from 1930 to about 1950 replaced the earlier naive Liberalism.

BARTOLI, DANIELLO (1608-1685), Italian Jesuit preacher and historian, born at Ferrara, studied under the Jesuits, then entered the novitiate of San Andrea, Rome, in 1623. Ordained in 1636. After spending some years as a teacher of rhetoric, he began preaching, meeting with great success in Ferrara, Genoa, Lucca, Florence, and Rome. He wrote a book, *The Learned Man*. It was received with such applause, his attention was turned to writing. Called to Rome by superiors in 1650; from that time until his death, thirty-five years later, he published many books of history in Italian.

Best known and most important work: *A History of the Company of Jesus,* covering the Jesuit history in India, China, Africa, England, and Italy. He also wrote biographies of Loyola, Caraffa, and other Jesuits.

BARTOLOMMEO DI PAGHOLO DEL FATTORINO, FRA (1475-1517), Florentine painter, born in Savignano, near Florence, Italy. Close student of the works of Leonardo da Vinci. Raphael gave him instruction in perspective, and in turn he gave Raphael lessons in coloring and handling of drapery. A follower of Savonarola, of whom he painted several pictures. Most of his paintings religious, particularly excellent in drapery.

BARTON, CLARA (CLARISSA HARLOWE BARTON) (1821-1912), American philanthropist and founder of the American Red Cross, born at North Oxford, Massachusetts. Began teaching at fifteen; fifteen years later entered the Liberal Institute, Clinton, New York, from which she graduated. During Civil War did heroic service aiding the wounded, often under heavy fire; 1864, appointed superintendent of nurses with the Army of the James. After the war, for four years, under President Lincoln's appointment, supervised the search for missing soldiers and the task of marking sixty thousand graves in Andersonville, Georgia. 1869, suffered a nervous collapse and went to Europe to recuperate. At outbreak of the Franco-Prussian War associated with the International Red Cross at Geneva and served on the actual battlefield. At close of the war organized and distributed relief, and aided in the rehabilitation of the war-torn country. 1873, returned to the United States a nervous invalid. In 1877, having regained her health, appointed by the International Red Cross to try to secure United States participation in the Geneva Convention of the Red Cross. When the American Red Cross was organized in 1881, was its first president (1881 to 1904). 1884, represented the United States at the Red Cross Conference and at the International Peace Convention at Geneva. The rest of her life busy mustering the Red Cross forces into action against floods, pestilences, tornadoes, hurricanes, earthquakes, explosions, wars, and other disasters. Food, clothing, shelter, medicines, and other vital necessities were provided. These activities took her not only to disaster areas in the United States, but also to Russia, Constantinople, South Africa, and Cuba. Took an active part in various women's movements, an earnest advocate of temperance, equal suffrage, and better social conditions for women. Her religious faith was Universalism.

BARTON, GEORGE AARON (1859-1942), American educator and author, born at East Farnham, Quebec, Canada, educated at Haverford College, Pennsylvania, and Harvard University. Appointed minister of the Society of Friends in 1879, and remained in that capacity until 1918, when he was ordained in the Protestant Episcopal church. Teacher of higher mathematics and classics at the Friends School, Providence, Rhode Island, 1884-1889; professor of biblical literature and Semitic languages at Bryn Mawr College, 1891-1922; professor of Semitic languages and history of religions at the University of Pennsylvania, 1922-1932; and professor of New Testament literature and language in the Divinity School of the Protestant Episcopal church in Philadelphia, 1921-1937. 1902-1903, director of the American School of Oriental Study and Research; director of the American School of Oriental Research in Baghdad, 1921-1934; a member of several learned societies, both American and foreign. Most writings were of archaeological nature of which *Archaeology and the Bible* was most important.

BARTON, WILLIAM ELEAZER (1861-1930), American Congregational clergyman and author, born at Sublette, Illinois, educated at Berea College and Oberlin Theological Seminary. Ordained to the Congregational ministry in 1885, held several pastorates in Tennessee and Ohio, then in Shawmut Congregational Church, Boston, 1893-1899; 1899-1924 was pastor of the First Congregational Church, Oak Park, Illinois. Served as associate editor of *Bibliotheca Sacra,* as editor-in-chief of *The Advance,* and a staff member of *Youth's Companion*. Lectured on practical theology in the Chicago Theological Seminary and at Vanderbilt University. Secretary of his church's commission on polity, and principal author of the Kansas City Creed of 1913. Moderator of the National Council of Christian Churches, 1921-1923, held several other important offices in the Congregational church. Wrote about sixty books: *A Hero in Homespun, The Psalms and Their Story, Jesus of Nazareth, The History and Religion of the Samaritans, Into All the World, Day by Day with Jesus, Congregational Creeds and Covenants, The Life of Clara Barton,* and *The Parables of Safed the Sage*. Made a special study of Abraham Lincoln, and wrote about a dozen volumes on the "Great Emancipator." Gave his library of about 4000 volumes about Lincoln to the library of the University of Chicago.

BASHFORD, JAMES WHITFORD (1849-1919), American Methodist missionary to

China, born at Fayette, Wisconsin, pursued education at the University of Wisconsin and in the school of Theology at Boston University. From college days his desire was to go to China as a missionary. The way opened for him to go only after he had held pastorates from 1876 to 1889 in Massachusetts, Maine, and New York, and after he had been president of Ohio Wesleyan University from 1889 to 1904. Following election to the bishopric in 1904, and upon his request that he be assigned to China, at the age of fifty-five, he began a period of fourteen years of active and effective missionary work in China. During pastorates and presidency he read much on China; and while yet in this country he formed the nucleus of an excellent library on China and the Chinese. Chinese leaders turned constantly to him for advice. Wrote half a dozen books, among them *China: An Interpretation, Wesley and Goethe, China and Methodism,* and *God's Missionary Plan for the World,* also many tracts and magazine articles. In 1907 he organized a China Centennial which raised $600,000 for missions.

BASIL THE GREAT (c. 329-379), administrator and prelate among the "Three Cappadocians," born at Caesarea in Cappadocia of a wealthy, pious family. A lover of nature, he wove this love and his spiritual aspiration into the dominating philosophy of life. Lived in Pontus and attended school in Caesarea, where he first met his lifelong friend, Gregory Nazianzen. He received the best education his day afforded, was a pupil of Libanius of Constantinople as was also John Chrysostom a little later. After completing education in Athens went into the practice of law and the teaching of rhetoric. He was not baptized until after he was through with his training. Inclined toward asceticism, took a journey into Syria, Palestine, and Egypt to study monastic institutions. Returning, gave up law, divided his wealth among the poor, and went to Pontus to form a monastery near the place where widowed mother and sister had already retired to enter a cloister. From the quiet cloister, much against his inclinations, he was called into active service, and was made presbyter at Caesarea in about 365. Preached often and with great effect. In 370 elected bishop of Caesarea and archbishop of all Cappadocia, which gave him oversight of fifty subordinate bishoprics. Entered upon his task with seriousness. Endeavored to fight Arianism by appointing orthodox bishops in all the churches. Appointed his brother, Gregory, as bishop of Nyssa and his friend Gregory as bishop of Sasima. Besides cares of administration and preaching, active in works of benevolence, founded a hospital, perhaps the first in Christian history, especially for the care of lepers to whom he often ministered in person. Severe ascetic practices and arduous labors took their toll and he died. Greatly loved in life and lamented at death, distinguished and remembered as a pulpit orator, an orthodox theologian, a tender and loving shepherd of souls, and a wise and beloved bishop. Wrote books in defense of the deity of Christ and of the Holy Spirit. First to formulate the idea of the Trinity as one essence *(ousia)* in three persons *(hypostases)*. Style pure, elegant, and vigorous.

BASILIDES (First half of second century), one of the most celebrated of the Gnostics, born in either Alexandria or Syria. A man well versed in Greek and Jewish Alexandrian philosophy, and in Egyptian theosophy, a pupil of Menander, who had been a pupil of Simon Magus. He appeared in Alexandria as a religious leader about A.D. 133, produced the first well-developed system of gnosis. His system, like the other Gnostic systems, grew out of the endeavor to explain the problems of God and the world, of good and evil. Seems to have started his system with God as the Non-existent One, as absolute void, and to have developed a creation on a somewhat evolutionary basis, through successive generations of seven intelligent or personified attributes. This was repeated successively until there were three hundred sixty-five heavens or orders, the last of which resulted in chaos of the earth and the human race. The system of salvation in this as in other Gnostic sects was the gaining of freedom by attaining truth—a knowledge of highest truth, an attainment which is possible for only the souls that are enlightened by knowledge—hence salvation by knowledge. The minds of all others shrouded in eternal night, the night of ignorance. Christ was human only in appearance; though He suffered, He did not die on the cross, Simon of Cyrene being crucified in His stead.

BAUER, BRUNO (1809-1882), German critic of Bible. Born at Eisenberg in the duchy of Saxe-Altenburg, Germany, received his education in Berlin. In 1839 was given a position in the University of Bonn. At first a conservative Hegelian, at Bonn changed views and became a critic of the most extreme radicalism. Extreme views soon cost him his position at the university. Contended that the gospels, the Acts, and the Pauline Epistles were second-century products. Stigmatized the evangelical sources of the gospels as mere fabrications. Attempted in his *Christus und die Cäsaren* to prove the connection between Graeco-Roman philosophy and Christianity. Tried to place the genesis of the Christian religion as late as the reign of Marcus Aurelius, and to attribute the foundation of Christianity to Seneca. A few works: *Critique of the Gospel of John, Critique of the Synoptic Gospels,* and *Critique of the Pauline Epistles,* in which he denied the authenticity of the Epistles of Paul.

BAUER, WALTER (1877-1960), German lexicographer. Taught at Göttingen from 1916 to 1945. He believed that heresy was not so much a departure from orthodoxy but Christian ideas that became heresy as the Roman Catholic church centralized polity and dogma. His Greek New Testament lexicon became the foundation on which W. F. Arndt and F. W. Gingrich built their *Greek-English Lexicon of the New Testament and other Christian Literature (1957).*

BAUR, FERDINAND CHRISTIAN (1792-1860), higher critic and church historian, born at Schmiden, Germany, educated at the Seminary of Blaubeugen and the University of Tübingen. In 1817 became professor of Latin and Greek in the Seminary of Blaubeugen, and in 1826 professor of church history in Tübingen. Remained at Tübingen the rest of his life. Borrowed Hegel's method of dialectical development based on thesis, antithesis, and synthesis, and applied it to the New Testament and the history of Christianity, particularly of early Christianity. Founded the famous Tübingen school of theology. Upon this theory he redated the writing of most of his books of the New Testament, setting the dates in the second century. Had no adequate conception of the significance of Christ in the development of the early church. Eliminated the supernatural and the miraculous from his theology.

BAVINCK, HERMAN (1854-1921), Dutch Reformed Theologian, born at Hoogeveen, province of Drenthe, Holland. Educated at gymnasium of Zwolle at Kampen and University of Leiden. Pastor at Franeker, Friesland (1881-1882); professor of dogmatic theology at the Theological School at Kampen (1883-1902); professor of dogmatics and apologetics at Free Reformed University, Amsterdam (1902-1921). In theology adhered to principles of Heidelberg Confession and canons of Synod of Dort. Conservative, modest and sensitive, and mild in criticism of others. Man of ecumenical sympathies; hoped to consolidate the Theological School and the Free University, but failed. Was a member of several scientific societies and was knighted into Order of the Dutch Lion. Chief writings: *The Ethics of H. Zwingli, The Science of the Holy Divinity, Reformed Dogmatics* (4 volumes, his magnum opus), *The Philosophy of Revelation* and *Christian Philosophy.*

BAXTER, RICHARD (1615-1691), English Puritan divine, born at Rowton, near Shrewsbury, Shropshire, England. Although without a university education and always sickly, he acquired great learning. By diligent private study, when twenty-three years of age, was able to pass a satisfactory examination and ordained in 1638 by the bishop of Worcester. Began preaching at Dudley and Bridgnorth. In 1640 began pastoral work at Kidderminster, near Birmingham; with some interruptions continued until 1660. Suffered a serious illness, at which time wrote his great devotional work, *The Saints' Everlasting Rest* (1650). No blind partisan, he boldly spoke out for moderation and fairness. This put him in a mediary position relative to the monarchy and the Commonwealth, to Episcopalianism and Presbyterianism, to the High church and the Independents, and to Calvinism and Arminianism. After the Restoration in 1660, he was denied the privilege of being pastor, and never again had a fixed pastorate. Became chaplain to Charles II for a time, and was offered the bishopric of Hereford, but declined. A leader on the nonconformist side of the Savoy Conference in 1661. In 1662 upon the passage of the Act of Uniformity he was forced out of the Church of England. In 1685 arraigned on a charge of preaching sedition. Trial was a travesty and he was condemned to imprisonment in the Tower for eighteen months. He continued his writing. Christianity to him was no mere set of doctrines or code of ethics, but the power of an endless life. Baxter was one of the most successful preachers and pastors of the Christian church. Wrote more than one hundred works. Chief among them: *The Saints' Everlasting Rest, The Reformed Pastor, A Call to the Unconverted, Dying Thoughts, Catholic Theology, Christian Directory.* Wrote several hymns such as "Ye Holy Angels Bright."

BEA, AUGUSTIN (1881-1968), German Roman Catholic scholar, cardinal, and ecumenical leader. Joined the Jesuit order in Holland and was ordained in 1912. Rector of the Pontifical Biblical Institute from 1930 to 1949. Appointed director of the Secretariat for Promoting Christian Unity in 1960 by John XXIII. Leader of the more liberal faction during the second Vatican Council and helped to develop the decrees on ecumenism and religious liberty.

BEACH, HARLAN PAGE (1854-1933), American Congregational missionary and professor of missions, born at South Orange, New Jersey, educated at Phillips Andover Academy, Yale College, and Andover Theological Seminary. Ordained to the Congregational ministry in 1883. Went as a missionary to China for six years, became associated with a school at T'ungchow where he organized one of the first two Young Men's Christian Associations in China. His wife's ill health prevented staying in China beyond 1889. Became the educational secretary of the Student Volunteer Movement for Foreign Missions, promoting that work from 1895 to 1906. In 1906 chosen professor of theory and practice of missions in Yale Divinity School, a post he held until 1921. From 1921 to 1928 professor of missions at Drew Theological Seminary. He was also librarian of the Day Library, which he made one of the two best collections in the world on Protestant foreign missions. A member of the American Board of Commissioners for Foreign Missions; chairman of the exhibit committee and executive committee of the Ecumenical Conference in 1900; member of the executive committee of the Yale Foreign Missionary Society; member of the advisory board of Canton Christian College; and trustee of the Hartford School of Religious Pedagogy. Theologically, a moderate conservative.

BEATON, DAVID (1494-1546), Roman Catholic cardinal and archbishop of St. Andrews, born at Fife, Ireland, studied at the universities of St. Andrews, Glasgow, and Paris, law in the latter. Became abbot of Arbroath in 1523; lord privy seal, 1528; ambassador to France 1533; bishop of Mirepoix 1537; cardinal in 1538; archbishop of St. Andrews 1539; Chancellor of Scotland in 1543. Lived in turbulent times of international strife. In the political contests between the French and English parties sided with the French. In religious contest between the Romanists and the Reformers, took a decided stand for the hierarchy and freely used intrigue and force when argument and persuasion failed. He induced the king to institute a Court of Inquisition to inquire after heretics in all parts of the kingdom. The trial of George Wishart before Cardinal Beaton and a court of priests; Wishart's sentence to death at the stake, without the aid of the civil power, in 1546 were the immediate cause of a conspiracy to put Beaton out of the way. Certain members of the Reform party, friends of Wishart, murdered him one morning in his bed chamber in the castle of St. Andrews a few weeks after he had ordered Wishart's death. A statesman, Beaton was able, resolute, and in general policy, patriotic. In the execution of his duties he sometimes resorted to extreme cruelty; in private life some of his acts were scandalous to the Christian religion.

BECKET, THOMAS à (c. 1118-1170), Archbishop of Canterbury, born in London, received good education in Merton Abbey, Surrey, London, and in Paris. About 1142 came into the service of the Archbishop of Canterbury, and was sent by the archbishop to Bologna and Auxere to study civil and canon law. He was soon made archdeacon and provost of Beverley. In 1154 King Henry II, in the second year of his reign, raised Becket to the chancellorship of England. Became one of England's best chancellors, served under the most powerful sovereign of Western Europe. He was elected Archbishop of Canterbury in 1162. In his new office he determined to be loyal to the church and give full allegiance to the pope, just as he had given supreme allegiance to the political sovereign when he was chancellor. When he became archbishop, he changed completely from luxurious and pompous statecraft to ascetic priesthood. Soon fell into bitter conflict with former friend and patron, the king. Becket strongly opposed the Constitutions of Clarendon limiting the right of appeal to Rome in ecclesiastical cases, restricting the power of excommunication, subjecting the clergy to civil courts, and putting the election of bishops under the control of the king. Determined to magnify new office and uphold all ecclesiastical claims, defend the church at the expense of the state. Henry was a strong nationalist, and Becket completely broke with the king. Obliged to flee to France, from 1164 to 1170. By the insistence of the pope, 1170, the king made peace with Becket, and the archbishop returned to England only to become involved in further controversy. In the latter part of the same year he was murdered by some of Henry's knights in the Cathedral of Canterbury. The pope used this deed skillfully; Henry was forced to abandon the Constitution and to do public penance at the grave of Becket. Two years later, 1172, Becket was canonized.

BEDE (bēd), **the Venerable** (c. 673-735) English monk, scholar, church historian. Born near Jarrow of North England. Early placed in a monastery, spent life as a teacher, preacher, and writer in monasteries near birthplace. An apt and diligent student, well versed in the Scriptures, in the Latin Fathers, and in other branches of current learning, is said to have been the most learned Englishman of his day. At nineteen he was made a deacon and at thirty a priest. He was a successful and much beloved teacher and a voluminous writer. Best known and most valuable writing: *Ecclesiastical History of the English Nation* (731), translated from the Latin by King Alfred into the Anglo-Saxon. Wrote a number of commentaries, homilies, hymns, and lives of the saints.

BEECHER, HENRY WARD (1813-1887),

American Congregational clergyman and reformer, born at Litchfield, Connecticut. Received education at Boston Latin School. Amherst College, and Lane Theological Seminary in Cincinnati under his father, then professor of theology and president of Lane. After holding two Presbyterian pastorates in Indiana (from 1837 to 1847), became pastor of the Plymouth Congregational Church in Brooklyn from 1847 to 1887. Beecher became the most popular and widely-known preacher in America. Became known as a revivalist of great power, and as a preacher of delightful humor and originality. A man of robust health and physical vigor, of strong courage and conviction, an oratorical giant, usually sweeping all before him. For years one of the most popular lecturers and after-dinner speakers in America. Active and courageous in the cause of antislavery, but deplored revolutionary measures. Publicly advocated, 1863, the cause of the American Union in a series of lectures in cities of England at a time when the sympathies of England were with the southern Confederacy. Able to carry his bitterly hostile audiences with him. Like father and brothers, unconventional in manners and speech. In theology, became more and more liberal, and in order not to cause faction within denomination, withdrew from the Congregational church. Accepted higher criticism and the theory of evolution as consistent with Biblical teaching. Messages were pre-eminently on the subject of love—love to God and love to man. For over twenty years a regular contributor to the *Independent,* a politico-religious journal; editor for two years. Founder of and from 1870 to 1881 editor of *The Christian* (later known as *The Outlook*), and made it a pioneer non-denominational paper. Wrote much for *The New York Ledger*. Sermons were published after 1859 as *The Plymouth Pulpit*. Among the other books: *Freedom and War, Aids of Prayer, Lecture Room Talks, Life of Jesus the Christ, Yale Lectures on Preaching, Norwood* (a novel), *Doctrinal Beliefs and Unbeliefs*.

BEECHER, LYMAN (1775-1863), American Presbyterian clergyman, and reformer, born at New Haven, Connecticut, educated at Yale College. Continued study of theology under President Dwight for a year. Ordained, 1799, became pastor of the Presbyterian Church of East Hampton, Long Island. Moved, 1810, to the Congregational Church at Litchfield, Connecticut, 1826 to Boston as pastor of the Hanover Street Congregational Church. Chosen president and professor of theology, 1832, of Lane Theological Seminary, Cincinnati, Ohio. Also served as pastor of the Second Presbyterian Church from 1833 to 1843. After twenty years at Lane retired. Returned to Boston in 1852; after 1856, in feeble health, lived with his son Henry Ward in Brooklyn until his death, 1863. A profound student of theology, but pre-eminently practical in preaching. A liberal in theology, rejecting stern Calvinism, but at the same time staunchly opposing Unitarianism. He was a trinitarian leader in the Unitarian controversy with Dr. Channing during his six years' pastorate in Boston. Later, while in Cincinnati, took part in the theological and ecclesiastical controversy that shook New England and divided the Presbyterian church. Charged with holding heretical views, he was tried, but acquitted by both the presbytery and the synod in 1835. Through the controversy, one of the New School leaders. Fervent in denouncing slavery, duelling, intemperance, and every form of immorality. Preached sermons against the Roman Catholics. Sermon preached on duelling, following the tragic death of Alexander Hamilton, did much to awaken the popular conscience on the subject, to make way for the ultimate law against duelling. Six sermons on intemperance exerted a world-wide influence. A believer in evangelism revivals and conversion. Seven sons all became clergymen. Three of the four daughters became famous for their literary and philanthropic activities.

BEECHER, WILLIS JUDSON (1838-1912), American Presbyterian theologian and educator, born at Hampden, Ohio, studied at Hamilton College, Ohio and Auburn Theological Seminary, New York. Ordained to the ministry, 1864, and filled two short Presbyterian pastorates. Professor of moral science and belles-lettres in Knox College, Galesburg, Illinois, 1865-1869. Professor of the Hebrew language and literature in Auburn Theological Seminary, 1871-1908. Beginning in 1893 prepared the Old Testament Sunday school lessons for the *Sunday School Times*. In 1902 delivered the Stone Lectures at Princeton Theological Seminary. 1904, was president of the Society of Biblical Literature and Exegesis. In theology a progressive conservative. Among his writings: *Reasonable Biblical Criticism, Drill Lessons in Hebrew, The Prophets and the Promise, Dated Events of the Old Testament,* and *The Teaching of Jesus Concerning the Future Life*.

BEET, JOSEPH AGAR (1840-1924), English Wesleyan theologian and author, born at Sheffield, England, attended Wesley College, Sheffield, took up mining engineering; afterward studied theology at Wesleyan College, Richmond. 1864-1885 a pastor; 1885-1905 professor of systematic theology in

Wesleyan College, Richmond; also from 1901 to 1905, a member of the faculty of theology, University of London, being one of the original members of the theology faculty. Came to the United States, 1896; delivered a series of lectures at the University of Chicago, and at the summer schools of Chautauqua and Ocean Grove. Long recognized as one of the ablest theologians and exegetes of his denomination, sympathy with the modern critical school of interpretation and particularly views on eschatology, as evidenced in *The Last Things* and *The Immortality of the Soul,* occasioned much criticism. Charges of heresy were brought against him in 1902, yet re-elected to the professorship on condition that he refrain from expressing his views on immortality and future punishment. To retain liberty of speech retired from professorship in 1905. Besides writing commentaries on several of Paul's epistles, he also wrote *Credentials of the Gospel; Through Christ to God; The New Life in Christ; Church, Churches, and Sacraments; The New Testament: Its Authority, Date, and Worth; The Old Testament: Its Contents, Truth, and Worth; A Key to Unlock the Bible;* and *A Theologian's Workshop, Tools, and Methods.*

BEETHOVEN (bā'tō ven), **LUDWIG VAN** (1770-1827), German composer of symphonies, born in a Roman Catholic home in Bonn, Germany. Father, though a drunkard, was a singer in the electoral chapel at Bonn, and wanted Ludwig to become a musician. Had the best teachers, and learned to play the organ so well that he often substituted for his teacher at the court church. Later led the band in the court theater. In 1787 Beethoven met Mozart, and possibly received a few lessons from him. Later met Haydn, who became his teacher at Vienna, his permanent home. From the time he was eleven years old until his death, a period of about forty-five years, most of his time was occupied with composing music. The world however was slow in giving recognition to his compositions. Before thirty he began to grow deaf. At fifty could hear nothing of the wonderful music he wrote and played. Composed some of his greatest works after deafness overtook him. He never married. Beethoven suffered much from ill health, increasing deafness, poverty, and unhappy family relationships. Finding no relief from them he became gloomy, distrustful, and solitary, even contemplated suicide. Yet, he felt he had something to live for—art. He said, "I owe it to myself, to mankind, and to the Almighty. I must write music to the glory of God." His passion was music. Had more thoroughgoing music development than any other of the composers, was more original and independent. He was an innovator. Wrote many symphonies, sonatas, masses, one oratorio, one opera, and many other compositions. He said, "Music is the only spiritual entrance to a higher world of knowledge."

BEGBIE, HAROLD (1871-1929), English author and journalist, born at Farnham St. Martin, Suffolk, England, educated entirely by private tutors and in private schools. Began to farm, but soon turned to journalism. Wrote novels, children's stories and biographical studies; then wrote concerning movements that were directed toward religious and social betterment. Authored nearly fifty books, some: *Broken Earthenware* (published in America as *Twice Born Men*), *Other Sheep, Life Changers* (on Buchmanism), *Life of William Booth* (two volumes), *and Broken Lights.*

BEISSEL (bī' sel), **JOHANN KONRAD** (1690-1768), mystic, founder of the Ephrata Society, born at Eberbach in the Palatinate, Germany. Education limited; became an expert baker. Plying his trade at Heidelberg, became acquainted with many learned Pietists, and he became an ardent Pietist. Early religious name was Father Friedsam. Fled to Crefeldt and Schwarzenau where he met some of German Baptist Brethren. 1720, came to America; 1724 was baptized by Peter Becker, the overseer of the German Baptist Brethren Church at Germantown. Soon made a minister and overseer of the Conestoga congregation, never in full sympathy with the Brethren. Began to teach strange doctrines. In 1728 carried away a few of the Brethren, rebaptized them, and organized the Ephrata Society, sometimes known as the Seventh Day German Baptists or Seventh Day Dunkers. His society erected several buildings, "Bethania," "Hebron," "Saron," and "Saal," in addition to a little hut in which he lived. These buildings are under the care of the Pennsylvania Historical Society. The sect has almost completely died out. Even within the Ephrata Society Beissel ruled with an iron hand. Mention should be made of the Sunday school at Ephrata, Pennsylvania, 1748, thirty years before the famous Robert Raikes Sunday school. These people were renowned for their singing and the hymnbooks which they published.

BELL, GEORGE KENNEDY ALLEN (1883-1958), Anglican bishop and ecumenist. Ordained in 1907, Oxford don in 1910 and chaplain to Archbishop of Canterbury, 1914-1924; 1924 dean of Canterbury, bishop of Chichester in 1929 to 1958. Leader in Lambeth Conferences and supported founding of World Council of Churches in 1948. Editor of multi-volume *Documents on*

Christian Unity. Author of *Randall Davidson* (1935) and *Christian Unity, the Anglican Position* (1948).

BELL, L. NELSON (1894-1973), missionary surgeon and editor. Born in Longdale, Virginia. Educated at the University of Virginia and Washington and Lee Medical College. Medical missionary and chief surgeon at Tsiangkiangpo General Hospital in China, 1916-1941. Practicing physician in Asheville, North Carolina, 1941-1956. Founder of the *Presbyterian Journal* of the Southern Presbyterian Church and founder with Billy Graham, husband of his daughter Ruth, of *Christianity Today*. Moderator of the General Assembly of his denomination in 1972. Contributor of articles to *Christianity Today*.

BELLAMY, JOSEPH (1719-1790), Congregational clergyman and educator, born in New Cheshire, Connecticut, graduated from Yale College. Studied theology under Jonathan Edwards at Northampton, Massachusetts. Ordained pastor of the church at Bethlehem, Connecticut in 1738. Served there until 1790. Took active part in the Great Awakening in New England, 1740-1744. Wrote *True Religion Delineated* in defense of the New or Edwardean Theology, also *The Wisdom of God in the Permission of Sin*. Writings were devoted mainly to the defense of Calvinism against antinomianism and Arminianism, and to the study of true piety. Influence on the religious thought of the time in America was probably surpassed only by that of his friend and teacher, Jonathan Edwards.

BELLARMINO (bĕl lär mēn'ō), **ROBERTO FRANCESCO ROMOLO** (St. Bellarmine) (1542-1621), Italian Roman Catholic theologian and cardinal, born at Montepulciano in Tuscany near Siena, Italy. Entered the Jesuit order at Rome in 1560. Began his theological study, 1567, at Padua; in 1569 continued his study at Louvain, becoming professor of theology there. In 1570 he was ordained priest. After seven years of study and teaching at Louvain, began eleven years of lecturing on controversial theology in the New Roman College, later the Gregorian University. At this time wrote celebrated *Disputationes de Controversis Christianae Fidei,* which is regarded by the Roman Catholics as containing the best arguments for their tenets, and which places the author as chief defender of papal authority and tenets of the Roman Catholic faith of the sixteenth and seventeenth centuries. In 1589 he was sent by the pope on a mission to Paris. In 1592 shared in the Sistine revision of the Vulgate, and was made rector of the Roman College; in 1597 was made personal theologian of the pope, and examiner of the bishops. Became cardinal-priest in 1599, archbishop of Capua in 1602, resigning the latter post in 1605. In 1606 entered into controversy with the Republic of Venice and in 1608 with King James I of England concerning the fundamental and primitive authority of the Catholic church. Wrote effective defenses against both. He was among the theologians consulted concerning the teaching of Galileo, which at first made a stir at Rome. Also opposed the "Malabar Customs" as practiced by his order. In old age returned to home at Montepulciano as its bishop for four years, afterward retired to the Jesuit College of St. Andrew in Rome. A rigorous ascetic, a controversialist and fighter of "heresy," and one of the greatest theologians that the Roman Catholic church has produced. He was canonized in 1930 and declared a doctor of the church in 1931.

BENDER, CARL J. (1869-1935), missionary to Cameroons in Africa. Born in Germany, came to the United States with family at age of twelve. Educated at the German Baptist Seminary in Buffalo, his home town. Spent his life as a missionary from 1899 in the Cameroons at Soppo under the German Baptist Missionary Society.

BENEDICT IX (THEOPHYLACT) (c. 1012-c. 1055), pope, 1032-1045. By simony and intrigue on the part of his father, Count Alberic of Tusculum, elected pope. He exasperated the Romans to such a degree by his scandalous life that a rebellion broke out in 1044. Sylvester III was elected. Twice deposed and twice regained the papacy; but in 1048 finally forced to retire.

BENEDICT XIII (PEDRO DE LUNA) (c. 1328-1423), last of the Avignon popes in the Western Schism, 1394-1417, born of noble family at Illucca, Aragon, Spain. Studied law at the University of Montpellier in France, later taught canon law. Made a cardinal deacon by Gregory XI in 1375 and elected pope to succeed Clement VII as Avignon pope in 1394 in time of the Western Schism. At the Council of Pisa in 1409 an effort was made to end the papal schism. The council deposed the two claimants to the throne and elected another. Although deposed he would not yield, persistently claiming to be the legitimate pope. The Council of Constance, 1414-1418, recommended the resignation of all three claimants to the papacy. John XXIII was deposed and Gregory XII resigned; but Benedict XIII refused to comply. The council declared him a perjurer, a heretic, and an obstacle to the union of the church and deposed him. Until death in 1423 insisted that he was the rightful pope. Martin V, who was declared pope, ruled over the subsequent sessions of the council. As the Roman Catholic historians deny his rightful place in the papal succession, considering him an anti-pope, the title Benedict XIII was attached to a pope who ruled in the eighteenth century.

BENEDICT OF NURSIA (c. 480-c. 543), founder of the Benedictine Order, born at Nursia in Umbria; parents were of the higher class. Pursued an education at Rome, but shocked by the immorality of companions; left school in later teens, retired to a dark, secluded cave at Subiaco as a hermit in isolation for three years. At invitation of other monks in neighborhood formed a cloister and became abbot. About 529 left Subiaco and found a picturesque mountain spot in the Neapolitan Province, between Rome and Naples, where he founded the renowned monastery of Monte Cassino. This was the beginning of organized monasticism and the beginning of the first great monastic order which bears his name. Presided over the order for fourteen years, and composed the Benedictine Rule. This rule soon superseded all former and contemporary rules of a similar nature, and became the code to be followed largely by all later monastic orders. The outline plan for the cenobitic and monastic life was fourfold: (1) Organization. At the head of each monastery, an abbot. (2) A threefold vow: (a) perpetual adherence to the order: (b) voluntary poverty and chastity (including celibacy): (c) obedience to a superior. (3) Exercise. Manual labor and educational instruction must accompany worship, meditation, and study. (4) Simplicity. Simplicity must obtain in every aspect of life. The Benedictine Order had great influence, was forerunner of other great religious orders. All added much power to the Roman Catholic church; restored to Europe the dignity of labor; linked work with worship; aided and fostered education; preserved the treasures of the old culture, and greatly fostered the copying of manuscripts of the Scriptures. Benedict lifted the ascetic and monastic spirit out of the selfish into the altruistic and philanthropic.

BENEZET, ANTHONY (1713-1784), Quaker abolitionist. Born in San Quentin, France and came to Philadelphia in 1731. School teacher in Philadelphia from 1742 to 1784. Helped French immigrants from Acadia in 1765. Desired to protect Indians but most ardent in his struggle against slavery. Wrote "A Caution to Britain and Her Colonies on the Calamitous State of Enslaved Negroes" in 1766 and a history of the Quakers.

BENGEL, JOHANN ALBRECHT (1687-1752), German Lutheran theologian and commentator, born near Stuttgart, Württemberg, and studied at Stuttgart, Halle, and Tübingen. Devoted himself strictly to the sacred text with the conviction that to understand the Bible nothing should be read into the text, nothing therein contained should be omitted, which might be drawn out by the most rigid application of grammatical principles. His New Testament text and critical apparatus, published in 1734, mark the beginning of modern scientific work in the field of textual criticism. 1713-1741, professor at the cloister-school at Denkendorf, Württemberg, a seminary established for the early training of candidates for the ministry. At this time wrote his *Gnomen Novi Testamenti,* a brief and widely used Latin exegetical commentary on the New Testament, published in 1742. Upon this work Bengel's fame chiefly rests, yet as lecturer and commentator on the Holy Scriptures he won and retains an exalted position among scholars. In 1741 made general superintendent of Herbrechtingen, and eight years later, until his death, was general superintendent at Alpirspach. Bengel was a man of eminent piety, of vast and sound learning. Teaching and character strongly and permanently influenced for good many preachers and did much to preserve in South Germany an evangelical type of preaching when evangelism sadly deteriorated in post-Pietistic days in the north. He was one of the eminent Pietistic successors of Spener. Very interested in eschatology.

BENSON, CLARENCE HERBERT (1879-1954), Presbyterian minister, educator, author. Father a Presbyterian minister, grandfather and great-grandfather, Moravian missionaries to the Indians. Received his education at the University of Minnesota, in preparation for theology, and at Macalester College, majoring in astronomy in both schools, and at Princeton Seminary. After graduating in 1908, ordained to the Reformed ministry, between 1908 and 1919 held five Presbyterian and Reformed church pastorates in New York and Pennsylvania. 1919-1922, pastor of the Union church in Kobe, Japan. In 1922 began a twenty-year period of teaching at the Moody Bible Institute. In 1924 Dr. Gray appointed him director of the Christian Education Department of the Institute. Because of no textbooks in the field of Christian education that fully harmonized with his ideas and ideals he produced textbooks, some: *A Popular History of Christian Education, The Christian Teacher, Techniques of a Working Church, An Introduction to Child Study, The Church at Work,* and *The Sunday School in Action.* Some earlier writings in Astronomy: *The*

Earth, the Theatre of the Universe, and *Immensity*. Thought Sunday school lessons in the churches were inadequate. Over a period of years with his students, produced the All Bible Graded Series used widely today, published by Scripture Press which he and Victor Cory founded in 1934. Founded the *Church School Promoter,* now *Christian Life,* later became its editor-in-chief. Made this paper the official organ of the Evangelical Teacher Training Association, of which he was one of the founders in 1931, subsequently executive secretary. In the scientific world, he was a member of the Bernard Astronomical Society of Chattanooga, and also of the Royal Astronomical Society of Canada.

BENSON, EDWARD WHITE (1829-1896), Archbishop of Canterbury, 1882-1896, born near Birmingham, England, studied at King Edward VI School, Birmingham, at Trinity College, Cambridge. Ordained priest in 1857. Became headmaster of the newly founded Wellington College 1859 to 1872. Excellent administrative ability in developing the college. After holding various minor ecclesiastical offices following headmastership, in 1875 became chaplain-in-ordinary to the queen, and in 1877 became first bishop of Truro in Cornwall. Here he formed a divinity school for the training of candidates for holy orders, began the erection of a cathedral, and founded and strengthened schools. In 1882 appointed archbishop of Canterbury. As primate of all England, he sought to restrain the more extreme followers of the Oxford movement, although a high churchman. Helped to effect a more settled relationship in the Church of England between the various parties. Manifested a friendly attitude toward the Eastern churches, but toward any suggestion of *rapprochement* with the Roman church, cold. Much interested in efforts toward social and civil betterment, introducing into parliament bills that might bring about reform. Published several volumes of sermons. After death his important study of Cyprian was published.

BENSON, LOUIS FITZGERALD (1855-1930), American Presbyterian minister and hymnologist, born in Philadelphia, Pennsylvania, educated at the University of Pennsylvania. Practiced law seven years before taking up theology at Princeton Theological Seminary. After graduation, ordained. Pastor of the Presbyterian Church of the Redeemer in Germantown, Philadelphia. Six years later resigned to devote time to hymnology and to the editing of the *Journal of the Presbyterian Historical Society*. Considered a leading authority on hymnology, and collected a library of nine thousand volumes on the subject. Author of *Hymns and Verses, The Best Church Hymns, Studies of Familiar Hymns* (two series), *The English Hymn: Its Development and Use in Worship, Hymns Original and Translated,* and *The Hymnody of the Christian Church*. Editor of *The Hymnal* for the Presbyterian Church, and editor also of *The Hymnal* of the Congregational Churches.

BERDYAEV (bir dyä'yĭf), **NIKOLAI ALEKSANDROVICH** (1874-1948), philosopher, born at Kiev, Russia. Studied science at the University of Kiev and philosophy at Heidelberg. Began as a Marxist; under influence of Kant and Jacob Boehme turned from Communism. Founded a free academy for spiritual culture in Moscow (1919). In 1922 exiled from Russia. In Berlin organized free courses in philosophy and religion under name of Academy; later transferred Academy to Paris from 1924 to 1948. Champion of Christian-Apocalyptic philosophy, with some pantheistic and theosophist leanings in his existential thought. Prolific writer in Russian. Chief works: *Freedom and the Spirit, Destiny of Man, Spirit and Reality, Solitude and Society, Slavery and Freedom, Origins of Russian Communism*.

BERENGAR OF TOURS (bā räɴ'zhā) (c. 1000-1088), French theologian and ecclesiastic, born at Tours, France, studied arts and theology at the School of Chartres under Fulbert. In 1031 became canon and director of the school of St. Martin of Tours, able dialectician, a popular teacher. His blameless, ascetic life, and spiritual aspirations won for him a wide reputation and following among the monks. About 1041 chosen archdeacon of Angers. In philosophy, a nominalist. In about 1047 it became noised that he opposed the view held by the church since the time of Radbertus in the ninth century that the eucharistic elements are changed as to substance into the actual body and blood of Christ. He held the view that was taught by Ratramnus and John Scotus Erigena, that it is necessary to distinguish between the symbol and the thing to be symbolized. Immediately opposed by Lanfranc, then prior of the monastery of Bec. Without a hearing or even a summons was condemned at the Roman synod of 1050. Conformed and restored only to reassert his opinions and condemned again. This occurred several times. Recantations forced, had rancor rather than sorrow or contrition. About 1080 another trial followed with another forced submission. Afterward kept silence, retiring to the island of Saint-Cosme, near Tours, to live in ascetic solitude until his death, convictions unchanged. Without purposing to be disobedient to the church, opposed a tradition and view of the Church that later, in the Fourth Lateran Council in 1215, was accepted as a dogma of the church, the doctrine of transubstantiation.

BERGGRAEV, EIVIND (1884-1959), patriotic Norwegian Lutheran bishop. Born at Stavanger. Ordained in 1908. Taught from 1909 to 1918. Pastor (1918-1924). Consecrated as bishop in 1929 and primate of the Norwegian church from 1937 to 1950. Led Norwegian church courageously in World War II even when interned (1940-1945). Wrote *Kirke og Kultur* in an attempt to relate religion and culture. Supported the ecumenical movement and one of the World Council of Churches presidents (1950-1954).

BERGSON, HENRI LOUIS (1859-1941), French philosopher, born of Anglo-Jewish parents in Paris, became French citizen, attended the Lycee Condorcet and the Ecole Normale Superiéure in Paris. After graduation taught philosophy successively at several schools, the Ecole Normale Superieure and the College de France in Paris from 1900 to 1921. At Clermont long walks in nature dissipated skepticism. Realized that there is a great Personality behind creation. In 1913 visited America where he delivered a course of lectures at Columbia University. Same year was president of the English Society for Psychical Research, and delivered lectures at London and Oxford. In 1901 elected a member of the Academy of Moral and Political Sciences, in 1914 a member of the French Academy of Science. About 1918 gave up teaching and devoted time to politics, to international affairs, as head of a mission to America. After the World War, president of the committee of international co-operation. In 1928 awarded the Nobel Prize for literature and in 1940 the Nicholas Murray Butler gold medal. Chief works translated into English. Some of them: *Time and Free Will, Creative Evolution, Mind Energy, Matter and Memory, Perception of Change, Introduction to Metaphysics, Spiritual Energy,* and *Sources of Morality and Religion*. Bergson's philosophy held that time or duration is the fundamental reality, and that intuition, as the completion of intellect, is humanity's most trustworthy guide. Furthermore, believing that the universe is in a state of creative evolution, he opposed strongly the materialistic philosophy.

BERKELEY, GEORGE (1685-1753), Irish philosopher and idealist; bishop of Cloyne, born near Thomastown, Kilkenny County, Ireland. Educated at Trinity College, Dublin. At Trinity, deeply influenced by the views of John Locke. In 1709 completed his *Essay Towards a New Theory of Vision,* in which he extended Locke's views on the character of matter, emphasizing that no object exists apart from the mind. A little later wrote *Treatise Concerning the Principles of Human Knowledge,* and *The Dialogues Between Hylas and Philonous.* Ordained in 1710 in the Church of England, and soon became prominent as a churchman. After two trips to the Continent, and after holding several college offices and teaching in Dublin, he was appointed dean of Derry in 1724. In 1728 resigned his deanery in the interest of a new venture establishing a college in the Bermuda Islands for the training of pastors and missionaries for the colonies. In 1728 came to Rhode Island, waited for the promised money for the projects to arrive. Finding his hopes gone, returned to England in 1732. In 1734, made bishop of Cloyne in the established church of Ireland, continued to serve until his retirement in 1752. Throughout his life wrote much, mostly on philosophical subjects. To him, only mind and ideas have real existence. Matter apart from experience is inconceivable and contradictory. Formulated a philosophical defense of Christianity, criticizing the "natural religion" of those who opposed revealed religion. Held that the whole of the natural order is a conversation between God and man. Thought both materialism and deism are false conceptions. Nature is the ordered succession of ideas produced by the Universal Spirit. Major work was *Alciphron*.

BERKHOF, LOUIS (1873-1957), Christian Reformed theologian. Born in Holland. Educated at Calvin Seminary. Teacher and later president of Calvin Seminary from 1906. Major work was *Reformed Dogmatics* (3 vols., 1932). More popular *Manual of Reformed Doctrine* was widely used by Calvinists, as well as his *The History of Christian Doctrine* (1937).

BERNADETTE (1844-1879), born to a poor miller's family with surname of Subirous at Lourdes. Claimed to have seen Virgin Mary in a cave near the Gave River in 1858. Entered the Convent of the Sisters of Charity near Lourdes. Site of her vision became an important center for Roman Catholic pilgrimages. Many claimed to be healed in the waters.

BERNARD, THOMAS DEHANY (1815-1904), Church of England clergyman, born at Clifton near Bristol, Gloucestershire, England, educated at Exeter College, Oxford. Ordained priest in 1841. Between the time of ordination and 1895 held various clerical positions in several different churches. Select preacher in Oxford in 1855, 1862, and

1882. Bampton lecturer in 1864, publishing lectures under the title *Progess of Doctrine in the New Testament*. Other writings: *The Witness of God, The Central Teaching of Jesus Christ,* and *Songs of the Holy Nativity.*

BERNARD OF CLAIRVAUX (ber närd′ kler vō′) (c. 1090-1153), schoolman, and mystic. Born at Fontaines, near Dijon, France. Weak of frame and unfit for military service, early destined for the church and given an education with religious service in view. About 1113 entered the famous monastery at Cîteaux or Cistercium, from which came the Cistercian order of monks. In 1115 ordained and founded the famous monastery of Clairvaux over which he was abbot until his death in 1153. From it his influence reached far and wide. Remembered as Abbot of Clairvaux, a pious mystic, a great schoolman, and a staunch defender of the orthodox Catholic faith. Practiced rigid asceticism, disciplined his monks with strict but loving care, preached to them and counseled them in the spiritual life. Outside the monastery, preached to great crowds. Became the most notable man in the church of France, and exerted great influence in Germany and Italy. Successful in healing disputes and was an able defender of Catholic orthodoxy against the scholastic subtleties of Peter Abelard, the anti-papal tendencies of Arnold of Brescia, and the popular evangelistic views of Peter de Bruys and Henry of Lausanne. Counsel sought in a dispute as to who should occupy the papal chair. In 1146 at the pope's request preached the second crusade. A man of deep mystical and spiritual capacity; life one of profound contemplation. His love was passionately centered in God and in Christ. A practical, creative mysticism led him into a passion to serve his fellow-men. Union in God must issue in creativeness. His teaching affected the whole spiritual life of the medieval church, and enriched the life of the whole church from his day to ours. Founded over 500 monasteries in Europe. Wrote such great hymns as "Jesus Thou Joy of Loving Hearts," "O Sacred Head Now Wounded" and "Jesus the Very Thought of Thee."

BERNARD OF CLUNY or MORLAIX (fl. c. 1140 or later.), Benedictine monk, poet, satirist, hymnist, born in Brittany, of English parentage, died at Cluny. Almost nothing is known except that he wrote a poem of nearly three thousand lines entitled *De Contemptu Mundi,* about 1140. It is a bitter satirical arraignment of the twelfth century for its vices in church and society, sparing not even monks or nuns, priests or bishops, not even Rome itself. One of the best known and most popular parts today is that which begins with "Jerusalem the Golden," and in the translation has become the beautiful hymn by that name. Two other hymns developed from this translation are: "The World is Very Evil," and "For Thee, O Dear, Dear Country" and "Brief Life is Here Our Portion."

BERNARDINO OF SIENA (1380-1444), Observant Franciscan preacher, born at Massa di Carara, Italy. 1402 entered the Franciscan order as an Observant, and became the first vicar-general of the Observants, who numbered only a few congregations then, but increased greatly under his administration. Restored the strictness of the earlier monastic rule of the Franciscans. Became a most famous preacher, preaching all over Italy, but centering labors chiefly in Siena. Like the most of the Franciscans, preached moral rather than religious sermons. Successful in attacking and overcoming gambling, refused three bishoprics that eagerly sought his service—Siena, Ferrara, and Urbino. Canonized in 1450.

BERSIER (bĕr syā′), **EUGENE ARTHUR FRANÇOIS** (1831-1889), French Reformed preacher, born near Geneva, Switzerland, spent most of his life in France. About 1850 made an extended visit to the United States. While here felt the call, and made the decision to go back to France to teach the gospel. Then pursued theological studies in Geneva, Göttingen, and Halle under such men as Merle D'Aubigné, Friedrich Tholuck, Julius Müller, and Isaac Dorner. From 1855 to 1877 was pastor of Free church of Paris. In 1877 he and congregation joined the Reformed (established) church of France. Took high rank as pulpit orator and used influence in every way possible against the war with Prussia in 1870. After the war spent about two decades building congregation, preaching with great power. Published seven or eight volumes of sermons. He ranks with such French preachers as Bossuet. Wrote a biography of Coligny.

BERTHOLD (bĕr′tōlt) **von REGENSBURG** (or **RATISBON**) (1210-1272), German Franciscan itinerant preacher, "The Chrysostom of the Middle Ages," born at Regensburg (or Ratisbon), entered the Franciscan order, and was ordained priest. A great preacher, traveled over much of the continent, preaching in Bavaria, Germany, Alsace, Switzerland, Austria, Hungary, Bohemia, Moravia, and Silesia. Great crowds gathered to hear him. Preached in the open air to as many as sixty thousand people at one time. Spoke both in German and in Latin, and often to Slavic groups through an interpreter. Preached unsparingly against such vices of the age as usury, avarice, dishonest trade, unchastity, drunkenness, gossip, vanity, the tournament, the dance, and anything that would tend to destroy the home. His preaching was strong, vivacious, picturesque, and compelling. He was strongly opposed to the preaching of indulgences, and to the false confidence in the prayers of intercession of the saints and of Mary. His chief appeal was to manifest true sorrow for sin, sincere confession, and penitence, as well as works of penance. A child of his age; he was hard on heretics. After several years of itinerant preaching returned to Regensburg (or Ratisbon).

BERYLLUS OF BOSTRA (Third Century), unorthodox theologian. Home in Bostra in Arabia, Petraea. Denied the personal preexistence and in general the independent deity of Christ, teaching a dynamistic monarchianism; at the same time asserted the indwelling of the divinity of the Father in Christ during his earthly life. Teaching was somewhat a connecting link between simple Patripassianism and Sabellian modalism. At a council held in Bostra, 244, the bishops condemned his teaching. Eusebius says that Origen, by discussion with Beryllus, brought him back to the faith.

BESANT (bĕz'ant), **ANNIE, nee WOOD** (1847-1933), British theosophist and nationalist leader in India, born in London and educated by private tutors and at London University. Originally a member of the Church of England and daughter of a minister. At twenty married Rev. Frank Besant, Vicar of Sibsey, Lincolnshire; after six years of inner, turbulent, spiritual struggles left the vicar and received a divorce, then left Christianity altogether. For three years served as a member of the school board of London. Became an ardent free thinker, a revolutionary socialist, and a member of the National Secular Society, and finally a disciple of Madame Blavatsky. 1889, joined the Theosophical Society, serving as president from 1907 until her death. She not only was probably the most prominent of all British theosophical luminaries, but was also destined to become a bright star in the political fortunes of India. In 1898 founded the Central Hindu College of Benares, India; in 1904, the Central Hindu Girls' School, Benares; in 1907 the University of India; in 1916 established the Indian Home Rule League, becoming its president; in 1917, elected president of the Indian National Congress. 1923, general secretary of the National Convention of India. Regarded as a powerful figure in Indian politics. 1926, traveled widely with her protégé and adopted son, Jidder Krishnamurti, an Indian mystic whom she declared the new Messiah and reincarnation of the World Teacher. Krishnamurti in 1931 repudiated Mrs. Besant's claims of his being the Messiah. She was the author of: *The Religious Problems of India, The Wisdom of the Upanishads, The Basis of Morality, A World Religion, India: Bond or Free?, World Problems of Today, Theosophy and the New Psychology, Re-incarnation,* and an autobiography, *Through Storm to Peace,* as well as many occult works.

BESSARION, JOHNNES (BASILIUS) (c. 1403-1472), Byzantine theologian. Born in Trebizond and studied in Constantinople. Became a monk in 1423 and took the name Bessarion. Ordained in 1431. Abbot of St. Basil's monastery. Archbishop of Nicaea 1439. In 1439 worked at Florence to unify the Latin and Greek Churches. Made cardinal in 1439. His library became the nucleus of the library of Marciana, Venice in 1453.

BEVERIDGE, WILLIAM (1637-1708), Anglican bishop of Asaph, born at Leicestershire, England, educated at St. John's College, Cambridge. 1660, ordained priest in 1660. From 1660 to 1672 vicar of Ealing, near London. Became rector of St. Peter's, Cornhill, London in 1672; prebendary of Canterbury in 1674; Archdeacon of Colchester in 1681. 1704, installed bishop of Asaph. His principal theological works: *An Exposition of the Thirty-nine Articles, Sermons on the Ministry and Ordinances of the Church of England, Duo, Private Thoughts upon Religion,* and *Doctrine of the Church of England.*

BEZA (bē'zȧ), **THEODORE** (1519-1605), reformer. Admirer, friend, associate and successor of John Calvin at Geneva, born at Vézelay, Burgundy, educated at Bourges and Orléans. Trained for the bar but preferred literature. An illness turned his thoughts in 1548 to God and the Reformed faith. Upon conversion came under the influence and teaching of Calvin. A place was soon found for him at Lausanne where he taught Greek, expounded the Scriptures, and assisted in translating the Psalms from 1549 to 1558. In 1558 called to Geneva to teach Greek, to become president of the college in 1559, and to help Calvin. Installed as one of the pastors of Geneva, did effective service. Learning and eloquence gave him great influence and power in preaching and in reform work. After Calvin's death, 1564, he was called by the city council to succeed Calvin as leader of the Geneva Reformation. Long and busy life as preacher, theologian, scholar, and reformer. Wrote a biography of Calvin (1564) and *Treatises* (1582) with harmony of fifteen Protestant Confessions.

BICKERSTETH (bĭk'ĕr stĕth), **EDWARD** (1786-1850), English Evangelical clergyman, born at Westmorland, England. For fifteen years clerk in a solicitor's office.

Studied law and began to practice at Norwich; but soon becoming deeply interested in spiritual matters, left the law practice, ordained in 1815, and entered the service of the Church Missionary Society. Traveling secretary for the society for about fifteen years. From 1830 until his death, rector of Watton, Hertfordshire. A strong Protestant, he consequently opposed the Tractarian Movement. Also strongly opposed the coming of Unitarianism into the church. In eschatology a millennialist. In 1840 took part in the formation of the Parker Society for republishing the works of the English reformers; assisted in the formation of the Evangelical Alliance; and took part in the establishment and promotion of the Irish Church Mission Society. Among writings: *A Help to the Study of the Scriptures, Guide to Prophecy,* etc., in sixteen volumes. Edited *The Christian Library* in fifty volumes; compiled an anthology *Christian psalmody* of more than seven hundred hymns, later adding two hundred more. For a long time this was the most popular hymnbook of the Evangelical party. Wrote the hymn, "Peace Perfect Peace." His son, Edward Henry Bickersteth (1825-1906), was also a prominent churchman, and a missionary in West Africa.

BIDDLE, JOHN (1615-1662), early English Unitarian. Born in Gloucestershire. Educated at Magdalen Hall, Oxford. Taught school in Gloucester. Write an anti-trinitarian work, *Twelve Questions* or *Arguments Denying the Deity of the Holy Spirit.* His views led to alternate periods of imprisonment and release.

BIEDERWOLF (bē'dẽr wo͝olf), **WILLIAM EDWARD** (1867-1939), American Presbyterian evangelist, born in Monticello, Indiana, educated at Wabash College, Indiana, Princeton University, Princeton Theological Seminary, the universities of Erlangen and Berlin, Germany, and the Sorbonne, France. Converted at twenty, while teaching school, ordained in 1897. Pastor of the Broadway Church, Logansport, Indiana, three years; chaplain in the Spanish-American War, one year, evangelist from 1900 to 1939. About three years worked with the J. W. Chapman evangelistic campaign in various parts of country. For the next third of a century conducted evangelistic campaigns in the United States; in company with Homer Rodeheaver and Miss Grace Saxe, made a world evangelistic tour in 1924. President of Winona College, 1917-1919. In 1922 became director of Winona Lake Bible Conference, "the world's largest Bible Conference." Raised the money to clear the conference of accumulated debts, saving it from bankruptcy. Reorganized with a new constitution, and renamed The Winona Lake Christian Assembly, Inc. Biederwolf was first president. 1923, also became director of The Winona Lake Bible School of Theology, holding this position until 1933, then became its president. In 1909 Dr. Biederwolf had started, and had become general director of the Family Altar League, in later years its president. When in Japan and Korea in 1920 he became much interested in the lepers and leper work, raised money which built "The Biederwolf Leper Home" in Korea. During last ten years, 1929-1939, pastor of the Royal Poinciana Chapel at Palm Beach, Florida. A few books from his pen: *A Help to the Study of the Holy Spirit, The Growing Christian, The Millennium Bible, Evangelism, Whipping Post Theology, The Great Tribulation, The New Paganism,* and *The Wonderful Christ.*

BIEL (bēl), **GABRIEL** (c. 1410-1495), schoolman, born at Speyer, Germany. Studied at Heidelberg and Erfurt. Filled, with distinction, the chair of philosophy and theology at the University of Tübingen. Biel was a diligent preacher as well as a noted teacher. In theology he followed the nominalism of William of Occam. He separated faith and reason. Like others among the scholastics he wrote a commentary on the *Sentences* of Peter the Lombard, which was perhaps his most important work. He also did some writing of note in the field of political economy. Held that supply and demand, not theology, should determine what was a just price. Though a churchman, not a rigid papist, held the authority of Church Councils above that of the pope. His doctrine of the eucharist also varied from the traditional view of the church. In his later years he joined the Brethren of the Common Life at Schönau. Greatly influenced Luther.

BIGG, CHARLES (1840-1908), Church of England theologian and historian, born near Manchester, England, studied at Christ College, Oxford. A brilliant academic career as a student, becoming tutor in the college in 1863. Ordained priest in 1864. Between 1866 and 1901 successively classical master in Cheltenham College, headmaster of Brighton College, chaplain of Corpus Christi, rector of Fenny Compton, Leamington, and honorary canon of Worchester. In 1901, elected Regius Professor of ecclesiastical history in Oxford University, thus coming into the main sphere of life work. The same year made canon of Christ Church, Oxford. Examining chaplain to the bishops of Worcester, Peterborough, London, and Man. In 1886 delivered the Bampton lectures on *The Christian Platonists of Alex-*

andria. Edited a number of Greek classics, the *Confession of Saint Augustine, The Didache,* and other works. Wrote *Neoplatonism, The Church's Task under the Roman Empire, Commentary on the Epistles of Peter and Jude (International Critical Commentary),* and *The Origins of Christianity,* perhaps his most important work.

BILDERDIJK (bĭl'dĕr dīk), **WILLEM** (1756-1831), Dutch poet and scholar, born in Amsterdam, Holland. Studied at the University of Leiden. Practiced law at the Hague. Exiled in 1795. Went to London and to Brunswick. Upon return to Holland in 1806, became state librarian. From 1817 to 1827 lectured on history in Leiden. After 1827 lived at Haarlem. His poetic masterpiece was *The Destruction of the First World*. Isaac de Costa, a Jew converted by Bilderdijk, started a strong Evangelical revival in Holland, repudiating both the eighteenth century rationalism and the extreme orthodoxy of Dort. The movement was carried on by Henry de Cock.

BILHORN, PETER PHILIP (1862-1936), American composer, singer, and publisher of music, born at Mendota, Illinois. When fifteen the family moved to Chicago and opened a carriage business. In 1881 Peter was converted at the Moody Church. Having discovered his talent for singing, began music study under George F. Root. Earnestly studied the Bible and began evangelistic preaching. Entered the Mount Hermon school at Northfield, Massachusetts; left the school to re-enter evangelistic work. Sold out carriage business and devoted himself to preaching and singing the gospel, becoming a noted evangelist. Compiler of several gospel song books; author of many gospel hymns, both words and music. Writer of tunes for many more. Among his hymns: "Peace, Peace, Sweet Peace," "I Will Sing the Wondrous Story," "Drinking at the Living Fountain." Inventor of the miniature organ known as "The Bilhorn Telescope Organ."

BINGHAM, HIRAM, Sr. (1789-1869), American Congregational clergyman and missionary, born at Bennington, Vermont. Graduated from Middlebury College in 1816 and from Andover Theological Seminary in 1819. 1819, ordained at Goshen, Connecticut, and sent that year by the American Board as one of their first missionaries to Hawaii, the land of Obookiah, a young native Hawaiian whose death in Connecticut led to Bingham's decision to go to Hawaii. Stationed at Honolulu from 1819 to 1840, became a leader of the mission and pastor of the first church. Prominent in the creation of a written language; and translated into that language most of the Scriptures from 1825 to 1839, hymns, the catechisms, and several text books. Trusted adviser of the king and of the chiefs in their hostile relations with foreigners. Remained in Honolulu until 1840, when he returned for a time to the States because of the ill health of his wife, who died in 1848. Returning to the field, he wrote *The Residence of Twenty-one Years in the Sandwich Islands* and completed translation of the Old Testament. As a missionary greatly beloved by the people among whom he worked. Made a significant contribution to the success of the mission.

BINGHAM, HIRAM, Jr. (1831-1908), Congregational missionary to Polynesia, born of missionary parents in Honolulu, Hawaii, educated at Yale College and Andover Theological Seminary. He was acting superintendent of the Northhampton High School, 1853-1854. In 1855 ordained. In 1857 Mr. and Mrs. Bingham were sent by the American Board to the Gilbert Islands as the first missionaries. Set himself to task of mastering the Gilbert Islands language, gathering a vocabulary and constructing a grammar. At the end of twenty years produced a New Testament in the Gilbertese. Then he and his scholarly, devoted wife began work on the Old Testament. Finally, in 1893 (after an absence of nearly thirty years from the United States) in New York he saw the last verse of the Old Testament being put into type. Next effort and accomplishment was a Gilbertese dictionary. Before publication the manuscript was loaned and lost beyond recovery. Bingham quietly began work once more, and in 1908, just before his death he completed the second copy. Also wrote some commentaries on portions of the New Testament, and a hymn and tune book in the Gilbertese. Many other activities filled the life of this missionary. From 1866-1868, in command of the missionary brig *Morning Star*. Corresponding secretary of the Board of the Hawaiian Evangelical Association, 1877-1880, and from 1880-1882 Hawaiian Government Protector of South Sea immigrants.

BINGHAM, ROWLAND VICTOR (1872-1942), born in East Grinstead, Sussex. Taught school at thirteen. Converted through the Salvation Army and became an officer. Missionary to Lagos in 1894. Went to USA in 1894 and took medical course in Cleveland and Bible training at Nyack. Served Church in Newburgh, New York (1895-1899). Went to Lagos and then Kano in 1900. Organized the Sudan Interior Mission in 1901, which had its origin in his first period in Lagos in 1893. Was responsible for development of Canadian Keswick at Muskoka. Founded and was editor from 1904 to 1929 of the *Evangelical Christian*. Helped found the Soldiers and Airmen's Christian Association. Evangelical Publishers was developed in 1912.

BINNEY, THOMAS (1798-1874), English Congregational preacher, born at Newcastle-on-Tyne, Northamptonshire, England. At seven years apprenticed to a bookseller where between the ages of fourteen and twenty did much reading. Studied Latin and Greek evenings with a Presbyterian minister. Attended a Congregational theological school at Wymondley, Hertfordshire for three years. Short pastorates at Bedford, and at Newport, Isle of Wight. In 1829 began his pastorate at the historic King's Weigh House Chapel, London, where he ministered until 1869. In 1845 he visited Canada, and the United States. In 1857 went to the Australian colonies, where he preached with power and acceptance. Became the leading figure of his denomination. In 1869 became professor of homiletics and pastoral theology at New College, London. Twice chairman of the Congregational Union in England and Wales. Among his writings are: *Is It Possible to Make the Best of Two Worlds?; Service of Song in the House of the Lord; Dissent not Schism; St. Paul, His Life and Ministry; Micah, the Priest-Maker;* and books of sermons and biography.

BIRKS, THOMAS RAWSON (1810-1883), English Evangelical divine and theologian, born at Staveley, Derbyshire, England; a nonconformist, educated at Chesterfield; at Dissenting College at Mill Hill; at Trinity College, Cambridge. Joined the Church of England, and settled first as tutor at Watton, and then as curate to Edward Bickersteth at Watton. From 1844 to 1866 preached at Kelshall in Hertfordshire; in 1866 accepted the important charge of Trinity Church, Cambridge, a position held until 1877. In 1871, installed honorary canon of Ely Cathedral, and the next year elected professor of moral philosophy at Cambridge. For twenty-one years honorary secretary to the Evangelical Alliance, active in all university affairs during connection with Cambridge. Some of his chief writings: *Modern Rationalism, Inspiration of the Scriptures, The Bible and Modern Thought, Commentary on the Book of Isaiah, Horae Apostolicae, The Scripture Doctrine of Creation,* and several lectures published in the Victoria Institute.

BIRNEY, JAMES GILLESPIE (1792-1857), reformer and abolitionist. Born Danville, Kentucky. Educated at the College of New Jersey (now Princeton University) and studied law. Admitted to the bar in 1814, practiced law in Danville and served as a legislator in 1816. Moved to Alabama in 1818. Served as state legislator in 1819 as well as public prosecutor from 1818 to 1826. Counsel for Cherokee Indians. Agent of American Colonization Society (1832-1834). Went to New York in 1837 as secretary of the American Anti-Slavery Society. Candidate for president for Liberty Party in 1840. Wanted abolition of slavery by legislative action.

BISMARCK, OTTO VON (1815-1898), Prussian statesman. Born in Prussia. Studied at Göttingen and Berlin. Judicial administrator in Aachen. Represented Prussia at Frankfurt Diet in 1851. Diplomat in St. Petersburg and Paris (1859-1862). Prime minister of Prussia in 1862. Arranged wars against Denmark, Austria, and France from 1864 to 1870 that led to the rise of the German Reich in 1871 and his chancellorship. During the 1880's obtained legislation to win workers away from socialism. Opposed papal control in Germany as hindering national spirit and obtained Falk laws (later repealed) to weaken the Roman Catholic church. He was the architect of a united German state.

BLACK, HUGH (1868-1953), Scottish-American preacher and author, born at Rothesay, Buteshire, Scotland, studied at the Free Church College and at the University of Glasgow. Ordained in 1891, and held charges at Sherwood Church, Paisley, 1891-1896; at St. George's United Free Church, Edinburgh, 1896-1906. Became professor of homiletics at Union Theological Seminary, New York, 1906-1938. Recognized as one of the world's great preachers. Several volumes of sermons published.

BLACK, JOHN (1818-1882), Canadian colonial missionary. Born at Dumfries, Scotland. Educated at Knox College, Toronto. Ordained 1851. Sent to Scottish Red River settlement, where he served the settlers until 1862.

BLACK, WILLIAM (1760-1834), Canadian Methodist leader. Born in Huddersfield, West Yorkshire. Moved to Nova Scotia in 1775. Became a Methodist preacher. Founded the Wesleyan Methodist Church in Nova Scotia and was general superintendent of Methodist work in America for a time.

BLACKSTONE, WILLIAM EUGENE (1841-1935), businessman, evangelist, Zionist, born at Adams, New York. Converted at eleven. Because of ill health formal education limited to that of a local academy. An inveterate reader and a deep student of the Bible and of world events. Served in U.S. Christian Commission during the Civil War. In 1870 settled in Oak Park, Illinois, where he became a successful businessman. Though a layman in the Methodist Episcopal Church, he was deeply interested in prophecy, which led to his writing the widely circulated *Jesus Is Coming*. He soon became interested in the Jews and in the re-establishing of Palestine as a Jewish state. In 1887 he helped start the Chicago Hebrew Mission, and was superintendent until 1891. In 1888 he made a trip to Palestine and Egypt. As a result of the trip he became much interested in the Zionist movement in re-establishing Palestine as a Jewish state, so that the Jews might be enabled to return to their fatherland. 1891 he sent a memorial signed by Jews and Christians to President Harrison asking the president to use his office to bring about an international conference to consider the Jews and their claims to Palestine. First conference of Jews and Christians held in Chicago in 1890.

BLACKWOOD, ANDREW WATTERSON (1882-1966), born at Clay Center, Kansas. Educated in Franklin College, Ohio and Princeton and Xenia Theological Seminaries. Ordained in 1908. Pastor in Pennsylvania, South Carolina, and Ohio (1908-1925). Taught homiletics and pastoral theology at the Presbyterian Seminary in Louisville, Kentucky (1925-1930), Princeton Theological Seminary (1930-1950), and at the School of Theology of Temple University (1950-1958). Advocated expository preaching based on a sound exegesis of Scripture. Wrote *Preaching From the Bible, The Preparation of Sermons, Expository Preaching for Today* and numerous other books on preaching.

BLAIKIE, WILLIAM GARDEN (1820-1899), clergyman, Free Church of Scotland, born at Aberdeen, Scotland, studied at Marischal College, and universities of Edinburgh and Aberdeen. He was ordained minister of the Established Church at Drumblade, Aberdeenshire in 1842, joined the Free Church of Scotland at the time of the Disruption in 1843. Most of his congregation seceded with him and erected a church for their use. Became minister of Pelrig, Edinburgh in 1844, remaining there twenty-four years. In 1868 Blaikie was chosen for the chair of apologetics and pastoral theology in New College, Edinburgh, filling this office until 1897. A delegate from the Free Church of Scotland to the General Assembly of the Presbyterian Church of the United States at Philadelphia in 1870. The actual founder of the Alliance of the Reformed churches with Presbyterian Form of Government. Active in home missions, temperance, and church extension for his denomination. 1892, he was the last of the Pre-Disruption ministers to be honored with the moderatorship of the General Assembly. The same year received the additional honor of being appointed president of the Presbyterian Alliance. Dr. Blaikie was editor of two different magazines, *The Sunday Magazine,* 1873-1874, and *The Catholic Presbyterian,* 1879-1883. Among his books: *Bible History, Bible Geography, Better Days for the Working People, For the Work of the Ministry, Glimpses of the Inner Life of Our Lord, The Public Ministry and Pastoral Methods of Our Lord, The Personal Life of David Livingstone,* and several biographies.

BLAIR, JAMES (c. 1655-1743), American clergyman and educator. Born in Alvah, Scotland. Educated at the University of Edinburgh. Minister in Scotland (1679-1681) and librarian in London (1682-1685). Minister at Henrico Parish, Virginia (1685-1694), Jamestown (1694-1710) and from 1710 until death at Bruton Parish Church in Williamsburg. Obtained charter for and became first president (1694-1743) of William and Mary College. Appointed commissary in 1680 by the bishop of London to oversee the churches in Virginia. Greatly strengthened the Anglican church in Virginia.

BLANCHARD, CHARLES ALBERT (1848-1925), president of Wheaton College, born at Galesburg, Illinois, where his father, Jonathan Blanchard, was president of Knox College (Presbyterian). Named after Charles Albert, Duke of Saxony. Attended Wheaton Academy, and entered Wheaton College, where his father had become president, in 1860. 1870, graduated from the college and entered Y.M.C.A. work, lecturing for the Association from 1870 to 1872. 1872, became principal of Wheaton Academy. 1878, became assistant to his father in the college. 1882, elected president of Wheaton College, which position he held until his death. In 1878, ordained pastor of the College Church in Wheaton. Served from 1878 to 1883. From 1883 until 1884 supply pastor of the Chicago Avenue Moody Church. During his administration the college took its place among the colleges of the country and became noted for its Christian principles and conservative teaching. In 1913 he was elected to the presidency of the Chicago Hebrew Mission, and continued in that capacity until his death.

BLANCHARD, JONATHAN (1811-1892), Presbyterian clergyman, born in Rockingham, Vermont; educated at Middlebury College, at Andover, and at Lane Theological Seminary. At Middlebury began one of the first student papers, the *Undergraduate*. Anti-slavery lecturer (1836-1837). Ordained pastor of the Sixth Presbyterian Church, Cincinnati, Ohio in 1838. Deeply interested in temperance, abolition, and antisecrecy. President of Knox College, Galesburg, Illinois, 1846-1857; president of Wheaton College, 1860-1882; president emeritus, 1882-1892. His son Charles succeeded him at Wheaton in 1882. Editor and publisher of *Free-Masonry Illustrated,* and *Christian*

Cynosure (1868). Attended second Anti-Slavery convention in London in 1843. President of National Christian Association.

BLAUROCK or CAJACOB, GEORG (c. 1492-1529), Swiss Anabaptist reformer, who though with little education was an effective preacher. By 1524, Blaurock, once a monk of Corie, had come to the conviction that infant baptism was unscriptural. Helped form the Anabaptist movement. In January, 1525 in the home of Felix Manz in Zurich, requested rebaptism at the hands of Conrad Grebel, the leader among the early Swiss Brethren. He then baptized by sprinkling others present, thus instituting believers baptism and crystalizing the Anabaptist movement. In spite of frequent imprisonments, Blaurock continued his preaching with great power of conviction. He was captured in Tyrol and burned at Innsbruck.

BLAVATSKY (blå väts'kĭ), **ELENA PETROVNA, nee HAHN** (1831-1891), founder of Theosophical Society, born in Ekaterinoslav, Russia, of noble descent. In 1848 married the aged General N. V. Blavatsky, but soon separated from him. For next twenty years traveled in many parts of the world studying spiritualism, Buddhistic philosophy, and other occult and esoteric doctrines. 1858, converted to spiritualism and started a spiritualistic movement in Russia. 1873, in the United States. 1875, in collaboration with Col. Henry Steel Olcott and William Judge, founded (New York) the Theosophical Society, a highly mystical, philosophical, and non-Christian cult. 1877, published *Isis Unveiled: The Master Key to Ancient and Modern Mysticism,* with some startling theories concerning the evolution of humanity and of religion. 1879, with Col. Olcott went to India where they founded the Theosophical Society's magazine, *The Theosophist,* and established their headquarters near Madras, herself secretary. Died in London in 1891, leaving the society a membership of nearly one hundred thousand in many parts of the world. While she lived she ruled the society with an iron hand. Upon her demise, one of her pupils, Annie Besant, took up the work of the society.

BLISS, DANIEL (1823-1916), American Congregational missionary educator, born at Georgia, Vermont, educated at Amherst College and Andover Theological Seminary. Ordained to the Congregational ministry and sent to Syria as a missionary of the American Board of Commissioners for Foreign Missions (1885). When the Syria Mission (1862) voted to start a "Literary Institution," Bliss was assigned the task and privilege of organizing and presiding over it. 1862, during the Civil War, Bliss in the United States raised one hundred thousand dollars to start the college, and in England raised another twenty thousand. In 1866 the school opened as the Syrian Protestant College of Beirut (now American University) with Bliss as president. Arabic was the medium of instruction for the first seventeen years, and English thereafter. Bliss also served as professor of Bible and ethics, and as treasurer. President of the college for thirty-six years, resigning in 1902 when the college had grown to a student body of over eight hundred with a faculty of about seventy-five members. He authored a number of textbooks in Arabic, particularly one on *Mental Philosophy* and one on *Natural Philosophy.*

BLISS, PHILIP PAUL (1838-1876), hymn and hymn-tune writer and gospel singer, born at Rome, Pennsylvania in a home of praying and singing parents. Made public confession of Christ at the age of twelve. Early years spent on a farm, early formal education very limited. Between 1856 and 1860 taught several terms of school while studying music. One of his public school pupils was Daniel Brink Towner. 1859, married a young woman, musician and poet, a great help to him. 1860, began teaching music professionally. 1864, produced first composition, 1865, moved to Chicago, became associated with Root and Cady, music publishers. Also conducted musical institutes, gave concerts, composed Sunday school melodies. For some time Dwight L. Moody urged him to give up his business for full time gospel singing. 1874, consented to join Major D. W. Whittle in evangelistic work as song leader and children's worker. Service in this field for the next two or three years was effective. Died in a train accident while trying to rescue his wife. A great gospel singer. Many of the hymns he had written and the melodies for them had been produced in a flash of inspiration: "Let the Lower Lights be Burning"; "Hold the Fort"; "Man of Sorrows! What a Name!"; "The Light of the World is Jesus"; "Almost Persuaded"; "I Will Sing of My Redeemer"; "Hallelujah What a Savior"; "I am so Glad that Jesus Loves Me"; "Hallelujah, 'Tis Done"; "Wonderful Words of Life"; "Whosoever Will May Come"; and "More Holiness Give Me." Julian says that P. P. Bliss stands next to Fanny Crosby for gospel hymns.

BLUMHARD, CHRISTIAN GOTTLIEB (1779-1838), born in home of pietistic cobbler in Stuttgart, Germany. Missionary, mainly in India, for the Basil Missionary Society from 1804. Was inspector for the Society from 1816 until his death.

BLUMHARDT, JOHANN CHRISTOPH (1805-1880), German evangelist and divine healer. Studied at Tübingen. Pastor at Basel

Mission Institute (1830-1838). Pastor at Möttlingen from 1838 to 1852, where healings took place. Moved in 1852 to Bad Boll which became a divine healing center.

BOARDMAN, GEORGE DANA, Sr. (1801-1831), American Baptist missionary to Burma, born at Livermore, Maine, educated at Waterville College and Andover Theological Seminary. Earned money to obtain education by teaching school for several years. Ordained in the Baptist church in 1825, same year sent by Baptist Board of Foreign Missions to India. After studying the Burmese language near Calcutta for about fifteen months, established a mission among the Burmese at Moulmein near the coast of Burma. This mission became the main Baptist headquarters in Burma. Founded a mission among the Karens at Tavoy, about one hundred fifty miles south of Moulmein. Worked with great success until his death. Few years on the field accompanied by much physical suffering.

BOARDMAN, GEORGE DANA, Jr. (1828-1903), American Baptist minister, born at Tavoy, British Burma, son of George Dana and Sarah Hall Boardman. Came to USA for education when six years old. Later studied at Brown University and at Newton Theological Institution. Held several pastorates, notably First Baptist Church, Philadelphia, 1864-1894. 1899, established a permanent lectureship at the University of Pennsylvania, known as the Boardman Foundation in Christian Ethics. President of the American Baptist Missionary Union, 1880-1884; of the Christian Arbitration and Peace Society of America. Most important production, *Titles of Wednesday Evening Lectures,* embracing nine hundred eighty-one lectures—a complete exegesis of the Bible. Other writings: *Studies in the Creative Week, Epiphanies of the Risen Lord, The Golden Rule, The Ten Commandments, The Church, The Kingdom, Our Risen King's Forty Days* and *Studies in the Model Prayer.*

BOARDMAN, RICHARD (1738-1782), early Methodist minister in America, born in Ireland. For several years a lay Methodist minister there. 1769, sent with Joseph Pilmoor as a missionary to America. Began mission in New York in the John Street Church established by Philip Embury. Did his chief work there, but exchanged pulpits periodically with Pilmoor of Philadelphia, and did some itinerant preaching in environs of New York City. After several years of successful work in New York, when the shadows of the Revolutionary War began to thicken, he returned to England in 1774. Continued his itinerant preaching in England and Ireland until his death in Ireland.

BOEGNER, MARC (1881-1967), pastor, professor, and ecumenist. Born in Epinal, France. Studied law and theology in Paris. Ordained in 1905 and became pastor at Aouste, Drôme, in 1911. Professor of theology in the Missionary School of Paris (1911-1918). Pastor of the Reformed church at Passy, Paris from 1918 to 1953. President of the French Protestant Church Federation from 1920 to 1939, the National Council of Reformed Churches of France from 1938 to 1950 and one of the presidents of the World Council of Churches from 1948 to 1954.

BOEHLER, PETER. *See* **BÖHLER, PETER**

BOEHM (bûm), **MARTIN** (1725-1812), with Philip Otterbein co-founder of the Church of the United Brethren in Christ, born in Lancaster County, Pennsylvania of Swiss Mennonite parentage. Education meager, elected to the ministry by his local Mennonite church. Experienced a spiritual awakening similar to that of German Reformed preacher, Philip William Otterbein. About 1768 joined Otterbein in many evangelistic campaigns, holding two-day "great meetings," among German-speaking people of Pennsylvania, Maryland, and Virginia. The earnest evangelistic preaching of these two men resulted in many converts, the final organization of a new denomination in 1800 under the name of the Church of the United Brethren in Christ. Boehm and Otterbein were elected as joint bishops, continuously re-elected until they died.

BOEHME (bû'mě), **JACOB** (1575-1624), profound German Lutheran mystic, born at Altseidenberg, near Görlitz, in upper Lusatia, Germany. Became a shoemaker, settled at Görlitz where he married and raised family of six. His neighbors thought him a model husband and father. A visionary and interested in theosophical speculations. In 1600, as in "a flash of lightning," he felt that "the gate of his soul was opened." He claimed after that to have had frequent visions and revelations. After ten years of these experiences, he wrote down in an unsystematic way some of his ideas and visions. Outwardly, continued a loyal Lutheran, inwardly, a mystic. Mystical writings offended the orthodox church authorities. Commanded in 1612 to cease writing. Complied for five years; then, conscience-stricken for keeping quiet, began to write again. From 1617 until his death in 1624, he wrote about thirty works, one of them *Aurora, oder die Morgenröte im Aufgang,* which contained "revelations and meditations upon God, man, and nature, and showing a remarkable knowledge of Scripture, and of the writings of the alchemists."

1623, persecution was renewed; fled to Dresden and then later to Silesia. 1624, overtaken with illness and died soon after his return to his old home at Görlitz. His mystical writings have had a great influence on many individuals and religious groups through the centuries. Latourette says his thought had wide influence in Germany, the Netherlands, Russia, and England; also influenced Isaac Newton and William Law.

BOETHIUS (bō ē'thĭ ŭs), **ANICIUS MANLIUS TORQUATUS SEVERINUS** (c. 480-524), Roman philospher, born in Rome, received the best education Rome could afford, becoming well acquainted with Greek philosophy. 510, became consul. Enjoyed esteem of people and confidence and friendship of Theodoric, the Ostrogothic king of Italy. When the king became suspicious of all Romans and Catholics he charged Boethius with treasonable relations with Emperor Justin of Constantinople. Exiled to Pavia, and imprisoned and finally beheaded in 524. A man of enormous learning and industry. Literary aim throughout life, to make all the writings of Plato and Aristotle available to Latin readers. In passing on to the schoolmen the Aristotelian ideas and methods he had a great influence upon the medieval church, being in a sense a forerunner of Thomas Aquinas. Became the connecting link between logical and metaphysical science of antiquity and scientific attempt of the middle age. Has been called the last of the Romans and the first of the Schoolmen. Great philosophical work. *On the Consolation of Philosophy,* written in prison shortly before his execution; translated into nearly every European language. Also wrote the more Christian *De Sancta Trinitate*.

BOGUE, DAVID (1750-1825), born in Scotland. Presbyterian and later Congregationalist minister. Helped to organize the interdenominational London Missionary Society in 1795. Blocked from missionary work in India by the British East India Company. Aided in the founding of the British and Foreign Bible Society and the Religious Tract Society.

BÖHLER, PETER (1712-1775), Moravian minister and missionary, born at Frankfort-on-Main. Studied theology at Jena, met Count Zinzendorf. In 1737 set apart by Zinzendorf, sent by way of London to the American colonies to work among the blacks of Georgia. In London, 1738, awaiting his sailing Böhler organized a society, later to be known as Fetter Lane Society. Met John Wesley, just returned from his mission in Georgia. Böhler taught a complete self-surrendering faith, an instantaneous conversion, and a joy in believing. Positive, assuring faith was just what Wesley was craving, and it greatly influenced him the rest of his life. Upon arrival in Georgia, Böhler found the mission in weak condition. As a result of the war between England and Spain, he gave up the mission. Led his members to Pennsylvania where a new settlement was founded at Bethlehem. Labored with diligence and success. 1747, made superintendent of the Moravian church in England, and the next year, consecrated bishop. 1753, again sent to America where he labored until 1764. 1756, appointed assistant superintendent of the Moravian church in America. On a trip to England in 1775 he died. His episcopal visitations had been extensive, including his oversight of and his traveling among the congregations in England, Ireland, Wales, and America.

BOMPAS, WILLIAM CARPENTER (1834-1906), pioneer Anglican bishop in the Canadian Northwest. Born and educated in London, England. Left England in 1865 as a volunteer missionary for work among the Eskimos and Indians in the Yukon. In 1874 became bishop of Athabaska and in 1881 sent to the Mackenzie River see. In 1891 became first bishop of Selkirk (now Yukon) and served until 1905. As "Apostle of the North" translated the New Testament into Indian dialects and founded schools.

BONAR (bŏn'er), **ANDREW ALEXANDER** (1810-1892), writer and minister in Free church of Scotland, born in Edinburgh, Scotland, the youngest brother of Horatius Bonar, studied in Edinburgh. Minister at Collace, Perthshire, 1838-1856, joining the Free Church when it began in 1843. Minister of Finnieston Church, Glasgow from 1856 until his death. In 1881, at the invitation of D. L. Moody, he was a speaker and counselor at Northfield Conference in America. His church chose him as its moderator in 1878. Andrew Bonar was a man of deep and fervent prayer which became a fixed habit of his life. Jesus Christ was a very real person to him. He was identified with evangelical and revival movements; like his brother Horatius he was an ardent premillennialist. In 1839 he and his very close friend, Robert Murray McCheyne, visited Palestine to inquire into the condition of the Jews. He then published *A Narrative of a Mission of Inquiry to the Jews for the Church of Scotland in 1839*. He also published a *Memoir* of R. M. McCheyne, *A Commentary on Leviticus,* and *Christ* and *His Church in the Book of the Psalms.*

BONAR, HORATIUS (1808-1889), Scottish Presbyterian poet-preacher, born at Old Broughton, Edinburgh, Scotland, from a line of ministers. An older brother of Andrew A. Bonar. Educated at the High School and the University of Edinburgh; a favorite pupil of Dr. Chalmers. Bonar was ordained minister of North Parish Church of Kelso in 1837. At the disruption of 1843 became minister of the newly formed Free Church, remained until 1866. In 1866 moved to the Chalmers Memorial Church, Edinburgh, where he built up a large congregation. In 1883 chosen moderator of the General Assembly of his church. Editor of and contributor to the *Quarterly Journal of Prophecy,* which he founded in 1849. In theology, a conservative and premillenarian. His best work was done in hymnody. He wrote "Go Labor on! Spend and be Spent!"; "I Heard the Voice of Jesus," and about six hundred other hymns and poems. He published three series of *Hymns of Faith and Hope* between 1857 and 1866. Later he published *The Song of the New Creation; Hymns of the Nativity; Songs of Love and Joy,* and others. His hymns are simple and lucid.

BONAVENTURA (bon ȧ vĕn tū′rȧ) **(FIDANZA), GIOVANNI** (c. 1217-1274), scholastic, mystic, cardinal. Born in Tuscany. About 1238 joined the Franciscan Order in which he became a power. In Paris studied under Alexander of Hales, and became a close friend of Thomas Aquinas. Both distinguished scholars and theologians studied under Albertus Magnus, and both died in 1274. Bonaventura was made general of his order in 1257. He was created cardinal by Gregory X in 1273. Numerous writings of his remain in which are clearly traced the scholastic method and the mystic spirit. Apart from his personal influence his writings had great influence in many of the church councils. Bonaventura marks a sort of transition in scholastic theology. Opposed to Aristotle. Christian illumination superior to human wisdom. He was canonized by Sixtus IV in 1482, and declared doctor of the church by Sixtus V in 1587.

BONHOEFFER, DIETRICH (1906-1945), Lutheran minister and author. Born in Germany. Studied at Tübingen and Berlin Universities and Union Theological Seminary, New York. Much influenced by Karl Barth, under whom he studied. Pastor of German churches in Barcelona, Spain and London. Taught at the University of Berlin (1930-1936). Helped in the drafting of the 1934 Barmen Declaration of the Confessing Church. Founded in 1935 and led until closed by the Nazis in 1937 Finkenwalde Seminary. Imprisoned as a member of the resistance movement in 1943 for supposed plotting against Hitler and hanged by the Nazis in 1945. Bonhoeffer opposed institutional religion and natural theology. He stressed God's self-disclosure in Christ, "the man for others," and existential "religionless" Christianity in an era when men "come of age" and act in a world where they link the religious and the secular.

BONIFACE (bŏn′ĭ fās), (or **WINFRID** or **WILFRITH**) (680-755), English Benedictine missionary—"The Apostle to the Germans." An Anglo-Saxon, born in Devonshire, England. Early entered monastic life, and at thirty he was ordained. Seemingly had before him an assured place in his church in England; but preferred to be a missionary. About 716 with a few companions he sailed for Frisia, a group of small islands off the Dutch coast, to help Willibrord in his difficult task. Meeting strong opposition from the local Frisian king, he returned to England. Soon he was back on the continent, going first to Rome from 718 to 719, there receiving from Pope Gregory II a commission to Germany. Began work in Thuringia; but before many months, hearing of the death of the hostile Frisian king, went back to Frisia to help Willibrord establish the church in Frisia. From 719-722 worked with Willibrord; then went to Germany and entered upon the main work of his life. He first went to Hesse, and then later back to Thuringia. His ten years' work in these two provinces was highly successful. Great numbers of pagans were converted, the Irish or Celtic monks were brought largely into obedience to Rome. In 732 Pope Gregory III made Boniface an archbishop with authority to establish new sees in Germany. In 738, after third and last trip to Rome, organized the church in Bavaria, and later in Thuringia. About 744 helped to establish the important and influential monastery of Fulda. A year or two later was made archbishop of Mainz, also worked among the Franks, trying to reform the Frankish church. Everywhere Boniface went, it was with papal sanction and authority. In 739 the pope named him apostolic vicar or papal legate. His authority and influence were tremendous. In 742 assembled the first German council, organized churches, schools and monasteries according to the Roman pattern. He trained and sent missionaries from the German churches, and did more than any other to instill into the hearts of the bishops and clergy of Central Europe permanent obedience to the pope, and did much to lay the foundation for the medieval papacy. In 753 he went back to preach to the Frisians; with a company of monks and priests spent about two years traveling among them, preaching to them, baptizing thousands of converts, destroying pagan temples, and building churches. In 755, a body of hostile pagans fell upon the group, and Boniface was slain.

He died with a copy of the gospels in his hands.

BONIFACE VIII (c. 1234-1303), Benedetto Gaetani, born at Anagni and was Pope Boniface VIII from 1294-1303. Before becoming pope had served in various capacities for the church in different countries and personally knew all the principal sovereigns of Europe. Was an able jurist and well-skilled in all the arts of curial diplomacy. From the onset he determined to give the papacy its full power. His coronation as pope was the most splendid ever seen in Rome. Innocent III (1198-1215) had made the highest claims for the papacy up to that time, and was successful in carrying them out. Boniface VIII a century later made not only the same claims, but even more ambitious claims for the papacy, but was unable to accomplish his purposes and ambitions. In 1296 he issued his famous *Clericis Laicos,* a bull directed against Philip IV of France, prohibiting the taxation of church property without the consent of the Holy See. Both France and England objected. When Boniface made further demands upon Philip, the king responded by burning the bull. In 1302 he issued the famous bull, *Unum Sanctum,* the highwater mark of papal claims, the claim of absolute authority over civil power and no salvation outside the church or without obeying the pope. When the king refused to accept it, both excommunication and interdict were exercised against him. Instead of bowing to the pope, the king had Boniface seized and confined to prison in Anagni for three days. Boniface was then rescued and taken to Rome where he died.

BOOTH, BALLINGTON (c. 1857-1940), founder of the Volunteers of America, born at Brighouse, Yorkshire, England. Second son of General William Booth, educated at Taunton Collegiate Institute, and at Nottingham Seminary. Trained by his father for the work of the Salvation Army. Was commander of the Salvation Army in Australia, 1884-1887, and with his wife Maud in the United States, 1887-1896. He and his wife seceded from the mother organization in 1896 and established the more democratic Volunteers of America of which he became the general-in-chief and president. To tie the new organization in more closely with the churches he was ordained presbyter in the Evangelical Church in Chicago. He wrote *From Ocean to Ocean.*

BOOTH, CATHERINE (MUMFORD) (MRS. WILLIAM) (1829-1890), British welfare worker and "Mother of the Salvation Army," born at Ashbourne, Derbyshire, England. A sickly child in her early years, she received her education largely from her mother at home. In 1844 Catherine Mumford moved with her parents to London. In same year joined the Wesleyan church at Brixton; four years later with a group of "Reformers" she was excommunicated. From 1852-1861 William Booth was pastor of these "Reformers." In 1855 Catherine and William were married. Catherine assisted her husband and in 1860 published a pamphlet defending the right of women to preach, also delivered her first sermon in her husband's pulpit. In 1861 they broke away from the Reformers. Between 1861 and 1877 the Salvation Army was gradually being molded. In 1877 it was organized along military lines. Mrs. Booth had an influential part and devoted much of her energy to improving the position of women and children. In 1885 she worked hard to secure the passage of the Criminal Law Amendment Act. Her public career reached its climax in 1886-1887 when she conducted a notable series of meetings throughout England. The next year she was stricken with cancer, and after two years of great suffering died in 1890. She wrote *Paper on Practical Religion, Papers on Godliness, Papers on Aggressive Christianity, Popular Christianity,* and *The Salvation Army in Relation to the Church and State.*

BOOTH, EVANGELINE CORY (1865-1950), General of Salvation Army, daughter of General William Booth, born and educated in London. Trained by her father for work in the Salvation Army. She supervised the field operations of the Salvation Army successively in Great Britain, Canada, and the Klondike. 1904, promoted to the command of the Salvation Army in the United States, during which time the Salvation Army made rapid progress and growth. Directed the Salvation Army war work during World War I. Was elected general of the World Wide Salvation Army in 1934, holding that position until she retired in 1939. She wrote *Songs of the Evangel, Love is All, Toward a Better World;* and *Women;* and was the author of many well-known Salvation Army hymns.

BOOTH, MAUD BALLINGTON (CHARLESWORTH) (1865-1948), leader of the Volunteers of America, born in Limpsfield, Surrey, England, daughter of a wealthy clergyman. At the age of seventeen joined Miss Catherine Booth in Salvation Army work in Paris and Switzerland. In 1886 married Ballington Booth and accompanied him to the United States, where they commanded the Salvation Army from 1887 to 1896. In the latter year she joined her husband in seceding from the Salvation Army and in forming the Volunteers of America of which they became directors. In

1940 upon the death of her husband she succeeded him as national president and commander-in-chief. Mrs. Booth turned her attention particularly to work in prisons and with released prisoners, which was carried on in the state and federal prisons of the United States. During World War I she served with the American Expeditionary Forces in France. Mrs. Booth was one of the founders of the Parent-Teachers Association. She attained a wide reputation as a lecturer. She wrote *Branded, Look up and Hope, After Prison—What?,* and *Twilight Fairy Tales.*

BOOTH, WILLIAM (1829-1912), founder and first general of the Salvation Army, born of Church of England parents near Nottingham, England. Converted in a little Methodist chapel, early became interested in both mission work and evangelistic preaching. For several years worked long days to make a livelihood, then spent evenings in visiting the sick, preaching on the street, and attending cottage meetings. Became a close student of the Bible. In his mission work he met and later married Catherine Mumford of London, who became an ideal co-worker with him in his great work in the Salvation Army. Ordained in 1858; from 1850 to 1861 he was in the New Connection Methodist Church. In 1861 he and Mrs. Booth became weary of the controversy in the Methodist Church, withdrew and launched into evangelistic work. About this same time the Booths were both led into a deeper Christian experience, following John Wesley's views and teachings on sanctification, heart purity, and holiness. In 1865 Booth began preaching and doing missionary work among the poor, lower classes in the Whitechapel neighborhood in East London. Here the Salvation Army had its beginning, first as the "East London Christian Revival Society," or "Christian Mission." By 1878 he had formed his society into an organization with military form, name, and discipline, calling it the Salvation Army. William Booth lived to see his organization spread into no less than fifty-five different countries, where it continued to be devoted to and engaged in practical philanthropy as well as in street preaching and personal evangelism. He travelled about 5 million miles and preached nearly 60,000 sermons. In 1890 he published his great book, *In Darkest England and the Way Out*. General Booth's eldest son, Bramwell Booth, succeeded him in the leadership of the Salvation Army after his death.

BORA, KATHERINE VON (1499-1552), German nun who became Martin Luther's wife. Supervised and cared for a large household of six children and orphaned nieces and nephews as well as boarders and poor students. Helped to soften Luther's rough temperament.

BORDEN, WILLIAM W. (1887-1913), born into a wealthy Chicago family. After high school traveled around the world (1904-1905). Educated at Yale University and Princeton Theological Seminary where Samuel Zwemer influenced him to think about the Muslim world. Believed he was called to work among Muslims in China. Ordained 1912. Went in 1913 to Egypt to study Arabic language and culture and died that same year of cerebral meningitis. Gave over $500,000 to educational institutions, churches and mission societies during his life and through his will. During 1910 he was a trustee of Moody Bible Institute, delegate to the Edinburgh Missionary Conference and a director of the National Bible Institute of New York City.

BOREHAM, FRANK WILLIAM (1871-1959), author of numerous devotional books and essays. Born Tunbridge Wells, England. Educated in Spurgeon's Pastors College, London. Wrote for London magazines. Pastor in Mosgiel, New Zealand (1895-1906), Hobart Tabernacle, Hobart, Tasmania (1906-1916) and Armadale, Melbourne from 1916. Wrote attractive devotional essays with much alliteration in titles which were collected and published in numerous books. Was a most ardent cricket fan.

BORGIA (bôr'jä), **CESARE (CAESAR)** (1475-1507), Duke of Valentinois and Romanga. An illegitimate son of Rodrigo Borgia (later Pope Alexander VI) and Vanozza dei Cattanei. At the age of six he was declared eligible for ordination. He was made a protonotary and bishop of Pampeluna by Pope Innocent VIII. At the age of sixteen appointed archbishop of Valencia, and then cardinal. In 1498 he resigned his eccleciastical offices to become a secular prince. His father then tried to create a dukedom in central Italy for his unscrupulous son, even appropriating for this purpose the states of the church. His father endowed him with the title of Duke of the Romanga, and made him captain general of the church. But Cesare failed in his attempt to establish an independent kingdom in central Italy, and played no prominent part in Italian affairs after his father's death in 1503. The annals of Rome and the Vatican for more than a decade were filled with his impiety, intrigue, sensuality, treachery, murders, and other crimes. Pope Julius II being utterly unable to condone his duplicity and crime, had him imprisoned. After two years in prison in Spain he escaped to the court of his brother-in-law, the king of

Navarre. In the king's service he was killed in the campaign against Castile in 1507 at the age of thirty-one. Cesare Borgia was held up by Machiavelli as the model prince.

BORIS (-d. 907) King of Bulgaria (852-889), was baptized into Greek Orthodox church in 864 or 865. Boris wanted Bulgarian church to be independent of the state. When the Byzantine emperor refused this, he supported German missionary work under Pope Nicholas I and expelled the Byzantine clergy. Later the patriarch agreed to a semi-autonomous Bulgarian archbishopric.

BORROMEO CHARLES (1538-1584), Archbishop of Milan and cardinal reformer. Born in Arona, Italy. Abbot of Arona at twelve. Ordained in 1563. Cardinal in 1559 and Archbishop of Milan in 1560. Helped reform the College of Cardinals and the clergy during the last session of the Council of Trent by strict discipline. Founded schools and orphanages for the young and in 1578 the order of Oblates of St. Ambrose. Canonized in 1610.

BORROW, GEORGE HENRY (1803-1881), English traveler, linguist and writer, born at East Dereham, Norfolk, England. The boy was placed in a lawyer's office at Norwich, but found greater interest in language study than in law. After the death of his father in 1824, Borrow went to London where he was barely able to support himself by hack writing. He then spent eight years traveling throughout England, chiefly on foot, gathering impressions which were later used in writings. From 1827 to 1840 he traveled in Russia, Spain, Portugal, Morocco, Germany, and Italy, first as an agent for the British and Foreign Bible Society, later as a newspaper correspondent, continuing, however, with the Bible Society until 1840. Having an aptitude for languages, he acquired a practical though somewhat superficial knowledge of many European and Eastern tongues, was particularly noted for his acquaintance with Romany, the dialect of the Gypsies, with whom he associated. While at St. Petersburg he edited the Manchu translation of the New Testament. In Madrid he edited the Spanish translation of the New Testament. His *Zincali, or an Account of the Gypsies in Spain,* (two volumes) and *Bible in Spain,* (three volumes), won a high place in literature, and his reputation as an authority on gypsy life. Among his other writings: *Targum, or Metrical Translations from Thirty Languages and Dialects; Romano Lavo-Lil* (Gypsy word-book); *Lavengro, the Scholar, the Gypsy, the Priest;* and its sequel *The Romany Rye*. Latter two constitute sort of autobiographical novels with a unique narrative style.

BOSSUET (bō so͞o ĕ'), **JACQUES BENIGNE** (1627-1704), French Roman Catholic and pulpit orator, born at Dijon, France. Educated in a Jesuit college in Dijon; in the College of Navarre, Paris, mastering the Latin and Greek classics in the former and studying theology in the latter. He was ordained deacon in 1649, lived in retirement for two years. In 1652 ordained priest and given the degree of Doctor of Divinity at the Sorbonne. He then moved to Metz where he preached for seven years, entered into controversies with the Reformed churches, and sought to convert the Protestants. In 1669 appointed Bishop of Condom, resigned in 1670 when he was appointed as preceptor to the young dauphin, the son of Louis XIV until 1681. Made bishop of Meaux (1681). Residing in his diocese, busied himself with the details of its administration, completed some long-interrupted historical works such as his *Discourse on Universal History* with its providential view of history (1681), gave spiritual care to people, wrote spiritual letters, and entered upon new polemical controversies with Fenelon and the Quietists, the Jansenists, the Reformed churches, and others. His *Histoire des Variations des Eglises Protestantes* (1688) was the greatest polemical work in French against the Reformation. Though a strong Roman Catholic he was not an ultramontanist. Presided over the assembly of the French clergy which the king had convened in 1682 to defend the royal prerogatives and the liberties of the Gallican church against the claims of the pope. Upheld royal absolutism in his *Politics Drawn from the Words of Holy Scripture*. A man of simplicity, piety, sincerity, and ability, one of the noted members of the French Academy. Soaring oratory made him one of the first-rank preachers of France of the seventeenth century. His sermons are works of real art and literature and fill forty-three volumes. Bossuet died in Paris in 1704.

BOSTON, THOMAS (1677-1732), Evangelical minister in Church of Scotland, born at Dunse, Berwickshire, Scotland. After receiving collegiate and theological education at the University of Edinburgh, became tutor. In 1699 after being ordained became pastor of a small community parish. He found in the home of one of his parishioners a copy of Edward Fisher's Arminian *The Marrow of Modern Divinity,* a seventeenth century book on Calvinism. He had the book reprinted; distributed it among his friends which started the famous "Marrow Controversy" involving the Erskine brothers and finally led to the formation of the Secession Church. In 1707 called to Ettrick, where he remained the rest of his life. Wrote voluminously, exercising great influence in the Presbyterian churches both in Scotland and England. A book that became famous and a much read classic of evangelical teaching was his book of sermons, published as *Human Nature in Its Four-fold State*. His *Crook in the Lot* or *The Sovereignty and Wisdom of God* also was an important work. He also wrote his *Memoirs.*

BOTTICELLI (bōt tē chĕl'lē), **ALESSANDRO di MARIANO de FILIPEPI (SANDRO)** (c. 1444-1510), Italian Renaissance painter, born in Florence, Italy, studied under and worked with Fra Filippo Lippi for about ten years, later with Leonardo. In early years an artist with a pagan love for worldly pageantry. His subjects then were mainly mythological, the two chief of which were *Primavera (Spring)* and *Birth of Venus,* painted for Lorenzo de Medici. In these early years he gained some fame also in painting Madonnas. The second phase of his painting was chiefly religious: *The Coronation of the Virgin, The Adoration of the Magi, The Annunciation,* and *The Nativity.* The most important productions were the frescoes illustrating episodes in the life of Moses, painted in the Sistine Chapel of the Vatican. His paintings are characterized by a graceful and flowing line, bright with color and poetic in atmosphere. After 1497 he became a follower of Savonarola; thereafter his paintings showed the influence of mysticism. Botticelli died in Florence.

BOUNDS, EDWARD McKENDREE (1835-1913), Methodist minister and devotional writer, born in Shelby County, Missouri. Studied law and was admitted to the bar at twenty-one years. After practicing law for three years, began preaching for the Methodist Episcopal Church, South. At the time of his pastorate at Brunswick, Missouri, war was declared, and he was made a prisoner of war for refusing to take the oath of allegiance to the Federal Government. After release he served as chaplain of the Fifth Missouri regiment until near the close of the war, when captured and held as prisoner at Nashville, Tennessee. After the war ended, Bounds served as pastor of churches in Tennessee, Alabama, and St. Louis, Missouri. Turned to special evangelistic work in his church. During a part of pastoral ministry was editor of the *St. Louis Advocate,* and later editor of the *Christian Advocate,* the organ of the Methodist Episcopal Church, South. Spent the last seventeen years of his life with his family in Washington, Georgia, writing his "Spiritual Life Books." Some of these were: *Preacher and Prayer, Purpose in Prayer, Prayer and Praying Men,* and *Power through Prayer.* He prayed each day from four to seven and then wrote for some hours. "He experienced and proclaimed entire sanctification as a second definite work of grace."

BOURDALOUE (bo͞or dȧ-lo͞o'), **LOUIS** (1632-1704), Jesuit court preacher in France, born at Bourges. Received his education at a Jesuit college in Bourges, becoming a member of the Jesuit order in 1648. For a time a teacher in literature and rhetoric. Quick and penetrating intelligence, tireless industry, and strict observance of religious discipline soon led to appointment as a professor of philosophy and moral theology. But when his fine oratorical ability was discovered, it was determined that he should devote himself altogether to preaching. In 1670 succeeded Bossuet as court preacher, and for thirty-four years (1670-1704) preached to the court of the king, being a favorite preacher in the reign of Louis XIV. Besides preaching his carefully prepared sermons, he served often as father confessor, spent many hours in visiting and consoling the poor and the sick, and in preparing the dying. He was the best spokesman the Jesuits had to oppose the Jansenism of Pascal and Arnauld. Held in high esteem as a man of sincerity and purity of character, and along with Bossuet and Massillon among the greatest of the French preachers. Many sermons translated into English.

BOURGEOIS bo͝or'zhwä), **LOUIS** (c. 1510-c. 1561), Calvin's choirmaster at Geneva, born at Paris. In Geneva, 1541-1557. Editor of the French Geneva Psalter about 1551, the composer of the tune, "Old Hundredth" for the hymn, "All People That on Earth Do Dwell," (Psalm 42) which had been written by John Knox's friend, William Kethe. One of the first to harmonize the melodies of the French version of the Psalms. Also the compiler of four psalteries, and author of a pedagogical treatise, *Le Droiet Chemin de Musique,* and the *Eighty-three Psalmes de David.*

BOURNE, HUGH (1772-1852), founder of Primitive Methodist Church. Born at Stoke-on-Trent. Joined and supported Wesleyan Methodists. Helped as a lay preacher to organize a camp meeting in 1807. Expelled by the Methodists, he organized the first conference of the Primitive Methodist Church in 1820. Church grew to over 100,000 by his death. Travelled widely in the British Isles and in the USA. Worked as carpenter and builder all his life in order not to burden the church.

BOVILLE, ROBERT G. (Late nineteenth—early twentieth centuries), executive secretary of New York City Baptist Board and popularizer of daily vacation Bible schools.

Mrs. Eliza Haines held first such school in Epiphany Baptist Church in New York. Spurred Boville to support this work. By 1901 he had five schools on the East Side, by 1902 ten and in 1903 seventeen. He created a National Vacation Bible School Committee, and schools started in Philadelphia and Boston. Organization became Daily Vacation Bible School Association in 1911. Such schools a major summer activity in many parts of the world.

BOWEN, GEORGE (1816-1888), American missionary to Bombay, India from 1848 to 1888, born at Middlebury, Vermont. Through self-study became an avid reader in several languages. In 1844, after death of his Christian fiancée, was converted to a vital Christian faith. Immediately began planning to be a missionary; graduated from Union Theological Seminary, New York (1847); same year ordained by New York Presbytery and sailed for India under the American Board. Soon declined salary; lived simply among natives; never married; took no furlough, change of climate, or vacation. Withdrew from board in 1855, supported himself by tutoring and by editing and publishing the *Bombay Guardian* (associate editor 1851-1854, editor 1854-1888). Selections of articles were later published in highly prized devotional books, *Daily Meditations, The Amens of Christ,* and *Love Revealed*. Became secretary of the Bombay Tract Society, serving without pay. In 1871 met and traveled with Bishop William Taylor, the well-known Methodist missionary evangelist; in 1873 joined the Methodist missionary society, working under that board the remaining years of his life. Known as "the white saint of India."

BOWNE (boun), **BORDEN PARKER** (1847-1910), American Methodist philosopher and educator, born at Leonardville, New Jersey, studied at Pennington Seminary, the University of the City of New York, and Halle and Göttingen. Before going abroad to study, taught school for one year and was pastor of a Methodist church in 1873. In 1875, after returning from Europe, became assistant professor of modern languages in the University of the City of New York for a year, during which time he was also religious editor of the New York *Independent*. From 1876 until 1910 professor of philosophy at Boston University. After 1888 until 1910 dean of the graduate school. At a time when a mechanistic determinism was popular, rejected every argument against the freedom of personality, never tired of maintaining the freedom of the self and its relation to the Unseen behind the universe. So insistent upon the central importance of personality that he came to believe that no other term so well defined his thought as Personalism. His philosophy contributed definitely to shaping much of contemporary Methodist theology. His religious faith colored his thought. He particularly stressed the personality of Jesus as the norm for all men. Bowne was chairman of the Philosophical Department at the St. Louis World's Fair, 1904, and honorary member of the Imperial Education Society of Japan. His writings include: *The Philosophy of Herbert Spencer, Studies in Theism, Philosophy of Theism, Metaphysics, The Theory of Thought and Knowledge, Principles of Ethics, The Atonement, The Christian Revelation, Personalism, The Immanence of God, The Christian Life,* and *Introduction to Psychological Theory.*

BOWRING, SIR JOHN (1792-1872), English public official, linguist, hymn writer, born at Exeter, England. The first editor of the "Westminster Review" and a member of Parliament for ten years. In 1849 appointed British consul at Hong Kong and chief superintendent of trade in China. Knighted in 1854, governor of Hong Kong, 1854-1856. Sent to Siam on a mission for the government, published *Kingdom of Siam and Its People;* in 1858 visited Manila, then published *A Visit to the Philippine Islands.* Bowring is known widely for his hymns, "In the Cross of Christ I Glory"; "Watchman Tell Us of the Night"; "God Is Love, His Mercy Brightens"; and "From the Recesses of a Lowly Spirit."

BRADBURY, WILLIAM BACHELDER (1816-1868), editor of Sunday school music books, born near York, Maine. Went to Boston to study music; for the first time had the privilege of hearing an organ or a piano. Became a pupil of Lowell Mason, who encouraged him to follow music as a profession. After several years of playing and directing in Boston, he, with his wife and daughter, went to Europe where he studied for two years. Returning became known as a composer of sacred tunes. After holding his first musical convention in 1851, he, Lowell Mason, Thomas Hastings, and George F. Root formed the faculty of the various institutes which they held in the East the next few years. A pioneer in holding musical conventions and also in publishing Sunday school music books. Ira D. Sankey received part of his musical inspiration from one of Bradbury's conventions. During twenty-six years of active life work, fifty-nine separate books appeared with his name on title page. Bradbury set beautiful music to many of the great hymns written by others: "'Tis Midnight and on Olive's Brow"; "The Solid Rock"; "He Leadeth Me"; "Saviour Like a

Shepherd"; "Holy Is the Lord"; "Depth of Mercy"; "Just As I Am."

BRADFORD, WILLIAM (1590-1657), Pilgrim father and second governor of Plymouth Colony, born in Austerfield, Yorkshire, England, received a good education, attended Separatist meetings and joined the Separatist church or Brownists at Scrooby in 1606. Imprisoned for trying to escape from England, later succeeded in 1609 in joining the Pilgrims in Leiden, Holland, where he attended the university and became an apprentice to a silk manufacturer. In 1620 sailed with the Pilgrims on the Mayflower, thus becoming one of the founders of Plymouth Colony, America. Chosen the second governor of the colony to succeed John Carver, held the office 1621 to 1656 except for five years when he declined to serve, but at which time he acted as deputy governor. Main problems during terms of office were the disease and famine which afflicted the colonists, hostile Indian attacks, persecution from England, the colony's debts, and rebellion from malcontents within their ranks. Tact, good judgment, and executive ability helped to make the colony a success. Especially sagacious in dealings with the Indians. His *History of the Plymouth Plantation,* covering the history of the colony from its inception in 1620 to 1646 has been the basis for all other histories of Plymouth colony. This history remained in manuscript form for over two hundred years, because it was lost until the mid-nineteenth century.

BRAHMS (brämz), **JOHANNES** (1833-1897), celebrated German musical composer, born in the slums of Hamburg. Recognizing the musical genius in his sons Johannes and Fritz, the father taught them violin and cello. At ten Johannes was placed under the instruction of the foremost musician in Hamburg. At twenty he left Hamburg and joined a concert tour of Europe, appearing as accompanist, soloist, and composer. On tour he met Joachim, Liszt, and Schumann. His meeting with the latter, who recognized in Brahms a new musical genius, resulted in a warm intimacy with the Schumann family. Brahms, a sensitive emotional young man, fell madly in love with Madame Schumann. By the time that Robert Schumann died in 1856, Brahms had learned to control his emotions and passions. He married neither the widow nor any other woman. He had other love affairs but he turned them into musical productions, or as he called it "Translation of emotion into song." From 1854 to 1858 conducted concerts for the Prince of Lippe-Delmold. Later conducted a women's choir in Hamburg. In 1863 made Vienna his home and became conductor of the Singakademic, a choral society. In 1868 his reputation firmly established, he first performed at Bremen his *German Requiem*. It is considered by many his masterpiece. In 1878 withdrew from society, lived in seclusive bachelor quarters, and devoted himself almost exclusively to composition. Wrote in almost every musical field except opera. His choral compositions are given the highest place by critics. Wrote nearly two hundred songs, of which "How Art Thou My Queen?" is best known. Given the degree of Doctor of Philosophy by Breslau in 1881. In 1886 made Knight of the Prussian Order.

BRAINERD, DAVID (1718-1747), missionary to the American Indians, born at Haddam, Connecticut, died at Northampton, Massachusetts in the home of Jonathan Edwards. Entered Yale in 1739, was expelled in 1742 in his junior year for persisting in attending meetings of the "New Lights," and for criticizing one of the tutors for having "no more grace than a chair." In 1742 licensed a minister by the Ministerial Association at Danbury, Connecticut, later appointed a missionary to the Indians by the Society in Scotland for the Propagation of Christian Knowledge. In 1744 ordained by the Presbytery of New York at Newark, New Jersey. April 1743-November 1746, worked most devotedly and heroically for the conversion of the Indians at Kaunaumeek, New York, along the Delaware, Lehigh, and Susquehanna rivers in eastern Pennsylvania. Met greatest success in ministry among the Indians at Crossweeksung and Cranberry, near Newark, New Jersey; baptized eighty-five Indians, about half of whom were adults. In 1747 relinquished his missionary work because of tuberculosis. Jonathan Edwards preached the funeral sermon from II Corinthians 5:8. David had kept a diary of his life and work among the Indians, of hardship and suffering borne with heroic devotion. This diary, published by Jonathan Edwards as *Brainerd's Journal,* turned many to missions.

BRAMWELL, WILLIAM (1759-1818), English Methodist preacher and revivalist, born at Elswick, Lancashire, England. Received very limited education. Served as a choir boy in the Church of England. After a thoroughgoing conversion at one of Wesley's meetings, soon became an active and earnest personal worker. Became a class leader and Wesley made him an itinerant preacher. Persistently sought and received by faith the experience of sanctification as taught by Wesley. In 1785 he entered upon his travels as a preacher. For more than thirty years he was one of the most successful preachers of English Methodism. A man of prayer and faith, he lived very close to God.

BRAY, WILLIAM (BILLY) (1794-1868), Methodist evangelist, born in the village of Twelveheads, Cornwall, England. In early years an inveterate smoker and a drunken, profligate miner. In 1823 he was converted by reading Bunyan's *Visions of Heaven and Hell*. Many fellow-miners were moved by his concern for them. He not only became a teetotaler but also became an active fighter of tobacco and alcohol. About a year after his conversion Billy was placed on the local preachers' roll of the Bible Christian church (Methodist). Was more of an exhorter than a preacher, and principal work in soul-winning was done outside the pulpit. A man of strong faith in God, knew how to expect answers to his prayers.

BRAY, THOMAS (1656-1730), Church of England divine, born at Marton, Shropshire, England, studied at Oswestry School, at All Souls and Hart Hall, Oxford University. Received the degree of D.D. from the latter. Took orders about 1680, and served a small parish at Over Whitacre for a time. In 1690 became rector of Sheldon, Warwickshire. Later Henry Compton, bishop of London, sent Bray as commissary from 1696-1706 to organize the Anglican church in Maryland. However, after a few months in America (1699-1700), decided he could better promote the interests of the province from England. Returned to London, bearing the whole expense of the mission himself. Became interested in missions among the American Indians. About 1699 became one of the founders of the Society for the Propagation of the Gospel, also projected a successful scheme for establishing parish libraries in England, Wales, and America. Out of that grew the Society for Promoting Christian Knowledge in 1701. Hence Bray may almost be regarded as the founder of the two oldest English missionary societies. His efforts resulted in the founding of nearly forty libraries in America, the one at Annapolis, Maryland being the largest collection of books in the plantations at the time, the first lending library in the British colonies. More than 500 libraries were founded in Great Britain, about 120 by Dr. Bray himself. Collected and managed a fund for instructing of the Negroes in the West Indies and in America. At seventy-one became interested in prisoners in London jails and undertook to ameliorate their condition. In 1723 planned for the continuance of his work by founding the society that came to be known as "Dr. Bray's Associates for Founding Clerical Libraries and Supporting Negro Schools." From 1706 till his death in 1730, Dr. Bray was rector of St. Butolph-Without, Algate, London. The work of Thomas Bray had wide influence in extending the Anglican church in the American colonies. Dr. Bray wrote several books: *A Course of Lectures upon the Church Catechism; Bibliotheca Parochialis;* and *A Martyrology, or History of the Papal Usurpation*.

BREASTED, JAMES HENRY (1865-1935), American historian and archeologist, born at Rockford, Illinois, studied at North Central College, Naperville, Illinois; Chicago Theological Seminary; Yale University; and the University of Berlin. 1894-1933 was associated with the University of Chicago, teaching Egyptology, Semitic languages, and Oriental history. From 1895 associated with the Haskell Oriental Museum, and from 1901-1931 was its director. Led numerous research projects in the Near East and in the museums of Europe. With the aid of a large subsidy from John D. Rockefeller, Jr., founded and became the first director of the Oriental Institute of the University of Chicago in 1919, a position held the rest of his life. In 1925 released from all teaching responsibility to make it possible to devote full time to the Institute. Honored with medals from several societies, and held membership in all the important academies and societies including the Royal Academy of Berlin. Called upon to deliver lectures in various colleges and universities. Some of his chief writings are *A History of Egypt, Ancient Records of Egypt* (five volumes), *A History of the Ancient Egyptians, Survey of the Ancient World, The Temples of Lower Nubia, Conquest of Civilization, Ancient Times,* and *The Dawn of Conscience*.

BRÉBEUF, JEAN DE (1593-1649), born at Conde-sur Vire, France. Entered Society of Jesus and ordained in 1612. Went to Quebec in 1625 and worked among the Hurons (1626-1629). After brief stay in France founded a permanent Huron Mission of which he was superior from 1633 to 1649. Died of torture by the Indians at St. Ignace near Georgian Bay. His work recorded in the Jesuit *Relations*.

BRENT, CHARLES HENRY (1862-1929), American Protestant Episcopal Bishop, born in Newcastle, Ontario, Canada, educated at Trinity College, Toronto. Ordained priest in 1887. After serving a pastorate in Boston, 1891-1901, made bishop of the Philippines (1901-1918), bishop of western New York (1918-1926), and bishop in charge of the Episcopal churches in Europe (1926-1928). During his last thirty years developed a strong interest in the reunion of the churches. Attended the World Missionary Conference in Edinburgh in 1910. Out of this conference grew the World Conference on Faith and Order of which Bishop Brent was one of the chief initiators. Attended the ecumenical conference at Stockholm, Sweden, and at Lausanne, Switzerland, and became chairman of the committee for the continuance of these conferences. Took an active part in the fight against narcotics and the opium traffic, serving as chief commissioner of the United States and as president of the International Opium Commission in Shanghai, 1908-1909; chairman of the United States delegation to the International Opium Conference at The Hague, and president of the conference, 1911-1912. In World War I, chief of the chaplain service of the A.E.F. in France. Author of several books on theology and practical Christian life, one being *With God in the World*.

BRENZ (brĕnts), **JOHANN** (1499-1570), German Protestant Reformer, born in Weil, Württemberg. He was a student of Oecolampadius at the University of Heidelberg and a fellow-student with Martin Bucer and Phillip Melanchthon. Ordained priest in 1520 by the bishop of Spires. and appointed priest of the free city of Hall near Stuttgart in 1522. Came under the teaching of Luther and gradually espoused all the ideas of the Reformation. With great wisdom and moderation, yet with undisguised zeal preached the evangelical doctrine and led his people into reformation views and order. In 1525 did away with the mass, and soon reorganized the church at Hall along evangelical lines. Preached that the body of the Lord is everywhere present, giving rise to his followers being called Ubiquitarians. Opposed the Peasants' War and did not favor the killing of Anabaptists and others who did not accept his views. Assisted in the writing of Reformation tracts, took part in the Marburg Colloquy in 1529, was present at the Augsberg Conference when the Augsburg Confession was written and accepted by the Lutherans. At the time of the Schmalkaldic War in 1546, Hall was taken by imperial troops and Brenz had to flee in 1548. Found refuge with Duke Ulrich of Württemberg, who welcomed him as a leader of the Reformation at Württemberg, and solicited his help in reforming the University according to Lutheran ideas. When better times came in 1553 he became the leading Lutheran preacher at the Collegiate Church at Stuttgart. There distinguished himself as an author, organizer, and administrator, and carried on an able ministry for many years. Co-author of the Württemberg Confession.

BREWSTER, WILLIAM (c. 1563-1644), Pilgrim Father, Elder of Plymouth, born at Scrooby, Nottinghamshire, England. Studied at Peterhouse, Cambridge. A man of education, culture and piety. From 1583 to 1589 served William Davidson, the ambassador to Holland. About 1602 Scrooby Puritans wishing to have a special place of meeting began assembling in the Scrooby manor-house, the home of William Brewster. The movement grew and persecution forced them out of the church. In 1606 Brewster and others organized the Separatist Church of Scrooby. About 1609 they moved to Amsterdam, Holland to obtain fuller freedom of worship, and the next year moved to Leiden, where he was in the printing business. Chosen ruling elder and John Robinson, pastor. After twelve years of exile in Holland and after many difficulties in a strange land and under a foreign government, they made up their minds to seek a home in the new world. Brewster was one of the leading promoters of the project. In 1620 they sailed to England in the *Speedwell* and then to America in the *Mayflower.* They became the founders of Plymouth Colony. Their pastor, John Robinson, remained behind. William Brewster became leader and counselor. He continued as ruling elder; but more, he preached regularly until the first ordained minister came in 1629. When the first dreadful winter was past and half the company were swept away by death and the rest were prostrate from disease and hunger he was their comforter and "pastor."

BRIÇONNET (brē sō nā′), **WILLIAM** (1472-1534), Bishop of Meaux, born in Tours, France, son of Cardinal Briçonnet, Archbishop of Narbonne. Made bishop of Lodeve in 1504 and bishop of Meaux in 1516. In 1507 also became abbot of St. Germain des Pres, and gave his teacher, Jacques Lefèvre an appointment as teacher in the abbey. Had encouraged Lefèvre to turn from secular interests to theology and the Scriptures. Was then influenced by Lefèvre's warm reformatory preaching and tended to accept these reformatory views, all of which gave decided impetus to the new movement. After becoming bishop of Meaux, invited Farel and other reformers to preach and expound the Scriptures in the new way in his diocese hoping to bring reform within the church. When the Parlement of Paris started severe persecution against all who departed from the accepted doctrines of the Roman Catholic church, Briçonnet, bowing before the storm, forsook evangelical friends. Not ready to break with the Roman church and become a reformer, he definitely silenced his friend William Farel whose preaching had become vigorously reformatory. Farel and Lefèvre had to flee for safety. Meaux, as it seemed, had been about to become a second Wittenberg; but with Briçonnet's defection, the efforts of the Meaux group were completely arrested.

BRIDAINE (brē dān′), **JACQUES** (1701-1767), French Jesuit preacher, born in the little village of Chusclon near Avignon in the south of France. Educated at the Jesuit College and the Mission Seminary of St. Charles de la Croix in Avignon, ordained a priest in 1725, but began his preaching while still in minor orders when he was a mere youth. In spite of and partly because of extremely unusual and sensational methods, gained a large following, had many converts, and was given permission by Pope Benedict XIV to preach anywhere in Christendom. In the course of his life preached to almost every town in France. One of the greatest evangelistic preachers of his day, and thousands were led to the faith by his preaching. His *Cantiques Spirituels* passed through forty-seven editions. Five volumes of his sermons have been published. He was greatly loved and admired by the French people, both Catholic and Protestant.

BRIDGET (BIRGITTA) OF SWEDEN (1303-1373), founder of Brigittine Order. Became a nun on death of husband in 1344. Because of a vision founded the Brigittines in 1350 and received papal approval in 1370. Went to Rome about 1350. Helped persuade Gregory XI to return to Rome from Avignon. Canonized in 1391.

BRIDGMAN, ELIJAH COLEMAN (1801-1861), American Congregational missionary, born at Belchertown, Massachusetts. Converted at eleven, and joined Congregational church in his twelfth year. A graduate of Amherst College and of Andover Theological Seminary, joined Robert Morrison in Canton, China in 1830, the first missionary sent by the American Board to China. Accompanied by David Abeel, both young men being supported for one year by R. M. Olyphant, a Christian merchant engaged in the China trade. Bridgman resided in the foreign factories of Canton. Learned to speak and write the Chinese language, became an official interpreter for both high Chinese and American officials. Held daily services in Dr. Peter Parker's Hospital in Canton, preached on the streets, presented Christ to the Chinese coolies, soldiers, or officials who came to his home. Mrs. Bridgman established a girls' school. Dr. Bridgman devoted many long hours to the translation of the Scriptures. In 1847 he and his wife removed to Shanghai where he founded a new mission and supervised the translation, revising, and printing of the Bible. In 1832 he began the monthly, *The Chinese Repository,* an English periodical that dealt with missionary news, information on the history and culture of China, and political and commercial news. Continued as its editor until 1851. Bridgman prepared the *Chinese Chrestomathy,* a seven hundred thirty page manual of the Cantonese dialect, the first book of its kind. He and his wife made one visit to America in 1852. Returning to China in 1853, he took part in the dedication of a church built for the Chinese in San Francisco.

BRIGGS, CHARLES AUGUSTUS (1841-1913), American clergyman and theologian, born in New York City, educated at the University of Virginia, Union Theological Seminary, and the University of Berlin. Ordained in the Presbyterian ministry in 1870 and pastor at Roselle, New Jersey from 1870 to 1874, when appointed professor of Hebrew and cognate languages at Union Theological Seminary. Remained there until 1913. In 1891 transferred to the chair of Biblical theology, and in 1904 became professor of theological encyclopaedia and symbolics. In 1892 he was tried for denial of verbal inspiration by the Presbytery of New York and was acquitted. The following year the prosecution appealed to the General Assembly which condemned him and suspended him from the ministry. About 1900 he took orders with the Protestant Episcopal Church. The Board of Directors of the seminary, however, voted to retain Briggs in his professorship, and the seminary itself severed its relation with the Assembly, becoming independent and undenominational. A strong advocate of church unity or reunion of all Christendom. One of the founders, and for ten years (1880-1890) editor of the *Presbyterian Review,* and one of the editors of the *International Theological Library* and of the *International Critical Commentary.* He was also one of the editors of the *Hebrew and English Lexicon of the Old Testament.* He wrote *Theological Symbolics, American Presbyterianism, Messianic Prophecy, History of the Study of Theology, General Introduction to the Study of the Holy Scriptures, The Authority of the Holy Scriptures, The Fundamental Christian Faith, The Higher Criticism of the Hexateuch, The Messiah of the Gospels, The Messiah of the Apostles, The Incarnation of the Lord, New Light on the Life of Jesus, Ethical Teachings of Jesus, and Critical and Exegetical Commentary on the Psalms.* Died of pneumonia in 1913.

BRIGHTMAN, EDGAR SHEFFIELD (1884-1953), Personalistic philosopher, born in Holbrook, Massachusetts, educated at Brown University, Boston University, University of Berlin, and University of Marburg. Ordained a Methodist minister in 1912. 1916-1919 taught philosophy and Greek at Brown University; professor of philosophy and Bible at Nebraska Wesleyan University; professor of ethics and religion at Wesleyan University, Connecticut. 1919-1953 occupied the Borden P. Bowne chair of philosophy at the Boston University Graduate School. Leading exponent of Bowne's Personalism. Author of several books on philosophy and religion, chief among them: *An Introduction to Philosophy, Nature and Values, A Philosophy of Ideals,* and *A Philosophy of Religion.*

BRIGID (brĭj'ĭd), **(BRIDGET, BRIGIT, BRIDE)** (c. 455-523), Saint of Kildare, born at Fochart, Ireland. After conversion founded and presided over a monastic community, which became a model and pattern for monasteries and nunneries throughout Ireland. Brigid's influence in the monastic life of Ireland is perhaps next to that of Patrick and Columba. Became a patron saint of Ireland with February 1, the day of her death, her festive day. Many monasteries, churches, and villages named after her in Ireland, Scotland, and England.

BROADUS (brôd'ŭs), **JOHN ALBERT** (1827-1895), American Baptist scholar, teacher, preacher, born in Culpeper County, Virginia. Educated at the University of Virginia. For a time assistant professor of Latin and Greek at the University of Virginia and pastor of the Baptist Church at Charlottesville, Virginia. At organization of the Southern Baptist Theological Seminary at Greenville, South Carolina in 1859, became professor of New Testament Interpretation and of Homiletics. After the removal of the seminary to Louisville, Kentucky, he became president in 1889 until 1895. A member of the International Lesson Committee from 1878 until his death. Attained high rank as teacher, preacher, and scholar. Published two notable books in the field of homiletics: *The Preparation and Delivery of Sermons* and *Lectures on the History of Preaching.* Wrote also a *Commentary on the Gospel of Matthew,* and *Harmony of the Gospels According to the Revised Version.*

BROOKES, JAMES HALL (1830-1897), American preacher, author, editor, born in North Carolina, attended Miami University at Oxford, Ohio, Princeton Theological Seminary. After graduation, 1854, within a week he was ordained to the Presbyterian ministry, installed in his pastorate at Dayton, Ohio. Held pastorate four years, then (1858) became pastor in St. Louis, Missouri, remained there until his death, 1897. He founded, edited, and wrote much of the content of *Truth or Testimony for Christ* for twenty-three years. Some of his books: *The Way Made Plain, Maranatha or The Lord Cometh, Israel and the Church, Till He Come, The Mystery of Suffering,* and *Is the Bible Inspired?* He wrote between two hundred fifty and three hundred tracts and pamphlets.

BROOKS, PHILLIPS (1835-1893), American Protestant Episcopal minister and author, born in Boston, Massachusetts of distinguished New England Congregational ancestry. Entered the liberal Unitarian university of Harvard on his sixteenth birthday, graduated at twenty. After a short, unpleasant experience as a teacher in the Boston Latin School studied at the theological seminary of the Protestant Episcopal Church in Alexandria, Virginia, 1856-1859. In 1859 he began his first rectorate in Philadelphia. Ordained priest in 1860. In 1869 received a call from Trinity Church in Boston, where he remained until 1891, becoming famous as a preacher of rare personality, charm, and spiritual force. Liberal in theology, belonged to the broad-church school of theology. Central message was that all men are the children of God. Church in Boston took a leading part in the movement for Christian unity. He was consecrated Protestant Episcopal bishop of Massachusetts in 1891. During his ministry traveled abroad frequently and preached before the Queen of England. He gave the Lyman Beecher lectures before the Yale Divinity School, 1877 (published as *Lectures on Preaching*), and the Bohlen lectures at the Philadelphia Divinity School, 1879 (published as *The Influence of Jesus*). Produced five volumes of sermons during his life, and five more were published after his death, 1893. He wrote the hymn, "O Little Town of Bethlehem."

BROTHER LAWRENCE. *See* **HERMAN, NICHOLAS.**

BROWN, CHARLES REYNOLDS (1862-1950), American Congregational clergyman and educator, born at Bethany, West Virginia, educated at the University of Iowa, School of Theology, Boston University. Ordained in 1889. Held pastorates at Wesley Chapel Methodist Episcopal Church, Cincinnati, Ohio; Winthrop Congregational Church, Boston, Massachusetts, and the First Congregational Church, Oakland, California. Special lecturer on ethics in Leland Stanford University, 1900-1906; Lyman Beecher lecturer at Yale, 1905-1906; lecturer on ethics in Mills College, 1906-1908; lectured also at Cornell, Harvard, Columbia and University of North Carolina. From 1911 to 1928, dean of Yale Divinity School. Moderator of the National

Council of Congregational Churches, 1913-1915. In theology Brown was a liberal, was nationally known as a preacher, teacher, and author. Writings include *The Art of Preaching, Why I Believe in Religion, The Social Message of the Modern Pulpit, The Making of a Minister,* and *My Own Yesterdays*.

BROWN, DAVID (1803-1897), Free church of Scotland minister, born in Aberdeen, Scotland, graduated from Aberdeen University, 1821. Served as associate to Edward Irving in London 1830-1832. Ordained minister of a country chapel, 1836. At time of Disruption, 1843, he went with the Free church, same year became minister of St. James's, Glasgow. Elected professor of apologetics, church history, and exegesis of the gospels in the Free Church College, Aberdeen, 1857; held post for thirty years, made principal of the college in 1876, position held until his death. Was a director of the National Bible Society of Scotland, one of the founders of the Evangelical Alliance, 1888, member of the New Testament Revision Company. At age of eighty-two made moderator of the General Assembly of the Free church. Chief writings were *Christ's Second Coming: Will It Be Premillennial?* (a post-millennial view); *The Restoration of the Jews: The History, Principles, and Bearings of the Question; The Apocalypse: It's Structure and Preliminary Predictions*. Collaborated with R. Jamieson and A. R. Fausett in preparing the *Commentary, Critical, Experimental, and Practical on the Old and New Testaments*.

BROWN, JOHN (1800-1859), radical American abolitionist, born in Torrington, Connecticut. When five years old family moved to Ohio. Turned to land surveying. Unsuccessful in every business venture attempted. Resided in several different states, often in lawsuits because of debts; inherited a hatred for slavery. Initiated in Pennsylvania, 1834, where he was then living, a project among abolitionists to educate blacks. Devoted the next twenty years to this and other abolitionist ventures. Followed five sons to Kansas, 1855, a center of strong contention between the "free state" and the pro-slavery settlers. Settled at Osawatomie. Ordered five proslavery men shot in cold blood, in retaliation for five "free state" settlers who earlier had been murdered. With a small band of armed men resisted an attack on Osawatomie, gaining for himself the name "Old Brown of Osawatomie." Then went to Virginia, where on October 16, 1859, attempted to carry out a plan to free the slaves. With about twenty followers led an attack upon Harper's Ferry, seizing federal arsenal, believing this would result in an immediate uprising of the slaves. A day or two later, under the command of Colonel Robert E. Lee, the arsenal was taken, several of Brown's men including two sons were killed. Brown was wounded and captured. He was taken to Charleston, where he was imprisoned on charge of insurrection, murder, and treason. He was tried, sentenced to death, then hanged on December 2, 1859.

BROWN, JOHN ELWARD (1879-1957), evangelist and college president. Born in Oskaloosa, Iowa. Served in Spanish-American war. President of Scarritt Collegiate Institute (1901-1903) in Neosho, Missouri, of Summer Bible Conference, Lebanon Springs (1913-1940) and John Brown College (now University) (1919-1957) which he founded in 1919.

BROWN, SAMUEL ROBBINS (1810-1880), American missionary to China and Japan, born at East Windsor, Connecticut, received education at Yale University; Columbia Theological School, Columbia, South Carolina; and Union Theological Seminary, New York. Went to China, locating at Macao, 1838, removing to Hong Kong in 1842. In 1838 opened for the Morrison Education Society the first Protestant school in the Chinese Empire. Returning to America, 1847, because of his wife's ill health, brought three Chinese boys, one of whom, Yung Wing, became first Chinese graduate of Yale, and influential and prominent for his country in international affairs. Brown taught at Rome, New York 1848-1851, and was pastor of the Dutch Reformed Church and principal of a school at Owasco Outlet (Sand Beach), near Auburn, New York, 1851-1859. In 1851 one of the incorporators of Elmira College, the first chartered women's college in America. Upon the opening of Japan to the world, Dr. Brown in 1859 went as missionary to Japan for the Dutch Reformed church, pioneering in educational work there as in China and in America. Scores of his students became prominent in the life of the empire. Due to his wife's failing health returned to America and became a pastor and teacher of boys for two years at his old church at Owasco Outlet, then returned to Japan for another ten years (1869-1879), continuing his missionary educational work. Chairman of the committee which translated the New Testament, personally translated several of the books. Considered the advancement of civilization a part of the work of the Christian missionary. Wrote many articles and newspaper letters, and published *Colloquial Japanese* and *A Maker of the New Orient*.

BROWN, WILLIAM ADAMS (1865-1943), American Presbyterian theologian, born in

New York City, educated at Yale University, Union Theological Seminary, and the University of Berlin. Ordained to the Presbyterian ministry in 1893; Professor at Union Theological Seminary from 1892 to 1936. Very liberal tendencies as evidenced in his published contributions in the *American Journal of Theology,* and the *Harvard Theological Review,* made the Presbyterian church at the General Assembly, 1913, criticize him sharply. Held important positions in many organizations including the Federal Council of Churches of Christ in America, the World Council of Churches, the World Conference on Faith and Order, Religious Education Association, the Institute for the Deaf and Dumb in New York, the Near East College Association, the Grenfell Association of America, and the Commission of Higher Education, India. He wrote for Hastings' *Dictionary of the Bible,* and Hastings' *Encyclopedia of Religion and Ethics,* and published, among others, the following books: *Christian Theology in Outline; Modern Missions in the Far East; Modern Theology and the Preaching of the Gospel; The Church in America; Beliefs That Matter; The New Order in the Christian Church; The Minister—His World and His Work.*

BROWNE, ROBERT (c. 1550-1633), founder of the Brownists or Congregationalists, born at Tolethorp, Rutlandshire, England, studied at Corpus Christi College, Cambridge. For three years taught school in or near London. Began to preach against the discipline, government, and ceremonies of the Church of England. Repudiated a state church for autonomy of each church with members linked by a covenant. At Norwich several people followed in separating from the Anglican church. In 1580 organized his first church. This group of Separatists became known as Brownists. When the English church tried to silence him, he left Norwich in 1582 and traveled in England, Holland, and Scotland for several years preaching his views, suffering harsh treatment and imprisonments. By 1586 he submitted to the demands of the church and covenanted to cease propagating his peculiar doctrines and to live as a member of the church. He was then appointed to the mastership of Stamford grammar school; in 1591 ordained priest. From 1591 to 1631 served as rector of Achurch, Northants. Died in the Northampton jail, where held for assaulting a constable. Main work was *A Treatise of Reformation Without Tarrying for Any* (1582).

BROWNE, SIR THOMAS (1605-1682), English prose writer and physician, born in Cheapside, London. Studied at Winchester school, Pembroke College, Oxford, and later at Montpellier, Padua, and Leiden, receiving the degree doctor of medicine from the latter in 1633. After a short residency at Shipton Hall, near Halifax, settled at Norwich for the rest of his life. Became a physician of high standing and of large practice. He was a Royalist and Charles II, 1671, knighted him as the first citizen of his town. An Anglican, a physician, and scientist, his thinking was inclined toward the theological and his writing toward the religious. Wrote heavy Latinized prose. Most notable work was *Religio Medici,* the religion of a doctor, in which he strongly expressed his devotion to religion as well as to science and asserted the right to be guided by reason. Combined skepticism with faith in revelation. His longest work was *Pseudodoxia Epidemica* or *Inquiries into Vulgar and Common Errors,* which emphasized the transition from the age of authority to the scientific era. In his *Urn Burial (Hydriotaphia)* he made observations on time and immortality.

BROWNING, ELIZABETH BARRETT (1806-1861), English poet. Maiden name, Moulton. Born at Coxhoe Hall, Durham, England, grew up at Hope End in Herefordshire. As daughter of a wealthy West Indian landholder, was privately educated. Not until she was in her thirties was her poetry taken seriously. From the time she was fifteen when she injured her spine saddling a horse, she was a semi-invalid. After her favorite brother died, 1838, she weakened until her life was despaired of; rallied and began to write poetry again. *The Cry of the Children* and *Lady Geraldine's Courtship,* written in her sick room, are among her best known works; *Sonnets from the Portuguese* was one of her greatest. These were love sonnets written during the time of her engagement to Robert Browning. *Aurora Leigh,* which she ranked highest, is a narrative poem, presenting ideals and beliefs. Reference to Robert Browning in one of her poems led to their first meeting. In 1846 they were married. The two poets lived in Italy where Mrs. Browning's health improved for a time. She was buried in Florence. In religious conviction she leaned toward spiritualism.

BROWNING, ROBERT (1812-1889), English poet and philosopher, born at Camberwell, London, privately educated. After age fourteen largely self-taught, reading books in his home and studying nature. Spent a brief time at University College, London. In middle life, parents became Dissenters. Determinedly devoted himself to the art of poetry, making it the main work of his life. First published work in verse, *Pauline* (1833). Poetry marked with profound and subtle erudition; he ranks with Alfred Tennyson as greatest of the Victorian poets. First met Elizabeth Barrett when he called to thank her for a compliment she paid him in one of her poems. Call was followed by a friendship that ripened into courtship and marriage. They lived happily in Italy from 1846 until her death in 1861. After her death he returned to England to educate their only son. Later returned to Venice, where he died in 1889. Buried in Westminster Abbey. His masterpiece was *The Ring and the Book* (four volumes). Other works included *My Last Duchess, Andrea del Sarto, The Bishop Orders His Tomb at St. Praxed's, The Laboratory, The Last Ride Together, Fra Lippo Lippi, Rabbi Ben Ezra, Pippa Passes, The Pied Piper of Hamlin,* and *Christmas Eve and Easter Day*. A few of his widely used lines are:

Grow old along with me,
The best is yet to be. . . .
God's in His Heaven,
All's right with the world!

BRUCE, ALEXANDER BALMAIN (1831-1899), Free church of Scotland theological writer, born at Aberargie, Perthshire, Scotland. At the time of the Disruption, 1843, the father removed to Edinburgh where Bruce first entered the university then went to the divinity hall of the Free church. After serving in two assistant pastorates called to Cardross in Dumbartonshire, 1859; nine years later to Broughty Ferry in Forfarshire. During these years published some sermons and lectures under the titles *The Training of the Twelve,* and *The Humiliation of Christ,* which established reputation as a biblical scholar and a writer of ability. From 1875 until 1899, on the death of Patrick Fairbairn, Bruce filled the chair of apologetics and New Testament exegesis in the Free Church Hall, Glasgow. During this time did the most of his writing. Bruce may be recognized as one of the most distinguished biblical scholars of his time. The boldness of his views, especially expressed in *The Kingdom of God, or, Christ's Teachings According to the Synoptic Gospels,* brought him somewhat unfavorably to the notice of the General Assembly of his church in 1890. His writings were pronounced to be, not at variance with the standards of the church. Some of the more noteworthy were: *St. Paul's Conception of Christianity, Commentary on the Synoptic Gospels* (in the *Expositor's Greek Testament*), *The Epistle to the Hebrews, The Chief End of Revelation, The Parabolic Teaching of Christ,* and *The Miraculous Element in the Gospels*.

BRUCIOLI (broo chē ō'lē), **ANTONIO** (c. 1500-c. 1554), Italian Protestant reformer and scholar, born in Florence, Italy. Becoming implicated in a conspiracy in 1522 against Cardinal Giulio de Medici, ruler of Florence, Brucioli took refuge in France, embraced the doctrine of the reformers. Five years later ventured to return to Florence, but again found it necessary to leave. Resided in Venice where he published a number of works, some of them promoting reform doctrines. Chief among his works, a translation of the Bible into Tuscan, with commentaries on the whole Bible. The pope placed them on the Index.

BRUMBAUGH (broom'bä), **MARTIN GROVE** (1862-1930), American educator and governor of Pennsylvania, born in Huntingdon County, Pennsylvania, educated at Juniata College, Huntingdon, Pennsylvania, and University of Pennsylvania. He was ordained in the German Baptist Brethren Church. From 1884 to 1890, superintendent of schools in Huntingdon County, at the same time conductor of the teachers' institutes of Louisiana, 1886-1891. President of Juniata College from 1895 to 1906, meanwhile professor of pedagogy at the University of Pennsylvania, 1895-1900, 1902-1906. First commissioner of education in Puerto Rico, 1900-1902. From 1906 to 1915 Dr. Brumbaugh was superintendent of public schools in Philadelphia, and governor of Pennsylvania, 1915-1919. From 1924 to 1930, again president of Juniata College. Wrote *History of the Brethren in Europe and America,* and *Life and Works of Christopher Dock*.

BRUNNER, EMIL (1889-1966) Swiss theologian. Born in Winterthur. Pastor at Obstalden for about eight years. Professor of theology at Zurich (1924-1953) and of Christian philosophy at the International Christian University in Tokyo (1953-1955). A former colleague of Barth with whom he broke in 1934 by rejecting Barth's denial of general revelation and Barth's denial that man still had the image of God after the Fall. Influenced by Kierkegaard and Martin Buber. Revelation is encounter with a self-revealing God. Christ comes to us as the Mediator whom we obey. Opposed both Liberalism and evangelical orthodoxy. His most important work is the three volume *Dogmatics* (1946-1960). Other significant works are: *The Divine Imperative, Man in Revolt, The Divine-Human Encounter,* and *Natural Theology*.

BRUNO or **BERNO (?-927),** a Burgundian Benedictine monk, abbot of Cluny, trained at the monastery of Dijon, France. A successful abbot in several monasteries, made first abbot of the reform monastery started by William I, the Pious, Duke of Aquitaine, at Cluny in 910. Bruno enforced the strictest observance of the rules of St. Benedict. He was a man of remarkable character and ability, as was his notable disciple and successor, Odo, 927-941.

BRUNO, PHILIPPO GIORDANO (1548-1600), Neo-Platonic, humanistic, pantheistic philosopher of the later Renaissance period, born at Nola, near Naples, Italy. In 1562 joined the Dominican order at Naples. Later becoming restive under the strict rules of the order, and revolting against all asceticism and scholasticism, left the order about 1576 and fled to Rome. Led a wandering life in various countries of Europe, teaching, lecturing, and writing. The philosophers who influenced him most were Pythagoras, Plato, Plotinus, and Lucretius. He in turn influenced Descarte, Schelling, Spinoza, Leibnitz, Böhme, and Hegel. First philosopher to espouse the Copernican hypothesis. Mystic, poetic mind sought the beautiful in nature. To him philosophy, aesthetics, and religion were identical. Pantheistic view led him to see God in everything. The world is perfect because it is the life of God, that is, animated by the universal soul. Writings largely done in Italian in dialogue form, but philosophical or metaphysical and somewhat scientific in nature. In 1600, after lying in prison in Rome for seven years under the Inquisition, he was excommunicated and delivered to the state to be burned at the stake.

BRYAN, WILLIAM JENNINGS (1860-1925), American political leader, editor, lecturer, born at Salem, Illinois, converted at the age of fourteen, joined the Presbyterian Church. Educated at Whipple Academy, Illinois College, and the Chicago Union College of Law, all at Jacksonville, Illinois. Admitted to the Illinois Bar in 1883; in 1888 moved to Lincoln, Nebraska, where his law practice developed rapidly. In 1890, elected to Congress and served two terms. In 1896, 1900, and 1908, unsuccessful Democratic candidate for the presidency of the United States. He caused the nomination of Woodrow Wilson in 1912. In 1913 Wilson appointed him Secretary of State, in which position negotiated arbitration treaties with thirty nations. Strong belief in neutrality, and disagreement with Wilson's policy toward Germany led him to resign in 1915. After his resignation devoted himself largely to the cause of international peace, prohibition, and to lecturing on temperance and other civic and ethical reforms. From 1894 to 1896, editor of the Omaha *World-Herald*. In 1901 founded the *Commoner*, a political weekly in Lincoln, Nebraska, continued as its editor until 1913. In 1906 toured the world. A staunch Christian and an active member of the church. Believed implicitly in the inspiration of the Bible, and in the deity of Jesus Christ. A lay preacher, a patriotic leader, and servant of the people. The epithet, "Commoner" well suits the man. Bryan led the prosecution in the famous Scopes' trial in Dayton, Tennessee. John Scopes was arrested for teaching evolution and defended by Clarence Darrow. Bryan won the case for the state, but died a few days later.

BRYANT, WILLIAM CULLEN (1794-1878), pioneer American poet and journalist, born at Cummington, Massachusetts in a home of culture, literature, and religion. He spent a year at Williams College, but had to leave college. Studied a year at home, and Williams College later gave him his degree. He studied law and at twenty-one was admitted to the bar. However, in 1825, after ten years of practice he retired to enter upon journalism. In 1826 became assistant to the editor of the New York *Evening Post*. In 1829, promoted to the chief editorship; bought one-half interest in the paper. When he died his two thousand dollar share was worth close to half a million. An honest, conscientious editor, gave to paper and patrons his best. Made acquaintance with many distinguished men in his seven trips abroad. Interest in poetry began early and continued throughout his long life. The poem that made him famous, *Thanatopsis,* which remained practically his masterpiece, was written before he was nineteen. He was pre-eminently a poet of nature, recognizing the presence of God in nature. In his laters year he translated into English the Iliad and the Odyssey of Homer and collaborated in writing *History of the United States*. Physically, mentally, and religiously he lived a well-disciplined life. When well in the ninth decade of life he was robust, agile, and alert, and could outwalk younger men. Brought up a Unitarian, maintained connection with that church nearly all his life. Active and robust, he had good hearing and eyesight, and retained a keen mind until the last.

BUBER, MARTIN (1878-1965) Jewish theological philosopher. Born in Vienna and educated there and in Berlin. From 1916 to 1924 edited *Der Jude* for German-speaking Jews. Professor of philosophy at Frankfurt University (1923-1933) and of religion at the University of Jerusalem (1933-1951). Followed existentialism of Kierkegaard. Viewed God as one who may be known but not known about. Influenced Neo-orthodoxy with ideas of discontinuity between God and man and God as transcendent.

BUCER (bōō'tsĕr), **MARTIN** (1491-1551), the chief reformer of Strassburg, born near

Strassburg. In 1506, became a Dominican monk and was later ordained priest. In 1517, went to Heidelberg where he studied the Bible and the writings of both the humanists and Luther. Met Luther at Heidelberg, 1518, began to correspond with him in 1520. In 1521, left his order and the Catholic church. Married a nun, 1522, among the first of the reformers to break the celibate rule. In 1523, accepted a call to Strassburg where the Reformation was already in progress. Labored as minister for twenty-five years. Bucer was an important figure in the Reformation as arbiter and mediary between Luther and Zwingli; between the Lutherans and the Calvinists. His motto was: "We believe in Christ, not in the church." But importance was more than being a mere arbiter. Wrote several catechisms, introduced the lay presbytery and inaugurated confirmation in Strassburg. He and friend Sturm laid the foundations of the Protestant educational system in Strassburg, founding the Gymnasium in 1538 and the seminary in 1544. Arranged for pastoral conventions, introduced a sound church discipline, organized works of charity, effected a close cooperation between secular and religious government, introduced a simple liturgy, and arranged for congregational singing. Calvin in three years at Strassburg (1538-1541) was greatly impressed and influenced by Bucer's pastoral work and church organization. Serious political troubles finally arose which made further stay at Strassburg dangerous and at last impossible. Finally accepted a call from Cranmer to England in 1549 where he aided the English Reformation, forming a connecting link between the German and the English Reformation. Highly esteemed by both the archbishop and King Edward VI. Spent the last months of his life as professor of theology and lecturer in Cambridge. At the request of the young king, wrote *De Regno Christi,* which proved to be his last work, and the university conferred the degree bachelor of divinity.

BUCHANAN, CLAUDIUS (1766-1815), born in Cambuslang near Glasgow, Anglican missionary to India. Educated at Glasgow University and Queen's College, Cambridge where influenced by John Newton and Charles Simeon. Ordained in 1796. Became a chaplain in Bengal and in Calcutta for the British East India Company. From 1799 to 1807 was vice-principal of Fort William College. Translated the Bible into Hindustani and the Persian language. In 1818 helped to set up the first Indian bishopric.

BUCHANAN, GEORGE (1507-1582) Scottish political theorist. Born at Killearn, Scotland. Educated at the Universities of St. Andrews and Paris. Writings critical of the Franciscans led to flight to France in 1537. Taught at Bordeaux, Paris, and teacher and regent of the University of Coimbra in Portugal. Principal of St. Leonard's College of St. Andrews University. Moderator of the General Assembly of the (present) Reformed Church of Scotland. In his 1577 *De Juri Reni Apud Scoti* argued that royal power is from the people and if abused may be subject to popular resistance.

BUCHMAN, FRANK NATHAN DANIEL (1878-1961), born at Pennsburg, Pennsylvania, educated at Muhlenberg College, Westminster College, and Cambridge University, receiving the A.M., D.D., and LL.D. degrees. Lectured at Hartford Theological Seminary (1916-1921). He traveled widely throughout the world. Visited Oxford in 1921 where in Christ Church College his "Oxford Group" began which he led until 1961 in its spread into more than sixty countries. His movement since 1938 is known as the Moral Re-Armament Movement (MRA). During World War II he initiated the "You Can Defend America" campaign for total defense and the campaign for industrial teamwork and production. After the war visited many countries, establishing missions and training assemblies. Group held house parties at good hotels marked by sharing or confession publicly and practiced the "Quiet Time for God to speak." Upheld four absolutes of love, purity, honesty, and unselfishness. A few of the books Buchman wrote are: *Rising Tide, Moral Re-Armament, You Can Defend America, Remaking the World, The World Rebuilt, Battle Line of American Industry,* and *The Oxford Group and Its Work of Moral Re-Armament.*

BUCK, DUDLEY (1839-1909), American composer, organist, and music teacher, born in Hartford, Connecticut, attended Trinity College, Hartford, studied in Leipzig, Dresden, and Paris. Between 1862 and 1875 while teaching and composing, was organist at North Congregational Church, Hartford, Connecticut; St. James Episcopal Church, Chicago; St. Paul's Church, Boston; and the Music Hall Association in Boston. From 1875 until retirement in 1903, organist in churches in New York and Brooklyn, serving twenty-five years at the Holy Trinity Church, Brooklyn; about the same time also organist and conductor of the Brooklyn Apollo Club. One hundred forty excellent anthems, solos, cantatas, hymns, *Te Deums,* for both liturgical and choir use, were fluent, attractive, well-constructed, with many of them having depth and fervor. Religious compositions frequently made use of dramatic effect. Also wrote a valuable handbook, *Illustrations for Choir Accompaniment, with Hints on Registration; The Influence of the Organ in History;* and *A Dictionary of Musical Terms*. A member of the National Institute of Arts and Letters.

BUDÉ (bōō dā′), **GUILLAUME (BUDAEUS)** (1468-1540), French scholar, friend of Erasmus, born at Paris, studied at Paris and Orleans. After leading a dissipated life for several years began to apply himself to Greek, philosophy, theology, law, medicine, and science. Louis XII sent him (1505) as ambassador to Leo X at Rome; later became royal librarian under Francis I, whom he induced not to prohibit printing in France. Became an eminent Greek scholar and a man of influence. Instrumental in establishing (1530) the Collegium Trilingue, later to become the College de France, for the study of the Greek, Hebrew, and Latin languages. Also founded the royal library at Fontainebleau, which later was moved and became the Bibliotheque Nationale in Paris. A secret adherent of the Reformation, but afraid of an open rupture with the church. Before Luther's time he had written against the corruption of the clergy and the papacy, and for reform in the church. More important writings were a work on ancient coins and measures; a work on the study of law; work on morals and philosophy, and commentaries on the Greek language.

BUGENHAGEN (bōō′gĕn hä gĕn), **JOHANN** (1485-1558), a leader of the German Reformation, born at Wollin, Pomerania. Well-educated humanist, especially in the Latin classics. Ordained priest in 1509. Under the influence of Erasmus, he was led to the study of the Bible. In 1517, appointed to lecture on the Bible and the church Fathers in the monastery school of Belbuck. Read some of Luther's writings, then began a correspondence with him. In 1521, while Luther was at the Wartburg, Bugenhagen joined the Reformation and gave himself fully to it. Married in 1522. In 1525 officiated at Luther's wedding. Energetic as a teacher, lecturer, writer, translator, and pastor. From 1523 to 1527 pastor of the Collegate Church in Wittenberg and a member of the faculty of the University of Wittenberg. Especially gifted in government, organized many churches in Northern Germany and in Denmark. His church constitutions were models. Spent five years, 1537-1542, in Denmark supervising the Lutheran Reformation in that country. While there crowned the new king of Denmark, ordained seven evangelical theologians as superintendents of the new Lutheran Church, and reorganized the university. In 1530, assisted Luther and Melanchthon in drawing up the criticisms of the Roman Catholic practices; as worked over by Melanchthon then comprised the second part of the Augsburg Confession. He and Melanchthon largely instrumental in putting into effect the educational program for the people of Germany as idealized and planned by Luther. Remained at Wittenberg, a help and strength to Luther in his last years, and preached his funeral sermon on Feb. 22, 1546. In decade following Luther's death the Wittenberg Church suffered reverses at the hand of the Roman Catholics. Bugenhagen, desiring to serve the university, sought to reconcile himself to the new situation, consequently lost the confidence of some of more ardent evangelical friends. However, continued protest against the Roman Catholic church, and remained a staunch Reformation preacher until death in 1558. His best work was a commentary on the Psalms.

BULGAKOV, SERGIUS NIKOLAEVICH (1871-1944). Born in Russia. Studied at Orel, Moscow, Berlin, Paris, and London. Marxist in youth. Taught at Kiev Polytechnical Institute from 1901 to 1906 and the University of Moscow from 1906 to 1918. Elected to second Duma. Ordained priest 1918. Taught at the University of Simferopol in the Crimea. Exiled from Russia in 1922 and settled in Paris in 1925. Founder, professor of theology and dean of the Orthodox Theological Institute of St. Sergius. Believed the universe to be an organic whole with a world soul created out of nothing as an emanation from God, the third Sophia. His idealism and mysticism developed in *The Unfading Light* and *The God-Manhood*.

BULLINGER, JOHANN HEINRICH (1504-1575), Swiss reformer and successor to Zwingli, born at Bremgarten, near Zurich, Switzerland, son of a highly respected and beloved married Catholic priest. Sent to the school of the Brethren of Common Life at Emmerick in Westphalia. Entered the University of Cologne, after graduating began the study of theology (1520) at which time Luther's reformatory activity at Wittenberg was at its height. By reading the writings of the fathers, those of Luther and Melanchthon, and especially the Bible, came to the conviction that Luther was right, accepted the principles of the Reformation. When he heard Zwingli in 1527, cast in his lot with him. In 1529, made pastor at Bremgarten where his father had been priest until he too joined the evangelical faith and had resigned his charge. Same year married a former nun who bore him eleven children. In 1531, following the death of Zwingli, chosen pastor of the Great Minster Church in Zurich to succeed the great Swiss Reformer, carried on the work of Zwingli with great power and success for the rest of his life. In 1536, with several others drew up the First Helvetic Confession with the hope of finding an acceptable interpretation of the eucharist and of effecting a plan of union among the various Reformed groups, even with the Lutherans. In 1549 he, Calvin, and Farel wrote the Consensus of Zurich (Consensus Tigurinus), which ended dogmatic disputes in Protestant Switzerland. In 1566, drew up the Second Helvetic Confession which included much of the First Confession, united Zwinglianism and Calvinism, crystalized Reformed thought and cemented together the Evangelical Reformed churches. An indefatigable, expository preacher, esteemed and devoted pastor, a sympathetic counselor, an expert educationalist, a prolific writer, a conciliatory controversialist, a precautionary administrator, a man of strong convictions, and adamant Christian character. Bullinger succeeded Zwingli in the local leadership at Zurich.

BULTMANN, RUDOLF (1884-1976) German New Testament scholar and theologian. Born in Germany. Studied at Marburg, Tübingen, and Berlin. Professor of New Testament at Marburg from 1921 to 1951. Influenced by Martin Heiddiger. Elaborated form criticism by which the truth in the gospels enshrined in parabolic and other forms had to be demythologized. Little left of Jesus' words and deeds when the process was completed. Existential decision for Christ was to be based on the residue of truth. Important works were *The History of the Synoptic Tradition, New Testament Theology* and a commentary on John's gospel.

BUNTING, JABEZ (1779-1858) Methodist leader after Wesley. Minister by 1779. Minister of Oldham Street Chapel in Manchester by 1803. Called to London headquarters in 1833. Fourteen times president of the Methodist Conference. Secretary of Wesleyan Missionary Society for eighteen years. President of Theological College at Hoxton. Greatly influenced English Methodism in its transition from societies in chapels to members in Methodist churches.

BUNYAN, JOHN (1628-1688), Puritan preacher and writer, born at Elstow, near Bedford, England. Joined the army, probably the Parliamentary side, when sixteen or seventeen. On leaving the army, settled down as a tinker at Elstow, following the trade of his father. In 1647, married a praying Christian. She succeeded in leading her husband to Christ. In 1655, baptized and became a member of the Bedford Baptist Church. Soon after baptism began to preach. At the Restoration (1660) was arrested for preaching without receiving permission from the Established Church, thrown into the Bedford jail. Remained there for twelve and one-half years. His young wife and family suffered much during this time. Welcomed the visits of wife, children and friends, especially that of little blind daughter. While in this prison, wrote famous allegory, *The Pilgrim's Progress*. In last part of imprisonment, was given considerable freedom, allowed occasional visits out and even privilege of preaching at times. In 1672, the Act of Pardon freed him and gave liberty to preach. At once became pastor of the Bedford Baptist Church, served the rest of his days. In prison again, however, for a few months (1675). Buried at Bunhill Field. Besides the *Pilgrim's Progress,* Bunyan wrote *The Life and Death of Mr. Badman, The Holy War,* and *Grace Abounding*.

BURNET, GILBERT (1643-1715), British prelate and historian, born at Edinburgh, educated at Marischal College, Aberdeen. In 1661 became a probationer for the ministry of the Church of Scotland, studied and traveled in England, Holland, and France until 1664. Parish priest at Saltaun, 1664-1669, and professor of divinity at Glasgow University, 1669-1674. From 1674 to 1684 removed to England and became chaplain at the Rolls Chapel and lecturer at St. Clement. After reproving Charles II for his dissolute living, retired from the university; upon the accession of James II, settled at The Hague. Espoused the cause of William and Mary. In 1688, returned to England as chaplain to William and Mary, the next year made bishop of Salisbury. In this office, exemplary in zeal and activity, in pastoral and administrative ability, and in puritanic virtue. In politics, a Whig, in theology a latitudinarian or Broad Churchman. Endeavored to carry through plans that would allow the incorporation of the Nonconformists into the Church of England. Denounced by John Maitland (Duke of Lauderdale), Secretary of State for Scottish Affairs. Zealously anti-Roman Catholic. Most noted and praiseworthy writings: *History of the Reformation in England* and *History of My Own Times; Exposition of the Thirty-Nine Articles;* and *Infallibility of the Roman Church Confuted*. Helped to inaugurate provision for the augmentation of livings, generally known as Queen Anne's Bounty.

BURNS (bûrnz), **WILLIAM CHALMERS** (1815-1868), Scottish missionary to China, born at Dun, Forfarshire, Scotland, and died at Newchwang, Manchuria, studied at Marischal College in the University of Aberdeen, and at the University of Glasgow. Licensed to ministry in 1839, had first charge in Robert M. McCheyne's church at Dundee during McCheyne's visit to Palestine. For about seven years held successful evangelistic meetings in the British Isles and Canada. In 1846 sailed as the first missionary to China under the English Presbyterian Missionary Society. Soon achieved a remarkable fluency in the Chinese language, adopted Chinese dress and manner of living, and lived among the Chinese people. Lived for a period of a few months or a few years at most in each of the following places: Hong Kong, Canton, Foochow, Amoy, Swatow, Shanghai, Peking, and finally at Newchwang Manchuria, where he died. Labored for seven years before he gained his first convert. Results of labors in China counted by number of converts were meager, but the effect of personal influence was great. Translated Bunyan's *Pilgrim's Progress,* and many Christian hymns into the Chinese. The life of J. Hudson Taylor was profoundly influenced by Burns.

BURRELL (bûr′rĕl), **DAVID JAMES** (1844-1926), pastor of Reformed and Presbyterian churches, born at Mt. Pleasant, Pennsylvania, educated at Yale University and Union Theological Seminary. Between 1872 and 1926, held successive pastorates at the Westminster Presbyterian Church, Chicago; the Second Presbyterian Church, Dubuque, Iowa; Westminster Presbyterian Church, Minneapolis, Minnesota; and from 1891-1926 Marble Collegiate Reformed Church, Manhattan, New York City, the latter being the oldest church on the American continent, founded in 1628. In 1903 and several years following, also acting professor of homiletics, Princeton Theological Seminary. For a time associate editor of *The Presbyterian,* and also of the *Christian Herald*. President of the World's Council of Reformed and Presbyterian Churches; manager of the American Sabbath Union; one of the seven incorporators, a director, and a president of the Anti-Saloon League of New York; director of the Anti-Saloon League of America; a vice-president of the National Temperance Society; one of the Board of Regents of Theological Seminary of the Northwest, Bennett Female Seminary, Elmira Female Society, and McCormick Theological Seminary; member of the board of managers of the American Tract Society; a trustee of the United Society of Christian Endeavor; a trustee of the Board of Domestic Missions of the Reformed Church; and a member of the New York and the Pennsylvania Historical Societies. In theology, conservative. Publications were numerous and popular rather than scholarly. Some of his writings: *The Religions of the World, The Early Church, The Wondrous Cross, The Gospel of Certainty, Why I Believe the Bible, The Wonderful Teacher and What He Taught, Paul's Companions, Paul's Campaigns, Life and Letters of Paul, The Religion of the Future,* and *The Resurrection and the Life Beyond*.

BURTON, ERNEST DEWITT (1856-1925), Baptist theologian and educator, born at Granville, Ohio, studied at Denison University, Granville, Ohio; Rochester Theological Seminary, New York; Leipzig and Berlin, Germany. Instructor in Kalamazoo College, Kalamazoo, Michigan a year, then teacher in public schools in Ohio for two years; instructor in New Testament Greek in Rochester Theological Seminary for a year. In 1883 ordained to the Baptist ministry, elected associate professor of New Testament interpretation of Newton Theological Seminary, Massachusetts from 1883 to 1892. From 1892 to 1923, professor of New Testament literature and interpretation, head of the department of biblical and patristic Greek at the University of Chicago. From 1910 to 1925, also director of University Libraries. From 1923 until death in 1925, president of the university. Editor of the *Biblical World,* 1892-1920; the *American Journal of Theology,* 1907-1915. Among writings: *Syntax of the Moods and Tenses in New Testament Greek, Harmony of the Gospels for Historical Study* (in collaboration with W. A. Stevens), *Records and Letters of the Apostolic Age, Short Introduction to the Gospels, Studies in the Gospel of Mark,* and *Some Principles of Literary Criticism and Their Application to the Synoptic Problem*.

BURY, JOHN BAGNELL (1861-1927), Irish historian, born at Clogher, County Monaghan, Ireland, studied at Trinity College, Dublin. Became fellow of Trinity College, 1885, professor of modern history in Dublin, 1893, and regius professor of modern history in the University of Cambridge 1902 until his death in 1927. Best known for his work on the history of the Byzantine Empire, for studies and researches on the Roman Empire, and for edition of Gibbon's *Decline and Fall of the Roman Empire*. His writings include, *A History of the Later Roman Empire* (Three volumes), *History of the Eastern Roman Empire, A History of Greece to the Death of Alexander the Great, The Invasion of Europe by the Barbarians, The Constitution of the Later Roman Empire, A History of Freedom of Thought, The Life of St. Patrick and His Place in History, The Idea of Progress,* and *The Science of History.* One of the editors of the *Cambridge Ancient History,* and was one of the founders of the *Cambridge Modern History*.

BUSH, GEORGE (1796-1859), American Bible commentator and Hebrew scholar, born in Norwich, Vermont, studied at Dartmouth College and Princeton Theological Seminary. In 1824, went as a home missionary to Indiana. Ordained by the Salem Presbytery and became pastor of the Presbyterian church in Indianapolis, 1825-1828. From 1831 to 1847, professor of Hebrew and Oriental literature at the University of the City of New York, also serving, 1836-1837 as instructor of sacred literature at Union Theological Seminary. During this period wrote *A Grammar of the Hebrew Language;* most of the eight volumes of *Notes* on the Pentateuch and Joshua and Judges. In 1845 embraced the mystical doctrines of Swedenborgianism, and became an ardent defender of its tenets both by voice and by pen. Editor of the *New Church Repository and Monthly Review,* 1848-1855, preacher in the New Church Society in New York, 1848-1852 and in Brooklyn, 1854-1859. After change of faith wrote, *Mesmer and Swedenborg; New Church Miscellanies;* and *Priesthood and Clergy Unknown to Christianity, or the Church a Community of Co-equal Brethren.*

BUSHNELL, HORACE (1802-1876), Congregational minister, born near Litchfield, Connecticut, graduated at Yale University. After teaching two years at Norwich, Connecticut, and editing the *Journal of Commerce* in New York for ten months, entered the New Haven Law School, where he studied and taught for five years. When ready to enter the bar in 1831, converted and entered Yale Divinity School to prepare for the ministry. Upon graduation in 1833, became pastor of the North Church, Hartford, Connecticut. Remained until 1859. Nevertheless, continued preaching and writing the rest of his life. Among his writings: *Christian Nurture* (in which he advocated the leading of the children to Christ in the home rather than in revivals); *God in Christ* (showing affinities with Sabellianism); *The Vicarious Sacrifice,* his treatise on the atonement (Moral influence view); *Nature of the Supernatural* (in which he relates miracles to law); and *Christian Theology.* Criticized the nonliturgical churches for their reliance upon the emotional experiences of conversion. His theory in *Christian Nurture* was to let the child "grow up a Christian and never know himself as otherwise." Teaching that the child merely has to grow into grace in a Christian environment evidences a defective view of original sin, the moral influence theory of atonement, emphasis on divine love at the expense of divine justice, and sudden conversion as an abnormal experience. A liberal accused him of antitrinitarian heresy; he barely escaped formal trial for heresy. Bushnell was the interpreter and exponent of Schleiermacher's views in America as Coleridge was in England. In 1856 helped in founding the University of California at Oakland.

BUSWELL, JR., JAMES OLIVER (1895-1975), Theologian and college president. Born in Mellon, Wisconsin. Educated at the University of Minnesota, McCormick Theological Seminary, and New York University (Ph.D.). Chaplain United States Army (1917-1918). Pastorates in Minnesota, Wisconsin, and Brooklyn, New York from 1919 to 1926. President of Wheaton College from 1926 to 1939. Professor at Faith Theological Seminary (1939-1940), National Bible Institute in New York, now Shelton College (1941-1955), and Covenant Theological Seminary, St. Louis, Missouri (1956-1969). Major work was *A Systematic Theology of the Christian Religion* (2 vols., 1962-1963) with a premillennial Calvinistic viewpoint.

BUTLER, JOSEPH (1692-1752), English theologian and Bishop of Durham, born at Wantage, Berkshire, England in a Presbyterian home. Studied at the dissenting academy at Tewkesbury, and then at Oriel College, Oxford. In 1718 ordained in the Church of England. From 1719 to 1726, preacher at the Rolls Chapel, London. From 1721 to 1738 held various positions in the Church; and from 1738 to 1750, bishop of Bristol. Also from 1740 to 1750, Dean of St. Paul's; and from 1750 until death in 1752, bishop of Durham, the richest see in England. In 1747 he was offered, but declined to accept the archbishopric of Canterbury. Lived in the "golden age of English deism," and it was his great aim to combat the current deism and contempt for religion. To this end wrote in 1736 one of his most significant books, *The Analogy of Religion, Natural and Revealed, to the Constitution and Course of Nature.* Butler's *Analogy* showing the strong probabilities of the theistic existence of God as over against deism, was widely believed to be the answer to deism, and was long used as a required text in Christian apologetics in the universities of England and America. Sermons are classics of the English pulpit. Wrote *Fifteen Sermons Preached at the Rolls Chapel,* "to justify to practical men the practice of the common virtues, benevolence, compassion, and the like, . . . to bring to light the objectives of right living."

BUTLER, JOSEPHINE ELIZABETH (1828-1907), Evangelical social reformer. After conversion worked to reclaim prostitutes and end the white slave trade. Formed Ladies National Association in 1869 which obtained the Repeal of Contagious Diseases Act. Her 1875 calling of a meeting in Geneva led to the founding of the International Federation for the Abolition of State Regulation Of Vice. Woman of piety, prayer, and social compassion. Wrote *Life of Catherine of Siena* (1878).

BUTLER, WILLIAM (1818-1899), Methodist missionary, born in Dublin, Ireland, educated at Didsbury College, near Manchester, England. Joined the Irish Wesleyan Conference in 1844, came to America and joined the New England Conference in 1850. In 1856, while pastor of a church in Lynn, Massachusetts accepted a call to the superintendency of the proposed Indian mission of his church. Mission established in the province of Oudh in the northwest of India with headquarters at Bareilly. Established a girls' orphanage at Bareilly and a boys' orphanage at Lucknow. In 1864 fell ill and had to return to America. About that time the mission in Oudh was organized into a conference. Resumed pastoral duties in America until 1869, became secretary of the American and Foreign Christian Union in New York. When the Methodist Church decided to open a mission in Mexico, Butler at the age of fifty-five was asked to assume the superintendency, accepted and for six years carried on the work; forced by ill health to return to the States. In 1883-1884, visited his mission in India; in 1887, visited Mexico. Wrote *Compendium of Missions, Land of the Veda, From Boston to Bareilly and Back,* and *Mexico in Transition*.

BUXTON, THOMAS FOWELL (1786-1845) English brewer, evangelical philanthropist and abolitionist. Educated at Trinity College in Dublin. Member of Parliament from 1818 to 1837. Succeeded Wilberforce as the leader of a crusade that abolished slavery for 700,000 slaves at a cost of £20 million (or $100 million) to the British Treasury through the act of 1833. Supported naval patrols in the 30s and 40s to stop the slave trade off the west coast of Africa.

BYRENNIOS, PHILOTHEOS (1833-1914) Discoverer of the *Didache*. Born in Constantinople, educated at Halki, Leipzig, Berlin, and Munich. Professor at Halki in 1861. Metropolitan of Sevres in 1875 and of Nicomenda (1877-1909). In 1883 published the *Didache* from a manuscript he obtained from the residence of the visiting patriarch of Jerusalem. It gives information about Christian ethics, liturgy, and practice in the early second century.

C

CABRINI (kȧ brē′nĭ), **FRANCES XAVIER** (1850-1917), Catholic nun, "Mother Cabrini," born Mary Frances Cabrini in St. Angelo Lodigiano, Lombardy, Italy. In 1880 she founded the Missionary Sisters of the Sacred Heart in abandoned Franciscan convent. At order of Pope Leo XIII, she came to the United States in 1889, to do religious and charitable work among Italian immigrants, although originally planning to go to China as a missionary. Became American citizen in 1909. With great skill, energy, and business acumen she established hospitals, schools, orphanages, and convents in Brooklyn, Philadelphia, Chicago, Denver, Los Angeles, and other American cities; branches established in Madrid, Paris, London, Buenos Aires, Sao Paulo, Rio de Janeiro, and other cities of the world. Died in Columbus Hospital, Chicago, one of her hospitals. Buried in chapel of Saint Frances Xavier Cabrini High School, New York City. Canonized by Pope Pius XII in 1946, first American citizen ever to be canonized a saint of the Roman Catholic church.

CADBURY, HENRY JOEL (1883-1974), New Testament scholar. Born in Philadelphia. Educated at Haverford College and Harvard University. Professor at Haverford College (1910-1919), Andover Seminary (1919-1926), Bryn Mawr College (1926-1934), Harvard Divinity School (1934-1954) and lecturer at the Quaker School of Graduate Study at Wallingford, Pennsylvania (1954-1972). Member of the New Testament Revised Standard Version Committee and the committee on the Apocrypha. Helped organize the Friends Service Committee and was its chairman from 1928 to 1960, except from 1935 to 1943.

CADMAN, SAMUEL PARKES (1864-1936), Congregational minister and author, born at Wellington, Shropshire, England. Educated at Wesleyan College, Richmond, Surrey, England; at Wesleyan (Connecticut), Syracuse, Yale, and New York universities in the United States. Came to US in 1890. Held successive pastorates at Millbrook, Yonkers, and Metropolitan Temple, New York from 1895 to 1901. Became pastor of Central Congregational Church, Brooklyn, where he remained from 1901 to 1936. Began broadcasting his sermons in 1923 and received nationwide interest. President of Federal Council of Churches of Christ in America (1924-1928); named the Council's first radio minister (1928). Lectured in several different colleges and universities. Writings include *William Owens, a Biography; Ambassadors of God; Christianity and the State; Every Day Questions and Answers; The Pursuit of Happiness; The Prophets of Israel; The Parables of Jesus*. Theological position was liberal.

CAECILIAN (d. c. 345), Bishop of Carthage. His election as bishop about 311 by Felix, who was accused of giving up the Scriptures in persecution under Diocletian, brought about the Donatist schism. Opponents elected Majorinus as bishop and, on his death in 316, Donatus as the anti-bishop. Caecilian was the only African bishop at the Council of Nicaea in 325.

CAESARIUS OF ARLES (c. 470-542), born at Chalons. Studied in the monastery of Lerins. Ordained priest about 500. Consecrated bishop of Arles in 502. Held Synod or Council of Orange in 529 which ended the Semi-Pelagian controversy by assertion of a moderate position nearer to Augustine than that of John Cassian. He persuaded Pope Boniface II to endorse this position. An early advocate of the idea of purgatory.

CAEDMON (kĕd′mun), (fl. c. 670), one of the earliest English Christian poets, perhaps born in Northumbria. Was a poor, illiterate herdsman who worked on the Abbey lands at Streanaeshalech (Whitby) in Old Northumbria in 524. Venerable Bede reports Caedmon had a vision and was commanded to sing the creation story of Genesis. Soon, as if divinely inspired, began turning out early Bible stories into simple but vigorous verse; continued to write Old and New Testament stories in Anglo-Saxon verse. The Abbess Hilda and monks admitted him as an honored member of their order. His Bible poetry captured imagination of Anglo-Saxons and circulated among common people.

CAIRD (kârd), **JOHN** (1820-1898), Church of Scotland preacher, theologian and principal of Glasgow University, born at Greenock on the Clyde, Scotland, and educated at University of Glasgow. Pastor successively at Edinburgh, Errol, and Glasgow (1845-1862). Appointed professor of theology at Glasgow, 1862. Became principal and vice-chancellor in 1873, retaining both positions until death. In earlier years one of most powerful gospel preachers of his time; later came under influence of Hegel's philosophy and became liberal, being a member of Broad Church party. In philosophy an idealist. One of his sermons, *Religion in Common*

Life, pronounced by some as the greatest sermon of century, was preached before Queen Victoria and prince consort at Balmoral Castle, 1855; spread with favor throughout Protestant world. Wrote *Introduction to the Philosophy of Religion, Spinoza, The Fundamental Ideas of Christianity* (Gifford lectures), some books of sermons.

CAIRNS (kârnz), **JOHN** (1818-1892), Scottish United Presbyterian divine, born at Ayton Hill, Brunswickshire, Scotland, and educated at Edinburgh University and Secession Hall. Ordained minister of Golden Square Church, Berwick-on-Tweed, 1845. Traveled in Europe and America, representing this church, learned several languages, some late in life, to speak at special conferences. Professor of apologetics in Theological Hall of his denomination in Edinburgh (1867-1876). 1872, moderator of United Presbyterian Synod; same year represented his church in Paris at first meeting of Reformed Synod of France; 1876, became joint professor of systematic theology and apologetics with James Harper of United Presbyterian Theological College; 1879, became principal of the college. Best work done upon platform and in pulpit. Among his writings were: *Unbelief in the Eighteenth Century; False Christs and the True; Romanism and Rationalism;* books of sermons.

CAJETAN ST. GAETANO DA THIENE (1480-1547) Born near Venice. Studied law at Padua. Legal aide of Julius II in 1505. Ordained in 1516 and joined the Dominican order in Rome. Organized the Theatine Order in 1524.

CAJETAN (kăj ĕ tăn), **JACOPO TOMMASO DE VIO** (1469-1534), Italian theologian and Roman Catholic cardinal, born at Gaeta, Italy; studied at Naples, Bologna, Padua, and Ferrara. In 1486 entered Dominican order; in 1508 made general of his order. Was a zealous Thomist, changing his name from Jacopo to Tommaso in his reverence for Thomas Aquinas. Taught theology and philosophy in various universities of Italy. Made a cardinal in 1517; bishop of Gaeta following year. Sent as papal legate to Germany, 1518, to bring Emperor Maximilian and king of Denmark into league formed against Turks. At same time became pope's representative at German diet at Augsburg where Luther was tried in 1518; tried to reconcile Luther with the church. Luther resolutely refused to yield. Attributed Luther's superiority over himself to Luther's great knowledge of Bible. Spurred on, Cajetan resolved too to become a student of the Bible and pursued this study until he became a recognized biblical exegete. Never left track of tradition, but did depart from allegorical method of his predecessors; followed a freer method of interpretation of the Fathers. Made a translation of the Old Testament with a commentary; wrote a standard commentary on the *Summa* of Thomas Aquinas; labored with other Greek and Hebrew scholars in revising the Vulgate. Writings extensive, numbering about 115. Cajetan was one of nineteen cardinals who sat with Pope Clement VII and pronounced validity of the marriage of Henry VIII of England and Catherine of Aragon in 1534.

CALAMY, EDMUND (1600-1666), Puritan Theologian. Born at Walbrook. Educated at Pembroke Hall, Cambridge. From 1626 to 1636 lectured at Bury St. Edmunds and curate of St. Mary Aldermanbury in London from 1639. Member of the Westminster Assembly. Supported Presbyterianism but also wanted the restoration of Charles II. Jailed briefly in 1663 for disobeying the Act of Uniformity.

CALIXTUS, GEORGE (1586-1656), Ecumenical theologian. Born in Schleswig. Educated at the University of Helmstadt. Traveled from 1609 to 1613. Professor of theology at Helmstadt from 1614 to 1656. Influenced by Melanchthon, wanted a theology based on the Bible, the Apostles' Creed, and the church Fathers that he hoped would reconcile Roman Catholics, Lutherans, and Calvinists.

CALIXTUS (ká lĭks'tŭs), **I** (or **CALLISTUS**) (died c. 222), early pope of Rome. After the death of Zephyrinus in 217, Calixtus made bishop of Rome; occupied office for five years, being known as Pope Calixtus I. Counted as one of the greater popes of early centuries. Excommunicated Sabellius about 220 for heresy. Catacombs of "San Callisto" on Appian Way are named for him.

CALLIXTUS II or CALLISTUS (Guido of Burgundy) (d. 1124), Archbishop of Vienne. Papal legate in France 1106. Pope 1119. At Lateran Council ended long struggle of Holy Roman emperors and popes by promulgating the Cocordat of Worms 1122 which protected both royal and papal rights in clerical elections and banned lay investiture.

CALVERT, GEORGE (c. 1580-1632), First Baron or Lord Baltimore, English statesman who planned the colony of Maryland as a refuge for Roman Catholics. Born in Kipling, Yorkshire, England; graduated from Trinity College, Oxford. Was in Parliament from 1609 to 1624, and was knighted in 1617. Served as Secretary of State under James I from 1619 until 1625; resigned after becoming Roman Catholic. Retained, however, favor and confidence of the king and was raised to Irish peerage as Baron or Lord Baltimore. Founded a settlement in Newfoundland in 1621 but because of rigorous climate moved further south. In 1632 King Charles I granted him right to found colony of Maryland; before charter was signed Lord Baltimore died and charter rights passed to his son, Cecil Calvert (1606-1675), who became second Lord Baltimore and founded colony of Maryland. His second son, Leonard Calvert (1606-1647), became first governor of Maryland.

CALVERT, JAMES (1813-1892), Wesleyan missionary to Fiji, born at Pickering, England. Converted at eighteen; began to preach before age of twenty. Worked with a printer at Colchester for three years, preaching on Sundays in Exeter villages. Became a candidate for the ministry (1837) and entered Hoxton Academy for training. In 1838 Wesleyan Missionary Society appointed James Calvert, John Hunt, J. T. Jaggar and their wives to enter Fijian mission, organized in 1835 by David Cargill and William Cross. They landed on Lakemba, one of the eastern islands of the archipelago. He did his own printing in Fiji and issued many books, among them a translation of the New Testament in the vernacular. After more than twenty-five years, he and his wife returned to England. Supernumerary minister at Bromley, Kent, England (1867-1872). Again he and his wife went as missionaries to Kimberley and other areas in South African diamond fields (1872). Returned to England in 1881 and settled at Torquay. From 1882 to 1885 Mr. Calvert traveled in interest of foreign missions. In 1885 he visited Fiji and took part in golden jubilee of Christianity.

CALVIN, JOHN (1509-1564), French Reformer and theologian, born in Noyon, Picardy, France. Father, a lawyer, at first planned for John to be a priest and secured for him a chaplaincy with revenues sufficient for his support; was given the tonsure. In 1523 he began studies at University of Paris; in 1528 went to the University of Orléans upon his father's decision for him to study law. Later he attended University of Bourges. Came under spell of humanism in these universities. Upon father's death (1531), Calvin decided to become a man of letters and went to Paris to study the humanities. In 1532 he published text of Seneca's *De Clementia* with a commentary. Experienced "sudden conversion" in 1533 and whole course of life was changed. Came to have a new conviction of reality of God's sovereignty and of the importance of living according to His will. Without thought of leaving Catholic church he proceeded courageously to follow his convictions. Joined a group of Protestants in Paris and soon became their leader and preacher. Prepared most of inaugural address from a friend, Nicholas Cop, who had been chosen as rector of University of Paris. Message in 1533 was so evangelical and made such a stir in ecclesiastical circles that it became necessary for Cop and Calvin to leave Paris. Calvin went to Angouleme in France for a year and resigned benefices at Noyon, severing relations with Roman church. Went to Strassburg, then Basel (1535-1536), and wrote theological treatise to help and comfort persecuted brethren. In 1536 published first edition of this treatise, entitled *Institutes of the Christian Religion* with its emphasis on God's sovereignty, predestination, limited atonement, and irresistible grace. After this, went to Ferrara, Italy, where he spent a few months in interest of the Reformation. Intending to return to Strassburg or Basel to write and study, he stopped in Geneva on the way. Here William Farel was attempting to establish Reformation and prevailed upon Calvin to stay and help. Yielding, Calvin became moving leader of Genevan Reformation. After two years of progress, a group of Libertines gained control of city council and drove Calvin and Farel out because of disputes over the Communion. At Strassburg Calvin pastored a group of French evangelicals from 1538 to 1541 and made friendship with Bucer, great Strassburg Reformer. While here, in 1540, Calvin married Idelette de Bure and lived happily until her death in 1549. In Geneva Cardinal Sadoleto was trying to induce people to return to Roman church; this called forth Calvin's masterful literary reply, *Reply to Sadoleto*. Libertines were discredited and overturned. Calvin was urgently called to Geneva, where he spent rest of his days (1541-1564) making Geneva the "Rome of Protestantism." His 1541 *Ecclestical Ordinances* advocated church government by elected representatives. Organized and superintended church-state of Geneva against many obstacles, almost entirely changing complexion of city. His *Institutes* became the guide of all "Reformed" churches. Religious life was held on a high plane, and to follow Calvin meant to live a high degree of holiness, seeking to know and follow will of God. Began what became the University of Geneva.

CAMERON, RICHARD (c. 1648-1680) Scottish leader of Covenanters and founder of Cameronians. Born Falkland, Fifeshire. Schoolmaster Episcopalian but adopted Covenanter ideas and became a Presbyterian field preacher. Ordained and lived in Holland from 1678 to 1680. Killed in battle with royal forces of Charles II. Became a symbol for the "Cameronians" who formed the Reformed Presbyterian church.

CAMPANELLA (käm pȧ nĕl'lȧ), **TOMMASO** (1568-1639), Italian Dominican monk in 1582 and philosopher, born in Stilo,

Calabria, Italy and died in Paris, France. Studied at Naples and Cosenza; taught at Rome and Naples. Opposed Aristotelianism of his order, yet a loyal Catholic, almost ultramontane in convictions. Kept in prison by Spanish over twenty-seven years for involvement in a conspiracy to free Naples from Spanish dominion; finally rescued by Pope Urban VIII. During imprisonment in 1623 he wrote *Civitas Solis* (City of the Sun), his utopian vision of perfect society or theocratic monarchy under papal authority.

CAMPANIUS (kăm păn'ĭ ŭs), **JOHN** (1601-1683), Swedish Lutheran clergyman and missionary, born in Stockholm, Sweden, and came to New Sweden in America with Governor Printz (1642), ministering to Swedes on the Delaware until 1648. Here became interested in Delaware Indians, learned dialect, and translated Luther's *Small Catechism* into their tongue, fifteen years before John Eliot's Indian Bible appeared. Translation published in 1696, and later in Sweden. Returned to Sweden in 1649, pastoring in Upland; here revised Indian translation.

CAMPBELL, ALEXANDER (1788-1866) AND **THOMAS** (1763-1854), founders of the Disciples of Christ, Alexander born near Ballymena, Antrim County, Ireland, the son of Thomas Campbell, a Seceder minister. Educated at Glasgow University and there influenced by Haldane brothers. Came to America in 1809, two years after father's arrival; settled in western Pennsylvania. Both father and son much averse to rigid sectarianism, strongly advocating Christian liberty. Urged that Word of God be held as infallible all-sufficient standard for Christian union, using slogan, "Where the Scriptures speak, we speak; and where the Scriptures are silent, we are silent." At Brush Run Thomas organized First Christian Association of Washington, Pennsylvania, with twenty-nine members (1811). His *Declaration and Address* on the occasion has become an ecclesiastical document of historical importance. At Brush Run (1812) Alexander Campbell was ordained to the ministry. A study on baptism led Campbells to believe that immersion was scriptural mode; thus they were immersed in 1812. At that time Thomas conceded to son the leadership of movement. Brush Run Church in 1813 joined Redstone Baptist Association. About 1820 Alexander Campbell began series of debates with Presbyterians, Roman Catholics, and others; this publicized his doctrinal views. 1823, began publishing *Christian Baptist;* 1825, a series of articles entitled *A Restoration of the Ancient Order of Things* was published in this paper. These argued for the abandonment of everything not in use among early Christians, as creeds, confessions, unscriptural words, phrases, theological speculations, and for adoption of everything sanctioned by primitive practice, as weekly breaking of loaf, fellowship, simple order of worship, the independence of each church under the care of elders and deacons. His plea was not for a reformation, but restoration of original church. Hence his movement became known as the "Restoration Movement." In 1827 the Baptists became apprehensive of his views and his movement, and the two movements drifted apart. An organization developed which by 1827 was known as Disciples of Christ. In 1832 about 10,000 of Barton W. Stone's group of "Christians" joined. 1829, Campbell had begun to publish the *Millennial Harbinger,* a magazine he continued until his death in 1866. 1829, he sat as delegate in the Virginia State Constitutional Convention. Ex-President Madison, one of his fellow delegates, said, "I regard him as the ablest and most original expounder of the Scriptures I ever heard." 1840, founded Bethany College, served as its president until his death, 1847, preached in Britain and Ireland, and in 1850 spoke before both houses of Congress at the Capitol at Washington. Alexander Campbell was a prodigious writer, and eloquent preacher, an ardent debater, a strong missionary advocate, and an educator. He was an advocate of anti-slavery but not an abolitionist. His church did not divide because of slavery. Campbell believed in the inspiration of the Holy Scriptures and accepted the New Testament as the rule of faith and practice, giving it a higher inspirational value than the Old Testament.

CAMPEGGIO, LORENZO (c. 1472-1539) Born in Milan. Trained in civil and canon law at Bologna. Ordained in 1510. Bishop of Feltre in 1512. Papal nuncio to Holy Roman Emperor Maximilian I from 1513-1517 to get his aid for an anti-Turkish crusade. Archbishop of Bologna in 1523. Papal representative to England in 1528 to deal with the problem of Henry VIII and his desire to divorce Catherine. Cardinal in 1537. Helped to keep southern Germany in the Roman Catholic church during the German Reformation.

CAMUS, ALBERT (1913-1960) Novelist, essayist, and playwright. Born Mondovi, Algiers. Educated at Algiers University. Philosophy was atheistic and existentialist. Man is alienated from an irrational world in which he has no meaning except in man's own actions or experience. Nobel Peace prize in 1957.

CANDLISH, ROBERT SMITH (1806-1873), a founder and early leader of Free

Church of Scotland, born in Edinburgh, studied at Glasgow University, spent two years as tutor at Eaton, then licensed in 1828, served as assistant of St. Andrews, Glasgow and of Bonhill, Dumbartonshire. 1834, became minister of St. George's, Edinburgh, there became famous as a preacher. 1839, publicly identified himself with evangelical party of the Church of Scotland, which after 1843 became the Free church of Scotland. After the Disruption, Candlish was one of the foremost leaders in organizing and developing Free church. From death of Thomas Chalmers in 1847 until his own death in 1873 was the ruling spirit of the Free church. He was moderator of the Assembly in 1861. 1862, did accept the principalship of New College, Edinburgh, continuing ministry at St. George's. He was chief organizer and promoter of the school system of the Free church, which was later incorporated with the national system of education. He was also one of the founders of the Evangelical Alliance in 1846. Candlish was a voluminous writer, but books did not attain a very wide circulation. Among his works are: *Reason and Revelation, The Fatherhood of God, The Two Great Commandments, On the Atonement, The First Epistle of John, Life in a Risen Saviour,* and *Contributions towards the Exposition of the Book of Genesis* (three volumes).

CANISIUS, PETER (1521-1597) Roman Catholic lawyer, theologian, and leader in Counter-Reformation in Southern Germany and Austria. Born in Nijmegen. Educated in theology at Cologne. Ordained in 1546. Jesuit in 1543. Jesuit provincial leader for three years. Developed three *Catechisms* which went through 200 editions and were put into twelve languages.

CANSTEIN, KARL HILDEBRAND FRIEHER VON (1667-1719) Pietist patron of Bible distribution. Friend of Francke. Lived at Halle. Founded a Bible House in 1710 to print and circulate copies of the Bible.

CANUTE (kȧ nūt') **THE GREAT** (c. 994-1035), king of the Danes, English, and Norwegians. Son of Sweyn, king of Denmark. Though baptized as a child, no evidence of Christianity in his life until after he ascended the English throne in 1016. Under Canute the conversion of Denmark was practically completed. He filled Danish bishoprics with bishops from Canterbury, England, invited English monks to serve as ecclesiastics and missionaries in the Danish churches. Canute made pilgrimages to Rome, but he refused to permit the introduction of the Peter's pence in Denmark.

CAPISTRANO (kä pē strä'nō), **GIOVANNI di (JOHN CAPISTRAN)** (1385-1456), Italian Franciscan preacher and inquisitor, born in Capistrani in Abruzzi, Italy. Studied civil and canon law at Perugia. 1412, appointed by the king of Naples as governor of Perugia, and as such set himself against civic corruption and bribery. 1416, entered the Franciscan order; 1426, ordained a priest. Became a strict Franciscan, regarded in his native land as a preacher. 1446, made vicar-general of the Observantines in Italy. Because of his fanatic zeal against heretics, Jews, and unbelievers he was chosen by the pope to carry out important missions in various countries, including one as papal legate to Germany to war against the Hussites. On these tours preached with great effectiveness to great crowds, succeeded in winning many heretics back to the church. When he proceeded to Bohemia in campaign against the Hussites he met with little success. 1454, summoned to the Diet at Frankfurt to assist in planning a crusade against the Turks. He accompanied the forces throughout the campaign, leading one sector of the army himself, preaching, though with little success, to the Mohammedans. Died during the siege. During his lifetime revered as a saint. He was beatified in 1694, and canonized in 1724.

CAPITO (kä'pē tō), **WOLFGANG FABRICIUS** (Original name, Köpfel) (1478-1541), German clergyman and reformer, born at Hagenau, Alsace, Germany, studied at Freiburg, first studying medicine, then law, and finally theology. Entered the Benedictine Order, and in 1515 became cathedral preacher and professor of theology at Basel. 1519, came into the service of Archbishop Albrecht of Mainz, but adopting the ideas of the Reformation, went to Strassburg, 1523; chief preacher of the New St. Peter's Church, became one of the most prominent leaders of the reformatory movement in that part of Germany. He was both a friend of Martin Bucer, and an ardent supporter of Martin Luther. Like Bucer, possessed a comprising spirit and endeavored to reconcile the Lutheran and the Swiss reformers. His moderating and conciliatory influence was felt also in the Peasants' War, and in the Anabaptist disturbances. He and Martin Bucer, authors of the Tetrapolitan Confession which was submitted to the Diet of Augsburg in 1530.

CAREY, WILLIAM (1761-1834), "The father of modern missions," born in the home of a poor Northamptonshire weaver and schoolmaster in Paulersbury, England. Elementary schooling received under father's teaching in the village school. At fourteen apprenticed to a shoemaker and cobbler. Applied himself so diligently to study while working that he early learned Latin, Greek,

Hebrew, French, and Dutch, and in his teens could read the Bible in six languages. This bent toward language a great asset in his missionary life. In 1783 joined the Baptist church and shortly after began preaching. Along with his cobbling, teaching, and preaching, he continued his study of languages, he followed the missionary activities of John Eliot and David Brainerd, read with avidity the *Voyages* of Captain James Cook. As pastor at Moulton he preached missions and urged his neighboring ministers to do likewise. Wrote a treatise on "An Enquiry into the Obligations of Christians to Use Means for the Conversion of the Heathen." 1792, preached memorable sermon on "Expect Great Things from God; Attempt Great Things for God." In that year helped organize the English Baptist Missionary Society, the next year went to India as one of its first missionaries. His first plan had been to go to Tahiti. First years on the field developed for him many hardships and disappointments. Financial reverses due to Dr. Thomas' mismanagement, illness and death among his children, and the serious mental illness of his wife until her death in 1807, made his work difficult. Soon after arriving in India became superintendent of an indigo factory from 1794 to 1799. In 1799, purchased a small indigo plantation and started a mission. Because of opposition from East India Company, 1800, he moved to Serampore in Danish territory a short distance from Calcutta. William Ward and Joshua Marshman joined him to form the famous Serampore Trio, where teaching, preaching, and printing provided the chief missionary activity and also provided much of the fund for carrying on the mission. In 1800 Carey baptized first converts, among them his oldest son, Felix. From 1831, professor of Oriental languages in the newly founded Fort William College in Calcutta, a position held for thirty years. He and Marsham did much translating of the Scriptures. The Bible or portions of it were issued by the Serampore press in about thirty-six languages and dialects. Besides preaching and translating the Scriptures, they translated Indian classics into English, prepared grammars and dictionaries in various languages, opened many mission stations in India, Burma and East Indies, and established schools out of which in 1818 came Serampore College. Did much for the advancement of horticulture and agriculture in India. He advocated two important missionary principles, (1) equality of missionaries and natives, and (2) self-sustaining missions. Forty-one years of missionary life in India were crowded full. He was an indefatigable worker, even to death at age seventy-three. The labors of few missionaries have been more fruitful. "The Serampore Press under his direction rendered the Bible accessible to more than three hundred million people." Helped end the burning of child widows in 1829.

CARLILE, WILSON (1847-1942) Founder of Church Army of the Anglican Church. Businessman from 1862 to 1878. Studied theology in London College of Divinity. Ordained in 1880. As pastor in Kensington held open air and after service meetings. In 1882 founded the Church Army to assist the poor in emigration to the British colonies and dominions.

CARLSTADT (Originally Andreas Bodenstein) (c. 1480-1541), German reformer, born at Carlstadt in Franconia, Germany, studied at Erfurt, Cologne and in Italy and came in 1504 to Wittenberg, where in 1513 made professor of theology at the university and archdeacon in the collegiate church. Started teaching as a medieval scholastic. When, under Luther's influence, Wittenberg turned to Augustine and the Bible, threw himself into the opposite extreme, became a mystic and aggressive reformer, and for a while with Luther worked in harmony. Bold reformatory activity, 1519, brought him to his famous disputation with John Eck; but unable to cope with the arguments of his former teacher. A self-sufficient and vain man, having a poor memory, and having to depend on notes, became embarrassed and confused. Luther had to come to his aid. Foiled by Eck's skill and humiliated by Luther's assistance and superiority, Carlstadt became bitter, and turned against Luther. While Luther was at the Wartburg, Carlstadt found opportunity to seek to regain popularity. Claimed that Luther was compromising truth and principle, while he went all the way in the Reformation. He carried the populace, the city council, and the university into a most dangerous revolution. On Christmas Day, 1521, he celebrated the Lord's Supper, leaving out the most essential features of the Roman liturgy. A few weeks later he married in most ostentatious way. Proceeded with the destruction of images, the abolition of monasteries, and other sweeping reforms. Luther appeared and restored order. Again humiliated, shortly after left Wittenburg. In 1523 made pastor of Orlamunde and immediately repeated his experiment of Wittenberg. This took place at the same time that Thomas Munzer was causing great disturbance at Alstadt. The next year, 1524, Carlstadt banished from Saxony. For several years he wandered from place to place in great poverty. In 1530 he came to Strassburg. Following the Marburg Colloquy between Luther and Zwingli, he joined Zwingli and cast his lot with the Zwinglian Reformation. In 1531 he was appointed pastor at Altstatten and in 1534 professor at Basel. Here he spent his remaining years and died of the plague.

CARLYLE (kär līl'), **THOMAS** (1795-1881), Scottish historian, biographer, and essayist. Entered the University of Edinburgh in 1810 as a student of divinity, but after six years abandoned his purpose of studying for the ministry. Taught mathematics for two years in an academy, then in 1818 moved to Edinburgh where he supported himself by private teaching and literary work. In 1834 he removed to London where he resided until his death. In his autobiographical *Sartor Resartus,* a philosophic romance, and in his *Life of John Sterling,* he gave expression to his own religious views. Other writings of great importance were *The French Revolution, The Letters and Speeches of Oliver Cromwell, The History of Frederick the Great,* and *Heroes and Hero Worship* in which he developed "a great man" view of history. In 1866 Carlyle was chosen rector of the University of Edinburgh, delivered inaugural on *The Choice of Books.* As an historian he is distinguished by exact and laborious attention to detail. His histories are a series of striking portraits and pictures. In theology he may fairly be regarded as a theist.

CARMAN, ALBERT (1833-1917). Canadian educator and Methodist church superintendent. Born in Iroquois, Ontario. Educated at Victoria University, Cobourg. High school teacher. Head of Albert College, Belleville, which he had admitted to the University of Toronto federation. Helped found Alma Ladies College in St. Thomas in 1884. Methodist bishop in 1874 and in 1883 became superintendent of Methodist work in Canada until 1915. Opposed theological liberalism and had G. B. Workman dismissed from his position as professor of Old Testament. Much interested in Canadian church union.

CARMICHAEL, AMY WILSON (1867-1951), founder of the Dohnavur Fellowship, born at Millisle, County Down, Northern Ireland. Educated at Wesleyan Methodist Boarding School, Harrogate. In 1893-1894 she spent fifteen months as a missionary in Japan. Her health failed her and she went to Ceylon for a time, then to England. In 1895 Miss Carmichael went to Tinnevelly in South India as a missionary of the Church of England Zenana Missionary Society; remained in that land until her death. Adopted Indian dress. In 1901 found her distinctive work in rescuing girls who had been dedicated to a life of servitude and shame in Hindu temples. This led to the establishment of a home for children at Dohnavur, Tirunelveli (Tinnevelly) South India. The home later received boys as well as girls. The Dohnavur Fellowship, which began in 1925 as part of Miss Carmichael's work within her mission, was registered as an independent society in 1927. After breaking her leg in 1931 became an invalid and devoted her life to writing devotional books. A few of her books are *Lotus Buds, Gold Cord, Overweights of Joy, Things As They Are, Rose from Brier, Mimosa, The Widow of the Jewels, Windows, From the Forest, Gold by Moonlight, Kohila, This One Thing, Walker of Tinnevelly, Though the Mountains Shake,* and *Toward Jerusalem.*

CARNELL, EDWARD JOHN (1919-1967) Evangelical Baptist theologian. Born at Antigo, Wisconsin. Educated at Wheaton College and Westminster Seminary with doctorates from Harvard and Boston Universities. Professor of philosophy at Gordon College in 1945 and from 1947 to 1967 professor and from 1954 to 1959 president of Fuller Seminary in Pasadena, California. Important books upholding orthodox theology are *An Introduction Christian Apologetics, The Case for Conservatism* and *The Burden of Soren Kierkegaard.*

CARPOCRATES (kär pōk'rȧ tēz), (early second century), Alexandrian Gnostic, born in Alexandria and educated under the influence of Platonic philosophy. The system of Carpocrates and his son Epiphanes is one of the basest of Gnosticism, far more pagan than Christian. He taught that the world was created by angels out of harmony with and greatly inferior to the Supreme Unity; that Jesus was the son of Joseph, but was superior to other men in his memory of his preexistent stage, and in purity of soul, hence merited special honor from the Supreme Unity; that true religion consisted in the union of the soul with Monas or Primal Being or Supreme Unity, by means of contemplation, which elevated the soul above superstition and liberated it from the necessity of submitting to religious regulations or to the common laws of society. True religion abrogated the distinctions between right and wrong, leaving ethical standards to the opinion of men. Only he is wise who can attain this goal. Among those who have done so were Jesus, Pythagoras, Plato, and Aristotle. Also held to the doctrines of the preexistence and transmigration of souls. His disciples or followers were known as Carpocratians, surviving until the fourth century.

CARROLL, BENAJAH HARVEY (1843-

1914), Southern Baptist preacher, born near Carrollton, Carroll County, Mississippi. Educated at Baylor University; never attended seminary. Served in Confederate army through Civil War. Converted summer 1865 in Methodist camp meeting, ordained to ministry in 1866. Taught school three or four years. Pastor of Baptist church, Waco, Texas (1871-1899); was powerful preacher, keen debater, ready writer, widely-read historian. Influential in clearing Baylor University of debt and in creating Southwestern Baptist Theological Seminary (1910). Became principal of Bible Department at Baylor (1894); dean and professor of English Bible (1901-1910); president Southwestern Baptist Theological Seminary (1910-1914). Author: *Baptist Doctrines, Lectures on Revelation, Lectures on Genesis,* two volumes of sermons.

CARROLL, JOHN (1735-1815), American Roman Catholic prelate, born at Upper-Marlboro, Maryland, and became the First Roman Catholic bishop in the United States and first archbishop of Baltimore. Education at St. Omer's College in France, in 1753 joined the Society of Jesus, spent about five years teaching at St. Omer's and at Liege, and making a tour in Europe. In 1774, after the Jesuit Order had been suppressed by the pope (1773), returned to Maryland, and 1774 to 1784 engaged in missionary work in Maryland and adjoining states. In 1784 he was appointed by Pius VI as Prefect Apostolic for the United States. In 1789 he was chosen bishop of Baltimore and was consecrated in England in 1790. In 1805 he was made Administrator Apostolic of Louisiana and the Floridas. In 1808 when his see was created an archdiocese, became Archbishop of Baltimore with suffragan sees at New York, Philadelphia, Boston, and Bardstown, Kentucky. Two years later Bishop Carroll and the newly appointed suffragan bishops of these sees drew up uniform rules of Catholic discipline for the United States churches. Bishop Carroll opposed "trusteeism" and "nationalism." The former would lead to the loss of control of church property, the latter would greatly weaken the unity and catholicity of the Roman church. Although Carroll was deeply interested in the solidarity, continuity, and catholicity of the church, he was also determined to keep the American church free from all foreign entanglements, save the spiritual union with the Holy See. He endeavored to make and keep the American Roman Catholic church indigenously American, even to the selection of bishops for the churches in America, definitely approving, however, of papal appointments and consecration of the highest offices. It was largely through his efforts that Georgetown College in 1788 was established for the training of a native Catholic clergy. Many other schools and colleges were established during his archbishopric (1790-1815).

CARTWRIGHT, PETER (1785-1872), American Methodist pioneer preacher, born in Amherst County, Virginia, but in 1790 moved with parents to Logan County, Kentucky, where amid the rude surroundings of the frontier received but little education. Conversion took place in 1801, and the next year, at the age of seventeen, licensed as an exhorter. In 1808 ordained an elder by Bishop McKendree of the Methodist church. In 1812 he was made a presiding elder. He spent seventy years in the ministry, laboring in Kentucky, Tennessee, and Illinois, forty-eight years of this time in Illinois. At one time a member of the Illinois State Legislature, and defeated by Abraham Lincoln for Congress in 1846. Wrote his *Autobiography* (1857).

CARTWRIGHT, THOMAS (1535-1603), English Puritan divine, born in Hertfordshire, England, and educated at St. John's, Clare Hall and Trinity Colleges, Cambridge. In 1569 chosen Lady Margaret professor of divinity at Cambridge and began to lecture on the Acts of the Apostles, receiving great popularity. He so vigorously championed the cause of Puritanism that he came into a long and bitter conflict with Dr. Whitgift, head of the Prelatical party, and was by him deprived of his professorship in 1570. Following this went to the Continent where he conferred with Beza and other Reformed church leaders at Geneva. Upon advice of friends returned to England to continue the defense of Puritanism. Cartwright and his Puritan friends contended that the church government and the discipline, as well as the doctrine, must be reformed according to the Scriptures. Then followed an order for Cartwright's apprehension in 1574. Again he fled to the Continent, where for several years he ministered to the English residents at Antwerp, and then at Middelburg. In 1583-1584 Thomas Cartwright and Walter Travers formulated a Book of Discipline for the Puritans. By 1590 it had been distributed far and wide over England, subscribed to by as many as 500 ministers. The Puritans were gaining such headway that the English clergy became alarmed and determined to arrest Cartwright and other Puritan leaders and to destroy as many copies as possible of the *Holy Discipline*. In 1585 Cartwright returned to England without permission, and was twice briefly imprisoned. In 1590 summoned before the High Commission and committed to the Fleet. In 1592, broken in health, released from prison on the promise of quiet and peaceable behavior. Most of his remaining years lived quietly in Warwick on the Island of Guernsey. Thomas Cartwright is the hero of Presbyterianism in England.

CARVER, GEORGE WASHINGTON (c. 1864-1943), American educator and scientist, born at Diamond Grove, near Carthage, Missouri of slave parents on the farm of Moses Carver. With brother James, brought up by Mr. Carver, the mother's slave-owner of pre-emancipation days. Worked way through Iowa State College of Agriculture and Mechanic Arts in 1894, became a member of the faculty until 1896; joined Booker T. Washington's staff at Tuskegee Normal and Industrial Institute in Alabama, as director of the Department of Agricultural Research at Tuskegee. There he spent fifty years, developing hundreds of new uses for the peanut, the sweet potato, and other agricultural products. Carver wanted the Southern farmer to diversify his crops and he sought to discover some widespread uses for those crops. A unique scientist in that he professed to believe that all his products were the work of God, rather than of science. Never attempted to patent any of his discoveries. "My discoveries come like a direct revelation from God." In 1935 Dr. Carver was appointed collaborator in the Bureau of Plant Industry of the United States Department of Agriculture. Carver also won international recognition as a painter and in 1916 was elected a Fellow of the Royal Society of Arts in London, an honor given to few Americans. For many years Dr. Carver taught a Sunday school class at Tuskegee. Member of the Presbyterian church; in 1940 established the Carver Foundation with his life savings of thirty-three thousand dollars.

CARVER, JOHN (1575-1621), Pilgrim father, born in the province of Nottinghamshire, England. Joined the English Separatists in their migration to Leiden, Holland, elected a deacon. Became agent for the expedition to New England, chartering and helping to equip the "Mayflower" for the voyage in 1620. Elected the first governor of the Plymouth Colony in November, 1620. His short rule was wise and firm.

CARVER, WILLIAM OWEN (1868-1954), American Baptist theologian, born in Wilson County, Tennessee. Studied at Doyle College, Tennessee, Richmond College, Virginia, Southern Baptist Theological Seminary, and in Europe. Ordained to the Baptist ministry in 1891, served in several Baptist pastorates from 1889 to 1907. Professor of philosophy and ancient languages at Boscobel College, Nashville, Tennessee, 1893-1895; taught New Testament interpretation at Southern Theological Seminary, 1896-1923. Professor of comparative religions and missions at the same seminary, 1899-1943, retiring in 1943. Dr. Carver was managing editor of the *Review and Expositor,* 1919-1942; author of *Missions in the Plan of the Ages; Missions and Modern Thought; The Bible, a Missionary Message; The Course of Christian Missions; Christian Mission in Today's World;* and *All the World in All the Word.*

CARY, ALICE (1820-1871) and **PHOEBE** (1824-1871), American authors and hymn writers, born on a farm near Cincinnati, Ohio. In 1852 they moved to New York City where they lived the rest of their lives. Alice wrote and published several books of poetry, essays, stories, and fiction, her most important volume of verse being *Ballads, Lyrics, and Hymns.* Phoebe's most noted poem was "Nearer Home," or "One Sweetly Solemn Thought." In collaboration with Dr. Charles F. Deems she compiled *Hymns for All Christians.* Alice became a member of the Universalist church.

CASE, SHIRLEY JACKSON (1872-1947), American Baptist liberal theologian, born at Hatfield Point, New Brunswick, Canada, received education at Acadia University, Nova Scotia, Yale University, and University of Marburg, Germany. Ordained in 1900. Teaching career as follows: teacher in academies in New Brunswick and New Hampshire, 1893-1897; instructor in New Testament Greek in Yale, 1905-1906; professor of history and philosophy of religion in Bates College, Lewiston, Maine, 1906-1908; professor of New Testament interpretation at the University of Chicago, 1908-1917; professor of history of early Christianity, 1917-1938; dean of the Divinity School of the University of Chicago, 1933-1938; professor of religion and dean of the School of Religion in Florida Southern College, Lakeland, Florida, 1939-1947. Editor of the *American Journal of Theology* for eight years, and of the *Journal of Religion* for twelve years. Some of his most notable books were *The Historicity of Jesus, Evolution of Early Christianity, Makers of Christianity from Jesus to Charlemagne, The Millenial Hope, Christianity in a Changing World, The Christian Philosophy of History, The Revelation of John, Experience of the Supernatural in Early Christian Times, Through the Centuries,* and *Bibliographical Guide to the History of Christianity.*

CASSIANUS (kăs i ān'us), **JOHANNES** (or **CASSIAN**) (c. 360-c. 435), writer and monk, father of the semi-Pelagian school. Born in Scythia. Educated in a monastery in

Bethlehem. Became acquainted with Germanus with whom he traveled among the monks of Egypt for many years. About 403 they were in Constantinople where they studied under Chrysostom, who ordained Cassian as deacon. About 415 he founded the monastery of St. Victor, near Marseilles, France, and was a diligent promoter of monasticism in Western Europe. He wrote two books on Eastern monasticism, *De Institutis Coenobiorum,* and *Collationes Patrum*. Though Cassianus labored awhile in Rome with Pelagius, later in writings decidedly rejected the errors of Pelagius and affirmed the universal sinfulness of man, the introduction of sin by the Fall of Adam, and the necessity of divine grace to every individual act. Opposed Augustine's doctrine of election and of the irresistible and particular operation of grace. His doctrine lay somewhere between that of Augustine and that of Pelagius (hence called semi-Pelagian) and was not essentially different from the accepted Catholic doctrine. He was a man of thorough cultivation, rich experience, and unquestioned orthodoxy. Leo the Great commissioned him to write a work, *De Incarnatione Domini,* against Nestorianism, in which service he found excellent opportunity to establish his orthodoxy and to clear himself of all connections with the heresies of Pelagianism and Nestorianism. Though not formally canonized he has been honored as a saint by some dioceses.

CASSIODORUS (kăs ĭ ō dō'rus), **FLAVIUS MAGNUS AURELIUS** (c. 477-c. 570), Roman historian, statesman, monk, born at Scyllacium in Bruttium, of Syrian ancestry, and of noble, wealthy, and patriotic family. An administrative officer under Theodoric the Great and Athalaric, until he entered a monastery which he founded on his own estate. Devoted himself to literary work, and required his monks to copy and translate Greek works. Later he wrote many theological works. Of chief importance to posterity, however, is his abstract of the works of Socrates, Sozomen, and Theodoret, in twelve books under the title, *Historia Ecclesiastica Tripartita,* for the Latin Church of his day. Though incomplete, this history was the principal handbook used in the Middle Ages as a manual of church history. While still a Roman official wrote an important book of imperial edicts and decrees entitled *Variae*.

CASTELLIO, SEBASTIAN (1515-1563). Humanistic theologian. Born in Savoy. Became Protestant after meeting Calvin in Strassburg in 1540. Rector of college in Geneva about 1541 but problems over predestination and the interpretation of Song of Solomon led to his departure. Professor at Basel (1553). Translated Bible into Latin and French. Tolerant and opposed persecution of heretics in *De Haereticis.*

CASWALL, EDWARD (1814-1878), Roman Catholic hymn writer, born at Yately, Hampshire, England; studied at Marlborough and at Brasenose College, Oxford. In 1839 was priest in the Church of England. In 1840 became curate of Stratford-sub-Castle, near Salisbury, but resigned in 1847. Received into the Roman Catholic church. In 1850 joined the Oratory of St. Philip Neri under John Henry Newman, through whose influence he had been converted to Roman Catholicism. In 1852 ordained a priest. His original hymns and poems were mostly written in the Oratory. His fame rests, however, on his translations from the Roman Breviary and other Latin sources. His hymns appeared in *Lyra Catholica, Masque of Mary and Other Poems,* and *A May Pageant and Other Poems.* These three books were later combined in *Hymns and Poems,* with many of the hymns rewritten and revised, together with elaborate indices. Among popular translations were, "When Morning Gilds the Skies"; "Hark, a Thrilling Voice is Sounding"; "Bethlehem of Noblest Cities"; "Jesus, the Very Thought of Thee"; and "Jesus, King Most Wonderful." He also published several devotional works.

CATHERINE DE MEDICI (1519-1589), French Queen (1547-1559), born in Florence, Italy, daughter of Lorenzo (II) de Medici, Duke of Urbino and a niece of Pope Clement VII. In 1533 she was married to Henry the son of Francis I, Duke of Orleans, who became Henry II of France. She became mother of four sons, three of whom became kings of France in her lifetime, and of two daughters who became wives of royalty, Elizabeth the wife of Philip II of Spain, and Margaret, the wife of Henry of Navarre, afterward Henry IV. Her unbounded ambition, however, led her to sacrifice both France and her children for the passion of ruling. After the death of Henry II in 1559, her son Francis II, who had married Mary Stuart of Scotland, was king for one year. When Francis died in 1560, his ten-year-old brother came to the throne as Charles IX. Catherine ruled as queen regent. Though a Roman Catholic, Catherine sought to strengthen her own royal position by playing the Huguenots against the Catholics. At times she greatly worried the Catholics by her favors and concessions to the Protestants. She hated Admiral Coligny the leader of the Huguenots, fearing he might gain too much power and influence over the young king. She persuaded Charles IX to order the massacre of the Huguenots on St. Bartholomew's Day, 1572. Coligny was one of the first to be massacred; in all over 20,000 Huguenots were killed throughout France. When Charles IX died in 1574, his brother Henry (III) became king. Catherine's power over this favorite son of hers was somewhat limited. She continued to be the power behind the throne, her machinations greatly alienated all parties. In 1589 she died friendless and unmourned. The royal family of Valois thus came to an end. Catherine was dictatorial, unscrupulous, calculating, and crafty. A haughty lover of pomp and magnificence, a woman of the Renaissance, and a worthy disciple of Machiavelli. Her chief contributions to society and to civilization were by the way of art and literature.

CATHERINE OF GENOA (jĕn'ō å), (original name Caterinetta Fieschi (1447-1510), Roman Catholic Italian mystic, born at Genoa, Italy, of a noble Ligurian family, and named after Catherine of Siena. From the Guelph family. In 1463 married Giuliano Adorno. After ten years of worldly living she was converted to the contemplative life. Sometime later her husband lost his fortune. He too was converted, and became a member of the Franciscan tertiaries, joined her in doing works of charity. In 1479 they left their home to live in two rooms of St. Lazarus Hospital where they could give all their time in service to others. A mystic, able to tie her profound love of man and God to the world of practical philanthropy, perhaps best remembered by her deeds of mercy. Her writings were *Life and Teaching, Dialogues on the Soul and the Body, Treatise of Purgatory,* and other mysticoprophetical works. Canonized by Pope Clement XII in 1737.

CATHERINE OF SIENA (sy â'nä), **SAINT** (1347-1380), Roman Catholic Italian mystic, born at Siena, Italy, and died at Rome. Became a Dominican nun Tertiary in about 1365, and after a few years of strictest asceticism devoted herself to helping the sick and plague-stricken people and to the conversion of sinners. The chief cause of her fame was her reputation for visions and prophecies. Claimed that Christ appeared to her at Pisa that her union with Christ was confirmed by the espousal ring which she said He placed on her finger, and by the stigmata of the five wounds in her body. Despite renunciation of the world, was frequently called upon during the closing years of her life to take part in the political and ecclesiastical affairs of her country and church. In 1376-1378 instrumental in persuading Gregory XI, the seventh of the Avignon popes, to return to Rome. At the beginning of the Great Schism in 1378, became active in support of Urban VI urging cardinals and monarchs to return to his obedience. A healer of family quarrels and a fearless denouncer of clerical evils. The chief writings of Catherine of Siena were letters, prayers, and a Dialogue between her and God, the Father, dictated in 1378 while in a trance. This dialogue is considered one of the jewels of Italian literature. Canonized by Pope Pius II in 1461.

CAVALIER (kå vå lyā'), **JEAN** (1681-1740), French leader of the Camisards or "French Prophets," born at Ribaute, near Anduze in Languedoc, France, son of a peasant and brought up in the Huguenot faith. Driven from home by the pitiless persecution of the Protestants that followed the revocation of the Edict of Nantes (1685), took refuge in Geneva. When the persecution under Louis XIV drove the Camisards of the Cevennes to revolt, Cavalier, a young man in his early twenties, returned in 1702 to his country, and joining the insurgents, rose to command with incredible skill, courage, and success. Carried on the warfare against great odds, until 1704, when seeing that further resistance was futile, negotiated with the opposition and arranged for a capitulation. Denounced as a traitor, left France for Switzerland, and from there passed to Holland where he married. Then entered the service of England, became the head of a regiment of French Camisard refugees, and served with the English forces in Spain in 1707. After his return to England, made a major general and lieutenant governor of Jersey and finally governor of the Isle of Wight. Died at Chelsea in 1740. Wrote *Memoirs of the Wars of the Cevennes under Colonel Cavalier.*

CAVERT, SAMUEL MCCREA (1888-1976) Leader in ecumenism. Born in Charlton, N.Y. Educated Union College, Schenectady, N.Y., Columbia University and Union Theological Seminary. Y.M.C.A. secretary from 1910 to 1912. Professor at Union Theological Seminary from 1915 to 1916. Secretary of the Federal Council of Churches from 1921 to 1950, of the National Council of Churches from 1951 to 1954 and of the World Council of Churches from 1954 to 1957. First suggested the name World Council of Churches for the new organization. Wrote *The American Churches and the Ecumenical Movement, 1900-1968* and several others on the same topic of ecumenism. Editor of the *Pulpit Digest*.

CAXTON, WILLIAM (c. 1422-1491) First English printer. Born in Kent. Businessman in Bruges who later went into printing trade. Set up first press in England in 1476. Printed Chaucer's *Canterbury Tales.* His work helped in the spread of the ideas of the Reformation.

CECILIA (died c. 177), Christian martyr. Vowed virginity but her parents had her married to a pagan Roman nobleman. On the eve of marriage converted her husband Valerianus and his brother Tibertius from paganism to Christianity. The two brothers, as Christians, were beheaded, and a little later Cecilia's life was threatened in a scalding bath. When this failed she was killed by the sword. The remains of the three martyrs were buried in the catacomb of St. Callistus. A church was erected by Pope Urban in her house and called by her name. About 821 Pope Paschal removed her remains to the Church of St. Cecilia in Trastevere, Rome. She has been made a patron of music, particularly church music. Artists celebrate her in paintings and glass windows in churches, and writers refer to her in their works.

CELESTINE V (sĕl′ĕs tĭn or sel ĕs′tĭn), **PIETRO di MURRHONE** (c. 1215-1296), Hermit-Pope, July to December, 1294, born at Isernia, Province of Apulia. Became a Benedictine monk at seventeen, and later made a priest. Spent the most of his life as a hermit living in extreme asceticism. About 1254 founded an order known as the Hermits of St. Damian, but named themselves the order of Celestine when their founder ascended the papal throne as Celestine V. Celestine unacquainted with the ways of the papal court and of the world, was an easy prey to men of worldly and ecclesiastical ambition. He made many errors in judgment and administration. After a little more than five months in this high office, the aged pope in an unprecedented papal act, resigned from the papacy. The last act of his pontificate was to issue a constitution giving a pope the right to resign and the cardinals the right to accept the resignation. Celestine's successor, Boniface VIII, fearing a schism might result from his liberty, held him a prisoner in the castle of Fumone, near Anagni, until his death in 1296. Canonized in 1313 by Clement V.

CELESTIUS (early fifth century), advocate of Pelagianism. Born in Britain. An advocate in Rome. Opposed low morality of times in church with ideas of Pelagius. Asserted that man was born sinless, had free will which made him responsible morally, and could cooperate with the grace of God in salvation. His views condemned at councils in Carthage in 412 and at Ephesus in 431.

CELSUS (sĕl sus), (second century, d. about 180), eclectic Platonist and polemical writer against Christianity. His elaborate attacks upon the Christian faith anticipated the most of the objections of modern infidels and skeptics against Christianity. *The True Discourse* of Celsus was likely written in the latter years of Marcus Aurelius, about A.D. 178. In it opposes both Christianity and Judaism; familiar with both the Old Testament and the New Testament, and also with Gnosticism and its relation to Christianity. Origen felt it important enough to call forth his answer seventy years later, in *Against Celsus.* According to Origen the principal charges Celsus brought against Christianity were: the Christians were members of illegal secret associations; they were rebellious against the state; Christ could not be divine; the incarnation is absurd; the miracles are mere tricks; Jewish converts to Christianity were renegades; Christianity did not improve upon Judaism; Christians lack unity among themselves; the resurrection of the body is a corruption of the doctrine of transmigration; alleged theophanies were merely appearances of demons; and Christian eschatology is irrational and incredible. Origen copied verbatim so much of the work of Celsus that although the original work has been lost, about nine-tenths of it has been reconstructed. Celsus' criticism of Christianity, was the reasoning of a pious pagan philosopher of Platonic tendencies. Ends his work by inviting the Christians to join the religion of the majority, to become good citizens, to give thanks to the powers of nature and to abandon the idea of establishing the universal rule of their doctrines. One value to the church of the attacks of Celsus is that writings show the existence and recognize the importance of the New Testament writings in his day.

CERINTHUS (sē rĭn′thŭs), (second half of the first century), early Gnostic leader, born in Egypt of Jewish descent and studied in Alexandria. Became a teacher of own views in Judea and especially in Asia Minor with home in Ephesus. Held some of the general views of Gnostics, but also some of the Jewish Ebionite teachings. He held a strange admixture of Gnosticism, Judaism, Ebionitism, and Chiliasm. Borrowing from Philo as did other Gnostics, he held that the earth was not created by the Supreme God, but by the Demiurge who was ignorant of, though not hostile to, God. Denied the virgin birth; the Logos or "the Christ" who descended on Jesus at Baptism departed from Him before the crucifixion and went back to the Father or "Pleroma," only the human Jesus was crucified. Differed from both the Gnostics and the Ebionites on the matter of the millennium, holding that Christ would later set up a millennial kingdom. Accepted Christ as a teacher of enlightenment and speculative knowledge rather than as a Redeemer from sin. Rejected all the New Testament except a mutilated Matthew, and taught a modified validity of the Mosaic law. It was likely against the Cerinthian heresy that John wrote his gospel and his First Epistle.

CERULARIUS (sĕr ū lâr'i us), **MICHAEL** (died c. 1059), Patriarch of Constantinople. Born into one of the great families of Constantinople. Banished for conspiracy against the government, then became a monk and regained favor with the government, which he served in ecclesiastical capacity. When Alexius, a bishop under the patriarch of Constantinople, died in 1034, Cerularius was appointed to that office. In this position he began to widen the breach between the East and the West. May be considered the real author of the final Great Schism in 1054. The Normans were harassing both the East and the West, and the opportunity seemed ripe for the two areas of the church to be drawn together. The emperor of the East appealed to Leo IX, pope of Rome, to help rout the common foe. Leo was conciliatory but Michael Cerularius, who in 1043 had become patriarch of Constantinople, saw opportunity to carry out his designs to widen the breach to his advantage. He ordered the closing of all the Latin churches in the East, stirred up old differences between East and West, condemned the use of unleavened bread in the Eucharist. Pope Leo IX replied by sending Cardinal Humbert and others to Constantinople in 1054. After an extended controversy and unsuccessful attempt at reconciliation, the papal legates laid on the high altar of the church of St. Sophia a papal excommunication of Michael Cerularius and all his followers. The Eastern Patriarch answered by placing a counteranathema upon the papal legates. Cerularius was very powerful for several years, dethroning one emperor and crowning another. Died in exile.

CHAFER (chā' fer), **LEWIS SPERRY** (1871-1952), American Presbyterian clergyman and educator, born at Rock Creek, Ohio, studied at New Lyme Academy in Ohio, at Oberlin Conservatory and College, Ohio, and under C. I. Scofield. Ordained in 1900, traveling evangelist, 1900-1914, Bible lecturer, 1914-1924. Also taught music at Mt. Hermon Boys School (1903-1914) and Bible at the Philadelphia School of Bible (1914-1923). In 1924 founded the Evangelical Theological College (now Dallas Theological Seminary), Dallas, Texas. From that time until his death president and professor of systematic theology. Conservative and dispensational in theology. Author of *Satan, True Evangelism, The Kingdom in History and Prophecy, Salvation, He That Is Spiritual, Grace, Major Bible Themes, The Ephesian Letter,* and premillennial *Systematic Theology* (8 volumes). For many years editor of *Bibliotheca Sacra*.

CHALMERS, JAMES (alias **TAMATE**) (1841-1901), Scottish missionary to the South Sea Islands, born in Ardrishaig, Argyllshire, Scotland. Heard first call to the mission field when his pastor read a letter from a missionary in the Fiji Islands telling of the power of the gospel over the cannibals, followed with an appeal for someone to go. James secretly pledged himself to answer the appeal. When he became a Christian at the age of eighteen, he at once began to prepare for active Christian service. Worked with the Glasgow City Mission. Then after spending two years at Cheshunt College and taking some special training at Highgate, appointed by the London Missionary Society to go to Rarotonga in the South Sea Islands. Accepting the appointment as God's will for him, began an intensive study of the Rarotongan language. Two days after his marriage in 1865 he was ordained. Early the next year the Chalmers sailed on the *John William II*. They reached Sydney, Australia late in 1866 and arrived at Rarotonga early in 1867. Here he labored for ten years, seeing wonderful changes on the island during this time. In 1877 transferred to New Guinea or Papua to open up work on that island. Chalmers' heroism, firmness, and kindness won the hearts of these natives and they respected him highly. Life and preaching won many of them to Christ. As Christian settlements were established he pressed on farther interior to reach other tribes. Upon the solicitation of his society returned to England in 1886 for a furlough. A Mrs. Harrison, who in 1888 followed him to the field became his wife, his first wife having died. In 1891, after an absence of thirteen years, he with his wife visited Rarotonga. In 1891 they returned to Port Moresby and Chalmerses began touring new areas. Cannibals became Christians. Churches were built and paid for by these new Christians. In 1894 the society called him home to England for a second furlough to help celebrate the hundredth anniversary of the London Missionary Society. Upon return to New Guinea entered upon new explorations thinking this might be his last and greatest work. On April 4, 1901 Mr. Chalmers and a brother missionary, Mr. Oliver Tomkins, and a band of twelve native Christians sailed away to visit Goaribari Island to make friends with the savages there. The whole band were massacred, beheaded, and their flesh eaten by the cannibals.

CHALMERS, THOMAS (1780-1847), leader of the Free church of Scotland, born at East Anstruther, Fifeshire, Scotland. Studied at the University of St. Andrews, and at the University of Edinburgh, licensed to preach in 1799. Became pastor at Kilmany in 1803, served there for twelve years, professor of mathematics for a while at St. Andrews, then taught for a time in a private school which he set up. Preaching and Christian life for him were only halfhearted until in 1811, following a serious illness, the death of a sister. A careful study of Christianity made in order to write an article for the Edinburgh Encyclopedia gave a deep religious experience which changed his life. He went to Glasgow in 1815 and for eight years he efficiently served successively in the Tron and the St. John's Churches. A part of this time associated with Edward Irving. In 1823 called to the University of St. Andrews to become professor of moral philosophy for five years. In 1828-1843 professor of theology at the University of Edinburgh. On three visits to England, 1830, 1837, and in 1847, he spoke to appreciative audiences. In 1831-1832 served the established church of Scotland as moderator. He held for the right of a congregation to choose its own minister, and was a proponent of the growing spirit of evangelism and revival in the church. In 1843 when the state refused these rights, Chalmers led about one third of the ministers of the church out of the General Assembly. They organized the Free church of Scotland and chose Chalmers as moderator of the new group. In 1843 Chalmers became professor and principal of the newly founded Free Church College in Edinburgh, held this position until his death. During last years, while writing *Institutes of Theology,* he was much interested in the general work of the church, and preached to a congregation of the Free church people at Westport. Thomas Chalmers was one of the greatest preachers of the age. Labors among the poor and admirable organization of charity work in his parish, and efforts to establish Sunday schools were impressive, efficient, and successful, yet these activities he always made subservient to his pulpit work. Among Chalmers's best and most famous sermons are his *Astronomical Discourses,* and *The Expulsive Power of a New Affection.*

CHAMBERLAIN, JACOB (1835-1908), American Dutch Reformed missionary to India, born at Sharon, Connecticut. In 1838 moved with parents to Hudson, Ohio. Received education at Western Reserve College at Hudson; the Dutch Reformed Theological Seminary at New Brunswick, New Jersey; and the College of Physicians and Surgeons, New York City, taking a medical degree from the latter. In 1859 ordained and sent as a medical missionary to Madras Presidency in Southern India, where he resided until death in 1908. Established two hospitals with their dispensaries, and was largely responsible for founding the first theological seminary on the mission field, which was founded in the Arcot mission at Palmaner in 1887. Lector of biblical language and prophecy and acting principal after 1891. Played an important part in translating the Scriptures, the Reformed church liturgy, and hymns into the Telugu language. He wrote, in English, *Native Churches and Foreign Missionary Societies, In the Tiger Jungle, The Cobra's Den, The Religions of the Orient,* and other books on missionary subjects. During much of missionary career Dr. Chamberlain had to contend with fever, spending ten years or more on furlough to regain health. During these years did much to promote the cause of missions. In 1878, made president of the General Synod of the Reformed Church in America, the first missionary to be accorded that distinction in his denomination. In 1902 the first moderator of the Synod of South India.

CHAMBERS, OSWALD (1874-1917) Born in Aberdeen, Scotland. Educated in The Art School in South Kensington, the University of Edinburgh, and in theology in Dunoon training school where he became a tutor in philosophy. From 1906 to 1907 engaged in a round the world tour preaching among Methodist and Holiness groups. Worked with the League of Prayer from 1907 to 1910. Principal of the League's Bible Training College from 1911 to 1915. From 1915 to his death served among soldiers in Egypt as a YMCA worker. A man of prayer who taught a life of victory in Christ. Most important book was *My Utmost for His Highest,* a devotional classic.

CHAMPLAIN, SAMUEL DE (c. 1570-1635) French explorer, colonizer, and supporter of Roman Catholic missions in Canada. Travelled to Canada in 1603 and set up a colony in Acadia in 1604 and another in Quebec for the fur trade in 1608. In 1615 helped the Recollects to come to Quebec for mission work. Governor of New France, (1633).

CHANNING (chăn'ing), **WILLIAM ELLERY** (1780-1842), American Unitarian clergyman and philanthropist, born at Newport, Rhode Island. At eighteen graduated in 1798 from Harvard, spent two years as a private tutor in Richmond, Virginia. Became so obsessed with religious doubts and so prone to follow ascetic practices that the experience permanently impaired health.

In 1802 returned to Harvard as regent, the next year was licensed to preach. In 1803 ordained and installed as minister of the Federal Street Congregational Church, Boston, a charge held the rest of his life. Preached and practiced Christian philanthropy and social reform. In 1822 visited Europe and began celebrated essays on Milton, Napoleon, and Fenelon. In 1830 visited the West Indies, and in 1835 commenced anti-slavery labors. In the time of his early ministry the "Unitarian Controversy" in New England was at its height in the Congregational church. Many of the Congregationalists became anti-Trinitarian and anti-Calvinistic. Channing allied himself with the liberal party and became its acknowledged head from 1819 onward. In that year he defended Unitarianism in a sermon. In 1820 he organized the Berry Street Conference of Ministers from which grew in 1825 the American Unitarian Association. His impact upon the views and writings of such literary men as Longfellow, Emerson, and Holmes was very great. Upheld the exercise of reason in religious matters, held that truth must be sought in the Bible much as it is sought in other books. Objected to the doctrine of the trinity, holding that Christ was sent to earth as a great moral teacher rather than as a mediator. At the same time he paradoxically spoke of Christ as a perfect manifestation of God to men, and maintained belief in the pre-existence, miracles, sinlessness, and resurrection of Christ. Said that Christ was the ideal of humanity who spoke with divine authority. Also rejected belief in the existence of evil spirits and in the personality of Satan. Channing was a preacher and philanthropist rather than a theologian. Labored for the purification of life and society, for the abolition of slavery, intemperance, prison abuse, and war. Among his written works are *Evidences of Revealed Religion, Negro Slavery, Self Culture,* and *Character of Christ.*

CHAPMAN, JOHN WILBUR (1859-1918), Presbyterian clergyman and evangelist, born in Richmond, Indiana, educated at Oberlin College, Lake Forest University, and Lane Seminary in Cincinnati. He was ordained in 1882. Married in 1882, but wife died about four years later, leaving him with a motherless child. Chapman held pastorates in four different states: Ohio, Indiana, New York, and Pennsylvania from 1884 to 1905 but devoted more than half of his ministry to evangelism. Associated with Dwight L. Moody, and worked with Charles M. Alexander for ten years, from 1908 until 1918. Evangelistic tours took him to many large cities of the United States, and to Canada, Hawaii, the Fiji Islands, Australia, Tasmania, New Zealand, the Philippines, China, Japan, Ceylon, England, Scotland, Ireland, and Wales. Became the first director of the newly founded Winona Lake Bible Conference and did much toward the development of the Conference. In later years had much to contribute to the progress of two other summer conferences, one at Montreat, North Carolina, and one at Stony Brook, Long Island, New York. From 1903 to 1918 was Executive Secretary of the Presbyterian General Assembly's committee on evangelistic work. In 1917 served as moderator of the Presbyterian General Assembly. Author of several books on evangelism. In preaching calm but forceful, emotional but not dramatic. In setting up campaigns planned well.

CHARLEMAGNE (shär′le mān), **(CHARLES THE GREAT)** (c. 742-814), King of the Franks from 768 to 814. Born perhaps at Aachen. He was a son of Pepin. Charles assumed control of the entire empire. In five campaigns completed the destruction of the Lombards and added materially to the donations Pepin had earlier made to the pope. The chief goal of this ambitious king seems to have been to unite under his civil rule all the Teutonic and Latin races, and to bring them under the spiritual domination of the pope of Rome. Over fifty military campaigns, nearly twenty of which were made against the Saxons, were significant. Like Constantine used the church to enhance civil rule, while at the same time gave the church increased temporal power and status. He increased the prestige and power of the church. He encouraged education by calling into his service some of the most eminent scholars, poets, and historians of Britain and Italy; called ecclesiastics into his court and counsel; attended church and encouraged subjects to attend; gave tithes for the support of the church and required subjects to do likewise; encouraged preaching and the writing of sermons and other books. Dictated the *Libri Carolingi* (Caroline Books) in which he opposed image worship in the churches, even doing this against the decision of the second Council of Nicea. In his Caroline Books introduced the *Filioque* controversy into the Frankish kingdom, favoring the teaching of the procession of the Holy Spirit from the Father "and the Son." Brought Christianity into the countries which he conquered, demanding of the conquered people that they submit to baptism. Finally subdued the Saxons, the last of the German tribes to accept the Christian religion. Charlemagne brought numbers into the church, however, not only by conquest, but also by sending out missionaries, such as Arno, bishop of Salzburg and Willihad, bishop of Bremen. Alcuin and Eginhard were his advisers on education and monastic life. On one of Charlemagne's many visits to Rome, while kneeling in prayer in St. Peter's Church on Christmas Day, 800, Pope Leo III crowned him emperor of the Roman Empire. Charlemagne believed that the church and state should rule side by side, each supreme in its own sphere; but the implications and the application of the principle led to much controversy and even warfare in the empire for many years. Shortly after his death the rapid decline of the empire began. Shared the weaknesses of his age. A cruel despot, demonstrated by cruelty to the Saxons, moral life no better. Married several women and divorced them at whim. Charlemagne was buried at Aixla-Chapelle (modern Aachen).

CHARLES I (1600-1649), King of England, Scotland, and Ireland (1625-1649), born at Dunfermline, Scotland, the second son of James VI (later James I of England) and Anne of Denmark. In 1625 became king. The first three or four years of reign saw England in several disastrous wars, for the prosecution of which the king and his officers levied heavy unjust taxes on the people. He had no Parliament from 1629 to 1640 and 40,000 Puritans migrated to New England and the Caribbean area. The king had the nobility, the gentry, and the clergy on his side, Archbishop Laud being the strong support of the king. Charles believed in the divine right of kings; Laud believed not only in the divine right of kings, but also of the divine right of bishops, and proceeded accordingly. The Puritans and the people of the important trading towns supported Parliament with Oliver Cromwell as the leader of the Puritan opposition. The archbishop and the king tried to force liturgical uniformity in England and Scotland, which led to Scottish invasions and the Civil War (1642-1646, 1648). In 1649 Charles was tried, condemned as a public enemy of the nation, and was beheaded at Whitehall. He faced the court with courage and met death bravely. He was buried in Henry VIII's vault at Windsor.

CHARLES II (1630-1685), King of England, Scotland, and Ireland (1660-1685), born at St. James' Palace, London, the son of Charles I, King of England, and of Henrietta Marie of France. Following his father's execution in 1649, during the time of the rule of Oliver Cromwell, Charles assumed the title of king, and was proclaimed such in Scotland, Ireland, the Channel Islands, and one or two places in England. Crowned at Scone, January 1, 1651. Shortly after the death of Cromwell, Charles was restored as king of England in 1660, crowned in 1661. In 1662 married Katharine of Portugal. Charles was profligate and was continually in need of money and in the 1670 Secret Treaty of Dover even sold some of his country's interests to France to replenish coffers. Charles' leanings were toward the Roman Catholic church, and in dying hours received absolution from a Roman Catholic priest. Though he had never vowed allegiance to that church, his brother, the Duke of York, and later King James II of England was publicly received into the Roman church. It was during the reign of Charles II that two great disasters befell London, the great plague in 1665, and the great fire in 1666.

CHARLES V (1500-1558), Emperor of the Holy Roman Empire (1519-1556), born at Ghent in Flanders. On paternal side, grandson of the Emperor Maximilian I, and on the maternal side, grandson of Ferdinand and Isabella of Spain. In 1516 succeeded Ferdinand as king of Spain, and in 1519, Maximilian as emperor. As king of Spain his role was difficult, and as emperor no less difficult. Came into power as a very young man and in the midst of the Protestant revolution and conflict with France and Turkey. A loyal Catholic and bitterly opposed to the Lutheran Reformation, but did not dare to carry the warfare against the Lutherans as vigorously as the papal authorities demanded. The Catholic League was formed in 1525. When the Lutheran Torgau Alliance came into being the following year, Charles felt forced to be conciliatory with German Reformers, even to granting leniency and favor to the Reformers at Spier in 1526. By 1529 Catholic pressure became so strong that in the second Diet of Spier Charles found it possible to abrogate much of the toleration extended to the Protestants three years before. He decided to call a diet at Augsburg in 1530, to which Catholics and Evangelicals were to come together to the end that Catholic unity might be attained for the strengthening of the empire. Failed in securing the unity, but worked for the next fifteen years to bring about conciliation and unity. Plans, however, constantly beset by the growing Protestant influence, by the stiff Catholic resistance, by interstate threats and conflicts within Europe, and by Turkish interference from without. By 1546 he determined to take sterner measures against the Protestants and yet was not able to extirpate the evangelical faith and bring about Catholic unity. In 1555 compelled to accept the Peace of the Augsburg. Abdicated throne in 1556 and retired to the monastery of Yuste. Broken in health and depressed in spirit, spent the remaining two years of his life there living in luxury and composure.

CHARLES, ELIZABETH (RUNDLE) (1828-1896), High Church Angelican author, born at Tavistock, near Plymouth, Devonshire, England. Educated at home and began to write at an early age. In 1851 married Andrew Paton Charles, a philanthropist among the poor at Hampstead. After his death in 1868 Mrs. Charles continued her interest in philanthropy. In 1885 founded at Hampstead a home for incurables, calling it Friedenheim. In all Mrs. Charles wrote about fifty books; but the work upon which her fame chiefly rests was *Chronicles of the Schönberg-Cotta Family,* an historical romance of the time of Martin Luther. Between 1885 and 1896 she wrote sixteen productions that were published by the Society for the Promotion of Christian Knowledge. *By the Mystery of Thy Holy Incarnation* contains the epitome of her religious faith. A few of her other works were: *Martyrs of Spain and Liberators of Holland* and *Tales and Sketches of Christian Life in Different Lands and Ages.*

CHARLES, ROBERT HENRY (1855-1931), Anglican theologian and biblical scholar, born at Cookstown, County Tyrone, Ireland, and educated at Trinity College, Dublin, Exeter College, Oxford, and Queen's University, Belfast. Ordained priest in 1884; served curacies at Whitechapel, Kensington, and Kennington. From 1898 to 1906 professor of biblical Greek in Trinity College, Dublin, and from 1906 to 1913 Grinfeld lecturer at Oxford. Hibbert lecturer at Oxford, Jowett lecturer in London, select preacher at Dublin, Speaker's lecturer in biblical studies, Oxford, and lecturer in advanced theology, London. Received the first award of the British Academy's Medal for biblical studies. From 1913 to 1931 canon of Westminster Abbey and archdeacon from 1919 to 1931. In matters of Jewish eschatology and apocalyptics the greatest authority of his day. Produced editions and translations of the *Book of Enoch,* the *Book of Jubilees, The Secrets of Enoch, The Apocalypse of Baruch, The Assumption of Moses, The Ascension of Isaiah, The Testament of the Twelve Patriarchs, Eschatology between the Old and New Testaments, The Apocrypha and Pseudepigrapha of the Old Testament,* and *The Zadokite Fragments.* Wrote articles for the *Encyclopaedia Britannica* and for Hastings' *Dictionary of the Bible,* and wrote *A Critical and Exegetical Commentary on the Book of Daniel; Lectures on the Apocalypse;* and several other works. Charles had command of not only Hebrew, Greek, and Latin, but also of Syriac, Armenian, and Ethiopic.

CHARLES MARTEL (688-741), Carolingian ruler of the Franks (714-741). Illegitimate son of Pepin of Heristal, who was duke of the Frankish kingdom of Austrasia and mayor of the palace under the last of the Merovingian kings. Upon Pepin's death in 714 Charles was proclaimed mayor of the palace, though in reality he possessed the power of a king and was the real ruler of the kingdom, yet never with the title of king. Charles subdued the rebellious Franks who were chafing under the rule of the weak Merovingian king Chilperic III; then in 732 defeated the invading Moslems in the historic and decisive Battle of Tours, France. Checking the advance that had threatened all Europe, gained the name Martel, the Hammer. Charles was willing to support the missionary work of Willibrord and Boniface in Frisia and Germany, knowing that their success would materially aid in the extension of Frankish political power. Died in 741, leaving his kingdom divided between his two sons, Carloman (741-747) and Pepin the Short (741-768). Carloman in 747 entered a monastery, leaving his brother Pepin to become ruler of the Franks.

CHARLES, THOMAS (1775-1814) Welsh revivalistic Methodist. Born Longmoor, Carmarthenshire. Educated at Jesus College, Oxford. Converted under Daniel Rowland and ordained as an Anglican priest. Served churches in Somerset and Mereroneth. Became Methodist at Bala in 1784. Developed a system of schools and Sunday schools. In 1804 edited a Welsh version of the Bible for the British and Foreign Bible Society which he helped found, a popular yet scholarly Bible dictionary and a catechism (over eighty editions).

CHARNOCK (chär′nŏk), **STEPHEN** (1628-1680), English Puritan theologian, born in London and studied at Emmanuel College, Cambridge, and at New College, Oxford. In 1652 became superior proctor of the university, when Oliver Cromwell was chancellor and John Owen was vice-chancellor. In 1655 went to Dublin as chaplain to Henry Cromwell, where he remained until 1660, when, upon the death of Oliver Cromwell, he was ejected by the Act of Uniformity, and then returned to England. Preached without a regular charge for fifteen years, and in 1675 pastor of a Presbyterian church in London which was held until death. A man of great piety and vast learning. Charnock is best known for *Discourses upon the Existence and Attributes of God,* which ranks with the greatest of the many great products of the Nonconformist clergy, and is one of the greatest treatises on the subject in the English language. He wrote also *A Discourse of Divine Providence.*

CHATEAUBRIAND (shä tō brē än′), **FRANCOIS AUGUSTE RENE, VICOMTE de**

(1768-1848), French writer, statesman, apologist of Christianity, born in devout Roman Catholic home, St. Malo, Brittany; educated at Dôle and Rennes. For a time skeptic, but returned to faith of early training. Exiled he toured the United States, and England from 1791 to 1800. While in England wrote *Essai Historique, Politique, et Moral sur les Révolutions Anciennes et Modernes* (1797). Returned to France, 1800; for a time held diplomatic post under Napoleon, then fell out with emperor. 1806, traveled in Holy Land and Near East; wrote *Les Martyrs, ou le Triomphe de la Réligion Chrétienne* (1809), picturing "rising Christianity and sinking paganism"; and *Itineraire de la Paris à Jerusalem et de Jerusalem à Paris* (1811). Drew attention to the literary sources of the Middle Ages and Christian antiquity. "His effect on morals and religion has been considered morbid and transitory; in literary art he marks an era." His *Le Genie du Christianisme* (1802), asserting superiority of Christianity over other religions, had profound influence on religious and literary life in France.

CHAUCER, GEOFFREY (c. 1340-1400), English poet, born in London. In 1359 fought in the English army. In 1386 elected to Parliament. Chaucer studied the Latin classics and composed poetry which has greatly enriched the English language. His *Canterbury Tales* furnish a remarkable account of the life of his time and are critical of the church. Credited with fixing, in a large degree, the form of the present English language. Chaucer is called the "Father of English Poetry." Though we think of Chaucer as a poet, he was also a man of affairs. Died in 1400, buried in Westminster Abbey. Some of his chief writings besides the *Canterbury Tales* were *Book of the Duchess, Legends of Good Women, Troilus and Criseyde, House of Fame,* and *The Parliament of Birds.*

CHAUNCY, CHARLES (1705-1787), Congregational leader of "Old Light" in opposition to American Great Awakening. Born in Boston. Educated at Harvard. Pastor of First Church, Boston. Criticized the revival in his *Seasonable Thoughts on the State of Religion in New England,* Edwardian theology in *Salvation for all Men,* and Anglican bishops in America in *Complete View of Episcopacy.*

CHELCICKY, PETER (c. 1390-1460), leader of the Chelcic Brethren, forerunners of the Bohemian Brethren. Influenced by John Wycliffe in Prague. About 1420 opposed the use of secular force in spiritual affairs.

CHEMNITZ (kĕm'nits), **(KEMNITZ), MARTIN** (1522-1586), Lutheran Reformation preacher and theologian, born at Treuenbrietzen, Brandenburg, and educated at Magdeburg, at the University of Frankfort-on-Oder, at Wittenberg, where he came under the influence of Luther and Melanchthon, and at the University of Königsberg. Ordained in 1554. After spending a short time teaching and lecturing at Wittenberg, and serving as rector at the cathedral school at Königsberg, and as librarian to Duke Albert of Prussia, in 1567 settled permanently in Brunswick, first as coadjutor to the superintendent, and then as superintendent of the church there. While there wrote a book in which he defended Luther's view of the Lord's Supper against that of the Swiss Reformers. In 1567 subsequent to the distraction caused by the divisions over Osiander's teaching, he helped reorganize the Church in Prussia. The next year, along with the help of Jakob Andreae and Nikalaus Selnecker, he induced the Lutherans of Saxony and Swabia to unite in adopting the Formula of Concord, himself being the chief architect of the instrument. Became known as one of the first theologians of his time and was called upon to take part in every controversy. Better known, however, through his polemics against the Roman Catholics and the Jesuits. He wrote *Examen Concilii Tridentini,* more damaging to the Roman claims than any other book of the period. Co-author of the 1577 *Formula of Concord.* The most important and the most learned successor of Luther and Melanchthon.

CHENEY (chē'nĭ), **CHARLES EDWARD** (1836-1916), American Reformed Episcopal bishop, born at Canandaigua, New York, and educated at Hobart College, Geneva, New York, and at the Protestant Episcopal Theological Seminary, Alexandria, Virginia. Ordained in 1858. After serving two churches in New York for a short time each, in 1860 accepted a call to the rectorship of Christ Church in Chicago, Illinois. His pronounced Low Church evangelicalism led to trial and suspension from the Protestant Episcopal church and to deposition from the priesthood. The court, however, decided that the church property belonged to the congregation and not to the diocese. At the urgent request of congregation Cheney remained rector of Christ Church. The congregation went with him into the new organization when in 1873 Cheney joined with Bishop George David Cummins and others in organizing the Reformed Episcopal church. Later the same year Cheney was consecrated missionary bishop of the Northwest. In 1878 made the first bishop of the Synod of Chicago, and in 1905-1917 was president of the Synod of the Reformed Episcopal churches of the Middle States. Bishop Cheney was strongly opposed to all high church leanings toward or compromise with Roman Catholicism, and was equally opposed to destructive higher criticism.

CHENG CHING-YI (chĕng jing yē), (1881-1940), Chinese pastor and ecumenicist. After graduating from a school of theology, left China because of persecution, engaged in translation of the New Testament while waiting in England for quieter conditions at home. Then became pastor of an independent church in Peking that was formerly connected with the London Missionary Society. Mr. Cheng soon became active for unity in the Christian church. Dr. Cheng was one of the few delegates who attended all three international missionary conferences, at Edinburgh in 1910, at Jerusalem in 1928, and at Tambaram in 1938, at each of which he made a notable contribution. Soon after the Edinburgh Conference he became the first secretary of the China Continuation Committee, and later of the National Christian Council, which grew out of the Continuation Committee. In 1918 Cheng became chairman of the newly organized but rapidly growing Chinese Home Missionary Society. As a vice-chairman of the International Missionary Council, 1928-1938, and as an extensive traveler through the churches of the Occident, helped to tie Chinese Protestantism into the world fellowship of Protestantism. When the first General Assembly of the Church of Christ in China was held in Shanghai in 1927, representing seventeen provinces and between one-fourth and one-third of the Protestant communicants of China, Dr. Cheng was elected Moderator. He remained in this position until 1934, and subsequently served as the general secretary. He also introduced the China for Christ Movement. In 1934 resigned as general secretary of the National Christian Council of China to head the Church of Christ in China.

CHEYNE (chān), **THOMAS KELLY** (1841-1915), Old Testament scholar and critic, born in London, England, and educated at Merchant Taylor's school, at Worcester College, Oxford, and in the University of Göttingen. Ordained in 1865 as priest. From 1868 to 1882 was fellow at Balliol College, Oxford. Rector at Tendring, Essex from 1880 to 1885, Oriel professor of the interpretation of Holy Scripture at Oxford 1885-1915, and canon of Rochester in 1885. Edited the Old Testament portion of the "Variorum Bible," was a member of the Old Testament Revision Committee in 1884, was Bampton lecturer in 1889, and American lecturer on the History of Religion in 1897-1898. Made English readers familiar with the results of German biblical research. He became one of the leaders of the "higher criticism" of the Bible in the English-speaking world. His numerous writings deal almost exclusively with the exposition and criticism of the Old Testament books, and reveal a scholarly and able attempt to reconcile the views of the advanced critics of the Bible with the evangelical school. He was chief editor of *Encyclopaedia Biblica*. Publications include commentaries on Isaiah, Jeremiah, Hosea, and Micah; *Jeremiah, His Life and Times, The Origin and Religious Contents of the Psalter, The Hallowing of Criticism, Aids to the Devout Study of Criticism, Founders of Old Testament Criticism, Traditions and Beliefs of Ancient Israel, The Two Religions of Israel, The Veil of Hebrew History,* and *The Reconciliation of Races and Religions.*

CHIANG KAI-SHEK (1887-1975) Christian president of mainland China and Taiwan. Born in Fenghua, Chekiang province. Educated at Paoting Military Academy and (1908-1910) Tokyo Military Staff College. Aided Sun Yat-Sen in 1911 revolution. Founded Whampoa Military Academy in 1924. Commander of Kuomintang armies (1926-1928). Married Soong Mei-ling in 1927 and baptized as a Methodist Christian in 1930. United China and defeated the Communists by 1930. Fought the Japanese invaders from 1939 to 1945. Elected president of mainland China 1948 but Communist victory led to his withdrawal to Taiwan as president of Republic of China. Sponsored Christianity on the mainland and in Taiwan by word, deed and example.

CHILLINGWORTH, WILLIAM (1602-1644), Church of England divine and controversialist, born at Oxford, and educated at Trinity College, Oxford. Falling under the influence of the Jesuit John Fisher, Chillingworth induced to become a Catholic and to go to a Catholic college at Douay in France in 1630 for further study. But upon the advice of godfather, Bishop William Laud, attempted to make an impartial inquiry into the claims of the two churches. On the grounds of Scripture and of reason declared for Protestantism and soon returned to Oxford. However, some of the claims of the Church of England seemed to him unreasonable and he declined to take orders; but later modified decision and accepted the Thirty-nine Articles. Then made prebendary of Chester (1635-1639). In 1637 published chief work, *The Religion of Protestants a Safe Way to Salvation*. Sought to vindicate the principle of the sole authority of the Bible in spiritual matters and of the free right of the individual conscience to interpret it. Declared also that the doctrine of the Church of England is essentially pure and orthodox and contains no serious error. The next year Chillingworth was made chancellor of Salisbury, prebendary of Brixworth, Northamptonshire, and master of Wigton's Hospital in Leicestershire. Being a strong royalist, made a chaplain of the royal army at the outbreak of the Civil War in 1643. Taken prisoner by the Parliamentarians, and died the next year at the Bishop's Palace, Chichester. His ministry was of short duration, only six years, but he ranks high as a preacher. Died at the age of forty-two.

CHINIQUY (shē nē kē'), **CHARLES PASCHAL TELESPHORE** (1809-1899), Canadian Presbyterian convert from Roman Catholicism, born at Kamouraska, Quebec, Canada of Roman Catholic parents, and studied at the college of Nicolet, Canada, professor of belles-lettres there after graduation until 1833. In 1833 ordained a Roman Catholic priest, and until 1846 was vicar and curate in the province of Quebec where he established the first temperance society, winning the title "Apostle of Temperance of Canada." In 1851 established an extensive Roman Catholic colony at Kankakee, Illinois. In 1858 left the church of Rome and joined the Canadian Presbyterian Church taking his congregation at Kankakee with him. Lectured in England and in Australia (1878-1882). Published a number of books and tracts on temperance and anti-Romanism, some of which became very popular and were translated into several languages. Among his writings we note the following: *The Priest, the Woman, and the Confessional; Fifty Years in the Church of Rome; Forty Years in the Church of Christ; Papal Idolatry.*

CHISHOLM, THOMAS O. (1866-1960), hymn writer, born near Franklin, Kentucky, and educated in a country schoolhouse. For a short time served as a newspaper reporter in Louisville, Kentucky. Became a Methodist preacher and was pastor of a church in Lexington, Kentucky. Preached and dealt in insurance until retirement in 1953. Mr. Chisholm wrote more than twelve hundred hymns and religious poems. The best known are "Great Is Thy Faithfulness" and "Living for Jesus."

CHRISTIAN III (1503-1559), King of Denmark and Norway (1536-1559). Educated by German Lutheran teachers; traveled in Germany and was present at the Diet of Worms (1521). Ardently embraced teachings of Luther and introduced the Reformation in Denmark (1536), establishing Lutheranism as the state church.

CHRISTLIEB (krĭst'lēp), **THEODOR** (1833-1889), German Lutheran theologian, born at Birkenfeld, near Stuttgart, Württemberg, Germany. Received theological education at Tübingen and taught for a time in France. Ordained in 1856 as assistant to father, and soon took charge of a church at Ruith, near Stuttgart. From 1858 to 1865, pastor of a German Lutheran church in London, where famous lectures on *Modern Doubt and Christian Belief* were published. In 1868 made professor of practical theology and university preacher at Bonn, and remained there until his death. Chief emphasis in preaching and writing was to present the great truths of Christianity, and to meet some of the modern objections to Christianity, dealing especially with materialism, pantheism, and deism. Paid particular attention to the doctrine of the Trinity and the possibility of miracles, and vigorously opposed the rationalistic conceptions of Strauss, Renan, and Baur. Worked for the spirit of unity among Christians of various denominations without specifically working for external union. Took part in the work of the Evangelical Alliance, being sent in 1873 to the United States as delegate to the meeting in New York City, and helped found the German Evangelistic Union. Established a training school for evangelists, and was an advocate for foreign missions.

CHRYSOLORAS, MANUEL (c. 1355-1415), Byzantine humanist who taught Greek in Italy. Born in Constantinople. Went to Italy in 1393 and in 1396 professor of Greek at the University of Florence. Back in Constantinople after three years. Travelled in western Europe after 1400. Promoted revival of study of Greek language and classics in Italy.

CHRYSOSTOM (krĭs'ŭs tŭm), **JOHN** (or **JOHN OF ANTIOCH**) (c. 347-407), born at Antioch in Syria, the son of Anthusa. She gave him the best educational training that the time and place afforded. For a time he studied rhetoric under the famed Libanius. Also had studied law, but preferred the ascetic life to the practice of law. After his mother's death entered a monastery near Antioch, remaining there from about 373 to about 381 studying the Scriptures under Ocodore of Tarsus. In 381 ordained by Bishop Meletius as a deacon of Antioch and served in this subordinate office for five years. Flavian, the new bishop of Antioch, recognizing John's excellent gift of speech, in 386 appointed him presbyter and chief preacher in the leading church in Antioch. He became the most popular preacher of the city and of the age with his careful exegesis and moral application. Golden eloquence won for him the title *Chrysostom*, golden-mouthed. In 387, when political fate of Antioch was hanging in ominous suspense, while Bishop Flavian was in Constantinople interceding with Emperor Theodosius, and mob violence was ruling at Antioch, John delivered his masterful series of *Homilies on the Statues.* The aged bishop returned from Constantinople with hopeful news of pardon from the emperor. Continued for the next ten years as preacher and teacher at Antioch. During this time wrote many famous commentaries on the Bible. In 398 when the archbishopric of Constantinople was left vacant, Chrysostom was called away from his church in Antioch to become archbishop of this strategic center. Here he preached for six years. Unsparing condemnation of sin sorely offended the unscrupulous queen, Eudoxia. She succeeded in persuading Theophilus the infamous bishop of Alexandria to call a synod in 403 to silence and condemn Chrysostom. False charges were brought up and he was condemned to banishment for life. The people were furious and tried to protect their bishop who during exile kept up correspondence with friends, continued the care of his flock, as well as benevolences and missions, and was much sought in counsel. The authorities soon intervened and determined to change his place of exile to a more remote area. On the way his weakened frame gave way, and the patient and humble great preacher died in a church along the way near Comana in Pontus.

CHURCH, RICHARD WILLIAM (1815-1890), Dean of St. Paul's and a liberal High Churchman, born at Lisbon. Because of ill health of father, was from 1818 to 1828 in Italy. A brilliant student, received education at Wadham College, Oxford, Fellow of Oriel College (1838-1852), being tutor (1839-1842), and junior proctor (1844-1845). In 1846 helped start the *Guardian* newspaper. Ordained in 1852 as priest, when he became rector of the small country church of Whately, near Frome in Somersetshire. Became dean of St. Paul's, London in 1871. Labored there for the rest of his life. Several times appointed select preacher at Oxford. While at the university he was drawn into the Oxford movement and came into close association with Newman. His perhaps most important work was his *History of the Oxford Movement*.

CLARA SCIFFI (SCEFI) (c. 1194-1253), founder of the order of Poor Clares or the Clarisses, born in a rich and noble family of Assisi, Italy. Diverted from being married when she heard a sermon of Francis showing her the vanity of earthly things. In 1212 took the three vows. Under the influence of Francis and with permission from the pope, she founded in 1215 a woman's order paralleling the Franciscans. Her mother and sister followed her, and she became head of the order until her death. Francis of Assisi made a little cloister for them near the Church of St. Damien. This was the first of such orders for women and grew rapidly. Before 1219 they followed the oral counsels of the friars, but at that time Cardinal Ugolino gave them the rules of St. Benedict, with some additional rules of severity. Later Francis and Ugolino drew up for them a rule of twelve chapters analagous to that of the Friars Minor, prescribing strictest poverty, confinement to the enclosure of the convent, fasting, and other rigid strictures or practices. After obtaining a reputation for sanctity, she died at Assisi and was canonized two years later by Pope Alexander IV.

CLARK, FRANCIS EDWARD (1851-1927), Congregational minister and founder of the Christian Endeavor, born Francis Edward Symmes in Aylmer, Quebec. Orphaned in childhood and legally adopted by his uncle, the Rev. Edward Warren Clark, a Congregational minister. After graduation at Dartmouth College and Andover Seminary, in 1876, became pastor of the Williston Church, Portland, Maine, where in 1881 he organized young people into the first Young People's Society of Christian Endeavor. From 1883 to 1887 pastor of the Phillips Church, South Boston, Massachusetts. In 1887 resigned the pastorate to become president of and to give full time to the United Society of Christian Endeavor until 1925. In 1895 the world Christian Endeavor Union was organized and he became president until 1925. In the interest of the Society made five trips around the world and many shorter trips.

CLARK, GLENN (1882-1956), college professor and founder of "The Camps Farthest Out," born in Des Moines, Iowa, studied at Grinnell College, Iowa, and Harvard University. After being principal of two different high schools for one year each, became professor of English and director of athletics at William and Vashti College, Aledo, Illinois (1908-1912), and professor of English and athletic coach at Macalester College, St. Paul, Minnesota (1912-1940), and professor of creative living (1940-1942). Founder and director of "The Camps Farthest Out," and editor of *Clear Horizons Magazine*. Author of several books on prayer and Christian living, some of them: *Souls Sincere Desire, The Thought Farthest Out, How to Find Health Through Prayer, Two or Three Gathered Together,* and *What Would Jesus Do?*

CLARKE, ADAM (c. 1762-1832), English Methodist preacher, commentator, and theologian, born at Moyberg, County Londonderry, Ireland, studied at John Wesley's school at Kingswood, near Bristol, England, received little further formal education. After the close of early school days diligently studied Hebrew and other Oriental languages by himself, as well as most of the languages of Western Europe. He became a Methodist preacher in 1778, and was appointed by Wesley to his first circuit at Bradford, Wiltshire in 1782. Became a successful and famous itinerant preacher, traveling throughout Great Britain, making conversion and sanctification of souls the great object of his preaching, and becoming one of the chief leaders of the Wesleyan Connection. Clarke was president of the British Conference three different times; a member of the committee of the British and Foreign Bible Society for several years, one of the advisers of its oriental publications; active in the Wesleyan Missionary Society; made two missionary journeys to the Shetland Islands, where he established two Methodist stations; a member of the Antiquarian Society; a member of the Royal Irish Academy; an associate member of the Geological Society of London; a fellow of the Royal Asiatic Society; and a member of the American Historical Institute. Chief literary works were a commentary on the Bible in eight volumes, a work of forty-five years of writing and publication; a *Biographical Dictionary* in six volumes; *The Biographical Miscellany,* in two volumes; *The Memoirs of the Wesley Family.* He also assisted in preparing an *Arabic Bible* for the British and Foreign Bible Society.

CLARKE, GEORGE R. (1827-1892), cofounder of the Pacific Garden Mission, born in Ostego County, New York and studied at Beloit College, Beloit, Wisconsin. After graduating from college became principal in Milton College, edited a paper, and studied law. Although admitted to the bar in 1853, turned attention to real estate. When the Civil War broke out raised recruits for the 113th Illinois Volunteers and became a colonel. After the war returned to Chicago to resume real estate activity; then spent two years in Denver, Colorado among the miners. Here he had a new and real conversion experience and became a flaming witness among the miners. Upon returning to Chicago married Sarah Dunn in 1873. Mrs. Clarke longed to get into mission work. She prayed that her husband might also become interested in rescue mission work; but he continued in business. Went to Denver to open a business there. Soon after arriving at destination telegraphed his wife that he had decided to enter the Lord's work, and asked her to locate a place for a mission at once. In 1877, in a tiny store at 386 South Clark Street, they opened a rescue mission to be known as "Colonel Clarke's Mission." After about three years the site was changed to 100 East Van Buren Street. At D. L. Moody's suggestion the name was changed to Pacific Garden Mission. In 1892 at the age of sixty-five, Colonel Clarke died, leaving the work to Mother Clarke and Harry Monroe, who became Clarke's successor as superintendent. During the fifteen years that Colonel and Mrs. Clarke worked together at the mission it is estimated that from twenty-five to thirty thousand people knelt at the altar in the Pacific Garden Mission. Though he continued successfully with his real estate business, his first love was the Pacific Garden Mission and the men and women who came there.

CLARKE, JAMES FREEMAN (1810-1888), American Unitarian theologian, born in Hanover, New Hampshire, educated in the Boston Latin School, at Harvard University, and at Cambridge Divinity School. Pastor in Louisville, Kentucky 1833-1840, and in 1841 helped establish a new Unitarian church in Boston, named the Church of the Disciples. He was pastor of this church from 1841 to 1850, and again from 1854 until his death. Clarke was a director of the Unitarian Association from 1845 and was chosen its secretary in 1859, and helped form the National Conference of Unitarian Churches in 1865. As a Unitarian Transcendentalist he believed in the universality of goodness and truth and practiced this belief in dealings with other people and with other denominations. Clarke was a member of the State Board of Education (1863-1869); trustee of Boston Public Library (1879-1888); nonresident professor of natural theology and Christian theology in Harvard Divinity School (1867-1871), and lecturer there on ethnic religions (1876-1877); member of the Board of Overseers of Harvard College most of the time from 1863 until 1888; and active in anti-slavery, temperance, and woman suffrage movements. A prolific writer; of his books we mention: *Ten Great Religions, The Christian Doctrine of Forgiveness, The Christian Doctrine of Prayer, Common Sense in Religion, Manual of Unitarian Belief, Anti-Slavery Days,* and *A Service and Hymn Book* (written for his congregation in Boston).

CLARKE, JOHN (1609-1676), early Baptist and a founder of Rhode Island. Born in Suffolk or Bedfordshire, England. Came to Boston in 1637, declaring concern for religious liberty, and being associated with the so-called antinomian, Anne Hutchinson, he was driven out of Massachusetts Bay colony; but was graciously received by Roger Williams of Providence, Rhode Island. Went to Aquidneck Island, Rhode Island, and established a settlement and founded a Baptist church at Newport about 1639. This was the earliest Baptist church in America, or at least next to Roger Williams' church in Providence, which may have been the earliest. In 1651, for preaching the Baptist faith in Lynn, Massachusetts, Dr. Clarke and two fellow workers were arrested and fined, and one of them whipped, whereupon Clarke the next year wrote and published *Ill News from New England; or a Narrative of New England Persecutions,* in which he vindicated the principle of religious liberty and believer's baptism. In 1652 he and Roger Williams were sent to England to protect the interests of the colony. After twelve years he returned to Rhode Island having obtained from Charles II the second charter for the colony, which secured the right of personal liberty in matters of religion. Assumed the pastoral care of the Newport church until death. From 1664 to 1669 and from 1671 to 1672, a member of the General Assembly, and Deputy Governor of Rhode Island in 1669 and 1671. Died suddenly, leaving most of property for religious and educational purposes. Well educated, and qualified both as a physician and as a preacher, as well as a political leader.

CLARKE, SARAH DUNN (1835-1917), cofounder of the Pacific Garden Mission, born in Cayuga County, New York. After teaching school for several years in Elmira, New York, moved to Waterloo, Iowa in 1861, then to Chicago where she became a "socialite." Deeply interested in spiritual things, started a mission Sunday school at State and Twenty-third Streets in 1869. For four years Colonel and Mrs. Clarke maintained a high social prestige. In 1877, however, she urged her husband to start a rescue mission; but he was intent on a business career and went to Denver, Colorado. Suddenly suggested that she find a location at once for a mission. They found a location at 386 South Clark Street, and opened the oldest rescue mission in the Northwest, the second oldest in America, and probably the best known in the world. After Colonel Clarke's death in 1892, Mother Clarke continued in the work for another twenty-five years.

CLARKE, WILLIAM NEWTON (1841-1912), American Baptist clergyman and theologian, born at Cazenovia, New York, studied at the Oneida Conference Seminary, Madison (now Colgate) University, and Hamilton Theological Seminary, Hamilton, New York. Ordained in 1863. Held pastorates at Baptist churches at Keene, New Hampshire, Newton Center, Massachusetts, and Olivet Baptist Church, Montreal, between 1863 and 1883. Professor of New Testament interpretation in Toronto Baptist College (1883-1887), pastor at Hamilton, New York (1887-1891), and professor of Christian theology in Colgate University (1890-1908), and of Christian ethics (1908-1912). Wrote *An Outline of Christian Theology;* his most important work. Helped to develop modernism in American theological seminaries. Linked evolution with theology.

CLARKSON, THOMAS (1760-1846) English opponent of the slave trade and slavery. Born in Wisbeach. Educated at St. John's College, Cambridge where his prize-winning essay in Latin on slavery led him to support a ban on it. Ordained as Anglican deacon. From 1787 he obtained data on the evils of the slave trade which led to its abolition for Englishmen in 1807 and for Europeans in principle at the Congress of Vienna in 1815. Helped to end slavery in British possessions in 1833.

CLAUDE, JEAN (1619-1687), French Calvinist preacher and controversialist, born near Agen, southwest France, where father as pastor taught son literature and theology. Also studied at Montauban. After ordination in 1645, charges at La Freyne and at St. Affrique, while continuing studies. In 1654 became pastor of Nîmes and professor of theology there. In 1661 presided over the provincial synod held at Nimes, strongly opposed the government's proposal of reunion of the Protestants with Roman Catholics. For this forbidden to preach in the province. The next year accepted the pastorate and professorship at Montauban, where he was forbidden to preach. He then went to Paris where he was pastor for the Protestants at Charenton from 1666 to 1685. Became engaged in several controversies with the Catholics and Jansenists, wrote famous Defense of the Reformation. Upon the revocation of the Edict of Nantes in 1685 he was ordered to leave France. Being welcomed by the Prince of Orange, went to The Hague, where he spent his last two years preaching to the Protestants of the Netherlands. Here at the request of the Prince of Orange, he wrote *Plaintes des Protestants* or *A Short Account of the Complaints and Cruel Persecutions of the Protestants in the Kingdom of France*. An eloquent preacher, the greatest leader of the French Reformed churches, their ablest disputant, their favorite preacher and one of the most profound thinkers of his day.

CLEMENS, TITUS FLAVIUS (CLEMENT OF ALEXANDRIA) (c. 150-c. 215), a father of the Eastern church, born in Athens. After conversion to Christianity in maturer years, came in touch with Pantaenus of Egypt, who strongly influenced life in Stoic morality, eclectic philosophy, and allegorical interpretation of the Scriptures. Pantaenus was head of the catechetical school at Alexandria. After the death of Pantaenus, A.D. c. 190, Clement succeeded as head of the school. Held this position until driven from his post in the persecution under Septimus Severus in 202. Origen and Alexander of Jerusalem were two of Clement's most noted pupils in the catechetical school, Origen later becoming Clement's successor. Early in Christian life Clement became a presbyter in the Church of Alexandria. A scholar of wide reading, versed in all branches of Greek literature and systems of philosophy, in the Old and the New Testament, in the apocryphal and spurious Christian writings, and in the writings of the Gnostics and other heresies. A great thinker and a Christian philosopher, eclectic in his philosophy and called his philosophy Christian Gnosticism. He said that Christianity has all the good of other philosophies and much truth they do not have. In *Paidagogos* he laid much stress on Christian ethics and the fulfillment of moral obligations. A copious writer; but writings such as *Miscellanies* are repetitious and lacking in clarity. The church has recognized him as a great scholar and Christian. We give credit to Clement for writing the oldest Christian hymn that has come to us, a poem entitled, "Shepherd of Tender Youth."

CLEMENT I (OF ROME) (c. 30-100), Bishop of Rome, the place of his birth is not known. One of the earliest bishops of Rome, and may possibly have been the Clement mentioned by Paul in Philippians 4:3. It is not certain, however, whether or not he was ever associated with either Peter or Paul. His Epistle to the Corinthians was written likely about A.D. 96 and is the oldest specimen of post-apostolic literature. It quotes profusely from the Old Testament and has many references to Paul and Peter. Valuable for information concerning the exalted position of the bishops or elders in the church and apostolic succession.

CLEMENT V (BERTRAND DE GOTOR GOTH) (1264-1314), Bishop of Bordeaux and first Avignon Pope (1305-1314), born of nobility in Aquitaine, France. Through influence of Philip the Fair, elected pope in 1305 and crowned at Lyons, France. Established the papal court at Avignon, France, 1309 which was the beginning of the "Babylonian Captivity" (1309-1377). Annulled the bulls of Boniface VIII, released Philip IV from the ban, dissolved the order of the Knights Templar, appointed relatives to high dignities, appointed mostly Frenchmen to the cardinalate, and called the ecumenical Council of Vienne in 1311. Founded Universities of Orléans and Perugia.

CLEMENT VII (ROBERT OF GENEVA), (1342-1394), anti-pope at beginning of Papal or Great Schism, 1378. Neapolitan Urban VI had been elected pope by college of cardinals. French cardinals dissented; demanded new election, electing a Frenchman, Cardinal Robert of Geneva. Took name Clement VII and returned to Avignon. France, Spain, Scotland, part of Germany, Southern Italy supported Clement; rest of Europe supported Urban. Europe was divided ecclesiastically and politically. Clement was diplomatic and versatile; his rival was unpolitic and intractable.

CLEMENT VIII (IPPOLITO ALDOBRANDINI), (1536-1605). Appointed cardinal in 1585. Revised the Vulgate (1592) Breviary and Missal. Expanded the Vatican Library. Notorious for nepotism with three nephews as cardinals.

CLEMENT XI (GIOVANNI FRANCESCO ALBANI) (1649-1721). Born in Urbino. Ordained in 1700. Educated at Rome in civil and canon law. Made cardinal in 1690 and pope in 1721. Helped to start the church in the Philippines. Expanded the Vatican Library with collections of manuscripts from the East. Beautified Rome. Decree condemning the Jansenists in 1718.

CLEMENT XIV (GIOVANNI VINCENZO ANTONIO GANGANELLI) (1705-1774). Born near Rimini. Became a Franciscan in 1723. Taught theology at convents in Oscoli, Milan and Bologna. Pope from 1769 to 1774. Suppressed Jesuit order in 1773 because of pressure from nations incensed at Jesuit intrusion into politics. Founded the Clementine Museum in the Vatican.

CLOTILDA (SAINT) (c. 475-c. 545), Queen of the Franks as wife of Clovis. Educated in the Christian faith, married to Clovis, 493, and led her husband to the orthodox faith. After the death of Clovis in 511, Clotilda entered the Abbey of St. Martin at Tours, where she remained until her death. Canonized a few years after her death.

CLOUGH (klŭf), **JOHN EVERETT** (1836-1910), American Baptist missionary, born near Frewsburg, New York, and later moved with parents to Iowa. Entered Burlington Institute, Iowa in 1857, joined the Baptist church in 1858, and finished college course at Upper Iowa University.

After teaching school a year, serving for a time as a colporter, and attending a "Ministers' Institute" in Chicago, offered himself as a foreign missionary. Accepted and assigned to the Telugu Mission in India. Ordained in 1864; went with family to India in 1865. The next year took up residence among the Telugus, a tribe of low caste people, at Ongole. A Baptist church was organized, and a mass movement was soon under way. The terrible famine of 1876-1878 spread its distress over the Telugu area; and Clough was able to give relief to great numbers. For a while during the famine Clough deemed it wise to refuse baptism to applicants; but in 1878 he resumed the rite, and within six weeks nearly nine thousand were baptized. By the close of 1879 there were about thirteen thousand baptized people, and by 1883 twenty-one thousand members. Work on the field was interrupted several times by furloughs to America, at which times he raised large sums for the work. In 1905, after forty years on the field, he found it necessary to retire.

CLOVIS (Clodwig) (c. 466-511), King of the Franks. Succeeded father Childeric in 481 as king of the Salic Franks. A capable, energetic ruler who rapidly rose to fame and power, and became the first real king of the Merovingian line and ruled from 481 to 511. Though pagans, he and his father maintained friendly relations with the bishops of Gaul. In 493 married Clotilda, a Catholic Burgundian princess. After a significant victory over the Alemanni, he and three thousand soldiers were baptized on Christmas day in 496. From capital at Paris Clovis manifested real administrative ability in ruling vast domains. Protected the church and seems to have founded many churches and monasteries throughout France.

COAN, TITUS (1801-1882), missionary to Hawaii, born at Killingworth, Connecticut, studied in a military school and at Auburn Theological Seminary. Following graduation in 1833 ordained, and later the same year sailed on a mission of exploration to Patagonia. Failing to make friendly contacts with the Patagonians the mission party returned. In 1835, he, his wife, and six other missionaries, reached the Hawaiian Islands. The missionaries who were already on the field assigned to young missionary Coan as his parish a one-hundred-mile strip of Hawaiian shore, including the towns of Hilo and Puna, with population of fifteen thousand. Mr. Coan soon learned the language and in three months from the time he set foot on the shores of Hawaii began to preach in the native tongue. Mr. Coan preached to great crowds and catechized and baptized many. During the three years ending April 1840, 7,382 persons were received into the church at Hilo. These people were baptized only after prolonged catechizing, and careful and exacting examination. By June 1841 about three-fourths of the adult population of Hilo had been received into the church. In 1867 the grand old church was divided into seven local churches, six of them with native pastors. The church buildings were erected with Hawaiian hands and money. In 1870 Mr. Coan reported that he had baptized and received into the church 11,960 members. From the first he taught the people to be self-supporting and self-sustaining, and to be a missionary church. He saw nearly a score of his people go as foreign missionaries to the dark islands of Micronesia. He lived and labored faithfully until 1882. The evening of his life was spent as a pastor of the large church at Hilo and as supervisor of his diocese which he had so magnificently developed. Following a revival late in 1882 he died. His book is *Life in Hawaii: an Autobiographic Sketch (1835-1881).*

COCCEIUS (kŏk sē'yŭs), **(KOCH), JOHANNES** (1603-1669), Dutch Protestant Hebraist, theologian, and Bible interpreter, born at Bremen, educated at Hamburg, and at the University of Franeker. In 1630 accepted the professorship of biblical philology at Bremen, in 1636 was called to the chair of Hebrew at Franeker, and in 1643 was appointed to the chair of theology. In 1650 accepted the chair of theology at Leiden, served with honor and fame until death. A distinguished interpreter, lecturer, and writer on the Scriptures, in preaching and teaching followed the expository method and insisted that it was the main business of the preacher faithfully and carefully to interpret and apply the Word of God. Held that the Bible is an organic whole. Developed the covenant or federal type of theology, which taught that the two covenants, "of works" and "of grace," were the basis of theology. Chief works were *Lexicon et Commentarius Sermonis Hebraici et Chaldaici Veteris Testamenti, Summa Doctrinae de Foedere Testamento Dei,* and commentaries on nearly all the books of the Bible. In the Dutch Reformed church the followers of Voetius represented the stronger Calvinistic central party, and the followers of Cocceius the modified Calvinistic Remonstrants.

COFFIN, HENRY SLOAN (1877-1954), American Presbyterian educator. Born in New York City. Educated at Yale, Edinburgh Marburg, and Union Theological Seminary, New York. Ordained in 1900. Founded and served at the Presbyterian Mission in the Bronx in 1900 and from 1900 to 1905 the

Bedford Park Church. From 1905 to 1926 he served the Madison Avenue Presbyterian church and taught practical theology at Union Theological Seminary of which he was president from 1926 to 1945. Moderator of the Presbyterian church, USA, in 1943. Liberal in theology and advocated the social gospel. Wrote *In a Day of Social Rebuilding* and *The Meaning of the Cross.*

COILLARD (kwä yär'), **FRANÇOIS** (1834-1904), pioneer missionary to Barotseland, Africa, born in Asnieres-les-Bourges in Central France. When twenty attended a seminary in Paris, and the next year enrolled in the University of Strassburg to prepare to be a foreign missionary. In 1857 ordained in Paris, and later the same year sailed under the Paris Evangelical Missionary Society for Basutoland in South Africa. When in 1864 war broke out (between the British and the Boers) was exiled from Basutoland to Natal. Labored among the Zulus for two years, then returned in 1869 to the Basutos and stayed there until 1874 when the old Basuto chief, Moshesh, became a Christian before he died. After twenty years of fruitful labor among the Basutos, Coillard was commissioned to open a new mission among the Barotses about five hundred miles to the north in Northern Rhodesia. After extreme hardships and dangers, traveling with a sick wife, he reached his new field in 1878. Then in 1879 after twenty-three years in Africa took his first furlough, during which time worked hard in campaigning France, England, and Scotland to raise the funds for his new mission. Two years later returned to Basutoland to find work there largely demolished. Did what he could to re-establish the church, and then two years later moved on to Barotseland again. Encountered the bitterest of pagan opposition. Health of both was often in precarious condition with life often hanging in the balance. In 1891 Madame Coillard died. Mr. Coillard continued the work for another thirteen years. About 1895 took second furlough, but returned in 1898 to spend his last six years laboring for the African church, chiefly among the Barotses. Died in Barotseland in 1904.

COKE, THOMAS (1747-1814), first bishop of the Methodist Episcopal Church, born at Brecon, Wales. Educated at Oxford, ordained deacon in the Church of England in 1770. Curate at South Petherton, Somerset from 1771-1777. In 1777 joined the Methodist movement and became Wesley's "right hand man," an indefatigable itinerant minister. In 1782 became the first president of the Irish Conference, and in 1784 was set apart by Wesley as "Superintendent" for America. Arrived in America in November, 1784, went to the famous Christian Conference at Baltimore, at which he ordained Francis Asbury as co-superintendent (or bishop, the term that in 1787 was adopted by the American Methodist Church, though never approved by Wesley). They adopted the order of worship, and Wesley's Articles of Religion for the church in America, and named the church the Methodist Episcopal church. For many years Coke visited Ireland annually and presided at its conferences. Several times president of the English Conference, crossed the Atlantic eighteen times at own expense, the last time in 1803. Went back to England to take up Wesley's work after the death of the latter in 1791. Deeply interested in the cause of missions, founded the black mission in the West Indies, where there were seventeen thousand members at the time of his death. He furnished the funds to establish a Methodist mission in India. In 1814 sailed with a band of helpers, but died on the voyage, and was buried at sea. His venture succeeded and the Wesleyan East Indian Mission became a reality. An opponent of slavery, wished to heal the breach between the Methodist and Anglican communions.

COLENSO, JOHN WILLIAM (1814-1883), first Anglican bishop of Natal, born at St. Austell, Cornwall, England, and died at Durban, Natal. After graduating from St. John's College, Cambridge, was assistant master at Harrow, 1839-1842, then returned to St. John's as tutor for four years. From 1846 to 1853, vicar of Forncett St. Mary in Norfolk, and in 1853 became the first bishop of the new see at Natal in South Africa. Worked zealously for the conversion of the Zulus for whom he translated portions of the Scripture, wrote manuals of instructions, and prepared a grammar and a dictionary in the Zulu language. Higher critical interpretation of the Bible evidenced in *The Pentateuch and the Book of Joshua Critically Examined* and *Commentary on the Epistle to the Romans,* along with denying eternal punishment and condoning polygamy among converts, led first to suspicion as to his orthodoxy, and finally to his deposition in 1863. Following appeal to the Privy Council, his deposition was pronounced null and void and he maintained his office. A rival bishop, however, was consecrated, and was stationed at Martizburg to take the place of Natal, leaving Colenso in a schismatic position the rest of his life. A warm friend of the Zulus favoring them in their conflict with the Boers, he stood boldly for right treatment of these people regardless of the fears and selfish interests of the Europeans in diocese and of being alienated from fellow Britishers.

COLERIDGE, SAMUEL TAYLOR (1772-1834) Poet and philosopher. Born in Ottery St. Mary, Devon. Educated at Jesus College, Cambridge. Travelled widely in Europe. Influenced by German idealism which he mediated to the English lake poets and American transcendentalists. Wrote *The Rime of the Ancient Mariner* and many other works.

COLET (kŏl′et), **JOHN** (c. 1467-1519), English humanist and theologian. Son of Henry Colet, several times Lord Mayor of London, born in London and studied at Magdalen College, Oxford, at Paris, and in Italy. In Italy became acquainted with Savonarola, and was influenced by his teachings. Upon return to Oxford in 1497 lectured with great favor and approval upon the Epistles of Paul. At Oxford became an intimate friend of Erasmus and More. As dean of St. Paul's, an appointment received in 1509, stood forth as a reformer of clerical abuses, a bold and scriptural preacher, and a liberal patron of education. Preached at the installation of Thomas Wolsey as cardinal. Spent much of the inheritance received from father in founding St. Paul's School, "where 153 boys, without restriction of nationality, could gain the rudiments of education, be brought up in a sound Christian way, and learn Greek as well as Latin." A man of high ethical character. Colet died of dropsy.

COLGATE, WILLIAM (1783-1857), American soap manufacturer and philanthropist, born at Hollingbourne, Kent, England, and came with his family to Baltimore in the United States in 1795. At age twenty-one he was apprenticed to a soap maker. In 1806 later established his own business in New York City. In 1847 moved plant from New York to Jersey City. From that time until the end of his life gave at least a tenth of profits to temperance, educational and religious purposes. A Baptist, he heavily supported Madison University, Hamilton, New York, later to be known as Colgate University. Helped found the first Bible Society in New York, and aided in the organization of the American Bible Society, and the American and Foreign Bible Society, for thirteen years was the treasurer of the latter. In 1838 he withdrew from his church, and helped organize the society which built the Tabernacle, a society which adopted no creed, but only a simple covenant.

COLIGNY (kô lē nyē′), **GASPARD DE** (1519-1572), French statesman and admiral; Huguenot leader, born at Chatillon-sur-Loing, France of noble family. A man of sterling character, devoted to Calvinism. Knighted in 1544 and admiral in 1552. Won distinction in the wars of Francis I and Henry II of France. He spent two years in a Spanish prison in the Netherlands. Emerged from the prison as a Protestant. He and Prince Conde became strong leaders and defenders of the Huguenots during the early stage of the Wars of Religion. On one side the Roman Catholics and the Guises; the other the Protestants, Coligny, Conde, and Henry of Navarre. When Conde was killed, Coligny assumed full command with the political support of Henry. Coligny held the good favor of King Charles IX, but Charles's mother, queen regent Catherine de Medici, hated the admiral. She plotted his destruction and that of his followers. The plot was carried out on St. Bartholomew's Day, August 24, 1572. Coligny was the first to fall. While upholding the Huguenot cause at home Coligny attempted to secure a safe asylum for them in the New World, sending expeditions of Huguenots to colonize in Brazil in 1555 and Florida in 1562.

COLLINS, ANTHONY (1676-1729), Prominent English Deist. Born at Keston, Middlesex. Educated at Eton and King's College, Cambridge. Lived in London until 1715 when he took a civil office in Essex. Influenced by John Locke. Stressed acquisition of truth by free inquiry in *A Discourse of Freethinking*. Attacked orthodox ideas in *Discourse on the Grounds and Reasons of the Christian Religion*.

COLMAN (d. 676) Bishop of Lindisfarne. Born in Ireland. A monk in Iona. Bishop of Lindisfarne in 661. Led Celtic Christians in Northumbria and at the Synod of Whitby in 663. Defended Celtic date for Easter. Returned to Iona in 664 and later to Ireland to found Innisboffin monastery in County Mayo.

COLUMBA or COLUMKILLE (c. 521-597), Irish Celtic missionary, "Apostle of Caledonia." Born of Royal stock at Gartan, a wild district in Donegal county, Ireland, son of an Ulster chief. Given an excellent education and in the Christian faith, early distinguishing himself for piety and zeal. Dedicated himself to monastic zeal. Ordained deacon and priest, about 551. In 563, at the age of forty-two, left Ireland with twelve companions, and landed on the small island of Iona, off the coast of Scotland. There founded his monastery from which center he and companions evangelized the Picts and more carefully taught the Scots who had already professed Christianity. He made Iona his chief abode and a great school and missionary training center. He made frequent visits to Scotland where he founded many churches. Also maintained a close connection with Ireland, making frequent visits there in behalf of his monasteries.

Soon smaller societies had to be formed and other monasteries founded. Accounted one of the poets of Ireland, being the author of three hymns. Finished his missionary career dying beside the altar in the church while engaged in his midnight devotions. A product of the Celtic church of the Isles, whereas Augustine was from Rome and represented the Catholic church.

COLUMBAN or COLUMBANUS (c. 543-615), Irish missionary, born in a Christian family in the Celtic church in Leinster, Ireland in the year that Benedict of Nursia died. A very studious lad, early entered the famous abbey of Bangor. Studied until he was thirty becoming a noted scholar. When about forty years of age he felt the missionary call to the people of central Europe. About 591 with a band of twelve companions went to the Germanic tribes in Burgundy, eastern Gaul. In the wilderness of the Vosges they founded several monasteries, the most famous of which was the one at Luxeuil. In these monasteries Columban established rules more strict than were those of the Benedictines. Trouble, however, arose over the tonsure and the date of Easter, and in 610 all the Irish monks were banished from Burgundy. They gained permission to go to the Alemanni and the Suevi (present-day Switzerland), where they remained for three years. A monastery was established and named St. Gall. But again in 613 difficulties arose, and Columban crossed the Alps and established himself in a new monastery at Bobbio in the Appennines. He spent two years in Italy, dying at Bobbio. He had lived a most rigorous and disciplined life. Although loyal to his Celtic heritage and teaching, he showed great respect for the pope and the church of Rome.

COLUMBUS, CHRISTOPHER (c. 1446-1506), explorer of the Americas, born at Genoa, Italy. Became a sailor at the age of fourteen; for twenty-five years sailed the Mediterranean, down the coast of Africa as far as Guinea, and north as far as England and Iceland. An excellent draftsman and skilled in making maps and charts. About 1470 moved to Lisbon, Portugal, the most enterprising seaport in the world. Appealed without success to the kings of Portugal and England for aid in seeking a passage to India by sailing west. Queen Isabella of Spain equipped Columbus for the voyage. Made admiral and to be governor general of the lands he would discover. On August 3, 1492 sailed from Palos, Spain with ninety men in three little sailing vessels, the *Nina,* the *Pinta,* and the *Santa Maria*. After a voyage of twenty-eight hundred miles, experiencing threatened mutiny among his men, on October 12, 1492, twenty-five years before the beginning of the Reformation, Columbus landed on a small island of the Bahamas, naming it San Salvador. Being a devout Roman Catholic, and a man of deep mystical piety, as well as being a commissioned officer of the court, took possession of the new country with religious solemnity. After finding and visiting Cuba and Haiti, calling the latter Hispaniola, he returned to Spain in great triumph and honor, with about half his men and with two of his vessels. His great aim had been to find a shorter way to the East and to present Christ to the natives. In three succeeding voyages, 1493, 1498, and 1502, maintained high aims, but fellowmen failed him. After his third voyage, Columbus was sent back to Spain in chains. Following fourth voyage in four small leaky vessels, shipwrecked, life endangered by mutineers, he was separated from his brother Bartholomew, his men were massacred, his settlements were sacked and burned by natives, he suffered from a painful disease, marooned for nearly a year in his worm-eaten ships, he finally returned to Spain in almost a dying condition. He could still say, "God has always been good to me!" He wrote his will on the pages of a prayer book. He signed his name, as was his custom, "Christ Bearer," and died reciting a psalm, May 20, 1506. His remains were buried at Valladolid, but were later removed to Seville, then to San Domingo in Haiti, thence to Havana, and finally back to the Cathedral in Seville. It was centuries before his native country gave Columbus the honor and acclaim that were due him.

COMBA, EMILIO (1839-1904) Waldensian theologian. Born at San Germano, Chisome, Italy. Educated at the theological school in Geneva under Merle d'Aubigne. Ordained in 1863. Worked in Brescia, established a Waldensian church in 1867. From 1872 to 1904 in Florence taught in the theological faculty. Edited the theological journal *La Rivista Cristiana*. Wrote *Who Are the Waldenses?* and a two-volume work on the Reformation in Italy.

COMBER (kōm'bĕr), **THOMAS JAMES** (1852-1887), English Baptist missionary to the Congo, born in Clarendon Street, Camberwell, Kent, England. When fifteen, attended evening classes in Greek and Latin in Mr. Spurgeon's school. At sixteen made public confession of faith, was baptized and joined the Baptist church. In 1871 Comber entered Regent's Park College with the purpose of preparing for the foreign mission field. Soon after graduation in 1875 accepted by the Baptist Missionary Society as a missionary to the Cameroons, West Africa.

Began his missionary work on the island of Fernando Po, and a little later on the mainland of the Cameroons. Enroute to the field, Comber met the veteran Alfred Saker of the Cameroons at Sierra Leone in 1876. In 1878 Thomas Comber and George Grenfell were the two first pioneer missionaries to enter the Congo. They explored the Congo River region. From that time until death ten years later Comber was the acknowledged leader of the mission. Later that year he returned to England to report on expedition into Congoland, secure new recruits for the mission, to marry the young woman who was his bride for only four months. Shortly after arriving on the field in 1879 Mrs. Comber died of meningitis. His missionary career was short, but he had done a significant work in helping establish the Congo Mission. Work in Africa was honored by his being made a fellow of the Royal Geographic Society.

COMENIUS (kō mē'nĭ ŭs), **(KOMENSKY, JAN AMOS) JOHANN AMOS** (1592-1671), Czech theologian and educational reformer, the last bishop of the Church of the Bohemian Brethren, born in Moravia. Studied theology at Herborn and Heidelberg, then took charge of a parish at Prerau, and a little later at Fulnek. When in 1621 he and co-religionists were expelled from Bohemia for their faith, they settled at Lissa in Poland. Driven from Poland went from place to place preaching and propagating his views. Though a noted preacher and the last bishop of the Bohemian Brethren, his greatest fame, however, rests in his system of pedagogy, especially in his methods of teaching languages. Some of his writings were translated into all the European languages, into Persian and Arabic, and were reprinted over and over for two centuries. Traveled much, presenting pedagogical views. Called especially to England, to Transylvania (1650-1654), and to Sweden to examine and reform their whole educational departments. Many of the ideas of Rousseau and Pestalozzi are found in his writings in fully developed form. Opposed coercion in education. Wanted to educate whole person for life with science and history and for eternity by biblical studies. After much unrest, he finally settled down at Amsterdam until his death. Comenius was the author of *Pansophiae Prodromus, Janua Linguarum Reserata, Orbis Sensualium Pictus,* and *Didactica Magna.*

COMMODIANUS (kŏ mō dĭ ā'nŭs), (c. 200-c. 275), Christian Latin poet, born in early third century in a pagan home, but won to Christianity through the reading of the Scriptures. He was the oldest known Christian poet writing in Latin, in the middle of the third century, likely in North Africa. As to literary form his poetry is rather worthless; but its apologetic nature has value to church history. He was an honest student of the Bible, but his theology is not reliable. He was a Chiliast and a Patripassianist.

COMPTON, HENRY (1632-1713), English bishop, born at Compton Wyngates, Warwickshire, England. Studied at Queen's College, Oxford, 1649-1652, then traveled on the Continent until the Restoration of Charles II. He decided to enter the church, studied at both Cambridge and Oxford, was ordained in 1662, consecrated bishop of Oxford, 1674, becoming bishop of London, 1675. Privy councilor and tutor for James II's two daughters, Mary and Anne, who through his teaching became attracted to the Protestant faith. An Anglican he maintained a conciliatory attitude toward the dissenters, and held several conferences with the clergy of his diocese relative to bringing about a reunion. In 1686, under James II, suspended from ecclesiastical functions for disobedience to the king's orders and for strong opposition to the papacy. Compton actively espoused the cause of William and Mary, crowning them king and queen in 1689. Reinstated in his old positions. In 1696 he commissioned Thomas Bray and William Blair to organize the Anglican church in Maryland and Virginia. During the reign of Anne put on a commission to arrange the union of England and Scotland. Later life was somewhat embittered by disappointment at not receiving the primacy. Gave liberally to all in need and for building churches and hospitals, and died poor in consequence. Writings include several theological books, *A Treatise on the Holy Communion,* and a *Translation from the French of the Jesuit Intrigues.*

COMTE, ISIDORE AUGUSTE MARIE FRANÇOIS XAVIER, (1798-1857), French philosopher, sociologist, and founder of positivism, born at Montpellier, France and educated at the Ecole Polytechnique, Paris. He held a position for twelve years in the Ecole Polytechnique as entrance examiner. His system of philosophy, known as positivism, gained a wide following. For many intellectuals, especially in Latin Europe and Latin America, it became a substitute for Christianity. He wished to apply scientific methods to the study of society and to have science serve the welfare of mankind. He created a cult in which humanity took the place of God, which had as its object, the progressive welfare of mankind. The "Religion of Humanity" was to him a necessary new religion, indeed replacing Christianity. To give practical expression to views he formed the "Positive Society."

Chief writings were *Cours de Philosophie Positive,* (Course of Positive Philosophy) six volumes; *Systeme de Politique,* (System of Positive Polity) four volumes; *Catechisme Positive, ou Sommaire Exposition de la Religion Universelle* (Positive Catechism).

CONSTANTINE THE GREAT (c. 280-337), First Christian Roman emperor, born at Naissus in Upper Moesia (Serbia). First became distinguished in imperial service in the Egyptian and Persian wars in the reign of Diocletian. Commissioned to Gaul and Britain, where in 306 he was proclaimed emperor both by dying father and by the Roman troops. Maxentius, aspiring to the throne occupied by Constantine in the West, rebelled against him. At Milvian Bridge in 312 Constantine defeated Maxentius. It was at the beginning of this battle with Maxentius that he is supposed to have seen in the heavens a cross with the inscription: "By This Conquer." This victory was a political and military victory of Christianity over heathenism as well as a victory over his foes. The year prior to this victory, in 311, Constantine, Galerius, and Licinius as co-emperors had signed the Edict of Toleration, which granted toleration to all religions, including Christianity. A short time after this Galerius died. In 313 Constantine as co-emperor in the West and Licinius as co-emperor in the East signed the Edict of Milan, which made Christianity a legal and official religion, though not yet the state religion. In 324 sole emperor in both the East and the West. Sensing that future success as emperor depended on uniting his subjects, he blended his interests in and built his policies around the Christian church as an aid to the unity and power of the Roman Empire. He used the term "catholic" in his imperial edicts, chose Christian men as advisers, gradually exempted the clergy from military and civil duty, legalized bequests to the churches, enjoined the civic observance of Sunday, contributed liberally to the building of churches, and gave his sons a Christian education. In 325 called the first ecumenical council at Nicea to settle disputed doctrines and to unify the church. In 330 moved the capital from pagan Rome to Byzantium on the Bosporus, naming it New Rome, later to be called Constantinople. Though favoring and encouraging Christianity and calling himself "bishop of bishops," retained pagan title Pontifex Maximus until the last. The emperor had a deep interest in the church; yet he was not a baptized member until his closing days. In 337 when he sensed the approach of death, admitted into full communion of the church by baptism at the hands of Eusebius of Nicomedia, a semi-Arian bishop.

CONTARINI (kon tȧ rē'nē), **GASPARO** (1483-1542), Venetian statesman and cardinal, born in Venice. Educated in and taught in Padua. Venetian ambassador to England, Spain and Italy. In 1535 Pope Paul III made him cardinal in the hope of using his evangelical disposition to conciliate and win back the evangelical or Reformation schismatics, and in the hope of using his reformatory spirit in bettering the inner condition of the church. In several colloquies that were held between the Protestants and the Catholics in effort to bring them together, especially at the Diet of Regensburg in 1541, Contarini represented the more moderate side of the Catholic view. He favored Luther's view on justification, but did not agree with Luther on his rejection of church authority. Served on Reform Commission of Paul III from 1536 to 1537. He wrote a treatise on *Immortality of the Soul* and a book directed against Luther.

CONWELL, RUSSELL HERMAN (1843-1925), lawyer, preacher, lecturer, writer, university president, philanthropist, born near South Worthington, Massachusetts. Worked way through Wilbraham Academy and Yale University. Began public speaking career while making sales of the *Life of John Brown,* giving speeches on "the Great Martyr." Used native oratorical ability also to raise volunteers for the federal army; and before age twenty commissioned captain and later lieutenant colonel. In college joined the Infidel Club of Yale. Entered the army an avowed infidel, but experiences in the service and a serious illness led to his conversion. He then entered the Albany Law School, New York, and upon graduation was admitted to the bar. He practiced law in Minneapolis, 1865-1868; and while there established the *Minneapolis Chronicle*. Also lectured, worked in Sunday schools, and worked for the Y.M.C.A. In 1867-1868 he was in Germany as immigration agent of Minnesota. The following two years foreign correspondent of the New York *Tribune* and of the *Boston Traveler.* Spent some time visiting in the Holy Land. After returning to America set up his practice in Boston for nine years. Began the *Somerville Journal*. Feeling the call to the ministry, in 1880 quit law practice, resigned all other activities, and was ordained a Baptist minister. Became pastor of a struggling Baptist church in Lexington, Massachusetts. The little church grew rapidly under his pastoral care. Two years later moved to Philadelphia to become pastor of the Grace Baptist Church. In 1891 a new church, the great Temple Baptist Church which he had built to seat thirty-five hundred people, was opened. He continued to pastor this church until 1925, as long as he lived. In

1888 he established and became president of Temple College (later Temple University), where poor students might have the privilege of attending. He soon added various departments including in 1891 Samaritan Hospital. Russell Conwell also gave lectures all over the country. His most famous lecture, *Acres of Diamonds,* was given more than five thousand times. Assisted Bishop J. H. Vincent in founding the Chautauqua. During fifty years of lecturing his income (perhaps eight million dollars) was all invested in education and other philanthropies. Wrote dozens of biographies and other books.

CONYBEARE (kŏn'ĭ bēr), **WILLIAM JOHN** (1815-1857), Church of England clergyman. Educated at Westminster and Trinity College, Cambridge. The first principal of Liverpool Collegiate Institute, 1842-1848, where he was joined in 1845 by his friend J. S. Howson. Failure of health forced him to resign his post at Liverpool, and he became vicar of Axminster, Devon (1848-1864). In 1854, illness again necessitated his resignation. Conybeare's fame rests chiefly on the *Life and Epistles of St. Paul,* written in collaboration with J. S. Howson.

COOK, DAVID CALEB (1850-1927), American editor and publisher of Sunday school literature, born at East Worcester, New York. At age of fourteen united with the Methodist church, and at seventeen became a Sunday school teacher. When about twenty he set up a small successful sewing machine business in Chicago. Became more and more interested in Sunday school work, organizing Sunday schools for underprivileged. Owing to lack of Sunday school materials and helps, decided to prepare and publish his own. Called his first publication *Our Sunday School Quarterly.* After surveying field well, published forty thousand copies of his first number and twice as many of his second. Soon sold his thriving sewing machine business, and gave all his effort to his Sunday school publications, at the same time conducting Sunday schools. Continually tested his publications and helps. In 1882 moved expanding publishing work to Elgin, Illinois. David C. Cook was constantly devising and forming new methods and new helps for the Sunday school and for Christian education. In truth a prophet, and pioneer, and a promoter, he became a national and international figure in Sunday school gatherings and conventions, active until the last.

COOK, CAPTAIN JAMES (1728-1779), English navigator and explorer, born at Marton, Yorkshire, England, son of a farm laborer. In 1755 joined the royal navy and in 1759 made master of the *Mercury,* and was sent on a mission to the Gulf of St. Lawrence. Between 1768 and 1779 given command of three important scientific expeditions. The first of these voyages brought to the civilized world much information concerning Australia, New Zealand, New Guinea, and many of the island groups of the South Pacific. The basis for England's later claim of Australia and New Zealand was laid by him. The second voyage was to Antarctica, covering seventy thousand miles; the third was to the Arctic regions, seeking a northwest passage from the Pacific to the Atlantic. On the third voyage he rediscovered the Sandwich Islands, and explored the west coast of North America from the Oregon coast through Bering Strait to the Arctic Ocean. In 1776 Cook was chosen Fellow of the Royal Society. In 1779 he was tragically killed by the natives of Hawaii. "Interest in non-Christian peoples and missions to them was aroused in Great Britain by the voyages of discovery in the Pacific conducted by Captain James Cook." Influenced by Cook's work Carey's purpose was to go to Tahiti as a missionary, until his attention was finally drawn to India.

COOPER, ANTHONY ASHLEY. *See* **SHAFTESBURY**

COORNHERT, DIRCK VOLKERTSZOON (1552-1590), Dutch humanist, engraver, moralist and theologian. Born in Amsterdam. Copper engraver in Harlem. Held several public offices. Influenced by Erasmus and the Reformers; emphasized the Bible for ethical instruction. Supported William of Orange against the Spaniards. Forced to flee to Emden (1585) and Gouda. Believed man is free to follow divine Christ who can after one chooses lead that one to an ethical life. Opposed to clerical or civil control of human free will. Opposed by Arminius. Translated several Latin classics into Dutch.

COP, NICHOLAS (Early sixteenth century), Rector of the University of Paris, son of a distinguished royal physician. Had been a member of the "Group of Meaux," and a leader among the humanists in the University of Paris. In October, 1533 he was elected rector of the university, and in November delivered his inaugural address, which was a bold statement of evangelical views, containing statements from both Erasmus and Luther, and was a strong plea for reformation on the basis of the New Testament. The address, which evidently had been prepared in part, if not entirely by Cop's friend, John Calvin, so stirred the church authorities that both Calvin and Cop were forced to leave the city to avoid arrest.

COPERNICUS (kō pûr'nĭ kŭs), **or KOPPERNIGK, NICOLAUS** (1473-1543), Polish astronomer and mathematician, born at Thorn, Prussian Poland, studied astronomy and other sciences at the University of

Cracow; astronomy and canon law at the University of Bologna; medicine at the University of Padua; and received the doctor's degree in canon law from Ferrara in 1503. In 1497 had been appointed canon at the cathedral of Frauenburg, East Prussia. Held this office until he died. For several years he was his uncle's physician in the episcopal palace of Heilsberg, Poland. Copernicus is best known for his promotion of the Copernican theory that the sun is the center of the universe, and that the earth rotates on its axis, as opposed to the Ptolomaic theory that the earth is the center, with the sun and the other planets revolving around it. The idea that the earth moved around the sun was developed in his *De Revolutionibus Orbium Coelestius (Concerning the Revolution of the Celestial Spheres),* which was dedicated to Pope Paul III. Died a few hours after his book was published and never knew the fame that was to come to him. Prepared the way for Kepler, Galileo and Newton. The "Galileo affair" led to the placing of Copernicus' writing on the Index in 1616, where it remained until 1757.

CORREGGIO (kōr rād′jō), **ANTONIO ALLEGRI DA** (1494-1534), Italian Renaissance painter, born at Correggio, Lombardy, Italy. Though receiving almost no training in painting, he became one of the great painters of Italy. He was of the so-called Lombard school, founding the school of painting at Parma. He was a master of delicacy, and of lights and shadows. His religious subjects were similar to those of Michelangelo, Raphael, Da Vinci, and Titian, and he may be ranked with them. His paintings are to be found in the galleries of Dresden, London, Paris, Naples, Florence, and Rome. Most of his work was done by way of decorations in the churches of Parma. Some of his characteristic paintings were *Ecce Homo, Holy Night, Adoration of the Shepherds, The Ascension of Christ, Il Giorro,* an exquisite picture of St. Jerome, *Ascension of the Virgin,* and several *Madonnas.*

COSIMO DE MEDICI (kō zē′mō dē mĕ′ dē chē) (the Elder) (1389-1464), rich banker and ruler of Florence, born in Florence, eldest son of Giovanni de Medici, wealthy banker who brought the Medici family into prominence. Cosimo was a Renaissance promoter of arts and letters, a founder of educational and charitable institutions, among which were the Platonic Academy, churches, and public libraries. He was scholarly and well read, traveled extensively in France and Germany. Though a layman of wealth and not a prince, he was the capable ruler of Florence for thirty years.

COTTON, JOHN (1584-1652), Puritan minister of Boston, born at Derby, England, studied at Derby Grammar School and at Trinity and Emmanuel Colleges, Cambridge. Became fellow, dean, and catechist at Emmanuel, and distinguished himself as tutor, orator and scholar from 1607 to 1612. He was ordained in the Church of England ministry in 1610, and was pastor of St. Botolph's Church at Boston, Lincolnshire from 1612 to 1633. In the latter year summoned before Archbishop Laud because of his Puritanic leanings, and for refusing to comply with certain phases of Anglican church ritual. To escape persecution fled to Boston, Massachusetts Bay Colony. Here ordained "teacher" of the First Church, Congregational, in Boston, where he served until his death nearly twenty years later. Both in England and in Massachusetts he wielded a powerful influence over affairs. Though he fled to this country to escape persecution, he sanctioned Williams' expulsion from Massachusetts in 1634, and also the next year approved the exile of Anne Hutchinson for not complying with the demands of the church authorities. John Cotton was a voluminous writer, being the author of perhaps more than fifty volumes, a few of them being, *The Keyes of the Kingdom of Heaven, The Way of the Churches of Christ in New England,* and *Spiritual Milk for Babes.*

COUGHLIN, CHARLES EDWARD (1891-1979), radical Roman Catholic radio preacher. Born in Hamilton, Ontario. Educated at St. Michael's College and Toronto University (Ph. D. 1911). Ordained in 1916. Taught at Assumption College from 1916 to 1926 and pastor in Kalamazoo and Detroit from 1922 to 1926. Priest of Shrine of the Little Flower, Royal Oak, Michigan from 1926 to 1966. Began radio preaching in 1926 and in 1930 began to promote political views on radio and later on the CBS network. Was anti-Semitic and opposed Communism and internationalism. Founded National Union for Social Justice and the magazine *Social Justice*. Critical of Roosevelt and the New Deal.

COURT, ANTOINE (1696-1760), reorganizer of the Reformed Church in France, born at Villeneuve-de-Berg, Ardeche (or Languedoc), France. In 1714-1715, defying the rigid anti-Protestant laws of Louis XIV, Court undertook first preaching tour. In 1716, even though the king declared Protestantism non-existent in France, Court convened his "first synod" in an abandoned quarry at Monobet where plans were laid for the reorganization and the propagation of the reformed faith in France. In 1718 ordained minister, and the new organization became known as "the Church of the Desert." In

1724 a heavy blow fell upon the Huguenots; a decree was issued again declaring the nonexistence of Protestantism in France. In 1730 Court fled to Lausanne, where with the aid of the government of Berne and of the Archbishop of Canterbury, he established a seminary for the training of Huguenot ministers. Court became its director for the next thirty years. He was busy maintaining an enormous correspondence, instructing candidates for the ministry, convening synods, preparing memorials to the king, and collecting documents for a history of his church. His principal writings were *An Historical Memorial of the Most Remarkable Proceedings against the Protestants in France from 1744 to 1751*, and *Historie des Troubles des Cevennes ou de la Guerredes des Camisards.*

COURTENAY, WILLIAM (c. 1341-1396), Archbishop of Canterbury, great grandson of Edward I, born at St. Martin's, near Exeter and studied law at Stapleton College, Oxford. After holding prebendaries in the churches of Exeter, Wells, and York, in 1369 consecrated bishop of Hereford. In 1375 became bishop of London, and in 1381 made archbishop of Canterbury and chancellor of England. He loyally obeyed the pope when the interests of the national church were not at stake. Bitterly opposed Wycliffe and the Lollards. While bishop of London, in 1377 and again in 1378 he tried in vain to suppress Wycliffe. In 1382, after he was archbishop of Canterbury, summoned an assembly in London. Here the doctrine of Wycliffe was condemned and Wycliffe was prohibited from preaching; but the archbishop was unable to secure the condemnation of Wycliffe himself or his Lollard followers. Courtenay founded the College of St. Mary and All Saints in the parish church of the arch-episcopal manor of Maidstone, and founded five scholarships in Canterbury College, Oxford.

COVERDALE, MILES (1488-1568), English translator of the first printed Bible, born at Coverham, Yorkshire, England, studied at Cambridge University. In 1514 ordained priest at Norwich, and later entered the Augustine monastery at Cambridge. Left the monastery and began evangelical preaching about 1528, spending the next seven years on the Continent where his Bible, the first complete translation in English, was published in 1535. Under commission of Thomas Cromwell he was in France (1538-1539) superintending the printing of a revised English version for the Anglican church, to be known as the "Great Bible." In 1540 he edited "Crammer's Bible," a revised edition of the "Great Bible." In 1540 Coverdale fled to the Continent where he spent the next eight years. Between 1543 and 1547 was Lutheran pastor and schoolmaster near Strassburg. Returning to England in 1548 he was well received and was made chaplain to King Edward VI and almoner to the queen dowager, Catherine Parr. In 1551 Coverdale was appointed bishop of Exeter, but was deprived of the office and imprisoned for two years when Mary came to the throne. In 1553 he owed his escape to the intercession of the Danish king, and spent some time in Denmark, Switzerland, and Germany. In 1559, two years after Elizabeth had come to the throne, he returned to England, but was not reinstated in his bishopric. From 1564 to 1566 he was rector of St. Magnus, near London Bridge. Due to infirmity and to his Puritanic leanings, he resigned the position. He did little original literary work, but was a good translator. He won remarkable popularity as a preacher.

COWMAN, CHARLES ELMER (1864-1924), born Toulon, Illinois. Railroad telegrapher in Iowa and Chicago for years. After conversion won hundreds of telegraphers to Christ. In 1894 experienced missionary call in meetings under A. B. Simpson. Studied at Moody Bible Institute from 1894 to 1900. Went to Tokyo in 1901. Set up Oriental Missionary Society and a Bible Training Institute in 1903. Work spread with success, and Bible institutes were established in Korea and after his death in China. Organized the Great Village Campaign from 1912 to 1918 to reach the villages of Japan. Served in Japan from 1901 to 1917.

COWPER (ko͞o'pĕr or kou'per), **WILLIAM** (1731-1800), English poet and hymnwriter, born at Great Berkhamstead, Hertfordshire, England, the son of a British chaplain, educated in a private school and at Westminster School, studied law in England. Though admitted to the bar, he never practiced law, preferring literature instead. Naturally inclined to morbid brooding and worry. Suffering from an unhappy love affair and worrying over an examination resulted in a mental break that took him to an asylum for a year and a half. After recovering somewhat he lived in the home of Morley Unwin, a retired clergyman of the evangelical party at Huntingdon. Five years after Unwin's death in 1767 Cowper became engaged to Unwin's widow; but his further derangement of mind interfered; they never married. In 1773 Cowper was seized by a fit of religious melancholia, from which his recovery was due partly to the patient care of Mrs. Unwin, who encouraged him to write poetry. Cowper moved with the Unwin family to Olney in

1767, where he became intimate with the pastor, John Newton, and helped him in parish work as a sort of lay curate. He assisted Newton in writing *The Olney Hymns* in 1779. Among the sixty-eight of Cowper's hymns are the following; "Oh! for a Closer Walk with God," "There is a Fountain Filled with Blood," "God Moves in a Mysterious Way," "Hark, My Soul, It is the Lord," and "Jesus, Where'er Thy People Meet." He became excessively pious and devout, yet was ever a prey to deep religious doubts and hallucinations and often fell into deep depression. The last decade or more of his life was a period of deep gloom and a settled notion that God had cast him off. In 1785 Cowper became famous upon the publication of his long poem in blank verse, *The Task*. He also wrote *To Mary,* a touching lyric tribute to Mrs. Unwin, and *On the Royal George*. Shortly before his death he wrote *The Castaway,* in which he expressed his spiritual torment.

CRANMER, THOMAS (1489-1556), English reformer, and first Protestant archbishop of Canterbury, born at Aslocton, Nottinghamshire, England, spent eight years at Jesus College, Cambridge. In 1523 he was ordained, became university preacher and examiner in theology. About 1529 Cranmer suggested that the question of the divorce of Henry and Catherine be referred to the theologians of the universities. The suggestion led to rapid political and ecclesiastical advancement for Cranmer, until the king in 1533 appointed him archbishop of Canterbury. Cranmer declared the marriage void from the beginning, and in five days declared the marriage with Anne Boleyn valid, then crowned her as queen. By 1534 he had enjoined silence in regard to masses for the dead, prayers to the saints, pilgrimages and celibacy. One of Cranmer's most important endeavors was to promote circulation of the Bible in the vernacular. He set on foot the translation of the Bible, the result of which came to be known as "Cranmer's Bible." When Henry died in 1547 Cranmer was named one of the regents of the kingdom. During the short reign of Edward VI (1547-1553), the First Prayer Book (1549), and the Second Prayer Book (1552), and the Forty-Two Articles (1553), later to become the Thirty-nine Articles, were largely the creation of Cranmer. When Catholic Mary came to the throne in 1553, he was arrested and sent to the tower in London, but his execution was delayed for more than a year. In the meantime the pope excommunicated him and appointed Reginald Pole to fill the vacant archbishopric. With the hope of receiving leniency Cranmer recanted the most of his Protestant views, and acknowledged papal supremacy. He publicly recanted all his recantations and heroically met his death, being burned at the stake at Oxford at the same spot where Ridley and Latimer had been martyred.

CRASHAW (krăsh'ô), **RICHARD** (c. 1613-1649), English lyrical and religious poet, born in London, educated at Charterhouse and at Pembroke Hall, Cambridge. Elected to a fellowship at Peterhouse, Cambridge, in 1637, expelled in 1644 because he refused to sign the national covenant. Fled to France where he embraced in 1645 the Roman Catholic faith. In 1646 he became secretary to Cardinal Palotta, and in 1649 removed to Italy and was made canon of the Basilica Church of Our Lady at Loreto; died there four months later. Crashaw wrote poetry in Greek and Latin as well as in English, and was familiar with the classical languages and Spanish and Italian. "His poetry collected in *Steps to the Temple* and *Carmen Deo Nostro,* is filled with a devotion nourished on the Song of Solomon and on the mysticism of St. Teresa." Some of his best poems were: "In the Holy Nativity," "The Flaming Heart or a Hymn to St. Theresa," "The Weeper," and "Song of Divine Love." Crashaw, sometimes termed metaphysical poet, exercised no small influence on later poets such as John Milton and Alexander Pope.

CRAWFORD, DANIEL (DAN) (1870-1926), missionary to Central Africa. Born at Gourock, on the Clyde, Scotland. His conversion followed a desperate soul struggle when he was seventeen years old. He was baptized and associated with the "Brethren" in 1887. Through his incessant street preaching in all kinds of weather, he developed a severe, hacking cough. In 1889 at age of nineteen, he started to Africa in company with the great missionary explorer F. S. Arnot. His work was to be at Katanga on the borderland of Northern Rhodesia and the Belgian Congo. In 1895 he formed his mission at the point where the Luanza River flows into Lake Mweru. A town sprang up which was called Luanza, fashioned after the towns of Crawford's home country. In 1895 Crawford wrote to Scotland to Miss Grace Tilsley asking her to become his wife. They were married in 1898 at the consulate in Blantyre, Nyasaland. In 1911 Dan Crawford took his first and only furlough home. In 1913 he visited the United States and Canada; and the next year Australia. In 1915 he was back at Luanza on Lake Mweru. During his absence the Roman Catholic Mission entered his territory and took advantage of the foundation he had laid. His rebuilding task was heavy, and he refused to take another furlough. In his *Thinking Black,* his missionary principle and practice is given, namely, that the missionary must think with the people and identify himself with them. He also wrote *Back to the Long Grass.* Other literary work was chiefly that of translating readers, prayer books, catechisms, and the Bible into Luba by 1926.

CREMER, AUGUST HERRMANN (1834-1903), German linguist and theologian. Professor of theology at Grefswald from 1870 to 1890 as well as being a pastor. Greatest work was *Biblico-Theological Lexicon of the New Testament* (1878, English translation), the forerunner of Kittel's later great work.

CROMWELL, OLIVER (1599-1658), soldier and statesman; Lord Protector of the Commonwealth, born in Huntingdon, England, educated at the free school of Huntingdon under an austere Puritan, and at Sidney Sussex College at Cambridge, a stronghold of Puritanism. In 1628 elected to Parliament from Huntingdon. Became a zealous advocate of toleration and freedom in religious matters. Inclined toward the Independents or Congregationalists. In 1640 sent by Cambridge as a member of the Short Parliament, where he joined in the protest against the abuses in church and state under King Charles I. In the Long Parliament (1640-1653) he early attracted attention by the vehemence of his oratory in attacking the arbitrary rule of the king and the abuses in the church, in demanding the abolition of episcopacy. In the ensuing First Civil War (1642-1646) Cromwell became the outstanding leader and won every battle with his cavalry. In 1648 ordered Pride, one of his generals, to purge Parliament of all the members who opposed the army's policies. Thus it was possible during the Second Civil War (1648-1649) for the purged Parliament to sentence Charles I to be executed, to abolish the office of king and the House of Lords, and to establish the Commonwealth. Cromwell was one of the signers of the king's death warrant. In 1649 after the establishment of the Commonwealth with Cromwell as Lord Protector, or President, Cromwell brought Scotland and Protestant Ireland under his sway. He pursued a vigorous policy at home and on the sea. He was considered a champion of religious liberty, yet ruled in church and state with a firm hand. Parliament made him in 1653 Lord Protector and in 1656 offered him the crown; but he refused it. Cruel, brutal treatment of the Catholic Irish leaves a dark stain on his memory. When Charles II raised the Stuart banner in Scotland, Cromwell defeated him. In 1660 Charles II was restored to the throne. One of the first acts of the restored king was to hang the body of Cromwell and then to bury it beneath the gallows. In 1899 Parliament erected a statue to Oliver Cromwell in Westminster.

CROMWELL, THOMAS (c. 1485-1540), Protestant Lord Chancellor under Henry VIII, born in Putney of humble parentage, and received a limited education, served as a soldier in the French army, and made somewhat of a fortune in money lending. On returning to England about 1513 he became legal adviser and supporter of Cardinal Wolsey until the Cardinal's death in 1530. In 1523 he sat in Parliament and supported King Henry VIII. Henry made him Lord Chancellor to succeed Thomas More in which capacity he attempted to support the absolute monarchy of Henry VIII. He supported the cause of the Reformation, urging the king to ignore the supremacy of the papacy and to declare himself the head of the Church of England. The Reformation Acts between 1532 and 1539 were largely Cromwell's work, and he dissolved the monasteries. He was an ardent advocate of the principle of supremacy of the temporal sovereign of the church in the matters of government. He overstepped wisdom when he persuaded Henry to marry Anne of Cleves in 1540. Henry developed a repugnance for her from the first. In 1540 was tried for treason, and beheaded on Tower Hill.

CROSBY, FANNY (MRS. FRANCES JANE CROSBY VAN ALSTYNE) (1820-1915), American hymn writer, born in Southeast, Putnam County, New York. She became blind at six weeks of age. She received her formal education from an institution for the blind in New York City, which she entered in 1835. She was student for twelve years, then a teacher from 1848 until her marriage in 1858. Though she had grown up with a strong religious bent, it was in 1850 at the age of thirty, during a revival meeting, she gave her heart to Christ. In 1858 she married Mr. Alexander Van Alstyne, a gifted blind teacher at the institute. Being a Christian organist he wrote the music for many of Fanny's songs. She greatly appreciated the spiritual fellowship, encouragement, and inspiration of D. L. Moody, I. D. Sankey, George B. Stebbins, William H. Doane and P. P. Bliss. When twenty-four she published her first book of poems, *The Blind Girl and Other Poems.* She wrote a large number of secular and religious poems, a few cantatas, and many songs. Her real contribution to musical literature lay in her beautiful, inspirational hymns. The total number of her hymns and poems likely exceeded eight thousand. Her outstanding hymns are "Safe in the Arms of Jesus," "Pass Me Not, O Gentle Saviour," "Rescue the Perishing," "Some Day the Silver Cord Will Break," "Blessed Assurance," "Thou, My Everlasting Portion," "Tell Me the Story of Jesus," "Will Jesus Find Us Watching?," "Jesus is Tenderly Calling," "Praise Him! Praise Him!," "To God Be the Glory," "Redeemed," "He Hideth My Soul," "All the Way My Saviour Leads Me," "Draw Me Nearer," "Close to Thee," "Near the Cross," "Saved by Grace," and "Saviour, More Than Life to Me."

CROWTHER (krou'ther), **SAMUEL ADJAI** (ăj'ī), (c. 1806-1891), first black bishop of the Anglican church, born at Oshogun in Yoruba, Nigeria, West Africa. In 1821 captured by Mohammedan slave raiders, sold to Portuguese slavers, and shipped from Lagos; but freed with other slaves by a British man-of-war in 1822. Placed in a mission school at Bathurst, Sierra Leone. An apt pupil, and at about age fifteen became a Christian, taking the name of Samuel Adjai Crowther. In 1826 taken to England on a visit where he spent part of a year in a parochial school at Islington, London. In 1827 one of the first natives to enter Fourah Bay College in Sierra Leone, where he was ordained, later became an instructor and subsequently was made principal. Finished his education in the Church Missionary College in London, and took orders in the Church of England in 1843. Became a missionary at Akessa in the Niger country. Having a talent for language, he studied Latin and Greek, and knew also several of the tribal languages. He was sent on several exploratory expeditions, then later frequently retraced his journeys teaching and preaching, continuing this preaching and the establishing of missions and schools the rest of his life. Made several trips to England in his endeavor to stop the slave trade among his people. After twenty-five years of separation, Crowther had the joy of being reunited with his mother and two sisters; two years later seeing them become Christians, the first fruits of his mission. He prepared a dictionary and grammar and translated part of the New Testament and the Prayer Book into the Yoruba language. He prepared vocabularies, grammars, and school books in several other languages also. In 1864 he was consecrated in Canterbury Cathedral in London as the first bishop of the Niger territories, and filled his position with honor. In 1888 Bishop Crowther was an outstanding personality in attendance at the World Missionary Convention in London.

CRUDEN, ALEXANDER (c. 1699-1770), Scottish bookseller and Bible concordance compiler, born in Aberdeen, Scotland, educated at Marischal College, Aberdeen University, with a view to the ministry. Aberration of mind led to confinement in 1720, 1738, and 1753 in an institution. Upon recovery became a private tutor for ten years, 1722-1732. Settled in London as a bookseller and a proof corrector; and after a time became bookseller to the queen. In 1737 issued his immortal work, *A Complete Concordance of the Holy Scriptures of the Old and New Testaments,* and dedicated it to Queen Caroline. Three editions were published between 1737 and 1769. Received only about $15,000 for his work. Considered it his divine call to correct the morals of the nation, especially with regard to profanity and Sabbath-breaking, and adopted for himself the title, "Alexander the Corrector." He solicited knighthood from the king; sought a seat in Parliament from the people; and courted the daughter of the Lord Mayor. In the last ten years of his life he twice revised his concordance, and seemed to enjoy a more nearly normal state of mental health. Among his other writings, *A Scripture Dictionary,* and an autobiography, *Adventures of Alexander the Corrector.* Cruden was a humble and devout Christian, a sincere lover of the Bible, a member of an Independent Church in London, and a public-spirited citizen. Found dead on his knees while engaged in prayer.

CRUGER (krü'gẽr), **JOHANN** (1598-1662), German composer of choral music and organist, born at Grossbresen, near Guben, Prussia, received education at the Jesuit college at Olmütz, the school of poetry at Regensburg, and at the University of Wittenberg. Organist of the St. Nicolai Church in Berlin the last forty years of his life. Composed fine chorals for the Protestant church. Best known of Crüger's works were published in 1644 in a volume entitled *Praxis Pietatis Melica,* which included "Nun Danket Alle Gott," "Jesu meine Freude," "Schmücke dich, O liebe Seele." He set a large number of Paul Gerhardt's hymns to music. Composed motets and concertos and was author of treatises on musical theory.

CUDWORTH, RALPH (1617-1688), English philosopher and chief Cambridge Platonist, born at Aller, Somersetshire, England, educated at Emmanuel College, Cambridge. Became successively fellow of Emmanuel College, rector of North Cadbury, master of Clare Hall, regius professor of Hebrew, master of Christ College, vicar of Ashwell, Herefordshire, and prebendary of Gloucester. In his sermons he advocated principles of tolerance and charity. Stood boldly as a champion of revealed religion as against the prevalent deism, fatalism, and irreligion of the age. Opposed to the materialistic philosophy of Thomas Hobbes. Chief work, *The True Intellectual System of the Universe, Wherein All the Reason and Philosophy of Atheism is Refuted,* in which he sought to establish a supreme divine intelligence, to refute determinism or materialistic atheism, and to show that the only real source of knowledge lies in the Christian religion. In posthumous *Treatise on Eternal and Immutable Morality,* and in *Treatise on Free Will* sought to justify moral ideals and to uphold the reality of moral freedom and responsibility of man for his own actions.

CULBERSTON, WILLIAM (1905-1971), born in Philadelphia, Pennsylvania. Educated at Temple University and the Reformed Episcopal Seminary. Ordained 1928. Became bishop in 1937. From 1927 to 1942 ministered in Collingsdale, Pennsylvania, Ventnor, New Jersey, and Germantown in Philadelphia. Taught at Reformed Episcopal Seminary from 1929 to 1942. Lecturer and dean at Moody Bible Institute from 1942 to 1947 and president from 1948 to 1971. Assistant editor of the *Episcopal Recorder* (1923-1927), associate and then editor of *Moody Monthly* from 1937 to 1971.

CUMMING, JOHN (1807-1881), Scottish preacher and writer on prophecy, born at Fintray, near Aberdeen, Scotland, educated at King's College, Aberdeen, served for a while as private tutor. In 1832 licensed to preach and called to the National Scottish Church at Crown Court Covent Garden, London, where he remained until near the end of his life. Preaching attracted such large congregations that church had to be rebuilt and enlarged. Popular as an effective and strong evangelical preacher; but attained greater popularity as a controversialist. He strongly opposed the disruption in 1843; and also attacked Roman Catholicism and papal aggression. Opposed those who differed from him on apocalyptic interpretation. Chief among his more than two hundred publications of various kinds are the following, *Is Christianity from God?; Apocalyptic Sketches; Prophetic Studies—Daniel; Signs of the Times, or Past, Present and Future; The Great Tribulation; The Millennial Rest; Redemption Draweth Nigh; Destiny of the Nations; The Seventh Vial; The Fall of Babylon, Forshadowed in her Teachings, in History, and in Prophecy; The Sounding of the Last Woe;* and *Ritualism, the Highway to Rome*.

CUMMINS, GEORGE DAVID (1822-1876), a founder of the Reformed Protestant Episcopal church, born near Smyrna, in Kent County, Delaware, educated at Dickinson College, Carlisle, Pennsylvania. Served two years as a Methodist minister, changed to the Protestant Episcopal church, and was ordained deacon in 1845. Between 1846 and 1863 held charges in several Protestant Episcopal churches in Baltimore, Norfolk, Richmond, Washington, and Chicago. In 1866 consecrated assistant bishop of Kentucky. A leader in the Low Church party, favored a revision of the prayer book. In 1873 officiated at a joint communion service held in connection with a conference of the Evangelical Alliance in New York, for which he was sharply criticized. A month later, he withdrew from the Protestant Episcopal church, declaring that he could no longer be bound by the rigid and exclusive ritualism. Later the same year (1873), after several conferences, eight clergymen and twenty laymen met in New York City and organized Reformed Protestant Episcopal church, of which he became the first presiding bishop. He was formally deposed by the Protestant Episcopal church in 1874.

CUNNINGHAM, WILLIAM (1805-1861), Scottish Free Church theologian, born at Hamilton near Glasgow, Scotland, studied at the University of Edinburgh under Dr. Thomas Chalmers, licensed in 1828 and became assistant minister of the Middle Church, Greenock in 1830. In 1834 received charge of Trinity College parish, Edinburgh. In the stormy discussion that preceded the disruption of 1843 he was a powerful advocate of the cause of the Free church. Appointed professor in 1845 of church history and divinity of the Free church's New College, Edinburgh, of which he followed Dr. Chalmers as principal in 1847. Before entering upon teaching, however, he was commissioned by the General Assembly to visit the United States to make a study of theological institutions and methods there. In the United States he formed a warm and sympathetic friendship with Dr. C. C. Hodge of Princeton. In 1859 he was moderator of the General Assembly. He was the founder of the Evangelical Alliance. In doctrine a thoroughgoing Calvinist; said to have been the ablest defender of Calvinism in his day. *The Reformers and the Theology of the Reformation, Discussions of Church Principles,* and *Historical Theology.*

CUTHBERT (d. c. 687), English monk, probably born near Melrose, Scotland. About 651 entered the famous monastery of Melrose, was made prior of the monastery about 661. After the Council of Whitby, 663, he seems to have accepted the Roman customs. He was then made prior of Lindisfarne. While at Lindisfarne spent much time evangelizing the people. In 676 decided to become a hermit, and retired to a cave and a very austere life. In 685 he was prevailed upon to return to Lindisfarne to be consecrated bishop. Within a few months, sensing that the end of life was near, he returned to his cell, died a few months later.

CYNEWULF (kĭn'e wŏŏlf), (or **CYNWULF**) (fl. from 750), early Anglo-Saxon poet, born in Northumbria or Mercia. He was a scholar, familiar with both Latin and religious literature. Late in life renounced the world and settled down in a quiet monastery or hermitage. Produced his four religious poems, *Juliana,* the story of the martyrdom of St. Juliana; *Elene* (Helena), a legend of the discovery of the true cross; *Christ,* celebrating the coming of Christ, His ascension, and the day of judgment; and *The Fates of the Apostles.*

CYPRIAN (sĭp'rĭ ăn), **THASCIUS CAECILIUS** (c. 200-258), Bishop of Carthage, born near Carthage, North Africa. Father a noble and wealthy Roman officer of high rank who gave his son a good Greek education. Became a Christian in middle life. Devoted himself to ascetic retirement, and to the study of the Scriptures and of great men of the church, especially Tertullian, whom he respected highly. In 248 or 249, after he had been a Christian only about a year, the church at Carthage made him a presbyter, and the next year prevailed upon him to occupy the vacant office of bishop. This placed him at the head of the North African clergy. It was a most stormy period with bitter persecutions raging without and schismatic agitations seething within the church. Administered his episcopal office with skill, energy, wisdom, and fidelity. When the onslaught of fierce persecution came many lapsed and denied the faith. Cyprian urged them to constancy. He retired from the public in order to escape seizure. He continued in his official capacity while in seclusion, writing to his presbyters, deacons, and laymen, encouraging them to be faithful and true. Assured them that he would return as soon as God showed him it was His will. In dealing with the lapsed after persecution was over, he was rigid, demanding confession and unmistakable evidence of penitence. Cyprian returned to Carthage A.D. 251, after the severe wave of persecution was past, having been in retirement about two years. In the same years presided over a council at Carthage, in which it was decided that pardon could be granted the lapsed, but only after a proper period of penitence. In 257 Valerian issued an edict that resulted in Cyprian's banishment. Then he was summoned to Utica to appear for trial. Refusing to deny the faith, he was ordered to be executed. That followed immediately. Cyprian wrote a number of epistles, the most important being *De Unitate Ecclesiae*. In this he declared that the unity of the church rested in episcopate, making the bishops representatives of the apostles, thus making the chair of Peter the center of episcopal unity. He gave Peter a primacy of honor in the church.

CYRIL (sĭ rĕl), or **CYRILLUS,** original name **CONSTANTINUS** (c. 826-869), missionary to the Slavs, born in Thessalonica, studied at Constantinople. He and brother Methodius (c. 815-885) both monks and priests in the Eastern Catholic church, in 860 went to the Khazars, a Tartar tribe on the northeast shore of the Black Sea, and planted a church. For a while they worked among the Bulgars whose king was Boris or Bogaris. About 862, in answer to an invitation from Duke Ratislav of Moravia, Emperor Michael III sent Cyril and his brother to Moravia, where they labored with great success. Cyril invented an alphabet and translated the Bible into the Slavic language. In 868 he and Methodius went to Rome and effected an agreement with Pope Adrian II for the use of the Slavic language; their work thus came under the supervision of the Roman church. In 869 Cyril died while in Rome. His brother returned to Moravia having been consecrated archbishop.

CYRIL OF ALEXANDRIA (376-444), patriarch of Alexandria and theologian. Succeeded his uncle as patriarch of Alexandria about 412. A member of the synod that condemned Chrysostom. Soon after taking office as archbishop he closed the doors and seized the property of the Novatians as heretics. When in 415 the Jews in Alexandria, because of his injustice toward them, raised a riot, Cyril authorized an armed onslaught on their synagogues. Before, at, and after the Council of Ephesus in 431, Cyril was the able and violent opponent of Nestorius and his teachings. Even convened the council before John of Antioch had arrived. The victory was at the cost of schism in the church. As preacher and theologian Cyril is entitled to consideration. He was an able exponent of the Alexandrian school. He wrote and sent out circle letters to the churches of his dioceses vigorously defending the doctrine of the trinity and the doctrine of Mary, Mother of God, which were being debated so heatedly between the orthodox party and the Nestorian party.

CYRIL OF JERUSALEM (c. 315-c. 386), Bishop, born at or near Jerusalem, well versed in the Scriptures and had broad, general education. About 330 ordained a deacon in the Jerusalem church, and about

342 appointed presbyter and charged with the task of instructing catechumens in preparation for baptism. The lectures he prepared for and gave to candidates for baptism, he also often preached to his congregation. In 350 Cyril was elected bishop of Jerusalem. His writings give strong evidence of orthodoxy. In 381, present at the second Council at Constantinople and stood in rank with the bishops of Alexandria and Antioch as chiefs among the metropolitans. Joined with them in declaring full adherence to the Nicene faith. Died having been bishop of Jerusalem thirty-five years, sixteen of which were passed in exile.

D

DABNEY, ROBERT (1820-1898) Theologian. Born in Louisa Co., Virginia. Graduated from the University of Virginia and Union Seminary, Richmond. Minister of Tinkling Springs Church (1847-1853). From 1853 to 1883 professor of theology in Union Seminary, and from 1883 to 1894 at the University of Texas. Helped found Austin Theological Seminary and important in the development of the Southern Presbyterian church. His *Syllabus and Notes of the Course of Systematic and Polemic Theology,* taught in the Union Seminary in Virginia, went through many editions until 1927. Served over a year as chaplain in the Confederate Army.

DA COSTA, IZAAK (1798-1860), Dutch poet and Reformed theologian, born in Amsterdam of Jewish parents of Portuguese ancestry. Studied at Amsterdam and at Leiden. In 1822 came under the impelling influence of the poet, Willem Bilderdijk, who won the young man from Voltaire's deism. Upon conversion and baptism in 1822, became an ardent Christian and defender of his new faith. Christian writing and influence made a vital contribution to the orthodoxy and spirituality of the Reformed church. In 1839 there resulted a schism that developed into a separate church to be known as the Christian Reformed church. Dr. Abraham Kuyper, who for a long time remained with the Orthodox wing of the established Reformed church, finally withdrew and united with the Da Costa separates. Toward the close of his life Da Costa became professor and director of the seminary established in Amsterdam in connection with the mission of the Free Church of Scotland. Da Costa ranked first among the poets of Holland after the death of Bilderdijk. Known largely for poetry, he also wrote theological books.

D'AILLY, *See* **AILLY, PIERRE DE.**

DALE, ROBERT WILLIAM (1829-1895), English Congregational preacher and educational reformer, born in London, England. Studied at Spring Hill College, Birmingham, received Master of Arts degree from the University of London, then taught school for a while. In 1854 ordained and became associate pastor with John Angell James in Carr's Lane chapel. In 1859, Dale became sole pastor, remaining in this position until 1895. Dr. Dale was distinguished as a preacher, author, educator and statesman. He was as deeply concerned about the salvation of the "up and out" as of the "down and out." A man of affairs, he lent his active service to national, municipal, educational, and philanthropic realms of life. He sat on the Birmingham school board, served on the royal commission of education, was one of the founders of Mansfield College, Oxford. At age forty he became chairman of the Congregational Union of England and Wales. For seven years he was editor of the *Congregationalist.* In 1875 he assisted D. L. Moody in his campaign in Birmingham. In 1877 delivered the Lyman Beecher lectures at Yale; in 1891 was president of the first International Council of Congregationalists. Some of his many writings were: *The Life and Letters of the Rev. John Angell James, On the Atonement* (his most important work), *Lectures on Preaching,* and *Christian Doctrine.*

DAMASUS I (c. 305-384), born in Rome of Spanish ancestry. Pope from 366. Condemned Apollinarianism and Macedonianism. Issued the Tome in 382 as a collection of the canons of councils against heresies. Asked Jerome, his secretary, to revise the inferior Latin translations of the Bible. Jerome's Vulgate, which included the Apocrypha became the official Roman Catholic Bible at the Council of Trent.

DAMIEN (då myăn') **de VEUSTER** (vûs târ'), **JOSEPH** (1840-1889), Roman Catholic missionary to Hawaii, born at Tremeloo, near Louvain, Belgium. Educated at Louvain and Paris. At twenty admitted to the Congregation of the Picpus Fathers. In 1864, as a substitute for his brother who had fallen ill with typhus fever on the eve of sailing for the mission field, he went to Hawaii as a missionary, and was there ordained a priest in 1864. After nine years of arduous missionary work, Father Damien offered to go to the island of Molokai where all the lepers of the islands were being forcibly segregated by law. Became not only priest, pastor, preacher, and catechist, but also doctor, nurse, undertaker, coffin-maker, and grave digger. Became head mason and carpenter-in-chief of the island. Got the people to do much of the work, but what they could not do, he did. He built two orphanages, one for the boys and one for the girls. One day made the discovery that the fatal disease had laid hold on him. Before his death, after sixteen years of labor on Molokai, he had the joy of knowing that the work started and carried on so well would be well cared for. A band of

Franciscan Sisters volunteered to serve as nurses among the lepers of Molokai; two young priests were ready to take over.

DANIEL-ROPS, (PETIOT) HENRI (1901-1965), French Roman Catholic church historian. Born Epinal, Vosges. Educated at the University of Grenoble in history. High School teacher from 1922 to 1946. Published novels, short stories, essays, and a twelve-volume history of the church.

DANTE ALIGHIERI (dăn′ty ä lē gyâ′rē) (1265-1321), the most eminent Italian poet, born at Florence, Italy, received a liberal education at Bologna, Padua, Naples, Paris, and Oxford. Belonged to the Guelph or papal family. At twenty-five became a soldier and helped in the war against the imperialistic Ghibellines. About 1302 his property was confiscated and he was banished from Florence. Dante's chief works were *Vita Nuova,* written in memory of Beatrice, and *De Monarchia.* In his *De Monarchia,* Dante held that empire is as necessary for man's temporal peace and happiness as papacy is for his eternal blessedness. Both are from God and neither should interfere with the other. Advocated the calling of a general council to settle the Great Schism. The pope placed *De Monarchia* on the Index. His *Divina Commedia,* the first great Christian poem, is a poetic view of the moral universe setting forth the three conditions of man—sin, repentance, and salvation. The great poem depicts Dante with the guidance of the shade of the poet Virgil ascending by stages from the lowest parts of Inferno up through Purgatory. At the very apex he met Beatrice who guided him up through Paradise. In the various sections of the three regions he placed the men and women of past generations according to their individual dues, whether popes, bishops, emperors, nobles, or common folk. This was work that brought him universal fame. As a theologian, the voice of medieval faith, following closely the thought and teaching of Thomas Aquinas. As a man of letters, the creator of Italian poetry.

DARBY, JOHN NELSON (1800-1882), chief founder and early leader of the Plymouth Brethren, born in London, graduated from Trinity College, Dublin, where he was educated for the bar. Admitted to the bar in 1825, began the practice of law, but soon gave it up, took orders, and served a curacy in the Church of Ireland for a short time. Doubts as to the scriptural authority for church establishments led him to resign his position and to leave the church in 1827. He joined with a little group of like-minded persons in Dublin, who were opposed to denominationalism, formal church membership, nonscriptural church names, and a one-man ministry. In 1830 he visited Paris, Cambridge, and Oxford to promote his views, and went to Plymouth, where an assembly of the Brethren had recently been formed. This group of worshipers became known as the Brethren from Plymouth, and finally, quite generally, as Plymouth Brethren. Between 1838 and 1845 Darby worked in France and Switzerland. There many congregations of the Brethren were formed. When through Jesuit intrigue revolution broke out in Switzerland in 1845, some of the Darbyites suffered persecution and Darby's life was in danger. He returned to England and became more active in behalf of the English Brethren though he longed to continue his work in Switzerland and France. At this time dissension broke out among the Brethren at Plymouth. B. W. Newton, one of the members in this congregation entertained views on prophecy and church order that differed from those held by Darby. A controversy arose and spread to other assemblies, and new controversies developed. Consequently there came into being exclusive or separate Brethren, as they exist today. Darby translated the New Testament into both German and French, as well as doing an English translation. He also assisted in translating the Old Testament into both German and French. Between 1853 and the time of his death in 1882 he made at least three trips to Germany, spent considerable time in France, made six journeys to Canada and the United States, and visited Italy, New Zealand, and the West Indies. He was a hymn-writer and edited the hymnbook generally used by the Brethren.

DARROW, CLARENCE (1857-1938), lawyer. Educated at Allegheny College and the University of Michigan. Practiced law in Chicago. Chief counsel for John T. Scopes in the 1925 evolution trial in Tennessee and bitter opponent of William Jennings Bryan, the opposing lawyer.

DARWIN, CHARLES ROBERT (1809-1882), English naturalist, born in Shrewsbury, England. After doing academy work at Shrewsbury, went to Edinburgh University to study medicine, and then Christ College, Cambridge to study theology. His father designed him for the ministry; eventually he turned from his Christian faith to agnosticism. His interest turned to geology and biology. In 1831 studied geology on an excursion in North Wales. He received an appointment as naturalist on board the "Beagle," which spent five years on a surveying trip around the world from 1831 to 1836. Darwin's views and writings on natural selection, and survival of the fittest were bitterly opposed by many Christians. Darwin substituted mechanical and natural for biblical and supernatural explanations of the origin of the forms of life. His theories tended to make the accepted Christian faith untenable for many Christians. Some of his writings resulted from his trip on the "Beagle": *Journal of Researches, Zoology of the Voyage of H.M.S. Beagle, Structure and Distribution of Coral Reefs, Volcanic Islands,* and *Geological Observations.* Later writings were *Origin of the Species by Means of Natural Selection,* and *The Descent of Man in Relation to Sex.*

D'AUBIGNE, JEAN HENRI MERLE (1794-1872), evangelical Swiss historian. Born near Geneva and educated there. Influenced by Scottish evangelical Robert Haldane. Ordained in Berlin in 1817. Pastor of churches in Switzerland and Belgium (1818-1830). Professor in theological school in Geneva after 1830. Wrote multivolume histories of the Reformation in Europe from an evangelical viewpoint.

DAVENPORT, JAMES (1716-1757), eccentric Presbyterian revivalist minister. Born Stamford, Connecticut. Graduate of Yale. Pastor of several churches from 1738 to 1757. Influenced by George Whitefield. Excess in revival preachings and his sermon on "Unconverted Ministers" led to his expulsion from churches. Repented of excesses in 1744 in *Confessions and Retractions* and returned to regular parish ministry.

DAVENPORT, JOHN (1597-1670), cofounder and first minister of New Haven Colony, born at Coventry, Warwickshire, England, studied at Merton and Magdalen Colleges, Oxford, held several pastorates as a Church of England minister; because of nonconformity tendencies, came into conflict with Archbishop Laud, withdrew from the Church of England, and went to Holland, where for a time he was co-pastor of the English church at Amsterdam. Due to his preaching against the baptism of children whose parents were not church members, he met strong opposition and in 1635 was back in England. In 1637 he and a friend and member of his church, Theophilus Eaton, sailed with a band of colonists for New England, in 1638 founding the colony of New Haven at Quinnipiac. Eaton became governor of the colony. Davenport became pastor of the church of the new colony exercising powerful influence in pastorate of thirty years. In 1642 he declined an invitation to attend the Westminster Assembly; opposed the union of New Haven colony with Connecticut in 1665; opposed the Half-Way Covenant, which caused a split in the Boston church to which he had been called in 1667, resulting in the formation of Old South Church.

DAVID (c. 520-589), ascetic patron saint of the Welsh. Founded many monasteries. Established an abby at Minervia (Mynyur), became its bishop abbot, and built up an unusual library there.

DAVID, CHRISTIAN (1691-1751), one of the founders of Herrnhut, born at Senftleben, Moravia, of a Bohemian father and a German mother. In 1722 a few families of German-speaking Moravians began to emigrate from Moravia to Saxony, seeking asylum from persecution. Led by carpenter David, they found a warm welcome on the private estate of Count Zinzendorf in Berthelsdorf. In the course of the next few years David brought several hundred of these persecuted Moravian and Bohemian Brethren to the Berthelsdorf estate, or Herrnhut, as it was soon named. When the church was organized at Herrnhut, David was elected in 1727 one of the first of twelve elders. In 1733 he led the first Moravian mission to Greenland to help Hans Egede. The major part of his life was spent in making trips to his native Moravia, and in visiting missions in Greenland and America. He died in Herrnhut.

DAVIDSON, ANDREW BRUCE (1831-1902). United Free Church of Scotland scholar, born at Kirkhill, Aberdeenshire, Scotland, studied at Marischal College, Aberdeen. After teaching for three years in the Free Church School of Ellon, studied at New College (the Divinity Hall of the Free Church), Edinburgh, and graduated in 1856. Filled several pulpits temporarily, preached with great acceptance, but never held a charge. In 1858 became assistant professor of Hebrew in New College, and from 1863 to 1902 full professor. An influential member of the Old Testament Revision company, and recognized as the foremost British Biblical scholar and critic of his day. George Adam Smith and W. Robertson Smith were among his pupils. His literary work was relatively small in amount, but superior in quality. For the Cambridge Bible series he wrote commentaries on Job, Ezekiel, Nahum, Habakkuk, and Zephaniah. Other works were *An Introductory Hebrew Grammar* (widely used), *A Hebrew Syntax, Theology of the Old Testament, Called of God,* and *Waiting Upon God.* Died unmarried at Edinburgh in 1902.

DAVIDSON, RANDALL THOMAS, First Baron Davidson of Lambeth (1848-1930), Archbishop of Canterbury and primate of all England (1903-1928). Born in Scotland, studied at Harrow and Trinity College, Oxford; had special training for orders under Dr. Charles John Vaughan; ordained priest

(1875) church in Dartford, Kent, (1874-1878) Chaplain and private secretary to archbishops Tait (1877-1882) and E. W. Benson (1882-1883). Dean of Windsor and domestic chaplain for Queen Victoria, who placed much confidence in his counsel, (1883-1891). Bishop of Rochester (1891-1895), of Winchester (1895-1903), Archbishop of Canterbury (1903-1928). Was with Edward VII at death (1910); crowned George V (1911). Resigned in 1928 in order to give successor time to prepare for 1930 Lambeth Conference; then was created First Baron Davidson of Lambeth. In the 1928 prayer book controversy took a middle course. Presided at Sixth Lambeth Conference (1920); favored reunion of Christendom. Supported League of Nations; made important contributions in debates on temperance, divorce, labor, race, education, religious persecution, and other religious and moral issues.

DAVIES, SAMUEL (1723-1761) Father of Southern Presbyterianism. Born near Summit Ridge, New Jersey. Trained in Samuel Blair's School at Foggs Manor, Pennsylvania. Ordained in 1747. Evangelist to Hanover County, Virginia from 1748 to 1759 and the organizer of Presbyterianism in Virginia. Went to England with Gilbert Tennent in 1753 and raised 3,000 pounds for the College of New Jersey (Princeton University) and its president from 1759 to 1761.

DECIUS (dē'shĭ ŭs or dē'shŭs), **GAIUS MESSIUS QUINTUS TRAJANUS** (d. 251) Emperor of Rome, 249-251, born at Budalia, near Sirmium in lower Pannonia. Earlier life largely military. Became emperor and at once set about to organize the empire and to restore the old pagan religion and the old political absolutism. In the carrying out of ambitious plans saw in Christianity a formidable adversary, and determined to destroy it. In 250 instituted the first empire-wide persecution in an all-out effort to eradicate Christianity, issuing an edict requiring all Roman subjects, without exception, throughout the provinces, to sacrifice to the gods. Origen was severely tortured in prison in Caesarea, dying later from the ill treatment. The life of Cyprian of Carthage was spared for the time by his concealing himself. The persecution suddenly ceased when Decius was killed in Thrace in battle with the Goths (251); but it was renewed with great vigor under Valerian in 257, at which time Cyprian was martyred. From the apostatizing and lapsing of Christians under the persecutions of Decius and Valerian, and the trend toward receiving them back into the church, there arose the puritanic Novatian schism to plague the Catholic church for several centuries following.

DEISSMANN (dīs'män), **GUSTAV ADOLF** 1866-1937), German Lutheran theologian and linguist, born at Langenscheid, Nassau, Germany; studied at the universities of Tübingen and Berlin, and at theological seminaries at Hebron and Marburg. Ordained in 1890; and, after teaching at Hebron and Marburg for a time, was professor of New Testament exegesis at Heidelberg (1897-1908), and at Berlin (1908-1934). He was rector of the university (1930-1931). In 1906 made an archaeological tour of Asia Minor and Greece, and the next year lectured at the University of Cambridge, and in 1910 at the University of Upsala. Did distinguished pioneer work in biblical philology; pointed out that the New Testament Greek was the common Greek of the papyri; and made extensive use of the material gathered from the recently discovered papyri. His many writings included *Light from the Ancient East; Philology of the Greek Bible; The Religion of Jesus and the Faith of Paul; The New Testament in the Light of Modern Research; New Light on the New Testament from Records of the Graeco-Roman Period; Paul, a Study in Social and Religious History.* Dr. Deissmann was an indefatigable worker for international church unity, and served as a delegate to the World Church Conference in Stockholm (1925) and to the Lausanne Conference (1927).

DELITZSCH (dā'lĭch), **FRANZ JULIUS** (1813-1890), Lutheran Old Testament scholar, theologian, and orientalist, born at Leipzig of Hebrew ancestry, studied at University of Leipzig, where he became a teacher for a time in 1842. Became professor of theology at Rostock in 1846, at Erlangen in 1850, returned to Leipzig in 1867. Became connected with the new theological school of Lutheran confessionalism that was developing at the University of Erlangen. Interested himself in the conversion of the Jews, founded the Jewish Missionary College in 1877 for this purpose. Intimately acquainted with rabbinical literature. His Hebrew translation of the New Testament was widely distributed in Russia and Galatia. Delitzsch made his chief contribution in Old Testament exegesis, writing several commentaries, Job, Isaiah, Habakkuk, Proverbs, Psalms, Song of Solomon and Ecclesiastes, Genesis, and also on Hebrews, besides several others in collaboration with J. F. K. Keil.

DEMETRIUS (dē mē'trĭ ŭs), **OF ALEXANDRIA** (d. 231), Bishop of Alexandria. Eleventh bishop of Alexandria in 189, and took an active interest in the catechetical school, appointing Origen to succeed Clement when the latter retired under persecution about 203. When Origen took refuge in Caesarea on the occasion of the persecution of the Christians under Caracalla in 215-216, and was invited by the bishops of Caesarea and Jerusalem to preach, Demetrius objected that a layman should preach, and called him back to Alexandria. About 230 when Origen was again in Caesarea on a business trip, the bishops there ordained him a presbyter. This greatly incensed Bishop Demetrius, and he called two synods in Alexandria which condemned and banished Origen.

DENCK (dĕngk), **JOHANNES (HANS)** (c. 1495-1527), a mystic, Anabaptist reformer. He taught an inner light superior to all Scriptures and saw in Christ the highest human example of love. In 1521 studying at Basel, he attended the lectures of Oecolampadius. In 1523 he was at Nürnberg as rector of the school of St. Sebaldus. For unorthodox views he was brought to trial at Nürnberg and expelled from the city for life. In 1525 in Augsburg he was baptized by Hübmaier and thus formally joined the Anabaptists. He was given a teaching position; and through his influence the number of Anabaptists increased rapidly. Opposition followed and in 1526 he moved to Strassburg. In the disputation with Bucer and Capito, he was defeated and driven from the city. He went to Worms, but there met the same fate. In 1527 he presided over the Synod of the Austrian Anabaptists. After the synod Denck went to Basel, Switzerland.

DENNEY, JAMES (1856-1917), United Free Church of Scotland theologian, born at Paisley, Scotland. After graduating from Glasgow University, studied theology at the Free Church College, Glasgow. Pastor of East Free Church, Broughty Ferry, Fifeshire, from 1886 to 1897; and from 1897 to 1915 professor of New Testament language, literature, and theology in the United Free Church College, and principal from 1915 to 1917. Wrote *The Epistles to the Thessalonians* and *The Second Epistle to the Corinthians* in the *Expositor's Bible;* and *The Epistle to the Romans* in the *Expositor's Greek Testament*. In theology he adhered firmly to the traditional doctrine of the Person of Christ, as seen in his works: *The Death of Christ, Jesus and the Gospel, The Atonement and the Modern Mind, The Doctrine of Reconciliation* and *Studies in Theology.* In later years Denney moved doctrinally from a somewhat liberal to an evangelical position, and became more and more involved in the administrative activities of the United Free Church after 1900. In his later years, too, he took a leading part in the negotiations for reunion with the Established Church of Scotland. These toils and anxieties probably shortened his life.

DE NOBILI, ROBERT (1577-1656), Jesuit missionary in India. Born at Montepulciano. Became a Jesuit about 1596 and went to India in 1605. Sought to separate Christianity from its western cultural dress by adopting Indian dress and customs. Served until he retired to Myalfore in 1654. Several thousand converts under his preaching.

DE ROSSI, GIOVANNI BATTISTA (1822-1894), archaeological rediscoverer of the catacombs. Born in Rome. Educated at the Collegio Romano and in law. Served as a scriptor in the Vatican Library. From 1841 explored the geology of and the inscriptions in the catacombs, on which he wrote extensively. Founded in 1863 and edited for 30 years the *Bulletino di Archeologia Cristiana*.

DESCARTES (dā kärt′), **RENE** (1596-1650), French philosopher and noted mathematician, born at La Haye, near Tours, France, educated at the Jesuit school of La Fleche. He served in the army from 1612 to 1615 and traveled for some years in France and Italy. Then in 1629, at the age of thirty-three he settled in Holland to study and to write. His philosophical system started with self-consciousness as the basis of all positive knowledge. Discarding all accepted or traditional ideas, he would seek knowledge and truth on the basis of provisional doubt. He would start with *Dubito ut intelligam* (I doubt that I might know). This led him to the conviction, *Cogito ergo sum* (I know, therefore I am). He proved to his own satisfaction the existence of his soul or mind. He assured himself of the existence of his body, thus arriving at the acceptance of the scholastic principle of *dualism* (both mind and body) as over against the *idealism* of Berkeley and the *materialism* of Thomas Huxley. From this point he proceeded to prove that God, the great cause of his existence, must exist. For twenty years Descartes lived in seclusion in various parts of Holland meditating, studying, writing his philosophy, and working out his mathematical system. His chief works were *La Monde,* which gives his views of the origin and nature of the universe; *Discussion on Method of Reasoning: Principles of Philosophy;* and *Geometry.* In 1649 he went to Sweden at the urgent invitation of Queen Christina, and died there a few months later.

DEWEY, JOHN (1859-1952), American philosopher, psychologist, educator, born at Burlington, Vermont, studied at the University of Vermont and at Johns Hopkins University. Taught philosophy at the University of Michigan (1884-1888 and 1889-1894) and at the University of Minnesota (1888-1889). Professor of philosophy, psychology, and pedagogy at the University of Chicago (1894-1904), and professor of philosophy at Columbia University (1904-1930). His philosophy of "progressive education," based on the theory of learning by doing, has had a great influence on teachers and schools across the country. Dewey traveled very widely visiting China, Japan, Turkey, Mexico, Russia, and England, studying their educational systems and their ways of living and thinking. He expressed the results of these studies in his *Reconstruction in Philosophy* and in *Impressions.* His major contributions to education include such ideas as that the child is more important than the subject matter; learning must be related to age; schools should be democratic and not authoritarian in spirit; discipline comes from within and not from without; learning can be taught by experience, "immediate empiricism" or "instrumentalism"; education must aim at developing character; and an adequate philosophy of education must underlie the whole educative process. His humanistic philosophy was basically a denial of the Christian faith. Many feel that his materialistic and humanistic approach to education has been inimical to religion, and that his failure to take religion seriously makes his educational philosophy inadequate. He published hundreds of articles and over twenty-five books, including, *Psychology, Critical Theory of Ethics, School and Society, How We Think, Influence of Darwin on Philosophy, Democracy and Education, Human Nature and Conduct, Experience and Education, Experience and Nature, The Quest for Certainty, Liberalism and Social Action, Freedom and Culture, Education Today,* and *Problems of Man*. "Among his philosophical colleagues he stands with William James as one of the two great American leaders of the pragmatic movement."

DIBELIUS, MARTIN (1883-1947), German theologian and New Testament scholar. Native of Dresden. Educated at the universities of Leipzig, Tubingen, and Berlin. Professor at the University of Berlin (1910-1915) and of Heidelberg (1915-1947). Moved from Semitic languages and cultural studies to New Testament studies. Pioneer of Form criticism. Believed that gospels have kernel of truth in forms such as myths and paradigms. Wrote *Die Formgeschichte des Evangeliums.* Leader in the Faith and Order movement.

DIBELIUS, OTTO (1880-1967), German Lutheran bishop. Born in Germany. Studied theology at Wittenberg. Reformed church pastor from 1915 to 1925. Lost his position as Lutheran superintendent (1925) in Berlin in 1933 when he refused to recognize the authority of Hitler's appointee. Supported the 1934 Barmen Declaration of Christ's primacy as Head of the church. Bishop of Berlin from 1945. Helped to create the German Evangelical Church and was its presiding bishop. Resisted both Nazis before 1945 and the Communists after 1945. One of the World Council of Churches presidents from 1954 to 1961. Present at the World Congress on Evangelism in 1966 in Berlin.

DICKINSON, JONATHAN (1688-1747), American Presbyterian clergyman, born at Hatfield, Massachusetts, attended college at Yale. After graduation ordained in the Congregational church, became pastor of Congregational churches in and near Elizabethtown, New Jersey; but soon went into the Presbyterian church in the Philadelphia Synod, taking with him the most of the members of these churches. Remained the pastor there until his death thirty years later. Twice moderator of his synod, a dynamic and aggressive leader of his denomination doing for the Middle Colonies much that Jonathan Edwards was doing for the church in New England. An acknowledged leader in the Philadelphia Synod, also later in the New York Synod, which he helped to organize. Dickinson did much to encourage revival in the Presbyterian church during the time of George Whitefield's revival preaching in the period of the Great Awakening. David Brainerd and Indian missions found a warm friend in him. He was a thoroughgoing Calvinist. Dickinson did much to effect harmony between factions in the Presbyterian church which resulted from controversy on the revival movement, then sweeping the area, and was largely influential in restoring unity and union after the short schism. He obtained the charter for opening the College of New Jersey in 1746 (now Princeton University). The first classes were opened in his home in Elizabethtown; he was elected first president, though he was privileged to serve less than a year. Wrote *Display of God's Special Grace, Vindication of God's Saving Free Grace,* and *True Scripture Doctrine Concerning Some Important Points in Christian Faith* (an able discussion of the five points of Calvinism).

DIDEROT (dē drō'), **DENIS** (1713-1784), French encyclopedist, born in Langres in Champagne, France, and educated by the Jesuits in Langres, also studied literature, languages, and science at the College d' Harcourt in Paris. In 1746 published *Pensees Philosophiques,* a work on natural religion, which was burned by order of the Parliament of Paris. Two years later published his *Lettre sur les Aveugles,* the materialistic doctrine of which led to three months of imprisonment at Vincennes. Then in collaboration with Jean le Rond d'Alembert, the mathematician, he began writing a large rationalistic, deistic encyclopedia of universal knowledge. The work was completed in 1772 as the *Encyclopedie, ou Dictionnarei Raisonne des Sciences, des Arts, et des Metiers* in twenty-eight volumes, eight more volumes being added later. Diderot received financial support from Catherine II of Russia who bought his valuable library, but left him the use of it for the rest of his life. Though educated by the Jesuits, he became one of the bitterest enemies of the church.

DIDYMUS (dĭd'ĭ mŭs) the Blind of Alexandria (c. 313-398), one of the last teachers of the Alexandrian catechetical school. He was connected with the catechetical school for more than fifty years, and had as one of his noted pupils the great Jerome. Didymus was a follower of Origen and adopted some of the errors into which Origen fell. Yet as was Origen, he was, in the main, a staunch defender of orthodox truth, being a firm Christian, and a man of excellent Christian character. He wrote commentaries on Micah, Hosea, and Zechariah.

DIFFENDORFER (dĭf fĕn dôrf' ẽr), **RALPH EUGENE** (1879-1951), American Methodist, born at Hayesville, Ohio, and received education at Ohio Wesleyan University, Drew Theological Seminary, and Union Theological Seminary. Began church activities as assistant secretary of the Epworth League. For the major part of his life was connected in one way or another with the Home and Foreign Missionary Program of the Methodist Episcopal Church, for about thirty-five years being a secretary of a missionary board. He was delegate for his church to the First International Conference on Missionary Education in Lunteren, Holland, 1911; to the International Missionary Council, Jerusalem, 1928; to the Life and Work Council, Oxford, England, 1937; and to the International Missionary Council, Madras, India, 1938. He was delegate also to the United Methodist Conference at Kansas City, Missouri in 1939. In 1941 he was a member of the Methodist Deputation to Japan. Diffendorfer was prominent also in the work of the Federal Council of the Churches of Christ in North America; on the Foreign Missions Conference of North America; on the Committee on Co-operation in Latin America; and in Church World Service. After 1949 he was director of the Japan International Christian University. Some of his writings: *A Modern Disciple of Jesus Christ: David Livingstone; Missionary Education in Home and School;* and *The Church and Missions in Japan.*

DIOCLETIAN (dī ō klē shăn) **or GAIUS AURELIUS VALERIUS DIOCLETIANUS** (c. 245-313), Roman emperor (284-305), born at Salona in Dalmatia. With Diocletian the absolute monarchy began. Diocletian appointed Maximian as co-emperor (Augustus) and Galerius and Constantius Chlorus as assistants (Caesars) in 292. Diocletian made Nicodemia rather than Rome his capital. The empire was divided into four parts. With the growing power and influence of the Christian church there seemed one of two procedures to follow, either to force the church into submission and break its power, or to enter into alliance with it and secure political control over it. Constantine pursued the latter course, and Diocletian the former. The fanatically pagan Galerius persuaded Diocletian that the total destruction of the church was necessary to the preservation of the empire; and in 303 the last and severest persecution against the Christians began suddenly and violently. Edicts against Christians were issued. The fourth edict in 304 ordered that all Christians without exception, upon pain of death, should be compelled to sacrifice to the gods. Many Christians yielded and lapsed. The persecution spread over the whole empire. Many of those who lapsed under the pressure later repented and sought re-admission to the church. In the interest of keeping the church pure there arose a schismatic movement known as Donatism which refused to receive these lapsed people back into the church. An edict of toleration was issued by Galerius and Constantine in 311. After a prosperous reign of twenty years, becoming weary of the cares of state, Diocletian abdicated the throne in 305.

DIODORUS (dī ō dō'rŭs), (d. c. 392), Bishop of Tarsus, born at Antioch, studied at Athens, and became a leader in the School of Antioch. He became head of a monastery in or near Antioch, and was also a presbyter there. Sometime after 378 he became bishop of Tarsus. He was a strong defender of the Nicene faith at the time that Arianism was raging and when the Melitian schism had rent the church of Antioch. A prominent churchman, taking an active part in the Council of Constantinople in 381, the teacher of two of the outstanding leaders of the church of his day, Theodore of Mopsuestia and John Chrysostom.

DIONYSIUS (dī ō nĭsh'ĭ ŭs) **THE AREOPAGITE** (First Century), Greek convert to Christianity. Probably born at Athens. Studied at Athens and in Egypt. According to

Dionysius of Corinth and Eusebius he was the first bishop of Athens. Became a judge in the Athenian court or the Areopagus. The writings often attributed to Dionysius were written by a pseudo-Dionysius in the fifth century, probably a Syrian mystic who lived about A.D. 500, and wrote under strong Neo-Platonic influence in the name of Dionysius. The language and figures of speech of this pseudo-Dionysius to link Christianity and Neo-Platonism found particular reception in the fourteenth century, at a time when mysticism reached its zenith. These mystical writings were: *On the Heavenly Hierarchy, On the Ecclesiastical Hierarchy, On the Names of God,* and *On Mystical Theology.* They exerted a deep influence upon Victor of St. Hugo, Albertus Magnus, and Thomas Aquinas.

DIONYSIUS THE GREAT OF ALEXANDRIA (c. 190-c. 264), Bishop of Alexandria, son of distinguished, wealthy, pagan parents. After his baptism by Bishop Demetrius of Alexandria, he entered the catechetical school, and became one of the most noted pupils of Origen. Then when Heraclas became bishop of Alexandria upon Demetrius' death, Dionysius succeeded as head of the Alexandrian catechetical school, which position he held for sixteen or seventeen years. In about 247 he became bishop of Alexandria. He was deeply involved in the Trinitarian controversies that raged from the middle of the third century on, and also in the controversy over receiving back the lapsed into the church. He was greatly influenced by Origen, and in the main upheld the views and teachings of Origen. He was more an administrator than he was a theologian.

DIONYSIUS OF CORINTH (d.c. 195), Bishop of Corinth about 170. A famous preacher and apologist in his day, distinguished for zeal, moderation, and a catholic and peaceful spirit. He wrote a number of pastoral letters to various congregations, which have unfortunately been lost. Honored as a martyr in the Greek, and as a confessor in the Roman church.

DIONYSIUS EXIGUUS (d. c. 527), Scythian monk. Residing in Rome when he constructed a church calender. Wrongly chose 753 A.U.C. instead of 749 A.U.C. as the year of Christ's birth, which would make Christ's birth about 5 B.C. Anglo-Saxons adopted his dating at Synod of Whitby in 663. Called Exiguus (the less) because of his humility.

DIOSCURUS (d. 454). Patriarch of Alexandria (444-451). As archdeacon he accompanied Cyril, then bishop of Alexandria, to the Council of Ephesus in 431. Upon Cyril's death in 444, Dioscurus succeeded to the patriarchal chair of Alexandria. A man of unbounded ambition and strong passion, he shrank from no measures to accomplish his personal designs, and to advance the Alexandrian see to the supremacy over the entire Eastern church. He put himself at the head of the Monophysite party, gave bitter opposition to orthodox Christianity. Eutyches was a leading advocate of the Monophysite doctrine (that is, a denial of the two natures of Christ) and was a close friend and collaborator of Dioscurus. Eutyches, through some influential friend, induced Emperor Theodosius II to call a council at Ephesus in 449. Dioscurus was moderator at this council, which because of its murderous, scandalous, unlawful procedure and character has been called the "Robber Synod." At the Council of Chalcedon, two years later, 451, the Eutychian doctrine was condemned and the Nicene-Chalcedon Creed was accepted. Dioscurus was deposed, excommunicated and banished to Gangra in Paphlagonia.

DIX, DOROTHEA LYNDE (1802-1887), social reformer. Born in Hampton, Maine but lived in Boston. From 1817 to 1835 headed a girls' school with a stress on moral character development. A Unitarian, she lived in the Channing family to teach the children. She set up a Sunday School in a women's prison in East Cambridge, investigated prison conditions from 1841 to 1843, and got beneficial legislation to improve prisons. From 1851 to 1852 worked to get state hospitals for the insane with much success in several states. Carried her campaign to Europe from 1854 to 1857. Was superintendent of Union nurses in the Civil War.

DIXON, AMZI CLARENCE (1854-1925), Baptist clergyman, born at Shelby, North Carolina, studied at Wake Forest College, Wake Forest, North Carolina, and Southern Baptist Theological Seminary. Ordained to the Baptist ministry in 1876, and held pastorates successively at Warsaw, North Carolina; Chapel Hill, North Carolina; Asheville, North Carolina; Immanuel Baptist Church, Baltimore; Hanson Place Baptist Church, Brooklyn; Ruggles Street Baptist Church, Boston; Moody Memorial Church, Chicago; Metropolitan Temple, London; and University Baptist Church, Baltimore. In theology Dixon was orthodox and a militant fundamentalist. Joined R. A. Torrey from 1909 on in editing *The Fundamentals,* a 12-volume set of paperbacks supporting orthodoxy.

DOANE, GEORGE WASHINGTON (1799-1859), American high churchman, Bishop of New Jersey, born at Trenton, New Jersey, educated at Union College, Schenectady, New York. Attended the General Theological Seminary of New York City. Following ordination in 1823 he was assistant minister at Trinity Church, New York, and later rector of Trinity Church, Boston. From 1832 he was bishop of the Protestant Episcopal Church in New Jersey. He was, for a time, professor in Trinity College, Hartford, Connecticut. Sometimes referred to in his church as the "Missionary Bishop of America." Founded St. Mary's Hall, Burlington, in 1837, and Burlington College in 1846. Bishop Doane made a strong impact upon his church through his emphasis upon church worship, and in particular upon church praise. He made a distinct contribution to hymnody in his *Songs By the Way,* published in 1824. Some of his hymns in this volume were "Thou Art the Way, to Thee Alone"; "Fling out the Banner, Let it Float"; "Father of Mercies Hear, Thy Pardon We Implore."

DOANE, WILLIAM HOWARD (1832-1916), composer, business man and inventor, born in Preston, Connecticut and studied at Woodstock Academy. At the age of eighteen he was elected director of the Norwich Harmonic Society. Educated for the musical profession by eminent American and German masters. Denison University gave him the Doctor of Music degree in 1875. For many years he was superintendent of the large Mt. Auburn Baptist Sunday school in Cincinnati, Ohio, and was an active member of the Young Men's Christian Association. His mechanical skill resulted in the patenting of more than seventy inventions in woodworking machinery. For some years he was engaged with manufacturing concerns, and was a successful business man and a generous benefactor, yet his interest in song worship and in Sunday school and church work never abated. A well-known trainer of choirs and a composer of some of the best modern devotional tunes; yet not a hymn writer himself. He composed the tunes for many of the hymns and gospel songs written by Frances Jane Crosby Van Alstyne (Fanny Crosby). Among his many musical editions of hymn books for Sunday school and evangelistic purposes are the following: *Silver Spray, Pure Gold, Royal Diadem, Welcome Tidings, Brightest and Best, Fountain of Song, Songs of Devotion,* and *Temple Anthems.* Some of his best known melodies are, "Jesus, Keep Me Near the Cross"; "Safe in the Arms of Jesus"; "Pass Me Not, O Gentle Saviour"; "More Love to Thee, O Christ"; "I Am Thine, O Lord"; "Rescue the Perishing"; "Tell Me the Old, Old Story"; "Take the Name of Jesus with You"; and "When Jesus Comes to Reward."

DOBER (dō'ber), **LEONARD JOHN** (1706-1766), Moravian missionary, born at Münchsroth, was a potter by trade. In 1732 he and David Nitschmann were sent as the first Moravian missionaries to the Negroes of St. Thomas in the Danish West Indies. After a few months on St. Thomas, Nitschmann returned to Europe and Dober was soon employed as a watchman on a plantation to earn his livelihood. Through his work and that of those who followed him, many slaves became Christians. After his return to Europe, he labored for sometime for the conversion of the Jews at Amsterdam; then became the superintending elder in the congregation at Herrnhut.

DOCK, CHRISTOPHER (1698-1771) Mennonite schoolmaster in colonial Pennsylvania, born in Germany and came from Hesse-Cassel, Germany to America about 1714. For the most of his life, a teacher in the schools of Skippack and Salford, in Montgomery County, Pennsylvania. Though a public school teacher, he added a Christian emphasis to the three R's and opened every school day with worship, used religious materials, such as the New Testament and the hymnal in regular classes. After school he often remained in the schoolroom for a time of prayer with his pupils. A teacher and a close friend of Christopher Saur, of Germantown, and a contributor to Saur's *Geistiches Magazien,* where his "Hundred Necessary Rules of Conduct for Children" appeared. He wrote the earliest American treatise on pedagogy, *Eine einfaeltige und gruendlich abgefasste Schulordnung (School-Management)* in 1750, first published twenty years later. He composed about ten hymns.

DODDRIDGE, PHILIP (1702-1751), dissenting (Congregationalist) divine, born in London. A pious mother gave him good care and education, but left him an orphan at thirteen. His friends provided for his entering the Dissenters Academy at Kibworth near Leicester about 1719. Here he became a teacher as well as pastor. In 1725 he was called to Harborough as pastor and head of an academy in 1729. Ordained in 1730, the same year was called to Northampton. He took his students with him and labored there for about twenty years as teacher, pastor, and writer. Many young men, especially Independents, were trained by him for the ministry. Dr. Doddridge was a man of deep piety, scrupulous in habits of study, a man of love and charity, always seeking to avoid controversy. Among his chief writings are his famous *Family Expositor,* and *the Rise and Progress of Religion in the Soul.* Also the author of many excellent spiritual hymns, such as: "How Gentle God's Commands"; "O Happy Day"; "Awake, My Soul, Stretch

Every Nerve"; and "Grace, 'Tis a Charming Sound."

DODD, CHARLES HAROLD (1884-1973), British Congregational New Testament scholar. Educated at University College, Oxford, and Berlin. Taught New Testament at Mansfield College (1915-1930), University of Manchester (1930-1935) and Norris-Hulse professor of theology at Cambridge (1935-1940). From 1950 directed the New English Bible project. Important books are *The Parables of the Kingdom, The Apostolic Preaching and Its Development,* and *According to the Scriptures.*

DODS, MARCUS (1834-1909), Scottish divine and biblical scholar, born at Belford, Northumberland, England, educated at Edinburgh University, and New College, Edinburgh. Ordained in 1864 and began ministry at Renfield Free Church, Glasgow; remained there until his appointment to the chair of New Testament criticism in New College, Edinburgh in 1889. Became principal in 1907, succeeding Robert Rainy. Did significant work in popularizing modern biblical scholarship. Brought before the General Assembly with the charge of denying biblical inerrancy, but exonerated by a large majority. Some of the most important of his published works; *Handbook on Genesis; Parables of Our Lord; The Gospel According to St. John; Commentary on Thessalonians; The First Epistle to the Corinthians; The Bible: Its Origin and Nature;* and *Introduction to The New Testament.* Dods was a contributor to the Encyclopedia Britannica and Hastings Dictionary of the Bible.

DÖLLINGER (dûl'lĭng er), **JOHANN JOSEPH IGNAZ von** (1799-1890), Bavarian Church historian, leader in the Old Catholic movement, born at Bamberg, Bavaria, educated at the Würzburg Gymnasium and at Bamberg. Ordained priest in the Roman church in 1822. In 1823 became professor of ecclesiastical history and canon law in the lyceum at Aschaffenburg, and in 1826 called to the newly opened University of Munich to become professor of theology and ecclesiastical history until his death. His strong liberalism, his opposition to the Jesuits, his critical attitude toward papal authority, and dislike of the promulgation of the dogma of the Immaculate Conception of the Virgin Mary (1854), all led Rome to distrust him. His relationship with Rome reached a crisis in 1870 when the Vatican Council declared the dogmas of papal infallibility and universal episcopacy of Rome. Döllinger protested against papal infallibility and insisted that the church councils should retain their traditional significance. He was declared a heretic and was excommunicated. He lent his influence toward the movement away from the Roman church, and worked for union of Anglicans, Eastern and Old Catholic churches. He took part in several conferences at Bonn (1872-1875) of these churches for the purpose of formulating plans for church unity, but was unable to get the churches to take any effective action. He presided over the conference of the Old Catholics in 1874. Writings were chiefly historical, dealing with general church history and with the problems relating to Rome. As a mark of general esteem, Döllinger in 1873 was appointed president of the Bavarian Royal Academy of Sciences.

DOMINIC de GUZMAN (1170-1221), founder of the Dominican Order, born at Calaroga in old Castile, Spain. Educated at the University of Palencia. Gave himself to an austere ascetic life. With the bishop of Osma, he made a trip through southern France about 1203 where he saw the missionary zeal of the Cathari or Albigenses who were then in the height of their power. Dominic purposed in his heart to seek to reform these people and to attempt to bring them back into the fold by preaching. He gathered about him a group of like-minded men, and adopted the so-called "Rule of St. Augustine." However, in 1216, after the death of Innocent III, Dominic appealed to Pope Honorius III for confirmation of his order and gained his desired wish. Thus the second great mendicant or begging order was formed, the chief work of which was to preach the doctrine of the church, to do mission work, and to fight heresy. Dominic's preaching friars, dressed in black, went everywhere preaching orthodoxy and fighting heresy. Dominic focused his attention on three great centers of education—Paris, Bologna, and Rome. The order grew with amazing rapidity. In 1220 mendicancy was made the rule of the order, and the following year the constitution for the "Order of Preachers or Dominicans" was developed. When Dominic died the Dominican Order or Order of Black Friars was well established, numbering sixty houses and over 500 friars. Dominic was canonized in 1234.

DOMITIAN (dō mĭsh'an), or **TITUS FLAVIUS DOMITIANUS AUGUSTUS** (51-96), Roman Emperor (81-91), born at Rome, the second son of Vespasian and the younger brother of Titus, whom he succeeded as emperor in 81. Domitian was the first of the Roman emperors to deify himself during his lifetime assuming the title of "Lord and God." The second so-called Roman persecution of the Christians took place under Domitian. His own niece Flavia

Domitilla was banished, and her husband, the consular Flavius Clemens, a cousin of Domitian, was put to death as a Christian. He also exiled the apostle John, bishop of Ephesus, to Patmos, where John remained until after the death of Domitian. The tyrant was assassinated, and the senate ordered his infamous name erased from the public documents.

DOMITILLA, FLAVIA (End of the First century). Christian matron of the imperial family; husband Titus Flavius Clemens, a consul and a first cousin of Domitian, accused of defection (likely for being a Christian), was beheaded. She was banished for the same reason about A.D. 95 to Pontia (or Pandaleria) in the Tyrrhenian Sea. One of the oldest catacombs, on the Via Ardeatina, near Terracina, known as the Cemetery of Domitilla, is traced back to Flavia Domitilla and may have been her gift to the church.

DONATUS (dō nā'tŭs), **THE GREAT** (d. 355), Bishop of Carthage. Born in Nomidia. After the persecution of Diocletian when the lapsed Christians were being received back into the church following persecution, a new puritanic, rigoristic movement came into being. It took its name from Donatus a rising leader in the puritanic party in the church in Carthage. About 313 this learned and gifted man of fiery energy and eloquence had been elected bishop of the puritanic minority in opposition to the Catholic bishop who had been elected by the more lenient majority. Donatus was banished, and later died in exile. Augustine devoted many years trying to win them back to the Catholic faith, and developed his ecclesiology while fighting them.

DONNE (dŏn), **JOHN** (1573-1631), English poet and divine, born in London and educated at Hart Hall, Oxford, and at Cambridge, studied law at Lincoln's Inn. Early Christian experience seems to have been unsettled and unhappy, and for some years led a worldly and rather reckless life. In 1596 and 1597 took part in an expedition to Cadiz and the Azores under the Earl of Essex. In 1598 became private secretary to Sir Thomas Egerton, Keeper of the Great Seal, but lost this post in 1601. In 1602 was imprisoned for secret marriage with Egerton's niece. In 1610 wrote a controversial treatise on Roman Catholicism, *Pseudo Martyr,* which won the attention and favor of King James I. In 1615 ordained, and successively given charges as minister of Keyston, Hunts; as rector of Sevenoaks, Kent; as reader in divinity at Lincoln's Inn; and finally in 1621 as dean of St. Paul's, where he preached his most celebrated sermons. Often preached before King Charles I. One of his greatest sermons, "Death's Duel," was preached just five weeks before his death. John Donne was one of the most remarkable poets as well as preachers of the seventeenth century. Usually classified as a "metaphysical poet," has occupied an important place in English literature. Other writings: *Divine Poems, Cycle of Holy Sonnets, Devotions upon Emergent Occasions, Essays in Divinity,* and several collections of sermons.

DOOYEWERD, HERMAN (1894-1977), Netherlands lawyer, political philosopher and theologian. Born in Amsterdam. Educated at the Free University. Government official from 1919 to 1922. Director of the Dr. A. Kuyper Foundation from 1922 to 1926. Professor in the Free University from 1926 until 1967. Editor of *Philosophia Reformata*.

DORNER, ISAAK AUGUST (1809-1884), German Lutheran theologian, born at Neuhausen-ob-Eck, Würtemberg, Germany, son of a Lutheran minister. Studied theology and philosophy at Tübingen where he was a pupil of F. C. Baur. For two years he assisted his father as pastor at Neuhausen. Then after filling chairs at Tübingen, Kiel, Königsberg, Bonn, and Göttingen between the years 1834 and 1860, in 1862 called to be professor of systematic theology and exegesis in the University of Berlin until his death. A strong upholder of Evangelical Christianity as opposed to German Rationalism. A leader of the mediating theologians who were interested in the Evangelical church of Prussia. He favored the Prussian Union of 1813. In 1873 visited America as delegate to the Conference of the Evangelical Union at New York. His theology was preeminently Christological. His greatest work, an answer to Strauss's rationalistic *Leben Jesu,* was *History of the Development of the Doctrines of the Person of Christ*. Among other works: *History of Protestant Theology, System of Christian Doctrine,* and *Christian Ethics.*

DOSITHEOS (1641-1707), patriarch of Jerusalem. Native of the Pelopennesus, Greece. Educated at Athens. Archdeacon of Jerusalem in 1661. Archbishop of Caeserea in 1666. Patriarch of Jerusalem in 1669. Proponent of Greek theology against western Protestant theology espoused by Cyril Lucar. President of Synod of Jerusalem in 1672 to eliminate any Protestant influence. It adopted his Confession of Dositheos. Wrote History of the Patriarchs of Jerusalem. Set up anti-Protestant printing press at Jassy in 1680.

DOSTOEVSKY, FYODOR MICHAEL (1821-1881), Russian novelist. Born in Moscow. Educated as a military engineer in the Military Engineering College. Resigned commission in 1846. In Siberia from about 1848 to 1854 and then travelled in Germany, Switzerland and Italy. Major works are *Crime and Punishment* and *The Brothers Karamazov,* probably his greatest work. In it with psychological insight he pictures emotions in the struggle between good and evil with salvation coming through suffering like Christ.

DOUGLAS, LLOYD CASSEL (1877-1951), American Lutheran minister and religious novelist, born in Columbia City, Indiana, and studied for the Lutheran ministry in Wittenberg College and Hamma Divinity School, Springfield, Ohio. Ordained in the Lutheran ministry in 1903, and from 1903 to 1933 held several pastorates in Indiana, Ohio, Washington, D.C., Michigan, California, and Montreal, Canada. Wrote *The Minister's Everyday Life*. Among novels with religious themes: *Magnificent Obsession, The Robe, The Big Fisherman,* and *Disputed Passage*.

DOUGLASS, FREDERICK (1817-1895), American abolitionist and orator, born at Tuchahoe, Maryland. In 1832 purchased by a Baltimore shipbuilder. Taught himself to read and to write. Following the suggestion of a black Christian peace and joy came into his heart. In 1838, escaping bondage, he changed his name from Frederick Augustus Washington Bailey to Frederick Douglass. He worked as a day laborer in New York City and in New Bedford, Massachusetts. When he attended and addressed an anti-slavery convention at Nantucket in 1841, his talent as an orator became known and he was employed by the Massachusetts Anti-Slavery Society as one of its lecturers. In 1845 he published his autobiography, *The Narrative of the Life of Frederick Douglass, An American Slave,* which he later revised and enlarged under the title, *Life and Times of Frederick Douglass.* To escape the danger of seizure he went to England (1845-1847), where he made a successful lecture tour. Some friends there collected money to buy his freedom. After return to the United States he began to publish a weekly abolitionist paper, first called *The North Star,* then renamed *The Frederick Douglass Paper.* At the outbreak of the Civil War he helped recruit black regiments. In 1870 he started and edited *The New National Era,* a journal devoted to the interests of his race. In 1871 appointed secretary of a commission to San Domingo; in 1872 presidential elector for the state of New York; in 1877-1881 United States marshall for the District of Columbia; and in 1889 the United States minister to Haiti. Douglass fought for the enactment of the Thirteenth, Fourteenth, and Fifteenth Amendments to the United States Constitution. He wrote *My Bondage and My Freedom* and *Narrative of My Experience in Slavery.*

DOUGLASS, HARLAN PAUL (1871-1953), Congregational Christian minister, born at Osage, Iowa, and studied at Grinnell College, Chicago Theological Seminary, and Andover Theological Seminary. Between 1894 and 1906 held pastorates at Manson, Iowa; Ames, Iowa; and Springfield, Missouri. Professor (1900-1906) at Drury College. For eleven years with the American Missionary Association, serving for a time as educational director of seventy-five schools for blacks and mountaineers of the south, and then as secretary for the Society. Spent a year with the American Expeditionary Forces in France as secretary of the Young Men's Christian Association; worked for a time for the Inter-Church World Movement; for twelve years research director for the Institute of Social and Religious Research; four years director of the China Survey of the Laymen's Foreign Mission Inquiry; on the Commission of Appraisal of the American Unitarian Association; for five years secretary of the Commission to Study Christian Unity in the Federal Council of Churches of Christ in America. Douglass was editor of *Christendom* (1938-1948), and was associate editor of the *Ecumenical Review* after 1948. Some of his writings: *Church Comity, Church Unity Movements in the United States,* and *Protestant Co-operation in American Cities.*

DOW, LORENZO (1777-1834), eccentric Methodist preacher, born at Coventry, Connecticut, received only the most elementary education. Felt the call to preach and in 1796 the Methodists granted him a license. In 1799 assigned to the Cambridge circuit. Within a year transferred to Pittsfield, Massachusetts, then "dropped" from the Conference. Thereafter worked independently. Believing himself called to preach to the Roman Catholics, made two trips to England and Ireland (1799 and 1805), where his methods of attack exposed him to personal danger. While in England he introduced camp meetings into that country, giving rise to a controversy that resulted in the formation of the Primitive Methodists. Eccentric manner in preaching, long hair and beard, and peculiar clothing gained him much prejudice, ridicule, and persecution, and the epithet, "Crazy Dow." The latter years of his life were devoted to fanatical attacks on the Jesuits.

DOWIE, JOHN ALEXANDER (1847-1907), founder of the Christian Catholic church, born in Edinburgh, Scotland. In 1860 emigrated with parents to South Australia. In 1867 returned to Edinburgh to continue education at the University of Edinburgh. Upon return to Australia, ordained a Congregational minister in 1870, and began preaching at Alma and Sydney. Dowie at this time began his ministry of divine healing. Early in his ministry Dowie developed a conviction that the use of alcohol, tobacco, drugs, and pork was sinful. In 1878 retired from the Congregational Church and took up healing and evangelistic work. In 1878 he moved to Melbourne where he organized the International Divine Healing Association, Dowie being president until 1888 when he came to the United States. In 1893 he located his headquarters in Chicago. In 1894 baptized by trine immersion; he organized the Zion Publishing House; began publishing "Leaves of Healing"; built Zion Tabernacle Number One; and established schools, a college and many industries. In 1896 the Christian Catholic church was organized on the basis of the trilogy, "Salvation, Healing, and Holy Living." Dowie was Overseer. Growing in power, notoriety, and wealth, he proclaimed himself to be Elijah the Restorer in 1901, and in 1914 as the First Apostle. In 1900 he purchased land forty-two miles north of Chicago on the shore of Lake Michigan and set up Zion city. His followers began to react against his financial administration of Zion. Through court procedures he was deposed. His successor as overseer was Wilbur Glenn Voliva.

DRIVER, SAMUEL ROLLES (1846-1914), Old Testament and Hebrew scholar, born at Southampton, England, studied at Winchester College, and at New College, Oxford. Fellow of the latter between 1870 and 1882, and tutor from 1875 to 1882. From 1883 Driver was regius professor of Hebrew and canon of Christ Church, Oxford. A member of the Old Testament Revision company (1876-1884), and examining chaplain to the bishop of Southwell (1884-1904). Devoted his life to the study, both textual and critical, of the Old Testament. Some of his books: *A Treatise on the Use of the Tenses in Hebrew; Isaiah: His Life and Times; Notes on the Hebrew Text of the Books of Samuel; Introduction to the Literature of the Old Testament;* commentaries on Leviticus, Deuteronomy, Joel and Amos, Daniel, Genesis and Exodus, in the Cambridge Bible series. He also collaborated with F. Brown and C. A. Briggs in the production of the *Hebrew and English Lexicon of the Old Testament,* and contributed extensively to Hastings' *Dictionary of the Bible*. He was one of the editors of the *Variorum Bible*.

DRUMMOND, HENRY (1786-1860), founder and "apostle" of the Catholic Apostolic or Irvingite church, born at Grange, Hampshire, England, educated at Harrow and Christ Church, Oxford. A banker and a member of Parliament (1810-1813 and 1847-1860). In 1817 met Robert Haldane in Geneva, and was led by him to support the evangelical Genevan clergy against the Socinians. In 1826 about fifty clergymen and laymen, among them Edward Irving, began meeting in Drummond's home at Albury Park, in Surrey, for the study of prophetic Scriptures. Five years later the Catholic Apostolic church was formed, and the following year Drummond was called to the apostolate. Wrote numerous works in defense of the new church and gave of his wealth toward its support.

DRUMMOND, HENRY (1851-1897), Scottish biologist, lecturer, and religious writer, born at Stirling, Scotland, studied at Edinburgh University, New College, Edinburgh, and the University of Tübingen. Took an active part in the meetings conducted by D. L. Moody and I. D. Sankey. In 1877 appointed lecturer in natural science at the Free Church College, Glasgow, Scotland, in 1884 was raised to full professorship and ordained to the ministry in the Free Church of Scotland. Made three visits to the United States in the interest of student missions giving lectures on scientific and religious subjects. In 1893 delivered the Lowell Lectures at Boston which later were published under the title of *The Ascent of Man*. Also visited the Australian colleges in the interest of student missions. In 1883 went to Africa for a scientific exploration of Lakes Nyasa and Tanganyika. One of his most popular books, *Natural Law in the Spiritual World,* was published in 1883 and reached its twenty-ninth printing in ten years. This work was an attempt to reconcile the doctrines of Christianity with the theory of evolution by arguments based on analogy. Another book from his pen that had a strong influence on the Christian world was *The Greatest Thing in the World*.

DUCHESNE (dōō shān'), **LOUIS MARIE OLIVIER** (1843-1922), Roman Catholic church historian, born at Saint Servan, Brittany, France; and educated at the seminary of St. Brieuc and at Rome. Ordained priest in 1867, and traveled for several years in Greece and Asia Minor. From 1877 to 1885 professor of Church history at the Institut Catholique at Paris; but when views on the history of doctrine offended the more conservative theologians, he resigned. For the next ten years a lecturer at the École Pratique des Hautes Études in Paris. From 1895 until his death, director of the French School at Rome, and in 1910 became a member of the French Academy. Eminent especially in the field of the early church. His best known works translated in English were: *Christian Worship: Its Origin and Evolution; Early History of the Christian Church from Its Foundation to the End of the Third Century,* which was put on the Roman Catholic Index. Other works were: *Memoire sur une Mission au Mont Athos, Liber Pontificalis, Origines du Culte Cretien,* and *Fastes Episcopaux de l'Ancienne Saule.*

DUFF, ALEXANDER (1806-1878), first missionary of the Church of Scotland to India, born at Auchnahyle, Perthshire, Scotland. Studied at St. Andrews under the famous Thomas Chalmers. In 1829 he was ordained, and in 1830 he and his wife sailed for Calcutta, India. One of his chief aims was to establish a collegiate institute through which he might educate the native youth. His school was to follow two main principles, to have the Scriptures read in all classes, and through the English language to teach the Western sciences. With the assistance of Ram Mohun Roy started the school (1830) which became the University of Calcutta. Within the first ten years the school grew from the original five to nearly one thousand pupils. When in 1834 he was furloughed home because of ill health, he toured Scotland promulgating missions, and won high acclaim for his eloquence. Pressure came to detain him in Scotland, but he returned to India in 1840. In the disruption in the Church of Scotland in 1843, as did most other missionaries, he cast his lot with the Free Church. In so doing he lost his beloved and thriving institution and its valuable library and equipment. He then set to work to build a new school and to equip it as well as the old had been. In 1850 he again returned to Scotland to promote the India missionary cause at home. In 1851 he was elected moderator of the General Assembly. Visited America in 1854, and made a deep impression on both the United States and Canada. In 1856 returned to India to continue labors there until 1864, when he had to take his final leave of the country, first visiting South Africa, then returning to Scotland. During the last fourteen years of his life, he urged upon the Scottish churches their duty to give the gospel to the millions of India. He was given the chief management of the foreign mission work of the Free Church; also did much to promote missions in Africa as well as in India. In 1867 he was appointed first professor of evangelistic theology in the Free Church, which office he held for eleven years. In 1873 he was again elected moderator of the Free Church Assembly. Dr. Duff was first of all a missionary and his principal publications pertained to the India Mission.

DUFFIELD, GEORGE (1818-1888). Born Carlisle, Pennsylvania. Educated at Yale and Union Theological Seminary, New York. Presbyterian pastor in New York, New Jersey, Pennsylvania, Illinois, and Michigan after his ordination in 1840. His hymn "Stand Up, Stand Up for Jesus" was based on the last words of Dudley A. Tyng of Epiphany Church in Philadelphia, who died from an accident in which the sleeve of his gown had caught in a machine.

DUNCAN, JOHN (1796-1870), Scottish Presbyterian clergyman and Hebraist, born at Gilcomston, near Aberdeen, Scotland. Studied at Marischal College; ordained in 1836 and preached for a time at Milton Church, Glasgow. In 1840 sent to Pesth (Budapest) as missionary to the Jews; celebrated converts, Dr. Alfred Edersheim and Dr. Adolph Saphir. From 1843 to 1870 held chair of Oriental languages in New College, Edinburgh (Free church). Published an edition of E. Robinson's *Greek and English Lexicon of the New Testament.*

DUNS SCOTUS (dŭnz skō tus), **JOHN** (c. 1266-1308), the "Subtle Doctor," was born in Scotland. Joined the Franciscan Order at Newcastle about 1290, studied theology at Oxford was ordained in 1291. He was teaching at Oxford somewhat before the close of the century. About 1304 he went to Paris where he received his doctor's degree and taught for a short time. In 1307 or 1308 was sent to Cologne as a professor or lecturer, dying there in 1308. Ready to criticize any of his predecessors, even the great Thomas Aquinas, whose dogmas were already being accepted by the Roman Catholic church as its representative theology. The mind of Duns Scotus was critical rather than constructive. It was his delight to disturb faith and to re-open questions to which Thomas Aquinas and other schoolmen were supposed to have given final statement. His philosophy was that of moderate realism similar to that of Albertus Magnus and Thomas Aquinas. He tended to separate reason and science from faith and revelation. He was the author of a philosophic grammar and commentaries on the Bible, Aristotle, and the *Sentences* of Peter Lombard.

DUNSTAN (d. 988), English prelate and statesman, born at Glastonbury in the south of England, where he received his early education from Irish scholars in an old monastery. He spent some time at the court of King Athelstan, and then became a monk at the monastery of Glastonbury. Then Athelstan's successor Edmund made him principal state treasurer and abbot of the monastery at Glastonbury. He made Glastonbury more of a school than a monastery. Glastonbury became the center of monastic reform in Britain, with the complete establishment of the Benedictine rules. He became adviser to Edmund's successor, the young and weak king Eldred, and was in all but name the ruler of the kingdom, a wise and vigorous administrator. Under Edgar, Dunstan became chief minister, and was made successively bishop of Winchester (957), bishop of London (959), and archbishop of Canterbury in 959 or 960. Under Edgar's successor Edward, Dunstan continued as principal minister of state; but upon the murder of Edward and the accession of Ethelred in 979, Dunstan passed his closing years in retirement, going back to the favorite studies and pursuits of his youth: music, painting, making musical instruments, and even the building of churches. His old zeal for religion, education, and charity continued. He had a powerful and beneficent influence upon the culture and laws of England of his day and of the days to follow. Died at Canterbury. One of the chief English saints until his glory was overshadowed by Thomas á Becket.

DUNSTER, HENRY (1609-1659), Congregational minister and first president of Harvard College, born at Bury, near Manchester, Lancashire, England, educated at Magdalen College, Cambridge. Took orders but in 1640 came to New England to escape High Church tyranny. Soon after arriving he was made president of Harvard College, which position he held until he was compelled to resign in 1654 because of his preaching against infant baptism. He then took a pastorate at Scituate where he labored until his death. Did much to give standing to Harvard College, and was greatly esteemed for piety and learning, and for excellent oriental scholarship.

DURER (dü'rĕr), **ALBRECHT** (1471-1528), German painter, engraver, and designer, born in Nuremberg, Germany, learned the goldsmith trade from his father. After spending four years as a traveling artist, returned to Nuremberg, married, and settled down as master of his art, wood engraving. Became the greatest German artist of the Renaissance period. Although he never renounced his Catholic faith, he showed a real sympathy with the Reformation. Friendship with Luther, Melanchthon, Pirkheimer, and Erasmus is well known. Enjoyed the friendship of the chancellor of the empire, the cardinal-archbishop of Mayence, Elector Frederick the Wise, and Emperor Maximilian. From 1512 to 1519 was court painter to Emperor Maximilian and, after Maximilian's death, to Emperor Charles V. Few artists have received more universal recognition. He introduced lights and shades into engraving, designed more than one hundred woodcuts, many of which were religious subjects. Did some beautiful work on copper plates. An inventor of etching, and some architectural work, emphasizing late Gothic style. Well known for his religious paintings, chief of which were altar pieces, such as "Adoration of the Christ Child," "Four Apostles," "The Adoration of the Magi," "Adoration of the Trinity," and "Descent from the Cross." In 1505 in Venice he studied the Venetian masters and painted. In 1520-1521 in Holland he exerted a marked influence on Flemish painters.

DURIE, JOHN (1596-1680), Scottish proponent of Protestant reunion. Studied during exile at Sedan and Leiden. In 1624 minister of English and Scottish Presbyterian church in Elburg, Prussia. In 1634 ordained in the Church of England and a chaplain at Rotterdam. Member of Westminster Assembly. From 1654 worked and traveled on behalf of reunion of the churches.

DWIGHT, TIMOTHY (1752-1817), American Congregational clergyman and educator. Eighth president of Yale College, born at Northampton, Massachusetts, a grandson of Jonathan Edwards, and graduated from Yale at seventeen. Headmaster at Hopkins Grammar School (1769-1771) and tutor at Yale (1771-1777). Licensed to preach and for more than a year was chaplain in the Continental army. For a while principal of a boys' school at Greenfield, Connecticut. From 1783 to 1795 pastor of the Congregational church at Greenfield. From 1795 until his death in 1817 president of Yale College. His remarkable ability as teacher and his evangelical Christian life and character did much to raise the standard of the college. He found in Yale many students professing infidelity; but through his preaching and influence, led many of them to an evangelical faith. College chapel sermons constituted a system of theology, and were published under the title of *Theology Explained and Defended,* and often reprinted. The work is a moderate Calvinism in agreement with the Edwardean or New England theology. Wrote several other works and was the author of the famous hymn, "I Love Thy Kingdom, Lord."

DYER, MARY (d. 1660), Quaker martyr. Came to Massachusetts in 1635. Helped found Portsmouth, Rhode Island in 1638. In England from 1652 to 1657 became a Quaker. Expelled from New Haven in 1658 for Quaker preaching. Jailed on three visits to Boston and hanged after the third visit.

E

EADIE (ē'dĭ), **JOHN** (1810-1876), Scottish pastor, professor, and commentator, born at Alva, Stirlingshire, Scotland, educated at University of Glasgow and theological seminary of the United Session, now United Presbyterian church. Ordained in 1835, entered the pastorate of the Cambridge Street Church, Glasgow. Moderator of his denomination's general assembly. In 1863 when he, with a portion of his congregation, removed to form the new Lansdowne Church of which he was minister until his death, 1876. His greatest success lay in field of exegesis. In 1843 elected to the professorship of biblical literature in divinity school of his church, and for thirty-three years both pastor and professor. Not eloquent as a preacher, but sermons instructive. In teaching and in writing clear, easy, and natural. Scholarship broad and accurate; he was accordingly chosen a member of the New Testament revision company. Among his writings are a *Biblical Cyclopaedia,* an *Ecclesiastical Cyclopaedia,* and an *Analytical Concordance to the Holy Scriptures,* besides sermons, commentaries, and biography.

EADMER (c. 1055-c. 1130), Anglo-Saxon historian. Grew up in a monastery at Christ church. Became secretary and chaplain to Anselm. Wrote *Life of Anselm, History of Recent Happenings,* and biographies of Wilfred and Dunstan.

EBRARD (ā'brärt), **JOHANNES HEINRICH AUGUST** (1818-1888), German Reformed theologian and clergyman, born of Huguenot ancestry at Erlangen, Germany, and educated at the universities of Erlangen and Berlin. Professor of theology at Zurich (1844-1847), and at Erlangen (1847-1861), and from 1875 pastor of the French Reformed church at Erlangen. Chief writings: *Christliche Dogmatik; The Gospel History; Vorlesungen über Praktische Theologie; Apologetik; Handbuch der Christlichen Kirchen- und Dogmengeschichte; Die Iroschottische Missionskirche des sechsten, siebenter, und achten Jahrhunderts*. Completed H. Olshausen's commentary, contributing the Epistle to the Hebrews, the Johannine Epistles, and Revelation.

ECK (ĕk), **JOHANN MAIER** (1486-1543), Roman Catholic theologian, born at Eck, near Augsburg in Swabia. Studied at the universities of Heidelberg, Tübingen, and Freiburg. In 1510 became professor of theology at the University of Ingolstadt in Bavaria. From 1512 until his death he had complete control of the destinies of Ingolstadt. In 1517, however, attacked Luther's ninety-five theses and accused Luther of heresy. Carlstadt, who vigorously defended Luther's theses, came into sharp controversy with him. In the debate between Eck and Carlstadt at Leipzig in 1519, Eck had little difficulty in subduing his opponent. When Luther appeared, Eck was far less successful. Confessed that Luther was superior in memory, acumen, and learning. Later he held disputations with Zwingli, Melanchthon, and Bucer. Among Eck's many writings, mention should be made of German translation of the New Testament which was first published in Ingolstadt in 1537.

ECKHART, MEISTER (JOHANN) (c. 1260-c. 1327), German mystic and theologian, born at Hochheim, near Gotha, in Saxony, Germany, educated at Cologne, Erfurt, and Paris. Joined the Dominican Order at Erfurt, held various offices for his order in Erfurt, Strassburg, Frankfort, Cologne, Paris, and Bohemia. Lectured and preached with much power in different parts of Germany. Preaching was mostly to monks and nuns, urging those who were already converted to attain to a full union with God. Burden of preaching was to bring the soul of man into conscious, mystic union with God; had little to say for the church, and laid no stress on the penitential system. For him good works do not make a man righteous, but a man must first be righteous in order to do righteous works. Most famous and important work *Opus Tripartitum,* only a fraction of which is extant, was written about 1314. It dealt with many phases of theology, biblical commentaries, and other subjects. A preacher, a scholastic, and a mystic theologian, but his mysticism on the verge of pantheism.

EDDY, MARY MORSE (BAKER) (1821-1910), founder of Christian Science, born at Bow, near Concord, New Hampshire. Received education at Sanbornton Academy at Tilton, New Hampshire, and from private tutors. In 1838 joined the Congregational church. In 1843 Mary Ann Morse Baker married Col. George Washington Glover. Soon after the death of husband the following year, her only child, a son, was born. In 1853 she married Daniel Patterson, an itinerant dentist, who deserted her and from whom she was divorced in 1873. Four years after this divorce she married Asa Gilbert Eddy. Her interest in "Christian Science" began about 1862 when she came in touch with Phineas Parkhurst Quimby, a magnetic healer of Portland, Maine. She had had a weakly constitution from childhood, had suffered much from illness, at times had been subject to violent hysteria. She went to Mr. Quimby and seemed to have received the restoration of her health. She gave herself to further study of the Bible and to the subjects of God, reality, sickness, health, and by 1866 made her "Discovery." In 1866, following a period of what seemed hopeless physical suffering, resulting from an accident, she believed herself miraculously healed. From that time she devoted her study and efforts to the development of Christian Science, and to practicing her system on others. In 1875 published *Science and Health with Key to the Scriptures.* In 1879 she founded the First Church of Christ, Scientist, in Boston, later to be known as the mother church, herself its pastor. In 1881 founded Massachusetts Metaphysical College, and in 1883 established the *Christian Science Journal* (monthly). Her other papers were: *Christian Science Sentinel* (weekly), and *Christian Science Monitor* (daily). Her doctrines deny the trinity, Christ's Deity, sin, death, disease, and Satan.

EDERSHEIM (ăd'ērs hīm), **ALFRED** (1825-1889) Bible scholar and theologian, born of Jewish parentage at Vienna, Austria, received earliest education in gymnasium of native city and in school attached to the Viennese synagogue. Attended University of Vienna. When a teacher of languages at Pest, Hungary, he was converted to Christianity by John Duncan, a Scottish Presbyterian chaplain. Edersheim later went with John Duncan to Scotland, studied theology at New College, Edinburgh, and at the University of Berlin. In 1846 ordained to the ministry in the Presbyterian church. After spending a year in missionary work among the Jews in Jassy, Rumania, and preaching for a time in Aberdeen, he was installed at the Free church, Old Aberdeen, in 1849. In 1861 due to failing health he was forced to resign, and the Church of St. Andrews was built for him at Torquay. Nine years later his health again failed and he lived four years quietly at Bournemouth. In 1875 he took orders in the Church of England, and was curate of one Anglican church for a year and vicar of another for six years. In 1882 resigned his living and moved to Oxford. From 1880 to 1884 he was Warburtonian Lecturer at Lincoln's Inn; from 1884 to 1885 was preacher to the University; and from 1886 to 1889 was Grinfield lecturer of the Septuagint. He made an intensive study of doctrines, practices, and conditions of Judaism as they illustrated and related to the New Testament. Wrote many books, among which are: *History of the Jewish Nation after the Destruction of Jerusalem by Titus, The Temple, Bible History* (in seven volumes), *Sketches of Jewish Social Life in the Days of Christ,* and *The Life and Times of Jesus the Messiah* (in two volumes, his greatest work).

EDDY, SHERWOOD (1871-1963), born Leavenworth, Kansas. Educated at Yale. Y.M.C.A. worker in India with students from 1896 to 1911. From 1911 to 1915 secretary for Y.M.C.A. in Japan, Korea, China, India, Near East, and Russia. Y.M.C.A. worker with the British and American armies from 1915 to 1917. Author of *God in History.*

EDMAN, VICTOR RAYMOND (1900-1967), American college president. Born in Chicago Heights, Illinois. From 1918 to 1919 in U.S. Army Medical Corp. Educated at the University of Illinois, Nyack Missionary Training Institute and Boston University. Missionary to Quechua Indians in Ecuador from 1923 to 1928. Forced home by illness, earned Ph.D. at Clark University in 1935 while a pastor in Worcester from 1929 to 1935. Taught in the institute at Nyack for one year. Professor of political science, Wheaton College from 1936 to 1940, president from 1940 and its chancellor from 1965 to 1967. Global traveler. Wrote over twenty popular devotional books.

EDWARD THE CONFESSOR (c. 1003-1066), King of England (1042-1066), born at Islip, Oxfordshire. Son of Ethelred II and Emma of Normandy. Educated in Normandy, his mother's homeland. On the death of his maternal brother, the Danish king Hardicanute in 1042, he returned to England and was acclaimed king, thus restoring the old Saxon line after a quarter of a century of Danish rule. A man of excellent personal qualities, but lacking in force and decisiveness. Edward was more monkish than kingly in disposition and occupied mainly with religious matters, building monasteries and churches, particularly the great abbey of St. Peter at Westminster, which was consecrated in 1065. He was succeeded by his wife's brother, the last of the Saxon line to rule in England. Harold was shortly to be overthrown by William the Conqueror. Edward caused a compilation of laws to be made, known as "The Laws of Edward the Confessor." He was canonized by Pope Alexander III in 1161.

EDWARD VI, TUDOR (1537-1553), King of England (1547-1553), born at Hampton Court, son of Henry VIII and Jane Seymour, Henry's third wife. Always sickly, yet given an excellent education. Upon Henry's death in 1547, Edward, the only male heir, succeeded to the throne. For a time he was under the protectorship of his Protestant maternal uncle, Edward Seymour, First Earl of Hertford, and later made Duke of Somerset. Both Edward and Somerset strongly favored the Reformation and did much to establish Protestantism in England. The Six Articles of Henry VIII were repealed. The Book of Common Prayer and the Forty-Two Articles were prepared and published largely by Cranmer. Somerset's bitter enemy, John Dudley, Earl of Warwick, but later Duke of Northumberland, persuaded the young king to consent to the execution of Somerset. Dudley became Edward's powerful protector. Before Edward died Northumberland induced him to assign the crown to Lady Jane Grey, Northumberland's daughter-in-law, to the exclusion of Henry VIII's children, Mary and Elizabeth. However, his older half-sister, Mary, succeeded him on the throne.

EDWARDS, JONATHAN (1703-1758), American theologian and philosopher, born at Windsor Farms (now East Windsor), Connecticut. His mother was a daughter of Solomon Stoddard, pastor of the Congregational church at Northfield, Massachusetts for fifty-seven years. He began study of Latin at six years of age under the tutorship of father and four older sisters. Before he was thirteen he had a good knowledge of Latin, Greek, and Hebrew, at which time he entered Yale College. In 1720, before age seventeen, he was graduated with the highest honors. Conversion took place when he was about seventeen. In 1722, before age nineteen, he was "approbated" as a preacher, and for about eight months preached in a small Presbyterian church in New York City. Then received a call to Yale to become tutor and remained at Yale for two years. In 1726 ordained as colleague with his grandfather and married later the same year. Two years after this, when his grandfather died, Edwards became pastor until 1750. The Great Awakening of 1734-1744 broke out in his and other New England churches. His Calvinistic sermons, such as "Sinners in the Hands of an Angry God," had a powerful influence upon audiences. In 1750, after he had been in the Northampton church for twenty-three years, an old controversy concerning the terms of admission to full membership in the church was revived. Edwards opposed the view and practice held by his predecessor, holding scrupulously to his own theological views. He was shortly ejected from the pastorate. The next year, 1751, he became pastor of the Congregational church at Stockbridge, Massachusetts, and missionary to the Housatonic Indians. In 1757 he was elected president of Princeton College in New Jersey. Five weeks after his inauguration in 1758, at the age of fifty-six, he died as a result of an inoculation for smallpox. Edwards was the outstanding preacher and theologian of colonial New England, founder and leader of the Edwardean or New England theology. His book, *Freedom of the Will,* is a defense of the doctrines of foreordination, original sin, and eternal punishment, and is a masterpiece of philosophical reasoning. Man's natural will is free in time but his depraved moral will can only choose grace when divinely inclined.

EDWARDS, JONATHAN (THE YOUNGER), (1745-1801), American Congregational theologian, born at Northampton, Massachusetts, son of President Edwards. Received education at Princeton College, where he also received the degree of doctor of divinity. After college studied theology with Dr. Joseph Bellamy, a friend of his father. He was tutor at Princeton (1767-1769). In 1769 he declined an offer to become professor of languages and logic at Princeton; in 1769 ordained pastor of White Haven Church in New Haven, Connecticut, where he remained until 1796. Opposition to the Half-way Covenant, the demoralizing influences of the Revolutionary War, and the dwindling membership of his congregation together made it necessary for him to leave in 1795. Installed pastor of the church in Colebrook, Connecticut, 1796, and in 1799 elected president of Union College, Schenectady, New York. His theology was a modified Calvinism that came to be known as "New England" theology. This included the acceptance of the "governmental" theory of the atonement, the theory accepted by the Presbyterians and Congregationalists for nearly a century following. Edwards's chief works were *A Dissertation Concerning Liberty and Necessity* and three sermons on *The Necessity of the Atonement*. Edited a number of his father's manuscripts for publication.

EDWARDS, LEWIS (1809-1897), Welsh Calvinistic Methodist pastor. Born at Cardiganshire. Educated at the University of Edinburgh. Opened school at Bala, later a training school for Welsh Calvinists of which he was principal from 1837 to 1887. Founded in 1845 the quarterly *Y Traethodydd*.

EGEDE (ā'gĕ dĕ), **HANS** (1686-1758), Norwegian apostle to Greenland, born in northern Norway, and completed studies at the University of Copenhagen. In 1707, at about age twenty-one, became pastor of a Lutheran parish which he served for about ten years. During this time he was seeking a way to go to Greenland as a missionary. He finally found a few friends who joined with him in forming the "Greenland Society." They bought a boat and named it the "Hope." In 1721 a band of forty-six, including the Egede family, left Bergen for Greenland. Instead of finding Norwegians on the island, they found only timid, unapproachable Eskimos. Through Egede's children's playing with the Eskimo children, friendly relations were gradually established. Egede set himself to the difficult task of learning the language. One of his early handicaps was the evil conduct of his own countrymen, especially after the government had transported a number of colonists and soldiers of doubtful character to the colony. In 1727 the trading-colonizing-missionary company was dissolved as an unprofitable venture. In 1731 the king commanded that the colony should be abandoned. Then in 1733-34 a smallpox epidemic practically wiped out his mission. In 1735 Egede's wife died, and he, broken in health, returned to Copenhagen, leaving the stricken land to his son Paul (c. 1708-1789). In Copenhagen he became director of the newly founded training school for missionaries to Greenland from 1740 to 1747.

EICHHORN, JOHANN GOTTFRIED (1752-1857), German biblical critic. Born at Dörrenzimmer. Educated at Göttingen. Professor of eastern languages at the University of Jena 1775 to 1788 and professor of philosophy at Göttingen in 1788. Compared books with other semitic writings and, following Astruc, divided the Pentateuch into *J* and *E* sources and added a *P* source. Most important works are *Einleitung in Alte Testament* and *Einleitung das Neue Testament*.

EINARSEN, GISSER (sixteenth century). Brought Reformation to Iceland. Studied in Germany under Reformation ideas. In 1540 began to reform the Icelandic church. Bishop of Iceland. Publication of Icelandic New Testament in 1540 helped to defeat the Catholic reaction under John Aresen in 1548 to 1554. Later Lutheranism was established by royal decree.

EINHARD (īn'härt), **(EGINHARD)** (c. 770-840), Frank historian and biographer of Charlemagne, born of a noble family in the valley of the Main in the Frankish empire. Received earliest education in the monastery of Fulda, and later studied at the palace school under Alcuin. He became one of the trusted counselors of Charlemagne. In 806 he was sent by the emperor to Rome to confer with the pope. He was retained as court adviser under Charlemagne's son and successor, Louis the Pious, who entrusted Einhard with the education of his son Lothair. About 829 he resigned court position. In 826 ordained presbyter; and after leaving the court assumed the abbacy of a Benedictine monastery at Seligenstadt, which he erected upon the estates that had been granted him as mark of imperial favor. Reputation rests chiefly upon his life of Charlemagne.

ELIOT, JOHN (1604-1690), apostle to the American Indians, born at Widford, Hertfordshire, England. Studied at Jesus College, Cambridge, and became distinguished for skill in languages. Unable to follow nonconformist principles under Archbishop Laud, he came to Boston in 1631. In 1632 became teacher in the Church of Christ in Roxbury. Continued in that office until his death. In collaboration with Thomas Weld, pastor of the Roxbury church, and Richard Mather, prepared for the press a new metrical version of the Psalms, *Bay Psalm Book*. This was the first book printed in the English Colonies, published in 1640. In 1637 Weld and Eliot opposed the antinomian teaching of Anne Hutchinson. Eliot soon became interested in the Algonquin Indians and started work among them, preaching for the first time to them in 1646. Villages of "praying Indians" were established, and in 1660 the first Indian church was organized. In 1653 published a catechism in the Algonquin language, by 1661 had the whole New Testament translated and printed at Cambridge, two years later the entire Bible. A little later with the assistance of his sons, John and Joseph, prepared *The Indian Grammar Begun, or an Essay to Bring the Indian Language into Rules.* Also wrote *The Christian Commonwealth, The Indian Primer,* and in 1678 *Harmony of the Gospels.* In 1674 the number of "praying Indians" was estimated at three thousand six hundred; but in the time of King Philip's War, they met many reverses. After Eliot's death their extinction proceeded rapidly. There is not a person living today who is able to read the Scriptures as translated by Eliot. His mission endeavors led to the formation of the Society for the Propagation of the Gospel in New England in 1649.

ELIOT, THOMAS STEARNS (1888-1965), pessimistic poet. Born St. Louis, Missouri. Educated Harvard, the Sorbonne and Merton College, Oxford. Taught in a grammar school and worked at Lloyd's bank in London. Assistant editor of *The Egoist* (1917-1919) and of *Criterion* (1923-1939). Lecturer at Harvard University from 1933 to 1936. Received Nobel Peace Prize for literature in 1948. Moved from agnosticism to High Church Anglicanism. Major works are *The Wasteland* and *Murder in the Cathedral*.

ELIZABETH I (TUDOR) (1533-1603), Queen of England (1558-1603), born in

Greenwich Palace, daughter of Henry VIII and Anne Boleyn. Received an excellent classical and humanistic education. In 1558 she succeeded Mary on the throne of England. She was the third and last of Henry's children to occupy the throne, and the last of the Tudor line. She preferred Protestantism because it gave her control of the church. She accordingly released imprisoned Protestants, chose strong and wise councilors to assist her in forming the policies for a rising modern political power, maintained the royal supremacy under the term Supreme Governor of the Realm, enforced the new Act of Uniformity, adopted the Thirty-Nine Articles of the Church of England as prepared by Archbishop of Canterbury Mathew Parker, and accepted the revised Second Prayer Book of Edward VI. Hers was one of the greatest reigns in English history, known as the Elizabethan age. She restored popular confidence in the monarchy. During her reign the Spanish Armada was defeated, the Spanish power was broken, and England entered upon a period of maritime power, commercial prosperity, progress, far-flung colonization and of world power. Her successor was James VI of Scotland who became James I of England, Scotland, and Ireland.

ELLICOTT (ĕl'ĭ kŭt), **CHARLES JOHN** (1819-1905), Anglican clergyman and Bible commentator, born at Whitwell, near Stamford, Rutlandshire, England, studied at St. John's College, Cambridge. Ordained priest in 1846. From 1848 to 1861 professor of divinity in King's College, London, also rector of Pilton, Rutlandshire, until 1858. In 1860 appointed Hulsean professor of divinity at Cambridge. In the following year resigned both professorships on being appointed dean of Exeter. In 1863 consecrated bishop of Gloucester and Bristol, and, on the division of the see in 1897, became bishop of Gloucester, resigning diocese in 1904 or 1905. During the forty-two years of his episcopate helped to establish the Gloucester Theological College and the Church Aid Society in Bristol (1867). Secretary of the Lambeth conferences of 1867, 1878, and 1888, chairman of the British New Testament Revision Company, 1870 to 1881. Most important work: *Critical and Grammatical Commentaries* on several of the New Testament epistles. Wrote *Historical Lectures on the Life of Our Lord Jesus Christ* (Hulsean lectures), *The Being of God, Aids to the Faith,* and *Christus Comprobatur.* He edited a *New Testament Commentary for English Readers* (three volumes), and *Old Testament Commentaries for English Readers* (five volumes).

ELLIOTT, CHARLOTTE (1789-1871), born in Brighton. Granddaughter of the evangelical pastor Henry Venn and influenced by the Swiss Caesar Malan, whom she met in 1871. When querying him on how one became a Christian, he urged her to "Come to Him just as you are." From this came her well-loved hymn, "Just As I Am." She wrote in all about 150 hymns.

ELLIOTT, HARRISON SACKET (1882-1951), Methodist theologian and educator, born at St. Clairsville, Ohio, studied at Antioch College, Valparaiso University, Ohio Wesleyan University, Drew Theological Seminary, Teachers College at Columbia University, Oxford University, and Yale University. Secretary to Bishop James W. Bashford of the Methodist Episcopal Church in China (1905-1908), secretary of the International Committee of the Young Men's Christian Association (1910-1922). Instructor in religious pedagogy in Drew Theological Seminary (1921-1923), Professor of practical theology and head of the Department of Religious Education at Union Theological Seminary (1925-1950), and member of the summer faculty at Teachers College, Columbia University (1923-1929). Ordained to the Methodist ministry in 1944. For many years secretary of the Religious Education Association. Outstanding leadership in the field of religious education, and in the area of group process and group discussion. Directed the first large-scale use of group discussion in several international conferences of the Young Men's Christian Association and in the Student Volunteer Convention in Indianapolis. Elliott was also greatly interested in mental hygiene and helped to introduce courses in mental hygiene in the curriculum of theological seminaries. Wrote *How Jesus Met Life Questions, The Bearing of Psychology upon Religion, The Process of Group Thinking, Group Discussion in Religious Education,* and *Can Religious Education Be Christian?*

ELLIOTT, JAMES (1927-1956), born in Portland, Oregon. Educated at Wheaton College and Summer Institute of Linguistics of Wycliffe Translators, Inc. (1950). Went to Ecuador in 1952. With four other missionaries tried to reach the Auca Indians. Nathanael Saint, (1923-1956), born in Huntingdon Valley, Pa. studied at Wheaton and was in the U.S. Army from 1942 to 1946. Flying for the Missionary Aviation Fellowship from 1948 he developed a bucket drop on a rope to give gifts to win Auca confidence. T. Edward McCully, a graduate of Wheaton College and Marquette Law School, Peter Fleming, educated at the University of Washington and Roger Youderian, of Montana and a World War II paratrooper worked with Elliott and Saint. After winning Auca friendship in 1956 they flew in, erected a prefabricated tree house, but were murdered by some of the Aucas. In 1958 Saint's sister Rachel and Elizabeth Howard Elliott went to live among the Aucas and won large numbers for Christ. The deaths of the five men also brought many missionary volunteers to take their place. Elizabeth Elliott's *Through Gates of Splendor,* telling Jim's story from his diary, was a best seller.

ELLIS, WILLIAM (1794-1872), English Congregational missionary, born in London, England, educated in the London Missionary Society Training School, in Gosport and Hamerton College, South Hampstead, England. Ordained in 1815; went to Polynesia. In 1816 sent by the London Missionary Society to the South Pacific, where he remained until 1824. In Tahiti he set up the first printing press in the South Sea islands, introduced many species of fruits and plants which became a source of revenue to the inhabitants. In 1822 Ellis, other missionaries, and several native chiefs and teachers made a visit to Honolulu. In 1823 he and his wife went to Oahu, remaining for eighteen months, assisting the missionaries in reducing the Hawaiian language to written form. From 1831 to 1839 Ellis was secretary of the London Missionary Society. From 1847 until his death he was pastor of the Congregational church in Hoddersdon, near London, except for four visits to Madagascar, which he made to help the mission which had suffered so terribly from persecution at the hands of the queen, Ranavolona. On fourth trip he stayed four years (1861-1865). Contributions to missionary literature and to Polynesian research are large. Wrote *Narrative of a Tour through Owhyhee* (Hawaii); *Polynesian Researches; The Martyr Church of Madagascar; History of Madagascar,* two volumes; and *Three Visits to Madagascar.* His Hawaiian hymns are still used in the native churches.

EMBURY, PHILIP (1728-1773), first Methodist minister in America, born of German parents in Ballingrane, Ireland. Converted and joined John Wesley's society in 1752, became a local preacher at Court-Mattress, Ireland, in 1758. Two years later emigrated to America. In 1766, stimulated by the advice of a cousin, Barbara Heck, and began to preach in his own house. A carpenter by trade, he soon erected a chapel on the site of the present John Street Church in New York City. In 1768 preached the dedicatory sermon in this, one of the oldest Methodist chapels, built in the New World. The next year, upon the arrival of several missionaries sent out by Wesley from England, he moved to Camden, New York. Living on a farm owned by his brother-in-law, formed a congregation which grew into the flourishing and influential Troy Conference. Here he did his greatest work, plying his trade during the week and preaching on Sundays.

EMERSON, RALPH WALDO (1803-1882), American philosopher, essayist, and poet, born in Boston, Massachusetts. He entered Harvard College at the age of fourteen. Poet of his class, 1821. Taught school and studied theology in Cambridge. In 1826 ordained to the Unitarian ministry, and in 1829 became pastor of one of the leading Unitarian churches of New England, the Second Church of Boston. Some of the church forms troubled him and in 1832 retired from the pastorate and became a lecturer and writer. Did some preaching for several years. For a time chaplain of the State Senate and member of the Boston School Board. Health failing, his wife and two brothers gone, spiritual problems were burdening him. He resorted to travel. In 1832 he made first trip to Europe, where he met Walter Savage Landor, Samuel Taylor Coleridge, William Wordsworth, and Thomas Carlyle. In America formed close friendships with Nathaniel Hawthorne, Henry David Thoreau, Henry Wadsworth Longfellow, Amos Bronson Alcott, Louisa May Alcott, William Ellery Channing, William Henry, Freeman Clarke, and Theodore Parker. In middle years of life he was a member of the group of New England idealists who were known as *Transcendentalists.* For a time the editor of their paper, *The Dial*. First published work, *Nature,* contained the gist of his transcendental philosophy. His philosophy may be described as ethical idealism with an undercurrent of stoicism; his religion as pantheistic unitarianism.

EMMONS, NATHANIEL (1745-1840), New England Congregationalist, born at East Haddam, Connecticut, educated at Yale. In 1773 ordained pastor of the Congregational church at Franklin, Massachusetts, pastor for fifty-four years, resigning in 1827. His house was a theological seminary where nearly one hundred young men were trained for the ministry. Emmons was one of the fathers of the Massachusetts Missionary Society, for the first twelve years of its existence its president. One of the original editors of the *Massachusetts Missionary Magazine* which later developed into the *Missionary Herald*. An intimate friend of Dr. Samuel Hopkins, a disciple of Jonathan Edwards, a pronounced anti-Mason, an abolitionist, and a Federalist.

ENDECOTT (ĕn′dĭ kŭt), (or **ENDICOTT**),

JOHN (c. 1589-1665), Puritan colonial governor of Massachusetts, born at Chagford, Devonshire, England. Sent to this country by the "Massachusetts Company" to manage the plantation at Salem. Arrived on the *Abigail* with his wife and about sixty others on September 6, 1628. The next year chosen governor of the Massachusetts Bay Colony, and served until the arrival of John Winthrop, who before leaving England had been appointed governor. After this Endecott served eleven years as assistant to the governor, four years as deputy governor, and from 1644, the death of Winthrop, thirteen years as governor. The United Colonies of New England elected him president in 1658. After Harvard was founded became a member of the Board of Overseers. He was a member of the congregation of Roger Williams, whom he resolutely defended. Cruel in his treatment of the Quakers, having several of them put to death. His unsuccessful expedition against the Indians in 1636 helped bring on the Pequot War.

ENGLE, JACOB (1753-1832), first overseer of the Brethren in Christ in Pennsylvania, born in Switzerland, came to America, the only infant who survived the voyage. At fourteen apprenticed to a weaver by the name of Witmer. Witmer joined with him in the belief that immersion was the proper mode of baptism. Seven years later, in 1778, they immersed each other. Shortly, about a dozen others were baptized by Engle. The little group then repaired to an upper room where they held their first love feast. Shortly afterward they met at the home of Henry Engle, at which meeting the Brethren in Christ Church was organized, and Jacob Engle was declared overseer or bishop.

EPHRAIM (EPHRAEM) THE SYRIAN (c. 300-373), hermit, writer, poet, apologist, preacher, born in Mesopotamia, probably in Nisibis. He was the most distinguished theologian, orator, and hymnist of the ancient Syrian church. As a young Christian he attended the Council of Nicea. He moved from Nisibis to Edessa, spent his time in a cave in ascetic exercises, and in reading, writing, preaching to the monks, and helping the poor. Wrote widely in the Syrian language, defended Nicene orthodoxy against all classes of heretics. Made a journey to Egypt where he spent several years among the hermits. Visited Basil the Great at Caesarea in Cappadocia. Basil ordained him deacon. After return to Edessa he gained a large following of disciples. His many exegetical, theological, controversial, and ascetical writings are mostly in verse. They include cycles of hymns on the great church feasts, eschatology, and the refutation of heretics. He was declared a doctor of the church by the pope in 1920.

EPIPHANIUS (ĕp ĭ fā′nĭ ŭs), (c. 315-403), Bishop of Salamis. Likely born of Jewish parentage at Besanduke, near Eleutheropolis in Palestine, and became a Christian at about age sixteen. Spent several years with the monks in Egypt, then returned home to establish a monastery, becoming its abbot. Labored diligently for the spread of monasticism in Palestine. First ordained presbyter, then in 367 elected bishop of Salamis (Constantia) in Cyprus, where he faithfully discharged episcopal duty for thirty-six years. Became an intimate friend of Jerome, true to the Nicene Creed, strongly opposing Gnosticism, Arianism, Origenism, and other heresies of the time. Written works are of considerable value as a storehouse of the history of ancient heresies and patristic polemics. His chief work was the *Panarium* or *Medicine-Chest,* in which he attempted to describe and to refute no less than eighty heresies, twenty of which were extant before the time of Christ.

EPISCOPIUS (ĕp ĭ skō′pĭ ŭs), **SIMON (SIMON BISCOP)** (1583-1643), Dutch theologian, born at Amsterdam, Holland, educated at Leiden, where he studied under Jacob Arminius and Francis Gomarus. When the great controversy broke out between the Arminians and the Gomarists, he joined with the former, and after the death of Arminius in 1609, became the leader of the Arminian doctrine; in fact became the real promoter of the doctrine. In 1610 ordained pastor of Bleyswick, a village near Rotterdam. In 1612 appointed professor of theology at the University of Leiden to succeed Gomarus. In 1618 chosen as chief spokesman to defend the Arminians at the Synod of Dort. The synod refused him a hearing, and with the other Remonstrant representatives he was condemned, expelled from the church, and banished from the country. He went to France from 1621 to 1626. In 1626 permitted to return to Holland, and in 1634 became director of the Remonstrant Theological Seminary at Amsterdam, a position he filled with much honor and renown for nine years. The systematizer of the Arminian theology.

ERASMUS, DESIDERIUS (c. 1466-1536), Dutch humanistic scholar of Greek. Born in Rotterdam, Holland. Educated in the school of the Brethren of the Common Life in Deventer from 1475 to 1484. Augustinian Monk from 1486 to 1491. Ordained in 1492. Studied at the universities of Paris and Orléans from 1495 to 1499. In England Thomas More, Linacre, Grocyn, and Colet influenced him against scholasticism. From 1506 to 1509 in Italy revelled in the classical past. Back in England from about 1509 to 1516 was for some years professor at Cambridge. He was in Basel from 1521 to 1529 in the home of the printer Froben. His biblical patristic and classical studies inclined him to reform in the church but not revolution. Thus in his book on free will he opposed Luther's ideas. From 1529 to 1535 he lived at Freiburg-im-Bresgau. His negative critical stire in *Colloquies* and in *In Praise of Folly* showed the need for reform, and his Greek New Testament in 1516 showed scholars what the church should be. His more humanistic ethical conception of Christianity is revealed in *Handbook of the Christian Soldier.* He paved the way for reform of the church, but he refused the revolutionary changes of the Reformers such as Luther.

ERDMAN, CHARLES ROSENBURY (1866-1960), Presbyterian teacher of homiletics and pastoral theology. Graduate of Princeton University and Theological Seminary. Ordained in 1891. Pastor in Pennsylvania from 1890 to 1905. Professor of practical theology in Princeton Theological Seminary from 1905. Moderator of General Assembly, Presbyterian Church, USA, 1925. President of the Presbyterian Board of Foreign Missions from 1928 to 1940. His many books as well as his classes on homiletics helped to train many pastors to become able biblical expositors.

ERIGENA (ĕ rĭj'ēnȧ), **JOHANNES SCOTUS** (c. 810-c. 877), medieval philosopher and theologian, born in Ireland, educated in one of its famous schools, where the Greek fathers, especially Origen, were studied. Became well acquainted with the Greek and with Greek philosophers, which greatly aided in his theological controversies and speculations. Went to France in 843, and Charles the Bald appointed him principal of the school of the palace. In his *Be Predestinate* (851) he opposed Gottschalk's predestinarian views and also opposed Ratramnus' view of the Lord's supper. Erigena wrote with much freshness, originality, and independence. Though the church councils judged his writings as erroneous, many of his philosophical views turn up later in Anselm, Alexander of Hales, Peter Abelard, Albertus Magnus, Thomas Aquinas, and others of the Schoolmen. Though neither a scholastic nor a mystic, the scholastics and the mystics both were influenced by him. He tended to blend philosophy with religion and to identify God with intellect. He was one of the most interesting figures among the medieval writers. Among his chief literary works were the translation into Latin of the works of Pseudo-Dionysius, and in *De Divisione Naturae* explained God and nature along neoplatonic lines that verged on pantheism.

ERNEST, JOHANN AUGUST (1707-1781). Born in Thuringia. Educated at Leipzig and Wittenberg in the classics. Produced many good editions of Greek classical writers. From 1742 to 1770 he taught ancient literature and later theology at the University of Leipzig. Stressed careful use of grammar and history in the interpretation of the New Testament. His major work was *Institutio Interpretes Novi Testamenti* in eight volumes in 1761.

ERSKINE (ûr'skĭn), **EBENEZER** (1680-1754), founder of the Scottish Secession church, born at Dryburgh, Berwickshire, Scotland. He was educated at the University of Edinburgh. Ordained and became pastor at Portmoak in Kinros from 1703 to 1731. In 1731 transferred to Stirling, where he was pastor until his deposition in 1740. Few men of his day enjoyed greater popularity as a preacher than he. In the conflict over the right of the congregation to elect its own ministers, took the affirmative and evangelical side, then led the Seceders out of the Established Church and helped form the Associate Reformed Presbytery in 1733, which in 1740 became the Secession church. Erskine's writings consist of his occasional sermons published after his death, and of his *Life and Diary.*

ESTIENNE, ROBERT (STEPHANUS) (1503-1559), printer and scholarly editor. Royal printer from 1539 to 1551 for Francis I of France. Fled to Geneva in 1551, joined the Reformed church and edited and printed several Latin Bibles and Hebrew Old Testaments (1539). Published first printed editions of Eusebius, Justin Martyr, and other church Fathers. Responsible for the verse divisions of the New Testament; done, according to his son Henri, on a trip from Paris to Lyons. Verse divisions first appeared in his fourth Geneva edition of 1551.

ETHELBERT or **AETHELBERT** (d. 616), King of Kent (560-616). Married Bertha, a Christian princess, daughter of the king of the Franks; permitted her to worship God in her own way and to bring along her bishop as private confessor. Also permitted Augustine and his missionary companions to settle and to preach in his capital, Canterbury. Before the end of the first year (597) he was converted; and he and thousands of his subjects were baptized by Augustine. He then helped Augustine convert a heathen temple into a church at Canterbury, and encouraged the people to become Christians. He was a lawgiver of importance. His code of laws, the dooms of Ethelbert, was the first of its kind in England.

EUCKEN (oi'ken), **RUDOLF CHRISTOPH** (1846-1926), German Protestant philosopher, born in Aurich, East Friesland, and educated at the universities of Göttingen and Berlin. After teaching in a gymnasium for four years he became professor of philosophy at Basel (1871-1874). In 1874 became professor of philosophy at Jena, remained until his retirement in 1920. The Nobel Prize winner in literature in 1908; exchange professor at Harvard, 1912-1913; in 1914, a visiting professor at the universities of Kyoto and Tokyo, Japan. Against the naturalistic positivism of his time he developed an ethical idealism with the concept of a spiritual activity that must make this ideal applicable to life. Some of his works have been translated into English: *Fundamental Concepts of Modern Philosophic Thought, Religion and Life, Christianity and the New Idealism, The Truth of Religion, Fundamental of a New Philosophy of Life,* and *The Transient in the Permanent in Christianity.*

EUGENIUS IV (Gabriele Condulmare) (1383-1447). Born in wealthy Venetian family. Became an Augustinian monk, cardinal in 1408, and pope from 1431 to 1447. Quarreled with the Council of Basel which elected Amadeus VII as FelixV, an antipope. Eugene moved the council to Ferrara and then Florence where in 1439 a short-lived paper reunion of the Eastern and Western churches was worked out, and the number of sacraments was set at seven.

EUNOMIUS (ū nō'mĭ ŭs), (d. c. 395), leader of Extreme Arianism after Nicea, born in Cappadocia. In 356 went to Alexandria to study under the Arian Aëtius, whose pupil and amanuensis he became and whose extreme Arian doctrine he accepted and popularized. They taught that the Son was of different and inferior substance and even was unlike the Father, and was created out of nothing, and denied that Christ had any divine nature. Early in 360 Euxodius, the Arian bishop of Constantinople, made Eunomius bishop of the orthodox see of Cyzicus. When his flock complained of his heresy, Euxodius was obliged to depose and banish him to Mauretania in 364. He lived the life of an exile. The adherents of Eunomius who had become very numerous along with the followers of Aëtius were condemned as heretics at the Council of Constantinople in 381.

EUSEBIUS (ū sē'bĭ ŭs), **OF CAESAREA (EUSEBIUS PAMPHILI)** (c. 263-c. 339), Bishop of Caesarea in Palestine, and the "Father of Church history," educated at Antioch and Caesarea. He formed an intimate friendship with the learned presbyter Pamphilius, whose name he attached to his own. After the martyrdom of Pamphilius about 310, he left Palestine and went to Tyre and later to Egypt. He met persecution and imprisonment for a while. Next we hear of Eusebius as bishop of Caesarea where he labored from between 313 and 315 until his death. He first comes into prominence as a learned man, a historian, and an author who enjoyed the high esteem and favor of Emperor Constantine. At the beginning of the Arian controversy Eusebius was strongly inclined toward the Arian view. He was at the same time an admirer of Origen, and tended toward Origen's error of subordination of the Son of God. When the charge of heresy was brought against him, he saved the day for himself by siding with the orthodox party in renouncing Arius and in making a creed of faith which became the basis for the Nicene formula. During the entire Arian controversy Eusebius followed a middle-of-the-way view. He was president of the synod at Tyre in 335 where Athanasius was condemned and exiled. Eusebius was a court adviser for Constantine; a prolific writer, though not a profound or original thinker. Eusebius wrote a very important and valuable history of the Christian church from the time of the apostles down to his own time (about 325). Many prominent men and facts are known to us today only from the pages of this history. His panegyric, *The Life of Constantine,* has much historical though little literary value. His *Chronicles* and his tract on *Martyrs of Palestine* also possess much historic value. His *Ecclesiastical History* is our best source for church history till A.D. 325 and a part of the *Chronicles* provided chronology for medieval church historians.

EUSEBIUS OF NICOMEDIA (d. c. 342), Arian Bishop of Nicomedia, appointed bishop of Berytus in Phoenicia, and later of Nicomedia, where the imperial court resided. Like Arius, he was a pupil of Lucian of Antioch. Appeared as the defender of Arius at the Council of Nicea in 325. Under the pressure of the occasion finally signed the Nicene Creed, though with definite reservations; would not sign the clause condemning Arius. Soon after the close of the council, he endeavored to revive the controversy, which incurred the anger of the emperor and resulted in his banishment for about three years. Sought and regained the favor of the emperor, and was permitted to return to his see. Again revived the controversy and placed himself at the head of the Arian party, continued to champion the Arian cause. He continued to hold the goodwill of the emperors; it was he who baptized Constantine in 337, and became patriarch of Constantinople in 339, holding the position until his death.

EUSTATHIUS (ū stā'thĭ ŭs), **OF SEBASTE** (c. 300-c. 377), bishop of Sebaste in Pontus, born at Sebaste, Pontus (Armenia), and a pupil of Arius of Alexandria. Whole life was strongly dominated by the ascetic or monastic ideal, and in this connection for some time an intimate friend of Basil the Great. Became bishop of Sebaste about 356; founded monasteries in Armenia, Pontus, and Paphlagonia. He also founded a hospital for the poor at Sebaste. The Eustathian order, which was likely of his founding, was based on asceticism and celibacy. The sect was condemned at the Synod of Gangra in 340, and he was deposed eighteen years later by the Synod of Militene in 358.

EUTHYMIUS (ū thĭm ĭ ŭs), **ZIGABENUS** (zĭg ȧ bē'nŭs) (fl. 1100), Byzantine theologian and exegete, a monk in a cloister near Constantinople. At the order of the emperor, Alexius Comnenus, he wrote against all heresies. The book was entitled *Panoplia Dogmatica*. The most interesting part of the book is the section on the Bogomiles, which gives us our chief information on this sect. Attack on the Roman Catholic doctrines is concerned chiefly with the Procession of the Holy Spirit and the use of unleavened bread. His other important works were extensive commentaries on the Psalms, the four gospels, and the epistles of Paul. In the commentaries on the epistles he utilizes mainly patristic sources, especially Chrysostom.

EUTYCHES (ū'tĭ kēz) (c. 378-454), an honorable and pious presbyter of strict monastic training, for thirty years head of a cloister of about three hundred monks near Constantinople. A zealous foe of Nestorianism; became a useful instrument in the hands of the anti-Nestorian party in Alexandria under the leadership of Cyril and Dioscurus. Though unwilling to leave his monastery and although he claimed Nicene orthodoxy, finally was drawn into the controversy and found to hold phases of the Apollinarian heresy. In 448 accordingly deposed from his priestly and monastic office and excommunicated. At the "Council of Robbers" the next year he was reinstated by the Alexandrians, and used as a tool to enhance their views. The tide soon turned against the Alexandrian or the so-called Eutychian party. In 451 at the Council of Chalcedon, though Eutyches, the nominal originator of the controversy, was not expressly anathematized, Eutychianism was condemned; and a year or so later Eutyches was banished. In a letter written in 454 we read for the last time of him. The Christological view of Eutyches was that the human nature of Christ is absorbed into the divine; yet Eutychianism holds after unions to *one* nature, the divine, in Christ. This made the humanity of Christ a mere accident of the immovable divine substance. His ideas resulted in Monophysitism, which was finally condemned at the second council of Constantinople in 553.

EVANS, CHRISTMAS (1766-1838), Welsh Baptist preacher, born near Cardigan, Wales. He was converted at age seventeen, and at that time first learned to read. Upon his becoming a Christian companions gave him such rough abuse that he lost an eye. In 1789 ordained by the Baptists. Traveled about preaching for two years, then began a ministry from 1791 to 1826 on the island of Anglesea on the Welsh coast. In great revival preaching he made several tours through South Wales, bringing the people under the spell of his dramatic but spiritual preaching, and winning great numbers to the Lord.

EVANS, WILLIAM (1870-1950), American Bible teacher, born in Liverpool, England, studied in private schools in England, Moody Bible Institute, Chicago, Lutheran Theological Seminary, Chicago, and Chicago Theological Seminary. Ordained in 1894 in the Presbyterian ministry, and served as pastor from 1895 to 1900 in Goshen, Indiana, Wheaton, Illinois, and Chicago. Director of the Bible Course of Moody Bible Institute (1901-1915); dean of the Bible Institute of Los Angeles (1915-1918); director of Bible Conferences for the United States and Canada from 1918 to 1950. A few of his writings were: *The Book of Books; How to Memorize; Personal Soul-Winning; The Great Doctrines of the Bible* and *Book Method of Bible Study.* Many of his books provided the material for The Evans Bible Correspondence Course.

EWING, FINIS (1773-1841), helped found Cumberland Presbyterian church. Born Brevard County, Virginia. Converted about 1800. Supported Second Awakening and when forced out of the Presbyterian church he and others in 1810 formed what became the Cumberland Presbyterian church by 1814.

EXCELL, EDWIN OTHELLO (1851-1921), American song composer, born at Uniontown, Stark County, Ohio, received education in the public schools of Ohio and Pennsylvania, spent some years as a mason and brick layer. Music director for many gospel meetings, laboring with many of the most famous evangelists of the country. For twenty years associated with Samuel Porter Jones as gospel singer, and later in life with Gipsy Smith. After 1881 engaged in the publication of church and Sunday school music books. Excell was the composer of the music for many gospel songs and hymns, such as "Let Him In," "Count Your Blessings," and the words of "Since I Have Been Redeemed." Belonged to the Methodist church, and took a prominent part in the prohibition movement.

EXELL, JOSEPH SAMUEL (1849-c. 1909), Church of England clergyman, born at Welksham, Wiltshire, England, studied at Taunton and Sheffield colleges. Ordained priest in 1882. From 1881 to 1884 he was curate of Weston-super-Mare, Somersetshire; from 1884 to 1890 he was vicar of Townstall with St. Saviour, Somersetshire; and after 1890, he was rector of Stoke-Fleming, Dartmouth, Devonshire. Excell compiled the *Biblical Illustrator,* a set covering nearly all the books of the Bible. Collaborated with Canon H.D.M. Spence in editing *The Pulpit Commentary,* and *The Homiletic Library,* and collaborated with Spence and C. Neil in editing *Thirty Thousand Thoughts* (six volumes).

F

FABER, FREDERICK WILLIAM (1814-1863), English Roman Catholic clergyman and hymn writer, born of Huguenot ancestry at Calverley, Yorkshire, England, studied at Harrow School and Balliol College, Oxford. Ordained priest in the Church of England in 1839 and appointed rector of Elton, Northamptonshire in 1842. An enthusiastic follower of John Henry Newman at Oxford and took active part in the Tractarian Movement. Spent several years on the Continent studying Roman Catholicism and in 1845 left Protestantism and joined the Roman Catholic church. Formed a religious society in 1846 at Birmingham, to be known as the Brothers of the Will of God. In 1847 was reordained priest and in 1848 joined the Oratory of St. Philip Neri at Birmingham. Became head the next year of Brompton Oratory which he founded in London. Faber's fame rests largely on his beautiful hymns such as "My God How Wonderful Thou Art," "Faith of Our Fathers," "There's A Wideness in God's Mercy," "The Pilgrims of the Night" and "The Land Beyond the Sea." He wrote also other works of religious and devotional nature.

FABER, JACOBUS. *See* **LÈFEVRE D'ÉTAPLES, JACQUES.**

FABIAN (FABIANUS) (d. 250), nineteenth bishop or pope of Rome (236-250). Little actually known of his pontificate. In Cyprian's letters to Fabian's successors, Fabian is often mentioned with respect. Improved the organization of the church of Rome. He divided the city of Rome into seven ecclesiastical regions with a deacon in charge of each. Considerable work was done in the catacombs. Killed in the Decian persecution in 250.

FAIRBAIRN, ANDREW MARTIN (1838-1912), English Congregationalist theologian, born at Inverkeithing, near Edinburgh, Scotland. Educated at Edinburgh University, Evangelical Union Theological Academy in Glasgow, and Berlin. In 1860 became minister at the Evangelical Union Church at Bathgate, West Lothian, and in 1872 of St. Paul's Congregational Church in Aberdeen, where he won great reputation as a preacher and as a lecturer on philosophical and theological subjects. In 1877 he became principal of the Congregational Airedale Theology College at Bradford, England. In 1883 became chairman of the Congregational Union of England and Wales. In 1886 was chosen to establish Mansfield, a Congregational college at Oxford, of which he was principal until his retirement in 1909. Substance of his teaching published in 1893 in *The Place of Christ in Modern Theology*. Later wrote *The Philosophy of the Christian Religion; Studies in Religious Thought; Catholicism, Roman and Anglican; Studies in the Life of Christ;* and two volumes of sermons, *The City of God* and *Catholicism, Roman and Anglican*. Made several visits to America, lecturing in many university centers. In 1898-1899 was Haskell lecturer in India.

FAIRBAIRN, PATRICK (1805-1874), Scottish Presbyterian theologian, born at Hallyburton, Berwickshire, Scotland, educated at the University of Edinburgh, licensed to preach in 1826. From 1830 to 1836 located in the Orkney Islands. In 1836 transferred to Bridgeton, Glasgow, and in 1840 to Salton, East Lothian. At the disruption in 1843 left the established church and helped form the Free church, remained at Salton as pastor of the newly established Free church. In 1853 appointed professor of divinity in the theological college of the Free church at Aberdeen. In 1856 transferred to the Free Church college at Glasgow, where appointed professor of systematic theology and New Testament exegesis, and principal of the college, holding these positions until his death. In 1865 moderator of the General Assembly, and in 1867 a member of the Scottish delegation appointed to visit Presbyterian churches in the United States. He was also a member of the Old Testament Revision Company. Principal writings: *The Typology of Scripture; Jonah, His Life, Character and Mission; Ezekiel and the Book of His Prophecy; Prophecy Viewed in Its Distinctive Nature, Its Special Function, and Its Proper Interpretation; Hermeneutical Manual;* and *Pastoral Theology*. He edited *The Imperial Bible Dictionary* and contributed important articles to the work.

FAREL (få rĕl′), **GUILLAUME** (1489-1565), French Reformer, born at Gap, Dauphine, France. Finishing his study of languages, philosophy, and theology at the University of Paris, taught in one of the colleges of the university. His teacher, Jacques Lèfevre d'Étaples, led him to adopt Reformed views, which he began to preach with great fervor. Became pioneer of Protestantism in western Switzerland. In 1521 he preached his new faith so vigorously at Meaux that Bishop

Briçonnet felt compelled to silence him. He then visited Paris and Gap, and went to Basel in 1524, where Oecolampadius received him as an ally. For awhile with Bucer and Caprini in Strassburg; in 1532 came to Geneva and succeeded in persuading the authorities there to adopt the Reforming edict in 1535. He was not able to carry through the program of organizing the Reformation. When John Calvin chanced through the city in 1536, Farel compelled him to join and help in the work. But the opposition was so strong that in 1538 Farel and Calvin were forced to leave Geneva abruptly. Farel went to Neuchatel, then to Metz and Gap, and back to Neuchatel, continuing to labor for the Reformation, preaching and writing to the day of his death at Neuchatel.

FARRAR (făr'er), **FREDERIC WILLIAM** (1831-1903), Dean of Canterbury and author, born in Bombay, India, where his father was a chaplain under the Church Missionary Society. Studied at King's College, University of London, and at Trinity College, Cambridge. Ordained priest in 1857; taught at Marlborough and Harrow, during which time he also was preaching and was doing some writing that gave him distinction. Select preacher at Cambridge on several occasions; was honorary chaplain to the queen; Hulsean Lecturer at Cambridge in 1870; and Bampton Lecturer at Oxford in 1885. In 1885 visited Canada and the United States, where he became a close friend of Phillips Brooks. In 1876 appointed by Disraeli as canon of Westminster and rector of St. Margaret's, where his preaching attracted great crowds. In 1883 made archdeacon of Westminster and rural dean; in 1890 became chaplain of the House of Commons; and in 1895 made dean of Canterbury, where he took great interest in the great, old cathedral. His publications were numerous: prepared commentaries for the *Expositor's Bible*, for Bishop Ellicott's Commentary, and for the Cambridge Bible series. Wrote the *Life and Work of St. Paul; Life of Christ; The Early Days of Christianity; Eternal Hope* (in which he called in question the doctrine of eternal punishment), *The Witness of History* (Hulsean Lectures), and *History of Interpretation* (Bampton lectures). Many of his books were published in America.

FAULHABER, MICHAEL VON (1869-1952), Archbishop of Munich. Born in Bavaria, educated at Schweinfurt and Würzburg. Ordained 1892. Lecturer at Würburg and from 1898 to 1911 professor at Strassburg. Bishop of Speyer 1911, Archbishop of Munich 1917, cardinal in 1921. World War I chaplain. Defended Roman Catholic church in Germany in Hitler regime. Worked out concordat between Vatican and Hitler in 1933.

FAUSSET (fô'set), **ANDREW ROBERT** (1821-1910), Church of England clergyman, born near Enniskillen, County Fermanagh, Ireland, studied at Trinity College, Dublin. Ordained priest in 1848. Curate of Bishop Middleham, Durham (1847-1859), rector of St. Cuthbert's, York (1859-1910), and canon of York after 1885. Chaplain at Bex, Switzerland, 1870 and at St. Goar on Rhine, 1873. He belonged to the premillennial Evangelical school of the Church of England. Some of his writings: *Scripture and Prayer Book in Harmony; The Englishman's Critical and Expository Cyclopaedia; The Church and the World; The Millennium; The Signs of the Times; Prophecy a Sure Light; The Latter Rain; The Personal Antichrist;* and *True Science Confirming Genesis*. He revised, edited, and published the first English translation of John Albert Bengel's *Gnomon of the New Testament*. Fausset collaborated with Jamieson and Brown in writing the set of commentaries commonly referred to as *Jamieson, Fausset, and Brown* or simply *J.F.B.* Fausset wrote the third, fourth, and sixth volumes of this six-volume set.

FAWCETT (fō'set), **JOHN** (1740-1817), English Baptist preacher, born near Bradford, Yorkshire, England. Converted under George Whitefield's preaching when about sixteen, joined the Baptist church at Bradford in 1759, being ordained a Baptist minister in 1764. Settled in Halifax and remained there until his death, preaching first at Wainsgate, then at Hebden Bridge, where a new church was built for him in 1777. In theology, a moderate Calvinist. In addition to preaching ministry, he conducted an academy at Brearley Hall the greater part of his ministry. In this institution William Ward of Serampore fame received a part of his training. He published several books, among them a collection of hymns. Included in this collection are such hymns as, "Lord Dismiss Us With Thy Blessing," "How Precious is the Book Divine," "Thus Far My God Hath Led Me On," and "Blest Be the Tie That Binds." His best known literary undertaking was a *Devotional Commentary on the Holy Scripture*, published in two large volumes.

FELICITAS (fē lĭs'ĭ tăs), (d. 203), early Christian martyr, from Carthage, North Africa. With Perpetua, following the rescript of Septimus Severus forbidding any conversions to Christianity, she was consigned to prison. Her child was born in prison shortly before her martyrdom and was placed in the hands of a Christian relative. After the trial she and Perpetua were led out to the amphitheater to be gored by an enraged cow. Being only wounded, she was put to death by the sword.

FELIX OF URGEL (d. 818), bishop of Urgel in Spain. Defended Elipandus of Toledo at Regensburg in 792 and before Pope Adrian I. Elipandus held that Christ was son of God by adoption. Elipandus later charged with heresy at Frankfurt and Aachen.

FELL, MARGARET (1614-1702), wife of Thomas Fell, vice-chancellor of the Duchy of Lancaster. Converted to Quakerism by George Fox in 1652. Married Fox in 1669. Her estate, Swarthmore Hall, became the center of Quaker activity.

FENELON (fān lôn′ or fā ne lôn′), **FRANÇOIS DE SALIGNAC DE LA MOTHE** (1651-1715), French quietist, born at the castle of Fenelon in Perigord, France. At twelve years of age sent to the Jesuit University of Cohors, then attended the Jesuit College du Plessis. Theological studies continued at the Seminary of St. Sulpice. Made an abbé and preached first sermon at the age of fifteen. Ordained to the priesthood in 1675. About 1678 appointed supervisor of the Nouvelles Conventies, an association of women, formed to educate and train young Protestant women inclined toward the Catholic faith. From 1686 to 1688 in a mission to the Huguenots. In 1695 consecrated to the archbishopric of Cambrai. In 1689 appointed preceptor to the young duke of Burgundy, the grandson of Louis XIV. When the mystical writings of Madam Guyon were being challenged by the church of France, Bossuet, bishop of Meaux, with the support of the court of France vigorously sought to suppress her teaching. When Fenelon championed her cause, he was bitterly assailed and his favor at court suddenly ceased. The controversy between Fenelon and Bossuet was long and vigorous. He answered with self-restraint and dignity, and meekly and patiently bore the accusation brought against him. Finally when the pope formally disapproved the twenty-three statements sent to him by Fenelon's accusers, Fenelon at once submitted and offered to burn with his own hands his book, *Maximes des Saints,* which contained the statements. The book was burned, but the copyist had made a duplicate, and it was printed again in Holland in 1699. Fenelon was allowed to continue his church work but was ordered to remain within his diocese, and forbidden all intercourse with his former pupil, the duke of Burgundy. Devoted the remainder of his life to the diligent care of his diocese and to literary labors. Founded a seminary at Cambrai. Though a mystic he nevertheless possessed remarkable insight in the practical affairs of his day. In the Jansenist controversy he took an active part as an opponent to the bishop of Ypres and fully upheld the papal decisions. He died at Cambrai. Fenelon's best known writing, *Telemaque,* caused him to fall into disgrace at the court.

FENG YU-HSIANG (fŭng′ yû shē äng′), (1882-1948), the "Christian General" of China, born in Ching-hsien, Anwhei, China. Graduated from the Paoting Military Academy with honors in 1910. At the early age of about twelve entered military service, and gradually rose in military power. At the time of the Boxer Rebellion, Feng as a young soldier, seeing the sacrificial, vicarious spirit of the missionaries, especially of Miss Mary Morill, who was killed by the Boxers, was greatly impressed and influenced toward Christianity. About ten years later at an evangelistic meeting conducted by Dr. John R. Mott, he made the decision to accept Christ publicly. Baptized by Rev. Liu Fang in the Methodist Episcopal church, and maintained his Christian testimony thereafter. For many years he had the reputation of having the model Christian army of the world, about half of his thirty thousand troops being baptized Christians. Military governor of Shensi in 1921, the first Christian governor in China. In 1922 appointed military governor of Honan, and in 1923 made field marshal. In 1924 commander-in-chief of the Peoples' Armies. The discipline of his men, and their confidence in him was most excellent. Bible reading, gospel singing, prayer, clean morals, and good will prevailed throughout his army. "In his religious life, perhaps above any other side of his character, General Feng shows his true greatness." As a prominent layman, Feng came to the United States in 1946 to study the Tennessee Valley Authority, and to visit missionary groups.

FERDINAND V of Castile; II of Aragon and Sicily; III of Naples (1452-1516), surnamed "the Catholic," born at Sos in Aragon, the son of John II of Navarre and Aragon. In 1469 married Isabella of Castile; and five years later Ferdinand and Isabella were crowned joint sovereigns of Leon and Castile. In 1479 Ferdinand also became king of Aragon. Thus was laid the foundation of modern Spain. The power of these sovereigns was greatly strengthened by the establishment of the Inquisition (1478-1480). The Inquisition or Holy Office had been established by the church for the purpose of detecting and punishing heresy. In Spain its chief victims were the Mohammedan Moors and the Jews; thousands were burned at the stake and most cruelly treated. The expulsion of the Jews and the driving out of the Mohammedan Moors from Granada in Southern Spain, and the discovery of America by Columbus—all in or by 1492—added to the prestige and power of Ferdinand. Cardinal Ximenes had great influence in helping Ferdinand to power, and also along with Isabella, was a great restraining moral influence in the kingdom. Isabella died in 1504; and two years later Ferdinand married the niece of Louis XII of France. Successful in uniting his own lands in Spain, he also added to them various fortresses of northern Africa, and much of the Kingdom of Navarre. Catherine, the daughter of Ferdinand and Isabella, became the wife of Henry VIII of England and had great influence on the history of the Reformation in England. "Ferdinand was unsurpassed in an age of cunning diplomatists. Spain owes her unity and greatness as a nation, and the imperial influence over Europe to Ferdinand and Isabella."

FICHTE (fĭk′tĕ), **JOHANN GOTTLIEB** (1762-1814), German philosopher, born in Rammenau, Upper Lusatia, studied at Meissen, Schulpforta, Jena, and Leipzig. Served for a number of years as tutor to several families in Leipzig, Zurich, and Warsaw. About 1791 he went to Königsberg to confer further with Kant on his system of philosophy. Fichte then wrote *The Essay toward a Critique of All Revelation,* published anonymously. When it became known that Fichte was the author, his reputation as a philosopher was at once established, and he was offered a position as professor in philosophy at Jena in 1794. Here he began to expound with extraordinary zeal his system of transcendentalism. A few years later (1799), however, he wrote a short essay in which he declared that the moral order of the world is God, and that there is no other God. This confirmed the charge of atheism against Fichte, and he was discharged from Jena. He spent nearly all the remainder of his life in Berlin. In 1805 he lectured for a few months in the University of Erlangen, and in 1806-1807 made a visit to Königsberg. Took a prominent part in the founding of the University of Berlin, and was rector and professor of philosophy there from its opening in 1809 until his death. On the faculty of the university were Schleiermacher and Neander. Napoleon's victories in Germany aroused the philosopher to action in behalf of his nation. In his *Address to the German Nation* he called upon fellow-countrymen to establish German freedom upon the highest moral basis, and especially upon genuine educational reform. Fichte's earliest interests were in theology, and a strong theological bent was manifest throughout his career. Writings and philosophy were largely an interpretation of Kant, especially laying emphasis on the practical and moral aspects of Kant's teaching. He did not accept the traditional orthodox doctrine of Christ. Among his other writings were *Science of Knowledge;* and *The Way Towards the Blessed Hope, or the Doctrine of Religion.*

FICINO, MARSILIO (1433-1499), humanist of Florence. Educated at Florence in classical learning. Ordained priest in 1473. Translated Plato, Plotinus, and Pseudo-Dionysius, works that were widely used in the Middle Ages. Taught at the Platonic Academy of Florence where Colet, Erasmus, and other scholars studied. Wrote *Theologia Platonia.* Believed there was truth in classics of Greek philosophy and sought to relate Platonic thought to biblical revelation. Also wrote *Of the Christian Religion.*

FILLMORE, CHARLES (1854-1948), co-founder (with his wife) of the Unity School of Christianity, born in Minnesota, crippled from childhood, and self-educated. The Fillmores, former Christian Scientists, began their "new revelation," healing cult in Kansas City, Missouri, in 1889 after they had been reduced to poverty, losing all their recently amassed wealth, and after being miraculously healed of their incurable diseases. That year they began publishing a magazine, *Modern Thought.* In 1903 the cult was incorporated under the name, "Unity School of Practical Christianity," organized to demonstrate "universal law." In 1906 Unity built and dedicated a church, which included a publishing house, a school, and a health dispensary. In 1914 its present name of Unity School of Christianity was adopted. Unity is a pantheistic cult based upon the idea of spiritual oneness of man with God. It is akin in some respects to Christian Science, Theosophy, and New Thought. Charles Fillmore supervised the entire facilities of this huge empire until his death in 1948. Myrtle, (1845-1931) his wife was partner, and co-founder of Unity. By tracts, books, the mail, and the radio the movement broadcasts its "soothing" remedies for everything from sin, sickness, and death to domestic troubles and the incessant demands of finance companies. The underlying idea of Unity is the concept that thought is omnipotent. Fillmore's writings include *Talks on Faith, Christian Healing, The Twelve Powers of Man,* and over one hundred tracts.

FINAN (d. 661), an Irish Celtic monk of Iona who was later ordained, and in 651 or 652 succeeded Aidan as bishop of Lindisfarne with charge of the whole of Northumbria.

Aided by Oswy, king of Northumbria, the brother of King Oswald who had aided Aidan, labored earnestly for the conversion of Northumbria, and extended missionary labors to other areas outside Northumbria. It was his privilege to baptize the kings of both Mercia and of the East Saxons, and to consecrate Caedmon. He was opposed to the Roman manner of observing Easter.

FINDLAY, GEORGE GILLANDERS (1849-1919), English Methodist educator and biblical scholar, born at Welshpool, Montgomeryshire, Wales, studied at Wesley College, Sheffield, at Richmond Theological College; and at London University. Assistant tutor at Headingley College (1870-1874), classical tutor at Richmond Theological College (1874-1881), and tutor in New Testament exegesis and classics at Headingley Theological Institution (1881-1917). Wrote several commentaries on Paul's Epistles for *The Expositor's Bible, The Expositor's Greek Testament, The Cambridge Bible,* and the *Pulpit Commentary.* He wrote *Epistles of the Apostle Paul, Their Origin and Content.*

FINNEY, CHARLES GRANDISON (1792-1875), Congregational revivalist, theologian, abolitionist and college president, born at Warren, Connecticut, at age of two moved with his parents to Oneida County, New York. When about twenty went to New Jersey where he attended high school and taught school from 1808 to 1816. In later years learned some Latin, Greek, and Hebrew. At age of twenty-six entered a law office in Adams, New York. Observing how often law books quoted from the Bible, he purchased the first copy of the Bible he had ever owned and began to read it. He also attended prayer meeting and church. In 1821 occurred his conversion, remarkable for its suddenness, and thoroughness. Almost immediately he resolved to give up law to accept a call to preach. He entered the Presbyterian church and in 1824 was ordained. Soon turned attention to revival labors, which he continued with few interruptions until 1860 when age prevented traveling. Preached in many of the cities in the eastern part of the United States, and made two revival trips to England. In 1832 assumed the pastorate of the Second Free (Presbyterian) Church of New York City, and in 1836 of the recently organized Congregational Broadway Tabernacle, organized especially for him. In 1835 he went to Oberlin College as professor of theology, continued until his death in 1875. In 1851 he became president of Oberlin. During these years he continued to hold revival meetings. He initiated the "anxious bench" and dwelt upon the importance of hearers coming to immediate decision and of rising in public attestation of their decision. His novel methods and his departure from certain Calvinistic emphases called forth the criticism of the more conventionally and doctrinally conservative leaders of the church. Unique methods of preaching prevailed and he continued revival labors. It is estimated that more than half a million people were converted through his ministry. As a teacher his influence was great, and had a shaping effect upon students and upon denomination. Among his writings are: *Lectures on Systematic Theology, Lectures on Revivals,* and *Autobiography.* As a revivalist, as a theologian, and as college president, he left the impress of his character upon thousands of lives and contributed not a little toward the shaping of Christianity in the American republic.

FISHER, GEORGE PARK (1827-1909), Congregational clergyman and historian, born at Wrentham, Massachusetts, studied at Brown University, Yale Divinity School, Auburn Theological Seminary, and Andover Theological Seminary, and then two years in Germany. Livingston professor of divinity and college preacher in Yale College (1854-1861). Professor of ecclesiastical history in Yale Divinity School for forty years (1861-1901), also serving as dean (1895-1901). In 1898 Fisher was president of the American Historical Association. He was also president of the American Society of Church History for a number of years. Some of his writings: *History of the Reformation, The Beginnings of Christianity, Grounds of Theistic and Christian Belief, History of the Christian Church, Manual of Christian Evidences,* and *History of Christian Doctrine.*

FISHER, JOHN (1459-1535), Bishop of Rochester and Roman Catholic martyr, born at Beverley, Yorkshire, England, educated at Michaelhouse, Cambridge. After taking orders appointed chaplain and confessor to Margaret, the mother of Henry VII, about 1497. In 1504 consecrated Bishop of Rochester and also president of Queen's College and chancellor of Cambridge University. He took a deep interest in revival of learning and began the study of Greek at the age of sixty. Among his friends were the humanists Reuchlin and Erasmus. He was not insensible of the clerical wrongs in the church, even sought reform within the church, but had no sympathy with the Protestant Reformation. One of the chief advisers of Henry VIII. In 1531 signed the formula constituting the political sovereign as the supreme head of the Church of

England, however, only "so far as the law of God permits." Refused further attempts to divorce the Church of England from the pope. Championed papal authority and strenuously opposed Henry's divorce from Catharine. In 1534 when he refused assent to the Supremacy Acts, he, along with Sir Thomas More, was sent to the Tower. To protect him, Pope Paul III, made him cardinal, but this incensed the king. Fisher was tried for treason, found guilty, and beheaded on Tower Hill. Several days later Sir Thomas More was beheaded at the same place and for the same reason. He was canonized in 1935.

FISK, PLINY (1792-1825), American Congregational missionary, born at Shelburne, Massachusetts. After graduating from Middlebury College, Vermont and Andover Theological Seminary, he was ordained in Salem, and preached in Wilmington, Vermont. In 1818 he and Levi Parsons were appointed by the American Board to go to the Near East to consider the opening of work in Palestine and Syria. They arrived in Smyrna in 1820, and began the study of modern Greek and Italian and the survey of the field. Early in 1822 they made a trip to Egypt, but Parsons died in Alexandria within a few weeks. Fisk continued traveling in Egypt, Greece, Palestine, and Syria, surveying the entire region, distributing tracts and Bibles, and studying Greek and Arabic. He did some preaching in Italian, French, Greek, and Arabic, and published a number of articles in the *Missionary Herald*. In May 1825 joined the mission which had shortly before been established at Beirut. On the day before his death he completed an English-Arabic Dictionary.

FISK, WILBUR (1792-1839), American Methodist educator and clergyman, born in Brattleboro, Vermont, received his education at the University of Vermont and Brown University. He took up the study of law, but soon changed to become an itinerant preacher in the Methodist church in 1818. Held pastorates at Craftsbury, Vermont, and at Charlestown, Massachusetts. For a time agent for the New Market Academy in New Hampshire, and in 1826 chaplain of the Vermont legislature. Chief contribution to the Methodist church and to American Christianity was through the advancement of Christian education. Helped found Wilbraham Academy, in 1825 became its first principal. Also helped found Wesleyan University at Middletown, Connecticut, and in 1830 became its first president. He was convinced that preachers must be trained to bring culture, education, and Christianity to the whole of the expanding nation. Interested in missions, and included them in his educational program. Originator of the Flathead Mission in Oregon. Offered to go as a missionary to the Indians. In 1828 elected bishop of the Methodist church in Canada, but declined the office. Wesleyan University sent him to Europe in 1835 for the benefit of his health and to study educational institutions. An early advocate of temperance and an opponent of abolitionism yet opposed slavery. After struggling with ill health all his life, he died in 1839. Chief writings: *The Science of Education, The Calvinistic Controversy,* and *Travels in Europe*.

FISKE, FIDELIA (1816-1864), missionary to Persia, born at Shelburne, Massachusetts, educated at Franklin Academy and at Mount Holyoke Seminary. Early in life became interested in missions through her uncle, Pliny Fisk, a missionary to Syria. Inspired by her seminary teacher, Miss Mary Lyon, in 1843 went to Urumia, Persia, as a missionary. Womanhood was in a state of utter degradation. Miss Fiske opened a boarding school and for fifteen years gave herself devotedly and unstintingly to these girls. Many became earnest Christians. During these fifteen years experiences of great spiritual awakening and of bitter persecution alternated with one another. Miss Fiske's missionary career was cut short by ill health, and in 1858 she was compelled to take a vacation in her homeland. Miss Fiske never returned to Persia.

FITZWATER, PERRY BRAXTON (1871-1957), theologian and clergyman, born in Hardy County, West Virginia. Educated at Bridgewater College, Virginia, Moody Bible Institute, Chicago, Xenia Theological Seminary, Ohio, Princeton Theological Seminary and Princeton University. Taught in public schools in West Virginia, Virginia, and Iowa. Pastor one year, Elkhart, Indiana, and worked in a city mission in Sidney, Ohio while at Xenia. Ordained in 1909. Years 1905-1911, Dean of Bible Department, Manchester College, Indiana; 1912-1913, taught Bible, LaVerne College, California; 1913-1954, member of faculty, Moody Bible Institute. Last twenty years at Moody was director of Pastor's Course. Writings: *Why God Became Man, The Doctrines of the Christian Faith, Christian Theology, Preaching the Bible, Preaching and Teaching the New Testament*. For twenty years wrote syndicated columns of Bible lessons for twenty-six hundred newspapers, and International Sunday School Lessons for *Moody Monthly* Magazine.

FLACIUS (flā'shĭ ŭs), **MATTHIAS ILLYRICUS (VLACICH)** (1520-1575), German Lutheran theologian and controversialist, born at Albona in Illyria, studied with a humanist teacher in Venice. Went to Basel in 1539, then to Tübingen in 1540, and to Wittenberg in 1541. Studied with Melanchthon and Luther. He began to preach the Evangelical doctrine. In 1544 became professor of Hebrew at Wittenberg, and the next year married. He lectured on the Old Testament, the Pauline epistles, and Aristotle. His activities were suddenly interrupted by the Schmalkald War, when he fled to Brunswick in 1547, where he lived by teaching. Bitterly opposed the Augsburg Interim (1548) and especially the Leipzig Interim which was a compromise proposed by Melanchthon the same year. Became involved in the several current Lutheran controversies. An opponent to the Adiaphoristic, Majoristic, Osiandrian, Schwenkfeldian and other views. This placed him in direct opposition to the Melanchthonian party. After he became professor in Jena in 1557, helped make Jena headquarters for the strict Lutheran party as Wittenberg had become the center of the Philippist party. In a short time he became involved in the synergistic controversy (relating to the function of the will in conversion), which arose in Jena. Flacius was criticized and deposed. For the rest of his life, a harried wanderer. Finally settled in Frankfort where he died. Not only the most learned Lutheran theologian, but also the promoter and founder of theological disciplines. Among chief writings were: thirteen volumes of *The Magdeburg Centuries,* written with help of others, the first Protestant church history; *Catalogus Testium Veritatus,* a catalog of witnesses against Roman Catholicism before Luther; *Clavis Scripturae Sacrae,* the basis of Biblical hermeneutics, and *Glossacompendaria in Novum Testamentum.*

FLANAGAN, EDWARD (1886-1948), founder of Boys Town, Omaha, Nebraska. Born Roscommon, Ireland. Came to the United States in 1904 and naturalized in 1919. Educated at St. Mary's College, Maryland; St. Joseph Seminary, Dunwoodie, New York; Gregorian University in Rome; and the Jesuit University in Innsbruck. Ordained priest in 1912. Served churches in Nebraska (1912-1916). Opened Workingman's Hotel in Omaha (1914-1917). Feeling need of helping boys before they became hardened in crime, he organized Home for Homeless Boys which he later moved outside Omaha and called Boys Town in 1922. Made monsignor in 1937. Helped set up similar institutions in Japan and Europe. Believed that there was "no such thing as a bad boy."

FLAVEL (flăv'ĕl), **JOHN** (c. 1630-1691), English Presbyterian clergyman, born at Bromsgrove, near Birmingham, Worcestershire, England, son of a minister, studied at University College, Oxford. In 1650 was ordained a Presbyterian minister, and became curate of Diptford in Devonshire; in 1656 of Dartmouth. Being ejected from his church by the Act of Uniformity he retired to Slapton, five miles distant, where he preached twice each Sunday, sometimes in the woods and remote open places, until 1671, when James II relaxed the penal laws, he was able to return to Dartmouth and to continue his self-sacrificing labors there. A prolific writer on practical religion and piety. A few of his many writings: *Treatise on the Soul of Man; Husbandry Spiritualized; The Fountain of Life Opened Up; The Soul of Man; Exposition of the Assembly's Shorter Catechism; The Methods of Grace; A Token for Mourners;* and *A Saint Indeed.*

FLÉCHIEE (flȧ shyā'), **VALENTIN ESPRIT** (1632-1710), French Roman Catholic panegyrist and Bishop of Nimes, born at Pernes near Avignon in the south of France, educated by the Jesuits at the College of the Congregation of Christian Doctrine at Tarascon. Taught rhetoric for a while at Narbonne, and in 1660 went to Paris and became a catechist in one of the parishes of the city. Gradually attracted attention to his preaching talents, rivaling Bossuet. Excellency and fame lay in his funeral orations. In 1673, became a member of the French Academy, wrote many poems in French and Latin and some political compositions, bringing him great fame and favor with Louis XIV, who gave him various ecclesiastical promotions, in 1685 naming him Bishop of Lavaur, and in 1687, Bishop of Nimes. Diocese included Languedoc, which contained many Calvinists. Revocation of the Edict of Nantes in 1685 made Fléchiee's work in this region especially difficult, because of the presence of the Protestants; but his gentle spirit, kind disposition, and mild attitude won for him the respect and affection of all.

FLEETWOOD, WILLIAM (1656-1723), English prelate, born in the Tower of London, and studied at Eton and at King's College, Cambridge. Soon after taking orders in 1689 won renown by a sermon delivered before King's College in commemoration of Henry VI, the founder of the college. In the same year given fellowship at Eton, and the chapter rectory of St. Augustine and St. Faith's, London. Held liberal political views and favored the Revolution. Shortly after accession of William and Mary in 1689 he was appointed chaplain to the king, and in 1702 was made canon of Windsor. In 1708 Queen Anne made him bishop of St. Asaph, and in 1714 King George I translated him to Ely, where he died in 1723. He was buried in that cathedral. One of the most eloquent preachers of his day. Besides sermons which he published wrote: *An Essay on Miracles, Inscriptionum Antiquarium Sylloge,* and *The Judgment of the Church of England Concerning Lay Baptism.*

FLETCHER or DE LA FLECHIERE, JOHN WILLIAM (1729-1785), Vicar of Madeley and early Methodist theologian, born at Nyon, Switzerland. Parents, whose original name was De la Flechiere, designed him for the ministry; he preferred the army. Received most of his education at Geneva. Went to England and acquired a good knowledge of the language, becoming a tutor. Came in touch with the Methodists and experienced a deep faith as taught and experienced by Wesley and others. In 1757 ordained priest and in 1760 became vicar of Madeley, a rough mining town in Shropshire. In 1768 Lady Huntington engaged Fletcher to be superintendent of her newly established seminary at Trevecca, Wales. Three years later because of doctrinal differences between himself and the trustees he resigned. Worked with John Wesley in evangelistic labors and journeys as much as he could while caring for pastorate. Fletcher was an Arminian, and was drawn into many controversies. Most of his writings, such as his best work *Checks to Antinomianism,* directed against Calvinism and in defense of Wesleyan doctrines. Treated opponents with fairness and courtesy, an eloquent preacher, a zealous evangelist, a man of saintly piety, one with rare devotion to God, beloved by all.

FLIEDNER (flēd'nār), **THEODOR** (1800-1864), founder of Protestant deaconess institutions, born at Epstein, near Wiesbaden, Germany, orphaned at thirteen, later studied at Giessen, Göttingen, and Herborn. Began ministry in a small Protestant church in a Roman Catholic community at Kaiserswerth. Began the use of deaconesses to assist him, and founded a training school for them in 1836. They nursed the sick as well as cared for the spiritually destitute. Fliedner visited many countries to raise money for his parish, and for his institution at Kaiserswerth, and for many others. At his death the number of deaconesses in connection with Kaiserswerth and its twenty-nine branch establishments exceeded six hundred. By 1878, fourteen years after his death, the number of institutions in Germany, Switzerland, France, Scandinavia, Russia, and Austria rose to fifty-two, and the number of sisters to nearly four thousand. He also organized the Prisoners Society of Germany. He and his wife inaugurated a home for discharged women convicts in 1833.

FLINT, ROBERT (1838-1910), Scottish philosopher and theologian, born at Dumfriesshire, Scotland, educated at the University of Glasgow, early trained in the Free church, turned to the Church of Scotland. Employed in lay mission work for a time, licensed to preach in 1858, was parish minister in Aberdeen and in Kilconquhar between 1859 and 1864. Flint was professor of moral philosophy and political economy at St. Andrews (1864-1876); and professor of divinity at the University of Edinburgh (1876-1903). In 1880 Stone lecturer at Princeton University. Wrote: *Philosophy of History in Europe; Theism; Anti-Theistic Theories; Hindu Pantheism;* and *On Theological, Biblical, and Other Subjects.*

FLORENTIUS RADEWIJNS (1350-1400), helped Gerhard Groot found the Brethren of the Common Life in order to cultivate practical piety. Educated at Prague. Canon at Utrecht. From 1387 organized the Congregation of Windesheim which as a unit of the Brethren promoted devotion to God and religious education.

FOAKES-JACKSON, F. S. *See* **JACKSON, F. J. F.**

FORSYTH, PETER TAYLOR (1848-1921), English Congregational clergyman, born in Aberdeen, Scotland, studied at the University of Aberdeen, (under Ritschl), University of Göttingen and New College, Hamstead, London. Professor of Latin at Aberdeen, later successively held five pastorates between the years 1876 and 1901 at Shipley, Hackney, Manchester, Leicester, and Cambridge. In 1899 sent as one of the English delegates to the International Congregational Council in Boston, Massachusetts, where the greatness of the man came to be recognized on this side of the Atlantic. From 1901 to 1921 principal of Hackney Theological College, Hamstead, London, and also a member of the theological faculty of London University. In 1905 elected chairman of the Congregational Union of England and Wales, the highest office with which his denomination could honor him. In 1907 delivered the Lyman Beecher lectures at Yale, *Positive Preaching and Modern Mind,* in which he brought together the evangelical power of the older school and the intellectual range of modern liberalism. He gave emphasis to the divine initiative of Christ. A prolific writer. Some of his works: *The Person and Place of Christ; The Work of Christ; The Cruciality of the Cross;* and *This Life and the Next.* He was greatly pained when the German theologians gave their support to the Kaiser in the invasion of Belgium. Out of this concern wrote: *The Christian Ethic of War.* Never a robust or well man, died on the fourth Armistice Day.

FOSDICK, HARRY EMERSON (1878-1969), American liberal Baptist minister. Born near Buffalo, New York. Educated at Colgate University, Columbia University, and Union Seminary, New York. Ordained in 1903. Pastor at Montclair, New Jersey from 1904 to 1915. Professor Union Seminary, New York (1908-1946). From 1919 to 1925 pulpit supply at First Presbyterian Church, New York, where he preached his famous sermon "Shall the Fundamentalists Win?" which led to his resignation in 1925. Became pastor of Riverside Church, financed partly by Rockefeller, from 1926 until 1946. Focused clash between Fundamentalists and Liberals in the 1920s. Emphasized problem-centered preaching. In 1927 began "National Vespers" on NBC. More important books: *The Modern Use of the Bible, A Guide to Understanding the Bible,* and his autobiography, *The Living of These Days*.

FOSTER, JOHN (1770-1843), English Baptist preacher and essayist, born at Wadsworth Lane, parish of Halifax, Yorkshire, England. Received education at Fawcett's academy at Brearley Hall and at the Baptist college in Bristol. Entered the ministry and for twenty-five years held pastorates in several places. Due to manifest lack of preaching ability, with unsettledness in his Christian life and experience, with sensitiveness and peculiarities in personal and social character, and with an aggravated throat ailment, he was compelled to give up preaching. Foster's denial of eternal punishment placed him at odds with all his Baptist brethren in the religious realm. For a time before leaving ministry gave instruction to some African youths who had been brought to England to be trained as missionaries. Published a volume of essays which included his famous essay, *On Decision of Character*.

FOX, GEORGE (1624-1691), Mystic, itinerant preacher, and founder of the Society of Friends, born at Drayton, Leicestershire, England. Puritan training in the home and association with Anabaptists had a marked influence on his life. Failing to find from the church leaders the serenity he sought, when twenty-two years old decided he must turn to God alone. Discovered in a vital way that the Spirit of God dwells in the spirit or heart of man, and that man can have direct communion with God. To him this was the real secret of perfect spiritual guidance. Intimate, direct fellowship with God led him to disparage external ordinances as unnecessary, tending only to formalism and hypocrisy. After receiving this light, Fox started out in 1647 on mission as a wandering preacher, and for the next forty years, by writing and itinerant preaching, heralded teachings and convictions far and wide. Traveled extensively in England and Scotland, also visited Holland and America. Refused to take any oath or to do any military service. Took persecution and maltreatment with meekness and non-retaliation. Fox and many of his followers suffered much persecution and imprisonment. His following grew rapidly. They spread to London, Bristol, and Norwich. One of Fox's early converts was Margaret Fell (1614-1702). One of his most eminent preachers and a literary defender of the Quaker faith was William Penn. In 1660 a constitution was prepared and local congregations were formed. The people, early known as "Children of Light" or "Friends of Truth," finally came to be known as Quakers, but accepted officially the name, "Society of Friends." Fox's teachings may be summarized: Great emphasis is placed on the immediate, personal teaching of the Holy Spirit or "inner light"; every member being a priest of God, a professional ministry is to be rejected; the sacraments, including baptism and the eucharist, are inner and spiritual verities only; oaths are needless and wrong for the Christian; war is unlawful for a Christian; slavery is abhorrent. Fox wrote little beyond his *Journal*.

FOX, MARGARET (1833-1893), American spiritualist medium, born in Bath, Canada, early moved with her parents to Hydesville, New York. In 1848 with younger sister Catherine (Kate) claimed to have heard supernatural rappings, and worked out a code which they claimed would permit communication with the spirit world. They went to Rochester with their older sister, Leah, where the rappings continued. Leah took the girls to New York, where Margaret and Catherine became spiritualist mediums, and held seances, said to have brought them one hundred dollars a night. "The Fox Sisters" with their mother then toured the United States and Europe, holding public seances marked with rappings, the mysterious movings of large objects, and supposed communications with the spirit world. They gained a large hearing, and many were converted to spiritualism. Among those interested abroad were such noted people as Harriet Martineau and Elizabeth Barrett Browning, and several men and women of note in the United States. Catherine was later married. Margaret claimed common-law marriage to Dr. Elisha Kent Kane, an Arctic explorer, who had tried to draw her away from spiritualism. She assumed his name and published his letters to her as *The Love Letters of Dr. Kane*. In 1888 Margaret became a convert to Roman Catholicism, made a confession of the fraud of spiritualism, but later retracted her confession, returned to the rappings for a living, and resorted to frequent and rather heavy drinking until the time of her death in squalor and obscurity.

FOXE, JOHN (1516-1587), English martyrologist, born at Boston, Lincolnshire, England, educated at Brasenose, Oxford. In 1539 elected a fellow of Magdalen College, 1539 to 1545, applying himself to church history. Among intimate friends were Hugh Latimer and William Tyndale. Study of the great controversy between the Roman Catholic church and Protestantism led him to become a convert to the principles of the Reformation. Expelled in 1545 from his fellowship, but restored by Edward VI. In 1550 ordained deacon by Nicholas Ridley, Bishop of London. During Mary's reign he sought asylum in Basel, Frankfurt, and Strassburg, returning to England on the accession of Elizabeth. In 1560 ordained priest and in 1563 prebendary in the cathedral of Salisbury, and vicar of Shipton. For a short time rector of Cripplegate, where he was buried in 1587. Foxe's fame rests upon *The Acts and the Monuments of the Church,* usually known as *Foxe's Book of Martyrs,* in the compilation of which he had the help of Cranmer and others. The work was first published in Latin in Basel in 1559, and in English in London in 1563.

FRANCIS OF ASSISI (äs sē'zē), (1182-1226), founder of the Franciscan order, Francesco (christened Giovanni) Bernardone born at Assisi in Umbria, Central Italy, son of a rich cloth merchant, but received little education. As a frivolous youth joined the army, but taken prisoner. After release experienced a deep religious awakening. Following this went into seclusion, made a pilgrimage to Rome. His strict asceticism estranged him from his father and divorced him from society. He devoted himself strictly to religious life. Dressed scantily, ate sparingly, took up abode with the lepers, and rebuilt several chapels, one of which became a holy place to him. In 1210, at age twenty-eight, drafted a set of rules for his life. With these rules and eleven companions, went to Rome to apply for papal approval for starting an order. Innocent III gave the little party his blessing, granted them the tonsure, and bade them go out and preach. Known as Friars Minor, two by two they went about preaching repentance, singing, aiding the peasants in their work, caring for the lepers, the sick, and the outcast. Francis resolved to enter into marriage with poverty. The brotherhood spread rapidly. Far-reaching missionary plans were made, including missions to the Mohammedans. He went to Morocco (1213-1214) and Syria and Egypt in 1219, where he preached before the Sultan of Egypt. During his stay in the East the order he had founded, the Franciscan Order, in 1222 was placed in other hands, and was given new rules. He yielded in humble submission but was brokenhearted. Indeed a man of purity and humility, a real preacher. Gave the gospel to the common people and served them freely. Canonized by Pope Gregory IX, 1228.

FRANCIS DE SALES (frän'sis de säl), (1567-1622), Roman Catholic preacher, devotional writer, and mystic, born at Thoren, Savoy. Educated by the Jesuits at the College of Clermont in Paris, and for law at the University of Padua. Strong bent toward theology and the religious life made him enter the church. Ordained a priest in 1593, against father's will, very active, acquired some fame as a missionary among the Protestants of Le Chablais. In 1602 bishop of Geneva, where he entered actively into the work of church reform. In 1610, together with Madame de Chantal, founded the Order of the Visitation of Mary. A writer and mystic, a precursor of Molinos and Fenelon, and the first representative of the so-called Quietism. Best remembered for discourses and writings on the life of the Spirit. Stressed the love of God and fidelity to God's will. Canonized in 1665, in 1677 made a doctor of the church. Best known works: *Introduction to a Devout Life,* a very popular book among the Roman Catholics in the present day, and *Le Treatise on the Love of God*.

FRANCIS XAVIER. *See* **XAVIER, FRANCIS**

FRANCK (fränk), **CESAR AUGUSTE JEAN GUILLAUME HUBERT** (1822-1890), French composer, born at Liége, Belgium, of German ancestry, an excellent pianist by the age of eleven. Following a concert tour through Belgium studied at the Paris Conservatoire. In 1844 settled in Paris, became an influential teacher of music, and also gained fame as a composer. Became a French citizen. In 1872 professor of the organ at the Paris Conservatoire; and from 1851 to 1858 organist at the Church of Saint-Jean-Saint-Francois, and from 1858 until his death in 1890, at the Church of Sainte Clotilde, Paris. Principal works were the oratorios of *Ruth, The Redeemer, The Beatitudes, Rebecca,* several symphonic poems, a mass, two operas, important works for the organ, and excellent chamber music. His *Symphony in D Minor* ranks among the most popular of all symphonies. Franck was an inspiring, lucid, patient man, teaching out of the overflow of a quiet, modest, fruitful, happy life. Affection for his disciples or pupils demonstrated the inherent love, goodness, and saintliness of the man. Writings were drawn out of a busy and full life.

FRANCK (FRANK) (frängk), **SEBASTIAN** (1499-c. 1542), German reformer, humanist, historian, mystic, and freethinker, born at Donauwörth, Germany, educated for the Roman Catholic priesthood at the University of Ingolstadt and at the Dominican Bethlehem College at the University of Heidelberg. Ordained in 1524, held a curacy near Augsburg; the following year joined Reformation party at Nürnberg, and became a Protestant preacher at Gustenfelden. At first he allied himself with the Lutherans, but soon became interested in the Anabaptists. In 1528 abandoned all organized religion. Since his liberal religious ideas antagonized the authorities, removed from Nuremberg to Strassburg in 1529, developed an intimacy with Caspar Schwenkfeld. Two years later, published his chief work, the critical *Chronica, Zeitbuch, und Geschichtsbibel*. Freedom of thought, and broad tolerance relative to a universal but invisible church, again brought him official condemnation. After a brief imprisonment, expelled from Strassburg. Life witnessed a series of polemical vicissitudes with removals to Esslingen, where he set up a soap factory; then to Ulm, where he established a printing press; finally in 1539 to Basel, where he continued his printing and publishing of books until his death. Franck combined the humanist's passion for freedom with the mystic's devotion to the religion of the spirit, denouncing all external ordinances, machinery, and organization.

FRANCKE, AUGUST HERMANN (1663-1727), German pietistic leader and founder of charitable institutions at Halle, born in a pious home in Lübeck, Germany, received education at Gotha, Erfurt, Kiel, and Leipzig. Developed a passion for Greek and Hebrew. Read the Hebrew Bible through seven times in one year. In university studies came under the influence of the pietistic teaching of some of Spener's pupils, in 1688 at Leipzig met Spener and definitely became an adherent of the great pietistic preacher. In 1684 became member of the faculty of the University of Leipzig. The next year he was glad to leave the university and accept a call to preach at Erfurt. A year later dismissed for the same reason. In 1691 called to a pastorate in a suburb of Halle, and a chair of Greek and Oriental languages and later theology in the University of Halle. In 1686 organized University teachers in a Bible study class. Became the outstanding lecturer at Halle; continued to pastor his church with great effect and earnestness. Promoted the regular program of Spener in the principles of instruction, especially in requiring a conversion experience, the use of the Bible, preparation for preaching, and prayer before and after classes. Through Francke's noble vision and indefatigable efforts there grew about the university a group of remarkable institutions of inner missions, with Francke as the governing spirit. Established also seven day schools for the children of Halle; a school for sons of noble families and men of wealth; a normal seminary which had great influence in Germany in popularizing Francke's improved pedagogical methods; a theological school which especially assisted poor students; a school for the study of Oriental tongues to elucidate the study of the Old Testament; a chemical laboratory and pharmacy; a Bible Society, a book store, and a printing establishment; a boarding school where poor students could get free board; and an infirmary, a home for widows, beggars, and other poor people. Francke's university and his other institutions were a great missionary training center. Ziegenbalg, Plutschau, Schwartz, Zeisberger, Egede, and Dober were a few of the missionary spirits trained at Halle under Francke's administration or shortly after his death.

FRANKLIN, BENJAMIN (1706-1790), American printer, journalist, diplomat, statesman, born in Boston. He taught himself arithmetic, navigation, grammar, logic, algebra, and geometry, learned several languages. In Philadelphia in 1728 set up printing house and published the *Pennsylvania Gazette* for thirty-five years. In 1727 organized the Junto Club, which grew into the American Philosophical Society; in 1731 founded the first circulating library in America; planned and helped establish the Academy of Pennsylvania, which later became the University of Pennsylvania. In 1732 and for twenty-five subsequent years wrote and from 1732 to 1757 published *Poor Richard's Almanac*. In 1752 proved the identity of electricity and lightning, and invented the lightning rod and other electrical devices. Invented an improved heating stove, made the first bifocals, introduced the culture of silkworms, and use of lime to improve the soil, made improvements in the printing press, ship rigging, carriage wheels, and windmills. Made a member of the Royal Society in London and of the Royal Academy of France. From 1753 to 1774 postmaster general of the colonies, and in 1774 elected a member of the Second Continental Congress, where he exerted a strong influence in favor of the Declaration of Independence. Helped draft the Declaration of Independence and was one of its signers. One of the drafters and signers of the Constitution of the

United States. His was the only signature on all four great documents that marked our nation's birth. Died in 1790 in his eighty-fourth year. Franklin's unfinished *Autobiography,* covering the first fifty years of his life, is considered one of the best autobiographies ever written. He ranks as one of the greatest and ablest men that the United States has produced. He believed in God and in prayer, but did not accept the redemptive work of Christ or His deity. His theology was essentially deism.

FRANSON, FREDRIK (1852-1908), founder of the Evangelical Alliance Mission, born in Sweden. At age seventeen settled in Nebraska. During a prolonged illness in 1871-1872 he had a profound religious experience which resulted in conversion. Joined the local Baptist church, but three years later came to Chicago and joined the Moody Church on Chicago Avenue, where he held his membership the rest of his life. Did much evangelistic preaching in Minnesota among the Scandinavians, then in Utah among the Mormons, and in other places in the United States. Ordained in 1881 in the Evangelical Free Church in Phelps Center, Nebraska. From 1881 to 1890 traveled much of the world as a missionary, carrying his dynamic evangelistic campaigns into various parts of America, the West Indies, the Scandinavian countries, Germany, Switzerland, France, Italy, Russia, Poland, Egypt, Palestine, Syria, Turkey, and South Africa. Preached the imminent second coming of Christ and repentance, and brought revival almost everywhere he went, often with opposition and persecution. Founded Scandinavian Alliance Mission (now TEAM) in 1890. Raised up and sent out scores of missionaries to China, Japan, India, and Africa. A man of faith, prayer, and piety, a dynamic preacher, and a winner of souls.

FRAZER, SIR JAMES GEORGE (1854-1941), Scottish anthropologist and folklore scholar, born in Glasgow, educated at Larchfield Academy, Helensburgh, at Glasgow University, at Trinity College, Cambridge; in the latter became a disciple of William Robertson Smith. In 1914 Frazer was created a knight, and in 1920 a fellow of the Royal Society. From 1907 to 1919 professor of social anthropology in the University of Liverpool, and in 1889 instrumental in founding the *Cambridge Review.* An original fellow of the British Academy, a Fellow of the Royal Society of Edinburgh, and a member of the Order of Merit. Works are of the greatest importance in the study of anthropology, and particularly of religion and myth. Between 1890 and 1912 produced a monumental work, *The Golden Bough* in twelve volumes concerning early religions.

FREDERICK I, BARBAROSSA (bär bȧ rŏs′ ȧ), (c. 1122-1190), Holy Roman Emperor (1155-1190) and a prominent figure in the Third Crusade. Became emperor when crowned by Pope Adrian IV in 1155. The greatest and strongest of the Hohenstaufen line and one of the ablest of the Holy Roman Emperors. He had much difficulty and trouble in subduing the cities of Italy. He needed new support, and found it necessary to come to terms and make peace with the pope. In 1177 he bowed at the feet of Pope Alexander III in humiliation and reconciliation. In 1190 Frederick Barbarossa of Germany, Philip Augustus of France, and Richard the Lion-Hearted of England took the cross, and at the head of three great armies set out for the Holy Land to recover the Holy City. In 1187 it had been captured by Saladin, master and sultan of Egypt, who had developed a strong Moslem state which enveloped the Latin kingdom of Palestine, established by Godfrey and Baldwin of Bouillon eighty-eight years before. Philip and Richard both reached the Holy Land by way of the sea, and captured Acre in 1191. Frederick, who with his army attempted the overland route, met with disaster. He was drowned in a stream in Cilicia.

FREDERICK II, THE MAGNIFICENT (1194-1250), Holy Roman Emperor (1220-1250), born at Jesi, near Ancona, Italy, the son of Emperor Henry VI and Constance of Sicily, and the grandson of Frederick Barbarossa. Placed under the guardianship of Pope Innocent III, crowned king of Sicily in 1198, and king of the Germans and Holy Roman Emperor in 1215. Frederick's education had been part Christian and part Arabic. Versed in geometry, astrology, and natural history; he could speak several languages. Most accomplished sovereign of the Middle Ages, and a patron of the arts and sciences, as well as a poet and scientist in own right. Ruled as an enlightened despot, his court resembling more that of an Oriental monarch than of a western Christian. His interest in Saracenic philosophy bespoke his Arabic training, and indicated a trend away from Christian thinking. In 1229, went on crusade, made a treaty with the Moslems, and was crowned king of Jerusalem and successor of King David. He returned to Italy and made a truce with the pope in 1230, which lasted four years, when the struggle between the pope and the emperor was renewed and continued from 1235 until the emperor's death in 1250. For a time Frederick seemed to be gaining prestige and favor. Through his death the papacy won the struggle with the empire.

FREDERICK III, THE PIOUS (1515-1576), elector of the Palatinate (1557-1576), born in Simmern and educated a Catholic by Bishop Eberhard of Liege and at the court of Charles V. Became impressed early by the ideals of the Reformation. In 1537 married a Lutheran princess, in 1549 openly embraced Lutheranism. In 1561 turned to Calvinism, thus arousing the hostility of the Lutheran princes, who had tried to eradicate Calvinism from the Palatinate. Calvinists were appointed teachers and preachers. In 1563 supervised Kaspar Olevianus and Zacharias Ursinus in writing the Heidelberg Catechism for the Reformed Churches. The catechism was soon adopted by almost the entire Reformed Church of Europe. To the end of his life, the great supporter by both troops and money of the Reformed church in both France and the Netherlands.

FREDERICK III, THE WISE (1463-1525), Elector of Saxony (1486-1525), born at Torgau, near Leipzig, Germany. Received first instruction in the school at Grimma, where the Augustinian Order had a flourishing monastery. In 1493 traveled to the Holy Land, bringing back a large part of the choice collection of relics he had in his church at Wittenberg. Through the influence of John von Staupitz, the elector became interested in the study of the Bible. In 1502 founded the University of Wittenberg, appointing Luther and Melanchthon to professorships. This act, however, was not with a desire to break with the past or from his church; for he still was a loyal patron of the Roman church. It was his sense of justice that caused him to protect Luther and demand for him fair treatment. When Luther was taken from Worms to Wartburg, it was Frederick who had charged soldiers to protect Luther from violence and to convey him away secretly. Frederick became more and more sympathetic with the evangelical doctrine. In 1523 he consented to make an end of the worship of relics, even though he by 1520 had collected over nineteen thousand relics. He was interested in the Word of God, and became more and more absorbed in the study of Luther's doctrine. Spalatin his adviser, faithful secretary, and chaplain, and at the same time a close friend and sympathizer of Luther, had a strong influence over Frederick. Before his death Frederick partook of the Lord's Supper in both kinds from full conviction. Thus he openly avowed the evangelical doctrines and joined himself to the evangelical church.

FREDERICK IV (1671-1730), King of Denmark and Norway (1699-1730), born at Copenhagen. Aided by Poland and Russia waged war with Charles XII of Sweden. Rebuilt Copenhagen and freed peasants from serfdom. The church remembers him for deep religious character, and for part in establishing missions in India. Believed with the Lutherans that it was the duty of monarchs to Christianize their non-Christian subjects. Through the influence of his court preacher, Dr. Lütken, Frederick called upon the pietistic leaders of Halle to provide missionaries. Bartholomew Ziegenbalg and Heinrich Plütschau answered the call and were sent to Tranquebar in 1706. They began the work of the famous Danish-Halle Mission in India. In 1714 King Frederick established a college of missions, and in 1716 sent missionaries to Lapland. Hans Egede appealed for aid to go to Greenland and was sent out in 1721.

FREEMAN, JAMES (1759-1835), American Unitarian clergyman, born in Charleston, Massachusetts. After attending Public Latin school of Boston, entered Harvard, graduating in 1777. During the Revolution, a prisoner of war at Quebec for two years. In 1782 lay leader in King's Chapel for six months, and in 1783 chosen pastor of the church, but with the stipulation that he might omit the Athanasian Creed from the service. A Unitarian he soon openly renounced the doctrine of the Trinity and in 1785 induced his church to alter the prayerbook to comply with his views. Thus the first Episcopal church in New England became the first Unitarian church in America. Freeman having been refused ordination by bishops Seabury and Provost, was ordained in 1787 by the senior warden of his congregation. He remained sole minister of the now Unitarian King's Chapel until 1826 when failing health compelled him to retire. Freeman was a man of fine social qualities, of excellent intellectual powers, and of much power in the pulpit. One of the founders of the Massachusetts Historical Society, a member of the American Academy of Arts and Sciences, and a member of the Massachusetts constitutional committee (1820-1821).

FREEMAN, THOMAS BIRCH (1809-1890), British Wesleyan Methodist missionary, born at Twyford, near Winchester, England. In 1837 offered himself for missionary service in West Africa to take the place of other missionaries who were not able to survive the physical rigors of climate and country. Arrived at Cape Coast in January 1838, and a little more than a year later made first appearance before the king of Kumasi. Through several visits to the king, and by courtesy, friendliness, and respect for the chiefs, he won the confidence of rulers and people, and accomplished a great work. Made visits to other parts of Gold Coast,

Nigeria, and areas between, establishing a firm work in that part of West Africa. Due to growing denominational disturbance at home, and a consequent flagging interest on the part of the people and the board, adequate support was denied the field and strictures were brought upon the mission. In 1857 Freeman resigned from mission and ministry and became civil commandant of the Accra District. Turning again to gardening, his early profession, he built a model farm, introducing coffee, cinnamon, ginger, mangoes, and olives. During these sixteen years preached regularly to the people, and maintained loyalty and membership in the Methodist church. In 1873 returned to the ministry, was received back in the mission, and devoted himself to the religious welfare of the people of Gold Coast. In 1885 retired and lived with his wife on a meager pension in a little house near Accra, Gold Coast.

FRELINGHUYSEN (frē'ling hī zn), **THEODORE JACOB** (1691-c. 1748), Dutch Calvinistic, pietistic revivalist, born at Lingen in East Friesland (now in Hanover, Prussia), ordained in 1717. German minister, in 1720 came from Amsterdam, Holland, to the Dutch Reformed of northern New Jersey. Revival ministry was effectively felt in New Jersey and New York. By 1726 it resulted in numerous conversions and accessions to the church. One of the revivalists who helped to bring about the Great Awakening. He labored in connection with such great preachers as Gilbert Tennant, Jonathan Edwards, and George Whitefield. Initiated the first formal move in 1737 to organize an Assembly for the Dutch Reformed in America.

FREUD (froidt), **SIGMUND** (1856-1939), Austrian physician and psychoanalyst, born of Jewish parents in Freiberg, Moravia, educated at the University of Vienna and in Paris. Lectured on diseases of nervous system at the Vienna General Hospital after graduation; and from 1902 to 1938 was professor of neuropathology in the University of Vienna. First to discover the anesthetic properties of cocaine in 1884. Visited the United States in 1909. Freud placed great emphasis on the existence of infantile sexuality, and the role of sexuality in the origin of neuroses. He used a psychoanalytic interpretation of dreams in treating neuroses. Also applied his principles to interpretation of mythology, religion, and the arts. Freud's work received much opposition from orthodox clinical psychologists and psychiatrists, as well as from orthodox Christians. In his *The Future of an Illusion,* describes religion as a neurosis of humanity in which the concept of God is a fictitious extension of the human father ideal as a refuge from fear. His writings further include *Studien über Hysterie, A General Introduction to Psychoanalysis, History of the Psychoanalytic Movement, Totem and Tabu,* and *Moses and Monotheism.* In 1938 Freud fled to London, after fifty years in Vienna, to seek refuge from the Nazi regime. Became a British citizen.

FRIDOLIN (frē'dō lēn), **(FRIDOLD)** (probably sixth century), first Celtic missionary to the Alamanni, born in Ireland of noble parents, received an excellent education. After preaching the gospel in his country for a time, went to the Upper Rhine in Gaul as a missionary, locating at Poitiers in the time of the Merovingians. After preaching and founding churches and monasteries along the Upper Rhine, founded, on the island of Säckingen, a church to St. Hilary and a famous nunnery. Represented on the coat-of-arms of Glarus. "The only historically tenable fact is that Fridolin was an Irish missionary who preached the Christian religion in Gaul, and founded a monastery on an island in the Rhine."

FRITH (FRYTH), JOHN (1503-1533), English reformer and Protestant martyr, born at Westerham, Kent, England, educated at Eton and King's College, Cambridge. Upon graduation appointed by Cardinal Wolsey as junior canon of Cardinal College (now Christ Church), Oxford. About 1525 met William Tyndale and assisted in the translation of the New Testament. For adopting Reformation principles and for aiding the Reformers, imprisoned for several months, until released by Wolsey. Went to Marburg, Germany, where he remained for about four years. Became acquainted with Patrick Hamilton and associated with Tyndale in literary labors. Upon returning to England again seized and imprisoned in the Tower. Burned at the stake at Smithfield in 1533. A scholar and prolific writer. First to declare the doctrine concerning the eucharist which ultimately became the accepted tenet of the anglican church as stated partially in his own words in the Book of Common Prayer.

FROBEN, JOHN (c. 1460-1527), German printer and publisher. Born at Hammelberg, Bavaria. Educated at Basel. Set up first printing press in Basel in 1490s. Printed Erasmus Greek New Testament in 1516 and also editions of the church Fathers.

FROMENT (frō mōn') **ANTOINE** (1509-1584), Genevan Reformer, born at Menz, near Grenoble, Dauphine, France, studied at Paris where he became acquainted with Lefèvre. Early converted to the evangelical faith. In 1529 became an ardent follower of William Farel, and preached the gospel in western Switzerland. In 1532 opened a

French language school in Geneva, using the Bible as textbook. Soon became a popular, daring preacher, and his school became a place of public worship. Assisted Farel and Viret in laying a foundation for the evangelical church that was to be established by Calvin in Geneva only a few years later. After leaving Geneva, a pastor of a church for a decade or more, then neglected his pastorate, fell into moral error, and gave up the ministry. He is remembered as one of the great reformers along with Viret, Farel, and Calvin. Wrote a history of the Reformation in Geneva.

FROUDE (frōōd), **RICHARD HURRELL** (1803-1836), Tractarian propagandist, born at Dartington, Devonshire, England. Educated at Eton and at Oriel College, Oxford. Tutor at Oriel (1827-1830). Ordained priest in 1829. Detested the reformers and admired the Catholic church. Accepted tradition as a main instrument of religious teaching. To him the church is in possession of the truth. A revival of fasting, clerical celibacy, reverence for the saints, and Catholic doctrines and usages he deemed imperative. With Newman he became one of the most influential leaders of the early Oxford or Tractarian Movement, and wrote several of the tracts of the times. Besides the tracts, he left behind two volumes of *Remains,* a spiritual diary.

FRUMENTIUS (frōō mĕn'shĭ ŭs), (c. 300-c. 380), first bishop of Axum and Apostle to Abyssinia. He and his brother Aedesius were Greeks from Tyre. As youths, about 316, accompanied their uncle on a voyage up the Red Sea to Abyssinia. When the ship stopped at one of the harbors, the boys were captured and taken to Axum as slaves to the king. They won confidence, favor and were given places of trust, also an education and were permitted to preach Christianity. Later the young men went to Alexandria to ask Athanasius to send missionaries to Abyssinia. Aedesius returned to Tyre and was ordained priest. About 339 Athanasius consecrated Frumentius as bishop and head of the Abyssinian church. There he established an episcopal see at Axum, baptized the king who had just come to the throne, built many churches, and spread the Christian faith throughout Abyssinia. Abyssinian tradition credits Frumentius with the first Ethiopian translation of the New Testament.

FRY, ELIZABETH GURNEY (1780-1845), English philanthropist and prison reformer, born in Earlham Hall in Norwich, Norfolk, daughter of John Gurney, a wealthy banker. In 1800 became the wife of Joseph Fry, a wealthy merchant. In 1811 acknowledged by the Friends (Quakers) as a "minister." Hearing of the wretched condition of inmates in the prisons of England, in 1813 visited the women's prison at Newgate, and found the prisoners in a crowded and deplorable condition. At once instituted measures for the amelioration of prison morals and life, daily visited the prison, read the Scriptures to the prisoners, and taught them to sew. In 1818, in company with her brother, visited the prisons in Northern England and Scotland, in 1827 those in Ireland. Efforts resulted in the formation of societies for the help of female prisoners in Great Britain. Made visits to the Continent in 1839-41 which resulted in remedial legislation and the organization of prison reform societies in Holland, Denmark, France, Prussia, Italy, and other continental countries. In 1839 secured the organization of a society for the care of criminals after their discharge from prison and for visitation of the vessels that carried the convicts to the colonies. Worked out a plan to supply coast vessels and seamen's hospitals with libraries. Established a "nightly shelter for the homeless" in London, and instituted a society in Brighton to discourage begging and to promote industry. A woman of even temper, practical skill, tenderness of heart, and deep knowledge of the Scriptures. Her maxim was "Charity to the soul is the soul of charity." Because of her great work in prison reform, she has been called "the female Howard."

FULLER, ANDREW (1754-1815), English Baptist preacher and theologian, born at Wicken in Cambridgeshire, England. Experienced conversion in 1769, baptized the next year in the Baptist church at Soham. Though without more than a common school education read widely. Profoundly influenced by John Owen, the Puritan, and Jonathan Edwards, the New England divine. In 1775 ordained and became pastor in the Soham Baptist Church, and in 1782 of the Baptist Church at Kettering, Northamptonshire, where he served until his death. Though a Calvinist theologian his moderate views disturbed some hyper-Calvinistic friends. He held a monthly concert or prayer meeting dedicated to praying for the conversion of the world. Out of this meeting developed, 1792, the Baptist Foreign Missionary Society, which sent William Carey to India as its first foreign missionary. Fuller was the secretary of the society from 1792 to 1815, and traveled through England, Scotland, and Ireland promoting the cause of missions and raising funds for the mission. Writings were popular and include, *The Calvinistic and Socinian Systems Examined and Compared As to Their Tendency; The Gospel: Its Own Witness; An Apology for the Christian Mission to India; Expository Notes* *on Genesis*, 2 Volumes; and *Letters on Communion*.

FULLER, CHARLES E. (1887-1968), American Baptist radio evangelist. Born in Los Angeles. Educated at Pomona College and Biola College from 1919 to 1922. Ordained in 1925 as pastor of Calvary Church (until 1933). Began radio preaching in 1937 over MBS, later on CBS until heard over six hundred stations from Long Beach Municipal Auditorium. Helped to found Fuller Seminary in 1947.

FULLER, RICHARD (1804-1876), American Baptist preacher, born in Beaufort, South Carolina, brought up as an Episcopalian. Graduating from Harvard, practiced law in home town, where he built up a lucrative practice. Converted in 1832, joined the Baptist church, ordained, and began ministry in Beaufort from 1833 to 1847. In 1847 began a twenty-four years' pastorate at the Seventh Baptist Church in Baltimore. More than once president of the Southern Baptist Convention. A leader of the pro-slavery party in the church, defending it as a divine and biblical institution. His argument was answered by a fellow Baptist, Francis Wayland, president of Brown University. Their ensuing argument was published: *Domestic Slavery Considered as a Scriptural Institution*. Promoted idea of what became Southern Baptist Seminary. His three volumes of *Sermons* were published posthumously. Wrote *Baptist and Close Communion, A City or House Divided Against Itself, On the Roman Chancery*, and *Correspondence on Domestic Slavery*. A born orator, the pulpit was his throne.

FULLER, THOMAS (1608-1661), English divine, born at Aldwinkle St. Peter's, Northamptonshire, England. Educated at Queen's College, Cambridge. In 1630 appointed to the curacy of St. Benet's, Cambridge; in 1631, prebendary at Salisbury Cathedral; and in 1634, rector of Broad-Windsor, Dorsetshire. In 1642 settled in London, where he became a popular preacher at the Chapel of St. Mary Savoy. Preached in favor of the signing of articles of peace by both royalists and parliamentarians in the Civil War. In 1643 joined the forces of King Charles I at Oxford as chaplain of one of the regiments. About 1648 presented to "the living" of Waltham in Essex; in 1658 received "the living" of Cranford, Middlesex; and at the Restoration in 1660 reinstated in his prebend of Salisbury. Appointed chaplain extraordinary to the king. Among writings: *The History of the Holy Warre*, (an account of the crusades), *The Holy State and the Profane State, A Pisgah-Sight of Palestine* (a history and biography of the Holy Land), *The Church History of Britain*, and *Mixed Contemplations of Better Times*.

G

GABRIEL, CHARLES HUTCHINSON (1856-1932), writer and composer of gospel hymns, born on a farm in Iowa. Early showed an interest in music. The day he was sixteen taught his first singing school. Same year began writing hymns. At seventeen started out to seek a career in California. A self-made man, became a prolific writer of anthems and cantatas for children and adults, and music for special occasions, as well as the author of hundreds of hymns, sometimes writing under the nome de plume, Charlotte G. Homer. Some of his best known tunes are, "I Need Jesus," "Higher Ground," "Send the Power Again," "Just When I Need Him Most," "Brighten the Corner," and "The Way of the Cross Leads Home." Wrote both words and music for the following: "O That Will Be Glory for Me," "Send the Light," "He Lifted Me," "He is So Precious to Me," "Oh, It is Wonderful," "More Like the Master," "My Savior's Love," "I'll Go Where You Want Me to Go," "Where the Gates Swing Outward Never." Wrote the music for Ada Ruth Habershon's beautiful hymn, "Will the Circle be Unbroken?" Devoted his last forty years wholly to composition and editorial work. Famous for duet singing with E. O. Excell, with whom he intimately worked for more than thirty years. Compiled or assisted in compiling thirty-five gospel songbooks.

GAEBELEIN (gā'bē līn), **ARNO CLEMENS** (1861-1945), American clergyman, author, and teacher of prophecy, born in Thuringia, Germany, came to America in 1879. Received education in the German gymnasium and in concentrated private studies. Ordained to the ministry of the Methodist Episcopal church in 1885; held various pastorates in Baltimore, Maryland, New York City, and Hoboken, New Jersey. His comprehensive knowledge of Hebrew and his prophetic vision of the needs of the Jews in this country led to his spending much time, thought, and effort in behalf of the Jewish people. Superintendent of the Hope of Israel Mission in connection with the City Mission of New York (1894-1899). Editor of *Our Hope* from 1894 until the time of his death. In later years carried his work interdenominationally. Conducted large and frequent conferences. He was author of many books on Bible study, prophecy, and the Jews, some of these: *An Annotated Bible* (nine volumes); *The Prophet Daniel; The Prophet Ezekiel; The Prophet Isaiah; Revelation, an Analysis and Exposition; Studies in Zechariah; Conflict of the Ages; Current Events in the Light of the Bible; Harmony of the Prophetic Word; The Healing Question; The Hope of the Ages; Studies in Prophecy; World Prospects; The Jewish Question; Hath God Cast His People Away?; Half a Century: the Autobiography of a Servant.*

GAIRDNER, WILLIAM HENRY TEMPLE (1873-1828), Anglican missionary and Arabic scholar, born at Ardrossan, Scotland. Educated at Rossall and at Trinity College, Oxford. Visit of John R. Mott and Robert E. Speer at Oxford had a vital influence on Gairdner's plans for his future. In 1899 sent by the Church Missionary Society as a missionary to Cairo. Ordained priest in Alexandria in 1901, and soon after made master of a school for little boys. He had begun the study of Arabic at Oxford, and intensively continued this study at Cairo. Became recognized as a foremost Arabic scholar. Founded a language school at Cairo for the service of fellow missionaries. Besides writing hymns, made a collection of Near East airs. Some of his chief writings: *Reproach of Islam, The Muslim Idea of God, The Phonetics of Arabic, Egyptian Colloquial Arabic,* and *Arabic Syntax*. The above in English; the following were in Arabic: *Passover Night; Saul and Stephen; Life of St. Paul; Life of the Messiah; Life of Joshua;* and *Inspiration, Christian and Islamic*.

GALERIUS (gȧ lēr'ĭ ŭs), **VALERIUS MAXIMIANUS** (died 311), Roman Emperor (305-311), born of humble parentage near Sardica in Dacia, entered the imperial army and rose rapidly to the highest ranks, until c. 293, when Diocletian confered on him the title of Caesar, gave daughter Valeria in marriage, and to him the government of the Roman province of Illyria. Fierce hatred of the Christians led him to persuade Diocletian in 303 to issue the edicts which inaugurated eight years of persecution. This proved to be the last of the Roman persecutions. Upon the death of Constantius in 306, his son Constantine became joint emperor with Galerius. Five years later on his deathbed, in conjunction with Constantine and Licinius, Galerius issued the Edict of Toleration of 311. Called upon all to "pray to their God for the welfare of the empire, of the state, and of themselves, that they might prosper in every respect, and that they might live quietly in their homes."

GALILEI (gä lē lĕ'ē), **GALILEO** (1564-

1642), Italian astronomer and mathematician, born at Pisa, Italy, received first education in Greek, Latin, and logic at the monastery of Vallombrosa, near Florence. In 1581 entered the University of Pisa to study medicine and Aristotelian philosophy; four years later turned from medicine to mathematics and physical science. In 1589, made professor of mathematics at the University of Pisa. Discoveries and conclusions differed widely from the traditions of the church and from the accepted teachings of Aristotle, and brought criticism upon him. Resigned from Pisa, and in 1592 made professor of mathematics at the University of Padua (1592-1610). Here made practical use of the telescope, which had been recently invented, and discovered important facts about the moon, the milky way, Jupiter, Venus, Saturn, sun spots, and the rotation of the earth. As a result of astronomical activities, appointed professor for life of the University of Florence, and appointed philosopher and mathematician to Cosimo Medici, grand duke of Tuscany. Galileo defended the Copernican theory of the solar system, attempting to show that there is scriptural confirmation of the system. However, the Copernican theory was condemned and the writing of Copernicus placed on the Index. Galileo was summoned to Rome in 1616, forbidden to hold, teach, or defend the heretical system. The publication of Galileo's *Dialogo . . . del Mondo* in 1632 brought down the wrath of the church on his head and he was again summoned to Rome, tried by the Inquisition, and under threat of torture, was forced to recant and deny his theory. His writing was placed on the Index; he was confined to his villa in Florence. Here wrote, *Dialogue on the Two New Sciences;* published in 1636, which summed up his work on motion, acceleration, and gravity. Before the publication of his latest work, five years before his death, Galileo went blind.

GALL (c. 550-c. 640), Irish missionary. Born of a good Irish family, a student of Columban at Bangor. The most famous of the companions and assistants of Columban in his missionary work in Central Europe. Gifted in language, learned with Alamanni language and preached with much effect. When persecution drove Columban into Italy about 612, Gall, prevented by illness, remained behind. Recovering his health continued missionary work and monastic life in what is today Switzerland. Established his cell in monastery and in town, both of which to this day bear his name—St. Gall. From this famous monastery continued work until his death, leaving behind a Christianized nation (the Alamanni).

GAMEWELL, FRANCIS (FRANK) DUNLAP (1857-1950), American Methodist missionary, born at Camden, South Carolina, studied civil engineering at the Rensselaer Polytechnic Institute, and at Cornell, Ithaca, New York. Graduated at Dickinson College, Pennsylvania. Went to China in 1881, and for three years engaged in educational work at Peking; for three years superintendent of the West China Mission; and from 1889 to 1900 professor of chemistry and physics at Peking University. Widely known for leadership as chief of staff at the fortifications of the British embassy during the siege of Peking in the Boxer Uprising in 1900. From 1901 to 1908, field secretary and executive secretary of the Board of Foreign Missions of the Methodist Episcopal church, New York. From 1909 to 1925 served the Methodist church in the capacity of secretary or superintendent of education for his church in China, also served as general secretary of the China Christian Educational Association from 1912 to 1925. Editor of the *Educational Review* and a member of the editorial board of the *Chinese Recorder.* Died at the age of ninety-two.

GANSFORT, WESSEL HARMENUS (c. 1420-1489), Dutch theologian. Educated at Deventer by the Brethren of the Common Life. In Paris sixteen years and became defender of nominalism. Visited Italy and spent last years in Germany. Anticipated Reformers in his challenge to papal and clerical authority.

GAPON, GEORGI APOLLONOVICH (c. 1870-1906), educated for Russian Orthodox priesthood. Mission work among St. Petersburg workers to organize labor unions. Organized the major strike of 1905. Led strikers on January 22, 1905 to the palace of the Czar to petition the Czar, and Cossacks fired on the crowd. Start of fall of Russian monarchy. Escaped to London but on return to Russia was executed by the government.

GARDINER, ALLEN FRANCIS (1794-1851), missionary to Terra del Fuego, born at Basildon, Berkshire, England, of godly parents. Preferring to serve the Lord as a layman, never was ordained. While a commander in the navy wandered away from his mother's Christian teaching; but at Penang, in 1820, gave his heart to God. Traveling in various parts of the world he saw the crying need of Christian missions and offered himself to the London Missionary Society. First went to Port Natal in the 1830s and worked for two or three years among the Zulus, the first missionary among these people. Instructed the natives and held services for the few Englishmen there. Helped found the town of Durban. All went well for awhile and new missionaries were sent out by the Church Missionary Society; when serious trouble broke out between the natives and the whites, the missionaries had to leave. Gardiner decided to go to the Indians of South America. In 1836 he married a second time. In 1838, taking his wife and children with him, he began a period of traveling and investigating amid great hardships and dangers in southern Chile. Returned with his family to England in 1844. His pleading resulted in the founding of the South American Missionary Society to Patagonia and Tierra Del Fuego. The establishing of a mission was most difficult. In 1846 he made his way through Bolivia, in spite of fever and opposition, to the Indians beyond. The next year he was back in England trying to stir up the society to action. Two years later he landed on Picton Island among the Fuegians. Shortly he was back in England. Finally in 1850 Captain Gardiner and six devoted companions set out for Picton Island on the "Ocean Queen" with two launches and provisions for six months. Arrangements had been made for provisions to follow for another six months. The second allotment never arrived. About a year after their arrival at Picton Island, in September 1851, the dauntless seven were all dead of disease and starvation. This sacrificial act of the deathless seven stirred the British people to action for the Indians of South America.

GARNIER-JEAN (1612-1681), Jesuit patristic scholar. Born in Paris, entered the Jesuit order in 1628. Professor of theology at the Collège de Clermont for ten years, then at Barrois until his death. Wrote useful works on Pelagianism and Nestorianism in 1680. Edited *Liber Diurnus* with much data on papal ordinations and professions of faith.

GARRETTSON, FREEBORN (1752-1827), American pioneer Methodist minister and abolitionist, born in Maryland, reared in the Church of England, but became a Methodist about 1775. Upon conversion freed slaves and entered upon over a half century of active itinerant preaching, making converts and establishing churches. Sent out the call for the Christmas Conference of 1784, which ordained him and sent him and James O. Cromwell as missionaries to Nova Scotia and New Brunswick, first foreign missionaries of the Methodists in America. Garrettson was charged with the oversight of the work. In 1787 recalled to the United States and spent the next forty years in vigorous preaching trips to the South and East. From 1788 to 1792 served as presiding elder over the area that late came to include New York and Troy conferences. In 1793 he married, establishing his home on the Hudson at Rhinebeck, which became a favorite resort for Methodist preachers. He was of mystic temperament and also was conscientiously opposed to oathtaking and war. As a church counselor his influence was perhaps second to none. At Wesley's request wrote, *The Experience and Travels of Freeborn Garrettson*. Wrote also *A Dialogue Between Do-Justice and Professing Christian,* a plea for black colonization and gradual emancipation by legal means. In his will left to the Missionary and Bible Society of which he was a founder, a sum "to support a single missionary until the millennium."

GARRISON, WILLIAM LLOYD (1805-1879), American journalist and abolitionist, born in Newburyport, Massachusetts. At nine apprenticed to a shoemaker and at thirteen to the Newburyport *Herald,* where he became an expert printer and foreman. Edited several newspapers in Massachusetts and Vermont before 1829, and then joined Benjamin Lundy in Baltimore, and started the *Genius of Universal Emancipation*. Became one of the earliest and most vigorous advocates of immediate and complete emancipation of slaves. In 1830 sued for libel by a slave dealer, in jail for seven weeks until Arthur Tappan of New York paid his fine. In 1831 he and Isaac Knapp founded and published the *Liberator*, in the first number of which appeared the keynote of the editor: "I will be as harsh as truth, and as uncompromising as justice. On this subject [abolition of slavery] I do not wish to think, or speak, or write with moderation. I am in earnest—I will not equivocate—I will not excuse—I will not retreat a single inch—I will be heard!" In paper not only advocated abolition, but also attacked war, alcoholic beverage, tobacco and the lottery. He also assailed free masonry, capital punishment, imprisonment for debt, advocated woman suffrage and justice to the American Indian. A pacifist, he was deeply convinced that slavery had to be abolished by moral force alone. Articles and lectures aroused great opposition. In 1835 a mob broke up one of his meetings in Boston. He was so roughly handled that he had to be rescued by the police and lodged in jail for safety. In 1832 wrote: *Thoughts on African Colonization*. Later the same year he and eleven associates founded the New England Anti-Slavery Society. The next year he was conspicuous among the organizers of the American Anti-Slavery Society, of which he was president from 1843 to 1865. During the Civil War period he supported President Lincoln. Upon adoption of the Thirteenth Amendment in 1865, feeling that his work as an abolitionist was done, he discontinued the

Liberator and resigned from the presidency of the American Anti-Slavery Society.

GARVIE, ALFRED ERNEST (1861-1945), English Congregationalist minister and educator, born at Zyrardow, Russian Poland, studied at George Watson's College, Edinburgh, the universities of Edinburgh, Glasgow, and Oxford. Lecturer in Mansfield College in 1892, and held pastorates from 1893 to 1903 at Macduff and Montrose Congregational churches. From 1903 to 1907 professor of philosophy of theism, comparative religions, and Christian ethics in Hackney College and New College, London. After 1907 was principal of the latter, after 1924, principal of both. Examiner in Biblical languages and literatures in Edinburgh Congregational Hall (1895-1902), president of the Congregational Union of Scotland in 1902, president of the Hampstead Free Church Council (1906-1907), chairman of the Congregational Union of England and Wales (1920), president of the National Free Church Council (1923), deputy chairman of the Lausanne Conference of Faith and Order (1927), and moderator of the Federal Council of Free Churches (1928). In theology moderately progressive and liberal, Lutheran rather than Calvinistic. Some of his writings: *Commentary on Romans, Commentary on Luke, The Christian Preacher, Studies in the Inner Life of Jesus, Studies of Paul and His Gospel, Handbook of Christian Apologetics, The Christian Belief in God.*

GASQUET, FRANCIS AIDAN (1846-1929), Benedictine historian and cardinal. Born in London. Entered Benedictine order in 1866. Prior of Downside from 1878 to 1885. Research in the British Museum and in Rome. Abbot-president of English Benedictine congregation from 1900 to 1914. From 1914 cardinal in Rome. Vatican Librarian in 1919. Wrote *Henry VIII and the English Monasteries* (1888-1889) to show reasons Henry VIII took over the monasteries. Wrote *Monastic Life in the Middle Ages* (1922). Defended the monasteries against charges made against them in the sixteenth century.

GAUSSEN (gō sŏɴ'), **FRANÇOIS SAMUEL ROBERT LOUIS** (1790-1863), Swiss Reformed preacher and theologian, born at Geneva, Switzerland, where he received education. In 1816 appointed pastor at Satigny, a suburb of Geneva, Gaussen belonged to the evangelical school of Haldane, Malan, Monod, Vinet, and Merle d'Aubigné. Each of these men preached the evangelical gospel in spite of bitter opposition of their established churches. Gaussen sought to revivify the national church, but did not advocate a break from the church. When he was ejected from his pastorate at Satigny and forbidden in 1831 to preach in any of the churches in the canton, he, Merle d'Aubigné and other like-minded men founded the Evangelical Society of Geneva to distribute Bibles and tracts, and to develop a missionary interest in the heathen. The Evangelical Society soon established a school for training young ministers according to their views, and for preaching the gospel in Switzerland. After being deposed Gaussen spent some time traveling and preaching in Italy and England. In 1834 returned to Geneva and became professor of Dogmatics at the new evangelical seminary there. At this school Gaussen did the principal work of his life, continuing to teach and defend the evangelical faith, until his death. Three points of evangelical theology were especially treated by him: the divinity of Christ, the prophecies, and the divine authority of the Holy Scriptures. Among his writings was *Theopneustia, the Plenary Inspiration of the Holy Scriptures* in which he upheld verbal inspiration. His works enjoyed a wide circulation.

GEDDIE (gĕd'ĭ), **JOHN** (1815-1872), Canadian missionary to New Hebrides, born in Banff, Scotland. Brought by his parents to Pictou, Nova Scotia, Canada. In 1838 ordained to the ministry of the Presbyterian church. Began ministry as pastor at Cavendish on Prince Edward Island. Appointed by the Presbyterian Church in Nova Scotia as the first missionary from Canada to foreign lands. Sent to the New Hebrides. In 1848 came to the island of Aneityum, most southerly island of the New Hebrides, where he did heroic service for nearly twenty years. Won the confidence of these wild, dangerous, cannibalistic people, built an alphabet and translated into their language school books, hymnals, and the New Testament. A church house was built and a Christian church was soon established. Schools were established throughout the island and large churches were built. In 1852 Mr. and Mrs. Inglis joined the Geddies. By 1854 more than one half of the four thousand people had become Christians. Teachers from the island were going out to other islands. Due to the perpetrations of the white sandalwood traders, measles was introduced onto the island, carrying off a third of the population. Persecutions and martyrdoms followed, but the Christians, especially those on Aneityum, remained loyal and the church grew. After eighteen years, in 1864, with impaired health, Mr. Geddie started home for a furlough. In 1866 he returned to his work in Aneityum. But the ill health of both himself and Mrs. Geddie made it necessary for them to go to Australia where he took charge of Scripture translating, and made yearly voyages to the New Hebrides acting as a visiting missionary among the islands. On one of these trips he contracted influenza which was followed by paralysis.

GEIKIE (gē'kĭ), **JOHN CUNNINGHAM** (1824-1906), English clergyman and writer, born in Edinburgh, educated at the University of Edinburgh, and Queen's College, Kingston, Ontario, Canada. Ordained to the Presbyterian ministry in 1848, and between the years 1851 and 1873 pastor of Presbyterian churches in Halifax and Toronto, Canada; and in Sunderland and London, England. Entered the Church of England; ordained priest in 1877. Between the years 1876 and 1890 successively curate of St. Peter's, Dulwich; rector of Christ's Church, Nuilly, Paris; vicar of St. Mary's Church, Barnstaple; and vicar of St. Martin-of-Palace, Norwich, retiring from active service in the church in the latter year. In theology adhered to the evangelical school of the Church of England. Earned wide popularity as a writer on biblical and religious subjects. Works include: *The Life and Words of Christ; Hours with the Bible,* twelve volumes; and *The English Reformation*.

GELASIUS I (d. 496), probably Roman citizen of North Africa. Early assertion of papal supremacy in letter to the Roman emperor Anastasius I. Wrote that there are two earthly powers, the state and the church. The church is above the state because it is responsible for the souls of the rulers, although each is independent in its sphere. Wrote against Pelagianism and on the two natures of Christ.

GEORGE, SAINT (c. 303), Christian martyr, born of noble Cappadocian family. Martyrdom at Lydda, Palestine, in the reign of Diocletian, on April 23, is generally considered a matter of historical fact. Became the patron saint of Portugal and of Genoa as well as of the English Order of the Garter (1350), and of many military orders. The English Crusaders of Richard Coeur de Lion were under this saint's protection. A decree of a national council held at Oxford in 1222 made his day, April 23, a national festival. However, he did not become the patron saint of England until the fourteenth century in the reign of Edward III. Since the later Middle Ages the Western universities have regarded him as the patron of artists.

GEORGE OF BRANDENBURG (1484-1543), margrave of Brandenburg-Ansbach-Kulmbach, born at Onolzbach, Middle Franconia, early embraced the Lutheran Reformation, maintained very intimate relations with Luther, and helped his brother Albrecht to introduce Lutheranism into Prussia.

GERHARD (gär'härt), **JOHANN** (1582-1637), German Lutheran dogmatician, born at Quedlinburg, Germany, studied philosophy and theology at Wittenberg, Jena, and Marburg, also studied medicine for two years. After lecturing for a year on theology at Jena, given the degree of doctor of divinity, made general superintendent of the duchy of Coburg, entrusted with the visitation of the realm and the drawing up of a new church order. In 1616 became professor at Jena, where he spent the rest of his life, attracting crowds of students. Contemporaries considered him the greatest theologian of his time. While at Jena received no fewer than twenty-four calls from different universities, but chose to remain at Jena until his death. Loved and respected by students and fellow teachers. Useful and helpful, not only in class and lecture room, but also in church and politics. Counsel sought in many realms and on many questions. A prolific writer, but chief work which established Gerhard's reputation was his *Loci Theologici,* nine volumes. Of great value to Reformed and Roman Catholic as well as to Lutheran theologians, but of special value as an exposition of Lutheran high orthodoxy. Gerhard was the scholastic Protestant for the Lutherans as Voetius was for the Reformed. Other works written by Gerhard were *Doctrina Catholica et Evangelica; Confession Catholica;* and *Meditationes Sacrae,* which was translated into the most of the languages of Europe; and various commentaries.

GERHARDT, PAUL (c. 1607-1676), German Lutheran hymn writer, born at Gräfenhainichen, near Wittenberg, Saxony, studied at Wittenberg. Studied music under Ruthardt, Homeyer, and Jadassohn. Tutor in Berlin 1643 to 1651. In 1651 became pastor at Mittenwalde, and in 1657 called to the Church of St. Nicholas in Berlin. Dismissed in 1666 because unwilling to consider union with the Reformed church. From 1668 until his death, pastor of Lübben, Saxe-Mersburg. The greatest German hymn writer after Luther. With him sacred poetry assumed a strongly personal character, a new strain in religious poetry. His compositions included sacred songs, choral, organ, piano, and ensemble works. Author of one hundred thirty hymns. His excellent book of hymns, *Geistlich Andachten,* appeared in Berlin in 1667. His best known hymns are "O Sacred Head Now Wounded" and "Jesus Thy Boundless Love to Me."

GERMANUS (zhĕr män'ŭs), **OF CONSTANTINOPLE** (c. 634-c. 733), patriarch of Constantinople (715-730), born at Constantinople, consecrated bishop of Cyzicus;

in 715 raised to the patriarchate of Constantinople. Almost immediately he convened a council to deal with the Monothelete heresy. Entered into communication with the Armenian Monophysites with hope of restoring them to unity with the church, but without success. Germanus was a zealous defender of image worship, strongly opposed the policy of iconoclasm held by Emperor Leo III, the Isaurian. In 730 emperor summoned a council in Constantinople, before which Germanus was cited to subscribe to an imperial decree prohibiting images. He resolutely refused and was compelled to resign patriarchal office. Retired to the home of his family, where he died.

GERSON (zhĕr sôN), **JEAN CHARLIER** (shȧr lyā), **DE** (1363-1429), French conciliarist, mystic and scholar, born at Gerson-les-Barry, near Reims, studied at the University of Paris. In 1381 took up theology. At the university elected procurator of the French or Gallic nation. He became doctor of theology in 1392; and in 1395 succeeded his teacher, Pierre d'Ailly, as chancellor of the University of Paris, and was made a canon of Notre Dame. The Church was rent by the great papal schism (1378-1414). His great hope was to effect a compromise and heal the schism. One of the late scholastics, a nominalist, and a moderate mystic. To him the task of theology was a practical one and true theology was mysticism. He said that the essence of mysticism is the art of love. Perception of God was through experience. Took part in the so-called reformatory councils of Pisa (1409) and Constance (1414-1418). He expressed the desire of the true reformers of his day. Believed that (a) a visible head of the church at Rome was necessary, but that a General Council was superior to the pope, (b) a genuine reformation was necessary in "head and members" of the church, and (c) the Bible was the only source and rule of Christian knowledge. At the trials of Huss and Jerome of Prague, he cast his influence for their condemnation. His last ten years were spent in a monastery at Lyons, teaching little children, and writing books on mystical devotion and hymns.

GESENIUS (gā zā'né o͞os), **HEINRICH FRIEDRICH WILHELM** (1786-1842), German Protestant Hebraist, born at Nordhausen, educated at the universities of Helmstedt and Göttingen. From 1811 to 1842 professor of theology at Halle. But Gesenius was a teacher of great power and attraction. Students flocked to his courses on Hebrew and on Old Testament introduction and exegesis. First student of Hebrew under him was Neander. He was a student of linguistics rather than of theology. His chief works were lexicographical. Remembered chiefly for oriental philology. Some of his works: *Hebrew and Chaldaean Hand Dictionary; Elementary Hebrew; Critical History of the Hebrew Language and Literature; On the Origin, Genius, and Authority of the Samaritan Pentateuch; A Critical Grammatical System of the Hebrew Language; Hebrew Thesaurus;* and *Hebrew Lexicon.* His only exegetical work was his *Commentary on Isaiah*.

GIBBON, EDWARD (1737-1794), English historian, born at Putney, Surrey. Owing to poor health and much sufering in early childhood, formal education consisted of two years at Westminster. Entered Magdalen College, Oxford in 1752. While there he began to read history. At Magdalen temporarily converted to Roman Catholicism and in 1753 received into the Roman fold. Because of this dismissed from Oxford. His father send him to Lausanne, Switzerland, to be under the guidance and instruction of M. Pavilliard, a Calvinist pastor. Soon renounced Catholicism and outwardly again accepted Protestantism though he subsequently renounced all forms of religion. He next spent five profitable years of study at Lausanne, studying French, Latin and Greek, and reading history. Then for two and a half years was a captain in the South Hampshire militia. As soon as he was released from the militia, began traveling in France, Lausanne and Italy. While in Rome began to plan, and between 1776 and 1788 wrote his monumental six-volume work, *The History of the Decline and Fall of the Roman Empire*. This history covers a period extending from the middle of the second century to the year 1453. The work has been admired as good literature as well as well-written history, and has been translated into many languages. It betrays an unfriendly animus to Christianity as the "triumph of religion and barbarism." Wrote also *Memoirs of My Life and Writings.* A member of parliament between the years 1774 and 1783, during the years of the American Revolution.

GIBBONS (gĭb'ünz), **JAMES** (1834-1921), Roman Catholic Cardinal, Archbishop of Baltimore, born at Baltimore, Maryland, received early education in Ireland, returned to the United States in 1851, studied at St. Charles College, Ellicott City, Maryland, the Seminary of Saint Sulpice, and St. Mary's Seminary, Baltimore. Ordained priest in 1861, then served a few months as assistant at St. Patrick's Church in Baltimore, and for several years was rector of St. Bridget's Church in Canton, near Baltimore. Between 1865 and 1868 secretary to Archbishop Spalding. In 1868 consecrated titular bishop of Adramytum, and appointed vicar apostolic of North Carolina. At Vatican Council in 1870 the youngest bishop present. In 1872 moved to the see of Richmond, Virginia, and 1877 became archbishop of Baltimore, thus becoming primate of the Roman Catholic church in the United States. In 1882 sanctioned the founding of the Knights of Columbus. Prepared for and presided over the third plenary council in 1884, whose decrees were so comprehensive and practical that they have ever since served as a regulative norm for the work of the Roman Catholic church in America. In 1886 created cardinal. In 1888 laid the cornerstone of the Catholic University of America at Washington, D.C.; was its chancellor until his death. In time of war he was president of the Catholic National War Council. A model Roman Catholic churchman, but also a typical American citizen, loyal, progressive, and public-spirited. Wrote the *Faith of Our Fathers; Our Christian Heritage;* and *The Ambassador of Christ: a Retrospect of Fifty Years.*

GILLESPIE (gĭ lĕs′pĭ), **THOMAS** (1708-1774), Scottish founder of the Relief church in Scotland, born at Clearburn, near Edinburgh, Scotland, studied at the University of Edinburgh and Doddridge's academy, Northampton. Ordained in 1741. From 1741 to 1752, pastor of Carnock near Dunfermline. In 1752 deposed by the General Assembly for refusing to participate in the installation of a minister over an unwilling congregation. Soon founded a new independent congregation in Dunfermline. He and Thomas Boston the Younger of Jedburgh later ordained another independent minister at Colinsburgh. These three independent congregations: Dunfermline, Jedburgh, and Colinsburgh, in 1761 formed themselves into a presbytery for the relief of the Christians deprived of their church privileges. In 1847 they united with the Secession church of 1733 to form the United Presbyterian Church of Scotland.

GILMOUR, JAMES (1843-1891), Scottish Congregationalist, missionary to Mongolia, born at Cathkin, near Glasgow, studied at the University of Glasgow, Theological Hall of the Congregational Church of Scotland, Cheshunt Congregational Theological College near London, and the L.M.S. Missionary Seminary at Highgate. Appointed by the London Missionary Society to reopen the long suspended mission in Mongolia. In 1870 left for the field. After a brief study of the Chinese language plunged into Mongolia. For twelve years spent summers with the nomadic Mongols on the plains of Mongolia, acquiring their language by listening to their conversations and conversing with them, adopting their dress, living in their tents, and eating their food, seeking to make himself one of them. Dispensing simple medicines to them helped win their confidence. In the winters lived at Peking, seeking out the Mongols who came to the city, selling them gospels and tracts for cash or produce, reading or explaining to them the contents of their purchase. In 1882 due to wife's failing health made a trip to England, at which time wrote, *Among the Mongols.* After return to the field in 1883, welcomed his first convert, his only convert among the nomadic Mongols. In 1885 Mrs. Gilmour's health gave way and she died, leaving him with three little boys. He sent the boys back to England, and took up his work with the agricultural Mongols of Eastern Mongolia. As a lay doctor without any formal medical training, entered into a medical ministry that was no less extensive and effective than that of many a trained physician. Continued rugged missionary labors until his death in 1891, except for a short trip to England in 1889 to be with his sons, and to write: *Gilmour and His Boys.*

GILSON, ÉTIENNE HENRI (1884-1978), philospher, educator, and author. Born in Paris. Educated at the Sorbonne. In French army from 1914 to 1918. Professor at Strassburg (1919-1921), of medieval philosophy at the Sorbonne (1921-1932), and at the Collége de France (1923-1951) Director of Pontifical Institute of Medieval Studies, Toronto, Ontario. Able books on medieval philosophy and on the lives and work of Augustine and Aquinas.

GIOTTO (jôt′tō) **di BONDONE** (bōn dō′nā) (c. 1266-1337), Italian painter, sculptor, and architect, born at Vespignano, near Florence, Italy, the greatest pre-Renaissance Italian painter. Great achievement was the revitalizing of Italian art. Prepared the plans for the beautiful bell tower of Florence, known as Giotto's Tower. Pictures were mostly religious in theme and figures had a grace of form and color that made them especially appealing. Decorated with wonderful paintings a part of the Church of St. Francis at Assisi, depicting scenes from the life of St. Francis; the entire Arena Chapel at Padua, depicting scenes from the life of the Virgin and of Christ; and part of St. Peter's at Rome, depicting Peter walking on the waves and the martyrdom of Peter and Paul. Among best known works are the four allegorical frescoes in honor of St. Francis: *Marriage of St. Francis with Poverty; Triumph of Charity; Triumph of Obedience; Glorification of St. Francis;* and scenes from the life of Christ: *Last Supper,* and *Presentation of*

Christ in the Temple. A chief architect of the Duomo in Florence, designed the campanile and the facade.

GIRDLESTONE, ROBERT BAKER (1836-1923), Church of England clergyman, born at Sedgley near Birmingham, Staffordshire, England, studied at Charterhouse, London, and at Christ Church, Oxford. Superintendent of the translation department of the British and Foreign Bible Society (1866-1876); principal of Wycliffe Hall, Oxford (1877-1889); minister of St. John's, Downshire Hill, Hampshire (1889-1901). Served on various committees connected with the Church Missionary Society, the Society for the Promotion of Christian Knowledge, the British and Foreign Bible Society, the London Jews' Society, the National Protestant Christian Union, and other similar organizations. Writings include *Synonyms of the Old Testament, Old Testament Theology, Duplicate Passages in the Old Testament, Age and Trustworthiness of the Old Testament, Why Do I Believe in Jesus Christ?, Outlines of Bible Chronology,* and *Grammar of Prophecy.*

GLADDEN, WASHINGTON (1836-1918), advocate of social gospel. Born Pottsgrove, Pennsylvania. Educated at Williams College. Ordained in 1860. Pastor of churches in New York and Massachusetts (1860-1882). Editor of the *Independent* (1871-1874). Long pastorate at First Congregational Church of Columbus, Ohio from 1882 to 1914. Served on the city council. In 1915 tried to stop his denomination from taking a large gift of "tainted money" from Standard Oil. Moderator of National Council of Churches from 1904 to 1907. Supported union rights, profit sharing, and industrial arbitration. Leader in formulation of the social gospel. Wrote hymn "O Master, Let Me Walk with Thee."

GLADSTONE, WILLIAM EWART (1809-1898), British statesman, born in Liverpool, England, of Scottish parents, educated at Eton and Christ Church College, Oxford. A devout High Church but evangelical Christian, an earnest student of the Bible, and man of prayer. Associated with the political life of England as member of parliament from 1832 to 1895 and on the cabinet, three times chancellor of the exchequer, and four times prime minister. In public service endeavored to act as a Christian. In public career started out as a conservative but gradually changes his views, finally becoming a leader of the liberal party. For many years a political opponent of Benjamin Disraeli. A champion of the rights of the common people, advocate of justice, friend of liberty, known as the Great Commoner. Strove honestly to achieve, and did achieve reform at home. Disestablished Anglican Church in Ireland in 1869. In foreign policy was less successful. An able classical scholar, a theologian of wide and generous opinions. During busiest years as a politician wrote extensively, often on religious subjects. *The State in Its Relation with the Church, Church Principles Considered in their Results,* which upheld high church ideas, and *The Impregnable Rock of Holy Scripture* are three of religious writings. All his work and thought were undergirded by a firm faith in Christ.

GLEGG, ALEXANDER (1882-1975), lay evangelist. Born into a Scottish family in London. Educated as an electrical engineer in London University. Successful in business, but his evangelism won thousands in England. Meetings in Albert Hall in 1940s. Helped start Christian holiday camp at Filey. Influenced Billy Graham.

GLOAG (glōg), **PATON JAMES** (1823-1906). Scottish Presbyterian exegete and theologian, born at Perth, Scotland, studied at Edinburgh and St. Andrews. From 1840 to 1890 held pastorates successively at Dunning, Perthshire, Blantyre, Lanarkshire, and Galashiels in Selkirkshire. Moderator of the General Assembly of the Church of Scotland in 1889. After retirement from the active ministry in 1890, temporary professor of biblical criticism in the University of Aberdeen (1896-1899). Wrote: *Commentary on Acts, Introduction to the Pauline Epistles, Life of Paul, Commentary of James, Commentary on the Epistles to the Thessalonians, Introduction to the Catholic Epistles, Introduction to the Johannine Writings, Subjects and Modes of Baptism, Life of St. John,* and several other books.

GLOVER, TERROT REAVELEY (1869-1943), English Baptist classicist, born in Bristol, England, educated at St. John's College, Cambridge. Professor of Latin at Queen's University, Kingston, Canada (1896-1901); classical lecturer at St. John's College (1901-1939); public orator at the University of Cambridge (1920-1939); and Sather Professor at the University of California (1923). President of the Baptist Union of Great Britain and Ireland (1924). Author of many works on classical and early Christian times. Some writings: *The Conflict of Religions in the Early Roman Empire, The Jesus of History, Paul of Tarsus, The Influence of Christ in the Ancient World,* and *The World of the New Testament*.

GOBAT (gô bȧ'), **SAMUEL** (1799-1879), missionary to Abyssinia and bishop of Jerusalem, born at Crémine, Bern, Switzerland, studied theology, Arabic, Ethiopic, and Amharic at the Missionhaus in Basel, and at the missionary Institution in Paris. Ordained in the Lutheran church, Baden, went to England to seek appointment by the Church Missionary Society. After three years of waiting in Egypt, gained admittance to Abyssinia in 1830. Well received and labored successfully for three years, when the king was killed in war and Gobat had to flee from the country. Between 1839 and 1842 associated with the society's mission at Malta where he superintended the translation of the Bible into Arabic and took charge of the printing press. Appointed in 1845 vice-president of the Malta Protestant College; within a year appointed by Frederick William IV of Prussia as archbishop of Christ Church, the Anglican Cathedral Church in Jerusalem, and at Lambeth in 1846 consecrated bishop in Church of England. Work in Jerusalem where he remained until his death in 1879 was vigorous and successful. Especially worthy of mention are the diocesan school and the Orphanage of Mount Zion. Before his death there were thirty-seven schools and fourteen hundred children under his care, as well as twelve native churches. Wrote: *Journal of a Three Year Residence in Abyssinia*.

GOCH (gōkh), **JOHANN VON (JOHANN PUPPER)** (c. 1400-1475), pre-Reformation reformer, born at Goch on the Lower Rhine; studied at Cologne and Paris. Founded a house of Augustinians over which he was head until death. Chief contribution to the Reformation lay in positive teaching of the supreme authority of the Bible. As a nominalist strongly emphasized the authority of the church, and as a mystic aimed at a close and intimate union with God.

GODET (gô dě′), **FREDERIC LOUIS** (1812-1900), Swiss Reformed theologian, born at Neuchatel, Switzerland, educated in his native city, and at the universities of Bonn and Berlin, in the latter of which he studied under Dr. Neander. After ordination in 1836, an assistant pastor for a year, and then tutor to Crown Prince Frederick William of Prussia for six years (1838-1844). In pastoral work for twenty-two years, the last fifteen years at Neuchatel. From 1851 to 1873 professor of exegetical and critical theology in the theological school of the state church in Neuchatel; but withdrew from the state church in 1873, taking part in the founding of the Free Evangelical church of Neuchatel, and becoming a professor on the faculty of its new theological academy. Held this position until 1887, when he retired from active life. As a prominent representative of the Reformed theology, Godet exercised a wholesome influence on the development of conservative religious thought in Switzerland. Best known work: *Commentary on the Gospel of St. John*. Wrote also commentaries on Luke, Romans, and Corinthians, and *Studies on the Old Testament, Studies on the New Testament, Introduction to Paul's Epistles,* and *Lectures in Defense of the Christian Faith*.

GODFREY (gŏd′frĭ), **OF BOUILLON** (bōō-yôɴ′), (c. 1060-1100), leader of the First Crusade, born at Baisy in Belgium. One of the several leaders of the first crusade which started to the Holy Land in 1096. Godfrey's army reached Constantinople by Christmas 1096, and crossed over to Asia in 1097, capturing Nicea by mid-summer, taking Antioch a year later. By mid-year 1099, after a siege of five weeks, Godfrey captured Jerusalem, and slaughtered the inhabitants of the city. Accepted the title of "Advocate of the Holy Sepulchre." Succeeded by abler brother Baldwin, who had established a Latin county in Edessa, and took the title of King Baldwin I. This Latin Kingdom of Jerusalem with its Latin Patriarchate lasted eighty-eight years. In 1187 Jerusalem was recaptured by the Mohammedan Turks under Saladin.

GOFORTH, JONATHAN (1859-1936), Canadian Presbyterian missionary to China, born near Thorndale in Western Ontario, Canada. As soon as he entered Knox College, he began to engage in city mission work. In 1887 ordained, married to Miss Florence Rosalind Bell-Smith; they went to Honan, China, where they labored several years to gain a foothold in new area. Mr. Goforth saw the need of reaching not only the illiterate and moderately educated, but also the scholars and literati, if China were to be won. Opened a station at Changte where they labored for many years. In the Boxer uprising of 1900 Goforths succeeded in escaping with their lives, but not without severe wounds and serious personal losses. Jonathan Goforth's great strength lay in evangelistic and revival work, especially in training Chinese evangelists and preachers to do much of the work. Spent a few weeks opening up and establishing a new mission, then left native preachers to carry on while he went to new fields. Itinerating became the settled policy of the mission. During missionary career it was his privilege and joy to send out fifty Chinese converts as ministers or evangelists. In 1907 he visited Korea when that country was experiencing its great spiritual revival, and brought back the spirit of revival to China, first to Mukden, Manchuria, and then to his station at Changte. In 1925 when the Church Union movement in Canada divided the Presbyterian church, the Goforths chose to remain with the Presbyterian Church of Canada. Leaving their mission in Honan, which was taken over by the United church, they began anew in Manchuria, where they worked for the next seven or eight years. Spent the last two years in Canada, traveling and preaching up to the very last day of his life. Wrote *By My Spirit,* the story of Chinese revivals.

GOMAR (GOMARUS) FRANCIS (1563-1641), Dutch supralapsarian Calvinist. Born in Bruges. Studied at Strassburg, Neustadt, Oxford, Cambridge, and Heidelberg. Pastor of Dutch church in Frankfurt. From 1594 to 1611 professor of theology at the University of Leyden. Upheld rigid Calvinism in dispute with colleague Arminius in 1603. Pastor at Middleburg (1614-1618). Professor at Samaur and at Gronigen (1618-1641). Helped to revise the Dutch Old Testament.

GOODELL, WILLIAM (1792-1867), American Congregational missionary, born at Templeton, Massachusetts, educated at Phillips Academy, Dartmouth College, and Andover Theological Seminary. Graduated from seminary he studied medicine, spent a year visiting among the churches for the American Board of Commissioners for Foreign Missions. In 1822 ordained in the Congregational ministry, and in 1823 at Beirut under the American Board, where he aided in establishing the station which was to become the center of the Syrian Mission. In 1828 the missionaries removed to Malta. He remained for three years. In 1831 the board sent him to Constantinople where he started a new mission among the Armenians, and labored there with diligence and success amid many trials and perils until his retirement in 1865. One of the most important results of his labors was the translation by 1842 of the entire Bible from the Hebrew and Greek into Armeno-Turkish, a task of twenty years. In 1865 after forty-three years of missionary service he and his wife returned to the United States. His efficiency in preaching the gospel in six languages, his knowledge of the biblical languages, and cheerful disposition under all circumstances, even under bitterest trial and persecution, produced a great scholar and an effective and successful missionary.

GOODSPEED, EDGAR JOHNSON (1871-1962), American Greek Scholar and Bible translator; born at Quincy, Illinois. Studied at Denison University, Yale University, University of Chicago, University of Berlin. Traveled in Europe, Egypt, and Palestine. From about 1898 to 1915 assistant or associate professor of biblical and patristic Greek in University of Chicago, full professor, 1915-1937, and professor emeritus after 1937. Chairman of department of New Testament (1923-1937). From 1938 to 1951 lectured on history in the University of California, Los Angeles and in other universities. Author of over sixty books and about two hundred scholarly articles. Among his books: *The Story of the New Testament, The Story of the Old Testament, Strange New Gospels, Apostolic Fathers: An American Translation, An Introduction to the New Testament, New Chapters in New Testament Study, Epistle to the Hebrews, How Came the Bible, History of Early Christian Literature, Complete Bible: An American Translation* (including the Apocrypha), *How to Read the Bible, Paul, A Life of Jesus.* "He was active in beginning to collate the New Testament Greek manuscripts in America, and in introducing study of Greek Papyri in America." Best known for *The New Testament: An American Translation*. One of the nine scholars who worked on the Revised Standard Version of the New Testament in 1930 and after. Early student in USA of study of Greek Papyri and collation of Greek New Testament manuscripts.

GOODWIN, THOMAS (1600-1680), English Nonconformist preacher, born at Rollesby, Norfolk, England, educated at Christ's College and Catherine's Hall, Cambridge. In 1625 licensed to preach, in 1628 was appointed lecturer at Trinity Church, and vicar in 1632. In 1634 under the influence of John Cotton of Boston, New England, became a Separatist preacher and removed to London where he preached until 1639. Because of Laud's interference resigned position and went to Holland where he became pastor of the English merchants and refugees at Arnhem. Soon after Laud's impeachment by the Long Parliament in 1640 he returned to London, gathered an independent congregation at St. Dunstan's-in-the-East, ministering to them for ten years. In 1643 became a member of the Westminster Assembly, identified himself with the Congregational party, known as the "dissenting brethren," became their leader, and edited *The Reasons Presented by the Dissenting Brethren*. Made chaplain to the Council of State in 1649, and president of Magdalen College, Oxford, in 1650. Became one of Cromwell's chief advisers, served on important commissions, and attended the Protector on his death bed. Deprived of the presidency of Magdalen College at the Restoration, returned to London as an Independent minister. From 1660 until his death devoted himself exclusively to theological study and to the charge of the Fetter Lane Independent Church. Written works consist mainly of sermons and expositions on parts of Scripture.

GORDON, ADONIRAM JUDSON (1836-1895). Baptist minister, educator and author, born at New Hampton, New Hampshire, and converted when fifteen years old. Educated at Brown University and Newton Theological Seminary. In 1863 became pastor at Jamaica Plain, Massachusetts, where he remained for six years. From 1869 until 1895 pastor of the Clarendon Street Baptist Church in Boston. His dream that Christ sat in his congregation one Sunday morning; the prayers and spiritual activities over a period of several years of the famous Uncle John Vassar in Clarendon Church; and the great evangelistic effort of D. L. Moody in Tremont Temple in 1877 near A. J. Gordon's church all did much to raise the spiritual tone and the evangelistic zeal of both pastor and church on Clarendon Street. He began to preach with new power; the church became "a salvation station in Boston," and a center of missionary support and activitiy. Great sums of money were raised for missions, and many types of mission work were carried on in his church, including missions for the Jews, the Chinese, and blacks, Boston Industrial Home, rescue work for fallen women, evangelistic work on the wharves, in hospitals, in street car stables, and in weak churches. He also established in 1889 a school for the training of missionaries and pastors' assistants which became Gordon College. Among Gordon's writings are his *When Christ Came to Church, The Ministry of the Spirit; The Two-fold Life; Ecce Venit: Behold He Cometh; The Ministry of Healing;* and *The Holy Spirit in Missions.* Wrote music for "My Jesus I Love Thee" and editor of *Watchword* (1878-1895).

GORDON, CHARLES GEORGE (CHINESE GORDON and GORDON PASHA) (1833-1885), British colonial soldier and administrator, born at Woolwich, Kent, England, educated at Taunton and the Royal Military Academy at Woolwich. Served in the Crimean War against Russia (1854-1856). After the war served for two years on the boundary commission in Bessarabia and Armenia. In 1860 went to North China to join the British force then engaged with the French in war with China. Participated in the siege of Peking. In 1863 made commander of the "Ever Victorious Army," which the next year completely suppressed the Taiping rebellion. Gordon spent the next ten years in military service in England and in commissions on the Continent. Then for six years he was in the service of the khedive of Egypt, being appointed governor-general of the Sudan. During the next few years served the British government in various administrative positions in India, China, South Africa, and Mauritius, in the latter of which he was made major general. In 1884 visited Palestine. His last year was spent in the defense of the Anglo-British forces against a Moslem rebellion in the Sudan. For ten months he held out in the siege of Khartoum; but two days before British relief arrived, Khartoum fell and Gordon was killed. His passion was to glorify God and to please Jesus Christ. A constant student of the Bible, carried his Bible more often than a gun or sword. Endeavored to deal with all men in the spirit of love and justice, and was trusted by all classes. A man of humility, honesty, truth, and unselfishness, seeking at all times to combat falsehood, selfishness and hatred. Wrote *Reflections in Palestine* and *Last Journal,* a sort of spiritual biography.

GORDON, CHARLES WILLIAM (RALPH CONNOR) (1860-1937), Presbyterian minister, teacher, missionary, writer, born in Indian Lands, Glengarry, Ontario, Canada, educated at the University of Toronto, Knox College, Toronto, and New College, Edinburgh. In educational work from 1883 to 1887 in Toronto; ordained in the Presbyterian ministry in 1890; a missionary in the mining and lumbering regions of Northwest Territories, Alberta, 1890-1893. Minister of St. Stephen's Church, Winnipeg, from 1894 until death. Moderator of the General Assembly of the Presbyterian Church of Canada in 1922. Played an important part in effecting the merger of the Methodist, Presbyterian, and Congregational churches into the United Church of Canada. Held many public offices in his city; served as chaplain with the Canadian Expeditionary Forces in World War I; manifested much interest in social work. Under pseudonym "Ralph Connor" he was the author of several novels which had their setting in the regions of Western Canada. Among them are: *Black Rock, The Sky Pilot, The Man from Glengarry, The Girl from Glengarry;* and *Glengarry School Days.* Novels are of high moral tone. In them he displays his love of human nature in a combination of humor and pathos that won for them a wide acceptance.

GORDON, SAMUEL DICKEY (1859-1936), devotional lecturer and writer, born in Philadelphia, Pennsylvania, educated in the public schools of Philadelphia. In 1884 became an assistant secretary in the Philadelphia Young Men's Christian Association, and a short time later called to the position of state secretary of the Ohio Young Men's Christian Association. After ten years of service began a career of public speaking. Traveled for four years in the Orient addressing student assemblies and religious gatherings. Unique style in public address led him into a distinctive field in Bible conferences and missionary conventions. In theology orthodox and conservative. Author of many books of the *Quiet Talk* series, books of a devotional nature and of the deeper religious experience.

GORE (gōr), **CHARLES** (1853-1932), High Church Anglican bishop, born in Wimbledon, near London, England, educated at Harrow, and at Balliol College, Oxford. Elected fellow of Trinity College, Oxford and ordained in 1875. Served as vice-principal of Cuddeston Theological College from 1880 to 1883, and librarian of Pusey Library, Oxford, from 1884 to 1893. A leader of the liberal group of the High church or Anglo-Catholic party. Questioning of the orthodoxy of his views led to his resignation from Oxford in 1893, to his acceptance of the small parish of Radley, near Oxford, where he founded a community called the Society of the Resurrection. From 1894 to 1902 he was canon of Westminster, also chaplain to the queen from 1898 to 1901. In 1902 consecrated bishop of Worcester, and in 1905 was transferred to the new see of Birmingham, where he remained until 1911. Bishop of Oxford from 1911 until 1919. Taught in King's College, London (1924-1928). Wrote many books on theology and creed, especially pertaining to the Church of England. Some books were: *Belief in God, Belief in Christ, The Holy Spirit and the Church, The Anglo-Catholic Movement Today, Religion of the Church,* and *Jesus of Nazareth*. Dr. Gore linked Tractarian ideas with biblical criticism and social consciousness.

GOSSNER (gōs'nēr), **JOHANNES EVANGELISTA** (1773-1858), German minister, founder of the Gossner Foreign Missionary Society, born in Hausen, near Augsburg, Germany. Studied at the University of Dillingen and the college at Ingolstadt. Ordained priest in 1796 and served as a Catholic pastor until in 1826 he left Romanism and joined the Evangelical church. From 1829 to 1846 pastor of Bethlehem Church, the Bohemian Protestant church in Berlin. Developed a great and beneficial activity founding schools and asylums, and sending out missionaries to the heathen. In 1842 established the Gossner Foreign Missionary Society, which during his lifetime sent out more than one hundred and forty missionaries, principally to the Khols of East India. After 1846 ceased pastoral activity. Preaching was plain, popular, effective, and thoroughly evangelical. Wrote several books, founded and edited a missionary journal.

GOTTSCHALK (gōt'shŏlk), (c. 805-c. 868), German Benedictine monk and theologian, born near Mainz, Germany. A monk of Fulda, Germany. When tired of monastic life was restrained from leaving the monastery by his abbot, Rabanus Maurus. Began to study Augustine, and to support the doctrine of absolute double predestination. Made two trips to Italy, and wandered through Dalmatia, Pannonia, and Noricum, preaching his doctrine and writing. In meantime made priest. For teaching, condemned by Rabanus Maurus, now archbishop of Mainz, and by Hincmar, archbishop of Rheims who adhered to the church's generally accepted semi-Pelagian views. The first condemnation was at a council in Mainz, 848, and the second at a council called at Quiercy, 849. Deprived of his priesthood and confined to monastic imprisonment for the last twenty years. Spent time studying, writing, and carrying on an extensive correspondence. In purity of life, knowledge, and natural endowments, Gottschalk was one of the foremost men of his time. Among extant writings are a letter to Ratramnus, and a work attacking Hincmar's doctrine of the trinity.

GOULBURN (go͞ol'bērn), **EDWARD MEYRICK** (1818-1897), Church of England divine, dean of Norwich, born at Chelsea, London, England, educated at Röttingdean, Eton College, and Balliol College, Oxford. Fellow of Merton College, Oxford (1841-1846), tutor and dean (1843-1845). In 1843 ordained priest. Between the years 1844 and 1889, successively curate of Holywell, Oxford; chaplain to the bishop of Oxford; headmaster of Rugby; minister of Quebec Chapel; vicar of St. John's, Paddington, London; and finally dean of Norwich. Served in the latter capacity for twenty-three years. In theology changed gradually from the evangelical to the High church position. Regarded with abhorrence latitudinarianism and rationalism. Author of numerous sermons, lectures, commentaries, and theological manuals. More important works: *The Doctrine of the Resurrection of the Body* (Bampton lectures); *A Manual of Confirmation; Thoughts on Personal Religion; The Holy Catholic Church: Its Divine Ideal, Ministry, and Institutions; Everlasting Punishment; An Introduction to the Doctrinal Study of the Holy Scripture;* and *The Acts of the Deacons.*

GOUNOD (go͞o nō'), **CHARLES FRANÇOIS** (1818-1893), French composer, born in Paris, studied at Paris Conservatoire and Rome. Won Grand Prix de Rome in 1839. In Rome devoted much time to the study of Italian church music, being especially attracted to Palestrina. Composed his own first important piece, *Messe a Tre,* which was performed in Rome in 1841. Following was organist and choirmaster at the Eglise des Missions Estrangeres, Paris; and for a time studied for the priesthood. In 1851 gave up this study to devote himself to musical composition, especially to that of opera. Operatic music is distinguished for lyric more than for dramatic quality. Produced several operas, the most famous being *Faust* and *Romeo et Juliette*. For several years conductor of the Orpheon in Paris, for which society he composed several choruses and masses. The composer of distinguished sacred music, including the oratorios *Tobie; La Redemption,* dedicated to Queen Victoria; *Mors et Vita,* dedicated to Pope Leo XIII; the cantata *Gallia;* several masses, motets, symphonies, anthems, and hymns. One of his hymn tunes was "Send Out Thy Light." He wrote the "Ave Maria." One of his most beautiful and famous masses was "St. Cecilia." During the Franco-Prussian War (1870-1871) resided in England where he formed the Gounod Choir, a popular choral society of mixed voices, and in 1871 was succeeded as conductor by Sir Joseph Barnby.

GRACE, CHARLES EMMANUEL (1881-1960). Born at Brava, Cape Verde Islands. Set up Pentecostal-holiness black sect wih first house of prayer in Charlotte, North Carolina in 1926. Later moved to Newark, New Jersey. Church ran cafeterias and retirement homes. National headquarters were placed in Washington, D.C. with a claimed membership of over one million.

GRAF (grōf), **KARL HEINRICH** (1815-1869), German Protestant Old Testament Critic and Orientalist, born at Mühlhausen in Alsace, studied at the Protestant Seminary and the University of Strassburg. In 1844 became teacher in a gymnasium at Leipzig, and from 1847 until 1868 teacher of French and Hebrew in the gymnasium at Meissen. While a student sitting in the classroom under E. G. E. Reuss, Graf accepted his teacher's theory of post-exilic origin of the Pentateuch. This view was then passed on by Graf to Kuenen and Wellhausen, all of whom became proponents of this critical, historical view of the Pentateuch. Some of his writings: *Der Segen Moses, Der Prophet Jeremia erklärt,* and *Die Geschichtlichen Bücher des Alten Testaments.*

GRANT, CHARLES (1746-1823), statesman and reformer. Born at Aldourne in Inverness Shire, Scotland. Educated at Elgin. Went to India as a soldier in 1767. Made a factor in 1773. From 1781 resident in charge of silk manufacture and in 1784 a senior merchant who built a fortune. From 1787 until his return to England in 1790 member of the Board of Trade at Calcutta. From 1802 to 1818 a member of the British Parliament. On Board of Directors of the British East India Company (1806). When charter of the company was up for renewal, worked to get clauses for education of natives and admission of missionaries to India and succeeded in 1813. Chairman of Commission for issue of exchequer bills from 1818 to 1823. Introduced Sunday Schools into Scotland. Director of Sierra Leone Company. As member of Clapham Sect helped to send such chaplains to India as Henry Martyn in 1805.

GRANT, GEORGE MONRO (1835-1902), Canadian clergyman and educator. Born in Nova Scotia. Educated at Pictou Academy, West River Seminary, and Glasgow University. Ordained in 1860 in the Church of Scotland. From 1863 to 1877 pastor of influential St. Matthews Church in Halifax. From 1877 until his death was head of Queens' University, Kingston, Ontario. Gained national reputation in 1873 with his book *Ocean to Ocean* and social and political involvement. Honored with moderatorship of the General Assembly of the Presbyterian church in Canada in 1899. President of Royal Society of Canada in 1900.

GRATIAN (Twelfth century), systematizer of canon law. Born in Chiusi, Italy. Became a monk of the Camoldese Order and resided in a monastery. His *Decretum* was the compilation of canon law based on Roman law. It has been used by the Roman Catholic church as ecclesiastical law.

GRAY, JAMES MARTIN (1851-1935), clergyman, author, Bible teacher, and Bible school president, born in New York City. Received education in New England. In 1879 became the rector of the First Reformed Episcopal Church in Boston, served there for fourteen years, resigning in 1894. For a time taught Bible in Dr. A. J. Gordon's Missionary and Training School. Beginning in 1893 a special Bible teacher at the summer sessions at the Moody Bible Institute. In 1904, when Dr. R. A. Torrey began his worldwide evangelistic campaigns, Dr. Gray was called to the office of dean at the Institute. In 1925 became president. A man of breadth and vision; though a conservative theologian, Bible teacher, and Sunday school promoter, manifested an interest in civic affairs, in national patriotism, in social betterment, in public education, and in prohibition. A successful pastor and church builder, a good expository preacher, an active evangelist, an excellent Bible teacher, and a capable administrator. A deep student and a profound scholar. Served as one of the seven editors of the Scofield Reference Bible. His interests were worldwide. Helped make the Institute a great missionary training school.

Made nine teaching and preaching trips to Great Britain, and had planned another when he died. Author of about twenty books and many booklets and pamphlets. A few titles: *How to Master the English Bible, Synthetic Bible Studies, Christian Worker's Commentary, Text Book of Prophecy, Bible Problems Explained, Great Epochs of Sacred History, Satan and the Saint, Why a Christian Cannot be an Evolutionist,* and *Spiritism and the Fallen Angels.* Among the hymns he wrote: "Nor Silver nor Gold," "What Did He Do?", "Lord, Send a Revival," "Bringing Back the King," and "I Find Thee So Precious."

GREBEL (grā'běl), **CONRAD** (c. 1498-1526), Swiss Anabaptist preacher and reformer, born in Zurich, Switzerland, educated at Basel, Vienna, and Paris. For eight years a humanist. In 1522 had a spiritual awakening, and soon became a disciple of Zwingli. By 1525 he and several others came to the conviction that infant baptism was unscriptural and criticized Zwingli for his stand. Early in 1525 a group of these men met in the home of Felix Manz in Zurich. At the spontaneous request of Georg Blaurock, Conrad Grebel rebaptized him, and the same evening Blaurock baptized the others present. In the following days these Swiss Brethren went from house to house in Zurich teaching and baptizing. Grebel participated, but Blaurock did the most of the preaching and administering the sacraments. This was the beginning of the reformation Anabaptist movement. A heated disputation arose between these Brethren and Zwingli. In 1525 The Zurich Council ordered a final disputation between the parties with the hope of arriving at a settlement of the dispute. Though these men ably defended their position, the council decided in favor of Zwingli, ordered all the children to be baptized, and ordered Grebel and his friends to cease from disputing. The Zurich Council in 1526 ordered Anabaptists to be drowned; and in the next few years many Anabaptists were drowned or otherwise martyred. Grebel left Zurich and spent brief periods in several centers of Switzerland, preaching and visiting the brethren. Before the year had passed, he, Manz, and Blaurock were imprisoned in the tower at Zurich for several months. In March, 1526 all escaped. Later the same year Grebel died of the plague.

GREEN, SAMUEL GOSNELL (1822-1905), English Baptist minister, born at Falmouth, England, educated at Stepney (now Regent's Park College) and at the University of London. Between 1844 and 1851 held two ministerial posts. From 1851 until 1863 a tutor, and from 1863 to 1876 president of Horton (now Rawdon) College, Bradford. In 1876 chosen book editor of the Religious Tract Society, London, and later became secretary, retiring from active life in 1899. A trustee of the John Rylands Library, Manchester, and a vice-president of the British and Foreign Bible Society. President of the Baptist Union of Portsmouth in 1895. Author of many books on Bible, church history, theology, and other subjects. Most important work, *Handbook to the Grammar of the Greek Testament*. Among other books: *Hebrew of the Old Testament,* his Angus lecture on *The Christian Creed and the Creeds of Christendom, A Handbook of Church History,* and a revision of Dr. Angus' *Bible Handbook*.

GREENWOOD, JOHN (d. 1593). Educated at Corpus Christi College, Cambridge. Ordained as an Anglican. Chaplain to Robert Rich in Essex. In 1581 in London became a separatist. In prison 1582. Helped Francis Johnson organize the "Ancient Church" which moved to Holland. Arrested in 1592 and hanged for writing and distributing "seditious" books.

GREGORY THE GREAT (GREGORY I) (540-604). Occupied the papal chair (590-604), born in an old, senatorial family of Rome, educated for government service, held the highest civil office in Rome. After father's death when Gregory inherited father's wealth, he quit government position, turned father's home into a monastery about 575 and became a monk. Then built six other monasteries in Sicily. Lived in such strict abstinence and austerity that he seriously undermined health. Chosen as one of the seven cardinal deacons of Rome. Before long the pope appointed him ambassador to the imperial court at Constantinople where he served from 578 until 585. Upon return to Rome, made abbot of the monastery which he had earlier founded. In him monasticism for the first time ascended the papal throne, for in 590, he was unanimously elected by the senate, the clergy, and the people to become bishop or pope of Rome. Gregory was an organizer and an administrator. He did much to make the Western church strong. There was no emperor in the West and Gregory became the strong man there. Raised an army and defeated the Arian Lombards and made peace with them. Had charge of the patrimony of St. Peter, vast estates in Sicily, Italy, Southern France, and North Africa. Used the income from possessions for the advancement and strengthening of the church. Though Gregory was considered with Augustine, Jerome, and Ambrose as one of the four great doctors of the church, he was not an original theologian, but rather a transmitter. Glorified the past and held tradition on a par with the Scriptures. Promoted the doctrines and practices of good works and penance, of purgatory, veneration of relics, mass, and transubstantiation, of celibacy of the clergy, of liturgy in worship, of the traditional historic episcopacy, largely as they had been originated or instituted before his day. A missionary-minded man. Sent Augustine of Canterbury to England and made him the first Roman Catholic archbishop in the British Isles. Emphasized the parity of the bishops, yet at the same time tended to raise the authority of the bishop of Rome above that of the other churches. Sought to give church and state each its proper place, but held tenaciously to what he thought was the church's rightful place in relation to the State. This opened up the way for much difficulty and conflict. He created the popular medieval theology. Interpreted Bible allegorically in his *Moralia* (on Job). His *Liber Regula Pastoralis,* is helpful for pastor's life and work.

GREGORY VII (HILDEBRAND) (c. 1023-c. 1085), pope (1073-1085), one of the greatest popes of the Roman Catholic church, born at Siena in Tuscany, Italy. Educated in a Benedictine monastery in Rome, later becoming a Benedictine monk. In 1047 spent a year in Cluny, in 1059 became cardinal, and from that time until 1073 the power behind the papal throne, adviser of no less than five popes. His great concern was for the reform of the Catholic church. Definitely influenced by the Cluniac Reform movement and had brought Cluniac reformers to the papal throne. The day following the death of Alexander II in 1073 during the funeral ceremonies in the Church of the Lateran, Hildebrand, the cardinal archdeacon, the great Cluniac reformer himself was singled out by the people and the clergy for the highest office in the Roman Catholic church. Gregory believed in the position and authority of the papacy, and at once exerted administrative and hierarchial powers to bring the papal power to a new height. He wrote in *Dictatus vs. Papae:* "The Roman Church was founded by God alone; the Roman pope alone can with right be called universal; he alone may use the imperial insignia; his feet only shall be kissed by all princes; he may depose the emperors; he himself may be judged by no one; the Roman Church has never erred; nor will it err in all eternity." Gregory maintained a strong stand for reform in the church. Determined to rule out simony. He had in mind to initiate a crusade to deliver the Christians of the East from the oppression of the Seljukian Turks, and attempt uniting the Eastern and the Western church. Having denied all monarchs the right of investiture by the ring and the staff, he so informed Henry IV of Germany. A struggle began that ended with tragedy for both. Henry was excommunicated, his prestige lowered among his subjects and his tenure of rule endangered. The pope was coming to Germany to bring further pressure to bear upon Henry, whereupon Henry hastened to meet Gregory at Canossa in 1077, to plead for forgiveness and reinstatement. After three days of waiting in the snow before the castle it was granted. This was a humiliation for the king, a victory for the pope. When Henry had gained sufficient strength he marched on Rome, reduced it almost to ruins and drove Gregory into exile. In Salerno, heartbroken, Gregory died.

GREGORY IX (c. 1145-1241), pope (1227-1241), born Ugolino, Count of Segni at Anagni, Italy, educated at the universities of Paris and Bologna. First created cardinal deacon, and in 1206, cardinal bishop of Ostia. As cardinal supported Francis of Assisi in establishing the Franciscan Order. As pope, Gregory also befriended the early Dominicans to whom in 1233 he gave the commission to operate the Inquisition which he had recognized and centralized as the Holy Office, established to eradicate heresy. In 1234, canonized Dominic. Clara and the Clarissines also stood under the protection of Gregory. During his pontificate engaged in two bitter conflicts with Emperor Frederick II. Because Frederick failed to go on a crusade as he had promised, the pope excommunicated him. In 1228 Frederick did proceed with an army to the Holy Land, but without the pope's consent or blessing. Upon his return to Europe the next year he marched upon Rome and the pope was obliged to flee. A treaty of peace was effected between the pope and the emperor in 1230. Trouble again broke out between them in 1239. Gregory again excommunicated Frederick whom he styled "blasphemous beast of the Apocalypse." This led to open war, which, while Gregory lived, was favorable to Frederick. Noted also for collection of papal decretals, the work being completed in 1234.

GREGORY XI (PIERRE ROGER de BEAUFORT (c. 1329-1378), pope (1370-1378). Born near Limoges, France, son of a French count. At age seventeen made cardinal by his uncle, Pope Clement VI. Attended the University of Perugia. In January 1371 ordained priest and shortly after crowned pope and continued the papacy at Avignon. Reign was a constant warfare with cities of Italy. Through the persistent entreaties of

Catherine of Siena (1347-1380), he returned from Avignon to Rome in 1377, thus ending the "Babylonian Captivity." That year he issued five bulls ordering the arrest and examination of John Wycliffe of England as a heretic. After his death a Neapolitan, Urban VI, was elected to succeed him, and the papacy remained at Rome.

GREGORY XII (ANGELO CORRARIO) (c. 1326-1417), last of Roman popes in the Papal Schism, ruled 1406-1415, born in Venice of a noble Venetian family. In 1380 became bishop of Castello, and in 1390, titular patriarch of Constantinople. In 1405 elected to the cardinalate as cardinal priest of San Marco, Venice; in 1406 elected pope at the age of eighty, succeeding Innocent VII. The council of Pisa in 1409 deposed him and elected Alexander V. Like his rival and enemy, the ambitious Benedict XIII (Pedro de Luna), he protested the right of the council to take this action. Ultimately at the Council of Constance in 1415 all three popes were deposed. Martin V was elected, reuniting the papacy under one head once more. Martin V made Gregory cardinal bishop of Oporto, Portugal, where he died in 1417. Gregory XII generally is considered by the Roman church as the true pope during the years of his pontificate, his rivals as antipopes.

GREGORY XIII (UGO BUONCOMPAGNI) (1502-1585), pope (1572-1585), born at Bologna, studied canon law and taught at the University of Bologna from 1531 to 1539. Held various appointments under popes Paul III, Julius III, and Paul IV, being the latter's confidential deputy at the Council of Trent (1545-1563). Learning and service at Trent procured for him the cardinal's hat in 1564. Spanish influence made him pope in 1572 at the age of seventy. In his ardor to combat Protestantism, he founded twenty-three colleges and seminaries within and outside Rome to train the youth of the Catholic nations, assigning the educational program largely to the Jesuits. Promoted missions in Japan and India; attempted to effect a union with the Eastern church to work against Protestantism; adorned Rome with magnificent churches and other public buildings; and issued a new edition of the *Corpus Juris Canonici* (1582). Work, however, for which he is chiefly remembered was the reformation of the Julian calendar in 1582 introducing leap year to correct the inaccuracy of the year's length.

GREGORY THE ILLUMINATOR (c. 240-c. 332), the Apostle of Armenia. Rescued and taken to Caesarea in Cappadocia, Asia Minor, was brought up in the Christian faith and given a good education. He went to Armenia and won the high esteem of King Tiridates III. Had become a trusted servant of the king until he not only refused to worship the pagan idols of Tiridates, but also confessed his Christian faith. The king, became enraged and cast him into a dungeon where for about fourteen years he was daily supplied with food by a Christian of the community. When the king was afflicted with a terrible disease, Gregory was released and the king and his family and many of his retainers were converted. About 302, Gregory was sent to Caesarea, his old home, to be consecrated as bishop. Upon return to Armenia with a band of fellow missionaries, within a short time thousands accepted the faith and were baptized. Tiridates made Christianity the national religion, making Armenia the first Christian state. Gregory went throughout the land preaching the gospel and destroying pagan temples or converting them into churches. He secured his first helpers and co-laborers from Cappadocia. As fast as possible he built up a native ministry. Preached in the language of the people. Schools were established under the patronage of the king. Twelve episcopal sees were established by Gregory.

GREGORY OF NAZIANZUS (c. 330-c. 390), poet and orator of the "Three Cappadocians." Received the best of education in schools at Caesarea in Cappadocia, at Caesarea in Palestine, at Alexandria, at Athens, and at other places. After completing education in 358 was baptized by his father. Joined his friend Basil in a monastery in Pontus for a few months, on another visit home was ordained a presbyter by his father whom he assisted until his father's death in 374. Meantime Basil the Great as metropolitan of Cappadocia, about 372 appointed him bishop over a little insignificant church at Sasima. Upon father's death in 374 he exercised the office of bishop at Nazianzus for a time. In 379 Basil's death greatly saddened and depressed him. It called forth the famous and eloquent panegyric on Basil. Within a year called to the decadent church at Constantinople. He built a large church, and preached to enormous crowds. At the Ecumenical Council at Constantinople in 381 released from his former bishoprics and formally declared the archbishop of Constantinople, and inaugurated with great pomp. Gregory resigned before the year was out. Retired to seclusion on the paternal estate near Nazianzus, he devoted the last decade of his life to religious exercises and to literary pursuits. Exerted great influence upon the church, and shared with Chrysostom, who followed him as bishop of Constantinople, the honor of being one of the greatest orators of the Greek Church. Wrote five *Theological Orations* against the Arians.

GREGORY OF NYSSA (nĭs′a) (c. 330-c. 394), philosopher and student of the "Three Cappadocians." Educated in rhetoric and taught same. Unlike his older brother Basil and his friend Gregory Nazianzen, he married. Maintained strong tendencies toward the ascetic life, exalting the celibate life and spending some time in retirement. After Basil became metropolitan of Cappadocia about 371, he appointed Gregory to the small bishopric of Nyssa. Strong defense of the church against Arianism led the imperial government, which favored Arianism at this time, to replace him with an Arian bishop. After two years, under a new emperor, permitted to return to his church. After Basil's death he became one of the strongest defenders of the faith against Arianism. In 381 attended the Council of Constantinople and had much influence in the decisions of the council. The council commissioned him, "one of the pillars of Catholic orthodoxy," to visit churches in Arabia and Jerusalem where disturbances had broken out and where schism had threatened. Of the Nicene age teachers he was the most like Origen. First to clearly distinguish between *ousia* (essence) and *hypostasis* (persons) in Trinity. Held ransom theory of atonement.

GREGORY THAUMATURGUS (thô må tûr′gus), (Wonderworker) (c. 213-c. 270), Greek church Father and Bishop of Neo-Caesarea. Born at Neo-Caesarea in Pontus. As young men he and brother Athenodorus made a trip to Palestine on family business. There they heard of Origen's lectures at his school in Caesarea. They were captivated by his teaching, and accepted the Christian faith. They remained in Caesarea for several years to receive teaching from Origen. Upon his return to Neo-Caesarea he is said to have found seventeen Christians in the city. He entered upon Christian work among them, and was soon, though against his will, made their bishop. Gregory attended the Synod of Antioch in 265, which condemned Paul of Samosata.

GREGORY OF TOURS (GEORGIUS FLORENTIUS) (c. 538-594), Frankish bishop and historian, born at city in the Auvergne, France, and educated by uncle Gallus, bishop of Clermont. Ordained priest in 569, and called to succeed Euphronius as bishop of tours in 573. Governed diocese from 573 to 594 with great ability and sympathetic concern, though under adverse and very difficult circumstances in the period of Merovingian intrigues and warfare. Owes his great celebrity, however, to writing of the *Historia Francorum*, a *History of the Franks,* ten volumes, the last six of which deal comprehensively with the history of his time. This history is the most important, if not the only source of the history, of Gaul in the dark and stormy time of the Merovingian kings. It describes the settlement, history, and conversion of the Franks down to his time. His history is somewhat colored by the fact that his mind was always busied with extraordinary events—crimes, miracles, wars, and excesses of every kind more than with commonplace occurrences; yet he attempted to be exact and impartial. Also promoted the tradition of the assumption of Mary or her miraculous ascent to Heaven. His theological work was a commentary on the Psalms, also wrote, *Seven Books of Miracles, Book of Glories of the Martyrs, Book of Glories of the Confessors,* and *Book of Lives of the Fathers.* Canonized by acclamation shortly after his death.

GREGORY OF UTRECHT (c. 701-776), early Frankish missionary, related to the royal Merovingian house, born near Trier, educated at the court school and in the monastery of Pfalze in the diocese of Treves. Met Boniface the missionary to the Germans, and became his constant companion. When Boniface was martyred in 755, Gregory took upon himself the care of the Frisian mission, but declined the episcopal dignity. From his monastery preachers were sent to tribes of the Frisians who had not yet heard the gospel, as well as to those who had recently been Christianized. Gregory continued work of counseling and teaching until death.

GRELLET (grā lĕ′), **STEPHEN (ETIENNE DE)** (1773-1855), Quaker minister, missionary and philanthropist, born in Limoges, France. Originally a Roman Catholic, educated under Catholic auspices at the College of the Oratorians in Lyons. At seventeen entered the bodyguard of Louis XVI. During the Revolution, captured and sentenced to be shot, escaped, going first to South America in 1793, and to the United States in 1795. A protege of Voltaire, but through the writings of William Penn led to join the Friends. During the yellow fever epidemic in Philadelphia in 1798 ministered to the stricken until laid low with the fever. In same year recommended by the Yearly Meeting for the ministry. After 1799 traveled as a missionary and philanthropic worker over much of the United States, Canada, and Haiti; made three visits to Europe, preaching in nearly every country in Europe. Not only held religious meetings, but also visited mines, hospitals, prisons, and asylums, seeking to ameliorate social conditions generally.

Boldly preached to the Roman Catholics, even to Pope Pius VII, to kings, to Czar Alexander I; to his unsaved relatives, to the Indians, to slaveholders against slavery, to militarists against war. At age eighty-two, he died at Burlington, New Jersey, where he had spent several years. Interested Elizabeth Fry in prison work.

GRENFELL, GEORGE (1849-1906), British Baptist missionary and explorer of the Congo, born near Penzance, Cornwall, England. Educated at King Edward's School in Birmingham and apprenticed to a Birmingham hardware and machinery firm. In 1873 entered the Baptist College at Bristol, the following year sent by the Baptist Missionary Society to the Cameroons, Africa, to work with Alfred Saker. First three years of mission work in the Cameroons were an apprenticeship for great work on the Congo, worked for ten years with Thomas J. Comber, exploring the river and establishing mission stations. Grenfell continued to manage several expeditions, and discovered more of the tributaries of the Congo. In 1884 launched a river steamer, the "Peace," brought from England dismantled. He put it together above the river rapids. This large boat facilitated expeditions, and provided a home for his family for many years. He explored 15,000 miles of the Congo River. In 1890, the Belgians demanded possession of "Peace" and the charts and maps. In 1893 launched a new steamer, the "Goodwill." The Belgian government later returned his "Peace," though badly worn. In 1887 he was awarded the Founder's Medal by the Royal Geographic Society for his articles written on his explorations, and for his maps of the Congo Basin. In 1891, with the consent of the mission, he was appointed a plenipotentiary from Belgium to negotiate the settlement of the boundary between Belgian and Portuguese territories. Grenfell continued cruising and building mission stations until his death. His last trip went farther interior than he had gone before, past burial places of numerous fellow workers and of his children. For thirty-two years he had labored in Africa, planting the gospel on the Congo.

GRENFELL, WILFRED THOMASON (1866-1940), physician and missionary to Labrador, born at Parkgate, Cheshire, England, educated at Marlborough and Oxford taking M.D. degree from Oxford in 1889. Studied medicine at the London Hospital under Sir Frederick Treves, later personal physician to Edward VII. After conversion at a Moody Mission service in 1885, and in 1890 joined the Royal National Mission for Deep Sea Fishermen, and for three years cruised with it as medical missionary. In 1892 he began his famous work in Labrador as missionary and physician for forty-two years among the fisherfolk. Instrumental in building hospitals, orphanages, boarding schools, agricultural stations, cooperative stores, and other community enterprises. Located his hospitals along the coast of Labrador and Newfoundland about one hundred fifty miles apart, nursing stations between them, equipping the entire organization with dog teams and motor boats. In 1912 the International Grenfell Association was organized to aid in the execution of his work. The same year the George V Seamen's Institute at St. John's, Newfoundland was established. Grenfell was a fellow of both the Royal and the American College of Surgeons, received honors from the National Academy of Social Science, the Royal Geographic Society of England, and the Royal Scottish Geographic Society. In 1927 he was knighted by King George V of England. In 1929 rector of St. Andrews University. Wrote many books about his missionary experiences, such as *Forty Years for Labrador.*

GRIESBACH, JOHANN JACOB (1745-1812), New Testament textual critic. Born at Butzbach. Studied at Frankfurt-am-Main, Tübingen, Leipzig, and Halle. From 1773 professor at Halle and Jena. First to use literary analysis of the gospels and promote the synoptic concept to relate the first three gospels. In his great critical edition of the Greek New Testament (1774-1777) developed three "families" of Greek texts—the Alexandrian, the Western, and the Byzantine.

GRIGG (grĭg), **JOSEPH** (1720-1768), Presbyterian hymn writer, probably born in London, England, trained for mechanical pursuits, early forsook his trade to become assistant minister in a Presbyterian church, Silver Street, London. Four years later, when the minister died, retired from the ministry. As a hymn writer, is known chiefly by two hymns: "Behold a Stranger at the Door," and "Jesus, Can It Ever Be?" Published works of various kinds numbering over forty.

GRIMKE, SARAH MOORE ANGELINA (1792-1873) and **EMILY** (1805-1879), abolitionists. Born in Charleston, South Carolina. Sisters freed family slaves after father's death and moved to Philadelphia in 1821 to get away from slavery. Joined the Quakers in 1823 and also the Anti-Slavery Society a little later. Angelina spoke for women's rights as well as abolition. Wrote *Epistle to the Clergy of the Southern States* and *Letters of the Equality of the Sexes and the Condition* *of Women*. Angelina married Theodore Dwight Weld.

GRIMSHAW, WILLIAM (1708-1763), evangelical Anglican minister. Born Brindle, Lancashire. Educated at Christ's College, Cambridge. After a short chaplaincy at Todmorden, became minister at Haworth in 1742 until the end of his life. His reading of the Bible at Todmorden led to his conversion, and his athletic ability and humorous preaching won the confidence of his rough Yorkshire congregation. Helped poor, sick, and lonely. Preached in nearby parishes. Helped the Wesleys and Whitefield.

GROCYN (grō'sĭn), **WILLIAM** (c. 1446-1519), English humanist, renaissance scholar, born at Colerne, Wiltshire, England, educated at Winchester College, and at New College, Oxford. After occupying a pastorate for a year or two, and being prebendary at Lincoln Cathedral in 1485, spent about two years traveling and studying in Italy. After return to England lectured on the classics at Exeter College, Oxford. Later became professor of Greek at Oxford, being perhaps the first one who publicly taught Greek at Oxford. Sir Thomas More was a pupil of Grocyn, and Erasmus while at Oxford lived in Grocyn's house. In 1496 became rector of St. Lawrence Jewry. In 1506 became master of All-Hallows' College, near Maidstone, still held the rectory, and obtained in addition the rectory of Shepperton. In religious attitudes more conservative than were many of the humanists and renaissance scholars. Continued study of and interest in the Schoolmen.

GROOT (grōt), **GERARD (GEERT) DE** (1340-1384), founder of the Brethren of the Common Life, and Dutch religious reformer, born at Deventer, Holland. A brilliant scholar, studied at Paris, taught at Cologne, and appointed canon of Utrecht and Aachen. After experiencing a sudden conversion about 1374, with the longing to live a deeper Christian life, gave up ecclesiastical appointments and income, and withdrew for ascetic practice, devotion, and further study, spending three years in a Carthusian monastery. Ordained a deacon, but not a priest. At age forty began preaching. Great throngs gathered to hear him in the churches and churchyards of Deventer, Zwolle, Leiden, and other towns of Holland. Always loyal to doctrines of the Catholic church, but strongly denounced the low morals of the clergy. Laid the foundation for the Brethren of the Common Life, a free association based upon the community of property, occupation, and station, but not requiring monastic vows. The people sought to develop the inner life of piety and mystic communion with God, and to glorify and exemplify the life of Christ. Though deeply mystical they escaped the pantheistic and antinomistic tendencies so often prevalent in mysticism. Influenced by the teaching of Johann Ruysbroeck, Groot himself strongly influenced Florentius Radewyn, Thomas à Kempis, and Johann of Wessel, who carried on and helped spread the teachings and practices of the Brethren of the Common Life.

GROSSETESTE (grōs'tĕst), **ROBERT** (c. 1175-1253), bishop of Lincoln, reformer of ecclesiastical abuses, born at Stradbrook, Suffolk, England, studied at Oxford and Paris. An able teacher at the Franciscan School, Oxford, for several years, also chancellor at Oxford. At the same time held several preferments. In 1235 elected bishop of Lincoln. Schemes of moral reform and clerical discipline brought him into conflict with the clergy as well as with the civil and ecclesiastical authorities. In 1250 delivered a sermon in which he arraigned the fountain and origin of the papal system as all the evils of the Church. In impetuous and fearless temper resembled Luther. Noted student of the sciences, a mathematician and physicist. Among students was Roger Bacon. Wrote voluminously on philosophy and theology, and translated from the Greek. Wrote commentaries on Aristotle and Boethius. In earlier life preached in the Latin; in the latter part often used the vernacular.

GROTIUS (grō'shĭ ŭs), **(DeGROOT), HUGO** (1583-1645), Dutch statesman, jurist, theologian, author, born at Delft, Holland. Studied law under his father and continued his study at Leiden, taking his degree in law at the age of fifteen. At age twenty-three became advocate-general of Holland. Rapidly rose to prominence in the political world, being appointed pensionary of Rotterdam in 1613. Both legal and literary interests and abilities soon became involved in the theological controversies which were agitating Holland, centering around the conflict between Calvinism and Arminianism. He favored the views of Arminius as to man's freedom to accept or refuse grace. He wrote a eulogy on Arminius in 1609, undertook to defend the Remonstrant or Arminian party, which was under the leadership of Oldenbarnevelt. At the Council of Dort in 1619 the Arminians were condemned. Oldenbarnevelt had been beheaded and Grotius was sentenced to life imprisonment in the castle of Loevenstein, his wife being allowed to share her husband's confinement. Occupied for about two years in philological and theological studies, and in the writing of several books. In 1621, through his wife's machinations, able to escape, fled to Paris where he remained with his wife and children until 1631. Finally forced to leave France. Went to Hamburg where he remained until 1634. Spent the last ten years of his life in the service of the Swedish government. In 1645, left Sweden. On journey back to Holland he became ill and died. Body was carried to Delft and buried in the grave of ancestors. Wrote: *De Veritate Religiones Christianae, Via ad Pacem Ecclesiasticam,* and *Votum pro Pace Ecclesiastica* in which he sought to unite all denominations. In his *Annotationes in Vetus et Novum Testamentum* used the historico-philological method in Scripture interpretation. As a jurist wrote: *De Jure Belli et Pacis.* In theology originated and developed the governmental theory of atonement. As an historian wrote: *Historie Gothorum, Vandalorum, et Longebardorum.* Early developer of idea of international law and world organization.

GROVES, ANTHONY NORRIS (1795-1853), joint founder of Plymouth Brethren movement, missionary to Bagdad and India, born at Newton, Hampshire, England. Studied chemistry in London, took up dentistry under his uncle, and at the same time studied surgery in the London hospitals. In 1813, settled as a dentist at Plymouth, three years later moved to Exeter. In 1825 took charge of a small church at Poltimore, near Exeter. Later, with a view to taking orders, studied at Trinity College, Dublin, where he associated with John Nelson Darby. Went to the foreign field as an independent minister and missionary. In 1829 with several others set out for Bagdad in Mesopotamia as the Brethren's first foreign missionaries. In 1833 removed to India, spending the next nineteen years in effective missionary work. There attempt was made to make the mission self-supporting by engaging in agriculture. Died in the home of his brother-in-law, George Müller, in Bristol, England. Wrote: *Journal during a Journey from London to Bagdad* and *Journal of Residence at Bagdad during the Years 1830 and 1831.*

GRUBB, WILFRID BARBROOKE (1865-1930), Scottish missionary to Paraguay, born in Liberton, near Edinburgh, Scotland, educated at George Watson's College, Edinburgh. At nineteen applied to the South American Missionary Society to go out as a pioneer missionary. After period of preparation in England and of preaching in a village of Surrey, sent to Keppel Island in the West Falklands in 1886. In 1889 asked to open pioneer work among the Indians in Paraguayan Chaco. Entered work with much zeal and eagerness; explored the country, living among the people as they lived; by demonstration of great courage won the good will of the Indians; and built a lasting work among them, though it took seven or eight years to win his first converts and to build the first church among them. Called by fellow-workers "The Livingstone of South America," and by the people of Paraguay "The Peacemaker of the Indians."

GRUBER (grōō'bĕr), **FRANZ XAVIER** (1787-1863), Austrian church organist, composer of music for "Silent Night, Holy Night," born in Unterweizburg, Upper Austria, the son of a poor linen weaver, who refused to permit his son to study music. Secretly, in the evenings, Franz took lessons in organ playing and composition from a local school teacher and organist. Became an organist and school teacher. The night before Christmas, December 24, 1818, the pastor wrote the words of "Stille Nacht, Heilige Nacht," and the next morning Gruber played the music. The song was sung by these two men, accompaniment by guitar, since the church organ was broken at the time. It was first sung in the quiet little chapel at Oberndorf on Christmas day, 1818. Gruber is known for this tune alone. He died in Hallein, Austria, where he had founded and directed the now famous Hallein Choral Society and had been choir leader and organist for thirty years.

GRUNDTVIG (grŏŏnt'vīg), **NIKOLAI FREDERIK SEVERIN** (1783-1872), Danish bishop, poet, hymn writer, born at Ubdy on the island of Zealand, Denmark, the son of a clergyman. Received theological education at the University of Copenhagen. Spent years 1805 to 1821 as teacher and as writer of poetry and history, except for years 1808-1810, when assistant minister to his father at Ubdy. In 1811 he was ordained; in 1821 became pastor at Praesto in southern Zealand. Believed himself called to be a religious reformer. In 1822 he was called to chaplaincy at the Church of Our Saviour in Copenhagen. Becoming deeply disturbed over the rationalism and liberalism among the Lutheran clergy, also their deviation from the teachings of the Bible, he started a reforming movement in Danish Lutheranism. In 1825 became involved in a bitter and personal controversy with H. N. Clausen, a professor in Copenhagen, and representative of the rational school. A lawsuit followed with the case going against Grundtvig. Sentenced to pay a fine, he was forced out of his position, and forbidden to publish anything more without royal permission. He retired from active preaching, and devoted himself to the study of the history of the world, making several visits to England pursuing this study. He was impressed with the individual liberty he witnessed in England. It renewed interest in bringing reform to the Danish church. In 1839 made chaplain of Vartov, a home for the aged in Copenhagen, where he ministered until his death. Grundtvig was a deeply spiritual man and his influence upon the church increased greatly during the last thirty years of his life. At the fiftieth anniversary of his ordination (1861) the king conferred on him the title of bishop, with the rank, Bishop of Zealand. Wrote more than fourteen hundred hymns, over 250 of them finding their way into the hymnal of the Church of Denmark. Founder of folk high schools.

GUBER, EBERHARD LUDWIG (1665-1728), Lutheran clergyman, co-founder of Amana Church Society. See Rock, Johann Frederick.

GUINNESS (gĭn'ĭs), **HENRY GRATTAN** (1835-1910), foreign missions promoter, born at Montpelier House, near Kingstown, Ireland, received early education in private schools. At age seventeen went to sea, traveled through Mexico and West Indies. Upon his return to England, 1853, converted. In 1856 entered New College, St. John's Wood, London. The next year ordained an evangelist. Married in 1860; with wife spent twelve years traveling and preaching in the British Isles, France, America, and the Near East. Conducted in Dublin the Merrion Hall Mission, where he helped bring Thomas John Barnardo under religious influence in 1866. In 1873 founded, and directed until his death, the East London Institute for Home and Foreign Missions. It has trained over a thousand missionaries. In 1878 started a foreign missions magazine, "The Regions Beyond"; in 1880 made director of the Livingstone Inland Mission, with Mrs. Guinness as secretary. New missions were founded in the Congo in Peru and in Argentina. In 1899 united these organizations into "The Regions Beyond Missionary Union." In 1901 a mission in India was added. He spent five years (1903-1907) in world missionary tours, after which he retired and resided at Bath, Ireland, where he died. Guinness was a Fellow of the Royal Geographic Society, also a Fellow of the Royal Asiatic Society. Wrote grammars of Congo languages and other books.

GUIZOT (gē zō'), **FRANÇOIS PIERRE GUILLAUME** (1787-1874), French historian and statesman, descended from family of Huguenot pastors, born at Nimes, near Avignon, France. His mother took him to Geneva for his early education. In 1805 went to Paris to study law, history, and philosophy. Interest soon turned to literature and education. The first period of his life (1812 to 1830) was principally literary. In 1812 he became professor of modern history at the Sorbonne, University of France. At this time wrote historical works, *History of Civilization in Europe,* and *History of Civilization in France*. The second period (1830-1848) was political. During this time he held two important posts, minister of public instruction (1832-1834) and minister of foreign affairs (1840-1848), in 1847 becoming official head of the cabinet. Effected a thoroughgoing reform in the educational system of France; but during revolution of 1848, popular indignation rose so high against him that he was obliged to seek asylum in England. After political fall entered his third period, that of interest in religious affairs, and became the chief support of orthodoxy in the Reformed church. For him religion was, above all else, the sanction of order and authority. Desired unity in the Reformed church and sought to unite liberalism and conservatism in order to maintain for the French people the liberties gained in the Reformation. In 1852 chosen president of the consistory. He clung tenaciously to the Calvinistic system of the sixteenth century. Largely responsible for the division of the church which was occasioned about the time of the Synod of 1872. Helped found the French Bible Society in 1826 and the Society of the History of Protestantism in 1857.

GUNKEL, HERMANN (1862-1932), Protestant biblical critic. Born at Springe in Hanover. Taught Old and New Testament exegesis at Göttingen, Halle, Berlin, and Giessen from 1888 to 1927. Key advocate of comparative religion school which found roots of Old Testament religion in the religions of surrounding peoples. Used Form Criticism in his study of the Old Testament. The former idea he developed in *Schopfüng Und Chaos Im Urzeit Und Endzeit*. Wrote commentaries on Genesis, Psalms, and 1 Peter.

GUNSAULUS (gŭn sô'lus), **FRANK WAKELEY** (1856-1921), Congregational minister, born at Chesterville, Ohio, educated at Ohio Wesleyan University. Ordained a Methodist Episcopal minister in 1875. Preached for four years on a Methodist circuit with headquarters at Harrisburg, Ohio. Changed to the Congregational ministry. Held four pastorates in four different states—Columbus, Ohio (1879-1881), Newtonville, Massachusetts (1881-1885), Baltimore, Maryland (1885-1887), and Plymouth Church, Chicago (1887-1899). In 1899 succeeded Newell Dwight Hillis as pastor of the independent Central Church in Chicago, where for twenty years his preaching drew great crowds. In 1893 appointed president of the Armour Institute of Technology, which he and Philip Danforth Armour jointly founded. Held this position until his death in 1921. Lectured regularly at the University of Chicago, and conducted several other lectureships. Author of *Metamorphoses of a Creed, Transfiguration of Christ, The Man of Galilee, Paths to the City of God, Paths to Power, Life of William Ewart Gladstone, The Minister and the Spiritual Life,* and *Songs of Night and Day.* A civic leader and reformer as well as a preacher.

GUSTAVUS (gŭs tā'vus) **ADOLPHUS** (1594-1632), Gustavus II of Sweden (1611-1632), "Lion of the North," born in Stockholm, grandson of Gustavus Vasa. Trained in military skill from childhood, and highly educated. Ascended the throne in 1611. Inherited from father, Charles IX, three wars with Russia, Denmark, and Poland. When German emperor in the Thirty Years' War was aiming to root Protestantism out of Europe, Gustavus Adolphus in 1630 led well-trained army into Germany as the champion of northern Protestantism. Won victory over the Catholic League commanded by the great imperial general, Tilly, in 1631 at the Battle of Breitenfeld. The next year defeated the famous Wallenstein in the Battle of Lützen, near Leipzig. Gustavus was mortally wounded, but the victory of his army saved Protestantism in Germany, and also saved the Baltic for Sweden. Due to the efforts of Gustavus Sweden gained a supreme position in commerce and industry among the nations of the North. Gustavus Adolphus ranks among the great soldiers of the world. Taught Europe that a small well-disciplined army is superior to an armed mob. A great warrior, also a man of deep-seated piety and high moral character. Raised Sweden to a commanding position as the great power of the North. Succeeded on the throne by his daughter Christina.

GUSTAVUS VASA (1496-1560), King Gustavus I of Sweden (1523-1560), born at Lindholmen, the son of a Swedish nobleman, studied at Upsala. Sweden had been united with Denmark for a century and a quarter. Gustavus Vasa (real name Gustavus Ericksson), then a young man in late teens, had been treacherously imprisoned by the Danish king, but had escaped after a year. Having lost his father and brother-in-law in the shocking and shameful "Stockholm blood bath" under Christian II of Denmark in 1520, the next year he raised a peasant army and drove the Danes out of Sweden. Elected king in 1523. Following the practice of other monarchs, sought to bring the church in his realm under the control of the crown. At the time he came to the throne, the Reformation was entering Denmark through the preaching of Olaus Petri. In 1527 made the Swedish bishops subject to the royal crown, in the following year crowned by the Protestant archbishop of Upsala. In 1529 Lutheranism was proclaimed the state religion. During long reign of thirty-seven years, the Lutheran Reformation was thoroughly established in Sweden. Venerated as the founder of Swedish independence.

GUTENBERG (gootĕn bĕrk), **JOHANN** (c. 1398-1468), German inventor of printing with movable type, born in Mainz, Germany. Father's name was Gensfleisch. Johann took the name of Gutenberg. Family later settled at Strassburg, where about 1438 he seems to have become a printer. About 1448 returned to Mainz, about 1450 formed a partnership with Johann Fust, a wealthy, shrewd goldsmith. Peter Schöffer later joined the partnership. They set up a printing press and started printing a Latin Bible. This Bible, known as the "Gutenberg Bible" or the "Mazarin Bible" was completed about 1456, the earliest book printed on the new movable type press. Business and legal complications developed between Gutenberg and Fust. The latter having the money, gained possession of the type and the press. Gutenberg died poor, childless, friendless, and practically unknown. Most of the books which Gutenberg is believed to have printed were religious.

GUTHRIE, THOMAS (1803-1873), Free Church of Scotland clergyman and philanthropist, born at Brechin, Forfarshire, Scotland, educated in Edinburgh and Paris. Became parish minister of Arbirlot, Forfarshire in 1830. Strong evangelical preaching and pastoral zeal led to call in 1837 to the Collegiate Church of Old Greyfriars, Edinburgh. In 1840 became pastor of St. John's Church in Edinburgh. When the "Disruption" took place in 1843, Thomas Chalmers, Robert Smith Candlish, and Thomas Guthrie organized the Free church, and Guthrie became minister of the Free St. John's Church, which was erected fifty yards from former church. For about twenty years he ministered to a large and influential congregation, and attracted crowds of strangers from all over the world. In 1862 elected moderator of the Free church Assembly. Ill health due to overwork led to retirement in 1864, after which, until his death in 1873, his was a prolific ministry of writing especially as editor of the *Sunday Magazine*. Wrote books of devotion and studies of the Scripture. Zealous advocate of union with the United Presbyterian Church. Most signal philanthropic service was the institution of the "Ragged Schools" for the reclamation of juvenile delinquents. Ardent advocate of total abstinence, warm friend of foreign missions, and defender of the Waldensians and their mission.

GUSTZLAFF (güts'läf), **KARL FRIEDRICH AUGUST** (1803-1851), German Lutheran missionary to China, born at Pyritz, near Stettin, Pomerania. Died at Hong Kong. Through meeting Robert Morrison in England his attention was directed toward China. In 1823 went to Singapore in the service of the Netherlands Missionary Society, then to Batavia, 1826, where he learned several of the more common dialects of the Chinese language. In 1828 severed connection with the Netherlands Missionary Society, and went to Bangkok, Siam as an independent missionary. Helped translate the Bible into the Siamese, and also practiced his profession as a physician. In 1831 he went to China, residing first at Macao, afterward at Hong Kong. Made numerous journeys to various parts of the Chinese empire, published accounts of his observations. Assosiated W. H. Medhurst and Robert Morrison in translating the Bible into the Chinese, wrote in Chinese several tracts of useful information, edited a monthly magazine in Chinese. In 1844 founded at Hong Kong an association for the training of Chinese converts to become missionaries to their own people. Except for the first few years in China, not connected with any missionary society. In 1834, upon the death of Robert Morrison, appointed interpreter and secretary of the East India Company at Canton, rendering valuable help to the British during the Opium War. With all his literary and political activities, was first of all a missionary, and greatly beloved by the Chinese people. Among writings: *Sketch of Chinese History* (two volumes), *China Opened* (two volumes), and *Journal of Three Voyages along the Coast of China.*

GUYON (güē yôɴ'), **JEANNE MARIE BOUVIER** (bo͞o vyā'), **DE LA MOTTE** (1648-1717), French quietist writer, born at Montargis near Orleans, earliest education received in convents. Early showed strong tendencies toward asceticism and mysticism. Marked by a fervent devotion to the name of Jesus. Her mother married her in 1644 to a rich invalid, twenty-two years her senior. She was loyal to her husband, but was most unhappy, finding her only consolation in close communion with God dwelling within her heart. After twelve years her husband died, leaving her in 1676 with three young children. She vowed never to marry again, but to devote herself to spiritual service. Her life began to be a continuous series of visions, revelations, and spiritual experiences, and she turned to writing. Her commentary of the Scriptures made her an object of wide attention. She was soon denounced as a dangerous person and charged with being a follower of Molinos and his mystic quietism. She was arrested and held in prison for months. From 1688 to 1694 she lived with her married daughter. At this time she began a close fellowship with Archbishop Fenelon. Propositions from her writings were examined by Bossuet, archbishop of Meaux, and were condemned. The same fate befell the writings of Fenelon. She too revoked the condemned propositions. However, she continued her spiritual teachings and was again arrested and imprisoned from 1694 to 1702 in the Bastile, until she again signed a recantation of her theories, promising to refrain from spreading them. For the last fifteen years of her life she was permitted to live in Blois in silence and isolation with her son, spending time in charitable and pious excercises, in the composition of religious verse, and maintaining a voluminous correspondence with her admirers, both Catholic and Protestant, in France, Germany, Holland, and England.

H

HAAKON (hô'kǒn), the Good (c. 914-961), King of Norway (935-961). Educated and converted to Christianity in England. Led expedition against half-brother Erik, who had been proclaimed King, and won the crown. Upon return to Norway attempted to introduce the Christian faith into Norway. Acted prudently in quietly winning those next to him, and in calling Christian priests from England. Built church at Drontheim. In time felt safe to make public appeal for subjects to accept Christian religion. They suspected his motives and turned against him, forcing him to sacrifice to heathen gods. Was successful in series of battles with sons of Erik and their Danish allies, but died of wounds received in battle.

HADRIAN (hā'drĭ an), **(PUBLIUS AELIUS HADRIANUS)** (76-138), Emperor of Rome (117-138), born in Spain, accompanied Trajan in his wars. Though a trained soldier, loved peace and spent much time touring provinces and consolidating empire. Prudently abandoned territory Trajan had acquired beyond Euphrates; made that river empire's eastern boundary. One chief accomplishment was wall constructed across Scotland as rampart of protection against barbarian marauders of Caledonia. About 132-135 suppressed revolt of Jews which broke out in Palestine following planting of Roman colony in Jerusalem and prohibition of circumcision. Protected Christians against popular outbursts of fury but continued Trajan's policy of punishing all who were convicted by ordinary legal procedures.

HAECKEL (hĕk'l), **ERNST HEINRICH** (1834-1919), German biologist and natural philosopher, born at Potsdam, Germany, studied medicine and natural sciences at universities of Berlin, Würzburg, Vienna. After practicing medicine for about a year, turned wholly to natural science; in 1862 became professor of zoology at University of Jena, teaching there until 1909. Was first German biologist to give wholehearted adherence to Darwinian theory of evolution; proceeded to apply findings to religion and philosophy, and thus brought upon himself anathemas of the church. Views set forth in *The Riddle of the Universe*, where he epitomizes speculative views as to man's position in universe; gives final exposition of theories relative to evolution of organic life. In his uncompromising monistic philosophy asserted essential unity of all organic and inorganic nature; held to materialistic determinism. Consequently denied immortality of soul, freedom of will, and existence of a personal God.

HAGENBACH, KARL RUDOLPH (1801-1874), German-Swiss church historian. Born at Basel, Switzerland, where father was physician. Attended Pestalozzian school, and gymnasium of Basel. Studied theology at Basel, Bonn, and Berlin, at the latter under teaching of Neander and Schleiermacher. Special interest was church history; in 1823 accepted position in University of Basel, where he remained till death, lecturing on and teaching church history and history of dogma. Increasingly laid stress upon independent objective reality of Christian revelation, and emphasized confessions of the church. Was a powerful preacher; nine volumes of sermons appeared between 1858 and 1875. Also wrote and published two volumes of poems and a helpful multi-volume biblical theology. Was president of Protestant Relief Society for Switzerland.

HALDANE, JAMES ALEXANDER (1768-1851). Born in Dundee, educated in Dundee and Edinburgh University. From 1785 to 1794 in the navy where he became commander of a ship. Settled in Scotland, was converted and became an evangelist. Founded the Society for the Propagation of the Gospel at Home in 1797. Became a Congregational minister in 1799 and in 1804 pastor of a tabernacle seating 3,000 built for him by his older brother Robert. Ideas were similar to those of the Plymouth Brethren.

HALDANE (hôl'dān), **ROBERT** (1764-1842), Scottish philanthropist and evangelist, born in London, educated at Dundee and Edinburgh, distinguished himself in the British navy from 1770 to 1783. He and brother, James Alexander Haldane (1768-1851), were converted about 1795, and became interested in lay evangelical preaching. James left his business and Robert sold his estate in 1789 to preach the gospel. James became a Congregational preacher, and served for fifty years in a Tabernacle in Edinburgh which his brother Robert had built for him. After a few years the brothers became Baptists. Robert purposed to go to India as a missionary at own expense, but was hindered by the East India Company. Then, in conjunction with Rowland Hill and other eminent evangelicals, he carried on extensive revival work throughout Scotland. When established church forbade their field preaching and revivals, Robert Haldane left the established church, and at a cost to him of $350,000 built chapels known as "tabernacles" in the large cities. In 1816 went to Geneva, spent three years teaching the Bible at his famous Home Bible College. Also taught and preached at Montauban, France. Among converts and pupils were such men as Jean Henri, Merle d'Aubigné, S. R. L. Gaussen, Cesar Malan, and Adolphe Monod. They helped to introduce evangelical thought in rationalistic circles in Europe. Haldane conceived the idea of procuring native children from Sierra Leone to educate for missionary work in their homeland. Prominent in the management of the Bible Society of Edinburgh. Helped form the Society for the Propagation of the Gospel at Home. It was Robert Haldane's privilege to educate three hundred young men for the ministry. Wrote *Exposition of the Epistle to the Romans* frequently reprinted.

HALE, EDWARD EVERETT (1822-1909), American author and philanthropist, born in Boston. Educated at the Boston Latin School and Harvard College. Was class valedictorian at Harvard in 1839. Taught at the Boston Latin School while studying theology and doing some journalistic writing. Became pastor of the Unitarian church in Worcester, Massachusetts about 1846. In 1856 called to the South Congregational (Unitarian) Church, Boston, where he was pastor until 1901. From 1903 to 1909 served as chaplain of the United States Senate. He was a prolific writer of poetry, short stories, essays, and magazine articles. Devoted much of his energy to helping people individually, whether in social, economic, or spiritual realm. An aggressive abolitionist, out of which concern he wrote stirring story, *The Man Without a Country*. Out of his great purpose to help others organized the "Lend a Hand" clubs, and edited the magazine *Lend a Hand*. Edited several other papers. Was a prolific writer, the author of more than sixty books.

HALLESBY, OLE KRISTIAN (1879-1961), Norwegian theologian. Became a Liberal in school but converted in 1902. Served as an itinerant lay preacher. After obtaining his doctorate in Berlin, professor of theology at the Free Faculty of Theology from 1909 to 1952. Chairman of Norwegian Lutheran Home Mission. A leader in the resistance during the Nazi occupation in World War II and in concentration camp from 1943 to 1945. First president of International Fellowship of Evangelical Students in 1947. Wrote devotional *Prayer, Why I Am a Christian,* and texts on theology and ethics.

HALL, GORDON (1784-1826), American Congregational missionary to India, born near Tolland, Massachusetts. While in Williams College he was directly influenced by the famous haystack prayer meeting, himself a leader of the haystack band. After graduation from Williams College in 1808 studied theology at Andover. Later pursued a short course in medicine in Philadelphia. In 1809 licensed to preach; and for a few months ministered to the Congregational church at Woodbury, Connecticut. When asked to become its permanent pastor, refused, having already decided for the foreign mission field. Ordained at Salem early in 1812, and was sent out by the newly organized American Board of Commissioners for Foreign Missions to Calcutta, India. Refused permanent residence in Calcutta by the British East India Company, he went to western India, the first American missionary to Bombay. He and Samuel Newell established schools and churches and published gospel tracts and other works. An eloquent preacher in the Marathi language. Best achievement was the Marathi translation of the New Testament.

HALL, JOSEPH (1574-1656), Church of England prelate, born at Bristow Park in Leicestershire, England, educated at Emmanuel College, Cambridge. Took orders about 1600, and for a time held a living at Halsted, and a canonry at Wolverhampton. Won favor with James I, who in 1616 made him dean of Worcester. In 1618 sent him as his representative to the Synod of Dort to assist in moderating the bitterness in the Arminian-Calvinistic controversy. Wrote *Via Media, The Way of Peace*. In 1627 promoted to the see of Exeter, and in 1641 transferred to Norwich. Having incurred the displeasure of Archbishop Laud for leanings toward Puritanism and Calvinism, and having joined the bishops who protested against their expulsion from the House of Peers, with ten other bishops in 1642 he was sent to the Tower for high treason. In his *Episcopacy by Divine Right Asserted,* defended loyalty to the Church of England. Upon release six or seven months later he returned to Norwich to find revenue impounded and property pillaged. In 1647 moved to a small farm at Higham near Norwich, where he spent his last ten years in retirement and poverty. Wrote *A Century of Meditations,* his best work, and *Paraphrase of Hard Times,* an autobiographic account of experience of persecution under Parliament; and several satirical works.

HALL, ROBERT (1764-1831), Baptist preacher, born at Arnesby, Leicestershire, England. Before nine years read Jonathan Edwards' *On the Will,* and Joseph Butler's

Analogy with understanding and appreciation. At age fourteen baptized in the Baptist church, and entered Bristol College. Received M.A. degree from King's College, Aberdeen University. Began preaching in 1779. Assumed first pastorate in 1785 at Broadmead Church, Bristol, where he attracted great audiences. Liberal tone of teaching and preaching alarmed the more conservative brethren, and in 1790 withdrew from Broadmead. Spent fifteen years of brilliant, liberal preaching at the Baptist church at Cambridge during which time he became very popular. During his latter years at Cambridge he suffered severely from physical and mental ill-health. Following resignation from Cambridge, in 1807 became minister at Harvey Lane, Leicester. Coincident with these physical changes he experienced a change of religious views, which he called his "conversion," became much more conservative in theology. After twenty years at Leicester, where he preached with remarkable power, in 1826 returned to Broadmead and spent the last five years of his life amid the scenes of earliest ministry. Writings including his *Apology for the Freedom of the Press; Reflections on War;* and noted sermon on *Modern Infidelity* were collected in six volumes in 1800.

HALLOCK, GERHARD BENJAMIN FLEET (1856-1953), Presbyterian clergyman and author, born at Holiday's Cove, West Virginia, graduated from Princeton College and Princeton Theological Seminary. Ordained to Presbyterian ministry in 1885. Until 1890 pastor of the Wheatland Presbyterian Church, Scottsville, New York, after which time he was co-pastor of the Brick Presbyterian, Rochester, New York. Served at one time as moderator of the New York Synod of the Presbyterian church of the United States of America. Stated clerk for forty-two years. Editor of *The Expositor* for three years. Compiler of Doran's *Ministers' Manual;* the compiler and editor of a number of cyclopedias of illustrations and sermons for special occasions; author of a dozen religious books, among them: *The Model Prayer, The Homiletic Year, Growing Toward God,* and *Journeyings in the Land Where Jesus Lived.*

HAMILTON, PATRICK (c. 1504-1528), proto-martyr of the Scottish Reformation, born of nobility and royalty at or near Glasgow, Scotland. While still a boy, in 1517 appointed abbot of Fern; in 1520 graduated in Paris; then to Louvain where he came under the spell of Erasmus and humanism. Upon return to Scotland in 1523 matriculated at the University of St. Andrews, in 1524 received as a member of the Faculty of Arts. By 1527 charges of promoting heretical views were brought against him. Fled in 1527 to Germany where he spent some time with Luther and Melanchthon at Wittenberg, and studied at Marburg where he met William Tyndale. Returned to Scotland and to St. Andrews, proclaiming vigorously the doctrines of the Reformation. Cardinal Beaton, archbishop of St. Andrews, brought him to trial, and he was burned at the stake.

HAMLIN, CYRUS (1811-1900), American Congregational missionary educator, born near Waterford, Maine, educated at Bowdoin College, and Bangor Theological Seminary. In 1838, married, ordained, and went to Turkey under the auspices of the American Board of Commissioners for Foreign Missions. In 1840, Hamlin opened Bebek Seminary on the shores of the Bosporus, which he successfully operated until 1860. During the Crimean War in 1853 gave the English valuable help in the hospital established at Scutari. In 1860 resigned from the service of the American Board; and along with Mr. Christopher R. Robert, a merchant from New York, founded Robert College, first in Bebek, the doors of which were first opened in 1863. After using the old seminary buildings at Bebek for eight years, was granted permission by the Turkish government to move the location of the college and to build it in Constantinople. Served as president of the college from 1860 to 1877. In 1877 returned to the United States. Became professor of dogmatic theology in Bangor Theological Seminary, which position he held from 1877 to 1880. From 1881 to 1885, president of Middlebury College, Middlebury, Vermont. In 1885 resigned to retire to private life. Spent the last fifteen years of his life preaching, lecturing, and writing in behalf of missions. Work included *Among the Turks,* written after his return to America in 1878, and *My Life and Times,* published in 1893.

HANDEL (hăn'dl), **GEORGE FREDERICK** (1685-1759), German musical composer, born at Halle, Germany, early showed a love of music but his father had set his mind on the son becoming a lawyer. When nine he was writing spiritual cantatas; the next year composed a set of sonatas. At twelve went to Berlin to continue musical education. Played before Elector Frederick of Brandenburg, later king of Prussia, to the elector's great satisfaction. Went to Hamburg where he continued studies and became second violinist in an orchestra, and also demonstrated high accomplishment in the harpsichord. Spent three years in Italy writing operas. In 1710 went to England where he received fame presenting operas. In 1712 made London his permanent home, becoming a British subject. The people tired of Italian operas and he became bankrupt. Partially retrieved fortune by writing oratorios, three of the greatest of which were *Israel in Egypt, Judas Maccabaeus,* and *Messiah*. The *Messiah,* his masterpiece, was composed in 1741, first publicly performed in 1742. People were so charmed and moved by its presentation that when the Hallelujah Chorus was sung, the king and the entire audience arose and stood for the remainder of the performance. Last six years of Handel's life were spent in blindness. He continued to write, and to play the piano. Died in 1759. Buried in Westminster Abbey. A man of high character, intelligence and broad interest. Compositions included about two dozen oratorios, more than forty operas, about forty concertos, and many sonatas, cantatas, chamber duets, and other pieces of church music.

HANNINGTON, JAMES (1847-1885), Anglican missionary bishop to Eastern Equatorial Africa, born at St. George, Hurstpierpoint, near Brighton, England. Died in Uganda, Africa. After two years in Temple School at Brighton worked for six years in father's countinghouse. In 1868, when twenty years of age, entered St. Mary's Hall, Oxford, and received his B.A. degree in 1873 and M.A. in 1875. Became curate at Martinhoe in 1874; of St. George, Hurstpierpoint, 1875. Ordained priest in 1876. Offered himself to the Church Missionary Society for the Central African Mission in Uganda. Accepted, and after a most difficult journey, more than once being near death from fever and dysentery, reached Lake Nyanza in 1882. He was so exhausted that almost immediately he was forced to return to England. He reached England, rapidly recovered and soon resumed his duties at Hurst. The ensuing year made such marvelous recovery that he was consecrated bishop of Eastern Equatorial Africa and started back to mission field in 1884. After a few months' stay at the coast, on July 23, Bishop Hannington started for Uganda, determined to open up a new and more healthful route to Lake Nyanza and Uganda. The route lay through the land of the Masai, a lawless and dangerous tribe. He and fifty porters who accompanied him on the last lap of the journey were murdered on October 29. The bishop died a martyr at the hands of the people whom he loved and longed to save.

HARMS, CLAUS (1778-1855), German Lutheran evangelical theologian, born at Fahrstedt, Schleswig-Holstein, Germany. In 1799 went to the University of Kiel to study theology. Began preaching while still a student at Kiel. In 1806 made a deacon, and called as pastor to the church in Lunden in Ditmarsch. In 1816 appointed archdeacon in St. Nicolai Church in Kiel. Held this position until 1835 when made chief pastor and provost in the church. In 1817 on the three-hundredth anniversary of the beginning of the German Reformation, he called special attention to Luther's Ninety-five Theses and added his own Ninety-five Theses in an endeavor to counteract prevailing religious indifferentism and rationalism, to defend and promote the evangelical faith, also to oppose the growing effort to unite the Reformed and the Lutheran churches. In 1849 partial blindness and advancing age made it necessary for him to resign at Kiel. Wrote sermons, hymns, catechisms, and other books for religious instruction, among them the *Pastoraltheologie*.

HARNACK (här'nŏk), **KARL GUSTAV ADOLPH VON** (1851-1930), German Lutheran theologian and Church historian, born at Dorpat, Livonia (now Estonia), received education at the universities of Dorpat and Leipzig. In 1874 became privatdocent at Leipzig and professor in 1876. From 1879 to 1886, professor of Church history at the University of Giessen, from 1886 to 1889 at Marburg. In 1890 he was called to serve on the faculty of the University of Berlin, a position he held for thirty-eight years. From 1905 to 1921, director of the Prussian Royal Library, later called the Prussian State Library, and from 1902 to 1912, president of the Evangelical Congress. At Leipzig Harnack became an ardent follower of Albrecht Ritschl. Recognized as one of the leaders of the critical school of theology, applying the critical method to both church history and theological dogma, and also became an authority on Ante-Nicene church history. Wrote multi-volume works, *History of Dogma* and *Luther's Theology.* Able scholar of patristics.

HARPER, WILLIAM RAINEY (1856-1906), Hebrew scholar and educator, born at New Concord, Ohio. Educated at Muskingum College, Ohio, and Yale University. After teaching five years in preparatory schools, became professor of Hebrew and Old Testament exegesis in the Baptist Union Theological Seminary in Chicago (1879) then professor of Semitic languages in Yale (1886-1891). He was also principal of the Chautauqua College of Liberal Arts (1885-1891). From 1891 to the time of his death he was professor of Semitic languages and literature, and also president of the newly established University of Chicago. He developed the University of Chicago into one of the leading universities of America. A member of the Chicago Board of Education (1896-1898). In 1881 commenced to teach Hebrew by correspondence, thus inaugurating a movement which culminated in the organization of the American Institute of Sacred Literature. In 1884 founded the American Institute of Hebrew. Author of several Hebrew textbooks emphasizing the inductive method of study. Wrote *The Trend in Higher Education, Religion and the Higher Life, Elements of Hebrew, Elements of Hebrew Syntax, Hebrew Vocabularies, Hebrew Method and Manual,* and *Amos and Hosea* (in the International Critical Commentary). Was one of the editors of the *Biblical World, The American Journal of Theology,* and *American Journal of Semitic Language and Literature*.

HARRIS, HOWELL (1714-1773), Welsh lay evangelist. Born at Talgarth, Breconshire. School teacher from 1730 to 1735 when he was converted. From 1736 to 1752 was a powerful impassioned evangelist. Main founder of Welsh Calvinistic Methodism. In 1752 at Trevecca, a school for evangelists where the Countess of Huntington sent many students. Wrote many popular Welsh hymns. Aided for some years by Daniel Rowlands.

HARVARD, JOHN (1607-1638), Congregationalist minister, born in Southwark, London, England, received education at Emmanuel College, Cambridge. In 1637 came to Charlestown on the Massachusetts Bay as minister for that settlement. Died, leaving his library of about three hundred volumes, and half of his estate, nearly eight hundred pounds, to the newly organized college at New Towne. In 1639 the name of the town was changed to Cambridge and the Court of Massachusetts Colony named the college Harvard in his honor.

HASE (hä'zĕ), **KARL AUGUST VON** (1800-1890), German church historian, born at Steinbech, Saxony, studied theology at Leipzig and Erlangen. In 1823 began lecturing on theology and philosophy at Tübingen. In 1826 began lecturing and teaching on the philosophical faculty at Leipzig, and in 1829 became professor extraordinary at Jena. Attempted to bring historical theology into harmony with modern thought and at the same time keep the warmth of religious life. Wrote his *Leben Jesu* six years before Strauss wrote his book of the same title. Opposed supernaturalism in his *Leipzig Disputation,* and extreme rationalism in *Theologische Streitschriften,* and in *Tübingen School*. Besides his *History of the Christian Church,* written in a moderately rationalistic spirit, also wrote special church history treatises on *New Prophets, Life of Francis Assisi, A Handbook of Protestant Polemical Theology,* and *A Life of Saint Catherine of Siena*.

HASTINGS, HORACE LORENZO (1831-1899), American minister and writer, born at Blandford, Massachusetts. Began writing hymns and preaching in seventeenth year, labored as an evangelist in various parts of the United States. In 1866 established and published *The Christian,* a monthly paper in which appeared many of his hymns. Published *Social Hymns, Original and Selected* and *Songs of Pilgrimage, a Hymnal for the Churches of Christ*. Wrote and published many anti-infidel booklets, tracts and about four hundred fifty hymns, best known hymn being, "Shall We Meet Beyond the River?"

HASTINGS, JAMES (1852-1922), Scottish clergyman and biblical scholar, born at Huntley, Scotland, educated at Aberdeen University and the Free Church Divinity College in Aberdeen. Ordained in 1884 and held pastorates in three different churches between 1884 and 1911. In 1911 retired from pastoral work to devote himself to literary activities. Founder in 1889 and editor of *The Expository Times.* Hastings is best known for the religious dictionaries and encyclopedias that he edited, including *Encyclopaedia of Religion and Ethics* (twelve volumes), *Dictionary of the Bible* (five volumes), *The Dictionary of the Apostolic Church* (two volumes), *Dictionary of Christ and the Gospels* (two volumes), *Dictionary of the Bible* (one volume), and *Great Texts of the Bible*.

HASTINGS, THOMAS (1784-1872), American hymn writer and composer, Presbyterian layman, born at Washington, Litchfield County, Connecticut. When twelve years his family moved to Clinton, New York. As a boy showed musical taste and took every opportunity to secure a musical education. At eighteen led the village choir and at twenty-two began to teach music. From 1823 to 1832 edited the *Western Recorder,* a religious paper published at Utica, through the columns of which he brought to the public his views on music. From 1835 to 1837 edited the *Musical Magazine*. In 1832 moved to New York. There until his death as musical leader. In 1858 University of the City of New York conferred on him the degree, Doctor of Music. He, Lowell Mason, and William B. Bradbury did much to give church music a dignified, artistic character. In all, Hastings is said to have written six hundred hymns, composed about one thousand hymn tunes, and issued fifty volumes of music. Nearly all recent hymnbooks contain both hymns and music of his composition. In his *Church Melodies,* published in 1858, he adopted the plan of having words and music printed on the same page, a plan that soon became well-nigh universal.

HAUGE (hou'gĕ), **HANS NIELSEN** (1771-1824), Norwegian Pietist lay evangelist, born in the parish of Thunö in Norway. From early youth a zealous student of the Bible and of such religious books as his parents could provide. Converted in 1796 through reading Luther's works began to preach, first in home community, then from 1798 to 1804 through Norway, forming little religious brotherhoods for prayer, conversations, and exhortation, somewhat like the "collegia pietatis" of Germany. He was not a separatist and sought to keep his brotherhoods closely linked with the state church. Yet pietistic lay preaching and religious zeal brought strong opposition from the clergy and the state officials. Imprisoned from 1804 to 1811 on the charge of violating the conventicle acts which forbade lay preaching. In 1814 again seized, and sentenced to two years of hard labor. Initiated a voluntary lay activity which has ever since characterized religious life of Norway.

HAVERGAL, FRANCES RIDLEY (1836-1879), English hymn and devotional writer, born in the rectory at Astley, Worcestershire, England. Receiving education at home, in private schools at Worcester, and in Düsseldorf, Germany. Attained proficiency in several modern languages, also in Latin, Greek, and Hebrew. Conversion took place when she was about fifteen. Began writing verse at the age of seven. Quite early her poems were being published in *Good Words* and other religious periodicals. For her hymns she furnished some of her own tunes, her father wrote the music for others. Her first accepted poem was the well-known, and much loved hymn, "I Gave My Life for Thee" but her best and perhaps most widely used hymn is "Take My Life and Let it Be." Her relatively short life was spent in doing aggressive religious and philanthropic work, in singing the love of God and the way of salvation. Prose writings include *My King, Kept for the Master's Use, Royal Commandments and Royal Bounty*. Wrote hymns "Lord Speak To Me," "Who is on the Lord's Side," and "I Am Trusting Thee, Lord Jesus."

HAWEIS, THOMAS (1734-1820). Born Redwith, Cornwall. Educated at Christ Church, Oxford where he helped set up a second "Holy Club." Ordained in 1757. Served at St. Mary Magdalene (1757-1762), chaplain at Loch Hospital, London (1762-1764), pastor at All Saints, Aldwinkle, Northhamptonshire (1764-1768), then chaplain to Lady Huntington from 1768. Helped manage Trevecca Hall. Helped found the London Missionary Society in 1795.

HAYDN (hī'dn), **FRANZ JOSEF** (1732-1809), Austrian composer, and great master of the symphony, born at Rohrau, Austria, near the border of Austria and Hungary. As a small boy he learned to play the violin and the harpsichord. At eight received into the boys' choir of St. Stephen's Cathedral, Vienna, which helped to earn his education. When his voice changed dismissed. It was through much hardship and poverty that he secured musical education. In 1758 appointed master of the chapel of Count de Mortzin, where in 1759 he wrote his first symphony. In 1760 appointed chapel master to Prince Estenhazy of Hungary, a position held for thirty years. For this chapel he wrote some wonderful symphonies and some of his masterly quartets and many instrumental pieces. In 1791 met Beethoven, who later became his pupil. Mozart also was a pupil of Haydn. Haydn's great master work was his oratorio, *The Creation*. Other great work the cantata, *The Seasons* and *Seven Last Words.* Wrote the *Austrian Hymn,* a national anthem, and perhaps seven hundred instrumental works, among them about one hundred twenty-five symphonies upon which his fame chiefly rests.

HEBER, REGINALD (1783-1826), Anglican Bishop of Calcutta, born at Malpas, Cheshire, England. Educated at Brasenose College, Oxford. In 1805 elected fellow of All Souls. After a year or two of traveling on the Continent, ordained priest in 1807, succeeded his father as rector of Hodnet, Shropshire. In 1812 made prebendary of St. Asaph; three years later appointed Bampton lecturer at Oxford; in 1822 became preacher at Lincoln's Inn. In 1822, following the death of Bishop Middleton, consecrated by the archbishop of Canterbury to succeed as second bishop of Calcutta, which then comprised the whole of India, Ceylon, Mauritius, and Australasia. In 1824 started on a sixteen-month tour of diocese, visiting the mission stations of Northern Bengal, Bombay, and Ceylon. Then in February, 1826 left Calcutta for a second tour, this time in South India. He died at Trichinopoly. A liberal high-churchman and a Tory, an Arminian in theology, and a man of profound faith in the fundamental doctrines of the gospels and of their adaptation to the heathen. Wrote many poems and about sixty hymns, some of which are conspicuous for their beauty and devotional quality. They have attained high popularity. Some of these are: "From Greenland's Icy Mountains," "Holy, Holy, Holy," and "The Son of God Goes Forth to War."

HECK, BARBARA RUCKLE (1734-1804). Born in Limerick County, Ireland in a family of German refugee stock. Converted to Methodism by Wesley's preaching. Migrated to the Thirteen Colonies in 1760. Encouraged her cousin Philip Embury in 1766 to hold the first Methodist meeting in his home. Later he built the John Street Chapel in New York in 1768. Tory sympathies forced her to migrate to Canada during the American Revolution. There she also sponsored Methodist societies.

HECKER, ISAAC THOMAS (1819-1888), founder of the Paulists, born in New York City of German parentage, reared a Protestant. Early became an advocate of the Workingmen's party, later led into sympathy with the Transcendentalist movement; for awhile was a Brook Farm socialist. In 1844 became a convert to the Roman church, and was baptized by Bishop McCloskey. Went to Europe for study and mission work for several years. In 1846 joined the Redemptorist Fathers in Belgium; studied for two years at Wittem, Holland, and a year at Clapham, England. In 1849 was ordained to the priesthood in London by Cardinal Wiseman. Returning to the United States in 1851, devoted himself wholeheartedly to the many German Roman Catholic immigrants then entering the United States of America. A misunderstanding developed with his Redemptorist superiors, and he was excluded from the order. Went to Rome about the matter and was released by Pope Pius IX from his vows, and was encouraged by the pope to form a new congregation. In 1858 formed the Missionary Society of St. Paul the Apostle, known as Paulists or Paulist Fathers. He was the society's superior for thirty years (1858-1888). The object of the order was the conversion of Protestants. In 1865 Hecker founded *The Catholic World,* the chief Roman Catholic organ in the United States, and edited it until his death. Also founded and directed a paper for children. In 1866 organized the Catholic Publication Society. Wrote *Catholicity in the United States;* and *The Church of the Age: Exposition of the Catholic Church.*

HEFELE (hā'fĕ lĕ), **KARL JOSEPH VON** (1809-1893), ecclesiastical historian, born at Unterkochen, Württemberg, Germany, studied at the University of Tübingen and the clerical seminary of Rottenburg. At the university, a pupil of Johann Adam Möhler, greatly influenced by him. Ordained to the priesthood in 1833. Succeeded Möhler at Tübingen as church history lecturer in 1836. Became full professor in 1840. From 1839 editor of *Theological Quarterly.* In 1869 elected Bishop of Rottenburg. Spent the winter of 1868-1869 at Rome. Took a prominent part as consultor in preparation for the Vatican Council of 1870. At the council he was a strenuous opponent of the Vatican decree concerning papal infallibility. Most important work, *History of the Councils,* nine volumes. Wrote also a monograph on *Cardinal Ximines, Works of the Apostolic Fathers,* and *History of the Introduction of Christianity in Southwest Germany.*

HEGEL (hā'gĕl), **GEORG WILHELM FRIEDRICH** (1770-1831), German philosopher, born at Stuttgart. Educated at Tübingen, studied theology, philosophy, and natural science. In university years showed little aptitude for philosophy, but did seek to fathom the true meaning of Christianity. Wrote a life of Jesus in which he portrayed Jesus as the son of Mary and Joseph. Private tutor, first at Bern, then at Frankfurt, from 1793 to 1801. Taught at Jena (1801-1807), where for a short time was a close friend of Schelling. In 1808 became director of the gymnasium of Nürnberg, a post held for eight years. In 1816-1817 professor of philosophy at Heidelberg. In 1818 succeeded Fichte at Berlin, where his fame rapidly rose to that of the first philosopher of his day in Germany. Hegel identified being with thought. To him God was the Absolute seeking to manifest himself in history by a logical process of reconciliation of contradictions which Hegel called thesis and antithesis resulting in synthesis. Thus, the world was created by a philosophical evolution, with God involved in history rather than being Lord over history. Hegel thus conceived religion as arising out of tension between the individual and the world, with Christianity being the highest development of religion. These ideas in his *Philosophy of History,* which verged on pantheism. Hegel's influence grew strong in England and America, and gave background for the philosophy of Karl Marx and Hitler's Germany. Hegel's works were all philosophical writings.

HEGESIPPUS (Hĕj-ē-sĭp'-pŭs) (second century), Church historian. Likely of orthodox Jewish origin. In extensive travels through Syria, Greece, and Italy, collected "memorials" of the apostolic and post-apostolic churches written to prove the purity of the faith and doctrine of orthodox Christianity, and the apostolic succession and catholicity of the Church. Appropriated both available written sources and oral traditions to compile work. It is the first known historical attempt after the writing of Acts by Luke, and was extensively used by Eusebius in his history.

HELENA (hĕl'ē nȧ), (c. 250-c. 330), mother of Constantine the Great, born at Drepanum in Bithynia, Asia Minor. Wife of Constantius Chlorus. Constantius divorced her for political reasons in order to marry Theodora, the stepdaughter of Emperor Maximian; Helena retired to obscurity. Constantine, however, recalled her to court after his accession in

306, heaped honors upon her, among them the title of Augusta. About 325, when well advanced in years, she visited Palestine, and is said to have discovered the sepulcher and the cross of Christ, and built there the Church of the Holy Sepulcher and the Church of the Nativity.

HÉLÖISE (c. 1098-1164), learned and beautiful niece of Fulbert, a canon of Notre Dame. Secretly married her tutor Abelard and fled. Fulbert had ruffians emasculate Abelard. After their son was born, she retired to a convent in order not to hinder his career. Became Superior of the Convent of the Paraclete about 1129. Wrote moving love letters to Abelard.

HELWYS (hĕl'wĭs), **THOMAS** (c. 1550-c. 1616), founder of the first English Baptist church, a country gentleman of England who had been educated in law at Gray's Inn, London. Under leadership and influence of John Smyth he became a Separatist and about 1607, with Smyth, seeking relief from persecution, migrated to Amsterdam. In 1608 or 1609 he and others, having rejected infant baptism, joined the Anabaptists and were baptized by Smyth by pouring. When differences developed between Helwys and Smyth, Helwys with John Murton and several other members of the congregation returned to London and organized the first Baptist congregation on English soil about 1611 or 1612. They practiced affusion as the form of baptism and continued to hold Arminian doctrines which they had accepted in Holland, and became known as General Baptists. His *Declaration of the Mystery of Iniquity,* pleading for liberty of conscience, landed him in Newgate Prison.

HENDERSON, ALEXANDER (c. 1583-1646). Born in Criech, Fifeshire. Educated at St. Andrews where he briefly taught philosophy. Pastor at Leuchars. After conversion became a Presbyterian. Helped draft the National Covenant of 1638 and the Solemn League and Covenant in 1643. Moderator of the Scottish General Assembly of his church in 1639. Rector of Edinburgh University from 1640 to 1646. Drafted the Directory of Worship of the Westminster Assembly.

HENGSTENBERG (hĕng'stĕn bĕrk) **ERNST WILHELM** (1802-1869), German Lutheran theologian and exegete, born at Fröndenberg, Westphalia, Germany. Ready to enter the newly founded University of Bonn at age nineteen. In preparation for his studies grounded himself thoroughly in philology and philosophy. Gave particular attention to the Aristotelian philosophy. Above all else devoted himself to Arabic. From 1824 to 1829, a professor of theology at Berlin. Rigid orthodox doctrine and protest against rationalism and higher criticism brought him into disfavor with the ministry of worship at the university. In 1827, became editor of the *Evangelische Lutherische Kirckenzeitung,* a medium through which he had a wide influence on the religious life of his time. Entered vigorously upon this task, continued until 1869. Maintained interest in defending evangelical truth with fearless daring, undaunted by the attacks of critics. He also wrote several volumes of theology and exegesis, his *Christology of the Old Testament* (four volumes) being the best known.

HENRY III (1017-1056), King of Germany (1039-1056) and Holy Roman Emperor (1046-1056), born at Osterbeck, Netherlands. In 1039 became king of Germany; upon the death of father crowned Holy Roman Emperor in 1046. During his reign enforced German authority throughout all the territories of the Holy Roman Empire. Being a deeply religious man, also supported ecclesiastical reform, especially as it was being promoted at Cluny. On first visit to Rome in 1046 called the Synod of Sutri that put an end to the intrigue of the three rival popes, Silvester III, Benedict IX, and Gregory VI, and elected Clement II in their stead. Clement then crowned Henry as Holy Roman Emperor. After Clement's death Henry named Damasus II to be pope. This pope lived only a few months; and Henry then nominated his cousin Bruno, who became the powerful Cluniac reform pope, Leo IX. Upon Leo's death in 1054 Henry appointed a fourth German pope. Then in 1056 the able emperor died, leaving the throne and a struggle over the papacy to six-year-old son, Henry IV. Henry III did much to help check the clerical abuses of the church and to strengthen the power of the papacy. He was also a patron of the arts and sciences. Founded numerous monastery schools and built the cathedrals at Worms, Mainz, and Spiers.

HENRY IV (1050-1106), German king and Holy Roman Emperor, born at Goslar, Prussia, son of Emperor Henry III, succeeded to the German throne in 1056 upon death of father. Reign was beset with difficulties owing to the rebellious Saxons on the one hand, and to the question of investiture with Pope Gregory VII on the other. Having conquered the Saxons in 1075, refused obedience to the pope, answered the pope's threat of excommunication in 1076 by declaring Gregory deposed. Gregory released Henry's subjects from their oath of allegiance; and the Saxons refused obedience to Henry unless he became reconciled to the pope within one year. Henry decided upon the strategy of meeting the pope before he could come to Germany. He crossed the Alps in mid-winter, and met the pope at Canossa. Henry is said to have stood three days in the snow in 1077 begging the pope's forgiveness. The pope was persuaded to yield, and Henry was released from the excommunication. Henry returned to Germany to subdue Rudolph, counter king who had been set up in his absence. Succeeding in his endeavor, and flushed with the victory, Henry broke his pledge to the pope and rebelled. The pope again excommunicated the king, but not with the same success as formerly. Henry marched into Italy to take vengeance on Gregory. He finally seized the pope (1084) and imprisoned him. Appointed an anti-pope, Clement III, who crowned Henry as Holy Roman Emperor in 1084. He was taken prisoner and dethroned by his younger son, Henry V, in 1105, escaped and began to raise an army. Premature death in 1106 saved Germany from civil war.

HENRY IV (1553-1610), **HENRY BOURBON OF NAVARRE,** first Bourbon king of France, born at Pau in Bearn, France, educated under the supervision of mother, Jeanne d'Albret, who was a zealous Calvinist. Though a Protestant, Henry in 1572 married Catholic Marguerite of Valois, daughter of Catharine de Medici, and sister of King Charles IX of France. In early Wars of Religion Henry was on the side of the Protestants with Admiral Coligny and Prince Conde. At the time of the Massacre of St. Bartholomew's Day in 1572, he saved himself by abjuring Protestantism. In 1576, reasserted Protestant faith, and was made political head of the Huguenots. Henry Bourbon, upon the death of Henry III, became Henry IV of France, first of the Bourbon line. Henry in 1593 declared himself a Catholic, and the Wars of Religion came to a close. In 1598 the Edict of Nantes gave the Huguenots a large degree of religious and political freedom. Henry was assassinated by a religious fanatic.

HENRY II (1133-1189), English king (1154-1189), made his playboy friend Thomas à Becket archbishop of Canterbury to help him bring the Roman Catholic church in England under royal control. Becket in his new office upheld the church and opposed the 1164 Constitutions of Clarendon. Murdered by Henry's henchmen on the chancel steps of Canterbury in 1170. Henry did penance and rescinded the unwanted legislation because of public disapproval. Henry was important in the rise of common law, jury trial, and travelling judges.

HENRY VIII (1491-1547), King of England (1509 to 1547). Of the house of Tudor, younger son of Henry VII and Elizabeth of York. In 1503, upon the death of Prince Arthur, Henry VII secured from Pope Julius II a dispensation for the betrothal of young Henry to Arthur's widow, Catherine of Aragon. In 1509 Henry succeeded his father to the throne, and subsequently married Catherine. Attractiveness of person, interest in sports, the hunt, and military prowess, and a genial personality, early endeared him to his subjects. He was an obstinate, egotistic, self-seeking, autocratic man. Sought to use parliament, the tribunals, and even national freedom as tools to attain his ends. At the same time educated in theology and a devoted son of the church of Rome. His *Defense of the Seven Sacraments,* written in 1521 against Luther's *Babylonian Captivity,* led Pope Leo X to give him the title, "Defender of the Faith," a title used by Protestant rulers of England since that time. The one surviving child of Henry and Catherine was Mary Tudor queen of England, popularly known as "Bloody Mary." When it became apparent that there could be no son from this marriage, and having fallen in love with Anne Boleyn, Henry ordered Thomas Cardinal Wolsey, his Lord chancellor, to negotiate with Pope Clement VII for a divorce from Catherine. Wolsey, unable to secure the divorce, was charged by Henry with high treason. Wolsey died before Henry could have him tried and executed. Thomas More, also a Roman Catholic, followed as lord chancellor, but refused to secure the divorce for Henry, and was consequently executed. Thomas Cromwell became lord chancellor, and Thomas Cranmer, archbishop of Canterbury, both of them Protestants. The divorce was secured and Henry soon married Anne Boleyn (1533). To this union was born a girl, princess Elizabeth, later queen of England. When Henry tired of Anne Boleyn he charged her with adultery and had her executed. Married Jane Seymour who bore him the son he desired, but she died a few days later. Later married Anne of Cleves whom he divorced within a few months, and married Catherine Howard. Soon had her executed, and then married Catherine Parr, who outlived him. He wanted and secured in 1534, through his political maneuvers, a national Catholic church independent of Rome, with himself "the only supreme head on earth of the Church of England." Strengthened the English position and weakened Rome by confiscating the monasteries of England. At the same time, however, was not only willing but eager to retain much of Rome's theology and form of worship. Through the work of Cranmer the "Great Bible" was put in the churches. He reinstated many Catholic practices in the Six Articles. It was left for his son Edward VI to recover lost ground and to give the Reformation in England a firmer stand.

HENRY OF LAUSANNE (d. about 1145), medieval dissenter, originator of the Henricians, born probably in Italy near the close of the eleventh century, and for a time a Benedictine monk at Cluny. Left the monastery, put off the cowl, and began itinerary preaching of penitence in the diocese of Le Mans. His doctrine seems to have been an insistence upon personal responsibility in religion, and rejection of the rites and authority of the church. Attacks on the corruption of the church and the depravity of the clergy brought the wrath of the church upon him. Arrested and imprisoned, but subsequently released. The bishop expelled him from the diocese and he went to Lausanne, thence to southern France, joining in the spiritual crusade opened by Peter of Bruys. By 1135 he was practicing and teaching celibacy and poverty; and teaching that the sacraments were valid only when administered by priests who led a life of asceticism and poverty. Preached to the laity, among whom he gained large following. Bernard of Clairvaux preached against Henry and his views. Henry was arrested and condemned to lifelong imprisonment. His followers, known as Henricians, were gradually absorbed by the Waldenses.

HENRY THE NAVIGATOR (1394-1460), patron of Portuguese exploration by sea. Born Oporto, Portugal. In 1418 set up at Ceuta an observatory and school for navigators, and improved the compass. Directed voyages to win new lands for the church and wealth for Portugal. Laid foundations for later Portuguese empire in Brazil and the Far East.

HENRY, MATTHEW (1662-1714), Nonconformist Bible commentator, born at Broad Oak, Flintshire, Wales. Educated privately in the home of father, Philip Henry, a distinguished Nonconformist minister, and at an academy at Islington. Studies included Latin, Greek, Hebrew, and French. He went to London and began the study of law at Gray's Inn. In 1687 ordained a Presbyterian minister, became pastor at Chester, where he labored from 1687 to 1712. The last two years of his life was pastor at Hackney, near London. In 1714 while on a preaching mission at Chester he died and was buried there. Married twice and father of nine daughters and one son. Matthew Henry was a faithful, humble, devout, orthodox minister of the gospel, a loving pastor of souls, and a wise spiritual father. Famous for his *Exposition of the Old and New Testaments,* now commonly known as *Matthew Henry's Commentaries* (six volumes). The last volume was completed after his death by thirteen Nonconformist ministers from his manuscripts and notes. The value of his Commentaries lies not in their critical, but in their practical and devotional emphasis.

HEPBURN, JAMES CURTIS (1815-1911), American Presbyterian medical missionary to the Far East, born in Milton, Pennsylvania, educated at Princeton and the University of Pennsylvania (in medicine). In 1840 went to China as a medical missionary, at Singapore from 1841 to 1843, at Amoy from 1843 to 1846. Due to the ill health of wife, he returned to the States, and from 1846 to 1859 was in New York. In 1859 the Presbyterian Board asked them to go to Japan. With headquarters at Yokohama, Dr. Hepburn remained in Japan until 1902 when he returned to New York. Won his way into the hearts of the people by medical skill and practices. Was also an educator of the first rank. In Tokyo founded a medical school and Meiji Gakuin University where he taught both medicine and surgery. His able wife, a capable teacher, opened a school for girls which is said to have been the first Western-type school for women. She also taught young men, some of whom later came into prominent public life. In 1859 Hepburn became a member of the American Geographical Society, and in 1881 a member of the American Bible Society. In 1905, decorated by the emperor with the Third Order of the Rising Sun. Writings were chiefly in the Japanese language: the first *Japanese-English Dictionary,* a *Grammar of the Japanese Language, Dictionary of the Bible* (in Japanese), translations of the Westminster Confession, the Shorter Catechism, the Lord's Prayer, and the creed. Also assisted in translating the Bible.

HERACLAS (hē răk'las), (c. 170-248), Bishop of Alexandria. He and his brother Plutarch, who died a martyr, were the oldest distinguished converts and pupils of Origen. Like Origen, Heraclas studied the Neo-Platonic philosophy under Ammonius Saccas. A promising theologian, he was appointed by Origen as his assistant, and then became his successor for about two years until his election to the bishopric of Alexandria in 232. In the Origenistic controversy he sided with Bishop Demetrius in opposing and in excommunicating Origen.

HERBERT, EDWARD (1583-1648), First Lord Herbert of Cherbury, diplomat, philosopher and forerunner of Deists. Born near Wroxeter. Educated at University College, Oxford. Much travelled soldier and diplomat. Elevated to the peerage in 1629. In

1624 published his *De Veritate* in which he said that God is, God ought to be worshiped, virtue is worship, repentance from sin is needed, and reward and punishment come in the next life. The later Deists had similar ideas about what was common in all religions.

HERBERT, GEORGE (1593-1633), English poet and divine, born at the Castle of Montgomery, Wales, educated at Westminster School and at Trinity College, Cambridge. A fellow of Trinity College (1615) and public orator of the university (1619-1627). For a time courtier to King James I; but upon the king's death took holy orders, and in 1626 was given a prebend in Huntingdonshire. In 1630 ordained priest and made rector of Fugglestone and Bemerton, Wiltshire. Life as minister was exemplary and devoted. Passionately fond of music, and his hymns were written to the accompaniment of his lute and viol. His fame rests largely upon poems, *The Temple, Sacred Poems,* and *Private Ejaculations.* His most famous prose work, *A Priest to the Temple, or the Character of a Country Parson,* is an excellent treatise upon pastoral theology. Wrote the hymn, "The God of Love My Shepherd Is."

HERDER, JOHANN GOTTFRIED VON (1744-1803), German theologian, critic, preacher, and man of letters, born at Mohrungen, East Prussia, in a humble Lutheran home, studied theology, philosophy, languages, and literature at Königsberg, and later taught there. Became an eager supporter of the Romantic movement, and helped emancipate German literature from all foreign influences. A liberal Bible scholar, opposing rigid orthodoxy. His creed was more humanitarian than Christian. From 1764 to 1769 teacher in the cathedral school of Riga, where he distinguished himself as a pulpit orator, drawing large audiences. In 1771 appointed court preacher and councilor of the consistory at Bückelburg. Became the friend and source of inspiration of Goethe, who in turn helped him in 1776 to gain appointment as court preacher and general superintendent at Weimar, a position held the rest of his life. To him religion, especially Christianity, is the embodiment of that which is deepest in the feelings of mankind. Understanding of the Scriptures must be interpreted according to the views and feelings of the time of writing. Chief among writings are: *Spirit of Hebrew Poetry, Ideas on the Philosophy of Mankind, Fragments of Recent German Literature,* and *The Oldest Record of the Human Race*.

HERMAN (är män'), **NICHOLAS (BROTHER LAWRENCE)** (c. 1611-1691), Carmelite mystic, born in Lorraine, France, received very little education, and spent eighteen years as a soldier, fighting in wars waged in the name of the Holy Roman Emperor against the Protestant sovereigns of the North. Converted at age eighteen. Became a lay brother of the Discalced Carmelites in Paris. Worked in the kitchen as a "servant of the servants of God" until his death. In the monastery he became known as Brother Lawrence. "He wedded work with prayer." He is best known for his little posthumous book of maxims, *The Practice of the Presence of God*. Sought to do everything for the love of and to the glory of God with a consciousness of God's presence.

HERMAS (Second century), writer of *The Shepherd*. A Christian slave in Rome of Rhoda. Freed and became a wealthy merchant. Lost money in persecution and his family. Finally all converted. Key idea of this book of this apostolic father is repentance and holy living set forth in vision, command, and similitude.

HERRICK, ROBERT (1591-1674), English poet and clergyman, born in Cheapside, London, educated at St. John's and Trinity Hall, Cambridge, studied law for a time. In 1629 he took orders; was rural vicar of Dean Prior in Devonshire (1629-1647), but ejected for royalist sympathies in 1647. Retired to London, but reinstated in his parish after the Restoration (1662). In 1648 his collected poems were published under the title, *Hesperides, or the Works Both Human and Divine, of Robert Herrick, Esq*. Collection of sacred poems bears separate title, *Noble Numbers, or Pious Pieces.* Among religious poems: "The Litany" was his masterpiece. Greatest of the Caroline or Cavalier poets. "As a writer of pastoral lyrics Herrick has never been excelled by any English author."

HERRON, GEORGE D. (1862-1925), exponent of the social gospel. Born in Montezuma, Indiana. Pastor in Minnesota and Iowa from 1883 to 1889. Professor at Iowa (Grinell) College from 1893 to 1899. Deposed from the ministry. Joined the Socialist party. With Mrs. Edith Rand organized the School of Social Sciences in New York in 1906. Was Wilson's personal representative in peace negotiations.

HERVEY, JAMES (1714-1758), Anglican clergyman and devotional writer, born in Hardingstone, near Northampton, England. Studied at Lincoln College, Oxford. Ordained in 1736 and held curacies in Weston Favell, Dummer, and Biddeford, then in 1752 succeeded to the family livings of Weston Favell and Collingtree. George Whitefield was the chief instrument used in Hervey's conversion. Writings were evangelical and full of the love of nature. Made a notable contribution to the church of his day. His Calvinistic *Dialogue Between Theron and Aspasio* provoked the active opposition of John Wesley. Hervey's chief work was *Meditations and Contemplations Among the Tombs.* A man of great sincerity, purity of life, high moral character, extreme gentleness, and deep mystic piety.

HERZOG (hĕr'tsōk), **JOHANN JAKOB** (1805-1882), German Reformed theologian, born at Basel, Switzerland, received education at Basel and Berlin. At Basel until 1835 when he became professor of historical theology in the Academy at Lausanne. In 1847 professor of church history at the University of Halle; in 1854 became professor of Reformed theology and church history at Erlangen. In 1877, retired to devote the remainder of time to the editing of church history, and to the new edition of his theological encyclopedia, to which he contributed 529 articles. *Realencyclopädie für Protestantische Theologie und Kirche* (twenty-two volumes) was his greatest contribution to the Protestant church. After his death a condensed edition was prepared by Philip Schaff (3 volumes) and later revised. *The New Schaff-Herzog Encyclopedia of Religious Knowledge* (thirteen volumes) is widely used. Herzog also wrote *Calvin and Zwingli, Life of Oecolampadius and the Reformation in Basel,* and books on the Waldenses.

HEURNIUS (hûr'nĭ ŭs), **JUSTUS** (c. 1585-1656), Dutch missionary, born in Holland, son of medical professor at the University of Leiden. After taking a medical course he traveled in France for five years. Returned to take a theological course, wished to go to India, but both the Dutch and the Engish East India Companies were opposed to Christian missions. In 1624 the East India Company sent him to Batavia. Began to do mission work among both the Malayans and the Chinese. Did some translating into Chinese and prepared a Dutch-Latin-Chinese dictionary. When he advocated the independence of the church from the East India Company, arrested and imprisoned. Upon release went to the island of Amboyna and did missionary work. Broken in health, obliged to return to Holland, where he continued writing and translating into Malayanese.

HICKS, ELIAS (1748-1830), American Quaker, born at Hempstead, Long Island, New York, received only a meager formal education. Early life served as a mechanic, then a farmer. From 1799 began to have "openings leading to the ministry" and soon became a noted preacher among the Friends. When liberal element of the Society of Friends broke off in 1827, they became popularly, though not officially, known as Hicksites. Hicks held liberal, rationalistic, anti-evangelical, and unorthodox views, speaking depreciatively of the Bible and of the historical work of Christ. Opposed external authority, and taught that obedience to the Spirit of God in the heart of man is sufficient for salvation and for Christian walk. A vigorous abolitionist in New York.

HIGGINBOTHAM, SAM (1874-1958), agricultural missionary to India. Born in Manchester, England and came to the United States in 1894. Educated at Amherst College, Princeton University, and Ohio State University (in agriculture). Missionary in India from 1903 to 1945. Organized Agricultural Institute at Allahabad and Allahabad Christian College of which he became president. Moderator of his denomination in 1939. Wrote *The Gospel and the Plow.*

HIGGINSON, FRANCIS (c. 1587-1630), Anglican pastor and later American Congregationalist. Born Claybrooke, England. Educated at Jesus College, Cambridge. Minister at Claybrooke (1615-1617). Lecturer at St. Nicholas (1617-1629). Went to America in 1629 and became minister at Salem (1629-1630).

HILARION (hĭ lâr'ĭ ŏn), (c. 291-371), Palestinian hermit, born of heathen parents near Gaza, Palestine, died on the island of Cyprus. Educated in Alexandria after becoming a Christian. Hearing Anthony in Alexandria, chose to live the life of an anchorite. At age fifteen began the rigid, ascetic life of a solitary. Later, because of the persecution of the Christians, he permanently left Palestine, going first to Egypt, thence to Sicily and to Dalmatia, and finally to Cyprus. Hilarion is credited with having been one of the first to transplant the hermit life to Palestine, especially the southern part.

HILARY OF POITIERS (c. 315-368), Bishop of Poitiers, born at Poitiers, southwestern France. In adult life he became a Christian convert from Neo-Platonism. About 353 became bishop of his native city. Took a decided stand against Arianism. For opposition to Arianism banished by the Arian emperor Constantius to the Arian stronghold of Phrygia in Asia Minor. Between 356 and 361 wrote his main work against Arianism, *De Trinitate*. About 361, recalled to Gaul, but before long again banished. Spent the remaining years of his life in rural exile. Besides work on the Trinity, also wrote *De Synodis,* commentaries, polemic works against Arius and Arians, and some original hymns. Hymn writing places him next to Ambrose among lyric poets of the ancient church. A man of thorough Biblical knowledge, theological depth, and earnest piety, and the leading and most respected Latin theologian of his age.

HILDA (HILD), ST. (614-680), Anglo-Saxon abbess, born in Northumbria, England, daughter of a nephew of Edwin, king of Northumbria, and converted to Christianity along with the king about 627 and baptized by Paulinus. Early devoted herself to monastic religious life. She was recalled by Bishop Aidan from a French monastery in 650 to become abbess of Heorta (Hartlepool). In 659 founded the celebrated abbey of Streoneshalh or Whitby, a double house for nuns and monks over which she ruled for twenty-two years, where some of the chief ecclesiastics of the day, including the poet Caedmon, were trained. Following the Synod of Whitby Hilda accepted the Roman date for Easter.

HILDEGARD (hĭl′dĕ gärd), (1098-1179), German Benedictine abbess, prophetess, and mystic, born in Böckelheim, educated in a Benedictine convent where she became abbess. Between 1147 and 1152 founded the convent of Rupertsberg, and later, one at Eibingen. When older, mystic, prophetic insight was used to denounce evil in ecclesiastical and civil government. Most renowned for her 26 mystical experiences which were recorded between 1141 and 1150, and which were later published under the title *Scivias.* A close friend of Bernard of Clairvaux.

HILL, ROWLAND (1744-1833), Nonconformist English preacher, born at Hawkstone Park, Shropshire, England, educated at Eton and at St. John's College, Cambridge. During college career, active in religious work, helping the poor and engaging in lay-preaching. When about to receive M.A. degree at Cambridge, applied for ordination. Ordained priest in 1773 in the Anglican church and obtained a small curacy at Kingston which he held for many years. He began preaching for the Calvinistic Methodists and pursued his itinerant ministry with much success. In 1783, with money he had inherited built the famous Surrey Chapel in London. Preached to immense audiences until near the end of his life. During summers made preaching tours through Ireland and Scotland. Attached to chapel were thirteen Sunday schools with over three thousand children. One of the founders of the Religious Tract Society, and an active promoter of the work of the London Missionary Society, and of the British and Foreign Bible Society. Preaching was earnest and evangelical, original and often quaint. His best known writing was *Village Dialogues.*

HILLIS, NEWELL DWIGHT (1858-1929), Presbyterian clergyman and author, born at Magnolia, Iowa in a deeply religious Quaker home. Received education at Iowa College, Lake Forest University, and McCormick Theological Seminary. The summer before he entered college he drove in a horse and buggy through Nebraska, Colorado, and Wyoming organizing Sunday schools for the American Sunday School Union, organizing forty-four schools in one summer. Ordained in 1887. From 1887 to 1899 held pastorates in Peoria and Evanston, Illinois, and in the Independent Central Church in Chicago. From 1899 to 1924 pastor of the Plymouth Congregational Church, Brooklyn, New York. Under ministry of Henry Ward Beecher the Plymouth church had become a strong institutional church, much interested in the social side of Christianity. Organized Plymouth Institute to educate young people. In theology he was very liberal and resigned from the Presbyterian church before a heresy trial was instigated. At the beginning of World War I he strongly advocated the entrance of the United States into the war against Germany. Assisted in many states by sermon and lecture in promoting the Liberty Loan drive. In his later years he gave a series of "Better American Lectures," touring every state in the Union. One of the most popular preachers, lecturers, and after-dinner speakers in this country. Retired in 1924, continued to do some preaching, traveling, and writing. Writings include: *A Man's Value to Society, Great Books as Life Teachers, Influence of Christ in Modern Life, Contagion of Character, Prophets of a New Era, How the Inner Light Failed, The Quest of Happiness,* and *The Investment of Influence.*

HINCMAR (hĭngk′mär), **OF RHEIMS** (c. 806-882), French Roman Catholic prelate and theological controversialist, born in France, educated in the Benedictine Abbey of St. Denis, near Paris. As a young man served both in the abbey and at court. In 844 ordained priest. In 845 Hincmar was regularly elected and consecrated as archbishop of Rheims. Soon became involved in the predestination controversy started by Gottschalk. In this controversy he supported Paschasius Radbertus. At a synod which he called Hincmar condemned Gottschalk. Meantime there had arisen a more serious struggle in the form of a rival claim by Ebbo to the see at Rheims. Although the synod at Soissons in 853 decided against Ebbo and confirmed Hincmar, the difficulty was not settled. Pope Nicholas I later reproved Hincmar, bringing estrangement between them until Nicholas needed the services of Hincmar in his struggle with the Eastern church. With difficulty and struggle he successfully held his position of ecclesiastical power and supremacy at Rheims. Also held a very prominent place in the sphere of politics. The most faithful counselor of the West-

Frankish kings, Louis the Pious and Charles the Bald, and their successors, and more than once saved the Frankish kingdom from downfall. Likewise acknowledged leader of the Gallican church, and strongly asserted the liberty of the Gallican church, tirelessly opposing both royal and papal tyranny over the Church of France. Firmly defended the principle that the spiritual power takes precedence over royal authority. Finally driven from Rheims when the Normans came a short time before his death. Found refuge in Epernay where he died.

HIPPOLYTUS (hĭ pŏl'ĭ tŭs), (c. 170-c. 236), apologist, writer and bishop, probably born of Greek parentage. A younger contemporary of Tertullian, and an older contemporary of Cyprian, like them belonged to North African or Western school of thought. Did all his writing in the Greek language. Writings dealt at length with the heresies that were plaguing the Christian church. Most important book was *Philosophumena,* or *Adversus Omnes Haereses,* or *Refutation of All Heresies.* A preacher of note, bishop of Pontus, near Rome. Hippolytus reproved Zephyrinus and Callistus, contemporary bishops of Rome, for leniency in dealing with church members, and for their Patripassian leanings. In his writings especially severe with Callistus. Hippolytus refused to recognize Callistus as bishop. Some of his followers set him up as rival bishop or antipope. In doctrine and discipline he resembled the Montanists before him and the Novatian schism after him. It seems that he was banished by Emperor Maximin to the mines of Sardinia, where he died, and was therefore considered a martyr.

HOBBES (hŏbz), **THOMAS** (1588-1679), English philosopher, political theorist, and forerunner of modern materialism, born in Malmesbury, Wiltshire, England, son of a dissolute clergyman. Educated at Magdalen Hall, Oxford. For several years after leaving the University tutored for various noble families, often traveling with pupils on the Continent. For a while he was tutor of the Prince of Wales, afterward Charles II. About 1640 wrote *The Elements of Law, Natural and Political,* then for fear of arrest, fled to Paris where he was in exile from 1640 to 1651. When in 1651 he produced his best-known work, *Leviathan, Or the Matter, Form, and Power of a Commonwealth,* it aroused the suspicions of the French authorities and the Roman Catholics. In fear he fled back to England. In the *Leviathan* he advocated pure and unrestrained monarchy as the best form of government, and held that the state was superior to the church and must decide religious issues. In 1660 when Charles II was restored, Hobbes came into favor with the new government. Chief claims to fame were works in the analysis of human nature and political institutions. Among those are *De Cive, De Corpore Politico, De Homine,* and *Behomoth.* In epistemology and psychology Hobbes was a sensationalist, in metaphysics a materialist, and in ethics a hedonist. Maintained that nothing is spiritual, but everything material, even God, "the first cause of the universe." Maintained also that the only source of knowledge is sensation, that the only objects of knowledge are bodies, either natural or political, and that the only end of action is self-interest.

HOCHMANN (hōk'măn), **ERNST CHRISTOPH (VON HOCHENAU)** (1670-1721), Pietist, born in a distinguished noble family at Lauenburg near Hamburg, Germany, father's later years were spent at Nüremberg as Secretary of War. He went to Halle to study law. In 1693, expelled from Halle because of eccentric views. In 1697 went to Giessen and became associated with Gottfried Arnold. Then went to Frankfurt as a missionary to the Jews. Soon driven from Frankfurt, and in 1700 was beaten almost to death. From 1700 to 1711 became a homeless, persecuted wanderer, roaming throughout Germany, preaching, protesting, and suffering scourgings and imprisonments. Finally settled in village of Schwarzenau and built himself a little home, named Friedensburg. A man of deep piety and persuasive personality, won many friends and adherents. Among intimate friends were Gottfried Arnold, Pietist and church historian; Gerhard Tersteegen, mystic and hymnist; Alexander Mack, founder of the German Baptist Brethren. Hochman opposed infant baptism, and held that the Lord's Supper should be administered only to the faithful disciples of Christ. He advocated complete separation of church and state. Held to the doctrine of Christian perfection.

HOCKING, WILLIAM ERNEST (1873-1966), philosopher and educator. Born in Cleveland, Ohio. Educated at Harvard, Göttingen, and Heidelberg (Ph.D., 1904). Teacher of philosophy at Andover Theological Seminary, University of California, Yale, and from 1914 to 1943 Harvard. Edited in 1932 *Rethinking Missions,* the final report of a study of Far East missions financed by John D. Rockefeller, which stressed education and philanthropy as the task of missions and opposed "conscious evangelism" in favor of crosscultural interpenetration for a synthesis of religion.

HODGE, ARCHIBALD ALEXANDER (1823-1886), American Presbyterian theologian, son of Charles Hodge; born at Princeton, New Jersey. Educated at Princeton College and Princeton Theological Seminary. After spending three years (1847-1850) as missionary in Allahabad, India. From 1851 to 1862 held pastorates in Maryland, Virginia, and Pennsylvania. From 1864 to 1877 held the chair of systematic theology at the Western Theological Seminary at Allegheny, Pennsylvania. From 1878 to 1886 professor at Princeton in the chair of didactic and exegetical theology. A leader in the Presbyterian church, trustee of Princeton College; editor of the *Presbyterian Review;* author of some important encyclopedia articles in Johnson's *Universal Cyclopaedia,* in McClintock and Strong's *Cyclopaedia of Biblical Literature,* and in Schaff-Herzog *Encyclopaedia of Religious Knowledge.* Hodge was a forceful preacher, a great teacher, and a good writer—preaching, lecturing, and writing almost to the time of death. Author of *Outlines of Theology, The Atonement, The Life of Charles Hodge, A Commentary on the Confession of Faith,* and *Popular Lectures on Theological Themes.*

HODGE, CHARLES (1797-1878), American Presbyterian theologian, born at Philadelphia, Pennsylvania, and educated at the College of New Jersey and Princeton Seminary. In 1820 appointed instructor, in 1822 professor of biblical and Oriental literature and in 1840 of New Testament exegesis. In 1821 ordained to the Presbyterian ministry. In 1825 started the *Biblical Repository,* which later was renamed the *Princeton Review*—about forty-five years its editor and principal contributor. In 1826 went abroad to study in Paris, Halle, and Berlin. Two of his sons also were teachers of theology at Princeton, Dr. C. W. Hodge in the department of exegetical theology, and Dr. Archibald Alexander Hodge succeeding him in didactic theology. Dr. Hodge belonged to the Old School group in the Presbyterian church, and in 1846 was moderator of their General Assembly. A voluminous writer, greatest work, three-volume set of *Systematic Theology,* extending to 2260 pages. Literary powers were seen at their best in contributions to the *Biblical Repository* and *Princeton Review.* As a teacher had few equals. His enviable privilege was to have had three thousand ministers pass under his instruction at Princeton from 1820 to 1848. Had rare privilege of achieving distinction as a teacher, exegete, preacher, controversialist, ecclesiastic, and systematic theologian. A man of warm affection and piety. Devoted to Christ and the truth. He had no mind to strike out in new paths, intent on establishing the old landmarks. Came to be considered the greatest American Calvinist theologian since Jonathan Edwards.

HOFFMAN, ELISHA A. (1839-1929), Presbyterian minister and hymn writer, born in Orwigsburg, Pennsylvania, educated in the Philadelphia public schools. Graduated from a scientific course, then pursued the study of the classics in Union Seminary of the Evangelical Association. For eleven years connected with the Association's publishing house in Cleveland, Ohio. For more than thirty-three years pastor of the Benton Harbor Presbyterian Church. His pastime was writing hymns, setting them to music of his own composition. Wrote more than one thousand songs or hymns, some of the more popular: "What a Wonderful Saviour," "Are You Washed in the Blood?", "I Must Tell Jesus," "Breathe upon Us Holy Spirit," "Precious Is the Blood," and "Vale of Beulah."

HOFFMANN, MELCHIOR (c. 1500-c. 1543), German mystic and Anabaptist, born at Schwäbisch-Hall, Württemberg, Germany. A leather dresser by trade, in the interest of which he went to Livonia. Began to preach Luther's doctrine mingled with a strain of mysticism. Though an untrained layman, his religious fervor, vehemence of speech, and directness of appeal presented a formidable competition to the educated clergy. Preaching was so effective that he was driven from Wolmar in 1524. Went to Dorpat where the efforts of the state-church authorities to seize him led to the iconoclastic uprising of 1525. His growing revolutionary and ultra-prophetic and eschatological teaching led the Reformers to look askance of his motives and efforts, and finally to oppose him. In 1526 left Dorpat and became a preacher among the Germans of Stockholm. In 1527 he left Stockholm to spend two years in preaching at Kiel in Holstein, Denmark, then went to Strassburg where he joined the Anabaptists. Continued shifting from place to place, agitating revolutionary ideas. Became known as "the evil genius of the Anabaptists." Hoffmann claimed to be one of the two witnesses of Revelation 11:3. Predicted that Christ would reign over the saints in 1533, and that Strassburg was to be the New Jerusalem, the seat of Christ's universal kingdom. Soon gained a large following, known as "Melchiorites." Said that non-resistance might be given up, and led the Anabaptists into evil ways. The authorities had him arrested in 1533. He died in prison ten years later. After his imprisonment movement was carried on by Jan Matthys and John of Leiden.

HOFMANN, JOHANN MICHAEL FERDINAND HEINRICH (1824-1902), German painter, born in Darmstadt, Germany; studied in Düsseldorf, Germany, and Antwerp, Belgium. Early turned to painting, and after making a residence of four years in

Italy, and practicing in various German cities, settled at Dresden in 1862 as professor of painting in the academy there. Best pictures were of religious subjects, also painted scenes from Greek mythology and from Shakespeare. His painting was a free departure from strict classicism with a romantic tendency. Works include "Christ in the Temple"; "Christ Taken Prisoner"; "Christ's Sermon on Lake Genessaret"; "Christ in Gethsemane"; "The Adulteress before Christ"; "The Burial of Christ"; "The Betrayal of Christ." His works are popular and have been engraved and photographed more extensively than those of most other German painters.

HOLMES, JOHN HAYNES (1879-1964), Pacifist minister. Born in Philadelphia, educated at Harvard College and Divinity School. Unitarian minister of churches in New York from 1907 to 1949. Opposed Tammany Hall from 1929-1938. Supported the NAACP. Pacifist in World War I. Helped found the American Civil Liberties Union and supported cultural Zionism.

HONE (hōn), **WILLIAM** (1780-1842), independent preacher, writer, and bookdealer, born at Bath, England, studied law for a while, but became a bookseller. Failing in this took up writing to earn a livelihood for himself and family. He translated and collected into one volume, with prefaces and tables and various notes and references, the *Apocryphal New Testament,* "being all the gospels, epistles, and other pieces now extant, attributed in the first four centuries to Jesus Christ, his apostles, and their companions, and not included in the New Testament by its compilers." In the latter part of his life he frequently preached in Weigh House Chapel, Eastcheap, London.

HOOKER, RICHARD (c. 1553-1600), Church of England writer on ecclesiastical polity, born near Exeter, Devonshire, England, educated at Corpus Christi College, Oxford. Ordained in 1581 and held pastorates in Wiltshire and Kent. His reputation rests upon his great work, *The Laws of Ecclesiastical Polity,* written in the 1590s in defense of the High Church polity of Anglicanism, and as an answer to Calvinistic Puritanism or Presbyterianism. Its object is to explain and defend the episcopal system of government on the basis of Scripture and reason. The work is one of the most important contributions of early English ecclesiastical writing of the sixteenth century. It really stands as a tolerant, moderate view of historic episcopacy. His work remains as one of the classics of English literature.

HOOKER, THOMAS (1586-1647), founder of the colony of Hartford, Connecticut, born at Markfield, Tilton, Leicestershire, England. Educated at Emmanuel College, Cambridge, the intellectual center of Puritanism, and from 1611 to 1618 fellow of college. From 1620 to 1626 preached at Esher, Surrey. Then accepted a position as supplementary Puritan preacher at St. Mary's Church at Chelmsford, Essex; but due to his Puritanism came into conflict with Archbishop Laud. Later opened a school at Little Baddow, Essex, with John Eliot as assistant. In 1630 upon renewed charges against him for Puritanism, left England for Holland, where for three years preached at Amsterdam, Delft, and Rotterdam. In 1633 sailed with John Cotton to New England. Almost immediately chosen pastor of the first church at Newtowne (now Cambridge). Rivalry and friction in the churches in Massachusetts led Hooker and the greater part of his congregation to move to the Connecticut Valley, where they founded Hartford in 1636. Hooker was pastor of the Hartford church until his death in 1647. Helped draft Connecticut Constitution of 1639. In 1639 advocated to Governor Winthrop a confederation for mutual protection against the Dutch, French, and Indians. This proposal resulted four years later in the organization of the "United Colonies of New England," the earliest system of federal government in America.

HOOPER, JOHN (c. 1495-1555), English bishop and martyr, born in Somersetshire. Studied at Merton College, Oxford, entered a Cistercian monastery. A diligent study of Scripture and the works of Zwingli and Bullinger on the Pauline Epistles convinced him of errors of the Roman church and made him an ardent advocate of the Reformation. Opposed the Six Articles issued by Henry VIII and brought upon himself severe persecution. In 1537 fled to Zurich, Switzerland, coming into close association with Bullinger. Studied theology and Greek, adopted in full the Zwinglian view of Reformation, and married. In 1547 after the death of King Henry returned to England, where warmly received by King Edward's Protestant council. Made the chaplain of the Earl of Warwick, and then Bishop of Gloucester (1550), and later Bishop of Worcester also. Helped greatly in the progress of the Reformation in England. But when Mary ascended the throne he was called to London, tried for heresy, then sent to Gloucester, stripped of all priestly vestments, and led to the stake where he was burned, meeting death firmly and cheerfully.

HOPKINS, SAMUEL (1721-1803), American theologian, born at Waterbury, Connecticut, converted under the preaching of

George Whitefield and Gilbert Tennent. Attended Yale College and then studied theology under Jonathan Edwards at Northampton, Massachusetts. Pastor at Great Barrington, Massachusetts from 1743 to 1769, where he often preached to the Indians. From 1769 to 1803 pastor of the First Congregational Church at Newport, Rhode Island, for last thirty years of his ministry preached and wrote against slavery. Theology was essentially Calvinistic. In attempt to reconcile sin with the Calvinistic dogma of predestination, and to blend the new spirit of revivalism with Calvinistic doctrine, he developed what is often referred to as Hopkinsianism, a modified form of Calvinism. Besides writings on slavery, chief work was *System of Doctrines.*

HORNE, CHARLES SILVESTER (1865-1914), English Congregationalist minister, born at Cuckfield, Sussex, England, educated at Glasgow University and Mansfield College, Oxford. In 1889-1903 minister of Kensington Chapel, from 1903 until 1914 of Whitefield's Chapel, Tottenham Court Road, retiring from the pastorate in 1914. In 1910-1911 chairman of the Congregational Union; 1910 and following a liberal member of the House of Commons, the only clergyman in the House who at the same time held a church charge. Held the conviction that religion had an obligation to render to politics and that politics needed the impact of religion. Established a number of social agencies which were designed to work in connection with the church. In the spring of 1914 delivered the Lyman Beecher lectures on *The Romance of Preaching* at Yale University. In addition to his Lyman Beecher lectures wrote *David Livingstone; A Popular History of the Free Churches; The Story of the London Missionary Society; and Pulpit, Platform, and Parliament.*

HORNE, THOMAS HARTWELL (1780-1862), English biblical scholar and bibliographer, born in Chancery Lane, London. Educated at Christ's Hospital. Became clerk to a barrister, using spare time for study and literary activities. In 1818 published *Introduction to the Critical Study and Knowledge of the Holy Scriptures,* three volumes. Covers the entire field of biblical learning—hermeneutics, apologetics, biblical geography and natural history. As a result of this work King's College conferred on him the degree of M.A., and the Bishop of London ordained him to the curacy of Christ Church, Newgate Street. In earlier years was active in the Methodist church, later entered the ministry of the Church of England, admitted to holy orders in 1819. Following six years at Christ Church, became successively assistant minister at Welbeck Chapel, prebend at St. Paul's Cathedral, and rector of the united parishes of St. Edmund the King, and St. Nicholas Acons, London. Was also senior assistant librarian in the department of printed books in the British Museum from 1824 to 1860. Resigned librarianship in 1860 and died in London in 1862.

HORNER, RALPH (1853-1921), founder of the Canadian Holiness Movement Church. Born Shawville, Quebec and converted to Methodism in 1876. Educated at Victoria College. Began evangelistic ministry in 1886 but deposed from the Methodist church in 1895 for allowing tongues speaking in his meetings. Organized the Holiness Movement Church that same year at Ottawa and was its bishop from 1895 to 1916. In 1916 he set up the Standard Church of America because of differences over sanctification.

HORT, FENTON JOHN ANTHONY (1828-1892), English theologian and biblical scholar, born in Dublin, Ireland. Educated at Rugby, and Trinity College, Cambridge, becoming fellow in 1853. In 1853 began to prepare with B. F. Westcott an edition of the Greek New Testament. In 1854, with J. E. B. Mayor and J. B. Lightfoot, began publishing the *Journal of Classical and Sacred Philology.* Ordained priest in 1856, and in 1857 became vicar of St. Ippolyts near Cambridge, where he remained until 1872. His great work was biblical scholarship. Cambridge frequently called upon him to serve as examiner, lecturer, and professor. Finally in 1872 he moved to Cambridge. For six years lectured on New Testament and patristic subjects at Emmanuel College. In 1878 made Hulsean professor of divinity and in 1887 Lady Margaret reader in divinity. During this time a member of fifteen boards and committees, all of which made heavy claim upon his time, strength, and health. In 1881 appeared monumental text of the Greek New Testament by Westcott and Hort, and the revised edition of the English New Testament, on which he as a leading member of the committee had worked from 1870 to 1881, also Hort's *Introduction to the New Testament in Greek.* Died worn out by intense mental labor.

HORTON, DOUGLAS (1891-1968) Congregational ecumenical leader. Born Brooklyn, New York. Educated at Princeton University, Edinburgh (New College), Mansfield (Oxford) Tübingen and Hartford. Taught at Newton, Chicago, Union and Harvard theological schools. From 1938 to 1955 led the General Council of Congregational Churches. From 1957 to 1963 served as Chairman of the Faith and Order Commission of the World Council of Churches. He had earlier served from 1915 to 1938 as pastor of churches in Massachusetts and Illinois after his ordination in 1915.

HOSIUS (hō′zhĭ ŭs), **OF CORDOVA** (c. 257-c. 357), Bishop of Cordova, place of birth and early life unknown. Consecrated Bishop of Cordova, Spain, about 296. For several years chief ecclesiastical adviser to Emperor Constantine. In 323 or 324 the emperor sent him to Alexandria to settle difficulties between Arius and Alexander. At the Council of Nicea in 325 a leader of influence, likely one of the moderators of the council; and is said to have helped prepare the Nicene Creed. Next hear of him at the Council of Sardica in 343. Emperor Constantius, the Arian son of Constantine the Great, tried unsuccessfully to induce Hosius to declare himself against Athanasius, until he finally did succeed in getting him to sign the compromising "Second Sirmian formula," which removed him from his rigid orthodoxy. He was restored to his see and died a centenarian, in Spain.

HOUGHTON (ho′t′n), **WILL H. (WILLIAM HENRY)** (1887-1946), Baptist evangelist, pastor; president of Moody Bible Institute, born in South Boston, Massachusetts, educated in Boston, and Providence, Rhode Island. Early interested in song and drama and had begun an actor's career. Upon his dedication at once gave up the stage and entered the Eastern Nazarene College in Boston. Six months later left college to join Reuben A. Torrey as evangelistic song leader. Ordained in 1915 at the First Baptist Church at Canton, Pennsylvania. After two years became pastor at New Bethlehem, and a little later at Norristown, Pennsylvania. In 1924 conducted an evangelistic campaign in Ireland. From 1925 to 1930 he was pastor of the Baptist Tabernacle in Atlanta, Georgia. From 1930-1934, pastor of the Calvary Baptist Church in New York. In 1934 succeeded Dr. James M. Gray as president of the Moody Bible Institute, filling that office until his death. A man of vision, dedication, devotion, faith, and humility. A poet, singer, pulpiteer, soul-winner, able administrator, and Christian gentleman. Edited Moody Monthly from 1934 to 1936. Began what became Moody Institute of Science in 1938.

HOW, WILLIAM WALSHAM (1823-1897), Anglican bishop and hymn writer, born at Shrewsbury, Shropshire, England, educated at Wadham College, Oxford. Ordained priest in 1846. Between 1846 and 1879 successively curate of St. George's at Kidderminster, Holy Cross at Shrewsbury and rector of Whittington. He accepted the suffragan see of Bedford with episcopal supervision of East London. Consecrated in 1879 and held the position until 1888 when he was translated to the newly created see of Wakefield. In theology, a rather modernistic Broad churchman; in practice, a man of the people, always seeking to help, often at great cost to himself. He was called "the poor man's bishop." Among his numerous writings special mention of the following: *Commentary upon St. John, Commentary on the Four Gospels, Lectures on Pastoral Work* and *Notes on the Church Service*. An excellent hymn writer. Other hymns were written between 1858 and 1871 while he was rector at Whittington. Best known hymns are: "O Jesus Thou Art Standing"; "For All the Saints Who from Their Labor Rest"; "We Give Thee but Thine Own"; "O Word of God Incarnate"; and "Before Thine Awful Presence, Lord."

HOWARD, JOHN (c. 1726-1790), English philanthropist, apostle of prison reform, born at Hackney, near London, educated in private schools at Hertford and London. Inheriting considerable property in 1742 from his father, made a tour of the Continent. In 1756 started for Lisbon which was lying in ruins from a recent earthquake. His vessel was captured by a French privateer, the crew and passengers were cast into a dungeon at Brest where they underwent terrible hardship and suffering. Upon release returned to England, where in 1759 he was made a member of the Royal Society. In 1769 made an extensive tour of the Continent. In 1773 became high sheriff of Bedfordshire. Visited the Bedford jail and found prison conditions unspeakably bad. Began a nation-wide and continent-wide investigation of prisons. Found the most of the prisons both in England and on the Continent in a most filthy and deplorable condition. In 1774 gave evidence of this before a committee of the House of Commons, and in 1777 wrote, *The State of the Prisons in England and Wales, with Preliminary Observations and an Account of some Foreign Prisons.* Devoted the rest of his life, largely at own expense (about thirty thousand pounds of inheritance money), working in behalf of prison reform measures. In further study of prisons and pesthouses in Italy voluntarily subjected himself to the inhuman quarantine system that was being practiced there in order to learn first hand the existing conditions in the pesthouses. In ten months' confinement learned the horrible condition of these places and wrote an *Account of the Principal Lazarettos in Europe*. Had also studied medicine, which had been a help in his travels. In 1790 went to South Russia to study military hospitals, and died there from camp fever which he contracted from a patient he was treating. Helped found the Howard League of Penal Reform.

HOWE, JOHN (1630-1706), English Puritan divine and author, born at Loughborough, Leicestershire, England, where his clergyman father was thrust out of the pastorate by Laud for his espousal of Puritanism. Educated at Christ's College, Cambridge, and at Magdalen College, Oxford, being for a while fellow and chaplain at Magdalen College. Ordained by Nonconformist divines. About 1654 appointed perpetual curate of Great Torrington, Devonshire, two years later domestic chaplain to Oliver Cromwell, and subsequently to Richard. Upon Richard Cromwell's deposition, Howe returned to former parish at Great Torrington and preached there with the permission of the king. Though urged by friends in high position to conform, refused, left Great Torrington (1662). For several years led a wandering and uncertain life but chaplain in Antrim Castle from 1670 to 1676. In 1676 became pastor of a dissenting congregation in London. In 1685 went to the Continent, settling for a time at Utrecht, where he officiated in the English chapel. The "Declaration for Liberty of Conscience" in 1687 induced him to return to London. He was conciliatory in disposition, catholic in spirit, and anxious to promote Christian unity. Frequently styled, "The Platonic Puritan" and ranked as the greatest of the Puritan divines. An eloquent preacher and a prolific writer. Writings were among the most suggestive and profound of the Puritan works. Some of chief writings were: *Blessedness of the Righteous; Union Among Protestants;* and *Future Blessedness.*

HOWE, JULIA WARD (1819-1910), American writer, and social reformer, born in New York City, educated privately. Following marriage to the abolitionist, Dr. Samuel Gridley Howe in 1843, they moved to Boston. Became a member of the church of which James Freeman Clarke was pastor. Belonged to the Radical Club, yet maintained a strong faith in God. Prior to the Civil War assisted her husband in editing the antislavery paper, the *Boston Commonwealth.* Early in the war wrote her famous hymn, *The Battle Hymn of the Republic*. The editor of the *Atlantic Monthly* accepted it and published it, paying her five dollars. It at once was widely accepted and soon became a national hymn. After marriage of her children and death of her husband, she turned her attention and her interest to such social reforms as women's suffrage, prison reform, international peace, and children's welfare. As a Unitarian occasionally preached in Unitarian and other churches. She was the only woman ever elected to the American Academy of Arts and Letters.

HOWSON, JOHN SAUL (1816-1885), Dean of Chester, born at Giggleswick-in-Craven, Yorkshire, England, educated at Giggleswick School and Trinity College, Cambridge. Ordained in 1846 as priest. In 1845 taught at Liverpool Collegiate Institute, where W. J. Conybeare was headmaster. On Conybeare's resignation in 1849, Howson succeeded him. Held this position until elected vicar of Wisbech in 1866. From 1867 until his death, dean of Chester. Practically restored the cathedral and also founded the Chester King's School and Queen's School. Best known for his *Life and Epistles of St. Paul,* which he wrote in collaboration with Conybeare. Most of the descriptive passages were done by Howson. He also wrote several other books on the Apostle Paul.

HROMADKA, JOSEF (1889-1969), Czech theologian. Born in Hodslavice, Moravia. Educated in Vienna, Basel, and Heidelberg. In 1912 pastor of an Evangelical Church of the Czech Brethren. Professor of theology at Jan Hus Theological Faculty, Prague (1920-1939) and Princeton Theological Seminary (1939-1947). Dean of Comenius Faculty of Theology in Prague in 1950. Urged on return to Czechoslovakia in 1947 dialogue between Christians and Communists through the Christian Peace Conference. Helped found the World Council of Churches and was a member of its central committee. Received Lenin Peace Prize in 1958.

HÜBMAIER (hueb'mī er), **BALTHASAR** (c. 1480-1528), German Anabaptist. Born near Augsburg, Germany, and as an ardent Catholic studied under Dr. John Eck. At age thirty became professor of theology at the University of Ingolstadt and pastor of the town church. Secured a pastoral position, became a famous preacher at the cathedral of Regensburg. In 1521 embraced Protestant opinions and became pastor at Waldshut on the Rhine on the northern edge of Switzerland. For a while a staunch supporter of the latter in the Swiss Reformation. Soon disagreed with Zwingli on the subject of infant baptism. In place of baptism instituted a solemn consecration of children before the congregation. Wholeheartedly joined the rising Anabaptist movement in 1523. Entered sympathetic agreement with Thomas Münzer who kindled the Peasants' War, also became a pronounced mystic. Hübmaier became such an ardent leader of the Anabaptists that he led nearly all the citizens of Waldshut to accept the new movement. On Easter 1525 he and three hundred followers were rebaptized by William Reublin. The defeat of the rebellious peasants in 1525 forced him to flee to Zurich. The Zwinglians, as well as the Catholics, strongly opposed him and his radical movement. He fled to Moravia where he continued preaching and writing with signal effect and gathered a large following from among the "Brethren." Became pastor of a congregation and purchased a printing press to publish writings. Political changes, however, soon developed in Moravia. The Catholics came into power and Hübmaier and his wife were arrested and thrown into prison. Refusing to retract convictions, he was condemned. On a public square in Vienna in 1528 he was burned. His wife who encouraged him to remain firm was drowned in the Danube.

HÜGEL (hüe'gĕl), **BARON FRIEDRICH VON** (1852-1925), Roman Catholic lay theologian, born in Florence, Italy, the son of an Austrian ambassador. Family moved to England in 1867 where he made his home the rest of his life. In 1914 became a naturalized British subject, but received education in Florence and in Brussels. Von Hügel is remembered as a liberal Catholic scholar, a higher critic of the Bible. He believed in the decentralization of the Roman church, yet did not radically revolt from Rome. Advocated the holding of three principal elements of religion: "The mystical, the institutional, and the intellectual together in a dynamic tension." Influence on Protestant theology in England was great. In 1905 founded the London Society for the Study of Religion, which became the center of the modernist group, and brought him in touch with thinkers and scholars of the most diverse views, some of whom were Alfred Loisy, George Tyrrell, Ernst Troeltsch, and Rudolf Euchen. Wrote several books. Died, leaving library to the University of St. Andrews.

HUGHES, JOHN JOSEPH (1797-1864), first Roman Catholic Archbishop of New York, born at Annaloghan, County Tyrone, Ireland. Came to America in 1817, entered Mount St. Mary's Catholic College, Emmittsburg, Maryland. In 1826, ordained priest, soon took charge of two different parishes in Philadelphia, where he remained until 1837 when appointed coadjutor bishop of New York, and in 1842 succeeded to the bishopric. In 1850 when the see of New York was made an archbishopric Hughes went to Rome to receive the pallium from the pope in 1850. He took the Roman Catholic view of the public school system. In his regime the problem of "trusteeism" was finally settled in the Roman Catholic church in America; that is, the holding of church property by lay trustees was finally ended and the title was secured over the name of the archbishop himself for and in the name of the church. During twenty-five years of service as bishop and archbishop organized and built more than one hundred churches. Also introduced or organized several Roman Catholic societies in his diocese. Established St. John's College (now Fordham University) at Fordham, New York, in 1861, St. Joseph's Seminary at Troy, New York, and helped establish North American College in Rome. Began the erection of St. Patrick's Cathedral in 1858. During Civil War he was sent by the United States government as a special envoy to Europe to promote the cause of the Union. He was successful in gaining the political sympathies of France, Ireland, and Italy.

HUGO OF ST. VICTOR (c. 1096-1141), theologian and mystic, born in Saxony. In 1115 he entered the monastery of St. Victor in Paris, where he spent the rest of his life studying, teaching, and writing. In 1133 he was chosen as head of the school. One of the most notable of the medieval mystics. His mysticism was strongly influenced by the scholastic thinking of the age. Argued that the soul has a threefold faculty of apprehension and vision; flesh, the reason, and contemplation. This faculty can have stages of activity: *cogitatio,* or apprehension of objects in their external forms; *meditatio,* study of the inner meaning and essence; and *contemplatio,* insight into the truth and the vision of God.

HUMBERT (d. 1061), Roman Catholic reform leader and cardinal, a monk of Moyenmoutier, Lorraine, called to Rome by Pope Leo IX in 1049. In 1050 appointed archbishop of Sicily, and cardinal bishop of Silva Candida. In 1053 Leo IX sent Humbert as a member of an embassy to the emperor at Constantinople to effect an ecclesiastical peace treaty between the East and the West. The patriarch of Constantinople, Michael Cerularius, treated the Roman legates with contempt, burning in their presence a controversial tractate which Cardinal Humbert had prepared. Following this on July 16, 1054 the Roman legates, on behalf of the pope, placed on the altar of the Church of St. Sophia a decree of excommunication against the patriarch and his adherents. The patriarch in turn excommunicated the pope and his followers. This act led to the final severance of the Eastern church from the Western. Cardinal Humbert was intent on reform. In 1056 published his *Three Books against Simoniacs;* in this he expanded simony to include lay investiture, thus expressing opposition to secular interference in the appointments of church offices. In 1059 Humbert also wrote the revised decree for election of the pope, which is essentially the plan in use by the Roman Catholic church today. A strong opponent of Berengar of Tours in the Eucharistic Controversy. Humbert's influence upon the papacy and on the church was strong until the time of his death, 1061. For several years he was chancellor and librarian at the Vatican. Next to Cardinal Hildebrand, who became Pope Gregory VII; he was perhaps the most influential cardinal of his day.

HUME (hūm), **DAVID** (1711-1776), Scottish philosopher and historian, born in Edinburgh, studied at home and at the University of Edinburgh. Went to France, and there completed his chief philosophical work, *Treatise of Human Nature,* which embodied the essence of his skeptical philosophy. He turned his attention to ethics and political economy, writing *Essays Moral and Political*. It attained immediate success. He turned to tutoring, then took up residence for twelve years in Edinburgh and became librarian of the Faculty of Advocates during which time he worked on his multi-volume Tory oriented *History of England*. Sought to restate his *Treatise* in more acceptable fashion by writing *Philosophical Essays Concerning Human Understanding,* in 1748. Wrote also an autobiography, *My Own Life,* which was published posthumously. Years 1762 to 1765 he served as secretary of the British embassy in Paris. From 1767 to 1768 was undersecretary of state in London. Retired to Edinburgh to spend the rest of his life. Hume's philosophy was essentially an extension of John Locke and George Berkeley, and a foundation for Immanuel Kant. Accepted the theory of evolutionary development of religion. His philosophy had no place for miracles. It was a skeptical philosophy denying the existence of the individual self, holding that men are nothing but a bundle or collection of different perceptions. Nothing exists but perceptions (impressions and ideas). All existing ideas are derived from impressions; that is, from external sensations, and inner feelings or emotions. Hume's philosophy has been carried forward in empiricism and positivism which undercut revealed theology.

HUNT, JOHN (1812-1848), English missionary to Fiji, born at Hykeham Moor, near Lincoln, England. After conversion at age seventeen joined the Wesleyan society, and turned to preaching and missionary work. Studied for about three years (1835-1838) at Wesleyan Theological Institute at Hoxton. Ordained, 1838, married, and appointed by the Wesleyan Missionary Society of London to go to Fiji. The Hunts, the James Calverts, and the J. T. Jaggars arrived in Fiji early in 1839. Hunt and his wife were appointed to an isolated station at Rewa, but seven months later were transferred to Somosomo, both very difficult and dangerous areas in which to work. After three years of unremitting toil at the latter station the Hunts removed to Viwa to spend his last six years. In 1845 a great religious awakening took place, including the conversion of the queen of Viwa. Hunt "became a living example to all missionaries through those islands." A hardworking missionary, by 1853 translated the New Testament and Old Testament by 1864 administered medicine to the sick, wrote books, taught the people, and preached.

HUNT, ROBERT (c. 1568-1608), First Episcopal clergyman in America. Born in Reculverin, Kent. Educated in Cambridge. Served in two English parishes. Went under the Virginia Company to America as chaplain in 1606 with expedition that founded Jamestown. Held first service in America under a sailcloth hung from trees and a board nailed to two trees for the pulpit.

HUNT, WILLIAM HOLMAN (1827-1910), English painter of religious subjects, born in London, England, began early to study art at the Royal Academy, and was admitted as a member in 1844. Possessed an essentially pious nature and early evinced a taste for morality in painting, revolting against the popular art tastes of the time. In 1848, along with D. G. Rossetti and J. E. Millais and a few other young painters, initiated the Pre-Raphaelite Brotherhood. In 1854 painted his famous "The Light of the World." In 1854 and again in 1875, went to Palestine to get local color for Bible paintings. Other religious pictures which he painted were: "The Scapegoat," "Triumph of the Innocents," "The Awakened Conscience," "Our Saviour Entering the Temple," "The Shadow of Death," "Nazareth," "Christ among the Doctors," "Shadow of the Cross," and "Plains of Esdraelon." In 1904 reproduced a life-size copy of "The Light of the World" for St. Paul's Cathedral. The original painting hangs in Keble College, Oxford. Wrote *Pre-Raphaelism and the Pre-Raphaelite Brotherhood*. He was a member of the Order of Merit.

HUNTINGDON, SELINA HASTINGS, COUNTESS (1707-1791), founder of Countess of Huntingdon's Connection or Calvinistic Methodists, born at Stanton Harold, Leicestershire, England. Maiden name was Shirley, and in 1728 married Hastings, ninth earl of Huntingdon. Converted through the influence of her sister-in-law, Lady Margaret Hastings, allied herself with the Methodists, attended regularly the meetings held by the Wesleys in Fetter Lane, and joined the first society formed there in 1738. After death of her two sons in 1743 and of her husband in 1746 devoted herself and her wealth enthusiastically to the advancement of Methodism. In 1747 she made George Whitefield one of her chaplains and threw open her London house for religious services to win upper class. She built or acquired numerous chapels in various parts of England and placed chaplains in them. In 1768 established at Trevecca in South Wales a special seminary for the training of chaplains. Appointed Fletcher of Madelay to have oversight of this work. Until 1780 Lady Huntingdon and her chaplains continued as members of the Church of England, but in that year they were declared dissenters and her chapels were registered as dissenting places of worship in 1781. In 1790 she formed an association. When the breach occurred between Wesley and Whitefield, Lady Huntingdon sided with Whitefield, at his death becoming sole trustee of his institutions in Georgia. In 1790 she created a trust for the management of the chapels and college after her death.

HUNTINGTON, WILLIAM REED (1838-1909), American Protestant Episcopal ecumenist. Born Lowell, Mass. Educated at Harvard and ordained in 1862. Served churches in Massachusetts and New York City from 1862 to 1909. Helped in the construction of the Cathedral of St. John the Divine in New York City. Responsible for the "Lambeth Quadrilateral" in 1884 of Lambeth Conference for unity on the bases of the Bible, Apostles' and Nicene Creeds, two sacraments, and the historic episcopate.

HURLBUT, JESSE LYMAN (1843-1930), American Methodist Episcopal clergyman, born in New York City, educated in Wesleyan University, Middleton, Connecticut, and in Pennington, New Jersey. After entering the Methodist ministry held various pastorates between 1865 and 1879 in New Jersey and New York. Appointed an agent of the Sunday School Union of his denomination for five years. From 1884 to 1888 assistant Sunday school literature editor, and from 1888 to 1900 editor and secretary of the Sunday School Union and Tract Society. Hurlbut was one of the founders of the Epworth League of which he was the secretary (1889-1892). For some years associated with Dr. J. H. Vincent in the direction of the Chautauqua Literary and Scientific Circle. In 1901 resumed the active ministry, and was successively pastor at Morristown, South Orange, and Bloomfield in New Jersey, until 1909, when he was named district superintendent of the Newark district (1909-1914). From 1914 until retirement in 1918, director of the Biblical Institute of Newark. Wrote thirty books on Bible study, Bible history, and Sunday school work. Some of chief works were: *Bible Atlas: A Manual of Bible Geography and History; Studies in the Four Gospels; Studies in the Old Testament;* and *Story of Jesus.* Died in 1930, age eighty-eight.

HURST (hûrst), **JOHN FLETCHER** (1834-1903), American Methodist clergyman and church historian, born near Salem, Maryland, educated at Dickinson College, Carlisle, Pennsylvania, and at universities of Halle and Heidelberg, Germany. Taught classics two years at Dickinson College, was pastor in Newark, New Jersey for eight years. From 1866 to 1871 professor of theology in the Mission Institute of the Methodist Episcopal Church for the training of German ministers, first at Bremen and then at Frankfurt. Traveled extensively in Europe, Syria, and Egypt. Returning to the United States, was professor of historical theology in Drew Theological Seminary, Madison, New Jersey from 1871 to 1880, also president from 1873 to 1880. In 1880 elected bishop of his denomination, and subsequently spent much time visiting missions and conferences in Europe and India. In 1898 elected chancellor of the American University (Methodist Episcopal), Washington, D.C., an institution he had helped to found. Translated K. R. Hagenbach's *History of the Church in the Eighteenth and Nineteenth Centuries,* and J. J. Van Oosterzee's *Apologetical Letters on John's Gospel*. Some of his many books are: *Short History of the Church in the United States, History of the Christian Church, History of Methodism,* and *The Literature of Theology.*

HUS, JOHN (c. 1373-1415), Bohemian Reformer, born of peasant parentage in Husinec, Bohemia, received bachelor's and master's degrees at the University of Prague, and by 1396 was lecturing on theology at the university. In 1402 ordained to the priesthood and became rector of the University of Prague. A powerful preacher and occupied Bethlehem Chapel, most influential pulpit in Prague. A loyal member of the Roman Catholic church, but had the same desire for church reform and doctrinal purity as Wycliffe of England. Translated the *Trialogues* of Wycliffe from English into the common language of the people of Bohemia, preached to them the same doctrine Wycliffe had preached in England. This movement in Bohemia was at first known as Wycliffism, but as Hus gained the confidence and respect of the people, his movement became popularly known as Hussitism. By 1409 Hus came to be the leader of the national Bohemian party at the university. Became outspoken for church reform, and for political and religious rights of people. Clergy branded him a heretic and his teaching heresy. The whole nation rallied around him. Hus was excommunicated, yet continued to write and preach. Wrote in 1413 *Of the Church,* in which he attacked transubstantiation, subservience to the pope, the popular belief in saints, the efficacy of the absolution of a so-called vicarious priest, unconditional obedience to earthly rulers, and simony, all of which were extremely prevalent. He made the Holy Scriptures the only rule in matters of religion and faith. In 1414, summoned before the Council of Constance. Though promised safe conduct and fair treatment by King Wenceslaus and Emperor Sigismund and also by the pope, he was hastily prosecuted, condemned, and imprisoned. Year 1415, he was burned at the stake. When the news reached Bohemia it incited great indignation throughout the country. Hus became not only a national hero, but a martyr as well.

HUTCHINSON, ANNE (1591-1643), American colonial religious leader, born in Alford, Lincolnshire, England, daughter of Rev. Francis Marbury, married William Hutchinson in 1612, and became mother of fourteen children. In 1634 migrated to Boston with her husband and family. A thorough student of the Bible. Began to propagate the "antinomian" doctrine of the "covenant of grace" in contradistinction to the current preaching of the "covenant of works," or in other words, to teach redemption through faith rather than through deeds. Gained a considerable following and great controversies ensued. In a synod called to try her, she was charged with heresy and sedition, and was banished from the Massachusetts Bay colony. With friends she fled to Rhode Island, where Dr. John Clarke and others had recently established a colony. They purchased from the Narragansett Indians the island of Aquidneck and set up a community on the principle that no one was to be "accounted a delinquent for doctrine," and called the place Portsmouth. Her husband shared her views and after his death, 1642, she and her family of fifteen persons moved to a Dutch colony in New York for greater security. In 1643 she and all but one daughter were murdered by the Indians, who were at war with the Dutch.

HUTTEN, ULRICH VON (1488-1523), Humanist, poet, satirist, and German Renaissance Reformer, born at Steckelberg, near Fulda in Hesse. Placed in a Benedictine monastery at Fulda at the age of eleven. Six years later fled from the monastery to enter upon humanistic studies at Erfurt, Cologne, and Frankfurt-on-the-Oder. Visited Wittenberg, Leipzig, and Vienna (1510-1512), then in order to be reconciled to estranged father began the study of law at Pavia and Bologna. In 1517 returned to Germany, and settled there permanently, receiving a position at the court of elector Albert of Brandenburg, Archbishop of Mainz, and a patron of the new learning. In the same year crowned poet laureate and was knighted by Emperor Maximilian. The great aim of his life was to aid Luther in freeing Germany from the yoke of Rome. For this cause wrote and fought with great valor. For a while was under the protection of, and worked with, Franz von Sickingen, an imperial soldier and a protector of the Reformers. Though often working in unison with the Reformers, and greatly assisting them in their efforts, he was not a Reformer himself, but rather a satirist and a knight-errant. In the conflict of Reuchlin with Pfefferkorn and the Dominicans, he defended Reuchlin and favored the punishment of Pfefferkorn. Hutten's plans for uniting Germany against the pope failed and former friend Erasmus turned against him.

HUTTER (HUTER), JACOB (d. 1536). Anabaptist minister, from Moos in the Tyrol. A minister of a group of Swiss Brethren. Went to Moravia where Hübmaier and others were preaching Anabaptist doctrines, and were baptizing large numbers of converts. Several hundred, following the leadership of Jacob Widermann, separated from the rest, and established a common household (Bruderhof) or "community of goods." Hutter united with this branch of the Anabaptists. In 1535 was chosen their head pastor. In months following brought many hundreds of Brethren from Tyrol to Moravia. Hutter continued to advocate communal ownership of property, a principle to which his followers adhere today. From the beginning of their movement, they repudiated infant baptism, the alliance of church and state, and participation in war. They believed in religious freedom and consequently, in common with other Anabaptists, suffered much persecution from the state and the Roman Catholic church, as well as from other Reformation groups. In 1536, the very year that Menno Simons renounced the Roman Catholic church, Hutter was burned at the stake at Innsbruck in the Tyrol. Followers were scattered in Moravia, then went to Russia and Rumania. Finally, together with many Russian Mennonites, came to South Dakota in the United States. In the early days they were strongly evangelistic and missionary minded. Today the Hutterites, and the body closely related to them, the Bruderhof settlements, are found in several localities in North America, and even in South America.

HUXLEY, THOMAS HENRY (1825-1895), English biologist, born at Ealing, a suburb of London, studied medicine at Charing Cross

Hospital, took his medical degree from the University of London, admitted to the Royal College of Surgeons in 1845. In 1846-1850, assistant surgeon on the *Rattlesnake* of the royal navy which was sent on an expedition in Australian waters. During these four years he intimately studied the animal life of the sea in this area. In 1851 elected a Fellow of the Royal Society. In 1854 Huxley became professor of natural history and paleontology at the Royal School of Mines where he taught for thirty-one years. Lectured on biology at the Royal College of Surgeons, held several governmental and educational positions, and made a member of various scientific societies. In 1883 Huxley received the crowning honor of his life when elected president of the Royal Society. He came to America in 1876 and delivered lectures on evolution in New York, and at Johns Hopkins University. In later years attacks on Christian orthodoxy became more persistent. He carried his agnosticism into the field of New Testament study, holding that one could not be certain of knowledge as to the teachings and doctrine of Christ. Between 1885 and 1895 wrote many essays on the relation of science to Hebrew and Christian tradition, and on the evolution of theology and ethics. His chief writings: *Zoological Evidence of Man's Place in Nature; Lay Sermons, Essays and Reviews; Manual of the Comparative Anatomy of Vertebrated Animals; Elementary Psychology; Science and Culture;* and *Evolution and Ethics.*

HYDE, JOHN (1865-1912), born in Carrolton, Illinois. Educated at Carthage College and McCormick Seminary in Chicago. Went to India as a village missionary in 1892. In 1904 helped found the Punjab Prayer Union. Returned to the USA via England in 1911. Prayed for and won several persons a day to faith in Christ.

HYPATIA (hī pā'shĭ ȧ), (c. 375-415), Neoplatonic philosopher, famous woman teacher of pagan philosophy, born in Alexandria. Studied in Athens and became a distinguished lecturer on philosophy, and ultimately the recognized head of the Neoplatonic school in Alexandria. Among her students was Synesius, who later became bishop of Ptolemais. Incurred the enmity of Cyril, bishop of Alexandria, who suspicioned her of inciting Orestes, the pagan prefect of Alexandria, against the Christians. In the name of Christianity Cyril is said to have stirred up a fanatical mob against her under the leadership of Peter, a reader in his church. She was brutally murdered in the street. Her tragic fate provides the theme for the novel *Hypatia* by Charles Kingsley.

I

IBAS (ī'băs) **of Edessa** (d. 457) Bishop of Edessa (435-457), born in Syria. A friend of Nestorius and an ardent admirer of Theodore of Mopsuestia, whose writings he translated into Syrian. He strongly opposed the Monophysites. As a presbyter had attended the Council of Ephesus in 431. Later when a bishop, having charged Cyril of Alexandria with the heresy of Apollinarianism, he was called to appear at the "Council of Robbers" in 449. Here he was condemned on the charge of following the Nestorians and was deposed without even a trial. Two years later at the Council of Chalcedon (451) Ibas was restored to the Church and to his charge, on condition of his anathematizing Nestorius and Eutyches, and was declared orthodox. Ibas was a translator and transmitter rather than an original author. Had a great and lasting influence upon the school at Edessa.

IGNATIUS (d. 117), Bishop of Antioch. He was likely a native of Syria, a pupil of the apostle John, and the second or the third bishop of the church at Antioch, Syria. We know little of Ignatius except what he tells us in the seven genuine letters to the churches that are ascribed to him. A man of apostolic character, governed the church with care. A devoted son of the church, loving Christ supremely and honoring Him as God incarnate. Spoke of Christ as the God-Man. Ignatius had a positive part in the development of the episcopacy in the church, and was the first to use the term, "Catholic church." Lived in an age when it seemed proper to glorify and even court martyrdom. His *Epistles* were written during his journey from Antioch to his martyrdom. First to speak of a threefold order of deacon, elder, and monarchical bishop.

IGNATIUS OF LOYOLA (INIGO LOPEZ DE RECALDE) (1491-1556), founder of the Society of Jesus, born of a noble family at the castle of Loyola in the province of Guipuzcoa, Spain. Spent youth in the court of Ferdinand. In 1521 in the battle of Pampelona wounded and lamed for life. Through reading the lives of Christ, St. Dominic, and St. Francis led to dedicate his life to the service of Jesus Christ and the Holy Virgin. At age thirty went to a Dominican monastery at Manresa. Like Luther he found that mortifying the flesh could not bring peace to his troubled soul. He finally found peace and satisfaction in yielding himself with full abandon to the church and its traditions and to the authority of the pope. His practice of severe self-discipline and the remarkable divine visions which he claimed to have received after his dedication to the church, provided the background and the experiences which he recorded in his *Spiritual Exercises* (1522). He first made a pilgrimage to Palestine, decided to turn from begging and rigid asceticism to study. In 1524 at age thirty-three began to prepare for the priesthood. In pursuit of his education first went to Barcelona where he sat among the schoolboys to study Latin. Went to the Universities of Alcala and Salamanca in Spain, thence to the University of Paris. At Paris gathered around him a little band of younger students whose lives were molded by his dynamic personality, spiritual devotion, and deep religious life. Among them was the great and famous future missionary, Francis Xavier. During these years of study, Loyola constantly visited the hospitals, ministering to the sick and poor. In 1529 finished his Latin course and by 1534 received his master's degree in philosophy. After two more years in theology, at age forty-five, after fifteen years of preparation he was ready for a life career. In 1534, Ignatius and his six companions took the vows of poverty, chastity, and obedience, and formed the Society of Jesus (Jesuit Order). They added to these three vows, their purpose to do mission work for the church. With these four vows, and the *Spiritual Exercises,* they were ready to seek the pope's approval and benediction. This was received from Pope Paul III in 1540. Loyola soon after was made the first general of the new order. They became active teachers, preachers, confessors, and workers of mercy. They became a great power for the papacy and for the Catholic church, and leaders in the Counter Reformation. Loyola was canonized by Pope Gregory XV in 1622. In 1551 he founded the Roman College.

INGE (ĭng), **WILLIAM RALPH** (1860-1954), Anglican divine, born at Craike, Yorkshire, England, educated at Eton and at King's College, Cambridge. In 1884-1888 assistant master at Eton; and fellow and tutor at Hertford College, Oxford (1889-1905). Vicar of All Saints Church, Ennismore Garden (1905-1907); Lady Margaret professor of divinity and fellow of Jesus College, Cambridge (1907-1911); and dean of St. Paul's cathedral (1911-1934). Inge attracted attention as a prophet of doom, who denounced the present and had little hope for the future in either religion, democracy, or contemporary civilization. Over the years special lecturer in Scotland, England, and the United States. Select preacher at both Cambridge and Oxford on several occasions. In 1902 examining chaplain for the Bishop of Lichfield. Dean Inge held many honorary degrees and was knighted in 1930. He retired in 1934 and died in 1954 at the age of ninety-three. A few of his many books: *Faith and Knowledge, Christian Mysticism, Types of Christian Saintliness, Personal Religion and the Life of Devotion, The Church in the World,* and *Lay Thoughts of a Dean*.

INGERSOLL (ĭng′ gẽr sôl), **ROBERT GREEN** (1833-1899), American lawyer, politician, orator, and agnostic, born at Dresden, New York, son of a Congregational minister. Studied law and admitted to the Illinois bar in 1854. Lawyer in Illinois, Washington, D.C. and New York. Soon became prominent in the courts and in Democratic politics. In 1860 nominated for Congress by the Democratic party. From 1861 to 1863 served as colonel of the Eleventh Illinois Cavalry in the Civil War. After the war turned Republican, and in 1867 appointed Attorney General of Illinois. Became campaign speaker for the party and made the presidential nomination speech for James G. Blaine in 1876. Moved to Washington, D.C. to engage in the practice of federal law, and later to New York City, where he became a brilliant corporation and trial lawyer. From 1856 till death turned the powers of his oratory to attacking Christianity. Some of his lectures: *What is Religion? Some Mistakes of Moses, The Gods, The Ghosts, About the Holy Bible, Why I am an Agnostic*.

INGLIS, CHARLES (1734-1816), first North American colonial Anglican bishop. Born and educated in Donegal, Ireland. Taught school some years and ordained in 1758 in London in the Anglican church. Anglican missionary to Dover, Delaware. Assistant in Trinity Church, New York from 1765. Lost church and property during the American Revolution and fled to Nova Scotia in 1783. Consecrated bishop in England for Nova Scotia in 1787. In 1788 founded King's College at Windsor, Nova Scotia.

INNOCENT III (LOTARIO DE CONTI) (1161-1216), pope (1198-1216), born at Anagni, educated in Rome, Paris, and Bologna. In 1190, at age 29 made cardinal deacon. In 1198 at age thirty-seven became pope. As pope, saw his first task that of restoring the prestige of the papacy. He had completely grasped the papal idea of absolute civil and ecclesiastical control. He wanted to make the church a theocracy with the pope as absolute ruler over both church and state. He excommunicated John of England and Philip of France, annulled royal marriages, removed bishops from their congregations, crowned kings, mediated between kings, permitted a new crusade to the Holy Land (the fourth), and attempted to reunite the Greek and the Latin churches. Added to the list of the pope's titles that of "Vicar of God." Developed and used the dreadful instrument of the interdict. The crowning act of his reign was the convening and directing of the Fourth Lateran Council in 1215, the greatest church council of the Middle Ages. Council established annual confession and mass and fixed the dogma of transubstantiation. Sanctioned and gave his blessing to the organization of the Franciscan Order. A zealous protector of the orthodox faith, and an opponent of heresy, especially among the Albigenses. Turned the spirit and power of the crusades against the Moslems into a war against heretics. His great political and ecclesiastical achievements brought the papacy to the very pinnacle of its power and prestige.

IRENAEUS (fl. last quarter of second century), Bishop of Lyons, probably born in Smyrna in western Asia Minor, early education seems to have included a study of the Greek poets and philosophers to whom he often referred in his writings. Early Christian training was under Polycarp, Bishop of Smyrna, and other presbyters of Asia Minor. May have assisted Polycarp in earlier years. The Asia Minor churches planted Christianity in Gaul, and Irenaeus may have been sent there as a missionary. He had been serving the church at Lugdunum for several years as presbyter, when in 177 aged Pothinus, bishop of Lyons, fell victim to the persecution under Marcus Aurelius. The next year Irenaeus was elected to succeed Pothinus in this difficult and dangerous post. He labored for many years with zeal and success, in literary activity, pastoral work, and missionary preaching. According to Gregory of Tours he converted almost the entire population of Lyons and sent other missionaries to other parts of pagan Europe. His greatest literary work, written in Gaul about 185, was *Against All Heresies,* a defense of the faith against the Gnostics and other heretics in which he upheld Christ's Incarnation as flesh, His Crucifixion and resurrection as history. He had a Rule of faith and upheld apostolic succession. His writings freely used the Bible. First of the Fathers to make full use of the New Testament. Also showed the unity of the Old and New Testaments.

IRELAND, JOHN (1838-1918). Born Burnchurch, Ireland. Educated in USA and France. Ordained in 1861. Attended Vatican

I. Chaplain in Union Army (1861-1862). Bishop of Moronea (1875-1884) and bishop of St. Paul (1884) and archbishop (1888). Opposed ultramontanism and ethnic divisions in the church. Promoted parochial school system and founded the Catholic University of America in Washington, D.C. in 1889.

IRELAND, JOHN (1761-1842), Anglican minister, dean of Westminster, and philanthropist, born at Ashburton, Devonshire, England; after studying at the free grammar school at Ashburton, attended Oriel College, Oxford. Successively curate of a small church near Ashburton, vicar of Croydon, reader and chaplain to the earl of Liverpool, prebendery in Westminster Abbey, and subdeacon of Westminster. In 1813 declined an invitation to become regius professor of divinity at Oxford. In 1816 became dean of Westminster, rector of Islip in Oxfordshire, and dean of the order of Bath. Having acquired considerable wealth used it generously in founding scholarships at Oxford and prizes at Westminster School, and in furthering free education. Also set aside funds for several old persons of his home town. Left ten thousand pounds to establish a professorship of biblical exegesis at Oxford, a professorship held for years by H. P. Liddon, also left a sum for a new church at Westminster. He wrote *Paganism and Christianity Compared*.

IRENE (c. 752-803), Byzantine empress. Married Leo IV in 769 and on his death in 780 became sole empress until about the end of the century. Brought back worship of icons and called second Niceean Council in 787 which established veneration but not worship of icons.

IRONSIDE, HENRY ALLAN ("Harry") (1878-1951), American clergyman, born in Toronto, Canada. Before the age of two his father died. His mother moved the family to Los Angeles, California in 1886. From the time he was eight read the Bible through at least once each year. Conversion took place at age fourteen. He began preaching immediately. Joined the Salvation Army, and entered the Oakland Training Garrison to become an officer. This was his only formal education beyond the grammar school. Became known as the "Boy Preacher of Los Angeles." After six years with the Salvation Army, in 1896, joined the Plymouth Brethren. Spent thirty-four years in preaching and Bible Conference teaching, traveling over the United States and Canada. During two months each summer for a dozen or more years worked among the Indians of the Southwest. After 1924 held many meetings under the direction of the Moody Bible Institute. Visiting professor at Dallas Theological Seminary from 1925 to 1943. In 1914 became president of the Western Book and Tract Company, which he had helped organize. From 1930 to 1948 pastor at the Moody Memorial Church in Chicago, his only pastorate. His preaching, radio, and writing ministry were very fruitful. During time of his pastorate traveled much in the United States and Canada, and in the British Isles preaching. Resigned from pastorate in 1948. Died in Cambridge, New Zealand in 1951 while on a preaching tour. At own request was buried there. Author of more than sixty volumes, many of which were pulpit messages comprising notes, lectures, and expositions of the books of the Bible. Other books: *Things Seen and Heard in Bible Lands, In the Heavenlies, Lamp of Prophecy, Changed by Beholding, The Way of Peace,* and *The Great Parenthesis*. Widely known as Harry Ironside.

IRVING, EDWARD (1792-1834), leader of the Catholic Apostolic or Irvingite church, born at Annan, Dumfriesshire, Scotland, educated at Edinburgh. In 1815 received license to preach in the Scottish Presbyterian church and became an assistant to Thomas Chalmers, Glasgow. In 1822 became pastor of a small congregation in the Caledonian Chapel in London. A popular preacher, attracting large crowds, especially among the educated classes. Began to publish books, thus adding to his popularity. In later years he, Henry Drummond, and others became deeply interested in the study of apocalypticism, including gifts, tongues, prophecies, healings, and raising the dead. Irving was forced to retire from his church at Regent Square and was deposed from the Presbyterian ministry in 1832 as a heretic. He, Drummond, Cardale, Taplin, and about eight hundred others in 1832 formed a new religious body, seeking to model it exactly on the line of apostolic Christianity, naming it the Catholic Apostolic church, known popularly as the Irvingite church. The church "set aside" twelve apostles who were "divinely called," and not elected by the church. Edward Irving was not one of those "called" to the apostleship. The other "prophets" of the new order took over and relegated Irving to a minor place.

ISABELLA OF CASTILE (1451-1504), Queen of Castile, daughter of John II, king of Castile and Leon, and niece of Henry IV. In 1469 married Ferdinand II of Aragon. Isabella retained sole authority in Castilian affairs as long as she lived. The chief events of her reign were the discovery of America by Columbus, the conquest of Granada, and the expulsion of the Moors. Her confessor,

Cardinal Ximenes had a strong influence on her life and her reign.

ISIDORE (ĭz′y dōr) **of Seville** (sĕ vĭl′), (c. 560-636), born at Seville or Carthagena in southeastern Spain, of a distinguished Roman family of the orthodox Christian faith. He received education from his brother Leander, Archbishop of Seville from about 579 to 600. In 600 Isidore succeeded his brother as Archbishop of Seville. In this position became the great leader of the Spanish Church. He presided over the second council of Seville in 619, and over the largest council ever held in Spain, the fourth council of Toledo in 633. Was teacher, administrator, controversialist, and the greatest scholar of his day. Established a highly successful school at Seville. Through his influence other seminaries were established in different cities of Spain. Lived in a time of transition from the old Spanish to the new Hispano-Gothic culture. Did much to weld into a homogeneous nation the various peoples who had moved into Spain. Helped to eradicate Arianism and other heresies and to strengthen religious discipline. Greatest distinction, however, lay in literary endeavors. As a writer he was prolific and versatile. Is sometimes considered the father of Spanish literature. Was the first to attempt to write a universal encyclopedia, a work that preserved fragments of classical learning for posterity. Greatest work, the encyclopedic twenty books of *Origines* or *Etymologiarium Sive Originum Libri Viginti* in which he quoted 150 authors, both Christian and non-Christian. Work became the most used textbook of the Middle Ages.

IVERACH (ē′vĕ räkh), **JAMES** (1839-1922), Scottish theologian born in Caithness, Scotland, educated at the University also at New College, Edinburgh. Ordained to the ministry in 1869, held pastorates at West Calder, Edinburgh (1869-1874) and at Ferryhill, Aberdeen (1874-1887). Professor of apologetics and dogmatics in United Free Church College, Aberdeen (1887-1907), principal (1905-1907), professor of New Testament language and literature after 1907. Was moderator of the United Free Church in 1912-1913. Writings include *Life of Moses, Is God Knowable?,* and *Christianity and Evolution*. Also a contributor to the *Spectator*.

J

JABLONSKI, DANIEL ERNST (1660-1741), German Reformed theologian and Bishop of the Moravians, born at Nassenhuben, near Danzig, a maternal grandson of Johann Amos Comenius. Educated at the gymnasium of Lissa, Poland, at the University of Frankfurt-on-the-Oder, and at Oxford. In 1683 appointed Reformed preacher at Magdeburg, in 1686 became pastor of the Polish congregation and rector of the Moravian gymnasium at Lissa. In 1691 he became court preacher for Frederick I at Königsberg, in 1693 became court preacher at Berlin. In 1699 ordained Bishop of the Unity of the Brethren of Moravia and Bohemia, thus becoming one of last bishops of historic succession of the old Hussite Bohemian church. When Jablonski ordained David Nitschmann in 1735 and Count Zinzendorf in 1737 as bishops, he transferred the historic succession from the old line of Moravian and Bohemian Brethren to the younger branch of the Herrnhutters or the Reorganized Unity of the Brethren. Jablonski had great influence in Prussia, but he and Leibnitz failed in their attempt to unite all Protestants under the leadership of Prussia, and to introduce the episcopate into the Evangelical church. In 1733 he became president of the Berlin Academy of Sciences of which he had been one of the founders.

JACKSON, FREDERICK JOHN FOAKES (1855-1941), Anglican theologian and church historian, born in Ipswich, England, educated at Eton College and Trinity College, Cambridge. Ordained in 1880, became divinity lecturer in 1882, and fellow in 1886. From 1895 to 1916 dean and tutor in Jesus College, Cambridge; then Briggs Graduate Professor of Christian Institutions at Union Theological Seminary, New York (1916-1934). Also lectured in the Jewish Institute of Religion in New York and in the General Theological Seminary. Among books published after coming to America were: *History of the Christian Church, Biblical History of the Hebrews, Introduction to Church History, Studies in the Life of the Early Church,* and *Josephus of the Jews.* He collaborated with Kirsop Lake in writing *Origins of Christianity.*

JACKSON, SAMUEL MACAULAY (1851-1912), American Presbyterian clergyman, editor, educator, and philanthropist, born in New York City, educated at the College of New York City, Princeton Theological Seminary, Union Theological Seminary, and the universities of Leipzig and Berlin. Ordained in the Presbyterian ministry in 1876, and pastor of the Presbyterian Church in Norwood, New Jersey (1876-1880), after which time engaged in philanthropic, educational, and literary work. From 1885 onward served in various capacities in the Charity Organization Society, and also became recording secretary of the Prison Association of the State of New York. Edited nine volumes of *Handbooks for Practical Workers in Church and Philanthropy* (1898-1904). From 1895 until 1912, professor of church history at New York University. Jackson was a devoted disciple of Dr. Schaff, for whom he prepared material for a *Dictionary of the Bible*. Associated with Schaff in producing *A Religious Encyclopedia* in three volumes. Later editor-in-chief of the expansion of this encyclopedia in the *New Schaff-Herzog Encyclopedia of Religious Knowledge* (1907-1911). Editor for the religious literature in *Johnson's Universal Cyclopaedia,* and for Protestant theology and religious biography of the *New International Encyclopedia*. Wrote *A Concise Dictionary of Religious Knowledge,* and *Huldreich Zwingli, the Reformer of German Switzerland*. Secretary of American Society of Church History from 1888 to 1912.

JACKSON, SHELDON (1834-1909), Presbyterian educator and missionary to the American Indians and Eskimos, born at Minaville, New York, educated at Union College, Schenectady, New York, and Princeton Theological Seminary. Ordained in 1858. Ambition from childhood was to become a foreign missionary. A minister and missionary to both Indians and whites in western Wisconsin and southern Minnesota (1859-1869) and from 1870 to 1882 superintendent of Presbyterian missions over a vast area from Iowa and Minnesota to Nevada, New Mexico, and Arizona. Developed prefabricated churches. Railways and stage coach lines, as a matter of good business, gladly provided him free travel. With his family living in Denver he made sixteen round trips to and from home in five years. In one twelve-month period (1869-1870) covered twenty-nine thousand miles and organized twenty-three churches. Sheldon Jackson worked in Alaska where he labored from 1884 until retirement in 1907. In various places started schools for the natives, thus introducing the public school system, and opened many mission stations, one being near Point Barrow in the farthest north. In

1885 the United States government made him general agent of education for Alaska. In 1887 organized the Alaskan Society of Natural History and Ethnology at Sitka; in 1892 began the successful introduction of Siberian reindeer into Alaska; in 1896 aided in the founding of Westminster College at Salt Lake City, Utah; in 1897 was a special agent of the United States Government in transporting a colony of Laplanders with their reindeer to Alaska; in 1897 was Moderator of the Presbyterian General Assembly; and in 1899 established the first reindeer post office routes in America. Began a religious periodical, *The Rocky Mountain Presbyterian,* and edited the *North Star* at Sitka from 1887 to 1897. Wrote *Alaska and Missions on the North Pacific Coast; Education in Alaska,* and many annual reports for the government on education and domestic reindeer in Alaska. Few men in missionary history have accomplished so much in planting the Christian faith over so wide an area. Biographer summarizes the results of his work by stating that in nine states and three territories where he labored there had been organized before the time of his death six synods, thirty-one presbyteries, eight hundred eighty-six churches with 77,105 communicants. Sheldon Jackson was one "of the most apostolic men of modern times."

JACOB, HENRY(1563-1624), English Congregational leader. Born in Cheriton, Kent. Educated at St. Mary's Hall, Oxford. Joined the Brownists about 1590. Fled to Leiden in 1593 where he became a member of John Robinson's church. Founded the first permanent English Congregational church at Southwark in London in 1616 and issued a confession.

JACOBS, CHARLES MICHAEL (1875-1938), American Lutheran clergyman and educator, born at Gettysburg, Pennsylvania, studied at the University of Pennsylvania, the Lutheran Theological Seminary, Mt. Airy, Philadelphia; and at Leipzig, Germany. Ordained in the Lutheran ministry in 1899, served in pastorates in North Wales and Allentown, Pennsylvania (1899-1913). Professor of church history and director of the graduate school at the Lutheran Theological Seminary, Philadelphia (1913-1938), president, (1927-1938). An active churchman in the Lutheran church. Coeditor of *Luther's Works in English,* six volumes, *Luther's Correspondence, The Story of the Church—an Outline of Its History; Helps on the Road;* and *An Outline of Christian Doctrine*.

JAMES I (1566-1625), King of Scotland (1567-1603) and King of England (1603-1625), only son of Mary Stuart, Queen of Scots and Henry Stuart, Lord Darnley, born in Edinburgh Castle. Though a weakly child, received a good education in the classics and theology, and lived till nearly sixty. Upon mother's forced abdication in 1567, became James VI of Scotland, but a succession of regents ruled the kingdom until 1575 when he became nominal ruler. For twenty years he gave Scotland a good rule. His grandfather, James IV, had been married to Margaret, daughter of Henry VII of England. Elizabeth's death in 1603 left the English throne without an heir any closer than the Scottish king. Thus James VI of Scotland became James I of England, the first ruler of Great Britain and Ireland. The Puritans, hoping to gain his ear, presented him with the Millenary Petition, a petition supposedly signed by one thousand Puritan ministers. James, having decided to support the established church, gave answer that Presbyterianism "agreeth as well with monarchy as God and the devil," and that if the Puritans would not conform, he "would harry them out of the kingdom." He set forth in his 1598 *Trew Law of Free Monarchies* his divine right of kings concept. Permission to make a new translation of the Scriptures was the net gain of the Puritan ministers. In accordance with the king's promise, a group of learned divines were chosen to begin work on the translation of the Bible, which, completed in 1611, has become known as the Authorized or King James Version. James believed, as did his son Charles I (1625-1649), that the monarch and not Parliament was sovereign, holding that the king was divinely appointed to rule the people. Divided Ireland caused by his settling of Scots in northern Ireland. Through his poor planning England was drawn into the Thirty Years War. As a Scot and a ruler who showed little dignity of kingship, James was never popular or highly respected by the people of England. As a scholar James was interested in literature and did some writing, publishing a few works both in verse and in prose.

JAMES II (1633-1701), King of England, Scotland, and Ireland, born at St. James' Palace, London; son of Charles I and Henrietta Marie. Upon the restoration of his brother Charles II in 1660 became Duke of York and lord high admiral of England, which position he was forced to resign about 1671 when he embraced the Roman Catholic faith. Upon accession at the death of Charles in 1685, began almost at once to show special favor to the Roman Catholics, and showed evidence of intention to restore the Roman Catholic church in England. In 1687 published a declaration of liberty of conscience for all denominations in England and Scotland. The next year ordered it read in all the churches. The English bishops opposed this move and invited William of Orange, James' son-in-law to come to save the country from Roman Catholic tyranny. When William landed at Torbay in 1688, James escaped to France, was welcomed and given a place of refuge by Louis XIV. In 1689, with troops provided by Louis, James attacked Ireland, but was totally defeated by William at the battle of Boyne. James returned to France and resided at St. Germain's until his death in 1701. Last four years he spent in religious observances. Two of his daughters, Queen Mary and Princess Anne, survived him.

JAMES, WILLIAM (1842-1910), American psychologist and philosopher; one of the founders of pragmatism or empiricism, born in New York City, son of Henry James, a Swedenborgian theologian. Parents took him and his brother Henry to Europe, enrolled them in school in London, Paris, Boullogne-sur-mer, Geneva, and Bonn. Returning to America, James entered Lawrence Scientific School of Harvard University, and Harvard Medical School. Stopped schoolwork for a while to make a trip with Professor Agassiz to South America to study natural history. Then made a trip to Europe where he studied psychology and philosophy. Back in America in 1872 began a thirty-five-year period of teaching at Harvard, chiefly physiology, philosophy, and psychology. Continued until 1907 when he resigned because of ill health, becoming professor emeritus. Chief writing, *Principles of Psychology,* published in 1890, established him as one of the most influential thinkers of the day, and placed him in the front rank of modern psychologists. Placed psychology among the laboratory sciences based on experimental method, and then applied the empirical method also to religion and philosophy. In philosophy represented empirical idealism as opposed to absolute idealism. It was a philosophy of *meliorism* or betterment. To him the practical duty of man is to make himself and the world better. All depends on man's will. In 1899-1901 he was Gifford Lecturer on *Natural Religion* at the University of Edinburgh, and in 1908 Hibbert Lecturer on philosophy at Oxford. After writing and gaining world renown in his *Principles of Psychology* wrote *The Will to Believe, Human Immortality, Talks to Students and Teachers, The Varieties of Religious Experience,* and *The Meaning of Truth.* He popularized philosophy through his lectures on *Pragmatism: a New Name for Some Old Ways of Thinking,* which he delivered in the late years of his life.

JAMIESON, ROBERT (1802-1880), Scottish divine, born in Edinburgh, went to Edinburgh University to study medicine, but before completing course decided to prepare for the ministry and entered Divinity Hall. After graduation and ordination served for seven years in the parish of Weststruther, and for seven years in the parish of Currie Street, Edinburgh. At the time of the Disruption in 1843 tried to prevent a schism. In 1844 became minister of St. Paul's Free Church in Glasgow, continuing there until 1880. Jamieson was collaborator with A. R. Faucett and David Brown in preparing *A Commentary Critical, Experimental, and Practical on the Old and New Testaments.* Wrote about one-third of the commentary, the Pentateuch, and Joshua to Esther.

JANSEN, CORNELIUS OTTO (1585-1638), Dutch Roman Catholic theologian, Bishop of Ypres, father of Jansenism, born at Acquoi, in Utrecht province, Holland, studied theology at the College of Adrian VI in Louvain, where a dispute was going on between the Jesuits and those who held to a strict Augustinianism. Studied Greek for a time in Paris. Became president in 1617 and teacher of theology at the College of St. Pulcheria at Louvain. Through incessant study of Augustine, he and Du Vergier became more and more convinced that the Catholic church had deviated from the doctrine of the early church, and resolved to work for reform in the church. Jansen and his movement were somewhat to the Roman Catholic church what the Puritan movement was to the Anglican church. They strongly opposed the semi-Pelagian doctrine of the Jesuits with their "Jesuitical casuistry," and the Aristotelian philosophy of Thomas Aquinas and the church. Urged a return to an acceptance of the Pauline and Augustinian view of conversion or salvation through irresistible grace. In 1630 appointed regius professor of Holy Scriptures in Louvain, and in 1636 Bishop of Ypres. Toward the end of his life, after twenty-two years of study of Augustine, produced *Augustinus,* intended to be a digest of Augustine's teaching, a presentation of his own views, and a thrust at the Jesuits. Influence was strong and many deeply religious Catholics accepted his views, notably in the convent of Port Royal, near Paris. In fact Port Royal became a Jansenist convent. He tried to make it clear that he was not a Protestant, and endeavored to show that he did not accept the Reformation view of Augustine's doctrine of grace. Condemned by the pope, yet his influence continued in many quarters, especially through his pupil, Arnauld, through Pascal and Quesnel, also the Jansenists and Old Catholics of Holland.

JARRATT (jăr'rat), **DEVEREUX** (1733-1801), Episcopal minister, born in New Kent County, Virginia. Before nineteen he improved his education sufficiently to be able to take charge of a neighborhood school. About this time stayed in a home where it became his duty to read one of Flavel's sermons every night. These discourses helped lead to conversion during the great awakening in the colonies. Resolving to enter the ministry, went to England and was ordained by the Bishop of Chester in 1763. Upon return to the colonies in 1763 began service of nearly thirty years at Bath, Virginia. Though an Episcopalian minister he was very friendly with the Methodist leaders and much influenced by them. Courageously led in a revival movement that won thousands of converts. In the revival co-operated freely with the Methodists, who looked to him to administer the sacraments to their converts, since they as yet had no ordained ministers. To meet increasing need traveled continually, visiting twenty-nine counties for the purpose of ministering to the needs of Methodist converts.

JASPER, JOHN (1812-1901), Black Baptist preacher, born a slave on a plantation on the James River, Fluvanna County, Virginia. From a fellow slave learned to read only six months before time of conversion, 1839. Followed the example of father in becoming a preacher, became a favorite among the black people of Richmond, becoming famous over the state as a funeral preacher. Made himself master of the Bible and well able to defend his views, singular though some of them were. After emancipation gathered a congregation, and was preaching to several thousand people every Sunday. In 1878 preached a sermon on the power of God. The sermon, entitled, "The Sun Do Move," created a sensation, and he was called to preach it again and again, not only in Richmond but outside that city. Said to have preached this sermon two hundred fifty times. Jasper was the pre-eminent and last antebellum preacher among the blacks of the South.

JASPERS, CARL (1883-1969), German existentialist philosopher. Studied at Heidelberg. Taught philosophy at Heidelberg from 1921 to 1948 except when suspended by the Nazis from 1937 to 1945. From 1948 to 1969 taught at Basel. Taught that philosophy comes from within man to give ultimate meaning as man tries to become himself. Future comes through the decisions and actions of man. Source and goal of our existence is the transcendent within, around and beyond us. The key is human action.

JEFFERSON, CHARLES EDWARD (1860-1937), Congregational minister and author, born at Cambridge, Ohio, educated at Ohio Wesleyan University and School of Theology, Boston University. For two years superintendent of public schools in Worthington, Ohio. Ordained in 1887; after serving a few months in a little summer resort town church in New Hampshire, became pastor of the Central Congregational Church, Chelsea, Massachusetts, where he ministered from 1887 to 1898. From 1898 until death was pastor of the cosmopolitan Broadway Tabernacle, New York City. In 1914 became chairman of the executive committee of the Church Peace Union. Among his writings are *Quiet Hints to Growing Preachers, Doctrine and Deed, Things Fundamental, The Minister as Prophet, The Minister as Shepherd, The Building of the Church*.

JEFFERSON, THOMAS (1743-1826). Third president of the United States, born at Shadwell, Virginia. Educated at first privately, then at William and Mary College, admitted to the bar in 1767, becoming a successful lawyer. In 1769 elected to the House of Burgesses where he became a zealous member of the revolutionary party. Took a prominent part in the calling of the First Continental Congress in 1774, sent as delegate in 1775 and 1776; again in 1783-1784. Writer of the Declaration of Independence. In 1786 Jefferson's views on religious freedom were embodied in United States law in the famous Statute for Religious Freedom, by which separation of Church and State was accomplished. In 1779, became the second governor of Virginia. In 1784 sent to France to join Benjamin Franklin and John Adams in negotiating commercial matters with foreign countries, then succeeded Franklin as our minister plenipotentiary in the French court (1785-1789). In 1789 President Washington appointed Jefferson as Secretary of State. In controversy with Alexander Hamilton, he originated the Democratic party with emphasis on state's rights. Hamilton was the originator of the Federalist party. In 1801 elected to the presidency of the United States, in which office he served two terms. A great achievement of his administration was the purchase of Louisiana. Dispatched the Lewis and Clark Expedition; ordered war against the Algerian pirates; advocated the abolition of slavery. The foundation of the University of Virginia was the main achievement of his career. Rector of the university until his death. In religion, as well as in politics, Jefferson was a radical, an adherent of deism. Published: *Notes on the State of Virginia;* and *The Life and Morals of Jesus of Nazareth: Extracted Textually from the Gospels in Greek, Latin, French, and English*.

JEROME (HIERONYMUS, SOPHRONIUS EUSEBIUS) (c. 345-420), Bible translator, advocate of monasticism. Biblical scholar, born of Christian parents in Stridon, Dalmatia, at age twelve went to Rome for eight years of study, becoming proficient in Latin, Greek, and pagan authors. At nineteen became a Christian and was baptized by the pope. Spent two or three years in Gaul. Spent several years in semi-asceticism in Aquilea near Rome. Longing for a still deeper experience of God, made a long lonesome journey through the Orient to Antioch. In a severe illness while there, had a vision of Christ, who reproached him for his devotion to the Greek and Latin classics. Turning from them gave himself with new zeal to the study of the Christian Scriptures. Retired to a limestone cave in the desert of Chalcis southwest of Antioch, and employed a Jewish rabbi to assist him in learning Hebrew. Remaining at Antioch awhile, ordained a presbyter, though he was not required to fill the function of the office. Went in 379 to Constantinople to sit under the teaching of Gregory Nazianzen. In 382 Pope Damasus called Jerome to Rome to become papal secretary. When the pope decided to have a new translation of the Scriptures made from the original Hebrew and Greek, he commissioned Jerome to the task. Work of translating begun in Rome and completed years later in his monastery in Bethlehem. By the eighth century Jerome's translation of Old and New Testaments and the Apocrypha, known as the Latin Vulgate, became the officially recognized and authorized version of the Bible for the Catholic church, replacing all other Latin translations. Jerome spent last thirty-five years of his life (386-420) in his Bethlehem monastery meditating, studying, writing, translating, and supervising his monks. His *De Viris Illustribus* was a bibliography with biographic sketches of Christian writers.

JEROME OF PRAGUE (c. 1370-1416), Bohemian reformer, born at Prague in a well-to-do family, educated at University of Prague. A knight at the court of the King of Bohemia; and a well educated, much traveled, and highly eloquent man. On a visit to England in 1398 became interested in the *Dialogues* and *Trialogues* of Wycliffe. On his return to Bohemia in 1407 he carried back to his house the teachings of Wycliffe. Though not a priest he sometimes preached. Went from university to university proclaiming the views of Wycliffe, often being driven away. Finally returned to Prague, joined with John Hus in teaching Wycliffe's doctrines. In 1415 followed Hus to Constance to aid his friend if possible. When Hus was condemned Jerome was captured and taken to Constance. Under trial his courage failed and he recanted. In an eloquent address renounced his weak renunciation. The next year after Hus's death, 1416, he was burned on the same spot where Hus had died just one year prior.

JESSUP, HENRY HARRIS (1832-1910), American Presbyterian missionary to Syria, born at Montrose, Pennsylvania, graduated from Yale University and Union Theological Seminary. In 1855 ordained, and went to Tripoli, Syria, the next year under auspices of American Board of Commissioners for Foreign Missions. Remained there until 1860, then went to Beirut. In 1870 transferred to the Presbyterian Board of Foreign Missions, and became professor of church history, theology, and homiletics in the Syria Theological Seminary, Beirut. A member of the Turco-American commission on indemnities after the massacres of 1860-1861. A missionary editor of the Arabic journal, *El-Nesrah*. Wrote *Women of the Arabs; The Mohammedan Missionary Problem; The Greek Church and Protestant Missions; Autobiography and History of the Syrian Mission; Fifty-Three Years in Syria*. Jessup was moderator of the General Assembly of the Presbyterian church in 1879.

JEWEL, JOHN (1522-1571), Bishop of Salisbury. Born in Devonshire. Educated at Merton and Corpus Christi Colleges, Oxford. Fellow at latter from 1542 to 1553. Mary's accession to the English throne forced him to flee in 1555 to Frankfurt and then Strassburg. Bishop of Lambeth in 1560 on his return to England. Built cathedral Library and helped educate Richard Hooker. In his *Apology for the Anglican Church* in 1562 pointed out the need of the Reformation and described the beliefs and rites of his denomination. He set forth the Anglican position as opposed to the Roman Catholic.

JIMENES DE CISNEROS, FRANCISCO. See **XIMENES.**

JOACHIM OF FIORE (c. 1135-1202), eschatological philosopher of history. Born in Calabria, Italy. Became Cistercian monk on pilgrimage to Palestine. Bishop of Arezzo in 1177. In 1192 founded the order of San Giovanni del Fiore which received papal approval in 1196. Taught three ages, the first of the Old Testament under the law and Moses which was the age of God the Father, the second age of the son, Christ with New Testament grace of Paul until 1260, and the third age of the Holy Spirit with John's stress on love from 1260 when the whole world would be won. These and other ideas set forth in *The Eternal Gospel*.

JOGUES, ISAAC (1607-1646), Jesuit missionary martyr. Born in Orleans, France. Educated by the Jesuits at Rouen, La Fleche, and Paris. Became Jesuit in 1624 and ordained in 1636 as a missionary to the Huron Indians in Canada. Tortured by the Iroquois but saved by the Dutch and returned to France. Returned to Quebec in 1644 and in 1646 was taken and killed by the Iroquois.

JOAN of ARC or JEANNE D'ARC or JEANNE LA PUCELLE (1412-1431), "The Maid of Orleans," heroine of France, born in Domremy, Champagne. As a child of thirteen believed she heard celestial voices. In 1428 when the English were about to capture Orleans in the Hundred Years War, the voices exhorted her to come to her country's aid. She convinced Charles that she had a divine commission to aid the dauphin and to liberate France. She was given troops to command. She led them to a decisive victory. At the subsequent coronation of Charles VII at Rheims, she was given the place of honor beside the king. In 1430 she was captured by the Burgundians, allies of the English, and sold to the English, who in turn surrendered her to the ecclesiastical court at Rouen. There she was tried for heresy and sorcery, and for wearing masculine dress, then sentenced to death. Upon a forced confession of her error her sentence was cummuted to life imprisonment. When she recanted her confession, she was treated as a relapsed heretic, condemned to death, and burned at the stake as a witch and heretic in the old Market Square at Rouen at the age of nineteen. A quarter of a century later Charles VII ordered a retrial, when she was pronounced innocent and orthodox. In 1920 canonized by Pope Benedict XV. To this day Jeanne d'Arc is a national heroine of France. Literature and sculpture in France and in other countries have memorialized the name of Joan of Arc.

JOHN XXIII (CARDINAL BALDASSARE COSSA) (c. 1370-1419), one of three simultaneous popes in the papal schism, holding office 1410-1415, born in Naples of a noble Neapolitan family. In youth entered a military career, but later entered the service of the church. Studied law at Bologna; then entered the service of the papal curia. In 1402 became cardinal deacon, and the next year legate of Bologna. Fell out with rival Gregory XII, and became the leading spirit in the Council of Pisa (1409). Alexander V was made pope at this time, but died the year following, and Baldassare Cossa was elected to succeed him as John XXIII. In 1414 John called the council of Constance; but the council affirmed its superiority over the pope and proceeded to try Pope John on seventy charges which included almost every crime known to man. Deposed in 1415. Upon hearing of deposition, he submitted to his successor Martin V, and was imprisoned for four years. He was then released from prison and was appointed by Martin as Cardinal-bishop of Tusculum, and dean of the sacred college (college of cardinals). Survived his appointment only six months. Gregory XII resigned following his deposition, and was made Cardinal-bishop of Oporto, Portugal; but Benedict XIII (Pedro de Luna) refused to resign claim. As Roman Catholic historians deny John a rightful place in the papal succession and consider him an anti-pope, his title was taken by the pope who succeeded Pius XII in 1958.

JOHN XXIII (ANGELO GUISEPPE RONCALLI) (1881-1963), pope from 1958 to 1963. Born in Italy. Ordained in 1904. Became secretary to the bishop of Bergamo. In 1921 director of the Congregation for the Propagation of the faith in Italy. Papal diplomat in Bulgaria, Turkey, Greece, and France from 1925 to 1953. Cardinal and patriarch of Venice in 1953. Most important work was the calling of Vatican II for *aggiornamento* (renewal) of the church. Issued important encyclials on world peace, social justice and Christian unity. Had Protestant observers at the Vatican council.

JOHN (LACKLAND) (c. 1167-1216), King of England (1199-1216), born probably at Oxford, the youngest son of Henry II. A man of decided ability, and rapid in action but of ignoble spirit, low morals, and despotic temper. His reign was a succession of wrongs and insults to the English people and the English church. During absence of his brother Richard I, Coeur de Leon, on the Third Crusade in the East, John plotted to take the throne, but failed in attempt. On the death of Richard, 1199, however, being heir, he ascended the throne. Upon John's accession the people of France favored John's nephew Arthur, whereupon France opened war on England and deprived John of all his French possessions. In 1206 when the powerful Pope Innocent III appointed Cardinal Stephen Langton Archbishop of Canterbury, John refused to recognize the appointment. England was accordingly placed under the interdict in 1208, and John excommunicated and deposed, his throne transferred to Philip Augustus of France, until John consented to yield England as a fief to the pope of Rome, and agreed to pay an annual tribute of one thousand marks to Rome. John's autocratic rule led to an uprising among the nobles of England which culminated at Runnymede, where he was forced to sign the Magna Charta on June 15, 1215, in which he promised to levy no taxes without consent of those taxed and to permit fair trials by one's peers.

JOHN OF ANTIOCH (died 441), Bishop of Antioch (429-441), friend, fellow-townsman, and fellow-student of Nestorius. Became involved in the controversy over "Mary, Mother of God," the question that caused the condemnation of Nestorius. John opposed Cyril's invectives and accusations. John then began to incite other Asian bishops against Cyril. The breach between the two patriarchs became complete. Each denounced the other as heretical. When the Council of Ephesus was to be held in 431, Cyril took occasion to convene it before John could arrive, and hastily pushed through the condemnation of Nestorius. When John arrived he called a counter-council, claiming it to be the legitimate council. The two bishops anathemized each other. John openly defended Nestorious. Both John and Cyril gradually modified their views, each yielding to the other until an outward peace was effected in 433. John's action displeased some of the eastern pro-Nestorian bishops, and they broke off from John. John remained true to the orthodox party, even began a persecution of the Nestorians, which drove them across the border into Persia.

JOHN OF AVILA (JUAN DE AVILA) (1500-1569), Spanish mystic, the Apostle of Andalusia, born near Toledo, Spain, of humble but respectable birth. Educated at Salamanca and Alcala, being the pupil of the famous Dominican, Domingo de Soto. Ordained in 1525. For several years led a life of severest asceticism, a pious Catholic who urged the study of the Bible and preached a much purer gospel than did the most of the Catholic preachers of his day. Loved to preach to the common people and his converts were numbered among the thousands. He had intended to do missionary work in Mexico, but was persuaded by the Archbishop of Seville to turn his attention to work at home. Began his chief work as apostolic preacher of Andalusia in 1527. For nearly forty years was an indefatigable preacher among the cities of Andalusia, everywhere producing the deepest impression on the people. Health failed, he spent his last twenty years teaching in a monastery. John was the author of *Audi Filia* on Christian perfection.

JOHN OF THE CROSS (JUAN DE LA CRUZ (Baptized **JUAN DE YEPIS)** (1542-1591), Spanish Carmelite mystic and poet, born at Hontiveros (or Fontiveros), Avila, Spain. For seven years worked in a hospital while attending a Jesuit school. Received his higher education at Salamanca. In 1563, at age twenty-one, joined the Carmelite order. In 1567 ordained, calling himself "John of the Cross." The following year became a close friend and associate of Teresa of Avila, and helped her organize many Discalced Carmelite monasteries. Imprisoned for nine months at Toledo by some fellow Carmelites who opposed the reform orders. After escaping from prison became vicar-general of the order he had founded. Went from monastery to monastery strengthening the brethren and founding new houses. John's mysticism, like that of St. Teresa's, may be called empirical mysticism. They both started with the experience of their own meditation and thought. His axiom was: The soul must be emptied of self in order to be filled with God. His whole life and all his writings attested to that goal. Chief writings: *The Dark Night of the Soul, The Flame of Living Love, The Spiritual Canticle, The Ascent of Mount Carmel,* and *In an Obscure Night.*

JOHN OF DAMASCUS (or **John Damascene**) (c. 675-c. 749), Greek theologian. Personal history largely veiled in obscurity. Born in Damascus of Christian parents; his father though a Christian was treasurer to the Saracenic caliph. Received education from an Italian monk whom John's father had ransomed from salvery. Upon the death of father, John was given a higher position under the caliph than his father had held. When the emperor, Leo the Isaurian, in spite of the protests of Germanus, patriarch of Constantinople, issued his first edict against images in the churches (726), John came to the vigorous defense of image veneration; in this was enthusiastically supported by the monks. About 730 was a monk in the monastery of St. Sabas (or Mar Saba) in a desolate valley of the Kidron between Jerusalem and the Dead Sea. A few years later ordained priest. Last years were spent in study and literary labor. For writings in favor of images, he was enthusiastically lauded at the second Council of Nicea (787). The fame of John of Damascus as one of the greatest theologians of history, however, rests chiefly on his three-part work entitled, *Fount of Knowledge*. The third part, *De Fude Orthodoxa,* is a systematization of Greek theology as Thomas Aquinas' *Summa Theologiae* was of Latin theology five centuries later. Since John's time there has been little change in the doctrinal statement of the Eastern church. Furthermore it was to John that the Eastern church turned for its interpretation of the procession of the Holy Spirit when the Western church added "Filioque" to the doctrine of the Holy Spirit. One of the great hymnists of Middle Ages, wrote "The Day of Resurrection" and "Come ye Faithful, Raise the Strain."

JOHN OF GAUNT (1340-1399), Duke of

Lancaster, born in Ghent or Gaunt, Flanders (Belgium), fourth son of Edward III of England. Through marriage became Earl of Lancaster in 1361, and the next year created duke. Prominent in domestic affairs in England. He dominated English government and enriched himself by corrupt practices. Became involved in a conflict with the church over the church's right to exercise authority in temporal matters. Allied himself with the noted religious reformer John Wycliffe and for a time supported Wycliffe in attacks upon the church, and protected him from the attempted attacks of the Bishop of London and the Archbishop of Canterbury. Yet John had little sympathy with Wycliffe's religious or political opinions. Foremost patron of art and literature of his day, a friend of the poet Geoffrey Chaucer. His eldest son, Bolingbroke, in 1399 became Henry IV of England.

JOHN OF JANDUN (died 1328), Averroistic theologian and political writer, born at Jandun, Champagne, France. Educated at the College of Navarre (University of Paris), he became an outstanding teacher at the University. He wrote *De Laudibus Parisiis* and (in collaboration with Marsilius of Padua) *Defensor Pacis* in 1324 against Pope John XXII to defend the emperor Louis the Bavarian by asserting popular sovereignty in a council over the pope.

JOHN OF LEYDEN, properly **JAN BEUKELSZOON** or **BOCKELSON** or **BOCKHOLD** (c. 1509-1536), Dutch Anabaptist, born in Leiden, Netherlands, received little education, and wandered about as a journeyman tailor. Adopted opinions of the Anabaptists and joined Jan Matthys at Münster, the "New Jerusalem." When Matthys was killed in 1534 after a brief leadership, became his successor. Changed the Anabaptist government at Münster, setting up the "Kingdom of Zion" with himself as "King of Zion," appointed twelve elders or judges, established the practice of polygamy, himself selecting from among his many wives, the beautiful widow of Jan Matthys to be the queen, continued the community of goods. Fanaticism, cruelty, and licentiousness ruled in the city. In 1535 the town was taken by the soldiers of the bishop of Münster. John and accomplices were cruelly put to death; and Münster was restored to the Catholic fold.

JOHN OF MONTECORVINO (c. 1247-1330), Franciscan missionary, born at Montecorvino in southern Italy. He went to Peking in 1291 at a time when China was opening to the West. The Mongol, Kublai Khan, was on the throne. Marco Polo and father, Maffeo Polo and a fellow merchant Nicolo had opened the country to trade and to good will to the extent that Kublai Khan in 1270 asked for one hundred missionaries from the West. The popes were too busy quarrelling over the papacy to hear and answer the call. In 1291 John of Montecorvino started for Peking with a letter from the pope to Kublai Khan. He went by way of India, enroute preaching more than a year there. He arrived in China in 1294. During his early years in Peking, John must have been a lonely man, for in 1305 he wrote that for twelve years he had received no letters from the pope or from his order. By 1300 he had established a church. John learned to preach in the Chinese language and translated into Chinese the New Testament and the Psalms. Christianity flourished for awhile. In 1307 Pope Clement V sent out several bishops to assist him, and appointed John as archbishop over the whole area. Some of these bishops, however, perished on the way, only three arriving in China. A regrettable phase of his work in China, however, was the confusion and distress caused by his efforts to proselytize the Nestorian Christians whom he found in great numbers. His work and that of the Nestorians seem to have come to an end when the Mongols and other foreigners were expelled from China by the victorious native Ming Dynasty in 1368.

JOHN OF PARIS (c. 1250-1306), Dominican born at Paris, received a good education, taught philosophy and theology at Paris. John owes renown to the part taken in controversy between his king, Philip the Fair of France, and Pope Boniface VIII. In his tract, *Authority of the Pope and the King,* held that both papal and royal power are based on the sovereignty of the people, both receive their authority and power directly from God, neither power has a right to interfere in the sphere of the other. Held that the general council is superior in authority to the pope, and in civil affairs the king is superior to the pope. Joined with others in calling for a general council to settle current problems. His doctrine of the eucharist varied from the traditional viewpoint of transubstantiation, leaning toward the doctrine of impanation. Prohibited by the Bishop of Paris from preaching, lecturing, and hearing confessions. Appealed to the pope but died before the matter was settled.

JOHN OF WESSEL (JOHANNES RUCHRAT) (c. 1400-1481), Medieval reformer. Born in OberWesel-Am-Rhein. Educated at Erfurt, where he received his doctorate and became rector in 1456. Canon at Worms in 1460 and the next year professor at Basel. Cathedral preacher at Worms in 1463. When invited to become cathedral pastor at Mainz, he was accused of Hussite teaching, deposed and tried by the Inquisition, forced to recant and retire to an Augustinian monastery at Mainz. As a nominalist criticized penance, the abuse of indulgences, extreme unction, and making the church rather than the Bible the final authority.

JOHN THE CONSTANT (1468-1532), Elector of Saxony (1525-1532), born in Meissen, brother of Frederick III, the Wise of Saxony, whom he succeeded as elector. An intimate friend and admirer of Luther. From the beginning a staunch defender of the Reformation, declaring resolved "to stand by the imperishable Word of God." In 1526 joined the Torgau Union, and at the Second Diet of Spires in 1529 one of the signers of the protest. In 1530 at the Diet of Augsburg fearlessly opposed the emperor on the question of the confession. In 1531, one of the organizers of Schmalkaldic League. Acknowledged obedience to the emperor except where it conflicted with the honor of God and his soul's welfare. In 1531 entered into league of defense with Protestant cities and princes for six years which forced upon the emperor the religious peace of Nürnberg (1532). Luther preached his funeral sermon and Melanchthon delivered memorial address in Latin.

JOHN, GRIFFITH (1831-1912), Welsh Congregational missionary to China, born at Swansea, Wales, 1831, the next year mother died of cholera. From 1850-1854 studied at Brecon College, and then for a few months at the Missionary College at Bedford, England. Following college refused a pastorate in an important Congregational church that he might go under the London Missionary Society as a missionary to China. In 1855 appointed to China, ordained, was married. Just a little later Mr. and Mrs. John reached Shanghai, where they began language study. Within six months able to preach in the Chinese language. Until 1861 headquarters at Shanghai, and then until 1906 at Hankow, where he established the Hankow Mission. During missionary career made many extensive journeys preaching, distributing tracts and books, and establishing or helping to establish more than one hundred missions and churches in the surrounding country, and in nearby provinces. One of longest expeditions was the one made in 1868 with close friend and colleague, James Wylie, into the far west of China. During the Tai Ping rebellion John visited Soochow, Nanking, and Hankow in the interest of the Christian mission. Soon helped establish the Hankow Mission where many of his long years in China were spent. In 1870 he and family returned to their homeland. For three years preached in England, making vigorous appeals for China. In 1873 the Johns were permitted to return to China. Mrs. John died enroute near Singapore. Saddened and lonely he plunged into work again at Hankow. In the Yangtze Valley founded a theological college that bears his name. In 1881-82 took second furlough in England and the United States. In 1906 retired from active missionary life and resided in the United States until death in 1912. John was a highly efficient and indefatigable worker. An active evangelist, but chiefly through literary efforts that his name became so well known in the Celestial Empire. Many of his books and tracts were written and sent out over China. Translated the New and the Old Testament into "easy Wen-li." Also wrote several books on China in English.

JOHNSON, GISLE (1822-1894), Norwegian theologian and evangelist. Taught church history at the University of Christiana, Oslo from 1849 to 1894. Leader of the second Norwegian awakening in the late 1850's. Worked for reform in the church. Founded *Lutherstiftelsen* in 1868 to send out Bible colporteurs with Bibles and literature to educate the laity in Lutheran doctrine.

JOHNSON, HERRICK (1832-1913), American Presbyterian educator and clergyman, born at Kaughnewaga, New York, graduated from Hamilton College and Auburn Theological Seminary. After ordination to the Presbyterian ministry in 1860 became associate pastor of the First Presbyterian Church, Troy, New York, for two years, then pastor of the Third Presbyterian Church, Pittsburgh, Pennsylvania, and later of the First Presbyterian Church, Philadelphia. From 1874 to 1880, professor of homiletics and pastoral theology in Auburn Theological Seminary. Taught sacred rhetoric and pastoral theology in McCormick Seminary, Chicago (1880-1906), part time serving as pastor of the Fourth Presbyterian Church in Chicago (1880-1883). For several years president of the Presbyterian Board of Ministerial Education, and of the Presbyterian Board of Aid for Colleges and Academies, moderator of the General Assembly in 1882. Served as president of the Board of Publications, and as member of two different committees of the Presbyterian Church for the revision of the Confession of Faith.

JOHNSON, RICHARD (1753-1827), first chaplain to convicts in Australia from 1788, where he preached conversion, aided the sick among prisoners and aborigines while farming for a living. He returned to England by 1800 and in 1810 was given a parish in London. Aided by the Clapham sect.

JONAS, JUSTUS, real name **JODOCUS**

KOCH (1493-1555), German Reformer, born at Nordhausen in Saxony, had been professor and canon at Erfurt. Studied at Wittenberg and Erfurt. Came under the influence of Erasmus whom he called his "father in Christ." In 1521 at Wittenberg as professor of church law and provost, and became one of the most intimate friends and co-workers of Luther. While Luther was at the Wartburg, Jonas was of great assistance at Wittenberg. For ten years (1523-1533) dean of the theological faculty at Wittenberg. Translated some of Luther's and Melanchthon's works, and played an active part in the Marburg Colloquy in 1529 and in the Diet of Augsburg in 1530. Assisted Melanchthon and others in forming the Augsburg Confession. In Luther's declining years, Jonas helped carry on the organization of the Protestant church with resolute energy. In 1546 accompanied Luther on last trip to Eisleben, stood beside his death bed, delivered his funeral oration, and left us an account of Luther's last days. He came into conflict with the civil authorities and his relations with Melanchthon became strained.

JONES, ABNER (1772-c. 1841), New England Baptist minister, born at Royalton, Massachusetts, but moved with parents to the backwoods of Vermont. Joined the Baptists. Had but a meager education, but taught school for a time. Spent a few weeks studying medicine. Also preached as opportunity afforded. Left the Vermont Baptists, and in 1801 organized an independent church at Lyndon, Vermont, calling it simply a "Christian church," insisting that piety and character be the sole test of Christian fellowship. In 1802 ordained by three Freewill Baptist ministers but as a "Christian." Organized many independent "Christian" churches. Intermittently practiced medicine to augment his income. For forty years these men continued their work, and as a result independent churches with a loose fellowship among them sprang up throughout New England, New York, New Jersey, Pennsylvania, northern Ohio, and Canada. In time three similar movements, one in New England under Abner Jones, one in Virginia under the Methodist minister, James O'Kelley, and another in Kentucky under the Presbyterian minister, Barton W. Stone, joined and adopted the name "Christian."

JONES, DAVID (1796-1841), missionary pioneer to Madagascar, born at Neuaddlwyd, Cardiganshire, Wales, David Jones and Thomas Bevan offered themselves as missionaries to Madagascar. Soon ordained, accepted by the London Missionary Society, and sent to the college at Gosport for a year of training. In 1818 the two with their wives sailed for Mauritius, where they remained with missionaries for a time. When ready to proceed to Madagascar left their wives at Mauritius and ventured forth by themselves. A school was successfully started, with some of the chieftains' sons attending. The wives then came to the new field. Within a few months the Malagasy fever claimed the lives of Mrs. Jones and their baby leaving David Jones alone. After more than a year of recurring fever, and after partially recovering health, Jones with government assistance finally reached the capital of Madagascar. In 1820 slave trading was outlawed. Jones became a warm friend of King Radama. Under royal patronage a school was opened and named by the king himself, the Royal School. Originating an alphabet, translating the Scriptures, and preparing grammars, dictionaries, and textbooks occupied much time and that of missionary recruits for several years. No public confessions to Christian faith had yet taken place. In 1828 King Radama died. In 1831 after thirteen years on the field, David Jones exhausted and ill, had to return to England. About the same time the first twenty converts were baptized. When some government officers, some of them of royal blood applied for baptism, Queen Ranavalona, who had succeeded King Radama, refused to permit officers and soldiers to become Christians. In a few months, February 26, 1835, an edict went forth from the queen forbidding Christianity to continue, and a severe persecution ensued. The church, numbering nearly one thousand, was scattered far and wide, to England, to Mauritius, and to the caves and forests of Madagascar. After six years at his home, Jones returned to Mauritius. The next year went to the capital of Madagascar to plead for the persecuted church, but to no avail. The foundations had been laid and the Christians remained faithful. The church grew until within a few years the one thousand had become seven thousand.

JONES, E. STANLEY (1884-1973), missionary to India. Born in Baltimore. Educated at Asbury College, Duke and Syracuse Universities. Missionary evangelist to upper caste Indians from 1907 to 1973 after 1907 ordination. Created Christian Ashrams in India to reach Indians in 1917. Wrote *The Way, Mahatma Gandhi, An Interpretation* and the *Christ of the Indian Road*.

JONES, GRIFFITH (1683-1761), Welsh pastor. Born Carmarthenshire. Ordained an Anglican clergyman in 1709. Pastor at Abercowyn and Llandowror from 1716 to 1761. In 1730 he established charity schools to teach people to read the Welsh Bible. Between three and four thousand were opened with 150,000 pupils. Pioneered field preaching and a system of circuits. Calvinist in theology. Influenced Daniel Rowland, Howell Harris, and Howell Davies. From 1748 associated with Lady Huntington. Wrote story of his schools in *Welsh Piety.*

JONES, ROBERT (BOB) Sr. (1883-1968), American evangelist and college president. Born in Skipperville, Alabama. Educated at Southern University in Greensboro, Alabama. Licensed by Methodists at 15 to preach. From 1920 to 1968 an ardent evangelist and militant Fundamentalist. Founded his own college in Florida in 1926 in Florida, Tennessee, and later Greenville, South Carolina. College opened in 1927. Preached over 12,000 sermons in fifty states and thirty foreign countries.

JONES, RUFUS MATTHEW (1863-1948), American Quaker, born at South China, Maine, studied at Haverford College, Pennsylvania; the University of Heidelberg, Germany; and the University of Pennsylvania. Principal of Oak Grove Seminary, Vassalboro, Maine (1889-1893). From 1893 to 1934 on faculty of Haverford. Became the first editor of the *American Friend* from 1894 to 1912. One of the organizers of the Five Years Meeting of Friends; one of the persons responsible for the development of the American Friends Service Committee in 1917 and its chairman for twenty years. Conceived the idea of the Wider Quaker Fellowship. Influence reached outside own Quaker fellowship. A lecturer of national fame, speaking in many American colleges. One semester lectured in various colleges and missions in China. A member of the American Philosophical Society. For more than forty years taught psychology, philosophy, ethics, Bible, and the development of Christian thought at Haverford College. The author of hundreds of editorials, articles, and pamphlets, and of fifty-six books. In writings interpreted to the Christian world the life of mystic relation with Christ as he felt it could be practically lived in the modern world. Also wrote on Quaker history.

JONES, SAMUEL PORTER (SAM JONES) (1847-1906), American evangelist, born at Oak Bowery in Chambers County, Alabama, reared at Cartersville, Georgia. After attending a private school and Euharlee Academy, health broke, and discouraged, sought relief in drink. Studied law and showed promise of success in legal endeavor. Admitted to the Georgia bar in 1869. Continued life of dissipation until stirred by his father's dying words. The young man promised to quit his drinking, kept his word and became a Christian. Decided to become a preacher, and preached first sermon one week after conversion, three months before he was licensed. Held several pastorates in the Methodist church during eight years, beginning in 1872 in the Van Wert circuit, one of the poorest in Georgia. From 1880 to 1892 financial agent of the North Georgia Orphanage. He began evangelistic preaching in Nashville, Tennessee in 1892 until his death. Gained fame in preaching in the Midwest. Soon was going to important cities all over the nation. Crude wit, coarse stories, and rural life drollery captured hearers everywhere, even in the cultured audiences of Boston. Preached with such vigor that health broke and he had to rest from evangelistic preaching for several years. In the meantime turned to lecturing, using influence and oratory against the liquor traffic. In closing years resumed evangelistic preaching, and in one of these campaigns came to the end of his career.

JORDANUS or JORDAN (Fourteenth Century), Dominican missionary. About 1319 Jordanus, a Dominican monk, along with several other Dominican and Franciscan monks, left Avignon, France, then the seat of the papacy, for the Far East. Jordanus and a few others succeeded in reaching Thana District, Bombay Presidency, India, where they found a few Nestorian Christians largely ignorant of the Christian faith. Also came into controversy with the Moslems who had recently made conquest in that part of India. Companions were murdered. Jordanus remained afterward for two years in India. Claims to have baptized about three hundred, some of whom were pagans and some of whom were likely Nestorians. Returned to Europe, and in 1328 consecrated Bishop of Quilon by Pope John XXII. About 1330 returned to India and worked on the Malabar Coast in South India. Claimed that he and companions won to the Catholic faith ten thousand schismatics (likely Thomas or Malabar Christians) and unbelievers. Jordanus returned later to Europe, but when or why is unknown.

JOSEPHUS, FLAVIUS (original name **JOSEPH ben MATTATHIAS**) (c. 37-c. 100), Jewish historian, born in Jerusalem in a rich, distinguished, priestly family. Lived three years with a hermit, studied in the various schools of Judaism, then joined the sect of Pharisees. In 64 made a trip to Rome to seek the release of some imprisoned Jewish priests who were friends. Took part in the revolt of the Jews against Rome in 66, and was given command of the army of Galilee. Captured and imprisoned for awhile, but later released by Emperor Vespasian and given royal favor, not only by Vespasian, but also by Titus and Domitian. Made a Roman citizen, given a royal residence, an annual stipend, and a tract of land in Judea. Living at Rome, adopted the name Flavius Josephus, and devoted himself to studies and literary pursuits. In life and in writings pursued a policy midway between Jewish and pagan culture. Wrote his first work, *Jewish War* in seven volumes, in Aramaic, translated it into the Greek and did the rest of his writing in Greek. Chief among other writings are *Antiquities of the Jews* in twenty books, containing the history of the Jews from creation to A.D. 66, using both biblical and legendary sources. The early Christians and the Fathers of the church were zealous readers of Josephus's works. Also wrote *Contra Apionem,* an apology for Judaism. In his writings Josephus refers to Christ, John the Baptist, and the early Christians. The writings of Josephus were used extensively by the Fathers for their apologetics.

JOVIAN (jō'vyăn), **JOVIANUS** or **FLAVIUS CLAUDIUS** (c. 332-364), Roman Emperor (363-364), born at Singidunum, Pannonia (now Belgrade, Servia), commander of the imperial life-guard when Julian died fighting the Persians, 363, and proclaimed emperor by the army. Made a hasty treaty with the Persians. On arrival at Antioch publicly declared himself a Christian and rescinded the edicts of Julian against the Christians, revived the monogram of Christ on the imperial standards, and restored to the clergy their privileges and revenues. Stated publicly attitude toward the controversies in the church. Took the side of the Nicene party, reinstated Athanasius in his episcopal see at Alexandria, and asked to be remembered in the bishop's prayers. Also commanded Athanasius to issue a new statement of the orthodox creed. At the same time Jovian showed great tolerance toward pagans, neo-Platonists, and Arians. In a general edict of toleration established freedom for all forms of worship, even for pagans, but forbade magical sacrifices. Reintroduced the religious freedom proclaimed by Constantine in the Edict of Milan of 313.

JOVINIAN (died c. 405), unorthodox monk. Though an unmarried monk, wrote and argued against certain phases of monasticism. His views were: (1) A virgin is no better in the sight of God than a married woman; (2) Abstinence is no better than partaking of food with thankfulness; (3) A person who is born again by baptism cannot be overcome by the devil; (4) All sins are equal; (5) Rewards are equal in Heaven. Through Jovinian's writings and influence many monks and nuns left their celibate life and married. Jerome, in his *Adversus Jovinianum,* bitterly opposed Jovinian. Probably the excessive praise of monasticism on the part of Jerome and other monks led Jovinian to oppose monasticism so strongly. When he was excommunicated and banished for heresy about the year 390, he went to Milan. Here Ambrose held a council against him. Died in exile.

JOWETT, BENJAMIN (1817-1893), English educator and Greek scholar, born in Camberwell, London, studied at St. Paul's School, London, and at Balliol College, Oxford. In 1842 became tutor at Balliol College, Oxford; in 1845 ordained priest, and in 1855 became regius professor of Greek at Oxford. At Oxford had fallen into the Tractarian Movement. His earlier evangelical views were shaken. It was probably his close fellowship with A. P. Stanley, the leader of the Broad church school, that kept him from going into the Roman Catholic church. Liberal theology as expressed in his *The Epistles of St. Paul,* and an essay on *Interpretation of Scripture* committed him more definitely to the Broad church movement, and consequently led to his trial for heresy. Though acquitted in the trial, forbidden to preach from the university pulpit. After this refrained from writing on subjects of a theological nature. In 1870 became master of Balliol College. Writings, in addition to the above were chiefly translations and editions of Greek works: Plato's *Dialogues,* Thucydides' *History of the Peloponnesian War,* and Aristotle's *Politics.* Educational views led to reforms in the university, in the secondary school system in England, and in the colonial service in India.

JOWETT, JOHN HENRY (1864-1923), English Congregational clergyman, born near Halifax, Yorkshire, England, educated at Airedale College, Bradford, at the University of Edinburgh, and at Mansfield College, Oxford. In 1889 ordained a Congregational minister, and became minister of St. James Congregational Church in Newcastle-on-Tyne (1889-1895). Succeeded Robert William Dale as minister at Carr's Lane Congregational Church in Birmingham (1895-1911). While at Carr's Lane built Digbeth Institute and supported other efforts for the welfare of the poor. In 1909 visited the United States, and was a prominent speaker in the Northfield Conference. In 1910 served as president of the Free Church Council. In 1911 answered a call to America and became pastor of the Fifth Avenue Presbyterian Church in New York City for seven years (1911-1918). Returned to England to be minister of the Westminster Chapel, Buckingham Gate, London from 1918 to 1923. Among writings are: *Passion* *for Souls; My Daily Meditation; The Preacher: His Life and Work; Things That Matter Most;* and *Epistles of St. Peter.* Gave Yale lectures on preaching in 1912.

JUD (yo͞ot), **LEO (JUDAE)** (1482-1542), Swiss reformer, born at Gemar in Alsace. In 1499 entered the University of Basel where he first studied medicine; then through the influence of Zwingli, with whom he formed an intimate friendship, he turned to the study of theology. Ordained parish priest of St. Hippolyte in 1512 in Alsace. Along with Zwingli preached the evangelical doctrine. In 1518 when Zwingli left Einsiedeln to become pastor of the Great Minster Church at Zurich, Jud succeeded Zwingli at Einsiedeln from 1519 to 1522. In 1523 Jud was made pastor of St. Peter's in Zurich, continuing increasingly to preach the evangelical doctrine. In first year of pastorate married a former nun. After Zwingli's death in 1531, called to succeed the great reformer, but declined. Continued to preach the evangelical faith, and along with Bullinger, to oppose the Catholics, the Lutherans, and the Anabaptists. One of the greatest services rendered to the Reformation was assistance in the translation of the New Testament from the Greek, and his translation of the greater part of the Old Testament from the Hebrew text. A faithful pastor, an instructive preacher, a diligent and laborious scholar, and a lovable and pious man.

JUDSON, ADONIRAM (1788-1850), American Baptist lexicographer and Bible translator in Burma, born at Malden, Massachusetts. Graduated valedictorian at Brown University and went to Andover Theological Seminary. Following college found himself falling into the clutches of infidelity. The death of an intimate infidel friend, however, shocked him into a living faith in Christ. Two years later, in 1810, he and a group of fellow Congregational seminary students became interested in foreign missions and presented their concern to the General Association. Sent to England to seek to effect a working relationship with the London Missionary Society, but failed in attempt. In 1812 the American Board of Commissioners for Foreign Missions was incorporated, and Judson, Rice, Nott, Newell, and Hall were appointed by the board to go to India. In February Judson married Anne Hasseltine; and twelve days later the party embarked for Calcutta. Enroute to India Judson's and Rice's views on baptism changed and they severed connection with the American Board and joined the Baptists in 1812. Rice came back to America and helped to organize the American Baptist Missionary Union. The Judsons, in spite of much opposition from the East India Company, in 1813 went to Rangoon, Burma, where they found a home in the English Baptist mission house with the Felix Carey family. Devoted himself to the study of the difficult Burmese language, and after exactly three years in Burma, completed a well-written grammar. Six years after going to Rangoon ventured to preach first sermon in the Burmese tongue. It was also six years before he baptized first convert. Within a few years Mr. and Mrs. Judson went to Ava the capital to open work. Shortly after this the Anglo-Burmese War broke out. 1824-1826 were terrible years for the missionaries. For seventeen months Judson suffered almost incredible hardships in prison. In 1830 began great ministry among the Karens. In 1834 completed the translation of the whole Bible into the Burmese language. From 1845 to 1847, after more than thirty years in Burma, took first and only furlough to his native land. Judson remained in America more than a year. Back in Burma spent remaining years in revising the English-Burmese dictionary and starting on the Burmese-English section. In hope of regaining fast-failing health undertook a sea voyage, but died on the trip and was buried at sea.

JULIAN THE APOSTATE (JULIANUS, FLAVIUS CLAUDIUS) (c. 331-363), Roman Emperor (361-363), born at Constantinople, the son of Julius Constantius, a half brother of Constantine the Great. Given a nominal Christian training under the direction of Eusebius of Nicomedia and several eunuchs, was baptized, and was being trained for ecclesiastic life. Before twenty-five years he was deeply interested in Grecian and other pagan philosophies, having spent several months in Athens in the study of Greek philosophy. Had secretly turned from Christianity, and had been initiated into the Eleusinian mysteries. Emperor Constantius II, though jealous and suspicious of Julian, gave him his sister Helena in marriage, conferred on him title of Caesar, and in 355 sent him to Gaul to check the inroads of the Germans. Successful in his mission, a good administrator, won the affections of soldiers. Constantius, becoming alarmed at his growing success and popularity, in 360 ordered some of Julian's troops to be dispatched to the East. The soldiers rose in insurrection, and Julian ere long set out with his army for Constantinople. Then entered Constantinople as undisputed emperor (361), and set about to reform the government on paganistic ideals. Hated and rejected Christianity as a mere superstition, yet demonstrated a tolerant and a liberal attitude during short rule. Seeking to quell external opposition in the empire, headed an expedition against the hostile Persians. Mortally wounded in a battle with the Persians at Ctesiphon, the Persian capital. Brilliant but short reign of eighteen months came to an end, attempt to re-establish heathenism in the Roman government failed. Some of writings and orations were directed against Christianity and in praise of pagan religion.

JULIANA OF NORWICH (c. 1342-c. 1413), English mystic, little known of life except that she was a Benedictine nun, an anchoress outside the walls of St. Julian's Church, Norwich, England. In 1373, claimed to have received a series of fifteen revelations in state of ecstasy, lasting five hours. One other vision followed the next day. Twenty years later wrote *The Sixteen Revelations of Divine Love*. Laid stress upon love and presented the joyful aspect of religion. God revealed Himself to her in three properties: life, light, and love. Influenced by Neo-Platonism.

JULICHER (yüe'lĭk ẽr), **GUSTAV ADOLF** (1857-1938), German New Testament scholar, born at Falkenberg, a suburb of Berlin, educated at the University of Berlin, chaplain of the orphan asylum at Rummelsburg, near Berlin (1882-1888). In 1887 became a teacher of New Testament history and church history at the University of Berlin. Teacher at the University of Marburg from 1889 to 1923. After 1889 full professor. Became a member of the committee on church Fathers of the Royal Prussian Academy of Berlin, engaged in the preparation of a *Prosopographia Imperii Romani* from the reign of Diocletian to Justinian. A liberal theologian and an historical critic. Principal writings were *Introduction to the New Testament* and *Parables of the Lord*.

JULIUS AFRICANUS SEXTUS (d. c. 240). Born in Palestine. Travelled widely but finally settled in Rome. Built sewers and organized public library in Rome and helped rebuild Nicopolis. Wrote *Chronographia* to synchronize sacred and secular history. His chronology was carried over in Eusebius' *Chronicles* and became the basis for medieval historical writer's chronology.

JULIUS II (GIULIANO DELLA ROVERE) (1443-1513), Pope (1503-1513), born at Albisola near Savona, Italy. After the short reign of Pius III, was elected pope. Took the name Julius II and is known as the "Warrior Pope." As a cardinal for thirty-two years had shown himself a diplomat and a warrior rather than the priest. Headed an army to drive out foes and to restore the papal states. In clever diplomatic and military fashion pitted one force against another until ends were accomplished. First set out to eliminate Caesar Borgia. In 1509 joined the League of Cambrai to subdue the Venetians. In 1511 formed the Holy League in order to repulse the French from Italy. Succeeded in removing foreign domination from Italy and in restoring papal sovereignty in the ancient territory. Laid the cornerstone of St. Peter's Church, and ordered the renewal of the preaching of indulgences to raise the money. One of his last important acts was to call the Fifth Lateran Council (1512-1517), the last ecumenical council of the Middle Ages. His objective was to counter the purposes of Louis XII of France as set forth in the Council of Pisa, which Louis had called in 1511. Sent missionaries to America, India, and Africa. On the whole, if less concerned with spiritual affairs than the office demanded, a good statesman and general and an outstanding patron of the Renaissance fine arts, Michelangelo and Raphael being among close friends. The Vatican museum was his creation.

JUSTIN MARTYR (c. 100-165), philosopher, martyr, apologist, born at Flavia Neapolis, (the ancient Shechem) in Samaria of heathen parents. Well educated, seems to have had sufficient means to lead a life of study and travel. Being an eager seeker for truth, knocked successively at the doors of Stoicism, Aristotelianism, Pythagoreanism and Platonism, but hated Epicureanism. Platonism appealed the most and he thought he was about to reach the goal of his philosophy—the vision of God—when one day in a solitary walk along the seashore, the young philosopher met a venerable old Christian. This humble Christian shook his confidence in human wisdom, and pointed him to the Hebrew prophets, "men more ancient than all those who were esteemed philosophers," whose writings and teachings foretold the coming of Christ. Following his advice this zealous Platonist became a believing Christian. After conversion, which occurred in early manhood, devoted himself wholeheartedly to the vindication and spread of the Christian religion. With the conviction that Christianity is the oldest, truest, and most divine of philosophies; continuing to wear his philosopher's robe; having no fixed abode and holding no regular church office; went about as an itinerant lay evangelist or teaching missionary, with awareness of commission being from the Holy Spirit. Spent some time in Rome where he met and combated Marcion, one of the leading gnostics of the day. In Ephesus made an effort to gain the Jew, Trypho, and friends to the Christian faith. On a second sojourn to Rome, about the year 166, he and six other Christians were seized, scourged, and beheaded. In his *First Apology* shows Christianity is superior to paganism by priority in time, prophecy, miracles and purity of life. Shows Christianity is superior to Judaism in *Dialogue with Trypho*.

JUSTINIAN I (JUSTINIANUS, FLAVIUS ANICIUS JULIANUS (483-565), emperor of the East (527-565), born in Tauresium, Illyricum, of Gothic extraction, educated in Constantinople. Name was Uprauda, but changed by uncle to Justinianus. In 527 elected as emperor, and along with wife, Theodora, crowned in 527. Long reign the most brilliant in the history of the Byzantine empire. Attempted to restore the Roman Empire to its former glory. Throughout reign costly warfare carried on almost constantly, under his able generals Belisarius and Narses. Among conquests were the Vandals in northern Africa, the Ostrogoths in Italy, and the Franks in Spain. Carried on wars also with the Persians, the Huns, the Bulgars, and the Slavs. He sought to extirpate what remained of paganism. In 529 closed the ancient pagan philosophical school of Athens. Most famous architectural achievement was Saint Sophia, the cathedral church at Constantinople. As an adherent of the orthodox faith and as an advocate of unity within the church, called the Fifth Ecumenical Council at Constantinople in 553, which dealt with the Monophysite problem. Wished to have an empire that would be solidly united and orthodox. Famous *Institutes* of Justinian were laws that regulated ethical and ecclesiastical affairs as well as political. Roman law over the centuries collected under the title, *Corpus Juris Civilis.* This codification of Roman law has made his name memorable. Persecuted and punished not only the pagans, but also the Manichaeans, Arians, and other heretics, his wrath falling heavily upon the Montanists. He condemned Origen and his doctrines. Greatly accelerated the trend for the domination of the church by the emperor and for making the church an instrument of the state.

K

KAGAWA, TOYOHIKO (1888-1960), Japanese Christian social reformer. Born in Kobe and adopted by his father, a rich Buddhist official. Educated at Presbyterian College, Tokyo. Disinherited when converted. At Princeton Theological Seminary from 1914 to 1917. At Kobe Theological Seminary on return until 1934. Worked in Tokyo slums after 1909. Obtained right of unions to organize by 1926. After 1945 leader in setting up Japanese settlement houses and farm cooperatives. Imprisoned in World War II as a pacifist. Wrote *Christ and Japan* and *Love the Law of Life*.

KAHN (kän), **IDA (K'ANG C'HENG)** (1872-1932), Chinese physician and surgeon, Chinese home in Kiukiang, Kiangsu Province. At two months she was adopted by Miss Gertrude Howe of the Methodist Mission. Miss Howe educated her in mission schools, and in 1892 brought Ida and Mary Stone, Ida's life-long friend, to America to enter medical school at the University of Michigan, Ann Arbor. After four years of study both women were graduated with honors, and returned to serve their people at Kiukiang as a regularly appointed medical missionary. In 1899 Dr. Kahn represented the women of China at the World's Congress held in London. She shared with Dr. Stone in the work in the new Danforth Hospital, opened in 1900 in Kiukiang. In 1903, Dr. Kahn responded to a call to Nanchang, a city of three hundred thousand in Kiangsi. Here the Chinese citizens provided a hospital for women and children, of which she became chief, the only trained physician in that populous city. In 1907, she took a two-year leave to the United States, during which time she completed a three-year literary course at Northwestern and Chicago universities. In 1910 attended the Conference of the World's Young Women's Christian Association in Berlin, and then spent six months studying tropical diseases in London before returning to work in China. Miss Howe spent her last years in the home of Dr. Kahn.

KANAMORI (kän ȧ môr'ī), **TSURIN PAUL** (c. 1856-c. 1928), Japanese evangelist. He and several other Japanese boys were converted in 1875 by Captain L. L. Janes, who had gone to Japan to teach in a military school, then for seven years had taught an English school at Kumamoto. The Captain taught the boys to read the English Bible. Such a spirit of Bible reading, conviction, and conversion broke out, so much preaching and testifying by the young converts took place that a great "revival" was in progress even before these boys knew anything about foreign missionaries or about a church. In 1876 about forty of these enthusiastic Japanese Christians formed the world-renowned Kumamoto Band, Paul Kanamori being one of the leaders. These young Christians suffered severe persecution, Kanamori being one of the most bitterly attacked. In the band's early days, Joseph Hardy Neeshima was organizing Doshisha University. Paul Kanamori was the first of the Kumamoto Band to enter Doshisha University in the summer of 1876. A member of the first graduating class in 1879. Then started a Congregational Church in Okayama Province and became first pastor. Under Kanamori's preaching and influence this province became one of the strongest Christian centers in Japan. Kanamori was called by Dr. Neeshima to become professor of theology at Doshisha. While teaching in 1891 read books of German New Theology and Higher Criticism and was turned to socialism and liberalism, finally from the Christian ministry. Entered into political and social reform for the next twenty years. Aired liberal theological and critical views in *Christianity, Present and Future*. The Church was greatly influenced toward liberalism because of him. The death of his beloved and faithful Christian wife, the mother of his nine children, led him back to the gospel. Soon became known the world over for his three-hour sermon on "God, Sin, and Salvation," which he preached to multitudes throughout Japan, Formosa, and Korea. It guided tens of thousands of people to the Christian faith. Wrote *The Christian Belief* and *Kanamori's Life Story*.

KANT (känt), **IMMANUEL** (1724-1804), German philosopher, born in Königsberg, East Prussia, educated in the Pietistic schools at Halle, and at the University of Königsberg. From 1755 to 1770 lectured at the University of Königsberg on logic, metaphysics, physics, mathematics, ethics, anthropology, and physical geography. Completed theological course and did some preaching, though he never entered the ministry. In 1770 made professor of logic and metaphysics at Königsberg, and continued there until retirement in 1797. Whole life was absorbed in teaching and writing. Perhaps greatest and best known work was

Critique of Pure Reason, written in 1781 which limited rational certainty to the material world. He actually pointed reason back to its own territory by showing that pure reason could neither demonstrate nor overthrow the objects of belief. Even rose to the support of Christianity by emphasizing the validity of Christian experience. "We can know only what we experience," he said. We know objects or principles only as they affect our lives. Our reason interprets for us. Reason gives us our ideas of God, the universe, and self. Thus the idea of God is in our mind; but we do not thereby have any real knowledge of God or certainty of his external existence. Yet Kant reasoned that there must be a God who has provided man with his reason and his moral sense. But there is no place in Kant's system for an objective, historical revelation of God, therefore no place for Christ, the God-man. The Bible is only a man-made book of history to be subjected to historical criticism as any other book. In 1788 he published his second critique, *The Critique of Practical Reason.* He gave in it the view of moral obligation or conscience, which he called the "categorical imperative," and which he held to be the starting point of religion. This necessitates God, the soul, and immortality. Man with his free will and with his imminent sense of what is right becomes the creator of a religion in which he develops the morality inherent in himself. Kant helped to prepare the way for both biblical criticism and modern liberal theology. Kant's philosophy introduced a new epoch in the history of thought, and has influenced all subsequent philosophy.

KEBLE (kē'bl), **JOHN** (1792-1866), leader of the Oxford Movement and a poet, born at Fairford, Gloucestershire, England. Educated at Corpus Christi College, Oxford. In 1811 made fellow of Oriel College, Oxford, and tutor (1818-1823). By 1814 appointed by the University of Oxford as one of its public examiners. Ordained priest in 1816. In 1818 became curate of East Leach and Burthorpe. In 1825 became curate of Hursley and vicar in 1836, remaining at Hursley the remainder of his life. Gladly carried on ministry among the poorer, humbler folk; but made parish one of the model parishes of England. Held the professorship of poetry at Oxford from 1831 to 1841. His sermon, "National Apostasy" preached in 1833, in which he dealt with the question of the church and the state, really set in motion the Anglo Catholic party, known also as the Oxford Movement or Tractarianism. The movement was organized by Keble, Froude, and Newman, with Pusey joining two years later. Keble formulated the principles for which he and associates stood. Wrote nine of the ninety *Tracts for the Times*. While some of the Tractarians went over to the Roman church Keble remained in the Anglican church. In literature best known for book of religious lyrics, *The Church Year,* published in 1827 and issued in over one hundred editions before the expiration of the copyright. One of the hymns in book is "Sun of My Soul, Thou Saviour Dear." Among other works were a three-volume edition of the *Works of Richard Hooker,* several volumes of sermons, and a translation of Irenaeus in the *Works of the Fathers of the Holy Catholic Church.* Shortly after his death Keble College at Oxford was erected by friends to his memory and was opened in 1869.

KEIL (kīl), **JOHANN KARL FRIEDRICH** (1807-1888), German Lutheran exegete, born at Lauterbach, Saxony. Studied theology in Dorpat and Berlin, in 1833 accepted call to the theological faculty of Dorpat as teacher and professor of Old and New Testament exegesis and Oriental languages. Remained until retirement in 1858. Settled then in 1859 at Leipzig where he devoted himself to literary work and to the practical affairs of the Lutheran church. Belonged to the strictly orthodox and conservative school of theology. Ignored the modern criticism, holding that books of the Old and New Testaments are to be retained as the revealed Word of God. Chief work was commentary on the Old Testament in collaboration with Franz Delitzsch. Keil contributed Genesis to Esther, Jeremiah, Ezekiel, Daniel, and the Minor Prophets. Also published commentaries on Maccabees, Matthew, Mark, Luke, John, Peter, Jude, and Hebrews.

KEITH, GEORGE (c. 1639-1716), Scottish Quaker leader. Born Aberdeenshire. Educated at Marischal College and Aberdeen University. Quaker minister from 1664 to 1695. In Philadelphia as teacher (1687 to 1694). Ordained as an Anglican minister in 1700.

KEITH-FALCONER (fôk'nẽr), **ION GRANT NEVILLE** (1856-1887), Scottish Arabic scholar, born in Edinburgh, Scotland, educated at Harrow public school, and at Trinity College, Cambridge. During college days a noted bicyclist. While at Cambridge worked with Mr. F. N. Charrington in temperance and city mission work among the neglected poor. In 1880 turned attention to oriental languages, Hebrew and Syriac, especially Arabic, including the study of the Koran. Spent from 1881 to 1882 at Assiout in Egypt acquiring the colloquial Arabic language, learning the temper of the

Arabic mind, and studying the Moslem faith. Spent three more years at Cambridge University studying and translating Arabic. In 1885 went to Aden in South Arabia to investigate the prospect of opening a mission for the Free Church of Scotland among the Moslems. Appointed Lord Almoner's professor of Arabic at Cambridge in 1886. Prepared a series of lectures on the *Pilgrimage to Mecca*. On the eve of third and last lecture, with the conviction that life should be dedicated to mission work among the Moslems, he and his wife, accompanied by a medical doctor by the name of Cowan, in 1886 started on their mission to Arabia. The following February, both he and his wife fell victims to the Aden fever, and Keith-Falconer died in May. This young scholar and missionary enthusiast destined to be of more consequence in inciting others to labor for the conversion of the Moslems and other non-Christian peoples than as a worker. Great work had been "to call attention to Arabia."

KELLOGG, SAMUEL HENRY (1839-1899), American Presbyterian scholar and missionary, born at Quogue, Long Island, New York. Graduated with honors from Princeton College and Princeton Theological Seminary. Ordained in 1864 and in 1865 went as a Presbyterian missionary to India. During this time studied Hindi dialects and taught theology in the new Theological School of the India Synod of his church at Allahabad. Following death of wife in 1875 returned with family to the United States, became pastor of the Third Presbyterian Church of Pittsburgh until 1885 and later professor of systematic theology in the Allegheny Theological Seminary. In 1886 became pastor of St. James's Square Presbyterian Church in Toronto. In 1892 returned to India to aid in the revision of the Hindi Old Testament. Writings include *A Grammar of the Hindi Language and Dialects; The Jews: or Prediction and Fulfillment; An Exposition of the Book of Leviticus* (in the *Expositor's Bible*); and *Handbook of Comparative Religion*.

KELLY, HOWARD ATWOOD (1858-1943), American surgeon and gynecologist, born in Camden, New Jersey, in 1871 confirmed in Episcopal Church of the Epiphany. Completing a college course at the University of Pennsylvania, entered upon medical course there. Health failing, went West, where he spent a year as a cowboy in Colorado. Returned to complete work and to receive medical degree. After serving internship at Episcopal Hospital in Philadelphia, founded Kensington Hospital in the same city, spending eight years there ministering to the physical and spiritual needs of the millworkers in area. In 1888 became associate professor of obstetrics at the University of Pennsylvania. The next year joined the medical staff of the newly organized Johns Hopkins Hospital, and in 1889, the faculty of the Johns Hopkins Medical School as professor of gynecology and obstetrics, until 1919 remained there to do the main work of his life. Also surgeon at Howard A. Kelly Hospital, Baltimore, a private institution he founded in 1892. Huntarian Lecturer at the Mansion of the Mayor of London in 1928; one of the pioneers in employing radium for the treatment of cancer; and a cofounder of the National Radium Institute. A devout Christian and profound student of the Bible. Along with professional work devoted much time to Christian work, establishing classes for the training of Bible teachers in Sunday schools. Besides extensive writing for the medical world, we have from his pen such religious writings as *A Scientific Man and His Bible*, and *How I Study My Bible*.

KELLY, WILLIAM (1821-1906), Plymouth Brethren scholar, born in the north of Ireland, a graduate with highest honors in the classics at Trinity College, Dublin. Made confession of Christ, and joined the Brethren. Identified himself with the doctrine held by John Nelson Darby, with whom he worked for many years. Kelly edited the *Collected Writings* of Mr. Darby. An uncompromising opponent of all forms of higher biblical criticism. Editor of *The Prospect* (1848-1850), then of the *Bible Treasury* from 1856 until his death. Aided Dr. S. P. Tregelles in his investigations as a Biblical textual critic, wrote lectures, expositions, and notes on all the books of the Bible. Among other writings are *The Church of God, The New Testament Doctrine of the Holy Spirit, God's Inspiration of the Scriptures, Christ's Coming Again, The Day of Atonement*, and *Elements of Prophecy*. Shortly before his death in 1906 presented his library of fifteen thousand volumes to the town of Middlesborough, England.

KELVIN, First Baron, WILLIAM THOMSON (LORD KELVIN) (1824-1907), British mathematician, physicist, and inventor, born at Belfast, Ireland, educated at Glasgow and Cambridge. Brought up in the Established (Presbyterian) Church of Scotland; but at Cambridge conformed to the Church of England, and subscribed to the Thirty-nine Articles. Also when professor at Glasgow subscribed to the Westminster Confession. Elected professor of natural philosophy at Glasgow University, which position he held from 1846 until 1899. Studies, research, and teaching included all branches of mathematics and practical physics. A ruling scientific figure in the laying of the transatlantic cable, for which service knighted in 1866. In 1892 created a peer with the title Baron or Lord Kelvin of Largs. Researches and inventions led to many improvements in the mariner's compass, a tidal predictor, heat measurement, electrical measurements, and to developments of many pieces of electrical apparatus. Became recognized as the leading physical scientist and the greatest science teacher of the time. Published more than three hundred papers covering scientific findings. President of the Royal Society in 1890, and recipient of the Order of Merit in 1902. In religious life a man of strong faith in God and in the Bible.

KEMPE, MARGERY (c. 1373-1433), mystic. Born Bishop's Lynn, Norfolk. Vowed chastity in 1413 after she had fourteen children. Pilgrimage to Palestine in that year. Wrote *Book of Margery Kempe* in which she describes her travels and mystical experiences.

KEMPIS, THOMAS a (THOMAS HAMMERKEN) (c. 1380-1471), compiler of *Imitation of Christ,* born in Kempen, in the diocese of Cologne, Germany. Received early education from the Brethren of the Common Life at Deventer, Holland, through whom he was drawn to the life of contemplation, and upon whose advice entered a monastery. About 1400 entered the Augustinian convent of Mount Saint Agnes, near Zwolle, Holland. In 1413 ordained priest, in 1429 chosen subprior. Quietly lived to the age of more than ninety in exercises of devotion, writing and copying, reading, preaching, and exhorting novices and inquirers who came to him. Copied the Bible no less than four times. Though outward life was uneventful, inner life was one of simple, mystical devotion to Christ, evidenced by literary masterpiece, *The Imitation of Christ,* likely by him, one of Christendom's front rank manuals of devotion, originally written in Latin, later translated into many languages. Leans to quietism and is calculated to promote personal piety for those who dwell much alone rather than for those who are busy in life's activities.

KEN, THOMAS (1637-1711), English bishop and hymn writer, born at Little Berkhampstead, Hertfordshire, England. Educated at Winchester College and at Hart Hall and New College, Oxford. Tutor at New College (1661). Ordained in 1662; held several preferments until 1675 when he and his brother-in-law, Izaak Walton, toured Europe. Taught at Winchester College from 1672. In 1679 became chaplain to Mary, sister of king and wife of William of Orange, at the Hague; in 1680 chaplain to Charles II of England, and in 1683 chaplain to Lord Dartmouth, commander of the fleet at Tangier. In 1684 the king chose him bishop of Bath and Wells; the next year he attended Charles II on his deathbed. Was loyal to James II; but in 1688 was one of the seven bishops thrown into the Tower for refusing to accept and publish the second Declaration of Indulgence of James II to appease the Catholics; tried for treason, but was acquitted. Refused to give allegiance to William and Mary; consequently deprived of bishopric in 1691. Ken occupies important place in English hymnody. Most widely known hymns: "Awake My Soul," "Glory to Thee, My God, This Night," and "Praise God from Whom All Blessings Flow." Other writings were few: *Manual of Prayers for the Use of the Scholars of Winchester College, Practice of Divine Love,* an exposition of the catechism, *Prayers for the Use of All Persons Who Come to the Baths for Cure,* and a few letters and sermons.

KENNEDY, JOHN FITZGERALD (1917-1963), First Roman Catholic president of the United States. Educated at Harvard. In US navy from 1941 to 1945. Member of House of Representatives from 1947 to 1953 and of the United States Senate from 1953 to 1961. President from 1961 until his assassination at Dallas in 1963. Wrote *Why England Slept, Profiles in Courage, Strategy of Peace* and *To Turn the Tide*.

KENRICK, FRANCIS PATRICK (1796-1863), Roman Catholic Archbishop of Baltimore, born in Dublin, Ireland, received theological training in the College of the Propaganda in Rome, ordained in 1821, and immediately sent to America. Became head of the newly established Roman Catholic seminary at Bardstown, Kentucky (1821-1830); coadjutor bishop of Philadelphia (1830-1842); Bishop of Philadelphia (1842-1851); and Archbishop of Baltimore (1851-1863). While at Philadelphia founded the Seminary of St. Charles Borromeo. In 1854 called upon by the pope to collect and forward the respective opinions of the American bishops relative to the doctrine of the Immaculate Conception. As apostolic delegate presided over the first plenary council of the United States, at Baltimore (1852); and in 1859 the pope conferred upon him and succeeding archbishops of Baltimore the "primacy of honor" over other American archbishops. He was regarded as one of the most learned theologians of the Roman Catholic church in America. Wrote several polemic and apologetic books, such as *Primacy of the Apostolic See Vindicated; Vindication of the Catholic Church;* and *Pri-*

macy of the Holy See and the Authority of the General Councils. Chief writings, however, were *Theologia Dogmatica* and *Theologia Moralis*. He was making a revision of the Douay English Bible, with notes, when he died. Instrumental in helping to bring to an end the system of "trusteeism" in the young Roman Catholic church in America.

KENTIGERN (kĕn'ti gürn) (known also as **ST. MUNGO**) (c. 518-c. 603), Celtic missionary, patron saint of Glasgow, born at Culcross, Perthshire, Scotland, trained at the monastery there. Founder and first bishop of the diocese of Glasgow, labored for the conversion of the people of Cumberland. Driven from Cumberland by persecution, went to Wales, where he is said to have founded a monastery, and to have converted many people. Returned to Scotland in 570, left the work in Wales to trusted pupil Asaph, who became the first bishop of the Welsh see. Founded a college of monks and built several churches. Shortly before the death of Columba, Kentigern met the aged missionary of North Scotland, and they exchanged staves. Buried in a crypt of the cathedral of St. Mungo in Glasgow.

KENYON, SIR FREDERICK GEORGE (1863-1952), British archaeologist and philologist, born in London, England, and educated at Winchester, New College, Oxford, and Halle, Germany. Assistant in the British Museum (1889-1898), and assistant keeper of manuscripts (1898-1909), director and principal librarian at the British Museum (1909-1930). President of the British Academy (1917-1921); a member or chairman of several learned societies in the field of archaeology, and special university lecturer on several occasions. In World War I served with the territorial forces in France. One of Britain's foremost Bible scholars and authorities who devoted most of life to making biblical discoveries in New Testament Greek papri intelligible to laymen and convincing them that science does not disprove the Bible. A few of many books were *Our Bible and the Ancient Manuscripts, Handbook of the Textual Criticism of the New Testament, Recent Developments of Textual Criticism of the Greek Bible, The Text of the Greek Bible, The Story of the Bible, The Bible and Archaeology,* and *The Bible and Modern Scholarship*.

KERR, HUGH THOMPSON (1871-1950), Presbyterian clergyman, born at Elora, Ontario, Canada, educated at Knox College, Toronto, and Western Theological Seminary. Ordained in the Presbyterian ministry in 1897, and from 1897 to 1946 held subsequent pastorates in Oakland Church, Pittsburgh; First Church, Hutchinson, Kansas; Fullerton Avenue Church, Chicago; and Shadyside Presbyterian Church, Pittsburgh. Chairman of the Alliance of Reformed Churches (1913-1947); moderator of the General Assembly (1930); president of the Board of Christian Education (1923-1940); and Executive Secretary of the Pitcairn-Crabb Foundation. One of the first radio preachers in America (1922-1942). Among his more than twenty books wrote several children's story sermon books, *The Christian Mission in America, The Gospel in Modern Poetry, A God-centered Faith, The Christian Sacraments, Helpful Prayers for All Occasions,* and *Preaching in the Early Church*.

KEY, FRANCIS SCOTT (1779-1843), author of "The Star Spangled Banner," born in what is now Carroll County, Maryland, attended St. John's College, Annapolis, later studied law in Annapolis. In 1801 opened a law practice in Frederick. Moved to Georgetown, District of Columbia, became an influential young Washington attorney. During the British retreat from Washington in 1814 Dr. William Beanes was seized and confined aboard the British fleet. Key was asked to undertake his release. He obtained the release but was detained on British vessel off shore pending the projected attack on Baltimore. Through the night bombardment of September 13-14, Key remained on deck in agonized suspense, but at daybreak was overjoyed to see the American flag still flying over Fort McHenry. In intense emotional excitement composed the poem, "The Star Spangled Banner," scribbling it on the back of an envelope. It was published in the Baltimore *American* on September 21, and soon gained nationwide popularity. It became our national anthem in 1931. Key was a devout Christian, member of the Protestant Episcopal church. From 1814 to 1826 a delegate to the general conventions of his church, for many years a lay reader in St. John's Church in Georgetown. An early worker in the American Sunday School Union, and a United States Attorney for the District of Columbia from 1833 to 1841. Author of *The Power of Literature and Its Connection with Religion*.

KHAMA (kä'mȧ) **or KGAMA III** (c. 1828-1923), chief of the Bamangwato tribe of Northern Bechuanaland. Older son of the African chief, Sekhome, who with the lad Khama first met David Livingstone when he visited the Bamangwato tribe. Khama attended a mission school and in 1862 became a Christian. Married a Christian and established a Christian home. In 1872, three years before the death of Sekhome, the tribesmen chose Khama as their chief. The father became angry and tried to destroy Khama. The people honored and protected their young chief, loyal to his tribe. Ruled this people from 1875 with justice and equity and on high Christian principle. Sought to abolish the purchase of slaves, and ruled strong drink out of his tribe. Advocated marriage by free choice of the young people. Loyal to both tribe and Christ, demonstrated how good tribal traditions and Christian ideals can both operate at one and the same time. In 1885, after twelve years of struggle against the Boers, the whole of Bechuanaland was taken under British protection, but with the distinct understanding that the people were to be free in their own right to rule. In 1893 assisted the British South Africa Company in overthrowing the Matabele, two years later visited England to protest against his country being subjected to foreign power. Khama remained the firm friend of the British and assisted them in subduing other insurgent tribes.

KIDD, BERESFORD JAMES (1864-1948), Anglican church historian, born in Birmingham, England, and educated at Keble College, Oxford. Ordained in 1887; assistant curate of SS. Philip and James, Oxford (1887-1900); vicar of St. Paul's, Oxford (1904-1920); chaplain and lecturer in theology at Pembroke College, Oxford, and warden of Keble College, Oxford (1920-1939). Taught and examined in the school of theology at Oxford. Wrote *The Thirty-nine Articles: Their History and Explanation; The Continental Reformation; Documents Illustrative of the History of the Church to* A.D. *461; A History of the Church to* A.D. *461; The Churches of Eastern Christendom from 451; The Counter Reformation;* and *The Primacy of the Roman See.*

KIERKEGAARD (kĭ'kĕ gâr), **SOREN AABY** (1813-1855), Danish philosopher, born in Copenhagen, Denmark, took degrees in theology and philosophy in the University of Copenhagen, never ordained. Spent several months in Berlin studying under Schelling, otherwise spending whole life in native city. Constant ill health made him morbid and seclusive. Earlier writings (1843-1846) principally concerned with the nature of religion and man's relation to it. Through the early part of life suffered a sense of deep sin and guilt because of his father's and his own moral failure. In 1843 published pseudonymously first large work, *Either-Or,* representing respectively the aesthetical and the ethical type of life, placing indirectly before the reader the question: Which of these two types ought to be chosen? On the same day published also, over his own name, a small collection of sermons, thus answering the question. He said, "neither," for religion alone contains the truth of life. Other of earlier writings were *Fear and Trembling, Bits of Philosophy, What Is Fear?, Stations on the Path of Life,* and *Concluding Unscientific Postscript.* In the latter part of his life waged war upon Hegelian philosophy and religion as exemplified in the national Danish church. Writings bear the imprint of his attitudes. Stressed "otherness" of God and high ethics. A Christian was an isolated individual, alone with God, and in contact with the world only through suffering. The word "existential" is closely associated with Kierkegaard. "By it 'existence' is contrasted with mere 'life.'" "Existence is reached by the inner decisions of the individual." "Religion is a matter of the individual soul." He made a distinction between essence and existence. "In his view, the realm of essence is arrived at by thought and logic; the realm of existence by decision, always of a moral and religious character." His influence is seen in Neo-orthodoxy.

KILIAN (died c. 689), Irish apostle to Franconia, Germany, native of Ireland. In youth entered the monastic life. With eleven companions went to Franconia to preach the gospel. Crossing Gaul and the Rhine, reached Würzburg on the Main, continuing preaching. After a time made a pilgrimage to Rome, consecrated the first bishop of Würzburg. After returning to Germany, and preaching for a time, winning Duke Gozbert and many of his subjects to Christianity, he and two companions, were murdered at Würzburg at the instigation of Geilana, the pagan wife of Gozbert, because Kilian had reproved him for having married her.

KIMURA (kĭ mōō'rȧ), **HENRY SEIMATSU** (1875-1958), Japanese Congregational minister, sometimes called "The Moody of Japan," or "The Billy Sunday of Japan." Born in Japan and studied Bible at the Moody Bible Institute, Chicago (1900-1901). After return to Japan conducted extensive revivals and evangelistic campaigns in cities throughout Japan and among his nationals in Manchuria, Korea, Hawaii, and the South Sea Islands. Preaching was effective.

KING, HENRY CHURCHILL (1858-1934), American Congregational theologian and educator, born at Hillsdale, Michigan, educated at Hillsdale College, Oberlin College, Oberlin Theological Seminary, Harvard University, and University of Berlin. In 1884 returned to Oberlin as associate professor of mathematics; in 1891 became professor of philosophy; in 1897, professor of theology; and from 1902 to 1927, president of the college. Considered one of the ablest educators of the Middle West, and during incumbency completely rebuilt Oberlin. A religious philosopher of the idealistic school, and theologian of a liberal evangelicalism which accepts biological evolution and biblical criticism. Theology was influenced in Berlin by Lotze's personalism and Ritschl's theology of the social gospel.

KING, JONAS (1792-1869), American missionary, born at Hawley, Massachusetts; graduated from Williams College (1816) and Andover Seminary. Ordained (1819). In 1823 joined Pliny Fisk in mission in Holy Land and in expeditionary travels. From 1823 to 1869 had main interest in Greece. Married an influential Greek lady; built home, school, and church in Athens. Preached, gave Christian instruction, and disseminated Scriptures. In 1830 mission was transferred to the American Board. He served as mediating agent between the United States and Greek governments, 1851-1857. Was anathematized by the Holy Synod of Athens (1863). Reconciliation was effected shortly before his death.

KING, MARTIN LUTHER, JR. (1929-1968), black civil rights leader. Born at Atlanta, Georgia. Educated at Morehouse College, Crozer Theological Seminary, and Boston University (Ph.D. 1955). Pastor in Montgomery, Alabama (1954-1960). Co-pastor with father of Ebenezer Baptist Church in Atlanta from 1960 to 1968. National figure after non-violent mass black demonstrations in Montgomery in 1956. Organizer and president of the Southern Christian Leadership Conference from 1957 until his death. Main figure in march on Washington in 1963 that helped in the passage of Civil Rights Acts in 1964 and 1965. Won Nobel Peace Prize in 1964. Assassinated in Memphis in 1968.

KINGSLEY, CHARLES (1819-1875), Christian socialist and writer of novels. Born at Holne, Devonshire. Educated at King's College, London and Magdalene College, Cambridge. Ordained in 1842. Pastor at Eversley, Hants from 1842. Professor of modern history at Cambridge from 1860 to 1869. Canon of Chester and later Westminster from 1869 to 1875. Wrote for the Christian Socialists. Favored cooperatives and wanted to reform education and promote sanitation. *Herward the Wake* and *The Water Babies* are examples of his novels.

KIRKPATRICK, WILLIAM JAMES (1838-1921), American sacred music composer and publisher, born in Ireland, came with parents to America, becoming a resident of Philadelphia. In the Civil War served as a fife major. After the war gave up secular pursuits to write and publish sacred music. For many years director of music of the Grace Methodist Episcopal Church, Philadelphia, and organist and choirmaster of the Ebenezer Church of the same city. In connection with composition devoted much time to the conducting of music in conventions and camp meetings. First collection of songs was published in 1859 as Devotional Melodies. In seventeen years he and John R. Sweeny published over eighty gospel song collections. Among his tunes are "Jesus Saves," "Blessed Be the Name," "He Hideth My Soul," "'Tis So Sweet to Trust in Jesus," and "When Love Shines In." Wrote words and music of "Lord, I'm Coming Home."

KITTEL, GERHARD (1888-1948), German biblical scholar. Born at Breslau, Germany. He was an instructor at Kiel (1913) and Leipzig (1917), professor of New Testament at Greifswalg (1921-1926), and Tübingen (1926-1945). The Jewish background of the New Testament was Kittel's main interest. He believed that the Jewish element prevailed over the Greek element in the writing of the New Testament. Kittel became famous as the editor of the voluminous *Theological Wordbook of the New Testament*. This work utilizes secular usage in classical Greek, the religious connotations of the Septuagint, and Hebrew background to determine the meaning and significance of New Testament words. *The Jewish Question,* a pamphlet written by Kittel in 1934, led to his being imprisoned by the Allies in 1945. He was the author of several other works on the Jewish background of the New Testament.

KITTEL, RUDOLF (1853-1929), German theologian and Old Testament scholar. Born at Ehningen, Württemberg, and studied at Tübingen, receiving his Ph.D. in 1879. He was the pastor (1876-1879), lecturer at Tübingen (1879-1881), professor in a gymnasium at Stuttgart (1881-1888), professor of Old Testament Exegesis at the University of Breslau (1888-1897), and professor of Old Testament Exegesis at Leipzig (1898-1924). Kittel was the author or editor of several outstanding and scholarly works on the Old Testament and Apocrypha. Kittel's best known work is *Biblia Hebraica,* an edition of the Hebrew Old Testament prepared in collaboration with several German scholars.

KITTO (kĭt'ō), **JOHN** (1804-1854), Bible scholar, born at Plymouth, England. At age twelve became totally and permanently deaf in consequence of a fall. Through what education he had received and could obtain by himself, became a great lover of books, read much and began to write. An article written and published in the *Plymouth Weekly Journal* attracted wide attention. In 1824 went to Exeter to study dentistry with Anthony Norris Groves, one of the founders of the Plymouth Brethren. Later a missionary in the East. Kitto wrote a book, *Essays and Letters, with a Short Memoir of the Author*. Through Mr. Grove's mediation Kitto was engaged by the Church Missionary Association as printer, and was sent to the society's missionary college at Islington to learn printer's trade. In 1827 went to Malta for the missionary society, but returned in 1829 to England. Engaged to go with Mr. Groves as tutor to his family upon a missionary tour of the East. Toured several countries and Kitto was from 1829 to 1832 a missionary in Bagdad. Returned to England in 1833, found employment with Charles Knight, publisher, and wrote industriously for Knight's *Penny Magazine* and his *Penny Cyclopaedia,* a *Pictorial Bible* in four volumes. This was the beginning of the literary work by which Kitto became popular. Then wrote *Uncle Oliver's Travels* depicting his experiences and travels in Persia. Following this wrote *A Pictorial History of Palestine and the Holy Land, Gallery of Scripture Engravings* and *A History of Palestine from the Patriarchal Age to the Present*. His *Cyclopaedia of Biblical Literature* and his *Daily Bible Illustrations* (eight volumes) comprise two most popular works. Through kindness and help of friends went to Germany where he spent his last three months. Died at Cannstadt, Württemberg.

KLOPSTOCK, FRIEDRICH GOTTLIEB (1724-1803), German religious poet, born at Quedlinburg, Germany, early educated at Quedlinburg, at the Gymnasium of Naumburg, and at the famous classical school at Schulpforta, studied theology at Jena and Leipzig. Early became interested in the writings of Tasso, Virgil, and Milton, and purposed to write a religious epic for the Germans comparable to Milton's *Paradise Lost*. The great task of his life was to produce epic, *The Messiah,* the first German epic, written in blank hexameter verse in twenty cantos, a task which required twenty-seven years for its completion. Though written in an age of rationalism and infidelity, the epic gives expression of the faith in Christ of its author. The action of the poem opens after the triumphal entry into Jerusalem, and closes with the Savior sitting down at the right hand of God. His poem of importance next to *The Messiah* was his *Hermmann's Schlacht* (the Battle of Arminius). Also wrote *Odes,* lyric poetry, and religious dramas.

KNIBB, WILLIAM (1803-1845), Baptist missionary to Jamaica. Sent to Jamaica in 1824 to superintend Kingston School. Pastor at Montego Bay from 1830 to 1845. Became an anti-slavery propagandist by pen and word. Helped to make Jamaica Baptist churches independent of the Baptist Missionary Society, to create Calabar College to educate ministers and to form a West Indian Mission to Africa.

KNOX, JOHN (c. 1514-1572), Scottish Reformer, born at Haddington, Scotland. After grammar schooling at Haddington, went to the University of Glasgow and St. Andrews. Ordained priest about 1536. When Wishart was tried for heresy and burned at the stake in 1546, Knox escaped apprehension. When Beaton was assassinated shortly after the death of Wishart, some of the rebels took possession of St. Andrews, where Knox was preaching, and held it for three months in 1547. Then the leaders were captured and taken to France to be punished. Among those taken to France was John Knox. Held as a galley slave for nineteen months. As soon as released in 1549 he returned to England, and for about five years preached the doctrines of the Reformation with great eloquence as royal chaplain and minister at Berwick. When Catholic Queen Mary ascended the throne in 1553, he fled to Frankfurt, Germany, where he pastored a group of English refugees. Went to Geneva where he was with Calvin, learning thoroughly the Presbyterian-Calvinistic doctrines. For about ten years in voluntary exile, preaching in Germany, Switzerland, and France, and on occasional trips preaching in England and Scotland. On one of these trips home, about 1555, he married Marjorie Bowes. Together they returned to Geneva, remaining on the continent until 1559. While on the continent wrote elaborate treatise on *Predestination* and his *First Blast of the Trumpet against the Monstrous Regiment of Women*. During absence from Scotland the Reform party had grown and become more and more consolidated. The Catholic party was becoming more and more hostile. In this tense situation, with the Catholic queen regent, Mary of Lorraine, still on the throne, Knox returned home in 1559. He declared boldly that the mass was idolatry, and that Catholic churches and monasteries should be closed. In 1560 the queen regent died. Protestantism was established as the national religion, a confession of faith was formulated, and a constitution for the new church was drawn up. He had to face the new queen, Mary Stuart, who occupied the throne from 1560 to 1567. She had Knox arrested for treason, but the court acquitted him. Last years were devoted primarily to ministry of preaching and counseling in Edinburgh and St. Andrews. The triumph of the Scottish Reformation was complete.

KNUDSON, ALBERT CORNELIUS (1873-1953), Methodist theologian and philosopher, born at Grand Meadow, Minnesota, studied at the University of Minnesota, Boston University, and the universities of Jena and Berlin. Professor of church history at Denver University for two years, professor of philosophy and English Bible at Baker University for two years, and then professor at Allegheny College for four years. Professor of Hebrew and Old Testament exegesis at Boston University School of Theology (1906-1921), professor of systematic theology (1921-1943), dean (1926-1938). Early in career wrote *The Old Testament Problem,* and *The Religious Teaching of the Old Testament.* Under influence of Borden Parker Bowne turned attention to personalistic philosophy, and wrote the *Philosophy of Personalism, The Validity of Religious Experience,* and *Present Tendencies in Religious Thought.* Also wrote *The Doctrine of God, The Doctrine of Redemption, The Principles of Christian Ethics,* and *The Philosophy of Peace and War.*

KRAEMER, HENDRIK (1888-1965), lay educator, author, missionary, missionary anthropologist, and ecumenical leader. Specialized in Oriental languages and cultures in his education in Holland. Sent to Indonesia by the Dutch Bible Society as linguistics and translation advisor to the Reformed churches from 1921 to 1937. From 1937 to 1948 professor at Leiden. From 1948 to 1956 director of the Ecumenical Institute of the World Council of Churches at Bossey, Switzerland. Professor at Union Seminary, New York from 1955 to 1957. Lived in Holland until his death. His most famous work was *The Christian Message for a Non-Christian World* (1938), a study guide for the third World Missionary Conference at Tambaram, in which he stressed the uniqueness of the biblical revelation against the syncretism of Hocking's *Rethinking Missions.*

KRAPF (kräpf), **JOHANN LUDWIG** (1810-1881), pioneer German missionary-explorer in East Africa, born in Derendingen, near Tübingen, Württemberg, Germany, studied at the Latin School at Tübingen, school of the Basel Mission in Switzerland, and University of Tübingen. After a short experience as vicar and teacher in Germany, sent in 1838 to Abyssinia by the British Church Missionary Society, but due to continued hostile Roman Catholic influence, effort proved unsuccessful. In 1843 went to British East Africa to open work among the Moslems. In 1848-49, along with Johannes Rebmann and others, entered upon the first of several great expeditions into the heart of Africa. On this trip he discovered Mount Kenya. In 1850 visited England and Germany to print Bible translations, lecture on explorations, and find new missionary recruits. In 1851 made second great journey into the heart of Africa. Conceived idea of building a chain of missions across Africa from the east to the west coast. In 1854 made a trip to Palestine and began to promote his famous plan for "Apostles' Street" in which he would attempt to build a line of missions from Jerusalem to the capital of Abyssinia, naming the stations after the twelve apostles, this line and the proposed line east and west to form a great cross of missions in Africa. In 1857, 1861-65, and 1866-68 made further expeditions into the interior of Africa. He secured many valuable Ethiopian manuscripts, and African ethnology and philology are indebted to him for important contributions. On the last of these journeys met Henry M. Stanley in Africa. Through the work of Johannes Rebmann, Stanley, Grattan Guinness, H. K. F. Kumm and hundreds of others this vision of Johann Ludwig Krapf was further realized until Africa became an open mission field. Outstanding work was the translating of the Bible in Swahili, the opening of East Africa to Protestant missionary work. Weakened, had to retire from the field and to seek rest in Europe. Chose for home the little village of Kornthal near the place of his birth. Continued lexicographical and translating work until his death.

KRÜDENER, BARBARA JULIANA, BARONESS VON (1764-1824), mystic and Chiliast who greatly influenced Alexander I of Russia. Unfaithful to Russian diplomat husband, converted in 1804 at Riga by a Moravian shoemaker to Pietism. Urged Holy Alliance, a union of Christian rulers against revolution and atheism. Idea adopted by Alexander, whom she first met at Heilbron, and signed by several rulers of European states in 1814. Wrote a novel, *Valérie,* in 1804.

KRUMMACHER (kro͞om'ä kĕr), **FRIEDRICH WILHELM** (1796-1868), German Reformed preacher, born at Mörs on the Rhine, the birthplace of the German hymnist, Tersteegen, whose writings greatly influenced him. Studied at the University of Halle and at the University of Jena. One of the most influential and eloquent preachers of Germany of his century. Began ministry in 1819 as assistant pastor of Reformed congregation at Frankfurt-on-the-Main. Next went to Ruhrort, near Dusseldorf, then to Barmen in the Wupperthal, then to Elberfeld. In 1844 received a call to the seminary at Mercersburg, Pennsylvania, but declined in favor of Dr. Philip Schaff. In 1847 accepted a call to the Trinity Church, Berlin, in 1853 appointed court chaplain at Potsdam, where he died in 1868. A bitter opponent of rationalism, but warm friend of the Prussian Union and the Evangelical Alliance. Perhaps better known in England and America than any other German preacher. Some of his best known writings were *Elijah the Tishbite, The Prophet Elisha, Solomon and Shulamite, The Suffering Saviour,* and *David the King of Israel.*

KURTZ, JOHANN HEINRICH (1809-1890), German exegete and church historian, born at Montjoie near Achen in Rhenish Prussia, studied theology at the universities of Halle and Bonn, became the teacher of religion at the gymnasium of Mitau in 1835, and professor of Church history at the University of Dorpat in 1849, where he continued teaching for twenty years, becoming professor of Old Testament exegesis in 1859. In 1870 pensioned and the next year settled at Marburg where he spent the rest of his life in literary labor. In his works on Old Testament makes many concessions to modern higher criticism. First book was *The Bible and Astronomy*. Later wrote *Sacrificial Worship of the Old Testament, Manual of Sacred History, Bible History* (the book that made the name of Kurtz most widely known), *History of the Old Covenant, The Unity of the Book of Genesis,* and *Manual of Church History* (three volumes).

KUYPER (koi'pẽr), **ABRAHAM** (1837-1920), Dutch theologian and statesman, born at Maassluis, near Rotterdam, Holland. Instructed in the theology of the Dutch Reformed church at the University of Leiden. Members of first parish (1863-1868), a little country church at Beesd, challenged him to an orthodox Calvinistic faith. For many years after that represented and promoted orthodox Calvinism within the established church, seeking to hold it to the orthodox faith. Kuyper was pastor at Utrecht (1868-1870), and at Amsterdam (1870-1874). For nearly fifty years editor of the daily *De Standaard,* making it a power for Christ on the life of the nation, a fighting organ for evangelical Christianity. Also carried religious principles into politics, advocating the necessity of the church's using its influence for a purer public national life. In 1874 became an active participant in the political life of Holland, being a member of the States-General on two occasions and prime minister (1901-1905). In 1880 founded the Free Reformed University at Amsterdam, and was professor there for many years. In 1886 founded the Free Reformed church. In 1898 Stone Lecturer at Princeton University and his lectures were published under the title, *Calvinism.* Wrote many valuable theological and devotional books, among them, *The Work of the Holy Spirit* and *The Encyclopedia of Theology.*

KYLE, MELVIN GROVE (1858-1933), clergyman and archaeologist, born near Cadiz, Ohio, educated at Muskingum College and Allegheny Theological Seminary, taught Biblical theology and archaeology at Xenia Theology Seminary in St. Louis (1908-1930), president from 1922 to 1930. For years president of the Board of Foreign Missions, and in 1927 moderator of the United Presbyterian church. In visiting the mission work of his church in Egypt became interested in archaeology. A friend of men like Maspero, Sayce, Petrie, and Max Müller. As time passed received international recognition in the field of biblical archaeology, first Egyptian and later Palestinian. In 1921 editor-in-chief of *Bibliotheca Sacra,* the same year lecturer in the American School of Oriental Research in Jerusalem. Editor of the archaeological department of the Sunday School Times from 1915. Made explorations at Sodom and Gomorrah (1924) and Kirjath-sepher (1926-1928). He wrote *The Deciding Voice of the Monuments in Biblical Criticism, Moses and the Monuments, The Problem of the Pentateuch,* and *Explorations at Sodom.* Also was revision editor of the *International Standard Bible Encyclopedia,* (five volumes) the standard conservative work in its field.

L

LACORDAIRE (lȧ kôr dâr′), **JEAN BAPTISTE HENRI** (1802-1861), Roman Catholic Dominican monk, preacher, and theologian, born at Recey-sur-Ource, cote-d'Or, near Dijon, France; studied law at Dijon and at Paris, entering the profession for a short time. Under the influence of Rousseau's writings became a pronounced deist of the Voltaire school. Realizing that Christianity was the indispensable basis of modern society, decided to become a priest; in 1824 entered the seminary of St. Sulpice; took holy orders in 1827. First appointment was that of almoner in the College of Juilly, also known as College of Henry IV. After the July Revolution, 1830, he and Montalembert joined Lamennais in establishing the *Journal l'Avenir,* with its motto "God and Liberty." Their intention was to regenerate Catholic opinion in France and seal its union with liberal progress. They believed that Roman Catholicism was consistent with slogans of the Revolution: "liberty, equality, and fraternity." They believed that Catholicism must not depend on monarchial support in France, but must ally itself with the people of a republican government. Articles in *l'Avenir* speedily provoked the displeasure of the episcopate. These men attempted to open a free school in Paris upon the principles of the Revolution. The police at once closed the school and the pope condemned the Journal. Lacordaire went to Rome and submitted unconditionally to the pope. Upon return to Paris took up a defense of the church's doctrine setting forth in most eloquent oratory the Ultramontane view of history and the church. Became one of the greatest Roman Catholic preachers. At Rome in 1839 donned the habit of the Dominicans and joined the monastery of Minerva. When France was constituted a separate province of the Dominican order, Lacordaire became provincial. Unable to continue preaching in France, returned to Rome and was made provincial of the Dominican order. For four years labored to make the Dominicans a powerful religious order. In 1854 retired from active public life and withdrew to Soreze where he died.

LACHMANN, KARL (1793-1851), German textual critic and philologist. Born at Brunswick. He studied classical and Germanic philology at Leipzig and Göttingen. He served as private lecturer at Göttingen (1815), Berlin (1816), professor of philology at Konigsberg (1818), and Berlin (1825), he was extraordinary professor of classical and German philology at Berlin (1825-1827), and ordinary professor (1827-1851). Lachmann was the founder of modern texual criticism, making the restoration of ancient texts the area of his special study. He edited many Latin and old German works. To Lachmann scholarship owes the first edition of the Greek New Testament text in which the Textus Receptus is abandoned in favor of older Greek manuscripts. His attempt was to restore the text used in the Eastern church in the fourth century. Tischendorf, Westcott-Hort, and others found impetus in Lachmann's pioneer work. He has also exerted a considerable influence on modern Homeric criticism.

LACTANTIUS (lăk tăn′shĭŭs), **LUCIUS CAECILIUS FIRMIANUS** (c. 240-c. 320), born in Italy, studied in the school of the rhetorician and apologist Arnobius of Sicca; taught rhetoric in Diocletian's School in Nicomedia and became a Christian in adult life, brought to the imperial court at Treves by Constantine to teach one of his sons. Jerome called him the most learned man of his time. Lactantius is more the rhetorician than the philosopher or theologian, and is stronger in the refutation of error than in the establishment of truth. Most important work is *Seven Books of The Divine Institutions,* a comprehensive refutation of heathenism and a defense of Christianity, essentially an historic apology for the Christian church.

LAKE, KIRSOPP (1872-1946), Liberal English-American archaeologist and historian, born in Southampton, England, educated at St. Paul's School, London, and at London College, Oxford. Served curacies at Lumley in Durham, and at St. Mary the Virgin, Oxford between 1895 and 1904. From 1904 to 1914 taught New Testament exegesis and early Christian literature at the University of Leiden, Holland. Professor of Christian literature at Harvard University (1914-1938). Visited Mt. Athos, Greece, and Mount Sinai, and libraries of other monasteries to investigate Greek manuscripts; director of several archaelogical expeditions. A member of expeditions which discovered the site of the oldest Semitic cult on Serabit Plateau in Egypt and fragments of the "ivory house" of biblical history at Samaria. Among writings: *Texts of the New Testament, Texts from Mt. Athos, The Historical Evidence for the Resurrection of Jesus Christ* in which he challenged the sufficiency of the open tomb as evidence of Christ's resurrection, *The Early Days of Monasticism on Mt. Athos, The Athos Leaves of the Shepherd of Hermas, The Earlier Epistles of St. Paul, The Codex Sinaiticus, The Beginnings of Christianity, An Introduction to the New Testament*. Edited and translated several books.

LAMBERT, FRANÇIS (1486-1530), Reformer in Hesse, born at Avignon, in 1501 entered the cloister of the Franciscan Observants at Avignon. Became "apostolic preacher," gave himself to the study of the Holy Scripture. Influenced by writings of Luther, left the cloister and went to Geneva and Lausanne, then to Zurich. With credentials from George Spalatin to Luther and the elector, went to Wittenberg in 1523, remained for more than a year. Advanced the Reformation by lecturing on the prophets, translating several of the Reformers' books into French and Italian, and by writing. One of the first Reformation monks to marry. In 1527 made professor of theology at the University of Marburg, and had a large role in establishing the Reformation in Hesse. At Synod of Homberg advocated a Presbyterian form of church government, and at Marburg professed conversion to the Zwinglian view of the Lord's Supper. Devoted his last three or four years to teaching the Old and the New Testament.

LAMENNAIS (lȧ mĕ nĕ'), **HUGUES FÉLICITE ROBERT De** (1782-1854), French Roman Catholic writer and philosopher, born at Saint Molo in Brittany, France. Through influence of brother, an ordained priest, decided in 1804 to devote himself to the service of the church. Became a pronounced Ultramontanist. In 1811 received the tonsure, and then became professor of mathematics at an ecclesiastical college at Saint Molo. In 1816 ordained priest, began writing in defense of papal authority as against civil or imperial authority. Though writings were very acceptable to the pope, they were increasingly offensive to the Gallican clergy, the Sorbonne, and the imperial government. Between 1817 and 1824 wrote principal work, a four-volume set, which rallied and consolidated the Ultramontanist party and produced a kind of revival in the Church. On a trip to Rome, 1824, he was greeted with a warm welcome from Pope Leo XII; but declined to accept the pope's offer of the cardinal's hat. The next year wrote another book still more vehemently denouncing Gallicanism. This incurred much opposition from the French bishops and led to an open break with the monarchy. With hope of holding unity and authority of the church and at the same time of holding to the principles of democracy advocated a theocratic democracy in which there would be extension of suffrage, freedom of worship, liberty of conscience, and freedom of the press; at the same time the spiritual supremacy of the papacy. With this end in view, 1830, he, with Montalembert and Lacordaire, founded the journal, *L'Avenir* (The Future), with the motto, "God and Liberty." Loyalty to Rome and the papacy, and continued attacks on Gallicanism increased the hatred of the French toward him. At the same time Rome was beginning to question his orthodoxy. The editors felt obliged to suspend the publication of *L'Avenir,* and made a trip to Rome. Lamennais did not find under the new pope, Gregory XVI, the kind of welcome he had received in 1824. Now found himself opposed both by clergy and by papacy. Finally broke with the Catholic church and pursued an independent course, tending to social radicalism, which he combined with his religious radicalism. Wrote several works on liberty and democracy. In 1848 elected a member of the National Assembly. Died refusing to the last to be reconciled to the church.

LANFRANC (lăn'frăngk), (c. 1005-1089), Prior of Bec and Archbishop of Canterbury, born at Pavia, Italy, educated in rhetoric and law at Bologne. As a young man started out as a teacher and master; but in 1042 became a monk in a Benedictine monastery at Bec, Normandy. About 1045 became prior of the monastery, where Anselm his noted pupil later succeeded him. In 1049 when Berenger of Tours began to attack transubstantiation, Lanfranc was commissioned to combat the "heresy." Did the job so zealously and efficiently he grew in favor and strength in church and with pope. In 1063 William made Lanfranc abbot of St. Stephen monastery at Caen, Anselm succeeding at Bec. In 1070 made Archbishop of Canterbury, became William's right-hand man. Did much to strengthen the Catholic church in England and at the same time was able to help the English church maintain a strong national spirit. William entrusted to Lanfranc the administration of the kingdom during William's own absence on the Continent. After William I died in 1087, he crowned William II and continued as his adviser until his own death.

LANGE (läng'ĕ), **JOHANN PETER** (1802-1884), German Reformed theologian and exegete, born in Sonnborn, near Elberfeld, Prussia, educated at the gymnasium in Düsseldorf and the University of Bonn. Held pastorates in Reformed churches between 1825 and 1841. While at Duisburg, attracted attention by essays on theological and practical subjects which appeared in Hengstenberg's and other periodicals; by volumes of poems; by his book written in answer to Strauss's *Leben Jesu.* In 1841 called to the University of Zurich. Taught until called to Bonn in 1854 as professor of dogmatic theology. Made consistorial councilor in 1860. As a theologian, one of the most original and fertile authors of the nineteenth century. His theology is biblical, evangelical, and catholic. His *Theologische-homiletisches Bibelwerk,* later edited in its English form by Philip Schaff in twenty-five volumes as *A Commentary on the Holy Scriptures, Critical, Doctrinal, and Homiletic,* made his name familiar in England and America. *Life of Jesus According to the Gospels* is perhaps his greatest work. Other works: *History of the Apostolic Age, A System of Christian Dogmatics, A System of Theological Hermeneutics,* and *A System of Biblical Hermeneutics.*

LANGTON, STEPHEN (d. 1228), English theologian, cardinal, and archbishop of Canterbury (1207-1228), born in Yorkshire, England, educated chiefly at Paris, where he spent twenty-five years, studying and lecturing on theology. In 1206 Innocent III made Langton a cardinal, and in 1207, Archbishop of Canterbury. Excluded from his see by King John until 1213. Then, under the pressure of excommunication by Pope Innocent III, John yielded, and permitted Langton to be seated. Stood firmly both for country's liberty, and against royal tyranny. Had no small part in adopting the Magna Charta in 1215, and was the first to sign the document. As a Catholic bishop labored loyally for church and as an English patriot stood firm for country. In later years busied himself chiefly with the affairs of the church and instituted many reforms. Attended the Fourth Lateran Council in 1215. Langton is given the credit for dividing the Old Testament Vulgate into chapters.

LANPHIER (lăn′fēr), **JEREMIAH C.** (1809-?), founder and Superintendent of the Fulton Street prayer meeting, born at Coxsackie, New York, made a public profession of Christ in the Broadway Tabernacle Church in 1842. For more than twenty years engaged in mercantile business in New York City. In 1857, employed by the Old North Dutch Church at the corner of Fulton and Williams Streets, New York City to serve as lay missionary to reach the unchurched in the neighborhood. A man of much prayer, best remembered for his calling a noonday business men's prayer meeting at the Fulton Street Church on September 23, 1857, which engendered the Revival of 1857-1858.

LAS CASAS (läs kä′sȧs), **BARTOLOMÉ DE** (1474-1566), Spanish priest and missionary to the American Indians of the West Indies. Born at Seville, Spain, studied the humanities and law at the universities of Seville and Salamanca, and entered the Dominican order in 1523. He and father were companions of Columbus on the latter's second voyage to America in 1498. Bartolome made his second trip to the New World when he came with Columbus to Haiti in 1502. As a planter owned Indian slaves as did the other colonists. In 1510 ordained priest, the first to be ordained in the New World. Soon saw the evil of enslaving the Indians, and released his slaves. Las Casas then returned to Spain to seek amelioration for the ill-treated Indians. Cardinal Ximenés appointed him Protector General of the Indians, and he returned with this commission to the New World. Spent the most of a long life preaching to the American Indians and defending them against the cruelties of their conquerors. Nine times he traveled between America and Spain seeking respite for the horrible miseries which the Spaniards were inflicting upon the Indians. Efforts were in behalf of the Indians, not only in Haiti, but in Cuba, Peru, Guatemala, Nicaragua, St. Domingo, and Mexico. In 1544 at age seventy became bishop of Chiapa, Mexico. In 1547 returned to Spain and completed *Historia General de las Indias,* the source of much valuable information on the Spanish discoveries and conquests in the New World.

LASCO, JOHANNES À (Jan Laski) (1499-1560), Polish reformer, scholar and theologian, born in Warsaw, Poland, probably educated at Bologna for priesthood by uncle of the same name, a primate of the Polish church. Ordained in 1521 and served as a priest for a time in native land. Became bishop of Wesdrim in 1529 and archbishop of Warsaw in 1538. Became a friend of Erasmus; under the influence of Humanism became dissatisfied with the views of the Roman church. At age twenty-five began to travel, and came in touch with the German and Swiss Reformers, being especially drawn to Zwingli. About 1538 broke completely with the Roman church, resigned offices in the church, left Poland, and married a woman of humble rank. Went to Friesland, made superintendent of all the Evangelical churches of that country, became known as the founder of the Protestant Church of Friesland. About 1550 went to England where King Edward VI entrusted him with the organization of a congregation of all the foreign Protestants in London. Upon the accession of Mary three years later he and his congregation had to flee the country. In 1556, after twenty years' absence from Poland upon the urgent request of the Evangelicals, and with the welcome of the king of Poland returned to homeland to establish the Reformation there. In order to establish the Evangelical church in Poland he needed to guard against the influence and attacks of the Roman Catholics; to break the alliance that had been made with the Bohemian Brethren; and to counter the growing influence of the Unitarians. Also tried to effect a union between the Lutherans and the Reformed, but failed. There was a brief period when it seemed that Protestantism would sweep the country; but division in Protestant ranks, a strong Catholic reaction, and the missionary zeal of the Jesuits resulted in the cessation of the Reformation there and the return of Roman Catholicism.

LATHBURY, MARY ARTEMISIA (1841-1913), Hymn writer. Born in Manchester, New Hampshire. Daughter of a Methodist Episcopal pastor. In 1874 assistant to John Vincent. Spent much time at Chautauqua, New York under him. Wrote "Break Thou the Bread of Life" and "Day is Dying in the West" for Chautauqua meetings.

LATIMER, HUGH (c. 1485-1555), English bishop, reformer and martyr, born at Thurcaston, Leicestershire, England in a well-to-do farmer's home. Received his B.A., M.A., and B.D. degrees at Christ's College, Cambridge. In 1530 appointed royal chaplain, and the next year given a pastorate at West Kington, Wiltshire. Preached reform doctrines with such earnestness and vigor that he was cited to London, threatened with excommunication. Freed only at the intervention of the King, who was pleased with his attitudes and talents. Under Cranmer's influence, Latimer was again appointed a royal chaplain, and then in 1535 made bishop of Worcester, actively promoted the Reformation. Four years later refused to sign the King's Six Articles, which represented a return to the Romanist position. Latimer resigned from the bishopric, lived several years in privacy, then confined to the Tower where he remained until the accession of Edward VI in 1547. Declined to accept invitation to return to the bishopric. Theology was a mixture of Lutheran and Calvinistic teachings. Upon Mary's accession in 1553 he was imprisoned in the Tower; in 1555 he and Ridley were burned at the stake in front of Balliol College.

LATOURETTE, KENNETH SCOTT (1884-1968), church history and missions expert and ecumenist. Born in Oregon. Educated at Yale University. Taught in China till forced home by ill health in 1912. Professor at Yale from 1921 to 1953. President of the American Baptist Convention and of the American Historical Association. Major works are *History of the Expansion of Christianity* (7 vols., 1937-1945), *Christianity in a Revolutionary Age* (5 vols., 1958-1962), *A History of Christianity, The Development of Japan* and *The Development of China* and his autobiographical *Beyond the Ranges.*

LAUBACH, FRANK CHARLES (1884-1970), American Congregational missionary and linguist. Born in Pennsylvania. Educated at Princeton and Columbia universities and Union Seminary, New York. Ordained in 1914. Dean of Union Seminary, Manila from 1922 to 1926. By 1929 stressed teaching of reading by phonetic symbols, pictures and primers. His books were put into 300 languages and dialects in over 100 lands in Africa, Asia and South America. His Laubach Method had as its slogan "Each one teach one."

LAUD (lôd), **WILLIAM** (1573-1645), Archbishop of Canterbury, born at Reading, Berkshire, England, studied at St. John's College, Oxford. In 1601 ordained and in 1603 became a chaplain. In 1611 elected head of St. John's College. In 1616 made deacon of Gloucester, and in 1621 appointed bishop of St. David's. With accession of Charles I in 1625, real power in the Church of England began. Believed in the divine right of kings, but also believed in the divine right of bishops, and exercised authority accordingly. In 1626 became bishop of Bath and Wells, in 1628, bishop of London. In 1629 made Chancellor of the University of Oxford where he pursued a program of scholarly reform, founded a school of Arabic which is still in existence. In 1633 made Archbishop of Canterbury and began work as head of the church with great zeal and determination. In 1637 attempted to force ritualism on the Scottish Presbyterian church. This led to rebellion in the entire Scottish nation. When the king endeavored to squelch the rebellion, trouble broke out at home, and the Civil War of 1642-1649 followed. Laud's severe program against the Puritans led to migration of 400,000 of them to New England and the Caribbean. In 1640 impeached for treason, placed in confinement, and sent to the Tower in 1641. Tried later, and in 1645 with great firmness he met his death on the scaffold at the Tower. A High churchman and early exponent of what later came to be known as the Anglo-Catholic school.

LAW, WILLIAM (1686-1761), English divine and mystic, born at King's Cliffe, Northamptonshire, England, educated at Emmanuel College, Cambridge, became a fellow, and in 1711 received holy orders. On refusing to take the oath of allegiance upon the accession of George I, forfeited fellowship and all prospects of advancement in the church. Days were occupied largely in retirement and meditation, in literary labors, and in good works. Organized schools and almshouses in his hometown. In later years became a great admirer of Jacob Boehme. Law was a man of genius, a saint, a mystic, and a writer of great power. Best known for his *Serious Call to a Devout and Holy Life*, a masterpiece on devotion. Also wrote *On Christian Perfection*. To defend the Christian faith against the prevailing Deism, wrote *The Case of Reason*. Writings were highly valued by men like Philip Doddridge, and John Wesley.

LAWRANCE, (URIAH) MARION (1850-1924), promoter of organized Sunday school activity, born in Winchester, Ohio, studied at Antioch College. At sixteen chorister, at nineteen Sunday school superintendent in home church of the Christian denomination. In 1871 went to Syracuse, New York, and two years later to Toledo, Ohio, where he lived for the next thirty-four years. In 1876 became Sunday school superintendent of the Washington Street Congregational Church, which, under his guidance, developed into the model Sunday school of the country. In 1888 engaged by the church as superintendent on half time, in 1889 elected secretary of the Ohio Sunday School Association, and from 1893 to 1896 served as president of the International Field Worker's Association. In 1899 chosen General Secretary of the International Sunday School Association; and from 1910 to 1914 General Secretary of the World's Sunday School Association. After 1914 devoted entire time to the International Association, which largely owed to him its compact organization, the use of the uniform lessons, teacher training courses, and summer conferences. In 1922, largely responsible for completely reorganizing on interdenominational lines the International Council of Religious Education, of which made secretary emeritus. Some of best known works: *How to Conduct a Sunday School, The Working Manual of a Successful Sunday School, The Sunday School Organized for Service, Housing the Sunday School, Special Days in the Sunday School,* and *Practical Study of Sunday School Buildings.*

LAWS, CURTIS LEE (1868-1946), editor. Educated Richmond College and Crozer Theological Seminary. Ordained Baptist minister in 1892. Pastor in Baltimore from 1893 to 1913. Editor of *The Watchman-Examiner* from 1913 to 1940 and its publisher after 1940. Coined the word "Fundamentalist" in the July 1, 1920 issue of his magazine.

LAWS, ROBERT (1851-1934), medical missionary to Nyasaland, builder of Livingstonia, born in Aberdeen, Scotland. Apprenticed as a cabinet maker and attended evening school. Later entered Aberdeen University, enrolling in arts, medicine, and divinity. By hard work finished them all in seven years. In 1875 took his degree in medicine, was ordained in the United Presbyterian Church of Scotland, and sailed for Africa under the United Free Church of Scotland. The region about Lake Nyasa was his field of labor and was named Livingstonia in honor of the great explorer. In 1881, after being on the field for six years, Laws baptized his first convert; but when he left the field in 1927 there were sixty thousand Christians with thirteen ordained African pastors. In the year 1886-1887, there were severe sieges of fever, hostility of the natives, vigorous revival of the slave trade, finally the Portuguese claim to the whole of Nyasaland. In 1891 Great Britain declared a protectorate over Nyasaland, in 1895 ended the nefarious, inhuman slave trade. Dr. Laws' failing health made it obligatory that he return to Scotland for a while. While there in 1891 the home committee granted him permission to build an educational institution in Central Africa comparable to the institution at Lovedale in South Africa. Raised funds and went back to Nyasaland, built Livingstonia Institution, a spacious and beautiful Christian institution in the heart of Africa which he superintended from 1894 to 1927. Years following 1894 saw a steady development of the mission. Before World War I broke out, Livingstonia and its adjacent territory counted fourteen large, organized mission stations, seven hundred forty-one outstations with a Christian community of thirty thousand. Nine hundred seven schools with sixty thousand children being taught the Christian faith. When the war came the work was badly disrupted. Many of the mission stations were destroyed; after the war Dr. Laws had to begin much of his work anew. In 1908 called back to Scotland to serve as Moderator of the General Assembly of the United Free Church of Scotland. From 1912 to 1916 served at the governor's request as senior unofficial member of the legislative council of Nyasaland. In 1884 elected Fellow of the Royal Geographical Society. Permitted to labor in Africa for fifty-two years, retiring from the field in 1928.

LAVAL-MONTMORENCY, FRANCOIS XAVIER (1623-1708), born Montigny-sur-Avre France. Educated at La Fleche and Paris by the Jesuits. Ordained in 1647 Bishop and apostolic vicar by 1653. From 1663 a member of the governing council of Quebec and opposed the sale of liquor to the Indians. Organized parochial system of Quebec and bishop of Quebec from 1674 to 1688. Retired to Quebec Seminary (now Laval University) which he had founded. Dominated the spiritual life of Quebec from 1659 to 1688.

LEA (lē), **HENRY CHARLES** (1825-1909), American publisher and ecclesiastical historian, born in Philadelphia, Pennsylvania, educated privately. Early entered father's publishing business from 1843 until 1880. Constantly engaged in public affairs; active in support of the Federal Government during the Civil War; one of the first to support civil service reform; throughout life interested in good government in city, state, and nation. Active member of the Committee of One Hundred, formed in 1880 for the purification of politics, and was president of the Reform Club. Between 1840 and 1860 wrote many articles on chemistry and conchology; but after that chief intellectual interest was history. Entered into the study of medieval church history, specializing on the Inquisition. Acquired more than a million dollars in real estate, but used wealth in writing and publishing and collecting a large library. Collection of books and manuscripts, the finest of its kind in existence, bequeathed to the University of Pennsylvania. A member of the American Academy of Arts and Letters, a fellow of the British Academy; in 1909 served as president of the American Historical Association. Chief among his writings: *Superstition and Force, Studies in Church History, A History of Sacerdotal Celibacy in the Christian Church, History of the Inquisition in the Middle Ages, History of the Inquisition in Spain Connected with the Inquisition, History of Auricular Confession and Indulgences in the Latin Church, The Moriscos in Spain,* and *History of Witchcraft.*

LEANDER OF SEVILLE (c. 550-c. 600), Archbishop of Seville, born at Cartagena, Spain. Spent some years at Constantinople. On return to Seville appointed Archbishop of Seville, about 584, instrumental in converting Recared, King of the Visigoths, and his people from Arianism to Catholic orthodoxy. In 589 Leander presided over the famous Council of Toledo which condemned Arianism. It was at this council also that the "Filioque" was introduced into the creed of the Western church. Leander received the pallium in 599.

LECLERC (lē klĕr'), **JEAN** (1657-1736), Swiss Protestant theologian and scholar, born at Geneva, Switzerland, studied theology at Geneva, Grenoble, Saumur, Paris, and London. Preached in London for several months to the Reformed fugitives from Savoy. By studying works of Episcopius and other Remonstrants, was drawn from former Calvinism over to the Dutch Remonstrants (Arminians). In 1684 became professor of philosophy, and later of Church history at the Remonstrant Theological Seminary at Amsterdam. Leclerc held advanced and critical views on the inspiration of the Scripture, denying altogether the inspiration of Job, Proverbs, Ecclesiastes, and Song of Songs. Commentaries on the Old Testament were rationalistic and critical. Edited the bibliographical *Bibliotheque Universelle et Historique* (twenty-five volumes), which was his greatest work.

LEE, ANN (1736-1784), religious mystic and founder of the Shakers in America, born in Manchester, England, received little education, in 1762 married Abraham Standley, a blacksmith. In 1758 joined a society called the "Shaking Quakers," which eleven years before, under the influence of the Camisards or "French Prophets," had seceded from the Society of Friends. By 1770 she had become one of the leading spirits of the new sect. She advocated and preached mystic and ascetic doctrines; the early second coming of Christ through a woman. Persecuted and several times imprisoned for sabbath-breaking, alleged visions, prophecies, and miracle working, speaking in tongues, preaching against marriage, and a communistic way of life. Called herself "Ann the Word." Followers called her "Mother Ann." To escape persecution, to propagate her ideas she, her husband and a small group of followers came to New York in 1774; in 1776 founded the Shaker community at Watervliet, near Troy. Separated herself from her husband and continued to have visions and revelations. Her sect became known as "The United Society of True Believers in Christ's Second Appearing," or "Millennial Church," but popularly, "Shakers." During Revolutionary War she and some followers were imprisoned for refusing to bear arms, for alleged treasonable correspondence with England. After Governor Clinton released her from prison in 1781 she traveled on a missionary tour. Died in 1784. "Although originating in England, the sect is wholly American, and presents in its several communities an interesting example of thrift, industry, and good morals." Sect at present has become almost, if not entirely, extinct.

LEE, JASON (1803-1845). Born Stansteed, Vermont. Ordained in the Methodist Episcopal church in 1832. Founded Indian mission near present Salem, Oregon. Petitioned for territorial government in 1836. Founded Willamette University.

LEE, JESSE (1758-1816). Born in Prince George County, Virginia. From 1783 to 1789 was Methodist circuit rider in Virginia,

Maryland, and North Carolina. Ordained in 1790. From 1789 to 1798 was assistant to Asbury. Presiding elder in Virginia from 1801 to 1815. Chaplain of House of Representatives from 1809 to 1813 and one term in the senate. Wrote *Short History of Methodism in the USA*.

LEFÈVRE d'ÉTAPLES (lē fĕ'vr dē tȧ'pl), **JACQUES (Faber STAPULENSIS)** (c. 1455-1536.) French humanist, theologian, reformer, born at Etaples, France and early ordained priest. Pursued classical studies in Italy and in Paris. Under the influence of former pupil, William Briçonnet, Bishop of Meaux, turned attention from secular studies to theology and the Scriptures. His purpose was to offset the *Sentences* of Peter the Lombard by a system of theology that would present only what the Scriptures teach. In his revised Latin translation and commentary on the Pauline Epistles, 1512, declared for the authority of the Bible and the doctrine of justification by faith. In 1523 he completed French translation of the New Testament, in 1528 of the Old Testament. In 1522 his commentary appeared on the four gospels, in 1525, a commentary on the catholic epistles. Farel and Calvin, the Reformers of Geneva, were much influenced by the work of Lefèvre.

LEGGE (lĕg), **JAMES** (1815-1897), British Congregational missionary and Sinologist, born at Huntly, Aberdeenshire, Scotland, educated at King's College, Aberdeen, and Highbury Theological School, London. In 1839, ordained and sent by the London Missionary Society to Malacca as missionary to the Chinese. In 1840 appointed principal of the Anglo-Chinese College at Malacca, founded by Robert Morrison in 1825. When Hong Kong became a British colony, 1842, he moved there and helped plan for the transference of the college to Hong Kong. College was then converted into a theological seminary with Legge still its principal. Largely responsible for the founding and planning of the educational system of the colony. In addition to active and devoted missionary labor, took pastoral charge of the English-speaking Union Church. In 1873 after thirty-four years in China, returned permanently to England. In 1875 became the first professor of Chinese language and literature at Corpus Christi College, Oxford, a chair that was established for him. Remained there until death. Did much to instruct occidentals in the literature and religious beliefs of China. Greatest work and almost lifelong literary labor, his edition of the Chinese classics in the Chinese text, with translation, notes, and prolegomena. His other writings include: *The Life and Teaching of Confucius, The Life and Teaching of Mencius; The Religions of China; Confucianism and Taoism; The Record of Buddhistic Kingdoms; The Notions of the Chinese concerning God and Spirits;* and *The Nestorian Monument of Hsi-an-fu.*

LEIBNITZ (līp'nĭts), **GOTTFRIED WILHELM,** Baron von (1646-1716), German philosopher and mathematician, born in Leipzig. At age fifteen entered the local university, later studied jurisprudence, mathematics, and philosophy at Leipzig and Jena, received doctorate from Altdorf. Offered a professorship at the university, but refused, choosing rather to enter the service of the Elector of Mainz. From 1676 to 1716 at Hanover as librarian and historiographer. Visited the principal cities of Europe collecting materials for historical studies. Shared with Newton the honor of discovering differential calculus, each making the discovery independently. In 1700 induced Frederick I of Prussia to found the Society of Science in Berlin, was its first president. Through Leibnitz German philosophy came into its own. Unlike Spinoza, who saw the universe as one substance, Leibnitz saw an infinite number of monads or atoms, each an independent, indivisible center of active force, with God as the original, perfect, supreme monad. Theory of monads all working with preestablished harmony presents a doctrine of necessity or determinism. Each monad mirrors the universe, and man also is a microcosm reflecting the universe. To him there is no basic evil in the world. Moral life is gradually advancing toward perfection. Development or evolution becomes a progressive growth of what already existed in embryo. In chief religious work, *Theodicy,* attempted to demonstrate the agreement of reason with faith, presented the best possible world with Christianity merely as the purest and noblest of all religions. Along with Bossuet, was a strong advocate of the union of all Christendom, to this end wrote, *System of Theology.* Among his writings are: *Preestablished Harmony, Principles of Contradiction,* and *Principles of Sufficient Reason.*

LEIGHTON, ROBERT (1611-1684), Scottish preacher and theologian, educated at the University of Edinburgh. Traveled on continent, spending several years in France. After return to Scotland, 1641, ordained a Presbyterian clergyman, for several years minister in Newbattle, Midlothian. Resigning, 1652, turned from the Presbyterian church to the Anglican church. The next year became principal and professor of divinity at the University of Edinburgh. After the Restoration, Charles II, 1661, made him Bishop of

Dunblane, in 1670, Archbishop of Glasgow. Leighton labored for the restoration of church unity in Scotland. Neither a consistent Presbyterian nor a typical Anglican, failed in hopes of harmonizing the two systems, resigned in 1674; went to live with his sister at Broadhurst, Sussex. Bequeathed library to the diocese of Dunblane. Works consisted of *Sermons and Charges to the Clergy,* and *A Commentary on the First Epistle of Peter,* all published after his death.

LENSKI, RICHARD CHARLES HENRY (1864-1936), Lutheran clergyman and theologian, born at Greifenberg, Prussia, studied at Capital University and Lutheran Seminary, Columbus, Ohio. Ordained to the Lutheran ministry in the Ohio Synod, held pastorates at Baltimore, Maryland, Trenton, Springfield and Anna, Ohio (1887-1911). Professor of languages and theology at Capital University, Columbus, Ohio (1916-1921); professor of dogmatics, New Testament exegesis, and homiletics (1921-1928); professor of systematic theology (1928-1936); and dean (1919-1935). For twenty years editor of the *Lutherische Kirchenzeitung*. Main literary work a monumental commentary on the entire Greek Testament (eleven volumes).

LEO I, The Great (d. 461), Pope(440-461), probably a native Roman, by 431 a deacon and a man of influence and standing. Before long an archdeacon and a legate of the Roman church. His pontificate of twenty-one years, next to that of Gregory I, is most significant and important in the early history of Roman church. In many respects the real maker of the papacy. Chief aim was to sustain the unity of the church. Strongest man in the West, and made his authority and power bring glory and power to church. Laid great stress on the primacy of Peter among the apostles, taught that what Peter possessed had been passed on to Peter's successors, that is, to all the bishops or popes of Rome. This gave Rome of Leo's day special rank and authority. Persuaded Huns and Vandals not to sack Rome in 452 and 455. Exercised authority not only in Rome, but in Spain and North Africa. Reproved the bishops of Alexandria, Tuscany, Sicily, and others for alleged errors, especially for disregard for the authority of the Roman See. Had Emperor Valentinian III in 451 mandate by law the supremacy of the Roman bishop. Sought to assert authority over Illyria, Constantinople, and Gaul. His *Tome,* especially emphasized the doctrine that the two natures are complete and full in Christ. Accepted as the orthodox doctrine of the church at the Ecumenical council at Chalcedon two years later, 451. As an uncompromising foe of heresy became involved in the fight against the Pelagians, the Manichaeans, and the Priscillianists. He claimed to be Peter's successor.

LEO III (d. 816), Pope (795-816). A Roman by birth. Because of the hostility of the Roman aristocracy toward him at first, appealed to Charlemagne for support. Charlemagne expressed readiness to renew the alliance between the Frankish state and the church. In 799 enemies abused him and declared him deposed. When he fled to France, Charlemagne recognized him as the rightful pope, after careful investigation considered him acquitted of any charges. A few days later, Christmas day (800), while Charlemagne was kneeling in prayer in St. Peter's, Leo crowned him emperor. This was the beginning of the Roman Empire of Italians and Germans.

LEO IX (BRUNO) (1002-1054), pope (1049-1054), born in the noble family of Bruno at Egisheim, Alsace, received excellent clerical education from Berthold, Bishop of Toul, whom he succeeded in 1027. In sympathy with the reform that emanated from Cluny. Twenty-one years of successful administration as Bishop of Toul led cousin, Emperor Henry III of Germany, in December, 1048, to appoint him pope. His pontificate was devoted to reform; bettered the College of Cardinals by including in it distinguished men outside the environs of Rome, also men of reforming zeal. Knew how to combine monastic simplicity with papal dignity and splendor. Did much to strengthen the papacy. Opposed simony and clerical corruption. In 1050 condemned Berengar for his denial of the doctrine of transubstantiation. Took vital interest in the campaign against the Normans in southern Italy. Led the army. In 1053 army defeated and he fell into the hands of the Normans. Though treated with respect by captors, was seriously ill when released. Pontifical reign short, but significant. In effort to strengthen the papacy used the Pseudo-Isidorian Decretals to good effect. Laid much stress on church councils and used them to good advantage. Maintained good relations with Henry III of Germany to whom greatly indebted for position and power. Had bitter controversy, however, with Michael Cerularius, patriarch of Constantinople, which finally resulted in the Great Schism of 1054.

LEO X, (GIOVANNI DE MEDICI) (1475-1521), Pope (1513-1521). Born in Florence, Italy. Educated privately at Pisa. Appointments were heaped upon him until he possessed twenty-seven different charges, one of them the abbacy of Monte Cassino. Before he was fourteen made cardinal-deacon, then for three years was given a thorough training in Humanism, theology, and canon law. In 1513 at age thirty-seven, though not yet a priest, elected pope. "Let us enjoy the papacy, for God has given it to us," he wrote to his brother. Freely made apointments and created cardinalates for nephews and other relatives, which cost papal treasury a handsome sum. Highest ecclesiastical offices were for sale at exorbitant prices. Leo revived the sale of indulgences to finance the building of the Church of St. Peter's in Rome in Luther's time which was a direct factor in the coming of the Reformation. It was in his pontificate that the Reformation broke forth under Luther's rebellion.

LEO XIII (GIOACCHINO, VINCENZO RAFFELLO LUIGI PECCI (1810-1903), Pope (1878-1903), born at Carpineto, Italy, of a noble Sienese family, studied in the Jesuit colleges at Viterbo and in Rome. In 1837 ordained a priest and named domestic prelate to Pope Gregory XVI. Later a delegate at Benevento, Spoleto, and Perugia, and for a time was nuncio to Belgium. In 1843 consecrated titular archbishop of Dalmietta, and a little later appointed Bishop of Perugia. In 1853 created cardinal and in 1878 elected pope to succeed Pius IX. Displayed marked diplomatic and administrative ability. Restored the hierarchy in Scotland, established one in India, and successfully ended the religious struggle of the papacy with Germany. To the last regarded himself as a prisoner in the Vatican but in *Immortale Dei* in 1885 came to terms with democratic states. Definitely interested in reviving and promoting Thomistic Scholasticism. In 1883 opened the Vatican archives and library to scholars. Founded the Catholic University in Washington, D.C., 1899. In 1892 founded the apostolic delegation at Washington. Also took a lively interest in social betterment and reform. Famous encyclical, *Rerum Novarum,* 1891, supported unions, state intervention to help needy and upheld private property. In *Providentissimus Deus* (in 1893) permitted critical biblical scholarship in Old Testament studies and in *Aeterni Patris* in 1879 declared Thomism as the best theology to deal with science.

LEO III the ISAURIAN (ī sô rĭ'ăn) (c. 680-740), Byzantine emperor (717-740), born a peasant at Germanicia, in the mountains of Isauria (Armenia Minor), in early life a soldier. In 717 overthrew Theodosius III and became the first of the Isaurian dynasty. The same year saved Constantinople from the attacks of a powerful Moslem Arab army. From 726 to 739 he campaigned against the Moslems, finally defeating them in decisive battle of Acroinum in 739. Best known in church history for long struggle against the use of images in the churches. In an edict issued in 726 he forbade the veneration of images. In a second edict (730) ordered the removal or destruction of all images in the churches. The pictured walls were to be whitewashed. Removed the magnificent image of Christ over the gate of the imperial palace, replacing it with a plain cross. Successful in clearing the churches in the East of images; but the West revolted. Summoned a council at Constantinople in 730, deposed Germanus, the aged patriarch of Constantinople, and put iconoclastic Anastasius in his place. In 731 Pope Gregory III of the West held a synod in which opponents of pictures and images were excommunicated. This included Leo and all his iconoclastic churches of the East. Leo then attempted to transfer the bishoprics of Sicily and Southern Italy from the jurisdiction of the pope to that of the patriarch of Constantinople. A long iconoclastic struggle followed, which resulted in greater cleavage between the East and the West.

LEONARDO DA VINCI (lā ō när'dō dä vēn'chē), (1452-1519), Italian Renaissance painter, sculptor, architect, musician, and art critic; also inventor, civil and military engineer, botanist, astronomer, geologist, and anatomist. A profound thinker and scholar, one of the greatest minds of the Renaissance. Born at Vinci, near Florence, Italy, illegitimate son of a Florentine notary, received the best education Florence could give. In 1482 entered the service of Ludovico il Moro, Duke of Milan, as engineer and architect, painted for the duke his famous "The Last Supper." After the duke's expulsion in 1499, da Vinci spent some time in Venice and Florence continuing his painting. In 1502 became military engineer for Caesar Borgia, had opportunity to do much traveling. About this time painted his most famous picture, the portrait of Mona Lisa del Giocondo, a prominent Florentine woman. Sometime after Caesar Borgia's downfall da Vinci was appointed court painter for Louis XII of France, and later of Francis I. He both taught painting and did some further painting himself. Da Vinci pioneered in color blending, play of light and shade, and in "true to life and nature" painting. Expert both in portrait and in landscape painting. He was one of the greatest art masters of the High Renaissance, and scarcely less famous and influential as a scientist and inventor. Famous statues were his *David* and the *Pietá* in St. Peters. His dome of St. Peters was his architectural masterpiece. Has been classed with Dante, Beethoven, and Shakespeare among the four great intellects in the world of art and literature.

LEONIDES (lēŏn'ĭ dēs) (d. 202), father of Origen and a Christian martyr of Alexandria. In 202, when Septimus Severus enacted a rigid law against the spread of Christianity and of Judaism, Leonides was one early victim of the enactment. He was beheaded, dying a martyr to his faith. His young son, Origen, encouraged him to faithfulness and desired to be martyred with his father. The property of Leonides was confiscated, leaving his family of wife and seven sons in poverty. Origen supported and cared for his mother and brothers.

LESSING, GOTTHOLD EPHRAIM (1729-1781), German critic and dramatist and skeptical philosophical theologian, born at Kamenz in Upper Lusatia, Saxony. Studied theology, philosophy, philology, and medicine at the University of Leipzig, and also at the University of Wittenberg, interest early turned to aesthetics, literature, and especially drama. He made a name for himself as dramatist and art critic from 1748 to 1760 in Berlin where he became a journalist and critic. Was employed for a time by Voltaire. In 1760 became secretary to the governor of Breslau, a post at which he remained for more than four years. Librarian for the Duke of Brunswick (1774-1778). Became known as the "Father of German Criticism." He wanted "to free German taste and thought from French influence." One of best known dramas was *Minna von Barnhelm,* and Germany's greatest work of art criticism was Lessing's *Laokoon*. His religious ideas are in *Nathan the Wise*. In later years chiefly concerned with theological and philosophical problems. Saw the essence of religion in a purely humanitarian morality of tolerance and giving which was independent of all historical revelation. Became one of the principal leaders of the Aufklärung or Enlightenment, laying the foundations of the Protestant liberalism that was to hold sway in Germany throughout the nineteenth century. He dismissed Christianity as an historical religion because "accidental truths of history can never become proof of necessary truths of reason."

LETOURNEAU, ROBERT GILMOUR (1888-1969), manufacturer and inventor. Born Richford, Vermont. Little formal education. Ran garage from 1917 to 1929. Contractor and builder of land-breaking equipment (1962-1969). Founder and president of R.G. LeTourneau Inc. (1962-1969). Set up companies in Peru and Liberia to exploit natural resources, help the nationals and proclaim the gospel. Member of the Christian and Missionary Alliance.

LEWIS, CLIVE STAPLES (1898-1963), mystical novelist, poet, and professor. Born Belfast, Ireland. Educated at Malvern and Oxford. Served in World War I. Taught at University College, Cambridge, and from 1925 to 1954 at Magdalen College, Oxford. Among his religious works were *The Screwtape Letters, Mere Christianity,* and *Miracles.* Most popular mystical novels were *Out of the Silent Planet, Perelandra* and *That Hidden Strength*. The seven *Chronicles of Narnia* are children's classics. *Surprised by Joy* is his autobiography of his journey from atheism to theism. Influenced many intellectuals to accept Christianity. Main recreation was walking.

LIDDELL, HENRY GEORGE (1811-1898), dean of Christ Church and Greek lexicographer, born at Binchester, Durham, England, educated at Charterhouse School and Christ Church, Oxford. In 1836 became a tutor, and in 1845, professor of moral philosophy of his college. During residence as tutor at Oxford (1836-1845) prepared and published his *Greek-English Lexicon,* which was undertaken in conjunction with a fellow-student, Robert Scott (1811-1887). In 1838 ordained, and in 1846 was made domestic chaplain of Prince Albert, and later the same year headmaster of the Westminister school. Under his wise guidance the earlier reputation and standing of the school was restored. In 1852 appointed a member of the first Oxford University Commission; but in 1855 appointed to the deanery of Christ Church, a position he held until 1891, being also vice chancellor from 1870 to 1874. In 1862 became chaplain extraordinary to the queen. After resignation as dean in 1891 lived in retirement at Ascot where he died. In addition to his Greek Lexicon he published a *History of Ancient Rome*. It was for Liddell's daughter Alice that Charles L. Dodgson (Lewis Carroll) wrote *Alice's Adventures in Wonderland* and *Through the Looking Glass.*

LIDDON (lĭd'n), **HENRY PARRY** (1829-1890), High Church Anglican divine, born at North Stoneham, Hampshire, England, received higher education at King's College, London, and Christ Church, Oxford. In 1853 ordained priest. After two very brief pastorates made vice-principal of the college at Cuddesdon. Because of his High Church leanings left Cuddesdon after five years and became vice-principal of St. Edmund's Hall, Oxford. For many years a power in the pulpits of St. Mary's and Christ Church, Oxford, in his Sunday evening lectures on the New Testament. In 1864 became prebendary of Salisbury cathedral. In 1866 he delivered the Bampton lecture, *The Divinity of Our Lord and Saviour Jesus Christ,* his best known work. From 1870 to 1890 canon of St. Paul's, London. At the same time he was made Ireland professor of exegesis at Oxford. This position he held for twelve years. Early inclined toward High

Church principles, a warm friend and admirer of Pusey. Entertained strong hopes of a reunion of the Church of England and the Church of Rome. Opposed the German higher criticism. In 1866-1870 active in founding Keble College, in 1883-1884 in founding Pusey House, both of which were High church. He took a trip to Egypt ad Palestine. Because of interest in the Old Catholic movement stopped to see Döllinger in Munich. Writings were chiefly several volumes of sermons and a biography of his honored friend Pusey.

LIETZMANN, HANS (1875-1942), New Testament and patristic scholar and church historian. Educated in philosophy and theology at Jena and Bonn. Taught at Bonn, Jena (1905-1924) and Berlin (1924-1942). *Handbook of New Testament* concerned Greek patristic manuscripts. Main work was a four volume *History of the Early Church*. From 1920 to 1942 edited *Zeitschrift für Neutestamentliche Wissenschaft*.

LIGHTFOOT, JOSEPH BARBER (1828-1889), English scholar, textual critic, and Bishop of Durham, born in Liverpool, England, educated at King Edward VI's School, Birmingham, and at Trinity College, Cambridge. In 1854 with J. E. B. Mayer, and F. J. A. Hort became founder of the *Journal of Classical and Sacred Philology*. Also ordained in 1858 as presbyter. In 1857 became tutor at Trinity and in 1858, select preacher at Cambridge. Between 1858 and 1859 filled various posts as minister, chaplain, and Hulsean professor at Cambridge from 1861, and canon of St. Paul's from 1871 to 1879. In 1879 consecrated Bishop of Durham, filled that office until his death in 1889. From 1870 to 1880 a member of the New Testament revision committee. Quiet and shy, a successful teacher and preacher as well as writer. A generous giver, did much to enhance diocese by building new churches and mission chapels, using much of own money for these purposes. Lightfoot's enduring critical works on the New Testament and the church Fathers won him great fame. Commentaries: *Galatians, Philippians, Colossians with Philemon* and editions of the *Apostolic Fathers* are valued even today for "wide and original Patristic and classical erudition, lucid presentation, freedom from technicalities and avoidance of sectional controversies." Other works include *A Fresh Revision of the New Testament*.

LIGUORI (lē gwô′rē), **ALPHONSUS (MARIA ANTONY JOHN COSMAS DAMIAN MICHAEL GASPARD de')** (1696-1787), Italian Roman Catholic churchman and theologian. Commonly known as St. Alphonsus, born near Naples, Italy, received education at home, and by the priests of the oratory of Philip of Neri. Took degree of Doctor of Laws at age sixteen, was successfully practicing at the bar at age nineteen. Before age thirty left the legal profession, received the tonsure, and joined the association of missionary secular priests called the "Neapolitan Propaganda." In 1726 ordained priest. Soon became an earnest preacher, and devoted much time to relief of the poor. In 1732 founded the Redemptorist Order (Congregation of the Most Holy Redeemer), the purpose of which was "to preach the Word of God to the poor." Not until 1749 did the order receive the confirmation of the pope. The order conducted missions and retreats, eventually became widespread. In 1762 with much reluctance Liguori accepted appointment to the bishopric of St. Agatha of the Goths in the kingdom of Naples, retired in 1775 to live the rest of his days at the Redemptorist Institute near Nocera. Most important writing was *Theologia Moralis,* in which the principles of the Jesuits are enunciated. Used as the basis of moral instruction in many Roman Catholic institutions. The best known of popular works was *Le Glorie di Maria* (The Glories of Mary). Did much to promote the teachings of Jesuitical casuistry, the Immaculate Conception, and Papal Infallibility. Canonized in 1839. In 1871 Pope Pius IX added his name to the list of doctors of the church. Works were specially commended by Leo XIII in 1879. Thought of Mary as a semi-divine mediatrix.

LILBURNE, JOHN (c. 1614-1657), Leveller leader. Born at Greenwich. In Parliamentary army (1624-1645). Imprisoned for unlicensed printing from 1645 to 1648. Later became a Quaker. Advocated as leader of the Leveller party the sovereignty of the people, freedom of religion, universal manhood suffrage and equality before the law. Movement suppressed by Oliver Cromwell.

LINACRE, THOMAS (c. 1460-1524), English Renaissance Humanist and physician, born at Canterbury, England, educated at Canterbury Cathedral School, Oxford University, and the University of Padua, where he took degree in medicine. In 1484 became Fellow of All Souls. Upon the accession of Henry VIII, became his physician. Founder of the Royal College of Physicians in London; also founded chairs or lectureships of medicine in Oxford and Cambridge. One of the first Englishmen to study Greek in Italy, one of the earliest champions of the new learning, becoming recognized as one of the foremost Humanist scholars of England. An intimate friend of John Colet, Erasmus,

Thomas More, and William Grocyn. In 1520 at age sixty ordained priest. Famous for translations of the works of Galen, the Greek physician.

LINCOLN, ABRAHAM (1809-1865), sixteenth president of the United States, born near Hodgenville, Kentucky. The son of uneducated farmer and noble mother who died when Abraham was nine years old. When seven they moved to Indiana where they lived for about fifteen years. Learned the little that was taught in the backwoods schools, but secured education largely through books he was able to borrow in community. Read the Bible until he knew much of it by heart. Read such books as *Aesop's Fables, Robinson Crusoe, Pilgrim's Progress,* the lives of Washington, Clay, and Franklin. At nineteen took cargo down the Mississippi to New Orleans. Got his first unfavorable impression of slavery. Helped father for a year in felling trees, building a new log house, and splitting rails for fences in their new home in Illinois; then he located at New Salem, where he stayed for six years. Clerked in a store, served as postmaster and deputy to the county surveyor, and began to study law. Entered the bar in 1836. Elected captain of a company of riflemen in the time of the Black Hawk War in 1832. Elected to the State Legislature in 1834, served until 1842, when he declined further nomination. Became leader of the Whigs, led a successful campaign for removing the State capital from Vandalia to Springfield, where he had fixed his residence. While in the State Legislature, frequently lifted his voice in opposition to slavery. In 1842 married Mary Todd. In 1846 elected to the national House of Representatives where he served one term. Returned to private law practice and became recognized as the leading member of the Illinois bar. In 1854 in debate opposed Stephen A. Douglas on the question of slavery entering free territory. In 1856 became one of the founders of the Republican Party, which was organized to oppose slavery; became its foremost leader in Illinois. In 1858 by only a few votes lost to Douglas election to the Senate. In 1860 won the Republican presidential nomination, elected to the presidency by a strong vote. In inaugural address declared the Union perpetual and argued the futility of secession. Several states had already seceded, and a few weeks later Civil War was declared. In the midst of the four years' war, January 1, 1863, issued the famous, world-moving Emancipation Proclamation. It soon led to the writing of the Thirteenth Amendment to the Constitution. Delivered famous *Gettysburg Address,* November, 1863. In 1864 unanimously nominated for a second term, received an overwhelming majority in the election. Five weeks after Lincoln's second inaugural address Lee surrendered and the war was over. Only a few days later Lincoln was assassinated by John Wilkes Booth. Lincoln is revered throughout the world as "the great emancipator, champion of freedom, and hero of American history." Lincoln was a religious man, a man of the Bible. From childhood until the end of life he read it, and often referred to it in speeches. Wrote to a friend: "Take all of this book upon reason that you can, and the balance on faith, and you will live and die a better man." Also wrote; "I decided a long time ago that it was less difficult to believe that the Bible was what it claimed to be, than to disbelieve it. It is a good Book for us to obey." Often prayed and exhorted others to pray. Joined a church in Springfield, Ilinois. Many of his close friends considered him a believing Christian, and more than once he expressed his faith in Christ as God and Savior.

LINCOLN, WILLIAM (1825-1888), Plymouth Brethren preacher and writer, born in the east of London, converted through the reading of Philip Doddridge's *Rise and Progress of Religion*. Ordained in 1849, preached in the established church until 1862, last charge at Beresford Chapel at Walworth. Attempt to refute C. H. Spurgeon's memorable discussion on baptismal regeneration led him to change his view on baptism and other positions of the established church. Consequently broke connection with the Church of England. Immediately after his secession he wrote *Javelin of Phinehas,* which dealt with the evil of the union of church and state. Joined with the Brethren movement and continued ministry at Beresford. Preached much on the second coming, separation from evil, and the apostasy of Christendom. Prepared lectures on several of the books of the New Testament.

LINDSAY, THOMAS MARTIN (1843-1914), church historian, born at Lesmahagow, Lanarkshire, Scotland, educated at the universities of Glasgow and Edinburgh. Examiner at Edinburgh, and later assistant to the professor of logic and metaphysics. Soon abandoned career as a university teacher to study for the ministry. After completing theological course served as an assistant minister for a time. In 1873 the general assembly elected him to the chair of church history in the theological college at Glasgow, where he remained until death. Also principal (1902-1914) and for fifteen years convener of the Foreign Missions Committee of the Free Church of Scotland (1886-1900). Wrote many important articles for the *En-*

cyclopaedia Britannica, Cambridge Modern History, Cambridge Mediaeval History, Cambridge History of English Literature. Chief among books: *Luther and the German Reformation, The History of the Reformation in Europe,* and *The Church and the Ministry in the Early Centuries.* In the heresy trial of friend, William Robertson Smith, Lindsay ably defended Smith (1877-1881).

LINDSEY, THEOPHILUS (1723-1808), Unitarian leader. Born Middlewich, Cheshire. Educated at Leeds and St. Johns College, Cambridge. Pastorates in Yorkshire and Dorset from 1753 to 1763. Vicar of Catterick from 1763 to 1773. Adopted Unitarian ideas and held services in London from 1774. Preached in a chapel from 1778.

LIPPI (lēp′pe), **FRA FILIPPO** (fē lēp′pō), or **LIPPO** (c. 1406-1469), Florentine painter of religious subjects, in 1421 entered the Carmelite order, eleven years later left the monastery to specialize in art. Zealously patronized by the Medici family. In 1455 created most important series of frescoes, *The Life of St. John the Baptist,* and *Life of St. Stephen* in the Prato Cathedral, where he later became prior. Work shows gentleness and sympathy in treatment with color soft and clear. Among most famous paintings are *The Coronation of the Virgin, Virgin Adoring the Christ Child, Madonna and Child with Angels.*

LISLE, GEORGE (c. 1750-c. 1845), first black preacher in America and first black missionary (Jamaica). Founder of the first Baptist church in Savannah, Georgia and the first Negro Baptist church in Jamaica.

LISZT (lĭst), **FRANZ** (1811-1886), Hungarian pianist, teacher, and composer, born in Raiding, Hungary, studied in Vienna and Paris. He gave his first public performance when nine years, made concert tours through Europe when twelve years, everywhere receiving great acclaim. Beethoven was thrilled by his playing. Several Hungarian nobles captured by performances pledged to support him for six years in study. The family moved to Vienna where Franz studied piano under Czerny and Saliere. Following this settled in Paris. Began to teach others, and publicly, to interpret the music of the great musicians. As a young man formed a close friendship with such men as Hector Berlioz, Frederic Chopin, Nicolo Paganini, and Richard Wagner. Spent several years touring Europe giving concerts to enthusiastic crowds. In 1848 at height of popularity retired to Weimar, Thuringia, to direct the opera and concerts, and devote time to composition and teaching. Youthful sensitive spiritual nature, mother's early religious training, a disappointment in love drove him to extravagant ascetic practices that almost cost his life. After regaining health, gave himself to much travel, to public performances, and to liaison with women to whom he was not married, one woman bearing him three children. In 1858 he became a Franciscan tertiary, and in 1861 went to Rome to devote himself to religious study. In 1865 joined the Franciscan order and was made an abbot. Though fulfilling ecclesiastical duties continued his music with unabated interest. In 1870 became director of the Conservatory of Music at Budapest; in 1875 elected president of the Hungarian Academy of Music. Perhaps the greatest pianist of all time, writer of more than twelve hundred works. Originated the form of Symphonic Poem, of which *Faust* and *Dante* were two of his greatest. *St. Elizabeth* and *Christus* were two of his finest oratorios. Wrote some literary works, such as the *Life of Chopin.* Represented in music the nineteenth century Romanticism.

LITTLE, PAUL (1928-1975). Born in Philadelphia. Educated at the Wharton School of Finance of the University of Pennsylvania, Wheaton College, Chicago Lutheran Seminary, and New York University. Assistant to the president of Inter-Varsity Christian Fellowship and associate professor of Evangelism in the World School of Missions of Trinity Evangelical Divinity School, Deerfield, Illinois. Associate director of program of the 1974 Lausanne Conference on World Evangelism. Wrote *Know What You Believe, Know Why You Believe,* and *How to Give Away Your Faith.*

LIUDGER (lĭ o͞ot′gẽr), **or LUDGER, SAINT** (c. 744-809), first Bishop of Münster, Germany, born at Zeilen, near Utrecht, Frisia. Educated at Utrecht, studied for a year at York, England under Alcuin. After being ordained priest (777) returned to Frisia where for seven years labored as a missionary among fellow countrymen. When an invasion of the Saxons forced him to leave Frisia in 784, went to Rome and lived at the monastery of Monte Cassino for two and a half years, studying the Benedictine rule but not joining the order. On return, Charlemagne gave him an enlarged field in Frisia. He had eminent success, extending labors as far as the island of Helligoland. Later consecrated Bishop of Southern Westphalia with episcopal seat at Münster. Founded a monastery at Werden and built a cathedral. Only extant writing of Liudger is the *Life of St. Gregory,* his teacher at Utrecht. Also wrote a life of Albric.

LIVINGSTONE, DAVID (1813-1873), missionary and explorer. Born near Glasgow, Scotland, in poor family. With first wages bought a Latin grammar. By studying while at work and at home secured an early education. In 1830 at age seventeen entered the University of Glasgow, began the study of medicine and theology. Goal was missionary in China. In 1838 accepted by the London Missionary Society. The Opium War in China was on, and the society sent him to Africa in 1840. Went to Robert Moffat's station in South Africa, but soon pushed on to the tribes farther north. In 1843 started a mission at Mabotsa, two hundred miles north of Moffat. In 1845 married Mary Moffat and built a home. The next year found it necessary to move forty miles farther north; built second home and established a station. Because of a long, continued drought soon had to move again. Went forty miles farther north to Kolebeng and built third and last house for himself and family. When Boers sacked this house he built no more. Began great work of missionary and colonial exploration, saying, "The end of the geographical feat is the beginning of the missionary enterprise." He discovered Lake N'gami in 1849 and the Victoria Falls in 1853. Sent his family to England; then made hazardous fourteen hundred mile trip to Loanda and back. In 1856 returned to England with high acclaim as a world-renowned explorer. Opened Africa both to missions and to civilization. In 1857 resigned from the London Missionary Society, returned to Africa under the British government, with the three-fold goal: (1) to make Christ known to Africa; (2) to find the source of the Nile and open Africa to the west; and (3) to eradicate pernicious slave traffic. In 1858 discovered great lakes of East Africa. In 1864 he was back in England; but in 1865 returned to Africa to spend his last eight years. On this trip, 1871, Stanley found him when lost to the world. In 1873 his native helpers found him on his knees in the posture of prayer, his spirit having departed from the body. Body was taken to England and buried in Westminster Abbey.

LOCK, WALTER (1846-1933), warden of Keble College, Oxford, born at Dorchester, Dorsetshire, England, educated at Marlborough College and Corpus Christi, Oxford, fellow of Magdalen College, Oxford (1869-1892). Ordained priest in 1873. An assistant professor at St. Andrews University for one year, then 1870 to 1897 tutor and assistant warden of Keble College, Oxford, and from 1897 to 1921 warden of the college. From 1895 to 1919 Dean Ireland professor of exegesis in the University of Oxford. Appointed Canon of Christ Church and Lady Margaret professor of divinity in 1919, holding the latter until retirement in 1927. As a liberal post-Tractarian theologian wrote *The Church* in *Lux Mundi*. Wrote also *John Keble, a Biography; The Bible and the Christian Life;* and *Critical and Exegetical Commentary on the Pastoral Epistles.* Was also general editor of the *Westminster Commentaries on the Revised Version*.

LOCKE, JOHN (1632-1704), English philosopher, political theorist, father of the Enlightenment in England, born in Wrington, Somersetshire, England, of Puritan ancestry, educated at Westminster School, London, and Christ Church College, Oxford. For the first thirty-four years of life little more than a student of medicine and an unperturbed scholar, showing some interest in theology. From 1660 to 1666 lectured at Oxford on Greek, rhetoric, and philosophy. Next seventeen years were molded largely by association with Lord Ashley, later first Earl of Shaftesbury, whom he served from 1666 to 1683. During these years chief interest was politics. Became a strong advocate of political liberty. Then under the suspicion of government as a supposed radical, he sought refuge in Holland from 1683 to 1689. Returned when the "Glorious Revolution" (1688-1689) brought William and Mary to England. Up to this time had published nothing. Now, chief works were rapidly published, some of his books being the product of twenty years of thinking and writing. Chief among these, *Essay on Human Understanding,* in which he sought the origin, certainty, and extent of human knowledge, in which he also sought to prove that innate ideas do not exist, but that all knowledge comes through experience by sensation and reflection. Had no place for objective revelation. Wrote *Two Essays on Government,* in which he upheld popular sovereignty, *Letters on Toleration,* and *Some Thoughts on Education,* the latter a book which greatly influenced modern education. In 1695 appeared *The Reasonableness of Christianity as Delivered in the Scriptures,* a plea for a rational religion. Along with other English moralists, conceived of a basis for morality outside of church dogma. In the main his faith and philosophy seemed to be largely in line with orthodox Christianity. And though his philosophical thought contained nothing fundamentally new, it did provide seed thoughts for four major philosophical areas which were later developed by the empiricists, the English sensationalists, the English deists, and the English moralists.

LÖHE (lē′e), **JOHANN KONRAD WILHELM** (1808-1872), Lutheran theologian and philanthropist, born in Fürth, near Nuremberg, Germany, studied theology at the universities of Erlangen and Berlin. In 1831 became vicar of Kirchenlamitz, and two years later became assistant pastor of St.

Giles, Nürnberg. In 1837 settled at Neuendettelsau, a small and unattractive place which he soon transformed into busy Christian colony. Planned not a reformation but a new formation of the church. Insistence upon the withdrawal of secular supremacy over the Protestant church, the complete purification of confesssion, and strictest adherence to the symbols of the church, all but led to secession. In great work, *Drei Bücher von der Kirche,* propounded the strictest Lutheran orthodoxy. Had no small part in establishing the Missouri Synod of the Lutheran church in America. Sent out about sixty missionaries to the new world. Also sent about fifty students to the seminary of the newly organized Missouri Synod, which originated in the school which he founded at Fort Wayne the year before, which was transferred to Springfield, Illinois upon the organization of the Missouri Synod in 1847. Differing from the Missouri Synod on doctrines of the church and of the ministerial office, in 1854 became the founder of the Iowa Synod. A philanthropist of remarkably fertile and creative talent. In 1849, founded the Lutheran Society of Home or Inner Missions, in 1853, organized a deaconness society in Bavaria, and a deaconness home at Neuendettelsau. Built an asylum for insane children, hospitals, industrial schools, and a chapel. Furthermore a gifted author, writing no fewer than sixty books which were of spiritual and of practical nature.

LOISY (lwä zē′), **ALFRED FIRMIN** (1857-1940), Liberal French theologian, born at Ambrieres, Marne, France, educated at the seminary of Chalons-sur-Marne. Ordained priest in 1879; after being parish priest successively of two village churches, in 1881 began studying for a degree at the Institut Catholique, Paris. The next year given a lectureship in the Institut in Hebrew, and later a course in Old Testament exegesis and a course in Assyriology. In doctoral dissertation written in 1890 and other works that followed, liberal tendencies were so marked that in 1893 removed from the Institut and was appointed to a chaplaincy of the girls' school under the direction of Dominican nuns at Neuilly-sur-Seine. From 1900 to 1904 lectured at the Sorbonne on Assyriology, when, because of his unorthodoxy obliged by his superiors to cease lecturing there in 1904. Became the most prominent representative of modernism in the Roman Catholic church. Accepted the theory of evolution in the interpretation of the Bible and even regarded the Roman Catholic church as a growth and subject to further change. In 1908 published books on higher criticism, which led to excommunication later, same year. In 1909, discarding the clerical garb, he became professor of history of religions at the College de France, where he taught from 1909 to 1930. Wrote several books, at least five of which were placed on the Index.

LONGFELLOW, SAMUEL (1819-1892), American Unitarian clergyman and hymn writer, born at Portland, Maine, brother of Henry Wadsworth Longfellow, and graduated from Harvard College and Harvard Divinity School. Held pastorates in Fall River, Massachusetts; Brooklyn, New York, and Germantown, Pennsylvania. Made one trip abroad. Besides being the author of many hymns and other poetry, also the author of *The Life of Henry Wadsworth Longfellow* (two volumes).

LORENZO (lō rĕn′zō) **II DE MEDICI** (mĕ′dē chē) (1449-1492), ruler of Florence, Lorenzo "the Magnificent" son of Piero (1414-1469), who was the son of Cosimo (1389-1464), who was in turn the son of Giovanni (1360-c. 1429), wealthy Florentine banker who became perhaps the richest man in Italy, and who gave the Medici family its fame and distinction. Lorenzo's father, Piero, ruled Florence for five years as his grandfather, Cosimo, had done for nearly thirty years. Lorenzo succeeded to the rule of Florence at the age of twenty. Became the virtual dictator of the Florentine republic; and though autocratic, tyrannical, and even immoral, retained hold on Florence by popular sanction in spite of bitter papal opposition. Under him the prosperity and power of Florence was unequaled by that of any other state of Europe; and the republic's prestige in foreign courts was unrivaled. Eminent in political judgment, just in government, magnanimous to enemies, one of the most versatile men of all time. Well educated in Latin and Greek, a magnificent patron of art and literature, himself a poet of no mean distinction. Devoted time and energy to the revival of classical learning, and was indeed a true son of the Renaissance. His influence and power were tremendous. Youngest son made a cardinal-deacon at thirteen, and at age thirty-seven became Pope Leo X. Daughter Catharine, wife of Henry II of France, was the most noted member of the Medici family after Lorenzo.

LOSEE, WILLIAM (c. 1764-?), a Methodist Episcopal itinerant preacher from the Lake Champlain area in Vermont. Set up circuit in Canada in 1791 in the Bay of Quinte area of Ontario. First Methodist church built at Adolphustown in 1792. Helped to carry the Second Awakening revival to Canada.

LOTZE (lōt′sĕ), **RUDOLPH HERMANN** (1817-1881), German philosopher, born at Bautzen, Saxony, studied philosophy and medicine at the University of Leipzig. After teaching at Leipzig from 1839 to 1842, professor of philosophy at the University of Göttingen from 1842 to 1881. Called to Berlin in 1881, a few months before death. His teleological idealism ethical rather than intellectual, making metaphysics fully dependent upon ethics. Had a firm faith in theism; believing in the validity of moral judgments, became an early exponent of "value philosophy." Writings were chiefly in the fields of logic and metaphysics. As a psychologist he opposed the theory of "vital force." Declared against Hegel's pantheism, and no less against materialism, which was then becoming rampant in Germany. His whole conception of the universe was essentially ethical. Among works: *Metaphysics, Logic, Microcosmos: Thoughts Bearing upon Natural Philosophy and the History of the Human Race, General Pathology and Therapy as Mechanical Natural Sciences, Essay on the Idea of the Beautiful in Art, History of Aesthetics in Germany, Medical Psychology,* and *On the Conditions of Artistic Beauty.*

LOUIS I, THE PIOUS (778-840), King of the Franks and Holy Roman Emperor, (813-840). Born at Chasseneuil in central France, youngest son and successor of Charlemagne, received a good education. Earned the surname, "Pious," by banishing his sisters and others of immoral life from court; by attempting to reform and purify monastic life; by showing great liberality to the church. Like his father, interested in extending kingdom in close association with the spread of Christianity. Induced Anskar (801-865) to go on a mission to the Danes of the North. Created an archbishopric with Hamburg as center; later associated with Bremen, over which had Anskar appointed as archbishop. Also established the monastery of Corvey which became the best school for education in the country. Kind treatment of the Jews deserves special mention. Louis the Pious, a deeply religious man did not possess the administrative strength of father. He was active in ecclesiastical affairs, and through synods continued the reform movement. Various plans were made by him for the succession. Finally divided empire among his three sons. Lothair the older son received the central portion, including Italy and the imperial title. Louis II received Germany.

LOUIS VII, THE YOUNG or **LE JEUNE** (c. 1121-1180), King of France (1137-1180). Soon came into disfavor with Pope Innocent II, and excommunicated, kingdom placed under the interdict. Remorse for gross sins committed led to the heed of urgent call of Bernard of Clairvaux to go on a crusade to the Holy Land. In 1147 embarked on the Second Crusade at the head of a large army. Crusade proved unsuccessful. Louis divorced wife Eleanor. By third wife in 1165 he had an heir, Philip Augustus, who succeeded to the throne in 1180. Louis carried on long wars with Henry II of England who had married the divorced Eleanor.

LOUIS IX, SAINT LOUIS (1214-1270), King of France (1226-1270), born at Poissy, near Paris. Son ascended the throne under the regency of mother, Blanche of Castile, in 1226. His mother, a pious and capable woman, had Louis educated by the brothers of the Franciscan and Dominican orders, and Louis became a Franciscan tertiary. In 1248 in fulfillment of a vow, made at a time of serious illness, leaving his mother in the regency, he collected an army of between forty and fifty thousand, and undertook a crusade to the Holy Land. Though at first he captured Damietta in Egypt, his army was later cut down by the Moslem Saracens and reduced to scarcely six thousand men. Louis remained in Palestine for four years, then returned in 1254 following the death of his regent mother. Returned to France to give his country a wise and efficient administration. In 1259 made the Treaty of Paris with Henry III of England. In 1270 embarked on a new crusade and got as far as Tunis when dysentery broke out and the greater part of the army and the king himself succumbed. Louis IX was the founder of the Sorbonne in Paris.

LOUIS XIII (1601-1643), King of France (1610-1643), born at Fontainebleau. Realm at beginning of his reign was in a very turbulent state. The Huguenots were threatening and a great part of the kingdom rebelled. In 1624 Louis chose Cardinal Richelieu as prime minister. He largely took over the administration of the kingdom. Under him the Huguenot power was completely broken by the capture of La Rochelle in 1628. The monarchical power grew at the expense of Protestants, nobles, and parliaments.

LOUIS XIV (1638-1715), King of France (1643-1715), "The Grand Monarch," born at Saint-Germain-en-laye, France. Became king at the age of five, his mother being regent during his minority, and the premier, Cardinal Jules Mazarin caring for the administrative affairs of the realm. When Mazarin died in 1661, he left to the young monarch the richest, most powerful, and best organized state in Europe. Louis took control of country with the declared intention of being his own prime minister, of ruling by divine right, and of being supreme in realm. His ambition to add many foreign territories to France led to many devastating and costly wars. Also determined to extend absolute authority over the church as well as over the state. This brought on a controversy with the papacy. During this time, however, the king held the respect and confidence of the French clergy who supported him in the enactment of the four Articles of Gallican Freedom. His great champion of the cause of the Gallican Liberties was the eloquent theologian and preacher, Bossuet, Bishop of Meaux. Louis XIV was particularly fond of taking a hand in doctrinal matters; and those who surrounded him came to the belief that the king could well supervise the church and supply it with information on religious questions. Loved good preaching, but would not condone Protestant preaching. His policy called for the destruction of Protestant churches, forcible removal of Protestant children from their parents to be reared in Roman Catholic homes, the revocation in 1685 of the Edict of Nantes, making Protestantism illegal under the severest penalties. Supported the Jesuits in their bitter and cruel opposition to Jansenism and encouraged the persecution of its followers. Through excessive extravagance at court, costly wars of expansion, and ejection of many of his best subjects, he threw away the internal prosperity of country, and consequently all possibility of effective external expansion. Died after a reign of seventy-two years, the longest in all recorded European history. Built beautiful palace complex at Versailles.

LOUIS XVI (1754-1793), King of France (1774-1792), born at Versailles, grandson and successor of Louis XV. In midst of corrupt court grew up temperate, honest, moral, and religious, being a devoted and sincere Roman Catholic. A weak and incapable ruler. Married Marie Antoinette, the youngest daughter of the Empress of Austria, and often followed her counsel to his sorrow and detriment. Royal family had to flee from Versailles, and for a while were under guard in the Tuileries in Paris. In 1791 king and family tried to escape from France, but were arrested and brought back. In 1792 a mob stormed the Tuileries, and massacred the Swiss guard. The king was deposed a month later when France was declared a republic. In December, 1792 he was brought to trial for treason against the state, declared guilty, and condemned to death. The next month he and Marie Antoinette were guillotined on Concord Square.

LOVEJOY, ELIJAH PARISH (1802-1837), abolitionist printer. Born in Albion, Maine. Educated at Waterville (Colby) College, Maine and Princeton Theological Seminary. In 1835 licensed as a Presbyterian preacher after teaching school in Maine and Missouri. As editor from 1833 to 1836 of the *St. Louis Observer* advocated temperance and abolition. Moved to Alton, Illinois in 1836 and edited the *Alton Observer.* His opposition to slavery led to attacks upon his press, and he was killed by a mob in 1837. Founded Illinois Anti-Slavery Society in 1837. Advocated freedom of the press.

LOWRY, ROBERT (1826-1899), composer and pastor, born in Philadelphia, and at seventeen became a member of the First Baptist Church. After graduating from a six-year course in Lewisburg University in 1854 ordained a Baptist minister. From that time until death successfully pastored Baptist churches in West Chester, Pennsylvania, New York City, Brooklyn, New York, Lewisburg, Pennsylvania, and Plainfield, New Jersey. For the six years at Lewisburg occupied the chair of letters at his alma mater. Considered preaching his first love and supreme task, music being but a "side issue." Dr. Lowry is remembered for hymns rather than for sermons. Succeeded William B. Bradbury as editor of Sunday school song books published by Bigelow and Main, collaborating with William Howard Doane in this enterprise. Author of both words and music of many of his hymns, some of the best known and most widely used: "Shall We Gather at The River?", "Where is My Wandering Boy?", "Nothing But the Blood of Jesus," "Up From the Grave He Arose." He wrote the music for "I Need Thee Every Hour," "Saviour, Thy Dying Love," "We're Marching to Zion," "The Mistakes of My Life Have Been Many," "One More Day's Work for Jesus."

LOYOLA, see IGNATIUS OF LOYOLA

LUCIAN (lū'shăn), **OF ANTIOCH** (c. 240-312), presbyter of Antioch, born at Samosata in Syria, educated at Edessa, perhaps studying also at Caesarea, became a celebrated biblical scholar, settled at Antioch, where he founded a literal school of exegesis. Here Arius and Eusebius of Nicomedia became pupils of Lucian, who is considered by some as the founder of the Arian heresy. In the reign of Diocletian arrested for being a Christian. Made a noble and impressive confession of faith before the judge. Died under torture in prison in Nicomedia in 312. Eusebius praised him for sanctity and purity of life, his knowledge of the Scriptures, and noble martyrdom. Also recognized as a holy ascetic. The creed that goes by his name and was accepted at Antioch in 341 bears the marks of orthodoxy. Known for critical version of the text of the Greek Bible.

LUCIAN (OF SAMOSATA) (c. 125-190), Greek rhetorician, satirist, and writer. Born at Samosata on the Euphrates, Syria. Studied and practiced law for a time, then turned to teaching rhetoric. At about age forty gave up rhetoric and turned interest to traveling and writing dialogues which consisted largely in attacks upon the religion and philosophy of his age. Finally received a lucrative legal position in Egypt, held until his death. From superficial and fragmentary acquaintance with Christianity, attacked the Christian religion with ridicule, mockery, and wit, as he did all other phases of religion and worship. Among his writings: *Dialogues of the Gods, Dialogues of the Dead, Banquet of Philosophers, Auction of Philosophers,* and *Of The Death of Peregrinus.*

LUCAR, CYRIL (1572-1638), Greek Orthodox theologian. Born in Crete. Studied at Venice and Padua. Taught theology at Vilna and Lvov. Patriarch in Alexandria from 1602 to 1620 and of Constantinople from about 1620. Sent Codex Alexandrinus of Bible to the Archbishop of Canterbury about 1625. Had Bible put into the vernacular. In 1629 published a Calvinistic *Confession*. Sultan Murad had the Janizzaries strangle him, and the Synod of Jerusalem in 1672 rejected his doctrines.

LULL, RAYMOND (c. 1235-c. 1315), missionary to the Moslems. Born at Palma, capital of Majorca, one of the Baleric Islands. Lived a worldly life in the court of King James of Aragon until he was about thirty. Turned to the ascetic life and became a Franciscan tertiary. Began zealous preparation for missionary work among the Moslems, first learning the Arabic from a Moorish slave, then starting the College of Miramar to teach the Arabic and Chaldean tongues. For several years lectured in Paris and Montpellier. Wrote a book of diagrams and arguments to prove the truth and superiority of Christianity. In 1291, when about fifty-five, made first missionary trip to the Moslems. In Tunis, North Africa challenged the fanatical Moslems to a public disputation, which resulted in banishment. Back home spent several years lecturing and writing. In 1305 or 1306 made a second attempt to convert the Moslems of Tunis, but was again banished. Back in Europe succeeded in securing a council decree to establish professorships of oriental languages at Avignon, Paris, Bologna, Oxford, and Salamanca. In 1315 at age 80 made third attempt to penetrate the Moslem lines of North Africa. The Moslem population rose against him and drove him from the city with sticks and stones. The next day, on way back to Majorca, he died. Lull had introduced some new principles into the missionary enterprise by studying the Arabic language at home, writing and lecturing on missions, seeking to establish schools of oriental languages, and substituting love for force in missionary labors. His theologico-philosophical works were many, reaching perhaps the number of three hundred.

LUTHARDT (lo͞ot'härt), **CHRISTOPH ERNST** (1823-1902), German confessional Lutheran theologian, born at Maroldsweisach, Germany, studied at Erlangen and Berlin. A teacher at the gymnasium at Munich in 1847, teacher at Erlangen in 1851, professor extraordinary at Marburg in 1854, ordinary professor of systematic theology and New Testament exegesis at Leipzig from 1856 until the end of his life. Became an outstanding opponent and critic of the liberal and rationalistic school of Ritschl, charging that its unorthodox views on the deity of Christ, the atonement and other doctrines tended to undermine Christianity. Along with Delitzsch and other orthodox theologians became an exponent of Hofmann's new theological school of confessional Lutheranism developing at the University of Erlangen. A voluminous theological writer, an eloquent preacher, an ecclesiastical statesman, for forty-six years influential professor and an attraction at the University of Leipzig. Wrote a well-known commentary on John's gospel.

LUTHER, KATHARINA (VON BORA) (1499-1552), Martin Luther's wife, born near Bitterfeldt in Meissen, Saxony. At early age placed in the Cistercian convent of Nimbschen near Grimma, Saxony, became a nun in 1515. Learning of Luther's Reformation doctrines, she and eight other nuns, with Luther's help, consequently fled form the convent in 1523 and took refuge in Wittenberg. In 1525 became the wife of Luther. Katharina became the mother of three sons and three daughters, was a true wife and a good housekeeper—the marriage was a happy one. After Luther's death in 1546 she remained in Wittenberg, sparingly supported by the Danish king, Christian III. Her death was due to an accident which occurred as she was on the way with her children to Torgau to escape the plague at Wittenberg.

LUTHER, MARTIN (1483-1546), German Reformer, born at Eisleben, Germany, the eldest of seven children, to peasant parents. He received early religious education. Between six and fourteen received elementary education in the local school at Mansfeld. In 1497 sent to Magdeburg where he studied under the mystical teachings of the Brethren of the Common Life. The next three years resided in the home of Frau Ursula Cotta and studied at Eisenach. At eighteen, in 1501, went to the University of Erfurt. A narrow escape from death led Luther to enter a monastery of the Augustinian Order in Erfurt in 1505. Here was his first opportunity of possessing a Bible, which he studied most diligently under the supervision of Johann Von Staupitz. Soon became known as one of the most learned Augustinians. In his study gave special attention to the New Testament books of Romans and Galatians and to works of William of Occam and Augustine. Had the reputation of being a man of 1) singular piety, 2) devotion, and 3) monastic zeal. After finishing this probationary period in the monastery consecrated a monk in 1506, and a priest the next year. In 1508 called to teach at the newly founded University of Wittenberg. In 1510 the Augustinian Order sent him on a special mission to Rome. He had long wished to visit the Holy See. He was surprised and troubled by the corruption that existed at the papal court. In 1512 became professor of theology at the University of Wittenberg, which position he held the rest of his life. Between 1512 and 1517 his fame spread far and wide as he lectured on the Psalms, Romans, Galatians, and Hebrews. Lectured on theology in native language, and so simply that the common people could understand. As he studied the Scriptures he saw the truth of justification by faith as over against the Roman church's doctrine of work-righteousness. The Bible now began to bring new light. In his wide reading and study he was greatly influenced by 1) Occam's school of theology, 2) Augustine's writings, 3) Paul's epistles, and 4) German mysticism. Luther was having deep vital experiences and was rapidly receiving new light and new convictions, but as yet had not consciously worked out a system of theology. By 1517 fully accepted what have come to be known as the three great Reformation principles; 1) Man is justified by faith alone; 2) Every believer has direct access to God; and 3) the Bible is the sole source of authority for faith and life. On October 31, 1517, nailed on the church door at Wittenberg his *Ninety-five Theses* as a challenge to debate the abuses of indulgences. This event greatly stirred the Roman Catholic church, reaching even the papal court. Events moved rapidly after that. In 1518 Pope Leo X summoned him to appear at Rome. In 1519 he met John Eck in debate. In 1520 issued his three tracts attacking the sacraments and hierarchy, asserting the Bible as only authority for faith, and upholding justification by faith and the priesthood of believers. In 1520 he burned the bull which the pope had issued against him. In 1521 excommunicated, and at Worms made his actual break with Rome. He translated the New Testament in 1522 and by 1534 the Old Testament into German. From this point on he was forced to provide a system of worship and a clarified doctrine for the masses who were looking to him for guidance. A system gradually unfolded. In 1525 he married and established an exemplary evangelical pastor's home. In 1529 wrote two catechisms. The next year approved the Augsburg Confession and the Augsburg Apology as written by Philip Melanchthon. In 1537 restated his doctrines in the Schmalkald Articles. Luther's remaining years were spent in active and productive service. He composed the hymn, "A Mighty Fortress," numerous tracts, letters, and treatises. His biblical commentaries, especially on Galatians, and his *On the Bondage of the Will* are widely read to this day. After mediating a quarrel among the princes of Mansfeld, Luther experienced severe chest pains and died the following morning.

LUTKIN, PETER CHRISTIAN (1857-1931), American organist and hymnologist, born at Thompsonville, Wisconsin, studied music in Chicago, Berlin, Paris, and Vienna. Filled various posts as organist in Chicago; in 1888 began teaching theory at the American Conservatory of Music in Chicago; and in 1891 at the Music School of Northwestern University, Evanston. Dean of the School of Music from 1897 to 1928. In addition to these duties, for twenty seasons conducted the annual Chicago North Shore Festival at Evanston (1909-1930). In 1908 lectured at the Western Theological Seminary, Chicago, lectures appearing in print as *Music in the Church*. Edited the *Methodist Sunday School Hymnal*, and was co-editor of the *Episcopal Church Hymnal*. Wrote much church music, including a Communion Service, four Te Deums, four magnificats, many anthems, part-songs and songs, preludes, and other pieces; and published pedagogical works. Lutkin was the founder of the American Guild of Organists.

LYON, MARY (1797-1849), American Christian educator, born at Buckland, Massachusetts, educated at several schools and academies. Beginning at age seventeen, taught at several places, including the Adams Female Seminary at Londonderry, New Hampshire and Miss Grant's school in Ipswich. In 1834, after nearly sixteen years of teaching, left the school room to raise funds for the building of an academy for girls. It was not an easy task in those days to establish a school for women. Her school was finally opened in 1837 at South Hadley, Massachusetts, about ten miles south of Amherst, the first school of higher learning for women in Massachusetts. The school was named

Mount Holyoke Seminary (now College), and Miss Lyon was principal for twelve years, until early death in 1849. The institution, as her life, was consecrated to the Lord. Through her effort and influence it became a training school for missionaries and Christian workers, and continued for many years in the spirit and purpose of its founder. Mary Lyon was elected to the American Hall of Fame in 1905.

LYTTELTON (lĭt'l tŭn), **GEORGE, FIRST BARON LYTTELTON** (1709-1773), English statesman and man of letters, son of Sir Thomas Lyttelton, born at Hagley, Worcestershire, England, studied at Eton and Christ Church, Oxford, but took no degrees. Elected to the House of Commons in 1735, where he was a member until 1756, when elevated to the House of Lords. Lord commissioner of the treasury from 1744 to 1754 and chancellor of the exchequer the next two years. When about thirty-eight began a serious and honest study to ascertain the truth of Christianity. The result was conviction of the truth, his conversion, and writing of *Observations on the Conversion and Apostleship of St. Paul*.

LYTE, HENRY FRANCIS (1793-1847), hymn writer. Born near Kelso, Scotland. Educated at Trinity College, Dublin. Pastor of churches at Marazion, Cornwall, Lower Brixham, and Devon. Poems were chiefly religious. Wrote the hymns: "Abide With Me," "Praise My Soul the King of Heaven," "Jesus I My Cross Have Taken," and "God of Mercy, God of Grace."

M

MABILLON, JEAN (1632-1707). Born Saint-Pierremont, France. Member of the Benedictine Order. Belonged to the Congregation of St Maur, a Benedictine group who studied and wrote church history. His *De Re Diplomatica* of 1681 concerned diplomatics, the dating of manuscripts by paleography and paper. Put diplomatics on a scientific base. Collected writings of many medieval scholars and saints.

McALL (mȧ kôl'), **ROBERT WHITAKER** (1821-1893), English Congregationalist. Founder of McAll Mission, born at Macclesfield, Cheshire, England, educated at the University of London. After studying at Free College of Theology at Whalley Range, near Manchester, ordained in 1905 and held pastoral charges at Sunderland, Leicester, Manchester, Birmingham, and Hadleigh. While on holiday visit with wife to France in 1871 saw the religious destitution of the working men of Paris, who had broken with the Roman Catholic church and had drifted into irreligion. Early in 1872, at age fifty, began evangelistic work in the communistic quarter of Belleville, a suburb of Paris. In 1882 this interdenominational mission organized on a permanent foundation with McAll as honorary life director. By 1892 the mission reached far outside of Paris, even to Tunis and Algeria. The McAll Mission had had much influence upon native French Protestantism. Resigning the directorship in 1892, McAll went to England to collect funds for the work. The same year decorated with the cross of the Legion of Honor. The next year returned to Paris where he died. Wrote nearly one hundred tracts, and being an accomplished musician, with his wife prepared a hymnbook that was much used by French Protestants.

MACARIUS (mȧ kā'rĭ ŭs) (d. c. 390), Egyptian hermit, born in Upper Egypt, won to religious life at early age by Saint Anthony. When thirty years became a monk. At forty ordained a priest, for the remainder of long life presided over the monastic community in the desert of Scete or Scetis, a part of the great Libyan desert. The teachings of Macarius are characterized by a mystical and spiritual mode of thought which has classed him among mystics and has endeared him to the mystics of all ages. In theology, somewhat semi-Pelagian, ascribing to man the power to attain a degree of readiness to receive salvation. Fifty homilies, an *Epistola ad Filios Dei,* and several letters and prayers are attributed to him.

McCARRELL, WILLIAM (1896-1979). Born near Chicago. Educated at Moody Bible Institute. Pastor of Cicero Bible Church from 1913. Ordained 1915. Founder of Independent Fundamentalist Churches of America in 1930. Member of the official board of Wheaton College.

MACARTNEY, CLARENCE EDWARD NOBLE (1879-1957), Presbyterian minister, born in Northwood, Ohio, studied at University of Wisconsin, Princeton University, and Princeton Theological Seminary, later received honorary degrees from several colleges. Pastor of the First Church, Paterson, New Jersey (1904-1914), Arch Street Church, Philadelphia (1914-1927), First Church, Pittsburgh, Pennsylvania (1927-1953), retired in 1953. In 1924 moderator of the General Assembly of the Presbyterian Church in the United States of America. Lectured at many conferences, colleges, and seminaries; author of over forty books, consisting mainly of sermons, Bible studies, and works on Lincoln and other historical subjects.

MACAULAY (mȧ kô'lĭ), **ZACHARY** (1768-1838), philanthropist and abolitionist, governor of Sierra Leone (1793-1799); secretary of the chartered company which had founded the Sierra Leone colony (1799-1808); secretary of Africa Institute (1807-1812). Saw evils of slavery while a bookkeeper in Jamaica from 1784 to 1792. Editor of the abolitionist journal, *The Christian Observer* (1802-1816), sought to abolish the British slave trade, and to halt the slave trade abroad. Worked many years with William Wilberforce in this great endeavor. In 1823 Macaulay aided in organizing the Anti-Slavery Society; one of the founders of the London University. Macaulay was a member of the "Clapham Sect," an informal group of wealthy Anglican evangelicals who were interested in active participation in social and moral betterment projects. Deeply interested in the work of the British and Foreign Bible Society, and of the Church Missionary Society. A Fellow of the Royal Society. His son, Thomas Babington Macaulay (1800-1859), was a prominent historian.

McAULEY (măk ô'lĭ), **JEREMIAH (JERRY)** (1839-1884), founder of the first rescue mission in the United States, born in Ireland, cared for by Roman Catholic grandmother, father having left home to escape apprehension for crime of counterfeiting. Never went to school, was treated harshly, grew up in idleness and mischief. Came to New York when thirteen, soon joined with other criminals and became a river thief and a prizefighter. At nineteen arrested on false charge for highway robbery, sent to Sing Sing for fifteen years. While there he was converted and won several others to Christ. In 1864, after seven years of sentence, Governor Dix recognized his innocence and pardoned him. Leaving the prison, but finding no friend to help him lead an honest life, again fell into old ways of sin and crime. Through the efforts of Water Street Mission workers, led back to Christ. Experienced several failures in attempt to live the Christian life. Finally united with the Methodist church, found complete victory over former evil habits. In 1872 opened at 316 Water Street in New York "The Helping Hand" mission, the first rescue mission in the United States. Four years later this mission was incorporated as the McAuley Water Street Mission and a three-story brick building erected for its work. His wife, Maria, who also had been rescued from a life of degradation, was a devoted co-laborer. In 1882 McAuley founded the Jerry McAuley Cremorne Mission on West Thirty-Second Street, which he conducted until his death two years later. In 1883 began publishing *Jerry McAuley's Newspaper*. He dictated his autobiography, *Transformed, or the History of a River Thief*. His missions were continued by Samuel H. Hadley and John H. Wyburn.

McCABE, CHARLES CARDWELL (1836-1906), Methodist Episcopal bishop and home missionary. Born Athens, Ohio. Educated at Ohio Wesleyan College. Minister at Putnam, Ohio and then chaplain in the army from 1862 to 1864. US Christian commissioner from 1864 to 1865. Minister at Portsmouth, Ohio from 1865 to 1868. Secretary and organizing superintendent for his church from 1868 to 1896. Bishop from 1896 to 1906. Chancellor of American University from 1902 to 1906.

McCHEYNE (măk shān′), **ROBERT MURRAY** (1813-1843), Church of Scotland minister, born at Dundee, Scotland, studied at the University of Edinburgh, where he was distinguished for poetical talent, and at the divinity hall of the university, under Dr. Thomas Chalmers. In 1835 licensed to preach, assisted the Rev. A. A. Bonar, minister of the united parishes of Larbert and Dunipace. In 1836 ordained to the pastorate of St. Peter's Church, Dundee, which he held until death. A member of a committee sent to Palestine in 1839 to collect information respecting a mission to Jews. On return entered upon a successful evangelistic campaign in Scotland and North England. In the disruption controversy of 1843 took a decided stand on the non-intrusion side. Principal writings were: *Narrative of a Mission of Inquiry to the Jews—in 1839*, in collaboration with A. A. Bonar; *Expositions of the Epistles to the Seven Churches of Asia;* and *The Eternal Inheritance*.

McCLINTOCK (mȧ klĭn′ tŭk), **JOHN** (1814-1870), Methodist scholar and preacher, born in Philadelphia, graduated from the University of Pennsylvania, professor of mathematics and classics in Dickinson College, Carlisle, Pennsylvania, for twelve years, editor of the *Methodist Quarterly Review* (1848-1856). Pastor of St. Paul's Methodist Church, New York (1857-1860 and 1864). During the Civil War (1860-1864) in charge of the American Chapel in Paris. On two or more occasions elected president of a college, but declined each call. From 1867 until death three years later, president of the newly established Drew Theological Seminary, Madison, New Jersey. Most important work: the *Cyclopaedia of Biblical, Theological, and Ecclesiastical Literature* (twelve volumes), written in collaboration with James Strong, only three volumes of which were published before McClintock's death.

McCLOSKEY (mȧ klŏs′kĭ), **JOHN** (1810-1885), first American Roman Catholic cardinal, born in Brooklyn, New York, attended school in New York and at Mount Saint Mary's College, Emmitsburg, Maryland, ordained priest in 1834. From 1834 to 1837 studied in Rome and traveled in Europe. Upon return to America assigned for parish duty to St. Joseph's Church, New York City, meanwhile, during 1841-42, served as organizer and president of the newly founded St. John's College at Fordham. In 1844 appointed co-adjutor to Bishop Hughes of the diocese of New York with the right of succession, still retaining position at St. Joseph's parish. In 1847 became first bishop of the newly created diocese of Albany. Established the Cathedral of the Immaculate Conception at Albany, St. Joseph's Theological Seminary at Troy, several new parishes, and educational and charitable institutions, including hospitals, orphanages, homes for the aged and reformatories, introduced monastic orders and lay communities. In 1864 succeeded Archbishop Hughes in the archdiocese of New York, then including New York, New Jersey, and New England. In attendance at the Vatican Council in 1870, serving there as a member of the committee on ecclesiastical discipline. Made a cardinal in 1875, being the first American citizen to receive this dignity. Noted for gentleness, profound scholarship, effective preaching, rare executive and administrative ability and his earnest piety. Completed St. Patrick's Cathedral in New York.

McCORMICK, CYRUS HALL (1809-1884), American inventor and manufacturer, born at Walnut Grove, Virginia, received a common school education. Removed to Cincinnati in 1845, to Chicago in 1847. In 1831, continuing father's efforts, constructed a reaping machine which subsequently was patented and further improved, and which brought great wealth and world-wide fame. A pioneer in the creation of modern business methods. By nature deeply religious and keenly interested in the work of the Presbyterian church. In 1859 contributed one hundred thousand dollars to the establishment in Chicago of the Presbyterian Theological Seminary of the Northwest, later renamed McCormick Theological Seminary. His wife Nettie (Fowler) McCormick (1835-1933) of Brownville, New York provided two more buildings after his death. He endowed a chair in Washington and Lee University, Virginia, and made gifts to the Union Theological Seminary in Virginia. Gave thought and effort to bring about a reunion of the northern and southern branches of the Presbyterian church. Made an officer in the Legion of Honor, and a corresponding member of the French Academy of Sciences.

McCOSH (mȧ kŏsh′), **JAMES** (1811-1894), Free Church of Scotland philosopher and educator, born at Carskeoch, Ayrshire, Scotland, educated in the universities of Glasgow and Edinburgh. Licensed in the Church of Scotland in 1834, served in two different parishes (Arbroath and Brechin). At the disruption in 1843, entered the Free Church of Scotland and became superintendent of mountainous Brechen district until 1853. From 1852 to 1868, professor of logic and metaphysics in Queen's College, Belfast. Much interested in bettering the national system of schools, and in this interest visited Germany and the United States. In 1868 elected president of Princeton College, New Jersey, holding that office until resignation in 1888. Retained the chair of philosophy until 1890. Introduced the elective system in the college, and prepared the way for the college to become a university. As a philosopher takes a high rank; a firm believer in realism and strongly opposed to both idealism and materialism. Theology strictly on the lines of the Westminster Confession; but one of the first orthodox clergymen in America to accept and defend the theory of evolution in biology. Wrote voluminously; some of more important works: *The Method of Divine Government, Physical and Moral; Typical Forms and Special Ends in Creation* (written in collaboration with Dr. Dickie); *An Examination of Dr. J. S. Mill's Philosophy: Being a Defense of Fundamental Truth; The Supernatural in Relation to the Natural; Christianity and Positivism; The Intuitions of the Mind, Inductively Investigated; Scottish Philosophy, Biographical, Expository, Critical; Realistic Philosophy Defended;* and *Religious Aspects of Evolution*.

McCRIE (mȧ krē′), **THOMAS** (1772-1835), Scottish seceding divine and church historian, born at Duns, Berwickshire, Scotland, educated at the University of Edinburgh. In 1796 ordained minister of the Second Associate Congregation at Potterrow, Edinburgh, where he served from 1796 to 1809. In 1806 he and three other ministers left the General Association Synod and formed the Constitutional Association Presbytery, which later merged in the "Original Seceders." These ministers were deposed by the associate synod, and McCrie was ejected from the Potterrow Presbytery; but congregation withdrew with him and built for him the new West Richmond Street Church, where he continued from 1809 until death to minister. From 1816 to 1818 filled the chair of divinity in the theological seminary of denomination. During the controversy devoted himself to the study of the history, constitution, and polity of the churches of the Reformation, and came to admire the great Scottish Reformer so much that he wrote a masterly biography, *The Life of John Knox*. This work, two volumes, was chief literary achievement. It is believed that his studies and writing on the Scottish Reformation did much to bring about the disruption of 1843. Other works: *The Life of Andrew Melville, History of the Progess and Suppression of the Reformation in Italy,* and *History of the Progress and Suppression of the Reformation in Spain*.

McCULLY, T. EDWARD, *See* **ELLIOTT, JAMES**

McDOWELL, WILLIAM FRASER (1858-1937), Methodist bishop, born at Millersburg, Ohio, educated at Ohio Wesleyan University, Boston School of Theology, and Boston University. Ordained in 1882, held pastorates at Lodi, Oberlin, and Tiffin, Ohio, between 1882 and 1890. Chancellor of the University of Denver (1890-1899); then was corresponding secretary of the Board of Education of the Methodist Episcopal Church (1899-1904). Became a member of the International Committee of the Young Men's Christian Association (1899), and president of the board of trustees of Northwestern University (1906). Elected bishop (1904) and served in Chicago until 1916, and then in Washington, D.C., until retirement in 1932. Head of the commission formed in 1936 to draw up terms of unification for the three branches of Methodism that were contemplating union, and which were finally united in 1939. Active also in peace and temperance organizations, serving for several years as chairman of the Methodist Board of Temperance, Prohibition, and Public Morals. McDowell was regarded as one of Methodism's greatest preachers as well as one of the most influential and creative bishops in the history of denomination.

MCDONALD, GEORGE (1824-1905), Scottish poet and novelist. Born Huntley, Aberdeenshire. Educated at King's College and Highbury Theological College. Pastor of church in Arundel, Sussex until his resignation to write and lecture. Novels centered on northeastern Scottish life. *Phantastes* and *Lilith* are among his more imaginative works. Influenced C. S. Lewis.

MACEDONIUS (măs ĕ dō'nĭ ŭs), (died c. 362), Patriarch of Constantinople and founder of the Macedonian sect. In 342, upon the death of Eusebius of Nicomedia, Macedonius, the Arian bishop of Constantinople, made patriarch of Constantinople by the Arian party and enthroned by Emperor Constantius, an Arian. Held this position for about eighteen years. A moderate semi-Arian, teaching that the Holy Spirit is "a minister and a servant" on a level with the angels, and a creature subordinate to both the Father and the Son, thus rejecting the deity of the Holy Spirit. Became founder of the semi-Arian sect sometimes called Macedonians or Pneumatomachi (Adversaries of the Spirit). Being in good graces with neither the Athanasian nor the Arian party, really represented a third party. At an Arian council at Constantinople in 360 deposed. Lived but a short time after this. In 381 at the ecumenical Council of Constantinople his doctrine was condemned, and the clause defining the nature of the Holy Spirit was added to the Nicene Creed.

McGIFFERT, ARTHUR CUSHMAN (1861-1933), American Congregationalist church historian, born at Sauquoit, New York, studied at Western Reserve College, Union Theological Seminary, New York, University of Berlin, University of Marburg (studying under Harnack), in Paris, and in Rome. Upon return to the United States ordained to the presbyterian ministry in 1888, became a member of the faculty of Lane Theological Seminary at Cincinnati, Ohio, teaching Church history there until 1893, became Washburn professor of church history in and president of (1917 to 1926) Union Theological Seminary, retiring in 1927. *A History of Christianity in the Apostolic Age,* caused such criticism that he withdrew from the Presbyterian ministry to avoid an inevitable heresy trial. Retained position at the seminary, however, and joined the Congregational church. Some of his other writings were a translation of *Eusebius' Church History; A History of Christian Thought; The Apostles' Creed; Protestant Thought Before Kant; Martin Luther, the Man and His Work; The Rise of Modern Religious Ideas;* and *Christianity as History and Faith.*

McGRANAHAN (må grăn'å hăn), **JAMES** (1840-1907), gospel hymn and tune writer, born near Adamsville, Pennsylvania. Received education mainly in the public schools. As a lad learned to read notes and to sing alto, at nineteen began teaching music classes in the neighborhood, using the money thus earned to further musical education. At twenty-five began to write compositions and for many years wrote anthems and music for gospel songs. For a few years one of the managers and a teacher of Dr. George F. Root's Normal Musical Institute. Shortly after the tragic death of P. P. Bliss in 1876 decided to give up teaching in institutes and conventions and devote full time to evangelistic singing. Succeeded Mr. Bliss as singing evangelist with Major D. W. Whittle, employing his tenor voice in America, England, Scotland, and Ireland. On tour in Great Britain in 1881 edited *Songs of the Gospel,* much of the music being his own. Wrote many hymns along with melodies, also wrote many tunes for lyrics written by others. In all edited fifteen hymn books. In music and evangelistic work associated with such men as D. L. Moody, Ira D. Sankey, George F. Root, and Lowell Mason. Some of the great gospel hymns for which he wrote the music are: "Showers of Blessing," "The Crowning Day Is Coming," "Hallelujah for the Cross," "I Know Whom I Have Believed," "Christ Returneth," "Bringing Back the King," "O How I Love Thy Law," "Christ Receiveth Sinful Men," and "I Will Sing of My Redeemer." Both the words and the music of "Go Ye Into all the World" were written by Mr. McGranahan.

MCGREADY, JAMES (c. 1758-1817), Scotch-Irish Presbyterian preacher and founder of the camp meeting. Born in Western Pennsylvania. Studied theology under John McMillan. Spiritually energized by a visit to Hampden-Sydney College. Ministered in North Carolina from c. 1790 to 1796 and from 1796 to 1811 was pastor of three churches in Logan County, preached during Kentucky revival in 1797. In a camp meeting at Gaspar River in 1800 to prepare people for communion the camp meeting seems to have originated. From 1811 to 1817 an itinerant preacher, part of the time in Indiana.

MACHEN (mā'chĕn), **JOHN GRESHAM** (1881-1937), Presbyterian theologian, born at Baltimore, Maryland, studied at Johns Hopkins, Princeton University, Princeton Theological Seminary, and the universities of Marburg and Göttingen, Germany. Ordained to the Presbyterian ministry in 1914, after teaching at Princeton for eight years. Taught New Testament literature and exegesis in Princeton Theological Seminary (1906-1929), at Westminster Theological Seminary (1929-1937). In World War I worked with the Young Men's Christian Association in the French Army and with the American Expeditionary Force (1918-1919). An outstanding conservative apologist and theologian at Princeton Theological Seminary, but left because of modernism. Offered the presidency of several schools; but refused each offer. In 1929 founded Westminster Theological Seminary and became president and professor of New Testament from 1929 to 1937. Protesting against the liberalism of the Presbyterian Board of Foreign Missions, established an independent mission board. Charged with insubordination, tried, found guilty, and suspended from the Presbyterian ministry. Group of sixteen other clergymen and laymen with Dr. Machen withdrew in 1936 to found the Orthodox Presbyterian church. Chosen the first moderator. Wrote: *The Origin of Paul's Religion, Christianity and Liberalism, New Testament Greek for Beginners, What is Faith?, The Virgin Birth of Christ, The Christian View of Man,* and *The Christian Faith in the Modern World.* Never married. Died of pneumonia on a preaching engagement.

MACHIAVELLI (mä kyä vĕl'lē), **NICCOLO** (1469-1527), Italian statesman and political philosopher, born in Florence, Italy, received a good humanistic education, secretary of the Florentine Republic after the repulsion of the Medici family in 1498, carried out several diplomatic missions in the Italian States, France, and Germany from 1498 to 1512. Came under the influence and intrigues of Cesare Borgia, whose evil purpose colored his life and writings. In *Il Principe* (The Prince), Machiavelli set forth a moral political philosophy. Held that the ideal ruler must be absolute, and must use any means, however unscrupulous and unethical and however much he may perjure the truth or break promises to protect his state.

MACHRAY, ROBERT (1831-1904), primate of Anglican Church in Canada. Born in Scotland. Educated at the University of Aberdeen and Sidney Sussex, Cambridge. Ordained in 1856, then travelled for three years. Dean of Sidney Sussex from 1858 to 1862. Pastor at Madingley until appointed bishop of Rupertsland from 1866 to 1904. Helped revive St. Johns College in Winnipeg, Manitoba. From 1877 to 1904 worked to establish the University of Manitoba of which he was chancellor during that period. Made metropolitan bishop of Western Canada in 1875 and primate in 1893 of the Anglican Church in Canada. Under him the church moved from dependence upon the church in England to an independent national status.

MACINTOSH, DOUGLAS CLYDE (1877-1948), Canadian Baptist clergyman, liberal pacifist, and theologian, born in Breadalbane, Ontario, Canada, educated at McMaster University, Toronto, and University of Chicago. From 1897 to 1899 minister of the Baptist church of Marthaville, Ontario; 1903-1904 taught philosophy at McMaster University; professor of theology at Brandon College, Brandon, Manitoba (1907-1909). Associate professor of theology at Yale University (1909-1916), Dwight professor of theology and philosophy (1916-1942), and chairman of the department of religion (1920-1938). In time of World War I chaplain of the Canadian Expeditionary Forces in 1916; secretary of the Young Men's Christian Association with the American Expeditionary Forces in 1918. Writings comprise: *Theology as an Empirical Science, The Reasonableness of Christianity, The Pilgrimage of Faith, Religious Realism, Social Religion, The Problem of Religious Knowledge, Personal Religion,* and *Thinking About God.* In 1930 became widely known in the celebrated Macintosh Case in which he was denied United States citizenship for having affirmed scruples against promising to bear arms in defense of this country. Theology was of the liberal strain.

MACK, ALEXANDER (1679-1735), founder of the German Baptist Brethren (Dunkers), or Church of the Brethren. Born at Schriesheim, Germany, of pious parents of the Reformed church, early became dissatisfied with the formalism of the state church and became a separatist. Located at Schwarzenau in the Palatinate in close fellowship with other separatists, especially with Ernst Christoph Hochmann, an ardent Pietist. Together they made many preaching trips along the Rhine. Along with Hochmann felt that the Christian should stress right living as well as right doctrine. Convinced that the keeping of the New Testament ordinances was an essential part of the New Testament teaching and that an organized church is necessary. Parted company with ultra-pietistic friend, Hochmann; along with seven others organized a new denomination. In 1708 one of their number baptized Alexander Mack, and he baptized the other seven. Thus the German Baptist Brethren church had its beginning. Became the first pastor and the guiding spirit of the new church. About 1720 when the Schwarzenau congregation was sorely persecuted, Mack and members fled to Westervain, Friesland (Holland). Here the congregation flourished for nine years. In 1729 the little congregation came to America. They were joyfully met by the first party that had come under the leadership of Peter Becker from Krefeld, Germany to Germantown, Pennsylvania, ten years before. Saddened to find faction existing in the young church in America. Lived only six years after coming to America.

MACKAY (mȧ kī′), **ALEXANDER MURDOCH** (1849-1890), missionary to Uganda, born at Rhynie, Scotland, studied in Edinburgh and engineering in Berlin. Sent to Central Africa by the Church Missionary Society at own urgent request. Reached Zanzibar in 1876, in 1878, despite many hazards, delays, and unforeseen difficulties, with more than two hundred carriers, made his notable expedition from the east coast to Uganda. At first enjoyed the protection of King Mutesa. But when Mwanga came to the throne in 1884 and Kiwewa in 1888, he suffered much opposition and persecution; yet with courage, energy, and devotion held to purpose, and the Uganda Mission was firmly established. After several years of bitter persecution, in 1887 moved mission station to Usambiro, and there labored, preached, translated, and printed for three years. Built 230 miles of road to Uganda from coast. He died having spent fourteen years in Africa without once returning to native Scotland.

MACKAY, GEORGE LESLIE (1844-1901), missionary to Formosa, born in Zorra, Oxford County, Ontario, Canada, of Scottish Highland descent. Studied in Knox College, Toronto, and Princeton Seminary. After graduation from the seminary appointed by the Presbyterian church in Canada as missionary to China. Went to the field and ordained in 1871, decided to begin work in northern Formosa. Able to preach first sermon in Chinese at the end of five months. First convert became an ardent Christian preacher, and along with other converts started stable churches. When Mackay was in Canada on first furlough money was given him for a college to be named Oxford. Many young men were trained in this college, and many young women in the attached girls' school. Fully identified himself with the Chinese people, dressing and eating as they did. To carry this principle still farther, in 1878 married a Chinese lady. Mackay chose to train native workers rather than to depend on recruits from abroad. Wanted his church to be self-supporting and self-propagating. The church grew, and people in great numbers burned their idols and accepted Christ. Though he had had no formal training in medicine, he built a central hospital, and also did much dispensing of simple medicines during tours. During the Sino-Japanese War in 1895-1896 the Formosa church passed through affliction, losing about seven hundred. Before Mackay concluded his work in North Formosa, sixty churches had been established, with a native pastor in each, and with almost two thousand on the church rolls.

McKENDREE (mȧ kĕn′drē), **WILLIAM** (1757-1835), first American bishop of the Methodist Episcopal church, born in King William County, Virginia, received an elementary education, served in the American Revolution, and later was a school teacher. Conversion took place under the preaching of the Methodists when nearly thirty. In 1791 Asbury ordained him elder. Shortly after this Asbury barely restrained him from joining James O'Kelly when the latter seceded to start the Republican Methodist church, the first serious schism in American Methodism. Intinerant minister in Virginia (1788-1796) and presiding elder (1796-1799). Became an important factor in the Great Revival at the beginning of the nineteenth century. In 1801 appointed the presiding elder of the Western Conference, which included all circuits west of the Alleghenies, from Central Ohio to the borders of Georgia. In 1808 elected and ordained bishop. This event was a turning point in American Methodism, for it was a change from the one-man autocracy to a constitutional order. He was Asbury's assistant for Asbury's last eight years, succeeding him as the leading bishop in America. McKendree College in Lebanon, Illinois, formerly Lebanon Seminary, was named in his honor. He gave 480 acres to the seminary.

MACKENZIE (mȧ kĕn′zĭ), **JOHN** (1835-1899), missionary and statesman, born at Knockando, Morayshire, Scotland. After studying at Anderson Institute at Elgin, apprenticed to the printer of the *Elgin Courant*. At age eighteen experienced both conversion and desire to become a missionary. From 1853 to 1857 a student at Bedford Academy, a training school for the London Missionary Society. Took a short course in medicine. In 1858 ordained for service in South Africa, in July landed in Cape Town. With several fellow missionaries, proceeded to Robert Moffat's mission at Kuruman, and from there north to the Matabele and the Makololo tribes. The party spent six years of wandering, prospecting, and waiting. Finally in 1864 were able to settle at Shoshong, the capital of Bamangwato section of the Bechuana people, beginning a ten-year period of devoted service among these people. His privilege was to work with and be counselor to Khama, the Christian king of the Bamangwato people. In 1870-71 on furlough, spending much time in deputation work, and writing *Ten Years North of the Orange River*. In 1871 returned to Shoshong to finish work there. In 1876 moved to Kuruman, Dr. Moffat's station, to take charge of the Moffat Institution, a school to train native evangelists. Also pastor of the Kuruman church. At this place worked until 1882, returned to England, from 1882 to 1884 to plead with the Government for protection of the Bechuanas against unscrupulous landgrabbers and the Boers. Gave up mission work to devote entire time to statesmanship. Bechuanaland in 1885 was finally placed under British protectorate according to plans promulgated by Mackenzie appointed the first Deputy-Commissioner. After finishing several years of work with the government, called back by the London Missionary Society as a regular missionary, to be stationed at Hankey about fifty miles from Port Elizabeth. Spent last seven years at this mission station devotedly, laboriously, and whole-heartedly building up the church there.

MACKENZIE, JOHN KENNETH (1850-1888), medical missionary to China, born in Yarmouth, Norfolk, England. Joined the Presbyterian church, became active in open air preaching and city mission work. Becoming interested in foreign missions, 1870, went to Bristol Medical School for four years, took postgraduate work at the Royal Ophthalmic Hospital in London. In 1875 went to Hankow, and for three and one half years did some very intensive and fruitful medical and surgical work. Had as one close colleague Griffith John of the London Missionary Society, with whom he often traveled to interior villages on evangelistic tours. In 1879 because of unfavorable health conditions on the part of both wife and himself transferred to Tientsin. Great difficulty was encountered in getting work started until, through the restoring to health of the dying wife of Viceroy Li Hung Chang, he gained the favor of the Viceroy and thereby gained national fame and influence. Li Hung Chang and other wealthy Chinese provided funds for a hospital, dedicated by the Viceroy December 2, 1880. About a year later, under the support of Li Hung Chang, Dr. Mackenzie started a medical school for the training of native doctors. His wife proved to be a very great help in the work until her health failed. Twice she was invalided home. The second time Dr. Mackenzie went with her and spent five months in England and on the Continent. He then returned to China to spend last five years alone. Planned work so that he and assistants and co-workers could be most effective in meeting the spiritual needs of the people and in leading them to Christ. In 1885 the emperor conferred upon him "The Star of the Order of the Double Dragon." The next year he helped to organize the "Medical Missionary Association of China," and became one of the editors of its journal. In 1888 contracted smallpox from a patient and died a few days later.

MACKINTOSH (măk'ĭn tŏsh), **CHARLES HENRY** (1820-1896), Plymouth Brethren preacher and Bible expositor, born in Glenmalure Barracks, County Wicklow, Ireland. At age eighteen experienced a deep spiritual awakening. In 1844 opened a school in Westport, and taught for nine years. In 1853 went to Dublin to devote time to evangelism, pastoral ministry, and religious journalism. Very active in the revival that swept Ireland in 1859-1860. Edited monthly periodical, *Things New and Old,* wrote other religious literature. Author of *Notes* on the five books of the Pentateuch, which have enjoyed wide popularity. Gladstone and Spurgeon both commended his *Notes*. His *Miscellaneous Writings* have been printed in six volumes.

MACKINTOSH, HUGH ROSS (1870-1936), Church of Scotland theologian, born at Paisley, Scotland, educated at George Watson's College, Edinburgh; Edinburgh University; New College, Edinburgh; and the universities of Freiburg, Halle, and Marburg. Ordained in the Free Church of Scotland in 1896, and from 1897 to 1904 successively minister of Queen Street Church, Tayport, and Beechgrove Church, Aberdeen. Professor of systematic theology at New College, Edinburgh, from 1904 until 1935, then became professor of dogmatics in the University of Edinburgh. At different times examiner in theology in the universities of London, Wales, and Edinburgh. Moderator of the General Assembly of the Church of Scotland, 1932. In early studies strongly influenced by the Ritschlian theology, and later leaned somewhat toward the position of Karl Barth. Main emphasis was on the forgiveness of sins as the center of the gospel. Better known for the kenotic

Christology developed in *The Doctrine of the Person of Jesus Christ*. Other more important works were *Types of Modern Theology* and *The Christian Experience of Forgiveness*. He also wrote *The Person of Jesus Christ, Studies in Christian Truth, Immortality and the Future, The Originality of the Christian Message, The Divine Initiative, Some Aspects of Christian Belief,* and *The Christian Apprehension of God*.

MACLAREN, ALEXANDER (1826-1910), English Baptist expository preacher, born at Glasgow, Scotland. Educated at the University of Glasgow and the Baptist College of Stepney (now Regents Park College). In the Portland Baptist Chapel, from 1846 to 1858, built up a flourishing congregation. From 1858 to 1903 in Manchester as pastor of the Union Chapel on Oxford Road. Though a pastor, his chief role was that of scholar and preacher, and out of this dual interest came helpful and scholarly commentaries and expositions. Maclaren's expository sermons have, perhaps next to Spurgeon's, been the most widely read sermons of their time, and are still greatly appreciated. Twice president of the Baptist Union of England, and in 1905 president of the Baptist World Alliance meeting in London. Traveled much in Great Britain, the Continent, Australia, and America. A humble, modest man who shrank from publicity. A profound and instructive Bible scholar. Theological position was thoughtfully and candidly evangelical. In 1886, secured a summer home at Carr Bridge in the Highlands near Edinburgh where he spent his last months.

MACLEOD (măk loud'), **NORMAN** (1812-1872), Scottish clergyman and author, born at Campbeltown, Argyllshire, Scotland, attended the universities of Glasgow and Edinburgh. Ordained in 1838 after holding appointments at Loudoun, Ayrshire, and at Dalkeith, near Edinburgh, in 1851 became minister of the important parish of Barony, Glasgow. In 1857 became chaplain to Queen Victoria, with whom he was a great favorite. Remained in the established church at the time of the Disruption in 1843; became one of the founders of the Evangelical Alliance in 1847. In 1869 elected moderator of the General Assembly of the Church of Scotland. Edited *Christian Instructor* from 1849, and *Good Words* from 1860, and wrote several books.

MCNICOL, JOHN (1869-1956). Born in Ottawa. Educated at Toronto University and Knox College. Pastor of Presbyterian church at Aylmer, Quebec (1896-1900). In 1902 teacher and from 1906 to 1946 principal of Toronto Bible College. Wrote *The Bible's Philosophy of History* and a four-volume *Thinking Through the Bible*.

McPHERSON (măk fĕr'sn), **AIMEE SEMPLE** (1890-1944), founder of the International Church of the Four Square Gospel, born near Ingersol, Ontario, Canada. Came from Methodist background. In teens converted under the preaching of Robert Semple, a Baptist evangelist, her future husband. She went with him as a missionary from 1910 to 1911 to Hong Kong where he died. Returned with her infant daughter. A few years later married McPherson, a New England wholesale groceryman. Following a serious illness and a miraculous healing, felt and answered the call to preach. Began her career as an evangelist against her husband's wishes; he left her. Began evangelistic preaching, covering various parts of the United States until she located in California. In Los Angeles built her famous Angelus Temple, which was dedicated January 1, 1923. Opposite this site, about two years later founded and built the Lighthouse of International Foursquare Evangelism College, as a part of her Echo Park Evangelistic Association. The denomination known as the International Church of the Foursquare Gospel was organized in 1927. With clever use of psychology, pageantry, lighting effects, colorful costumes, healing, and evangelistic preaching, she attracted thousands and rapidly gained a following. Her Foursquare doctrine included the tongues, divine healing, Christ as Savior and a strong emphasis on adventism. The story of Mrs. McPherson's kidnapping in 1926 and the wide publicity it received deepened the conviction of her followers that she was a chosen messenger of God. Upon the death of Mrs. McPherson, her son, Dr. Rolf K. McPherson, according to her wishes and appointment, assumed the pastorate of the Angelus Temple and the presidency of the International Church of the Foursquare Gospel, and L.I.F.E. Bible College.

MAHAN (mȧ hăn'), **ASA** (1800-1889), American Congregational clergyman and educator, born at Vernon, New York, graduated from Hamilton College and Andover Theological Seminary. Between 1829 and 1835 served as pastor at Pittsford, New York, and at Cincinnati, Ohio. He was for a time trustee of Lane Theological Seminary in Cincinnati. From 1835 to 1850 president of Oberlin College, also teaching philosophy there. Eighty of the Lane students followed him to Oberlin, which fact led to the establishment of a theological department in the college. He required that new college be interracial, and was the first to give degrees to women on the same condition as men. From 1850 to 1854 president of Cleveland University. After a pastorate at Jackson and Adrian, Michigan between 1855 and 1860, president of Adrian College from 1860 to 1871, then retired and moved to Castbourne, Essex, England to do literary work, but continued to preach to large congregations. Wrote *Scripture Doctrine of Christian Perfection; Doctrine of the Will; The True Believer; Science of Moral Philosophy; Election and Influence of the Holy Spirit; Science of Natural Theology; Theism and Anti-Theism; Critical History of Philosophy and Autobiography—Intellectual, Moral and Spiritual.*

MAIER (mī'yẽr), **WALTER ARTHUR** (1893-1950), Missouri Synod Lutheran radio preacher and college professor, born in Boston, Massachusetts, educated at Concordia Collegiate Institute, Bronxville, New York; Boston University; Concordia Seminary, St. Louis, Missouri; and Harvard University. Ordained in 1917 and did relief work among German war prisoners and served as camp pastor at several places between 1917 and 1919. Executive secretary of the International Walther League (1920-1922); professor of semitic languages and Old Testament interpretation in Concordia Seminary, St. Louis (1922-1944); radio speaker on the International Lutheran Hour (1930-1931) and (1935-1946). Editor of the *Walther League Messenger* (1920-1945). Heard over twelve hundred stations throughout the world. Messages were strongly evangelical. Writings were largely publications of radio messages, some: *For Better, not for Worse; The Lutheran Hour; Christ for Every Crisis; Christ for the Nation; Peace Through Christ; Winged Words for Christ; The Radio for Christ; For Christ and Country; Victory through Christ;* and *America, Turn to Christ.*

MAIMONIDES (mī mŏn'ĭ dēz); properly **MOSES BEN MAIMON BEN JOSEPH** (1135-1204), Jewish Rabbi and philosopher, born in Cordova, Spain, received early education from father, and later, natural science and philosophy from Mohammedan scholars; a pupil and friend of the Spanish-Arabian scholar, Averroes. Persecution in 1149 forced him to leave native city, after wandering from 1149 to 1165 the family settled at Fez, Morocco, where outwardly they conformed to Mohammedanism. In 1165 the family left Morocco, and after a short residence in Palestine, settled at Old Cairo, Egypt, where he lived the rest of his life. For a time physician to Saladin, the sultan of Egypt and Syria, and also by appointment rabbi of Cairo. Founded a Jewish college at Alexandria, but chief reputation lies in writings. Writings have been an influential force in Jewish thought and ritual. Principal philosophical work, *The Guide of the Perplexed,* has had a striking influence not only on the progress of rational reformatory efforts in Judaism, but also had a strong influence on Christian scholasticism, especially that of Albertus Magnus and Thomas Aquinas. He attempted to reconcile Rabbinic Judaism with Aristotelian philosophy as modified by Arabic interpretation. Chief works: *Mishneh Torah; Commentary on the Mishnah;* and his main work *Guide to the Perplexed;* and *Book of Precepts.*

MAITLAND (māt'lănd), **SAMUEL ROFFEY** (1792-1866), Church of England clergyman and historian, born in London, educated at St. John's and Trinity Colleges, Cambridge. Called to the bar in 1816, but in 1821 took holy orders in the Church of England. From 1823 to 1827 perpetual curate of Christ Church, Glasgow. Traveled abroad, taking a keen interest in mission work among the Jews in Germany and Poland. A controversialist of no mean ability. Successfully combatted the "Year-day Theory" of Abbot Joachim (later taken up by Edward Irving). Also took sharp issue with Joseph Milner's view of the history of the Waldenses and Albigenses, as well as John Foxe's chapter on the Waldenses in *Book of Martyrs.* In 1838 Archbishop Howley of Canterbury appointed him librarian and keeper of the Lambeth manuscripts. Resigned in 1848 upon the death of the archbishop and settled at Gloucester. Editor of the *British Magazine* (1839-1849). Among many writings: *Facts and Documents Illustrative of the History, Doctrines, and Rites of the Ancient Albigenses and Waldenses; A Review of Fox the Martyrologist's "History of the Waldenses"; The Dark Ages.*

MAJOR, GEORGE (1502-1574), Lutheran controversialist. Born in Germany. Educated at Wittenberg. Professor at Wittenberg in 1544 after service as court preacher and ordination in 1537. Superintendent at Eisleben for a couple of years then dean at Wittenberg from 1558 to 1574. Believed good works necessary for salvation but not for justification. Created Majoristic controversy in the Lutheran church.

MAKEMIE (mä kĕm'ĭ), **FRANCIS** (1658-1708), American Presbyterian minister, born at Ramelton, Donegal County, Ireland, educated at Glasgow University, and ordained as a missionary to America in 1683. Itinerated in Barbados, Virginia, Maryland and South Carolina. Married a Virginian lady of wealth. In 1684 organized the first Presbyterian church in the colonies, at Snow Hill on the Chesapeake. In 1704 made a visit to London to secure aid for the church in America, and on return in 1706, with two ministers from Ireland, helped to organize at Philadelphia, the first presbytery in America, becoming its moderator. In 1707 at

Newtown, Long Island, arrested, fined, and imprisoned for several weeks for preaching without a license. Defended right of free speech. Regarded as the founder of Presbyterianism in America.

MALAN (må län′), **CESAR HENRI ABRAHAM** (1787-1864), Swiss Reformed preacher, born of French ancestry, and studied in Geneva, Switzerland. After graduation a successful teacher. Though ordained in 1810 his conversion did not take place until 1816 or 1817. He was vitally moved by the preaching of the Haldane brothers when they visited Geneva in 1817. His strong witness led the clergy of Geneva to forbid his preaching in the canton. Also dismissed from teaching position in the Latin school in Geneva. Built a chapel which rapidly grew into a church, which was still, however, a part of the national church. Fervent evangelical preaching caused a rupture in congregation about 1830. Then became a missionary, traveling into parts of Switzerland, France, Belgium, Holland, Germany, and through the valleys of the Waldenses in the Piedmont. Through preaching and influence an independent evangelical church was established. This movement gained the sympathy and adherence of such men as Gaussen, Vinet, Merle d'Aubigné, and the Monod brothers. Though silenced from preaching and severed from the state church, maintained a readiness to re-enter it whenever the free preaching of the Gospel would be permitted. Did become a member of the Scottish Church. Among writings are several polemics, many tracts, and perhaps a thousand hymns and hymn melodies.

MANALO, FELIX (1886-1963), founder of Philippine *Iglesia ni Kristo*. Born near Manila as a Roman Catholic but became a Disciple and then a Seventh Day Adventist minister. Founded his own church in 1914. Denied Christ's diety and justification by faith. Built many splendid churches and controlled clergy and people closely. Appealed to nationalism.

MANNING, HENRY EDWARD (1808-1892), Archbishop of Westminster, born in Totteridge, Hertfordshire, England, educated at Harrow and at Balliol College, Oxford. After holding minor appointments in the church, made archdeacon of Chichester in 1840, and two years later select preacher at Oxford. Became a strong High Churchman and a Tractarian. In 1851 left the Anglican church and ordained in the Roman Catholic church. In 1857 developed and became superior of the Congregation of the Oblates of St. Charles in London. In 1865 succeeded Cardinal Wiseman as the second Archbishop of Westminster since the Reformation. As a strong ultramontanist labored diligently for Catholic church in England. Successful in promoting parochial schools. Gained prominence in 1870 by advocacy of the dogma of papal infallibility, and five years later, in 1875, created cardinal. In conclave of 1878 supported the election of Leo XIII. Turned attention chiefly to social, educational, and temperance activities. For the last twenty years a total abstainer. Became founder of a temperance society known as the League of the Cross. A writer on ecclesiastical and polemical subjects. Some of his works: *The Temporal Mission of the Holy Ghost, The Internal Mission of the Holy Ghost, The Eternal Priesthood, The Unity of the Church,* and *The True Story of the Vatican Council*.

MANNING, JAMES (1735-1791), founder and first president of Brown University, Rhode Island. Born at Piscataway, New Jersey. Educated at the College of New Jersey (Princeton University) and in 1763 ordained. From 1763 to 1765 worked to get a charter for Rhode Island College (Brown). President in 1765 and professor to 1791. Became pastor of the First Baptist Church. Represented Rhode Island in the Congress in 1786 and in 1791 made a report outlining the free public school system for Rhode Island.

MANZ (măns), **FELIX** (1498-1527), Swiss Anabaptist. By 1524 with several others came to the conclusion that infant baptism was unscriptural. Early in 1525 the Zurich Council ordered a final disputation between the parties with the hope of arriving at a settlement of the dispute. The council decided in favor of Zwingli and ordered children baptized, and ordered Manz and his colleagues to cease from disputing. In January, 1525, when about a dozen of Manz's friends gathered in his home in Zurich, Georg Blaurock, who had just been rebaptized by Conrad Grebel, rebaptized the rest of the Brethren present, instituting believer's baptism by sprinkling. This step was also the beginning of the Anabaptists. The Zurich Council in March, 1526 ordered Anabaptists drowned. In 1527, Manz was drowned, becoming the first of a long line of Anabaptist martyrs.

MARCELLA (325-410), ascetic, born in a wealthy Roman family and married early; husband died soon after the marriage and she refused to remarry. Made a vow of perpetual celibacy and gave her goods to relatives and to the poor. When Jerome came to Rome in 382 became his friend and studied the Scripture with him. Home became a sort of convent dedicated to the study of the Scriptures, to psalmody, and to prayer. Later retired to a little house outside the city, where she devoted her whole time to good works. Induced Pope Anastasius to condemn the doctrines of Origen as heretical. At the sack of Rome by Alaric in 410 tortured by the Goths and died shortly after.

MARCELLUS OF ANCYRA (died c. 374), Bishop of Ancyra in Galatia (modern Angora). Present at the Council of Nicea, 325. A strong opponent of Arianism, and in zeal to combat the heresy adopted the opposite extreme of a modified or refined form of Sabellianism. Made a rigid distinction between Son and Logos, saying that before the incarnation the Logos *was*, but the Son *was not;* and after the work of redemption was completed, the Son resigned His kingdom, and returned again into the repose of God. Since views and writings were considered heretical, he was deposed and condemned several times between 336 and the time of his death.

MARCION (mär'shĭ ŏn), (died c. 160), founder of an early heretical sect. The son of a bishop, born at Sinope on the south coast of the Black Sea, where he became wealthy ship builder. Went to Rome about A.D. 139 and made a generous gift to the church. Was excommunicated about A.D. 144 and his donation to the church was returned to him. Soon founded a separate church which merged Gnosticism and orthodox Christianity. Like the Gnostics and the Manichaeans sharply dualistic, and violently antagonistic to Judaism and anything that savored of Judaism. Completely rejected the Old Testament. Therefore formed a canon which consisted of only eleven books—an expurgated gospel of Luke and ten of the Pauline epistles. This forced the church to decide what New Testament books were canonical. In chief writing, the *Antitheses,* propounded the ideas of the eternity of matter, rationalistic dualism, the docetic view of Christ, a demiurgic notion of God, and an extremely ascetic way of life. Polycarp called him the "first-born of Satan." He had an anti-Jewish and pseudo-Pauline tendency, and a supernaturalism, which in zeal for a pure primitive Christianity, nullified all history. The Marcionite church differed from Gnosticism in that it was completely organized, having clergy, rites, and its scriptures. In his churches enjoined strict asceticism, chastity, and celibacy, and martyrdom was prized. System grew, especially in the eastern part of the empire, and wielded a wide and destructive influence in Christendom, until in the fifth or sixth century, when it seems to have been absorbed in Manichaeism.

MARCUS AURELIUS (ô rē'lĭ ŭs) **ANTONINUS** (121-180), nickname, Caracalla. Roman emperor (161-180), born in Rome, carefully educated, disciplined in Stoic wisdom. At the death of his uncle, the emperor, he became emperor in 161. Forced to spend much of reign in camp, protecting Rome against the barbarians, who were already beginning to press hard against the frontier. One of the best of the pagan emperors, though a loyal emperor and a vigilant general, continued to be a stoic philosopher. Wrote a sort of autobiography or diary, *Meditations*. Stoicism was a religion or philosophy of fatalism, which required that one be indifferent to his fate. The best one can do is to accept the laws of nature and be neither sad nor happy. Nothing changes; the course of nature goes on. Would govern own soul and Roman subjects firmly but fairly. Justice to fellows, indifference to own fate —this was the highest virtue in the philosophy of Marcus Aurelius. It is a question as to how much the emperor sanctioned the persecution of the Christians during his reign; but sense of justice did call for fair dealing with them. They were to be punished only if they could be proved to have committed political offenses against the Roman state. Governors in distant provinces, however, often were not so discreet, and persecution and martyrdom of the Christians did take place. Some of the Christians who became martyrs during his reign were Justin Martyr in Rome, Polycarp of Smyrna, and Pothinus of Gaul.

MARGARET OF NAVARRE (1492-1549), supporter of French Reformers. Set up center at Meaux where Lefèvre, Vatable and others were protected. She became a Calvinist. Grandmother of Henry IV who issued the tolerant Edict of Nantes in 1598. Sister of Francis I of France.

MARITAIN, JACQUES (1882-1973), French Roman Catholic philosopher. Born in Paris. Educated at the Sorbonne, Heidelberg, and Rome. Became a Roman Catholic in 1906. Professor of philosophy at Institut Catholique de Paris in 1914. Helped to organize Thomist Society in 1923. From 1933 to 1939 taught at the University of Toronto Institute of Medieval Studies and at Princeton and Columbia during World War II. From 1945 to 1948 French ambassador to the Vatican. Professor at Princeton from 1948 to 1954. Wrote *An Introduction to Philosophy* and *Art and Scholasticism*.

MAROT (mȧ rō'), **CLEMENS** (c. 1497-1544), French poet and a hymnist, born at Cahors, France. Long a resident in the court of Francis I and in 1524 accompanied the king on a campaign to Italy, where he was wounded. Upon return to France, began to attack the abuses of the Roman church and was imprisoned. On release inclined toward

Protestantism, if not openly declaring adhesion to it. When a special wave of persecution befell Protestantism, fled to Ferrara, Italy. Following return to Lyons in 1536 renounced Protestantism. After this time he did the most of translating of the Psalms into poetic meter, many of which were used by Calvin in his French Protestant hymnal. Hymns were popular and very helpful to the Reformation cause.

MARQUETTE (mär kĕt′), **JACQUES** (1637-1675), French Jesuit missionary and explorer, born at Laon, Piccardy, France. In 1654 entered Jesuit college at Nancy with the intention of joining the order. After twelve years of study and teaching in various Jesuit colleges of France made priest in 1666, and sent to labor among the Indians in Canada. Spent two years studying the language, learning to converse fluently in six different dialects. In 1669 founded a mission at Sault Ste. Marie and the following year moved to the mission at La Pointe du St. Esprit on the southern shore of Lake Superior. In 1671 he moved to the northern side of the Straits of Mackinac and erected a mission at St. Ignace. In 1673 was instructed to accompany Louis Joliet on an expedition to find the mouth of the Mississippi. This gave a coveted opportunity to visit the Indians along the Mississippi, especially the Illinois Indians of whom he had already met representatives. On May 17, 1673, Marquette and Joliet and five other Frenchmen left St. Ignace in two birchbark canoes carrying with them only a meager supply of food. Skirting the northern shore of Lake Michigan, they entered Green Bay and pushed up the Fox River. Crossing a short portage they entered the Wisconsin River from which they glided into the broad expanse of the Mississippi, and sailed down the river to about three hundred miles beyond the mouth of the Arkansas, establishing the fact that the Mississippi flows into the Gulf of Mexico. Fearing that they might be captured by the Spaniards, they proceeded no further, but returned to report their findings. Arriving at the mouth of the Illinois they paddled up river and crossed to the Des Plaines, entering Lake Michigan at the point where Chicago now stands. Then paddled up the lake until they came to the mission of Saint Francis Xavier at the head of Green Bay. After an absence of four months from this mission and a voyage of over twenty-five hundred miles, they had returned to the mission. Marquette remained for a year endeavoring to regain health, while Joliet went on to Montreal to report. Spent the winter of 1674 at the mouth of the Chicago River, built a log cabin, the first house built on the site of Chicago. The next spring started for the Indian village, having earlier promised them he would return to build a mission. Proceeded about as far as Kaskaskia, but ill and exhausted had to return, and started for St. Ignace, coasting along the eastern shore of the lake. Got as far as Ludington, Michigan, where he died.

MARSHALL, DANIEL (1768-1837). Born at Windsor, Connecticut. Worked with Susquehenna River Indians for two years. Baptist minister working with Shubal Stearns in Virginia, Georgia and North Carolina from 1747 to 1784. Helped organize the Georgia Baptist Association and the Separate Baptist denomination.

MARSHALL, PETER (1902-1949), Presbyterian Chaplain of the United States Senate; born in Coatbridge, Scotland, studied at Coatbridge Technical School and Mining College, and at Columbia Theological Seminary, Decatur, Georgia. Came to the United States in 1927, naturalized in 1938. Ordained to the Presbyterian ministry in 1931, held pastorates in Covington, Georgia; Atlanta, Georgia; and Washington, D.C. From 1947 to 1949 Chaplain of the United States Senate. Died of heart attack, at age forty-six. Senator Arthur H. Vandenberg, of Michigan, said, "Dr. Marshall was a rugged Christian with dynamic faith . . . an eloquent and relentless crusader for righteousness in the lives of men and nations. He always spoke with courage, with deepest human understanding, and with stimulating hope. To know him was to love him." Some prayers and sermons as well as his biography were published subsequent to his death. Best known book, *Mr. Jones, Meet the Master*.

MARSHMAN, JOSHUA (1768-1837), English Baptist missionary, linguist and printer, born of godly parents at Westbury Leigh, Wiltshire, England, worked at father's trade of weaving, using every spare moment studying and reading. Said to have read more than five hundred books before he was eighteen. In 1794 appointed master of a Bristol school, and studied Latin, Greek, Hebrew, and Syriac languages. After reading of Carey's work in India dedicated his life to that field. In 1799 with Mrs. Marshman, with William Ward and others went to India to join Carey. Marshman, Ward, and Carey formed the famous Serampore Trio of the mission at Serampore. He was teacher, Ward printer, and Carey chief translator and preacher. The Marshmans operated two boarding schools, the proceeds from which helped support the Serampore Mission. In 1814 printed first complete Chinese Bible. Edited a newspaper in Bengali, the *Mirror of News,* translated parts of the Bible into several languages and some Indian and Chinese works into English. Died at age sixty-nine.

MARSIGLIO (MARSILIUS) MAINARDINO of PADUA (c. 1275-1342), principal author of *Defensor Pacis,* born at Padua, Italy, studied medicine. By 1312 had master's degree and priest's orders. Became a professor of philosophy, and was for a brief time rector of the University of Paris. He and John of Jandun collaborated in the controversy that raged between Pope John XXII and the emperor Louis IV of Bavaria. In 1324 Marsilius and John of Jandun prepared a book called *Defensor Pacis,* the most important contribution on the relation between church and state in the later Middle Ages. A bold attack against the spiritual as well as the temporal assumptions of the papacy and against the hierarchical organization of the Church. In summary, the book asserted (1) the need of reform; (2) the supremacy of state over church, the clergy being subservient to civil law; (3) democratic rights of the people in both state and church; (4) limitation of the sphere of priestly functions to spiritual matters, both in ownership of property and in possession of powers; (5) purity of all clergy and priesthood, from the papacy down; (6) denial of divine origin, infallibility, or absolute power of the papacy; and (7) the Holy Scriptures as the ultimate source of authority. Marsilius went to court of Louis of Bavaria for protection. The *Defensor Pacis* was of positive help to William of Occam and other pre-reformation Reformers as well as to the Reformers themselves.

MARSDEN (märz'dn), **SAMUEL** (1764-1838), apostle to the Maoris of New Zealand, born at Horsforth, near Leeds, Yorkshire, England. Educated at Hull Free Grammar School under Dr. Joseph Milner, and at Magdalene College, Cambridge. Ordained in the Anglican church in 1793, married a little later. In 1794 sailed with wife to New South Wales, Australia as chaplain of the penal colony, which England had started at Parramatta, near Sydney. The charge at Parramatta was a difficult one, dogged with much opposition, even by the authorities of the institution. He established a farm which eventually became one of the finest in Australia. Imported Spanish sheep in 1807 to help found Australian sheep ranching. Endeavored to train the convicts to habits of industry, conducted schools for orphans, and planned for social and moral improvement of women, aborigines, and convicts. On the occasion of first and only trip to England (1807-1808), made a report of work at the colony, and sought improvements for carrying on the work there, and also made an appeal to the Church Missionary Society to open a mission for the savage, cannibalistic Maoris of New Zealand. In 1814, after fitting up a small vessel at personal expense, with two mechanics sailed to New Zealand to prospect. Natives who had learned to know him previously, and whose confidence he had already secured, welcomed him gladly. In the little vessel *Active,* made seven different trips to the island over a period of twenty-three years, opening a mission, settling tribal disputes, placing new missionaries, superintending the language study, building schools, and civilizing and evangelizing the people. The first baptism was that of a chief in 1825. At age seventy-two, Marsden made seventh and last visit to the Maoris. Found a well organized church. Returned to Parramatta where he died. Two years after his death the British took over the protectorate of New Zealand and its people.

MARTENSEN, HANS LASSEN (1808-1884), Danish Lutheran theologian, born at Flensburg, Schleswig, educated at Copenhagen and in Berlin, Heidelberg, and Paris. Ordained in 1832, in 1840 became professor in the University of Copenhagen and court preacher in 1845. In 1854, appointed Bishop of Zealand, the highest ecclesiastical office of Denmark, holding the office until death. In 1865 made private chaplain to the king and to the royal family. One of the greatest preachers of his day. His writings show a modified mysticism, the result of study of the Medieval mystics. As a thinker and theologian became known far beyond his own land through strong works on *Dogmatics* and *Ethics*.

MARTIN, WILLIAM ALEXANDER PARSONS (1827-1916), American Presbyterian missionary and educator to China, born in Livonia, Indiana, educated at Indiana State University, and the Presbyterian Seminary at New Albany, Indiana. After teaching classics for a year went to China in 1850, missionary at Ningpo (1850-1859). Mastered the local language and the Mandarin as well. In 1858 acted as interpreter to the United States minister, William B. Reed, in negotiating the treaty of Tientsin. After a furlough to America in 1863 located at Peking, founded the Presbyterian Mission; and remained there for five years. From 1869 to 1894 president and professor of international law in the Tung-wen College in Peking, served as adviser in international law to the Chinese government on several occasions. President of the Imperial University of China from the time of its founding in 1898 until it was destroyed in the siege of Peking in the Boxer uprising in 1900. From 1902 to 1905 president of the University of Wuchang; following 1905 engaged in literary work, in 1911 rejoining the staff of the Presbyterian Mission and serving it until death. Wrote several books in Chinese, one *Evidences of Christianity*. Some of his English writings were: *The Chinese: Their Education, Philosophy, and Letters; Essays on the History, Philosophy, and Religion of the Chinese; The Siege in Peking;* and *Awakening of China*.

MARTIN OF TOURS (c. 335-c. 400), soldier, monk, saint, bishop, and missionary, born at Sabaria, Pannonia of pagan parents. A soldier for about eight years. Became a pupil of Hilary of Poitiers, converted his mother to Christianity. About 361 established a monastery of Marmoutier, near Poitiers. About the year 372 unanimously elected bishop of Tours. In this episcopal office maintained strict monastic mode of life until death. Also established a monastery beyond the Loire. While bishop, was missionary to the Franks and other northern tribes who had invaded that region. Having been a soldier, adopted military methods in missionary work. Out from Tours as a center led army of monks through the land, destroying idols, pagan temples, and graves, and preaching. Held as the patron saint of France.

MARTINEAU (mär'tĭ nō), **JAMES** (1805-1900), English Unitarian clergyman, born at Norwich, England, of Huguenot ancestry, educated for the ministry at the Unitarian Manchester New College, ordained to the Presbyterian ministry in Dublin. Preached in Dublin (1828), Liverpool (1832-1857), and London (1858-1872). While serving in Liverpool appointed in 1840 as professor of mental and moral philosophy at Manchester New College, a position held until retirement in 1885. From 1869 to 1885 principal of the college. Writings are extensive and treat on a wide range of topics from the viewpoint of ethical theism.

MARTYN (mär'tĭn), **HENRY** (1781-1812), missionary to India and Persia, born at Truro, England, mother died when he was one year old. After finishing grammar school in 1797, entered St. John's College, Cambridge. In 1803 ordained deacon in the Church of England at Ely. Assisted in the Church of the Holy Trinity at Cambridge, had charge of the small parish of Lolworth not far away. Reading of Baxter's *Saint's Rest,* Brainerd's *Journal,* and accounts of William Carey's work in India, led to a deepening of mystical fellowship with his Master and to the offering of his services to the mission field in India. Obtained a chaplaincy in 1805 from the East India Company, and reached India in 1806. Found great comfort in the Serampore Trio. After finishing first period of service at Calcutta, preaching in a ruined pagoda, transferred by the Company to Dinapore in 1806, and in 1809, to Cawnpore. At these places engaged in language study, street preaching, doing aggressive missionary work, and translating. Translated the New Testament and the Prayer Book into Hindustani. Had to leave work and congregation at Cawnpore, which often reached eight hundred, for a rest in 1810. Decided to go to Persia rather than back to England. In 1811 arrived in Tabriz where he witnessed to Christ among the Mohammedans, and finished translation of the New Testament and Psalms into Persian. In September 1812 started last journey across Persia, reaching Tokat in Pontus, Turkey, in mid-October 1812. Here succumbed to fever, ague, and tuberculosis. His *Journals* reveal his devotion to Christ and missions.

MARX (märks), **HEINRICH KARL** (1818-1883), founder of modern socialism, born in Treves, in Rhenish Prussia, the son of a middle-class Jew, who had been converted to the Protestant faith. Studied at the universities of Bonn and Berlin, and took Ph.D. at Jena. In university life came under the influence of Hegel. In 1842 had become the editor of the *Rheinische Zeitung,* a paper of liberal tendencies. His paper was suppressed, he went to Paris and continued journalism. Formed an enduring friendship with Friedrich Engles (1820-1895). In 1845 expelled from France, went to Brussels, where he organized a German Working Men's Association. In 1848 Marx published the *Communist Manifesto,* which became practically the creed of socialistic revolutionaries. In 1848 returned to Germany, and revived *Zeitung;* but its revolutionary character led to his banishment from Germany the next year. Went to Paris, then to London, where he remained the rest of his life, writing books and articles for the *New York Tribune*. In 1864 led in organizing the International Working Men's Association, known as the "International," or the "First International." In 1869 helped found the Social Democratic Party in Germany. In 1867 appeared the first volume of *Das Kapital* in which he advocated the management of all industries by the state or government rather than by individuals. Wage earners should have all the profit, if any, so that capitalists as a class might cease to exist. After his death the second, third and fourth volumes were edited and published by Engels. These books became the standard for the kind of socialism which was to be known by his name, and the basic philosophy of Communism. His atheistic philosophy included ideas of matter in motion,

Hegel's dialectic of change, class war, dictatorship of the workers, and a classless society as the final goal. His followers have consistently opposed religion, especially Christianity. Over a third of the world's people are under the control of this dogma.

MARY STUART (1542-1587), "Queen of Scots," born at Linlithgow Palace, the daughter of James V of Scotland and Mary of Guise (Mary of Lorraine), granddaughter of Margaret Tudor, the daughter of Henry VII of England. Infant Mary crowned Queen of Scotland, but her mother Mary of Lorraine acted as regent until her death in 1560. Married Francis, who became king of France in 1559, but died in 1560. In 1561 Mary Stuart, the widow of the late Francis II, returned to Scotland to claim the crown. In 1565 married cousin Henry Stuart, better known as Lord Darnley (1545-1567). In 1567 Darnley was killed in an explosion. Three months later Mary and Bothwell were married. This caused a national revolt; Mary was imprisoned and forced to abdicate in favor of her one-year-old son, James, who became James VI of Scotland and later James I of England. Mary in 1568 fled for safety to her Cousin Queen Elizabeth in England. Elizabeth kept her in captivity in the Fotheringay Castle until she was induced to sign Mary's warrant for execution for treason in 1587. Mary opposed efforts of John Knox.

MARY TUDOR (1516-1558), Queen of England (1553-1558), born in Greenwich, London, the daughter of Henry VIII and Catherine of Aragon, educated a zealous Roman Catholic. During the short reign of Protestant half-brother Edward she was in retirement. Upon the death of Edward VI in 1553, however, she ascended the throne, although Duke of Northumberland had attempted, without success, to place Mary's Protestant cousin, Lady Jane Grey, on the throne. Mary executed Jane Grey, her husband, the Duke of Northumberland, and his son. The pope sent the exiled English cardinal Pole back to England to become Mary's adviser. Pole also became Archbishop of Canterbury to succeed Cranmer. In 1554 Mary married the Catholic Philip II of Spain. She fully purposed to restore Roman Catholicism in England. Mary had Thomas Cranmer, Hugh Latimer, Nicholas Ridley and nearly three hundred other Protestant leaders burned at the stake, whereupon she became known as "Bloody Mary." Also took steps to have the old heresy laws of earlier days revived, and to have all the anti-papal statutes since 1528 repealed. Joined her husband in war against France and thereby in 1558 lost Calais to England. Grief over this loss, over failure to win the love of her husband, and failure to win the hearts of the English people likely contributed to early death.

MASON, C. H. (died after 1907), founder of the Church of God in Christ. A black, received early training in the Missionary Baptist Church in Tennessee. Became dissatisfied with the Baptist church of which he was a member, and in 1897 separated from the Baptists, and in collaboration with C. P. Jones started another organization. He and C. P. Jones disagreed, in 1907, with many members withdrew. Called a meeting of all ministers who believed as he did; they formed the first general assembly of the Church of God in Christ with Mason as the general overseer and chief apostle. The church believes in entire sanctification, and speaking in tongues, and accepts three ordinances: baptism, the Lord's Supper, and foot-washing.

MASON, LOWELL (1792-1872), American musical composer and educator, born and educated in Medfield, Massachusetts. In 1812 began to give public music instruction in Savannah, Georgia, and there completed his first book of *Psalmody*. In 1827 moved back to Boston, and devoted himself to the musical instruction of children in the public schools. Traveled widely in New England, exciting popular interest in music and in organizing choirs. He founded the Boston Academy, and early became an advocate of the Pestalozzian method of teaching music. In 1837 studied in Europe, did much to stimulate an interest in music as a part of the community life by organizing church choirs and fostering congregational singing. Made more than forty collections of music and wrote or arranged more than one thousand hymn tunes. In later years devoted much attention to congregational singing in the churches, and did much to advance the interests of church music in general. Founder of the Orange Valley Church, New Jersey and superintendent of its Sunday school, as well as its music leader. His hymns include "Nearer My God to Thee," and "My Faith Looks Up to Thee."

MASSILLON (må sē'yôɴ'), **JEAN BAPTISTE** (1663-1742), French preacher, born at Hyères, Provence, France, studied in the colleges of Hyères and Marseilles. Entered the Congregation of the Oratory in 1681, ordained priest in 1691. Spent several years teaching theology at Montbrison, Vienne, and Paris before persuaded he should preach. Preached for several years before King Louis XIV. One of these sermons, "On the Fewness of the Elect," is considered a masterpiece. The king is said to have remarked that he had been pleased with his court preachers, but when he heard Massillon he was dissatisfied with himself. Massillon in 1715 delivered the funeral oration of Louis XIV. About 1717 named Bishop of Clermont. The next year preached a series of ten lenten sermons before young Louis XV, urging upon him and his court the obligation of morality and just government. These sermons became his most famous work. His sermons were of such beautiful style that they comprise some of the finest of French literature. Greatly interested in his people and did much for their welfare. Sought to maintain good morals and ecclesiastical discipline among his clergy. Posterity has classed him among the greatest of the French bishops and preachers of the eighteenth century.

MATEER (mȧ tĕr′), **CALVIN WILSON** (1836-1908), missionary to China, born near Harrisburg, Pennsylvania. Studied at Jefferson College (later Washington and Jefferson) and at Allegheny (Western) Theological Seminary. Principal of Beaver Academy (1857-1859), ordained in 1861 and pastor of the Presbyterian church, Delaware, Ohio (1861 to 1863). In 1863 appointed to China as a missionary and sailed for Tengchow, Shantung. Spent the most of his life there. In 1864 established a school for boys, which in 1878 developed into Tengchow Christian College of which he was president until 1895. Also had a church at Tengchow until 1906. A missionary devoted to work and to people, an extraordinarily versatile man, master of language, born teacher, skillful mechanic, electrician, college administrator, eloquent preacher, and Bible translator. Voluminous *Course of Mandarin Lessons* for many years the standard text for introducing Protestant missionaries to the various forms of Mandarin.

MATHER (măth′ẽr), **COTTON** (1663-1728), colonial historian and theologian, born in Boston, Massachusetts. Entered Harvard at eleven, took B.A. when fifteen. Conquered his stammering, and preached his first sermon at seventeen, then became an assistant to father. Ordained in 1685 as joint pastor with father of the Second or North Church, Boston. Held joint or sole pastorate of the church from 1685 to 1728. Widely celebrated as a scholar, a member of the Royal Society in 1713, the obvious leader of the conservative element among the Puritans of the day. Strove to maintain the theocratic rule which had developed among the New England clergy, but then on the decline. Became involved in the Salem witchcraft prosecution of 1692, advocated it, wrote extensively on the subject. Some books on the subject were: *Memorable Providences Relating to Witchcraft and Possessions* and *Wonders of the Invisible World*. Also wrote *Magnalia Christi Americana,* an ecclesiastical history of New England. Wrote nearly four hundred works in all. Most tangible public service was advocacy of inoculation for smallpox in 1721. His own library of 450 books was the largest private library of the continent.

MATHER, INCREASE (1639-1723), colonial minister, born in Dorchester, Massachusetts. Educated at Harvard College, and at Trinity College, Dublin. After graduation ministered to several congregations in England and on the island of Guernsey; returned to Massachusetts in 1661 after the Restoration. Ordained in 1657, became pastor of Second or North Church, Boston in 1664, and served there until death in 1723. Leading clergyman in the development of the Half-way Covenant. Along with pastorate, president of Harvard College from 1684 to 1701. Received the first diploma granting the degree of D.D. in America. In 1688 went as a special agent of the Massachusetts colony to England to secure a new charter for the colony. Published nearly one hundred books, among them: *A Brief History of the Wars with the Indians, A Relation of the Troubles of New England with the Indians, An Essay for the Recording of Illustrious Providences,* and *Cases of Conscience concerning Witchcraft*. He is credited with ending executions for witchcraft.

MATHER, RICHARD (1596-1669), colonial clergyman, born at Lowton, Lancashire, England, at fifteen began teaching school at Toxteth Park, near Liverpool. Studied for a few months for the ministry at Brasenose, Oxford. In 1619 received ordination from the Bishop of Chester and became minister at the Toxteth Chapel. In 1633 suspended because of Puritan tendencies, and in 1635 left for New England. Gathered a church at Dorchester, Massachusetts and became its pastor, from 1636 to 1669. An active advocate of the Half-Way Covenant, a plan which provided for a modified form of church membership for third generation children who were unable to meet the tests prescribed by the original Congregational polity. Had a share in the framing of the Cambridge Platform in 1648. Joined Thomas Welde and John Eliot in the translation of *The Whole Booke of Psalmes,* known as the *Bay Psalm Book,* the first book printed in the English colonies—a translation designed for use in the colonies.

MATHESON, GEORGE (1842-1906), Church of Scotland minister and hymn writer, born in Glasgow, Scotland. Became blind at 18, finished Glasgow University course with honors. Licensed to preach in

1866 and the next year was assistant to John Ross McDuff of the Sandyford Church, Glasgow. From 1868 until 1886 minister of Innellan, Argyllshire, and from 1886 until retirement in 1899, minister of St. Bernard's Edinburgh. Out of long study of comparative religions wrote *The Psalmist and the Scientist;* and *Can the Old Faith Live with the New? or Evolution and Revelation*. Answered the question in the affirmative. *Aids to the Study of German Theology* reflected Hegelian thought. Titles of other books: *The Growth of the Spirit of Christianity from the First Century to the Dawn of the Lutheran Era, Studies of the Portrait of Christ, Natural Elements of Revealed Theology* and *Distinctive Messages of the Old Religion*. Many of his brief devotional treatises have been widely read. Some of these are *My Aspirations, Leaves for Quiet Hours, Rest by the River, Messages of Hope, Moments on the Mount, Times of Retirement,* and *Searchings in the Silence*. Author of the much loved and popular hymn, "O Love That Will Not Let Me Go," and "Make Me a Captive, Lord." Invitation to preach before the queen at Balmoral; to be fellow of the Royal Society of Edinburgh.

MATHEWS, BASIL JOSEPH (1879-1951), Methodist educator and writer, born at Oxford, England, graduated from Oxford University. He was a member of the literary staff of *The Christian World* (1904-1910); editorial secretary of the London Missionary Society (1910-1919), director of Press Bureau of the Conference of Representatives of British Missionary Societies (1920-1924), international literature secretary of the World's Commission of the Young Men's Christian Association, Geneva (1924-1928), professor of Christian world relations at Andover Newton Theological Seminary and Boston University (1931-1944), and professor of world relations at Union College, University of British Columbia, Canada (1944-1949). Among more than forty books are: *Livingstone the Pathfinder; Paul the Dauntless; The Clash of World Forces; A Study of the Race Problem; The Church Takes Root in India; The Jew and World Ferment; Booker T. Washington; John R. Mott: World Citizen,* and *Supreme Encounter*.

MATHEWS, SHAILER (1863-1941), Baptist educator, born at Portland, Maine, studied at Colby College, Newton Theological Institute, and the University of Berlin. Professor of rhetoric (1887-1889), of history and political economy (1889-1893) at Colby College. In 1894 went to the University of Chicago to teach New Testament history and interpretation, later systematic theology and comparative theology until 1933. From 1908 until 1933 dean of the divinity school. President of the Federal Council of the Churches of Christ in America (1912-1916), as its representative visited Japan in 1915. In 1915 president of the Northern Baptist Convention. He was director of the religious department of the Chautauqua Institute from 1912 to 1934. From 1903 to 1911 was editor of *The World Today,* and from 1913 to 1920, of *The Biblical World*. Author of about thirty books, among them: *The Social Teachings of Jesus, The Spiritual Interpretation of History, The Faith of Modernism, The Social Gospel, The Church and the Changing Order, The Gospel and the Churches, The Atonement and the Social Process, Creative Christianity, The Messianic Hope in the New Testament,* and *New Faith for Old: An Autobiography*. Joint compiler with Gerald Birney Smith of *Dictionary of Religion and Ethics*. Champion of liberalism and the Social Gospel.

MATTHYS, JAN (died 1534), Münsterite leader of the Anabaptists. A baker from Haarlem, Holland, joined the Anabaptists at Strassburg, claimed to be the second of the witnesses of Rev. 11:3. In 1533 Matthys moved the headquarters of the Anabaptists from Strassburg to Münster in Westphalia, and proceeded to set up his kingdom. After about three months he was killed in a sally against the bishop's soldiers. John of Leiden, one of his strongest followers, became the new leader of the "New Jerusalem." Within two years he too was killed and Münster was restored to the Roman Catholics.

MAURICE (MORITZ) OF SAXONY (1521-1553), Duke and Elector of Saxony, born at Freiberg, Germany. In 1541 succeeded father as Duke of Saxony. Joined the Reformation, and along with father signed the Lutheran Schmalkald Articles; he did not join the Schmalkald League. Finally won over by the emperor, Charles V, and promised the electoral dignity if Elector John Frederick could be dispossessed. In the battle of Mühlburg, which followed in 1547, Elector John was defeated, Maurice was granted all the lands then held by Elector John. Made elector of Saxony. John Frederick soon gained back territory, electorship, and invaded Maurice's territory. When bitter feeling before long arose between them, Maurice betrayed Charles, and returned to the Protestants. In 1552 almost captured the aging and sick emperor, and did force him to sign the Treaty of Passau, which was favorable to the Lutherans. Established reputation as one of the ablest generals, diplomats, and administrators of his day.

MAURICE (mô'rĭs), **JOHN FREDERICK**

DENISON (1805-1872), Church of England theologian, born at Normanston, Suffolk, England, the son of a Unitarian minister, studied law at Trinity College and Trinity Hall, Cambridge, and theology at Exeter College, Oxford. Ordained priest in 1834 in the Church of England, and served two years as a curate. Chaplain of Guy's Hospital (1836-1846), chaplain of Lincoln's Inn (1846-1860), incumbent of St. Peter's, Vere Street, (1860-1869). Became professor of English history and literature at King's College, London (1840) and of theology (1846-1853). Deprived of the latter in 1853 for alleged unorthodoxy on the atonement and eternal life in *Theological Essays*. Had helped found Queen's College for women in London in 1848, and in 1854 founded Working Men's College, of which he became principal, and which helped promote his socialistic ideals. In 1866 became professor of moral philosophy at Cambridge, appointed to St. Edward's, Cambridge in 1870, preacher at Whitehall (1871-1872). Strongly in sympathy with the Broad church; along with Thomas Hughes and Charles Kingsley founded the Christian Socialist movement. Author of many books, some of the more important being: *The Claims of the Bible and Science, The Kingdom of Christ, The Doctrine of Sacrifice, Social Morality, The Old Testament, The Unity of the New Testament, The Epistles of St. John, The Gospel of St. John, Epistle to the Hebrews, The Gospel of the Kingdom of Heaven,* and *Ecclesiastical History of the First and Second Centuries.*

MAXIMILLA (died 179), Montanist prophetess. Maximilla and Priscilla were two Phrygian women who accompanied Montanus and helped propagate his teaching. Proclaimed the near approach of the age of the Holy Spirit and of the millennial reign in Pepuza, a small village in Phrygia. Gave her wealth to the church and lived on grateful free-will offerings. Believed herself to be a prophetess fully under the guidance and power of the Holy Spirit. Maximilla was a woman of high and noble character, earnestly seeking to restore the discipline and practices of primitive Christianity, even as Montanus was seeking to do.

MAXIMUS CONFESSOR (c. 580-662), theologian of the Eastern Church, born of a distinguished family in Constantinople and received a good education. Became the orthodox leader, hero, and martyr of the Monothelite controversy in the seventh century. For some time private secretary of Emperor Heraclius, but left this position of honor to enter the monastery of Chrysopolis near Seutari. Soon became abbot of the monastery; one of the most prolific writers of the Greek church, an able debater, a writer of a few hymns. Elucidated and developed the ideas of Dionysius Areopagitica. Writings in turn greatly influenced John of Damascus in the East and John Scotus Erigena in the West. Maximus valiantly stood for the orthodox faith, also, most cruelly treated and died of the injuries. The persecution of these martyrs, however, prepared the way for the triumph of the orthodox doctrine. In 680 at the sixth Ecumenical Council of Constantinople the question was settled and Monothelitism was condemned.

MAX MÜLLER (mül'ẽr), **FRIEDRICH** (1823-1900), Anglo-German Orientalist and philologist, born at Dessau, Germany, studied at Dessau, Leipzig, and Berlin, taking degree of doctor of philosophy before age twenty. Specialized in Sanskrit and went to Paris and London to prepare an edition of the *Rig Veda*. Between 1849 and 1874 six volumes of the *Rig Veda* were published. In 1850 appointed deputy Taylorian professor of modern language at Oxford, in 1854 became full professor, and in 1858 elected fellow of All Souls' College. He turned from Sanskrit to comparative philology, and in 1868 was given the chair of comparative philology at Oxford, which he held until 1875. Became a pioneer in the science of comparative mythology and comparative religion. In 1878 delivered the first Hibbert lectures on *The Origin and Growth of Religion,* and later the Gifford lectures on *Natural Religion*. In 1875 gave up professional duties to assume the greatest single work of his life, the editing of *The Sacred Books of the East,* a series of English versions of oriental scriptures, translated by different scholars. Fifty-one volumes including indexes were published, including three volumes which Dr. Max Müller himself wrote. All but three appeared under his supervision during his lifetime. Became a naturalized English citizen.

MAYHEW (mā'hū) **EXPERIENCE** (1673-1758), New England pastor and missionary to the Indians, born at Chilmark on Martha's Vineyard Island, Massachusetts. Began preaching to the Indians in 1694, devoting life to this service, having oversight of six congregations of Indians. In 1709 under direction of the Society for the Propagation of the Gospel in New England, translated into the Indian language the Psalms and the gospel of John, prepared the work in parallel columns of English and Algonquin. Experience Mayhew is considered as one of the great philologists of the Algonquin dialect. Wrote *Indian Converts* which contained accounts of thirty Indian ministers and eighty other Indian Christians.

MAYHEW, JONATHAN (1720-1766), New

England clergyman, born at Chilmark, Martha's Vineyard, a son of Experience Mayhew, graduated from Harvard in 1744, minister of the West Church in Boston from 1747 until death in 1766. This church was probably the first Unitarian Congregational church in New England. Liberal views led to his exclusion from the Boston Association of Congregational Ministers. Opposed the measures of the British Society for the Propagation of the Gospel in Foreign Parts because he regarded it as a pretext for introducing prelacy. In both pulpit and press an earnest American patriot, and did much to hasten the Revolution. From him came the suggestion for uniting the colonies against England. Among writings were several volumes of sermons, and *Discourse Concerning Unlimited Submission and Non-resistance to Higher Powers*.

MEARS, HENRIETTA CORNELIA (1890-1963). Born in Fargo, North Dakota. Educated at the University of Nova Scotia. Taught school in Beardsley and North Branch, Minnesota and organized a Sunday School in each place. Became director of Christian Education in First Presbyterian Church of Hollywood in 1928 and under her the Sunday School grew from 1450 to 4200 in two and a half years. Wrote her own Sunday School curricula. She and Cary Griffin started Gospel Light Press (later Publications) in 1933 to print her materials. Organized three camps in the mountains and in 1937 Forest Home as a conference center. Founded Gospel Literature in National Tongues in 1961 to send Sunday School literature all over the world. Sent 400 young people into Christian service among whom were Bill Bright, founder of Campus Crusade, Don Moomaw, and Louis H. Evans, Jr.

MEDHURST, WALTER HENRY (1796-1857), missionary and Oriental scholar, born in London, England, studied at St. Paul's School and Hackney College. In 1816 appointed by the London Missionary Society to Malacca as a missionary printer, three years later was ordained in 1819 by William Milne at Malacca. Worked in India, Borneo, Java, and on the Chinese coast, spending several years working among the Chinese emigrants in Java. On opening of Shanghai as a treaty port in 1842, Medhurst settled there, and from 1843 until death, had Shanghai as headquarters. Besides printing, writing and translating, did much itinerary preaching. On the Shanghai revision committee, helping to revise both the New and the Old Testament in High Wen-li. Accomplished in several oriental languages as well as in English, Dutch, and French. He published the *Chinese Repository,* twenty volumes, 1838-1867. Among his books: *English and Japanese Vocabulary; Dictionary of the Hok-kien Dialect of the Chinese Language; Chinese-English Dictionary; English-Chinese Dictionary; Chinese Dialogues; Dissertation on the Theology of the Chinese;* and *China: State and Prospects with Especial Reference to the Diffusion of the Gospel*. Left Shanghai in 1856 impaired in health, and died in London.

MEDICI FAMILY (See Catharine de Medici, Lorenzo de Medici, Clement VII, Leo X, Cosimo de Medici.)

MELANCHTHON (mĕ lăngk'thŭn), **PHILIPP** (original name **PHILIPP SCHWARZERD**) (1497-1560), German humanist and Reformer, born at Bretten, Germany, before age thirteen entered the University of Heidelberg, where he excelled in Greek. In 1512 studied at Tübingen. In 1518 accepted a call to become the professor of Greek at Wittenberg, where almost immediately he cast lot with Luther and the German Reformation. In fact he became Luther's right-hand fellow-worker, and became known as the formulating genius of the Reformation. Present at the Leipzig disputation between Luther and Eck in 1519, at the Diet of Spier in 1529, and at the colloquy of Marburg, 1529. In 1520 was married to Katharina Krapp, the daughter of the mayor of Wittenberg. In spite of irenic attitude composed the Augsburg Confession and the Augsburg Apology, both of sufficient soundness to secure Luther's stamp of approval. After Luther's death in 1546 Melanchthon became the leader of the German Reformation. Melanchthon had a tendency to try to compromise and make peace with opposing parties whether Calvinistic or Catholic, sometimes to the jeopardy of the Lutheran cause. Late in Melanchthon's life a rift came in the Lutheran church, and one group known as Philippists or Melanchthonians became a schism in the Lutheran ranks. As a Reformer Melanchthon was characterized by moderation, conscientiousness, caution, and love of peace. Chief writing was *Loci Communes,* a commentary on Romans. He also developed the German system of schools.

MELITIUS of ANTIOCH (mē lē'shĭ ŭs), (died 381), Bishop of Antioch, born in Melitene, Armenia Minor, received a good education, studied three years under Chrysostom, and baptized by him. About 357 became Bishop of Sebaste, Armenia, and about 360, bishop of Antioch, succeeding the deposed, extremely orthodox Eustathius. He represented the mediating position between the extreme Arian and the extreme orthodox positions, stating position as follows: "Three persons are conceived in the mind, but it is as though we addressed one only." Within a month the angered Arians banished him to his native Melitene, Armenia. A schism known as the Melitian Schism thus developed at Antioch. (This is not to be confused with the Melitian Schism of Egypt a few decades earlier.) With the most of the orthodox party in the East, held a position of high esteem. In 361 recalled from exile by Julian, but the schism continued for over a half century. Exerted great effort and energy to bring about peace in the church. As senior bishop presided at the ecumenical council at Constantinople in 381, but died suddenly a few days after the opening of the council.

MELITIUS OF LYCOPOLIS (died c. 325), Bishop of Lycopolis and originator of the Melitian Schism, in the reign of Diocletian, about 305. During the persecution, both Peter, Archbishop of Alexandria, and Melitius were imprisoned and many of the Christians lapsed. Then when the backsliders wished to be reinstated, Peter was willing to receive them back into the church upon their doing penance; Melitius refused to receive them so freely. Peter excommunicated him, a schism resulted, known as the Egyptian Melitians or the "Church of the Martyrs." Made himself primate over Egypt. Ordained several bishops; the schism was rapidly spreading, he was encroaching upon the jurisdiction of Peter. The Council of Nicea in 325 took notice of the schism, tried to conciliate and compromise in order to heal the schism, but to no avail. The Council seemingly did not condemn Melitius for heresy, but for schism only. The council recognized the bishops whom Melitius had ordained, but required that he remain at Lycopolis as a titular bishop with merely nominal authority or jurisdiction. Died shortly after this, but the schism continued throughout the fourth century.

MELITO (mĕl ĭ'tō), (died c. 190), early apologist, Bishop of Sardis. He flourished during the reign of Marcus Aurelius (161-180). According to Eusebius wrote many works, but today we know little more than their titles. He is best known perhaps for the *Apology*. An ascetic, perhaps even a celibate.

MELVILLE, ANDREW (1545-1622), Scottish theologian. Successor of John Knox in the Scottish Reformation and "Father of Scottish Presbytery," born at Baldovie, Forfarshire, Scotland. Studied at Melrose, St. Andrews, Paris and Poitiers. Due to political disturbance had to leave France, so went to Geneva, spending five years teaching at Geneva and studying theology under Beza. After ten years absence from Scotland, returned in 1574 and became principal of Glasgow University. Achieved great success in raising the educational standards in the university. Distinguished himself as a scholar and administrator. Became vitally interested in reforming the system of church government. By 1575 became member of the General Assembly of the Presbyterian church; and in 1582 and 1587 presided over the assembly. Installed in 1580 as principal of the new College of St. Mary's in the University of St. Andrews. Assisted in drafting the second book of discipline in 1581. James VI of Scotland, then James I of England, an ardent Episcopalian, sought to obstruct him; while he boldly preached reform and stood high in position in the Presbyterian church. From 1607 to 1611 imprisoned in the Tower in London. Upon release desired to return to Scotland, but James refused. Forced to live in exile in old age. Professor of biblical theology in the University of Sedan from 1611 to 1622. Helped to save Presbyterian system in Scotland from bishops.

MENDELSSOHN-BARTHOLDY (mĕn'dĕl-zōn-bär tōl'dē), **JAKOB LUDWIG FELIX** (1809-1847), German composer, pianist, and conductor, born at Hamburg, Germany, son of wealthy, cultured Jewish parents who had become Lutherans. Grandson of the noted philosopher, Moses Mendelssohn. Received a broad and varied education, was taught music by mother. Began to compose at ten. Began an extensive tour of England, Scotland, France, Austria, and Italy. After returning to Germany, at age twenty-four appointed musical director in Düsseldorf. Two years later in 1835, became conductor of the famous Gewandhaus orchestra in Leipzig, and brought the orchestra to a high state of perfection. Held this position until 1847 except for a year when under the appointment of the King of Prussia he served as chapel master in Berlin. Made ten trips to England where he presented own musical compositions. Helped found the Berlin Academy of Arts, and in 1842, the Leipzig Conservatory. In 1835 wrote the oratorio, *St. Paul,* and after nine years of work produced *Elijah,* which is considered by many his masterpiece, second only to Handel's *Messiah*. Remembered also for his *Songs without Words* besides many symphonies, overtures, concertos, sonatas, and other pieces. Formed a warm friendship with Schumann and Goethe, and was a great admirer of Bach and Beethoven. Compositions were light and easily understood. Works were noted for their grace, delicacy, and sweet melody.

MENNO SIMONS (mĕn'ō sē'mônz) (1496-1559), Dutch Anabaptist, the early leader of the Mennonite churches, born at Witmarsum, Holland, educated for the priesthood and ordained in 1524. Located at the village of Pingjum. In 1532 named pastor of native place, which he served until 1536. Handling the bread and wine the thought suddenly flashed into his mind that these could not possibly be the real body and blood of Christ. He went to the New Testament for light; the more he read, the more light came. Began an intensive study of the Bible and of writings of Luther and other Reformers. Attention was drawn to the question of infant baptism, began a serious study of this. Anabaptists were being very bitterly persecuted. In 1531 witnessed the martyrdom of a man in the capital of province for having been rebaptized by an Anabaptist. Four years later several hundred Münsterite Anabaptists, among them his own brother, were killed in a cloister near his home. These events brought him to serious reflection. The next year, 1536, at age forty, impelled to yield, he publicly renounced the Roman Catholic church. The Anabaptists seemed to be the nearest the truth. Accordingly in 1537 cast lot with them and was baptized by Obbe Philip, a leading Anabaptist in those regions. Soon became the leader of the Anabaptists. In this role met tremendous difficulties, among the first of which was encountering the corrupt and fanatical so-called Anabaptist groups. In rejecting their error and in conserving the good in their movement, he made his invaluable contribution to the Anabaptist cause. From 1554 to 1559 at Wüstenfelde in Holstein. An ardent preacher and a voluminous writer. During later years owned a printing press and published his own pamphlets. Among most important writings are: *Renunciation of Rome, Testimony against Jan van Leyden,* and *Foundation Book*. Although not the originator of the Mennonite churches, he had such a vital part in their early history that since 1550 they have borne the name.

MERCATOR (mûr kā'tẽr) **MARIUS** (early fifth century), Latin ecclesiastical writer. Very little known of personal life but probably was of North African birth. Lived at Rome and Constantinople. Cultivated layman, well read in the Scriptures and able in polemics. Wrote tracts against the Pelagians and took part in the Nestorian controversy, a loyal defender of orthodox Roman Catholic doctrine. An ardent admirer of Augustine of Hippo and Cyril of Alexandria.

MERCIER DÉSIRÉ JOSEPH (1851-1926) Belgian cardinal and philosopher. Born at Braine-de-Alleud. Educated at Malines and Louvain. Ordained in 1874 and from then until 1882 professor at Malines and from 1882 to 1906 at Louvain. Archbishop of Malines and Belgian primate in 1906 and cardinal in 1907. Tried to reconcile science and religion as Aquinas did Greek philosophy and theology. Founded Higher Institute of Philosophy at Louvain in 1894. Opposed Tyrrell's modernism. Represented the Roman Catholic church at the Malines Conversations with the Anglicans from 1921 to 1926. Upheld Belgian morale in World War I.

MERLE D'AUBIGNÉ (mĕrl'dō bē nyā'), **JEAN HENRI** (1794-1872), Swiss evangelical preacher and Reformation historian, born at Eaux-Vives on Lake Leman, Switzerland, family name Merle received the addition of d'Aubigné from grandmother. Studied at Geneva and Berlin, but received deepest and most decisive religious impressions from Robert Haldane. Ordained in 1817. A visit to Eisenach in October, 1817, helped toward a decision to write an exhaustive history of the Reformation. In 1818 appointed pastor of the Reformed congregation in Hamburg, and in 1824 court preacher in Brussels. About 1831 left Belgium and returned to Geneva to spend the rest of life as professor in the newly established evangelical theological school. Lectured chiefly on church history, but also on symbolics, homiletics, catechetics, ecclesiology, and pastoral theology. Took turns with Gaussen and Galland preaching at the Chapel of the Oratory. When the Company of Pastors forbade the pulpit to Merle d'Aubigné and evangelical associates he permitted the Church of the Oratory to be separated from the state church, and the Evangelical church was founded about 1849. A very strong advocate of the separation of church and state. Closely associated with Malan, Vinet, Gaussen, and others of the Evangelical movement in Geneva. Published the Protestant evangelical partisan *History of the Reformation,* of which the thirteenth and last volume appeared after his death more than thirty-five years later. This history had wide use and circulation in Great Britain, America, Germany, and France.

METHODIUS (mē thō'dĭ ŭs) (d. 885), "Apostle to the Slavs," born in Thessalonica, son of a military officer, educated in Constantinople. In 860 with his brother Cyril (d. 869) began mission work on the northeast shore of the Black Sea. Later at the invitation of Duke Ratislav, they were sent to the Moravians. Great success attended their labors. In 868 the brothers, representatives of the Eastern church, went to Rome to effect an agreement with Pope Adrian II relative to their work. Cyril died in Rome the next year, and Methodius returned to Moravia. After the death of Ratislav of Moravia and of Pope

Adrian II of Rome, the attitude of both Rome and the people of Moravia changed. In 879 again summoned to Rome, and though the independence of the Slavic church was confirmed, the status of the church became insecure. After the death of Methodius, Latin replaced the Slavic language and the church deteriorated and paganism again became dominant.

MEYER, FREDERICK BROTHERTON (1847-1929), English Baptist clergyman, born London, England, educated at Brighton College and Regent's Park Baptist College. Between 1870 and 1895 held pastorates successfully at Pembroke Baptist Chapel, Liverpool; York; Victoria Road Baptist Church, Leicester; Melbourne Hall, Leicester; Regent's Park Chapel, London; and Christ Church, Westminster Bridge Road, Lambuth. While at York, between 1872 and 1874, met Dwight L. Moody and introduced him to the British churches, beginning a lifelong friendship with the evangelist. During much of Meyer's ministry he engaged in social, temperance, and reclamation work. Became a politician and Borough Councilor; headed a movement to close saloons; was the means of shutting up nearly five hundred immoral houses; labored for the reclamation of released prisoners; and effected organizations for all ages and classes of members. President of the National Federation of Free Churches (1904-1905), following that time, general evangelist of the Federation of Free Churches, conducting missions in South Africa and the far East, returning to England in 1909. Visited the Continent, the United States, Canada, Jamaica, Australia, and the Near East. Author of several excellent devotional, biographical, and interpretative books that have to the present time had much popularity. For many years closely associated with Keswick.

MEYER, HEINRICH AUGUST WILHELM (1800-1873), German biblical scholar, born at Gotha, Germany, studied theology at the University of Jena. After teaching for a while in a private school at Grone, near Göttingen, pastor successively at Osthausen, Meiningen, Harste near Göttingen, Hoya, and Neustadt, Hanover, between the years 1822 and 1848. At Neustadt had a parish of five thousand. During these years wrote commentaries. In 1848 resigned pastorate to give time to consistorial and exegetical duties, with residence at Hanover. In 1861 created a councilor of the supreme consistory, but in 1865 retired on a pension. Was most industrious in his writing. He shared in the revision of Martin Luther's version of the New Testament. Reputation, however, rests largely on the commentary on the New Testament which he edited. Meyer himself wrote on the gospels, Acts, and several Pauline epistles.

MICHELANGELO (mī kĕl ăn'jĕ lō), **BUONARROTI** (bwô'när rô'tē) (1475-1564), Italian Renaissance sculptor, painter, architect, and poet, born at Caprese, Tuscany, Italy, and studied in the school of Lorenzo de Medici in Florence. Pope Julius II (1303-1313), a patron of artists, in 1508 commissioned him to decorate the ceiling of the Sistine chapel in the Vatican. This painting, which depicts various scenes from the Old Testament, required four years to complete. From 1535 to 1541 painted the *Last Judgment* for the altar of the chapel. Michelangelo excelled as a sculptor, yet not many of completed works have come down to us. *David* in Florence and *Moses* and *Pietà* in Rome are his chief marble sculptures. Last years were given largely to architecture. Appointed architect of St. Peter's in 1547, and designed the present dome, which was completed in accordance with his plans after his death. Classed with Dante, Shakespeare, and Beethoven as one of the four great intellects in the world of art and literature.

MIGNE, JACQUES PAUL (1800-1875). Born near and educated in Orleans. Ordained in 1824. Parish priest for over a decade near Orleans and in Paris. Established in 1836 his own publishing house called *Ateliers Catholique*. Published *Latina Patrologia* (221 volumes), the writings of Latin ecclesiastical writers to Innocent III and *Patrologia Graeca* (161 volumes) of the Greek Fathers.

MILEY, JOHN (1813-1895), American Methodist Episcopal theologian and minister, born near Hamilton, Ohio, graduated from Augusta College, Kentucky. Entered the Methodist ministry in 1838 and served in the circuits of Ohio and Eastern New York until 1873. Taught in Wesley Female College, Cincinnati, Ohio (1849-1850); and in 1873 became professor of systematic theology at Drew Theological Seminary, continuing there until death in 1895. Held in high respect by theologians of church, as a "progressive conservative" leader. Writings were: *A Treatise on Class Meetings, Atonement in Christ,* and *Systematic Theology.*

MILLER, JAMES RUSSELL (1840-1912), American Presbyterian clergyman and author, born at Harshaville, Pennsylvania, moving with parents to Calcutta, Ohio in 1854. Educated at Westminster College, New Wilmington, Pennsylvania, and United Presbyterian Seminary, Alleghany. Before going to college spent some time teaching in public school, and between college and seminary for two and a half years served with the United States Christian Commission connected with the Army of the Potomac. Ordained a Presbyterian minister and held successive pastorates in Pennsylvania and Illinois. In all pastorates his churches grew rapidly and substantially. In 1880 began editorial work for the Presbyterian Board of Publication, Philadelphia, and was the board's editorial superintendent from 1887 until death. A prolific writer, authoring more than sixty devotional books. Some of them have been translated into many languages. One of his best known writings was eight-volume *Devotional Hours with the Bible,* of which more than two million copies have been sold.

MILLER, LEWIS (1829-1899), manufacturer and Sunday School promoter. Born Greentown, Ohio. Partner in an agricultural machinery company in 1852 and helped in the development of farm machines. Worked with J. H. Vincent to set up educational courses for Sunday School teachers during the summer at Lake Chautauqua in New York.

MILLER, WILLIAM (1782-1849), early advocate of the Adventist movement, born at Pittsfield, Massachusetts, a farmer, deputy sheriff, and justice of the peace from 1803 at Poultney, Vermont. Was a diligent student and a great reader. In the War of 1812 served as a captain of volunteers. From 1815 to 1849 a farmer at Low Hampton, New York. He became a skeptic through reading Hume, Voltaire, and Paine, but was converted and joined the Baptist church in 1816. Became a licensed minister and entered upon a careful study of Scriptures. Through this study arrived at the premillennial position, and then after further comparisons of the apocalyptic Scriptures concluded that Christ would return to this earth to cleanse with fire the sanctuary mentioned in Daniel 8:14; that this return would be in 1843. After 1831 lectured widely on Adventism. Joshua Himes publicized these ideas. He published a book *Evidence from Scripture and History of the Second Coming of Christ about the Year 1843*. Had more than fifty thousand adherents in this country gathered from the various denominations. Resting on Miller the movement probably soon would have come to naught. But a few followers reinterpreted the prophecy and effected an organization from which there developed several Adventist groups with somewhat varying teachings, the largest and most significant of which, under the leadership of Mrs. Ellen G. White, became the Seventh Day Adventist denomination. Known at first as the American Millennial Association, this movement held generally to Miller's position and theology, emphasizing personal and premillennial character of the second coming of Christ, the resurrection of the dead—the faithful to be raised at Christ's coming and the rest a thousand years later—the renewal of the earth as the abode of the redeemed. Although Miller at first held that the sanctuary to which Christ was to come was on earth, later Adventist leaders, such as Ellen G. White, claimed it to be a heavenly rather than an earthly sanctuary, and that Christ did come in 1843 to cleanse this sanctuary.

MILLIGAN (mĭl'ĭ găn), **GEORGE** (1860-1934), Scottish biblical scholar, born at Kilconquhar, Fife, Scotland, studied at Aberdeen, Edinburgh, Göttingen, and Bonn universities; minister at St. Matthew's, Morningside (1883-1894); Caputh, Perthshire (1894-1910); regius professor of divinity and Biblical criticism at Glasgow University (1910-1932). President of the Oxford Society of Historical Theology (1915-1916), moderator of the General Assembly of the Church of Scotland (1923), first chairman of the Scottish Sunday School Union for Christian Education (1926). Main writings: *History of the English Bible; The Theology of the Epistle to the Hebrews; The Twelve Apostles; St. Paul's Epistles to the Thessalonians; Selections from the Greek Papyri; The New Testament Documents: Their Origin and Early History; Here and There among the Papyri;* and *The Vocabulary of the Greek Testament* (part one and two in collaboration with James Hope Moulton).

MILLIGAN, WILLIAM (1821-1893), Church of Scotland clergyman, born in Edinburgh, Scotland, educated at St. Andrews University, the University of Edinburgh, and Halle, Germany. During the disruption controversy of 1843, adhered to the established church. Entered the ministry of the established church, held pastorates at Cameron and Kilconquhar in Fifeshire (1844-1860). In 1860 became professor of Biblical criticism at Aberdeen University. In 1870 chosen as one of the revisers of the New Testament. In 1882 moderator of the General Assembly and in 1886 appointed principal clerk to the assembly. Among numerous works: *The Resurrection of Our Lord; Revelation of St. John; Commentary on the Revelation; Elijah: His Life and Times; Ascension and Heavenly Priesthood of Our Lord; Discussions on the Apocalypse;* and *Resurrection of the Dead*.

MILLS, BENJAMIN FAY (1857-1916), American evangelist and social reformer, born at Rahway, New Jersey, received education at Phillips Academy, Andover, Hamilton College, and Lake Forest University. Ordained to the Congregational ministry in 1878, served Congregational churches at Cannon Falls, Minnesota, and Rutland, Vermont, and the Fourth Presbyterian Church, Albany, New York. Extensively and successfully engaged in evangelistic work from 1886 to 1897, making thousands of converts in campaigns. In 1897, owing to a change of religious views, withdrew from the Congregational church and for two years conducted independent religious meetings in Boston, preaching social gospel. From 1899 to 1903, pastor of the First Unitarian Church in Oakland, California. In 1904 organized a new liberal religious society in Los Angeles known as the Los Angeles Fellowship, edited the *Fellowship Magazine*. From 1911 to 1916 founder and leader of the Chicago Fellowship. From 1903 to 1915 delivered courses of lectures on philosophy, psychology, and sociology in leading cities throughout the United States. In 1915 experienced a reconversion to the Christian faith, and sought re-admission to the evangelical ministry, received into the Chicago Presbytery, again conducted evangelistic meetings in various cities. Died in Grand Rapids, Michigan. Among writings: *Power from on High, Victory through Surrender, A Message to Mothers, God's World and Other Sermons, The Divine Adventure*, and *The New Revelation*.

MILLS, SAMUEL JOHN (1783-1818), promoter of foreign missions, born in Torringford, Connecticut. Graduated from Williams College and Andover Theological Seminary, and spent a short time at Yale. While in college a member of the famous haystack prayer group. During brief stay at Yale met and befriended young Henry Obookiah from the Sandwich Islands, who found a home and a genial fellowship with Samuel and his parents. In the seminary became a part of the prayer meeting and msision study group that resulted in the organization of the American Board of Commissioners for Foreign Missions in 1810, and in the sending of Judson, Rice, Nott, Hall, and Newell to India in 1812. He also helped start a mission to the Sandwich Islands. Licensed to preach in 1812, and made two missionary tours through the midwestern and southern states between 1812 and 1815, distributing Bibles and visiting sick soldiers. In 1815 ordained. The next year agent for the School for Educating Colored Men. Exerted some influence in the founding of the United Foreign Missionary Society for the Presbyterian and Reformed Churches, in the organization of the American Bible Society in 1816, and in the starting of an African school near Newark. In 1817 went as an agent of the colonization society to Western Africa, which led to the formulation of the Republic of Liberia.

MILMAN, HENRY HART (1791-1868), Anglican church historian and poet, born in London, England, educated at Greenwich, Eton, and at Brasenose College, Oxford. Professor of poetry at Oxford (1821-1831). Became a fellow of Brasenose College in 1814. Ordained priest in 1816, and vicar of St. Mary's, Reading (1818-1835), rector of St. Margaret's, Westminster and canon of Westminster (1835-1849), and dean of St. Paul's, London (1849-1868), holding the deanery until death. In theology a liberal, belonging to the Broad church party, advocating the abolition of subscribing to the Thirty-nine Articles of the Anglican church, and writing church history and Jewish history from the critical viewpoint. A friend of Reginald Heber, composed several popular hymns for Heber's hymn book. Wrote *The Character and Conduct of the Apostles Considered as an Evidence of Christianity* (Bampton Lectures), *The History of the Jews, The History of Christianity from the Birth of Christ to the Abolition of Paganism in the Roman Empire* (three volumes), *History of Latin Christianity* (six volumes), *Life of E. Gibbon* and *Annals of St. Paul's Cathedral*. Also edited Gibbon's *Decline and Fall of the Roman Empire*.

MILNE (mĭln), **WILLIAM** (1785-1822), missionary to China, born near Aberdeen, Scotland. Lack of education was partially made up by much reading. After deciding to become a missionary, studied at the London Missionary Society's College at Gosport, where ordained in 1812. In 1813 with his wife went to Macao, and after spending some time with Robert Morrison in Canton, made a tour through the Malay Archipelago. After tour settled down at Malacca, mastered the Chinese language, opened a school for Chinese converts, set up a printing press on which he issued the *Chinese Gleaner*. Assisted Robert Morrison in translating parts of the Bible into the Chinese, completing it in 1819. Chief founder of the Anglo-Chinese College of Malacca, became its principal. Because of his own ill health visited Singapore and Penang in 1822, but died a few days after return to Malacca. Wrote: *The Sacred Edict* and *A Retrospect of the First Ten Years of the Protestant Mission in China*.

MILNER (mĭl′nẽr), **ISAAC** (1750-1820), English mathematician and church historian, born in Leeds, England, educated at the grammar school at Hull where older brother Joseph was headmaster, and at Queen's College, Cambridge, where attained high academic honors. In 1774 appointed tutor, in

1776 elected fellow of his college and also fellow of the Royal Society, in 1777 made priest. In 1783, returning to the university, chosen professor of natural philosophy, and in 1788 elected president of Queen's College. At once set about to raise educational standards and did much to make the college and the university a center of Evangelicalism. In 1791 appointed dean of Carlisle, in 1792 was elected vice-chancellor of Cambridge, six years later succeeded Dr. John Newton as Lucasian professor of mathematics. Upon brother Joseph's death in 1797 prepared the unfinished manuscript of *The History of the Church of Christ* for publication and continued the history to 1530. This history, the most popular manual on church history until Neander brought out more scholarly church history. Died in 1820 in the home of intimate friend, William Wilberforce, whose conversion was due largely to his influence during a trip in Europe from 1784 to 1785. Published a *Life* of brother Joseph, and edited *Sermons of the Late Joseph Milner* in two volumes.

MILNER, JOSEPH (1744-1797), English church historian, born at Leeds, England, studied at Catharine Hall, Cambridge. Became headmaster of the Hull grammar school, lectured at Holy Trinity or High Church, Hull. After thirty years' service almost unanimously chosen vicar of Trinity Church, though he died a few weeks later. About 1770 underwent a deep spiritual experience and became a powerful preacher of repentance and revival. Became an ardent evangelical and soon lost many of richer members, but gained a strong following among the lower classes. May be regarded as one of the founders of the evangelical school of the Church of England. Chief work was *The History of the Church of Christ,* in which brother Isaac was a collaborator. In it he emphasized the biographical approach, though facts are often inaccurate. Wrote *Gibbon's Account of Christianity Considered, Some Remarkable Passages in the Life of William Howard,* and *Essays on the Influence of the Holy Spirit.*

MILTIADES (mĭl tĭ'ă dēz), (second century), apologist, a philosopher of Asia Minor who became a Christian. Wrote an apology against both pagans and Jews, addressing it to the rulers of this world, referring to perhaps either Antoninus Pius or Marcus Aurelius. Scant excerpts of his writings are in Eusebius.

MILTITZ (mĭl'tĭts), **KARL VON** (c. 1490-1529), Saxon Roman Catholic ecclesiastic and chamberlain of Pope Leo X. Born at Rabenaus near Dresden. Son of a Saxon noble, became canon of Mainz, Treves, and Meissen. In 1515 became papal chamberlain, and in 1518 sent by Pope Leo X as nuncio to negotiate with Frederick the Wise, Luther's friend and protector. Also held a conference with Luther in the house of Spalatin in January, 1519. Hoped that by politeness and friendliness with Luther, and by throwing the blame for the theses-controversy on Tetzel he might win Luther and save the unity of the Catholic church. The truce suddenly ended when the pope became alarmed and stepped in and denounced Luther. Miltitz could go no further. He returned to Rome for awhile, then went back to Germany where he was accidentally drowned.

MILTON, JOHN (1608-1674), English poet, theologian, and pamphleteer. Born in London, educated at St. Paul's Grammar School, and in Christ's College, Cambridge. While in college and shortly after, wrote *On the Morning of Christ's Nativity, L'Allegro, de Penseroso, Comus, and Lycidas.* After college spent six years on father's estate in study and in writing verse, both English and Latin. Spent fifteen months traveling in Europe, mostly in Italy where he met Galileo, who was then under restraint by the Inquisition for publishing theory on the celestial system. Started out as an Anglican with moderate Puritan leanings, then turned Presbyterian, and finally Independent, inclining toward Arianism in later years. Intended to become a clergyman, but was diverted from this because of the absolutist principles of William Laud, Archbishop of Canterbury in 1633. During the last eight years of the reign of Charles I, and the tumultuous years of the rule of Oliver Cromwell, active in public affairs, serving as Secretary to the Council of State, though he became blind about 1652. During period wrote a notable series of pamphlets on ecclesiastical, social, and political subjects. In the religious area wrote in defense of the Presbyterian system of government against the Episcopal. Wrote *The Doctrine and Discipline of Divorce,* advocating divorce on the ground of incompatibility as well as adultery. Also wrote *Areopagitica; a Speech for the Liberty of Unlicensed Printing,* and *De Doctrina Christiana* in which soul sleep and subordination of Christ appear was a major theological treatise. After he became blind did literary work with the assistance of a secretary. With the Restoration in 1660 was punished for support of Parliament by a fine and a short term in prison. From the Restoration to the time of death lived in retirement, during which time wrote greatest work, *Paradise Lost,* and also two works of lesser magnitude, *Paradise Regained* and *Samson*

Agonistes. A product equally of the Renaissance and of the Protestant Reformation. Beliefs in the freedom of the human will made him take stand against the Calvinist doctrine of predestination.

MINUCIUS (mĭ nū'shĭ ŭs) **FELIX MARCUS** (second or third Century A.D.), Latin Christian apologist, born a pagan, likely in North Africa, though living the most of life in Rome. Minucius was one of the very early Latin writers, chief apology being a dialogue under the title, *Octavius.* A dialogue between two friends of Minucius, one Octavius, like himself, a convert from paganism, and the other an argumentative pagan. By the end of the dialogue Caecilius, the pagan friend confessed his error, resolved to embrace Christianity, and asked for Christian instruction. The literary form of the dialogue is pleasing and elegant, and is valuable as an apology.

MIRZA ALI MOHAMMED (mēr'zä ä'lē mō hăm'ed) (1819-1850), a reformer in the Shiite sect of Islam, born probably in Shiraz, Persia, claimed to be the "Bab" or door, succeeding the last of the twelve Immams who had disappeared about nine hundred years before. Became known as "Bab ed Din" or Gate of Righteousness. Stirred up among Muslim population of Persia a new spiritual life, but incurred the fanatical hatred of the local Muslim clergy, and the desperate fear of the civil rulers. His execution took place in the city of Tabriz, where in 1850, he was shot in the barrack square. One of his chief followers was Mirza Hussein Ali, better known as Bahaullah, the founder of Bahaism.

MOFFAT, ROBERT (1795-1883), pioneer translator and missionary, born at Ormiston, Scotland. At fourteen apprenticed as a gardener; formal education meager. Soon after conversion became interested in missions, and applied to the London Missionary Society. After some special instruction accepted and sent to Cape Town, South Africa, arriving there in 1817. Thrust into the center of several cannibalistic tribes in this colony which had just, three years before, come under the British. The next year, 1817, set out for Namaqualand, the home of the notorious outlaw, Afrikaner. To the surprise and marvel of everyone, won the dreaded outlaw to Christ. In 1817 brought him to Capetown. Moffat next went to Lattakoo in 1820. Mary Smith came from London to become Moffat's wife, and the couple settled at Kuruman in Bechuanaland in 1825, where a mission was soon established. Later, with much hard work and many obstacles, organized a mission station at Inyati among the Matabele. The Moffats spent the years 1839-1843 in England furthering the cause of missions in Africa. It was at this time that Livingstone was inspired by Moffat to go to Africa. After arriving on the field Livingstone married Moffat's daughter, Mary. In 1870 the aged missionaries returned to England. During last years in England labored untiringly for the cause to which he had devoted his earlier life and talents. While on the field translated the Bible into Sechvana by 1859, authored a hymn book, and wrote two missionary books on South Africa: *Labors and Scenes in South Africa* and *Rivers of Water in a Dry Place*.

MOFFATT, JAMES (1870-1944), New Testament scholar, born in Glasgow, Scotland, educated at the University and the Free Church College in Glasgow. Between 1894 and 1907 served successively as minister at Dundonald Church, Ayrshire, and at Broughty Ferry, ordained in 1896. Bruce Lecturer in the United Free Church College, Glasgow (1906), Jowett Lecturer in London (1907), Yates professor of Greek and New Testament exegesis at Mansfield College (1911-1915), Oxford, and professor of church history in the United Free Church, Glasgow (1915-1927). From 1927 to 1939 in the United States to be Washburn professor of church history at Union Theological Seminary, New York. Moffatt translated the Old and New Testaments into modern English, and translated Adolf Harnack's *Expansion of Christianity* from the German into the English. Wrote *The Historical New Testament, Paul and Paulinism, Critical Introduction to the New Testament Literature, Theology of the Gospels, The Approach to the New Testament,* and *Epistle to the Hebrews* (International Critical Commentary).

MOHAMMED (mō hăm'ĕd) (c. 570-632), founder of Islam, born in Mecca in South Arabia, of the tribe of the Koreish, the custodian of the sacred shrine of the Kaaba. Cared for by grandfather for two years, then by uncle, Abu Talib. At age twenty-five became a camel driver for Kadijah, a wealthy widow of Mecca, whom he married a little later. Of this union one child, Fatima, survived infancy, later became the wife of Ali, one of Mohammed's followers and later his successor. Trading trips took him to Syria, where he came in touch with both Judaism and a degenerate form of Christianity. At age forty claimed to have received a vision and a call to preach. Began a new religion of mingled Judaism, Christianity, and Arabian paganism, blended together by his imaginative mind. First converts were Kadijah his wife, Ali and Zaid, two adopted sons, and Abu Bekr, a close friend. Persecuted in Mecca, in 622 fled to Medina; this flight, the Hegira, dated the beginning of Islam and its calendar. Gained strength at Medina, established a theocratic state, eliminated internal strife in the city, repulsed attacks of the Meccans, and before long returned to and gained possession of Mecca, which became the holy place of Islam. Became judge, lawgiver, and administrator among followers, and built up a strong state and a mighty religion. By 632, time of death, nearly all of Arabia was at his feet; by 750 North Africa, Palestine, Asia Minor, Persia, and Spain were conquered for Islam. Essential doctrines of Mohammed's religion are (1) Allah, an absolute, all-powerful creator God; (2) angels, the sinless servants of Allah; (3) books, chief of which is the Koran; (4) prophets, of whom Mohammed was the last and most important; and (5) the resurrection and last day. The five practical duties or "pillars of faith" are (1) recital of the creed; (2) prayers five times daily; (3) fast of Ramadan; (4) almsgiving; and (5) pilgrimage to Mecca. Being built on truth and fiction, religion became strong, became one of Christianity's greatest foes, and has had worldwide consequences.

MOHLER, JOHANN ADAM (1796-1838), German Roman Catholic historian and theologian, born at Igersheim, Württemburg, Germany, studied at the lyceum of Ellwangen and the University of Tübingen. Took orders in 1819, served as vicar at Weilerstadt and Riedlingen for a short time. In 1822 began to lecture on church history, patrology, and church polity; became full professor of church history and patrology at Tübingen in 1828. Most important writing: *Symbolism: or the Doctrinal Differences between Catholics and Protestants as Represented by their Public Confessions of Faith,* in which he attacked Protestantism and sought to idealize the Council of Trent. In 1835 accepted the chair of biblical exegesis at Munich, but devoted himself chiefly to church history, and wrote a *Church History* (three volumes). Shortly before death appointed Dean of Würzburg Cathedral. Sometimes called the "Catholic Schleiermacher." Recognized as the greatest theologian of the Roman Catholic church since Bellarmine and Bossuet. Work contributed much toward the theological revival in his church. Wrote also *Unity of the Church,* and *Athanasius the Great and the Church of His Time.*

MOHR, JOSEPH (1792-1848). Born at Salzburg where he became a cathedral chorister. Ordained in 1815. Was pastor of several churches. Composed hymn, "Silent Night" in 1818 for a Christmas Eve service, and the teacher and organist Franz Grüber set it to guitar music. Sung often by wandering Tyrolean minstrels.

MOLINOS (mō lē'nos), **MIGUEL DE** (c. 1640-1697), Spanish Quietist, born near Saragossa, Spain, educated at Valencia, where he was ordained priest. Settled in Rome about 1663. Fame rests largely on *Spiritual Guide,* which was published about 1675. The *Guide* proved to be popular among Protestants as well as among Roman Catholics. Endeavoring to reconcile the life of active service with the life of contemplation, sought to show the fourfold way to inward peace, prayer, obedience, frequent communions, and inward mortification. To him the mystical union with God tended to render superfluous the rites, ceremonies, and institutions of the Roman church. Because of this tendency, mystical teachings were spreading far and wide, endangering the very traditions and authority of the church, and because of the close affinity of writings and those of the Protestant mystics and the pietists, the Jesuits sought and secured from the pope his condemnation. In 1685 placed in confinement until he should recant. Two years later, when two hundred people were arrested by the Inquisition for "Quietism," and were later condemned by the pope, he escaped the stake by recantation, but was confined in a Dominican monastery until death in 1697. Taught that perfection and spiritual peace are attained by annihilation of the will and passive absorption in the contemplation of God and divine things until the soul is indifferent both to the world, to sense and desire, and to virtue and morality.

MOMMSEN (mōm'zĕn) **(CHRISTIAN MATHIAS) THEODOR** (1817-1903), German classical scholar and historian born in Garding, Schleswig, the son of a pastor, educated at Kiel University. In 1848 elected professor of Roman law at Leipzig University, remained two years. For two years professor at the University of Zurich, following which, history professor at the University of Breslau. From 1858 until 1903 professor of ancient history at the University of Berlin. A famous archaeologist in the field of Roman inscriptions, spending many years editing the monumental *Corpus Inscriptionum Latinarum.* Greatest work was the *Romisch Geschichte* in three volumes. It was translated into English in 1861, and became a standard college textbook. Wrote also *Provinces of the Roman Empire,* and *History of the Roman Coinage.* In 1902 awarded the Nobel Prize in literature. Very interested in politics. A strong opponent of Bismarck.

MONICA or **MONNICA** (c. 331-387), mother of Augustine of Hippo, born of Christian parents in the Numidian town of

Tagaste in North Africa where she continued to live after marriage to Patricius. A woman of devoted piety. Her faith, her prayers, and her Christian life helped influence her whole family to become Christians. Before conversion Augustine loved his mother, but he evaded and spurned her Christian teachings and prayers. When he decided to leave Carthage and go to Rome, Monica wished to accompany him; went with him as far as to the port. He tricked her into spending the night in a church, and by morning he was on his way to Rome. Sorrowfully but prayerfully, she went home. Her prayers were answered when Augustine later and finally in Milan accepted Christ. After conversion and baptism, the family started to Rome; but Monica died on the way, at Ostia at age fifty-six.

MONIER-WILLIAMS (mŭn'ĭ ĕr-wĭl'yămz), **SIR MONIER** (1819-1899), British Sanskrit scholar, born in Bombay, India, studied at King's College, London, at Baliol and University colleges, Oxford, and at the East India Company's college, Haileybury, graduating from Oxford in 1844. At Oxford studied under the noted Indiologist, Prof. H. H. Wilson. Taught oriental languages at Haileybury and at Cheltenham; and in 1860 upon the death of H. H. Wilson chosen Boden professor of Sanskrit at Oxford, in preference to Max Müller. Taught until failing health necessitated resignation in 1887. Main work while at Oxford was the founding of the India Institute, an institution which was to become a focus for the concentration and dissemination of correct information about Indian literature and culture, a project begun in 1875, completed in 1896. He made three journeys to India to enlist the sympathetic cooperation of the leading native princes. Curator of the Institute until death; gave to the Institute his valuable books and manuscript collection numbering three thousand. Knighted in 1886. Among works are: *A Practical Grammar of the Sanskrit Language, An English and Sanskrit Dictionary, A Sanskrit and English Dictionary, Practical Hindustani Grammar, Indian Wisdom, Buddhism, Brahmanism and Hinduism,* and *Modern India and The Indians.*

MONOD (mô nō'), **ADOLPHE THEODORE** (1802-1856), French Evangelical preacher, Brother of Frederic Monod, born at Copenhagen, Denmark. Educated at the College of Bourbon at Paris, studied theology at Geneva (1820-1824). Conversion took place about 1825, from which time he possessed a firm evangelical faith. In 1825 visited Italy and soon founded a Protestant congregation at Naples, where he remained pastor until 1827. Returning to France became pastor of the Reformed church at Lyons. Being deposed because of orthodoxy in 1831, founded a Free church at Lyons which still exists. In 1836 called to a theological professorship at Montauban, where he taught and preached until 1847. Upon the retirement in 1847 of his brother Frederic, called to the principal Reformed church, the Orataire in Paris. Labored there until death in 1856. Unquestionably the foremost pulpit orator of the French Reformed church in the nineteenth century. Messages given during his last illness were taken down and published in a little volume under the title, *The Farewell of Adolphe Monod.* His masterpiece, *Five Sermons on the Apostle Paul,* has been translated into many languages and widely read.

MONOD (mô'nō'), **FREDERIC JOËL JEAN GERARD** (1794-1863), Evangelical French Protestant, brother of Adolphe Monod, born in Monnaz, Canton of Vaud, Switzerland, educated at Geneva. Came under the evangelical influence of Robert Haldane, ordained in 1817. In 1820 entered the active ministry and succeeded father as pastor of the Orataire in Paris, continuing there until 1849. In 1824 established the *Archives du Christianisme,* the chief organ of the Evangelical French Protestants, and continued as editor until death in 1863. Leader of a movement that attempted to exclude Rationalists. When this attempt failed Monod and some friends in 1849 left the state church and organized an independent organization. Succeeded in welding together the free, independent congregations and formed the Eglise Libre de France, or the Union of Evangelical Free Churches of France. Remained pastor of church until death; guided the alliance of the French free churches with consummate skill. Died in 1863, recognized as a champion of the evangelical cause the world over.

MONROE, HARRY (1853-1916), American rescue mission worker, born at Exeter, New Hampshire. Early an alcoholic, became associated with counterfeiters and arrested in Detroit. Left Detroit and went to Chicago, where at the Pacific Garden Mission Colonel Clarke led him to Christ. In a few weeks became the song leader and soloist in the mission. He assisted in the work of the mission for twelve years; when Colonel Clarke died in 1892 he became superintendent, a position held for twenty-four years.

MONTALEMBERT (môn tȧ län bĕr'), **CHARLES FORBES RENE, COMTE DE** (1810-1870), French Roman Catholic historian, born in London, studied at Fulham near London, and the College Saint Barbe in Paris. Became imbued with the Catholic faith and the idea of popular freedom. Spent the rest of life endeavoring to bring about a reconciliation between the two. About 1830 joined with Lamennais and Lacordaire in the publishing of the newspaper, *L' Avenir.* In 1832, when the pope condemned the newspaper along with Lamennais and his friends, he with Lacordaire made formal submission to the pope and remained within the Catholic church. Montalembert spent several years in Italy and Germany particularly in the study of early legend, medieval history, and medieval religious art. In 1837 took his seat in the chamber of Peers, where he stood as a champion of religion. From 1848 to 1857 sat in the Chamber of Deputies. In 1851 elected to the French Academy, after 1857 devoted himself to literature and traveling. Though a devoted son of the Roman church, a liberal, clung to early passion for freedom of thought. Earnestly opposed the Papal Syllabus of 1864, also the doctrine of infallibility of the pope.

MONTANUS (Second century), heretic. Became a Christian about the middle of the second century. Soon after conversion appeared in a small town, Pepuza, Phrygia as a prophet and reformer of Christianity. Since coldness, worldliness and laxity were creeping into the church, felt it his duty to recall the church to primitive purity and holiness. Considered himself to be the passive instrument or inspired organ of the Holy Spirit. Associated were two so-called prophetesses, Priscilla and Maximilla, also of Asia Minor, with the center of their activity in the village of Pepuza. His movement spread rapidly and gained a large following among the excitable and religiously sensitive people of Asia Minor. By 170 Montanism had penetrated Rome, and by 200 had claimed Tertullian as an adherent. Some who wrote against Montanism were Miltiades in the second century and Augustine in the fifth century. In doctrine Montanus was essentially orthodox, though strongly chiliastic, laying great stress on miraculous gifts, especially prophecy, and progressive revelation. The movement also laid great stress on severe asceticism and strict church discipline.

MONTGOMERY, HELEN BARRETT (1861-1934), modern speech New Testament translator. Born in Kingsville, Ohio. Educated at Wellesley College and Brown University in classical languages. From 1913 to 1924 president of Women's American Baptist Foreign Mission Society. Licensed as Baptist minister in 1892. Had large women's Bible classes. President of Northern Baptist Convention in 1921. Translator of an English modern speech version of the New Testament from the Greek.

MONTGOMERY, JAMES (1771-1854), British poet and hymn writer, born at Irvine, Ayrshire, Scotland. Sent to the Moravian school in Fulneck, near Leeds, Yorkshire, England. Parents later became missionaries to the West Indies, where they both died. James was for thirty-one years, beginning in 1796, editor of the *Sheffield Iris,* originally called the *Sheffield Register.* As editor twice fined and imprisoned for trivial offenses, but reputation was so little affected thereby that when he retired from the editorship in 1825 he received public honors. In 1830 delivered a series of lectures on poetry and literature before the Royal Institution, London. An earnest advocate of foreign missions and of the Bible Society. Reputation, however, rests chiefly upon four hundred hymns of which nearly one hundred are still in use. In English hymnody he stands next to Isaac Watts and Charles Wesley. Among his great hymns are "O Spirit of the Living God," "Hail to the Lord's Anointed," "Angels from the Realms of Glory," "Forever with the Lord," "Songs of Praise the Angels Sing," "Come Ye That Fear the Lord," "Prayer is the Soul's Sincere Desire," "Go to Dark Gethsemane," and "In the Hour of Trial." He published two volumes of poems, *Prison Amusements* and *The Switzerland Wanderer.* First public profession of religion was when he joined the Moravian church in forty-third year, after which time was eminent for piety and goodness; active in religious and philanthropic work.

MOODY, DWIGHT LYMAN (1837-1899), evangelist, born at Northfield, Massachusetts. Had only a few terms of school. He left home and went to Boston to seek employment. Living with his uncle, he became a shoe clerk. The next year he was led to Christ by his Sunday school teacher, Edward Kimball. In 1856 left Boston for Chicago, where he became a successful shoe salesman. Became interested in church work, soon joined the Plymouth Congregational Church. When he asked for a Sunday school class, he was charged with the responsible task of gathering the children for it. Brought in children enough for several classes. Soon organized a Sunday school of his own in North Market Hall that grew in attendance to about fifteen hundred. When twenty-three Moody answered the call of God to leave secular employment. This was the beginning of a life of great influence, popularity, and power. In Sunday school conventions he came to be much in demand. In the Civil War gave time to personal work among the soldiers. Injected new life into the Young Men's Christian Association, and in 1865 was made president of the Association. Had a part in erecting the first and second Y.M.C.A. buildings in Chicago. Though not an ordained minister, he was a great and effective preacher and evangelist. A builder of churches, in 1863 when only twenty-six he erected a church building at a cost of twenty thousand dollars on Illinois Street between LaSalle and Wells Streets in Chicago. After its loss by fire in 1871 he erected a new building on the corner of Chicago Avenue and LaSalle Street. These edifices were the forerunners of the great Moody Memorial Church now located on North Avenue and LaSalle Street. Though having only a meager education, he became a noted educator and builder of schools. In 1879 began the erection of Northfield Seminary for girls, and in 1881 Mount Hermon School for boys. In 1886 started the first Bible school of its kind in this country, the Chicago Evangelization Society, later to be known as the Moody Bible Institute. Between 1880 and 1886 inaugurated summer conferences and student conferences at Northfield, out of the latter came the Student Volunteer Movement in 1886. Perhaps Moody's largest contribution, however, to the Christian world was his far-flung evangelistic work. A trip to England in 1873 was the beginning of the many Moody-Sankey campaigns in England, Ireland, Scotland, and especially in America. Engaged in itinerant mass urban professional organized evangelism from 1871 to 1899. Hundreds of thousands, if not millions of people, became Christians through the ministry of Moody's preaching and Sankey's singing. Founded Colportage Association in 1895 to provide inexpensive religious literature. In the midst of last evangelistic campaign in Kansas City he became ill and died a few days later.

MOORE, GEORGE FOOTE (1851-1931), American theologian and scholar, born at West Chester, Pennsylvania, educated at Yale University and Union Theological Seminary, New York and Tübingen University. Ordained to the Presbyterian ministry, pastor of the Presbyterian church at Bloomington, Ohio, and of the Putnam Presbyterian Church, Zanesville, Ohio, for several years; became Hitchcock professor of the Hebrew language and literature in Andover Theological Seminary (1883-1902). In 1902 professor of history of religion in Harvard University, and in 1904 Frothingham professor of history of religion at Harvard. In theology belongs to critical school. For some years edited the *Journal of the American Oriental Society.* President of the American Academy of Arts and Sciences (1921-1924). Besides writing articles for the *Encyclopaedia Biblia* wrote: *Commentary on Judges; The Book of Judges in Hebrew, Critical Edition of the Hebrew Text; The Literature of the Old Testament; History of Religions; Judaism in the Christian Era.*

MOOREHEAD, WILLIAM GALLOGLY (1836-1914), United Presbyterian minister and scholar, born at Rix Mills, Ohio, educated at Muskingum College, Allegheny Theological Seminary, and Xenia Theological Seminary. Ordained to the United Presbyterian ministry in 1862, served as a missionary of the American and Foreign Union in Italy (1862-1869). Pastor of First Church, Xenia, Ohio (1870-1875), Fourth Church in Allegheny (1875-1876), and Third United Presbyterian Church of Xenia (1878-1885). Became professor of New Testament literature and exegesis of Xenia Theological Seminary in 1873, and president of the seminary in 1899, occupying both positions until death in 1914. In 1908 chosen to represent the United Presbyterian body on the International Sunday School Committee. Writings include: *Studies in Mosaic Institutions, Outline Studies in Old Testament, Studies in the Gospels, Outline Studies in Acts to Ephesians, Outline Studies in Philippians to Hebrews, Outline Studies in the New Testament Catholic Epistles,* and *Outline Studies in the Book of Revelation.* An editor of the Scofield Reference Bible. A conservative and evangelical theological writer and teacher.

MOORHOUSE, HENRY (HARRY) (1840-1880), evangelist, born in Manchester, England. The first half of his life lived in wickedness. Converted when about twenty-one and immediately decided to become a preacher. Entered heartily into Christian service distributing tracts, speaking personally with individuals, and preaching in streets and market places. In spite of frail body labored incessantly for his Master until early death. Made four trips to America, on the first preached in D. L. Moody's church. Recommendation of intensive Bible study challenged Mr. Moody.

MORE, HANNAH (1745-1833), English religious writer and philanthropist, born in Stapleton, near Bristol, England, educated in the school in Bristol kept by older sisters. Began writing verse at a very early age, and soon was writing dramas. In 1762 completed *The Search After Happiness,* a pastoral drama. In 1773 or 1774 went to London, introduced to David Garrick, noted English actor. He encouraged her in her drama writing. When he died five years later (1779), she renounced the stage, retired to Cowslip Green near Bristol, and turned to writing religious literature. Her *Village Politics* and *Shepherd of Salisbury Plain* written during the French Revolution "helped to maintain the cause of order and true religion against Deism from France." *Coelebs in Search of a Wife* was her most famous book of fiction. Wrote a series of tracts known as the *Cheap Repository Tracts* in which she sought to counteract the influence of the French Revolution. Tracts reached a circulation of nearly two million, and laid the foundation for the Religious Tract Society. A few of her books on moral and religious subjects: *Slavery, The Religion of the Fashionable World, On Female Education, Practical Piety, Christian Morals, Character and Writings of St. Paul, Moral Sketches,* and *Spirit of Prayer*. In later years, under the influence of William Wilberforce and John Newton, and with four older sisters established Sunday schools for the poor children at Cheddar in the mining districts of the Mendip Hills. Also established friendly societies and other philanthropic organizations for the relief and education of adults.

MORE, SIR THOMAS (1478-1535), humanist and lord chancellor of England, born in London. Studied at Canterbury Hall (now Christ College), Oxford, came into close fellowship with the humanists, Grocyn, Linacre, Colet, and Erasmus. At father's solicitation studied law at New Inn and Lincoln's Inn; later became a top-ranking lawyer of England. For four or five years subjected himself to ascetic living, and considered joining the Franciscans. In 1503 gave up the thought of entering a monastery, and returning with ardor to his profession, entered the field of politics. Became a member of Parliament in 1504. Henry VIII sent him on several missions abroad. In 1507 married, in 1514 made privy councilor, in 1521 knighted. Supported Henry's defense of the Roman Catholic church, and always remained loyal to pope and to church. Henry had great confidence in Thomas, and in 1529 made him his lord chancellor, successor of the demoted Cardinal Wolsey. Before long, when More refused to obtain the divorce that Henry desired from Catharine, when he refused to recognize Henry as head of the Church of England, he felt obliged to resign as Chancellor. Resigned in 1532 under the ruse of ill health, withdrew from public notice. Fearing the influence More might have in the kingdom, the king had him arrested and committed to the Tower in 1534. He then tried and beheaded him for treason the following year. More's personal life had been one of honesty and uprightness. An educated and cultured man, well versed in Greek and Latin. Best known writing was *Utopia,* a Latin treatise of the ideal political state. Beatified by Leo XIII in 1886 and canonized in 1935. Friend of and influenced Erasmus.

MORGAN, GEORGE CAMPBELL (1863-1945), British Congregational minister, born at Tetbury, Gloucestershire, England, educated at the Cheltenham Douglas School. In 1882 taught in the Islington Wesleyan day schools in Birmingham; from 1883 to 1886 master in the Jewish Collegiate School in Birmingham; from 1886 to 1888 mission preacher. Ordained to the ministry in the Congregational Church; held pastorates at Stone in Staffordshire, Rugeley in Birmingham, and New Court, Tollington Park in London, between the years 1889 and 1901. Worked with Moody and Sankey in evangelistic tour of Great Britain in 1883. Visited Northfield, Massachusetts in 1896. These contacts with D. L. Moody opened the way for next three years of service in the United States. From 1901 to 1904 a Northfield Bible Conference lecturer. In 1904 back in England, as pastor of the Westminster Congregational Chapel, Buckingham Gate, London, a dying church. With well-planned organization, Bible-centered preaching and teaching, meaningful week-day and Sunday activities and services, and excellent cooperation of people, in 1917 left Westminster Chapel one of England's most active and best known churches. Soon after arrival at Westminster established Mundesley Bible Conference, a "British Northfield" which drew to its annual conferences eminent ministers and Christian workers from the various denominations and from several countries. Mundesley became a vital part of Westminster Chapel. During these years Morgan made many, almost annual trips to America. In 1916 resigned from Westminster Chapel to do itinerant preaching. Between 1919 and 1932 traveled widely in evangelistic and preaching tours in the United States and Canada. For a year (1927-1928) served on the faculty of the Bible Institute of Los Angeles, and for a year (1930-1931) was Bible lecturer at Gordon College of Theology and Missions, Boston. Between 1929 and 1932 he was pastor of the Tabernacle Presbyterian Church in Philadelphia, Pennsylvania. In 1935, began second pastoral period at Westminster Chapel, London, resigning from that position in 1943. Work lives on today in a real way in his many writings. Edited the *Westminster Bible Record,* and the *Westminster Pulpit,* authored a large number of Bible commentaries, sermons, and other books on theology. A complete list shows sixty books and a dozen booklets.

MORISON, JAMES (1816-1893), Scottish minister of the United Secession church and founder of the Evangelical Union, born at Bathgate, Linlithgowshire, Scotland, studied at Divinity Hall of the United Secession church at the University of Edinburgh. Licensed as a probationer in 1839, appointed to an agricultural parish at Cabrach, Banffshire. Preaching helped bring about a widespread revival. Service sought in many parts in the north of Scotland. A tract, *The Question, "What Must I Do to Be Saved?" Answered,* in which he advocated the anti-Calvinistic doctrine of universal atonement brought reproof from the church. Upon promise to withdraw the tract from circulation, ordained in 1840 as pastor of Clerks Lane Secession Church, Kilmarnock. Continued, however, to preach universal atonement, suspended from the ministry, and eventually expelled from the United Secession church. In 1843 he, his father and two other ministers founded the Evangelical Union, which in 1896 merged with the Congregational Union of Scotland. At same time instituted a theological academy of which he was principal and professor of New Testament exegesis for fifty years (1843-1893). In 1851 became pastor of North Dundas Street Evangelical Union Church, Glasgow, and remained in this pastorate until retirement from active pastoral duties in 1884. Among extensive writings were *The Nature of the Atonement, The Extent of the Atonement, Vindication of the Universality of the Atonement, Saving Faith, St. Paul's Teaching on Sanctification,* and commentaries on Matthew and Mark.

MORRIS, SAMUEL (c. 1700-c. 1770). Born in Hanover County, Virginia, became a Presbyterian and held house meetings where he read religious literature to his neighbors which included such things as Luther's *Commentary on Galatians*. Crowds grew so much that he had to build log "reading houses," and revival came about 1740. May be called the father of Virginian Presbyterianism. Converts were organized into churches and the Presbytery of Hanover by Samuel Davies.

MORRISON, CHARLES CLAYTON (1874-1966). Born Harrison, Ohio. Educated at Drake University. Pastor in Iowa and Illinois from 1892 to 1908. Founder and editor from 1908 to 1947 of the liberally oriented *Christian Century*. Edited *Pulpit* from 1929 to 1956 and *Christendom* from 1935 to 1941. Minister of the Disciples of Christ church.

MORRISON, ROBERT (1782-1834), first Protestant missionary to China, born in Morpeth, Northumbria, England of Scottish father and English mother. In childhood an industrious student, as a man a learned scholar. In preparation for life work gave special attention to the study of theology, medicine, astronomy, and the Chinese language, the latter learned from a Chinese scholar who was living in London, and from some Chinese manuscripts in the British museum. In 1807 the London Missionary Society ordained and sent Morrison to Canton, China, first Protestant missionary to that land. The East India Company refused him passage; he went to Canton by way of New York. In China lived in a cellar and was rarely seen in public. He made such good progress in his mastery of the language that in 1809 he was employed by the British East India Company as an interpreter, a position held for the next twenty-five years. Worked assiduously for the mission, but labors were confined largely to literary activities, writing a Chinese grammar, preparing the standard Anglo-Chinese dictionary and encyclopedia, writing tracts and books, preparing a hymn book, translating morning and evening prayers from the Book of Common Prayer, and translating the entire Bible by 1823. Work was that of foundation laying, a very necessary part of the work of introducing missions in China. Number of converts as a result of twenty-seven years of labor perhaps did not exceed three or four, the first of which was not until after he had been seven years in China. Activities other than serving as interpreter for the East India Company, and translating and writing for the mission, consisted in treating the sick in his dispensary, and the founding of an Anglo-Chinese school at Malacca to train missionaries for the Far East. Made a trip to England in 1824, at which time he was made a fellow of the Royal Society. Promoted the cause of missions in China. In 1826 returned to China. As interpreter for the East India Company forced to become negotiator in the Anglo-Chinese War that had broken out about that time.

MOSHEIM (mōs'hīm), **JOHANN LORENZ VON** (1694-1755), church historian and theologian, born at Lübeck, Germany. Educated at the Gymnasium of Lübeck, and at the University of Kiel, where ordained. Also served as professor of logic and metaphysics, and as assistant to the pastor. In 1723 accepted a call as professor of philosophy and preacher at Helmstädt, Brunswick, where he remained for twenty-two years. In 1747 called to the newly organized University of Göttingen as professor and chancellor, where he remained until death eight years later. Though never a pastor, he became distinguished as an ardent and eloquent preacher. The most learned theologian in the Lutheran church of his day as well as one of the foremost German authors and scholars of his age. As theologian a latitudinarian, occupied an intermediate position between the extremes of pietism and deism. Opposed dogmatism of confessional orthodoxy on the one hand and extreme rationalism on the other. Wrote commentaries on the New Testament, dogmatics, polemics, church polity, and homiletics. Great work is the *Institutiones Historiae Ecclesiasticae*. His church history is noted for its erudition, fullness, accuracy, and objectivity.

MOTON, ROBERT RUSSA (1867-1940), Black American educator, born in Amelia County, Virginia, educated at Hampton Institute. Working way through school learned the principles of farming and other types of industry which aided him in future educational work. Studied law but decided that he could do more good for his people by following the teaching rather than the legal profession. After graduating from Hampton became a teacher at the Institute for twenty-five years. In 1915 elected to succeed Booker T. Washington as president of Tuskegee Normal and Industrial Institute, where he remained until his retirement in 1935. In addition to position as educator, Chairman of the United States Commission on Education in Haiti; a member of the National Advisory Commission on Education in Liberia. In 1930 awarded the Harmon Award on Race Relation, and in 1932 the Spingarn Medal. Robert Russa Moton developed a pride of both race and country. Wrote *What the Negro Thinks, Racial Good Will,* and an autobiography, *Finding a Way Out*.

MOTT, JOHN RALEIGH (1865-1955), Methodist layman, leader in the Y.M.C.A., founder of the Christian Student Movement, born at Livingston Manor, New York. A student at Upper Iowa University, but graduated from Cornell University in 1888. During college days active in Y.M.C.A. work. In 1888 chosen Student Secretary for the National Committee for the Association until 1915 when until 1931 he was general secretary. In that day the Y.M.C.A. was strongly evangelistic and Mr. Mott was zealous soul-winner. His influence upon college men was impelling. About same time made chairman of the newly formed Student Volunteer Movement. This brought him into close relations with the Christian missionary program. From 1895 to 1920 was General Secretary of the World's Student Christian Federation, an organization attributed to Mott's genius and foresight and its chairman from 1920 to 1928. In 1898 made secretary of the Foreign Department of the International Young Men's Christian Association, at the same time Chairman of the American Council of the Y.M.C.A. In 1901 became associate general secretary of the International Committee, in 1910 was Chairman of the World's Missionary Conference at Edinburgh and from 1928 to 1946 was Chairman of the International Missionary Council and in 1948 one of the presidents of the World Council of Churches. These positions made him the most distinctive international figure in the entire church. Most efficient in promoting foreign missionary enthusiasm among young people. Enjoyed a commanding position among the leaders of modern evangelization. Traveled in the interest of the Student Christian Movement in practically every land on the earth, and lectured before students and Christian workers of every nationality. Organized, lectured before, and presided at the greatest church and missionary gatherings of the world. Doubtful whether there has been in America preacher or layman who has wielded a wider influence in the religious circles of the world. Considered by many as the leading Christian statesman of the world. During Woodrow Wilson's presidency Mott was a leading counselor on international affairs. Served on US governmental missions to Mexico and Russia. Offered the presidency of Princeton University as Wilson's successor, but refused. Received more than a dozen decorations from foreign governments, as well as the Distinguished Service Medal of the United States. Co-recipient of Nobel Peace prize in 1946. Among the several books written in his busy life note the following: *The Evangelization of the World in this Generation, The Pastor and Modern Missions, The Future Leadership of the Church,* and *The Larger Evangelism*.

MOULE (moul), **HANDLEY CARR GLYN** (1841-1920), Bishop of Durham, born at Fordington, Dorset, England, educated at Trinity College, Cambridge, where he was fellow from 1865 to 1881. Assistant master at Marlborough College (1865-1867), ordained in 1867, assistant curate for his father at Fordington, Dorset (1867-1873), curate for him (1877-1880), dean of Trinity College (1873-1877), first principal of Ridley Hall, Cambridge (1881-1899), and Norrisian professor of divinity at Cambridge (1899-1901). In 1901 consecrated Bishop of Durham. Nine times select preacher at Cambridge and once at Oxford, honorary chaplain to the queen (1898-1901). In theology Moule was attached to the English Reformation, a believer in the authority of the Scriptures, and in later years linked with the Keswick Movement. Often spoke at Keswick and church congresses. Throughout his ministry an evangelical churchman. Writings were spiritual and scholarly. Some of his works: *Thoughts on Union with Christ, Veni Crea-*

tor, Christus Consolator, Outlines of Christian Doctrine, Life in Christ and for Christ, Charles Simeon, Philippian Studies, Ephesian Studies, Colossian Studies, and *Second Epistle to Timothy*.

MOULTON, JAMES HOPE (1863-1917), Methodist theologian; Greek and Iranian scholar, born at Richmond, Surrey, England, son of William Fiddian Moulton, studied at the Leys School and at King's College, Cambridge. Entered the ministry in 1886; assisted father at the Leys School (1886-1902), lecturing on classics at the same time at Girton and Newnham colleges; tutor at Wesleyan College, Didsbury (1902-1917); in addition Greenwood professor of Hellenistic Greek and Indo-European philology at Manchester University (1908-1917). Died from exposure at sea while returning from a missionary tour to India after his ship had been torpedoed and sunk. Noted for contribution to the study of the Greek Koine. Main writings: *An Introduction to the Study of New Testament Greek, The Science of Language and the Study of the New Testament, Grammar of the New Testament Greek* (Vol. 1), *Early Religious Poetry of Persia, Early Zorastrianism, Religions and Religion, The Treasure of the Magi,* and *British and German Scholarship*. Collaborated with George Milligan in compiling parts one and two of *Vocabulary of the Greek Testament*.

MOULTON, RICHARD GREEN (1849-1924), Anglo-American educator and literary critic, born at Preston, England, brother of William Fiddian Moulton. Studied at the University of London, Christ College, Cambridge, and University of Pennsylvania. Cambridge University extension lecturer in literature (1874-1890), and professor of literature in English at the newly founded University of Chicago (1892-1919), in 1919 retired and returned to England; professor emeritus (1920-1924). He specialized in Shakespearean and biblical literature. Chief biblical writings: *The Literary Study of the Bible, A Short Introduction to the Literature of the Bible, The Whole Bible at a Single View,* and *The Modern Reader's Bible*.

MOULTON, WILLIAM FIDDIAN (1835-1898), Bible scholar, born at Leek, England, received elementary education in Methodist schools, entered Wesley College, Sheffield, and later London University. For a while master in a private school in Davonport. After receiving B.A. and M.A. degrees from London, from 1854 to 1858 master of mathematics at Queen's College, Taunton. In 1858 entered the Wesleyan ministry; but in judgment of conference was better fitted for teaching than for preaching. Tutor at Richmond College, Surrey from 1858 to 1874. In 1872 chosen a member of the Legal Hundred of the Wesleyan connection, a rare occurrence for a man so young. In 1874 called to be the founder and headmaster of the Leys School, Cambridge, which he developed into a great school, remaining there till death thirty years later. In 1890 elected president of the Wesleyan Conference. From 1870 to 1881 a member of the New Testament Revision Company, the youngest member of the committee. Made an excellent translation of Winer's *Grammar of New Testament Greek*. Wrote *A History of the English Bible,* a commentary on Hebrews in C. J. Ellicott's *New Testament Commentary for English Readers,* and with A. S. Gedden compiled *A Concordance to the New Testament Greek*. As a Greek scholar among the foremost of his day and at the same time was a learned Hebraist, an able mathematician, and a devoted student of English literature. His son James Hope Moulton (1863-1917) also did important work in the same field, being collaborator with G. Milligan in producing the *Vocabulary of the Greek Testament*.

MOUNTAIN, JACOB (1749-1825), first Anglican bishop of Quebec. Born Thwaite Hall, Norfolk, England. Educated at Caius College. Cambridge. Ordained in 1780 and served churches in England until from 1793 to 1825 he served as the first Anglican bishop of Quebec over Upper (Ontario) and Lower (Quebec) Canada. His claim to exclusive use of land reserved for the clergy by the state for the Anglican church led to controversy with the Roman Catholics, Methodists, and other Protestant groups.

MOZART (mō'tsärt), **JOHANN CHRYSOSTOM WOLFGANG** (1756-1791), Austrian musician and composer, born in a Roman Catholic home in Salzburg, Austria. Since Johann early showed signs of musical ability, his father, himself a musician, decided to devote all his time and means to the education of his son. After teaching him violin, organ, and singing, the father began a tour of Europe with Johann, age six, and his sister, five years older, going from court to court and from city to city, giving concerts. During this time young Mozart wrote sonatas, a symphony, an oratorio, and an opera. While they were in Italy the pope decorated the lad with the Order of the Golden Spur, and at Bologna he was elected a member of the Philharmonic Society. Europe was extravagant with its praises for his prodigious playing, but gave little recognition to his compositions. Consequently later life was not filled with the glory and acclaim that filled his younger years. In 1778 went to Paris, but was disappointed in the response he received. In 1782 married Constance, a grandniece of the composer Weber, making Vienna home thereafter. Mozart met and learned many things from Haydn, who praised the young composer. Mozart was a poor businessman, again and again cheated out of an income that should have been his. In spite of poverty, ill health, abuse, melancholy, and depression, continued to compose. Died at the age of thirty-five, buried in an unmarked grave in a pauper's cemetery. Composed over six hundred works, many of which were not published during his lifetime. Wrote music for the church, the opera, and the concert. Wrote masses, cantatas, operas, symphonies, marches, dances, serenades, concertos, quartets, and choral and chamber works. Among chief works were his opera, *Don Giovanni,* and his unfinished religious work *Requiem*. In character kindhearted, guileless, cheerful, and void of envy.

MOZLEY, JAMES BOWLING (1813-1878), Church of England theologian and Tractarian, born at Gainsborough, Lincolnshire, England, studied at Oriel College, Oxford, in 1840 elected fellow at Magdalen College, Oxford, where he resided until 1856, when he accepted the living of Old Shoreham, Sussex. Through Mr. Gladstone made canon of Worcester in 1869, and in 1871 regius professor of divinity at Oxford, which positions he held until death. Appointed Bampton lecturer in 1865 and select university preacher in 1869. In student days at Oxford came under influence of Newman, Pusey, Keble, and Froude, and took an active part in the Tractarian movement. Yet when Newman entered the Roman Catholic church, Mozley remained a high churchman in the Anglican church. He could not agree fully with the High Church party, neither could he ally himself with the evangelicals. For ten years or more a prominent contributor to *The Critic* and *The Christian Remembrancer,* organs of the High Church party, writing on critical, dogmatic, and apologetic subjects. Published sermons show profound thought and depth, great candor, and clear style. Among works: *A Treatise on the Augustinian Doctrine of Predestination, The Primitive Doctrine of Baptismal Regeneration, A Review of the Baptismal Controversy, Eight Lectures on Miracles* (Bampton lectures), *Ruling Ideas in Early Ages and Their Relation to the Old Testament Faith, Essays Historical and Theological,* and other volumes on sermons and lectures.

MÜHLENBERG (mü'lĕn bĕrk), **HENRY MELCHIOR** (1711-1787), patriarch of the Lutheran Church in America, born at Eimbeck, Hanover, Prussia. Received theological training at Göttingen and Halle. While at Halle employed as a teacher in Francke's Orphan Home. Ordained in 1739 and served as pastor of Grosshennersdorf, Lusatia (1739-1741). Came to America in 1742 at the recommendation of Francke to organize and pastor the Lutheran church. A pleasant, cordial, tactful man, a good organizer and a good linguist, able to speak English, Dutch, and Latin in addition to native German. Mühlenberg came with the motto: "The Church must be planted." Ministered in Philadelphia area from 1742 to 1779. In 1748 organized the second Lutheran synod in America, known as the Evangelical Lutheran Ministerium of Pennsylvania and Adjacent States. In 1762 prepared a constitution for Philadelphia congregation by which all officers were chosen by the congregation, giving the American Lutheran church a semi-congregational form of government. In 1774-1775 spent a few months in Georgia reestablishing Lutheran unity and work there. Pietistic training had a wholesome effect on the Lutheran church under his ministry. Whitefield preached in his church in 1763. By time of death the Lutheran church had been well established in America. Had three notable sons who also were Lutheran clergymen: John Peter Gabriel Mühlenberg (1746-1807) who became Major-General of the United States Army in the Revolutionary War; Frederick August Conrad Mühlenberg (1750-1801), who was repeatedly chosen to Congress, serving twice as Speaker of the House; and Gotthilf Henry Ernst Mühlenberg (1753-1815), who served the Holy Trinity Church at Lancaster, Pennsylvania for thirty-five years.

MÜHLENBERG, WILLIAM AUGUST (1796-1877), Protestant Episcopal clergyman, poet, philanthropist, born in Philadelphia, Pennsylvania, great-grandson of Henry Melchior Mühlenberg. Baptized into the Lutheran church. As a boy made choice of the Protestant Episcopal church. Graduated from the University of Pennsylvania in 1814, at once entered theological studies under Bishop William White whose assistant he became in Christ Church. In 1820 ordained priest, and became rector of St. James, Lancaster, Pennsylvania until 1858. Exhibited much interest in public education in his town, also wrote many hymns. In 1826 became rector of St. George's, Flushing, Long Island, New York. Entered upon the pastorate of the Free Church of the Holy Communion, New York, 1846. Pastor, organizer and superintendent from 1857 to 1877. From this time on most active in philanthropic work along with pastoral activities. Founded St. Luke's Hospital, New York. During ministry in New York headed a group of ministers who presented the *Mühlenberg Memorial* which urged a "broader and more comprehensive ecclesiastical system" with more "freedom in opinion, discipline, and worship" in the church.

MÜLLER, GEORGE (1805-1898), evangelist and philanthropist in England, born at Kroppenstadt, near Magdeburg, Germany. Attended Halle and other schools, and received a fairly good education, but not in religion or ethics. Had been confirmed and even took communion, but was not a Christian. Living deep in sin, he had spent a time in jail in 1821 to 1822. In 1825 visited a Moravian mission and was soundly converted. Returned to Halle University to prepare for definite Christian work. In 1826 began to preach. In 1829 at the invitation of the Society for the Propagation of the Gospel went to England to do mission work among the Jews. In 1830 became pastor of Ebenezer Chapel at Teignmouth, Derbyshire, England, in connection with the Plymouth Brethren. Believing that through faith and prayer God would supply temporal as well as spiritual needs, refused a fixed salary and abolished pew rents. Wanting to help the poor children of England, in 1832 moved to Bristol where he made his home the rest of his life. Organized in 1834 the *Scriptural Knowledge Institution for Home and Abroad,* which was to be distinctly a faith venture. In 1836 in a house on Wilson Street opened an orphanage on a strict faith basis with twenty-six orphan girls. Through prayer and faith, but with no money of his own, other houses, more workers, and an increasing number of children came to the orphanage. Through prayer and with strong faith, but no money in hand, telling no one but God of the need for funds, the project went forward. A home was built in the country at Ashley Down, and in 1849 over 100 children were moved into the two buildings erected there. By 1866 "house number three" was built and "house number four" was started to accommodate one thousand orphans. By 1875 in the orphanage at Ashley Down over two thousand children were cared for, given a happy home, and instructed in the Christian life. At this time, when Müller was seventy years old, he and his wife started on an evangelistic tour which lasted nearly seventeen years. It took him to Europe, America, Asia, and Australia. They visited forty-two countries, traveled over two hundred thousand miles, and preached to three million hearers. Though having handled nearly eight million dollars sent in for the work when George Müller fell asleep at the age of ninety-three, his worldly possessions were valued at about $800. More than ten thousand orphans had been cared for in the orphanage homes. Wrote *The Narration of Some of the Lord's Dealings with George Müller,* (five volumes).

MULLER, JULIUS (1801-1878), German theologian, born at Brieg, Silesia, Prussia, studied law and theology at Breslau,, Göttingen, and Berlin. Decided to give his whole attention to theology. Ordained in 1825 and served for a few years as pastor at Schönbrunn and Rosen, and then in 1831 became preacher and lecturer on practical theology and pedagogics at Göttingen University and professor of theology in 1834. From 1835 to 1839 professor of dogmatics at Marburg University. Opposed the rationalistic tendencies of the day and took stand on the immutable basis of the Bible as a liberal evangelical. From 1839 to the end of life professor of theology at Halle. During the latter half of his life an advocate of the Prussian Union, as established by the government in 1817. Wrote a book on *The Evangelical Union*. Chief writing, however, was *Die Christliche Lehre von der Sünde* (The Christian Doctrine of Sin), one of the most exhaustive treatments of the subject in all theology.

MULLINS, EDGAR YOUNG (1860-1928), Baptist clergyman and theologian, born in Franklin County, Mississippi. At the age of eight moved with his parents to Texas. Received higher education at the Agricultural and Mechanical College of Texas, the Southern Baptist Theological Seminary, Louisville, Kentucky, and Johns Hopkins University, Baltimore, Maryland. Ordained to the Baptist ministry in 1885, pastor at Harrodsburg, Kentucky (1885-1888), of the Lee Street Baptist Church, Baltimore (1888-1895), and First Church, Newton, Massachusetts (1896-1899). From 1899 until 1928 president and professor of theology of the Southern Baptist Theological Seminary. In theology a moderate Calvinist, and a careful Bible student, holding a conservative, evangelical position. President of the Southern Baptist Convention from 1921 to 1924, of the Baptist World Alliance from 1923 to 1928. Wrote *Why Is Christianity True?; The Axioms of Religion: A New Interpretation of the Baptist Faith; The Christian Religion in Its Doctrinal Expression, Christianity at the Crossroads; Freedom and Authority in Religion;* and *The Life in Christ*. The Foundation on Preaching was established at the Southern Baptist Theological Seminary, Louisville, Kentucky, with a gift from Dr. and Mrs. Edgar Young Mullins.

MUNDELEIN (mŭn'dĕ līn), **GEORGE WILLIAM** (1872-1939), American cardinal of the Roman Catholic church, born in New York City, graduated from Manhattan College, New York, studied for the priesthood at the Urban College of the Propaganda in Rome. Ordained priest in 1895. He was consecrated Auxiliary Bishop of Brooklyn in 1909, and Archbishop of Chicago in 1915, which by the time of his death had become an archdiocese of perhaps one million, four hundred thousand communicants. The builder of over six hundred church edifices, and founder of the Seminary of St. Mary of the Lake at Area, Illinois (1921), which was renamed Mundelein in his honor in 1925. Also established Mundelein College for women in Chicago. Made cardinal by Pope Pius XI in 1924. He was the outstanding figure of the Eucharistic Congress in Chicago in 1926. Two years later presented to Pope Pius XI the sum of one and a half million dollars, which money was used to buy ground near the Vatican for the new University of Propaganda Fide. Cardinal Mundelein was famous also for charities. Established a series of homes for working girls, built up the Associated Catholic Charities of Chicago, founded the Mission of the Holy Ghost for the unemployed, and founded the Catholic Big Brother Movement and the Catholic Youth Organization in his archdiocese. Died at Mundelein, Illinois.

MÜNZER (mün'tsẽr), **THOMAS** (c. 1490-1525), German Anabaptist, born at Stolberg in the Harz Mountains, studied theology at Leipzig, embraced doctrines of the Reformation and preached them in the chief church at Zwickau, but carried them to such excess that he was deposed. Appeared at Wittenberg at the time that Luther was at the Wartburg (1521-1522), and joined with Carlstadt in the revolutionary turmoil that the latter was inciting. Luther's sudden appearance put a stop to their revolutionary behavior. Between 1523 and 1525 Münzer was pastor for a short time at each of the following places: Altstadt, Muhlhausen in Thuringia, Nürnberg, and Basel. At enmity with the whole order of existing society, imagined himself the divinely inspired prophet of a new dispensation, of a sort of communistic millennium in which there should be no priests, no princes, no nobles, and no private property, but complete democratic equality. Led in riotous attacks on monasteries and preached the ruthless killing of all the ungodly. He helped to inspire the peasants to revolt in what is known as the Peasants' War (1524-1525). Münzer and his revolutionaries called themselves Anabaptists and brought the name Anabaptist into ill repute. Beheaded in the course of the Peasants' War.

MURILLO (mōō rē'lyō), **BARTOLOME ESTEBAN** (1617-1682), Spanish painter of Andalusian school, born of poor parents in Seville, Spain, studied at Madrid. In the early days of poverty painted small madonnas by the dozen for sale to the churches in Mexico and Peru. Most of themes were religious, but in earlier life did paint some pictures of ragged street children, gypsies, and rural life. In 1645 painted a series of pictures for the Franciscan monastery in Seville. In 1648 married a lady of wealth and rank; their home became a meeting place for artists. In 1660 he founded and became president of the Academy of Arts at Seville. Murillo painted religious pictures in accordance with the dictates of the church and the Inquisition. Noted for several versions in painting of *The Immaculate Conception*. Some of his more famous paintings were *St. Anthony of Padua, Moses Striking the Rock, Return of the Prodigal, Abraham Receiving the Three Angels, The Miracle of the Loaves and Fishes, St. Peter Released from Prison, The Flight into Egypt*, and *St. Elizabeth*. While painting an altar piece for the church of the Capuchins at Cadiz, he fell from a scaffold, and died as a result of the injuries.

MURRAY, ANDREW (1828-1917), Dutch Reformed minister in South Africa, born at Graaff-Reinet, South Africa. He was sent to Aberdeen to study. For seven years lived with uncle. In 1845 received masters' degree from Aberdeen University. Following this went to Utrecht University to pursue theological education. While there helped to form a Students' Missionary Society. In 1828 ordained. Soon after returned to South Africa, and Andrew was appointed to a charge in Bloemfontein in the Orange River Sovereignty, where he labored for eleven years. Also made trips into the Transvaal to minister to several thousand immigrants who had no pastoral care. In the midst of this ministry spent over a year in England while convalescing from a severe attack of fever, at the same time represented his people in the Privy Council of the British Parliament seeking to help solve some of the existent problems and difficulties. During stay in England met and married Miss Rutherford of Capetown. In 1860 accepted a call to Worcester, an important inland town of Cape Colony. This was the time of the great revival in America and Ireland. It reached his country making a great impact on his church. During pastorate at Worcester, Mr. Murray began the writing of his many devotional books. Some of the books written at this time: *The Children for Christ, Abide in Christ,* and *Why Do You Not Believe?* After four years at Worcester, in 1864 took up a pastorate in Capetown where he labored for seven years (1864-1871). During this time he was moderator of his church. Made an official visit to England, started a branch of the Y.M.C.A. in Capetown, and did some writing besides the carrying on of his heavy pastoral duties. In 1871 accepted a call to a Huguenot community at Wellington, about forty-five miles from Capetown, where he labored until 1906. Mr. Murray was also deeply interested in the social and educational betterment of his people. In 1874 founded the Huguenot Seminary at Wellington after the pattern of Mary Lyon's Mount Holyoke Seminary. Also established at Wellington a missionary training school for missionaries to the Kaffirs and other tribes. Mr. Murray's time was in much demand among the churches of Cape Colony, Orange Free State, Transvaal, and Natal. At his insistence his Church consented to permit him to use half of his time in itinerant evangelism. He laid much emphasis on the deepening of the spiritual life of Christians, which brought an abundant fruitage, both through speaking and through books. *Like Christ, With Christ in the School of Prayer, Holy in Christ; and the Spirit of Christ* were written during his ministry at Wellington. Introduced the Keswick spirit into South Africa, and from 1889 until death in 1917 was the father of South African Keswick. Moderator of his Synod three times. Following Mrs. Murray's death in 1906 he resigned his pastorate at Wellington, and devoted his last twelve years to Keswick, Northfield, and other conventions and evangelistic meetings in the United States, Canada, England, Ireland, Scotland, Holland, and South Africa.

MURRAY, JOHN (1741-1815), founder of the Universalist denomination in America, born at Alton, Hampshire, England; at eleven moved with his parents to Cork, Ireland. About 1760 became a Calvinistic Methodist, joining Whitefield's congregation. Then somewhat later, coming under the influence of James Relly, a Universalist minister, and embracing the Universalist doctrine, excommunicated from the Methodist church. Came to America in 1770 and began preaching the Universalist doctrine from New England to Virginia. In 1774 he settled at Gloucester, Massachusetts and established a congregation there. In 1775 appointed chaplain of a Rhode Island brigade encamped near Boston. Ill health compelled him to leave the army; he returned to Gloucester, where he settled with a society of the Universalists. Ten years later, in 1785, he was largely responsible for the founding of the Independent Christian Universalists at Oxford, Massachusetts. In 1793 became pastor of a society of Universalists in Boston, where he remained until death, serving as their pastor, however, only until 1809 when paralysis compelled him to give up preaching. A man of great courage and eloquence, and in the defense of his peculiar views suffered much abuse. He was also a hymn writer and a compiler of hymnals.

MURRAY, JOHN COURTNEY (1904-1967), Roman Catholic theologian. Born New York City. Educated at Boston College, Woodstock Seminary, and the Gregorian University, Rome. Professor at Ateneo University in Manila from 1927 to 1930. Professor of theology at Woodstock Seminary from 1937 to 1967. Edited *Theological Studies* from 1941 to 1967. Held that religious authority in the state was indirect and direct in the church. Helped develop Vatican II decree on religious freedom.

MURTON, JOHN (?-1625), English separatist preacher, went to John Smyth's separatist congregation and fled with it to Amsterdam about 1607. When Smyth joined the Mennonites, Murton and Thomas Helwys about 1611 came back to England with part of the congregation and formed the first Arminian and affusionist Baptist congregation in England.

MYCONIUS (mü kō'nē o͞os), **FRIEDRICH** (1491-1546), German Lutheran Reformer, born at Lichtenfels in Thuringia, studied at the Latin school in Annaberg. In 1510 entered the Franciscan Order and studied the works of Peter Lombard, Alexander of Hales, Bonaventura, Gabriel Biel, and Augustine. Found no satisfaction in the scholastic theology, but was deeply impressed with Augustine. In 1516 ordained priest, and soon became known as a persuasive preacher; but in 1517 became sympathetic with Martin Luther's attack on Indulgences. In 1524 left his order and married. Soon joined wholeheartedly with Luther and Melanchthon in the Reformation movement, especially in Thuringia, remaining a devoted and positive factor in the Reformation. Went to Gotha and reformed the schools of the city and awakened the interest of the citizens in them. Became an influential reform preacher in Gotha and other cities. Took part in several important Lutheran conferences, including those at Marburg in 1529, Wittenberg in 1536, Schmalkald in 1537, and Hagenau in 1540. In 1538 accompanied the embassy to England to seek to win Henry VIII for the Augsburg Confession. Main writing: *Historia Reformationis*.

MYCONIUS, OSWALD (real name **OSWALD GEISHAUSLER**) (1488-1552), Swiss reformer, born at Lucerne, Switzerland, a student and a teacher at Basel, a friend of Erasmus, Zwingli, and Jud. Returned to Lucerne for a time, but his preaching of the evangelical doctrine in his native city resulted in his being driven from home as a "Lutheran heretic." From 1516 to 1531 taught ancient languages in a school in Zurich at which time threw strong support to Zwingli and the Reformation. Following the death of Zwingli he moved to Basel and became pastor of the Church of St. Alban; then a few months later upon the death of Oecolampadius, appointed successor at Basel. Latter position held until death twenty years later. During this time also professor of New Testament exegesis at the University of Basel. Under the leadership of Myconius the First Basel Confession of Faith in twelve articles was completed in 1532. Following the life and work of Zwingli, he was to the church at Basel what Bullinger was to the church at Zurich. Less a partisan and more a mediator and unionist than was true of many of the Reformers. Though a strong supporter of Zwingli, he was charged with pro-Lutheranism. Among his chief contributions were the reform of the Swiss schools, and a biography of Zwingli.

MYNSTER (mĭn'stẽr), **JAKOB PIER** (1775-1854), conservative Danish bishop and theologian, born at Copenhagen, Denmark, studied theology at the University of Copenhagen. In 1802 became pastor at Spjellerup on the island of Zealand. In early ministry profoundly influenced by Kant and showed strong leanings toward pantheism. Before thirty years of age he had a heartwarming and tranforming experience, following which his life was a positive witness for evangelical Christianity. In 1811 became chaplain of the Church of Our Lady in Copenhagen. Gathered large congregations and won fame as a preacher. For several years teacher of psychology in the theological seminary in Copenhagen, in 1826 court preacher. In 1834 Bishop of Zealand, the highest ecclesiastical office of Denmark, holding office to the end of his life. During incumbency of the bishopric ardently opposed N. F. S. Grundtvig's efforts toward religious liberalism in the Danish Lutheran church. Kierkegaard, once his student, also was at variance with his former teacher. Grundtvig succeeded in preventing the introduction of a revised ritual proposed by Mynster, also gained more and more adherents to his liberal views. Mynster gradually gave up struggle against liberalism and turned attention more to literary pursuits. Published numerous collections of sermons, *Thoughts on Christian Dogmas,* and an autobiography. One of the men who helped bring the Church of Denmark out of nationalism.

N

NAPOLEON I, BONAPARTE (1769-1821), Emperor of France (1804-1814). Born at Ajaccio, Corsica, studied at the military schools of Brienne le Chateau and Paris. Commissioned second lieutenant in 1785, gradually promoted until in 1795 made commander of the Army of the Interior. Through many campaigns and conquests in Europe gained wide influence and power. Extended the boundaries of France and reorganized the financial, educational, legal and governmental system on a grand scale. Secured the cession of Louisiana from Spain in 1800, but sold it to the United States in 1803. In 1804 with the consent of the French people terminated the republic, and had himself crowned emperor at Paris. In 1806 dissolved the Holy Roman Empire, and became virtual master of the continent; but lost the supremacy of the seas to England in defeat by Nelson at Cape Trafalgar in 1805. Made his brothers and other relatives kings of various states of Europe, and continued campaigns of conquest until finally defeated by Wellington at Waterloo, 1815. Surrendered to the British, and sent to St. Helena, where he died in 1821. Remains were removed to the Hotel des Invalides, Paris in 1840. Though a nominal Roman Catholic, he was wise enough to see that it was to his distinct advantage to recognize the church and to use it for his political purposes. Seeking to restore a certain liaison between state and chuch effected the Concordat of 1801 with the papacy. Had bishops named by the state but consecrated by the pope. The clergy was paid by the state. In all his measures, however, careful to guard the supremacy of the civil power and himself as its head. The church would thus be ruled by the state. The final result was a complete break between Napoleon and the pope, Pius VII. The pope then excommunicated the emperor and the emperor in turn imprisoned the pope. After Napoleon's fall in 1814, the pope returned to Rome amid great popular acclaim. He possessed undoubted military genius and almost equally great organizing and administrative ability.

NATION, CARY AMELIA (MOORE) (1846-1911). Born Garrard County, Kentucky. Unhappy marriage to drunkard Dr. Charles Gloyd in 1867. Taught school after his death until she married David Nation in 1877. Ran hotels in Columbia and Richmond, Texas. Joined Prohibition Party in 1908. Kansas in 1880 passed a constitutional amendment and enforcing act. In 1899 Cary, now living in Kansas, wrecked all the saloons in Medicine Lodge. In 1901 began to use a hatchet to expedite the wrecking in Wichita and Topeka. Went on similar destructive trail in Iowa and Illinois. Lectured on prohibition in England. Helped the prohibition cause in the United States.

NEAL, DANIEL (1678-1743), historian of the Puritans, born in London; educated as a dissenting minister at Merchant Taylor's School, London; Rev. Thomas Rowe's academy, Little Britain; at the universities of Utrecht and Leiden. Ordained in 1706 and became assistant pastor of independent congregation on Aldersgate Street, London; full pastor from 1706 to 1743. Recognized as one of best Puritan preachers of his day. Chief writings, *History of New England* and *History of the Puritans,* the latter somewhat biased, but of historic value.

NEALE, JOHN MASON (1818-1866), Anglican ecclesiastical historian and hymnologist, born in London, educated at Trinity College, Cambridge, ordained deacon in 1841 and priest in 1842. After a very short pastorate in Crawley, Sussex, health failed, he retired for a few years to Madeira. In 1845 returned to England and from 1846 until death warden of Sackville College, East Grinstead, a charitable foundation. His life was divided between literary toil and labors of piety and benevolence. In 1854 founded the Sisterhood of St. Margaret, which before he died was furnishing the best nurses in England. As an author his productiveness has few parallels. Some of the chief of his seventy publications: *History of the Holy Eastern Church, Commentary on the Psalms from Primitive and Mediaeval Writers, History of the So-Called Jansenist Church of Holland, Voices from the East, Mediaeval Preachers and Mediaeval Preaching, History of the Jews, Essays on Liturgiology and Church History, Sermons for Children,* and *Stories for Children from Church History.* Books of faith and intention, so strongly expressed that almost everything he wrote provoked controversy. His poetry was different. Here he worked in a field entirely congenial. Greatest services have been rendered, and widest fame won, through his hymns. He knew about twenty languages and translated many hymns from their original Latin and Greek. One of his best known translations was Bernard of Cluny's *De Contemptu Mundi,* which included "To Thee, O Dear, Dear Country," "Jerusalem the Golden," and "Brief Life Is Here Our

Portion." Others he translated were "O Come, O Come, Emmanuel," "All Glory Laud and Honor," "The Day of Resurrection," "Come ye Faithful, Raise the Strain," and "Christian Dost Thou See Them." As a poet Neale eleven times won the Seatonian prize.

NEANDER (nā än′dẽr), **JOACHIM NEUMANN** (1650-1680), German Reformed poet, born and educated at Bremen. Following conversion in 1670 from a life of youthful laxity, entered a life of religious devotion and became an ardent adherent of Philip Jakob Spener, the founder of the Pietistic movement in Germany. Went to Heidelberg to continue studies, and while there served as a children's tutor. The Reformed congregation of Düsseldorf called him as rector of the Latin school in 1674. In 1679 called to Bremen as third preacher of the Church of St. Martini, but died the next year. Chief contribution to the church was through about seventy hymns, many of which were gradually included in the hymnbooks, one of his best known hymns, "Praise Ye the Lord, the Almighty." He also wrote the music for many of his hymns. Published volumes were *Covenant Songs* and *Psalms of Thanksgiving*.

NEANDER, JOHANN AUGUST WILHELM (original name, **DAVID MENDEL**) (1789-1850), German Lutheran theologian and church historian, born at Göttingen, Germany of Jewish parents. Hamburg became his home and place of education. Schleiermacher's *Discourse on Religion* led him to break with Judaism and to become a Christian. In 1806, in seventeenth year, baptized under the name of Neander (new man). Purpose to study law led him to leave Hamburg and go to the University of Halle. Because of war conditions soon left Halle and went to the University of Göttingen. Became deeply interested in the study of the New Testament and the Church Fathers and soon declared purpose to study church history. In 1809 returned to Hamburg, where he taught for a year and a half, preached from time to time, and continued study of church history. In 1812 made professor extraordinary at the University of Heidelberg. Next year called to Berlin to labor as a colleague with Schleiermacher. Lectured the rest of his life with great success on church history, the exegesis of the New Testament, Christian ethics, and systematic theology. Among writings were biographies of Julian the Apostate, Bernard, and Chrysostom; *General History of the Christian Religion and Church* (six volumes), *History of the Planting and Training of the Christian Church by the Apostles, Life of Jesus Christ, History of Christian Ethics,* and some commentaries. Conception of church history a picture gallery of the history of the divine life of Christ pervading humanity. Regarded Christianity as also a force, a life, and not alone as a dogma. One of his important characteristics as a historian was his talent for portraying individual traits of character and life. Saw the history of Christianity as the permeation of human life by the divine life, stressed the place of the individual rather than the community or institutions. Sacrificed the conquering power of Christ in the universal church to the pervading power of Christ in the individual. This was perhaps his greatest weakness as an historian. He is known as one of the mediating school in Lutheranism.

NECTARIUS (nĕk tar′rĭ ŭs) **OF CONSTANTINOPLE** (d. 397), Patriarch of Constantinople (381-397). A native of Tarsus, Cilicia, a senator living at Constantinople, a praetor, and a catechumen. At the time of the Second Ecumenical Council at Constantinople in 381, paid a visit to his old bishop, Diodorus of Tarsus, who was attending the council. Gregory of Nazianzen had resigned as patriarch of Constantinople; and it was necessary at this time to fill the vacancy. At the recommendation of Bishop Diodorus the name of Nectarius, the venerable, white-haired senator, was placed at the bottom of the list of candidates. Emperor Theodosius at once declared that the senator should be made bishop. Nectarius was baptized and became at once patriarch of Constantinople and president of the Second General Council, then in session at Constantinople. The third canon of the council declared that the "bishop of Constantinople shall hold the rank after the bishop of Rome, because Constantinople is New Rome." Nectarius was thus the first bishop to hold that honor. Toward the close of his episcopate, about 391, he abolished the Presbyter Penitentiary, an office that had been established to receive the secret confession of such as fell into heavy sins after baptism. Died after a patriarchate of sixteen years, and was succeeded by John Chrysostom.

NEE, HENRY OR WATCHMAN (NI SHU-TSU), RENAMED NI CHING-FU, NI TO-SHENG or WATCHMAN NEE) (1903-1972). Born in Swatow. Educated at Trinity College, Foochow. Did student street preaching from 1924. Adopted Plymouth Brethren teachings of victorious life, local assembly, local unpaid ministers, weekly communion, and conferences of local groups (Shanghai in 1928). Church known as the Little Flock. Spread from Foochow and Shanghai to the north by 1932. Nee visited several times in Britain and the USA.

Ran a successful chemical business with his family from 1942 until 1948 when he turned it over to the Little Flock. Opposed Communist Three Self religious movement and in prison from 1952 until shortly before his death in 1972. Wrote *The Spiritual Man* and *Rethinking the Work*.

NEESIMA YUZURU (nē shē'mȧ), **JOSEPH HARDY** (1843-1890), founder of Doshisha College in Japan, born at Yedo (Tokyo), Japan in Buddhist samurai family. As a samurai received good Japanese education. Commodore Perry's coming into Yedo Bay in 1853 stirred Neesima's desire to know more about the outside world. In 1864, he made up his mind to counter custom, to risk facing the death penalty for leaving Japan, and to go to America. He was hidden by a captain who gave him the name Joe. The owner of the boat that carried him from Shanghai to Boston was Alphaeus Hardy, a Christian philanthropist, who took the young man to his home in Boston, and gave him a good education. Neesima attended Philipps Academy at Andover, where he publicly accepted Christ. He studied at Amherst College, and Andover Theological Seminary, graduating from the latter. He was ordained by the Mount Vernon Church, Boston, in 1874. He returned to Japan; and in the following year, surmounting much opposition and difficulty, succeeded in founding a Christian college, Doshisha, in Kyoto. In 1883 he began to plan for Doshisha to become a Christian university. Upon the urgent invitation and generous offer of Mr. Hardy, his benefactor and friend, he came to America in 1884 for a year of rest. The following year he returned to Japan somewhat improved in health, and continued his effort to make Doshisha a university. He saw money coming in for the growth and development of the school, new buildings erected, and a growing student body.

NERI (nā'rē), **PHILIP** (1515-1595), Italian saint, born at Florence, Italy; educated by Dominicans in Florence and Augustinians in Rome. Cofounder of the Confraternity of the Most Holy Trinity Hospital (1548) to aid pilgrims to Rome and convalescents. In 1551 ordained priest. Emphasized joyfulness and gentleness in service, yet maintained severe ascetic sternness; type of religious singing used gave rise to our "oratorio." Palestrina was his spiritual child. Teachings, humanitarian service, and spiritual conferences drew many priests to community and gave rise to the Congregation of the Oratory in 1564 which was confirmed by Gregory XIII in 1575. In 1593 resigned place as superior to Baronius. Canonized in 1622.

NERO CLAUDIUS CAESAR DRUSUS GERMANICUS (37-68), Roman emperor (54-68 A.D.). The last emperor of the Julian-Claudian line, born in Anzio on the coast of Latium. Nephew of Caligula Cesar and the great-great-grandson of Augustus Caesar. In 49 Nero's mother married her uncle, the Emperor Claudius, who adopted her son, Lucius Domitius Ahenobarbus, whose name was changed to Nero Claudius Caesar Drusus Germanicus. In 53, at the age of sixteen, Nero married Octavia the daughter of Claudius, and the next year upon the death of Claudius was chosen emperor by both the Roman Senate and by the provinces. The first five years of Nero's reign were called the golden *quinquennium Neronis.* The philosophy and guidance of his teacher Seneca bore fruits for a while. However, in 55 he caused the death of his step-brother Britannicus. By 59 his vanity, selfishness, and cruelty had become apparent to all. Murdered his mother, Agrippina, his wife, Octavia, and later his teacher, Seneca, by ordering him to commit suicide, his second wife, Poppea, and many others. By 61 affairs in the empire were in turmoil. An insurrection took place in Britain, and war broke out against the Parthians in Armenia. In 64 two-thirds of Rome burned. The blame was commonly laid upon Nero; to turn the attention from himself he blamed the Christians and persecuted them with fury and madness. History records this as the first great Roman persecution of the Christians. According to legend it was in his reign that both Peter and Paul were martyred. Nero rebuilt Rome with great magnificence and at great cost, and provided the populace of Rome with free grain, plundering Italy and the provinces to secure the means. Conspiracy after conspiracy was raised against Nero and murder after murder was perpetrated by him until in 68 the Gallic and Spanish legions and the Praetorian Guard rose against him and Nero fled. The Senate declared him a public enemy; the tyrant saved himself from execution by committing suicide.

NESTLE, EBERHARD (1851-1913), German biblical scholar. He held professorships at Ulm and Tübingen (1883-1898), and appointments at the Evangelical Theological Seminary at Maulbronn from 1898. His early work was done on the text of the Greek Old Testament. In 1898 Nestle published the first edition of his Greek New Testament based on the work of leading German and British textual critics. In 1904 his text was adopted by the British and Foreign Bible Society in place of the Textus Receptus, upon which the King James Version is based. Nestle's Greek Text has been constantly revised through twenty-five editions since

1914 by his son, Erwin Nestle. Nestle's Greek Text is probably the most widely used edition of the Greek New Testament.

NESTORIUS (nĕs tō'rĭ ŭs) (died c. 451), Patriarch of Constantinople (428-431), founder of the Nestorian church, born in Germanicia, Syria, near the boundary between Cilicia and Cappadocia, probably educated at Antioch under Theodore of Mopsuestia. Ordained to the priesthood and made presbyter at Antioch. Appointed Patriarch of Constantinople in 428, and very soon gained great popularity as a preacher, demonstrating much zeal in fighting the heretics of Constantinople—the Arians, the Novatians, the Macedonians, and the Quartodecimanians. In 430 a controversy began between Nestorius and Cyril, Bishop of Alexandria, over the doctrine of "Mother of God." The counter-accusations of the two men were mutually personal and acrimonious. Cyril stirred up strong antagonism among the churches of Egypt, Asia Minor, Constantinople, and Rome. Cyril's charges were that Nestorius was teaching that Christ had two natures, and that Christ was in reality two persons linked in a mechanical union. The dispute waxed so warm that Emperor Theodosius II directed that a council be called at Ephesus in 431. By scheme and trickery Cyril succeeded in outwitting Nestorius and his party and in carrying the council and popular opinion with him. The imperial court decided in favor of Cyril, and requested Nestorius to reenter his monastery at Antioch where he was permitted to remain in quiet for the next four years. Maximian was consecrated Patriarch of Constantinople to replace Nestorius. The Persian Nestorians broke off and became a separate, schismatic church as they have remained to this day. In 433 when Maximian died, the people of Constantinople demanded the restoration of Nestorius as patriarch. This threatened new trouble, and Cyril continued trying to get rid of Nestorius. Nestorius was permanently exiled to the Great Oasis in Upper Egypt. He busied himself writing several theological works, among which was *Tragedy,* a history of his life and of his theological controversy. In it he sought to vindicate himself. The last that we hear of him is in the year 451, soon after which he likely died in exile. There are still Nestorians in Persia.

NETTLETON, ASAHEL (1783-1844), American Congregational minister and revivalist, born at North Killingworth, Connecticut. Graduated from Yale College in 1809, licensed to preach in 1811. From 1811 to 1822 an effective traveling evangelist in Connecticut, Massachusetts, and New York. In 1822 he suffered a severe and almost fatal attack of typhus fever, from which he never fully recovered; yet he continued to preach with much success the rest of his life. Visited Great Britain in 1831. Preaching was simple, direct, and powerful; theology was Calvinistic, and sermons doctrinal. Large numbers won to the Lord and added to the church through his preaching. A decided opponent of the New Haven theology; opposed Dr. Finney's innovations of the "anxious seat," of calling on women to pray in public, and of praying for people by name. Published *Village Hymns,* an excellent American collection of hymns. Never married. Died of tuberculosis.

NEVE (nē'vĕ), **JUERGEN LUDWIG** (1865-1943), Lutheran theologian and church historian, born at Schleswig, Germany, educated at Breklum, Schleswig, and at the University of Kiel, Germany. Ordained to the Evangelical Lutheran ministry in 1883. Professor of church history in the Chicago Theological Seminary (1887-1892); Western Theological Seminary, Atchison, Kansas (1898-1909); professor of symbolics and history of doctrine at Hamma Divinity School, Wittenberg College, Springfield, Ohio (1909-1943). Served as pastor at Chester, Illinois for a time after 1892. Author of *Brief History of the Lutheran Church in America; Churches and Sects of Christendom; History of Christian Thought; Lutherans in the Movements for Church Union; The Augsburg Confession, Its History and Interpretation;* and *Story and Significance of the Augsburg Confession.*

NEVIN (nĕv'ĭn), **JOHN WILLIAMS** (1803-1886), German Reformed theologian, born in Franklin County, Pennsylvania. Graduated from Union College (1821), Princeton Theological Seminary (1826). Taught Greek at Princeton, 1826-1828, occupying chair during Dr. Charles Hodge's absence; professor of Hebrew and biblical literature at Western Theological Seminary, 1830-1840; professor of theology at Mercersburg Theological Seminary, 1840-1853, and acting president of Marshall College at Mercersburg, Pennsylvania, 1841-1853; lecturer on aesthetics and history in Franklin and Marshall College, Lancaster, Pennsylvania, 1861-1866; president of Franklin and Marshall, 1866-1876. Gradually abandoned Old School Calvinistic theology because not in sympathy with growing revivalistic methods of the Protestant churches; wrote *The Anxious Bench.* Nevin and Dr. Philip Schaff were founders of the Mercersburg Theology. Their teaching on the Real Presence in the sacrament and on more sacramental conception of Christianity led to fear of pro-Romanism and charge of heresy. Editor and principal contributor of the *Mercersburg Review.* Chief writings: *Summary of Biblical Antiquities, The Mystical Presence, The History and Genesis of the Heidelberg Catechism.*

NEVIUS (nē'vĭ ŭs), **JOHN LIVINGSTON** (1829-1893), American Presbyterian missionary to China, born near Ovid, New York, educated at Ovid Academy, Union College, Schenectady, and Princeton Theological Seminary. In 1849 taught school in Georgia for a year and became a Christian. Upon conversion decided to prepare for the ministry; while in the seminary decided to be a missionary. In 1853 completed seminary course, ordained, married, appointed by the Presbyterian Mission Board, and assigned to Ningpo, China. They arrived in China when the Tai Ping Rebellion was in progress and found much difficulty in establishing work. Nevius was in Ningpo, Chekiang Province (1854-1859); in Japan (1859-1861), preparing a *Compendium of Theology* for Chinese students; at Tungchow, Shantung Province (1861-1864); in America (1864-1868); and at Chefoo, Shantung (1871-1893), where he spent last days in Bible translation. Wrote *China and the Chinese* and *Demon Possession and Allied Themes.* Noted especially for the "Nevius Method," which places strong emphasis on the training of the Chinese Christians as much as possible to carry on their own work, with their own resources and from their own homes. Built churches in native style, and trained ablest nationals in Bible and prayer to be leaders. In 1890 Dr. Nevius met in conference with the Korean missionaries to explain the plan, following which time it was effectively applied in that country. Also introduced into China Western fruits and vegetables, Jersey cows for milk, and full tires for the wheels on their carts.

NEWBERRY, THOMAS (1811-1901), editor of the Englishman's Bible, born in England. From childhood a Christian with a deep love and reverence for the Holy Scriptures. In early Christian life read the Bible for comfort and instruction; later began a twenty-five-year period of diligent study of the Bible in the original Hebrew and Greek. Then commenced the main literary work of his life, *The Englishman's Bible* (often called *The Newberry Bible*). Contributed valuable articles to the *Witness* and to other religious magazines. Books, *Notes on the Temple, Notes on the Tabernacle, The Parables of Our Lord, The Temples of Solomon and Ezekiel,* and *Types of the Levitical Offerings,* have had a strong influence on many.

NEWELL, SAMUEL (1785-1821), American missionary to India, born at Durham, Maine. Educated at Harvard College and Andover Theological Seminary. Came into fellowship with Judson and Nott. Newell was one of the four students who presented the petition which contributed so largely to the formation of the American Board of Commissioners for Foreign Missions; became one of the board's first missionaries. In 1810 left the seminary and preached for some time at Rowley, Massachusetts. In the summer of 1811 spent some time studying medicine in Philadelphia. Ordained at Salem with Judson, Nott, Rice, and Hall, and on February 19, sailed with Judson for Calcutta. After a short stay at Serampore the missionaries were ordered to leave India. The Newells went to the Isle de France (Mauritius). He then went to Ceylon with the hope of opening a mission there. In January, 1814 he joined Hall and Nott at Bombay, and worked with them preaching, translating, and teaching when he fell victim to the cholera epidemic in Bombay.

NEWELL, WILLIAM REED (1865-1956), Plymouth Brethren Bible teacher. Born Savannah, Ohio. Educated at College of Wooster and Princeton Theological Seminary. After a brief pastorate, assistant superintendent at Moody Bible Institute from 1896 to 1898. Interdenominational Bible teacher in many parts of the world from 1897. Taught international Sunday classes with up to about 1,000 members. Wrote *Revelation, Romans* and *Hebrews.*

NEWMAN (nū'măn), **ALBERT HENRY** (1852-1933), American Baptist church historian, born near Edgefield Court House, South Carolina, educated at Mercer University, Macon, Georgia, Rochester Theological Seminary, and Southern Baptist Theological Seminary, Greenville, South Carolina. Acting professor of church history (1877-1880); Pettingill professor of church history (1880-1881), Rochester Theological Seminary; professor of church history in McMaster University, later Toronto Baptist College, Toronto, Canada (1881-1901); professor of church history in the new theological seminary that Dr. B. H. Carroll established at Baylor University, Waco, Texas (1901-1908); professor of Church history and dean of the faculty of the Western Baptist Theological Seminary, Ft. Worth, Texas (1908-1913). Again at Baylor (1913-1921); occupied the chair of church history at the newly organized seminary at Mercer University (1921-1929); his last four years professor emeritus. In 1906 and 1926 guest professor at the University of Chicago; in 1917-1918 at Vanderbilt; 1927-1929 at McMaster University. In theology a moderate conservative. Wrote *The Baptist Churches in the United States, A History of*

Anti-Pedobaptism from the Rise of Pedobaptism to A.D. 1609, widely used *Manual of Church History* (two volumes), and *A Century of Baptist Achievement.*

NEWMAN, JOHN HENRY (1801-1890), Roman Catholic Cardinal, born in London, England and reared an Evangelical. Graduating from Trinity College, Oxford. In 1822 elected fellow of Oriel College, Oxford. In 1824 ordained deacon in the Anglican church, soon became curate of St. Clement's Church, Oxford. In 1828 vicar of St. Mary's, the university church; adjudged one of the ablest and most influential preachers of Oxford. In 1833 wrote *Arians of the Fourth Century,* a writing that established his fame. At this time Newman, Keble, and Froude started the Oxford or Tractarian movement, Pusey joining them a little later. Newman began writing the *Tracts of the Times,* in defense of the Anglo-Catholic movement, and in opposition to the growing laxity of the church. Wrote twenty-four of the ninety tracts before the Bishop of Oxford forbade their continuance. Became editor of the *British Critic,* the chief organ of Tractarianism. In 1841 published memorable pro-Catholic *Tract Ninety,* which resulted in his being put under the ban in the Church of England. In rapid succession relinquished editorship of the *British Critic,* withdrew from Oxford, went into a period of seclusion, retracted severe language against the Church of Rome, resigned living in St. Mary's. In 1845 received into the Roman Catholic Church. Nearly two hundred fifty clergy of the Church of England followed him between 1845 and 1862. In 1847 ordained priest and given the doctorate. The year following Pius IX commissioned him to introduce the Oratory into his mother country. In 1854 went to Dublin as rector of the Catholic University, but returned to Birmingham in 1858. In 1864 in reply to harsh criticism of Charles Kingsley wrote greatest work, a religious biography, *Apologia pro Vita Sua*. Leo XIII in 1879 raised Newman to the cardinalate. Author of "Lead, Kindly Light."

NEWTON, BENJAMIN WILLS (1807-1899), member of Plymouth Brethren, born at Plymouth, England, studied at Exeter College, Cambridge. In the "Assembly" of the Plymouth Brethren labored for seventeen years as a teacher, contributed articles of value to *The Christian Witness.* Held a place of influence in the Plymouth "gathering" until 1845 when he and Mr. Darby came to a definite variance with each other as regards prophetic teaching (especially the "secret rapture" theory of Darby) and church order. The chasm so widened that Darby started another meeting at Plymouth. Newton continued in original meeting until some of his writings displeased many of his members. They charged him with being heterodox and withdrew from him. Left Plymouth in 1847, took up residence and pastorate in London.

NEWTON, SIR ISAAC (1642-1727), English mathematician and natural philosopher, born at Woolsthorpe, Lincolnshire, England, the year that Galileo died, studied at Grantham School and Trinity College, Cambridge University. In 1667 became a fellow, in 1669 succeeded Dr. Barrow, his former teacher, as Lucasian professor of mathematics. Warden in 1696 and in 1699 Master of the Mint. A member of the Royal Society, being president of the Society from 1703 to 1727. Member of Parliament in 1689 and again in 1701, knighted by Queen Anne in 1705. Discovery of the law of gravitation, the laws of motion, and the law of the composition of light revolutionized the scientific world. In *Philosophiae Naturalis Principia Mathematica* showed that the motion of the heavenly bodies is to be explained by the law of gravitation. The idea of natural law opened the way for deism. To him observation and experience were the only basis of knowledge. No wonder that Voltaire became one of his most effective disciples. He was interested in the Bible and in Bible study. Wrote *Chronology of Ancient Kingdoms Amended, Observations on the Prophecy of Daniel and the Apocalypse of St.John,* and *A Historical Account of Two Notable Corruptions of Scripture*.

NEWTON, JOHN (1725-1807), Evangelical hymn writer, born in London, England. He sailed for six years with father, a shipmaster on the Mediterranean. Early life was one of sad and wanton profligacy with intermittent but unsuccessful attempts to live an upright life. For ten years or more he engaged in the African slave trade. His conversion took place about 1748. From 1755 to 1760 surveyor of tides at Liverpool. Decided to take orders in the Church of England and began the study of Greek, Hebrew, and Syriac, and was ordained deacon in 1764. Given a curacy at Olney, Buckinghamshire, became an intimate friend and adviser of William Cowper, and a collaborator with him in the production of *Olney Hymns,* a collection that ranks high in English hymnody. In 1779 appointed rector of St. Mary's Woolnoth, London, a post held until death. Main pillar of the Evangelical party in the Church of England. Among choicest writings were *Omicron* and his *Cardiphonia*. Also wrote *A Review of Ecclesiastical History.* Among better known and best loved hymns are "Glorious Things of Thee Are Spoken,"

"Amazing Grace," "Safely Thro Another Week," and "How Sweet the Name of Jesus Sounds." In theology a pronounced Calvinist; had strong influence on some religious leaders of his time, such as Thomas Scott, William Wilberforce, Charles Simeon, and Hannah More.

NICHOLAS I (c. 800-867), pope from 858 to 867. Born in Rome. Demonstrated his belief in absolute papal authority. Rule marked by several issues: long struggle with the Eastern church; support of Ignatius against Photius as Patriarch of Constantinople (excommunicated Photius, Photius deposed Nicholas); opposition to bigamous marriage of Lothair II of Lorraine; suppression of archbishops John of Ravenna and Hincmar of Reims for disregarding papal authority; first using of Pseudo-Isidorian Decretals to strong papal advantage. Promoted missionary work in establishing the Hamburg-Bremen archbishopric with Ansgar in oversight. One of the great popes of the Middle Ages.

NICHOLAS II (c. 980-1061), pope 1059-1061. Born in Savoy. Influenced by Humbert and Hildebrand (later Gregory VII). In the Lateran Council of 1059 issued the decree that put the election of a pope in the hands of the cardinals with acclamation (not election) by the Romans and recognitions by the Holy Roman Emperor.

NICHOLAS V (TOMMASSO PARENTUCELLI) (1397-1455), pope from 1447 to 1455. Born at Sarzana, Italy. Studied theology at Bologna and Florence. Bishop of Bologna in 1444. Anti-pope Felix V and Council of Basel submitted to him. Crowned Frederick II in 1452. Planned the rebuilding of St. Peters and founded the Vatican Library. Blameless personal life but a nepotist. Tried to link Roman Catholicism with Humanism.

NICHOLAS (nĭk'ō lăs) **OF CUSA** (kū'sȧ) **(CUSANUS)** (c. 1401-1464), German cardinal, born at Kues or Cusa on the Moselle in the diocese of Treves. Educated in a school conducted by the Brethren of the Common Life at Deventer, then studied law at Padua, later entered Cologne to study theology. Studied Latin, Greek, Hebrew, and Arabic, also mathematics, astronomy, and philosophy with greal zeal. Ordained in 1430. An archdeacon at Liege when in 1433 he was sent to the Council of Basel. There wrote *De Concordantia Catholica* and *De Auctoritati Praesidendi in Concilio Generali,* in which advocated the supremacy of the general council over the pope, and the equal authority and dignity of all bishops of the church. Also expressed belief that the Donation of Constantine was a fraud, and the Isidorian Decretals spurious. Secured the prohibition of new brotherhoods and the condemnation of the sale of indulgences for money—was becoming a reformer of the church. A little later reversed course and became an obedient son of the church, an obsequious servant of the papacy, for which he was rewarded by promotion to the cardinalate (1448), and by appointment to the bishopric of Brixen on the Tyrol in 1450. A great scholar, one of the most universal since Albertus Magnus, and one of the earliest philosophers to break from the formalistic doctrines of scholasticism. Anticipated Copernicus in his belief that the earth rotated on its axis; he anticipated Bruno in conceiving space to be boundless and time unending; proposed a reform in the calendar; the first to have a map of Germany engraved. Held that the world of natural phenomena must be accounted for by the spiritual world, that the world is a mirror of God, and man is an epitome of the universe. His chief philosophical works: *De Docta Ignorantia* and *De Conjecturis.* Among mystic writings, *De Visione Dei*.

NICHOLAS OF HEREFORD or **NICHOLAS HERFORD** (died c. 1420), Lollard writer, studied at Queen's College, Oxford. While a fellow there became an ardent supporter of Wycliffe. Took part in the translation of the Bible into English, Wycliffe translating the new and a portion of the Old Testament, and Nicholas of Hereford completing the Old Testament in 1384. In 1382 he began preaching Wycliffe's reform doctrines for which he was condemned and excommunicated. Appealed to Rome but condemned by cardinals and pope, sentenced to imprisonment. Escaped from imprisonment in 1385; returning to England, resumed his Lollard activity. About two years later captured and again imprisoned, being kept in prison until he in 1391 finally recanted. Taken under royal protection and made chancellor. Later treasurer of Hereford cathedral. In 1417 resigned these posts and became a Carthusian monk at Coventry.

NICOLAI (nē kō lä'ē) or **KASATKIN, IVAN** (c. 1835-1912), Russian Orthodox missionary to Japan, name as priest was Nicolai; and he is thus popularly known, though his family name was Kasatkin. In 1861 went as a chaplain to the Russian Consulate at Hakodate in the northern island of Hokkaido, and made a careful study of the Japanese language. One of his early teachers was Joseph Neesima before he came to America. His first convert was a Buddhist priest. After a furlough in Russia, returned to Japan in 1871 to establish a mission for his synod at Tokyo. Organized a church of about one hundred members in 1872; taught the Russian language and Christianity. Before long more and more converts were being made and baptized. He longed to see the church have a Japanese rather than a Russian aspect, and wished to have Christianity promoted by the Japanese rather than by the Russians. His was the most successful Russian mission outside the Russian Empire. Nicolai was made successively bishop and archbishop; and at the time of death in 1912 there were more than thirty thousand converts. Stood in the front rank of modern missionary statesmen; in the translation of the Bible, in the education of the clergy, and in preaching, labors were abundantly fruitful.

NICOLL, SIR WILLIAM ROBERTSON (Pseudonym, Claudius Clear) (1851-1923), theologian and editor, born at Lumsden, Aberdeenshire, Scotland, graduated from the University of Aberdeen. Ordained in 1874 and minister of Dufftown, Banffshire (1874-1877), and of Kelso, Roxburghshire (1877-1885). Became editor of the following periodicals: *Household Library of Exposition, British Weekly, English Bookman, Expositor,* and *British Monthly.* Collaborated with others on preparing *The Expositor's Dictionary of Texts* and *The Expositor's Treasury of Children's Sermons.* He edited *The Expositor's Greek Testament*. Library adviser to the publishing house of Hodder and Stoughton. Knighted in 1909. Nicoll was eminent as a literary critic, brilliant as a theological writer and apologist, and was a preacher of recognized ability and power.

NIEBUHR, KARL PAUL REINHOLD (1892-1971), theologian. Born Wright City, Missouri. Educated at Elmhurst College, Eden Theological Seminary, and Yale University. Ordained in 1915 and pastor of Bethel Evangelical Church in Detroit from 1915 to 1928. From 1928 to 1960 professor of applied Christianity at Union Theological Seminary, New York. Influenced by Barth but rejected his non-participation in society. Emphasized the sin of man and his institutions but thought that the sovereign God in Christ would confront the individual with saving grace who would then work out proximate, not final, solutions in time to social problems. Founded and from 1941 to 1966 edited *Christianity and Crisis.* Most important works: *Moral Man and Immoral Society, Faith and History,* and *The Nature and Destiny of Man*.

NIEBUHR, RICHARD HELMUT (1894-1962), social ethics and theology. Born Wright City, Missouri. Educated at Elmhurst College, Eden, Yale Divinity School, Berlin and Marburg. Professor at Eden (1919-1922, 1927-1931), and Yale Divinity School from 1931 to 1962. Felt Christians should be involved in the social reconstruction of society. Wrote widely-known *Social Sources of Denominationalism* (denominations rooted in sociological considerations) and *Christ and Culture*.

NIELSEN, FREDRIK KRISTIAN (1846-1907), Danish church historian, born at Aalborg, Denmark, educated at the University of Copenhagen, taught privately for a few years, then in 1873 made catechist at Our Savior's Church, Copenhagen. In 1877 became professor of church history in the University of Copenhagen, taught until 1900. Then resigned to become Bishop of Aalborg and Aarhus in 1905. May be regarded as the greatest of church historians produced in the Scandinavian countries. Nielson stood high in the councils of church, where his advice was constantly sought. Leading written works: *History of the Papacy in the Nineteenth Century* (two volumes), *Haandbog i Kirkens Historie* (two volumes), *Ledetraad i Kirkens Historie* (two volumes), and *Kirkehistorie* (two volumes).

NIETZSCHE (nē'chĕ), **FRIEDRICH WILHELM** (1844-1900), German philosopher, born in Röcken, near Leipzig, Saxony, educated at Bonn, and Leipzig. Studied under Ritschl, on whose recommendation he was made professor of classics at Basel in 1869. Ritschl, Schopenhauer, and Wagner all had marked influence on his life and philosophy. Throughout life suffered from ill health, finally suffering a complete mental and physical collapse in 1889. Philosophy is that of an individualist, anarchist, anti-democrat and pessimist. Held up to ridicule the accepted ideas of the Christian religion and ethic. Would replace humility with pride, sympathy with contempt and cruelty, love for neighbor with ruthless exploitation, peace with war, equality with competition. Conception of evolution was an aggressive "will to power," with the *superman* as the next stage in human development. What men call morality he would dismiss as a hindrance to the achievement of the superman. Doctrines profoundly influenced the offical philosophy and propaganda of National Socialism in the German Third Reich. *Thus Spake Zarathustra* and *Will to Power* sum up his whole life, philosophy, and ethic.

NIGHTINGALE, FLORENCE (1820-1910), English nurse and hospital reformer, born in Florence, Italy in the home of a wealthy English gentleman. Most of childhood spent on her father's estate in Derbyshire, England, where she received a thorough classical education. Early became interested in nursing and hospital work, aroused by the ills and suffering she saw in her travels in Europe, also by the unhygienic conditions of the English hospitals. Entered upon a course of nurse training at Theodore Fliedner's Deaconess Institution of Kaiserswerth and in the Institute of St. Vincent de Paul in Paris. In 1853 reorganized the Governesses' Sanitorium in London. Reports of the sad condition of the hospitals in Crimea, when the war between Russia and England broke out there in 1854, led her to volunteer to give her assistance as a nurse from 1854 to 1856. Found the hospital at Scutari, Turkey in lamentable condition, and the soldiers very poorly cared for. With the thirty-eight nurses she brought to Scutari, she plunged into the work with all her might, and organized a barrack hospital. Filth, vermin, fever, overcrowding, scarcity of vitally needed food, lack of attention and care, and lack of hospital supplies had resulted in a death rate of forty-two percent. Her energy and tact brought order out of chaos and practical efficiency out of hopeless failure, and reduced the death rate to only two percent. During the war she suffered an attack of the Crimean fever, but remained at her post until the war was over. Laid the foundation for modern scientific nursing. The report of the success of her methods spread throughout the world. Became known as "the Lady with the Lamp," and "the Angel of Crimea." Fifty thousand pounds were raised by popular subscription in recognition of her heroic service. She used the money to build the Nightingale Home and School in 1860 for training nurses at St. Thomas' and King's College hospitals. After the war Miss Nightingale returned to England but continued to lend her support to the reform of sanitary conditions in the army. During the Sepoy Mutiny, the American Civil War, and the Franco-Prussian War she was frequently consulted concerning camp hospital matters. Her influence had some bearing upon the founding of the Red Cross. She did considerable writing on hospitals, nursing, and health. Although she lived to be ninety years of age, her last forty years were years of invalidism.

NIKON (nyē'kôn) **(NIKITA MININ)** (1605-1681), Patriarch of Moscow, born in a village near Nishnei Novgorod, Russia. Received a monastic education, then married and became a local priest. After ten years of married life and after all his children had died, persuaded his wife to enter a convent, while he became a monk on an island in the White Sea. In 1646 on a visit to Moscow he made such a deep impression on the young Czar Alexis that he appointed him archimandrite of a monastery in Moscow, three years later metropolitan of Novgorod, and in 1652 persuaded him, much against his will, to be Patriarch of Moscow. As patriarch at once began many important reforms, and for several years held the good favor of and maintained a strong influence over the Czar. His power in the kingdom became tremendous. His influence with the Czar was so great that he was called to be his official representative in the absence of the Czar. He assumed too much. He ignored the fact that he owed his power to the Czar and to his favor. Nikon declared that the church and state were two separate and distinct powers, and held that the state should in no way interfere with the affairs of the church. When friction developed between them Nikon resigned and retired to the monastery of the New Jerusalem, which he had founded earlier. Not called back as he had expected, he tried to regain his post. However, he was later deposed and sentenced to banishment. After fourteen years of severe imprisonment he was recalled to his monastery at Moscow, by Alexis' successor, Feodor II, but died on the way. Buried with patriarchal honors in the cathedral church at Moscow. Subsequently all decrees against him were revoked at the bidding of the Czar, and he is now recognized as one of the greatest bishops of the Russian church. Nikon's patriarchate marks the only epoch in the history of the Russian church in which a rivalry between the spiritual and the secular powers existed. He was an ardent upholder of monasteries, and was noted for benevolent life and character, showing much kindness to the poor and unfortunate.

NINIAN (nĭn'ĭ ăn) (c. 360-c. 432), the first missionary and monastic bishop of North Britain, though the son of a British chieftain, early devoted himself to the Christian ministry. Spent about fifteen years in Rome. Ordained and commissioned to evangelize the heathen of Caledonia, and to work with Martin of Tours in Gaul. Bishop in 394. Began the evangelization of the Picts in what is now eastern Scotland. Built the white stone church at Whithorn, southwestern Scotland, dedicated the church to Martin of Tours. The "Church of St. Martin" was the beginning of "the Great Monastery" at Rosnat, which exerted a very wholesome influence in the surrounding country and which annually attracted many pilgrims from England and Scotland as the shrine of St. Ninian. His work among the southern Picts seems to have had short-lived success.

NITSCHMANN (nĭtch'män), **DAVID** (1696-1772), pioneer missionary and first Bishop of the Renewed Moravian church, born in Zauchtenthal, Moravia. Because of persecution fled from native country to Herrnhut, became a leader in the evangelistic work of the Moravians. In 1732 accompanied Leonard Dober to St. Thomas in the Danish West Indies, where they started a mission among the black slaves. After a few months returned to Europe, and in 1735 consecrated bishop by Bishop Daniel Ernst Jablonsky at Berlin, thus establishing historic succession and becoming the first bishop in the Reorganized Moravian church. A little later the same year, led a group of about twenty-five Moravians to Georgia. Influenced John and Charles Wesley, who were on their mission to Georgia also. Nitschmann returned to Europe in 1736. His next twenty-five years were spent in episcopal journeys. Labored in Germany, Livonia, Denmark, Sweden, Norway, Great Britain, West Indies, Georgia, North Carolina, New York, and Pennsylvania. Made at least fifty sea voyages. Died at Bethlehem, Pennsylvania, one of the settlements he had founded in 1740.

NOBILI (nô'bē lē), **ROBERT de** (1577-1656), born at Montepulciano, Tuscany, of aristocratic birth, a relative of Pope Marcellus II. Joined Jesuits about 1597. Became a Jesuit missionary in Goa, India in 1605; in 1606 went to Madura and learned the language, literature, and customs of the people, then conformed strictly to the social requirements of caste, living like a rigid, ascetic Brahmin devotee, cutting himself off from fellow missionaries, and identifying himself with the high caste people of Madura. By recognizing caste distinctions and by accommodating to Indian prejudices, he tried to separate Christianity and culture. His practice of compromise and adaptation of the Christian doctrines to Hindu customs and rites, known as *Malabar Rites,* led to a long controversy in the Catholic church which helped to bring about a papal suppression of the Jesuit Order in 1773 which lasted for forty-one years. In the Madura mission, of which Nobili was head, there were one hundred thousand converts; but how thoroughly they were converted to true Christianity remains a question. A real scholar. Mastered Tamil, Telugu, and Sanscrit. Wrote many works in these languages.

NOMMENSEN, LUDWIG ENGER (1834-1918), Dutch missionary to Indonesia. Born at Nordstrand, Holland. Educated at the Rhine Mission School at Barmen from 1857 to 1861. Sent to Sumatra in 1861. Won chiefs and then people of Bataks entirely by 1911 with over 100,000 Christians. Created an indigeneous church with Batak preachers, lay elders and application of the Bible to Batak culture by the Bataks.

NORRIS, J. FRANK (1877-1952). Born in Dadeville, Alabama. Educated in Baylor University and Southern Baptist Seminary. Ordained in 1899. Pastor in Dallas from 1905 to 1908 where he stopped racetrack gambling at the State Fair by editorials in *The Baptist Standard*. Helped to start Southwestern Baptist Seminary. From 1909 to 1952 pastor of First Baptist Church in Fort Worth. Supported World Christian Fundamentals Association and Baptist Bible Union from 1932. Also, commuting by air pastored a church in Detroit from 1935 to 1948. From 1939 president of the Baptist Bible Seminary, a Bible school in his church.

NORTH, FRANK MASON (1850-1935), American Methodist clergyman, born in New York City, studied at Wesleyan University, Middletown, Connecticut; entered the Methodist ministry in 1873; from that time until 1892 held several pastorates in New York and Connecticut. From 1892 until 1912 corresponding secretary of the New York City Church Extension and Missionary Society of the Methodist Episcopal church; was corresponding secretary of the Board of Foreign Missions of the Methodist Episcopal Church (1912-1924), and secretary (1924-1928). Also corresponding secretary of the Methodist National City Evangelization Union. In 1894 one of the founders of the Open and Institutional Church League, a forerunner of the Federal Council of the Churches of Christ in America. North formed the social creed of the churches, which was adopted first by the Methodist conference, and shortly after by the Federal Council (1908). Chairman of the executive committee of the Federal Council (1912-1916), and president (1916-1920). Served as a trustee for both Wesleyan University and Drew University; a lecturer on missions at Drew during the last ten years of his life. Founded *The Christian City* and was its editor for twenty years. Perhaps the best known of his many hymns, "Where Cross the Crowded Ways of Life."

NORTON, RALPH (1868-1934). Born in Indiana. Educated at De Pauw University. Salesman for some years. Studied at the Moody Bible Institute. Evangelist in Kansas from 1901 to 1904. From 1906 to 1915 worked with J. Wilbur Chapman in his world evangelistic tours. During World War I worked with soldiers in England and Belgium. Founded the Belgian Gospel Mission in 1918 and in 1919 a Bible school with Donald Grey Barnhouse as a teacher. By 1934 there were 66 preaching centers and over 100 workers.

NOTT, SAMUEL, JR. (1788-1869), American Congregational missionary to India, born at Franklin, Connecticut, educated at Union College and Andover Theological Seminary. At Andover he and Adoniram

Judson became the chief promoters of missions to India and of the mission board which sent them. He and Judson, Hall, Newell, and Rice were ordained early in 1812, shortly before they sailed for India as the first missionaries of the newly organized American Board of Commissioners for Foreign Missions. After some delays caused by the East India Company, they reached Bombay, where they commenced the first mission of the board in India. Sickness in 1815 necessitated Nott's return to America. Taught school in New York for a while. From 1822-1829 he was pastor at Galway, New York, and from 1829 to 1849 was pastor at Wareham, Massachusetts. Died in Hartford, Connecticut.

NOVATIAN (nō vā'shŭn) (third century), Roman presbyter, a priest in the church at Rome. In adulthood came to the Christian faith during a severe sickness. He was a man of learning and skill in the middle of the third century, and was the most distinguished theologian in Rome and one of the very first to use Latin rather than Greek in his writing. In doctrinal views essentially orthodox. Held firmly to the full deity and to the full humanity of Jesus Christ. One of the strongest churchmen in Rome, he was deeply offended when Cornelius, a man of lesser ability, was elected Bishop (pope) of Rome in 251. This and his strong opposition to the church's growing tendency to become less rigid in receiving back into the church those who lapsed during persecution, especially in the Decian persecutions led to a new schism. This schism centered in Novatian, and become known as Novatianism. Although he was excommunicated as a schismatic and a heretic, and even as an antipope, by several councils that were called by the Bishop of Rome, the schism continued until the sixth century. Most important work was his treatise *Of the Trinity,* in which he refuted the Sabellians and the Monarchians. According to tradition, died a martyr.

NOVATUS (nō vā'tŭs), (died after 251), stood at the head of schism of Felicissimus at Carthage about 250. A presbyter of Carthage, seems to have opposed the election of Cyprian to the office of Bishop of Carthage. Headed the party that insisted on receiving back into the church those who had lapsed during persecution. The church of Novatus and Felicissimus became a resort for all careless lapsed Christians. Made his fellow schismatic, Felicissimus, a deacon without the permission or the knowledge of the bishop. He was excommunicated. In later life seems for some reason to have changed his policy and views, and to have joined in with the puritanic Novantianist party.

NOYES, JOHN HUMPHREY (1811-1886), American social reformer; born at Brattleboro, Vermont; graduated from Dartmouth (1830); studied law for one year; then went to Andover and Yale to prepare for the ministry; licensed to Congregational ministry (1833). His advocating of adventism and perfectionism necessitated his withdrawal from Yale in 1834, from the church, and from the ministry in 1836; started a Bible school in his home at Putney, Vermont. Opposition developed against his irregular views on marriage; arrested for adultery, he fled to northern New York and in 1848 established the Oneida Community noted for animal trap and later silverware production. Besides holding doctrines of adventism and perfectionism, the society practiced community of goods, complex marriage in which every man was "married to every woman" and sex was group controlled, miraculous healing, and mutual criticism of members. Public opinion against Noyes' practices led to abandonment of mixed marriage in 1880.

O

OASTLER, RICHARD (1789-1861), social reformer. Born at Leeds. Educated at Fulnek Moravian School. Manager of an estate. In prison for a time for debt. Early advocated abolition of West Indian slavery. Supported Shaftesbury's factory bill to protect children working in factories.

OATES, TITUS (1649-1705). Born into a Baptist home in Oakham. Educated at Caius and St. John's Colleges, Cambridge. Ordained an Anglican cleric in 1673. Fabricated story in 1678 of a Jesuit plot to murder Charles II and put his openly Roman Catholic brother James on the throne. Jailed for perjury in 1685 but pardoned and pensioned under William III in 1689. Many innocent people were executed because of false testimony by this unsavory cleric.

OBERLIN (ô bĕr lăɴ'), **JEAN FREDERIC** (1740-1826), Lutheran philanthropist, born at Strassburg, studied at the gymnasium and the university in Strassburg. Until 1767 supported himself by teaching. At age twenty-seven began ministry at Waldersbach, in the rough, desolate mountainous district of Steinthal, a poverty-stricken community in the Vosges on the boundary between Alsace and Lorraine. In short time married a daughter of one of the Strassburg professors, and with the help and support of his wife gradually effected a wonderful improvement in the morals, industry, thrift, and spirit of the community. Over a period of sixty years preached, organized Christian Societies and Sunday schools; also built a good school system, developed agriculture, constructed roads and bridges, established hospitals and orphanages, instituted a circulating library, a small museum of natural history and philosophy, loan associations, savings banks, and agricultural societies. Imprisoned a few days before the fall of Robespierre. First foreign member of the London Bible Society and took a vital interest in its work. When he could no longer labor physically, prayed with unfaltering devotion for his people. Name is memorialized in America by the town and the college of Oberlin, Ohio.

OBOOKIAH (ōb o͞o kī'ȧ), **HENRY** (1792-1818), Hawaiian convert to Christianity, born at Kau, Owhyhee, one of the Sandwich (Hawaiian) Islands; died at Cornwall, Connecticut. About 1808 came to New England. Edwin W. Dwight, one of the tutors at Yale College, helped him learn English. Young Samuel J. Mills became interested and took him to his father's home at Torringford, Connecticut, near Yale. He went with Mills to Andover Seminary for a short time. Learned rapidly and soon became a Christian, perhaps the first Hawaiian convert to Christianity. In 1815 received into the Congregational church, of which Mills was a member. The next year a school was opened by the American Board in Cornwall, Connecticut for the missionary training of American Indians, Pacific Islanders and Orientals. One of the first to enter was Henry Obookiah. Had a great longing to go to Hawaii to tell his people about Christ. Inspired S. J. Mills to greater missionary zeal; encouraged the philanthropist William E. Dodge to greater missionary giving. His death from typhoid fever in 1818 challenged Hiram Bingham and Asa Thurston, students at Andover Seminary, to decide to go to Hawaii in his stead. The next year a company of seventeen, including three Hawaiian students from Cornwall, started for Hawaii.

OCCOM, SAMSON (1723-1792), Mohican Indian preacher and missionary, born in pagan home at Mohegan, New London County, Connecticut. He and mother converted to Christianity in Great Awakening (1740). From 1743 to 1747 lived in home of and was pupil of Eleazar Wheelock, Congregational minister and educator; learned English, Latin, Greek, and Hebrew; eye weakness prevented further study. Schoolmaster and minister to Montauk tribe on Long Island, 1749-1764; preaching for Congregationalists. In 1759 ordained Presbyterian minister; 1761-1763, missionary to Oneida Indians. In England and Scotland, 1765-1768, raising funds for Dr. Wheelock's Indian school. Preached nearly four hundred sermons in George Whitefield's tabernacle, in prominent pulpits in London, and throughout England and Scotland; raised over $60,000 for Wheelock's school. Differences developed and Occom broke relations with Wheelock. From 1768 to end of life worked with Oneidas, established Brothertown, a purely Indian town, was pastor and adviser, resided with Stockbridge Indians. Published an Indian hymnal, some of the hymns being his own. Died at Stockbridge, New York.

OCHINO (ōk kē'nō), **BERNARDINO** (1487-1564), Italian reformer, born at Siena, Italy, and because of Savonarola's influence, joined the Franciscan Observants while still a young man. In 1534 joined the more ascetic Capuchins, and was twice elected vicar-general of the order. Recognized as a man of sanctity and piety. Coming under the preaching and influence of Juan de Valdes, led to accept the evangelical views of the Reformation. Also came into close association with Pietro Martire Vermigli. About 1541, joined the Protestants. When the Catholics were about to bring him to trial in the newly reorganized Inquisition, fled Italy, first finding refuge for two years in Geneva. Subscribed to Calvin's system, preached to the Italian refugees, wrote some books, and published some sermons for distribution in Italy. Then went to Basel, and spent two years at Augsburg as pastor of the Italian Protestant refugees there until again forced to flee. In 1547, he and Vermigli accepted Cranmer's invitation. Appointed canon of Canterbury. When Mary came to the throne in 1553, he fled to Zurich in 1555 where again he became pastor of an Italian congregation. Some doctrinal difference developed between him and Beza and Bullinger. The Zurich council denied him the privilege of preaching and he took refuge among Italian friends in Poland. Through Catholic influence he was soon forced to leave the country. Found asylum among Hutterian Anabaptists, died in Austerlitz.

OCKHAM, WILLIAM OF (c. 1280 or 1300-1349), English scholastic philosopher, the "Invincible Doctor," born at Ockham, near London. About 1310 entered the Franciscan Order, and took bachelor's degree at Oxford and master's at Paris. Likely a pupil of Duns Scotus. May have taught in Oxford, but most of career was tied up with Paris. The most influential theologian of his time, but many views were out of harmony with the church. In 1324 called before the pope, imprisoned for four years, and then excommunicated. Became one of the emperor's principal advisers and literary defender of Emperor Louis the Bavarian in his conflict with Pope John XXII; one of the most significant forerunners of the English Reformation. Spoke out against some of the long-established doctrines of the Roman Catholic church. Held that Christ was head of church, that the pope was not infallible, that the general council and not the pope was the highest ruling authority of the church, that the Bible was the only infallible source of authority in matters of faith and life, and that in secular matters the pope and the church were subordinate to the state. Teaching made strong impact on thinking and convictions of John Wycliffe and Martin Luther. While he was a medieval monk and churchman, reformatory principles made him a bridge between the period of scholasticism and the Renaissance.

O'CONNELL, DANIEL (1775-1847), Irish political leader. Born in Kerry County, Ireland. Educated at St. Omer, Douay, and Lincoln's Inn. Admitted to Irish bar in 1798. In 1823 formed the Catholic Association to get Roman Catholic emancipation by law from legal restrictions. Refused seat as member of Parliament in 1829, but the Emancipation Act was passed in 1829, opening all offices in the British Isles except four to Roman Catholics.

ODO OF CLUNY (879-942), abbot, born near Le Mans, France, educated at the monastery of St. Martin of Tours and at Paris. As a monk, noted for learning, wisdom, piety, and saintly character; became abbot and reformer of several Cistercian and Benedictine monasteries. Rule was very rigid; ideal was reformatory. From 927 to 942 succeeded Count Bruno (Berno), the first abbot of Cluny monastery. This monastery, located at Cluny in eastern France, had been founded in 910 by Duke William the Pious of Aquitaine. His strict reform program consisted of: (1) absolute liberation of the church from secular control, (2) the abolition of simony, (3) the abolition of clerical marriages, and (4) the elevation of the papacy as the real governing power of the church. Traveled extensively in France and Italy to promote the reform of monasteries in accordance with that of Cluny. By time of his death the Cluny movement had spread widely in these countries, and about a century later, Cluny-trained monks were becoming popes.

OECOLAMPADIUS (ē kō lăm pā'dĭ ŭs), **JOHANNES** (real name **HUSSGEN**) (1482-1531), Swiss reformer, born at Weinsberg, Württemberg, Germany, studied law at Bologna, later went to Heidelberg and Tübingen; turned to scholastic philosophy and theology, studying Thomas Aquinas and the mystics. At Stuttgart met Reuchlin. At Tübingen formed a close fellowship with Melanchthon. In 1515 called to Basel as preacher; met and formed an intimate friendship with Erasmus, whom he assisted in the publication of his Greek New Testament. When he left Basel, Oswald Myconius succeeded him there. By 1518 he was coming somewhat under the influence of Luther's teaching. In 1520 surprised friends by entering a monastery near Augsburg. Reserved the right, even in this monastery, to do independent thinking. Soon renounced some of the Catholic doctrines and boldly preached against them. In 1522, left the monastery and rapidly developed Reformation ideas. The same year went to Basel, remained until death as preacher of the Church of St. Martin and as professor of theology in the university. Was Zwingli's right-hand helper. Present with Zwingli and assisted him in the Marburg Colloquy with Luther and Melanchthon in 1529.

OEHLER (ē'lẽr), **GUSTAV FRIEDRICH VON** (1812-1872), German Old Testament theologian, born at Ebingen, Württemberg, Germany, studied at Tübingen and Berlin; for several years served as teacher in the Missionary Institute at Basel and at the theological seminary in Tübingen. Became professor at the theological seminary at Schönthal in Württemberg and also pastor there (1840). In 1845 went to Breslau, spoke against the union of the Lutheran and Reformed churches. Held aloof from the old Lutheran party. In 1852 went back to Tübingen as head of the seminary and teacher of Old Testament at university. Wrote *Prolegomena zur Theologie des Alten Testaments, Theologie des Alten Testaments* (two volumes) and *Lehrbuch der Symbolik*. One of the foremost conservative Old Testament scholars of his time. To him the New Testament was the fulfillment of the Old Testament in which God's plan was partially revealed. Although a conservative, clung to some modern ideas. Believed that several authors wrote the Pentateuch, and that two authors wrote Isaiah.

OESTERLEY (ēs'tẽr lĭ), **WILLIAM OSCAR EMIL** (1866-1950), Church of England theologian, born at Calcutta, India, received education at Brighton College, Jesus College, Cambridge and Wells Theological College. Became curate at Houghton-le-Spring, Durham (1891), at St. Botolph, Colchester (1895), secretary of Parochial Missions to the Jews at Home and Abroad (1897), secretary and sub-warden of the Society of Sacred Study, London (1908), warden of the International Society of the Apocrypha (1908), examiner in the Hebrew and Greek Testaments for the University of London (1909), and rector of St. Mary Aldermary (1923). Professor of Hebrew and Old Testament History at King's College, University of London (1926-1936), and after 1936 professor emeritus and examining chaplain to the bishop of London; became prebendary of St. Paul's cathedral in 1936. Wrote: *St. Francis of Assisi; Studies in the Greek and Latin Versions of Amos; Old Latin Texts of the Minor Prophets; The Religion and Worship of the Synagogue; The Doctrine of Last Things: Jewish and Christian; The Psalms in the Jewish Church; The Evolution of the Messianic Idea; A History of Israel; An Introduction to the Old Testament; An Introduction to the Apocrypha; A New Approach to the Psalms* and *Old Testament Backgrounds of Christianity.*

O'KELLY, JAMES (c. 1757-1826), Methodist minister, born in Ireland; came to the United States in 1778; an itinerant Methodist preacher before 1780. When the Methodist church was organized in the United States in 1785 was one of the elders ordained; later held the position of presiding elder in the district of South Virginia. Opposing the church's stand on the powers of the bishops, withdrew from the Methodists in 1792, leading several ministers and their congregations from the denomination, to form "the Republican Methodist church." Shortly after the turn of the century James O'Kelly joined with Abner Jones, who had left the Vermont Baptists, and Barton W. Stone, who had seceded from the Kentucky Presbyterians, and formed the "Christian church." This new church insisted that the Bible be taken as the only rule of faith and discipline, and that Christian character be made the only requirement for church membership. In 1929 this body of Christians merged with Congregational churches to form the Congregational Christian churches. O'Kelly, preacher and writer, was an active opponent of slavery.

OLAF II, HARALDSSON or **OLAY** (c. 995-1030), King of Norway (c. 1015-1030). At age twelve began Viking career. Fought in England and France and raided the shores of Sweden. While in England became a Christian, baptized in France. In 1015, returned to Norway to claim throne. Once securely in power proceeded to establish Christianity in realm and to reorganize the government. Often employed means that were violent and even cruel. Was defeated and killed in battle in 1030. In 1031 a great assembly of clergymen and laymen declared Olaf a saint. In 1164 canonized as the first Norwegian saint and has become the national hero and most celebrated saint in Scandinavia.

OLAF I, TRYGGVESSON (trüg'vĕ sŏn) (c. 969-1000), King of Norway (995-1000), educated at the court of Vladimir, grand prince of Russia. Early lived the adventurous life of a viking, raided England and France, but was baptized by a hermit on the Scilly Islands. In 995 returned to Norway, native home, elected king. Set about bringing all the Norwegians to acknowledge his rule and receive baptism. Proceeded with persuasion where possible and by force when necessary. Destroyed pagan temples and slew members of the opposition. Made Trondheim his capital; is said to have erected the earliest Norwegian cathedral. Established Christianity in Iceland and Greenland.

OLDCASTLE, SIR JOHN (c. 1378-1417), Lollard leader. Became one of Wycliffe's Lollard lay preachers in 1410. Had held government posts and headed the army of Henry V in Wales and France. Member of Parliament in 1404 and a baron in 1408. In 1413 accused of Lollard heresy and hanged and burned in 1417.

OLDENBARNEVELDT, JAN VAN

(BARNEVELDT, JAN VAN OLDEN) (1547-1619), Dutch statesman and champion of Dutch independence. Grand pensionary in 1586. Negotiated treaty with Spain in 1609. Sided with Arminian Remonstrants against Maurice and Calvinists in 1617. Arrested in 1618 and in the next year executed as a traitor.

OLDHAM, JOSEPH HOULDSWORTH (1874-1969), ecumenical leader. Educated at Trinity College, Oxford. Secretary of the Student Christian movement in 1896. Secretary of the World Missionary Conference, opening way for the 1910 missionary conference at Edinburgh. Joint secretary of the International Missionary Council from 1921 to 1938. Edited *International Review of Missions* in the thirties. Set up the Oxford Conference on Life and Work in 1937. Worked for betterment of educational and social life of Africans during the latter part of his life.

OLEVIANUS (ō lā vē ä′ no͞os), **KASPAR** (1536-1587), early German reformer and theologian, born at Treves, Germany, studied law at Paris, Orleans, and Bourges, where he came in touch with the Reformers and attached himself to the Reformation. In 1558 went to Geneva to study theology and became intimately acquainted with Calvin, Beza, Farel, and Bullinger. In 1559 returned to Treves to teach in the Latin School. Began to explain the principles of the Reformation, to bare the errors of Rome, and to preach the evangelical faith. Fearless preaching and teaching caused both state and church to restrict and finally to imprison him. After a short imprisonment released upon the payment of a sum of money. Invited by Elector Frederick III to become professor of theology at the University of Heidelberg. The next year became pastor of St. Peter Church where he exercised considerable influence upon the reconstruction of the church regime along Reformed lines. He and Zacharias Ursinus were the drafters of the final revision of the Heidelberg Catechism. Also became involved in the Arian controversy, and gave his vote for the death penalty against the "blasphemers." Later banished by Louis VI, went to Berleberg, where he wrote some New Testament commentaries. Developed idea of covenant of grace.

OLGA (d. 969), widow of Igor, ruler of Khiev. Baptized in Constantinople in 957 and tried to introduce Christianity into Russia. Accepted by her grandson Vladimir about 988.

OLIVÉTAN (ô lē vā täɴ′) **PIERRE ROBERT** (c. 1506-1538), French Protestant biblical scholar, one of the first translators of the Bible into French. Born at Noyon in Picardy, France, a cousin of John Calvin. Studied law at the University of Paris, and later at Orléans, converted to Protestantism. Later brought Calvin to adopt the evangelical doctrine. Suspected of Lutheran heresy, fled to Strassburg about 1528, began the study of Hebrew and Greek. In 1533 went to Geneva; with his meager knowledge of Hebrew and Greek and with the help of Lefèvre's translation began to translate the Scriptures into the French. Later Calvin corrected this 1535 translation, and his labors thus became the foundation for the Geneva Bible. Obliged to leave Switzerland, went to Italy. Died there in 1538.

OLOPUN *See* **ALOPEN**

OLSHAUSEN, HERMANN (1796-1839), mediating Lutheran theologian and New Testament exegete, born at Oldesloe in Holstein, Germany. First studied at the University of Kiel, then at the University of Berlin, where the teaching of Schleiermacher and Neander gave direction to his studies and writings. In 1821 elected professor at Königsberg, where he taught until 1834, when called to Erlangen, Bavaria. Answered this call hoping that he might regain his health, but he died of tuberculosis. Special field was New Testament exegesis, and fame rests on Commentary of the New Testament, which he was able to complete as far as the epistles to the Thessalonians before death. Approached the Bible as the divine Word of the Living God, and upheld the genuineness of the gospels but did not accept the doctrine of verbal inspiration. A brother, Justus Olshausen, was a prominent German orientalist, and wrote a widely-used commentary of the Psalms.

OOSTERZEE, JAN JAKOB VAN (1817-1882), Dutch Reformed preacher and theologian of the mediating school, born at Rotterdam, Holland, educated at the University of Utrecht. Held three pastorates between the years of 1840 and 1862, the third being the principal church in Rotterdam of which he was pastor for eighteen years. From 1863 to the end of life he was professor at University of Utrecht, teaching first Biblical, systematic, and practical theology and homiletics, and later, New Testament Introduction, history of doctrine, and philosophy of religion. The recognized leader of the evangelical school in Holland. In sermons laid entire stress on the preaching of the Gospel, the proclamation of Christ according to the Scriptures, and the announcing of salvation. Avowed aim as a preacher was to edify rather than to instruct; preached mainly expository sermons. He was a voluminous writer. Among works: *Life of Jesus, Christology, Pastoral Epistles, Theology of the New Testament, Christian Dogmatics, Year of Salva-*

tion, Practical Theology, Person and Work of the Redeemer, and commentaries on several of the books of the New Testament.

ORIGEN (ŏr'ĭ jĕn), or **ORIGENES ADAMANTIUS** (c. 185-c. 254), Christian writer and teacher, born of Christian parents in Alexandria, educated there. His father, Leonidas, was martyred in the persecution of Septimus Severus in 202. Origen had wished to go to prison and suffer for his faith with his father, but his mother restrained him. Property that was left by Leonidas was confiscated, family had to struggle with poverty. Origen immediately assumed their support by teaching Greek philology and literature and by copying manuscripts. When eighteen, scholarship and piety led to appointment as a catechist. New responsibility resulted in his reopening the Catechetical School, which had been closed upon Clement's departure and the scattering of the students a year or two previously. Assumed the superintendency of the school. This brought him no emolument, so sold library, and thus provided funds for meager subsistence for several years. As teacher and catechist, in spite of great danger to his life in periods of persecution, visited imprisoned Christians. Lived an extremely ascetic life, became a eunuch about 210, indefatigable in study, teaching, and writing. Commentaries are voluminous, covering nearly all the books of the Bible. Wrote many dogmatic works and many practical works. One literary contribution was *Hexapla,* a Bible in six columns, which has been said to be the greatest textual enterprise of ancient times. His great work, *De Principiis,* was the first Christian treatise of systematic theology, in which he developed his allegorical system of interpretation. Also wrote an apologetic against the pagan skeptic Celsus. Held to universal salvation, subordination of Christ to Father and souls created before embodiment in men. After forty years of devoted service at Alexandria was ordained in Palestine about 230 but was later deprived of office of presbyter and expelled from the church. Retired to Caesarea where he opened another theological school that for twenty years surpassed his catechetical school in Alexandria. In Decian persecution, imprisoned and so maltreated that he died from the effects.

OROSIUS (ō rō'sĭ ŭs), **PAULUS** (c. 385-after 417), historian and Christian apologist, born in Bracara (now Braga), Portugal. As a young presbyter went to Hippo, North Africa, collaborated with Augustine in opposing Priscillianists and Origenists in their teaching on the nature and origin of the soul. Went to Bethlehem, Palestine to consult Jerome (415) concerning Pelagius' teaching on original sin and grace. On return to Hippo in 416, wrote *Adversus Paganos Historiarum Libri Septem,* using as sources the Holy Scriptures, Eusebius, Jerome, Livy, Eutropius, Caesar, Florus, Suetonius, and Justin. Writing was hastily completed by 418. Popular for centuries as apology and textbook, and was translated into English by Alfred the Great. Historical counterpart to Augustine's *City of God* shows God controls history and Roman calamities not caused by deserting paganism.

ORR, JAMES (1844-1913), Scottish theologian, born in Glasgow, educated at Glasgow University and the Theological Hall of the United Presbyterian Church, Scotland. Entered ministry in 1874, pastor of the East Bank United Presbyterian Church, Hawich, for seventeen years (1874-1891). Professor of church history in the United Presbyterian Theological College, Scotland (1891-1901); and from 1901 until death professor of apologetics and theology in the Glasgow College of the United Free Church. In 1895, in 1897, and again in 1903 lectured in the United States. In 1909 lectured in Toronto, Canada. Took a prominent part in the uniting of the United Presbyterian and Free churches. Published writings include *The Christian View of God and the World, The Supernatural in Christianity, Early Church History and Literature, The Progress of Dogma, The Bible under Trial, The Image of God, Problems of the Old Testament, Sin as a Problem of Today, The Virgin Birth,* and *The Resurrection of Jesus.*

OSIANDER (ō zē än'dẽr), **ANDREAS** (original name **HOSEMANN**) (1498-1552), German theologian and Reformer, born at Gunzenhausen in Brandenburg, studied at Leipzig, Altenburg, and Ingolstadt, acquiring great proficiency in Hebrew, theology, mathematics, and medicine. Ordained priest at Nürnberg in 1520, appointed Hebrew tutor in the Augustine convent at Nürnberg and from 1522 to 1548 preacher in the St. Lorenz Church. Joined the Lutheran party in 1522. Married in 1525, attended the Marburg Colloquy in 1529, the Augsburg Diet in 1530, and the signing of the Schmalkald Articles in 1537. Opinionated, arrogant, impulsive, polemic, contentious, but a learned theologian. Refusing to consent to the Augsburg Interim in 1548, forced to leave Nürnberg. The next year became professor of theology at the newly founded Protestant university at Königsberg. Stirred up a bitter theological controversy with the Wittenberg divines, advocating mystical doctrine of an effective and progressive justification by the indwelling of Christ, rather than by an imputed righteousness of Christ through His death. Differed in that from Luther, but otherwise agreed in the main with the great German Reformer, both in doctrine, also in opposition to both Romanism and Calvinism. In 1537 wrote a harmony of the gospels.

OSWALD (c. 605-642), King of Northumbria (634-642). When father, King Ethelfrith of Bernicia, died in 616, Oswald was forced to flee to Iona in Scotland, because his uncle Edwin seized the kingdom. He was won to Christianity and baptized by monks. After Edwin's death in the battle of Heavenfeld in 633, he returned to the north of England and conquered Northumbria. Also united Deira and Bernicia with Northumbria and became king; brought the kingdom into a position of eminence. Received Aidan with a band of Celtic missionaries from Iona, about 635, and presented him with the island of Lindisfarne as a place to establish monastery and base of operation. Aidan succeeded in converting the larger part of the country to Christianity. Oswald was killed in the battle of Maserfield by the pagan king Penda of Mercia.

OTTERBEIN (ŏt'ĕr bīn), **PHILIP WILLIAM** (1726-1813), co-founder of the Church of the United Brethren in Christ, born at Dillenburg, Germany, educated at Herborn. Preceptor of Herborn for a year, then ordained in the German Reformed church, served as a pastor for a time in Germany. Came to America in 1752 at the invitation of Michael Schlatter, minister of the Reformed Church of Holland. Held charges among the German Reformed in Lancaster, Tulpehocken, and York, Pennsylvania, and in Frederick and Baltimore, Maryland. Went to Baltimore in 1774, remained there until 1813. Following a deep personal religious experience, did much itinerary preaching among the German settlers in Pennsylvania, Maryland, and Virginia. Martin Boehm, a Mennonite preacher who had experienced an awakening similar to that of Otterbein, joined him in holding two-day "great meetings" which produced thousands of converts. This co-operative effort in evangelistiic preaching continued for over fifteen years. Though these evangelists had no intention or desire of creating a new denomination, the increasing number of converts resulting from their preaching required spiritual care. At suggestion of Francis Asbury they organized their followers into Reformed church societies of the Wesleyan type for the promotion of personal piety. In 1800 a conference was held in Frederick County, Maryland, which resulted in the forming of the Church of the United Brethren in Christ, somewhat along Methodistic lines. Otterbein and Boehm were elected as joint bishops, and continuously reelected until both died. In 1946 this church united with the Evangelical church to form the Evangelical United Brethren church.

OTTO I, THE GREAT (912-973), Holy Roman Emperor of German nation from 962, son of Henry I (the Fowler) a powerful duke of Saxony. Came to the throne in 936 and continued to bring German duchies and principalities under the control of his family, and by establishing a revived Holy Roman Empire upon the power of the church. Master of the pope and defender of the Roman church, left everywhere the impress of a heroic character, second only to Charlemagne. Subdued the Danes, the Slavonians, and the Hungarians, converted the barbarians on the frontier, established order, restored the power of the Carolingian empire. In 962, Pope John XII crowned Otto emperor, thus reviving the Roman Empire under the name "Holy Roman Empire." Otto accepted the theory handed down from Constantine's time that the state and church were two independent arms of divine government, one ruling over the temporal, and the other over the spiritual affairs, the two working together, but each in its own sphere. The emperors were gaining more and more power over the church, and the church leaders were looking more and more to the civil power for protection. Otto was a wise, strong ruler and statesman.

OTTO or **OTHO OF BAMBERG** (c. 1060-1139), Apostle of Pomerania, born in Suabia, early began to plan life for the church. First worked as a teacher in Poland. Later entered the service of Emperor Henry IV, who in 1101 made him chancellor of the empire; the following year, Bishop of Bamberg, Germany, employed chiefly in administering diocese, increasing its territories, churches, castles, and especially its monasteries, of which he built or restored twenty. In 1124 chosen to bring Christianity to Pomerania. Before he returned to Bamberg the next year, baptized over 22,000 persons and established eleven churches in nine cities. Three years later returned to Pomerania for a short time and converted many nobles of the land. After founding new churches in the land and strengthening the people in the faith and in the knowledge of the Bible returned again to Bamberg, where he discharged duties until death in 1139.

OTTO, RUDOLF (1869-1937), German philosopher. Born in Hanover. Educated at Erlangen and Göttingen. Taught theology at Göttingen and Marburg in succession from 1907 to 1937. Stressed the "otherness" of

God as revealed in his holiness. Main work was *The Idea of the Holy.*

OTTO OF FREISING (c. 1110/1115-1158), church historian and bishop of Freising. Of royal birth. Studied at Paris under Abelard. Became a Cistercian about 1132 at Morimund and its abbot about 1137. Bishop of Freising in the next year. Participated in the second crusade. Wrote *History of the Two Cities.* Like Augustine's *City of God,* but saw the culmination of the divine city in the medieval Roman Catholic Church, and Holy Roman Empire as the continuation of the Roman Empire.

OVERHOLZER, J. IRWIN, JR. (1877-1955), child evangelist. Began the Child Evangelism Fellowship in Los Angeles in 1936 and associated with it until 1952.

OWEN, JOHN (1616-1683), Puritan divine, born at Stadhampton, Oxfordshire, England, age twelve entered Queen's College, Oxford, and received B.A. in 1632 and M.A. in 1635. Received orders while yet at Oxford, but left the university in 1637 rather than submit to Laud's High Church discipline. Then served two different private chaplainships for a time. Early espoused the Parliamentarian cause, and when the Civil War broke out removed to Charterhouse Yard, London. Wrote a decidedly Calvinistic book entitled *Display of Arminianism.* Called to become pastor of a congregation at Fordham, Essex in 1642. In 1646 preached before Long Parliament a sermon that clearly displayed tendencies toward the Independent or Congregational system of government; ejected from Fordham. Soon after this took charge of a Presbyterian congregation at Coggeshall, Essex, introduced independent church government. At the request of Parliament preached a sermon before that body in 1649 on the day following the execution of Charles I. Thus thoroughly identified himself with Parliamentarianism and soon became a fast friend and chaplain of Cromwell. Chaplain in his army in Ireland and Scotland from 1649 to 1651. In 1651, by vote of the House of Commons appointed dean of Christ Church College, Oxford. In 1654 made vice chancellor of the university. With determination and zeal, and relying on Calvinistic convictions, carried the university through difficult days. After the Restoration in 1660, tolerated, and even treated with respect by the royal government. Permitted to continue his preaching. In 1673 became minister of a large congregation in Leadenhall Street, London. Ranks with Baxter and Howe among the most eminent of the Puritan divines. Wrote: *Epistle to the Hebrews, Doctrine of Justification by Faith, On the Holy Spirit, The Divine Origin of the Scriptures, Saint's Perseverance, Union among Protestants, Meditation on the Glory of Christ,* and *Christologia.*

P

PACHOMIUS (på kō′mĭ ŭs) (c. 290-c. 346), founder of the cloister system, born of wealthy heathen parents in Lower Egypt. In youth served in the army. Contacts with Christian ascetics led him to become a Christian at about twenty. Early attracted to hermit life, and about 320 became the founder of the famous monasteries of Tabenna on the bank of the Nile in Southern Egypt. Here solitary monks or hermits were invited to assemble in groups or cloisters. He assigned them work, regular hours of worship, and uniform dress, and taught them to live in common under an abbot, Pachomius being the first and chief. Also established a cloister for his sister. At death there were nine of his cloisters for men and two for women. His rule of order influenced Eastern monasticism through Basil the Great.

PAGE, KIRBY (1890-1957), pacifist and social reformer, born in Tyler County, Texas, educated at Drake University, University of Chicago, Columbia University, and Union Theological Seminary. He was student pastor at Monteith, Iowa (1912-1915). Ordained to the ministry in the Disciples of Christ Church (1915). Pastor of the Morgan Park Church, Chicago (1915); 1916-1918, Young Men's Christian Association worker in France and British Isles. Traveled with Sherwood Eddy in evangelistic campaigns in America, China, Japan, and Korea. Pastor of the Ridgewood Church of Christ in New York (1918-1921). Following 1921 a lecturer on behalf of American Friends Service Commission and the Fellowship of Reconciliation. Through the years was a consistent pacifist. Among writings: *The Sword or the Cross; War: Its Causes, Consequences, and Cure; An American Peace Policy; Dollars and World Peace; National Defense; Industrialism and Socialism* and *Must We Go to War?*

PAINE, THOMAS (1737-1809), Anglo-American political philosopher, born at Thetford, Norfolk, England, father an English Quaker. At the invitation of Benjamin Franklin came to America in 1774; at once began writing. Became a warm advocate of American independence, aided the cause through 500,000 copies of *Common Sense* in 1792. Served for about six months in Washington's army, and then for about ten years served the new republic in various other capacities. Spent years 1787-1802 in Europe, mostly in France, where he was naturalized and elected to the National Assembly. He wrote *The Rights of Man,* defending the French Revolution, and also appealing to the English to overthrow their monarchy and organize a republic. He was tried, convicted of treason, and outlawed from England. He was also arrested and imprisoned for ten months in Paris as an Englishman. He was released through the intercession of the American minister, James Madison, who said Paine was an American citizen. In *Age of Reason* made an uncompromising, ignorant, and audacious attack on the Bible. Paine was not an atheist, but a deist. His *Age of Reason* helped to popularize the deistic theology in the United States and abroad. Paine's last years were lived in and near New York in social ostracism, loneliness, poor health, and relative poverty.

PALESTRINA (pä lā strē′nä), **GIOVANNI PIERLUIGI DA** (c. 1525-1594), Italian polyphonic composer, born at Palestrina, near Rome, studied music in Rome. Given various important positions among the musicians by Pope Julius III. Continued to fill important music positions throughout life. In turn organist of the principal church of his native city (1544-1551); director of music at Giulia Chapel of St. Peter's in the Vatican; director of the Julian Chapel after he had written his first masses and had dedicated them to Julius III; singer in the Sistine Chapel (1555); chapelmaster of the Basilica of St. John the Lateran (1555-1561); master of the Liberian Chapel in Santa Maria Maggiore (1561-1571), where he did some of his most enduring work; choirmaster of St. Peter's; composer to the papal chapel; director of music at St. Philip's Oratory; teacher at the school of music of Giovanni Maria Nanini. In 1564 called upon by Pope Pius IV to assist in bringing about important reforms in church music as had been decreed by the Council of Trent sometime before. Submitted three masses, one of which was his masterpiece, *Missa Papae Marcelli*. Had shown that church music could be both dignified and artistic as well as worshipful. For this accomplishment, in 1565, honored and elevated to a new position created for him, Special Composer of the Pontifical Chair which he held during the reigns of six succeeding popes. In 1577 Gregory XIII commissioned him to assist in a complete revision of the Gregorian Chant. His appointment as director of music to the pope's nephew, started him on perhaps the most brilliant period of his life. His compositions produced a complete revolution in the history of church music. Composed masses, madrigals, choir music, motets, hymns and offertories, litanies, lamentations, magnificats, and psalms, writing almost the entire duration of his life. He was a sensitively religious man.

PALEY, WILLIAM (1743-1805), English theologian and philosopher, born at Peterborough, England, received higher education at Christ Church College, Cambridge. Lectured on metaphysics, morals, and the Greek Testament at Cambridge for a while. Between 1767 and 1795 served in various churches as rector, vicar, and prebendary. In 1782 became arch-deacon, three years later was made chancellor of diocese. In 1795 appointed prebendary of St. Paul's, and a little later became subdeacon of Lincoln and then rector of Bishop Wearmouth, where he remained the rest of his life. Using the teleological argument in his books, *View of the Evidences of Christianity* (1794), and *Natural Theology* (1802), he attempted to prove the existence of God, who reveals Himself in the Bible, in Christ, and in miracles. Another important work from his pen was *Principles of Moral and Political Philosophy,* setting forth his ethical theory, which is a modified form of utilitarianism.

PALLADIUS (pă lā'dĭ ŭs), **PETER (PEDER PLADE)** (1504-1560), Danish leader of the Reformation, born at Ribe; for a short time a schoolmaster in Odense. In 1531 went to Wittenberg, spent six years studying under Luther and Melanchthon, obtaining doctorate in theology. From 1537 to 1560 appointed by King Christian III as first Protestant bishop of Zealand, and professor of theology in the University of Copenhagen from 1538 on. Ordained by John Bugenhagen and became the most influential man in Denmark. Introduced the Lutheran Reformation in Denmark, Norway, and Iceland. Helped to reorganize the University of Copenhagen, instructed ministers, made frequent visits to the more than three hundred churches in diocese, translated Luther's shorter catechism, compiled the first Danish ritual, assisted in the translation of the so-called Christian III's Bible in 1550.

PALMER, ELIHU (1764-1806), popularized Deism in America. Born Canterbury, Connecticut. Educated at Dartmouth. Pastoral career in Presbyterian, Baptist, and then Universalist circles. Deistic leader from 1793 to 1806. Wrote *Principles of Nature* in 1802 in which he argued that religion is ethics that man can discover by reason in the laws of nature.

PALMER, PHOEBE WORRAL (1807-1884). Born New York City. Wife of a doctor. Became Methodist exponent of perfectionism about 1835 both in meetings and writings. Main work was *The Way to Holiness*. Founded Hedding Church in the New York slums and in 1850 Five Point Mission, the forerunner of settlement houses. Supported equal rights for women in the 1840s.

PALMER, RAY (1808-1887), American Congregational clergyman and hymn writer, born at Little Compton, Rhode Island, educated at Phillip's Academy, Andover, and Yale College. Studied theology privately and entered the Congregational ministry. In 1835 became pastor of the Central Congregational Church, Bath, Maine, and in 1850 of the First Congregational Church, Albany, New York, serving the two churches a total of thirty years. In 1865 became Corresponding Secretary to the American Congregational Union, New York. Resigned in 1878, retired to Newark, New Jersey, served as associate pastor of the Bellevue Avenue Congregational Church (1881-1884). A hymn writer; most widely known hymns, "My Faith Looks up to Thee" and "Jesu, Thou Joy of Loving Hearts."

PAMPHILUS (păm'fĭ lŭs), (c. 250-310), early Christian teacher, born at Berytus (now Beirut), Phoenicia, of noble birth and wealthy parents. First studied philosophy in native city, then entered the catechetical school at Alexandria, where he became a great admirer of Origen, a former teacher there. Later ordained a presbyter, also became a theological teacher and a promoter of Christian learning at Caesarea in Palestine. A warm friend of Eusebius of Caesarea. He did little original writing, but did much transcribing from other books, especially from the Septuagint of Origen's Hexapla. Aided poor students, distributed the Scriptures, and wrote a defense of the orthodoxy of Origen. Did valuable service to future generations by founding a theological school and by collecting a large library, which was built upon the foundation of Origen's library at Caesarea. From this library Eusebius, Jerome, and many others found valuable help for their writing. After two years of imprisonment, he and eleven others suffered martyrdom in the persecution of Maximinus.

PANTAENUS (păn tē'nŭs) (died c. 190), first known head of Catechetical School at Alexandria (180-190). Probably born in Sicily or Athens. Stoic philosopher before conversion to Christianity. Teacher of Clement of Alexandria. Preached the gospel in "India" (Persia or South Arabia).

PAPIAS (pā'pĭ ăs) (c. 60-c. 130), Bishop of Hierapolis. He is thought to have been a disciple of the apostle John, a friend of Polycarp, and Bishop of Hierapolis in Phrygia, Asia Minor. A pious, devout, and learned student of the Scriptures. Seems to have written an important work, *Exposition of the Lord's Oracles,* the object of which was to throw light on the gospel history. Only meager fragments have come down to us through the writings of Irenaeus and Eusebius. About all we know of his theology is that he held millennarian views.

PARACELSUS (păr å sĕl'sŭs), **VAN HOHENHEIM THEOPHRASTUS BOMBASTUS** (1493-1541), Swiss Renaissance physician and philosopher, born in Einsiedeln, Switzerland, studied at Basel University, at one time professor of medical science at Basel. Deep religious nature led him to consider his medical calling as a divine mission of love. Theology based on the Bible as interpreted through his natural philosophy, rather than from a historical viewpoint. System was a combination of the theosophy of cabala and natural science, resulting in a kind of pantheism, bordering on the superstitious, and laid foundations for future Protestant nature mysticism.

PARHAM, CHARLES FOX (1873-1929), Charismatic educator. Born in Muscatine, Iowa. Educated at Southwestern College, Winfield, Kansas and a Methodist minister until 1894. Opened Bethel Bible School in 1900 at Topeka with only the Bible as the text, prayer and practical service. In this school Agnes Ozman spoke in tongues on January 1, 1901 which marked the beginning of classic Pentecostalism. School closed in 1901, and Parham held meetings in Kansas, Missouri, and Texas. William J. Seymour, who carried "tongues" to Los Angeles, was trained for a time in Parham's Houston Bible school.

PARKER, DANIEL (1781-1834), founder of the Two-Seed-in-the-Spirit-Predestinarian-Baptists, born in Virginia, ordained in 1806, and labored in Virginia, Illinois, and Texas. Early in the 1820s began a crusade of opposition to all forms of organized church work, including missionary, Bible, and temperance societies, as well as Sunday schools, colleges, theological seminaries, and instrumental music in the churches. An ultra-Calvinist predestinarian, and promulgated the theory that two seeds were planted in Eve, one by God and one by the devil. The "good seed" were elected to salvation, and the "bad seed" were destined to be damned. "The atonement, according to Parker, applies only to those born of the good seed, those born of the bad seed being absolutely lost." In pamphlet and magazine he vigorously opposed missions. Edited the *Church Advocate* for two years when it ceased for want of patronage.

PARKER, JOSEPH (1830-1902), English Congregational preacher, born at Hexham on the Tyne, Northumberland, England. Early developed the desire to preach; when eighteen was doing local, voluntary preaching. At same time was gathering his education by much reading. In 1852 went to London to seek the advice of John Campbell of Moorfields Tabernacle, and became his assistant. Studied a short time at University College, London in 1853, and then became pastor of the Banbury Congregational Church in Oxfordshire. In 1858 he moved to the Cavendish Street Congregational Church, Manchester, became the pastor, and was accorded the leadership of the Congregational denomination. In 1869 called to the pastorate of Poultry Church, London, an old but declining church. The church building soon proved to be too small, and the City Temple was erected on Holborn Viaduct, and was opened in 1874. In this church he preached there until his death. Though living in England in a period of liberalism he remained staunchly Nonconformist and evangelical. Twice chairman of the London Congregational Board, and twice chairman of the Congregational Union of England and Wales. He published *Parker's People's Bible* in twenty-five large volumes (sermons he had preached over a period of many years). He also published *Ecce Deus, Autobiography,* and *The Evils of Rum*.

PARKER, MATTHEW (1504-1575), Archbishop of Canterbury; born at Norwich, graduate of Corpus Christi College, Cambridge (1525). Ordained priest (1527), chaplain to Queen Anne Boleyn (1535), married in 1547. Received several preferments under Henry VIII and Edward VI, but was denied them under Mary. Elizabeth made him archbishop of Canterbury (1559). A conciliatory churchman, evangelical and conservative, but strongly opposed to Puritanism. Had a part in drawing up the Book of Common Prayer. Revision of the Thirty-Nine Articles done under his direction, also publication of the Bishop's Bible. More a scholar than an administrator.

PARKER, PETER (1804-1888), American medical missionary and diplomat, born in Framingham, Massachusetts, educated at Wrentham Academy, Amherst College, and Yale University, studying theology and medicine at the latter. Ordained to the Presbyterian ministry and sent by the American Board to China in 1834, as first Protestant medical missionary to China. In 1835 opened Ophthalmic Hospital in Canton, which rapidly grew into a general hospital and dispensary. Patients soon came from all of the eighteen provinces. In 1838 the Medical Missionary Society in China was founded at Canton. In 1840 the bitter feeling caused by the Opium War between China and

England made it necessary to close the hospital for a time. Dr. Parker spent this time on furlough in the United States. Urged the government at Washington to establish friendly relations with China. In 1842 reopened his hospital at Canton. More and more drawn into diplomatic service, soon asked to assist Mr. Caleb Cushing in negotiating a treaty between China and the United States. In 1845 resigned position with the American Board, appointed by President Tyler as secretary and Chinese interpreter to the legation in China. Gave much attention to the development of right relations with the Chinese empire, yet continuing with medical work at Canton. In 1855 in ill health returned to America. Soon sent back to China as United States Commissioner, helped in the revision of the treaty of 1844, which resulted in the treaty of 1858. From this time until death thirty years later Dr. Parker resided in Washington, D.C., interesting himself in such enterprises as the American Evangelical Alliance and the Smithsonian Institution, regent of the latter until his death in 1888. Wrote a few books pertaining to medical work in China.

PARKER, THEODORE (1810-1860), Unitarian clergyman, born at Lexington, Massachusetts. For several years taught school, studied at Harvard College and Divinity School. In 1837 ordained and accepted the pastorate of the West Roxbury Unitarian Church (near Boston). Sermons were liberal and latitudinarian. To him religion was mainly morality. The Boston Association of Ministers, of which he was a member, took prompt action of dissent and disapproval. Among the laity he had a strong following. He maintained membership with the Unitarians for twenty years, preached and lectured independently. First independent charge was with a congregation that assumed the name, Twenty-eighth Congregational Society of Boston from 1846 to 1859. Became one of the most popular preachers of the city, often speaking on the social questions. Directed eloquence against the Mexican War, slavery and intemperance. Name is associated with those of Garrison and Wendell Phillips. He was thoroughly hated by the South. Parker was one of the secret committee that aided John Brown's scheme for a raid on Harper's Ferry. His theology was antisupernaturalistic. Bequeathed thirteen thousand valuable books to the Boston Public Library. Among writings: *A Discourse of Matters Pertaining to Religion; Sermons on Theism, Atheism, and the Popular Theology; Ten Sermons on Religion;* and *Critical and Miscellaneous Writings.*

PARSONS, LEVI (1792-1822), pioneer missionary to Palestine, born in Goshen, Massachusetts, attended Middlebury College and Andover Theological Seminary. Ordained in 1817, labored a year under the Vermont Missionary Society. In 1819 he and Pliny Fisk were sent by the American Board of Commissioners for Foreign Missions to Palestine to survey the field, looking toward opening a mission at Jerusalem. They arrived in Smyrna, and after doing some surveying in Asia Minor studying modern Greek and Italian at Scio, Mr. Parsons made a special survey in Palestine. After spending about a year prospecting, three months of this time in Jerusalem, he decided that the Board should open a mission in Jerusalem. Arrived in Jerusalem on February 17, 1820, the first Protestant missionary to enter that city to make it the permanent field of his labor. However, ill health overtook him, and in search of recovery, with the doctor's advice, made a voyage, accompanied by fellow missionary, Pliny Fisk, to Alexandria, Egypt, where he died early in 1822 at the age of thirty. A good scholar, a devout Christian; his life fully devoted to Christian work.

PASCAL (pȧs kȧl'), **BLAISE** (1623-1662), French philosopher, mathematician, and mystic, born at Clermont-Ferrand, France. Father moved to Paris to give son and two daughters a good education. In 1654 an accident that all but cost his life, brought him to a thoroughgoing conversion. Pascal's religion centered on the Person of Christ as Savior and based on personal experience. Along with the Jansenists came into combat with the Jesuits concerning teaching of the doctrine of probabalism. When the Jesuits condemned the writing of Antoine Arnauld, a friend and pupil of Cornelius Jansen, and sought to have him expelled from the Sorbonne, Pascal under an assumed name wrote a series of letters in defense of the Jansenist doctrine of grace, and against the casuistry of the Jesuits. These nineteen letters were later collected and published as the *Provincial Letters of Pascal.* They were a moral achievement, and written in the finest literary style. Pascal had come out as a champion of freedom of conscience, of truth, and of justice against the powerful Jesuits. After this achievement he wanted to write a great work on apologetics, and attempted to do so; but rapidly failing health made it impossible to do more than to write a few scattered, elegantly written "Thoughts." These were later collected, arranged, and published as *The Thoughts of Pascal.* He spent his last months as an ascetic and mystic, living in retirement, following devotional exercises, and doing charitable acts.

PASSAVANT, WILLIAM ALFRED (1821-1894), Lutheran clergyman and philanthropist, born at Zelienople, Pennsylvania. After graduation from Jefferson College in 1840 and the Lutheran Theological Seminary at Gettysburg in 1842, ordained and became pastor in Canton, near Baltimore. From about 1844 to 1855 in charge of a parish in Pittsburgh. Founded *The Missionary* in 1848 and was its editor until 1861 when it merged to form *The Lutheran and Missionary*. He was one of its editors. In 1881 founded *The Workman,* which he and his son edited until his death. Gradually became a champion of Old Lutheranism, and became one of the founders of the conservative General Council of the Evangelical Lutheran Church in North America in 1867. In 1870 with A. Louis Thiel, founded Thiel College at Greenville, Pennsylvania, and assisted in founding the Chicago Lutheran Theological Seminary in 1879. In 1848 helped introduce the Kaiserwerth system of deaconesses in the United States. He was responsible for the establishment of hospitals and orphanages in several midwestern and eastern states.

PASTORIUS, FRANCIS DANIEL (1651-c. 1720), Mennonite emigration agent. Born in Sommerhausen. Educated at the universities of Altdorf, Wurzberg, Strassburg, and Jena and the German University in Rome. Served as lawyer from 1676 to 1679 and tutor from 1680 to 1682. Land agent for the Frankfurt Land Company from 1683 to 1700. Mayor of Germantown, Philadelphia from 1702 to 1719, and a teacher in Germantown from 1702-1719. Helped Mennonites and other persecuted minorities in Europe to move to Pennsylvania.

PATON, JOHN GIBSON (1824-1907), Presbyterian missionary to the New Hebrides, born at Kirkmahoe, near Dumfries, Scotland in a poor home. He later studied at the University of Glasgow, the divinity hall of the Reformed Presbyterian church, and the Andersonian Medical University, all in Glasgow, where he was a city missionary from 1847 to 1857. Ordained a missionary in March, 1858, and with newly wed wife sailed to the New Hebrides. Began work on Tanna, an island inhabited by most ferocious savage cannibals. A few months later his wife and infant son died. The savages of Tanna proved intractable, and after nearly four years of heroic and patient effort among them he was forced to leave his station in February, 1862. Left behind all his possessions except his Bible and a few things he could carry with him. (Later, a son resumed the work on Tanna, and that island was won for Christ.) Began extensive tours in behalf of New Hebrides mission work, going first to Australia, then to Scotland. In 1864 in Scotland, elected Moderator of the General Synod of the Reformed Presbyterian church, also secured seven new missionaries. In January 1865 returned from Scotland to the New Hebrides with his second wife. Began work on Aniwa, a small island near Tanna. He held his first communion in 1869 in a new house of worship built by native Christians. Gave to the Aniwan people the first hymnbook in their own language. Finally, saw the whole island become Christian. During the last quarter of the century, along with mission work, he traveled much in Australasia, Great Britain, United States, and Canada, raising money and promoting the cause of missions. In the United States he pleaded before vast audiences for a reversal of the national policy that tolerated the liquor traffic and the trade in firearms among the Melanesians. In 1886 elected Moderator of the Presbyterian Church of Victoria. In 1897, in Melbourne carrying through the press the New Testament which he had translated into the Aniwan language. His autobiography, carefully edited by his brother James, was published in two volumes in 1889. In 1900 attended the Ecumenical Missionary Conference in New York City, where he was hailed a great missionary hero. In 1904 privileged to visit the islands and his beloved Hebridean brethren.

PATRICK or **PATRICIUS** (c. 389-c. 461), Celtic missionary to Ireland. His father, Calpurnius, seems to have been a deacon in the local Celtic church, his grandfather a priest. When sixteen years old he was taken captive in one of the Irish pirate raids, and was sold as a slave to a herdsman in North Ireland, where he was held for six years. He escaped and somehow found his way to Gaul, where he spent some time in a monastic school. After returning home he saw a vision and heard voices from the Irish coast, crying, "We beseech thee, child of God, come and walk again among us." Answering the call, he set out for Ireland. About 432 he gathered people about him in the open fields and preached Christ to them. His burning zeal, deep sincerity, and gentleness of manner won peasants and nobility alike. Planted scores of churches and baptized over 100,000 converts. At Armagh he founded a monastery which was to become important and historic in the annals of the Christian church. His preaching made a strong impact, not only upon the Ireland of his day, but upon all medieval missions and church life of Ireland, of Great Britain, and of Continental Europe. Both Catholics and Protestants like to claim Patrick, but he was neither. He was a Celtic missionary in the British Isles before the time of either Protestants or Roman Catholics. Chief writing and our chief source of information concerning his life is his *Confessions*.

PATTESON, JOHN COLERIDGE (1827-1871), missionary bishop to Melanesia. Born in London and studied at Eton, Balliol College, Oxford, and in 1852 elected fellow of Merton College, Oxford. At Merton studied theology, Hebrew, and Arabic in order to prepare for holy orders. In 1853 ordained to the priesthood and was made curate or country parson of Alfington, Devonshire. In 1855 went to New Zealand to assist Bishop George Augustus Selwyn in his work among the South Sea Islands. In 1861 consecrated Bishop of Melanesia. His great linguistic ability made it possible for him to conduct worship in many of the languages, to write grammars and to translate the Scriptures into several languages, and to reduce many of the various dialects to written language. He spoke twenty-three of the dialects. An evidence of his success is the fact that after twenty years of work, only forty of the eight hundred natives on the chief island, Mota, remained unbaptized. Early death came about due to vengeance for the kidnapping of several islanders by unscrupulous traders some time earlier. Not aware of the ill-feeling existing among the islanders, he landed at Nukapu on one of the Santa Cruz Islands and was killed.

PATTON, FRANCIS LANDEY (1843-1932), Presbyterian educator. Born in Warwick, Bermuda. Educated at Knox College, Toronto, the University of Toronto and Princeton Theological Seminary. Ordained in 1865. Served churches in New York City and in Nyack from 1865 to 1871. Professor at McCormick Theological Seminary, Chicago from 1872 to 1881 and at Princeton Theological Seminary from 1881 to 1888. Professor and president of Princeton University from 1888 to 1902 and professor and president of Princeton Theological Seminary from 1902 to 1913. Moderator of his denomination's general assembly in 1878. Wrote conservative books, such as *Summary of Christian Doctrine* and *The Inspiration of the Scriptures* and articles for the *Fundamentals*.

PAUL III (ALESSANDRO FARNESE) (1468-1549), pope 1534 to 1549. Born in Italy and educated at Rome, Florence, and Pisa. Cardinal in 1493 and later ordained in 1519. In 1536 set up a commission that reported in 1537 and was critical of himself and the papal hierarchy. The report was placed on the Index. Approved the Society of Jesus in 1540 and convened the Council of Trent in 1545. Restored the Inquisition in 1542. Hired Michaelangelo to decorate the Vatican.

PAUL IV (GIOVANNI PIETRO CARAFFA) (1476-1559), pope from 1555. Born in Naples, educated in uncle's home. Bishop of Chiete in 1506. Papal envoy in succession to England, Flanders, and Spain from 1513 to 1520. He was a member of Oratory of Divine Love from 1520 to 1527 and helped found the Theatines in 1524. Made cardinal in 1536. Published the Index of Prohibited Books.

PAUL VI (GIOVANNI BATTISTA MONTINI) (1897-1968), pope from 1963. Educated at the Jesuit Institute, and in the Gregorian university and the University of Rome. Chaplain at the latter university. He was archbishop of Milan in 1954 and cardinal in 1958. As pope promulgated the decrees of the second and third session of Vatican II. Travelled in the Holy Land and the Philippines. Opposed birth control in the 1968 encyclical *Humanae Vitae*.

PAUL, KANAKARAYAN TIRUSELVAM (1876-1931), Indian Christian leader, born of Christian parents and educated in Madras arts and law colleges. He and Bishop Azariah were leaders in organizing the National Missionary Society of India in 1905; and he was its secretary from 1906 to 1913. In 1912 he became the well-known national general secretary of the Young Men's Christian Association of India, Burma, and Ceylon. Resigned his Young Men's Christian Association connections in order to devote himself to the political uplift of India as a representative of Christian communities. At the Round Table Conference in London he was trusted by Hindus and Moslems as well as by Christians. He represented the National Christian Council of India at the Jerusalem Missionary Council in 1928. President of United Church of South India in 1925 and 1930 and member of first Round Table Conference on future political evolution of India.

PAULINUS (pô lī'nŭs) **OF YORK** (c. 584-644), Roman missionary to Britain, likely born in Rome, was a monk in St. Andrews monastery at Rome. Sent by Pope Gregory I in 601 to assist Augustine until 625 when consecrated bishop by the Archbishop of Canterbury, and sent on a mission to Northumbria. In 627 baptized Edwin, king of the Northumbrians, whereupon Edwin assigned Paulinus to York, where he founded a cathedral. Continued to preach throughout Northumbria and to win converts until Edwin's death in 633. One of these converts was Hilda who became Abbess of Whitby. He fled back in 633 to Kent taking with him the widowed queen and her children, became

Bishop of Rochester. After making this flight, in 634, received the pallium from Rome, sent to him as Archbishop of York.

PEAKE ARTHUR SAMUEL (1865-1929), Nonconformist biblical critic. Born in Leek, Staffordshire. Educated at Oxford. From 1899 to 1919 lectured at Mansfield College, Merton College, Hartley College, Manchester, and was Rylands professor at Manchester University. Wrote a popular one-volume commentary setting forth his critical views.

PEARSON, JOHN (1613-1686), Church of England bishop and scholar, born at Great Snoring, Norfolk, England, educated at Eton and at Queen's College, Cambridge. Elected scholar and fellow at King's College, Cambridge, ordained in 1639. In 1640 became prebendary of Salisbury and rector of Thorington in Suffolk. During Civil War supported the royalist cause; under the Commonwealth lived in semi-retirement in London; and after the Restoration became rector of Christopher-le-Stocks, London, prebendary of Ely, archdeacon of Surrey, royal chaplain and master of Jesus College, Cambridge. In 1661 chosen to superintend the translation of the Prayer Book into Latin, and became Margaret professor of divinity at Cambridge; in the same year championed the cause of episcopacy at the Savoy Conference. The next year made master of Trinity College, Cambridge. He was consecrated Bishop of Chester in 1673. Has been considered the ablest theological scholar of the seventeenth century English church. His best known work, *An Exposition of the Creed,* won him fame. Also wrote a defense of the genuineness of the Ignatian epistles, and many minor works largely defending the Church of England against the attacks of both the Romanists and the Puritans. Probably never married.

PECK, JOHN MASON (1789-1858), Baptist minister and home missionary, born at Litchfield, Connecticut in a Puritan home. Received very little formal education beyond the elementary grades. In 1811 moved to Windham, New York. He and his wife joined the Baptist church. In 1813 ordained. Began to preach in a little church at Catskill, New York, supplementing living expenses by teaching school. Pastor of a church at Amena, New York (1814-1816), here coming in touch with Luther Rice who was creating missionary interest and raising support for the young Baptist mission in India. Greatly influenced by reading David Brainerd's Journal. In 1817 he and James E. Welsh accepted the call of the Baptist Philadelphia Board of Missions to open home mission work in Illinois and Missouri. Spent nine fruitful years as a pioneer itinerant missionary, and another ten years editing papers and founding schools for his mission field, along with much preaching. In 1829 began and continued for several years *The Pioneer,* the first Baptist journal published in the West. Principal of the newly established theological seminary in Rock Spring, Illinois (1830-1831); assisted in originating the American Baptist Home Missionary Society (1832); helped establish in 1819 the first college in Illinois, which became Shurtleff College at Upper Alton, Illinois (1835). He was its first president. Aided in establishing a theological seminary at Covington, Kentucky.

PELAGIUS (pē lā'jĭ ŭs) (early fifth century), early British theologian, born in Britain. An English monk of culture and education, of devout and virtuous character, but developed unorthodox views on the dignity and self-sufficiency of man, and on original sin and divine grace. At Rome about 400 came into intimate fellowship with Celestius, a lawyer of noble descent. Together they developed this doctrine, Celestius being the chief proponent of it, though the heresy took the name from Pelagius. Faith with them was hardly more than a theoretical belief; the main thing in religion was moral action, the keeping of the commandments of God by one's own strength. They were more concerned with the ethical side of religion than with the dogmatic. Pelagianism is summed up as follows: (1) Man has no original sin inherited from Adam. Sin is a matter of will and not of nature. (2) Each person is created with perfect freedom to do good or evil. Hence a sinless life is possible, and salvation can come by good works. (3) Infant baptism is unnecessary, since there is no original sin. (4) Although salvation is possible without the law and the gospel, or divine grace, these greatly facilitate the attainment of salvation. Christ helps by his good example. The Pelagian heresy spread in North Africa so widely and so effectively that Augustine felt it necessary to oppose it. Pelagianism was essentially defeated by the council of Ephesus in 431. After Augustine's time a modified form of Pelagianism continued for many years in the church as Semi-Pelagianism. This heresy never formed an ecclesiastical sect, but simply a theological school or movement that did make a powerful impact upon later Methodists, Salvation Army, and holiness groups. Pelagius wrote several treatises: *On the Trinity, On Free Will* and *Commentary on Paul's Epistles*.

PELOUBET (pĕ lo͞o'bĕt), **FRANCIS NATHAN** (1831-1920), American Congregational minister and Sunday school writer, born in New York City, studied at Williams

College and Bangor Theological Seminary, Bangor, Maine. Ordained a Congregational minister in 1857, and between 1857 and 1883 pastor of four different churches in Massachusetts. Author of forty-four annual volumes of *Select Notes on the International Sunday School Lessons* (1875-1920); author of many Sunday school publications. Among writings: *Suggestive Illustrations on Matthew; on John;* and *on Acts; Loom of Life; The Teacher's Commentary on Matthew;* and *on Acts; Studies on the Book of Job;* and a revision of Smith's *Bible Dictionary*. He also edited two volumes of *Select Songs for the Sunday School*.

PENN, WILLIAM (1644-1718), founder of Pennsylvania, son of Admiral Sir William Penn, born in London. Studied at Oxford and Lincoln's Inn. He joined the Society of Friends in 1666, consequently suffered much persecution and imprisonment. Becoming a non-conformist greatly displeased his father, and upon his becoming a Quaker, he was turned out of home and was sent to France. In 1664 returned to London a good French scholar and a polished gentleman. He traveled in Holland and Germany preaching fidelity to the light of Christ in the soul. From early years Penn had nourished the hope of seeing a home established for the oppressed in America. He helped to send more than eight hundred Quakers to New Jersey between 1677 and 1678. In 1681 received from King Charles II of England a grant of land now constituting Pennsylvania and Delaware in consideration of a royal debt of $80,000 to his father. Founded the colony of Pennsylvania as a "holy experiment" for the establishing of freedom and equality in the exercise of religion in 1682. Large numbers of emigrants of various denominations were attracted. He made peace treaties with the Indians; and granted a liberal charter to the colony. Except for 1683 was governor of Pennsylvania from 1682 to 1718. Upon the accession of William and Mary he was charged with being a papist, arrested and imprisoned; but later established innocency and came into favor with the king and queen as well as their successor, Queen Anne. Enjoyed the personal friendship of five English sovereigns. Penn became one of the most prominent preachers and literary defenders of the Quaker faith. Among his writings: *No Cross, No Crown; The Fruits of Solitude;* and *Primitive Christianity*.

PENNINGTON (pĕn'ĭng tŭn), or **PENINGTON, ISAAC** (1616-1679), Quaker mystic, born in a Puritan home, the Lord Mayor of London, educated privately and at Catherine Hall, Cambridge. For a time attached himself to the Independents, then in 1657, through the preaching of George Fox, he and his wife joined the Quaker movement. Quaker worship after 1658 was held in his house at Chalfont Grange. Six times between 1660 and the time of his death he was imprisoned for not conforming to the state church and for refusing to take the oath of allegiance, spending in all perhaps as much as eleven years in prison. House and property were confiscated. Preached powerful and spiritual sermons and wrote many books, pamphlets, and letters which were of great assistance in the building up of the new Quaker society.

PENTECOST, GEORGE FREDERICK (1842-1920), American Presbyterian clergyman, born at Albion, Illinois, and educated at Georgetown College, Georgetown, Kentucky; left college in 1862 after one year to enter the Eighth Kentucky (Union) Cavalry as chaplain. In 1864 returned from the army and entered the Baptist ministry. Held pastorates between 1864 and 1887 at Greencastle, Indiana; Evansville, Indiana; Covington, Kentucky; Hanson Place Baptist Church, Brooklyn, New York; and Warren Avenue Baptist Church, Boston. Spent a year in evangelistic work in Scotland in association with Dwight L. Moody (1887-1888), conducted a special mission for the English-speaking Brahmins in India (1889-1891), and was minister in the Marylebone Church, London (1891-1897). From 1897 to 1920 held pastorates in First Presbyterian Church, Yonkers, New York and the Bethany Presbyterian Church, Philadelphia, Pennsylvania. Devoted later years largely to Bible teaching and evangelistic work. Became a member of the American Board of Commissioners for Foreign Missions (1884). A special commissioner of that organization to the Philippines, China, Japan, and Korea (1902-1904). Among writings: *In the Volume of the Book, Systematic Beneficence, Bible Studies* (ten volumes), and *Precious Truths*.

PEPIN III (PIPPIN), THE SHORT (c. 714-768), First Carolingian king of the Franks (751-768), mayor of the palace and aspiring ruler of the Franks. Desiring the title and crown as well as the kingly power in France, determined upon a revolution which would eliminate Childeric III, the last feeble Merovingian king, and place himself upon the throne. In 751 coronation by Boniface secured the papal recognition and in 754 was again crowned by Pope Stephen III as "Patrician of the Romans." It was the beginning of an interplay of authority of papacy and empire that had many grave consequences through the middle ages. The pope had given

Pepin a significant boost to power. Now he would do the pope a service by giving him vast estates in 756 which had been promised in the 754 Donation of Pepin and which he had taken from the Lombards, over which the pope would have political sovereignty. These temporal possessions became known as the Papal States, the "States of the Church" or the "Patrimony of St. Peter." Only the Vatican State is left of those lands.

PERKINS, JUSTIN (1805-1869), American Congregational missionary to Persia, born at West Springfield, Massachusetts, converted at the age of eighteen, at twenty joined the Congregational church. Studied at Amherst College and Andover Theological Seminary, and after graduation became a tutor at Amherst. In 1833 ordained to the ministry, and sent by the American Board to the Nestorians at Urumiah, Persia, where he worked from 1833 to 1869. He and his wife took a furlough home in 1842-1843 for the sake of his wife's health, and were accompanied by the former Nestorian bishop, Mar Johannan, an early convert. Several new missionaries accompanied them back to the field. Perkins established several schools, some of which became seminaries. He also established a printing press. His great work was to build a written language for the Nestorians and to translate the Bible into the modern Syriac. Wrote commentaries on Genesis and Daniel, *Residence of Eight Years in Persia,* and *Missionary Life in Persia*.

PEROWNE, EDWARD HENRY (1826-1906), born at Burdwan, Bengal, India, the son of a missionary of the Church Missionary Society, and a younger brother of John James Stewart Perowne. After private education attended Corpus Christi College, Cambridge. Ordained priest in 1851. Among the positions filled were the following: curate of Maddermarket, Norfolk; fellow and tutor and later master of Corpus Christi College; examining chaplain to the Bishop of St. Asaph; prebendary of St. Asaph; vice-chancellor of Cambridge University; honorary chaplain to Queen Victoria; examining chaplain to the Bishop of Worcester. Strongly evangelical, unmarried. Principal writings: *The Christian's Daily Life, a Life of Faith; Corporate Responsibility; Counsel to Undergraduates on Entering the University; The Godhead of Jesus; Commentary on Galatians* (Cambridge Bible for Schools); and *Savonarola*.

PEROWNE, JOHN JAMES STEWART (1823-1904), Church of England bishop, born at Burdwan, Bengal, India, where father was a missionary of the Church Missionary Society. Educated at Corpus Christi College, Cambridge, and ordained priest in 1848. In seven different years select preacher to the university, and for ten years vice-principal of St. David's College, Lampeter, Wales. Held positions as master of King Edward's School, Birmingham; lecturer in divinity at King's College, London; examining chaplain to the Bishop of Norwich; prebendary of St. Andrew's; canon of Llandaff cathedral; prelector in theology in Trinity College, Cambridge; fellow Trinity College; and Hulsean professor of divinity. In 1875 appointed honorary chaplain to the Queen; in 1878 dean of Peterborough; in 1891 consecrated Bishop of Worcester, retiring in 1901 to be succeeded by Charles Gore. From 1870 to 1884 a member of the Old Testament company of Bible revisers. The author of *The Book of Psalms, a New Translation with Notes Critical and exegetical* (two volumes); *Immortality* (Hulsean lectures); *Sermons; The Church, the Ministry, and the Sacraments; The Doctrine of the Lord's Supper;* and an elementary Arabic grammar, *Al Adjrumiieh*. General editor of *The Cambridge Bible for Schools,* of which Haggai and Zechariah, Obadiah and Jonah, and Micah were his work.

PETER DAMIAN (dā'mĭ ăn), **(PIETRO DAMIANI)** (1007-1072), Cardinal, Bishop of Ostia, and Roman Catholic reformer, born at Ravenna, and studied at Ravenna, Faenza, and Parma. A successful teacher for several years, then he suddenly and unexpectedly retired to become a hermit. Became a prior and abbot in 1043 and introduced a new system of flogging penance, severely flogging himself with the accompaniment of the recitation of the Psalms. A friend and an able ally of Cardinal Hildebrand in the great cardinal's work of reform. Then against his will he was made a cardinal in 1057, and 1058 the pope called him from the hermitage to the papal court, and compelled him to assume the offices of Bishop of Ostia and head of the College of Cardinals. Only a short time later, however, he fled to his hermitage. The next year the pope sent him as papal legate to Milan where he succeeded in bringing reform to the corrupt church, and in bringing it into submission to the papal see. The pope sent him on various other missions on which he sought faithfully to work for the church's highest interests and to effect reform. Among his writings we find many hymns.

PETER OF BLOIS (blwȧ), (c. 1130-c. 1200), ecclesiastical writer, born at Blois, France. Early educated at Tours, studied canon law and medicine at Bologna, and theology at Paris. Lived several years in Sicily where he was tutor to the royal prince, William II, and then held several church appointments in France. Later went to England, became chief counselor of Henry II and filled various church posts, among them chancellor to the Archbishop of Canterbury, archdeacon of Bath, and archdeacon of London. Adviser to many bishops, writer of sermons, histories, commentaries, and moral and ascetic treatises. His *Epistolae* is an important historical source. He may have been the first theologian to use the word "transubstantiation." Though a loyal Catholic he had the courage to speak out against abuses in school, church, or state.

PETER OF BRUYS (brü ē′), **PIERRE DE BRUYS** (died c. 1140), medieval dissenter and originator of the Petrobrusians. Born at Bruis in southeastern France in the middle or latter part of the eleventh century. Appeared as a reformer in the Roman Catholic church about 1105. A pupil of Peter Abelard. Peter's chief aim seems to have been to restore Christianity to its original purity and simplicity. Rejected infant baptism, transubstantiation, the sacrifice of the mass, church buildings, ecclesiastical ceremonies, the veneration of the cross, and prayers for the dead. About 1140 seized and burned at St. Gilles as a heretic. After his death his followers joined Henry of Lausanne, the so-called Henricians, all of whom were later absorbed by the more widespread and better organized Waldenses.

PETER (THE GREAT) (1672-1725), czar of Russia from 1682 to 1725. Travelled in Western Europe from 1696 to 1697 to learn western culture in order to modernize Russia. Engaged in major war with Sweden to enlarge his country. Founded new capital at St. Petersburg in 1703. Created the Holy Synod which put the Russian Orthodox church under civil control.

PETER THE HERMIT (PETER OF AMIENS) (c. 1050-1115), French monk and preacher of the First Crusade, born at Amiens, France, where he became a monk. Returning in 1093 from a pilgrimage to Jerusalem, reported to Pope Urban II the brutalities inflicted by the Mohammedan Seljuk Turks upon the Christian pilgrims to the Holy Land. Urban's fiery sermon preached at the Council of Clermont in 1095 set Europe aflame. Peter went throughout France, even across the borders into Spain, Germany, and Italy stirring the people with his intense enthusiasm. In 1096 he started at the head of one untrained, improvised army, while Walter the Penniless started at the head of another for Palestine. Many perished along the way. Most of those who finally reached Constantinople or Asia Minor were cut to pieces by the Turks in 1096; Walter the Penniless was killed along with them. Peter escaped and waited at Constantinople for Godfrey of Bouillon with his army, and accompanied Godfrey to Nicea, Antioch, and Jerusalem (1097-1099). He later returned to Europe, and became prior of an Augustinian monastery which he earlier had helped to found.

PETER THE LOMBARD (c. 1095-c. 1159), Latin theologian and schoolman, born in Lombardy in Northern Italy, educated at Bologna, Rheims, and Paris, distinguishing himself as an excellent student and scholar. In Paris, a pupil of Peter Abelard. In 1159 made Bishop of Paris, but resigned his see the next year. The greatest teacher and representative of scholastic philosophy in his time. His *Four Books of Sentences* made a tremendous impact on the theology of his century and of the centuries following. These four books were *The Trinity, The Creation and Sin, The Incarnation and the Virtues,* and *The Sacraments and the Four Last Things*. The leading schoolmen who followed him lectured and wrote commentaries on these *Sentences*. His book became the popular textbook of the Middle Ages. Considered the father of systematic theology in the Roman Catholic church. Accepted and taught the seven sacraments as they were fully authorized later at the Fourth Lateran Council in 1215, and as they are now taught and practiced by the Roman Catholic church.

PETER THE VENERABLE (PIERRE MAURICE DE MONTBOISSIER) (c. 1092-1156), Abbot of Cluny, born at Montboissier in Auvergne, France, and trained in a Cistercian monastery. In 1109 became a monk at Cluny and from 1122-1156 was chief abbot, succeeding Hugo II. Did much to restore the discipline of Cluny and its over 2,000 affiliated houses, bringing to Cluny a new glory and prosperity. He wrote a strict discipline for the order and visited the Cluniac houses abroad in England and Spain. He opposed heretics and unbelievers, writing tracts against the Petrobrusians, the Jews, and the Mohammedans. In 1130 supported Innocent II against the antipope Anacletus II. He was a friend of Bernard of Clairvaux, yet was tolerant and kindly disposed toward Peter Abelard after Abelard had been opposed and condemned by Bernard. One of Peter's finest writings was his Epistle to Heloise after Abelard's death. Made first Latin translation of the Koran.

PETRARCH or **PETRARCA** (pā trär′kä), **FRANCESCO** (originally **PETRACCO**), (1304-1374), Italian lyric poet and Humanist, son of an exiled Florentine Guelph, born at Arezzo, south of Florence, but parents soon moved to Avignon, France, where he received his earliest education. Studied law at the universities of Montpellier and Bologna. Took minor orders in the church, and received a benefice at Avignon in 1326. In 1327 met Laura, a married woman, who became the inspiration for much of his lyric writing. He then spent several years in traveling, delving into old libraries of convents and monasteries, unearthing valuable Latin manuscripts, and engaging in writing. In 1341 accepted a call to Rome to receive the crown of poet laureate at the Capitol. Formed a warm friendship with Boccaccio. In later years turned from the glories and the immoralities of the world and became a monk and confessed his acceptance of Jesus Christ as his liberator. He has been called the first modern scholar and man of letters, the inaugurator of the Italian Renaissance, and the "Father of Humanism." First to collect a private library of two hundred volumes. Wrote poetry in Italian; both poetry and prose in the Latin. Though sharing with Dante and Boccaccio as makers of modern Italian, he took great delight in writing in Old Latin. Chaucer and other greater writers following him were much influenced by his writings. Had a great concern that the papacy be returned from Avignon to Rome, but died shortly before its accomplishment.

PETRI (pā'trĭ), **OLAUS (OLAVUS** or **OLAF)** (1493-1552), Swedish reformer, "the Luther of Sweden," born at Oerebro and studied at Upsala and Leipzig. He and his brother Laurentius Petri (1499-1573), went to Wittenberg where they studied under Luther and Melanchthon. Came back in 1519 to labor for the Reformation in their own country. Sweden had become independent of Denmark during the reign of Christian II of Denmark; Sweden's new king Gustavus Vasa also favored the Reformation and encouraged the Petri brothers in preaching the evangelical doctrine and in bringing the Reformation to Sweden. In 1523 Olaus became rector of a school at Strengnas where he combined fiery reformatory preaching with work. In 1524 Gustavus appointed him town clerk of Stockholm and opened the way for him to preach the Reformation there. In 1531 Petri became chancellor of the kingdom. In 1539 resigned state post to become the first Reformation pastor of Stockholm. Stockholm thus became the center of reformatory action and the center of Olaus's main life work. Served until his death in 1552. Olaus compiled the first Swedish hymn book. Younger brother, who was more of a scholar and of milder temperament, was appointed by Gustavus Vasa as preacher at Upsala, in 1531 made archbishop, becoming the first evangelical archbishop of Sweden. Materially aided the Reformation through assisting Olaus in Bible translation, and also in writing many theological treatises defending the principles of the Reformation.

PETRIE (pē'trĭ), **WILLIAM MATTHEW FLINDERS** (1853-1942), English Egyptologist, born at Charlton, Kent, England; died in Jerusalem. Educated in private schools. From 1874 to 1880 interested in British archaeology and surveyed ancient British earthworks. From 1880 to 1924, carried on excavations of the utmost importance in Egypt, at first under the auspices of the Egyptian Exploration Fund Committee, then under the Palestine Exploration Fund, uncovering valuable historical records of ancient Egypt. From 1927 to 1938 excavated in Palestine, working under the Palestine Exploration Fund. From 1892 to 1933 Edwards professor of Egyptology at the University College, London. In 1894 founded the Egyptian Research Account, which in 1905 became the British School of Archaeology in Egypt. Served on the committees of both the Palestine Exploration Fund and the Royal Anthropological Institute, knighted in 1923. Author of about seventy-five volumes, a few of which were *Pyramids and Temples of Gizeh, Ten Years Digging in Egypt, Tel el Amarna, Hyksos and Israelite Cities, Religion of Ancient Egypt, The Arts and Crafts of Ancient Egypt, Six Temples at Thebes, Religion and Conscience in Egypt, Methods and Aims in Archaeology, Egypt and Israel,* and *Seventy Years in Archaeology*.

PFEFFERKORN (pfĕf'ĕr kŏrn), **JOHANNES (JOSEPH)** (1469-1524), Jewish convert to Roman Catholicism, born in Germany or Moravia. He and his family were baptized in Cologne in 1505. Zeal to convert the Jews to Christianity caused him to try to force them to give up the practice of usury, to attend Christian sermons, and to do away with the Books of the Talmud. In 1509, with the aid of the Dominican monks, secured permission from Emperor Maximilian to confiscate and burn all Jewish books except the Old Testament, as being a dishonor to Christianity. In this came into sharp conflict with Johann Reuchlin, who had become a professor of Hebrew and an advocate of missions to the Jews. Pfefferkorn wrote several bitter polemics against both Reuchlin and the Jews. Reuchlin answered in his *Augenspiegel*. The conflict between Pfefferkorn and Reuchlin now became a fight between the Dominicans representing the clerical party, and the Humanists representing the liberal party of the church. The pope at Rome finally condemned Reuchlin's *Augenspiegel,* and Pfefferkorn accordingly wrote a triumphal panegyric, *Ein Mittleidliche Klag*.

PHELPS, AUSTIN (1820-1890), American Congregational clergyman and author, born at West Brookfield, Massachusetts, studied at Hobart College, Amherst College, the University of Pennsylvania, Union Theological Seminary, and Yale Theological School. Licensed to preach in 1840, pastor of the Pine Street Congregational Church, Boston (1842-1848). Professor of sacred rhetoric at Andover Theological Seminary (1848-1879), and president of the seminary from 1869 until retirement due to ill health in 1879. In the theological war at Andover during his last years aligned himself with the conservatives. Chief among publications: *The New Birth, Studies of the Old Testament, The Theory and Practice of Preaching,* and *My Study and Other Essays.*

PHILASTER (fĭ lăs'tĕr), (died c. 397), Bishop of Brescia, born possibly in Italy or in Egypt, education seems to have been slight. One of the bishops present at the Synod of Aquileia in 381; about 384 wrote *Diversarum Haereoseon Liber,* a book of one hundred fifty-six heresies, twenty-eight before Christ, and one hundred twenty-eight of the Christian era. This compilation in itself has little intrinsic worth; but Augustine cited Philaster and his book, thus giving it some importance in the Middle Ages. Probably after the writing of this book he was ordained priest and traveled widely preaching against pagans, Jews, and heretics, especially the Arians.

PHILIP II (1527-1598), King of Spain, Naples, Sicily, and Portugal, born at Valladolid, Spain, the only son and successor of Charles I (Charles V of the Holy Roman Empire). Educated by the clergy of Spain, and throughout life maintained a strong religious zeal. He had two passionate purposes: one was to exterminate Protestantism and make the Roman Catholic church the only religion throughout all the lands he could rule. The other was to make his will supreme throughout vast realm. Ruthlessly employed the instrument of the Inquisition against Protestants, Mohammedans, and Jews alike. To conquer England and to carry policy and purpose into that country, married Mary Tudor in 1554, and after her death proposed to marry Elizabeth. Inability to win the hearts of the English people and the urgent need of his presence at home led him to leave England forever. Following the abdication of Charles V in 1555, Philip became the greatest potentate on earth with seemingly unlimited resources. Built El Escorial, a great monastery-cathedral-palace. Became one of the chief actors of the Counter Reformation. Promoted the progress and multiplication of monastic orders and took the keenest interest in papal elections, but insisted upon his right to nominate to the papal office. Would oppose even the pope himself when his own Spanish power and authority seemed threatened or questioned. Ended Turkish threat to Europe by 1571 naval victory at Lepanto. Through Philip's intolerant warfare, disaffection with the pope, failure to win the English, the revolt of the Netherlands against his cruel agent, the Duke of Alva, and their subsequent loss to the crown, and his loss of the Spanish Armada in 1588 at the hands of the English, Spain was left a second-rate power with much of its hereditary possessions gone, and the people far behind the age in free institutions and in civilization.

PHILIP II, AUGUSTUS (1165-1223), King of France (1180-1223), crowned king in 1179. In war with Flanders gained considerable territory for France. Then drove the Jews from France and confiscated their wealth. In 1190 joined hostile neighbor king, Richard the Lion-Hearted of England, in the Third Crusade, but quarrelled with him on the way, and returned to France, schemed to secure some of Richard's territories in France. Succeeded in retaking Normandy and adjacent provinces from England. Philip's accession of new territory was tremendous, greatly enlarging French dominion. Brought France to a commanding position among the nations; improved the administration of the royal affairs. Devoted the last part of his reign to consolidating the gains of earlier years. Made Paris the administrative center of the nation, built the Louvre, encouraged commercial associations, issued the first charter for the University of Paris; made Paris a royal residence.

PHILIP IV, THE FAIR (1268-1314), King of France (1285-1314), son of Philip III, born in Fontainebleau, France. Stood for the unity and strength of the state, marked the beginning of the modern French nation. The great event in his reign was struggle with Pope Boniface VIII. Wanted to levy taxes on the clergy to raise money to wage war against Edward I of England. Pope Boniface, however, in his endeavor to protect the clergy from taxation issued the bull, *Clericis Laicos,* in 1296. Philip defiantly replied by forbidding the exporting of any money to Rome, defeating the pope's hope of raising money for the church. The king arrested and imprisoned the papal legate. To insure for himself the support of the nation called an assembly of the three estates—the clergy, the nobility, and the middle class. Then in 1302 Boniface issued his famous *Unum*

Sanctum, asserting no salvation outside the church or apart from obedience to the pope. The pope then excommunicated the king, put the French nation under the interdict; but the king seized and imprisoned the pope, who died shortly after in great humiliation. After the brief pontificate of Benedict XI, Boniface's successor, Philip, succeeded in 1305 in electing Bertrand de Goth, the Bishop of Bordeaux, as pope, who took the name Clement V. Forced suppression of the Templars in 1312 and induced Clement in 1309 to set up the papal court at Avignon, France. This was the beginning of the "Babylonian Captivity."

PHILIP OF HESSE (THE MAGNANIMOUS) (1504-1567), Landgrave of Hesse (1509-1567), born at Marburg. Education had been very imperfect, and religious and moral training had been neglected; yet he developed rapidly as a statesman. First met Luther at Worms in 1521, and disapproved of the breaking of the pledge of safe conduct. Began to read the New Testament and to study Luther's works. After he married Christina, daughter of George of Saxony, in 1524, began to take an active part in the Reformation, introducing reform in Hesse. Vanquished Franz von Sickingen in 1523, and joined the princes who went out in 1525 to quell the insurrection of the peasants. In 1527 founded the University of Marburg to be a school for Protestant theologians. After the protest of Spires in 1529, of which he was a signatory, tried to unite the Protestants, and planned the unsuccessful meeting of Luther and Zwingli at his castle at Marburg. Signed the Augsburg Confession, though with certain reservations, and was one of the founders of the Schmalkald League. Became Elector of Saxony in 1531. His bigamous marriage to Margaret of Saale played him into the hands of Charles; he had openly violated the emperor's law against bigamy in Hesse. Bucer, Luther, and Melanchthon had unfortunately and unwisely given consent to the marriage, providing he would keep it a secret. His compromise with the emperor greatly weakened his position in the Reformation. For several years he wavered and compromised between the two sides. In the Schmalkaldic War in 1546-1547 the Protestants were defeated, and the Schmalkald League was dissolved. Both John Frederick of Saxony and Philip of Hesse were captured and imprisoned, though Philip had banked on his treaty with Charles to save him. Upon release at the Treaty of Passau in 1552 he returned home and devoted his remaining years to his people, endeavoring to work a reunion between the Catholics and the Protestants.

PHILIP, JOHN (1775-1851), British Congregational missionary to South Africa, born at Kirkcaldy, Fife, Scotland. Studied at Hoxton Theological Academy, London; following graduation in 1802 began preaching at Newbury Congregational Church in Berkshire. In 1804 became minister of a Congregational church in Aberdeen until 1819. In 1818 joined John Campbell in conducting an inquiry into the mission stations of the London Missionary Society in South Africa. In 1822 began a period of nearly thirty years of pastoral care of the new Union Congregational Church at Capetown, and of the superintendency of the society's more than thirty stations in South Africa. Responsible for the placement and adjustments of the personnel of all these stations. Along with missionary and pastoral labors, made vigorous, persevering, and successful efforts in the interests of the oppressed and exploited tribes of South Africa. In program of protecting the South Africans from the abuses and exploitation of the colonists became a strong advocate of African tribal states protected by treaty with England. Won ordinance 50 to protect the Cape Colony Hottentots. Success in this regard was so great that he gained the title of "Liberator of Africa." Published a book entitled *Researches in South Africa*. His championship of the African brought against him the bitter hatred of many in Cape Colony, especially the Boers.

PHILIPS, OBBE (c. 1500-c. 1568), Anabaptist preacher, born at Leuwarden, Friesland, Holland. Through the preaching of Melchior Hoffmann converted from Roman Catholicism to the Anabaptist cause in 1533 and became a preacher. Led his brother Dirck, a Franciscan monk, to the same faith and into the ministry. The two brothers soon came to disagree with Hoffmann's extravagant views and to share no sympathy with the Münster movement. They withdrew from Hoffmann. In 1534 Obbe organized the first Anabaptist congregation in West Friesland, only a short time before Menno Simons' renunciation of Romanism. Obbe's followers became known as Obbennites. In 1536 baptized Menno Simons, and the next year ordained him in the ministry. By 1540 Menno Simons had taken over the leadership and the group gradually became known as Mennonites. Obbe left the Mennonite movement. His brother Dirck, however, became an intimate friend and most efficient co-laborer with Menno Simons. Dirck was a capable and educated man, and was the author of various books and pamphlets which were later collected and printed in one volume: *Handbook of the Christian Doctrine and Religion*.

PHILLIPS, WENDELL (1811-1884), American orator and abolitionist, born in Boston, Massachusetts, educated at Boston Latin School and Harvard College. Studied law and admitted to the bar in 1834, but took little interest in profession, even withdrew from the bar. He became an ardent abolitionist in 1835 after witnessing a mob attack on William Lloyd Garrison, because of his stand on the slave issue. Became one of the most eloquent anti-slavery orators in America. Favored the doing away with slavery even at the cost of the dissolution of the Union. Advocated the expulsion of the slave states and opposed Lincoln's policy in the Civil War. Even opposed the Constitution of the United States insofar as it recognized and sanctioned slavery. In 1865 succeeded Garrison as president of the Antislavery Society, led the society in the struggle for the enactment of the Thirteenth, Fourteenth, and Fifteenth Amendments to the Constitution. During the last years of his life devoted energies to prison reform, organization of the working classes, women's rights, prohibition, and fair treatment of the American Indian.

PHILO JUDAEUS (fī'lō jo͞o dē'ŭs), or **PHILO OF ALEXANDRIA** (c. 20 B.C.-c. A.D. 50), Jewish Hellenistic philosopher, born at Alexandria and received a thorough education in the Septuagint Old Testament, and in Greek literature and philosophy. Profoundly influenced by Greek thought, especially by Platonism, Stoicism, and Pythagoreanism. As a philosopher sought to reconcile Greek philosophy and the Old Testament by means of allegorical interpretation, or to reinterpret Judaism in terms of Hellenistic philosophy, holding that Moses was the source of much of Greek philosophy. In fact he tried to identify the God of Israel with the divine being of Plato, and with the *Logos* of the Stoics. His doctrine of God and God's relation to the world had a marked influence upon the Gnostic teachings in the first two or three centuries of the Christian era, the heresy which exerted such a threat to Christianity. The doctrine of "Logos," derived from the Old Testament "Wisdom" and from Plato's "Ideas," became a basis for the interpretation of John's "Word becoming flesh." Philo's method of allegorical interpretation had much influence on the allegorical method of interpretation followed by the Alexandrian church Fathers, especially by Clement and Origen.

PHILOSTORGIUS (fĭl ō stôr'jĭ ŭs), (c. 368-c. 430), Arian controversialist and ecclesiastical historian, born at Borissus in Cappadocia, son of a strict Arian by the name of Cartesius, educated in mathematics, astronomy, and medicine, at Constantinople, and studied the works of Eunomius whose doctrine he embraced. Chiefly remembered for his biased, often erroneous church history covering era from 300 to about 425. His latitudinarian history began with the controversy between Arius and Alexander about 300 and extended to the reign of Valentinian III, about 425. The work was read and used during the Middle Ages, but unfortunately has been lost.

PHOTIUS (fō'shĭ ŭs), (c. 820-891), Patriarch of Constantinople, born in a rich and distinguished family, Patriarch of the Eastern church 858-867 and again 877-886. Greatest scholar of his age. Read and studied with independent judgment both heathen and Christian books on philology, philosophy, theology, canon law, history, medicine, and general literature. Not originally trained to be a theologian, but was rather a courtier and a diplomat. When as a layman chosen to become Patriarch of Constantinople, in five days was hurried through the five orders of monk, lector, sub-deacon, deacon, and presbyter, and on the sixth day was consecrated patriarch. Became one of the greatest patriarchs of the Eastern church as Nicholas, his contemporary, became one of the greatest popes of the Western. Strengthened his position as Patriarch of Constantinople and pressed his claims against the Western church in two ways: (1) By Greek missionary expansion among the Slavs; and (2) by bold and powerful attacks on the pope's claim to primacy. The quarrel between Photius of the East and Nicholas of the West was bitter and long. It began when Photius was consecrated Patriarch of Constantinople. Nicholas refused to support Photius, declared himself favorable to Ignatius. Photius in turn pronounced sentence of condemnation on the pope. In Encyclical Letter, issued in 867, Photius magnified the differences in worship and practice between the Eastern and Western churches into a difference between *orthodox* and *heretical* Christianity. To minor differences in observance of fasts, celibacy, anointing with oil, and the like, he added the outstanding doctrinal difference implied in the *filioque*. Photius made *filioque* and *papacy* the two impossible barriers in bridging the chasm that was developed between the Eastern and the Western church. Photius was banished by Emperor Leo VI to an Armenian monastery in 886 and died there in 891.

PICO DELLA MIRANDOLA, GIOVANNI (1463-1494), Italian theologian and philosopher. Studied at Bologna, Ferrara Padua, and Paris. Knew Hebrew literature and Greek philosophy. At the Platonic Academy in

Florence after 1484 sought to link biblical truth and Greek philosophy. Many later northern European Reformers studied in this academy.

PIDGEON, GEORGE C. (1872-1971), first moderator of the United Church of Canada. Born in Grand Cascapedia, Quebec. Educated at McGill University and Presbyterian College in Montreal. Pastor in Ontario for fifty years except from 1909 to 1915 when he taught practical theology at Westminster Hall, Vancouver, British Columbia. Moderator of the Canadian Presbyterian church in 1924 and of the United Church of Canada in 1925. Advocated the social gospel to bring help to the poor in the cities.

PIERCE, ROBERT WILLARD (1914-1978), evangelist, exponent of Christian social service and founder of World Vision International, an evangelical relief organization. Born in Fort Dodge, Iowa. Family moved to California in 1924. Educated at Pasadena College. From 1937 an evangelist in California and later in Japan, Korea, and the Philippines. Ordained in 1940. As early leader in Youth For Christ to Asia in 1947 saw suffering and in 1950 incorporated World Vision International. Used documentary films, radio, and personal appearances to arouse evangelical social consciousness. By 1965 was supporting about 65,000 children in twenty countries. Resigned presidency of his organization in 1967. He then began the Samaritan's Purse to raise money for evangelism and relief in Asia. Died of leukemia.

PIERSON, ARTHUR TAPPAN (1837-1911), American Presbyterian pastor, missionary advocate, editor, and writer, born in New York City and graduated from Hamilton College, Clinton, New York and Union Theological Seminary. In 1860 he was married and was ordained to the ministry in the Presbyterian church. His first pastorate was in the First Congregational Church, Binghamton, New York. Served the Presbyterian Church at Waterford, New York; the Fort Street Church, Detroit; the Second Presbyterian Church, Indianapolis; and the Bethany Church, Philadelphia; terminating this last pastorate in 1891. When Charles H. Spurgeon became ill in 1891, Dr. Pierson filled the Metropolitan Tabernacle pulpit until 1893. Becoming convinced that the views held by the Baptists on baptism were biblical, he was immersed in 1896, separated his connection with the Philadelphia Presbytery, where he had been ordained to the ministry. In 1901-1903 and again in 1907-1908, pastor of Christ Church, London. During ministry he devoted himself to evangelistic activity, scriptural preaching, and missionary promotion. Helped establish the Student Volunteer Movement for Foreign Missions. From 1888 until the time of death in 1911, editor of the *Missionary Review of the World,* editor-in-chief after 1890. An expository preacher, an enthusiastic missionary leader, a noted Keswick speaker, a faithful Bible teacher, and an able writer. Pierson Bible Institute in Seoul, Korea, is an outgrowth of his ministry. Consulting editor of the Scofield Bible. First Penny Saving Bank organized by him. A few of his many books: *The Crisis of Missions, Many Infallible Proofs, Evangelistic Work in Principle and Practice, Keys to the Word, Divine Enterprise of Missions, Miracle of Missions* (four volumes), *New Acts of the Apostles, Acts of the Holy Spirit, The Coming of the Lord, Forward Movements of the Last Century, Bible and Spiritual Life, The Bible and Spiritual Criticism.*

PIERSON, DELAVAN LEONARD (1867-1938), American religious editor, born at Waterford, New York, son of Arthur Tappan Pierson, and graduated from Princeton University and Princeton Theological Seminary. From 1891 to 1911 managing editor of the *Missionary Review of the World,* and in 1911 upon father's death became editor-in-chief. In 1894-1904 editor of *Northfield Echoes,* was editorial writer for the *Record of Christian Work* after 1905, and editorial writer for the *Sunday School Times* from 1907 to 1935. Wrote *The Pacific Islanders, A Spiritual Warrior,* and *Life of Arthur T. Pierson.* Died at age eighty-five.

PIKE, JAMES ALNERT (1913-1969), liberal episcopal bishop. Born in Oklahoma City. Educated in arts and law at the University of Southern California and Yale and in theology in Union Seminary, New York. Lawyer with Securities and Exchange Commission and teacher of law from 1938 to 1942. From 1942 to 1945 an officer in the US navy. Ordained to the Protestant Episcopal priesthood in 1946. Chaplain and professor at Columbia University from 1949 to 1958. Dean of the Cathedral of St. John the Divine from 1952 to 1958. Bishop of California from 1958 until his resignation in 1966. From 1966 to 1969 on the staff of the Center for Democratic Studies. In his Grace Cathedral Eugene Carson Blake proposed the Consultation (of the major denominations) on church union in 1960. Supported civil rights, planned parenthood, and social reform. Turned to Spiritualism after his son's death by suicide in 1966. Died in the Judean desert while gathering material for a book about Christ.

PILKINGTON (pĭlk′ĭng tŭn), **GEORGE LAWRENCE** (1865-1897), missionary to

Uganda, born in Dublin, Ireland and attended Pembroke College, Cambridge. Two years after graduation answered a challenge of the Church Missionary Society to go to Africa. Early in 1890 arrived on the coast of Africa, but it was nearly a year before he and his party reached Uganda, where Alexander Mackay had labored so successfully, but where he had died a few months before. The months following were a time of language study in the midst of civil war and outbreaks of hostility. Uganda was finally made a part of the British Empire. He translated the Bible into Luganda. In 1893-1894 a great spiritual revival broke out in the Uganda church, with Pilkington at the center of the movement. Near the end of 1897, in one of the Sudanese raids against the government, Pilkington was killed in a skirmish, cutting short a promising missionary career.

PILMOOR (pĭl'mo͝or), **JOSEPH** (1739-1825), early lay preacher of Methodism in America, later a Protestant Episcopal clergyman, born at Tadmouth, Yorkshire, England. At age sixteen converted by Wesley's preaching and attended John Wesley's school at Kingswood. In 1765 became an itinerant Methodist preacher, traveling in Cornwall and Wales. In 1769 Wesley sent him and Richard Boardman as missionaries to the American colonies. Labored in Philadelphia for several years, sometimes exchanging pulpits with Boardman of New York. Returned to England in 1774 when the Revolutionary war clouds thickened. Unable to agree with either Asbury or Wesley, left the Methodist church, returned to America, became a member of the Protestant Episcopal church. Ordained deacon, then priest by Bishop Seabury, and given charges in New York and Philadelphia. Last twenty years spent as rector of St. Paul's Church in Philadelphia.

PIRCKHEIMER (pĭrk'hī mẽr), **WILLIBALD** (1470-1530), German Humanist and scholar, born at Einstätt, Germany, studied the classics, music, and jurisprudence at the universities of Pavia and Padua in Italy, for about seven years, became a leader of the Renaissance. From 1497 to 1523 city councilor at Nürnberg, Germany, and did much for the schools. Served in the war against the Swiss as imperial councilor to Maximilian I and Charles V; wrote *Historia Belli Suitensis sive Helvetici,* the history of the campaign against the Swiss. Famous for versatile scholarship, one of the most learned and eloquent laymen in Germany. Identified with the German Humanistic revival, sharing the leadership with Erasmus, Hutten, and Reuchlin. Translated wholly or in part the works of Euclid, Xenophon, Plato, Ptolemy, Theophrastus, Plutarch, Lucian of Samosata; Gregory Nazianzen, and John of Damascus. A friend of Alfred Dürer, who painted his picture. At the beginning of the Reformation took position with Luther, calling himself "a good Lutheran" in 1522, and defended Luther on several occasions. After 1524 gradually fell away from Protestantism, turning more and more to the Roman Catholic church, as many of the Humanists did. This defection was due in part to his strong Humanistic tendencies, and in part to the fact that his sister Charitas was a devoted abbess of the nunnery of St. Clara at Nürnberg. Though he finally disclaimed all fellowship with Luther, he remained on friendly terms with Melanchthon up to the time of the writing of the Augsburg Confession and the time of his death.

PIUS IX (pī'ŭs) **(GIOVANNI MARIA MASTAI-FERRETTI)** (1792-1878), pope (1846-1878), born in Sinigaglia of a noble Lombard family, studied at the Collegium Romanum. After being made priest in 1818, became head of a large orphanage in Rome; labored for two years in Chile. Became Archbishop of Spoleto in 1827, and of Imola in 1832; made cardinal in 1840, and elected pope in 1846, succeeding Gregory XVI. In 1847 established new dioceses in the United States, at Albany, Buffalo, Cleveland, and Galveston; in later years fifty others in medium-sized American cities. Also reestablished the hierarchy in England and in Holland. His purpose was to free Italy and to make her united and strong. At first the new pope was the idol of the populace. But he found much difficulty in dealing with the revolutionary party, and consequently lost the favor of the Roman people. In 1848 forced to flee into exile; returned two years later and in his 1864 *Syllabus of Errors* devoted himself to opposing liberalism in church and state, claiming for the church all control of science, culture, and education, and fully supported the principle of ultramontanism. Two important achievements of administration were the acceptance of the dogma of Immaculate Conception in 1854, and the establishing of the dogma of Papal Infallibility at the Vatican Council in 1870. The temporal rule of the papacy was finally abolished in 1870, when the Papal States became a part of the unified kingdom of Italy. Pius IX refusing to accept this mandate, voluntarily retired as a prisoner to the Vatican, where he remained until his death.

PIUS X (GIUSEPPE MELCHIOR SARTO) (1835-1914), pope (1903-1914), born at Riese in Upper Venetia, Italy, in a humble peasant family, spent seven years in the seminary at Padua. Ordained priest in 1858; immediately appointed to parish of Tombolo, and later to Salzano. In 1884 became Bishop of Mantua, where he found conditions in low state. Within the nine years of his bishopric, Mantua became a model see. In 1893 created Patriarch of Venice and cardinal priest of San Bernardo. In 1903 elected pope to succeed Leo XIII, became known as the "peasant pope." As pope devoted himself to charitable work and ecclesiastical reforms, the latter including abolition of the traditional veto at papal elections; the codification of canon law; reform of the breviary; restoration of the Gregorian Chant to its traditional place in the liturgy; condemnation of modernism and recommendation of the study of Thomism; refusal to consent to the separation of church and state; and the raising of the Roman Catholic church in the United States to an autonomous position. Founded Pontifical Bible Institute in 1909. Canonized in 1954.

PIUS XI (ACHILLE AMBROGIO DOMINIANO RATTI) (1857-1939), pope (1922-1939), born at Desio, near Milan, Italy, studied theology at Saint Charles Seminary in Milan, and at Lombard College and the Gregorian seminary in Rome. Ordained priest in 1879, obtained doctorates in theology, canon law, and philosophy. After serving a few months in the parish ministry, from 1883 to 1888 professor of dogmatic theology at the seminary in Milan. For several years director and prefect of the Ambrosian library of Milan, and then for several years prefect of the Vatican library at Rome. In 1919 appointed papal nuncio to Poland. In 1921 consecrated Archbishop of Milan, created cardinal, the following year elected pope to succeed Benedict XV. Reign was notable for the signing of the Lateran Treaty with Mussolini in 1929, whereby the fifty-nine-year retirement of the popes in the Vatican was brought to an end, and the temporal authority of the papacy over the Vatican City in Rome, an area of over 100 acres, was restored. The treaty gave the pope renewed power and influence in world affairs, especially in World War I; restored the position of the church in Italy; established the validity of church marriage, which for the Catholics was to precede the civil ceremony; provided for compulsory religious instruction in school for the children of Catholic parents; and declared Catholicism to be the exclusive religion of the state. From 1929 onward a series of concordats and agreements were concluded between the Vatican and several European powers to uphold the independence of the Roman Catholic church, and to safeguard the liberty of her administration, worship, and propagation. Roosevelt's sending of Myron Taylor as his personal representative to the Vatican in 1930 was highly pleasing to Pius. Remembered for his many encyclicals, the best known and most significant being his *Quadragesimo Anno,* in which he condemned laissez-faire capitalism.

PIUS XII (EUGENIO PACELLI) (1876-1958), pope (1939-1958), born in Rome of a middle-class Roman family, studied theology in the Gregorian University and at the Pontifical Athenaeum of the Roman Seminary. Ordained priest in 1899. Subsequently professor of canon law and of diplomacy and international law in Rome. In 1914 secretary of the papal department of extraordinary affairs; and in 1917 consecrated titular archbishop of Sardes and sent to Munich as papal nuncio to Bavaria. In 1920 appointed papal nuncio to Germany. In 1929 created cardinal, the next year became Secretary of State to Pius XI, ably serving the pope and the church in this capacity. In the period of World War II, Pope Pius XII, having failed to preserve the peace, sought to keep in close contact with the nations. His relation with the United States was especially cordial through the instrumentality of President Roosevelt's personal envoy, Myron Taylor, of his own apostolic delegate at Washington, and Cardinal Spellman. Pius XII made many efforts to negotiate peace and to conclude World War II. He was a strong advocate of peace and justice. Again and again he denounced Communism, and threatened with excommunication members of his church who would take up or retain membership in communist organizations. During the war and after the cessation of hostilities contributed to the relief of civilian populations, especially in Rome and Italy, and set up an office for gathering information on displaced persons, prisoners of war, and civilian internees. Opposed the separation of church and state, and defended the Roman Catholic policies of Italy and Spain in restricting the liberties of non-Catholic churches. Strongly protested the arrest or condemnation of cardinals and archbishops in Hungary, Czechoslovakia, and Yugoslavia. His purpose was constantly to strengthen the church in Italy, and also to stress the universal character of the church. In his 1943 encyclical *Divino Afflante Spiritu* approved literary and historical study of the Bible. In 1946 Pius XII named thirty-two new cardinals, the most ever appointed at one time, bringing the college to its full number of seventy, with representatives from every one of the six continents for the first time in history. In 1950 he proclaimed the dogma of the bodily assumption of the Virgin Mary to Heaven.

PLATO (ARISTOCLES) (427-347 B.C.), Greek philosopher, born in a noble family and educated in grammar, music, and gymnasium. Became a follower of Socrates. When Socrates was condemned to death for heretical teaching, Plato withdrew from public life and left Athens, traveling widely. Returning c. 387, he established his "Academy," where he taught and wrote for forty years until his death in 347. Wrote *Republic* in which he portrayed his view of the ideal state. Wrote a series of dialogues, most of which present Socrates as chief speaker. Among these dialogues: *Apology, Crito,* and *Phaedo*. Written on a lofty moral plane, unsurpassed outside of Holy Writ. Truthfulness, right-living, honesty, justice, kindness to all creatures, piety, and belief in the immortality of the soul are all stressed. To Plato as well as to Socrates the spiritual world is far superior to the material world. In him the Greek mind reached its highest spiritual attainment. To him salvation was the recovery of the vision of eternal goodness and beauty. The Alexandrian church Fathers thought they recognized an element of Christianity in Plato, and associated his idealism with Christian philosophy. To them Plato's teachings were a sort of preparation for the teachings of Christ. The pupil of Socrates, the teacher of Aristotle. Both Plato's and Aristotle's teachings had great influence on medieval theological and ecclesiastical developments of Christianity.

PLINY (plĭn'y), **THE YOUNGER (GAIUS PLINIUS CAECILIUS SECUNDUS)** (62-113), Roman statesman, orator, letter writer, born Novum Comum (Como) in Cisalpine Gaul or in Northern Italy. A pupil of Quintilian of Rome, became a noted orator. Held numerous public offices, serving as military tribune, tribune of the people, prefect of the treasury, consul, proconsul in Bithynia and Pontus, and augur. He seems to have written for publication. One of his most interesting letters was the one telling of the death of his uncle in A.D. 79 at the eruption of Vesuvius. Pliny is of special interest to the Christian church on account of the testimony which he bore concerning the Christians of his day in Bithynia, Asia Minor. Wrote a long letter (Epistle X:96:7) to Trajan concerning the Christians in Bithynia where he was proconsul, asking for instructions in regard to the policy to be pursued in dealing with them. These letters are the earliest account of Christians to be given by pagan writers.

PLOTINUS (plō tī'nŭs), (c. 205-270), Neo-Platonic philosopher and mystic, born of Roman parents at Lycopolis, Egypt, studied under Ammonius Saccas at Alexandria about 245, set up a school at Rome, lectured to eager listeners and gained numerous adherents, among whom was Porphyry. Considered himself a strict adherent of Plato. It was a last great attempt of the ancient Greek world to explain the mystery of the creation and of existence. His teaching was the quintescence of Neo-Platonism. All comes from and returns to one by contemplation and asceticism. His philosophy left a permanent impress upon Christianity partly through Augustine of Hippo and partly through contributions to Christian asceticism and Christian mysticism. Through his pupil Porphyry his teaching presented a real polemic against Christianity in the third century. Writings, the six *Enneads,* were edited and arranged by Porphyry, his pupil and biographer.

PLUMMER, ALFRED (1841-1926), Church of England theologian and church historian, born at Heworth, Durhamshire, England, educated at Exeter College, Oxford. Ordained deacon in 1866, never ordained to the priesthood. Fellow at Trinity College, Oxford (1865-1875). One of the last pupils of J. J. I. von Döllinger. Translated Döllinger's *Fables Respecting the Popes of the Middle Ages,* and other of his writings. Wrote *The Church of the Early Fathers; Lectures on English Church History* (three volumes); *The Church of England in the Eighteenth Century; English Church History from the Death of Henry VIII to the Death of William III;* and *The Churches in Britain before A.D. 1000*. He also wrote several commentaries for the *Cambridge Bible for Colleges; Expositor's Bible; The International Critical Commentary;* and *The Pulpit Commentary*.

PLUMPTRE, EDWARD HAYES (1821-1891), Church of England clergyman and theologian, born in London, studied at University College, Oxford, fellow at Brasenose College (1844-1847). Ordained in 1846. Among many appointments of long church life are: assistant preacher from 1847 to 1868 at Lincoln's Inn; select preacher at Oxford from 1847-1868; chaplain of King's College, London; dean of Queen's College, London; prebendary of St. Paul's, London; rector of Pluckley, Kent; vicar of Bickley, Kent; examining chaplain to the Bishop of Gloucester and Bristol and also to the Archbishop of Canterbury; from 1853 to 1881 professor of pastoral theology and of New Testament exegesis in King's College, London; principal of Queen's College, London; and finally dean of Wells from 1881 until death ten years later. Member of the Old Testament Translation Company of Revisers (1869-1874). Known also as a hymnist, two of his well-known hymns being "Rejoice, Ye Pure in Heart," and "Thine Arm, O Lord, in Days of Old." Contributed to the *Speakers' Bible Commentary, Ellicott's New Testament Commentary for English Readers, The Cambridge Bible for Colleges, Schaff's*

Popular Commentary on the New Testament; edited the *Bible Educator* (four volumes). Published *King's College, The Epistles of the Seven Churches, Introduction to the New Testament,* and several other books.

PLUTSCHAU (plü chō'), **HEINRICH** (c. 1677-1747), German Lutheran missionary to India, born at Wesenberg, Germany, student of Francke's pietistic school at Halle, Germany. In 1705 at instigation of Dr. Lutkens, chaplain to King Frederick IV of Denmark, Plütschau and Ziegenbalg were sent as the earliest of the German pietistic missionaries to the Danish colonies in West India. In July 1706 they landed at Tranquebar, one hundred forty miles south of Madras. The missionaries were opposed and even persecuted by the Danish authorities who were already there. These missionaries went to school with the native children to learn the Tamil language. They also learned Portuguese and won to Lutheranism some of the nominal Roman Catholics of mixed Portuguese and Indian blood. They translated into Tamil and Portuguese the Lutheran catechism and Lutheran prayers and hymns. Translated Bible into cultural idioms of people to create an indigenous church. Converts were made from Hinduism, and the mission slowly grew. In 1711 Plütschau returned to Europe to become pastor at Itzehoe.

POLE, REGINALD (1500-1558), cardinal and Archbishop of Canterbury, born at Stourton Castle, Staffordshire, England, a kinsman of the royal Tudor family. Educated at Magdalen College, Oxford, and at Padua. In 1531 came into King Henry VIII's disfavor, would not assist the king in securing a divorce from Catherine. He then went to the Continent where he remained for some time. When Pope Paul III invited him to Rome, he decided to accept the invitation; in 1536 he, Contarini, Caraffa, and Sadoleto, were created cardinals. Pole desired reform in morals, zeal, and administration in the Roman church. On Henry's death on 1547, Pole endeavored, though unsuccessfully, to have the Protestant leaders of England negotiate with the Holy See. Edward VI's death and Mary's accession to the throne in 1553 once more restored Pole to a very active life in England. In 1557 made priest and two days later was made Archbishop of Canterbury, thus succeeding the deposed and executed Thomas Cranmer in that office. His position and influence as cardinal and later as archbishop assisted Mary in the restoration of Catholic practices and worship in England. Died very shortly after Elizabeth came to the throne.

POLLARD (pŏl'ẽrd), **SAMUEL** (1864-1915), English missionary to the Miao in Southwest China, born at Camelford, Cornwall, England, the son of a minister. After leaving Oxford worked for six years in London; then in 1887 sailed for China. After than a year of language study, he and another young missionary appointed by the United Methodist Church Mission to Chaotung in Yunnan Province, fifteen hundred miles up the Yangtze. Stationed at Chaotung, labored there for the next fifteen years, but with meager numerical results. The harvest came, however, for the Pollards, after the downtrodden and enslaved Miao, another aboriginal tribe from Kweichow Province, began to come up to the Chaotung mission and to petition the missionaries to teach them. As many as one thousand came in one day. In 1905 the Pollards were released from Chaotung to move to Miaoland where a marvelous work, almost a mass movement, began. Overlords were greatly displeased to have their slaves taught, and consequently caused much trouble, one time beating Mr. Pollard almost to death. After a year and a half of furlough in England following the ordeal they returned to the Miao people and continued their work, building a church of several thousand Christians. In his labors among the Miao he mastered their language, created a script, gave them their first books, and was for nearly thirty years a typical pioneer missionary. Wrote *In Unknown China*.

POLYCARP (pŏl'ĭ kärp), (c. 69-c. 155-160), church father. Was a disciple of the apostle John, a friend of Ignatius, and a teacher of Pothinus and Irenaeus. Born at Smyrna. Being a definite connecting link between the apostles and the second century Christianity, had a distinct and unique contribution to make to the church of the second century. One extant letter of Polycarp, a letter written to the Philippian church, makes many references to various parts of the New Testament, and speaks of Paul's earlier epistle to that church. Late in his bishopric Polycarp is said to have made a trip to Rome apparently to discuss some matters of theological or ecclesiastical nature with Anicletus, the Bishop of Rome. Writings and life breathe a spirit of deep devotion. About 155, in the reign of Antoninus Pius, when a local persecution was taking place in Smyrna and several of his members had been martyred, he was singled out as the leader of the church, and marked for martyrdom. When asked to recant and live, he is reputed to have said, "Eighty and six years have I served Him, and He hath done me no wrong. How can I speak evil of my King who saved me?" He was burned at the stake, dying a heroic martyr for his faith.

POLYCRATES (pō lĭk'rȧ tēz) (c. 125-c. 195), Bishop of Ephesus. Remembered chiefly for part in the Easter controversy in the last two decades of the second century. Asked by Pope Victor to call a council to settle the Easter problem in Asia Minor. This synod was called about 190. It adopted the Quartodeciman view, that is, that Easter should be observed on the fourteenth of Nisan, regardless of the day of the week on which it might fall. This was not in accord with the Roman view and the pope excommunicated Polycrates and the recalcitrant congregations; but the Asia Minor churches continued that observance and a quartodeciman schism developed that lasted to the fifth century.

POND, ENOCH (1791-1882), Congregational clergyman and professor, born at Wrentham, Massachusetts. Entered Brown University. Ordained as pastor of the Congregational church in Ward, Massachusetts in 1815. Along with arduous ministerial duties did a great deal of writing. From 1828 to 1832, editor of *The Spirit of the Pilgrims,* an orthodox religious monthly that had been started for the purpose of controverting Unitarianism. After four years of editing the journal, called to Bangor Theological Seminary in Maine in 1832 where he was professor from 1832 to 1882. From 1856 until death was president of the faculty. A voluminous writer, writing about forty books: *The Young Pastor's Guide, Lectures on Pastoral Theology, Lectures on Christian Theology, A History of God's Church, The Seals Opened, The Mather Family, and Swedenborgianism Reviewed* and many more.

PORPHYRY (pôr'fĭ rĭ), (original name **MALCHUS**) (c. 234-c. 305), Greek scholar, Neo-Platonic philosopher, born at Tyre, Syria. After studying at Athens, at age thirty went to Rome, studied Neo-Platonism under Plotinus for six years. Spent five years in Sicily recovering health. Returned to Rome to lecture on Neo-Platonism, becoming the chief disciple and successor of Plotinus. Edited the six *Enneads* which Plotinus had written and also wrote lives of Plotinus and Pythagoras. Philosophy and deep religious nature led him to lay great stress upon asceticism and self-contemplation thereby to attain perfection. Regarded the national religions, whether Greek or barbarian, as justifiable; he strongly opposed Gnosticism and Christianity, apprehensive lest they seriously threaten the position of Hellenism and Neo-Platonism. He wrote fifteen books *Against the Christians*. His fifteen books were all destroyed by Theodosius II in 448, and we know his works only from the fragments as preserved in the writings of the fathers. He sought to depreciate Christianity and the Christian Scriptures by pointing out the inconsistencies of the Scriptures, both the Old and the New Testament, and by emphasizing the incongruities in the lives of the apostles, of Paul, and of Jesus himself. Yet in the end, seeing the value of the true teachings of Jesus, he, in rationalistic fashion, tried to show that the true doctrine of Christ was effaced by the adulterated teachings of the apostles.

POTHINUS (pŏth'ĭ nŭs), (c. 87-177), disciple of Polycarp, Bishop of Smyrna. Became the first bishop of the church at Lyons, Gaul. Death took place in the bitter persecution in Gaul under Marcus Aurelius. After martyrdom, his post was filled by Irenaeus, who also came from the churches in Asia Minor.

POTT, FRANCIS LISTER HAWKS (1864-1947), Protestant Episcopal missionary and educator in China, born in New York City, studied at Columbia University and General Theological Seminary, New York. While in the seminary became interested in China through teaching a class of Chinese laundrymen and others to speak and read the English language. Went to China in 1886. In 1888 ordained priest. After studying the language entered evangelistic work, but became president of St. John's University, Shanghai, from 1888 to 1914. Elected missionary bishop of Wuhu, China, in 1910, but declined the office in order to complete great lifework as Christian educator. Translated several works into Chinese. Author of *The Outbreak in China, A Sketch of Chinese History, The Emergency in China,* and *Short History of Shanghai*.

PRATT, WALDO SELDEN (1857-1939), American music educator, born in Philadelphia, educated at Williams College, Syracuse University, and Johns Hopkins University. Assistant director of the Metropolitan Museum of Art from 1880 to 1882. From 1882 until 1925 professor of music and hymnology at Hartford Theological Seminary, Hartford, Connecticut; from 1891 to 1905 instructor in elocution in Trinity College, Hartford; for years lecturer in musical history and science at Smith College, Mount Holyoke College, and the Institute of Musical Art, New York City. From 1880 to 1892 organist of Asylum Hill Congregational Church, Hartford, and conductor of the Hosmer Hall Choral Union in the same city, conductor of the St. Cecilia Club from 1884 to 1888. Honorary associate of the American Guild of Organists, a member of the Music Teachers' National Association, and president of the latter (1906-1909). Writings include *Musical Ministries in the Church, History of Music,* and *Music of the Pilgrims*. Musical editor of *Aids to Common Worship, The Century Dictionary,* and the American supplement of Grove's *Dictionary of Music and Musicians*.

PRAXEAS (prăk'sē ăs), (c. 200), heretic of

Asia Minor. The first prominent advocate of Patripassian or modalistic Monarchianism. Came to Rome in the time of Marcus Aurelius as a confessor; procured the condemnation of the Montanists; propounded Patripassian heresy. Tertullian opposed him in *Against Praxeas* saying he was guilty of teaching two grave errors: "He drove away prophecy, and he introduced heresy. He put to flight the Paraclete, and crucified the Father." Conceived the relationship of Father and Son to be the same as that of Spirit and flesh.

PRENTISS, ELIZABETH PAYSON (1818-1878), American author. Born at Portland, Maine. Taught school for a few years in Richmond, Virginia; first school was one she opened for small children in her mother's home in 1838. In 1845 married George Lewis Prentiss. While in her teens her literary work began with the writing of short articles for the *Youth's Companion*. In 1853 turned her attention to writing and published articles and stories for the *Youth's Companion,* the *New York Observer,* and the *Advance* (Chicago). Wrote hymns, poems, and children's fiction. Published more than twenty volumes. In 1856, a year in which she experienced severe physical suffering and sharp spiritual conflicts, wrote her beautiful prayer hymn, "More Love to Thee, O Christ." Her very popular and deeply devotional book, *Stepping Heavenward,* was written in 1869.

PRESSENCE (prā säɴ sā′), **EDMOND DEHAULT de** (1824-1891), French Protestant theologian and politician, born in Paris, France, attended the College Bourbon and the College Sainte Foy, studied theology at Lausanne, Halle, and Berlin, under Vinet, Tholuck, and Neander. From 1847 to 1871, pastor of the Free Evangelical Congregation of the Taitbout, Paris. Throughout whole career an eloquent opponent of the connection of church and state, and an able supporter of evangelical Christianity. From 1871 to 1876 a deputy to the National Assembly, and in 1883 was elected a life senator. Though resigning his pastorate in 1871, preached continually throughout France and French Switzerland. Founded the Protestant journal *Revue Chretienne* in 1854 (conducting it until death), the *Bulletin Theologique,* and a great many popular works.

PRESSLY, JOHN TAYLOR (1795-1870), organizer of the United Presbyterian Church in America, born at Abbeville District, South Carolina, graduated from Transylvania College, Kentucky, and from Dr. John Mitchell Mason's theological seminary in New York. Licensed to preach in 1815, spent a year in missionary work, then ordained and installed in 1816 as pastor of the Cedar Spring congregation in native village. In 1832 called to the professorship in the theological seminary, newly organized, and to the pastorate of the First Associate Reformed Church in Allegheny, Pennsylvania. Took a leading part in the organizing and the subsequent leadership of the United Presbyterian Church in North America, which in 1858 was formed out of the Associate Synod and the Associate Reformed Presbyterian churches. Elected the moderator of this newly formed church. As preacher, pastor, and professor exerted a significant and lasting influence upon his denomination.

PRESTER JOHN (Twelfth century), legendary priest and king, supposed to have conquered the Mohammedans and protected the crusaders. Esteemed to be the greatest Christian monarch of the world. Various legends developed concerning this mythical monarch. In thirteenth century Prester John was identified with early Nestorian history in China, later with ancient history of Abyssinia.

PRICE, IRA MAURICE (1856-1939), American Baptist Semitic scholar, born near Newark, Ohio, received education at Denison University, Granville, Ohio, the Baptist Union Theological Seminary, Morgan Park, Illinois, the University of Leipzig, Germany. Served short professorships in languages in Des Moines College, Des Moines, Iowa; Morgan Park Military Academy; Wheaton Theological Seminary, Wheaton, Illinois; and in Baptist Union Theological Seminary, before appointment in 1892 as professor of Semitic languages and literature in the University of Chicago until 1925. From 1900 to 1902 a member of the International Sunday School Lesson Association. Associate editor for many years of the *Biblical World,* the *American Journal of Semitic Languages and Literature,* and the *American Journal of Theology.* Also a contributor to Hastings' *Dictionary of the Bible and Dictionary of Religion and Ethics, The Jewish Encyclopaedia, The Standard Bible Dictionary,* and the *Encyclopedia Americana.* Wrote *Syllabus of the Old Testament History, The Monuments of the Old Testament, The Ancestry of Our English Bible,* and *Dramatic Story of the Old Testament.* A cofounder and for many years secretary of the Theological Faculties Union of Chicago and vicinity.

PRIESTLEY (prēst′lĭ), **JOSEPH** (1733-1804), Unitarian preacher and scientist, born at Fieldhead, near Leeds, Yorkshire, England, and entered the Dissenting academy at Daventry to prepare for the Presbyterian ministry. Early wrote *The Scripture Doctrine of Remission,* denying that Christ's death was a sacrifice and rejecting the trinity and the atonement. Held short pastorates at Needham Market, Suffolk and at Nantwich. In 1761 tutor in an academy at Warrington. Began the *Theological Repository,* a critical periodical that aroused much hostility. Favored the autonomy of the individual congregation, an increase in the number of sects, and complete toleration of Roman Catholicism, and attacked the idea of a national church. In 1791 became one of the founders of the Unitarian Society, and in the same year defended the French Revolution in *Letters to Burke*. Such hostility was raised against him in England that in 1794 he came to America, and spent his last ten years at Northumberland, Pennsylvania. Then adopted the doctrines of universal restitution and of moral progress in life after death. Established a Unitarian Society in Philadelphia. In the realm of science, known chiefly for discovery of oxygen in 1774 and for great work on *Experiments and Observations in Different Kinds of Air.* Other of his writings while in England: *Institutes of Natural and Revealed Religion, Disquisitions Relating to Matter and Spirit, A Harmony of the Evangelists, History of the Corruptions of Christianity,* and *History of Early Opinions Concerning Jesus Christ*. In the latter denied the impeccability and infallibility of our Lord. In America completed *General History of the Christian Church,* and wrote *Notes on All the Books of Scripture*.

PRISCILLA or **PRISCA** (second century), Montanist prophetess. Priscilla and Maximilla were two Phrygian women who are said to have left their husbands to accompany Montanus and help propagate his teaching. They proclaimed the near approach of the millennial reign in Perpuza, a village in Phrygia. So far as we know Priscilla was a woman of high, noble character, earnestly seeking to help restore the discipline and practices of the early church, even as Montanus and Maximilla were evidently seeking to do. They stressed chiliasm and charismatic gifts.

PRISCILLIAN (prĭ syl'yăn), (died 385), Spanish secretary and Bishop of Avila, born in Spain; a rich and gifted man of a distinguished family, devoted to philosophical and theological studies, but fell under the influence of Marcus, a teacher from Egypt. Being both a mystic and a rigid ascetic he did not wish to ally himself with any existing church or sect, but purposed to start a reform movement for the deepening of the Christian life and encouraging asceticism. Combining various elements of Gnosticism and Manichaeism and other esoteric teachings with Christianity, developed a sect of his own. His system had elements of dualism mingled with monism, with Manichaean and Gnostic doctrines clearly evident. His concept of Christ was a combination of Docetism, Sabellianism and Arianism. Apocryphal books were accepted as inspired and genuine. Wanted to appear as an orthodox Christian, and rapidly gained a following for his movement. In 380 a council was convened at Saragossa at which he was charged with all sorts of heresy. Meanwhile consecrated Bishop of Avila. Then he went to Rome to seek to win the support of Pope Damasus and to Milan to persuade Bishop Ambrose of his innocence. Rebuffed by both. Emperor Maximus condemned him and his associates to death as heretics. They were executed at Treves in 385. Priscillian at once was looked upon as a martyr. This was the first time that Christians were punished with death on account of heresy, and all Christendom felt the shock. The church soon took up the practice and promotion of persecution and execution for heresy. After his death and that of his fellow bishops, the sect continued in Spain and Gaul for nearly two centuries.

PROCOPIUS (prō kō'pĭ ŭs), **OF CAESAREA** (c. 490-562), Byzantine historian, born at Caesarea in Palestine, went to Constantinople, taught rhetoric and pleaded in the courts. In 527 sent as secretary and councillor to Belisarius in expedition against the Persians. In 533 during the war against the Vandals he was in North Africa. In 536 in Sicily at the time of the war against the Goths. By 542 back in Constantinople, remained the rest of his life writing the *Wars,* history of these expeditions. His *Anecdotes* is a gossipy history of the doings of the Byzantine court. His works have been consulted by later historians for information of both secular and ecclesiastical history. It is not certain that he was a Christian, yet his writings have aided church historians.

PROSPER OF AQUITAINE (c. 390-c. 463), an Augustinian divine and poet, born in Aquitaine; moved to Marseilles where he lived as a monk until 440. When Leo returned from Gaul to Rome in 440 to become pope, Prosper accompanied him as secretary. In Rome confuted the Pelagian heresy. Wrote a book upon grace and freedom in which he criticized the writings of Cassian and expressed favor of the Augustinian doctrines. Also composed a long poem in defense of Augustine and his system.

PROVOOST (prō'vōst), **SAMUEL** (1742-1815), first bishop of the Protestant Episcopal Church in New York, born and died in New York City. A member of the first graduating class of King's College (now Columbia University), and continued studies at St. Peter's House (now St. Peter's College), Cambridge University, England. Made deacon and priest in London in 1766; on return to America became assistant minister of Trinity Church, New York, and then of St. George's and later of St. Paul's, New York. During the time of the American Revolution (1771-1784), retired from church life to a small country estate. In 1784 became rector of Trinity Church, New York, and in 1785 chaplain of the Continental Congress; in 1789 of the United States Senate. In 1786 elected first Bishop of New York. In 1787 he and Dr. William White, Bishop of Pennsylvania, were consecrated by the archbishops of Canterbury and York, and the bishops of Bath, Wells, and Peterborough in the chapel of Lambeth Palace, London. Conducted the service at St. Paul's Chapel following Washington's inauguration in 1789, also officiated at the memorial service for Washington in 1799. In 1800, because of failing health, resigned rectorship but retained as bishop, a coadjutor being provided to assist him.

PRUDENTIUS (proo dĕn'shĭ ŭs), **AURELIUS CLEMENS** (348-c. 410), Latin poet and hymnist, born probably at Saragossa, Spain. A lawyer and provincial governor in Spain before called to occupy a military post at the court of Theodosius I. After conversion to Christianity devoted himself to the service of the church and to writing sacred poetry. At age fifty-seven retired to a monastery to spend last days in strict asceticism and contemplation. His poems, of which we have about 385, were chiefly devotional, praises to martyrs, doctrinal or didactic, apologetic, and polemic. Wrote *Psychomachia,* the earliest religious allegory in the Western church, picturing the battle waged by Virtue and Vice for the soul of a Christian. Wrote hymns about the same time that Ambrose was writing; but developed a new type of hymn with more warmth and glow than those of Ambrose, yet not as well suited for liturgical use. An example is *"Of the Father's Love Begotten."*

PRYNNE, WILLIAM (1600-1669), Puritan pamphleteer. Born in Somerset. Educated at Oriel College, Oxford and Lincoln's Inn. Became a barrister in 1628. Wrote against the stage and the High church in *Histromastix* in 1632 and expelled from the Inn and lost his law degree. In pillory and ears cropped in 1634. A member of Parliament in 1648 and Keeper of Tower Records under Charles II. Wrote about 200 books and pamphlets.

PUNSHON (pŭn'shŭn), **WILLIAM MORLEY** (1824-1881), English Wesleyan Methodist minister, born at Doncaster, Yorkshire, England, studied for short time at Wesleyan College, Richmond. Entered the Methodist Society in 1838, ordained in 1849, and from 1849 to 1867 served as pastor successively at New Castle-on-Tyne, Sheffield, Leeds, London, and Bristol. From 1860 to 1873 pastor of Metropolitan Church in Toronto. From 1867 to 1873 presided over the general conferences and had great influence upon Methodism in Canada. Helped to unify Methodists in the Methodist Church of Canada in 1874. In 1873 returned to England to be superintendent of Kensington district for two years, and then to become one of the secretaries of the Wesleyan Missionary Society until death in 1881. Published several volumes of sermons, lectures, and poems.

PURCELL, HENRY (c. 1659-1695), English composer, born at Westminster, England. At ten became a choir boy at the Chapel Royal. About 1680 chosen organist of Westminster Abbey and in 1682 held also the post of organist to the chapel. He showed such great skill in writing church music that he is regarded as "Father of Anglican Church Music." Work was characterized by inspirational and emotional qualities, by technical ingenuity, and by certain austerity of melody. Wrote numerous anthems, cantatas, and chants for the church which were eagerly sought after for use in the various cathedrals. Studied Italian masters carefully, and often expressed obligations to them. Best known works are *Te Deum Jubilate* and the hymn, "Rejoice in the Lord Always."

PURDIE, JAMES EUSTACE (1880-1977), Canadian Anglican clergyman. Born in Charlottetown, Prince Edward Island. Educated at Wycliffe Theological College and ordained in 1907. Anglican pastor in New Brunswick, Saskatchewan, and Stearns Memorial Church in Germantown, Philadelphia. Drafted by the Pentecostal Assemblies to head their Bible schools in Winnipeg and Toronto. Trained PAOC leaders in moderate Calvinism from 1925 to 1950. His notes became basis for curriculums in other schools. Wrote *Concerning the Faith* and *What We Believe*.

PURNELL, BENJAMIN (1861-1927), founder of The House of David, born in Fleming County, Kentucky. His parents belonged to a religious sect known as Carmelites. Had very little education. After moving from state to state, in 1903 settled at Benton Harbor, Michigan. Set up a communal system calling it a "commonwealth according to the apostolic plan," with himself the supreme ruler over all the community's spiritual and temporal interests. Proclaimed himself to be the seventh messenger as prophesied in Micah 3:1 and Revelation

10:7, and to be the younger brother of Christ; founded the Israelite House of David. Claimed group to be the descendants of the twelve lost tribes of Israel, and promised followers that they should escape death. His communal system became a commercial pleasure resort and a social rather than a religious center. Charges of dishonesty and immorality were brought against "King Benjamin"; he died at the height of the scandal in 1927. His peculiar cult of only a few hundred members continues at Benton Harbor, where it originated.

PURVES (pûr'vĕs), **GEORGE TYBOUT** (1852-1901), American Presbyterian clergyman, born in Philadelphia, graduated from the University of Pennsylvania and Princeton Theological Seminary. From 1877 to 1892 successively pastor of the Presbyterian church at Wayne, Pennsylvania, Boundary Avenue Presbyterian Church, Baltimore, and the First Presbyterian Church, Pittsburgh. From 1892 to 1900 professor of New Testament literature and exegesis in Princeton Theological Seminary. From 1900 to the time of death in 1901, pastor of the Fifth Avenue Presbyterian Church, New York City. Writings include *The Testimony of Justin Martyr to Early Christianity, Christianity in the Apostolic Age,* and some books of sermons.

PURVEY, JOHN (c. 1353-1428), English biblical translator, born at Lathbury, Buckinghamshire, England, and likely educated at Oxford. Ordained in 1377. Associated with John Wycliffe at Lutterworth for sometime before 1384; after Wycliffe's death became a leader of the Lollard party. Preached at Bristol, silenced by the Bishop of Worcester in 1387 and later imprisoned. While in prison compiled from Wycliffe's translation a commentary on Revelation. In 1400 in fear of martyrdom recanted his Lollardy, and was given the vicarage of West Hythe, Kent. Resigned this charge in 1403, returned to preaching for the next eighteen years. Chiefly noted for revision of Wycliffe's and Hereford's translation of the Bible into a literal and unidiomatic style, which he completed in 1388. Wrote against the corruption of the church a work called the *Ecclesiae Regimen*.

PUSEY (pū'zĭ), **EDWARD BOUVERIE** (1800-1882), Tractarian leader and Hebrew scholar, born at Pusey near Oxford. Received education at Eton and Christ Church College, Oxford. In 1822 elected fellow of Oriel College, Oxford. In 1825 to 1827 studied languages and theology in Göttingen, Berlin, and Bonn, Germany. In 1829 appointed professor of Hebrew, ordained priest, and became canon of Christ Church. Became a noted scholar, especially in Hebrew and biblical learning. Joined and became an active supporter of the Oxford or Tractarian movement, which had been started by Keble, Froude, and Newman two years earlier. Wrote eight of the ninety *Tracts for the Times.* By some the movement became known as Puseyism. When in 1845 Newman joined the Roman church, Pusey remained in the Anglican church and was recognized as the head of the High church or Anglo-Catholic party. In 1843 suspended for three years from preaching at Oxford. In theology, essentially Catholic, but strongly opposed to Romanism on the subject of Mariolatry and the authority of the pope. Pusey's and Keble's loyalty to the Anglican church saved a larger number from becoming Roman Catholics. Pusey was instrumental in establishing several sisterhoods in the Anglican church. Among works are several volumes of sermons, some books of Anglo-Catholic doctrine and history, *The Minor Prophets, Daniel the Prophet,* and other doctrinal works. Helped to edit the fifty-volume set of *Oxford Library of the Fathers of the Holy Catholic Church*.

Q

QUADRATUS (kwäd rā'tŭs) (second century), early Christian apologist from Asia Minor. About A.D. 125 addressed an apology for the Christians to Emperor Hadrian. According to Eusebius, he claimed to have been a disciple of the apostles.

QUESNEL (kĕ nĕl'), **PASQUIER** (1634-1719), French Jansenist, born in Paris and educated by the Jesuits at the Sorbonne, entered the Congregation of the Oratory in 1657. Two years later became a priest and director of the Paris Institute, the seminary of his order. Began to write the main work of his life, *Moral Reflections on the New Testament,* which incurred against him the bitterest hatred of the Jesuits. The book was condemned by Pope Clement XI and was placed on the Index. It was a defense of Augustinian Jansenism and was so nearly identified with the movement that the name Jansenism nearly gave way to that of Quesnelism. In 1675 published a scholarly edition of the works of Leo the Great, which gave evidence of his Gallicanism and created for him the ill-will of the Archbishop of Paris. This writing, too, was placed on the Index. With this double odium, retired from the Oratory, fled the country, and joined the Jansenists at Brussels. Did his final work on his *Reflections,* by this time embracing the whole of the New Testament, and published this work in 1694. It incorporated the Jansenist doctrine, both dogmatic and practical. In 1703 arrested, but he escaped and fled to Holland out of reach of the Jesuits. Died in Amsterdam.

QUIMBY (kwĭm'by), **PHINEAS PARKHURST** (1802-1866), founder of mental healing in America, born at Lebanon, New Hampshire. When two years old his family moved to Belfast, Maine. By trade a clockmaker with no more than six weeks of schooling in his whole life. Apart from his trade he invented the band saw similar to the saw in use today. By 1838 had become deeply interested in mesmerism, and subsequently abandoned trade to give public exhibitions of hypnotic powers. Interest was then aroused by the seeming close relation between mesmerism and healing; in 1847 turned from mesmerism to mental healing, and set up practice at Portland, Maine, though still living at Belfast. Worked out a system of philosophy, which denied the reality of both illness and matter, and which on occasion he called, "Christian Science" or "mental science." Among his patients in the early 1860s was Mary Baker Patterson, later Mrs. Eddy, who became acquainted with the manuscripts which he had written on his philosophy. Many think that she appropriated and enlarged upon his principles in development of her cult of Christian Science. After his death Julius Dresser and Warren Felt Evans tried to continue his work. From their efforts there developed the New Thought movement. His philosophy lies at the basis also of the Unity movement.

R

RABANUS (rä bä'nōōs) **MAURUS** (c. 776-c. 856), Abbot of Fulda and Archbishop of Mainz, born at Mainz, educated at the Benedictine abbey of Fulda in Hesse, Germany, entered the Benedictine Order. Pupil of Alcuin, Charlemagne's court adviser and educator. Became a famed teacher and educator, a commentator on the Scriptures, a benefactor in time of famine, and author of what was well-nigh an encyclopedia. Ordained priest in 814, became abbot of Fulda in 822. Resigned in 842, divided time between devotional exercises and literary activity. Persuaded to accept the position of Archbishop of Mainz in 847. Took part in the predestination controversy, and became opposer and persecutor of Gottschalk who held an extreme predestinarian view. Took part in the eucharistic controversy, opposing the transubstantiation view of Radbertus. View was more clearly stated a little later by Ratramnus, who rather held to the symbolic view of the eucharist. Author of several biblical commentaries.

RABAUT (rä bō), **PAUL** (1718-1794), French Reformed pastor of "the Church of the Desert," born at Bedarieux, near Montpellier, France, in a Protestant family. At age twenty sent as preacher to Nimes, but chose first to study theology at Lausanne, where Antoine Court was director. Became pastor of Nimes in 1744, at time when the Protestant church in France was rallying from the fearful calamities following the revocation of the Edict of Nantes (1698), the War of the Camisards (1701-1706), and the issuance of new edicts against the Protestants. A younger associate with Court in the restoration of the Reformed Protestant church in France. Obliged to go into hiding and to perform pastoral duties under the utmost secrecy, preaching frequently in ravines and desert places, at times preaching to as many as ten thousand people. Two sons became pastors and assisted their father in his work. Though never appointed as official head of the Protestant Reformed Church of France, earned distinction of being the recognized leader in all matters of importance. Vice-president of the General Synod in 1744, and president of the National Synod in 1756 and again in 1763.

RADBERTUS, PASCHASIUS (păs kā'sĭ ŭs) (c. 785-c. 865) a distinguished Benedictine writer and theologian of the Carolingian period, and originator of the transubstantiation theory, born at or near Soissons, France. Brought up by Benedictine nuns at Soissons. Became a monk in the monastery of Corbie in Aquitaine, near Amiens, France. Though never a priest, he was abbot (844-c. 853). Most important writing was *De Corpore et Sanguine Domini,* written about 831. Taught with Augustine that only those who partake in faith receive the virtue of the sacrament, and with the Greek fathers that the eucharist is the food of immortality, and also that the substance is made the very body and blood of Christ. His view of the eucharist was opposed by Ratramnus and Rabanus Maurus. Transubstantiation was approved by the church at the Fourth Lateran Council nearly four centuries later. In 853 resigned office as abbot and died a simple monk at the abbey of St. Requier. Last years devoted to zealous study of theology and philosophy.

RADER, PAUL (1879-1938), evangelist. Born Denver, Colorado. Educated at the University of Denver and Colorado College. Pastor of Moody Memorial Church from 1914 to 1921 and Christian and Missionary Alliance churches in Pittsburgh, Los Angeles, and Ft. Wayne, Indiana. Pastor of Chicago Gospel Tabernacle from 1922 to 1929 and president of the Christian and Missionary Alliance (1921-1933). Pioneer in radio gospel broadcasting.

RADEWIJNS, FLORENTIUS (1350-1400), disciple of Gerard Groote and organizer of the Brethren of the Common Life. Educated at Prague. Became priest in 1377. Was the Canon at Utrecht. By 1384 leader of the Brethren. Founded the Congregation of Windesheim in 1387. Promoted devotional and educational activities in the Low Countries.

RAIKES (rāks), **ROBERT** (1735-1811), early Sunday school promoter; born at Gloucester, England. Educated at the Cathedral school. Inherited father's *Gloucester Journal,* continued it for forty years. Chief contribution to society, however, was giving of secular and religious instruction to poor and neglected children. Began this work about 1780 by employing a Mrs. King at about thirty cents a Sunday to teach boys and girls to read and to repeat the catechism. In 1783 began publicizing his Sunday school through the columns of his Journal. This was the beginning of a far-reaching movement which spread rapidly both within and without the churches. The Wesleys, Hannah More, and the other non-conformists became enthusiastic supporters of the Sunday school. The

Wesleyans began the practice of teaching gratuitously. This practice soon became the universal rule in Sunday school teaching. Also the teaching of the secular subjects rapidly declined. Robert Raikes persevered in undertaking for about thirty years during which time the Sunday schools were established extensively throughout England.

RAINY, ROBERT (1826-1906), United Free Church of Scotland leader, born at Glasgow, Scotland, educated at the University of Glasgow, and at New College, Edinburgh under Chalmers and Cunningham. Minister at the Free church at Huntly, Aberdeenshire (1851-1854), and the Free High Church, Edinburgh (1854-1862). From 1862 to 1900 Rainy was professor of Church history in New College, and principal from 1874 to 1906. Evangelical, a leading factor in the union of the Free church and the United Presbyterian church. Position soon became that of ecclesiastical statesman in church, in assembly a moderator three times. Collaborated in writing the *Life of William Cunningham;* wrote *Three Lectures on the Church of Scotland, The Delivery and Development of Christian Doctrine, The Bible and Criticism, The Epistle to the Philippians,* and *The Ancient Catholic Church.*

RAMABAI (räm'á bī), **PANDITA SARASVATI** (1858-1922), Indian educator, born in the forests of southern India of a learned but poor Brahmin who educated her. Keen intellect and memory, committed to memory thousands of verses from the sacred Hindu writings, and was adept in the Sanskrit, Marathi, Kanarese, Hindustani, and Bengali. During the famine of 1874 her parents and elder sister died of starvation, Ramabai and her brother barely surviving. In travels saw the sad plight of India's womanhood and gained a considerable reputation and earned livelihood by lecturing upon the importance of female education. Her brother died and she was left alone. In 1880 met and married a practicing lawyer and fellow of Calcutta University; in nineteen months a widow with an infant daughter. Resumed her lecturing, and established the Areja Mahita Samaj, a society whose object was to promote the education of women, and to discourage child marriage. In 1883 went to England to receive an English education. While there became a Christian; for three years taught Sanskrit in Cheltenham College. In 1886 visited America and raised money through lecturing to help establish in 1889 in Bombay a nonsectarian school for high caste Hindu girls, especially for child widows. In 1891 this school was moved to Poona. At Khedgaon a new building was erected and named Mukti (Salvation and Praise the Lord). Secured a farm which helped provide support for her orphanage and school. Her own life was greatly influenced by the lives of George Müller and Hudson Taylor. Translated the Bible into the Marathi tongue.

RAMSAY, SIR WILLIAM MITCHELL (1851-1939), Scottish archaeologist and church historian, born at Glasgow, educated at the universities of Aberdeen, Oxford, and Göttingen. From 1880 to 1886 in turn traveling scholar for Oxford University, research fellow for Exeter College, Oxford, and professor of classical art and archaeology in the University of Oxford. Professor of humanity in the University of Aberdeen (1886-1911), where he was also Wilson fellow (1901-1905); special lecturer in Mansfield College, Oxford, at John Hopkins, at Auburn Theological Seminary, in the University of Cambridge, and at the Southwestern Theological Seminary (1891-1910). Became widely known for researches in the history of the Christian Church, in the course of which traveled extensively in Asiatic Turkey, making a special study of the geography and topography of Asia Minor. Knighted in 1906. Received gold medals from Pope Leo XIII, the University of Pennsylvania, the Royal Geographic Society, and the Royal Scottish Geographic Society. Writings include: *The Historical Geography of Asia Minor, The Church in the Roman Empire, Before* A.D. *170, St. Paul the Traveler and Roman Citizen, Was Christ Born at Bethlehem?, Luke the Physician, The Education of Christ, Pictures of the Apostolic Church, Pauline and Other Studies in Early Christian History, Letters to the Seven Churches of Asia,* and *Historical Commentary on the Epistle to the Galatians.*

RAMUS, PETER (1515-1572), humanist. Born in Picardy. Educated at the Collège de France. Taught in a college for a time. Became Calvinist in 1561. After flight to Germany from 1568 until 1571 returned to France in the latter year and later killed. Taught Aristotelian logic. Held that universals are from eternal entities in the mind of God which are apprehensible by human deduction. Puritans in England and New England used his work.

RANDALL, BENJAMIN (1749-1808), founder and leader of the Freewill Baptists, born in New Castle, New Hampshire, son of a sea captain. Received little formal education, early learned the tailor's and sailmaker's trade. Attributed conversion to three sermons of George Whitefield in 1770 and shock received upon learning of sudden death of Whitefield. Joined the Congregational church; dissatisfied, left it two and a half years later, was immersed, began preaching. Associated with the Regular Baptists until disfellowshipped for rejecting Calvinism. In 1780, at New Durham, New Hampshire ordained "to the work of an evangelist." At this time drew up covenant which supporters signed. This became beginning of the New England Freewill Baptist Church, now known officially as the National Association of Freewill Baptists. While pastor at New Durham, traveled much in evangelistic labors. Doctrinal position was that of Arminianism, hence the name Freewill. Church government was congregational.

RANKE, LEOPOLD VON (1795-1886), German historian, born in Wiehe, Thuringia, Germany, educated at the universities of Halle and Leipzig. Taught for a time at Frankfurt-on-the-Oder, then professor of history at the University of Berlin (1825-1871), one of the leading historians of the nineteenth century. One of the originators of the modern historical school which relies on original sources rather than on tradition or legend for its material, stresses scientific objectivity in historical writing, also the understanding of national tendencies in their relation to the history of the age, but he did make providence the final cause. Most important of works was *Ecclesiastical and Political History of the Popes during the Sixteenth and Seventeenth Centuries,* which was based on extensive researches in the libraries of Italy, where he collected material for three years. Among nearly fifty historical works are: *German History in the Time of the Reformation, French History, English History,* and *Universal History,* the last begun in his eighty-first year. Though his academic activity ceased in 1871, work of research, writing, and revising continued almost to the very day of death in 1886.

RANKIN, THOMAS (1738-1810), early Methodist minister in America, born in Dunbar, Scotland. At age seventeen came under the influence of George Whitefield and decided to prepare for Christian work. Became an intimate associate and traveling preacher with John Wesley for eleven years. In 1773 Wesley sent him to America as superintendent of the work of Methodism in colonies. Soon after arrival in America called the first American Methodist Conference, July 4, 1773. In 1775 assisted in the great awakening in Virginia by making an extensive preaching tour in southern Virginia and northern North Carolina with Devereux Jarret, a revivalist of the Anglican church. Remained in this country about five years, when the Revolutionary struggle made further stay ill-advised, and returned to England. A truly pious man but too stern and uncompromising to succeed as a leader. Such a strong disciplinarian that he tended to estrange fellow-workers.

RAPHAEL, SANTI (RAFFAELLO SANZIO) (1483-1520), Italian Renaissance painter and architect, born in Urbino, first trained by father, Giovanni Santi, the painter, then taught by Perugino of Perugia. One of Raphael's earliest paintings was the *Marriage of the Virgin*. Studied the paintings of Leonardo da Vinci, Michelangelo, and Fra Bartolommeo, and greatly influenced by them. In 1508 commissioned by Pope Julius II to paint the frescoes in several of the rooms of the Vatican. After death of Julius II, continued to be the court painter under Leo X and in 1514 commissioned as chief architect of St. Peter's Church, succeeding Bramante. The year following appointed director of the excavations of antiquities in Rome and within a radius of ten miles around the city. During this time continued painting. His many paintings include several famous Madonnas. Paintings portray the historical, the classical and the allegorical; yet best works are devoted to religious and Biblical characters and events. The greatest of his paintings, the *Transfiguration* in the Vatican. In opinion of contemporaries, and of many critics of art since that day, Raphael, da Vinci and Michaelangelo were the greatest painters of the day. The distinguishing qualities of work were masterful composition, beauty and serenity of expression, harmony and purity of color, and refinement of taste.

RAPP, JOHANN GEORG (1757-1847), founder of the Harmony Society, born in Iptingen, Württemberg, Germany, received only a moderate education. A linen weaver by trade, under the influence of mysticism became a separatist, and held aloof from the public worship and communion of the church. By declaration of views and by eloquence attracted thousands who flocked to Iptingen where he established sect. Persecution from the government followed and he migrated to the United States in 1803, settled a community on a site of about five thousand acres in Butler County, Pennsylvania, building there the town of Harmony. The next year several hundred adherents followed from Germany, and organized the Harmony Society in 1805. In 1814 moved to a twenty-seven thousand acre section in Posey County in the Wabash Valley in Indiana, and founded New Harmony. In 1825 moved to Beaver County, Pennsylvania and started a town which he named Economy, and another which he named Harmony. He believed that attendance at school is wicked, baptism and the Lord's Supper are of the Devil, all people will ultimately be saved, all property should be held in common, and all members should practice celibacy. Rule of celibacy led to the sect's final extinction by the beginning of the present century.

RASPUTIN, GRIGORI YEFIMOVICH (c. 1871-1916), Russian monk and mystic greatly influencing Russian royalty. Born in the province of Tobolsk, Siberia. After 1907 due to reputed religious healing power to cure the haemophilia of the heir to the throne became the unofficial power behind the Russian throne. Interfered in church and secular matters. Notoriously immoral. Assassinated in 1916 by Russian nobles.

RATRAMNUS (rä trăm'nŭs), (died c. 868), theological writer. An Aquitanian monk of the monastery of Corbie near Amiens, France. Theologically a disciple of Augustine, following the double predestination of Gottschalk. Opinions frequently sought by Emperor Charles the Bald. His bishop delegated him to refute Photius, patriarch of the Eastern church in attacks on the Roman Catholic church. On the sacrament of the eucharist he opposed the transubstantiationary view of Radbertus. He held that the eucharistic elements are mystic symbols of remembrance, yet that the power of the divine Word, the body and blood of Christ, are truly present.

RAUSCHENBUSCH (rou'shĕn boosh), **WALTER** (1861-1918), American Baptist social gospel leader, born at Rochester, New York. Received first three years of schooling in Barmen, Germany, where mother spent the years 1866 to 1869. After graduating from Rochester Free Academy and Seminary in New York, spent four years traveling abroad, studying at the Evangelical Gymnasium of Gütersloh in Westphalia. Attended lectures for a few months at the University of Berlin. Following a short visit to England, returned to Rochester to enter simultaneously the senior year of the university and the junior year of the seminary. Rauschenbusch held a successful pastorate for two summers in a small German Baptist church in Louisville, Kentucky. From 1886 to 1897 pastor of the Second German Baptist Church in New York City. Did much religious work among the German immigrants. From 1897 to 1902 professor of New Testament in the German Department of Rochester Theological Seminary, and from 1902 to 1918 professor of church history in the English department. Rauschenbusch became much interested in a program of social betterment. Worked with Jacob Riis to secure playgrounds for children. Developed a strong interest in Christian socialism, and emphasized the necessity of economic as well as political democracy as a method of realizing the kingdom of God upon this earth. Wrote: *Prayers for the Social Awakening, Christianity and the Social Crisis,* and *A Theology for the Social Gospel*. Through these writings his teaching spread widely and caused some strong opposition.

RAWLINSON, GEORGE (1812-1902), English historian and orientalist, born at Chadlington, Oxfordshire, England, studied at Trinity College and Exeter College, Oxford. Ordained deacon in 1841 and priest the next year. After holding several lesser positions before 1861, from 1861 to 1889, Camden professor of ancient history at Oxford. After 1872 canon of Canterbury, and from 1888 until death in 1902 rector of All Hallows' Church, London. Wrote commentaries on Exodus, Joshua, I and II Kings, I and II Chronicles, Ezra, Nehemiah, Esther, Job, Psalms and Isaiah; *The Historical Evidences of the Truth of the Scripture Records* (Bamptom lectures); *The Seven Great Monarchies of the Ancient World; Manual of Ancient History; History of Ancient Egypt; The Religions of the Ancient World; History of Phoenicia; St. Paul in Damascus and Arabia; The Kings of Israel and Judah;* and several Old Testament biographies, and other histories of nations. Rawlinson championed a scholarly orthodoxy which opposed the literary higher critics with evidence from the monuments and archaeology. Fellow of the Royal Geographic Society, a corresponding member of the Royal Academy of Turin, and a corresponding member of the American Philosophical Society.

RAYBURN JR., JAMES C. (1909-1970). Born Newton, Kansas. Graduate of Dallas Theological Seminary. Sunday school missionary of Presbyterian Board of Missions in New Mexico. Founded Young Life (high school youngsters' Bible clubs) in 1940. Retired in 1964.

REBMANN (rāb'män), **JOHANNES** (c. 1819-1876), German missionary and East African explorer, born in Gerlingen, Württemberg, Germany, trained at the Basel Mission in Switzerland. Appointed in 1846 by the British Church Missionary Society to the East African Mission at Mombassa to assist Johann Ludwig Krapf. In 1848 accompanied Krapf on the first of those great missionary expeditions into the heart of Africa when they discovered Mount Kilimanjaro and later in 1849 Mt. Kenya and investigated Swahili and other native languages. When Krapf, through ill health, had to leave Africa temporarily, Rebmann remained to carry on the work. Devoted much time and energy to the study of the languages of this part of Africa and to publishing dictionaries for these languages. Becoming totally blind, had to resign his charge; returned to Germany 1875, taking up abode with Mr. Krapf at Kornthal. Died the next year. In twenty-nine years on the field without a furlough, Rebmann shared with Krapf in the preparation of dictionaries for three of the East African languages and in the opening of East Africa to Protestant missions.

RECARED I (rē kä'rěd), (died 601), King of the Visigoths, son of King Leovigild, one of the strongest kings of the Visigoths. At Council of Toledo in 589 formally renounced Arianism, and was followed by many of his bishops and nobles. Made orthodox Catholicism the official religion of the Visigoth kingdom. He also placed restrictions upon the Jews and commanded the baptism of children of mixed marriages. *Filioque* clause added to Nicaean creed in West.

REED, MARY (1854-1943), missionary to the lepers at Chandag, India, born at Lowell, Ohio. After college and ten years of teaching in America appointed missionary to the zenana women of India by the Women's Missionary Society of the Methodist Episcopal church. Soon after arriving in India in 1885 her health gave way and it became imperative that she go to the Himalayas to recuperate. Visiting the leper colony at Chandag, deeply moved by conditions, returning from the hills gave herself devotedly and vigorously to the teaching and evangelization of the Hindu women for four years, when again her health broke. In 1890 furloughed to America for rest. While at home it was discovered that she had contracted leprosy, consequently resolved to return to India. Accepted the invitation of the "Mission to the Lepers in India and the East" to become superintendent of the Leper Homes at Chandag. Under her supervision, without the assistance of any other missionary, a church, chapels, and homes were built and self-supporting industry was developed. Many lepers found Christ. By 1933 Rev. J. Singh, a retired preacher, was appointed to share with her the responsibility of the work. In 1938 at age eighty-four Miss Reed ended her active work when Miss K. Ogilvie was appointed to take over the administration of the Leper Homes. In April 1943, as the result of a fall attributed to her failing eyesight, she died after fifty-two years among the lepers.

REES, THOMAS BONNER (1911-1970), evangelist. Born in Blackburn, England. Became lay youth worker at St. Nicholas, an Anglican church, where he arranged camps for slum boys of London. On staff of *Christian Union*. Successful evangelist in England and Ulster with over 50 rallies at Albert Hall. Bible Conference leader with conferences at Hildenborough Hall. His book *Breakthrough* is a manual for home evangelism.

REIMARUS, HERMANN SAMUEL (1694-1768), German biblical critic. Born in Hamburg. Studied at Jena. Teacher of philosophy at Wittenberg and Hebrew at a gymnasium in Hamburg (1727-1768). In an essay in his *Wolfenbüttel Fragments* he anticipated Schweitzer with the idea that Jesus had taught the nearness of the Messianic age.

REINHARD, FRANZ VOLKMAR (1752-1812), German Lutheran preacher, born at Vohenstrauss in the duchy of Sulzbach, Germany, studied with father, a clergyman, until he was sixteen, then attended school at Ratisbon (or Regensburg) and Wittenberg. In 1782 he was appointed professor of theology, and two years later preacher to the University of Wittenberg. Recognized as one of the ablest preachers of his time, called in 1792 to be court preacher, ecclesiastical councilor, and member of the supreme consistory at Dresden. The distinguished court preacher at Dresden during the last twenty years of his life. Though at first a rationalist, became one of the leaders of the supernaturalistic school, defending the deity of Christ and the authority of the Bible. Preaching and experience both became more and more deeply Christocentric in latter years. Sermons were collected in thirty-nine volumes. Wrote *System der Christlichen Moral* in five volumes.

REMBRANDT, HARMENSZOON VAN RIJN (1606-1669), Dutch painter, born in Leiden, Holland, attended the University of Leiden. Became the greatest of all Dutch painters, painting religious scenes, portraits, scenes of everyday life, and landscapes. An accomplished etcher and draftsman. A master in painting light and shade. In 1631 removed to Amsterdam where he became the most fashionable portrait painter and had many pupils. In 1634 married the beautiful and wealthy Saskia Uylenborch; her death in 1642 cast a gloom over his life, and his fortune began to fail. He seems to have been a poor businessman and lavishly benevolent. Contracted debts, was declared bankrupt, and finally died in poverty. His sufferings seem to be the reason for his about ninety paintings of Christ's passion. Among principal paintings: "Sortie of the Civic Guard" commonly known as "Night Watch," "Anatomy Lecture," "Moses Descending from Sinai," "Pilgrims of Emmaus," "Simeon in the Temple," "The Sacrifice of Abraham," "The Woman Taken in Adultery," and "The Cloth Syndicates." Among etchings; "Descent from the Cross," "The Three Trees," "Christ Healing the Sick," "Christ Presented in the Temple," and "The Death of the Virgin." Preserved works total over six hundred oil paintings, two thousand drawings and studies, and three hundred etchings.

RENAN (rē nän′), **JOSEPH ERNEST** (1823-1892), French historian, critic, and essayist, born in Treguier, Brittany. Intending to enter the priesthood, studied theology in seminary, also Hebrew, Arabic, and Syriac. On the eve of ordination left the seminary (1845), having lost his faith in the teachings of the church. When twenty-five years old wrote *The Future of Science,* in which he declared that science is a religion that will some day displace all other religion. In 1862 appointed a teacher of the Collège de France, but after first lecture on the character of Jesus forced to resign. In 1870 reappointed and in 1882 became director of the college. In 1878 elected to the French Academy. Chief writings: *Life of Jesus, History of the Origins of Christianity, History of the People of Israel,* and *St. Paul.* Writings portray a thoroughly critical and rationalistic attitude. In *Life of Jesus,* which he wrote under the stimulus he received from reading D. C. Strauss's book by the same title, he depicted the purely human life of Jesus as a Galilean peasant prophet, distorting the historical facts of the gospels, thereby inviting the odium of both Catholics and Protestants by his denial of Christ's deity.

REUBLIN (REUBLI), WILHELM (c. 1480-c. 1529). Anabaptist. Studied at the universities of Freiburg and Tübingen, but seems to have been ordained a priest before completing course. He opposed the tithe, usury, military service, and the oath; refused to keep the church fasts; the carrying of relics in the processions instead of the Bible. Most likely met with the "brethren" for prayer and Scripture reading in the home of "Mother Manz" in Zurich. Opposed infant baptism and was an early advocate of believers' baptism. For these things deemed a heretic and banished from Zurich. Went to Waldshut where he met and baptized Dr. Balthassar Hübmaier. Widely known as "Pastor Wilhelm."

REUCHLIN (roikh′lĭn), **JOHANNES** (1455-1522), German Humanist scholar, born at Pforzheim, near Stuttgart, Germany, a granduncle of Philip Melanchthon, and regarded as one of the ablest Greek and Hebrew scholars of the closing years of the fifteenth century in Germany. Educated at Paris, Freiburg, Basel, and Orléans. Settled in Tübingen in 1481 as a teacher of jurisprudence and the liberal arts. Judge in the Swabian League from 1502 to 1512. His Renaissance desire to return to the sources led him to make a thorough study of Hebrew that he might better understand the Old Testament. After twenty years of study, in 1506 published Hebrew Grammar and Lexicon, which unlocked the treasures of the language to the Christian student. Reuchlin did much to win nephew Melanchthon to the evangelical faith. To the end he remained a staunch and loyal Roman Catholic, even attempting to destroy Melanchthon's friendship with Luther. In later years a quarrel arose between Reuchlin and Johann Pfefferkorn (1469-1522), a Christian convert from Judaism. Pfefferkorn secured from the emperor an order to confiscate Jewish books as doing dishonor to Christianity. Reuchlin opposed this action. The Humanists sided with Reuchlin, but the universities and the Dominicans were on the side of Pfefferkorn. A stormy controversy ensued, resulting in the case being appealed to the pope in Rome. Decided first in Reuchlin's favor, then against him. In 1521 appointed professor of Greek at Tübingen, but before entering upon duties there died in 1522.

REUSS (rois), **EDOUARD GUILLAME EUGENE** (1804-1891), Alsatian Protestant biblical scholar and theologian. Born at Strassburg, Alsace. After studying at the gymnasium and at the University of Strassburg studied theology and oriental languages at Göttingen, Halle, Jena, and Paris; took orders in the French Protestant church. Returned to Strassburg in 1828 where he taught for over fifty years and held many positions of importance. Chief interest was in the field of biblical science; became a pioneer in biblical criticism both in Old Testament and New Testament. Wrote in both French and German. Reuss, collaborating with others, edited the monumental edition of Calvin's works in thirty-eight volumes. Perhaps best known for complete French translation of the Bible with introductions (1874-1881) and commentaries in nineteen volumes. Wrote: *History of the Sacred Scriptures of the Old Testament, History of the Sacred Scriptures of the New Testament,* and *History of the Canon of the Holy Scriptures in the Christian Church.* His work had great importance as leading to the positions of Graf, Kuenen, and Wellhausen in historial criticism.

RICCI (rē′chē), **MATTEO** (1552-1610), Jesuit missionary to China born at Macerata, Italy; became a Jesuit in 1571. Sent as a missionary to Goa, India, in about 1578, about five years later went to Macao in South China. Desire to be "all things to all men" led him to adopt Chinese dress and customs. After years of work in southern China, near

Canton and Nanking, in 1601 made a hard, toilsome journey to Peking, where knowledge of geography, mathematics, and astronomy won for him employment in the government, repairing clocks and making maps. In 1610, when the Chinese astronomers failed to predict correctly the eclipse of the moon, the prediction of the missionaries proved to be correct, confidence was given the missionaries. Ricci's refusing any remuneration from the government for services resulted in his being given the privilege of promulgating Christianity. Before his death Ricci saw the conversion of a number of important persons, including an imperial prince; and he saw the coming of a number of other missionaries. Soon after his death the Jesuits under the leadership of Johann Adam Schall were given charge of a revision of the Chinese calendar, also charge of the bureau of astronomy. Ricci was the author of a work on Chinese geography and history and several works in Chinese.

RICE, JOHN R. (1895-1980). Born Cook County, Texas. Educated at Decatur Baptist College, Baylor University, and Southwestern Baptist Seminary, and the University of Chicago. After teaching for two years, a short pastorate, and over a year in the US Army, he became an evangelist with many city-wide campaigns across the country. He was also a radio pastor over his (at death) sixty stations. He was editor and publisher of *The Sword of the Lord* from 1934 and wrote over one hundred books and pamphlets.

RICE, LUTHER (1783-1836), Baptist minister and missionary promoter, born at Northbor, Massachusetts, converted in youth and united with the Congregational church. As a student at Williams College and at Andover Theological Seminary interested in foreign missions, and along with Adoniram Judson and others instituted a movement that resulted in the formation of the American Board of Commissioners for Foreign Missions in 1810. In 1812 Rice was ordained to the Congregational ministry; the same year, he and Nott, Newell, Hall, and Judson went to India as the first missionaries under the new board. On the way across the ocean the Judsons and Rice adopted Baptist views, and after landing were baptized. Rice returned to America the next year to help organize a Baptist foreign missionary society, and to raise funds for the Burmese Mission which the Judsons proceeded to inaugurate. In 1814 the General Convention of the Baptist Denomination in the United States for Foreign Missions was organized through his efforts. In 1817 under his leadership home mission work was undertaken, for which a separate society was later constituted. He helped establish a theological seminary at Philadelphia (1818), and Columbian University at Washington, D.C. (1822). In 1816 began the publication of a religious quarterly, *The Latter Day Luminary,* and in 1822 began to issue the first Baptist weekly, *The Columbian Star.*

RICHARD I, THE LION-HEARTED (1157-1199), King of England, surnamed Coeur de Lion, son of Henry II, whom he succeeded; crowned at Westminster in 1189. Almost immediately began preparations for a crusade against Saladin, the Kurdish general who had made himself master and sultan of Egypt and had captured Jerusalem in 1187. In 1190 he, as the central figure, along with Frederick Barbarossa of Germany and Philip Augustus of France, set out on the Third Crusade for the recovery of the Holy City. In 1191 Acre was captured; Jerusalem was not recovered. After a year or two of fruitless warfare with Saladin for the possession of the tomb of Christ, Richard made a truce with Saladin guaranteeing access to the Holy Places. Philip Augustus had returned to Europe, and in 1192 Richard set out for home. Seized on the way by Leopold, duke of Austria, he was turned over to the emperor Henry VI, held a captive for a time, and released only on the humiliating terms of paying a heavy ransom and consenting to hold his kingdom as a fief of the empire. Arrived in England in 1194, but soon involved in a war with Philip Augustus of France with whom he had quarrelled during the Crusade. Killed by an arrow while conducting a siege in 1199.

RICHARD OF ST. VICTOR (died 1173), theologian, schoolman, mystic, and ascetic. Born in Scotland; as pupil and disciple of Hugh of St. Victor, followed largely the same type of life, thought and teaching. Not interested in philosophy, but did follow the dialectics of Hugo and Abelard. In 1159 became sub-prior of the monastery of St. Victor and subsequently the prior.

RICHARD, TIMOTHY (1845-1919), Baptist missionary to China, born at Ffaldybrenin in Carmarthenshire, Wales. Converted in the Great Revival of 1859. In 1865 entered Haverfordwest Baptist College. Hearing Mrs. Grattan Guiness give an address on China led him to decide to go to that country as a missionary. In 1869 ordained and sailed to North China as a missionary of the Baptist Board. Reached Cheefoo, in Shantung in 1870, and worked there for five years, making several excursions to the interior. During this time studied the language, the New Testament, comparative religion, and the sacred books of the Chinese in preparation for work on the field. In 1875 moved to

Ch'ingchow, a city of Shantung, two hundred miles inland. Adopted Chinese dress, gained a reputation for medical skill through the use of quinine, and won friends among Buddhist, Confucian, and Moslem leaders. In famine of 1876-1878 helped the famine sufferers and built a growing church of seven hundred members in Ch'ingchow. Following this, bent his energies toward reaching the officials and literatti for Christianity. Considered by many as too liberal in his theology, and by his board as too tolerant with the non-Christian religions. In 1891 became director of the Society for the Diffusion of Christian and General Knowledge, later named the Christian Literature Society. This proved to be his main work for the remainder of life. Became an advocate of various reforms, and was a valued counselor to Chinese reform leaders. Following the Boxer massacre in Shansi, upon his recommendation the indemnity money was used to establish a university at Taiyuan to provide the Western type of education. For ten years he was to have supervision of the curriculum. During the Russo-Japanese War, Richard was made Secretary of the International Red Cross Society in Shanghai. Author and translator of many books.

RICHELIEU (rē shē lyû'), **ARMAN JEAN DU PLESSIS, DUC DE** (1585-1642), French cardinal and statesman, born in Paris. Educated at the College of Navarre in Paris, where he prepared for the army. Then turned toward the church and about 1607 consecrated Bishop of Lucon in Rome. Proved to be a successful pastor and administrator. Political career began in 1616 when he became the Secretary of State for War and Foreign Affairs. In 1622 made cardinal, from which time rose rapidly in positions of influence and power in the state, soon becoming Chief Minister of State under Louis XIII in 1624, retaining that position until death. The new minister's first important measure was the arrangement of a marriage between the royal houses of France and England, which assured friendly relations with England. Policies may be grouped under three heads: (1) to suppress the political power of the Huguenots; (2) to level the power of the nobility; and (3) to attack and destroy the power of the Hapsburgs in Austria and Spain. Purpose for carrying out these policies was to make France strong in Europe and to make the king absolute ruler in France. Established France as the first military power in Europe; creator of the French navy. More than any of its kings, the founder of the French monarchy. A liberal patron of literature and wrote voluminously. In 1636 Richelieu founded the French Academy. Died in 1642; buried in the chapel of the Sorbonne which he had built.

RICHTER (rĭkh'tẽr), **JULIUS** (1862-1940), German Lutheran missionary historian, pupil of Gustav Warneck. After fifteen years as a pastor, first professor of missions in the University of Berlin, holding the chair until 1910. After Warneck's death in 1910, he became joint editor of Warneck's missionary magazine, *Allgemeine Missions-Zeitschrift*, joint editor of the *Neue Allgemeine Missions-Zeitschrift*. From among thirty works the following is the chief: *Allegemeine Evangelische Missionsgeschichte* (five volumes, two of them being translated into English as *History of Missions in India* and *History of Protestant Missions in the Near East)*.

RIDLEY, NICHOLAS (c. 1500-1555), English Reformer and martyr, born in Northumberland, England, educated at Pembroke Hall, Cambridge, the Sorbonne in Paris, and the University of Louvain. In 1534 signed the decree against papal supremacy in England. In 1537 named chaplain to Thomas Cranmer, in 1538 master of Pembroke Hall; Archbishop of Canterbury; in 1541 made chaplain to King Henry VIII; in 1545 became canon of Westminster. More and more manifesting Protestant leanings, finally renounced transubstantiation. In 1547 named Bishop of Rochester; in 1549 deputed to place Protestantism on a firm basis at Cambridge; assisted Cranmer in the preparation of the English Prayer Book and the Thirty-nine Articles; and in 1550 became Bishop of London. Deep interest in the unfavored classes led to the establishment of three hospitals under royal direction. After the death of Edward VI in 1553, he espoused the cause of Lady Jane Grey as successor to the throne, and publicly pronounced both Mary and Elizabeth as illegitimate, therefore not eligible to the throne. When Mary Tudor, a Roman Catholic, was proclaimed queen, he was imprisoned in the tower of London, from which he was later removed to a jail in Oxford. In 1555, refusing to recant his written statements of defense, he was declared a heretic, excommunicated, and along with Hugh Latimer was burned at the stake, Thomas Cranmer meeting the same fate a little later.

RIGGS, ELIAS (1810-1901), American missionary and linguist, born at New Providence, New Jersey, graduated from Amherst College, and from Andover Theological Seminary, Massachusetts. A missionary of the American Board at Athens and Argos, Greece (1832-1838); Smyrna, Asia Minor (1838-1853); and Constantinople (1853-1901). For three years after going to Constantinople taught at the Bebek Theological Seminary; because of a breakdown in health was forced to take a two-year furlough home. On this (only) furlough he supervised the printing of his translation of the Bible in the Armenian, taught Hebrew in Union Theological Seminary, New York. A member of the committee appointed by the British and Foreign Bible Society and the American Bible Society to prepare a Turkish Bible in both the Arabic and the Armenian languages. Said to have had a working knowledge of twenty-one languages and mastery of twelve, to have written or translated 478 hymns in the Bulgarian language. Literary work consisted in preparing grammars and translations of the Scriptures, especially in the Armenian, Turkish, and Bulgarian languages. Wrote a *Harmony of the Gospels* and a *Biblical Dictionary* in Bulgarian, published a *Manual of the Chaldean Language*.

RILEY, WILLIAM BELL (1861-1947), Baptist minister and educator, born in Green County, Indiana. Educated at Valparaiso Normal School, Indiana, Hanover College, Indiana (B.A. and M.A.), Southern Baptist Theological Seminary (1883). Ordained to Baptist ministry (1883); pastor in several churches in Indiana and Illinois from 1884 to 1897; First Church in Minneapolis, 1897-1942. Founder and president of Northwestern Bible Training School (1902); Northwestern Evangelical Seminary (1935); and of Northwestern College of Liberal Arts (1944). Executive of the World Christian Fundamentalist Association and editor of *The Christian Fundamentalist* and *The Northwestern Pilot*. President of the Minnesota Baptist State Convention, 1944-1945. Wrote a series of forty volumes, *The Bible of the Expositor and the Evangelist, Greater Doctrines of Scriptures,* and many others.

RITSCHL (rĭch'l), **ALBRECHT BENJAMIN** (1822-1889), German Protestant theologian, born in Berlin, Germany; studied at the universities of Bonn, Halle, Heidelberg, and Tübingen. At Halle came under Hegelian influence and became a disciple of F. C. Baur; later broke with Baur. In 1859 was appointed professor at Bonn; from 1864 to 1889 at Göttingen. Early writings were theological, later ones of historical nature. Although his Christian views were Bible-centered, he interpreted theology and church history from pragmatic and historical or "higher critical" viewpoint. Later was strongly influenced by Kant, Schleiermacher, and Lotze; however stressed community consciousness (the church) rather than individual consciousness as did Schleiermacher. Faith rests on "value-judgments" rather than historical facts of Bible. The Bible being a record of community consciousness called for normal historical investigation, making unnecessary any theory of inspiration. The Ritschlian school thus made religion subjective, and opened the way for extreme critical study of the Bible, also promoted the social approach to religious problems, opening the way for stressing the social gospel. Ritschl stressed pragmatism to the point that he had little left for practical experience; greatly underestimated the "self-existence" and the infinity of God, but strongly emphasized the love of God. Helped to develop Liberalism.

ROBERT DE MOLESME (dē mô lām') (c. 1027-1111), founder of the Cistercian Order, known also as Robert of Citeaux. Born at Champagne, France; at age fifteen became a Benedictine monk in the abbey of Montier-la-Celle, where later elected prior. In 1068 appointed abbot of Saint Michael de Tonerre. Because of the recalcitrancy of the monks left them and joined some anchorites in the desert and became their superior. The band then removed in 1075 to Molesme in Burgundy and built cells and an oratory dedicated to the Holy Trinity. When this monastery became wealthy and lax in discipline, he left it and eventually settled at Cistercium or Citeaux in the diocese of Chalons near Dijon, joining with a group of devout members from the former abandoned community. In 1098 they established themselves and thus founded the Cistercian Order. But the next year he returned to Molesme, leaving Citeaux in charge of Alberic. Presided over Molesme until death in 1111. The rules established by him allotted four hours for sleep, four for singing, four for manual labor, and four for study. Bernard of Clairvaux joined the order in 1113 and brought the Cistercians into a place of prominence and influence in the Church.

ROBERTS, BENJAMIN TITUS (1823-1893), American Methodist clergyman and an organizer of the Free Methodist church, born at Gowanda, New York. At age sixteen taught school. Studied law for two or three years, then, following conversion, felt the call to ministry. In 1848 graduated from Wesleyan University, Middletown, Connecticut. Ordained in 1852 with pastorates until 1858. For ten years a member of the Genesee Conference of the Methodist Episcopal church; but in 1857 wrote an article on the "New-School Methodism" criticizing Methodist church for its departure from the early precepts and practices of the church. He and several who were causing agitation in the church were expelled from the Conference in 1858. In 1860 led in the organization of the Free Methodist church; became its first superintendent, holding that position until 1893. Began and was editor of a monthly magazine, *The Earnest Christian* (1860-1893); and edited *The Free Methodist* (1886-1890). He also took the leading part in founding Chesbrough Academy, now named Roberts Wesleyan College, at North Chili, New York, serving as its president. Wrote *Why Another Sect,* and *Ordaining Women,* advocated on scriptural grounds the right of women to be admitted to the ministry.

ROBERTS, EVAN JOHN (1875-1951), Welsh revivalist. Born in Glamorgan. Became a blacksmith's apprentice in 1902. Trained for ministry in Newcastle Emlyn. In 1904 after deep spiritual experience began revival ministry. Meetings in his home church, Moriah at Loughor, led to revival. Revival spread all over Wales from 1904 to 1906. Estimated 100,000 were converted. Health broke, and he retired from active ministry after 1906.

ROBERTSON, ARCHIBALD THOMAS (1863-1934), American Baptist theologian, born near Chatham, Virginia. When twelve years of age moved with parents to North Carolina. Converted at the age of thirteen and licensed to preach at sixteen. Educated at Wake Forest College, Wake Forest, North Carolina, and the Southern Baptist Theological Seminary, Louisville, Kentucky. During college and seminary days did a little preaching in various churches. After ordination in 1888 assumed a pastorate at the New Castle Church, but within a few months had to resign on account of a nervous breakdown. Later as a teacher, scholar, and preacher, in demand in many parts of the country. In 1894, about four months before the death of John A. Broadus, married a daughter of Broadus. Assistant to Broadus from 1888. In 1895 elected to succeed Dr. Broadus as Professor of New Testament interpretation in the seminary, which position he held until death in 1934. In 1916 and 1926 delivered the Stone Lectures at Princeton Theological Seminary and in 1927 the Wilkinson Lectures at the Northern Baptist Theological Seminary in Chicago. Spoke at twelve Northfield Conferences. Dr. Robertson's greatest contribution to biblical scholarship was in the field of New Testament Greek. In 1914 published his *A Grammar of the Greek New Testament,* the largest (1,454 pages), most comprehensive New Testament grammar in existence. Twenty-six years were spent in its preparation; it contains references to almost all relevant literature written before 1914. Outstanding among his forty-five books are: *Syllabus of New Testament Greek Syntax; Bibliography of New Testament Greek; Syllabus for New Testament Study; Epochs in the Life of Jesus; Epochs in the Life of Paul; Epochs in the Life of Simon Peter; Epochs in the Life of the Apostle John; Word Pictures in the New Testament* (six volumes); *The Minister and His Greek Testament;* and *Harmony of the Gospels.*

ROBERTSON, FREDERICK WILLIAM (1816-1853), English preacher, born in London into Evangelical atmosphere. Studied at the University of Edinburgh, and Brasenose College, Oxford, receiving B.A. in 1841; M.A. in 1844. In early life had planned to be soldier. Studied Platonic metaphysics and Aristotle. Ordained in 1840; same year took a curacy in the parish of St. Mary Kalendar, in poorest part of Winchester. Before long his health broke and he spent time in traveling. 1843 to 1846 curate at Christ Church, Cheltenham. Again health broke and he went to Germany; preached in 1846 to English congregation in Heidelberg. From 1847 to 1853 was minister of Trinity Chapel, Brighton. Successful in winning confidence of the people, especially the working classes. The power of his pathos, warm feeling, dignity, and beauty of language had marked effect. But his seriousness of temperament, intense sensitiveness and lack of humor militated against his health and evidently shortened his life. Nearly all of his writings were published posthumously, the most important were *Sermons Preached at Trinity Chapel, Brighton.* Wrote also *Lectures on the Influence of Poetry on the Working Classes,* and *Expository Lectures on St. Paul's Epistle to the Corinthians.*

ROBINSON, CHARLES SEYMOUR (1829-1899), American Presbyterian clergyman and hymnologist, born at Bennington, Vermont, studied at Williams College, Union Theological Seminary, New York, and Princeton Theological Seminary. Between 1855, when he was ordained, and 1868 pastor in Presbyterian churches at Troy, New York, and Brooklyn, New York. For three years (1868-1871), pastor at the American Chapel, Paris, France, which he organized into a church. Returning to the United States from 1871 to 1899 served successively the Madison Avenue and the Thirteenth Street Presbyterian churches in New York City. Most of his writings were of sermons and compilations of hymn books, some of which were *Hymns of the Church; Songs for the Sanctuary; Spiritual Songs; Laudes Domini;* and *New Laudes Domini.* Wrote only a few hymns. Also wrote *Simon Peter, His Early Life and Times; Simon Peter, His Later Life and Labors;* and *Studies in the New Testament.*

ROBINSON, EDWARD (1794-1863), American biblical scholar, born at Southington, Connecticut; received college education at Hamilton College; studied law for a year at Hudson, New York; studied Greek at Andover Theological Seminary. Tutor in mathematics at Hamilton College for a year. In 1823 made assistant professor of sacred theology at Andover. While here assisted Dr. Moses Stuart, the distinguished Hebraist, in preparing a *Greek Grammar of the New Testament*. From 1826 to 1830 studied philology at the universities of Göttingen, Halle, and Berlin; there made acquaintance with Gesenius, Tholuck, Neander, and Ritter. In 1830 became professor extraordinary of biblical literature at Andover Theological Seminary; from 1837 until death professor of biblical literature in Union Theological Seminary. In 1831 founded the *Biblical Repository,* which in 1851 was united with *Bibliotheca Sacra*. In 1838 and again in 1852, with Eli Smith, the accomplished Arabic scholar and faithful missionary of the American Board in Syria, made extensive and careful surveys and investigations in Palestine. Resulting from first visit, published his *Biblical Researches in Palestine; Mount Sinai; and Arabia Petraea* (three volumes), which gained Gold Medal of the Royal Geographic Society and established the author's reputation as geographer and Biblical scholar of the first rank. After second visit in 1852, wrote *Later Researches in Palestine and Adjacent Regions.* Hoped to publish a complete historical and topographical geography of the Holy Land. Repeated attacks of illness prevented accomplishing this; after death only the first part of the *Physical Geography of the Holy Land* was published. Also prepared a *Greek Harmony of the Gospels,* which was far superior to anything that had to that time appeared; also wrote an *English Harmony.*

ROBINSON, FRANK BRUCE (1886-1948), founder of Psychiana; studied awhile for the Baptist ministry. Became a pharmacist at Moscow, Idaho. Having come under the influence of New Thought, turned away from Christianity, railed against all churches, and repudiated Jesus Christ as the Son of God. Claimed a new experience with God, and began a vast mail evangelism for his new cult. His mail-order religion became a big and lucrative business. Ordained by one of the bishops of the Old Catholic church, he incorporated his movement with himself as Archbishop of Moscow. Teaching was a typical New Thought emphasis on health, prosperity, and happiness; strictly unitarian, highly mystical; sin, atonement, future life, inspiration of the Scriptures were all ruled out.

ROBINSON, GEORGE LIVINGSTONE (1864-1958), Presbyterian theologian and archaeologist, born at West Hebron, New York; received education at Fort Edward Collegiate Institute, Princeton College, Princeton Theological Seminary, at Berlin and Leipzig. After graduation from college became an instructor in the Syrian Protestant College, Beirut, Syria for three years (1887-1890). After return to the states took three-year theological course at Princeton (1890-1893), then spent two years in graduate study in Germany, where he received Ph.D. degree. After spending one year as pastor of the Roxbury Presbyterian Church, Boston, Massachusetts, became professor of Old Testament literature and exegesis at Knox College, Toronto for two years; took a similar position in McCormick Theological Seminary, Chicago, 1898, and held this position until retirement in 1939. In 1906 served as professor in the American School of Archaeology at Jerusalem. Made extensive explorations in Palestine, particularly in the peninsula of Sinai and Kadesh-Barnea. Discovered the high place of Petra and visited the Cave of Machpelah. In 1913-1914 director of the American School of Oriental Research in Jerusalem. Wrote: *The Sarcophagus of an Ancient Civilization; The Biblical Doctrine of Holiness; Leaders of Israel; History of the Hebrews from the Earliest Times to the Downfall of Jerusalem, A.D. 70; The Book of Isaiah; The Twelve Minor Prophets; Where Did We Get Our Bible?; The Bearing of Archaeology on the Old Testament; Live Out Your Years; Why I Am a Christian;* and *Autobiography.*

ROBINSON, JOHN (c. 1576-1625), English separatist and Pilgrim preacher, born probably in Lincolnshire, England. Educated at Cambridge, where Puritanism was exerting influence. Became curate at St. Andrews, Norwich about 1602, compelled to leave charge because of Puritanic leanings. Joined a congregation of separatists at Gainsborough, soon chosen as their pastor, the group becoming known as the "Pilgrim Fathers." In 1606 part of the group went to Amsterdam, Holland, under the leadership of John Smyth. Robinson and the remainder of the congregation met in William Brewster's house at Scrooby for a while; and then in 1608 went to Amsterdam. The next year chosen pastor with William Brewster as ruling elder of the Separatists at Leiden, where the congregation grew to three hundred. Became involved in the Arminian controversy that was prominent in Holland at that time, taking the Calvinistic side. Took an active interest promoting emigration to America. In 1620 a part of the congregation sailed to England on the "Speedwell" and then to America on the "Mayflower" under Brewster's guidance. Robinson, however, remained behind in Holland as pastor to the majority, who chose not to sail to America. Some of his congregation returned to England.

ROCK, JOHANN FREDERICK (1678-1749), co-founder of the Amana Church Society, born at Oberswälden, near Göppingen, Württemberg, Germany. He was a harness-maker. A mystic who came under the influence of the Camisards, the "French Prophets," and became a leader of the "Inspirationists." In 1714 he and Eberhard Ludwig Gruber (1665-1728) began to stir the German Pietists with their preaching, holding that the days of true inspiration from God had not ended. They gained adherents from among the Pietists, and at the same time were themselves influenced by the Pietists. These Inspirationists refused to take oaths, to participate in war, to send their children to state schools, and in their congregations had no office of teacher or preacher. At Himbach, Hesse, Germany, they loosely organized a group of their followers. For awhile kept close friendly relations with Count Zinzendorf. Controversy ensued, and Zinzendorf finally broke away. After the death of Rock in 1749, "the gift of inspiration ceased," the membership gradually dwindled until in 1817 under Michael Krausert, Barbara Heinemann, and Christian Metz, the movement was revived; the gift of inspiration and prophecy was renewed. Because of governmental opposition in Germany, they came to America in 1842 under the name of the Ebenezer Society, settling near Buffalo, New York. In 1855 removed to Iowa, and in 1859 organized themselves into the "Amana Church Society."

RODEHEAVER (rō'dĕ hā ver), **HOMER ALVAN** (1880-1955), music director, trombonist, hymn writer, and publisher of evangelistic hymns, born in Union Furnace, Ohio, studied at Ohio Wesleyan University. From 1909 to 1931 song and choir director for Billy Sunday in evangelistic campaigns. Also toured the world with Evangelist William E. Biederwolf (1923-1924), made a tour of Africa mission fields (1936). In 1942 became music director at Bob Jones College, Tennessee. Founded Summer School of Sacred Music at Winona Lake. President of the Rodeheaver Hall-Mack Company, publishers of gospel music, Winona Lake, Indiana. Prepared and published numerous compilations of gospel songs and wrote some hymns. Conducted a Florida ranch for underprivileged boys. Author of *Song Stories of the Sawdust Trail, Twenty Years with Billy Sunday, Hymnal Handbook for Standard Hymns and Gospel Songs.*

ROGERS, JOHN (c. 1500-1555), English Lutheran reformer and martyr, born at Deritend, near Birmingham, England, educated at Pembroke Hall, Cambridge. Ordained rector of Holy Trinity, London (1532-1534). Chaplain of the English merchants at Antwerp (1534-1536). Made the acquaintance of William Tyndale, and renounced the Roman Catholic faith. In 1537, under the pseudonymn of Thomas Matthew, issued a skillful combination of Bible translations of Tyndale and Coverdale, with preface and marginal notes, which has since been known as the Matthew's Bible. Work was largely used by those who prepared the Great Bible (1539-1540), out of which in turn came the Bishop's Bible in 1568 and the King James Version in 1611. Pastor at Wittenberg until the accession of Edward VI, when he returned to England by invitation of Bishop Ridley. Simultaneously made rector of St. Margaret Moyses and vicar of St. Sepulcher, London in 1550. In 1551 made prebendary of St. Pancras, St. Paul's. On the accession of Queen Mary in 1553 arrested for his vigorous denunciation of Romanism and later was burned at the stake at Smithfield, London, becoming the first martyr under Mary's reign.

ROLLE OF HAMPOLE, RICHARD (c. 1295-1349), mystical hermit. Born in Yorkshire. Student at Oxford and Paris. Ordained as priest about 1326. A hermit on John Dalton's estate and at Hampole. Wrote mystical books, *De Incendio Amoris* and *Melsos Amoris* in which he stated that Christ's love demanded all our love. The Lollards used some of his writings.

ROMAINE, WILLIAM (1714-1795), Church of England Evangelical divine, born at Hartlepool, Durham, England, educated at Hart Hall and Christ Church, Oxford. Ordained priest in 1738; held several curacies in and near London, including Banstead, Surrey, and Horton, Middlesex. In 1748 prepared for the press a new edition of the Hebrew Concordance and Lexicon of Marius de Calasio, which was a contribution to critical study in the scholarly traditions of the Church of England. In 1749 appointed lecturer at St. Dunstan's-in-the-West, and in 1850 at St. George's, Hanover Square. About the middle of his life came under the influence of George Whitefield, and for the rest of long life was one of the principal representatives of rigid Calvinism among the evangelicals. Consequently lost lectureship, and held several brief charges for a few years. In 1766 became the incumbent of the united parish of St. Anne's, Blackfriars and St. Andrews of the Wardrobe, where revivalistic preaching drew large congregations until the end of life. Had a deep sense of the value of the Church of England. A powerful preacher and a dynamic writer, expounded extreme Calvinism in three principal works, *The Life of Faith, The Walk of Faith,* and *The Triumph of Faith*.

ROOT, GEORGE FREDERICK (1820-1895), American composer, music publisher, and teacher, born in Sheffield, Massachusetts. In 1838 went to Boston, studied, played the organ, and began teaching. In 1841 became a teacher in Lowell Mason's musical conventions or "Teachers' Classes." In 1844 went to New York, taught and played for about ten years. Spent several months studying in Paris (1850-51). In 1853 originated the New York Normal Institute, himself, Lowell Mason, Thomas Hastings, and William B. Bradbury as the principal teachers. This was his most important contribution to the musical development of America. Many of the most eminent music teachers and composers of our country were students in Dr. Root's musical institute. In 1859 settled in Chicago, helped establish the firm, Root and Cady, in which Mr. Root's own compositions helped to enhance the firm, also brought his name as a composer more into the limelight. In the Chicago fire the firm of Root and Cady became engulfed in the general ruins. Became connected with John Church and Company of Cincinnati, able to give much of time to normal and convention work. Attained the highest place among American musicians as a teacher, a theorist, and a composer. Author of about seventy-five books, nearly two hundred song sheets, and many popular gospel songs. Wrote some music under the German equivalent of his name, Friedrich Wurzel. He composed the tune for Fanny J. Crosby's song, "There's Music in the Air." Perhaps best known sacred hymn tune is "The Shining Shore." Wrote both the words and the music for several patriotic songs, "Tramp, Tramp, Tramp, the Boys Are Marching," "Just Before the Battle, Mother," "The Battle Cry of Freedom," and "The Vacant Chair."

ROSCELLINUS (c. 1050-c. 1125), scholastic theologian and early nominalist. Born in Compiègne. Studied at Soissons and Rheims. In 1092 in England where Anselm opposed him. On return to France taught at Loches, Besancan, and Tours. His pupil Abelard attacked his views. Roscellinus taught that the only universal was our subjective idea of common characteristics of the thing.

ROSENIUS (rō zĕn'ĭ ŭs), **KARL OLOF** (1816-1868), founder of the Evangelical National Institution. Lay preacher in the Lutheran church in Sweden who had been generally influenced by the Methodist George Scott. Through magazine, *Pietisten,* and in sermons, exercised important influence on religious life of Sweden, paved the way for the Free church movement in Sweden. After 1842 until death was leader of the Free church movement. Sole dogma was the forgiveness of sins without merit on the part of the sinner. Movement led to formation of two national societies known as the National Evangelical Foundation, founded in 1856, and the Swedish Mission Covenant, founded in 1878. Immigrants from the latter came to America, and in 1885 organized into what is today known as the Evangelical Mission Covenant church of North America. After his death in 1868, Paul Peter Waldenström carried on Rosenius' movement in Sweden.

ROSSETTI, GABRIEL CHARLES DANTE (1828-1882), English poet and painter, born in London, well educated, studied at King's College School, in Cary's Art Academy, and at the Royal Academy, where associated with William Holman Hunt and J. E. Millais in the founding of the Pre-Raphaelite Brotherhood. Grief over wife's death, worry over a bitter attack made upon the morality of his later poems, and insomnia, led him to a drug habit which eventually gained the mastery. Rossetti gained distinction both as a painter and as a poet. Paintings may be divided into three groups—small biblical pictures, Dante pictures, and paintings representing the soul. In the first group, "Ecce Ancilla Domini" and "Girlhood of Mary Virgin" are the best known. In the second, "Dante's Dream," "Beata Beatrix," "Donna della Finestra," and "The Borgia Family." The third group includes "The Day Dream," "The Sphinx," and "The Blessed Damozel." At nineteen wrote poem also entitled "The Blessed Damozel." Most noted literary work was a group of beautiful love sonnets entitled *The House of Life*. *Ballads and Sonnets* contains some of his finest poetry. His sister, Christina Georgina Rossetti (1830-1894), a deeply spiritual woman and an invalid for the last twenty years of her life, was a famous English poetess.

ROUSSEAU (ro͞o sō'), **JEAN JACQUES** (1712-1778), French philosopher and author, born at Geneva, Switzerland, early orphaned. Became an ardent Roman Catholic, educated by them. Earlier years were devoted to political connections, to writing, teaching, and copying music, to reading philosophy and science, to wandering from place to place, and to reveling in the enjoyment of nature. Placed five children by Thérèse Lerasseur in orphanages. Wrote a prize essay on *Arts and Sciences* in which he proclaimed gospel of "back to nature," and conviction as to the corruption of society and civilization. Egotism, arrogance, and sensitive personality made their impact upon relations with people, and upon own life and writing. In book, *Social Contract,* he declared that man was born free and advocated representative government based on vote of the majority. This book became the ideology of the French Revolution. In *Emile, or an Essay on Education,* he would have children educated by experience of nature, or by "letting children be children." He said that the teacher should in no way restrict the child's personality or desires. Rousseau's *Confessions* are a revelation of his moral life. In religion he was a naturalist and a deist.

ROUTH, MARTIN JOSEPH (1755-1854), Patristic scholar and educator, born at South Elmham, Suffolk, England, educated at Queen's College and Magdalen College, Oxford. Elected fellow of Magdalen College and president of the college in 1791, holding the presidency until death. In 1810 received priest's orders and became rector of Tylehurst, near Reading. Respected and revered by the Tractarians. A special authority on ecclesiastical law and history. Published the valuable five-volume set of *Reliquiae Sacrae,* which was an edition of the scattered fragments of the writings of the less known fathers of the second and third centuries A.D. Published *Scriptorum Ecclesiasticorum Opuscula Praecipua Quaedam.* Valuable sixteen thousand volume library was bequeathed to Durham University. Works bear the stamp of profound erudition, critical ability, sagacity, accuracy, and clearness of expression. Opinions orthodox; sympathies were with the High church party.

ROWLAND, DANIEL (c. 1713-1790), Welsh Calvinistic Methodist, cofounder with Howell Harris of the Welsh Calvinistic Methodist church. Born at Pantybeudy, Cardiganshire. Ordained in 1736 and an associate of his clerical brother John in his church. Converted under Griffith Jones and began revival preaching in Llangeitho which became center of Welsh Methodism. Dispossessed of his church in 1763 and continued as pastor in the "New Church" built for him at Llangeitho.

ROWNTREE, JOSEPH (1801-1859), Quaker social reformer and philanthropist. Born in Scarborough. Entered grocery business. Alderman in York and in 1858 mayor. Founded schools for boys and girls in 1828 and 1830 and Flounders Institute at Ackworth to train teachers. Organized the Friends' Educational Society in 1837.

ROYCE, JOSIAH (1855-1916), American philosopher and teacher, born at Grass Valley, California, graduated from the University of California, studied at Leipzig, Göttingen, and Johns Hopkins. Instructor in English literature and logic in alma mater (1878-1882); professor at Harvard University (1882-1916). Author of *Religious Aspects of Philosophy, Spirit of Modern Philosophy, The Conception of God, The Conception of Immortality, The World and the Individual, Outlines of Psychology, Philosophy of Loyalty,* and *The Problem of Christianity* (two volumes). In metaphysics became one of the ablest exponents of absolute monistic idealism, "emphasizing individuality and will rather than intellect." Method was rationalistic. Mediated idealistic philosophy to America. Served as president of the American Philosophical Association and of the American Psychological Association. A member of the National Academy of Sciences, and of the National Institute of Arts and Letters.

RUBENS, PETER PAUL (1577-1640), celebrated Flemish painter, born in Siegen, Westphalia, Germany. At age ten began study at the Jesuit College in Antwerp, Belgium, and at thirteen began study of art. At twenty-one became a member of the Brotherhood of St. Luke in Antwerp, and was permitted to paint independently. Went to Italy, studied Titian, Paul Veronese, and Michelangelo. After spending some years in Italy, and making a trip to Spain, returned to home country, settled at Antwerp, became court preacher to Archduke Albrecht. From this time on became the most sought after painter in Europe. Pupils flocked to his studio. Most powerful sovereigns of Europe paid honor to his genius. Knighted by Charles I of England and by Philip IV of Spain. An accomplished scholar, proficient in Latin, French, German, Spanish, English, and Italian, acted many times in diplomatic capacity when England and Holland were involved. Life was extremely successful and happy throughout with never a sign of diminished artistic power or mental decline. In later years ill much of the time, but continued to paint on a large scale. Produced more than twelve hundred paintings, the greatest of which was "The Descent from the Cross." This painting is remarkable for its sympathy and religious spirit, faultless composition, color, and harmony, and hangs in the Antwerp Cathedral. Famous "Crucifixion" or "Elevation of the Cross" also hangs in the Antwerp Cathedral. Rubens did much portrait work; employed many students as assistants.

RUFINUS (ro͞o fī'nus), **TYRANNIUS** (c. 345-410), Latin theologian and church historian, born near Aquileia, Italy, at the head of the Adriatic, educated at Rome, where he met Jerome. Baptized about 370 at Aquileia where he lived for a time as a monk. In earlier years a warm friend of Jerome, but later became a bitter enemy through their controversy over Origen. About 371 left Aquileia for the East where he lived among the hermits in Egypt for about six years, and then may have lived with Jerome in his monastery at Bethlehem. In 381 he founded a monastery in Jerusalem. In 394 made a presbyter by Bishop John of Jerusalem. In 397 returned to Italy, translated Origen's *De Principiis,* the first attempt at a systematic theology. Also translated in nine books the Ecclesiastical History of Eusebius, which he did with abridgements and insertions. Then he continued the history to the time of Emperor Theodosius the Great (392).

RUSKIN, JOHN (1819-1900), English art critic and social reformer, born in London, studied at Christ Church, Oxford. Studied painting, claiming as his masters Rubens and Rembrandt. Expressed his art interests, however, with the pen rather than with the brush. The book that established his fame was his first volume of *Modern Painters* (1843), written to defend Turner. Four more volumes followed in subsequent years. The main principles of his moral and spiritual interpretation of art were summed up in *The Seven Lamps of Architecture,* as sacrifice, truth, power, beauty, life, memory, and obedience. Closely associated with his moral ideals were aesthetic views, truth and sincerity being the indispensable foundations of both; he held that the art and architecture of a people are the expression of its religion and morality. Other writings on art and architecture: *Stones of Venice, Pre-Raphaelitism,* and *Architecture of Venice.* Still others: *The Elements of Drawing, Sesame and Lilies,* and *Crown of Wild Olives.* After the middle years of life his evangelicalism gave place to a vague theism, his more deeply religious interests were turned to economic and social concerns. At this time wrote: *Letters to the Workingmen and Laborers of Great Britain.* In 1871 established the Guild of St. George, comprising agricultural and industrial settlements. Although those settlements did not prove a great success, they were a vital influence in leading to the establishment of university settlements later. From 1870 to 1879 and again 1883-1884, Ruskin was Slade professor of art at Oxford. In 1884 resigned, and lived in retirement the rest of life. In the closing years of life returned to a more Christian concern.

RUSSELL, CHARLES TAZE (1852-1916), founder of the "Jehovah's Witnesses," now International Bible Students Association. Born at Allegheny, Pennsylvania, and after receiving a common school education, entered the clothing business with his father and managed several stores. As a young man a member and earnest worker of the Congregational church and a member of the Young Men's Christian Association. Taught that Christ came to heavenly sanctuary and cast Satan out. About 1870 organized a Bible study group, which in 1878 elected him their "pastor." This was the beginning of a period of more than forty years of teaching his "new doctrine." By this time Russell totally rejected the Trinity, the deity of Christ, His physical resurrection and return, and the doctrine of eternal retribution for sin; denounced all existing churches as rejected of God, and all civil government as Satan's organization. In 1879 started a small magazine, *Zion's Watch Tower and Herald of Christ's Presence,* a year later published his first book, *Food for Thinking Christians.* In 1886 he incorporated the Watch Tower Society. Later published *Millennial Dawn,* later to be entitled *Studies in the Scriptures, Plan of the Ages.* Gradually began to establish churches throughout the United States, Canada, England, and the Continent, until there were more than twelve hundred congregations calling him "Pastor." Earlier years were spent in Pittsburgh and Allegheny, but in 1908 came to New York, where he bought Bethel Chapel, later rented Brooklyn Academy of Music for Sunday services. Later took over for his work the Brooklyn Tabernacle of Henry Ward Beecher and also the home of Beecher on Columbia Heights. Russell's career was highly colored with moral and legal irregularities—divorce when his wife left him in 1897, perjury in court, selling of "miracle wheat" seed in 1913, and a suit against the *Brooklyn Daily Eagle,* which he lost. He was a man of prodigious activity. Died while traveling in Texas on pastoral trip. Leadership was taken over by his trusted lawyer, Judge J. F. Rutherford. In addition to the seven volumes of *Studies in the Scriptures,* he was author of: *Why Evil Was Permitted* and *The Tabernacle Shadows of Better Sacrifices.*

RUTHERFORD, JOSEPH FRANKLIN (1869-1942), president of Jehovah's Witnesses, born at Boonville, Missouri. In addition to regular course in college, took shorthand and law. At twenty-two admitted to the bar in hometown, Boonville, and for fifteen years a Missouri lawyer. In 1909 became a member of the New York State Bar. While in Missouri appointed on occasion as special judge, thus coming to be known as "Judge" Rutherford. Early in the present century Rutherford came into fellowship with "Pastor" Charles Taze Russell, and soon became the chief legal adviser of his society. When Pastor Russell died in 1916, J. F. Rutherford was elected president from 1917 until 1942. An able and prolific writer and an effective orator. He and several others were imprisoned for nine months in 1918-1919 for urging Americans to refuse to take part in the World War. The change of name from *Watch Tower* to *Jehovah's Witnesses* (1931) was an occasion for renewed zeal and enthusiasm for the society. Rutherford died in 1942, left the active direction of the society in the hands of Mr. N. H. Knorr as president. Rutherford's writings were more voluminous than were those of Russell. A few of the more than one hundred titles: *Harp of God, Life, Comfort for the Jews, Where Are the Dead?, Our Lord's Return, Let God Be True, The New World, Children,* and *Can the Living Talk with the Dead?* One of Rutherford's widely advertised lectures: "Millions Now Living Will Never Die."

RUTHERFORD, SAMUEL (c. 1600-1661), Scottish theologian and Covenanter, born at Nisbet in Roxburghshire, Scotland, educated at Edinburgh University. In 1623 appointed professor of Latin in alma mater. Resigned in 1625 to devote himself to the study of theology. Took up a pastorate at Anwoth, Kirkcudbrightshire from 1627 until 1636. While serving at Anwoth wrote a book entitled *An Apology for Divine Grace,* which came to the attention of the bishop, Thomas Sydserf, who cited him before the High Commission Court to answer for his nonconformity to the Acts of Episcopacy, and for his writing against Arminians. Deprived of his parish at Anwoth he was banished to Aberdeen from 1636 to 1638. It was while in exile that he wrote many of his famous letters. After recall from exile he became professor at St. Mary's College, St. Andrews in 1638. In 1643 Rutherford took a prominent part in the preparation of the Westminster Confession and is credited with having written the Shorter Catechism. In 1647 he returned to St. Andrews and became principal at St. Mary's. In 1651 made rector of the University of St. Andrews. Upon the restoration of Charles II in 1660 his book *Lex Rex* (1644) was condemned to be burned, and Rutherford was deposed from all his offices, deprived of pastoral charge, and summoned to appear at the next Parliament on a charge of high treason. The messengers who brought the summons to him at St. Andrews found him on his deathbed.

RUYSBROECK (rois'bro͞ok), **JAN VAN** (1293-1381), Dutch mystic, born at Ruysbroeck, near Brussels, Belgium. He studied at Brussels, and was trained in piety by his mother, and by his uncle who was a priest. Through life more devoted to piety than to learning; associated much with other mystics. About 1317 ordained priest and appointed to a church at Groenendaal, near Brussels; served there until he was sixty. Retired from secular priesthood to give himself entirely to contemplation and thought on the inner life. Entered a newly founded Augustinian cloister near Brussels where he spent the remainder of his long life. Though deeply mystical, he warned against mere ecstatic mysticism, contended for a deep inward piety. In last years gave himself to meditation and writing, and to instructing the many who came to him to learn the way of piety and self-denial and love to God. He had been influenced by Eckhart and Tauler, and in turn left the impact of his mystical teaching on Gerard Groot, the founder of the Brethren of the Common Life.

RYERSON, ADOLPHUS EGERTON (1803-1882), Methodist educator. Born Charlotteville Township, Norfolk County, Upper Canada (Ontario). Ordained in 1824 and became missionary to Indians of Credit River. In 1829 editor of the *Christian Guardian*. Founded what became Victoria College in 1841 and was its principal. Secretary of Wesleyan Missionary Society. As superintendent of education for Upper Canada from 1844 to 1876 his 1846 *Report* influenced the educational organization of Ontario. From 1874 to 1878 first president of the General Conference of the Methodist Church of Canada.

RYLE (rīl), **JOHN CHARLES** (1816-1900), Low church Anglican bishop, born near Macclesfield, Cheshire, England, studied at Eton and at Christ Church, Oxford. After college ordained in 1842, pastored several lesser known churches, then in 1871 made honorary dean of Norwich. In 1880 nominated by Lord Beaconsfield as dean of Salisbury. Before he had taken office he was made the first bishop of the newly organized diocese of Liverpool where he served until his death. Wrote more than one hundred tracts and pamphlets on doctrinal and practical subjects which enjoyed a wide circulation in English and foreign languages. Published a number of books of sermons and devotional literature. Among published books are: *Christian Leaders of the Last Century; The Bishop, the Pastor and the Preacher; Is All Scripture Inspired?; Expository Thoughts on the Gospels* (seven volumes); *Light from Old Times; Hymns for the Church on Earth; Knots Untied; Lessons from English Church History;* and *What Do We Owe to the Reformation?* Thoroughly evangelical in doctrine; one of the most prominent members of the evangelical party.

S

SABATIER (så bä tyā'), **CHARLES PAUL MARIE** (1858-1928), French Protestant pastor and historian, born at St. Michael-de-Chabrillanoux, in the Cevennes. Studied at the lyceums of Besancon and Lille, and in the theological department of the University of Paris. Vicar of the Protestant Church of St. Nicholas at Strassburg from 1885 to 1889, when expelled from Germany because he refused to accept a position that would require him to become a German citizen. Returning to France became pastor at St. Cièrge-la-Serre, Ardêche (1889-1894). Retiring from the ministry because of ill health, devoted himself entirely to historical and theological studies. Spent much time at Assisi, Italy, and wrote much on St. Francis and the Franciscans. Chief work was *Vie de St. François d'Assise*. Also wrote *Modernism, Disestablishment in France,* and *La Didache*. In 1898, in recognition of studies created an honorary citizen of Assisi; and the following year elected a member of the Academia dei Lincei, Rome. In 1902 founded at Assisi the International Society of Franciscan Studies. Taught at the University of Strassburg from 1919 to 1928.

SABATIER (så bä tyā'), **LOUIS AUGUST** (1839-1901), French Protestant theologian, born at Vallon (Andreche) in the Cevennes, educated at the college of Montpellier and at Montauban; also studied at Basel, Tübingen, and Heidelberg. After four years of pastoral work became professor of Reformed dogmatics at Strassburg University (1867-1873), expelled because of animosity to the German regime. In 1877 became professor of Reformed dogmatics at the newly established Protestant theological faculty of the Sorbonne, Paris, and became dean of the faculty in 1895. Though conservative at first, later propagated the theories of Schleiermacher and Ritschl in France, applied the methods of historical criticism, and became extremely liberal, helping to prepare the way for the Modernistic movement. Writings were not well received in Germany, but welcomed in France by a section of French Roman Catholics, the general Protestant public, and even by circles that had broken with all religion. Among writings were *The Apostle Paul, Doctrine of the Atonement and Its Historical Evolution, Outlines of a Philosophy of Religion, Based on Psychology and History,* and *Religions of Authority and Religions of the Spirit*.

SABELLIUS (så bĕl'ĭ ŭs) (died after 260), founder of the Sabellians, probably born in the Pentapolis in Libya, North Africa; scene of greatest activity was in Rome about 215 during the episcopate of Zephyrinus, A.D. 198-217. He preceded Arius by half a century; and his heretical doctrine spread both in Rome and in Egypt. Bishop Calixtus of Rome excommunicated him about 220, and Bishop Dionysius of Alexandria excommunicated him in a council in that city about 260. Taught a trinity of successive revelations and not a simultaneous trinity of essence. Hence the Godhead reveals only one member at a time—God in the Old Testament, Jesus at the incarnation, and the Holy Spirit in inspiration. Thus Father, Son, and Holy Spirit are only temporary phenomena, or a temporary and modalistic Trinity, which fulfill their mission and then return into the abstract monad. The end of Sabellius' doctrine was dangerously near pantheism.

SADOLETO (sä dō lā'tō), **JACOPO** (1477-1547), Italian cardinal, born at Modena, Italy, studied philosophy and rhetoric in Pisa, Ferrara, and Rome. Ordained at Rome and became secretary to Pope Leo X about 1513 or 1514, and also later served as secretary to Pope Clement VII. Became Bishop of Carpentras in 1517. An admirer of Erasmus and Melanchthon; one of the founders of the Oratory of Divine Love. To counter the progress of the Protestant Reformation and to effect an element of reformation within the Roman Church, Pope Paul III in 1536 appointed him, Reginald Pole, Gasparo Contarini, and Giovanni Petro Caffa as cardinals. Though these men in 1538 laid before the pope extensive recommendations for ecclesiastical betterment, these recommendations were lightly passed over by the pope. Sadoleto prevented the spread of Calvinism in his diocese, but was opposed to any violent persecution. In 1537 Sadoleto addressed a letter to Melanchthon urging him to be reconciled with the Roman Catholic church, and in 1539 wrote to the municipal council of Geneva in an attempt to restore that city to the Roman Catholic faith. This brought him into sharp conflict with Calvin, who in six days wrote his famous *Reply to Sadoleto,* which was regarded as one of the ablest vindications of Protestantism, and one of Calvin's very important writings.

SAKER, ALFRED (1814-1880), English Baptist missionary to the Cameroons, born at Borough Green, Kent, England. Converted in a Baptist chapel. Soon became a teacher, a Sunday school superintendent, a member of the choir, and gradually deeply interested in mission work in West Africa. In 1843 Mr. and Mrs. Saker were accepted and went to the island of Fernando Po, West Africa, until 1853. In 1853, because of the opposition and persecution of the Jesuits, he moved the entire mission from the island of Fernando Po to the mainland, the native Christians moving with him. In 1862 Saker's translation of the New Testament into Dualla was completed. Completed the translation of the Old Testament in 1868. Constant work on translation and faithful visitation of outlying tribes taxed his strength to the limit. In 1869 he was again on furlough; but after a few months he, his wife, and one daughter returned to the field. In 1872 the whole Bible was published in Dualla. In 1874 he took his last furlough home, and on his return to Africa was accompanied by George Grenfell. In 1876, after thirty-two years of missionary labor, he made his final return to England. Encouraged founding of the Congo Mission of the Baptist Missionary Society.

SAMSON (SANSON), BERNHARDINO (sixteenth century), commissioner of indulgences in Switzerland. Guardian of the Observantist Franciscans at San Angelo, Milan, when he was commissioned by Cardinal Forli to preach indulgences in the Swiss cantons. Entered Switzerland in 1518 and met with success in the western cantons, but was less successful in the eastern cantons, where he met with the resistance and hostility of Zwingli, Dr. Faber, the vicar general, and Hugo, Bishop of Constance. He went to Baden, and in 1519 went to Bremgarten where he met with stiff opposition from Heinrich Bullinger. In answer to a complaint of the Swiss authorities, Pope Leo X recalled him from Switzerland.

SANCTIS (sängk'tēs), **LUIGI DE** (1808-1869), Italian Evangelical preacher and theologian, born in Rome. In youth became a Carmelite monk, ordained to the priesthood in 1831, devoted himself earnestly to the service of the Catholic church. Between 1840 and 1847 at the head of the parish of Santa Maddalena alla Rotonda in Rome where he gained renown as a pulpit orator. In 1849 he left the Roman Catholic church and married. In 1850 accepted a call to Geneva to preach among the Italian political refugees, workmen, and ex-priests. Went to Turin where he associated himself with Giovanni Pietro Meille (1817-1887) of the Waldensian Church and in 1853 was ordained to the Waldensian ministry. When a division occurred in the ranks of the Waldensians, he and Mazzarella founded the Free Italian church. Raised funds and established a Protestant school in Genoa. In 1864, when a rift developed in the Free church, he withdrew to Florence, returned to the Waldensians, and was appointed professor of apologetic, polemic, and practical theology in the Waldensian seminary, a position held until his death in 1869. Most of his books pertain to the papacy and the Roman Catholic church.

SANDAY, WILLIAM (1843-1920), New Testament scholar and theologian, born at Holme Pierrepont, Nottinghamshire, England, and educated at Balliol and Corpus Christi colleges, Oxford. Ordained priest in 1869. Principal of Hatfield's Hall, Durham (1876-1882). From 1882 to 1895 he was Dean Ireland's professor of exegesis of Holy Scripture in the University of Oxford and tutorial fellow of Exeter College, Oxford; and from 1895 to 1919 Lady Margaret professor of divinity and canon of Christ Church, Oxford. During those years at various times examining chaplain to the Bishop of Durham, select preacher at Cambridge, Bampton lecturer, chaplain to the king, and fellow of the British Academy. Some of Sanday's writings: *The Authorship and Historical Character of the Fourth Gospel, The Gospels in the Second Century, The Oracles of God, Two Present Day Questions, Inspiration, Criticism of the New Testament, Criticism of the Fourth Gospel,* and *The Life of Christ in Recent Research, Christologies, Ancient and Modern.* His influence won many Anglican clergy to accept modern, critical New Testament study.

SANDERS, FRANK KNIGHT (1861-1933), American Bible scholar and educator, born at Batticotta, Jaffna, Ceylon, educated at Ripon College, Ripon, Wisconsin, and at Yale University. Ordained in 1902. Instructor at Jaffna College, Ceylon (1882-1886). He was Woolsey professor of Biblical literature at Yale University (1891-1901), and professor of Bible history and archaeology and dean of Yale Divinity School (1901-1905). After serving as secretary of the Congregational Sunday School and Publishing Society (1905-1908), he was elected president of Washburn College, Kansas (1908-1914). Then became Director of Missionary Preparation for the Foreign Missions Conference of North America (1914-1927). Author of *The Teacher's Life of Christ, Studies in the Life of Paul, The Messages of the Earlier Prophets, The Messages of the Later Prophets, History of the Hebrews, The Program of Christianity, Old Testament Prophecy, Old Testament History, Historical Series for Bible Students* (nine volumes); and *The Messages of the Bible* (twelve volumes).

SAINT, NATHANAEL. *See* **ELLIOTT, JAMES.**

SANGSTER, WILLIAM EDWYN ROBERT (1900-1960), Methodist cleric and scholar. Born in London. Educated in Richmond College, Surrey. Served in the army in World War I. Ordained in 1926, served several churches before he came to Westminster Central Hall in London. President of Methodist Conference in 1950. Member of London University Senate. Wrote *The Path to Perfection* on Wesley's idea of perfection.

SANKEY, IRA DAVID (1840-1908), gospel singer and hymn composer, born at Edinburgh, Pennsylvania. Became a clerk in the bank in which his father had become president. Joined the Methodist church. Chosen as choir leader and superintendent of the Sunday school. Served in the Civil War from 1861 to 1863 and from 1863 to 1870 as a bank clerk and tax collector. In 1870 a delegate to the International Convention of the Young Men's Christian Association at Indianapolis, Indiana, where his singing attracted the attention of Dwight L. Moody, who persuaded Mr. Sankey to join him in the evangelistic work he was carrying on in Chicago. For the next quarter of a century assisted Mr. Moody in many great evangelistic campaigns in Great Britain from 1873 to 1875 and throughout America. Sankey's part in these revival efforts lay in his singing of solos, conducting the singing, composing music for the gospel hymns, and helping in the inquiry meetings. Mr. Sankey compiled *Gospel Hymns* and *Sacred Songs and Solos,* of which over fifty million copies were sold. The royalties were used for the support of the Christian institutions Moody established. Among the several tunes Mr. Sankey composed were "The Ninety and Nine," "When the Mists Have Rolled Away," and "Faith Is the Victory." Author of *My Life and the Story of the Gospel Hymns and of Sacred Songs and Solos.* In 1903 he became blind.

SAPHIR (säf'ĭr), **AARON ADOLPH** (1831-1891), Presbyterian clergyman and writer, born at Budapest, Hungary, son of a pious Jewish merchant. Converted to Christianity by John Duncan of the Jewish mission of the Church of Scotland. Studied at the University of Glasgow, Marischal College, Aberdeen, and the Free Church College, Edinburgh. Licensed to preach in 1854. From 1854 to 1856 worked among the Jews in Hamburg, Germany, and another brief period working among the Germans in Glasgow. In 1856 became pastor of the Presbyterian church, South Shields, where he remained for five years. In 1861 called to the St. Mark's Presbyterian Church, Greenwich, where he spent eleven successful years of service. At next pastorate, Notting Hill, delivered his lectures on the Epistle to the Hebrews, and on the divinity of our Lord. From 1875 to 1882 health was so poor that he held no regular charge. From 1887 to 1888 served the Belgrave Presbyterian Church, London. A theologian of the evangelical school. Like his friend, Alfred Edersheim, he threw much light on biblical study by his intimate knowledge of Jewish manners and literature. In later years took considerable interest in the efforts for the conversion of the Jews of Hungary and Southern Russia. Author of: *Christ and Israel, Christ and the Scriptures, Christ and the Church, Lectures on the Lord's Prayer, Christ Crucified, Expository Lectures on the Epistle to the Hebrews, The Divine Unity of the Scriptures, The Life of Faith, The Sinner and the Saviour,* and *Bible Records of Remarkable Conversions.*

SARTO, ANDREA del (sär'tō, än drā'ä dĕl) (1486-1531), Florentine painter Andrea Domenico d' Agnolo d' Francesco (family name, Vannucchi), born near Florence, Italy, son of a tailor. Trained by the best artists of his day; devoted much time to the study of the great masters da Vinci and Michelangelo. Known particularly as colorist and as master of chiaroscuro. In 1509-1514 painted a series of frescoes for the Servite church and convent at Florence, and later others for the Recollects. Became famous for frescoes, many of which were in Florence. The subjects of his frescoes were mostly religious. Some of his most celebrated pictures were several *Madonnas,* several *Holy Families,* two *Annunciations,* two *Assumptions, The Last Supper, Birth of Saint John, Procession of the Magi, Nativity of the Virgin, Adoration of the Virgin, The Marriage of St. Catherine,* and *The Fathers of the Church Disputing.* Owed much to Fra Bartolommeo. Also influenced by da Vinci and Dürer. Died of the plague in 1531.

SATURNINUS (săt ẽr nī'nŭs), or **SATORNILUS** (Second Century), leader of a Syrian Gnostic sect, born at Antioch. He studied under Simon and Menander, and was a contemporary of Basilides. Established school and taught at Antioch. Made great distinction between a supreme God or "one unknown Father" and the creations. Between them there is a great host of spiritual beings, at the bottom of which was the created world with the Jehovah or God of the Jews as the chief overseer. When man was created by the Demiurge he could but crawl upon the earth as a mere worm until the Father sent down a spark of his own divine light and stood him upright. Out of great pity for the human creatures who were oppressed by Satan's host, which the Jewish Demiurge and his prophets were unable to defeat, the Father finally sent down the aeon *Nous* or Christ, clothed with a phantom body to free men from their enemy. Saturninus was a rigorous ascetic, attributing marriage and procreation to Satan, and rejecting meat. He denied the human birth of Jesus, regarding His body as a mere appearance. He rejected the Old Testament. His sect did not extend beyond Syria, and was short-lived.

SAURIN (sō räɴ'), **JACQUES (JAMES)** (1677-1730), French Reformed preacher, born at Nimes; when eight years old, his parents fled France and settled at Geneva at the revocation of the Edict of Nantes. At the age of sixteen he quit school to serve for four years in a regiment of volunteers in the coalition against Louis XIV. When he returned home, continued his study of theology at Geneva, and was ordained and in 1701 chosen minister of the French Walloon (Reformed) congregation, London, where he remained for four years. In 1705 became pastor of the French Reformed Congregation at The Hague, where he labored the rest of his life. For twenty-five years his extraordinary gift of pulpit oratory, his agreeable personality, his high intellectual qualities, his deep religious conviction, his evangelicalism, and his adherence to the gospel attracted multitudes, and gained for him the admiration and love of many. Chief publications were: *Discourses Upon the More Memorable Events in the Bible,* and five volumes of Sermons.

SAVONAROLA (sä vō nä rô'lä), **GIROLAMO (JEROME OR HIERONYMUS)** (1452-1498), Italian Reformer, born at Ferrara, Italy, early felt the call of God to live a holy life; about 1474 secretly left home to enter a Dominican monastery at Bologna, remained there for seven years, becoming famous for this extraordinary piety and religious zeal. Studied Augustine, Aquinas, and the Bible. Was then sent to Ferrara to preach, but attained little success. About 1481 he began preaching in Florence, where during the next ten years became a great preacher of righteousness, attacking sin with much boldness. Became the most conspicuous figure in Italy. Great throngs came to hear him; preached against the evils of the day, especially against the sins of the clergy, not sparing the corrupt monks of his own monastery. About 1491 chosen prior of the monastery of San Marco. Gained such confidence and respect from the people of Florence by strong and straightforward preaching that upon the death of Lorenzo, a political leader of Florence, Lorenzo's son was set aside, and Savonarola was made manager of the city in 1494. The city became a republic, the reforming preacher at the head. A marked degree of reformation took place within the city. An adverse faction in the city and the pope, Alexander VI, became greatly disturbed. In the hope of diverting the reformer from his purpose, he offered him the cardinal's hat, which Savonarola refused. Savonarola's bitter attacks on the curia and Pope Alexander led to his excommunication and the public turned against him. He was arrested and found guilty of "heresy." He was hanged and his body burned.

SAYCE (sās), **ARCHIBALD HENRY** (1845-1933), English archaeologist and philologist, born at Shirehampton, near Bristol, Gloucestershire, England, educated at Grosvenor College, Bath, and at Queen's College, Oxford, where he became a fellow in 1869, and tutor in 1870. Ordained priest in 1871. From 1876 to 1890 deputy professor of comparative philology, and from 1891 until retirement in 1919 professor of Assyriology at Oxford. Scholarly activity covered a wide range—Assyriology, oriental history, biblical criticism, the Hittites, the Jewish people, comparative philology, and general archaeology—subjects on which he published the majority of his books. Member of the Old Testament Revision Company (1874-1884), Hibbert lecturer (1887), Gifford lecturer (1900-1902), and Rhind lecturer (1906). Sayce traveled much in the East (especially Egypt) and Europe. He suffered much from ill health and poor eyesight throughout life, he died at Bath, England. Among his writings: *Fresh Light from the Ancient Monuments, The Principles of Comparative Philology, Assyrian Grammar for Comparative Purposes, Introduction to the Science of Language, Lectures on Babylonian Literature, The Monuments of the Hittites, The Ancient Empires of the East, The Hittites, "The "Higher Criticism" and the Verdict of the Monuments, Life and Times of Israel, Babylonians and Assyrians, Patriarchal Palestine, Early Israel and the Surrounding Nations, Early History of the Hebrews, Records of the Past,* and *The Religions of Ancient Egypt and Babylonia.*

SCALIGER, JOSEPH JUSTUS (1540-1609), Huguenot historical scholar. Educated in the classics at Paris. Became a Protestant. Taught at Geneva, Valence, and from 1593 at Leiden. Laid the foundations of textual criticism for historical documents by developing rules. His 1583 book *On the Correction of Chronology* put historical chronology on a scientific basis after centuries of chronology dominated by Eusebius' system.

SCHAFF (shäf), **DAVID SCHLEY** (1852-1929), Presbyterian clergyman and historian, son of Philip Schaff, born at Mercersburg, Pennsylvania, graduated from

Yale University and Union Theological Seminary, ordained in the Presbyterian ministry. Between the years 1877 and 1907 pastor in three different churches in Nebraska, Missouri, and Illinois. Professor of church history at Lane Theological Seminary, Cincinnati, Ohio (1897-1903), and from 1903 until 1923 professor of ecclesiastical and doctrinal history at Western Theological Seminary, Pittsburgh, Pennsylvania. One of the editors of the *Schaff-Herzog Encyclopaedia* (four volumes, 1883), edited two volumes of his father's *History of the Christian Church;* wrote *The Life of Philip Schaff, John Huss, Our Fathers' Faith and Ours,* and *The Reformation and Its Influence*.

SCHAFF, PHILIP (1819-1893), ecumenist, theologian, and church historian, born at Chur, Switzerland, studied at the universities of Tübingen, Halle, and Berlin. In 1843 came to America and became professor of church history and biblical literature in the German Reformed church seminary at Mercersburg, Pennsylvania (1844-1863). He and John Williamson Nevin prepared a document, the so-called "Mercersburg Theology," which was charged with having a pro-Roman Catholic tendency. He became an outstanding leader in the German Reformed church. In 1859 brought out a *Gesangbuch* which introduced a new era in congregational singing of American German-speaking churches. Wielded a strong influence in shifting his school and his people from the German theology, traditions, and language to more democratic customs and to the English language. As a result of the Civil War, Mercersburg was forced to close for a time. From 1864 to 1869 he was secretary of the Sabbath Committee in New York City. From 1870 to 1893 professor in Union Theological Seminary, New York City, first holding the chair of theological encyclopedia and Christian symbolism, then of Hebrew and the cognate languages, later of sacred literature, and finally from 1887 until death, the chair of church history. He was one of the founders of the Evangelical Alliance, and was president of the American Old Testament Revision Committee. Founder of the American Society of Church History in 1888 and its president until his death. Strove earnestly to promote Christian unity and union, and showed a deep interest in the Parliament of Religions at the Chicago World's Fair. Represented the Evangelical type of German theology and was able to interpret German theology with authority. Through repeated visits to Germany was enabled to interpret American thought to Germany and German thought to America. His literary production was immense. He wrote *History of the Christian Church* (eight volumes), *The Creeds of Christendom* (three volumes), *A Companion to the Greek Testament and the English Version,* and other works. Edited *The Nicene and Post-Nicene Fathers,* the twenty-five volume American edition of Lange's *Bibelwerk (A Commentary on the Holy Scriptures),* and *The International Illustrated Commentary of the New Testament* (four volumes).

SCHALL (shäl), **JOHANN ADAM (VON BELL)** (1591-1666), German astronomer and Jesuit missionary, born at Cologne, Germany. Educated in the Collegium Germanicum in Rome, became a Jesuit, and in 1619 was sent as a missionary to China, first to Macao, and later to Peking in 1622 where he remained until his death. Invited to the imperial court at Peking, where he became astronomer royal and scientific adviser to the emperor and was entrusted with reforming and compiling the Chinese calendar, also with the direction of the public mathematical school that had been started by Matteo Ricci a bit earlier. Translated into Chinese many mathematical treatises into which he also injected many religious and Christian discussions. Created a mandarin by the emperor of China. Through favor with the emperor gained the privilege of building Roman Catholic churches, and was given the liberty of preaching throughout the empire. The Jesuits made great progress. Next emperor, however, opposed this policy, and Schall was imprisoned, dying a little later, in 1666. Wrote: *History of the Chinese Mission*.

SCHAUFFLER (shôf'lẽr), **ADOLF FREDERICK** (1845-1919), American Presbyterian clergyman, born at Constantinople, Turkey. Educated at Williams College, Union Theological Seminary, and Andover Theological Seminary. Ordained to the Congregational ministry in 1871. From 1873 to 1887 pastor of the Olivet Presbyterian Church, New York City. Superintendent of the New York City Missionary and Tract Society from 1887 to 1902, and president of the New York City Mission after 1902. Prominently connected with Sunday school work, chairman of the New York State Sunday School Association. For many years, a member of the International Sunday School Lesson Committee. Chief writings: *Training the Teacher; God's Book and God's Boy; Knowing and Teaching the Scholar; The Teacher, the Child, and the Book; Ways of Working;* and *Sparks from a Superintendent's Handbook*.

SCHAUFFLER, ALBERT HENRY (1837-1905), American missionary, born at Constantinople, Turkey. Came to America in

1855 to enter Williams College. Later studied two years at Andover Theological Seminary and one year at Harvard Law School. Professor of law at Robert College, Constantinople for two years; ordained in 1865 and served the American Board as a missionary in Constantinople for five years. From 1872 to 1874 served the American Board in Prague, Austria, and from 1874 to 1881 in Brünn. Affliction forced him to retire in America; in 1882 where he served until death as superintendent of missionary work under the Congregational Home Missionary Society among Bohemian and Polish peoples in various parts of the United States. Established missions and organized churches for these nationalities in several states. Probably his most important achievement was the Schauffler Missionary Training School in Cleveland, Ohio, founded in 1886 as the "Bible Readers' School" to train Slavic women for mission work among their own people.

SCHECHTER, SOLOMON (1847-1915). Born in Focsani, Romania. Educated as rabbi in Vienna and Berlin, and in England in 1882 under auspices of Goldsmid Montefiore. Professor at Cambridge from 1890 to 1902. President of Jewish Theological Seminary in New York from 1902 to 1915. Spread ideas of Conservative Judaism in seminary teaching. Edited *The Jewish Encyclopedia*.

SCHELLING, FRIEDRICH WILHELM JOSEPH VON (1775-1854), German philosopher, born at Leonberg, Württemberg, Germany, studied theology and philosophy at Tübingen, and science and mathematics at Leipzig. With the assistance of Fichte, Goethe, and Schiller, became professor at Jena (1798-1803), the center of Romanticism, which came to dominate much of his thinking at that time. Became professor of philosophy at Würzburg (1803-1806). In 1806 moved to Munich, where he became a state official and a member of the Academy of Science, in 1809 general secretary of the Academy of Arts. From 1820 to 1826 lectured at Erlangen, and from 1827 to 1841, professor at the newly established University of Munich. In 1841 called to the University of Berlin to lecture on mythology and revelation; but retired in 1846. Died in Switzerland. A brilliant writer, publishing several essays of the philosophy of Fichte before he was twenty years of age. Did most important writing between 1795 and 1810. Some of his writings were: *Idea of a Philosophy of Nature; Of the World Soul; System of Transcendental Idealism; Lectures on Mythology and Revelation*. The philosophy of Schelling is based chiefly on Fichte and Kant, along with Spinoza's doctrine of the oneness of all substance. The distinguishing tenet of his philosophy is the identity of subject and object. His philosophy, as he admitted, was a process of development, and his views a series of changes. At first he looked upon nature as rational, but later was impressed with its irrationality. For a time was under the influence of Jacob Boehme and turned noticeably to mysticism. While at Munich was much under the influence of Aristotle, Neo-Platonism, and the Gnostics. His philosophy has greatly influenced the rationalistic thinking of Christianity and the Christian church to this day.

SCHERESCHEWSKY, SAMUEL ISAAC JOSEPH (1831-1906), Protestant Episcopal missionary and bishop, born of orthodox Jewish parentage at Tanroggen, Lithuania. Educated at the Talmud Torah of Zhitomir, Russia, and at the University of Breslau. In 1854 came to the United States, accepted Christianity and was baptized in 1855. Studied theology at the Western Theological Seminary, Allegheny, Pennsylvania (1855-1858), and joined the Presbyterian church. In 1858 entered the Protestant Episcopal church, and studied another year at General Theological Seminary. In 1859 was sent by the Board of Foreign Missions of the Protestant Episcopal church as a missionary to China. In 1860 ordained priest. Spent a short time in Shanghai, then was transferred to Peking, where he remained from 1863 until 1875. During these years he translated the Bible and the Book of Common Prayer into the Mandarin. Did some mission work among the Jews in nearby areas. Spent two years in the United States, in 1875 becoming a naturalized citizen. In 1877 consecrated Bishop of Shanghai. In the States busy raising funds for St. John's College, which he opened in 1879. From 1883 continued literary work. Spent nine years in the United States preparing a revision of the Mandarin Bible which he had translated many years before. Returned to Shanghai for two years continuing work on the Mandarin Bible. From 1897 until his death resided in Japan preparing a reference Mandarin Bible and a translation of the Apocrypha.

SCHILLER, JOHANN CHRISTOPH FREIDRICH (1759-1805), German dramatist, poet, and historian, born in Marbach, Württemberg, Germany, attended a military academy at Ludwigsburg, studied jurisprudence and medicine at Stuttgart. He was for a while surgeon in a Württemberg regiment. Among poetical writings: *Wilhelm Tell*. Became professor of history at Jena where he formed an intimate friendhsip with Goethe. Wrote the *Defection of the Netherlands* and *History of the Thirty Years War*. These works hailed Protestantism as a defender of religious and "German" freedom. He is considered only second to Goethe in German literature and is to this day the most read of the great German writers.

SCHLATTER, MICHAEL (1716-1790), German Reformed clergyman, born at St. Gall, Switzerland, educated at the University of Helmstädt. Sent to the colonies in 1741 by the Synod of South and North Holland (Dutch Reformed) to organize and supervise the scattered groups of German Reformed people in the colonies. Pastor of the United Reformed churches in Philadelphia and Germantown (1746-1755). In 1747 organized the German Reformed members in Philadelphia into a missionary synod, and became supervisor under the support and authority of the Dutch Reformed church with its headquarters at Amsterdam. This arrangement continued until 1791 when the German Reformed church was separated and organized independently as the German Reformed church in the United States in 1793. He made extended missionary tours through Pennsylvania, Maryland, Virginia, New Jersey, and New York. In 1751 returned to Europe and secured six other ministers and about $60,000 for churches in the American Colonies. In 1755 became the superintendent of a system of schools among the Germans in America, but resigned in 1757 because of German opposition to the teaching of the English language in the schools. From 1757 to 1759 chaplain of the Royal American regiment. Supported the cause of the colonists when the Revolution broke out and imprisoned in 1777. Died near Philadelphia.

SCHLEIERMACHER (shlī'ĕr mä kĕr), **FRIEDRICH DANIEL ERNST** (1768-1834), German theologian and philosopher, born at Breslau, Germany, the son of a Reformed church army chaplain. Educated in Moravian schools and at the then rationalistic University of Halle. Ordained in 1794, and occupied a number of pulpits until he became professor and university preacher at Halle in 1804. In 1809 pastor in Berlin and the next year professor of theology at the newly founded university, holding those positions until 1834. He adhered to the mediating school with the ancient, orthodox creeds on the one hand, and German rationalism on the other. Friendly toward the Romantic movement, and perhaps introduced Romanticism into theology. Reconciled personal emotional religion with a modified adoption of the Kantian critical philosophy. Made personal and social ethics and morals an integral part of religion. His philosophy was built more around Kant than any other, yet being considerably influenced by early Moravian training and by the Romanticists, as well as by Spinoza and Plato. Kant had made religion a matter of the will, Schleiermacher defined religion as feeling, or as the immediate consciousness of absolute dependence upon God. The Christian consciousness thus alone became the interpreter of religion and the standard for testing the truth and knowing God. Schleiermacher's God was not a personal Being, rather an impersonal, pantheistic force, the universal, the absolute, the eternal principle which is immanent in the world. The life of this universe is mirrored in each individual. Man is thus finite, limited, temporary, and dependent. This feeling of dependence is the true basis of religion. Christianity is not the final religion, but is the best known to man. Jesus of Nazareth was his ideal. He was merely a superior, sinless man, unique in His God-consciousness. Christ redeemed man from ignorance rather than from sin. Schleiermacher's theology did not admit an orthodox view of the atonement. Man's God-Consciousness was somehow sustained by Christ through the church. Placed strong emphasis upon both Christ and the Church, but not in the orthodox sense. A pious and earnest man, with a warm faith in God, and a great admiration for Christ, though not in a personal God nor in Christ as Deity. Schleiermacher's influence upon the Christian thinking of the nineteenth century was pronounced. The impact of his *Reden,* published in 1799 and his most important work, *The Christian Faith,* was more permanent than immediate. He was the father of modern religious Liberalism.

SCHMIDT, GEORG (1709-1785), Moravian missionary to South Africa. Joined the Herrnhut group in 1727. In Roman Catholic prison for six years. Went as missionary to the Hottentots in 1737. Won some converts and returned to Holland in 1744.

SCHMUCKER (shmo͝ok'ĕr), **SAMUEL SIMON** (1799-1873), American Lutheran theologian and educator, born at Hagerstown, Maryland, studied at the University of Pennsylvania, and Princeton Theological Seminary. After ordination in 1821 served a parish in New Market, Virginia for five years. In 1826 became president and professor of theology at the newly organized theological seminary at Gettysburg, Pennsylvania, which he had helped to found, and where he taught until 1864. One of the most prolific writers of the American Lutheran church, some of his writings: *Elements of Popular Theology; Evangelical Lutheran Catechism; The Lutheran Manual on Scriptural Principles;* and *The Lutheran Symbols,* *or Vindication of American Lutheranism.* In his *Fraternal Appeal to the American Churches on Christian Union* and *The Unity of Christ's Church* he promoted church confederation. In 1846 largely instrumental in establishing a connection between the Lutheran churches in the United States and Europe, taking a prominent part in the organization of the Evangelical Alliance. Particularly interested in the problem of unity among all denominations in America, better known outside his communion than any other Lutheran minister. Though strongly nonconfessional and deeply interested in church unity, nevertheless did much to hold together the Lutheran church in America at a time when it was threatened with disintegration. His Lutheran indifferentism, however, led him to strive to eliminate everything distinctively Lutheran and to substitute the basis of the Evangelical Alliance for the Augsburg Confession and Luther's Catechisms.

SCHOPENHAUER (shō'pĕn hou ẽr), **ARTHUR** (1788-1860), German philosopher, born in Danzig, Germany. Studied at Gotha, Weimar, Göttingen, Berlin, and Jena; and in 1813 received degree from the latter, writing dissertation on *The Fourfold Root of the Principal of Sufficient Reason,* which contains the germ of his later philosophy. Endeavored to teach in 1820 in the University of Berlin, but failing to gain a hearing had to give it up. Settled down to many years of morose seclusion in Frankfurt-on-the-Main. Continued with his philosophy, which developed through three major influences: (1) Kant, from whom he got transcendental theory of knowledge; (2) Plato, from whom he got formulation of eternal ideas as offering an escape from the will; (3) the Buddhists from whom he got ethical-mysticism and the confirmation of his pessimism. Lived a long, lonely, isolated life, in which his inherited emotional and brooding nature became more and more cynical and pessimistic. To him the history of the cosmos is an endless struggle in which all reason is absent. Took no interest in history, phenomena being to him the surface illusions of an unreasoning will. Held that realization of desire only results in more desire, and the fulfillment of all desire in boredom. His principal work was *The World as Will and Idea.*

SCHUBERT (shōō'bĕrt), **FRANZ PETER** (1797-1828), Austrian composer, born in a suburb of Vienna, Austria. As a child learned to play violin, piano, and organ, also to sing. When fourteen began to compose, and before seventeen had written some of his finest and most celebrated songs. Also at that age produced symphonies, sacred music, and operatic works. A life of much disappointment. As a writer of songs, one of the masters. Wrote music freely and easily. Schubert's songs range from the simplicity of the folk song to the height of symphonic power. Left more than twelve hundred compositions, including more than six hundred songs and nine symphonies.

SCHUMANN (shōō'män), **ROBERT ALEXANDER** (1810-1856), German composer and music critic, born at Zwickau, Saxony. His mother sent him to Leipzig, then to Heidelberg, to study law. He turned to music with enthusiasm, coming under the personal influence of Mendelssohn and studying Bach. Permanently injured his hand, he turned from playing to composing. Married a pianist who played and popularized his compositions. Through his journal, *Die Neue Zeitschrift für Musik,* greatly influenced musical taste in Germany. Wrote many songs, four symphonies, and much chamber music.

SCHURER, EMIL (1844-1910), German Protestant scholar. Studied at Erlangen, Berlin, Heidelberg, and Leipzig. Professor from 1869 to 1910 in succession at Leipzig, Geissen, Keil and Gottingen universities. Specialized in Oriental Judaism and the early Christian era. His major work the five-volume *History of the Jewish People in the Time of Jesus.* Founded and edited the *Theologische Literaturzeitung* from 1876 to 1910.

SCHWARTZ, CHRISTIAN FREDERICK (1726-1798), German missionary to India, born in Sonnenburg, Prussia, educated at the University of Halle. Missionary influence led him to offer his service to the Danish Halle Mission, and to seek ordination. Along with several other missionaries, arrived in South India in 1750 where he served until 1798. Having learned the Tamil language from a returned missionary at Halle, four months after reaching India he was able to preach his first sermon in Tamil from Ziegenbalg's pulpit. Also learned the Hindustani and Persian languages. After laboring for ten years in Tranquebar moved to Trichinopoli where he labored for sixteen years. In 1767 he became an English chaplain and severed his connection with the Danish Mission, entered the service of the Society for Promoting Christian Knowledge at Tanjore from 1772 to 1798. Traveled extensively in Southern India, establishing schools and congregations, building houses of worship, and ministering to Europeans and natives alike. During strained relations between England and India, he was the only foreigner who was trusted by the Indians. A warm personal friend of the Rajah at Tanjore.

SCHWEITZER, ALBERT (1875-1965), theologian, musician, and medical missionary. Born in Alsace. Educated at the universities of Strassburg, Paris, and Berlin in theology and music, especially organ and that of J. S. Bach. Studied medicine from 1905 and in 1913 went to Lambarene, Gabon where he founded a hospital to serve Africans. In French prison in World War I. In his major book *The Quest of the Historical Jesus* argued Liberal idea of Jesus as mere man was wrong, that Jesus expected an early kingdom, and that the Gospel ethic was only an interim ethic.

SCHWENKFELD (shwĕngk'fĕlt), **CASPAR VON OSSIG** (1489-1561), founder of the Schwenkfelders, born in Silesia. A learned, pious nobleman, a friend of Luther, embracing enthusiastically the Lutheran Reformation. In common with the Mennonites, opposed participation in war, secret societies, and oath-taking. He denied to the state the right to dictate contrary to the conscience of citizens. Strong emphasis on an inward mystical religion caused him to sever relations with the Lutherans. In his 1340 *Great Confession* he held that regeneration is effected by grace through the definite work of the Spirit within. The believer by faith feeds on Christ's celestial flesh. Infant baptism is to be rejected, the sacraments are to be spiritually observed, outward church forms are to be rejected, members are to give experimental evidence of regeneration. He opposed forming believers into sects or denominations. He never organized his followers into a church. Schwenkfelders in America organized a church and formed a constitution for their body in 1734 at Philadelphia.

SCOFIELD (skō'fēld), **CYRUS INGERSON** (1843-1921), Bible student and author, born in Lenawee County, Michigan, reared in Wilson County, Tennessee, and privately educated. Fought in the Civil War from 1861 to 1865 under General Lee, his distinguished service earning him the Confederate Cross of Honor. Admitted to the Kansas bar in 1869, elected to the Kansas House of Representatives where he served for one year. President Grant appointed him United States Attorney for Kansas in 1873. Worked as lawyer in Kansas and Missouri from 1869 to 1882. Converted at 36, he was ordained to the Congregational ministry in 1882, and served as pastor of the First Church, Dallas, Texas (1882-1895), and again (1902-1907); and of the Moody Church, Northfield, Massachusetts (1895-1902). Later years were spent lecturing on biblical subjects on both sides of the Atlantic. The work for which he is best remembered is his 1909 dispensational premillennial *Scofield Reference Bible*. Also wrote *Rightly Dividing the Word of Truth, Addresses on Prophecy, The Doctrine of the Holy Spirit, Things New and Old,* and *Old and New Testament Studies*. Founder of the Central American Mission.

SCOPES, JOHN THOMAS (c. 1900-1970). Born Paducah, Kentucky. Educated at the University of Kentucky. In 1924 high school teacher of biology and football coach at Rhea Cocsi school. Tried in 1925 for planned violation of the Butler Act prohibiting the teaching of evolution in Tennessee schools. Oklahoma, Florida, and later Arkansas and Kansas had similar laws. William Jennings Bryan was prosecuting lawyer and Clarence Darrow was lawyer for the defense. Scopes was fined $100 but decision was reversed by the State Supreme Court. After study at the University of Chicago Scopes became a geologist in the south. Author with James Presley of *The Center of the Storm* (1967).

SCOTT, GEORGE (1804-1874), English Wesleyan minister and missionary, sent to Stockholm, Sweden, in 1830, as chaplain to a group of English laborers who were employed by a manufacturer. His preaching attracted large crowds; but the Swedish clergy and the secular press strongly opposed him. However, his efforts did much to further the distribution of Bibles and tracts, and the causes of foreign missions, Sunday schools, the temperance cause, and evangelical freedom. Joined by two young Swedish students, Carl O. Rosenius and Anders Wiberg. Began to hold services in Swedish, and in 1840 a chapel was erected for his work in Stockholm. When the authorities forced him out of the country in 1842, Rosenius took over the leadership, and for a time held followers in the state church. P. P. Waldenström was a little later associated with the movement, which gradually developed into the Evangelical Free church movement of Sweden, and resulted in separation from the state church. In 1866 Scott was appointed president of the conferences of Canada and Eastern British America.

SCOTT, THOMAS (1747-1821), clergyman and Bible commentator, born at Braytoft, Lincolnshire, England. Because of poverty in the home received very limited early education, compelled to earn a livelihood for nine years as a farmhand. Ordained priest in 1773 After holding curacies at Stoke Goldington and Gayhurst in Buckinghamshire, and at Ravenstone, in 1781 succeeded John Newton as curate at Olney. In 1785 he became chaplain of the Lock Hospital, London, and in 1801, vicar of Aston Sanford, Buckinghamshire. *The Force of Truth,* his first publication, was a description of his conversion from a rationalistic Unitarian philosophy to Calvinism. Most important work was *The Holy Bible with Notes* in five volumes. First published as a weekly newspaper series from 1788 to 1792 from which he received no royalties.

SCOTT, SIR WALTER (1771-1832), Scottish poet and historical novelist, born in Edinburgh, Scotland. Before two years he suffered an illness that left him lame for life. Educated at Edinburgh High school, and the University of Edinburgh. Neither at school nor at college was he distinguished for brilliance; but noted for courage, extraordinary memory, vast store of miscellaneous knowledge, and skill as a storyteller. A voracious reader, learning French, German, Italian, and Spanish in order to read the tales and ballads of other lands. Studied law and was admitted to the Scottish bar in 1792. A little later apointed sheriff of Selkirkshire and principal clerk of the Council of Session. About the turn of the century began literary activity, and for the next twenty-five or thirty years an immense amount of literary production came from his pen. Created baronet in 1820. Writings published by a firm of which he himself was a silent partner. For years he lived very comfortably at Abbotsford on the income from writing. Then adversities came. His firm failed, and though he was not responsible for that, he chose to assume the responsibility of paying in full the heavy indebtedness. Under the heavy strain his health broke in 1830, and he had to leave Scotland. Sometime before this his wife had died. He did not recover his health and returned to Abbotsford. Suffered several paralytic strokes and the partial loss of his mind. Author of *The Waverly Novels;* books of poetry, including *The Lay of the Last Minstrel, The Lady of the Lake,* and *Marmion;* and *The Life of Napoleon* in nine volumes. In spite of troubles, sorrows, and sufferings, Scott held to faith in God.

SCOTT, WALTER (1796-1861), co-founder of the Disciples of Christ, born at Moffat, Dumfriesshire, Scotland. Received good musical education and graduated from Edinburgh University in 1818. That same year came to New York, the next year moved to Pittsburgh. After teaching in an academy for a few months, moved to Ohio, where he became an evangelist in 1826. In his evangelistic campaigns many converts were won, not only from among the unchurched, but also from Baptist, Presbyterian, Methodist, and other Christian camps. Scott and the Campbells had originally been Presbyterians, but later associated themselves with the Baptists. Finally because of doctrinal differences they left the Baptists in 1830. Taking with them many Baptists who agreed with them in doctrinal views, Scott and the Campbells started the Disciples of Christ, and organized many new churches. Scott published the *Evangelist,* and from his home in Carthage, Ohio, for thirteen years traveled and preached in Ohio, Kentucky, Virginia, and Missouri. For a very short time, president of Bacon College. While continuing his preaching published *The Protestant Unionist,* a weekly paper. From 1852 to 1855 principal of a female academy in Covington, Kentucky.

SCOUGAL, HENRY (1650-1678), writer of devotional literature. Born Leuchars, Fife. Educated at King's College, Aberdeen. Ordained in 1672 and from 1673 to 1678 was pastor at Auchterloss when he returned to King's College to teach theology. His devotional classic *The Life of God in the Soul of Man* helped George Whitefield.

SCROGGIE (skrŏg'y), **WILLIAM GRAHAM** (1877-c.1959), Scottish minister and writer. Educated at Exeter, Malvern, Bath, and Spurgeon's College. Between 1902 and 1933 held pastorates successively at Leytonstone, London; Trinity Road, Halifax; Bethesda Free Chapel, Sunderland; and in Charlotte Chapel, Edinburgh from 1913 to 1933. Between 1933 and 1937 traveling ministry carried him to South Africa, Australia, New Zealand, United States, Canada, and the British Isles. From 1938 to 1944, minister at Spurgeon's Tabernacle, London and lectured on English Bible in Spurgeon's College from 1948 to 1952. Among many writings: *Bible Story and Study, Primeval and Patriarchal; Christ in the Creed; Facts of the Faith; The Fascination of the Old Testament, or How to Read It; The Great Unveiling, the Book of Revelation; The Book of the Acts; A Guide to the Gospels; Is the Bible the Word of God? Know Your Bible* (two volumes); *The Lord's Return; Method in Prayer; Prophecy and History; The Psalms* (four volumes); *The Unfolding Drama of Redemption* (two volumes); *Ruling Lines of Progressive Revelation;* and *A Note to a Friend: Paul to Philemon.*

SCUDDER, IDA (1870-1960), medical missionary to south India. Born at Ranipet near Madras. Educated in Moody's girls' school at Northfield. Back in India to help her mother was "called" to be a medical missionary. Studied medicine at Women's Medical College in Philadelphia and Cornell University Medical School. Returned to India in 1900. Founded Schall Hospital at Vellore, a nursing school, school of pharmacy, and a medical college in 1915 for women and one for men in 1947.

SCUDDER, JOHN (1793-1855), missionary to India, born at Freehold, New Jersey, trained in College of New Jersey and College of Physicians and Surgeons in New York; then followed a very succssful practice of medicine until 1819. One day, the young doctor picked up a tract entitled *The Conversion of the World or The Claims of Six Hundred Million,* which led him to decide to take the gospel and healing to the unreached. In 1819 he and his wife sailed for Ceylon as missionaries for the Dutch Reformed church, under the American Board of Commissioners for Foreign Missions. First revival took place on the boat "Indus" enroute to India, when many of the officers and crew on the boat confessed faith in Christ. After reaching Ceylon he was ordained. In 1821 established a hospital at Jaffnapatam, and the following year a college. Two years later a revival broke out under his preaching. In 1836 transferred by the American Board to Madras on the eastern shores of Peninsular India. Here he spent much time in printing Gospel portions in Tamil, and in distributing them among the villages. Under his care the Arcot mission was established and grew. In 1842-1845 went to America in the interest of the missionary work in India and to regain health. Soon after his return to India he was stationed at Madura; but in 1849 he returned to Madras. He died from apoplexy at Wynberg, Cape of Good Hope, South Africa. Seven of his sons became pastors and medical missionaries in India.

SEABURY, SAMUEL (1729-1796), first bishop of the Protestant Episcopal church in America, born at Groton, Connecticut. After graduation from Yale began the study of medicine, and in 1752 went to Edinburgh to finish the course. Ordained both deacon and priest in England in 1753, the next year arrived in New Brunswick, New Jersey as missionary for the Society for the Propogation of the Gospel. From 1757 to 1766 missionary rector at Jamaica, New York, and at Westchester, New York from 1766 to 1775. As a loyalist wrote some tracts that were very offensive to the American patriots. He was consequently imprisoned in Connecticut for six weeks. When freed took refuge in New York City, where from 1776 to 1783 he was chaplain to the King's American troops. He was elected Bishop of Connecticut in 1783, and sailed to England to be ordained. Because some complications over the civil oath of allegiance had not yet been resolved, he was refused ordination. Went to Scotland where in 1784 he was consecrated by three bishops who would not take a loyalty oath to the then ruler. He then returned to the States in 1785 and became rector of St. James' Church in New London, Connecticut. He resided as rector of St. James' Church, and bishop of Connecticut and Rhode Island until his death. Collaborated with three bishops in forming the new constitution which made the American Protestant Episcopal church independent and autonomous.

SEAGRAVE, GORDON STIFLER (1897-1965), American Baptist Medical missionary to Burma. Born in Rangoon, Burma. Educated at Denison University and Johns Hopkins University (M.D.). From 1921 to 1942 served as a faithful medical missionary to the Burmese, opening hospitals and training native nurses and orderlies. Served in the American Army in medical work in Burma in World War II and in the British military government (1945-1946). In prison in 1950 after trial in Rangoon. When freed continued medical mission. Wrote *Burma Surgeon* and *Burma Surgeon Returns.*

SEBASTIAN (sē băs′chăn), (Late Third and Early Fourth Century), Roman martyr. Likely born in Milan. He became a captain of the praetorian guard of Diocletian. The fact of his being a Christian, however, did not come to the emperor's attention until it was revealed by his encouragement and consolation in behalf of two young men upon their condemnation to death as Christians. By a miracle the guard was converted and the boys were spared temporarily. The emperor was angered, and Sebastian, though a friend of Domitian, was sentenced to death for his persistent stand as a Christian. Buried in the catacombs.

SEEBERG, REINHOLD (1859-1935), German Lutheran theologian, born at Pörrafer, Livonia, studied at the universities of Dorpat and Erlangen. A teacher at Dorpat for five years; professor at the University of Erlangen (1889-1898). From 1898 until death professor of systematic theology at the University of Berlin. Also director of the Institute of Social Ethics and Missionary Work in Berlin. Until 1933 president of the Christian Social Alliance. "He was an influential Lutheran theologian of the modern type." Author of several works on the history of dogma and on the relations of the church to the social life of the time, all of which are highly esteemed. Writings include *Compendium of the History of Doctrinal Theology, Fundamental Truth of the Christian Religion, Revelation and Inspiration, History of Dogma,* his most important work, and *System of Ethics.*

SEISS (sēs), **JOSEPH AUGUSTUS** (1823-1904), Lutheran minister, born at Graceham, Maryland, of Moravian parentage. Studied for two years at Pennsylvania College, Gettysburg, then received private instruction in theology. Held pastorates at Martinsburg and Shepherdstown, Virginia; Cumberland and Baltimore, Maryland; and St. Johns and Holy Communion, Philadelphia. Exerted a strong influence in the Ministerium of Pennsylvania and in the General Council, serving a number of terms as president in both bodies. One of the founders of the General Council; one of the committee that made the *Church Book*. For twelve years editor of the *Lutheran*, for a time, one of the editors of the *Prophetic Times*, author of many books. His writings include: *On the Last Times; Ecclesia Lutherana; Lectures on the Gospels; Lectures on the Epistles; On the Apocalypse; Holy Types; Digest of Christian Doctrine; The Gospel in the Stars; Voices from Babylon;* and *Church Song*.

SELWYN (sĕl'wĭn), **GEORGE AUGUSTUS** (1809-1878), missionary and first Anglican Bishop of New Zealand, born Hampstead, London, England. Educated at Eton and St. John's College, Cambridge. After graduation and foreign travel returned to Eton as private tutor. In 1834 ordained priest, then served for about three years as curate at Windsor. In 1839 married, and in 1841 when England decided to send a bishop to New Zealand, the choice fell upon him. A little later, same year, consecrated bishop. In 1842, reached his field. Became a busy, active missionary bishop. An able, devoted high churchman, man with an iron physical constitution, almost unlimited energy, and unflinching courage. Had a large share in establishing the church among both the Maori and the white settlers who were beginning to come from England in numbers. In addition to work in New Zealand, navigating his own little vessel, the *Southern Cross*, extended operations and helped organize Anglican missions on several of the Melanesian Islands north and east of Australia. Brought young men from Melanesia to New Zealand, who, after receiving instruction in his Polynesian College, set up in 1843, were sent back to teach their countrymen. In 1855 John Coleridge Patteson was made Bishop of the Melanesian Islands. It is said that in 1854 all but about one per cent of the Maoris in Selwyn's field were at least nominally Christian. In 1844 Selwyn called the first synod, and in 1858 was made metropolitan and had four bishoprics under him. In 1867 at the call of the queen and the archbishop, left bishopric and missionary work among the New Zealanders to become Bishop of Lichfield, England. In 1877 John Richardson Selwyn, his son, was dedicated Bishop of Melanesia to succeed the martyred bishop, Coleridge Patteson.

SERGEANT, JOHN (1710-1749), missionary to American Indians. Born in Newark, New Jersey. Educated at Yale and from 1731 to 1735 was a Yale tutor. Ordained in 1735 and worked among the Indians of Berkshire county, Massachusetts. Translated parts of the Bible into their language.

SERVETUS (sûr vē'tŭs), **MIGUEL** (1511-1553), Spanish physician and heretic, born in Aragon, Spain. First studied law and theology at Saragossa and Toulouse. Met several of the reformers and was interested in the study of the Bible. In 1531 published *De Trinatatis Erroribus, Libri VII*, questioning the doctrines of the Trinity and original sin. Later turned to the study of medicine and became the real discoverer of the pulmonary circulation of the blood. Settled in Vienne where he developed a large practice from 1541 to 1553. Later, while carrying on medical practice, secretly working on *Restitution of Christianity*, which he published in 1553. In this work advocated both Arian and Anabaptist views. He and Calvin became bitter enemies. He was imprisoned by the Inquisition, but fled to Geneva. Calvin had him arrested as a heretic. Convicted and burned to death.

SETON (sē'tn), **ELIZABETH ANN (BAYLEY)** (1774-1821), founder of the Sisters of Charity, born of non-Catholic parents in New York City. Educated largely by her father, Richard Bayley, a physician. Lived in Pisa, Italy for nearly ten years until 1803. The following year she returned to the United States. In 1805 she joined the Roman Catholic church, having become interested in that faith while abroad. Supported herself and her five children for awhile by teaching school. In 1809 with the assistance of her two sisters-in-law, Harriet and Cecelia Seton, she founded, near Emmitsburg, Maryland, a congregation of women for the care of poor widows with small children, and orphans. This community was patterned after the Sisters of Charity of St. Vincent de Paul in France. In 1812, the order having received the approval of Archbishop Carroll, became the Sisters of Charity in the United States. "Mother" Seton was made the first superior-general of the order, which position she held from 1809 to 1821. Mrs. Seton also may be said to have laid the foundation for the Catholic parochial school system in the United States, for about 1809 she established the first free parochial school in the United States. At the time of her death there were more than twenty Catholic communities, having charge of the free schools, orphanages and boarding schools, and hospitals in several different states. Her children joined her in the Catholic church, one of her sons becoming an archbishop.

SEVERUS (sē vĕr'ŭs) **SULPICIUS** (sŭl pĭsh'

iŭs) (c. 360-c. 420) Latin ecclesiastic historian. Born in Aquitaine, Gaul, educated for law. Upon the loss of his wife in 392 turned to a monastic life and settled somewhere in Aquitaine. Regarded Martin of Tours as his spiritual father, spending some time with him and writing a panegyric of his life, published after Martin's death. Another of chief works was his *Chronicle,* a history of the Old and New Testament and the early church from the creation to A.D. 400. For his history he borrowed liberally from earlier writers—Sallust, Tacitus, Velleius, Curtius, and Cicero. Sought to coordinate Bible and secular history. Life of Martin of Tours and his *Dialogues* were written largely to praise the ascetic or monastic life. In old age, temporarily won over to the Pelagian heresy, for which error he imposed on himself perpetual silence as a penance.

SEYMOUR, WILLIAM J. (?). Born in Louisiana. Studied in 1905 and 1906 in C. F. Parham's Bible School in Houston, Texas. A black named Neeley Terry visited Houston and on return to Los Angeles urged his call to her black Nazarene church. Locked out of the church because of tongues speaking, meetings were moved to a home and finally to 312 Azusa St., which became the home of a Pentecostal revival for three years from 1906 to 1908. Later leaders, such as T. B. Barratt of Norway, William Durham of Chicago, and E. N. Bell, had their Pentecostal experiences there.

SHAFTESBURY, ANTHONY ASHLEY COOPER, Seventh Earl of, (Lord Ashley) (1801-1885), philanthropist and social reformer, born in London, educated at Harrow and at Christ Church, Oxford. Of the evangelical party in the Church of England. In 1826, under the title of Lord Ashley, entered Parliament as a member of the conservative party, and was in the House of Commons until 1851, when he succeeded his father as earl and as a member of the House of Lords. First directed attention to the alleviation of the condition of the insane, and obtained complete reform of the Lunacy Acts. He was largely responsible for the legislation in behalf of employees in mills, factories, collieries, and mines, and especially for abolishing the apprentice system and the employment of women and small children in the mines between 1830 and 1850. Abolished the system of apprenticing small children as chimney sweeps, and helped remedy evils in connection with the slums. For thirty-nine years chairman of the Ragged School Union. Greatly improved the housing conditions of the poor with better lodging house regulations, and new and better tenement houses. Some of his other interests were the British and Foreign Bible Society, the National Society for the Prevention of Cruelty to Children, the Pastoral Aid Society, the Protestant Alliance, the London City Mission, the Church Missionary Society, and the Young Men's Christian Association.

SHARP, GRANVILLE (1735-1813), English abolitionist. Became ordinance clerk in the Tower of London in 1758. By legal reasoning in a case that concerned the slave James Somersett in 1772 obtained decision from the chief justice Mansfield that any slave stepping on the soil of England was free. Helped found Sierra Leone under a private evangelical company in 1787 to repatriate some of the approximately 14,000 slaves freed by this decision. Helped the British and Foreign Bible Society. Wrote important works on the Hebrew word *and* and the Greek definite article.

SHAW, BARNABAS (c. 1793-1857), Wesleyan missionary to South Africa, born on a farm at Elloughton, near Hull, England, joined the Methodists and employed as a local preacher. He was sent in 1816 as the first Wesleyan missionary to South Africa. Landing at Capetown, he was refused the liberty of preaching by the governor of the colony. He proceeded to preach without the consent of the governor. Went inland about two hundred miles, where he "providentially" met a Hottentot chief from Little Namaqualand coming to Capetown in search of white men to come to teach his people. Shaw and his wife followed the chief for another two hundred miles, and were led to their new mission field. They were well received, and established a thriving mission. Shaw taught the people and preached to them for eleven years before returning to England for a furlough. He gave over forty years in South Africa to missions. Died at Capetown.

SHAW, WILLIAM (1798-1872), Methodist missionary to South Africa, born in Glasgow, Scotland. In 1820 Shaw went to Grahamstown, Cape Colony, as a chaplain to the British colonists who had settled there, and traveled widely in work among them. In 1823 began missionary work among the Kaffirs. Early conceived the idea and the hope of building a chain of mission stations along the coast from Algoa Bay to Natal and Delagoa Bay. Within twenty-five years eight stations were built and his dream realized. During thirty-seven years of missionary activity, the mission grew from sixty-three to nearly five thousand church members. After thirty-seven years of labor in South Africa, returned to England, ministering to various Methodist circuits for eight years. Elected Conference president in 1865.

SHEDD, WILLIAM GREENOUGH THAYER (1820-1894), Presbyterian theologian and author, born at Acton, Massachusetts, educated at the University of Vermont and Andover Theological Seminary. In 1844-1845 pastor of the Congregational church in Brandon, Vermont. Professor of English literature, University of Vermont (1845-1852); of sacred rhetoric and pastoral theology, Auburn Theological Seminary (1852-1853); and professor of ecclesiastical history and lecturer on pastoral theology, Andover (1855-1862). For eighteen months (1862-1863) co-pastor with Dr. Gardiner Spring at the Brick Presbyterian Church, New York City. Taught in Union Theological Seminary, New York (1863-1890). Became known for his rigid logic, the compactness of his system, and his cogent defense of Calvinism, as embodied in his *Dogmatic Theology* (three volumes). Wrote also *A History of Christian Doctrine* (two volumes). A champion of rigid orthodoxy and opposed the higher criticism as expounded by his colleague, Charles A. Briggs.

SHEEN, FULTON JOHN (1895-1979), Roman Catholic radio preacher. Born El Paso, Ill. Educated at St. Viator's College, Kankakee, the Catholic University of America and Louvain (Ph.D. 1913). Ordained as priest in 1919. Professor of philosophy at the Catholic University of America from 1926 to 1950. Preacher at St. Patrick's Cathedral, New York City and preacher of the National Catholic Hour over NBC from 1930 to 1952. From 1950 director of the Society for the Propagation of the Faith. Bishop of New York in 1951 and Bishop of Rochester from 1966 to 1969.

SHELDON, CHARLES MONROE (1857-1946), minister and writer, born at Wellsville, New York, received education from Brown University and Andover Theological Seminary. Ordained to the Congregational ministry, pastor of the Congregational Church at Waterbury, Vermont (1886-1888), and Central Congregational Church, Topeka, Kansas (1889-1912). From 1912 to 1915 minister at large for his denomination. In 1915 called back to his church in Topeka. Wrote: *In His Steps, or What Would Jesus Do?* which sold over six million copies from which he received nothing. In 1900 received permission to edit for one week *The Topeka Daily Capital* as he "believed Jesus would have it run on earth," "in accordance with the principles of Christianity," an experiment that gained wide publicity. Editor of the *Christian Herald* from 1920 to 1925.

SHELDON, HENRY CLAY (1845-1928), theologian and church historian, born at Martinsburg, New York, studied at Yale University, Boston University School of Theology, and University of Leipzig, Germany. Ordained in the Methodist ministry and served as a pastor at St. Johnsbury, Vermont (1871-1872) and Brunswick, Maine (1872-1874). From 1875 to 1921 professor in Boston University. Among writings are *History of Christian Doctrine* (two volumes), *History of the Christian Church* (five volumes), *System of Christian Doctrine* and *New Testament Theology*.

SHEMBE, ISAIAH (c. 1870-1935), founder of Am-Nazereth cult of South Africa. Raised in Natal. Visions led to healing and preaching. Ordained in African Native Baptist church. Formed his own church near Durban and was looked upon as a Zulu Messiah. Major example of many African Christian cults founded by Africans and followed by millions of Africans.

SHIELDS, THOMAS TODHUNTER (1873-1955), Canadian Baptist fundamentalist preacher. Born in Bristol and educated in Maiden Kirk School and Roundhay Institute in Yorkshire. Migrated to Toronto and was ordained in 1897. Served churches in Ontario from 1894 to 1910 when he became pastor of Jarvis Street Baptist Church until 1955. Attacked modernism at McMasters University in 1927 in his *Gospel Witness* (editor from 1922). Helped found independent fundamental groupings of Baptists, especially the Baptist Bible Union of which he was president twice from 1923 to 1932. Unsuccessfully took over Des Moines University from 1927 to 1929. Founded in his church and president of Toronto Baptist Seminary from 1927 when it officially opened. Began broadcasting over the radio in 1936.

SHOEMAKER, SAMUEL MOOR (1893-1963), Episcopal supporter of the Oxford Group. Born in Baltimore. Educated at Princeton University and Union Theological Seminary. Ordained in 1921. Served two years as a YMCA worker in China. In 1925 became rector of Calvary Episcopal Church, New York. Worked for a time with Buchman's Oxford Group. Counsellor and radio speaker, stressing personal evangelism and everyday practice of Christianity. Assisted Alcoholics Anonymous develop their "Twelve Steps." Wrote *Twice Born Ministers* and *Realizing Religion*.

SHORE, JOHN (BARON TEIGNMOUTH) (1751-1834), Governor of India. Born in London. Educated at Harrow and a business school in London. From 1769 to 1775 filled clerical, financial, and political positions in the East India Company's offices in Calcutta. From 1775 to 1785 member of the revenue commission of that company. From 1787 to 1789 served as a member of the government of Bengal. From 1793 to 1798 governor-general of India. Given title Baron Teignmouth in 1798. From 1807 to 1828 a member of the British Privy Council. Lived in Clapham Commons and a member of the Clapham sect. President of the British and Foreign Bible Society from 1804 to 1834. Opposed the addition of the Apocrypha to the Society's Bibles.

SICKINGEN (zĭk'ĭng ĕn), **FRANZ VON** (1481-1523), knight, born at the Castle of Ebernburg, near Kreuznach, Germany. From early youth devoted himself to military life, protection of the oppressed his chief occupation. Defended Reuchlin against the monks of Cologne. His support of King Charles I of Spain aided in the king's election as Holy Roman Emperor, Charles V. As a reward for this service Charles made him commander of the imperial armies, councillor, and chamberlain. A little later, however, he became a strenuous advocate of the Reformation, placing himself at the head of a league formed by himself and Ulrich von Hutten in 1522 to 1523 for the forcible introduction of Reformation. In 1522 declared war against the elector and archbishop of Treves (Trier), who was one of Luther's most powerful enemies; but being defeated retired to his fortress at Ebernburg, and died of wounds, received in the war.

SIGISMUND (zē'gĭs mo͝ont) (1368-1437), King of Germany, Hungary, and Bohemia; and emperor of the Holy Roman Empire (1411-1437), born at Nürnberg. Educated at the Hungarian court from eleventh to sixteenth year, crowned king of Hungary in 1387. In 1396 with the Christian forces of Europe undertook a crusade against the Turks, but suffered a crushing defeat at Nicopolis. Upon death of the Holy Roman Emperor Rupert in 1410, chosen to succeed him, crowned at Aix-le-Chapelle in 1414, received the imperial crown at Milan in 1431 and at Rome in 1433. In 1414 convoked and guided the Council of Constance, which council settled the dispute involved in the Great Papal Schism, instituted various ecclesiastical reforms, and condemned John Huss and Jerome of Prague as heretics. Although he promised safe conduct to Huss, broke his pledge on the ground that it was right to break faith with a heretic. Upon death of his brother Wenceslaus (1361-1419), became king of Bohemia; yet his power was never more than nominal, as the Bohemians remembered his complicity in the death of Huss, and repeatedly rose in arms against him. Not until 1436 did they even recognize him as their king. One of the most farsighted statesmen of his day.

SIMEON (sĭm'ē ŭn), **CHARLES** (1759-1836), Church of England clergyman, born at Reading, England, educated at Eton and King's College, Cambridge. Ordained priest in 1783. From 1783 to 1836 was minister of the Church of the Holy Trinity in Cambridge. He became the center of evangelical infuence at Cambridge. May be regarded as the founder of the Low church party. An indefatigable Bible student and believer in prayer. An effective preacher. Best known written work is the *Horae Homiletica* or Discourses upon the whole Scripture. The three great purposes of his preaching were "to humble the sinner, to exalt the Saviour, and to promote holiness." One of the historic group that met in 1799 at Aldersgate to plan the founding of the Church Missionary Society, and to him in part is traceable Henry Martyn's inspiration and interest in missions while he was Simeon's curate. Helped the British and Foreign Bible Society at a time when it was viewed with suspicion by many churchmen.

SIMEON STYLITES (sĭm'e ŭn stī lī'tēz) (c. 390-459), the father of the pillar saints born at Sisan on the border of Cilicia and Syria. When about sixteen entered a monastery, and became an ascetic of the strictest order. For awhile lived as a hermit on a mountain. From 413 to 423 lived in an enclosed cell near Antioch. When people thronged to him for counsel and prayers, leaving scant time for his devotions, he resorted to pillar sitting. For thirty-six years, from 423 until his death, he lived on a platform at the top of a pillar over fifty feet above the ground.

SIMON MAGUS (mā'gŭs), (First Century), sorcerer, supposed-founder of the Simonian Gnostic sect, born at Gitta (or Gitton) in Samaria. Established himself in the city of Samaria as "the power of God which is called great" (Acts 8:10), and may even have been worshiped as a god. He professed conversion and was baptized by Philip about the year 40, and later sought from Peter and John the power of the Holy Spirit so that he might have more miraculous power and perhaps gain intercourse with the higher world. When Peter reproved him for this, he seemed to be repentant (Acts 8:4-24). His conception of Christianity was a mixture of pagan magic with scanty knowledge of the new Christian faith. Early writers say he perpetuated his confused religious concepts in what later came to be known as Simonianism, an early form of Gnosticism. According to some writers, he claimed himself to be the true Redeemer and a revelation of God. From Simon's request to buy the gift of the Holy Spirit (Acts 8:18-20), has come the word "simony" to represent the seeking or granting of ecclesiastical preference by means of purchase.

SIMPSON, ALBERT BENJAMIN (1843-1919), American Presbyterian minister and founder of Christian and Missionary Alliance, born on Prince Edward Island, Canada, of Scottish background, educated at Knox College, Toronto, Canada. Called in 1865 to become pastor of the Knox Presbyterian Church, Hamilton, Ontario. In 1879 went to the Chestnut Street Presbyterian Church in Louisville, Kentucky, one of the most important Northern Presbyterian churches. Here he promoted revival and the building of a new church. During the revival A. B. Simpson came into a new religious experience, the "fullness of the blessing of Christ," or sanctification "through faith in the provision of the atonement." Served the church in Louisville with success until 1881, when he resigned to accept the call to the Thirteenth Street Presbyterian Church in New York City. Sometime after he moved to New York his health completely gave way, and the doctors told him that he had but a few months to live. At this time after twenty years of suffering and definite periods of broken health, and in this particular crisis, the Lord gave him physical healing which carried him through thirty-five more years of most strenuous toil. By the time of his healing he had rounded out his doctrinal convictions and began preaching the "fourfold gospel," Jesus Christ as "Saviour, Sanctifier, Healer and Coming King." Dr. Simpson preached in the Thirteenth Street Presbyterian Church less than two years. In 1881 he left his lucrative position to begin a mission and service of faith. Dr. Simpson and a few associates opened the work in Caledonian Hall at Eighth Avenue and Thirteenth Street. The place of worship had to be shifted a dozen times until in 1889 a permanent house was built at Eighth Avenue and Forty-fourth Street. This tabernacle was one of the greatest evangelical centers of the city, and leading men of this and other nations were called to its pulpit. Early in his ministry Simpson began to use the printed page. Edited the *Alliance Weekly,* wrote more than seventy books on Bible, theology, missions, and the spiritual life, and wrote many beautiful poems and hymns. In 1883 opened a Bible and missionary training school which in 1897 was moved to Nyack on the Hudson. He organized two societies, the Christian Alliance in 1887, and the International Missionary Alliance in 1889. In 1897 the two were combined under the name, the Christian and Missionary Alliance.

SIMPSON, MATTHEW (1811-1884), American Methodist bishop and educator, born at Cadiz, Ohio. Converted at a camp meeting, early felt the call to preach. Studied medicine from 1830 to 1833 under a doctor at Cadiz, qualified as a practitioner, but soon abandoned medicine for the ministry. In 1837 ordained elder. In 1835 became pastor of the Liberty Street Church, Pittsburgh, and the next year pastor at Williamsport, Pennsylvania. In 1837 became vice-president and professor of natural sciences of Allegheny College, from 1839 to 1848 the first president of what is today DePauw University at Greencastle, Indiana. In 1848 his Conference appointed him editor of its paper, the *Western Christian Advocate.* In 1852 Simpson elected bishop with his residence at Philadelphia. In 1859 moved to Evanston, Illinois, became president of Garrett Biblical Institute. During the Civil War a friend and frequent adviser of President Lincoln, and at Lincoln's burial delivered the eulogy. Made several trips to Europe and one to Palestine. His chief publications were *Yale Lectures on Preaching, A Hundred Years of Methodism,* and *Cyclopedia of Methodism.*

SINGH (sĭng), **SADHU SUNDAR** (1889-c. 1929), Indian Christian, born in the home of high caste Sikh family at Rampur in North Punjab, India. Went to an American Presbyterian mission school, against his will was taught the Bible. One day in his hatred of this teaching, he burned a copy of the Bible in his father's courtyard. A vision of the Lord Jesus Christ, whom he had despised, made a very deep impression on him. Like the apostle Paul, he accepted and began enthusiastically to preach the Christian faith. Family forsook him and he was bitterly persecuted. His last meal at home was poisoned; he nearly died of the effects. When he reached Sabathu, he was welcomed and assisted by the Christians. In 1905, at age sixteen baptized in the Church of England. A month later donned the saffron robe of the "holy man," and for the rest of his days a Christian "sadhu," going from village to village, barefooted, as a messenger of Christ, carrying his New Testament. His missionary tours took him through Punjab, including his own native village, Kashmir, Baluchistan, Afghanistan, and Tibet. For the last twenty years of life he made regular tours into Tibet, suffering much for his faith and being bitterly persecuted, often miraculously delivered. Finally, 1929, made his last trip to Tibet. No trace was ever found of his closing days. In addition to his missionary trip in Asia, in his later years he traveled extensively in the United States, England, Scotland, Holland, Denmark, Sweden, Malabar, Japan, China, and Palestine. His father late in life became a Christian and paid his son's expenses to Europe. Wrote: *The Search After Reality,* and *With and Without Christ.*

SLESSOR, MARY (1848-1915), Scottish missionary to Africa. Born near Aberdeen, Scotland. Father died when she was a child and she became the main means of support for the family. The appeal of David Livingstone for missionaries to Africa intensified her desire to serve. With her mother's approval she sailed for Nigeria in 1876. For three years she labored so self-sacrificingly and strenuously that her health gave way. She had to return to Scotland and, when in 1880 she returned to Africa, she was assigned to Old Town and worked hard as before. In 1891 the British Government appointed her Vice-Consul for Okoyong. She knew the mind of the African well. In later years she chose to remain in Africa.

SMITH, ARTHUR HENDERSON (1845-1932), American Congregational missionary, born at Vernon, Connecticut, studied at Beloit College, Wisconsin, Andover Theological Seminary, Union Theological Seminary, and College of Physicians and Surgeons, New York City. Served in the armed services in the latter part of the Civil War. A missionary in Chicago and Clifton, Illinois (1871-1872); Tientsin, China, under the American Board of Commissioners for Foreign Missions (1872-1880); and P'ang Chuang, Shantung, China (1880-1890). Smith was in Peking during the Boxer siege of the city in 1900, after which he returned to P'ang Chuang for four years. Following 1906 a "missionary at large" in China, except for a brief visit to the United States. In later years engaged in literary work, in traveling and speaking in the interest of missions. Associate editor of the *Missionary Review of the World,* and author of *Proverbs and Common Sayings of the Chinese; Chinese Characteristics; Village Life in China; China in Convulsion; Rex Christus: an Outline Study of China;* and *Uplift of China.*

SMITH, EDWIN WILLIAM (1876-1957), missionary to South Africa, born in South Africa. After getting education abroad, returned to South Africa in 1898 to follow in his father's footsteps during seventeen years of active work as a missionary of the Primitive Methodist Church, first in Basutoland, and later at the Karenga in Northern Rhodesia. From 1902 to 1915 worked with the Ila tribe of Zambia. In 1916 joined the British and Foreign Bible Society as one of its secretaries until 1939. About 1927 played a leading part in the founding of the Industrial African Institute. In the late twenties and in the thirties, when closely associated with the Phelps-Stokes Foundation, became a leading figure in the promotion of research, publication, and teaching in African social and linguistic studies; and president of the Royal Anthropological Institute from 1933 to 1935. During the Second World War spent some time in North America as a visiting professor at Hartford Seminary, and later at Fisk University. Among best known books are: *Golden Stool* and *Aggrey of Africa.*

SMITH, ELI (1801-1857), American Protestant missionary translator and explorer, born in Northfield, Connecticut, educated at Yale College and Andover Seminary. In 1826, after ordination, the American Board sent him to superintend a missionary printing establishment in Malta. The next year transferred to Syria with headquarters at Beirut. In 1830 he and H. G. O. Dwight, under direction of the American Board, made a journey through Asia Minor, Armenia, Georgia, and Persia to secure information concerning the Nestorian Christians. The expedition, which lasted a year, resulted in the establishment of the Armenian and Nestorian missions by the American Board. Published an account of the journey in *Missionary Researches in Armenia* (two volumes). Between 1838 and 1852 assisted Edward Robinson in making lengthy journeys and extensive explorations in Palestine and Sinai. About 1847 began the translation of the Bible into Arabic, completing the New Testament and much of the Old Testament before he died in 1857.

SMITH, ELIAS (1769-1846), New England Baptist minister, born at Lyme, Connecticut, but spent boyhood days under very crude frontier conditions in Vermont. Joined the Baptist church and began to preach. In 1792 the Baptist ministers of Boston ordained him in spite of a very meager education. For about ten years preached for the Baptists, meanwhile securing an education by earnest, private study. As he studied the New Testament became disappointed with the doctrine of Calvinism, and also with the prevailing emphasis on denominationalism and church creeds. Advocated the restoration of the simple faith and practice of the primitive church. Joined with Abner Jones in preaching "Restoration." For forty years after 1801 they traveled and preached together. In 1808 established the *Herald of Gospel Liberty,* one of the first religious journals in America. In his paper advocated the following principles: (1) No head over the church but Christ; (2) no confession of faith, articles of religion, rubric, canons, creeds, etc., but the New Testament; (3) no religious names but Christian. In 1827-1829 edited the *Morning Star and City Watchman,* which was later absorbed in his *Herald of Gospel Liberty.*

SMITH, GEORGE (1840-1876), English Assyriologist, born at Chelsea, near London, England. In early life a banknote engraver. Became interested in the Oriental explorations of Layard and Rawlinson, and studiously devoted his spare time to research on Assyrian subjects. Taught himself the Oriental languages and studied the Niveveh sculptures in the British Museum. In 1867 appointed a senior assistant in the department of Egyptian and Oriental antiquities in the British Museum. Made several expeditions to Nineveh and obtained immense treasures in cuneiform transcriptions. Helped Sir Henry Rawlinson prepare the third volume of *Cuneiform Inscriptions,* discovered the *Chaldean Account of the Deluge,* and furnished the key to the interpretation of the Cypriote character and script. On third journey to Nineveh procured at Bagdad between two and three thousand tablets that had been discovered by some Arabs in an ancient Babylonian library. Stricken with fever and died at Aleppo. Published *The Phonetic Values of Cuneiform Characters, The Cuneiform Account of the Deluge, The Chaldean Account of Genesis, Assyrian Discoveries, Ancient History from the Monuments, Babylonian Fables and Legends of the Gods, From the Cuneiform Inscriptions, Early History of Assyria and Babylonia, History of Sennacherib,* and *Annals of Assurbanipal.*

SMITH, GEORGE ADAM (1856-1942), Scottish divine and Biblical scholar, born in Calcutta, India. Educated at Edinburgh University, at New College, Edinburgh, and in the Universities of Tübingen and Leipzig. After traveling for some time in Egypt and Syria, in 1880 became assistant minister at West Free Church, Brechin and also tutor in Hebrew in the Free Church College at Aberdeen. From 1882 to 1892 minister of Queen's Cross Free Church, Aberdeen. In 1892 appointed professor of Old Testament language, literature, and theology in the United Free Church College, Glasgow, and principal of Aberdeen University in 1909. Percy Trumbull lecturer at Johns Hopkins, Lyman Beecher lecturer at Yale, Jowett lecturer in London, Baird lecturer at Glasgow, and also lecturer in the University of California and the University of Chicago. In 1916 knighted and in 1916-1917 served as moderator of the United Free church. Writings include *The Book of Isaiah, The Preaching of the Old Testament to the Age, Historical Geography of the Holy Land, The Twelve Prophets, The Life of Henry Drummond, Modern Criticism and the Preaching of the Old Testament, The Early Poetry of Israel,* and *Jeremiah.*

SMITH, HANNAH WHITALL (1832-1911), American Quaker philanthropist and author, born in a Quaker home in Philadelphia, educated at the Quaker school of Miss Mary Anna Longstroth. In 1851 married Robert Pearsall Smith. Following death of her son Franklin Whitall in 1872 she wrote *The Record of a Happy Life: Being Memoirs of Franklin Whitall Smith.* Converted in 1858 she claimed to have a deeper spiritual life experience in 1867. For many years conducted Bible classes for women in her home in Philadelphia, which she made the center for various religious projects. In 1873-1874 she and her husband conducted a series of religious meetings in England. In 1888 moved with her family to England, and lived the remainder of her life in London. Wrote many religious tracts and was the author of *My Spiritual Autobiography or How I Discovered the Unselfishness of God; The Christian's Secret of a Happy Life; Everyday Religion; The God of All Comfort;* and *The Open Secret,* or the *Bible Explaining Itself.* Her teaching was similar to that of the Keswick conferences.

SMITH, HERBERT AUGUSTINE (1874-1952), American Congregationalist hymnologist, born at Naperville, Illinois, studied at North Central College, Naperville, and the Oberlin Conservatory of Music. Taught hymnology and church music at the Chicago Theological Seminary and Chicago Divinity School (1901-1916) and at Boston University (1917-1944), director of fine arts in religion (1921-1933) and director of the department of sacred music in the college of music (1934-1944). Also director of music, Chautauqua, New York (1921-1928). Founder of the New England Choir Directors' Guild. Compiled and edited eight hymnbooks: *The Hymnbook for American Youth, The Century Hymnal, The Army and Navy Hymnal, Hymns for the Living Age, The American Student Hymnal, The New Hymnal for American Youth, Praise and Service,* and *The New Church Hymnal.* He wrote also *Worship in the Church School through Music, Pageantry, and Pictures, Lyric Religion,* and *Organization and Administration of Choirs.* Smith was a pioneer in the field of church music and allied arts.

SMITH, HENRY BOYNTON (1815-1877), Presbyterian theologian, born in Portland, Maine, studied at Bowdoin College, Bangor, and Andover Theological Seminary. Tutor in Greek and librarian at Bowdoin for one year. Due to ill health spent three years in Europe. During the first year attended lectures at the Sorbonne in Paris, the Institute, and the Royal Academy. The next two years studied in Germany at Halle and Berlin. In 1840 returned to America and at once was licensed. Due to recurring ill health did not begin his five-year pastorate at the Congregational Church of Amesbury, Massachusetts until he was ordained in 1842. During two winters of this time also supply professor of Hebrew at Andover. In 1847 became professor in Amherst College. In 1850 accepted a call to the chair of church history in Union Theological Seminary, New York City, but transferred to the chair of systematic theology, which he occupied until 1874. Founded the *American Theological Review* in 1857 and edited it until 1862 when it merged with the *Presbyterian Review,* of which he was editor until 1871. Became an outstanding leader in the Presbyterian church, especially in shaping opinion in the New School branch at a crucial time in the life of the Presbyterian church. Moderator of the New School Assembly in 1863, delegate to the General Assembly at Philadelphia in 1867. Took an aggressive and leading part in the union of the New and Old Schools. He made several trips to Europe and one to the East. Wrote numerous books of high theological and inspirational value.

SMITH, HENRY PRESERVED (1847-1927), American educator, born at Troy, Ohio, educated at Marietta College, Amherst College, Lane Theological Seminary, and the universities of Berlin and Leipzig. Ordained in 1875. Instructor at Lane in church history and Hebrew, then professor of Hebrew and Old Testament (1877-1893); professor of Biblical literature at Amherst College (1898-1906), and professor of Old Testament literature and history of religions at the Unitarian Meadville Theological Seminary in Pennsylvania (1907-1913); and librarian at Union Theological Seminary (1913-1925). In 1875 ordained to the Presbyterian ministry, but as an exponent of higher biblical criticism was tried and suspended by the Cincinnati Presbytery in 1893 for heresy. In 1899 received into the Congregational ministry by the Hampshire Association. He wrote *Inspiration and Inerrancy, A Critical and Exegetical Commentary on the Books of Samuel, The Religion of Israel, Old Testament History, Essays on Biblical Interpretation,* and *The Heretics Dissent.*

SMITH, JOHN TAYLOR (1860-1907), British bishop and commanding army chaplain. Educated at St. John's Hall, Highbury. Curate in Norwood for five years. Canon missioner to Sierra Leone in 1891. Bishop in 1897. Chaplain general of British forces in World War I. Helped Children's Special Services Mission. Died on a ship in the Mediterranean and buried at sea.

SMITH, JOSEPH (1805-1844), founder of the Mormons, born at Sharon, Vermont. When ten years old moved with parents to Palmyra, New York, and later to Manchester, New York. Received little education. In the year 1820 several revival meetings were held near his home leaving him perplexed. Claimed to have received visions informing him he should join none of the existing churches, but establish the true church. On September 12, 1823, the angel Moroni is supposed to have revealed to him that on the side of the Hill Cumorah near his home some golden plates were hidden on which were engraved the true gospel. In 1827 claimed to have received these plates along with a pair of spectacles called "Urim and Thummim," by which he should read and translate the plates. The first publication of this translation was in 1830 and is known as the *Book of Mormon,* a supposed history of the early inhabitants of America and the plan of salvation for the American continent. In 1829 Smith and Oliver Cowdery received the priesthood, and on April 6, 1830, organized the Church of Jesus Christ of the Latter Day Saints with six members, Smith as leader. They claimed their church was a restoration of the religion of Jesus Christ Himself. In 1833 Smith published a *Book of Commandments,* and in 1835, *Doctrine and Covenants.* In 1831 he and his sect moved to Kirtland, Ohio, and later to Jackson County, Missouri. When driven from this county in 1833, they moved to Clay County, but in 1838 were expelled from the state. They then settled in Illinois in 1839 where they built the town of Nauvoo. Smith is said to have authorized the practice of polygamous marriage for the Mormon community in 1843. Charges of immorality were brought against him; he and his brother Hyrum were arrested and incarcerated at Carthage, Illinois. On June 27, 1844, a mob surrounded the jail and the brothers were taken out and murdered. Brigham Young assumed the leadership of the sect. In 1847 Young and his followers made their long historic trek to Utah. A smaller group rebelled against Young, and following Joseph Smith, Jr., organized the Reorganized Church of Jesus Christ of Latter Day Saints in Kansas.

SMITH, JOSEPH, JR. (1832-1914), first President of the Reorganized Church of Jesus Christ of Latter Day Saints, born at Kirtland, Ohio, the son of Joseph Smith, the founder of Mormonism. Moved with parents to Far West, Missouri in 1838. The following winter, expelled with other Mormons from Missouri, the family settled at Commerce, subsequently Nauvoo, Illinois. Grew to manhood and served several times as justice of peace. Studied law for a while, but gave it up. In 1860 became president of the Reorganized Church of Jesus Christ of Latter Day Saints; and the majority of the Mormons of the Middle West joined his church. Wrote tracts and books repudiating the doctrine and practice of polygamy. Also fought alcohol, tobacco, tea and coffee, and opposed Mormonism's later doctrines of polytheism and baptism for the dead. In 1865 the headquarters was moved to Plano, Illinois; in 1881 to Lamoni, Iowa, and in 1906 to Independence, Missouri, where it has since remained. Under his presidency the Reorganized Church grew to more than seventy thousand. Died at Independence.

SMITH, RODNEY (GIPSY) (1860-1947), British evangelist, born in a gipsy tent in the parish of Wanstead, near Epping Forest, England. Received no education. His father became a Christian when Rodney was in his early teens. When fifteen he accepted Christ. Joined William Booth's Christian Mission in 1877. Soon after their marriage in 1878, he and his wife were placed at Hull where as many as fifteen hundred people gathered to hear him. It was here that perhaps for the first time he became known as "Gipsy Smith." While preaching at Hanley he was dismissed from the Salvation Army for a technical breach of discipline in 1882. In 1889 made the first of his many trips to the United States. In 1889 became assistant to the Rev. F. S. Collier of the Manchester Mission. In 1892 conducted a series of services in Edinburgh, from which grew the Gipsy Gospel Wagon Mission, devoted to evangelistic work among his own people. After his fifth return from America, from 1897 to 1912, he was the special missioner of the National Free Church Council. He is best known for his active, seventy-year evangelistic work throughout the world. At age eighty-seven he died of a heart attack at sea en route to the US.

SMITH, SAMUEL FRANCIS (1808-1895), Baptist minister and hymnist, born in Boston, Massachusetts, educated at Harvard College and Andover Theological Seminary, and ordained in 1834. Pastor of the Baptist church at Waterville, Maine, and professor of modern languages in Waterville College (1834-1842), and pastor of the Baptist church in Newton, Massachusetts (1842-1854). Editor of the *Christian Review* of Boston (1842-1848), and edited the publications of the American Baptist Missionary Union (1854-1869). Author of many hymns, most famous of which are "My Country, 'tis of Thee" and "The Morning Light Is Breaking." A collection of his verse was published under the title *Poems of Home and Country*.

SMITH, WILBUR MOORHEAD (1894-1977), bibliographer, Bible teacher, and author. Born Chicago, Illinois. Educated at Moody Bible Institute and College of Wooster. Ordained by Presbyterians and pastor from 1913 to 1937 in Maryland, Virginia, and Pennsylvania. Professor of English Bible, Moody Bible Institute from 1938 to 1947. Professor at Fuller Seminary from 1947 to 1963 and at Trinity Evangelical Divinity School from 1963 to 1971. Edited *Peloubet Select Notes* for the International Sunday School Lessons from 1933 to 1972. Helped revise the Scofield Bible from 1954 to 1963. Gave his 25,000 volume library to Fuller Seminary. Wrote many booklets and articles on bibliography, such books as *Therefore Stand* and his autobiographical *Before I Forget*.

SMITH, SIR WILLIAM (1813-1893), English lexicographer and biblical scholar, born in Enfield, near London, England and educated at the University of London. Studied theology for a while; then turned to law. Meanwhile he also studied the Greek and Latin classics, becoming so proficient in his knowledge of them that he became professor of Greek and Latin in New College, London, and began writing on scholarly topics and editing Greek and Latin classics. Editor of the *Quarterly Review* from 1867 until his death. Knighted in 1892, the year before his death. Became the leading lexicographer of his day, and edited many dictionaries that were of great value to classical and biblical students, including *English-Latin Dictionary; Dictionary of Greek and Roman Antiquities; Dictionary of Greek and Roman Biography and Mythology; Dictionary of Greek and Roman Geography;* his most important, the *Dictionary of the Bible; Dictionary of Christian Antiquities,* written in collaboration with Archdeacon Cheetham; *Dictionary of Christian Biography,* written jointly with Dr. Henry Wace; *History of Greece; Illustrated History of the Bible; New Testament History;* and *Old Testament History*.

SMITH, WILLIAM ROBERTSON (1846-1894), Scottish biblical critic and Semitic scholar, born at New Farm, near Keig, Aberdeenshire, Scotland, where father was a Free church minister. Educated by father and at Aberdeen University, New College, Edinburgh, and in the universities of Bonn and Göttingen. In 1868 became assistant professor of physics at Edinburgh University, and in 1870 appointed professor of Hebrew and Old Testament exegesis in the Free church college at Aberdeen; in 1875 became a member of the Old Testament revision company. Free criticism of the Old Testament writings, and his articles, "Angels" and "Bible," prepared for the ninth revised *Encyclopaedia Britannica,* raised a storm of protest and led to a charge of heresy. In 1881 was suspended from his professorship, but was invited to become editor-in-chief of the new *Encyclopaedia Britannica,* to which he continued to contribute articles. Also continued his Semitic studies. Between 1879 and

1881 visited Egypt, Syria, Palestine, Tunis, Southern Spain, and Arabia. In 1883 called to be professor of Arabic in Cambridge University; in 1885 elected a fellow of Christ's College; and in 1886-1889 chief librarian of the university. In 1889 chosen Adams professor of Arabic, holding this position until death in 1894. His writings include: *What History Teaches Us to Look for in the Bible; The Old Testament in the Jewish Church; The Prophets of Israel; Kinship and Marriage in Early Arabia;* and *The Religion of the Semites.*

SMYTH (SMITH), JOHN (d.-1612), reputed founder of the General Baptists. A graduate of Christ's College, Cambridge, took orders in the established church. A preacher and lecturer at Lincoln about 1600-1602. About 1605 left the Church of England and became pastor of a Separatist congregation in Gainsborough, Lincolnshire, England. Because of persecution he and congregation migrated to Amsterdam about 1608, where he came in touch with the Mennonites. Smyth became convinced that infant baptism was without scriptural authority and did not represent primitive Christianity. In 1608 or 1609 baptized himself, Thomas Helwys, and about forty other members of his flock by pouring. His church in Holland is considered by some as the first Arminian Baptist or General Baptist Church. Smyth died of tuberculosis, and Thomas Helwys and John Murton returned to England and organized the first Baptist church (General Baptist) on English soil about 1611.

SOCRATES (sŏk'rȧ tēz) (surnamed **SCHOLASTICUS**) (380-450), Greek church historian, born at Constantinople, where he likely received education for the legal profession, where he lived most of his life. A lover of history and a warm admirer of Eusebius, he was impelled to continue the writing of the history of the Christian church where Eusebius left off. Overlapping the history somewhat he began his *Ecclesiastical History* with the accession to the throne of Constantine in 306, and carried the thread of history to 439. Wrote as a layman. His history is valuable for its numerous extracts from sources, and for its dispassionate and impartial presentation. As an example of historical composition the work of Socrates ranks very high.

SÖDERBLOOM (sö'dẽr bloōm), **LARS OLAF JONATHAN (NATHAN)** (1866-1931), Swedish Lutheran teacher, ecumenist and preacher; born at Trönö, Sweden; studied at universities of Uppsala and Paris. Ordained in 1893; pastor of Swedish parish and chaplain to legation in Paris from 1894 to 1901. 1901 to 1912, professor of religious history at Uppsala; 1912 to 1914 held lectureship at University of Leipzig. From 1914 to 1931, archbishop of Uppsala, thus primate of Sweden. Outstanding leader of the ecumenical movement; chief organizer of the first universal Conference of Life and Work in Stockholm (1925); moving spirit of the World Conference on Faith and Order in Lausanne, Switzerland (1927); these two movements later merged to bring into being the World Council of Churches. Elected to Swedish Academy in 1921; awarded Nobel Peace Prize in 1930. Wrote *Christian Fellowship, The Living God* (Gifford Lectures), *The Nature of Revelation, The Church and Peace, Religions of the World.*

SOHM (sōm), **RUDOLPH** (1841-1917), German Lutheran jurist and church historian, studied at Rostock, Berlin, Heidelberg, and Muenchen. Taught law at Göttingen, later professor of law at Strassburg, Freiburg, and Leipzig. Held the view that the church is wholly spiritual and law is wholly secular; hence the development of canon law in the Catholic church was an abandonment of the primitive ideal of the church, which was fundamentally a "charismatic" body of local churches. His chief works were *Verhaltnis von Staat und Kirche, Kirchenrecht, Wesen und Ursprung des Katholizismus, Outlines of Church History,* and *A History of Christianity.*

SORBON (sôr bôɴ'), **ROBERT de** (1201-1274), French theologian and founder of the Sorbonne, born at Sorbon, France. From the position of almoner student became successively preacher, doctor of theology, and canon of the Church of Cambray. Piety and sermons gained the notice of Louis IX, who made him his chaplain and confessor. About 1257 founded the Sorbonne in the Rue Coupe-Gorge for theological students who could not pay the high prices for food and lodging at other universities; for those who were not in sympathy with the scholastic subtleties propounded in other schools; and for the purpose of permitting teachers to reside in the same house with the students. It became a college of theology closely associated with the University of Paris. In time the Sorbonne became the center of the university; and before the Reformation it became the outstanding center of theology in Europe, and the strong arm of the Roman Catholic church in the defense against heresies. He made a small endowment to the institution; formulated the regulations for it which remained almost unchanged until the Revolution; founded a library; established an annex to the Sorbonne, the College de Calvi, to give literary preparation for theological study; and at his death willed all his property to the institution.

SOUTER, ALEXANDER (1873-1949), New

Testament and patristic writer. Educated at Aberdeen and Cambridge. Professor at Mansfield College, Oxford (1903-1911) and at Aberdeen (1911-1937). Books aid in the study of the Greek Testament and the Latin Fathers' commentaries on the epistles of Paul. Wrote *Oxford Greek Testament, The Text and Canon of the New Testament,* and *A Pocket Lexicon to the Greek New Testament.*

SOUTH, ROBERT (1634-1716), Church of England prelate and preacher, born at Hackney, Middlesex, near London, educated at Westminster school and at Christ Church, Oxford. He was ordained in 1658, and university orator (1660-1667). In 1663 became prebendary of St. Peter's, Westminster; in 1667 made chaplain to the Duke of York; in 1670 was made canon of Christ Church, Oxford; and in 1678 became rector of Islip. A zealous advocate of passive obedience to the established church and of the divine right of kings, and opposed the Toleration Act. Soon became one of the king's chaplains and won the high favor of Charles II. However, opposed the Roman Catholic leanings of Charles II and James II. After the abdication of James II, gave allegiance to the new government of William and Mary. A Calvinist at a time when the drift of the High church episcopacy was strongly toward Arminianism. About 1690 became deeply involved in the controversy with Dr. William Sherlock over the trinitarian question. He accused Sherlock of tritheism.

SOUTHWELL, ROBERT (c. 1561-1595), Roman Catholic poet and martyr, born at Horsham, Norfolk, England, educated at Douai, Paris, Tourney and Rome. Entered the Jesuit Order in 1578, and ordained priest in 1584 and prefect of the English College at Rome. In 1586 sent as missionary to England, where through his piety and winning manner gained many converts. In 1589 made chaplain to Anne, Countess of Arundle. In 1592 betrayed and tortured, and for three years was imprisoned in the Tower. After this hanged as a traitor. His poems were published after his death under the titles *St. Peter's Complaint and Other Poems;* and *Maeoniae*. Prose writings, designed to encourage Catholics under persecution, were *Consolations for Catholics; The Triumphs over Death; Mary Magdalene's Tears;* and *A Humble Supplication to Her Majesty.*

SOWER (sou'ẽr), **CHRISTOPHER (SAUR)** (1693-1758), German printer and publisher in colonial America, born in Laasphe in Wittgenstein, Westphalia, Germany, educated at Marburg and Halle. Protesting against coldness and formality was drawn to the new German Baptist Brethren church near his home. Came to Germantown in 1724. A man who could turn his hand to many trades and professions. Medical skill seems to have been out of the ordinary. Prepared his own medicines. Invented or made many of the materials he needed in his colonial home, including paper, ink, type, anvil, stoves, clocks. In 1738 he began printing in Germantown, Pennsylvania, on a printing press that likely had produced the early Berleberg Bibles in Germany. His press at once turned out an A B C and spelling book, and a twenty-four page almanac which became very popular, and was continued by his descendants for sixty years. Before long a hymnbook was published, and soon a newspaper that continued until the Revolutionary War. His monumental work, however, was the publishing of the Bible. In 1743 he published in America, in German language, the first Bible ever published in a European tongue.

SOZOMEN (sō'zō mĕn), **SALAMINIUS HERMIAS** (c. 375-c. 447), church historian, born in a Christian family at Bethelia, near Gaza in Palestine. Early education was directed by the monks near his home. Received legal training at Berytus, Phoenicia, where there was a famous law school, and then followed profession in Constantinople. Like Socrates purposed to continue the history of the Christian church from the time of Eusebius. Many scholars believe that he patterned his work after that of Socrates, and used that work as a secondary source. His history is divided into nine books and covers the period from 324 to 415, and dedicated to Emperor Theodosius the Younger. His history is similar to that of Socrates except that he gives more attention to the history of monasticism and to miracles of this period. Wrote much in favor and praise of asceticism and of the ascetics of the desert.

SOZZINI (sōt tsē'nē), **FAUSTO PAULO (SOCINUS)** (1539-1604), founder of Socinianism, born in Siena, Italy. Early became an orphan, received but scanty education. At age twenty he was denounced for holding heretical opinions, and took refuge for three years in Lyons. At this time produced a work on St. John's gospel in which he denied the essential deity of Christ. He then returned to Italy, living in Florence from 1563 to 1573, conforming outwardly to the regulations of the Roman Catholic church. Then went to Transylvania for a brief time, and for four years resided in Basel, where Unitarianism had gained a foothold. Under the influence of his uncle Lelio Sozzini (1525-1562), and in this Unitarian environment, developed a radical doctrinal system, denying the trinity and many other tenets of Catholicism. Also engaged in debate with Protestant leaders. Then after spending a short time in Transylvania went to Poland about 1579 where teaching gained a strong footing, and where he spent the remainder of his life. Extended the influence of Socinianism by his writing and his public debates. Also directed the anti-trinitarian movement in Transylvania, largely through correspondence. In 1598 was driven out of Cracow by a hostile mob. His last six years were spent in the village of Luclawice, where he died. His influence was strong in shaping the theology of the Unitarians in Poland. Gave to the movement its theological statement, the Racovian Catechism, which was published in 1605. He opposed all the chief Christian dogmas—the divinity of Christ, propitiatory sacrifice, original sin, human depravity, and justification by faith. Two of chief writings: *De Auctoritate S. Scripturae* and *De Jesu Christo Servatore*.

SPALATIN (shpä lä tēn′), **GEORG** (1484-1545), German Reformer, friend and associate of Luther, chaplain of Elector Frederick (the Wise) of Saxony. Born at Spalt, Germany, family name, Burkhardt. Educated at Erfurt and Wittenberg. In 1507 or 1508 ordained to the priesthood, and in 1509 appointed tutor to the young crown prince, John Frederick, son of Elector Frederick the Wise. Association with Luther at Wittenberg had a profound influence upon him. Spalatin won for Luther the sympathy and support of Frederick the Wise. Spalatin's living at the court, which was true much of his life, gave Luther and the Reformation much support, and his intimacy with Luther gave the government a better understanding of Luther and the Reformation program. In 1518 Spalatin accompanied the elector to the diet at Augsburg and conducted negotiations with Cajetan and Miltitz. While Luther was in concealment at the Wartburg, Spalatin helped Luther keep in touch with Wittenberg. After death of Frederick the Wise in 1525, Spalatin still remained at court; in same year also became a preacher in Alternburg, and married. In 1526 attended the Diet of Spires in the suite of Elector John, and in 1530 was at the Diet of Augsburg. At the Convention of Schweinfurt in 1532 contributed materially toward the securing of the Reformation in that vicinity. Traveled through many countries with the elector. A leading figure also in the formulating of the Schmalkald Articles in 1537, giving signature to the document. In all, Luther wrote Spalatin more than four hundred letters.

SPANGENBERG, AUGUST GOTTLIEB (1704-1792), Bishop of the Reorganized Moravian Brethren, and next to Zinzendorf its most illustrious leader, born at Klettenberg, Prussia. As a student in the University of Jena (1722-1726) and teacher from 1726 to 1732, came under the influence of Zinzendorf and Pietism, and by 1728 had become leader of the movement in Jena. For a year a member of the theological faculty at Halle. In 1733, due to differing viewpoints with Spener and Francke, both Spangenberg and Zinzendorf severed their relations with Halle. Spangenberg formally joined the Brethren and became Zinzendorf's assistant. Zinzendorf made him responsible for the Moravian colonization plans, which involved colonizing in Copenhagen, Georgia, and Pennsylvania between the years 1733 and 1739. In Georgia planning for the colony there when Nitschmann brought his colony of twenty-six members in 1735, where he also met the Wesleys when they made their mission to Georgia. Between 1739 and 1744 busy organizing the Brethren in Germany and England. In 1744 ordained Moravian Bishop and sent by Zinzendorf to America to oversee the work here. Organized and consolidated the Brethren colonists in Pennsylvania and New York, centering especially in Bethlehem and Nazareth, Pennsylvania, though the work spread to other parts also. In 1749 returned to England, but two years later resumed his work in America, founding a second complex of colonies in North Carolina. After Zinzendorf's death in 1760 the general leadership of the church fell to Spangenberg. In 1762 called back from America to Herrnhut, continued the guidance of the Brethren until his death thirty years later. He was a man of great devotion, strong and wise leadership; under his guidance the Moravians strengthened and grew. Sometimes called the "second founder" of the Brethren. Perfected the organization and assisted in the formulation of the doctrines as accepted by the Moravian Brethren through the years.

SPEER, ROBERT ELLIOTT (1867-1947), Presbyterian missionary secretary, layman, born at Huntingdon, Pennsylvania, educated at Princeton College, and Princeton Theological Seminary. Secretary of the Student Volunteer Movement for Foreign Missions (1889-1890), instructor in English Bible in Princeton College (1890-1891). For forty-six years (1891-1937), secretary of the Presbyterian Board of Foreign Missions. Made tours of visitation to mission fields, four to Asia and two to South America. President of the Foreign Mission Conference of North America, which represented over fifty mission boards in the United States and Canada. Chairman of the Committee on Cooperation in Latin America from its organization in 1916 until retirement in 1937. Served a four-year term as president of the Federal Council of the Churches of Christ in North America. In 1927 moderator of the Presbyterian

Church of the United States of America, being the second layman ever to be elected to that position. During First World War a member of the advisory committee on religious and moral activities of the army and navy; and was chairman of the General Wartime Commission of the Churches. In theology an evangelical. The author or editor of sixty-seven books, including: *The Man Christ Jesus, The Man Paul, Missions and Politics in Asia, Remember Jesus Christ, The Principles of Jesus, Missionary Principles and Practices, Light of the World, Race and Race Problems,* and *Marks of a Man*. Died of leukemia at age of eighty.

SPELLMAN, FRANCIS JOSEPH (1889-1967), Roman Catholic cardinal. Born in Whitman, Massachusetts. Educated at Fordham and North America College in Rome. Ordained in 1916. First American to serve on the Vatican Secretariat of State as translator of papal documents from 1925 to 1932. Bishop of Boston in 1932 and archbishop of New York from 1946 to 1967. Cardinal in 1947. Visited servicemen in distance places at Christmas in World War II.

SPENER (shpā'nẽr), **PHILIPP JACOB** (1635-1705), founder of German Pietism, born in Alsace. Studied at Strassburg, Basel, Geneva, and Tübingen. In 1663 became assistant preacher at Strassburg; then (1666-1686) engaged in preaching, teaching, and writing at Frankfurt. Called people together in semi-weekly meetings in his home for Bible study, prayer, and discussion of the Sunday sermon. These meetings, known as *Collegia Pietatis,* gave to the people the name of Pietists. In 1675 wrote a little book, *Pia Desideria* (Heart's Desires) in which he urged six means of spiritual instruction and improvement of the Christian life: (1) Meeting in groups to study the Bible; (2) application of the principle of the priesthood of all believers, by instructing others; (3) practical application of Christianity in a life of loving service; (4) sympathetic and kindly attitude in all religious controversies; (5) improvement in theological training in the universities, and insistence on personal conversion; and (6) reformation in the method and style of preaching. *Collegia Pietatis* and *Pia Desideria* caused such a storm among the clergy and in the church that in 1686 Spener was constrained to resign at Frankfurt and to accept a call to Dresden to become court preacher or chaplain for Elector John George III of Saxony. In 1688, August Hermann Francke joined him. Pietistic preaching caused great offense here also; after four years he had to leave. The following year accepted a call to Berlin, where he spent the last and most fruitful years of his ministry, and accomplished his greatest work. Achievements were many: founded the University of Halle in 1694, promoted the Sunday school, catechetical instruction, prayer meetings, and Bible study. Encouraged private devotional meetings. Stirred up interest in mission work among the heathen. Laid emphasis on a personal spiritual life rather than a merely intellectual acceptance of the doctrines of the church. In his preaching he denounced dancing, theatre-going, card playing, novel reading, elegant and gay clothing, light conversation, and immoderate eating and drinking. During the closing years of his life his mood fluctuated between hope for his cause and dejection caused by the many extravagances of friends and followers. Nevertheless, from first to last he conscientiously fulfilled his duties as preacher and catechizer.

SPINOZA (spĭ nō'zȧ), **BARUCH** or **BENEDICT** (1632-1677), Dutch philosopher, born in Amsterdam, Holland, to Jewish refugees from Portugal. Carefully educated in Jewish theology at the Jewish Academy in Amsterdam. Study of the physical sciences and the writings of Descartes led to his acceptance of heretical views; and in 1656, at the age of twenty-four, excommunicated from the Jewish synagogue. After this lived in quiet seclusion in or near The Hague, making a livelihood by grinding lenses and writing his philosophical works, the first being *Tract on God and Man and His Happiness.* Wrote also *Theologico-Political Tract, On the Improvement of the Intellect,* and *Ethics Demonstrated with Geometrical Order.* A thoroughgoing pantheist. To him God is not an individual but one absolute, infinite substance. All is God or nature, known in two modes or attributes, thought and extension, of which finite persons are but an expression. All is determined and no room is left for creation, divine purpose, or miracle. As to the future, believed in the immortality of the soul, though as a sort of absorption into an impersonal, pantheistic soul of God. Died of tuberculosis at The Hague.

SPRAGUE, WILLIAM BUELL (1795-1876), American Presbyterian pulpit orator, biographer, and collector, born in Andover, Connecticut, received education at Yale College and Princeton Theological Seminary. Pastor of the Congregational Church in West Springfield, Massachusetts, (1819-1829). Pastor of the Second Presbyterian Church in Albany for forty years (1829-1869). In 1869 retired to Flushing, Long Island, where he devoted last years to literary work. His great literary work was *The Annals of the American Pulpit: Notes of American Clergymen to 1855* (ten volumes).

SPURGEON, CHARLES HADDON (1834-

1892), English Baptist preacher, born at Kelvedon, Essex, London, of Huguenot origin. Attended school at Colchester, and spent a few months at an agriculture college at Maidstone. In 1849 became an usher in a Baptist school at Newmarket. Conversion took place in 1850 in Colchester. Study of the Scriptures led to the conviction that he should be immersed, consequently he united with the Baptist communion in 1857. The same year became usher in a school at Cambridge, entered the lay preachers association in connection with the Baptist church. Preached first sermon in a cottage at Teversham, near Cambridge at the age of sixteen. The fame of the "boy preacher" spread. Soon preaching in chapels, cottages, and in the open air in as many as thirteen stations in the villages surrounding Cambridge in the evenings after his school duties were over. In 1851 became pastor of a small Baptist church at Waterbeach, and in 1854 at age twenty became pastor of the New Park Street Church, Southwark, London. Congregation moved to Exeter Hall, then to Surrey Music Hall where he preached to audiences numbering ten thousand people. At twenty-two the most popular preacher of his day. The well-known Metropolitan Tabernacle seating six thousand people was built by the congregation and opened in 1861. Here he ministered with great popularity and power until his death. Besides regular pastoral and preaching duties and publishing of weekly sermons from 1855 on, founded the Pastors' College in 1856; built a circle of Sunday schools and churches; was president of a society for the dissemination of Bibles and tracts; and established Stockwell orphanage, with twelve houses, accommodating five hundred children. Opposed the evangelical party of the Church of England on the doctrine of baptism, and published a work on *Baptismal Regeneration*. Withdrew from the Evangelical Alliance. Deploring the Baptists' inclination toward biblical criticism, withdrew from the Baptist Union, yet remained an ardent Evangelical, a staunch Baptist, and a Calvinist. Writings reached an enormous circulation. Conducted the *Sword and the Trowel,* a monthly church magazine, published more than two thousand sermons. Forty-nine-volume set of *The Metropolitan Pulpit* was a mammoth work. Other writings: *The Treasury of David* (a homiletic commentary on the Psalms in seven volumes), *Lectures to My Students,* and *Commenting and Commentaries.* Died at Mentone, France, where he had gone for his health.

STAINER (stā'nẽr), **SIR JOHN** (1840-1901), English organist and composer of sacred music, born at Southwark, England, educated at Christ Church, Oxford. Between 1854 and 1888 he was organist in turn at Saint Benedict and Saint Peter's, Paul's Wharf; Saint Michael's, Tenbury; the University of Oxford; and St. Paul's Cathedral (1872-1888). Then was professor of music at Oxford University (1889-1899). Helped found the Musical Association in 1874, and in 1881 became principal of the National Training School for Music. Most widely known for his oratorios and sacred cantatas, the best known of which is "The Crucifixion." Among forty anthems: "Lead, Kindly Light," "O Clap Your Hands," "Sing a Song of Praise." Wrote two manuals, *Harmony* and *The Organ,* and collaborated with W. A. Barrett in editing a *Dictionary of Musical Terms.* Knighted in 1888 by Queen Victoria.

STALKER (stôk'ẽr), **JAMES** (1848-1927), minister and professor in the United Free Church of Scotland, born at Crieff, Perthshire, Scotland, educated at the University of Edinburgh and the universities of Berlin and Halle. Held pastorates at St. Brycedales, Kirkcaldy (1874-1887), and at St. Matthew's, Glasgow (1887-1902). Professor of Church history in the United Free Church College, Aberdeen (1902-1926). Lyman Beecher lecturer at Yale (1891) and Cunningham lecturer in New College, Edinburgh (1899); lecturer also at Louisville Baptist Seminary and at Richmond Presbyterian Seminary. He based his theology on the foundation of Scripture, tradition, and personal experience. Among many writings: *The Life of Jesus Christ, The Life of Paul, The Christology of Jesus, The Ethics of Jesus,* and *Men and Morals.*

STAM, JOHN (1907-1934) and **BETTY** (1906-1934). Martyred by Communists in China. John was born in Paterson, New Jersey. Worked in Star of Hope mission in home town. Educated at Wilson College, Pennsylvania and the Moody Bible Institute. Met Betty in Bible school. Betty went to China in 1931 and John went there under China Inland Mission in 1932. Married in 1933 and sent to Tsingteh. Martyred by Communists in 1934. Deaths brought in much money for missions and many new volunteers.

STANLEY, ARTHUR PENRHYN (1815-1881), Broad church Anglican divine, born at Alderley Rectory, Cheshire, England, educated at Rugby under Thomas Arnold, Balliol College, and University College. Ordained in 1839; after Dr. Arnold's death in 1842 Stanley wrote the biography of his teacher. In 1851 became Canon of Canterbury. Stanley made several trips to the Continent and to the Bible lands in the interest of historical studies. Made one trip to the United States. As a result of trip to Egypt and the Holy Land, wrote *Sinai and Palestine*. From 1856 to 1864, professor of ecclesiastical history at Oxford. At this time wrote: *Three Introductory Lectures on the Study of Ecclesiastical History, Lectures on the History of the Eastern Church,* and *Lectures on the History of the Jewish Church*. He also wrote *Essays on Church and State, The History of the Church of Scotland, Memorials of Canterbury* and *Commentary on the Epistles to the Corinthians.* In 1863 installed dean of Westminster. Member of the New Testament committee for the English Revised Version of the Bible. Favored both the union of the Anglican and the Eastern churches, also the return of the dissenters into the fold of the state church. Preaching was more ethical than doctrinal. From the evangelical or Low church was estranged because of his contempt of dogma and views of biblical criticism, inspiration, justification, and eternal punishment, and by his tolerance of ideas well-nigh Roman Catholic. From the High church differed on matters of ritual, vestments, lights, and traditional doctrines and practices. Chaplain for Queen Victoria for many years.

STANLEY, HENRY MORTON (1841-1904), African explorer and newspaper correspondent, born in Denbigh, Wales. Named after father, John Rowlands, who died when the lad was two years old. He spent his childhood in a poorhouse. When eighteen sailed as a cabin boy to New Orleans, Louisiana, where he was befriended and adopted in 1859 by a wealthy merchant, Henry Morton Stanley, whose name he took for his own. When twenty joined the Confederate army, taken prisoner at the battle of Shiloh in 1862. After release from prison made a visit to Wales, but soon returned to the United States. In 1864 joined the Union navy. After the war, took up newspaper work and became a foreign correspondent, first for the *New York Tribune* and the *Missouri Democrat,* and then for the *New York Herald* in 1868, traveling to many parts of the world. Real life work began when James Gordon Bennett, the proprietor of the *Herald* sent him to Africa to find David Livingstone, who for five years had been lost to the world. The story of his finding the long-lost missionary-explorer on Lake Tanganyika is told in his book, *How I Found Livingstone*. After spending four months with Livingstone in Africa, nursing him back to better health, leaving him supplies to continue his explorations, Stanley returned to Europe. In 1873 accompanied Lord Wolseley in his campaign against the Ashantis on the west coast of Africa. In 1874, hearing of Livingstone's death, determined to take up the unfinished task of the exploration. The *New York Herald* and the *London Daily Telegraph* shared the expense of fitting out the expedition. Crossed Africa from east to west. Though not a missionary, taught King Mtesa the principles of the Christian faith and translated part of the Bible for him, which led to Mtesa's acceptance of Christianity. Then Stanley called for missionaries to carry on the work, and missions were opened. Expeditions in Uganda covered a period of twenty years. Expedition down the Congo from its source to its mouth was the most dangerous and one of the most important expeditions. It led to the founding of the Congo Free State under the protection of the king of Belgium, also to the writing of *Through the Dark Continent*. In 1888 commanded an expedition for the relief of Emin Pasha, governor of the Egyptian Sudan. Following this period of exploration lectured in England, United States, and Australia. In 1892 repatriated himself and became a British subject. In 1895 entered parliament as a Liberal Unionist, working ardently to promote British interests in Africa. Knighted in 1899. Paid last visit to Africa in 1897. Another of his famous books: *In Darkest Africa*.

STAUPITZ (shtou'pĭts) **JOHANN VON** (c. 1469-1524), Augustinian vicar-general and a friend and spiritual guide of Martin Luther, born in Germany, educated at Leipzig and Tübingen. Prior of an Augustinian monastery, first at Tübingen and later at Munich. In 1502 Frederick the Wise appointed him dean and professor in the newly founded university at Wittenberg. The next year vicar-general of his order in Saxony. About this time Martin Luther came under his influence and direction. Advocated Bible study, reformation in morals in the church, and the strengthening of his order. In 1508 called Luther to teach at Wittenberg University. In 1510 sent him to Erfurt for advanced study. In 1512 Luther succeeded Staupitz as professor of theology at Wittenberg. By piety, personal influence, and most of all by his relation with Martin Luther, Staupitz occupies an important place in the early history of the Reformation. Evangelical without being a Protestant. In later years turned from the Augustinian order and joined the Benedictines. Theology was Augustinian, scriptural and mystical.

STEARNS, SHUBAL (1706-1771), Baptist minister. Born in Boston. Ordained as a Baptist minister in 1751. Worked in Virginia from 1754 to 1755. Greatest work at Sandy Creek, North Carolina after 1755. Helped to form Association of Separatist Baptists in 1706. Promoted spread of the Baptists in the South in the 1760s.

STEBBINS, GEORGE COLES (1846-1945), American gospel hymn writer, born on a farm near East Carlton, New York, educated at an academy in Albany. Soon after marriage in 1869 moved to Chicago where he worked for the Lyon and Healy Music Company. Became director of music in the First Baptist Church. In 1874 moved to Boston where he first led the singing in the church of Dr. A. J. Gordon; in 1876 became the music director in Tremont Temple. In these years began his lifelong acquaintance and fellowship with D. L. Moody, Ira D. Sankey, P. P. Bliss, and D. W. Whittle, then he began remarkable music career of Christian service. For many years one of the leading musical figures in the great evangelistic campaigns at home and abroad. He was the composer of over fifteen hundred hymns. In 1876 D. L. Moody induced Mr. Stebbins to join him in evangelistic work. He spent many years in this association, going with Mr. Moody three times abroad, twice to the Pacific Coast. Co-editor with Ira D. Sankey and James McGranahan of many widely accepted hymn books to which he contributed the music for such songs as "Some Day the Silver Cord Will Break," "Saved by Grace," "Have Thine Own Way, Lord," "Take Time to Be Holy," "True-Hearted, Whole-Hearted," "I Have Found a Friend," "Jesus, I Come," "Must I Go and Empty-Handed?" "There Is a Green Hill Far Away," "Ye Must Be Born Again," "Jesus Is Tenderly Calling."

STEPHEN, JAMES (1789-1859), Evangelical British Colonial Secretary. Born at Lambeth. Educated at Trinity Hall, Cambridge and Lincoln's Inn, London. Practiced law from 1811 to 1825. From 1813 to 1825 counsel to the Colonial Department and assistant (1834-1836) undersecretary and Secretary from 1836 to 1847. Drew up 1833 bill freeing slaves in the British Empire. From 1849 to 1850 professor of modern history at Cambridge and from 1855 professor at the East India College at Haileybury. An ardent Evangelical and strong supporter of missionaries while secretary for colonies.

STEWART, LYMAN (1840-1923), and **MILTON**. Headed what became the Union Oil Company, was its president and general manager from 1894 to 1905. Chairman of the board after 1905. Helped found and finance BIOLA (Bible Institute of Los Angeles). With Brother Milton gave $200,000 to finance the printing of *The Fundamentals* from 1910 to 1915.

STEWART, JAMES (1831-1905), missionary to South Africa, born in Edinburgh, Scotland. Studied at the University of Edinburgh, St. Andrews, and the divinity hall of the Free church. Studies covered a broad field, including arts, divinity, and medicine. In 1859 formally offered himself to his church for missionary service. In 1860 licensed as a probationary preacher of the Free church. In 1861, accompanied Mrs. David Livingstone to South Africa in her return from Scotland. Met Dr. Livingstone, and with him went up the Zambezi River. Several weeks later left to explore the Shire River, proceeding into the Nyasa territory in Central Africa, returning to Scotland in 1864 to report on discoveries. During the next two years he completed his medical studies, receiving medical degree. In 1866 married, and early the next year returned to Africa where he worked the rest of his life. Became an associate with William Govan, founder of Lovedale Institute in the northern part of Cape Colony; in 1870 became successor to Mr. Govan as principal of the Institute, serving in this capacity until his death in 1905. "Stewart of Lovedale" was the first great industrial and educational missionary in Africa, and developed the Institute until its influence was vitally felt among thousands of boys and girls of every tribe between the Cape and the Zambezi. First medical missionary to found a hospital for Africans and to train nurses and hospital assistants. In 1871-1872 founded the East Africa Mission of the Church of Scotland (the Kikuyu Mission). In 1873 started the Blythswood Institute, a second "Lovedale," in 1874 made a tour of Scotland in interest of these two institutions, and also proposed to the Union Free church the building of an institution in Nyasaland to be known as Livingstonia Institute, patterned after Lovedale Institute. In 1899 the United Free church of Scotland bestowed its highest honor by calling him to the moderatorship of the general assembly of the church. In 1902 delivered the Duff lectures on missions at the University of Edinburgh, the next year published as *Africa and Its Missions.* Also published *Lovedale, Past and Present; Dawn in the Dark Continent,* and *Livingstonia, Its Origin*. In 1904 back at Lovedale, telling students that he was home to stay. That year asked to preside over the first South African General Missionary Conference.

STILES (stīlz), **EZRA** (1727-1795), American Congregational minister and college president, born at North Haven, Connecticut, graduated from Yale College. Preached for a time to the Stockbridge Indians, tutor at Yale (1749-1755). Studied theology, but turned to law, admitted to the bar in 1753.

After practicing law for two years, was ordained in 1755 to the ministry and was pastor at Newport, Rhode Island (1755-1776). In 1776 congregation at Newport was broken up by the British occupation, moved to Portsmouth to become pastor; but in 1778 elected seventh president of Yale College, also professor of ecclesiastical history for fifteen years. Wrote much but published little; chief of published writings being a number of sermons, and *Literary Diary.* Left an unfinished *Ecclesiastical History of New England,* and more than forty manuscripts. Both during and preceding the Revolution, an ardent American patriot.

STILLINGFLEET (stĭl'ĭng flēt), **EDWARD** (1635-1699), Anglican prelate and theologian, born at Cranborne, Dorsetshire, England, studied at St. John's College, Cambridge, became a fellow in 1653. In 1657 became rector of Sutton, Bedfordshire, and in 1665 rector of St. Andrews, Holborn; two years later became chaplain to Charles II. Later became canon of Canterbury, archdeacon of London, canon of St. Paul's and later dean. After the revolution of 1689 appointed Bishop of Worcester. Stillingfleet was a man of latitudinarian views; in 1659 wrote his *Irenicon,* which advocated union between the Anglicans and the Presbyterians. His *Origines Sacrae,* and his *Rational Account of the Grounds of the Protestant Religion* were a defense of the Church of England against the charge of schism from the Catholic church. Two years before he died published *A Discourse in Vindication of the Doctrine of the Trinity.*

STODDARD (stŏd'ẽrd), **SOLOMON** (1643-1729), American Congregational minister, born in Boston, Massachusetts, graduated from Harvard College in 1662. First librarian of the college 1667-1674; for two years of this time chaplain in Barbados, preaching to the Dissenters of the island. Ordained in 1672. For many years (1670-1729) pastor at Northampton, Massachusetts. In 1727 grandson Jonathan Edwards became his colleague; upon the death of Stoddard in 1729, Edwards became sole pastor. Stoddard held the regenerating effect of the Lord's Supper, and its availability to the unconverted. Accepted the Half-Way Covenant as proposed by the synod of 1662, by which persons not sufficiently advanced in grace to qualify for full membership in the church may secure baptism for their children. Stoddard was the author of several theological works, among them: *A Guide to Christ, or the Way of Directing Souls in the Way of Conversion; The Doctrine of Instituted Churches;* and *A Treatise Concerning Conversion: The Way to Know Sincerity and Hypocrisy.* As a minister very successful in promoting revivals of religion in Northampton.

STONE, BARTON WARREN (1772-1844), co-founder of the Christian church, born near Port Tobacco, Maryland. Studied at David Caldwell's Academy at Guilford, North Carolina, and taught for a year in a Methodist academy in Washington, Georgia. Entered the Presbyterian ministry in 1796. In 1798 ordained, then became pastor at Cane Ridge, Kentucky which a short time later experienced a great revival and where a great camp meeting was held in 1801. Disagreement developed between him and the Presbyterian church; he with a few other ministers formed the Springfield Presbytery in 1803, but dissolved it a year later. His followers and those of Abner Jones and James O'Kelly together formed a body known as "Christians or Christian Church." Stone turned to farming and teaching for a while; spent the most of the next twenty years in forming churches in Ohio, Kentucky, and Tennessee. In 1826 began publishing the *Christian Messenger.* An ardent evangelist, became interested in the preaching of Alexander Campbell. In 1832 he and about ten thousand of his followers united with the Campbellites or Disciples of Christ. A majority of the "Stonites," who did not follow Barton Stone in this merger, continued as the Christian Church. This Christian Church continued as such until it merged with the Congregational church in 1931. Stone, Jones, and O'Kelly had formulated a set of six basic "Church Principles," the only statement or creed attempted for the Christian Church. In 1834 Stone moved to Jacksonville, Illinois, where he continued to preach and edit papers for the Disciples of Christ until his death ten years later.

STONE, JOHN TIMOTHY (1868-1954), American Presbyterian clergyman, born near Boston, Massachusetts, educated at Amherst College and at Auburn Theological Seminary. Ordained in the Presbyterian ministry in 1894 and held pastorates in the Olivet Church, Utica, New York; Courtland, New York; the Brown Memorial Church, Baltimore, Maryland, and the Fourth Presbyterian Church, Chicago, Illinois, serving in the last named from 1909 to 1930. During World War I served as chaplain, and was Y.M.C.A. religious director at Camp Grant, Illinois. From 1928 to 1940 president of McCormick Theological Seminary, becoming president emeritus in 1940. Moderator of the General Assembly (1913-1914). Author of *Footsteps in a Parish, Recruiting for Christ, Everyday Religion, Christianity in Action, Winning Men,* and *Places of Quiet Strength and Other Sermons.*

STONE, MARY (SHIH MAIYÜ) (1873-1954), born in Kiukiang, Kiangsi, China, daughter of a Chinese Methodist pastor who was the first ordained Chinese minister of Central China, and of a mother who was the first Chinese Christian woman of Central China. She and her sisters, Anna and Phoebe, were the first girls of that part of China to grow up with unbound feet. After receiving ten years of education in the Girls' Boarding School of the Methodist Mission at Kiukiang, in 1892, she and her friend Ida Kahn came with Miss Gertrude Howe, a missionary, to America to study medicine. In four years both graduated from the University of Michigan, becoming the first Chinese women to become doctors. After graduating they came to Chicago for several weeks to visit clinics. They met Dr. I. N. Danforth who took a special interest in them, and later made possible a modern hospital in Kiukiang for them. In the fall of 1896 Dr. Mary Stone and Dr. Ida Kahn returned to China. In 1900 the Elizabeth Skelton Danforth Hospital was built and opened with Dr. Stone as superintendent from 1902 to 1920. Kahn was soon called to Nanchang to open a medical work there. After spending eleven years of indefatigable labor, healing and training more than five hundred Chinese nurses, Dr. Stone found it necessary to return to the United States for an appendectomy and a needed rest. She then returned to her work in China. In 1917 she again returned to the United States for graduate work at Johns Hopkins. In 1920 Dr. Mary Stone and Miss Jennie V. Hughes founded Bethel Mission in Shanghai, with seven departments of work, including orphanages, grade and high schools, an evangelistic band, Bible schools for men and women, a hospital, and a nurses' training school. This nurses' training school was the largest such institution in China in that day, and has trained more than twenty-five thousand nurses. Bethel was moved to Hong Kong in 1938. Dr. Stone made several trips to the United States with Miss Hughes, and finally decided to select Pasadena, California as their headquarters. Here she died.

STONEHOUSE, NED BERNARD (1902-1962), New Testament scholar. Born in Grand Rapids, Michigan. Educated at Calvin College, Princeton Theological Seminary, Tübingen, and the Free University of Amsterdam (Ph.D.). Professor at Westminster Theological Seminary (1929-1962) and dean (1955-1962). Editor of the *New International Commentary* on the New Testament. Wrote the biography of J. Gresham Machen.

STOWE (stō), **HARRIET ELIZABETH BEECHER** (1811-1896), American author and abolitionist, born in Litchfield, Connecticut, daughter of Lyman Beecher, sister of Henry Ward Beecher. Attended school at Hartford, Connecticut where she studied for six years under her sister, Catherine, in the Female Seminary Catherine had started. Harriet was converted at the age of thirteen. Moved to Ohio with family in 1832. In 1836 she married Rev. Calvin Ellis Stowe, an ardent opponent of slavery, and professor of Hebrew at Lane Theological Seminary, where her father was president. In several trips to Kentucky with her husband she learned of the sad condition of many of the slaves. In 1852 she published the novel by which she is most widely known, *Uncle Tom's Cabin or Life Among the Lowly.* The novel was first published serially in 1851 in the *National Era,* an anti-slavery newspaper in Washington, D.C. Then in 1852 it was published in book form. Within five years five hundred thousand copies were sold in the United States, and many were sold in England also; it was translated into a score of languages. This book had perhaps more influence than anything else did in crystalizing anti-slavery sentiment, and had much bearing on precipitating the Civil War. In 1868 Mrs. Stowe became a joint editor of the *Hearth and Home* in Hartford. Among her many other books are *Dred: A Tale of the Great Dismal Swamp;* and *Footsteps of the Master.* Mother of seven children. Died in Hartford, Connecticut.

STRACHAN, JOHN (1778-1867), Bishop and educator. Born in Aberdeen, Scotland. School teacher in Kingston, Ontario (1799-1803). Ordained in 1803. Rector of St. James Church (1813-1867). Member for years of the legislative council of Upper Canada. First president of King's College, Toronto (later University of Toronto) in 1827. Bishop of Toronto in 1839. Founder and first president of Trinity College.

STRACHAN, ROBERT KENNETH (1910-1965). Born in Argentina of a missionary family which moved to Costa Rica. Educated at Wheaton College, Wheaton, Illinois and Dallas and Princeton theological seminaries. Returned to Costa Rica as a missionary under the Latin American Mission in 1936 to teach in the Bible seminary. Ordained in 1939. When his father died, he became general director of the mission from 1950 to 1965. Emphasized turning control of the work over to the Latin Americans. Developed Evangelism—in-depth, method of total mobilization of the Christian forces of the land by training, prayer, marches, personal work, and evangelism, to win the unconverted. Used first in Guatemala in 1962. Technique now used all over the world. Lecturer at Fuller Seminary from 1964-1965.

STRATON, JOHN ROACH (1875-1929), Fundamentalist Baptist clergyman. Born in Evansville, Indiana. Educated at Mercer and Baylor universities. Ordained in 1900. Pastor in Maryland, Virginia, and Illinois from 1903 to 1917 and from 1918 to 1929 of Calvary Baptist Church in New York City. Edited *The Calvary Pulpit* and *Faith Fundamentalist*. Organized the Fundamentalist League of New York state. Built Salisbury Hotel, which housed both the church and a hotel. Fought Modernism militantly. Upheld separation of church and state, justice for blacks, and women's rights.

STRAUSS, DAVID FRIEDRICH (1808-1874), German philosopher and theological writer, born near Stuttgart, Germany. Studied under Baur in the Protestant seminary at Blaubeuren, at Tübingen, and in Berlin under Schleiermacher and Hegel. Began his work as a country pastor. In 1830 taught for six months in the seminary at Maulbronn. In 1832 began to lecture at Tübingen; and in 1835 published his famous *Life of Jesus.* The book, patterned after the principles of Hegel, questioned the miracles, the inspiration of the Scriptures, the deity of Christ, the virgin birth, the facts of the crucifixion and the resurrection, and the post-resurrection appearances. He attempted to prove that the gospel narratives are of mythical origin and development. As a consequence of this writing lost his position at Tübingen. He was called to the professorship in Zurich in 1839. Strong opposition to his radical doctrines prevented his entering upon duties there; and in recompense he was given a small pension. Died of cancer, a materialist and pessimist; buried, by own request, without religious rites of any kind. Among other writings: *Christian Theology* and *Christ of Faith and the Jesus of History.*

STRAWBRIDGE, ROBERT (died 1781), early Methodist preacher in the American colonies, born at Drummersnave, County Antrim, Ireland, came to America between 1759-1766, settled on Sam's Creek, Frederick County, Maryland. Began to preach as a lay preacher in his own house, formed a society near Sam's Creek, where he erected a log chapel, which may have been the first Methodist meeting house built in America. Refused to submit to the rules of the Conference, which had been called and moderated by Thomas Rankin in 1773; named dropped from the minutes. In 1775 name reappears as second preacher in the Frederick Circuit. In 1776 moved family to a farm and continued to preach, leaving the care of the farm and family to his neighbors. Took charge of the Sam's Creek and Bush Forest societies, preaching for these people with great success for the next five years.

STREETER, BURNET HILLMAN (1874-1937), Anglican New Testament textual critic and religious philosopher, born at Croydon, England, educated at Queen's College, Oxford. Fellow and dean of Pembroke College, Oxford (1899-1905), fellow of Queen's College, Oxford (1905-1933), provost (1933-1937). Professor of exegesis at Oxford University (1932-1933), canon of Hereford (1915-1934). Sought to correlate science and theology, and was interested in contemporary problems confronting the Christian faith. An active supporter of Student Christian Movement, and Modern Churchmen's Union; later years of Oxford Group Movement, founded by Dr. Frank Buchman. His main interest was the philosophy of religion, but his most significant contribution was in the field of New Testament textual studies. Author of *The Four Gospels: a Study of Origins;* and *The Primitive Church.*

STRONG, AUGUSTUS HOPKINS (1836-1921), Baptist minister and theologian, born at Rochester, New York, educated at Yale University, Rochester Theological Seminary, and University of Berlin. While in Yale became a Christian under the preaching of Charles G. Finney; upon graduation went to the seminary to prepare for the ministry. After seminary spent two years traveling in Germany. Ordained in 1861. Upon return to America pastor for five years of a Baptist church in Haverhill, Massachusetts; for six years in Cleveland, Ohio. From 1872 to 1912 president of Rochester Theological Seminary. Taught systematic theology at seminary and preached largely on doctrinal subjects. Writings were likewise on theology and Christian philosophy. Wrote *Systematic Theology* (three volumes), *Philosophy and Religion, Christ in Creation and Ethical Monism, The Great Poets and Their Theology,* and *The American Poets and their Theology.* Theologically conservative but influenced by German philosophical idealism and theistic evolution. Augustus Strong exerted great influence upon the thought and theology of the Baptist church. Highly regarded as a teacher and leader, both by the North and South. As an administrator, kind and gracious. For many years also a trustee of Vassar College. Influenced John D. Rockefeller to support education in the Baptist church, and thus somewhat indirectly had a part in the founding of the University of Chicago. A churchman as well as a schoolman; kept in close touch with the Baptist churches throughout his life. From

1892 to 1895 president of the American Baptist Foreign Missionary Society. When the Northern Baptist Convention was formed in 1905, he became its first president until 1910.

STRONG, JAMES (1822-1894), Methodist biblical scholar and educator, born in New York City; after graduating from Wesleyan University, Middletown, Connecticut, taught ancient languages in the Troy Conference Academy, West Poultney, Vermont (1844-1846). Withdrawing from teaching for two years served as president of the Flushing Railroad Company. Also active in civic affairs; during these years continued study of ancient languages. In 1853 again entered the teaching profession as professor of biblical literature and acting president of Troy University (1858-1863), professor of exegetical theology in Drew Theological Seminary, Madison, New Jersey from 1868 until his retirement in 1893. Author of *English Harmony and Exposition of the Gospels; Harmony of the Gospels in the Greek of the Received Text;* and *Sketches of Jewish Life in the First Century.* Most important work, however, was editing of the ten-volume set of *Cyclopaedia of Biblical, Theological, and Ecclesiastical Literature,* with two supplementary volumes. Edited the first three volumes in collaboration with Dr. John McClintock, and the others alone. Another great work was his *Exhaustive Concordance of the Bible*. In theology, conservative. Strongly defended the Mosaic authorship of the Pentateuch and contended that there was but one Isaiah; also supported the theory that Paul was the author of Hebrews. A member of the Anglo-American Bible Revision Committee.

STRONG, JOSIAH (1847-1916), American clergyman, born at Naperville, Illinois, educated at Western Reserve College, Hudson, Ohio, and at Lane Theological Seminary, Cincinnati, Ohio. Home missionary at Cheyenne, Wyoming (1871-1873), chaplain and instructor in natural theology in Western Reserve College (1873-1876), pastor at Sandusky, Ohio (1876-1881), secretary of the Ohio Home Missionary Society (1881-1884), pastor in Cincinnati (1884-1886), and secretary of the Evangelical Alliance (1886-1898). In 1898 organized the League for Social Service which in 1902 was reorganized as the American Institute of Social Service. Remained head of this organization from its inception until his death in 1916. Became one of the leaders of the social gospel movement. Called to England to aid in the establishing of the British Institute for Social Service. In 1911 president of the Social Center Association of America. Urged that the churches cooperate in helping to Christianize the social order and in bringing to realization "the Kingdom" as an ideal society here upon the earth. Had an influential part in helping to form the Federal Council of the Churches of Christ in America (1901-1908). Coined the slogan "Safety First." Edited *Social Progress* (1904-1907) and after 1908 edited the *Gospel of the Kingdom*. Wrote *The New Era, The Twentieth Century City, Religious Movements for Social Betterment, The Next Great Awakening, The Challenge of the City,* and *Studies in the Gospel of the Kingdom*.

STUART, MOSES (1780-1852), American Congregational theologian and educator, born at Wilton, Connecticut, studied at Yale University, then studied law at Newton. Though admitted to the bar never practiced law. Under the influence of President Dwight of Yale entered the ministry. Ordained in 1806, became pastor of the First Church of Christ (Congregational) in New Haven. In 1810 called to the professorship of sacred literature at Andover Theological Seminary, where he remained until retirement in 1848. At once began the serious study of Hebrew, and in 1821 printed a large Hebrew grammar, the first to appear in America. Began the study of German in order to be able to read scholarly German literature, and was one of the first scholars to introduce German methods of scholarship in the United States. Translated Winer's *Greek Grammar of the New Testament,* and *Hebrew Grammar of Gesenius as Edited by Roediger* from the German. Wrote commentaries on *Hebrews, Romans, Revelation, Daniel, Ecclesiastes,* and *Proverbs.* He also wrote *Hebrew Chrestomathy; Grammar of the New Testament Dialect; Hints on the Prophecies;* and *Critical History and Defense of the Old Testament Canon*. Altogether produced more than forty works. In earlier ministry took part in the Unitarian controversy that was disrupting the Congregational church. He was for the defense of the old orthodox creed. In the course of labors taught more than fifteen hundred ministers, seventy men who became professors and presidents of colleges, a hundred foreign missionaries, and about thirty translators of the Bible into foreign languages.

STUDD, CHARLES T. (1862-1931), missionary pioneer, born in England. C. T. Studd's father, Edward, had been converted in the Moody-Sankey campaign in 1877. Father then became deeply concerned about the spiritual welfare of his three sons. By the time C. T. was sixteen he had become an expert cricket player; when nineteen captain of his team at Eton. After finishing Eton

College, attended Cambridge University (1880-1883), and here, too, was an outstanding cricketer. In 1883, while still at Cambridge, he heard Moody and Sankey and was converted, dedicating life and inherited wealth to Christ. He gave away about $150,000 while in China. He and six others, the famous "Cambridge Seven," offered themselves to Hudson Taylor for missionary service in the China Inland Mission and in 1885 sailed for China. They at once began the study of the language, donned Chinese garb, and ate with the Chinese, trying to substitute Chinese for Western ways, and to identify themselves with the natives. Three years later Studd married a young Irish missionary from Ulster. By 1894 the Studds were broken in health, and had to return to England. Unable to return to China they severed their connection with the China Inland Mission and turned their property over to the mission. In 1896-97 Mr. Studd toured the universities of America in behalf of the newly formed Student Volunteer Movement. In 1900 the family went to South India in search of a climate more conducive to Mr. Studd's health and for a place to serve. For six years C. T. Studd was pastor of the Union Church at Ootacamund, South India. After their return to England in 1906, he began to plan with Dr. Karl Kumm on a scheme of opening Africa from the Nile to the Niger for Christian missions. In 1910, leaving his wife and four daughters in England to care for the secretarial responsibilities for both the home base and the field, he started on his journey to penetrate the heart of Africa. On a part of the trip he was accompanied by Alfred Buxton, a young man who later became his son-in-law. The Heart of Africa Mission was organized in 1912. A mission was established at Niangara in 1913, in June 1915 twelve converts were baptized. Late in 1914 Studd returned to England for more missionaries, and in 1916 to Africa with a party of missionaries. In 1919 Gilbert Barclay, another son-in-law, joined the mission which was named the Worldwide Evangelization Crusade. Studd died in Africa two and a half years after Mrs. Studd, who had died in Malaga.

STURM, JAKOB (1498-1553), German reformer and statesman, born at Strassburg, Germany. Educated at Heidelberg and Freiburg. In 1506 became a member of the faculty at Freiburg. Later became a member of the city council; in 1526 chief magistrate of native city; represented Strassburg and other imperial cities in the imperial diet. Early became an adherent of the Reformation doctrine; and as a statesman advocated an alliance of all the evangelical groups in Germany and Switzerland into a political alliance based on a common anti-Roman confession of faith. In this ably seconded by Martin Bucer, the evangelical pastor at Strassburg. At Council of Spires in 1529 joined the evangelicals in their protest against the Catholic reaction, thus becoming one of the original "Protestants." The same year took part in the Marburg Colloquy. In 1530 presented to the Augsburg diet the Confessio Tetrapolitana, the first effort at a statement of the Reformed faith, but not accepted as was the Augsburg Confession of the Lutherans. Owing to Sturm's influence, Strassburg joined the Schmalkaldic League in 1531.

STURM, JOHANNES (1507-1589), German humanist and educational reformer, born at Schleiden (Sleida), received education at Liege and the University of Louvain. From 1530 to 1536 taught at Paris, where influenced by the writings of Martin Bucer, the evangelical pastor at Strassburg, he adopted the principles of the Reformation. Used his influence in the support of the Reformed church. Though a Protestant, ever cherished the hope of a reconciliation between the Reformation and the Roman Catholic parties. Reorganized the educational system of Strassburg; in 1538 founded the Gymnasium of Strassburg, which he directed for over forty years. It became the most famous classical school in Germany and a pattern for many other similar schools. Generally regarded as the greatest educator connected with the Reformed church, and influence has been potent in the German system of secondary education down to our day. His system also exercised considerable influence on the Jesuit system of education. Believed that all instruction should have an ethical and a spiritual side, aim being "piety, knowledge, and eloquence."

STURM OF FULDA (710-779), monk, born in Bavaria, worked with, studied under Boniface, Archbishop of Mainz. Received further education in Rome, ordained priest in 733, a missionary in Hesse for three years. In 744 founded the great Benedictine monastery at Fulda, which became a center for German Christianity and civilization of learning and priestly education. After the death of Boniface conflicts arose between Boniface's successor, Lullus, and Sturm, first concerning the remains of Boniface, and then concerning the administration of the property of Fulda. Banished, later recalled and restored to his monastery. Secured the remains of his beloved teacher and buried him at Fulda according to Boniface's wishes. Charlemagne, who highly regarded Sturm, employed him in diplomatic affairs and sent him as missionary among the Saxons. He made a distinct contribution to the general education and culture in the churches and schools of central Germany.

SUAREZ, FRANCISCO DE (1548-1617), Jesuit philosopher and theologian. Born in Granada, Spain. Studied at Salamanca. Entered Jesuit order in 1564. Ordained in 1572. Taught from 1571 except for 1580 to 1585 in the Roman College, Spanish universities and from 1597 to 1615 in Coimbra, Portugal. Helped develop basis for international law and opposed divine right theory. His *Metaphysical Disputations* which linked Aristotle and Aquinas was a standard text in both Protestant and Roman Catholic schools in the seventeenth century.

SUGER (c. 1081-1151) Abbot of St. Denis near Paris from 1122. In 1106 became provost of Berneval. Ordained priest in 1122. Regent of France during the Second Crusade. Wrote detailed record of the building of the abbey church which is an important record of the construction of the first major Gothic structure.

SULLIVAN, SIR ARTHUR SEYMOUR (1842-1900), English composer, born in Lambeth, London, sang in the Chapel Royal when twelve years old. When fourteen won the Mendelssohn scholarship at the Royal Academy of Music, and later continued studies at Leipzig Conservatory. From 1861 to 1872 organist at St. Michael's Church in London; in 1866 became professor of composition at the Royal Academy of Music. Set to music Adelaide Proctor's poem, "The Lost Chord." For two years conductor of the London Philharmonic Orchestra. Made a member of the Legion of Honor in 1878, principal of the National Training School for Music (1876-1881), knighted in 1883. Died in London, buried in St. Paul's Cathedral. Produced the cantata *Kenilworth,* the oratorios *The Prodigal Son* and *The Light of the World,* the overtures *The Martyr of Antioch* and *The Golden Legend,* and the grand opera *Ivanhoe*. To the general public, however, better known for his fifty-six hymn tunes and songs, some of them: "Onward, Christian Soldiers," "I've Found a Friend, O Such a Friend," and "Make Me a Captive, Lord." Much of his Church music is of high order. Collaborated with W. S. Gilbert in writing comic operas, two famous pieces being the *Mikado* and *H.M.S. Pinafore*.

SUNDAY, WILLIAM ASHLEY (1862-1935), evangelist, born at Ames, Iowa four months after his father had enlisted in the Union Army and a month before his father died. Spent part of his boyhood in two army orphanages. Studied for a short time at Northwestern University. From 1883 to 1891 was a professional baseball player with the Chicago, Pittsburgh, and Philadelphia teams of the National League. Converted in 1886 through the street preaching of Harry Monroe of the Pacific Garden Mission. From 1891 to 1893 assistant secretary of the Young Men's Christian Association in Chicago, leaving a five-thousand-dollar-a-year salary as a baseball player for seventy-five dollars a month in the Y.M.C.A. From 1893 to 1895 was associated with J. Wilbur Chapman. During World War I did some evangelistic work in the army camps. In 1903 ordained to the Presbyterian ministry in Chicago. Individualistic, unconventional, and sensational in his preaching, but did it with telling effect, attracting immense crowds. It is estimated that perhaps three hundred thousand converts were won through his efforts. In theology, a staunch conservative. Was evangelist from 1893 to 1935.

SUNG, JOHN (1901-1944), nationally famous Chinese evangelist; born at Hinghwa, Fukien, China; son of a Methodist pastor. Confessed Christ about age nine. Brilliant student; studied in Ohio Wesleyan University, Ohio State University, and Union Theological Seminary. Received Ph.D. in chemistry. Returned to China to preach the gospel rather than to teach science. Spent fifteen years in evangelistic preaching throughout China and surrounding countries with unique power and influence.

SUSO (zōō'zō), **HEINRICH (AMANDUS VON BERG)** (c. 1300-1366), German Dominican monk and mystic, born at Uberlingen, Baden, on Lake Constance. About 1313 entered a Dominican monastery at Constance. While studying in Cologne about 1328 became a disciple of Meister Eckhart. Subjected himself to the severest ordeals of asceticism until about 1340 when he became so weakened that he was compelled to discontinue it. He had a close fellowship with the Friends of God. In 1340 began traveling, preaching, hearing confessions, and winning many by his gentle, persuasive eloquence. About 1348 settled in Ulm, where he passed his last eighteen years in the Dominican monastery. His *Book of Eternal Wisdom,* a dialogue between Christ and himself, became one of the books on meditation of the Middle Ages. *Autobiography* portrays his meditations and experiences.

SWAIN (swān), **CLARA A.** (1834-1910), American Methodist pioneer missionary, born in Elmira, New York, family soon moving to Castile. Received education piecemeal and taught school at times. Studied for three years in the Castile Sanitarium under Dr. Cordelia A. Greene, then pursued a medical course at the Women's Medical College in Philadelphia, graduating in 1869. In 1869 appointed as a medical missionary to India under the sponsorship of the Women's Foreign Missionary Society of the Methodist church. Sailed with Miss Isabella Thoburn, arriving in Bareilly early the next year (1870). Work centered there for fourteen years, although she was back in the United States because of ill health from 1876 to 1879. Said to have been first fully accredited woman physician to be sent by any missionary society to the non-Christian world. Became associated with the girls' orphanage at Bareilly, and at once started a medical class of fourteen native girls, thirteen of whom in 1873 were granted certificates authorizing them to practice "in all ordinary diseases." Also carried on a large practice among women and children. In 1873 or 1874 the first women's hospital in India was opened, Miss Swain continuing her work there until 1885. At the request of the Mohammedan Rajah of Khetri, Rajputana, she became physican to the ladies of the palace from 1885 to 1896. In 1896 returned to the United States for her remaining years, revisiting India in 1906-1908 and attending the golden jubilee of the Methodist Mission.

SWEDENBORG (svā'dĕn bôrg), **EMMANUEL** (1688-1772), mystic and scientist; founder of the Church of the New Jerusalem, born in Stockholm, Sweden. He was given a good education, early developed a sensitive, spiritual nature. At twenty-one received his Ph.D. at Uppsala. Following graduation traveled extensively. Became especially interested in mathematics and the natural sciences. In 1716 the king appointed him to a responsible position in the College of Mines, which he held with success until 1747. After having attained the highest rank among the scientists and philosophers of his time, laid aside philosophical and scientific studies and turned attention to questions of spiritual and religious nature. In 1743, at the age of fifty-five, claimed to have had a revelation which opened to him a view of the spiritual world. This first revelation was followed by others between 1743 and 1749 in which he claimed that deep secrets of the universe were revealed to him. After a time he decided to give up his worldly learning and activities to devote himself to theological speculations and to recording his "revelations." This he did for the next thirty years. Became a prolific writer—claimed that his system was not a substitute for the Bible, but that it was the key to the true understanding of the Scriptures, which he interpreted allegorically. Revived some of the old Gnostic teachings. System had no place for original sin, justification by faith, atonement, bodily resurrection, future coming of Christ. Claimed that the second coming of Christ was a spiritual return, and that it had already occurred in 1757. Swendenborgian church, foretold in Revelation, he said, came to earth in 1771. In 1787 the New Jerusalem church was organized in London. The movement has not spread to any considerable extent.

SWEET, WILLIAM WARREN (1881-1959), Methodist minister, educator, historian, born at Baldwin, Kansas, studied at Ohio Wesleyan University, Drew Theological Seminary, Crozer Theological Seminary, and University of Pennsylvania. In 1906 ordained in the Methodist Episcopal church, served as pastor in Pennsylvania for five years. Professor of history in Ohio Wesleyan University and DePauw University between 1911 and 1927, dean of Liberal Arts in the latter (1926-1927). Professor of history of American Christianity at the University of Chicago (1927-1946), professor emeritus after 1946. Professor of church history at Garrett Biblical Institute (1946-1948) visiting professor or lecturer at a number of universities in the United States and England 1946-1957. Author of twenty-seven books on religion, specializing in the history of men and movements. Books include *The American Churches: An Interpretation; Religion in the Development of American Culture; Our American Churches; Makers of Christianity; Methodism in American History; The Story of Religion in America;* and *Religion in Colonial America*. His latest work was a four-volume set, *Religion on the American Frontier* (Baptists, Congregationalists, Methodists, and Presbyterians). Stressed influence of American frontier on religion.

SWETE (swēt), **HENRY BARCLAY** (1835-1917), Anglican biblical and Patristic scholar, born at Redlands, Bristol, England, educated at King's College, London, and at Gonville and Caius Colleges, Cambridge. Ordained priest in 1859, and served as pastor and as divinity lecturer in the University of Cambridge (1875-1877), rector of Ashdon, Essex (1877-1890). Examiner chaplain to the bishop of St. Albans (1881-1890) and professor of pastoral theology at King's College (1882-1890). From 1890 to 1915, when he retired, regius professor of divinity at Cambridge, also Lady Margaret preacher (1902-1903). In 1911 made honorary chaplain to the king. Perhaps the most important of his many works was *The Old Testament in Greek according to the Septuagint,* a masterpiece of sound scholarship. Wrote also *History of the Doctrine of the Procession of the Holy Spirit; The Holy Spirit in the Ancient*

Church; The Holy Spirit in the New Testament; An Introduction to the Old Testament in Greek; The Apostles' Creed in Relation to Primitive Christianity; The Apocalypse of John; The Appearances of Our Lord after the Passion; The Life of the World to Come; Patristic Study, and *The Gospel According to St. Mark*. Helped found *Journal of Theological Studies* in 1899.

SWIFT, JONATHAN (1667-1745), British satirist, born at Dublin, Ireland of English parents, studied at Trinity College, Dublin, and Oxford University. During Revolution of 1688 went to England and became secretary to Sir William Temple for six years. Returned to Ireland and ordained in 1695; for two years served a small country church at Kilroot, near Belfast; then returned to Temple, when he began his political writing. In 1713 Queen Anne appointed him dean of St. Patrick's in Dublin in the Established Church of Scotland, which position he held until death, and where he did greatest literary work. Died of a severe disease of the brain, leaving his fortune for the founding of an asylum for the insane. Buried in his own cathedral in Dublin. Though "the most thoroughgoing of pessimists," was a benevolent and charitable spirit. Spent a third of income on charities. The most famous of his nearly one hundred writings is *Gulliver's Travels.* Other notable works were: *The Battle of the Books, The Tale of a Tub, Drapier's Letters,* and *Journal to Stella*.

SWING, DAVID (1830-1894), American Presbyterian clergyman, born in Cincinnati, Ohio, grew up on a farm, and educated at Miami University, Oxford, Ohio, where he became professor of languages (1852-1864). Studied Old School theology for a while under Dr. Nathan L. Rice, but recoiling under this study, finished theological study under a local pastor, meanwhile supplying neighboring pulpits until 1866, when he accepted call to the Fourth Presbyterian Church in Chicago. Gained a reputation as a preacher of force and deep spirituality. Charged with heresy by Dr. Francis L. Patton in 1874, and though acquitted by the Chicago Presbytery, resigned his pastorate and withdrew from the Presbyterian ministry. Continued to hold meetings in a theater, and after 1878 to the end of his life was pastor of the Central Church, where he preached to one of the largest congregations in Chicago. Edited *The Alliance* (1873-1882) and *The Weekly Magazine* (1875-1894).

T

TACITUS, CORNELIUS (c. 55-117), pagan Latin historian. Best source of information on first century Roman rulers and their reigns and the pagan environment of the early church. Records Pilate's execution of Christ and the persecution in Rome in 64 of the church by Nero.

TAIT, ARCHIBALD CAMPBELL (1811-1882). Born in Scotland. Educated at Balliol College, Oxford and ordained as an Anglican in 1835. Principal of Rugby from 1842 to 1848. Archbishop of Canterbury in 1868. Chairman of Lambeth Conference in 1878. Supported disestablishment of the Anglican church in Ireland. Was a Broad churchman.

TALMAGE (tăl′mĭj), **THOMAS DeWITT** (1832-1902), American Presbyterian minister and lecturer, born near Bound Brook, New Jersey. Studied law for a time at the University of the City of New York, turned to theology and studied at the New Brunswick Theological Seminary of the Dutch Reformed church. In 1856 ordained and entered first pastorate at Belleville, New Jersey. From 1856 to 1869 served as pastor in three Reformed churches in New Jersey, New York, and Pennsylvania; from 1869 to 1899 pastor for the Presbyterians in New York and Washington, D.C. Chaplain in the Union Army during the Civil War. In 1870 his congregation erected the Brooklyn Tabernacle with a seating capacity of four thousand. This building and its two successive structures were destroyed by fires in 1872, 1889, and 1894. From 1895 to 1899 pastor of the First Presbyterian Church in Washington, D.C., retiring in 1899. In later years sermons were simultaneously published through newspaper syndicates in over thirty-five hundred papers in the United States and abroad. From 1890 to 1892 editor of *The Christian Herald*. Famous as a lecturer in the United States and Europe.

TAPPAN, ARTHUR (1786-1865), philanthropist and abolitionist. Born Northampton, Massachusetts. Silk merchant in Portland, Maine in 1807. By 1826 had a wholesale silk establishment in New York City. Founded *New York Journal of Commerce* in 1827. He and his brother Lewis built a tabernacle for Finney in New York. Helped found Oberlin College in 1835. Founder and president of American Anti-Slavery Society in 1833. Aided abolitionists with money and men.

TAPPAN, LEWIS (1788-1873). Born in Northampton, Massachusetts. Partner in silk business with brother Arthur from 1828 to 1841 after having his own hardware business from 1813 to 1828. Established first American credit rating organization in 1841, "The Mercantile Agy." Helped found the American Anti-Slavery Society in 1833.

TASSO (täs′sō), **TORQUATO** (1544-1595), Italian poet of the late Renaissance, born at Sorrento, near Naples, Italy. Educated by the Jesuits at Naples and Rome, pursued law at Padua and classical studies at Bologna. Chief work was *Jerusalem Delivered,* an epic poem celebrating the heroic deeds of Godfrey of Bouillon in the First Crusade. Shortly after completing epic in 1575, due to excessive religious scruples and an overwrought aesthetic sensitiveness, feared that he was being persecuted by critics. Delusions became so serious that for seven years (1579-1586) confined to the insane asylum of St. Anna in Ferrara. Upon final release he wandered from place to place in search of peace and satisfaction.

TATE, NAHUM (1652-1715), English psalmist, playwright and poet laureate, born in Dublin, Ireland, educated at Trinity College, Dublin. Went to London, in 1692 made poet laureate. Collaborated with Nicholas Brady (1695-1726) in producing *A New Version of the Psalms of David* in meter. His psalter found wide acceptance on both sides of the Atlantic. It contains some fairly poetical portions, some that are still well adapted to public worship where metrical psalms are preferred, and a few that are able to hold their own simply as hymns. In 1702 named historiographer-royal. "While Shepherds Watched Their Flocks by Night" is attributed to him.

TATIAN (tā′shăn), **THE APOLOGIST** (second century). Born in Assyria. When, in his travels, he stumbled upon the Bible, its simplicity and beauty attracted his attention and won him to the Christian faith. Became a pupil or disciple of Justin Martyr, and a teacher. Chief writing was his *Oratio,* a defense of the Christian faith and a condemnation of the pagan philosophies. Also wrote a harmony of the gospels, known as the *Diatessaron*.

TAULER (tou′lẽr), **JOHANN** (c. 1300-1361) medieval German mystic and preacher, born at Strassburg, Germany, about 1315 entered a Dominican monastery, and studied theology at Cologne, and perhaps at Paris. Most of his work was done at Strassburg, Cologne, and Basel. Became a friend and disciple of Meister Eckhart. He was, however, more practical, devotional, and evangelistic than Eckhart. In a distressed age, a preacher of helpfulness. Emphasized an inward religion and an immediate communion with God, unity of the soul with God. Condemned dependence on external ceremonies and dead works, preached against the abuses and sins of the times, and longed for a purified, reformed church. Held the admiration of Martin Luther. Associated for a time with the "Friends of God."

TAUSEN, HANS (1494-1561), Danish Reformer, born at Birkende on the island of Fünen, Denmark. After receiving early education in schools near home, including studying in the monastery of the Knights of St. John at Antoorskov, spent a year and a half at Wittenberg under Luther's teaching. After returning to native country became a popular Reformation preacher at Viborg. The Bible had been translated into the Danish language in 1523. In 1526 Frederick I came out openly in favor of the Reformation in Denmark, and made Tausen his royal chaplain. The clergy opposed Tausen's reformatory preaching and the archbishop imprisoned him. He tried to exclude Tausen from the churches; but the people broke open the doors of the Franciscan church. Also preached to large crowds in the open air, and lectured on theology at the University of Copenhagen. In 1528 published a baptismal formula for the evangelical church service, and introduced singing in the Danish tongue. The first Danish priest to marry, and first to use Danish instead of the Latin in the church service. In 1529 became pastor of the Church of St. Nicholas in Copenhagen. In 1530, under Tausen's leadership "the Forty-three Articles of Copenhagen," an independent counterpart of the Augsburg Confession, was laid before the assembly to become the Danish evangelical confession of faith. Tausen urged and practiced moderation in the process of changing from the old usages of the church to the new. In 1537 professor of Hebrew at the University of Copenhagen, and in 1542 consecrated Bishop of Ribe (Ripen), Jutland, a position held until death twenty years later. Under the evangelical king, Christian III, Tausen preached, translated the Psalms, wrote hymns, published sermons and Reformation treatises.

TAYLOR, GRAHAM (1851-1938), American sociologist, born at Schenectady, New York, received education at Rutgers College in New York, and at the Reformed Theological Seminary, New Brunswick, New Jersey. In 1873 ordained to the Dutch Reformed ministry, pastor of the Reformed church, Hopewell, New York for seven years, and then of the Fourth Congregational Church, Hartford, Connecticut for twelve years. Also professor of practical theology at the Hartford Theological Seminary (1888-1892). In 1892 became professor of social economics in the Chicago Theological Seminary. Founder and resident warden of the Chicago Commons Social Settlement, one of the most widely known social settlements in the United States. He exerted a wide influence as arbiter in labor troubles. He was president of the Chicago School of Civics and Philanthropy (1903-1920) and associate editor of *The Survey*. Wrote *Religion in Social Action, Pioneering on Social Frontiers,* and *Chicago Commons Through Forty Years*.

TAYLOR, JAMES HUDSON (1832-1905), founder of China Inland Mission, born in Barnsley, Yorkshire, England. After spending time in the study of medicine and theology, went to China under the newly formed China Evangelization Society, arriving in Shanghai in 1854. He stressed prayer and faith only in money raising. Adopted Chinese dress. For six months lived in the home of Dr. Medhurst of the London Missionary Society, whose book *China* had helped stir him to go to China. Spent years 1854 to 1860 working in Shanghai, Swatow, and Ningpo. Before long retired from the society which had sent him out and continued as an independent worker. At Ningpo he had charge of a hospital, in 1858 married Maria Dyer, the daughter of a missionary in China. In 1860 returned home, spent the next five years translating the New Testament into the Ningpo dialect, writing a book on China, and praying for missionaries for inland China. His definite planning in 1865 at Brighton to establish a society for the evangelizaton of inland China and return to China in 1866 with his wife and children and sixteen new missionaries was the beginning of the China Inland Mission. Became the director of the mission, traveled widely in China and Europe in its interest. Returned to China in 1872. At his death in 1905 at Changsha, there were 205 stations with 849 missionaries, and 125,000 Chinese Christians in the China Inland Mission.

TAYLOR, JEREMY (1613-1667), Anglican bishop and devotional writer, born in Cambridge, educated at Gaius College, Cambridge. In 1635 through Archbishop Laud, secured a fellowship at All Soul's College, Oxford. In 1638 Laud had him appointed rector of Uppingham, which preferment he held for four years, but lost it with Parliament's ascendency over the king.

During the Civil War chaplain in ordinary to King Charles I, and remained committed to the Royalist party. In 1643 appointed to the rectory of Overstone, Northamptonshire. In 1644 a prisoner of the army of the Commonwealth; but the next year released, and retired to Wales where he became principal in a school at Newton Hall, Carmarthenshire, and also chaplain to the earl of Carbery at Golden Grove. During these ten years of forced retirement in Wales, covering most of the period of the Commonwealth, produced the chief works that came from his pen. Best works were, *Life of Liberty, Life of Christ, Liberty of Prophesying, The Rule and Experience of Holy Living, The Rule and Experience of Holy Dying,* and *The Real Presence of Christ in the Sacrament,* and two series of sermons. In 1658 removed to Ireland and served an English church parish at Lisburn and at Portmore, near Dublin. For some strange reason, after the Restoration in 1660, instead of being given a prominent place in the English Church, made vice chancellor of the University of Dublin, and was elevated to the bishopric of Down and Connor in Ulster. Rendered distinguished service in the reorganization of the university, zealous and active as a bishop, serving church well.

TAYLOR, NATHANIEL WILLIAM (1786-1858), American Congregational preacher, teacher and theologian, born at New Milford, Connecticut, educated at Yale, studying theology under Timothy Dwight. Ordained in 1812 he became pastor of the First Church in New Haven (1811-1822), and then became Dwight professor of theology at Yale Divinity School from 1822 to 1858. As a preacher influential, especially in connection with "revivals." On the basis of the earlier Edwardean or New England Theology worked out an elaborate system of modified Calvinism with special insistence on the freedom of the will. System gained numerous adherents and powerfully affected the theological thought and preaching in America; came to be known as "The New Haven Theology," or "Taylorism." It was one of the most influential of the types of the so-called "New School Theology" pervading both the Presbyterian and the Congregational churches in Taylor's day. His "heretical" teaching at Yale Divinity School led to the founding of Hartford Theological Seminary in opposition to his views.

TAYLOR, WILLIAM (1821-1902), Methodist evangelist and missionary bishop of Africa, born in Rockbridge County, Virginia, of Scottish-Irish descent, received a very meager education. Ordained in 1847. Preached widely in many countries of the world. Made more than sixty sea voyages. Preached in the United States and Canada (1848-1861). Organized the first Methodist church in San Francisco. He spent eight years preaching, mostly in Australia; but also toured and preached in the British Isles, the Holy Land, Egypt, South Africa, West Indies, and Europe (1861-1870). Called to India by the young missionary, James M. Thoburn. From 1877-1884 started missions and sent missionaries to South America, urging self-support of missionaries on the field. The fifth and last period was the African period of thirteen years. From 1884 to 1897 he was missionary bishop of Africa. Established a chain of missions on the Congo. Because of failing health, retired in 1896, but made another tour and spent another year preaching in Africa. Last five years spent quietly with his family in California. Bishop Taylor was a strong advocate of the self-supporting, self-propagating, indigenous church.

TAYLOR, WILLIAM MACKERGO (1829-1895), Congregational minister, born at Kilmarnock, Scotland, graduated from the University of Glasgow and the Divinity Hall of the United Presbyterian Church, Edinburgh. Ordained in 1853 at Kilmaurs, Ayrshire, pastor there one year, then called to the Derby Road Church, Liverpool, England, where he labored for sixteen years. In 1871 visited the United States, the next year invited to become pastor of the Congregational Broadway Tabernacle, New York. Held this pastorate until 1892. Lyman Beecher lecturer in Yale Seminary in 1876 and in 1886, and the L. P. Stone lecturer in Princeton Seminary in 1880. Preacher of world renown. Suffering from a stroke in 1893, forced to retire, and died two years later. Editor of *The Christian at Work* (1876-1880). Wrote more than forty published works.

TCHAIKOVSKY (chī kôf′skĭ), **PETER ILICH** (1840-1893), Russian composer, born at Votkinsk, Ural region, Russia, began to take piano lessons at the age of four, began to compose music at ten. Studied law in St. Petersburg, and then worked for three years as a clerk in the Department of Justice, while studying music under Anton Rubinstein at St. Petersburg Conservatory. In 1866 became professor of harmony at the Moscow Conservatory. During next ten years he labored as a teacher, composer, and music critic. He suffered severely from nervous strain, and from 1875 to 1876 visited several countries of Europe. Following a brief unhappy marriage in 1877 suffered a nervous breakdown. After recovering there followed a stream of songs, symphonic poems, concertos, symphonies, operas, chamber music, overtures, and ballets. For thirteen years a wealthy widow and lover of music provided funds. He became one of Russia's greatest symphonic composers. Visited the United States in 1891. Died of cholera in St. Petersburg. Wrote a *Manual of Harmony* and *Musikalische Erinnerungen und Feuilletons*. A prolific songwriter; left in all about 107 songs. Possessed a melancholic nature, and many of his songs echo the morbidity of the writer. One later composition was "Nutcracker Suite," and his last was "Sixth Symphony," known as "Symphonie Pathetique." Religious music consisted of "Liturgy of St. John Chrysostom," "Vespers," "Hymn of St. Kyrilla and St. Mefodyi," and nine liturgical choruses. One of his beautiful anthems is "O Praise Ye the Name of the Lord."

TEILHARD DE CHARDIN, PIERRE (1881-1955), French Jesuit philosopher, geologist and palaeontologist. Born into a noble Auvergne family. Received doctorate from the Sorbonne. Ordained in 1911. Decorated heroic stretcher bearer in World War I. Helped discover the Peking man in frequent trips to China from 1923 to 1945. Forbidden by his superior to publish his findings. Linked Christ with the evolutionary process as its center.

TEMPLE, WILLIAM (1881-1944), Archbishop of Canterbury, born in the palace of the Bishop of Exeter, the son of Frederick Temple, the ninety-third Archbishop of Canterbury. Received education at Rugby and at Balliol College, Oxford, was fellow and lecturer at Queen's College, Oxford (1904-1910). Became deacon in 1908 and priest in 1909. From 1910 to 1921 chaplain to the Archbishop of Canterbury. For six years rector of St. James, Piccadilly. Then in successive periods canon of Westchester, bishop of Manchester (1921-1929), archbishop of York (1929-1942), and Archbishop of Canterbury (1942-1944). At the 1910 meeting at Edinburgh, dedicated himself to the spirit of Christian unity, and helped organize and promote the World Council of Churches. Leader of the Life and Liberty Movement, which was designed to inject new life into the Church of England and to free it of some of its incumbrances and abuses. Education of the masses, economic improvement, and better labor relations captured his imagination and sympathy. He became deeply interested and active in the Ecumenical Movement. He presided over the Edinburgh Conference in 1937. Largely instrumental in bringing about the British Council of Churches in 1942. Among best books he wrote are: *The Faith and Modern Thought; Church and Nation; Christianity and the State; Nature, Man and God; Christianity and the Social Order,* and *Readings in St. John's Gospel*.

TENNENT, GILBERT (1703-1764), Presbyterian preacher, born in the County of Armagh, Ireland and came with father to America about 1817. Educated by father, William Tennent, in the "log college" which his father founded, received the honorary master's degree from Yale, and studied theology privately. In 1726 ordained and installed minister of a Presbyterian congregation in New Brunswick, New Jersey. When George Whitefield came to the colonies holding his "Great Revival" meetings about 1740, Gilbert Tennent joined him, preaching with fiery zeal and deep moral earnestness. Many Presbyterian preachers being opposed to this type of revival preaching and also to the teachings and educational standards of the "log college" where he had received his training, clearly expressed their displeasure. He vigorously and abusively answered them in famous "Nottingham sermon" in 1740, which helped to bring about a division in the Presbyterian church. This division was known as the "Old Sides," the conservatives, and the "New Sides," those who favored these innovations. He helped to effect a reconciliation, bringing the two parties together in 1758. He raised money from 1753 to 1755 in England for the College of New Jersey (Princeton University). From 1743 until death in 1764, pastor of the newly organized Second Presbyterian Church of Philadelphia, a church composed largely of converts or followers of George Whitefield.

TENNENT, WILLIAM (1673-1746), Presbyterian clergyman and educator, born in Ireland graduating from the University of Edinburgh. Entered the ministry originally in the Episcopal church in Ireland, ordained priest in 1706. After coming to Philadelphia in 1718 received by the Presbyterian Synod of Philadelphia as a Presbyterian minister. For a short time supplied in two churches in New York, and in two churches in Pennsylvania, then in 1726 became pastor of a church at Neshaminy, Bucks County, near Philadelphia until 1746. Sensing the need of a place for training the young men of the colony for the work of the ministry, in 1736 established a school in a little log house on his own estate, for the training of his four sons and other young men of the church. This famous "log college" became the parent of all the secular and theological institutions of the Presbyterian church. Upon its closing in 1746, the College of New Jersey (Princeton College) began. The Tennents contributed in no small way to the "New Side" movement of the Presbyterian church. His four sons all followed the footsteps of the father into the Christian ministry. Died at his home in Neshaminy.

TENNISON, THOMAS (1636-1715), Archbishop of Canterbury. Educated at Corpus Christi College, Oxford and ordained in 1659. Rector of St. Martin-in-the-Fields, London in 1680. Bishop of Lincoln in 1692 and archbishop in 1695. Supporter of missions and the Society for the Propagation of the Gospel.

TENNYSON, ALFRED (LORD) (1809-1892), British Victorian poet, born at Somersby, Lincolnshire, England, the fourth of eight sons of an Anglican rector, studied at Trinity College, Cambridge, but left before graduating. He and bosom friend, Arthur Henry Hallam, joined a Spanish revolutionary army, and spent some time in the Pyrenees. Tennyson's spiritual development found its fullest expression in the long elegy, *In Memoriam,* a poem dedicated to and inspired by Hallam, in which he develops evolutionary ideology. This was published in 1850. In 1850 Tennyson made poet laureate to succeed Wordsworth. In 1864 appeared *Enoch Arden,* the most immediately popular of all his volumes of poetry. In 1884, eight years before his death, he was created a peer, taking his seat in the House of Lords as Baron Tennyson from Farringford and Aldworth. At eighty-one wrote *Crossing the Bar*. Tennyson's poetry is pervaded by a religious spirit.

TERESA (tā rā'sä), **(THERESA de JESUS) OF AVILA** (1515-1582), Spanish mystic, born at Avila, Old Castile, Spain. Early studied at an Augustinian convent. In teens withdrew from society and lived in strict asceticism within the walls of her own home. In 1533, leaving home secretly one morning, she entered the convent of the Incarnation of the Carmelite nuns at Avila. For more than twenty years suffered much from physical illness, and from constant inner spiritual conflicts. Subjected herself to excessively rigorous and horrible self-inflicted tortures and mortifications, bringing the severest of suffering. Her cry was, "Lord, either let me suffer or let me die." Finally claimed to have had a vision of the image of Christ, who came to be present in her in bodily form; she claimed to have found deep satisfaction in long uninterrupted periods of communion with God, and a sense of union and rapture. With the bishop's reluctant consent, in 1582 founded in Avila a Reformed (or Discalced) Carmelite house for nuns. Soon received permission from the general of the Carmelite order to establish new houses of her new order. Began to travel through Spain forming similar convents. Enlisted two monks, one of whom was Juan de la Cruz (John of the Cross) to organize Discalced Carmelite houses for the men. In 1576 there began a series of persecutions on the part of the older observant Carmelite order against Teresa, her friends, and her reforms. This stricture lasted for several years, but by 1580 or 1581 was removed, and the Discalced Carmelites were allowed to proceed with their activity. In her last twenty years she had founded seventeen Discalced Carmelite convents for nuns: and fifteen others due to her reform activity were formed for men. About forty years after her death Teresa was canonized by Pope Gregory XV. Today she is held as the patron saint of Spain. Her writings comprise chiefly her famous letters, ascetic and mystical treatises, among them: *The Way of Perfection, The Interior Castle,* and autobiography, *The Life of Saint Teresa of Jesus.*

TERRY, MILTON SPENSER (1840-1914), American Methodist minister and educator, born at Coeymans, New York, educated at the New York Conference Seminary at Charlotteville, New York, and Yale Divinity School. Between 1826 and 1884, pastor of several different Methodist Episcopal churches in the New York area, from 1879 to 1883 serving as presiding elder of New York City and Westchester County. In 1884 professor of Hebrew and Old Testament exegesis and Christian doctrine at the Garrett Bible Institute, Evanston, Illinois. In theology held to Wesleyan Arminianism, acknowledged the modern critical school, but steadfastly adhered to the fundamentals of evangelical Christianity. Writings include: *Commentary on Judges, Ruth, First and Second Samuel; Commentary on Kings, Chronicles, Ezra, Nehemiah, and Esther; Commentary on Genesis and Exodus; Biblical Hermeneutics; New Apologetics; The Prophecies of Daniel Expounded; Moses and the Prophets; Primer of Christian Doctrines* and *Biblical Dogmatics*.

TERSTEEGEN (tĕr stā'gĕn), **GERHARD (GERRIT)** (1697-1769), Reformed mystic and hymnist, born at Mörs, near Düsseldorf in Rhenish Prussia. Early came under the influence of mysticism and led a secluded life. Later he abandoned excessive asceticism and gave himself to mystical writing and to translating the writings of other mystics. About 1725 became a leader in private devotional meetings, and a little later established a semi-monastic community at Otterbeck from which his fame and influence extended throughout Germany, and to Denmark, Sweden, Holland, and the United States. For his physical support and for his benevolence he depended upon the contributions of friends, and on inheritance from his mother. His chief fame, however, rests upon 111 hymns, widely used in his day, and found in evangelical hymnbooks. Examples are "Lo, God is here" and "God Calling Yet! Shall I not Hear." He was a separatist and a decided mystic; but he never formed a separate sect.

TERTULLIAN (tûr tŭl yăn), **QUINTUS SEPTIMIUS FLORENS** (c. 160-c. 220), Latin church Father and apologist, born in Carthage, North Africa of heathen parents. Father was a man of rank in proconsular service. Thorough education prepared him for successful writing in both Greek and Latin, as well as for politics, the practice of law, and forensic eloquence. In about 195 he embraced Christianity with deep conviction. The rest of his life faithfully devoted to defending the Christian faith against heathen, Jew, and heretic, and to studying and pursuing the strictest morality of life. Married and considered the Christian marriage a very high and noble state. Wrote in Latin an apology about 197, in *Against Marcion* opposed Gnosticism and advocated the Traducian theory of the origin of the soul. About 206 cast his lot with the Montanist schism that was making itself so strongly felt in the church at this time. To him this growing sect seemed to be nearer to primitive Christianity than was the Catholic church. As a schismtic in the Montanist church used his great power of vindictiveness with both word and pen to reprove what he thought was compromise and worldliness in the Catholic church, and to defend Montanist puritanism. All this time he was bitterly attacking the heretics and false teachers in the church, seeking to defend pure Christianity. He was a prolific writer and ardent preacher and a strong defender of the faith. In his *Against Praxeas* he set forth the first statement of the trinity as one essence in three persons. He opposed infant baptism.

TETZEL (tĕt'sĕl), **JOHANN** (c. 1465-1519), commissioner of indulgences, born at Leipzig; became a doctor of philosophy. About 1490 entered the Dominican Order, later became prior of monastery. Achieved some success and popularity as a preacher. In 1501 began preaching indulgences and continued to do so the rest of his life. In 1516 Leo X made him commissioner of indulgences for all Germany and also inquisitor. It was in 1517 that Archbishop Albert of Brandenburg (or Mainz), obtained permission to have Tetzel dispense indulgences in his diocese to raise money to pay debts he had contracted in order to secure his archbishopric, and to provide funds for the building of St. Peter's Church in Rome. The unscrupulous and shameful manner in which these indulgences were sold led Martin Luther to post his Ninety-five Theses on the church door at Wittenberg on October 31, 1517.

THAYER (thâr), **JOSEPH HENRY** (1828-1901), New Testament lexicographer, born in Boston, Massachusetts, and attended college at Harvard and seminary at Andover. Ordained in 1859 was from 1859 to 1864, pastor of the Congregational church at Salem, Massachusetts, on leave, however, for nine months to serve as chaplain of the Fortieth Massachusetts Volunteers (1862-1863). Professor of sacred literature in Andover Theological Seminary (1864-1882), lecturer in Harvard Divinity School (1883-1884), and professor of New Testament criticism and interpretation at Harvard Divinity School (1884-1901). Main interest in the Greek language of the New Testament. Translated Winer's *Grammar of the New Testament Greek* and Buttmann's *Grammar of the Greek New Testament*. His greatest work was *A Greek-English Lexicon of the New Testament,* based on the work of Grimm. These publications established his reputation in the first rank in New Testament and Patristic scholarship, especially in textual criticism. A member of the Committee of Revision of the New Testament, and active in the preparation of the American Standard Version New Testament in 1901. Perhaps more than any other instrumental in founding the American School of Oriental Research in Jerusalem.

THEODORA (thē ō dō'rȧ), (c. 500-c. 548), Byzantine empress, wife of Justinian I. According to the dubious evidence of Procopius, she was of low birth, the daughter of the keeper of wild beasts at the circus at Constantinople; for a time a favorite on the stage and a famous courtesan. Beautiful, crafty, unscrupulous, and a lover of display. Justinian married her after which she led an exemplary domestic life. When he became emperor in 527 she shared the coronation and exerted a marked influence over her husband and his rule. Displayed great zeal for the church and for ascetic piety, and was especially interested in the Monophysite view; adroitly influenced the emperor in decisions and plans. Lovely mosaics in San Vitale Church in Ravenna depict and memorialize her and her husband.

THEODORE OF MOPSUESTIA (thē'ō dōr mŏp sū ĕs'chĭ ȧ) **(or of Antioch)** (c. 350-428), Greek theologian, born at Antioch, where father held an official position in the government. Attended the lectures of Libanius of Antioch. Upon becoming a Christian, as was a very common practice among young Christians, entered monastic life. Early made a presbyter at Antioch, and about 383 ordained a priest. In 392 consecrated bishop of Mopsuestia. Theodore was the ablest exegete and theologian of the Antiochian School. He was the able founder of the Antiochian or Nestorian Christology, which essentially advocated the duality of the person of Christ. He was the teacher of Nestorius, whose view was that Mary is the mother of Christ and not the mother of God. He wrote a book against the Augustinian anthropology. Later in life he became entangled also in the Pelagian as well as the Monophysite controversy. Stressed grammatical-historical interpretation and opposed allegorism.

THEODORE OF STUDIUM (759-826), Byzantine monastic and defender of image worship. Born in Constantinople. Became a monk in 787 and later in 797 abbot of a monastery in Bithynia. Thrice exiled for opposing the emperor's adulterous marriage. Adopted Rule of St. Basil which was widely used in the East. Wrote nearly 600 letters useful to church historians.

THEODORE OF TARSUS (c. 602-690), Archbishop of Canterbury, born at Tarsus in Cilicia and educated at Athens. Became a monk and early distinguished himself as a scholar. Consecrated at Rome as Archbishop of Canterbury by Pope Vitalian in 668, and arrived at his see the next year. Did a great work in reforming the English Church at a time when it had sunk to a low level of culture, order, and discipline. The first archbishop to whom all of the English church submitted. In 673 summoned and presided over the first important synod of the whole English church at Hertford; planned for other councils to follow. Divided his large diocese into smaller units; appointed worthy bishops; promoted learning, preparing the way for the parochial system; increased the number of monasteries; in fact he set the English church in order and united it with Rome under papal supremacy.

THEODORET (thē ŏd′ō rĕt) **OF CYRRHUS** (sĭr′ŭs) (c. 390-c. 458), Greek theologian and historian; born in Antioch. Belonged to the School of Antioch and was well trained in philosophy and literature. Entered a monastery. About 423 made Bishop of Cyrrhus, a small town of Syria, though his diocese included nearly eight hundred churches. About 430 became involved in the Christological controversies aroused by Cyril. Opposed the violent controversies aroused by Cyril with Nestorius; but did not accept the theory of the dual personality of Jesus as held by Nestorius. Through Cyril's influence Theodoret was condemned at the Council of Ephesus in 431. In 449 at the "Robbers' Synod," deposed from his bishopric; but at the Council of Chalcedon in 451 was acquitted and restored to his see, on the condition of his accepting the condemnation of Nestorius, and agreeing to the title, "Mother of God," as applied to Mary. This he did, likely with certain reservations. His *Ecclesiastical History,* in five volumes, continues the history of Eusebius from 325 to the year 429. His history, though shorter than those of Socrates and Sozomen, does furnish an essential supplement to their works. However, as an exegete and a preacher he has received high praise from the scholars.

THEODORIC (thē ŏd′ō rĭk), **THE GREAT** (c. 455-526), King of the Ostrogoths (475-526) and King of Italy (493-526), born in Pannonia. Received education at Constantinople while held there as a hostage by Emperor Leo, and acquired the refinement, culture, an education of the East. At eighteen allowed to return home. At about twenty succeeded his father as King of the Ostrogoths. Emperor Zeno gave him the title "Patricius and magister militum," and in 484 appointed him consul. He subdued and then, with his own hand, killed Odoacer, ruler of Italy, and established his seat of power at Ravenna in 493. Though himself a Goth, ruled the Italians in accordance with their own Roman law. Proud of his Gothic nationality and considered himself the restorer of the Western Empire. Believed it was possible to reconcile Roman and Germanic interests and ideals. Succeeded to the extent that history has given him the title, "the Great." An Arian Christian but lived on terms of amity with his Roman neighbors and subjects. Consolidated the empire to include Sicily and Dalmatia and parts of the German lands. The reign of Theodoric was a time of unexampled happiness for Italy. With one negligible exception unbroken peace reigned within her borders. His fame, however, was sullied by his execution of Boetius.

THEODOSIUS I (thē ō dō′shĭ ŭs) **(THE GREAT)**, Flavius (c. 346-395), Roman emperor (379-395), born in Spain. Upon the death of father, returned to family estate in Spain; but upon the death of Emperor Valens three years later, Gratian called him from his private life to declare him Emperor Augustus of the East. In 380 baptized as a Trinitarian or orthodox Christian. He then issued at Constantinople an edict solemnly acknowledging the Catholic faith and threatening heretics with punishment. In 379 appointed Gregory Nazianzus bishop of Constantinople. In rapid succession Theodosius issued edicts to strengthen Catholic orthodoxy, to expel Arian heretics, to extirpate Manichaeism and other heresies, and to suppress paganism. In 381 called the second general council at Constantinople, where the Nicene Creed was reconfirmed and Arianism received its death blow. For some time lived at Milan, enjoying the friendship and respect of Bishop Ambrose. A ruler of justice and deep convictions; but reign was not without the stain of cruelty. At one time responsible for the cruel massacre of the populace of Thessalonica. For this deed Bishop Ambrose withheld from him the communion until he would do penance. The heroic spirit of the emperor led him to comply and to receive forgiveness.

THEODOTUS (thē ŏd'ō tŭs), (Second Century), heretic, a tanner from Byzantium who denied Christ in time of persecution with the apology that he denied only a man, but did not deny God. Believed Jesus adopted by God at baptism and became divine. Gained followers in Rome and excommunicated by Bishop Victor (192-202). After his death many followers returned to the Catholic church.

THEODULF OF ORLEANS (c. 750-821), ecclesiastic and scholar, born in Spain of Gothic ancestry, and called to France by Charlemagne, first to be abbot of two or three monasteries, and later Bishop of Orleans. One of the most successful theologians of the Carolingian period, being regarded as second only to Alcuin for learning. Theodulf advanced education and culture and effected many reforms among the clergy and the laity through establishing schools, restoring convents, building churches, advocating high morals, and writing *Directions to the Priests of the Diocese* and doctrinal tracts. A lover of art, also wrote many hymns, including the much used "Gloria, Laud et Honor." He succeeded Alcuin, 804, as chief theological imperial counselor. In 809 sat in the council of Aix la Chapelle, and by request of the emperor wrote *De Spiritu Sancto* in which he collected the patristic quotations in defense of the *Filioque* clause. At the wish of the emperor wrote also *De Ordine Baptismi*. In 811 a witness to the emperor's will. After the death of Charlemagne accused of conspiracy with King Bernard of Italy against Louis the Pious, and was imprisoned in the monastery of Angers, 818. Louis later pardoned him.

THEOPHILUS (thē ŏf'ĭ lŭs) **OF ALEXANDRIA** (d. 412), Patriarch of Alexandria (385-412). A learned, gifted and broad-minded but unscrupulous, scheming and unspiritual bishop. With his name are associated three important historical events: the destruction of paganism in Egypt, the Origenistic controversy, and the deposition and banishment of Chrysostom. In each event he practiced violence and intrigue. During the first ten years of bishopric he gave a fairly good rule. But in the last decade and a half both his character and his rule seriously deteriorated.

THEOPHILUS OF ANTIOCH (Second Century), apologist, born near the Euphrates and Tigris Rivers, received a pagan Greek eduction. Converted from paganism in his later years by the reading of the Scriptures. About 169 became the sixth bishop of Antioch. Principal writing was an apology in three books addressed sometime after 180 to an educated pagan friend, seeking to convince him of the falsity of idolatry and of the truth of Christianity. One of these books was polemic, one was apologetic, and one a comparison of the Christian Scriptures with the pagan writings.

THOBURN (thō'bẽrn), **ISABELLA** (1840-1901), American missionary and educator in India, born at St. Clairsville, Ohio. Educated in the Wheeling Female Seminary and at the Cincinnati Academy of Design. Taught for several years. Ministered to soldiers in Civil War. Her brother James, who had been in India for ten years, appealed to her to come to India to work among the women. She volunteered and in 1869 the newly organized Women's Foreign Missionary Society of the Methodist Episcopal Church chose her as its first missionary. Her work was to be in the field of educating the womanhood of India. In 1870 she organized a school for Indian girls, and within a year established a Christian boarding school. Also engaged in evangelistic, Sunday school, and zenana work. Her school developed as the attendance increased, until a full high school course was offered. By 1887 a collegiate department was added to the high school. The college, the first Christian college for women in all Asia, rapidly developed until in 1895 the British Government granted a charter for the college to become the Lucknow Women's College, later to be known as the Isabella Thoburn College.

THOBURN, JAMES MILLS (1836-1922), American Methodist Episcopal bishop in India, born at St. Clairsville, Ohio, graduated from Allegheny College, Meadville, Pennsylvania. In 1858 admitted to the Pittsburgh Conference of the Methodist church. Traveled as a circuit preacher in Ohio for a year. In 1859 he was accepted for India. First place of labor was Naini Tal in the Himalayas. Learned the language quickly, and in six months was preaching. In 1870 joined sister Isabella at Lucknow. In 1871 began the *Lucknow Witness,* later to be named the

Indian Witness, and edited it for seven years. In 1888 elected missionary bishop of India and Malaysia with residence at Calcutta until 1896, and at Bombay until 1908, when he retired from active work. The Philippines were included in his bishopric after 1898. The bishop traveled widely throughout India preaching. After his retirement in 1908, he settled at Meadville, Pennsylvania. Authored several books, among them *India and Malaysia, Light in the East, The Church of Pentecost, India and Southern Asia, The Christian Conquest of India,* and *Life of Isabella Thoburn.*

THOLUCK, FRIEDRICH AUGUST GOTTREU (1799-1877), mediating German Lutheran theologian and Evangelical preacher, born at Breslau, studied there as well as under Neander at Berlin. At the University of Berlin, in twentieth year, through the influence of Pietism and of Neander and others, converted to faith in Christ. Became professor extraordinary of theology in Berlin in 1823, and in 1826 became professor of dogmatics and exegesis at Halle, where he taught until his death. In this time, however, spent two years (1827-1829) as chaplain to the Prussian embassy at Rome. Came to Halle at a time when spirituality and orthodoxy were at low ebb. Worked patiently, and rationalism was replaced by evangelicalism in both faculty and student body. As a preacher scriptural, earnest, and powerful. As a teacher presented a religion of experience. As a scholar a great linguist. Like others of his school, a member of the Evangelical Union, favoring the Prussian Union of 1817. As a theological writer devoted his best powers to Biblical exegesis, achieved his most enduring merits. Besides commentaries on John, Romans, Hebrews, and Psalms, wrote: *The Doctrine of Sin and Its Propitiation, Explanation of Christ's Sermon on the Mount, Hours of Christian Devotion, Credibility of the Scriptures, The Old Testament in the New,* and several volumes of sermons.

THOMAS, JOHN (1805-1871), founder of Christadelphians, born in London, studied medicine there. Came to Brooklyn, New York in 1832, for a time a member of the Disciples of Christ Church. Dissatisfied with the doctrines of that body and with all organized Christian churches, and attempting to restore primitive Christianity, organized several societies in the United States, Canada, and Great Britain. Applied for exemption from military service on grounds of conscientious scruples in the time of the Civil War, found it necessary to register as a member of an organized church body. He then organized his society and registered it under the name Christadelphians. Chief doctrinal beliefs: rejection of the doctrines of the trinity and deity, the pre-existence of Jesus, and a personal devil; baptism by immersion for salvation; a conditional immortality of the body; resurrection of the just to eternal salvation, and of the unjust to eternal punishment or utter annihilation, and nonresurrection for those who never heard the gospel; second coming of Christ to set up kingdom in Palestine for His millennial reign.

THOMAS, NORMAN (1884-1968), Presbyterian cleric, pacifist, and socialist. Born in Marion, Ohio. Educated at Bucknell University and Princeton and Union theological seminaries. Ordained in 1911. Pastor from 1905 to 1918. Executive secretary of the Fellowship of Reconciliation from 1918 to 1922. Member of the Socialist Party from 1918 to 1955. Advocated the League of Nations. Six times nominee of the Socialist Party for president from 1928 to 1948.

THOMAS, WILLIAM HENRY GRIFFITH (1861-1924), minister, scholar, teacher, born at Oswestry, Shropshire, England. Educated at King's College, London and Christ Church, Oxford. Ordained to the Anglican ministry in 1886, became vicar of St. Paul's eleven years later (1896). After nine years of fruitful ministry in St. Paul's, moved to Oxford and began a five year term of teaching at Wycliffe Hall, Oxford (1905-1910). In 1910 accepted a professorship at Wycliffe College, Toronto, Canada, where he spent nine years teaching Old Testament literature and exegesis. In 1919 began continent-wide ministry, moving to a new home in Philadelphia, Pennsylvania. Travels and activities were extensive: a trip to China, a third and last visit to England, conference work, Bible lecturing, teaching theological courses, lecturing in leading Bible schools and seminaries, Keswick and "Victorious Life" activities, contributing regularly to leading religious papers, and writing and publishing books. Together with Lewis Sperry Chafer and A. B. Winchester a cofounder of Dallas Theological Seminary in Texas. He was to have been a visiting professor there had he lived.

THOMPSON, FRANCIS (1859-1907), poet. Born in Preston and educated for the Roman Catholic priesthood at Ushaw near Durham and studied medicine at Owens College, Manchester. Became an opium addict in London until rescued by Wilfred Meynell in 1888. The "Hound of Heaven" in his *Poems* (1893) is his best known religious poem, which pictures God's pursuit of sinful man.

THOMSON, JAMES (died c. 1850), Scottish Baptist pioneer missionary to Latin America; the first evangelical missionary to introduce the Bible in Latin America; sent in 1818 by the British and Foreign Bible Society and by the English and Foreign School Society. The latter was a project formed by Joseph Lancaster in England for popular schools using the Bible as their main textbook. Opened a hundred Lancastrian schools in Buenos Aires with five thousand pupils. Used the New Testament as his textbook, and thus was able to get great numbers of Bibles into Catholic Latin America. Also prepared his more mature pupils to teach the younger pupils. Later opened schools in Chile, Peru, Ecuador, and Colombia, and circulated the Scriptures. Service was so highly valued in Argentina and Chile, made an honorary citizen in those countries. In 1826 returned to England to make a report of his eight years in Latin America; but unable to resume his work after that. It was another twenty years before a permanent evangelical body was formed in Chile, when David Trumbull was sent there in 1845.

THOMSON, WILLIAM McCLURE (1806-1894), Presbyterian missionary to Syria, born at Spring Dale, near Cincinnati, Ohio, studied at Miami University, Oxford, Ohio, and at Princeton Theological Seminary. In 1831 ordained an evangelist, sent the next year by the American Board of Commissioners for Foreign Missions to Jerusalem, where he worked for about a year, when an uprising made it necessary to leave Palestine. Transferred to Beirut, where (1835) he opened the first boys' boarding school in the Turkish Empire. Beirut became the general center of his missionary activity for years. Well read on Palestine and Syria; traveled much studying topography and people of the land; Knew language of the people; knew well the Bible. Used the best available archeological helps, hence well qualified to write books that made him famous: *The Land and the Book,* in three volumes. Very popular book.

THORNTON, HENRY (1760-1815), wealthy banker and philanthropist. Member of Parliament from Southwark after 1782. Important member of Clapham Sect, which met in his home in the oval library designed by William Pitt. Helped form the Sierra Leone Company to repatriate freed slaves in England to Africa. Treasurer of the Church Missionary Society and the British and Foreign Bible Society. Supported Hannah More's Sunday School work. Before marriage gave away six-sevenths of his income and one-third after his marriage.

THORNWELL, JAMES HENRY (1812-1862). Born in South Carolina. Educated at South Carolina College and Andover Theological Seminary. After some years as a Presbyterian pastor he became a professor (1837-1851) and in 1851 president of South Carolina College (later the University of South Carolina). From 1855 to 1862 served as professor of theology in Columbia Theological Seminary. Moderator of the General Assembly in 1847. Founder of *Southern Presbyterian Review*. Helped create a new southern Presbyterian church during the Civil War.

THORVALDSEN (to͝or'vȧl sn), **ALBERT BERTEL** (1770-1844), celebrated Danish sculptor, born in Copenhagen, Denmark, son of Icelandic wood carver. For twelve years studied at the school of art at Copenhagen, went to Rome to study in 1797, and maintained his home in Rome until 1838, then returned to Denmark. Most familiar of his sculptures is the world-famous "Lion of Lucerne" in Switzerland, near the home of William Tell. This work was executed in 1819 commemorating the killing of ten Swiss guards who were defending the French King, Louis XVI, in the Tuileries in 1792. His greatest religious work was his monumental group of *Christ and His Apostles,* executed for the cathedral at Copenhagen. Among other religious works were the tomb of Pope Pius VII in St. Peter's, "Entrance of Christ into Jerusalem"; "Christus Consolator." His last work was an unfinished bust of Martin Luther. The greatest sculptor that Northern Europe ever produced. Made a fortune by his art, the greater part of which he bequeathed to build and endow a museum in Copenhagen.

TIBERIUS (tī bĕr'ĭ ŭs), **CLAUDIUS NERO CAESAR** (42 B.C.-A.D. 37) the second emperor of Rome (A.D. 14-37) born in Rome. Four years after birth his mother divorced his father and married Octavianus, later Emperor Augustus, who carefully cared for the eduction of Tiberius. The boy early manifested intellectual power and military skill. In A.D. 4 formally adopted by Augustus; continued the military campaigns in which he had shown himself a commander of more than ordinary ability. Upon death of Augustus in A.D. 14, when fifty-five years old, he succeeded to the throne. The early part of reign was a period of general good government and good will; but the latter part of reign is notable for a series of conspiracies and consequent executions. Coldness, reserve, and suspicious nature, and strong desire for economy in government rendered him unpopular and even hated among the people. On the whole reign was just and beneficent in the empire, especially among the provinces. It was during the latter years of the reign of Tiberius that Jesus was crucified at Jerusalem, and the Christian church was born on Pentecost day.

TIILILA, OSMO ANTERO (1904-1972), ordained as a minister of the Finnish Lutheran church in 1926. Left ministry in 1960 in protest against the inroads of liberal theology and undue stress on social action in the church. Leader in the Lutheran World Federation.

TIKHON (tyē'kôn) (Monastic name), **BELAVIN, VASILI IVANOVITCH** (real name) (1865-1925), Patriarch of Moscow (1917-1925), born in Toropets, Pskov, Russia, son of a parish priest, spent five years in the Pskov Ecclesiastical Seminary, and in 1883 entered St. Petersburg Theological Academy. After graduating appointed to a position in the seminary at Cholm. In 1897 consecrated Bishop of Lublin, assistant to the Bishop of Warsaw. In 1899 transferred to San Francisco, California as Bishop of Alaska and the Aleutian Islands, and became presiding bishop of the Russian church in America in 1904. The next year became Archbishop of North America with residence in New York, introduced an innovation in his church when he held Sunday evening services in English in the New York cathedral. In 1907 he was appointed to Yaroslavl, one of the oldest archdioceses in Russia, and in 1913 to the see of Vilna in Russian Poland. In 1917 elected Patriarch of the revived patriarchate of Moscow, the first patriarch of the Russian church since 1721. Thus he became the head of the Russian Orthodox church. Took a strong stand against the persecutions of the Bolshevists, and issued pastoral letters denouncing Bolshevik cruelty, the suppression of liberty and faith, and blasphemy and sacrilege. Arrested and held in prison until 1923 when released through pressure from the pope, the Archbishop of Canterbury, and church leaders all over the world. Attempts were made to discredit the patriarch's loyalty through the so-called "Living Church" which the Soviet Government had attempted to establish. In 1923 signed a declaration professing loyalty to the Soviet Government, which improved his relationship with the government.

TILLICH, PAUL (1886-1965), teacher and philosophical theologian. Born in Starzeddel, Germany. Educated at Berlin, Tubingen, Halle, and Breslau (Ph.D.). Chaplain from 1914 to 1918 in German Army. Taught at Berlin, Marburg, Dresden and Leipzig universities and from 1919 to 1933 at Frankfurt University. Professor at Union Theological Seminary, New York (1933-1955), Harvard (1955-1962) and the University of Chicago (1962-1965). His three-volume *Systematic Theology* (1951-1963) depicts God as the "Ground of Being" to whom man relates existentially in action. To him the Bible was myth.

TIMOTHY I (728-823), Bishop of Bait Baghash before 769 and Patriarch of the East in 780. Built a palace at Bagdad in the era of Haroun-Al-Raschid. Translated Aristotle's writings into Arabic. Promoted missionary work around the Caspian Sea. Wrote about 200 letters.

TINGLEY, KATHERINE AUGUSTA WESTCOTT (1852-1929), American philanthropist and theosophist, born at Newburyport, Massachusetts. Educated in the public schools and by private tutors, became a professional spiritualist medium. In 1889 married P. B. Tingley, her third husband. Interested in humanitarian work and established the Emergency Relief Organization and the Do-Good Mission in New York. Became associated with the Theosophical Society and on the death of W. Q. Judge in 1896 succeeded him as head of the Theosophists; in 1897 founded the International Brotherhood League. The next year became the leader and official head of the Universal Brotherhood and Theosophical Society, established a sort of theosophical colony at Point Loma, California. Conducted two theosophical crusades around the world in 1896-1897 and in 1903-1904. In Point Loma established the Raja Yoga Academy, a School of Antiquity, and a home for orphan children. Also acquired educational sites in Cuba, Sweden, and England. In 1925 organized seven new theosophical centers in Europe. Under her leadership the Theosophical Movement spread around the world and gained many converts. Edited the *Theosophical or Century Path* and wrote *Mysteries of the Heart Doctrine, Pith and Marrow of Some Sacred Writings,* and *Theosophy and Some of the Vital Problems of the Day*.

TISCHENDORF (tĭsh'ĕn dōrf), **LOBEGOTT FRIEDRICH KONSTANTIN VON** (1815-1874), German biblical scholar and textual critic, born at Langenfeld, Saxony, educated at Leipzig, qualified as a lecturer at Leipzig. Became a count of the Russian Empire. Went to Paris in 1840 to study in the great library, and there deciphered the *Codex Ephraemi Syri,* which had been abandoned by earlier scholars as illegible. Later was made professor of theology at Leipzig, but spent much time traveling in Europe, Egypt, Sinai, and Palestine in search of biblical manuscripts, editing and publishing them. In these travels assisted by the Saxon and Russian governments. Discovered in 1844 at the monastery of St. Catharine at the foot of Mount Sinai, over forty leaves of a manuscript of the Greek Old Testament. Fifteen years later on third visit discovered and obtained the remainder of the manuscript, the famous *Codex Sinaiticus,* containing the New Testament, a large part of the Old Testament, the Epistle of Barnabas and a portion of Hermas. This was one of the oldest known manuscripts of the Greek Bible. Now in the British Museum. Published eight different editions of the Greek text of the New Testament, the crowning work of his life being his eighth edition (1869-1872) of the Greek Testament, with its large critical apparatus. It remains by reason of the abundance of its data a standard book of reference for the text of the New Testament. Also published an edition of the Septuagint, several editions of the Apocrypha, and many other works.

TISSOT (tē sō'), **JAMES JOSEPH JACQUES** (1863-1902), French painter, born in Nantes, France, studied at the Ecole des Beaux-Arts, Paris, a pupil of Ingres, Lamothe, and Flandrin. In 1870 opened a studio in London. Works characterized by care in drawing and exact coloring. Suddenly changed whole artistic aim in life under the stress of bereavement, and began to paint religious scenes. Spent ten years in Palestine obtaining material for his religious pictures on which he worked with painstaking attention to detail and with great realism. Tissot is noted chiefly for his series of 365 watercolor pictures and 150 pen-and-ink sketches, picturing the life of Christ and His environment. This series of pictures is in the Brooklyn, New York museum. At the time of death engaged in the painting of a series of pictures illustrating the Old Testament.

TITIAN (tĭsh'an) **(TIZIANO VECELLIO)** (1477-1576), painter of the Venetian Renaissance, born in Pieve di Cadore, a dsitrict in the Venetian Alps. A picture he painted of Charles V brought high honors from the emperor. Not a many-faceted genius like Michelangelo and Leonardo da Vinci, but attained supremacy in the field of painting. The greatest colorist in the whole galaxy of painters. During long span of life, painting up to the last, produced a vast number of outstanding works. Over 700 pictures in European and American galleries are attributed to Titian. Spent much of life in the commercial and worldly Venice. Painted many religious and Biblical pictures, some of the chief subjects being *Assumption of the Virgin, Pesaro Madonna, Entombment of Christ, Christ Crowned with Thorns, Descent from the Cross, Supper at Emmaus, St. Mark, Presentation in the Temple, Christ in the Garden,* and *St. Jerome.*

TOLSTOI (tŭl stoi'), **COUNT LYOV (LEO) NIKOLAYEICH** (1828-1910), Russian novelist, dramatist, essayist, social and moral reformer, born in Yasnaya Polyana, in south central Russia, studied at the University of Kazan, but did not graduate. In 1851 enlisted in the army and served for six years in the Caucasus, Turkey, and the Crimea. During this time wrote the "Sevastopol Sketches," in which he delineated the horrors of war. He went back to his four-thousand-acre estate to farm, freeing his serfs, and working side by side with them on the farm. Devoted himself also to educating peasant children in a school which he established on his estate, and to writing. Traveled in western Europe studying educational systems, and published a small pedagogical magazine. When about forty wrote his two greatest novels: *War and Peace,* and *Anna Karenina* in 1869 and 1877. When about fifty a profound spiritual interest led him to turn to Christianity and to an examination of the Russo-Greek church. Study resulted in his totally rejecting the Greek Orthodox church, the Roman Catholic and Protestant churches. For years then devoted himself to an ardent study of the gospels, especially the Sermon on the Mount. Rejected the miracles, the deity of Christ, the personality of God, and the New Testament plan of salvation; but ardently advocated the doctrine of non-resistance and the cultivation of a profound love for an impersonal God. Out of this background he framed own religion in which he held civil and criminal law; the prison system and executions; all police force, armies, navies, and war; all governments which employ police force; and all holding of property to be immoral. Rejected all political, ecclesiastical, or other authority that would permit one person in any way to rule over or dominate or subject another. Political views were essentially anarchistic; religious views unitarian. Influence in Russia and outside the country became tremendous. Finally excommunicated from the Russian church in 1901. In later years gave property and the copyrights of his writings to his wife and thirteen children; spent much of his time doing manual labor out of doors, living in his home merely as a welcome guest. In later years became more and more ascetic. Universally acknowledged to be his country's foremost writer and "living conscience."

TOMLINSON, AMBROSE JESSUP (1865-1943), leader of the Church of God movement, born in a Quaker home near Westfield, Indiana. Converted in Quaker meeting house in 1892. Became an American Bible Society colporter, moving to North Carolina. Came under the influence of the Rev. Richard G.

Spurling and others who had started the Pentecostal Church of God movement in Tennessee. In 1896 joined the movement, accepting with strong conviction the distinctive teachings of the Pentecostal movement. Rapidly rose in influence in the group to leadership, from 1903 to 1923, general overseer of the Church of God with headquarters at Cleveland, Tennessee. Friction and faction developing within the ranks of the Church of God movement, and a dispute arising over a successor following his death led to the rise of several new branches within the movement. The original group at Cleveland, Tennessee, attached the name "original" to its title. A branch under A. J. Tomlinson and his son Homer in New York has been designated as The Church of God (Tomlinson).

TOPLADY (tŏp'lā dĭ), **AUGUSTUS MONTAGUE** (1740-1778), Calvinist, hymnist, and clergyman of the Church of England, born at Farnham, Surrey, England, educated at Westminster School and Trinity College, Dublin. Converted in Ireland in 1755, turned to extreme Calvinism in 1758. Ordained in 1764 as priest. Held positions in several places, the longest of which was as vicar of Broad Hembury, Devonshire, from 1768 to 1775. In 1775 because of health moved to London and ministered in the French Calvinist Reformed church there. The great champion of Calvinism in the Church of England, clashed with John Wesley on Calvinism and Arminianism. Wrote some hymns, the chief and most popular of which is *Rock of Ages*.

TORQUEMADA (tôr kā mä'thä), **TOMAS DE** (1388-1468), first Spanish Inquisitor-General, born in Valladolid; became a friar preacher in the Dominican monastery where he studied philosophy and theology. For twenty-two years prior of the monastery of Santa Cruz at Segovia, confessor to Isabella and later to Ferdinand. Prominent in the establishment of the Inquisition in Spain, and in 1483 appointed Inquisitor-General of Castile and Aragon. Set up tribunals in various cities, and called a general assembly of Spanish inquisitors at Seville in 1484; presented an outline of twenty-eight articles for their guidance. In 1492 took part in the expulsion of the Moors from Spain and largely responsible for driving the Jews out of Spain. Is known for wanton cruelty in attempting to eradicate all heresy. During eighteen years of office thousands of persons were burned or otherwise killed. Toward the end of his life retired to a Dominican monastery at Avila where he died.

TORREY, CHARLES CUTLER (1863-1956), biblical linguist. Professor at Andover Seminary from 1892 to 1900 and at Yale University from 1900 to 1932. First director of the School of Oriental Research in Jerusalem. Wrote *The Four Gospels, The Apocryphal Literature* and *Documents of the Primitive Church*. Was liberal in his theology.

TORREY, REUBEN ARCHER (1856-1928), Congregational evangelist, teacher, author, born at Hoboken, New Jersey. Educated in Yale University and Divinity School. After having passed through a period of scholastic skepticism, ordained, became pastor of a Congregational church in Garrettsville, Ohio from 1878 to 1882. After four years in this pastorate resigned and went to Germany for his year of study in Leipzig and Erlangen. Upon return to America accepted a small city mission in Minneapolis. In 1889 Dwight L. Moody called Torrey to Chicago to superintend the new Bible Institute of the Chicago Evangelization Society, now The Moody Bible Institute. Remained until 1908. Also served as pastor of the Chicago Avenue Church, now the Moody Memorial Church, for twelve years. Wielded a tremendous influence in the development of these two institutions. Between 1902 and 1906 Dr. Torrey and Charles M. Alexander carried on a remarkable series of evangelistic campaigns of modern times, laboring in Australia, Tasmania, New Zealand, India, China, Japan, Britain, Germany, Canada, and the United States. From 1912 to 1924, dean of the Bible Institute of Los Angeles, the last ten years of which time he was also pastor of the Church of the Open Door, Los Angeles. During this time conducted several evangelistic campaigns in America and other lands. Also helped establish the Montrose, Pennsylvania Summer Bible Conference. During last four years (1924-1928) devoted his time to holding Bible conferences, teaching at Moody Bible Institute and filling various engagements. In this latter period of life made his home at Biltmore, North Carolina. He was the author of forty religious books such as *The Person and Work of the Holy Spirit* and *What the Bible Teaches*.

TOWNER (toun'ẽr), **DANIEL BRINK** (1850-1919), gospel music composer and teacher, born in Rome, Pennsylvania, son of a country singing-school teacher. A Methodist layman, moved to Cincinnati in 1882 to prepare to become a concert and oratorio singer, supporting himself by being a church soloist and choir director. In 1885 gave himself to full-time evangelistic work, assisted D. L. Moody in an evangelistic campaign in Cincinnati, then later in many other cities in the United States and Canada. Moved to Northfield, Massachusetts to take charge of the music in the Annual College Conferences, and aid Mr. Moody in other services. He was also associated with L. W. Munhall, Major D. W. Whittle, and other noted evangelists. In 1893 moved to Chicago to become director of the Moody Bible Institute music department, which position he held until his death in 1919. During these years probably trained and influenced more Gospel musicians than any other man. Universally acknowledged as a musician of the first rank and a leader of unusual ability. The University of Tennessee conferred upon him the Doctor of Music degree in 1900. As a composer is credited with more than two thousand published hymn tunes. A few of his most famous songs are the following: "Trust and Obey," "Full Surrender," "Anywhere with Jesus," "Move Forward," "My Anchor Holds," "Saved by the Blood," "Safe in Jehovah's Keeping," "Grace Greater Than Our Sin," "Only a Sinner," and "Christian Fellowship Song."

TOWNSEND (toun'zĕnd), **LUTHER TRACY** (1838-1922), American Methodist clergyman and writer, born at Orono, Maine, studied at the New Hampshire Conference Seminary, graduated from Dartmouth College and Andover Theological Seminary in 1859 and 1862 respectively. Served in the Federal army during a portion of the Civil War, and in 1864 entered the Methodist Episcopal ministry. For four years pastor in three different Massachusetts churches. Professor successively of Hebrew, Chaldee, and New Testament Greek; of historical theology, practical theology, and sacred rhetoric in the Boston University School of Theology from 1867 to 1893, resigning in the latter year to devote himself to writing. Among leading writings are *Credo, Lost Forever, The Supernatural Factor in Religious Revivals, The Story of Jonah in the Light of Higher Criticism,* and *Evolution or Creation*. Effective popular apologist for the traditional Evangelical theology.

TOY, CRAWFORD HOWELL (1836-1919), Hebrew scholar and critic, born at Norfolk, Virginia, graduated from the University of Virginia, studied at the Southern Baptist Theological Seminary and at the University of Berlin. Professor of Greek at Richmond College, Richmond, Virginia for one year, left to serve in the Confederate army from 1861 to 1865. In 1866, became professor in the University of Alabama for two years, later professor of Greek in Furman University, Greenville, South Carolina (1868-1869). From 1869 to 1878 professor of Old Testament at the Southern Baptist Theological Seminary, resigning in the latter year because of sympathy with Darwin's views on evolution, also because of inability to accept the seminary's view on the doctrine of inspiration of the Scriptures. In 1880 became professor of Hebrew and other Oriental languages at Harvard University, remaining there until his retirement in 1909. Editor of the *Jewish Encyclopedia* and author of *Quotations in the New Testament, Judaism and Christianity, Commentary on Proverbs, Introduction to the History of Religions,* and *History of the Religion of Israel*.

TRAJAN (trā'jăn), or **MARCUS ULPIUS TRAJANUS** (52-117), Roman Emperor (98-117), born at Italica, near Seville, Spain, son of a Roman commander and the first provincial to sit in the seat of the Caesars. A soldier by training and profession; but also a statesman and a good administrator. In 97 the emperor Nerva adopted him as his son, and upon the death of Nerva the next year, the senate chose him as emperor. In the early part of reign conquered Dacia (now Roumania), in the later years of reign conquered lands of the East and made three new provinces—Armenia, Mesopotamia, and Assyria. Extended the boundaries of the empire beyond the Euphrates, farther than any other emperor had been able to do. Rule was famous for building of roads and other useful works in the provinces, for the establishing of libraries and benevolent institutions. Policy was one of comparative toleration; yet when the Christians refused to obey the imperial laws concerning state worship he legalized their punishment. Letters of Pliny the Younger, governor of Pontus and Bithynia in Asia Minor, to him about 112 and the emperor's answers concerning the treatment that should be given to the Christians in the province give us some clear insight into the imperial policy of religious toleration on the one hand and of the determined effort to enforce recognition of state and state worship on the other. During his reign Ignatius of Antioch and Simeon of Jerusalem were martyred. He died in Cilicia in the midst of military campaigns and conquests.

TRAHERNE (trȧ hûrn'), **THOMAS** (c. 1637-1674), English metaphysical poet and religious writer, probably born in Hereford, and received education at Brasenose College, Oxford. Took orders in 1656, and in 1657 became rector of Credenhill, near Hereford, ten years later became chaplain to Sir Orlando Bridgeman, Lord Keeper of the Seals, and pastor of the parish of Teddington. Author of *Roman Forgeries, Christian Ethics,* and *Centuries of Meditations*. His poetry was published after his death.

TRAPP (trăp), **JOHN** (1601-1669), English Puritan divine, born at Croome d'Abitot, and graduated from Christ Church, Oxford.

Usher of the free school of Stratford-on-Avon and headmaster; preacher at Luddington, near Stratford, then vicar of Weston-on-Avon. From 1646 to 1660, rector of Welford, returning again to Weston 1660 to 1669. Most industrious and an excellent preacher. Fame rests upon his *Commentary* on the whole Bible, which furnishes a specimen of Puritan Bible study at its best; is characterized by quaint humor and profound scholarship.

TRAVERS, WALTER (c. 1548-1635), Puritan Presbyterian theologian. Born in Nottingham. Educated at Trinity College, Cambridge where he became a fellow in 1569. Visited Geneva and adopted Presbyterian polity which he set forth in his *Declaration of Ecclesiastical Discipline*. Provost of Trinity College, Dublin from 1594 to 1598.

TREGELLES (trē gĕl'ĭs), **SAMUEL PRIDEAUX** (1813-1875), English biblical scholar, born at Wodehouse Place, Falmouth, England, parents Quakers, but in earlier years he associated with the Plymouth Brethren, later worshiped with the Presbyterians. After attending the Falmouth classical school (1825-1828), went to the ironworks to earn livelihood, studying Greek, Hebrew, and Welsh in spare hours. In 1836 returned to Falmouth to become a private tutor for two years. Purposed to prepare a critical edition of the Greek New Testament. Began biblical studies early; from 1838 to the end of his life devoted himself to the study of the New Testament texts and related subjects. Made three trips to the Continent to collate ancient manuscripts, spending five months at the Vatican in Rome. In 1844 published first installment, *The Book of Revelation in Greek Edited from Ancient Authorities with a New England Version*. He worked on this New Testament the rest of his life. He superintended the publication of *The Englishman's Greek Concordance to the New Testament*, and *The Englishman's Hebrew and Chaldee Concordance to the Old Testament*. He translated *Gesenius' Hebrew and Chaldee Lexicon*. He wrote *Remarks on the Prophetic Visions in the Book of Daniel, On the Original Language of St. Matthew's Gospel, The Jansenists, Hebrew Reading Lessons, Heads of Hebrew Grammar,* and *The Hope of Christ's Second Coming*. About 1850 the University of Aberdeen conferred on him the degree of LL.D. Ill health prevented him from serving on the Bible revision committee.

TRENCH (trĕnch), **RICHARD CHENEVIX** (shĕn'ĕ vē) (1807-1886), Archbishop of Dublin, Church of Ireland, born in Dublin, Ireland, studied at Harrow and at Trinity College, Cambridge. Ordained priest in 1835. Between 1830 and 1845 curate or rector in several different churches. In 1845 became examining chaplain to Bishop Wilberforce of Oxford; Hulsean lecturer at Cambridge (1845-1846); professor of divinity at King's College (1846-1854); professor of exegesis of the New Testament (1854-1858); dean of Westminster (1858-1863); and Archbishop of Dublin (1864-1884). Owing to infirmity resigned his see in 1884. A devout and conservative High Churchman; though he strongly opposed disestablishment of the Anglican Church in Ireland, writings were free from sectional bias. Noted as a theologian, a religious poet, and a philologist. Noteworthy among theological works: *Notes on the Parables of Our Lord, Notes on the Miracles of Our Lord, Commentary on the Epistles to the Seven Churches in Asia, Studies in the Gospels,* and *Lectures on Medieval Church History*. Best known books on philology were *The Study of Words; English: Past and Present; Proverbs and Their Lessons;* and *New Testament Synonyms*. His poetry included many hymns and sonnets. He published several volumes of sermons. A member of the committee for the revision of the New Testament.

TROELTSCH (trĕlch), **ERNST** (1865-1923), German Protestant theologian and philosopher, born near Augsburg, Germany, educated at Erlangen, Berlin, and Göttingen. Became vicar at Munich in 1890 and later professor successively at Göttingen, Bonn, and Heidelberg. Succeeded Pfleiderer at the University of Berlin in 1908 as professor of theology. In theological outlook much influenced by Ritschl. In a sense he was in the succession of Schleiermacher. Taught that religions, including Christianity, are an outgrowth of inner religious feeling; hence to him religion was not a religion of revelation, and not necessarily the final religion; it is one of many religions; yet it is the loftiest and most spiritual experience we know. A theologian of the religio-historical school. To him religion and social culture are intimately related. At the close of World War I he entered politics under the democratic standard. In 1921 he was appointed minister of education in the German federal cabinet. In 1923 he wrote *Christian Thought*, and *The Social Teachings of the Christian Churches*.

TROTMAN, DAWSON EARLE (1906-1956), Founder of the Navigators. Born in Bisbee, Arizona. Raised in Los Angeles. Educated at the Los Angeles Baptist Seminary and Biola College. Became Presbyterian when converted. Left the Presbyterian church in 1931 because of Liberalism.

Stressed Scripture memorization, discipling of new converts and the Wheel (Bible, prayer, witness, and obedience) for those he discipled. Opened home in 1933 to disciple sailor converts. In 1934 called his group the Navigators and incorporated it in 1943. Traveled all over the world in his work. Set up a follow-up program for Billy Graham beginning in the Shreveport, Louisiana Crusade in 1951. Purchased Glen Eyrie in 1953 for his headquarters. Died saving a girl when she was thrown out of a motorboat.

TROTTER, ISABEL LILIAS (1853-1928), missionary. Born in London. Gave up painting of miniatures to become missionary in North Africa in 1888. Translated the New Testament into the Algerian dialect and wrote illustrated tracts to use in evangelism. Her Algiers Mission Band became a part of the North Africa Mission.

TROTTER (trŏt′ẽr), **MELVIN E.** (1870-1940), superintendent of city missions and evangelist, born at Orangeville, Illinois, received no early education. Converted by Harry Monroe one night in 1897 when he, a drunken barber, stumbled into the Pacific Garden Mission. Ordained to the Presbyterian ministry in 1905. Had a great passion to help men of skid rows, and became an outstanding evangelist among them. He conducted a rescue mission in Grand Rapids and superintended a chain of rescue missions from Boston to San Francisco. He founded more than sixty-seven missions in the United States.

TRUETT (tro͞o′ĕt), **GEORGE WASHINGTON** (1867-1944), Southern Baptist preacher, born in Clay County, North Carolina, educated at Baylor University. A high school principal from 1887 to 1889, and financial secretary of Baylor University from 1890 to 1892. In 1890 ordained to the Baptist ministry and served as pastor at Waco (1893-1897). In 1897 entered pastorate in the First Baptist Church of Dallas with seven hundred members, and continued in the same church until his death forty-seven years later, leaving the congregation wth a membership of seventy-eight hundred. One of the greatest preachers of his day and a great evangelist. His influence reached far beyond congregation or his city. Once president of the Southern Baptist Convention, and for five years president of the Baptist World Alliance.

TRUMBULL, CHARLES GALLAUDET (1872-1941), editor, born at Hartford, Connecticut, studied at Hamilton School, Philadelphia, and at Yale University. In senior year at Yale, superintendent of the Yale Mission Sunday School. Upon graduation in 1893 became associated with father in the editorial work of the *Sunday School Times*, in 1903 became the editor, also vice president, secretary, and director of the Sunday School Times Company. For many years a staff writer for the *Toronto Globe*, and each week wrote the Sunday school lessons for the *Philadelphia Evening Public Ledger* and several other daily newspapers in various parts of the United States. A member of the Victoria Institute, England, of the Palestine Exploration Fund, England, and of the Archeological Institute of America. Treasurer of the Belgian Gospel Mission, a director of the Pioneer Mission Agency, vice president of the World's Christian Fundamentals Association, and vice president of the American Tract Society. Author of *A Pilgrimage to Jerusalem, Taking Men Alive, Men Who Dared, Genesis and Yourself, Life Story of C. I. Scofield, What Is the Gospel?* and *Prophecy's Light on Today*.

TRUMBULL, DAVID (1819-1889), Congregational missionary, born in Elizabeth, New Jersey, studied at Yale and Princeton Theological Seminary. In 1845 ordained and went under the Foreign Evangelical Society as a pioneer missionary to Valparaiso, Chile. Part of his forty-four years there was under this society, part under the American Seamen's Friends Society, part under the Presbyterian Foreign Mission Board. A part of the time he was pastor of an independent church of English and American residents. However, chief ministry was among the seamen. At first it was difficult to gain an entrance to Chile because the country was so strongly Roman Catholic. But his service in the hospital and in the jail was so quiet and so effective that he soon was permitted to work openly. Established a school for girls, published and circulated periodicals, pamphlets, and tracts, advocated civil and religious liberty, circulated the Bible in Spanish, and established a Union church.

TRUMBULL, HENRY CLAY (1830-1903), Congregational clergyman and editor, born at Stonington, Connecticut, educated at Stonington Academy and at Williston Seminary, East Hampton, Massachusetts. In railroad business from 1851 until 1858 when he became state missionary of the American Sunday School Union for Connecticut. In 1862 ordained a Congregational minister in order to qualify for the chaplaincy in the Union army. Served through most of the war, and held a prisoner for several months in 1863. After the war, in 1865, became secretary for the New England department of the American Sunday School Union. As chairman of the National Sunday School Convention in 1872 issued the call for the meeting that established the International Uniform

Sunday School Lessons. In 1875 became editor of the *Sunday School Times*. Due to a break in health made a trip to Egypt and Palestine; then in 1880-1881 wrote *Kadesh-barnea* showing that he had located the site of biblical Kadesh-barnea. Wrote *The Blood Covenant; The Threshold Covenant;* and *The Covenant of Salt*. In 1888 delivered at Yale the Lyman Beecher lectures, which were published under the title *The Sunday School: Its Origin, Mission, Methods, and Auxiliaries*.

TRUTH, SOJOURNER ISABELLA (c. 1797-1883). Born Ulster County, New York. In 1843 began to preach against slavery and in 1851 for women's rights. Travelled through Connecticut, Massachusetts, Ohio, Indiana, Illinois, and Kansas speaking against slavery. Wanted to have a black state west of the Mississsippi.

TUCKER, ALFRED ROBERT (1849-1914), Anglican missionary to Uganda, born in Windermere, England, of artist parents; and became an artist of some distinction. At age twenty-nine entered Christ Church, Oxford, ordained in the Church of England ministry in 1882. After eight years of parish work in England, chosen to fill a vacant bishopric in Uganda, and was accordingly consecrated the third bishop of Eastern Equatorial Africa, succeeding bishops Hannington and Parker from 1890 to 1908 and bishop of Uganda from 1898 to 1911. Just fourteen years before this the mission had been opened by Alexander Mackay. Three weeks after arriving, he conducted first communion service, and only a few days later, the bishop was on his way back to England to make a personal appeal to the church for more help in Uganda. During his twenty-one years of episcopate the mission experienced a mass movement toward Christianity, and the Anglican church membership increased to over one hundred thousand. In 1911 when Bishop Tucker again visited England to plead for funds for the African church, he was offered the canonry of Durham which he accepted, and held until his death five years later. Chief literary work was *Eighteen Years in Uganda and East Africa*. The missionary bishop was largely responsible for bringing Uganda under the British crown and for instituting the progressive policies that have made that country one of the finest in Africa.

TULLOCH (tŭl'ŭk), **JOHN** (1823-1886), Scottish liberal theologian and educator, born at Dron, near Perth, Scotland, educated at St. Andrews and Edinburgh. Later studied theology in Germany where he came under the influence of Neander and Baur. After serving as a parish minister for a few years at Dundee and Kettins, Forfarshire, in 1854 became principal and professor of theology at St. Mary's College, St. Andrews University. In 1878 elected moderator of the General Assembly. In 1882 appointed dean of the chapel royal and dean of the Thistle. Tulloch is chiefly remembered for his endeavor to awaken a spirit of liberal orthodoxy in the Church of Scotland, yet as one who opposed disestablishment. Most important treatise was *Rational Theology and Christian Philosophy in England in the Seventeenth Century*, two volumes.

TYCONIUS (tĭk ō'nĭ ŭs) (d. c. 400), a moderate Donatist and scholarly theologian. In his two works, now lost, *De Bello intestino* and *Expositiones diversarum causarum,* he seems to have taught that the Church must be a society spread over the whole earth, and must contain both good and bad until the last judgment, since the church is a "twofold body of Christ," of which one part makes up the true Christians and the other those who appear to be. The church to him was the sole divinely provided institution into which all men have to enter for salvation. Chief writing was *Liber Regularum,* published about 382, now extant. In it he propounded seven rules for the interpretation of Scripture. Augustine greatly esteemed this book in spite of Tychonius' Donatism. Also wrote a Commentary on the Apocalypse. Augustine made much use of these latter writings.

TYNDALE (tĭn'dl), **WILLIAM** (c. 1494-1536), Bible translator, reformer and martyr, born probably at North Nibley, Gloucestershire, England. Was in orders, having been ordained about 1521. While attending Oxford and Cambridge, became very proficient Greek scholar. The Greek New Testament of Erasmus and the works of Luther awakened in him the desire to give the Bible to the common people in their own language. Went to Hamburg where he studied Hebrew with some prominent Jews. His English New Testament was printed in Worms, Germany (1525-1526). English merchants smuggled his New Testaments into England. This translation of the New Testament, and of the Pentateuch which he translated later, and his book, *The Obedience of a Christian Man,* had vital influence upon the English people. By 1534, believing that the Reformation in England had progressed far enough that it would be safe for him to come out of his concealment, he settled at Antwerp, Belgium, continuing his writing, and beginning the work of an evangelist. He was arrested, imprisoned in the castle of Vilvorde, near Brussels, Belgium, tried, either for heresy or treason, or both, and convicted. First strangled and then burned in the prison yard on October 6, 1536. Very few of the details of Tyndale's life and death are known, less than almost any of his contemporaries.

TYRREL (tĭr'ĕl), **GEORGE HENRY** (1861-1909), liberal Roman Catholic theologian, born in Dublin, Ireland. Enrolled in Trinity College, Dublin in 1878; strongly influenced by Cardinal Newman, the next year left the Anglican church and became a Roman Catholic, and joined the Jesuit Order in 1880, becoming a priest in 1891. Studied philosophy at Stonyhurst (1882-1885) and theology at St. Beuno's, Wales (1888-1892), and speedily became known as one of the ablest Roman Catholic writers in England. His modernistic leanings, his denial that the Roman Catholic theology was perfect and inerrant, and his teaching that the visible church is but a mutable organism subject to development and modification, incurred the extreme displeasure of the ecclesiastical authorities, and led to expulsion from the Jesuit Order. Later for criticizing the encyclical of Pope Pius X on modernism, he was virtually excommunicated from the Church. In 1908 in a volume entitled *Mediaevalism* he replied to an attack on him by Cardinal Mercier of Belgium. Described himself as a liberal Roman Catholic. Before he died received conditional absolution and extreme unction from the Catholic priests. Among publications are the following: *Christianity at the Crossroads, A Much-Abused Letter, Hard Sayings, External Religion, Faith of the Millions,* and *Through Scylla and Charybdis.*

U

UCHIMURA (o͞o chē mo͞o'rȧ), **KANZO** (1861-1930), Founder of no church movement in Japan, born in Satama, a Samurai, graduated from the Sapporo Agricultural College in 1881. Accepted Christ in freshman year. During college days established his life pattern of independency. Two years after graduation went to the United States to study at Amherst College in Massachusetts. Four years later, in 1888, back in Japan, taught in the first high school of Tokyo, until as a Christian he could not bow to the new Imperial Rescript on Education. Consequently forced to give up teaching. Became a journalist. In his *Tokyo Yorodzu* thundered out prophetic warnings against the sins of government and nation, until he was forced to cease writing. In 1926 became the founder and editor of the *Japan Christian Intelligencer*. A biblical teacher and writer of extraordinary power; and a pronounced independent, opposed to all religious organizations and rites, advocated the separation of Japanese Christians from foreign missions control. Headed an independent Japanese church, one of the largest groups of unbaptized believers in Japan. His magazine, *The Bible Study,* was a magazine of high quality and large circulation. Wrote *The Diary of a Japanese Convert or How I Became a Christian, Japan and the Japanese, Consolation of a Christian,* and *The Pursuit of Peace*.

UEMURA (ü mo͞o'rȧ), **MASAHISA** (1857-1925), Presbyterian Japanese pastor and theologian, born a Shintoist of Samurai rank in the Tokugawa clan. Studied at Dr. James Ballagh's school in Yokohama, and at the English college opened by Dr. S. R. Brown, later named Meiji Gakuin and moved to Tokyo. Ordained in 1879, began preaching in a little church in a poor part of Tokyo, where his father and mother were among his first converts. Shortly after ordination started the first Young Men's Christian Association in Japan, and assisted in publishing the Association's magazine. A few years later assisted Verbeck and Hepburn in translating the Old Testament into the Japanese. Made preaching tours to the large cities of Southern Japan while attending his own little church, and also was teaching future ministers at the Meiji Gakuin. In 1888 made a trip to England. Much of his energy and money went into weekly *Gospel Newsletter* which spoke against evil even in government headquarters. In 1905 started the independent Japan Theological Seminary that trained many of Japan's strongest Christian leaders. In 1922, as permanent chairman of the National Board of Missions of his denomination, went to America and Scotland on the occasion of the fiftieth anniversary of the founding of the Nihon Kirisuto Kyokai (The Church of Christ in Japan) of which he was for a long time the foremost promoter. A champion of self-supporting and indigenous Christianity in Japan. Pastor for over thirty years of the Fujimichi Church, one of the largest churches in Tokyo. His daughter became his successor at his church in Tokyo, has had a great influence on the Christian life of Japan.

ULFILAS (ŭl'fĭ lăs), (c. 311-c. 381), apostle to the Goths, born perhaps in the region of the Lower Danube, which, according to some historians, had become the home of his Cappadocian parents, who in 246 had been taken captive by the Goths in one of their raids in Asia Minor. When about twenty taken by the king of the Goths on an embassage to Constantinople, where he remained for ten years. There became a Christian and received a good education. In Constantinople became acquainted with the Arian bishop, Eusebius of Nicomedia, who with other bishops consecrated him to the episcopate in 341. He then returned as a missionary to the Goths. It is said that the whole tribe of the Visigoths were won to the Christian faith. For the first seven years (341-348), he labored in his native land beyond the Danube, until persecution compelled him and his fellow Christians to seek refuge on Roman soil. From here he continued work among the Goths. By force of circumstances Ulfilas had been won to Arian Christianity. As an Arian preached to the Goths and led them to the same doctrinal views of Christianity. Greatly enhanced missionary labors by inventing an alphabet for the Goths, and then by giving them most of the Bible in their own language.

ULLMANN (o͝ol mȧn), **KARL** (1796-1865), German Evangelical theologian, son of a clergyman, born at Epfenbach, near Heidelberg, Germany, educated at Heidelberg and Tübingen. In 1817 ordained vicar of Kirchham, in 1819 began lecturing at Heidelberg, and in 1821 was elected professor. In 1829 accepted a call to Halle, where he lectured until 1836 on church history, symbolics, and systematic theology. In 1836 returned to Heidelberg where he taught the next twenty years. Became a leader of the mediating school of theology, opposed rationalism, and favored union between the Lutherans and the Reformed churches in Baden. In 1853 appointed prelate of the Evangelical Church in Karlsruhe, Baden, and in 1856 was elected president of the supreme ecclesiastical council. Unable to carry his clergy with him, he resigned in 1861. Without any public office, devoted his time to the editing of the *Theologische Studien und Kritiken*. Most important writings were *Gregory of Nazianzen, Reformers before the Reformation, The Sinlessness of Jesus,* and *The Essence of Christianity*.

UNAMUNO, MIGUEL DE (1864-1937), philosopher and author. Born in Bilboa, Spain. Educated at the University of Madrid. Professor cf language at the University of Salamanca until he became rector in 1901. Exiled to Canary Islands in 1924 for political ideas. Upon return after six years in exile he denounced materialism he saw. Two best known books are *The Tragic Sense of Life in Men and Peoples* and *The Agony of Christianity*. In the latter he suggested that Christ brought a sword rather than peace.

UNDERHILL, EVELYN (MRS. HUBERT STUART MOORE) (1875-1941), born in Wolverhampton, Staffordshire, England; educated at King's College for women, London; in 1927 made a fellow of the college. In 1907 following an experience of conversion from agnosticism to Christianity, turned to study of mysticism. A friend and disciple of Baron Friedrich von Hügel. An Anglican of Catholic sympathies; in later years a keen pacifist. Some writings: *Mysticism, The Mystic Way, Man and the Supernatural, The Life of the Spirit and the Life of Today, Mystics of the Church, Practical Mysticism, The Mystery of Sacrifice, Essentials of Mysticism, Fruits of the Spirit, Immanence* (poetry).

UNDERWOOD, HORACE GRANT (1859-1916), pioneer Presbyterian missionary to Korea, born in London, England. In 1872 father emigrated to New Durham, New Jersey, and engaged in a business which developed into the Underwood Typewriter Company. Horace continued his studies at New York University, and at the New Brunswick Theological Seminary. Ordained in 1884 to the Dutch Reformed ministry, he was sent by the Presbyterian Board of Foreign Missions to Korea the next year. In 1886 opened an orphanage in Seoul, which became the John D. Wells Academy, of which he was principal for some years. From 1887 to 1911, chairman of the Board of Bible translators at Seoul and of the Korean Religious Tract Society. Instrumental in organizing the Seoul branch of the Young Men's Christian Association. Pastor of Sai Munan Church in Seoul from 1889 to 1916. For eight years (1907-1915) professor of theology in the Korean Theological Seminary at Pyeng Yang. Became the unofficial adviser of the king of Korea. Among writings: *English-Korean and Korean-English Dictionary, Korean Grammar, Call of Korea, Religions of Eastern Asia*.

UNGER, MERRILL F. (1909-1980), American educator and writer, born in Baltimore, Maryland. He received his A.B. from Johns Hopkins University in 1930, his Th.M. and Th.D. from Dallas Theological Seminary in 1943 and 1945, and his Ph.D. from Johns Hopkins University in 1947. He held pastorates in Buffalo, New York (1934-1940), Dallas, Texas (1943-1944), and Baltimore, Maryland (1944-1947). From 1947-1948 he was Associate Professor of Greek at Gordon College of Theology and Missions and Lecturer in Archaeology and Old Testament at Gordon Divinity School. In 1948 he joined the faculty of Dallas Theological Seminary as Professor and Chairman of the Department of Semitic Languages and Old Testament Exegesis. He served in this capacity from 1948 until 1967 when he retired from teaching. On his retirement he received the title Professor Emeritus of Semitics and Old Testament Studies. From the time of his retirement until his death he pursued an extensive writing and speaking career. He wrote numerous books on a wide spectrum of topics. These include *Archaeology and the Old Testament, Archaeology and the New Testament, The Baptizing Work of the Holy Spirit, Famous Archaeological Discoveries, Pathways to Power, The God-filled Life, Biblical Demonology, Unger's Bible Dictionary, Unger's Bible Handbook, Introductory Guide to the Old Testament, Principles of Expository Preaching, Israel and the Arameans of Damascus, Zechariah: Prophet of Messiah's Glory, Stop Existing and Start Living, New Testament Teaching on Tongues, Demons in the World Today, Beyond the Crystal Ball, The Mystery of Bishop Pike, Unger's Guide to the Bible, God Is Waiting to Meet You, The Baptism and Gifts of the Holy Spirit, Starlit Paths for Pilgrim Feet, What Demons Can Do to Saints,* and *God, Where Are You?*. At the time of his death Dr. Unger was writing *Unger's Bible Commentary,* a multivolume exposition of the entire Bible.

UPHAM, THOMAS COGSWELL (1799-1872), Congregational divine and philosopher, born in Deerfield, New Hampshire, graduated from Dartmouth College and Andover Theological Seminary. Taught Hebrew in Andover (1821-1823); was associate pastor in the Congregational church at Rochester, New York (1823-1824); professor of mental and moral philosophy at Bowdoin College from 1824 until retirement in 1867. After retirement lived in quiet study and writing at Kennebunkport, Maine. Wrote upwards of sixty volumes, some of the more important: *Manual of Peace, The Constitution of Congregational Churches, Elements of Mental Philosophy, Philosophical and Practical Treatise on the Will, Life and Religious Experience of Madame Guyon, Principles of the Interior or Hidden Life, A Treatise on Divine Union, Christ in the Soul, Method in Prayer*. One of the very earliest advocates of international peace by peace tribunals. A strong supporter of the temperance movement, and a liberal patron of the colonization of blacks.

URBAN II (OTTO or **ODO DE LAGNY)** (1042-1099), pope (1088-1099), born at Chatillon-sur-Marne, in the province of Champaigne, France. Studied at Rheims, there becoming monk, canon, and archdeacon. About 1070 entered the monastery of Cluny, where he became prior. A little later called by Gregory VII to Rome to become his chief adviser. In 1078 made Cardinal bishop of Ostia, and in 1088 elected to the papal throne. In 1089 excommunicated his two chief enemies, Emperor Henry IV and antipope Clement III. Then he was expelled from Rome by the emperor and the antipope. For three years an exile from Rome, but spent time holding reformatory councils and building up strength in Germany and Italy against Henry and Clement until he was able to return to Rome in 1093. About the same time appeal for help against the Moslems came from Emperor Alexis of Constantinople. Urban also heard the report of Peter the Hermit concerning the ill treatment of Christian pilgrims in Palestine. These incidents led him to call a Council at Clermont in 1095, where he preached his fiery sermon for a crusade against the "infidels." Urban's activity in preaching the first crusade started a series of crusades to the Holy Land, which lasted for a period of one hundred seventy-five years.

URBAN V (GUILLAUME de GRIMOARD) (1310-1370), pope (1362-1370), born at Grisac in Languedoc, became a Benedictine monk and studied in the Universities of Toulouse, Montpellier, Paris, and Avignon. After ordination taught canon law in these same universities, later became vicar general at Clermont and Uzes. In 1362 elected pope. In many ways, the best of the Avignon popes. In vain planned for a crusade against the Turks. In 1367, upon the urging of Emperor Charles IV, Urban returned to Rome, disregarding the remonstrances of the French court and cardinals. Enthusiastically received by the Roman people and began at once to restore the badly neglected city and reestablish discipline among clergy and laity. Chose as his residence the Vatican at St. Peter's. The next year crowned the consort of Charles IV as German empress; in 1369 received the Greek emperor John Palaeologus into communion. When Perugia revolted and war broke out between England and France he was urged to return to Avignon. In 1370 yielded and returned to the French city.

URBAN VI (BARTOLOMMEO PRIGNANI) (1318-1389), pope (1378-1389), born at Naples, Italy, studied canon law, and became Archbishop of Averenza and of Bari. In 1378 elected pope. Early in reign he estranged cardinals by violent and overbearing manner. The French members of the College announced his election null, and proceeded to elect Robert of Geneva as antipope, who took the title Clement VII and removed the papal court to Avignon again. Thus began what is known in history as the Great Schism. Excommunicated Clement VII and his followers. Supported by Catharine of Siena, Sweden, England, Ireland, and a great part of Germany. Clement was supported by all the cardinals except four Italians, by France, Scotland, Savoy, Castile, Aragon, Navarre and Lorraine.

URBAN VIII (MAFFEO BARBERINI) (1568-1644), pope (1623-1644), born in Florence, studied in Rome and Bologna under the Jesuits. Twice papal nuncio in France; Archbishop of Nazareth (1604); cardinal (1606); Bishop of Spoleto (1608); legate of Bologna (1617); elected pope succeeding Gregory XV. In policy an Italian prince rather than the head of the Roman Catholic church. Acquired the duchy of Urbino for the papacy; published a revision of the breviary; instituted the College of Propaganda; in the Thirty Years War sided with France against the emperor and Spain; denounced Jansenists; built Barberini Palace and founded the famous Barberini library, which later became a part of the Vatican library. Greatest fault was nepotism. Otherwise his morals and ideals were rather lofty. A gifted classical scholar.

URSINUS (o͞or sē′nŭs), **ZACHARIAS** (1534-1583), German theologian, born at Breslau, received education at Wittenberg, under Philip Melanchthon; in Geneva under John Calvin and in Paris under Jean Mercier. Taught for a year at Elisabethschule, but because of Calvinistic leanings was forced to leave Breslau. In 1561 Elector Frederick III, who had decided in favor of Calvinism, appointed him director of Collegium Sapientiae at the University of Heidelberg. From 1561 to 1568 was professor of dogmatics at the university. He and Kaspar Olevianus, a disciple of Calvin, were given the task of drawing up the Heidelberg Catechism. The catechism was officially adopted the next year as the offical creed of the German Reformed churches. Later became teacher at Neustadt-on-the-Hardt.

USSHER (ŭsh'ẽr) or **USHER, JAMES** (1581-1656), Archbishop of Armagh and primate of Ireland, born in Dublin, educated at Trinity College, Dublin. Ordained priest in 1601. About 1605 became chancellor of St. Patrick's; in 1607 professor of divinity at Trinity College; and in 1615 vice-chancellor of the University of Dublin. In 1620 made Bishop of Meath; in 1623 privy-councillor for Ireland; and in 1625, Archbishop of Armagh, succeeding uncle Henry Ussher (1550-1631). Left Ireland for England in 1640, and for about eight years preacher at Lincoln's Inn. Constant in loyalty to the crown, a strong advocate of episcopacy, and on cordial terms with Archbishop Laud. At the same time a Calvinist and stood in good favor with Oliver Cromwell. Held in respect by all classes—by the Puritans for his Calvinistic theology, by the churchmen for his reverence for antiquity and tradition, and by the royalists for steadfastness for the king. He wrote: *Annals of the Old and New Testament* which forms the basis of the Biblical chronology in the King James Version of the Bible.

V

VALDÉS (väl dās′), **JUAN DE** (c. 1500-1541), Spanish-Italian theologian, humanist, and reformer. Born at Cuenca, Spain, and educated at the University of Alcalá. Greatly influenced by Erasmus, became a Spanish humanist. Imbibed Reformation principles in Germany, accepted Luther's idea of justification by faith, preaching it and other evangelical doctrines, but remained a Catholic. About 1528 wrote a treatise, *A Dialogue between Mercury and Shannon,* criticizing the Church so severely that the Inquisition made Spain uncomfortable for him. Went to Italy shortly after 1534, and after some time in Rome and Bologna, went to Naples where he resided the rest of his life. Pietro Martire Vermigli came under the spell of his preaching, and he surpassed Valdes in becoming an evangelical. Valdes' influence was strong also upon Ochino. After his death, Vermigli and Ochino, abandoning the idea of regenerating Catholicism, left Italy. Valdes translated the Psalms from the Hebrew and much of the New Testament from the Greek into the Spanish.

VALENTINIAN III (FLAVIUS PLACIDIUS VALENTINIANUS) (419-455), Emperor of Rome (425-455), born at Ravenna. In 445 issued an edict which recognized the bishop of Rome as the primate of the whole Christian church, who should hold the highest judicial and legislative power in all church matters. Gave as his reasons for this enactment, the primacy of Peter, the dignity of the city, and the decree of the holy synod. Resistance to the Roman bishop was affirmed to be an offense against the Roman state. This decree, coming at the time that Leo I, The Great, was bishop of Rome, gave strong impetus to the development of papal authority and to the supremacy of the papacy. Upon consultation with Pope Leo, the emperor called the ecumenical council which met at Chalcedon in 451.

VALENTINUS (second century), founder of one of the Gnostic sects, born in Egypt. Hellenistic learning in Alexandria included both Pythagorean and Platonic philosophy, claimed also to have received instruction from one Theudas, a pupil of Paul. Went to Rome about 136 seemingly as an adherent of the orthodox church, and as a teacher. However, gradually drifted away from orthodoxy, began propagating his Gnostic heresy, finally was excommunicated and went to Cyprus where he continued his heresy. His religious system seems to have been derived from his fertile imagination, from oriental mythology and mysticism, from Hellenistic syncretism, from Platonic dualism, which separated the divine world of ideas from the material world of phenomena, and from Christian ideas. While alive he made many disciples; his system was the most widely diffused of all forms of Gnosticism. Ultimate salvation for the Valentinian Gnostics was for the few who were able to attain to the higher spiritual life and were privileged to enter the Pleroma, the ultimate fullness of the divine life.

VALERIAN (vȧ lēr′ĭ ăn) **(PUBLIUS LICINIUS VALERIANUS)** (193-c. 269), Roman emperor (253-260). Called by the army to become emperor. He issued a rescript in 257 which forbade the Christians to hold assemblies or to use the catacombs for burial, and which ordered the clergy into banishment. In 258 a very severe rescript was issued which ordered bishops, presbyters, and deacons at once to be executed. In this persecution Cyprian of Carthage and many others were martyred. In a war with the Persians, Valerian fell into the hands of the Persian king, and was held prisoner until his death.

VALLA, LORENZO (c. 1406-1457), Italian humanist and historical critic. Born in Rome. Taught classical languages in several Italian universities. Spent his last decade in Rome as secretary to Nicholas V. In his 1440 book on the Donation of Constantine he proved that document, formerly used to support papal claims to power, to be a forgery.

VANDERKEMP, JOHANNES THEODORUS (1747-1811), Dutch Reformed missionary to South Africa, born at Rotterdam, Holland. Educated at the University of Leiden. Entered the army but led a dissolute life. After sixteen years as a military officer, married, entered the University of Edinburgh, where he completed a medical course, then returned to Holland and began successful period of medical practice. Through the sad death by drowning of his wife and daughter he was brought to a humble faith, and soon offered himself to the London Missionary Society. Ordained and sent by the society to South Africa in 1799, when he was past fifty years of age. Before going, however, initiated a missionary society in his native land, the Netherlands Missionary Society at Rotterdam, for many years the only missionary society in Holland. After landing at Capetown, and during his stay at the Cape, helped form a society to be known as the South African Society for Promoting the Spread of Christ's Kingdom at the Cape of Good Hope. Decided to work among the Kaffirs and Hottentots, but to go farther interior than any others had gone. Was means of founding the Missionary Institute at Bethelsdorp, in 1803, about eight miles from Port Elizabeth. When Vanderkemp was about sixty he married a young slave, one of his native converts. The unsuitability of this union had an unwholesome influence on the mission.

VAN DUSEN, HENRY PITNEY (1897-1975). Born in Philadelphia. Educated at Princeton University, Union Seminary, and the University of Edinburgh. Professor of theology in Union Theological Seminary from 1926 to 1963 and its president from 1945 to 1963. Originated term "Third Force" for evangelical charismatic and holiness groups.

VANE (vān), **HENRY** (1613-1662), English statesman, born at Hadlow, Kent, England, and converted to Puritanism. Entered Magdalen College, Oxford, but refused to take the oath of supremacy and allegiance. Leaving the university traveled on the Continent, then in 1635 emigrated to New England. The next year elected governor of Massachusetts Bay Colony. Failed of re-election because of the religious disputes in which he became involved. Returned to England in 1637. Elected joint treasurer of the navy, entered Parliament, and was knighted by Charles I in 1640. From 1643 to 1646 leader in the House of Commons and was a member of the Westminster Assembly. Assisted Roger Williams in obtaining his charter for Rhode Island in 1643, and was influential in forming the Solemn League and Covenant with Scotland, and condemned Pride's Purge in 1648. Opposed Archbishop Laud, yet at the same time somewhat apprehensive of the growth toward power of Cromwell. When the Civil War broke out conspicuous in military and theological politics. On the establishment of the Commonwealth, appointed to the Council of State in 1649, and was one of its most active members. One of the commissioners who negotiated the union of England and Scotland in 1652. However, in 1653 broke with Cromwell when the latter dissolved the long Parliament, and withdrew from public life. In 1660, following the Restoration, arrested and sent to the Tower, in 1662 impeached for high treason, and beheaded on Tower Hill.

VAN RAALTE, ALBERTUS CHRISTIAN (1811-1876). Born in Holland. Educated in medicine and theology at the University of Leiden. Minister from 1834 to 1844. Led Dutch Reformed immigrants to Holland, Michigan about 1846. Part of them formed the Christian Reformed church in 1847. He founded Hope College and Seminary.

VAN TIL, CORNELIUS (1895-1964). Theological educator. Born in the Netherlands. Educated at Calvin College, Princeton Theological Seminary, and the University of Debrecen, Hungary. Came to America in 1905. Ordained in the Christian Reformed church in 1927. Professor at Princeton Theological Seminary from 1928 to 1929 and in Westminster Seminary from 1929. Supporter of presuppositional Calvinism and opponent of Neo-Orthodoxy as a new modernism from Kant. Wrote *The New Modernism, The Defense of the Faith, Christianity and Barthianism,* and several other theological works.

VARLEY, HENRY (1835-1912), British evangelist, born at Tattershall, Lincolnshire, England. Henry was converted at the age of sixteen. In 1854 at age nineteen he went to Australia for two or three years to get a start in business. Upon return to England he married, established a business, began preaching at Notting Dale as an unordained minister in a non-denominational church. In 1860 he and father-in-law built the West London Free Tabernacle, which could seat seventeen hundred people. Soon built the Working Men's Hall and the Tabernacle Schools in connection with his church. In 1868 gave up business and devoted time to evangelistic work, taking missions in the United Kingdom and abroad, visiting South Africa, India, the United States, Australia, New Zealand, and Canada, preaching wherever he went. In 1882, after a pastorate of more than twenty years, resigned from the West London Tabernacle that he might be more free to devote himself to world-wide evangelistic work. The last three years of life spent mostly at Brighton, where he continued preaching. It was Henry Varley who said, "It remains for the world to see what the Lord can do with a man wholly consecrated to Christ," a great challenge to D. L. Moody.

VASEY, THOMAS (1731-1826). Born in England. Ordained in 1784 by John Wesley to work in the Thirteen Colonies as a circuit rider. Helped to establish Methodism in America.

VAUGHAN, CHARLES JOHN (1816-1897), Church of England clergyman and educator, born at Leicester, England, educated at Rugby and Trinity College, Cambridge. Studied law for a time but turned to theology, ordained in 1841. For three years vicar of St. Martin's, Leicester, where father had been vicar several years earlier. From 1844-1859 headmaster of Harrow; and offered the bishopric of Rochester, but declined it to become (1860) the vicar of Doncaster, where in addition to pastoral duties, assumed the task of preparing hundreds of university graduates for the ministry. In 1869 master of the Temple, and in 1879 also dean of Llandaff, Wales. In 1883-1884 took a leading part in the founding of University College of Cardiff, became president in 1894. Had wide influence as a preacher and leader of the Broad Church party of the Anglican Church. Wrote commentaries of Greek text with notes on Romans, Philippians, Hebrews, and Revelation.

VEDDER (vĕd'ĕr), **HENRY CLAY** (1853-1935), Baptist clergyman and church historian, born at De Ruyter, New York, educated at the University of Rochester and at Rochester Theological Seminary. Licensed to preach in 1875, ordained in 1894. From 1876 to 1892 a member of the editorial staff of *The Examiner,* leading Baptist newspaper in New York; for two years editor-in-chief. From 1885-1892 editor also of the *Baptist Quarterly Review,* 1894-1926 professor of church history in Crozer Theological Seminary, Chester, Pennsylvania. After retirement from Crozer in 1926 he became associate editor of the *Chester Times*. His writings include: *Baptists and Liberty of Conscience* and *A Short History of the Baptists*.

VENN (vĕn), **SIR HENRY** (1725-1797), Church of England clergyman, born at Barnes, Surrey, near London, England, studied at St. John's College and Jesus College, Cambridge; elected fellow at Queen's College. Ordained in 1749. After holding several minor curacies, became curate of Clapham in 1754, vicar of Huddersfield, Yorkshire in 1759, and vicar of Yelling in 1771. He had a wholesome influence upon Charles Simeon and Joseph Jowett. A leader in carrying the gospel to the manufacturing classes in the large industrial town of Huddersfield. An indefatigable preacher of moderate Calvinistic theology. Became a warm friend of George Whitefield and Lady Huntingdon. Most popular work: *The Complete Duty of Man,* a sincere and vigorous work on practical piety.

VENN, HENRY (1796-1873). Born on Clapham Commons, London. Ordained in 1820 as an Anglican minister. After pastoral work appointed a fellow of Queen's College, Cambridge from 1824 to 1829. Secretary of the Church Missionary Society from 1841 to 1873. Advocated that national churches in mission fields should be self-governing, self-supporting, and self-propagating. Ideas developed before the indigeneous church concept of Rufus Anderson and Nevius. Wanted a "native clergy."

VENN, JOHN (1759-1813). Educated at Cambridge. After rectorship at Little Dunham, Norfolk for about ten years, he became rector of the Anglican church in Clapham Commons from 1792 to 1813 where the Evangelical Reformers, such as Wilberforce, attended. Helped found the Church Missionary Society in 1799.

VERBECK (vûr'bĕk), **GUIDO HERMAN FRIDOLIN** (1830-1898), Dutch American missionary to Japan, born at Zeist, Holland. Received earlier education in the Moravian Academy at Zeist and at the Utrecht Polytechnic Institute. In early life united with the Moravian Brethren. Their missionary zeal and his meeting with such men as Gützlaff of China greatly influenced his life. At twenty-two came to America, engaged as a mechanical engineer in Wisconsin and Arkansas. In 1855 entered the Theological Seminary in Auburn, New York to prepare for the ministry and for missionary work. In 1859 graduated from the seminary, married, ordained by the Presbyterian church, received into the Dutch Reformed church in America, appointed as a missionary to Japan by the Reformed Church Mission Board of New York, and reached Nagasaki as a missionary. His first efforts were limited largely to Bible distribution. The ban on Christianity in Japan was firm; very slow progress could be made. Not until 1866 did he secure his first converts, at which time three men of influence confessed Christ, and were baptized. In 1860 became principal of a school for foreign languages and sciences in Nagasaki, which was attended by Samurai. This led in 1863 to appointment by the Japanese government to engage in government educational work. For about sixteen years, with the consent of the home board, remained in this service, training young men who became leaders of the nation. Organized the national system of education, superintended the foreign teachers and instructors of the Imperial University of Tokyo, and translated many foreign constitutions, laws, and other documents into the Japanese language. By year of his death, 1898, Japan was admitted as an equal with modern nations. Much credit for this attainment was due to Verbeck's powerful influence for almost forty years over the government of Japan. Wrote a *History of Protestant Missions in Japan*. Went back to missionary activity from 1879.

VERBIEST (vĕr bēst'), **FERDINAND** (1623-1688), Flemish astronomer and Roman Catholic missionary to China, born at Pitthem, Belgium, studied at Coutrai, Louvain, and Seville. Became a Jesuit, received a thorough training in mathematics and astronomy under Schall, then went out to preach in China in 1657. Ordered to Peking to assist Schall, suffered imprisonment with Schall in the veteran missionary's latter days. Learned the Tartar language and demonstrated superior knowledge of mathematics and astronomy over Moslem rivals; put in charge of the calendar reform by the brilliant young emperor K'ang Hsi. At the emperor's command he constructed valuable astronomical instruments and prepared cannon for use against rebel forces. Instrumental in determining the boundary line between China and Russia. The hostile attitude that had been developed against Christianity was thus being reversed, and the Jesuits gained much favor at the court. Many Jesuits came to China and church accessions increased in many parts of the empire. Until the end of his life was highly respected and honored. At death an elaborate court funeral was given him.

VEREGIN, PETER (d. 1924), Doukhobor leader. Born in Russia and three times exiled to Siberia. Moved to Saskatchewan, Canada in 1903 to lead the Doukhobors there. Moved the colony to British Columbia. Opposed government education by nude demonstrations. Killed on a train by a time bomb explosion.

VERMIGLI (vār mē'lyē), **PIETRO MARTIRE (PETER MARTYR)** (1500-1562), Italian Reformer, born in Florence, Italy. At age sixteen entered an Augustinian cloister and later studied at Padua and Bologna. By 1541 elected visitor-general of order. In Italy came into close association with Valdes and Ochino, all of them adopting evangelical views of the Reformation. His conversion and evangelical preaching soon brought him under the ban of the Inquisition. Upon the death of Valdes in Italy, Vermigli and Ochino fled from Naples. First went to Switzerland, then located at Strassburg, where after the death of Capito in 1542 he filled the post of lecturer in theology for several years. In 1547 he and Ochino accepted Bishop Cranmer's invitation to become professors at Oxford. Took part in the preparation of the Book of Common Prayer. When forced by the persecution by Queen Mary to leave England, returned to Strassburg where he resumed position as professor of theology. In 1556 became professor of Hebrew at Zurich which position he then held until he died. Friend of Heinrich Bullinger of Zurich; before his death assisted Bullinger in preparing the Second Helvetic Confession which was adopted in 1566.

VIGILANTIUS (vĭj ĭ län'shĭ ŭs) (c. 370-c. 406), presbyter of Aquitaine, born at Calagurris in Western Gaul. Ordained presbyter at Barcelona, Spain about 395; visited Jerome in Bethlehem. A man of pious but vehement zeal, and of no little literary talent. In a book that is now lost wrote against monasticism and the superstition connected with it. Opposed celibacy and the vows of poverty of the priests, the worship of saints and relics, and the belief in the miracles of the martyrs. Rejected the double standard of morals, a higher standard for monks and clergy, and a lower for the laity. Jerome bitterly attacked him in his *Contra Vigilantium*.

VILATTE (vĭ lŏt'te), **JOSEPH RENE** (1854-1929), organizer of American Old Catholic Church, priest of French Canadian ancestry. About 1870 ordained by the Old Catholics of Switzerland, and sent to America to organize the scattered congregations of Old Catholics in America. Being unable to secure satisfactory episcopal leadership for the new movement, (1892) consecrated archbishop by Archbishop Francis Xavier Alvarez of the Syro-Jacobite Church of Malabar. On returning to America organized the Old Catholic church, himself its archbishop and primate. Later returned to the Roman Catholic church, but before doing so, about 1915, consecrated F. E. J. Floyd, a former Protestant Episcopal priest, as his successor. In 1921 consecrated Dr. George Alexander McGuire, for many years a priest in the Protestant Episcopal Church, as bishop of a Negro group of Episcopalians, who took the name of the African Orthodox church. Died in a French monastery.

VILLEGAIGNON (vēl gā nyôn'), **NICOLAS DURAND DE** (1510-1571), French soldier; founder and betrayer of the French Protestant Colony in Brazil, born in Provence, France of a noble family, educated for the navy. Distinguished himself in service for Charles V against the Turks and Algerians. In 1548 escorted Mary Stuart from Scotland to France, in 1550 took part in the defense of Malta; made a knight of the Order of Malta. In 1554 received appointment as vice-admiral of Brittany, and the next year, through the influence of Admiral Coligny, received the support of the king to found a French colony in Brazil as a refuge for Protestants as well as a colonizing project for France. John Calvin was interested in the expedition as a missionary colonizing project for the Reformed Church. In 1555 sailed from Havre to the bay of Rio de Janeiro. The following year in answer to letters he sent to Calvin and Coligny asking for more Protestants, men were sent and the colony was increased. But reverses came and disputes arose over doctrines and practices among the leaders; and Villegaignon betrayed the colony, favoring the Roman Catholics, and finally forbade all religious services and put to death as heretics those who disobeyed him. This first attempt of Calvinism to plant a colony in the new world came to naught. Finally retired to the estates of the Knights of Malta at Beauvais, where he died, loathed by the Protestants and suspected by the Roman Catholics.

VINCENT, JOHN HEYL (1832-1920), American Methodist Episcopal bishop and Sunday school promoter, born at Tuscaloosa, Alabama of Huguenot ancestry. At six moved with parents to Pennsylvania, and attended academies at Milton and Lewisburg, Pennsylvania, but received little formal college education. Began to preach at eighteen, preached in several churches in Pennsylvania and New Jersey. In 1855 ordained deacon, two years later received elder's orders and transferred to the Rock River Conference in Illinois, where he served as pastor in several Illinois churches; ordained bishop in 1888. Became vitally interested and active in training teachers for Sunday school work; in 1861 held the first Sunday school institute in America, at the same time began the publishing of an immense quantity of Sunday school literature, which included The *Sunday School Quarterly* and other helps. In 1872 the Uniform Sunday School lessons had their beginning, a result of Vincent's work. In 1874 he and Lewis Miller organized the Chautauqua Assembly to educate Sunday school teachers. From 1868 to 1888 corresponding secretary of the Sunday School Union and editor of the Methodist Episcopal Sunday school publications. In 1900 placed in charge of the European work of the denomination, with residence at Zurich, Switzerland. In 1904 retired from active life. Among writings are: *The Modern Sunday School, The Church School and Its Officers*.

VINCENT, MARVIN RICHARDSON (1834-1922), Presbyterian biblical scholar, born at Poughkeepsie, New York, educated at Columbia College, and Union Theological Seminary, New York City. Became the first classical instructor in a grammar school connected with the college, then four years later became professor of Latin at the Methodist University, Troy, New York. In 1860 entered the Methodist ministry, and served as a Methodist pastor for one year; but in 1863 was ordained by the Presbytery of Troy. For ten years pastor of the Presbyterian church at Troy, and for fourteen years of the Church of the Covenant, New York City. In 1887 became professor of New Testament exegesis and criticism in Union Theological Seminary, New York, becoming professor in 1916. Noted for his four-volume set of *Word Studies in the New Testament*. Translated Bengel's *Gnomon*. Wrote *Students' New Testament Handbook, Critical Commentary on Philippians and Philemon, Biblical Inspiration and Christ, History of the Textual Criticism of the New Testament,* and *Christ as Teacher*.

VINCENT DE PAUL (c. 1580-1660), "promoter of organized charity," born in Gascony, France, studied under the Franciscans at Toulouse, ordained priest in 1600. Captured by Mohammedan pirates and held as slave for three years. Vincent organized Parish Societies to care for the needy and for prisoners and for galley slaves, established homes for the aged and homes for unwanted babies. In 1633, he founded the Sisters of Charity, an organization that is devoted to the care and education of the sick, the poor, the aged, and the orphaned. He was canonized in 1737.

VINET (vē nĕ'), **ALEXANDRE RUDOLF** (1797-1847), Swiss evangelical preacher, professor, and literary critic, born in the canton of Vaud, near Lausanne, Switzerland of Huguenot heritage. Educated at the gymnasium and academy of Lausanne. In twentieth year appointed instructor in French at the gymnasium and normal school at Basel, where he lived and taught for the next twenty years. In 1819 ordained to the Reformed church ministry. During twenty years at Basel frequently preached in the French Reformed church, though he never was a pastor. In 1837 accepted a call to the chair of practical theology at the academy of Lausanne, where he labored the next nine years. Preaching was orthodox, but in his relation with others he was tolerant and liberal. A strong defender of freedom of thought and conscience. In 1846, because of the state church's opposition to Protestantism, he resigned theological professorship and soon joined the Free church which was begun at that time. Often preached for its congregations, acted as a member of its committee on organization, and helped prepare a confession of faith for the new church. Among published writings are: *The Treatise on Homiletics,* and *History of Preaching Among the Reformed During the Seventeenth Century*.

VIRET (vē rĕ'), **PIERRE** (1511-1571), Swiss Reformer, born at Orbe, Canton of Vaud, Switzerland, educated for the priesthood, studying for three years at Paris under Le Fèvre. Soon renounced Roman Catholicism, returned to native town, began to preach the evangelical faith, and in 1531 was ordained by Farel. Converted his parents and about two hundred persons in Orbe. Aroused many bitter enemies among Roman Catholic priests, one of whom attempted to poison him. The attempt left his health seriously impaired the rest of his life. Had a definite part in getting the Reformation established in Geneva. When Geneva tired of the anarchists and called the Reformers back to the city, he was the first to return, and helped to prepare the way for Calvin's return in 1541. Chief work, however, was accomplished at Lausanne, where he labored from 1536 to 1559 as pastor, teacher and writer. Pastor for a time at Lyons where he presided over the fourth national synod of the Huguenots in 1563, and preached there until the Catholics drove him out. He then went to Orthez, where he passed remaining days as preacher and theological teacher.

VLADIMIR I (vlăd'ĭ mĭr), **(SAINT, THE GREAT)** (956-1015), Russian emperor. In 980 he became sole emperor. By further conquest enlarged empire, and made Kiev capital. In the conquest of the town of Kherson in the Crimean Peninsula about 987, succeeded in obtaining Anna, a princess of the Byzantine imperial house, to add to his array of wives and concubines. Either through her or through some other influence decided to accept Christianity, choosing the Eastern or Greek Orthodox faith in 987 or 988. Undertook the mass conversion of his people. His character seems to have changed after his conversion. Greek Orthodox Christianity became the Russian official religion. By the end of Vladimir's reign Russia contained three bishoprics. He was later canonized by the Greek Church.

VOETIUS (vē'shĭ ŭs), **GISBERT (or VOET)** (1588-1676), Dutch Reformed dogmatic theologian, born at Heusden, Netherlands, educated at the University of Leiden. In 1611 became pastor of the church in the village of Vlymen, and in 1617 of the church in native town. In 1618 delegate to the Synod of Dort, where as a stern Calvinist he exercised a strong influence over the Remonstrants or Arminians. Continued to preach against Arminianism the rest of his life. Entered into persistent controversy with the liberal and moderately Calvinistic Cocceius. With much vigor also opposed the philosophy of Descartes. In 1634 accepted the professorship of theology and oriental languages at the newly founded academy of Utrecht (two years later, University of Utrecht), where he spent the last forty years of his life. In 1637 served also as pastor of the Utrecht congregation. A diligent scholar, and an earnest and sincere Christian. Works were published under the title of *Selectae Disputationes Theologicae*.

VOLIVA (vŏl'ĭ vȧ), **WILBUR GLENN** (1870-1942), overseer of Christian Catholic church in Zion, born near Newton, Indiana, educated at Hiram College, Ohio, and at Union Christian College, Marion, Indiana, studied privately at Stanfordville, New York. Ordained to the ministry in the Christian Connection (New Light) denomination in 1889, held pastorates in Linden, Indiana, and Urbana, Illinois, held supply charges at Albany, New York and York Harbor, Maine. In 1895 united with the Christian (Campbellite) church, and held a pastorate at Washington Court House, Ohio. In 1899 joined the Christian Catholic Church in Zion and for a short time was elder in charge of North Side Zion Tabernacle, Chicago. Then transferred to Cincinnati in 1900. From 1901 to 1906 overseer of the work of the denomination in Australia. In 1906 assistant to John Alexander Dowie in Zion City, Illinois; and upon Dowie's death in 1907, overseer of the Christian Catholic church in Zion. Continued the teaching and views of Dowie, but after his death many changes and modifications came into the tenets and practices of the denomination.

VOLTAIRE (assumed name of **JEAN FRANÇOIS MARIE AROUET**) (1694-1778), French writer, born of Jansenist parentage at Chalency near Paris, educated at the humanistic Jesuit College, Louis-le-Grand in Paris. His biting tongue and satirical verse got him into trouble frequently, twice landing him in the Bastille. Then forced to leave France, went to England and resided in London from 1726 to 1729. Came under the influence of Sir Isaac Newton, John Locke and the English deists. From 1734 to 1749 his principal place of residence was at Cirey in Lorraine, where he lived with the Marchioness du Chatelet. From 1750 to 1752 in Berlin at the invitation of Frederick the Great of Prussia. At Geneva he was a great benefactor to the poor people there; during his last twenty years at Ferney near the Swiss border, he was one of the most prominent men in Europe. Voltaire became most bitter against the Roman Catholic church. His whole life purpose came to be to "crush the infamous one." He opposed any state church, and finally all supernatural religion. He also bitterly attacked atheism. He was not an atheist, but a deist. A prolific though not a profound writer. Wrote seventy-two works embracing tragedy, epic and lyric poetry, oratory, essays, political pamphlets, history, novels, science, and philosophy. Away from Paris for many years, in 1778 returned to the city, received with great ovation.

VON HUGEL, FRIEDRICH (1852-1925), Roman Catholic theologian and mystic.

Born in Florence but went to England in 1873. Founded London Society for the Study of Religion. Wrote *Eternal Life* and *The Reality of God.*

VOS, GEERHARDUS (1862-1949), Presbyterian clergyman and theologian, born at Heerenveen, Holland, educated at the seminary of the Christian Reformed church at Grand Rapids, Michigan, Princeton Theological Seminary, the University of Berlin, and the University of Strassburg, where he received the degree of Ph.D. Professor of theology in the seminary of the Holland Christian Reformed church, Grand Rapids (1888-1893); of biblical theology at Princeton Seminary (1893-1932). Ordained Presbyterian minister in 1894. Chief writings: *The Mosaic Origins of the Pentateuchal Codes, Old and New Testament Biblical Theology, The Pauline Eschatology, The Self-Disclosure of Jesus, The Teaching of the Epistle to the Hebrews, The Teaching of Jesus Concerning the Kingdom of God and the Church, Grace and Glory,* and several volumes of poems.

VOSSIUS (vŏs'ē ŭs), **GERHARDUS JOHANNES (VOSS** [vŏs], **GERHARD JOHANN)** (1577-1649), Dutch humanist, theologian, and classical scholar, born near Heidelberg, Germany of Dutch parentage, studied at the universities of Dort and Leiden. A professor successively at Leiden (1598-1600), Dort (1600-1615), Leiden (1622-1632), and Amsterdam (1632-1649). In the latter, professor of general and church history. In 1618 became involved in the dispute of the Remonstrants and their opponents and published *Historia de Controversiis quas Pelagius ejusque Reliquiae Moverunt* in defense of Arminianism. In *Dissertationes Tres de Tribus Symbolis* he decisively disproves the traditional authorship of the Athanasian Creed. One of the first scholars to apply the historical method to Christian dogmatics.

WACE (wās), **HENRY** (1836-1924), Church of England clergyman, born in London, educated at Marlborough, Rugby, King's College in London, and Brasenose College, Oxford. Ordained in 1862. From 1861 to 1903 successively filled the following positions: curate of St. Luke's, Berwick Street, London; and of St. James, Westminster; lecturer of Grosvenor Chapel; chaplain and preacher of Lincoln's Inn; rector of St. Michael's, Cornhill. At various times during these years also Boyle lecturer at King's College, London, and Bampton lecturer at Oxford; professor of ecclesiastical history and principal at King's College; select preacher at Cambridge and Oxford; examining chaplain to the Archbishop of Canterbury; chaplain to the queen and to the king; prebendary in St. Paul's Cathedral; and rural dean of the East City. In 1903 became Dean of Canterbury, a position of honor which he held until his death. In collaboration with Sir William Smith edited *A Dictionary of Christian Biography, Literature, Sects, and Doctrines from the Time of the Apostles to the Age of Charlemagne;* in collaboration with Dr. Philip Schaff edited the second series of the *Nicene and Post-Nicene Fathers* (fourteen volumes); and edited *The Speaker's Commentary on the Apocalypse* (two volumes) and also *The Primary Works of Luther.* He wrote also *The Foundations of Faith, The Students' Manual of Evidences of Christianity, The Bible and Modern Investigation,* and *Prophecy, Jewish and Christian.*

WAGNER, CHARLES (1852-1918), French Protestant clergyman and moral essayist, born at Wibersviller, District of Chateau Salins, Lorraine, Germany, studied at Paris, Strassburg, and Göttingen. Preached for a year at Barr in the Vosges; in 1876 left the German language and the Lutheran church, and began ministerial service in connection with the liberal wing of the French Protestant church. In 1882 went to Paris where he opened a Sunday school and did pastoral work and preaching. Wrote a book, *Youth,* 1891, in which he attacked the degenerate tendencies in life and literature. Also took part in many philanthropic and charitable undertakings. Helped found "The Union for Moral Action," and cooperated in the university extension courses. Known especially for volume on *The Simple Life,* which gained a wide reading in the United States.

WALDENSTRÖM (väl′dĕn strûm), **PAUL PETER** (1838-1917), Swedish theologian and reformer, born at Lulea, Sweden, and studied at the University of Uppsala; became professor of Greek, Hebrew, and theology at Gävle College. Ordained in the Swedish Lutheran church in 1864, but never had a pastoral charge. Essentially evangelical in teaching, but differing from the National church (1) by insisting on going directly to the Scriptures for doctrinal truth rather than to the creed, which led to his subsequent derogation of the Augsburg Confession; and (2) by insisting that salvation comes as a subjective commitment to Christ rather than through the mediation of the church. This difference of view led to his consequent resignation from the ministerial rank in the state church in 1882, in order to be free to labor for the "Evangelical National Association," a movement for the reform of religion in Sweden. After the death of Rosenius, the founder of the movement, Waldenström became its leader, and the editor of the movement's literary organ, *Pietisten.* The movement became known as Waldenströmism, but later took the name of Swedish Mission Covenant. In its strong reaction against the hierarchy of the state church, it organized churches on essentially congregational principles. Emigrants from their churches to America organized what is today the Evangelical Covenant church in America. He began a new version of the New Testament. Visited the United States about 1890.

WALDO (VALDEZ), PETER (d. c. 1217), Founder of the Waldenses, a prosperous merchant of Lyons, France, who, upon conversion, decided to dispose of his property, to become a poor man, and to preach to the common people. Provided modestly for his wife and daughters, and gave the rest of his wealth to the poor. Took a formal vow of poverty and gathered about him a group of likeminded men, who became known as the "poor men of Lyons," and later as Waldenses, who went about preaching repentance. In 1179 at the Third Lateran Council in Rome they tried to secure permission to preach to the common people in the vernacular, and to work for reformation in the church. The pope confirmed their vow of poverty, but denied them the privilege of preaching unless they were expressly invited by the local priests. For awhile they obeyed the mandate of the pope, but finally becoming convinced that they were disobeying the voice of God in order to obey the word of man, they began to tour the country preaching repentance. The Lombard Humiliati joined them, and the movement spread rapidly. In 1184 they were excommunicated by Pope Lucius III. The Waldenses along with the Albigenses were officially condemned. The Council of Toulouse in 1229 decreed the forceful suppression of the heresy. The task of carrying out the decree was intrusted to the Dominican Order, and the Inquisition came down upon the Waldenses with great force and with much suffering. Peter Waldo died about 1217, but his movement has continued until this day.

WALKER, THOMAS (1859-1912), missionary in South India. Born in Derbyshire. Studied at St. John's College, Cambridge. Ordained in 1882 and commissioned to Tinnevelly, India. Evangelist and Bible conference speaker. Linked with the Amy Carmichael work at Dohnavur.

WALKER, WILLISTON (1860-1922), church historian, born at Portland, Maine, educated at Amherst College, Hartford Theological Seminary, and University of Leipzig. Appointed assistant professor of history at Bryn Mawr College for a year succeeding Woodrow Wilson; professor of Germanic and Western church history at Hartford Theological Seminary (1889-1901); and professor of ecclesiastical history in Yale University (1901-1922), succeeding George Park Fisher. For the school year 1916-1917, served as acting dean of Yale Graduate School, and as provost of the University from 1919 until his death. Active in his service in the interests of his denomination, the Congregational church. Among his writings are *A History of the Congregational Churches in the United States, The Creeds and Platforms of Congregationalism, The Reformation, Ten New England Leaders, John Calvin, The Greatest Men of the Christian Church,* and his most important work, *History of the Christian Church.*

WALLACE, LEWIS (1827-1905), soldier, lawyer, and novelist. Born in Brookville, Indiana. Admitted to the bar in 1849 and practiced law from 1849 to 1861. During the Civil War became an able general who saved Washington from capture. From 1878 to 1881 was governor of New Mexico. Ambassador to Turkey from 1881 to 1885. His novel *Ben Hur: A Tale of the Christ* sold over 300,000 copies in a decade.

WALLIN, JOHAN OLOF (1779-1839), Swedish poet, archbishop, and orator, born in Dalarna, Sweden, Sweden's greatest hymn writer. Gave himself to the revision of the Swedish Lutheran church hymn book. Wrote about one hundred fifty hymns, and has been called "David's Harp of the North." Held ministerial charges in various cities of Sweden, and in 1837 became Archbishop of Uppsala.

WALTER THE PENNILESS (GAUTIER SANS AVOIR) (gō tyā′ säɴ zȧ vwȧr) (died 1097), French knight; leader of the people's part of First Crusade. After the preaching of crusades to the Holy Land, masses of French peasants clamored for someone to lead them against the Turks. Walter the Penniless started out with an army of about fifteen thousand unorganized and undisciplined peasants, gathering numbers as they marched through France, Germany and Hungary until there were about forty thousand. The army was largely cut to pieces at the storming of Belgrade, and many were lost in the Bulgarian forests. Walter and a few stragglers reached Constantinople and were permitted by the emperor of Constantinople to cross the Straits of Asia Minor; but they were soon either massacred by the Turks, or taken prisoners and sold as slaves. Walter himself was slain in Palestine. This effort was but the vanguard move of the First Crusade. The real part of the crusade followed some months later, with much more success.

WALTHER, CARL FERDINAND WILHELM (1811-1887), founder of the Missouri Synod Lutheran church, born at Langenchursdorf, near Waldenburg, Saxony, Germany, educated at the University of Leipzig. Pastor at Braunsdorf, Saxony, for a year. Discouraged with the spiritual condition of congregation, came to America in 1839 with a colony of Lutherans. About eight hundred of them located at or near St. Louis, Missouri. From 1841 to 1847 he was pastor of Trinity Church in St. Louis, and in 1844 founded and edited a magazine, *De Lutheraner* until 1847. He founded a theological school at Altenburg, which later was moved to St. Louis to become Concordia Theological Seminary. He taught theology there from 1850 to 1887. In 1846 Walther and F. C. D. Wyneken took the lead in laying the foundation for the Missouri Synod on conservative confessional, democratic, congregational lines. In 1847 the first convention of the German Evangelical Lutheran Synod of Missouri, Ohio, and other states was held in Chicago. In 1853 the St. Louis Bible Society was founded and Walther became and remained its president until his death. In 1855 started the periodical, *Lehre und Wehre*. From 1868 to 1869 conducted conferences with the synods of Ohio, Wisconsin, and Illinois, which finally led to corporate union between these synods and the Missouri Synod. For several years president of the synodical conference of all

Western Lutherans in sympathy with the Missouri position.

WALTON, WILLIAM SPENCER (1850-1906), missionary in South Africa, born at Clare Cottage, Tulse Hill, London, England. After preparatory school days, went into business. In his teens made sea voyages to the Far East and to Africa for health. The years 1872 to 1882 were spent in business and in evangelistic efforts. Gave full time to evangelistic work with the Church Parochial Mission Society. In 1884 left the mission to become an independent evangelist. Four years later, 1888, went to South Africa, where he opened the nondenominational Cape General Mission in 1889, which in 1894 was amalgamated with the South East Africa Evangelistic Mission to form the South Africa General Mission. He became its director. Also editor of the *Pioneer*. After a decade and a half of fruitful service in mission on the field, in 1904 returned to England to devote his time to the promotion of the mission on a larger scale.

WANAMAKER (wŏn′ȧ mā′kẽr), **JOHN** (1838-1922), American merchant, philanthropist, and Sunday school promoter, born in Philadelphia. Became a Christian at twelve, and from that time until the end of his life was definitely connected with religious work. At fourteen began to work as an errand boy at one dollar and a quarter a week; a little later worked in a clothing store at twice that salary. At twenty became the first paid secretary of the Young Men's Christian Association in Philadelphia (1857-1861), and about the same time started Bethany Sunday School with twenty-seven pupils. Fifty years later this Sunday school, of which he was still superintendent, was the largest in the world. President of the Philadelphia Young Men's Christian Association from 1870 to 1883, and was one of the founders of the United States Christian Commission in 1861. In 1861 with his brother-in-law, Nathan Brown, started a clothing business in Philadelphia, which became the largest department store in the world. He became a pioneer in modern newspaper advertising; introduced educational and recreational benefits for employees, and conveniences and attractions for customers. Mr. Wanamaker was active in public life working for temperance and other reforms in city, state, and nation; took a prominent part in state and national politics. From 1889 to 1893 Postmaster General of the United States in President Harrison's cabinet. Aggressive in promoting improved postal measures.

WARBURTON (wôr′bẽr tn), **WILLIAM** (1698-1779), Church of England bishop, born at Newark-upon-Trent, Nottinghamshire, England. After studying and practicing law for five years, decided to enter the ministry; ordained priest in 1727. Served in several rectories until 1738 when made chaplain to the Prince of Wales. In 1746 named preacher to Lincoln's Inn; in 1754 became chaplain to the king; in 1757 made dean of Bristol; and in 1759 made Bishop of Gloucester. First theological work of importance was *The Alliance Between Church and State,* a defense of the existing established church, through which writing he gained court favor. Most famous book was *The Divine Legation of Moses,* in which he attacked the Deists' doctrine on the Old Testament. Also resented the enthusiasm of the Methodists and wrote *The Doctrine of Grace* against John Wesley. Wrote *Vindication of the Essay of Man,* by which he gained lasting friendship of Alexander Pope. Wrote also a work on Julian the Apostate; and *Principles of Natural and Revealed Religion*. Preached against the slave trade as early as 1766.

WARD, WILLIAM (1769-1823), missionary to India, born in Derby, England. After leaving formal school training apprenticed to a printer of a large printing establishment and received excellent training in chosen field of journalism. Edited the *Derby Messenger* until he felt the call of God to the mission field. Laid aside journalistic endeavors and gave himself to diligent theological training under John Fawcett. A search for missionaries to join Carey in India led Ward to accept the call and to become the printer of the Serampore Mission. With Marshman and several others sailed for India in 1799. Rendered valiant service in the Serampore Trio as the mission printer, with Marshman as teacher and Carey as chief translator and preacher.

WARE, HENRY (1764-1845), American Unitarian clergyman, born at Sherborn, Massachusetts. After graduating from Harvard in 1785 studied theology for two years. In 1787 became pastor of the First Church at Hingham, Massachusetts. In 1805 he accepted the Hollis professorship of divinity at Harvard. This was the time of the height of the Unitarian controversy in the Congregational Church, and his appointment to this professorship resulted in Harvard finally leaning toward the Unitarians; and from his courses developed Harvard Divinity School (organized 1816) in which he was professor of systematic theology and Christian evidences from the time of its organization until the time of his death.

WARFIELD, BENJAMIN BRECKINRIDGE (1851-1921), Presbyterian theologian and educator, born at Lexington,

Kentucky, studied at Princeton College, Princeton Theological Seminary, and the University of Leipzig. Ordained to the Presbyterian ministry in 1879. Served as supply at the First Presbyterian Church, Baltimore, for a year. In 1878, instructor in New Testament subjects at Western Theological Seminary, Allegheny, Pennsylvania, and in 1879 became professor of New Testament language and literature in the seminary. From 1887 to 1921 professor of theology in Princeton Theological Seminary, succeeding Dr. Archibald A. Hodge. Twice served as president of Princeton Theological Seminary, 1902-1903 and 1913-1914. Belonged to theologically conservative school. An enthusiastic Calvinist, particularly as stated in the Westminster Confession of Faith. He held to the plenary inspiration of the Bible. Editor of *The Presbyterian and Reformed Review* (1890-1903) and *Princeton Theological Review* for many years. He wrote *Introduction to the Textual Criticism of the New Testament, On the Revision of the Confession of Faith, The Gospel of the Incarnation, Two Studies in the History of Doctrine, The Right of Systematic Theology, The Divine Origin of the Bible, The Acts and Pastoral Epistles, The Power of God unto Salvation* (sermons), *The Plan of Salvation, The Saviour of the World, Calvin as a Theologian and Calvinism Today,* and *Inspiration.*

WARNECK (vär′nĕk), **GUSTAV ADOLF** (1834-1910), German Lutheran historian of missions, born at Naumburg, Germany, studied at the University of Halle. Served many years as a pastor, retiring in 1896; then became professor of missions in the University of Halle. In 1879 founded and became president of the Saxon Provincial Missionary Conference. He was secretary of the Committee of German Missions from 1885 to 1901. Until his death edited the missionary magazine *Allgemeine Missions Zeitschrift,* which he had founded in 1874. Among books translated into English: *Outline of the Protestant History of Missions from the Time of the Reformation to the Present Time,* and *Modern Missions and Culture.*

WARNER, DANIEL SIDNEY (1842-1925), founder of the Church of God (Anderson, Indiana), born at Bristol, Ohio (now Marshallville), then moved to Montpelier, Ohio. Converted in a schoolhouse revival in 1865 at the age of twenty-three. Became a member of the General Eldership of the Churches of God (Winebrennerian). Student at Oberlin College, and Vermillion College, Hayesville, Ohio. In 1872 licensed and preached for a time in Ohio and Nebraska. About 1877 he became an ardent advocate of "entire sanctification" as a second work of grace, for which he was brought to trial and ejected from the Winebrennerian church. Then for about two years wrote for a Holiness paper. About 1880 began publishing the *Gospel Trumpet* in Rome City, Indiana. Moved his publishing plant finally to Anderson, Indiana, the headquarters of the Church of God today. About 1880 Warner started a so-called "Reformation Movement" into which men of different denominations came. However, out of this movement there developed the present-day Church of God. Essentially orthodox and evangelical, differing from other fundamental churches mainly in that they emphasize the doctrine of sanctification. They are not premillennial. Warner emphasized three ordinances: baptism by immersion, the Lord's Supper, and the washing of feet.

WASHINGTON, BOOKER TALIAFERRO (c. 1856-1915), Black educator, lecturer and writer, son of a slave, born on a plantation near Hale's Ford in Franklin County, Virginia. After emancipation, when Booker was eight years old, his mother and family journeyed to Malden, West Virginia, where he worked in a salt furnace and in a coal mine. On the side able to pick up a little education. At this time he became a member of the Baptist church, in which he worked the rest of his life. Had a great desire to become educated. In 1872 traveled four hundred miles to Hampton Normal and Agricultural Institute, graduating there three years later. Then taught school for two years in Malden, West Virginia. Following this studied at Wayland Seminary, Washington, D.C. Called back to Hampton Institute and taught evening classes for a period of two years. In 1881 sent to Tuskegee, Alabama to organize a school for black youth. Founded Tuskegee Normal and Industrial Institute, and served as its principal for many years. In 1895 an important address immediately made him a national figure. In 1900 organized the National Negro Business League. The King of Denmark received him officially; the Queen of England welcomed him and Mrs. Washington at her palace; the presidents of the United States honored and respected him highly. Among his writings are the following books: *Future of the American Negro; Sowing and Reaping; Up From Slavery; Character Building; Story of My Life and Work; The Negro in Business; The Story of the Negro;* and *The Negro in the South.*

WASHINGTON, GEORGE (1732-1799), first president of the United States and "Father of His Country." Born at Bridge's Creek, Virginia, on the banks of the Potomac. When George was eight, the family moved to a farm on the Rappahannock. George received elementary education at home and in the common schools of the province until sixteen. Then he went to live with his older half-brother, Lawrence. When the brother died four years later, George took over Lawrence's plantation at Mt. Vernon and made it his permanent home, becoming a wealthy landowner. During these years gained the reputation of being a good surveyor. When hostilities arose between the French and Indians, and the English in 1752, Washington was pressed into military activity and leadership. In 1759 Washington married and for sixteen years lived happily on his Mt. Vernon estate. The mansion was a place of frequent social gatherings. In 1774 he was sent as delegate from Virginia to the First Continental Congress. The next year on June 15, following Lexington and Concord, Washington was elected commander-in-chief of the colonial army. The story of the incredible hardship of building and maintaining an army out of the raw colonial recruits, and of fighting the British in the Revolutionary War is the story of the next few years of Washington's life. Washington proved to be a master strategist and succeeded in driving the British out of the colonies. After the surrender of Yorktown, Washington resigned his commission, refusing any compensation for his military service, and retired to Mt. Vernon. He was soon called upon to help formulate a constitution, and then was unanimously elected to become the first president of the new republic. Again four years later he was re-elected; refused to accept a third term, and retired to Mt. Vernon to spend the last two years of his life. Made a member of the commission that located the proposed national capital. The city was named for him, an honor he greatly appreciated. A man of high moral standards. Did not swear and did not tolerate swearing among his men. Observed the Lord's day faithfully. Honesty, uprightness, justice, charity, and good will ruled his life.

WATSON, JOHN (pseud. IAN MACLAREN) (1850-1907), Scottish Presbyterian clergyman and writer, born at Manningtree, Essex, England. Studied at the University of Edinburgh, at New College, Edinburgh, and at Tübingen, Germany. Ordained by the Free Church of Scotland. Between years 1874 and 1905 successively minister at Barclay Church, Edinburgh; minister of Logiealmond Free Church; St. Matthew's Church, Glasgow; Sefton Park Presbyterian Church, Liverpool. Lyman Beecher lecturer at Yale in 1896. In 1906 moderator of the Synod of the Presbyterian Church of England. Became widely known for humorous, sympathetic, and entertaining stories descriptive of Scottish life and character. Among writings: *Beside the Bonnie Briar Bush, The Mind of the Master, The Cure of Souls, The Life of the Master,* and *Companions of the Sorrowful Way*.

WATTS, ISAAC (1674-1748), founder of modern English hymnody, born at Southampton, England. Began his study of Latin at the age of four and of Greek soon after. Went to a dissenters' academy at Stoke-Newington in London. After his school days became a tutor in a distinguished nonconformist family which attended a dissenting church in Mark Lane. Joined the church, became a teacher in it, then in 1698 assistant pastor, and in 1702 the pastor. Remained the pastor of this congregational church the rest of his life, but because of very poor health and because of the growing demands of the church, about 1712 an assistant was employed. Preached as often as he was able. Though he showed poetical talent from early boyhood, did not publish his first book of poetry until 1706. In 1707 published first hymn book. Opened a new path for English hymnody by introducing hymns whereas before this time only psalms had been sung in public worship. In 1719 came his *Psalms of David Imitated in the Language of the New Testament*. Next year appeared his *Divine and Moral Songs for the Use of Children,* which made him the founder of children's hymnody. Watts was one of the most popular song writers of the time. Wrote about six hundred hymns, some of which are among the finest in the English language. Considered one of the best preachers of his time, published three volumes of discourses. Writings were influential and helpful, and his learning and piety attracted many. Wrote "O God, Our Help in Ages Past," "When I Survey the Wondrous Cross," "There is a Land of Pure Delight," "Jesus Shall Reign," "Joy to the World," "Alas and Did My Savior Bleed," and "Am I a Soldier of the Cross."

WAYLAND, FRANCIS (1796-1865), American Baptist preacher and educator, born in New York, graduated from Union College, Schenectady, New York; studied medicine for three years. After experiencing conversion and uniting with the Baptist church, studied at Andover Theological Seminary, where he came under the influence of Moses Stuart. From 1817 to 1821 tutor in Union College, then ordained pastor of the First Baptist Church in Boston (1821-1826), where he gained reputation as a preacher. Sermon on *The Moral Dignity of the Missionary Enterprise* had a great influence.

Professor in Union College for one year (1826-1827), became president of Brown University, giving an administration of twenty-eight years of high achievement and wide recognition (1827-1855). Also encouraged the founding of public libraries. After retirement in 1855 devoted himself to literary, religious, and philanthropic labors, serving from 1855 to 1857 as pastor of the First Baptist Church in Providence. Engaged in prison reform and other philanthropic work.

WEBB, CAPTAIN THOMAS (1724-1796), soldier, Methodist preacher, born in England, served as an officer in the British army in America in the campaign against the French. Lost right eye and was wounded in right arm on the Plains of Abraham when Wolfe captured Quebec in 1759. Returned to England and was retired on captain's pay. About 1764 converted under Wesley's preaching in Bristol, soon licensed as a local preacher. Became an ardent preacher in England and Ireland, came to America about 1766 where he helped to establish Methodism. Assisted Philip Embury in preaching in New York, and in building the first Methodist chapel in New York on John Street. Established preaching places and organized classes in Jamaica, Long Island, Philadelphia, Baltimore, New Jersey, and Delaware. In 1772 returned to England to urge Wesley to send workers to the colonies, then accompanied Thomas Rankin and George Shadford when they came in 1773.

WEBB-PEPLOE (wĕb pĕp′lō), **HANMER WILLIAM** (1837-1923), Church of England clergyman, born at Woebley, Herfordshire, England, received education at Marlborough College, Cheltenham College, and Pembroke College, Cambridge. In 1863 ordained priest, and became curate of Woebley. In turn chaplain of Woebley Union, vicar of King's Pyon cum Birley, vicar of St. Paul's, Onslow Square from 1876 to 1919, and prebendary of St. Paul's Cathedral. Select preacher at Cambridge University; president of the Barbican Mission to the Jews; president of the London Clerical and Lay Union; chairman of the Council of the National Church League; vice-president of the Church Mission Society, of the Protestant Reformation Society, of the Mission to Seamen, and of the Spanish and Portuguese Church Aid Society; and chairman of the Waldensian Church Mission. Chief promoter of the Keswick Conference.

WEIDNER (wīd′nẽr), **REVERE FRANKLIN** (1851-1915), American Lutheran theologian and educator, born at Center Valley, Pennsylvania, educated at Muhlenberg College, Allentown, Pennsylvania, and at Lutheran Theological Seminary, Philadelphia. Ordained to the Lutheran ministry in 1873, pastor at Grace Church, Phillipsburg, New Jersey (1873-1878); from 1875 to 1877 spent a part of time also teaching English, logic, and history at Muhlenberg College. Second pastorate was at St. Luke's Church, Philadelphia (1878-1882). From 1882 to 1891, professor of dogmatics and exegesis in Augustana College and Seminary, Rock Island, Illinois; when the Evangelical Lutheran Theological Seminary was founded in Chicago in 1891 (now in Maywood), he was elected its first president, also professor of dogmatic theology and Hebrew exegesis, serving there until near the time of his death. Among writings: *Theological Encyclopaedia* (three volumes), *Biblical Theology of the New Testament* (two volumes), *Biblical Theology of the Old Testament, Introduction to Dogmatic Theology, Introductory New Testament Greek Method, A System of Christian Ethics, The Doctrine of God,* and *The Doctrine of the Church, Ministry*. Worked with Dwight L. Moody in Northfield, Massachusetts, and with William Rainy Harper on Chautauqua programs. An excellent expository preacher.

WEISS (vīs), **CARL PHILIPP BERNHARD** (1827-1918), German Protestant theologian and conservative critic, born at Königsberg, Germany, educated at Königsberg, Halle, and Berlin. Became privat-docent at the University of Königsberg (1852), associate professor (1857), divisional pastor (1861-1863). Professor of New Testament exegesis at Kiel (1865-1877). After 1877 professor of New Testament exegesis at the University of Berlin. Supreme consistorial councilor, and councilor to the department of public worship (1880-1899), president of the Central Committee for the Inner Mission of the German Evangelical church (1887-1896), and vice-president after 1896. Prepared the sixth to the ninth editions of several of H. A. W. Meyer's commentaries. Among his many writings: *A Manual of Introduction to the New Testament, Biblical Theology of the New Testament,* and an orthodox *Life of Jesus.*

WEISS, JOHANNES (1863-1914), German New Testament critic; born at Kiel, Germany. Educated in universities of Marburg, Berlin, Göttingen, and Breslau. Privat-docent at Göttingen (1888-1890); associate professor of New Testament exegesis at Göttingen (1890-1895); professor of same subject at Marburg (1895-1908); professor of same at Heidelberg (1908-1914). A theologian of the left wing of Ritschlian school, and applied Wellhausian theory in New Testament. In his *Die Predigt Jesu vom Reiche Gottes,* he expounded for the first time the principles of Form-criticism, which were further developed by Martin Dibelius and Rudolf Bultmann. Other writings: *Commentary on First Corinthians* (in the Meyer series) and *The History of Primitive Christianity*.

WELD, THEODORE DWIGHT (1803-1895), American abolitionist; born at Hampton, Connecticut; studied at Oneida Institute and at Lane and Oberlin theological seminaries. In 1825 became a member of Charles G. Finney's "holy band" of revivalists and preached in New York for two years. In 1830 turned to advocacy of the anti-slavery cause. Induced the New York merchants and philanthropists, Arthur and Lewis Tappan, to organize the American Anti-Slavery Society, of which he became one of the original founders, in 1833 its secretary, in 1836 publicity director, 1841-1843 lobbied in Washington, D.C. for anti-slavery. When his voice failed (1836), he turned to writing; edited the society's publications in Washington. Farmed from 1840 to 1854. In 1854 opened a school in Perth Amboy, New Jersey for boys and girls of both races; ten years later moved school to Hyde Park, Massachusetts, where he spent the remainder of his life. His book *American Slavery As It Is* had significant influence on Harriet Beecher Stowe's writing of *Uncle Tom's Cabin*. Wrote also *The Bible Against Slavery* and other anti-slavery books and pamphlets.

WELLHAUSEN (věl'hou zěn), **JULIUS** (1844-1918), German theologian, biblical critic and Orientalist, born at Hameln, Germany, studied at Göttingen. In 1870 became privat-docent at Göttingen. Two years later, appointed professor of theology in Greifswald University, resigned in 1882 because he could no longer hold the accepted views of the inspiration of Scripture. Went to Halle as associate professor of Oriental languages and in 1885, became full professor of same at Marburg. In 1892 went to Göttingen to occupy a similar position. Best known for elaboration of the theory that the Pentateuch is postexilic, and that it is of composite construction, that is, different parts were written by different authors and at different times. In this he carried out the views of Graf and Kuenen on Old Testament history. Wellhausen's writings were mainly Jewish history and Old Testament criticism. Wellhausen's theory was applied by Johannes Weiss to New Testament criticism. Interesting to note that archaeological discoveries of the past half century have done much to discredit the older forms of Wellhausianism.

WELLS, AMOS RUSSELL (1862-1933), American educator and author, born at Glens Falls, New York, attended college at Antioch College, Ohio. Professor of Greek and geology at Antioch from 1883 to 1891. From 1891 to 1933 he was the editorial secretary for the United Society of Christian Endeavor, also managing editor of the *Christian Endeavor World*. In this work associated with Rev. Francis E. Clark, the founder of the Christian Endeavor. Also a contributor to the *Christian Herald*. From 1901 until his death in 1933 editor of *Peloubet's Notes for the Sunday School Lessons*. A member of the International Sunday School Lesson Committee. Position theologically was that of a conservative Calvinist. Always an earnest advocate of prohibition, Wells served on the temperance committee of the Federal Council of the Churches of Christ in America.

WELTZ (vělts), **BARON JUSTINIAN ERNST VON** (1621-1688), Lutheran missionary pioneer to Dutch Guiana, born at Chemnitz, near Dresden, Saxony, Germany. In 1664 published the first general and vigorous appeal to the church, which had become lethargic in orthodoxy. In a series of three pamphlets boldly set forth the missionary duty of the church and called for the establishment of a college to train missionaries, and for the formation of a society to send them out. Failing to arouse others, he himelf proceeded to Holland, was ordained by a Lutheran preacher as "an apostle to the Gentiles," and sailed to Dutch Guiana. There he fell victim to the inhospitable climate and died.

WENCESLAUS (věn'tsěs lous), (c. 907-929) Bohemian prince and martyr; patron saint of Bohemia, son of Duke Wratislaw, received a good Christian education under the supervision of his grandmother Ludmilla. A man of deep piety and worked for the religious and cultural improvement of his people. After his Christian father died, and his pagan mother, acting as regent, opposed Christianity, he took over the reins of government and ruled until he was murdered by his mother and brother. Greatly venerated by the Bohemians, whose patron saint he became. The Crown of St. Wenceslaus came to be the symbol of Czech independence.

WESEL (vā'zěl), **JOHN (JOHN RUCHRATH von WESEL)** (c. 1400-c. 1481), reformer, born at Ober-Wesel on the Rhine. Both student and professor at the University of Erfurt, and for a time rector or vice-rector of the university. Distinguished himself both as professor and as preacher. About 1450 published a treatise against the current theory of indulgences. When the pope sent Cardinal Cuso and Capistiano to Erfurt to preach and sell indulgences, he opposed them after the fashion that Luther attacked

Tetzel. After about twenty years at Erfurt he became professor at Basel for a very short time. Following this he was for a brief period cathedral preacher at Mainz. Then preacher at Worms, where he preached for seventeen years against the doctrines of the Roman Church, the glaring corruptions of the time, basing convictions and preaching on the Scriptures and the Augustinian theology. In many respects anticipated Luther and his Reformation efforts. Accused of heresy, and in 1479 was brought to trial, imprisoned in an Augustinian convent. In consequence of harsh treatment, he died.

WESLEY, CHARLES (1708-1788), the hymnist of the English Revival, born eighteenth child and youngest son in family of nineteen in the home of Samuel and Susannah Wesley. Father rector of the poor and not too cultured town of Epworth. Studied at St. Peter's College, Westminster, London; and in 1726 began study at Christ Church, Oxford. While there helped form the Holy Club, of which George Whitefield and his brother John later became members. In 1735 ordained before he and John accepted the urgent invitation of General Oglethorpe to go with him as chaplain and teacher to his colony in Georgia. Dissatisfied and ill in health, Charles returned to England the next year. Greatest contribution to the Christian church was over six thousand hymns, four thousand of which were published. What John Wesley preached, Charles Wesley sang. Some of his greatest hymns are "Hark the Herald Angels Sing," "Jesus Lover of My Soul," "Love Divine, All Love Excelling," "O, For a Thousand Tongues," and "Christ the Lord is Risen Today." We often hear about John Wesley's heartwarming experience at Aldersgate on May 24, 1738. Charles had a similar experience only three days prior to John's experience. For a while Charles traveled with John in his preaching tours. After 1756 he itinerated little, not having the iron constitution of his brother and having a family of eight to provide for. From 1756 to 1771 preached at Bristol, and from 1771 until his death, in London.

WESLEY, JOHN (1703-1791), founder of Methodism, born at Epworth, England. At twenty-one John received his college degree from Oxford. After receiving his master's degree, spent two and one-half years as assistant to his father at Epworth, the only pastoral experience he ever had. In 1728, ordained a priest in the Anglican church. In 1729 joined the "Holy Club," which his brother Charles and others had formed a year earlier, and was at once made its leader. Because of their methodical procedure in meeting, study, prayer, and weekly celebration of the Lord's Supper, they were dubbed "Methodists." He had accepted the doctrine of justification by faith; yet it had not become to him an experiential fact. Partly in order to attain this he, along with his brother Charles, in 1735, answered a call of the Society for Propagating the Gospel in Foreign Parts for missionaries to come to Georgia. On this trip across the ocean, during a raging storm John was deeply impressed with peace and composure witnessed among a band of Moravians who were likewise coming to Georgia. The mission of the Wesleys was short. Discouraged and broken in health, Charles returned within a year. John was back in London early in 1738. In England he again met some Moravians who challenged his faith. On May 24, 1738, at a Moravian meeting on Aldersgate Street in London, the assurance of salvation finally became his experience. John Wesley felt greatly indebted to, and was greatly influenced by the Moravians; but he was too practical-minded to join their deeply mystical society. George Whitefield and Charles Wesley, both of whom had also undergone a deep heart-warming experience, joined John in a great revival campaign that soon flowed over the borders of England into Scotland, Ireland, and America. In their open-air preaching, pioneered by George Whitefield, great crowds came to hear and thousands were converted. Out of his great revival work and the organizing of his converts into classes and societies, there gradually developed the organization of the Methodist church around the pattern laid out by Wesley. Being forced out of the pulpits and the churches in the established Church of England, a separate denomination was inevitable after his death. In 1775 he began a series of preaching tours in Ireland and Scotland, but never returned to America. Appointed Dr. Thomas Coke as the first superintendent of the American work and a little later sent Francis Asbury to assist him. John Wesley was a great preacher, leader, and organizer, and a prolific writer. His life was one of great achievement. In his itinerant preaching he travelled chiefly on horseback, covering perhaps more than 250,000 miles, and preaching over 40,000 sermons. The number of works he wrote, translated, or edited exceeds two hundred. After a short illness in London in 1791 he died when almost eighty-eight years old. He wrote the hymn, "Jesus Thy Blood and Righteousness."

WESLEY, SAMUEL, SR. (1662-1735), rector at Epworth and father of John and Charles Wesley, born at Winterbourne-Whitchurch, Dorsetshire, England, of nonconformist descent. Early education was received among the dissenters; in 1683 renounced nonconformity and entered Oxford. In 1689 ordained priest and married Susannah Annesley, the daughter of an eminent nonconformist divine. Became the father of nineteen children, eleven of whom survived infancy. Held several pastoral appointments, the last and longest being the obscure country parish of Epworth, where he remained nearly forty years. For a little more than two years his son John assisted him. His earnest, faithful preaching created strong dislikes among his parishioners, and he suffered much harassment, even imprisonment because of debts. His rectory was burned. He did much writing which helped him stretch out his meager salary which never supported his large family. In 1702 he founded at Epworth one of the societies similar to Spener's *Collegia Pietatis* that were being organized here and there in England. A man of learning, benevolence, devotional habits, and liberal sentiments.

WESLEY, SUSANNAH, nee ANNESLEY (1669-1742), mother of John and Charles Wesley and one of notable and devoted mothers of Christendom. Born in London, father a nonconformist divine. Early in life renounced nonconformity and gave her adherence to the Church of England. In 1689 married Samuel Wesley. Mother of nineteen children; a woman of fine intellect and good education; ruled her house with singular diligence, system, and piety. The children who survived infancy were taught individually and punctiliously in the home, Mrs. Wesley doing most of the teaching. A woman of methodical and systematic habits, of loving Christian character. A tender mother and a good pastor's wife. Her piety and devotion and Christian character were implanted in the lives of her children; her impact on early Methodism through her children was significant. She died in London, her son John delivering the funeral discourse.

WESSEL (vĕs′sĕl), **JOHN (WESSELL HARMENESS GANSFORT)** (c. 1420-1489), teacher, mystic, and reformer, born of middle-class parents at Groningen, Holland, received early education in the school of the Brethren of the Common Life at Zwolle. Met Thomas a Kempis of the neighboring cloister of Mt. St. Agnes. Further pursued studies at Cologne, Lyons, Paris, Basel, and Italy, later taught and lectured at many of these places. Influential in building up the University of Heidelberg, where Melanchthon, Bucer, and other reformers studied shortly after his time and likely felt the influence of his teaching. At Paris he left influence on Reuchlin and Agricola. Many of his teachings and writings were against the basic teachings of the Roman Catholic church, and were a distinct preparation for the Reformation. His last years were spent with the Brethren of the Common Life at Mt. St. Agnes and at Groningen.

WEST, GILBERT (1703-1756), English writer; born at Wickham, Kent, England; educated at Eton and Christ Church, Oxford. Served for a time in the Royal Army. Dr. Johnson included West in his *Lives of the Poets*. Noted especially for his writing *Observations on the Resurrection*, the writing of which is said to have led to his conversion; won for him a high reputation, and from Oxford the degree D.C.L. His relatives William Pitt and George Lyttelton often visited in his home; he carried on extensive correspondence with Philip Doddridge.

WESTCOTT (wĕs(t)′kŭt), **BROOKE FOSS** (1825-1901), English scholar and divine, born near Birmingham, England, educated at King Edward VI's school at Birmingham and at Trinity College, Cambridge, graduating with highest honors. In 1849 obtained fellowship and ordained in 1851. Between 1850 and 1870 held various preaching posts. Writings created a new epoch in the history of modern English theological scholarship. Some of his greatest works: *The History of the New Testament Canon, Introduction to the Study of the Gospels, The Bible in the Church, The Gospel of the Resurrection,* and *A History of the English Bible*. The turning point of his life came in 1870 when he was appointed regius professor of Divinity at Cambridge. The same year he and F. J. A. Hort began ten-year work of revision of the Greek New Testament, completing their famous text in 1881. Between 1870 and 1890 held highest pulpit positions and continued with scholarly writing. His part in the bringing about of reform in the divinity school relative to degrees, preliminary examinations, and student and faculty meetings for discussion; in instituting new policies and broadening the scope of influence of the university was significant. In 1883 he became canon of Westminster, and in 1890 succeeded his friend J. B. Lightfoot as Bishop of Durham. During last ten years, vigorously and successfully participated in the social and industrial life of his people, and helped them in meeting and solving many of their problems. A staunch supporter of the cooperative movement, and also an ardent supporter of foreign missions. Westcott's commentaries on John, Ephesians, Hebrews, and the Johannine epistles have never been superseded.

WESTON, AGNES (1840-1918), "The Sailors' Friend," born in London, England.

Spent her childhood and youth in Bath. In her mid-twenties began active mission work among the poor, the sick, and the alcoholics in community; and about the same time began work among soldiers and sailors. In 1874 she and Miss Sophie Wintz opened the Royal Sailors' Rest at Devonport, which was gradually equipped for evangelistic work, Bible classes, reading, gatherings for wives and children of sailors, and temperance and other social gatherings. A little later they opened a similar Rest at Portsmouth. Miss Weston had tracts sent in her name to every ship touching at a port in the United Kingdom. Her work also benefited the "men of war" in many nations. Interest was always in evangelism, as well as in social and physical betterment. The Royal Naval Temperance Society and the Royal Naval Christian Union, numbering about twenty-five thousand members, scattered all over the world, have their headquarters at the Royal Sailors' Rests. Her chief writing: *My Life Among the Bluejackets.*

WEYMOUTH, RICHARD FRANCIS (1822-1902), English Baptist philologist and New Testament scholar, born at Plymouth Dock, Devonshire, England, educated at University College, London. After spending two years in France, assistant master in a private school at Leatherhead, Surrey, and later founded a school for boys at Plymouth. In 1869 elected fellow of University College, London, and appointed headmaster of a nonconformist school for boys at Mill Hill, London, where he remained until 1886. He then retired from active life to devote himself to biblical study and to textual criticism of the Greek Testament, which resulted in the *Resultant Greek Testament*. Among writings were: *Early English Pronunciation*. Especially remembered for *The New Testament in Modern Speech,* an idiomatic translation into everyday English from the text of *The Resultant Greek Testament,* which was not published until after Weymouth's death.

WHATCOAT, RICHARD (1736-1806), Methodist bishop in the United States, born in Quinton, Gloucestershire, England, reared an Anglican, entered the Wesleyan Conference in 1769. For sixteen years a lay preacher in England, Wales, and Ireland. In 1784 Wesley ordained him and sent him to America to aid in organizing the Methodist church. In 1800, at the age of sixty-four, he was elected bishop to assist Bishop Asbury.

WHATELEY (hwāt'lĭ), **RICHARD** (1787-1863), Archbishop of Dublin, born in London, educated at Oriel College, Oxford. Fellow of Oriel from 1811 to 1821, then for four years held the living of Halesworth, Suffolk. In 1825 returned to Oxford as principal of St. Alban's Hall; in 1830 was appointed Drummond professor of political economy at Oxford, but resigned two years later to become Archbishop of Dublin. As primate of Ireland sat in the House of Lords and made many speeches noticeable for their independence. Advocated a revision of the liturgy and of the King James Version of the Bible. Favored a gradual rather than a sudden emancipation of slaves. Strongly opposed Calvinism, and in writings fought against tractarianism. An early leader of the Broad church movement in the Anglican church. Wrote *The Errors of Romanism Traced to Their Origin in Human Nature*. His Bampton Lectures delivered in 1822 were published as *The Use and Abuse of Party Feeling in Matters of Religion*.

WHEELOCK (hwē'lŏk), **ELEAZAR** (1711-1779), Congregational minister and educator, born in Windham, Connecticut; graduated from Yale College (1733). Licensed to preach (1734); pastor Second Congregational Church, Lebanon, Connecticut (1735-1770); popular preacher and itinerant evangelist during Great Awakening. In 1743 took into his home and taught Samson Occom, a Mohican Indian. A number of Indians were trained and sent as missionaries, teachers, and leaders to their people. In 1765-1767, Samson Occom collected twelve thousand pounds in Great Britain for the school at Lebanon; but Wheelock, wishing to enlarge his program, moved his academy to Hanover, New Hampshire, and established Dartmouth College (1770), and became first president until 1779. Supervised building and farming operations, preached and taught, acted as justice of peace, and sent recruiting parties to Canada for Indian pupils. Remembered especially as friend and educator of Indian youth and as founder of Dartmouth College. He died at Hanover, son John succeeded as president. Published *A Plain and Faithful Narrative of the Indian School at Lebanon* and several sermons.

WHITBY, DANIEL (1638-1726), English theologian and writer. Developed the idea that Christ would return after the church had won the world to Christianity.

WHITE, ALMA (BRIDWELL) (1862-1946), founder of Pillar of Fire Church, born in Lewis County, Kentucky, educated at Millersburg Female College, Kentucky, and University of Denver. Put emphasis on regeneration and holiness, and her habit of organizing missions and camp meetings on her own authority and preaching in revival meetings brought her into sharp conflict with the bishops and presiding elders. Withdrew from the Methodist church, and in 1901 established the Pentecostal Union based on primitive Wesleyanism. The name of the church was changed in 1917 to Pillar of Fire. The headquarters of the church was later moved to Zerephath, New Jersey. First bishop of the Pillar of Fire, consecrated in 1918.

WHITE, ELLEN GOULD (HARMON), (MRS. JAMES WHITE) (1827-1915), chief leader of the Seventh Day Adventists, born at Gorham, Maine. Parents were ardent Methodists until disfellowshiped for adherence to the time-setting doctrines of William Miller. Had many dreams or visions which later she interpreted as new revelations from God. Miller's prophetic messages and Mrs. White's supposedly inspired visions or revelations in 1844 formed the basis for the Seventh Day Adventist church. Mrs. White became the inspired prophetess and leader of the group. In 1846 married "Elder" James White. In 1855 the Whites moved to Battle Creek, Michigan, which remained the headquarters for the denomination for about fifty years. In 1863 the Seventh Day Adventist church was organized. She spent two years visiting several European countries, and from 1891 to 1900 was in Australia.

WHITE, JOHN (1866-1933), English Wesleyan Methodist missionary to Southern Rhodesia, born in Cumberland, England. John's early education was very meager. Conversion to Christ at sixteen was followed by a determined commitment to Christian service. Offered to go as a lay evangelist to Australia; but upon advice from his minister entered Didsbury Wesleyan Methodist College in 1888 to prepare for the ministry. After training volunteered to go to China; but Africa was to be his field. For forty years worked among the Mashona people and was greatly loved and respected by them for his courageous championship of justice to them, even at the point of great personal danger to himself. Reduced Mashona to writing, and with the help of a devoted Mashona evangelist translated the New Testament.

WHITE, WILBERT WEBSTER (1863-1944), Presbyterian clergyman and educator, born at Ashland, Ohio, and studied at the University of Wooster, Xenia Theological Seminary, and Yale University. Ordained to the United Presbyterian ministry in 1885, pastor at Peotone, Illinois (1885-1886). Professor of Hebrew and Old Testament literature in Xenia Theological Seminary (1890-1895); taught in the Moody Bible Institute; engaged in Bible work in England and India (1897-1900). Founder of the Biblical Seminary in New York and president (1900-1940). Edited the *Biblical Review,* and was author of: *Thirty Studies in the Gospel of John, Thirty Studies in Jeremiah, Thirty Studies in Revelation, Thirty Studies in the Gospel of Matthew, Inductive Studies in the Minor Prophets,* and *How to Study.*

WHITE, WILLIAM (1748-1836), Patriarch of the Protestant Episcopal church, born in Philadelphia, educated in the schools of Pennsylvania, receiving college degree in the College of Philadelphia. After this theological education in 1770, went to England and was ordained priest in 1772. Returned to America and became assistant minister of Christ Church and St. Peter's in Philadelphia, in 1772, soon after was rector of the joint parishes of Christ, St. Peter's and St. James'. In the Revolutionary War sided with the colonies and chaplain of the Continental Congresses. Active during the War in trying to sustain the life of the Episcopal church, and later in obtaining the episcopate in order to effect the organization of the church. In 1782 wrote a pamphlet: *The Case of the Episcopal Churches in the United States Considered,* in which he advocated that an American Episcopal church be organized on a national basis even though there were as yet no ordained bishops. In 1775 chosen as president of the First General Conference held in Philadelphia. Constitution for the Protestant Episcopal church in the United States which the convention adopted was largely his work. It was he who suggested the name, Protestant Episcopal. In 1786 chosen the first bishop of the diocese of Pennsylvania; his consecration to the episcopacy took place in Lambeth Palace, England, a few months later in 1787. By 1789 the English church in America had been completely reorganized independent of state and of English church control. Exercised the episcopal office until his death almost fifty years after his consecration.

WHITEFIELD (hwĭt'fēld), **GEORGE** (1714-1770), English evangelist, son of an innkeeper, born in Gloucester, England. At twelve years of age placed in the school of St. Mary de Crypt at Gloucester, in 1733 entered Pembroke College, Oxford, where he became associated with Charles Wesley and later with John Wesley. Ordained a deacon in 1736, and took his B.A. the same year. Spent much time among the prisoners in Oxford, preached in London and elsewhere, and speedily rose to great prominence as a pulpit orator. Spent a few months in Georgia in 1738, arriving a short time after John Wesley had returned to England. After returning to England in 1738 to be ordained priest, and to raise money for an orphanage, which he later established in Savannah. Finding the church doors closed to him, he began his famous outdoor preaching, which John Wesley also took up. At Kingswood, near Bristol, laid the foundations for the Kingswood School, which became so important to Methodism. Whitefield now began his career as an itinerant evangelist. Back in America between 1739 and 1741. Association with Calvinistic divines while in America led him definitely to accept Calvinism. In 1743 he parted company with the Wesleys and started the Calvinistic Methodist Society. Following this spent most of his time in itinerant evangelism dividing his time between Europe and America. With great eloquence and power preached to multitudes in England, Scotland, and Wales, and paid seven visits to America.

WHITEHEAD (hwīt'hĕd), **ALFRED NORTH** (1861-1947), British mathematician and philosopher, born at Ramsgate, Kent, England. Studied at Trinity College, Cambridge. Lecturer in mathematics at Trinity (1885-1911), and at the University College, London (1911-1914); professor at Imperial College of Science and Technology (1914-1924); professor of philosophy at Harvard University (1924-1936), being professor emeritus after that. In later teachings and writings constructed an idealistic philosophical system, akin to Platonism, known as the "philosophy of organism." Brought to philosophy a mathematical analysis which led him to reject positivism. Elected to the British Academy of Sciences in 1931, and received the Order of Merit from the British Crown, the highest honor in learning in the world, in 1945, and also received several other awards and medals. In collaboration with his pupil, Bertrand Russell, he wrote the monumental *Principia Mathematica* in three volumes. Other writings include: *Universal Algebra, Principle of Relativity, Science and the Modern World, Religion in the Making, Process and Reality, Adventures of Ideas,* and *Modes of Thought*. Forerunner of process theology.

WHITGIFT (whĭt'gĭft), **JOHN** (c. 1530-1604), Archbishop of Canterbury, born at Great Grimsby, Lincolnshire, England; studied at Queen's College and Pembroke Hall, Cambridge. Took orders in 1560; gained distinction as a preacher; chaplain to the queen (1565). In 1563 received B.D. and was Lady Margaret professor of divinity (1563-1567); master of Trinity College (1567-1577); in 1570 vice-chancellor of the university; in 1577 appointed bishop of Worcester; in 1583 archbishop of Canterbury, till end of life. Adviser to Queen Elizabeth; vigorous supporter of her policies for religious uniformity; bitter opponent of Puritans as well as Catholics. In 1570 deprived Thomas Cartwright of his professorship at Cambridge and the next year expelled him from his fellowship at Trinity. In 1593 got law passed making Puritanism an offense against statute law. A thoroughgoing Calvinist in doctrine, moderately so in ritual, but not in church government. Whitgift attended Queen Elizabeth on her deathbed and crowned James I. A few weeks before his death attended and supported King James' Hampton Court Conference consisting of discussions between the Puritans and the High church party.

WHITMAN, MARCUS (1802-1847), pioneer missionary to the Oregon Territory, born at Rushville, New York. Converted and joined the Congregational church, later became an elder in the Presbyterian church. Studied medicine at the Berkshire Medical College at Pittsfield, Massachusetts, and practiced in Canada for four years. In 1835 offered services as a missionary to the American Board, and the next year with Samuel Parker set out to explore the regions west of the Mississippi River and the Rocky Mountains with the view of opening a mission among the Indians. Favorably impressed with the prospects, Parker stayed and Whitman returned to New York to report and to find more missionaries. In the meantime married and in 1835 Mr. and Mrs. Whitman and Mr. and Mrs. H. H. Spaulding set out on the new mission. They were the first persons to reach the Pacific Coast by wagon. Mrs. Whitman and Mrs. Spaulding were the first white women to cross the continent. They organized missions in Oregon Territory, the Territory then consisting of Washington, Oregon, Idaho, and parts of Montana and Wyoming. In 1838 reinforcements entered the mission. The Nez Perce, Cayuse, and Flathead tribes were showing an eagerness to receive the teaching of the missionaries. Many of them became Christians. In 1842-43 Dr. Whitman made another trip east to secure more help and to inform the government at Washington on the state of affairs in the Oregon Territory, and to "save Oregon to the United States." After interviewing President Tyler and Secretary of State Daniel Webster, and after conferring with the American Board concerning the future of the work, he returned to Oregon in 1843 with eight hundred immigrants. During his absence seemingly the Roman Catholics and the Hudson Bay Company were both manifesting hostility to the mission, and then in 1847 when an epidemic of measles broke out and some of the people died, the superstitious fears of the Indians led to open rebellion. A band of Cayuse Indians conspired against him and massacred Dr. Whitman and his wife and twelve other persons, and took the other residents prisoners. Oregon was saved but the work halted.

WHITTIER (hwĭt'ĭ ẽr), **JOHN GREENLEAF** (1807-1892), American Quaker poet and abolitionist, born near Haverhill, Massachusetts in a Quaker home of Huguenot ancestry. Formal education limited to a few terms of country school and two terms at Haverhill Academy. For thirty years after 1839 editor of several magazines and newspapers, and contributor to them, also several others. After the Civil War, became one of America's foremost abolitionists. Became a warm friend of William Lloyd Garrison, and supported Abraham Lincoln for the presidency; influential in the formation of the Republican party. Opposed to war as a means of solving the slave problem, but did ardently support the North and urged his Quaker friends to contribute their assistance by engaging in hospital service. Whittier had almost a constant struggle with his health, but continued to fight slavery, and to write poetry. After the Civil War, entered upon the peaceful part of his life and wrote his best poetry. Some of his best poems: *Snowbound, Maud Muller, Barefoot Boy, Ichabod, Pipes of Lucknow, My Psalm, Barbara Frietchie, The Pennsylvania Pilgrim,* and his early volume, *Voices of Freedom*. A much loved hymn is his "Dear Lord and Father of Mankind."

WHITTLE (hwĭt'l), **MAJOR DANIEL WEBSTER** (1840-1901), lay evangelist, Bible teacher, and hymn writer, born in Chicopee Falls, Massachusetts. As a young man came to Chicago and became cashier in the bank of Wells, Fargo and Company. In 1861 enlisted in the army, serving through the war; with Sherman on his march to the sea, wounded at Vicksburg, and at the close of the war was breveted "Major," a title he carried thereafter. After the war worked for the Elgin Watch Company, becoming its treasurer. In 1873, largely through the influence of D. L. Moody, entered fulltime evangelistic work, and worked with D. L. Moody, P. P. Bliss, James McGranahan, and George C. Stebbins. He and his singing companions conducted several campaigns in England as well as in various parts of the United States. Major Whittle did the last work of his life among the soldiers in camp during the Spanish American War, wearing himself out. His latter years were spent in Northfield, Massachusetts. Major Whittle wrote the words for about two hundred songs, some of the best known being the following: "Moment by Moment," "The Crowning Day Is Coming," "I Know Whom I Have Believed," "Showers of Blessing." Many of his hymns were written under the nom-de-plume, El Nathan. James McGranahan wrote the music for many of his hymns. His daughter, May Whittle Moody, wrote the music for many of his later hymns. Published a book of poems; *Life, Warfare, and Victory; Memoirs of Philip P. Bliss; Gospel Pictures and Story Sermons for Children;* and *The Wonders of Prayer.*

WHYTE (hwīt), **ALEXANDER** (1837-1921), Free Church of Scotland clergyman, born at Kirriemuir, Forfarshire, Scotland, educated at the University of Aberdeen, at New College, Edinburgh. In 1866 after graduation ordained deacon; assistant minister of Free St. John's, Glasgow, from 1866 to 1870, then was minister of Free St. George's, Edinburgh, until 1909, where he was colleague and successor to Dr. R. S. Candlish. Minister of the largest and most influential congregation of his church. From 1909 to 1918 professor of New Testament literature, and principal of New College, Edinburgh, succeeding Dr. Marcus Dods as principal. In 1898 moderator of the General Assembly. A great preacher, also a great writer. Some of his writings: *Bible Characters; Commentary on the Shorter Catechism; Bunyan Characters; Samuel Rutherford and Some of His Correspondents; Walk, Conversation, Character of Jesus Christ Our Lord; The Apostle Paul;* and *With Mercy and With Judgment*.

WICHERN, JOHANN HINRICH (1803-1881), founded German *Innere Mission*. Born in Hamburg. Studied theology at the universities of Göttingen and Berlin. In 1833 founded *Rauhes Haus* (Rough House) as a home and school for neglected children. Edited a monthly periodical whose influence led to the creation of the *Innere Mission* in 1848 to coordinate charitable work of the Prussian Evangelical churches. Supervised prison reform in Prussia in 1857. In Prussian wars in 1864, 1866 and 1870. Wichern organized workers to help the wounded.

WILBERFORCE, WILLIAM (1759-1833), English statesman, philanthropist, and abolitionist, born in Hull, Yorkshire, England, educated at St. John College, Cambridge. Entered politics in 1790, continued as a member of the House of Commons until 1825. Early became interested in various reforms. Through the influence of John Newton and Isaac Milner, his teacher at Hull grammar school, he became an advocate of evangelical Christianity. In 1777, assisted by Thomas Clarkson, William Pitt, Edmund Burke, and the Quakers, began his attack on the slave trade. Wrote his influential *A Practical view*—in 1797 on the application of Christianity to politics. After a twenty-year campaign in the House of Commons, in 1807 a bill abolishing traffic in slaves became law. Was one of the founders of the colony of Sierra Leone in 1787. In 1823 issued *An Appeal to the Religion, Justice, and Humanity of the Inhabitants of the British Empire on Behalf of the Negroes in the West Indies,* followed by the formation of the Anti-Slavery Society. Retired from Parliament in 1825, died in 1833 just a month before the Emancipation Bill was passed, freeing 700,000 slaves at a cost of $100,000,000. Partially responsible for the foundation of the bishopric of Calcutta, and for the founding and supporting of the Bible Society, the Church Missionary Society, and the Society for Bettering the Condition of the Poor. Generously assisted Hannah More in her good works and was a conspicuous member of the "Clapham Sect" of evangelicals. Founder of the Christian journal, the *Christian Observer.* He was buried in Westminster Abbey.

WILDER, ROBERT PARMALEE (1863-1938), chief founder of the Student Volunteer Movement, and a missionary to the students of India, born of missionary parents, the Royal Gould Wilders, in the city of Kolhapur, India. Early education received with Marathi children in the local native school. Early accepted Christ. At this time resolved to be a missionary. When twelve his parents returned to America, and in 1881 he entered Princeton College. In 1883 took the lead in organizing the Princeton Foreign Missionary Society and became its first secretary. For three and one half years the "Band" met in the Wilder home, Robert leading the men and his sister Grace, who had graduated from Mt. Holyoke College, leading the women. Just after graduation from Princeton, attended the College Students' Summer School for Bible Study held by D. L. Moody at Mt. Hermon in 1886. So persistently promoted foreign missions at this conference that one hundred students signed the declaration to become foreign missionaries. From the Princeton Foreign Missionary Society thus emerged the intercollegiate Student Volunteer Movement for Foreign Missions, with Wilder as its virtual founder. In 1887 entered the Union Theological Seminary in New York to prepare for work among the students of India. In 1888 again traveling secretary for the Movement, and John R. Mott became its first chairman. The next year Robert E. Speer became traveling secretary, and Wilder returned to the seminary, graduating with honors in 1891. That summer started for India under the Presbyterian Board, spent more than a year, however, in Europe, where he helped to organize the Student Volunteer Missionary Union of Great Britain and Ireland, and spent some time in Scandinavia. Almost immediately began work among the students of India, and pursued this task for several years. From 1897 to 1899 called by the International Committee of the Y.M.C.A. and by the Student Volunteer Movement to spend some time in America working in behalf of the newly formed World's Student Christian Federation. In 1899 returned to India as college secretary of the International Committee. In 1902 missionary career was brought to an abrupt close by a serious nervous breakdown. He and family returned to Norheim, Norway, where for several years they made their home. He then made tours among the students in the European countries in behalf of the World's Student Christian Federation and of foreign missions. In 1916 moved back to America, establishing his home at Montclair, New Jersey, and working among American youth. When the Near East Christian Council needed an executive secretary, it chose him, then sixty-five years of age. Again in 1929 established a new home, this time in Cairo, Egypt, to visit among the students and the missionaries of the countries of the Near East. In 1933 his health failed and he and his family returned to Norway, where he lived until his death.

WILFRID (634-709), Bishop of Northumbria. Educated at Lindisfarne monastery. Abbot of Ripon. Mainly responsible in 663 at the Synod of Whitby for the victory of the Roman Catholic form of Christianity over that of the Celtic. Spent his last years at Ripon.

WILKES, A. PAGET (1871-1934), Church of England missionary to Japan, born at Titchwell, Suffolk, England, educated at Lincoln College, Oxford, where he associated himself with the Oxford Intercollegiate Christian Union, well known for its evangelistic fervor and missionary zeal. In 1897 went under the Church Missionary Society to Japan where, except for several furloughs home, he spent the rest of his life in evangelistic service. Laid strong emphasis on the prayer life, Holy Spirit guidance, and sanctification. Passion for souls and willingness to sacrifice his own interests and pleasures for souls made him a great missionary. On first furlough home in 1903 organized the Japan Evangelistic Band, and labored in it the rest of his days. At this time he wrote a hymn, well known and well loved by many, "Jesus! Jesus! Jesus! Sweetest Name on Earth." He made Kobe his center, built the Kobe Mission Hall, opened a small Bible school there. Spent much time conducting conferences in various parts of the land for the deepening of the spiritual life. Best known works: *The Dynamic of Service; The Dynamic of Faith; The Dynamic of Redemption; Sanctification; So Great Salvation.* These books have been translated into Japanese and many other languages. Wrote also *Missionary Journeys in Japan.*

WILLARD, FRANCES ELIZABETH CAROLINE (1839-1898), American educator and temperance reformer, born at Churchville, New York; at seven moved with her parents to Ohio; later moved to a farm in Janesville, Wisconsin. Attended the Northwestern Female College in Evanston, Illinois, graduating in 1859 with honors as valedictorian. Taught a few terms of school, then went to Europe on a two-and-a-half-year tour. In 1869 appointed professor of aesthetics, in 1871 became dean of Northwestern Women's College at Evanston until 1874. Her interest, however, in the temperance movement being intensified when the anti-saloon crusade swept the country in 1874, carried on a fifty-day speaking tour that was far-reaching. Seeing that prohibition and woman suffrage went hand in hand, she became vitally interested also in promoting woman suffrage. Also became a strong supporter of the Prohibition Party in politics. Was president of the Chicago Women's Christian Temperance Union, and in 1879 was chosen as president of the National W.C.T.U., an office held until her death. Annual tours in the United States averaged thirty thousand miles, and over a period of ten years she averaged four hundred lectures a year. In 1883 founded the World's W.C.T.U. and from 1891 to 1898 was its president. The victory for the Eighteenth and Nineteenth Amendments to our Constitution (the Prohibition and Woman Suffrage Amendments) was greatly indebted to the work of Frances E. Willard. She wrote: *Woman and Temperance; Nineteen Beautiful Years; A Great Mother; Glimpses of Fifty Years;* and many magazine articles. She was the founder of *The Union Signal,* and its editor-in-chief from 1892 to 1898.

WILLIAM I, THE PIOUS (?-918), Count of Auvergne and Duke of Aquitaine (886-918), founder of Cluny monastery (910). Thinking to save monasticism by reforming it, provided the land for a new reform monastery, and placed at its head Berno, a Burgundian Benedictine monk. Then, to prevent successors from corrupting the foundation and diverting it from its original purpose, Duke William placed the monastery directly under the pope. Cluny monastery became the center of a reform movement of the Catholic church in the time of popes Alexander II and Gregory VII in the eleventh century.

WILLIAM I (WILLIAM THE CONQUEROR) (1027-1087), King of England (1066-1087), born in Falaise, Normandy, an illegitimate son of Robert, Duke of Normandy. Edward the Confessor, the English king, promised William that he should succeed him as king. Upon the death of Edward in 1066, however, Edward's brother Harold took the throne. Upon the advice and ardent support of Cardinal Hildebrand and Pope Alexander I, William the Conqueror claimed the throne, defeated Harold at the Battle of Hastings. Harold was slain and William was crowned as King William I, thus founding the Norman Dynasty in England in 1066. He created a strong state in England, and at the same time strengthened the Roman control of England. The English Parliament grew out of the feudal assembly known as the "Curia regis" that was introduced into England in William's reign.

WILLIAM I (THE SILENT) (1533-1584), Prince of Orange and Count of Nassau. Founder of the Dutch republic, born in Nassau, France, son of William, Count of Nassau. In 1544 inherited from his cousin the principality of Orange in Southern France and large estates in the Netherlands. Educated as a Catholic at the imperial court of Charles V. In 1555 the emperor appointed him governor of Holland, Zeeland, and Utrecht. After abdication of Charles, served Philip II, but began to resent Philip's arbitrary rule, and to sympathize with the Dutch Protestants. Resigned his offices and returned to his ancestral home in Nassau. The Dutch in the meantime had revolted against the Spanish, and in 1586 William placed himself at the head of Dutch forces, and entered upon the long struggle for Dutch independence. When Leiden was besieged by the Spanish, and the Dutch were starving, William cut the dikes and flooded the country, and the ships laden with food came through the city's gates. Leiden was saved and the struggle for Dutch independence took a favorable turn. His efforts to free the Netherlands were finally successful as far as the seven northern provinces were concerned. In 1579 he signed the Union of Utrecht and in 1581 formally repudiated the sovereignty of the king of Spain, and proclaimed the independence of the United Netherlands or the Dutch Republic. William became the new republic's first Stadholder. He fell victim of an assassin's dagger, at Delft, the result of a plot of King Philip, who had placed a price on the head of William. His place of leadership was then taken by Jan van Oldenbarnesveldt.

WILLIAM III (1650-1702), Stadholder of Holland (1672-1702), and King of England, Scotland, and Ireland from 1689 to 1702. Born at the Hague, the posthumous son of William II, Prince of Orange and of Mary, daughter of Charles I of England, and great-grandson of William the Silent. William III held the young Dutch Republic intact against the machinations of the French. In 1677 married Princess Mary, the Protestant daughter of James, Duke of York, later James II of England. When James showed his strong Catholic policy, William was invited to invade England. With an army he landed at Torbay in 1688, and James fled to France. Early the next year, 1689, after accepting the Declaration of Right, William and Mary were crowned as King and Queen of England. After Mary's death in 1694, William ruled as sole sovereign until his death at Kensington Palace in 1702. William was then succeeded by Anne, the younger daughter of James II and the last of the Stuarts. William and Mary College, the oldest educational institution in Virginia, was named in honor of the sovereigns.

WILLIAM OF CHAMPEAUX (shän pō′) (c. 1070-1121), French scholastic philosopher; born at Champeaux, near Melun, France. Studied under Anselm of Laon and Roscellinus, then taught rhetoric and logic in the cathedral of Notre Dame, Paris (1095). Teacher and rival of Abelard, who opposed and ridiculed William on his exaggerated realism. Retired to a suburb and founded abbey of Saint Victor; began teaching more modified doctrine; later abandoned his tenets of realism. Lifelong friend of Bernard of Clairvaux. Bishop of Chalons-sur-Marne (1112-1121).

WILLIAM OF TYRE (c. 1130-c. 1185), archbishop of Tyre and chronicler; born in Palestine; educated in Antioch, Jerusalem, and Europe. Ordained priest before 1161; studied in Europe before 1163. Appointed archdeacon of Tyre in 1167 by Amalric, king of Jerusalem. Tutor of king's son Baldwin (later Baldwin IV) (1170); chancellor of kingdom of Jerusalem; archbishop of Tyre (1175). One of the six bishops of the Latin church of the East to attend the Lateran Council in 1179. Wrote *Historia Rerum in Partibus Transmarinus Gestarum,* a well-written history of the First Crusade and of the Latin kingdom of Jerusalem, covering the period between 1095 and 1184.

WILLIAMS, GEORGE (1821-1905), Congregationalist, founder of Young Men's Christian Association, born at Dulverton, Somersetshire, England. At age twenty he went to London and became a clerk in a large draper's house. He helped to form a society for promoting foreign mission work. But the great work of his life began when he led in forming the Young Men's Christian Association. In 1844 twelve young men, all but one being his fellow employees, met in Williams' room and founded the Young Men's Christian Association to win other young men to the Christian faith. In 1851 Lord Shaftesbury, with whom Williams became closely associated, accepted the presidency, which he held until his death in 1886, when Williams became president for the rest of his life. The movement spread rapidly along interdenominational lines and branch organizations were formed throughout Britain and Ireland, on the Continent, in Australia, India, South Africa, the United States, and Canada. In 1855, only eleven years after the first association was formed, the World's Alliance of Young Men's Christian Associations was constituted in Paris by representatives from both sides of the Atlantic. In 1880 Williams gave five thousand pounds toward the purchase of Exeter Hall as the headquarters of the English work. In 1882 he led in the forming of English Associations over which he presided to the end of his life. In 1894 the London Association celebrated its golden jubilee with great demonstration, on which occasion Queen Victoria bestowed upon George Williams the honor of knighthood. Sir George's interests were wide and generous. He took active part in the British and Foreign Bible Society, the London City Missions, the Church Missionary Society, the Band of Hope Union, the Religious Tract Society, the Early Closing Association, and the Commercial Travelers' Christian Association. He served as president of several of these organizations. His life and labors were characterized by a fine public spirit, broad Christian sympathy, and the highest and truest philanthropy.

WILLIAMS, JOHN (1796-1839), missionary martyr of Erromanga in Polynesia, born at Tottenham, England, near London. Having been educated for business career, at fourteen apprenticed to an ironmonger in London. Soon after conversion at eighteen took a vital interest in things spiritual. Married before he was twenty-one, and appointed by the London Missionary Society to the South Sea Missions. Sailing by way of Sydney, Australia and New Zealand, arrived at Eimeo, one of the Society Islands, November 17, 1817, exactly one year after embarking from England. Almost immediately upon landing called upon to assist in building a ship, his part being the iron work. In June the following year it was decided to open work on Raiatea, which later became John Patterson's headquarters. Quickly learned the language and in ten months began to preach regularly in the native tongue. Most untiring in efforts to achieve the material as well as the spiritual advancement of the people. In May 1820 the first baptisms on the island took place. The people rapidly became Christianized and adopted many of the forms of civilization. In 1821 he bought a schooner, which he used in unceasing travels among the various island groups, planting stations and locating native mission workers whom he himself had trained. Visited the Hervey group of islands and established work on the island of Rarotonga in 1822. Built a sixty-foot ship naming it "The Messenger of Peace." Also extended labors to the Samoan Islands. After almost eighteen years of effective and faithful work in the South Seas, in 1834 took a four-year furlough to England to awaken new interest and to raise funds for mission. During stay in England wrote *A Narrative of Missionary Enterprises in the South Sea Islands,* and printed his translation of the New Testament in the Rarotongan language. After return to the Pacific with sixteen other missionaries, visited the stations he had already established, then sought to open new fields. While visiting Erromanga, one of the New Hebrides Islands, he and another of the group were murdered.

WILLIAMS, ROGER (c. 1603-c. 1683), founder of Rhode Island and of the first Baptist church in America. He was born in London. Educated at Sutton's Hospital (Charterhouse) and at Pembroke College, Cambridge University. Took orders in the Anglican Church but, rebelling against its organization and ceremonies, took membership in a separatist Puritan church. In 1631 he and his wife came to Massachusetts Bay Colony, seeking in New England the liberty of conscience. First went to Boston and became assistant pastor there; but coming into conflict with those about him, moved to Plymouth later the same year where separatist sentiments had preceded him. Became their teacher and pastor, and was greatly loved by the people. Also did much work among the Indians at this time. After a year or two there met with opposition from the authorities, and moved to Salem in 1633. After two years views on state-church relationships became too pronounced, and the authorities deprived him of his church and ordered him to leave the colony within six weeks; but they then extended his time until spring. He kept on preaching his views, insisting that the civil magistrates had no right to interfere in religious or ecclesiastical affairs. Hearing of a plan of the authorities to deport him to England, he at once left his home in the dead of winter and sought refuge among his Indian friends whose rights he was constantly seeking to protect. On the shores of Narragansett Bay purchased land from the Indians and founded a settlement in 1636, naming it Providence. Here he adopted Baptist views, was baptized, baptized eleven others, and founded at Providence about 1639 a Baptist church. A few months later withdrew from the Baptist group and became a "Seeker" or "Comeouter," yet remained most friendly with the Baptists. In 1643 returned to England to obtain from the crown a charter for his colony at Providence. From 1654 until 1657 he was president of the colony. Roger Williams' main goal seems to have been twofold: Freedom of worship and separation of church and state.

WILLIAMS, SAMUEL WELLS (1812-1884), American Congregational missionary, sinologist, and diplomat, born at Utica, New York. In 1831 he went to Rensselaer Polytechnic Institute at Troy, New York; in 1833 to Canton, China for the American Board of Commissioners for Foreign Missions as a printer. For fourteen years editor and printer of *The Chinese Repository.* In 1835, because of unsettled conditions, he was compelled to remove to Macao to complete the printing of Medhurst's *Dictionary of the Hokkien Dialect.* Learned Japanese language from some marooned Japanese sailors who were living in his home, thus equipped himself to translate into the Japanese the books of Genesis and Matthew, and to become interpreter for Commodore Perry in his expeditions of 1853-1854. In 1856 became, and for about twenty years remained, secretary and interpreter of the United States legation at Peking, and assisted in the negotiation and ratification of the Treaty of Tientsin in 1858, which provided for the toleration of both Chinese and foreign Christians. In 1877 returned to the United States to become professor of Chinese language and literature at Yale University. Became the ninth president of the American Bible Society (1881-1884). Chief writings were *The Middle Kingdom, Tonic Dictionary of the Chinese Language,* and *A Syllabic Dictionary of the Chinese Language.*

WILLIBRORD (wĭl'ĭ brôrd), (658-739), the apostle to the Frisians, born in Northumberland, England of devout Christian parents, reared in the Celtic church, early sent to the monastery at Ripon for education. Continued education in Ireland. About 690 the way opened for him to go to Frisia as a missionary. Embarked from England with eleven companions and landed near the mouth of the Rhine, and located in the land of the Frisians (present day Holland). In 695 he was in Rome to receive archepiscopal consecration. Established the headquarters of his archbishopric at Utretcht, where he labored for about forty-five years, giving Christianity firm footing in Southern Frisia. Made a trip to Denmark, but found the Danes as hostile as the Frisians. Spent the rest of his days laboring in Frisia. Boniface, the great missionary to Germany, was an assistant to Willibrord for three years.

WILSON, JOHN (1804-1875), British Presbyterian missionary to India and scholar, born at Lauder, Berwickshire, Scotland. Received education at the University of Edinburgh. Ordained in 1828 and in 1829 landed in Bombay as a missionary sent out by the Scottish Missionary Society; but shortly afterward the Church of Scotland took over the work of the Society. In 1831 organized a native church and was chosen as minister. In 1832 he helped to establish in Bombay an English college for the Christian education of the native youth. He contributed largely to the abolition of the practice of suttee. Much interested in the education of the common people in the vernacular as Alexander Duff was in the education of the upper classes in the English. In 1843 took his first furlough to his homeland, which was at the time of the disruption in the Scottish Church; and took his stand with the Free Church of Scotland and labored the rest of his life under the Free church. Twice president of the Bombay Branch of the Royal Asiatic Society, and vice chancellor of the Bombay University. On second furlough home, was in 1870, elected moderator of the General Assembly of the Free Church. After return to India in 1871 suffered several attacks of fever, and died. Active in many educational, literary, philological, archaeological, governmental, and social interests; but always pre-eminently a missionary and labored for the spread of the Gospel in India. Wrote *The Parsee Religion, The Lands of the Bible, History of the Suppression of Infanticide in Western India, India Three Thousand Years Ago,* and *Indian Caste.*

WILSON, ROBERT DICK (1856-1930), American Presbyterian philologist and theologian, born in Indiana, Pennsylvania, and attended Princeton University, Western Theological Seminary, and the University of Berlin. Instructor in Old Testament (1880-1881) and (1883-1885), and professor of Old Testament at the Western Theological Seminary (1885-1900); professor of Semitic philology and Old Testament introduction at Princeton Theological Seminary (1900-1929); and cofounder of Westminster Theological Seminary in 1929 and professor there (1929-1930). His writings include *Elements of Syriac Grammar, Hebrew Syntax, Hebrew Grammar for Beginners, Hebrew Illustrations, Studies in the Book of Daniel, Is the Higher Criticism Scholarly?* and *Scientific Investigation of the Old Testament.*

WILSON, WALTER LEWIS (1881-1969). Born in Aurora, Indiana. Educated at the University Medical College and Northwestern Medical College, Chicago. Briefly practiced medicine and then took over his father-in-law's tentmaking business from 1904 to 1929 in Kansas City. Founded the interdenominational Central Bible Church in 1920, the Flagstaff Indian Mission to the Navahos and Calvary Bible College, Kansas City. Travelled to British Isles, Europe and the Near East. Much in demand as an able Bible conference speaker.

WINEBRENNER (wīn'brĕn ẽr), **JOHN** (1797-1860), founder of the General Eldership of the Churches of God in North America, born at Glade Valley, Frederick County, Maryland, studied at Dickinson College, then studied theology in Philadelphia. While in Philadelphia in 1817 had a deep religious experience. Ordained by the German Reformed church and became pastor at Harrisburg, Pennsylvania in 1820. Emphasis on experiential religion, strong revivalistic preaching, and opposition to theaters, dancing, gambling, lotteries, and racing led to official charges against him. Severed relation with the denomination along with his pastoral charge, but continued evangelistic preaching in and around Harrisburg. Began to form independent congregations and to ordain elders. In 1830 he and six of these ministers met in Harrisburg and organized a new denomination ultimately to be known as the General Eldership of the Churches of God in North America. His doctrinal tenets were Arminian and premillennial. Accepted three sacraments: baptism by immersion, the evening observance of the Lord's Supper, and the washing of feet. Adopted the Presbyterial form of church government, formulated no written creed, accepting the Bible as the sole rule of faith and practice, adopting biblical names as much as possible in the organization. Held sectarianism to be unscriptural, yet founded a distinct denomination.

WINER (vē'nẽr), **JOHANN GEORG BENEDIKT** (1789-1858), German theologian and New Testament scholar, born at Leipzig, educated at the gymnasium in Leipzig. From 1817 to 1823 professor of theology at the University of Leipzig, then professor at Erlangen in 1823, returned to his chair at Leipzig in 1832, where he remained until his death in 1858. His *Biblisches Realwörterbuch,* a comprehensive handbook of biblical subjects, was a thesaurus of historical, geographical, archaeological, and scientific knowledge. His *Grammar of the Chaldee Language* was a work of importance. His masterwork was *Grammatik des Neutestamentlichen Sprachidioms* or *Grammar of the Idioms of the New Testament,* which was the standard work for the next seventy-five years, and repeatedly translated into English. Possessed a conscientious earnestness in seeking the truth and a pious reverence for the Holy Scriptures.

WINROD, GERALD (1900-1957). Born Wichita, Kansas. Founder of Defender of the Faith organization in 1925 and its magazine *The Defender* in 1938. Was anti-Semitic and opposed the New Deal. Indicted by the federal grand jury in 1942 for sedition by damaging morale of the armed services.

WINSLOW (wĭnz'lō), **EDWARD** (1595-1655), governor of Plymouth Colony, born at Droitwich, Worcestershire, England and received a good education. While making a tour on the Continent became a member of John Robinson's congregation at Leiden, then came to America on the Mayflower in 1620. Early won the confidence of the Indians, and made colonists' first treaty with the Indians. Winslow served as a member of the governor's council (1624-1646), and governor of Plymouth (1633, 1636, 1644). Made several trips to England in the interests of Plymouth and Massachusetts Bay Colonies. On another trip, following publishing of *The Glorious Progress of the Gospel among the Indians in New England,* he was instrumental in organizing the Society for the Propagation of the Gospel in New England in 1649. Activities for the colony kept him in England, and he did not again return to Plymouth. In 1654 Cromwell appointed him as one of the three commissioners to superintend an expedition against the Spaniards in the West Indies; but he died before its completion, dying at sea between Santo Domingo and Jamaica.

WINTHROP, JOHN (1588-1649), Puritan governor of Massachusetts Bay Colony, born at Edwardston, Suffolk, England, studied at Trinity College, Cambridge, and in 1613 entered Gray's Inn, where he studied law, and later became a successful lawyer in London. His sympathy with the Puritan and the Congregational movements led him to take an interest in American emigration. In 1629 he became associated with the Massachusetts Bay Company, and before the group set sail for America was chosen the first governor of their new colony in the New World. Came with a large group of colonists in 1630. Winthrop became one of the founders of Boston, which came to be his place of residence. He was annually elected governor of the colony during most of his time in America. In 1635 defended the banishment of Roger Williams, and in 1637 opposed Anne Hutchinson's antinomianism, and helped expel her from the colonies. In 1643 organized the New England Confederation, and served as its first president. Winthrop was conservative and somewhat aristocratic, and was opposed to unlimited democracy; but just and magnanimous in political guidance, even under circumstances of great difficulty. Despite colonial hardships and religious and political dissensions, showed skill and wisdom in keeping Massachusetts clear of English interference. On way across the ocean in 1630 wrote *A Model of Christian Charity.* His *Journal,* written during his life in the colony, sometimes called the *History of New England,* is considered one of the most valuable source books in American history.

WISE, ISAAC MEYER (1819-1900), Jewish rabbi. Born in Steingrub, Bohemia. Educated in Prague and Vienna as a rabbi. Rabbi in Bohemia. Rabbi of synagogues in New York and Ohio. President of Hebrew Union College from 1875 to 1900. Helped to found and became president of Hebrew Union College of Cincinnati from 1873 to 1900. Leader in the organization of the union of American Hebrew Congregations in 1873. Part of more liberal Reform Judaism.

WISE, STEPHEN SAMUEL (1874-1949). Born in Budapest, Hungary. Educated in Columbia University and for the rabbinate in New York, Oxford and Vienna. Rabbi mainly in New York and Portland, Oregon from 1893 to 1949. Established and served as president of the Jewish Institute of Religion from 1922 to 1948 for training rabbis. Helped create the American Jewish Congress and the World Jewish Congress. Editor of *Opinion* from 1936 to 1949. Favored Zionism. Helped found the NAACP in 1909 and the ACLU in 1920.

WISHART (wĭsh'ärt), **GEORGE** (c. 1513-1546), Scottish reformer and martyr, born near Montrose in Scotland. Early he began to teach doctrines of the Reformation at Montrose where he was master of a grammar school. In 1538 charged with heresy for teaching the Greek New Testament. Fled first to England, then to the continent, especially to Germany and Switzerland. In 1543 at Cambridge, and a little later ventured back to Scotland; continued his Reformation preaching. Continued preaching led to his arrest and trial for heresy. Condemned to be burned, the execution illegally taking place at St. Andrews in March 1546. In the last years of his life, John Knox accompanied him on some of his preaching tours and was greatly influenced by his reform preaching.

WITHERSPOON, JOHN (1723-1794), Presbyterian minister and signer of the Declaration of Independence, born near Edinburgh, Scotland. Graduated from Edinburgh University, licensed to preach in the Church of Scotland in 1743, and held two charges, one at Beith and one at Paisley, between 1745 and 1768. In 1768 accepted the invitation to the presidency of the College of New Jersey (now Princeton University). During presidency was also pastor of the church at Princeton. During the war the college was closed, and Witherspoon was selected by the citizens of New Jersey to represent the state in the General Congress from 1776 to 1782. Became one of the signers of the Declaration of Independence, the only clergyman accorded that privilege. Moderator of the Presbyterian General Assembly in 1789. In 1790 became totally blind. A versatile man, an able writer, and a leader in the conservative group in the church. Author of many theological books, several volumes of sermons, and of books dealing with civil government. Some of his writings wre *Ecclesiastical Characteristics, Essay on Justification,* and *Essays on Important Subjects.*

WOLSEY (wo͝ol′zĭ), **THOMAS** (c. 1474-1530), English cardinal and statesman, born at Ipswich, England, studied at Magdalen College, Oxford, ordained priest in 1498. By 1514 he was Bishop of Lincoln and Archbishop of York. In 1515 made cardinal by Pope Leo X and papal legate in 1518. In 1523 became Bishop of Durham and in 1529 Bishop of Winchester. First diplomatic employment was a mission to Scotland under Henry VII. Became privy councilor and lord chancellor, and from this time until death in 1530 his history largely the history of England. Wolsey's two great ambitions were to make England a great international power, and to become pope of Rome. In the former he succeeded. Began to use the balance of power in international relations. History scholars today recognize Wolsey as a statesman rather than as an ecclesiastic. Henry VIII assigned to Wolsey the very difficult task of negotiating with Pope Clement VII for a divorce from Catherine. The pope was not able to grant the divorce, because he was under the control of Catherine's nephew, the powerful Charles V, king of Spain and emperor of Germany. The failure greatly displeased Henry, who accused Wolsey of high treason. Wolsey became despondent, believing that the king was going to have him executed; but the great cardinal and chancellor died at Leicester on the way to trial at London.

WOOLMAN, JOHN (1720-1772), American Quaker preacher. Born in Rancocas, New Jersey. Taught school for a while, in 1741 began to preach. During the last thirty years of his life made journeys visiting and preaching among the Friends in different parts of the colonies, and in preaching to the Indians, supporting himself by work as a tailor. Deeply mystical, having been deeply influenced by the writings of Jacob Boehme, Thomas á Kempis, and Fenelon. His deep mystical consciousness of the unity of God and man led to vigorous and unpopular denunciations of intemperance, war, and slavery. After 1746 instrumental in helping Quakerism to purge itself of slave-holding, and through his disciple, Benjamin Lundy, in inspiring William Lloyd Garrison to devote his life to the cause of abolition. In 1772 Woolman made a trip to England where he died of smallpox. In addition to his main work, *A Journal of John Woolman's Life and Travels in the Service of the Gospel,* also wrote *Some Considerations in the Keeping of Negroes.*

WOODSWORTH, JAMES (d. 1917), Canadian Methodist home missionary. Born in Toronto. Ordained in 1864. Served the Portage La Prairie circuit the rest of his life. Superintendent of Methodist missions in the Northwest. Wrote Autobiographical *Thirty Years in the Canadian Northwest*.

WORDSWORTH, CHRISTOPHER (1807-1885), English prelate and scholar, born in Bocking, England, a nephew of the poet, William Wordsworth. Received education at Winchester and at Trinity College, Cambridge, a brilliant scholar. Headmaster of Harrow (1836-1844). While canon of Westminster, (1844-1869), also vicar of Stanford-in-the-Vale, Berkshire, and rural dean (1850-1869); was archdeacon of Westminster (1865-1869); and Bishop of Lincoln (1869-1885). Pronouncedly anti-Catholic and took part in the Old Catholic Congress held in Cologne in 1872. Belonged to the Low Church or Evangelical school. Most important writing was *The Greek New Testament with Prefaces, Introductions, and Notes,* and *The Old Testament in the Authorized Version, with Notes and Introductions.* Some of other many works: *Scripture Inspiration, or On the Canon of Holy Scripture* (Hulsean lectures); *On the Apocalypse* (Hulsean lectures); *The Harmony of the Apocalypse; On the Inspiration of the Bible; History of the Church of Ireland; A Church History to the Council of Chalcedon,* A.D. *481; Discourse of Scottish History,* and *St. Hippolytus and the Church of Rome*. He was the author of numerous hymns, one of which was "O Day of Rest and Gladness."

WORDSWORTH, WILLIAM (1770-1850), English poet, born at Cockermouth, Cumberland, England, graduated from St. John's College, Cambridge, then traveled in various countries of Europe. Then settled down making his home with his sister Dorothy at Grasmere in 1799 to be near his friend Carlyle. From 1808 to 1813 he lived at Allan Bank, and from 1813 to 1850 at Rydal Mount. Through frugal, simple living, able to devote the most of his life to writing poetry. On the death of Southey, 1843, he became poet laureate. The first of England's nature poets and depicted natural beauties simply, reverently, and faithfully. Wrote as though he believed that all nature was able to communicate with man. In later years returned to a more orthodox form of creed. Became loyal supporter of the Church of England, and was in sympathy with the Oxford movement, especially with John Keble, whose *Christian Year* he admired.

WREN, CHRISTOPHER (1632-1723), English architect, born at East Knoyle, Wiltshire, England, son of an Anglican clergyman. Educated at Westminster and at Wadham College, Oxford. Became a noted scientist and mathematician, and about 1660 became professor of astronomy at Oxford. During forty years following the great fire of 1666 in London, designed and rebuilt many buildings in London, notably the library at Trinity College, and the campanile of Christ's Church at Oxford. The great masterpiece of his architecture was St. Paul's Cathedral, considered by many as one of the great buildings of the world. Rebuilt more than fifty other churches and nearly all the other chief buildings of London that had been burned down in the fire. Originator of the new beautiful modern type of steeple. Work is noted for its simplicity and graceful lines. In 1673 knighted, and for many years was a member of Parliament. One of the founders of the Royal Society and was for a time president.

WRIGHT, CHARLES HENRY HAMILTON (1836-1909), Irish Anglican clergyman, born at Dublin, Ireland, educated at Trinity College, Dublin. Ordained deacon in 1859, and priest the next year. Besides holding various charges between 1859 and 1898, including being vicar of Saint John's Liverpool (1891-1898), Bampton lecturer at Oxford (1878), Donnellan lecturer at Dublin (1880), and Grinfield lecturer on the Septuagint at Oxford (1893-1897). At various times examiner in Hebrew in the universities of Oxford, London, Manchester, and Wales, and clerical superintendent of the Protestant Reformation Society (1898-1907). Militantly antagonistic to Roman Catholicism, writing many pamphlets denouncing the Roman church. In theology described himself as "evangelical and conservative, but quite willing to adopt opinions based on real evidence and not on mere conjecture or hypotheses of scholars however eminent." Publications include: *An Introduction to the Old Testament; Roman Catholicism; Zechariah and his Prophecies; Book of Genesis in Hebrew; Daniel and His Prophecies; Genuine Writings of St. Patrick, with Life;* and *The One Religion.*

WRIGHT, J. ELWIN (1896-1966). In 1929 founded the New England Fellowship for Evangelicals. Had a Boston bookstore. Had a summer Bible conference at Rumney, New Hampshire. Helped found the National Association of Evangelicals in 1942. Secretary of the World Evangelical Fellowship from 1951 to 1959.

WRIGHT, GEORGE FREDERICK (1838-1921), American Congregational clergyman and geologist, born at Whitehall, New York, and pursued education at Oberlin College and Oberlin Theological Seminary, Oberlin, Ohio. Served for five months as a private in the American Army in 1861. Between 1862 and 1881 held pastorates at Bakersfield, Vermont and Andover, Massachusetts. It was during his two pastorates that he developed an interest in geology, and attracted world attention through reportings of his findings and theories. Subsequently traveled extensively in Asiatic and European Russia and Greenland. Then professor of New Testament language and literature in Oberlin Theological Seminary from 1881 to 1892, and from 1892 to 1907 was professor of harmony of science and religion in the same institution, becoming professor emeritus. An expert in geology and from 1884 to 1892 was assistant geologist in the United States Geological Survey. In 1890 became a fellow of the Geological Society of America. Works include: *Studies in Science and Religion, Scientific Aspects of Christian Evidence, Scientific Confirmation of Old Testament History, Divine Authority of the Bible,* and several books on geology, among them *The Ice Age in North America.* Editor of *Bibliotheca Sacra* from 1884 until his death in 1921.

WYCLIFFE (wĭk'lĭf), **JOHN** (c. 1329-1384), "The Morning Star of the Reformation," born in Hipswell, near Richmond, Yorkshire, England. Entered Balliol College, Oxford as a student, and later became master. Seems to have been connected with Oxford the rest of his life, and esteemed the ablest member of the faculty. In philosophy a realist in contrast to the prevailing nominalism of the time. Augustine's writings had much infuence upon him. Seems to have become one of the king's chaplains; became a doctor of theology; and was given appointment by the king to the rectory of Lutterworth. Began to speak as a religious reformer, preaching in Oxford and London against the pope's secular sovereignty, and at the same time publicizing his ideas by tracts and leaflets. Soon became so outspoken against the church of Rome that in 1377 he was summoned before the tribunal of the Bishop of London at St. Paul's. The pope became alarmed and issued a document condemning many of Wycliffe's writings. Wycliffe, however, had strong support of the people, the scholars, and the nobles of England, and the pope was unable to quell the growing dissatisfaction over papal control and the growing reform sentiments in England. Also began to provide England with a new proclamation of the pure gospel, acknowledging the Bible as the only source of truth. Rejected the doctrine of infallibility of either pope or council, and held that papal decrees or pronouncements had authority only insofar as they were in harmony with the Scriptures. The clergy were not to rule, but to serve and help the people. Transubstantiation, purgatory, and other Roman dogmas were being examined and challenged. By 1380 enlisted from among Oxford graduates a body of "poor priests," later to be known as Lollards, to go out as evangelical preachers, proclaiming his views. In spite of England's sympathy with Wycliffe's position and teachings, the Archbishop of London succeeded in prohibiting him from preaching. He then retired to his rectory and devoted himself to writing, especially to the translation of the Bible, the first manuscript English Bible, and to writing and sending forth polemic tracts. At this time wrote *Trialogues,* in which he expressed supreme importance of obedience to the Bible and to conscience. Writings were rigidly repressed, and in 1415 at the Council of Constance his books were ordered burned and his remains to be exhumed and burned. This order was carried out in 1428.

XAVIER (zā'vĭ ĕr), **FRANCIS** (1506-1552), Jesuit missionary, born in an aristocratic family in Navarre, Northern Spain. As a student in the Univeristy of Paris distinguished himself in philosophical studies. Came under the influence of Ignatius Loyola who persuaded him in 1534 to become a charter member of what was later to become the Society of Jesus, popularly known as the Jesuit Order. Ordained priest in 1537. In 1540, at the request of King John III of Portugal, Loyola appointed Xavier to go to India as papal legate. Sailing from Lisbon, Portugal, the next year, he landed in the Portuguese colony of Goa in West India in 1542. He had the Creed, the Lord's Prayer, the Ave Maria, and the Decalogue translated into the vernacular, and committed them to memory. Dissatisfied with the results he was achieving in India, in 1545 turned to the East Indies. Worked for three years, returning to India in 1548. During seven years in India and the Indies, he baptized people by the thousands, both adults and infants. Founded a missionary school at Goa. Having been made a missionary bishop of the entire East, felt he must go to other lands too. Left to others his work in southern Asia and proceeded to Japan in 1549. Spent two years preaching through interpreters and baptizing. Then leaving to others this mission also, proceeded toward China to build a church, making a visit to Goa on the way, in 1552. But he died of a fever off the coast of the mainland of South China, near Canton. Work was superficial, an exploration rather than a structure. He was canonized in 1622.

XIMENES (hē mā'nās), **(JIMÉNES) DE CISNEROS FRANZISCO** (1436-1517), Spanish cardinal, inquisitor, born in Torrelaguna, Castile, Spain, received education at Salamanca. After rising into prominence as a churchman and a preacher, resigned all honors and became an Observant Franciscan monk in 1484 and for some years followed a rigorously ascetic regimen, and for years was a hermit living in solitude, prayer, and meditation. In 1492 Queen Isabella chose him for her confessor; but he continued to live in his monastery as a strict Franciscan monk, appearing in court only when called. In 1495 chosen Archbishop of Toledo, again wishing to continue living in his monastery. As confessor and chancellor of the queen during her lifetime, he was the guiding spirit of Spanish affairs and did much to unify and strengthen Spain. In 1507 created cardinal and grand inquisitor-general for Castile and Leon. Organized at his own expense an expedition for the conquest of the Moorish city of Oran and for the extirpation of piracy. A champion of reform in the Roman Catholic church in Spain, seeking to suppress heresy as well as to correct abuses in the monasteries, among the clergy, and in the church in general. In his reform efforts he had the support of Queen Isabella. On the death of Ferdinand in 1506, by the will of the king, he was made regent of all Castile during the absence in the Netherlands of his grandson Charles. A bold, stern, determined statesman. In the midst of a corrupt clergy his morals were irreproachable. Whole time was devoted to the State and to religion. About 1500 founded the University of Alcalá which became one of Spain's leading educational centers and a center of Catholic reform. Most famous literary service was the printing at Alcalá of the Complutensian Polyglot Bible and in 1514 the first printed Greek New Testament.

Y

YALE, ELIHU (1649-1721) Born in Boston, Massachusetts. Educated in England. Held high position in the British East India Company over twenty years. Gave money and goods for the school that was named for him.

YOUNG, ANDREW (1869-1922), missionary, born on a moorland farm, at Crossdykes, in Scotland. Early decided to be a missionary to the Congo, and in 1890 he was sent to the Congo as a layman to serve as a businessman at Tunduwa station in the Congo-Balolo mission. Spent six years in Africa with one furlough home. Though a busy and effective missionary, felt the handicap of having no professional training and resolved not to return to the field until he could secure such training. After three attacks of haematuric fever which almost cost him his life he returned to Scotland. He studied at Glasgow and took his degree in medicine. In 1905 the way opened for him to go to Shensi, China, under the Baptist Missionary Society where he spent his last seventeen years of missionary service. He was not only a surgeon but a preacher and an administrator as well.

YOUNG, BRIGHAM (1801-1877), president of the Mormon church (1844-1877), born in Whittingham, Vermont, one of a family of eleven children. Early in life moved to New York. By trade a painter and glazier. In 1832 joined the Latter Day Saints, ordained an elder; began active preaching and baptizing near his home in Mendon. In 1833 he moved to Kirtland, Ohio, the new center of Mormon activity. Helped build the Kirtland temple, and in 1835 was made an apostle, and in 1838 became the chief of the church's twelve apostles. Missionary in England from 1839 to 1844. At the time of the murder of Joseph Smith in 1844, Young was in Boston. He hurried back to Nauvoo, Illinois, and assumed the leadership of the sect. When the Mormons were ejected from the state of Illinois, Young decided to go to the valley of the Great Salt Lake. In the spring of 1847 Young began the long journey of eleven hundred miles across the plains and tablelands, arriving in the Great Salt Lake Valley in July. Most of the party, including Young, returned to the East for the winter, and then in 1848 he led four thousand of the faithful to their new home in the West. Here in the heart of an uninviting desert, he founded Salt Lake City and the political state of Deseret. In 1849 Young sought to have his state admitted into the Union. It was not admitted, but the United States government in 1850 organized the Territory of Utah, with Brigham Young as governor, which position he held for about seven years; in 1896 Utah was admitted into the Union as a state. In 1877 Brigham Young died, leaving an estate of two million dollars to be divided among his surviving. He had married over twenty wives, and fathered fifty-one children.

YOUNG, DINSDALE THOMAS (1861-1938), popular English Wesleyan preacher, born at Corbridge-on-Tyne, England. Educated in private schools and at Headingley Theological College, Leeds. Ordained in Wesleyan ministry, 1879, the youngest candidate accepted by the Wesleyan Conference. Held pastorates in London, Birmingham, York, Manchester, and Edinburgh, preaching in Wesley's Chapel, City Road, London, 1906-1914. In 1914, president of Wesleyan Conference; in that year was assigned to Westminster Central Hall, where he attracted capacity audiences. Writings include: *Neglected People of the Bible* and *Silver Charms, Stars of Retrospect* (an autobiography).

YOUNG, EDWARD JOSEPH (1907-1968), Old Testament scholar. Born in San Francisco. Educated at Stanford University, Madrid, Westminster Theological Seminary and Dropsie University (Ph.D.). Professor of Old Testament at Westminster Seminary from 1936 to 1968. Taught at Winona Lake School of Theology from 1950 to 1968. Moderator of Orthodox Presbyterian Church in 1956. Knew Semitic languages well. Major books are *An Introduction to the Old Testament, The Prophecy of Daniel* and a three-volume work on Isaiah.

YOUNG, EGERTON RYERSON (1840-1909), Canadian Methodist minister and missionary, born in Ontario, Canada, educated at the Normal School, Ontario. After teaching for several years, entered the ministry in 1863, ordained four years later. After one year of pastoral work at the First Methodist Episcopal Church, Hamilton, Ontario, sent as a missionary to Norway House, Northwest Territory, north of Lake Winnepeg, where he worked among the Indians for five years (1868-1873). Then to Beren's River, Northwest Territory, working in a similar capacity for three years. In 1876 returned to Ontario and worked at Port Perry, Colborne, Bowmanville, Medford, and St. Paul's, Brampton. After 1888 he made many tours speaking on the missionary work among the American Indians. Some of his writings: *By Canoe and Dogtrain, On the Indian Trail, The Apostle of the North, James Evans.*

YOUNG, ROBERT (1822-1888), lay theologian of the Scottish Free church, born at Edinburgh, Scotland, received his education in private schools, after which he served an apprenticeship to the printing business (1838-1845). In spare time studied oriental languages. In 1847 took up printing and selling of books pertaining especially to the Old Testament and its versions. Went to India as a literary missionary and superintendent of the mission press at Surat (1856-1861). Conducted the Missionary Institute back in Edinburgh (1864-1874). He was a strict textual critic and Calvinistic theologian. His most important contribution was the *Analytical Concordance of the Bible*. Wrote also *Two-Fold Concordance of the Greek New Testament; Grammatical Analysis of Hebrew, Chaldaic, and Greek Scriptures; Hebrew Vocabulary;* and a "literal" translation of the Bible.

Z

ZAHN, THEODOR (1838-1933), German biblical and patristic scholar, born at Mörs, Rhenish Prussia, educated at the universities of Basel, Erlangen, and Berlin. Teacher in the gymnasium of Neustrelitz (1861-1865); lecturer at the University of Göttingen (1865), and professor of theology (1871), professor at Keil (1877), at Erlangen (1878), and at Leipzig (1888), and returned to Erlangen to be professor of pedagogics and New Testament exegesis (1892-1909). A leader among the conservatives in New Testament criticism in opposition to the biblical criticism of the day. He also did basic work in the critical study of New Testament canon, its history, and authorship. Leading works were his monumental three-volume work, *The Introduction to the New Testament* and his *Commentary on the New Testament*.

ZEISBERGER (tsīs'bĕr gĕr), **DAVID** (1721-1808), Moravian missionary to American Indians, born in Zauchenthal, Moravia. When five years of age, fled with his Bohemian Brethren parents to the estate of Count Zinzendorf at Herrnhut, Germany. Then sent to a Moravian settlement in Holland to study, but in 1738 joined his parents, who in 1736 had settled in Georgia. Helped build the towns of Nazareth and Bethlehem, Pennsylvania. Became a missionary to the Indians, laboring among them from 1745 until 1808. Labored among many different tribes in New York, Pennsylvania, Ohio, Michigan, and Canada. Organized his first mission in Ohio, building a town called Schoenbrunn, on the Tuscarawas River. Here he was joined by all the Moravian converts from Pennsylvania. Built two more towns, other missionaries came, and many converts were added. Early in the Revolutionary War he was accused by British of favoring the American side. In 1781 the settlement was destroyed by a band of Wyandotte warriors at the instigation of the British. The next year nearly a hundred of the Christian Indians were massacred in cold blood at Gnadenhütten by a party of colonial militia. Disheartened, Zeisberger in 1782 led a small remnant of his converts to Michigan and built an Indian town. In 1786 went back to Ohio and founded New Salem near Cleveland. In 1790 impelled to migrate to Canada, but in 1798 returned with some of his Christians to the Tuscarawas Valley where Congress had granted his Indians their former lands. There they built a town, calling it Goshen. There he labored until his death ten years after. He prepared several grammars, lexicons, textbooks, hymn books, and Bible translations for the Indians.

ZENO (zē'nō) **OF CYPRUS** (died 264 B.C.), founder of Stoic philosophy, born at Citium, Cyprus, and studied under Cynic teachers. Came to Athens to open a school in the "painted porch" (stoa, hence Stoicism). Stoicism exacted absolute obedience and self-sacrifice for the sake of duty; and was admirably fitted to the Roman mind. The aim of life was virtue, not pleasure. The Stoics did not believe in immortality, but conceived of a final identification with God and nature. They had a high noble ethic, in many respects similar to the Christian.

ZENOS (zē'nŭs), **ANDREAS CONSTANTINIDES** (1855-1942), Presbyterian theologian, born at Constantinople, Turkey, educated at Robert College, Constantinople and at Princeton Theological Seminary. Ordained Presbyterian minister in 1881, then was pastor in Brandt, Pennsylvania (1881-1883). He was professor of Greek at Lake Forest University (1883-1888), professor of New Testament exegesis at Hartford Theological Seminary (1888-1891), professor of church history in McCormick Theological Seminary (1891-1894), and became professor of Biblical theology in 1894. Co-editor of the *Standard Bible Dictionary,* and author of *Elements of Higher Criticism, Compendium of Church History, The Teaching of Jesus Concerning Christian Conduct, The Son of Man,* and *Presbyterianism in America*.

ZIEGENBALG (tsē'gĕn bälg), **BARTHOLOMAEUS** (1682-1719), German missionary to India, born near Dresden, Saxony, Germany. Educated at the University of Halle, Germany, where he came under the influence and teaching of the pietist, August Hermann Francke. When King Frederick IV of Denmark appealed to Halle for missionaries to be sent to the Danish possessions in India, Bartholomaeus Ziegenbalg and Henry Plütschau were among the first to offer to go. Their commission to India in 1706 was the beginning of the famous Danish-Halle Mission. After a seven-month voyage, they arrived at the Danish port of Tranquebar, one hundred miles south of Madras. Within a year Ziegenbalg was preaching in the Tamil language, and baptized several converts. Though he met much opposition from the Dutch East India Company, and even suffered four months' imprisonment, he continued to preach; and between 1708 and 1711 he translated the New Testament into the Tamil. Began to translate the Old Testament and to prepare a Tamil dictionary and a Tamil-Latin grammar. In 1715 Ziegenbalg, too, had to return to Europe. While at home married, and in 1718, with his wife, returned to India. Early the next year his health broke, and he died in Tranquebar, leaving behind as a monument to his thirteen years of arduous and devoted missionary service over three hundred fifty converts, many catechumens and pupils, a missionary seminary, a Tamil lexicon, and a Tamil Bible. His mission continued under the patronage of the Danish kings for over one hundred twenty years.

ZINZENDORF (tsĭn'tsĕn dōrf), **NICKOLAUS LUDWIG, Count von** (1700-1760), Founder of the Moravian or Bohemian Brethren, born at Dresden, Germany of a Saxon nobleman and high official, who was a friend of Spener. He received his care and early training under his pietistic maternal grandmother. From age ten to sixteen a pupil in one of the Halle schools, where he came under the personal influence of Francke. The fundamental ideals of Pietism and a deep interest in foreign missions were inculcated in him at this time. After academic training at Halle, he desired to take up the study of theology; but deferring to the wishes of his family, pursued the study of law at Wittenberg (1716-1719). Then in 1721 accepted a civil office under the Saxon government at Dresden. With a part of his patrimony bought the estate of Berthelsdorf. He offered to use his estate as a home for religious refugees. In 1722, a carpenter, Christian David from Moravia, who had been doing some building for Zinzendorf, brought persecuted Hussite Bohemian families from Moravia to the Berthelsdorf estate until about three hundred of these persecuted people from Moravia and Bohemia migrated to Zinzendorf's estate. These settlers built the village of Herrnhut and established a little religious community, of which Zinzendorf himself soon became spiritual overseer. Other Protestants from various parts of Germany also joined this settlement, thus magnifying the problem of working out unity within the group. In 1727 he took occasion to resign official position in the state and to devote himself to full-time religious activities and leadership. Accepted the Augsburg Confession and was ordained as a Lutheran minister in 1734. It was his purpose to make his group of followers a little church within the church after Spener's pattern, thus keeping them loyal members of the Lutheran church. When the Lutheran church of Saxony, however, opposed him in this, a separate body became inevitable. They began a separate organization in 1732 with a foreign missionary program, going to Greenland, America, and to other parts of Europe, and before long to distant corners of the earth. In 1735 Nitschmann was ordained and in 1737 Zinzendorf was consecrated bishop by D. E. Jablonski, thus securing for the Brethren historic succession, and definitely linking Zinzendorf with the Hussite church. Since he was exiled from Lutheran Saxony in 1736 he made a visit to his mission fields in the West Indies. In 1741 came to America to do mission work and to attempt to unite Protestant Christianity in the colonies until 1743. Plan of union of the churches in the colonies, however, failed, and he returned to Europe. He was in England from 1749 to 1755. Appointed Spangenberg to be bishop over the Brethren in the United States and the West Indies. His last years were more or less depressing and unpleasant. It was difficult to maintain unity and piety among the Brethren, with all their divergent backgrounds. In 1752 his son, who he had hoped would be his successor, died. Four years later his wife died. A sincere and true pietist. From boyhood until death his goal was "heart religion" and "pure living." His motto was: "I have but one passion; it is He, He only." Wrote hymn "Jesus Thy Blood and Righteousness My Beauty Are."

ZIZKA (zhĭsh'kȧ) **JAN (JOANN ZISKA)** (c. 1360-1424), Bohemian general and Hussite leader, born at Trocznov, Bohemia; educated at court of King Wenceslaus. Disciple of John Hus. Had extensive military experience. After Hus's execution in 1415, became chief leader of the Hussites against Emperor Sigismund (1419); built a mountain stronghold, naming it Tabor. Repelled the Imperialists from Prague (1420). Blind after 1421, yet continued leading his army in victorious campaigns against Sigismund's armies (1421-1422). Headed the Taborites against the Utraquists in the Hussite civil wars (1423-1424). Died of plague. A high reputation as a patriot and champion of liberty and equality.

ZWEMER, SAMUEL MARINUS (1867-1952), American Dutch Reformed missionary to Moslems, born at Vriesland, Michigan, educated at Hope College, Holland, Michigan, and New Brunswick Theological Seminary in New Jersey. In college came under the influence of Robert Wilder, and became one of the first members of the Student Volunteer Movement, and one of its leaders. In 1888-1889 Zwemer and others formed a new missionary organization, The Arabian Mission. In 1889 James Cantine went to Arabia. The next year Zwemer was ordained and followed. In 1894 the regular board of the Dutch Reformed Church in America took over the mission. Between 1890 and 1905 Zwemer worked at Busrah, Bahrein Islands, and Muscat; later with headquarters at Cairo, Egypt, traveled over the most of the Islamic world, arousing in Europe and America interest in bringing the Christian faith to Moslems and in training missionaries. In spite of the firm hold of Islam on these lands a few converts were made. In 1906 organized and was chairman of the Conference on Islam at Cairo, but maintained his residence in the United States from 1905 to 1910 while promoting missions in his denomination. In 1910 returned to missionary field on the Arabian Gulf. Visited many missions over the Moslem world, making notable contributions to the cause in South Africa and the Netherlands Indies, where he preached in Dutch, English, and Arabic. Also visited India and China several times. In 1911 started the *Moslem World,* and was its editor for about forty years. For nearly a decade after returning from the mission field, professor of missions and comparative religions at Princeton Theological Seminary. Author of about fifty volumes in English, and a number in Arabic. A few of his works: *Arabia the Cradle of Islam, Moslem Doctrine of God, Islam a Challenge to Faith, The Unoccupied Mission Fields of Africa and Asia, The Moslem World,* and *Mohammed or Christ.*

ZWILLING, GABRIEL (DIDYMUS) (c. 1487-1558), the most noted of the thirty monks who left the Augustinian monastery at Wittenberg in 1521. Preached in the parish church at Wittenberg during Luther's absence at the Wartburg, greeted by some as a second Luther. Fiercely attacked the mass, the adoration of the sacrament, and the whole system of monasticism as dangerous to salvation. With equal zeal soon attacked images. Views were similar to those of Carlstadt. Their radical revolutionary movement rapidly grew and was greatly increased in radicalism under the added impetus of Thomas Münzer and the Zwickau prophets, who joined forces with them about this time.

ZWINGLI (tsvĭng'lē), **ULRICH (HULDREICH)** (1484-1531), Swiss Reformer, born into a well-to-do home at Wildhaus in the valley of the Toggenburg, Switzerland. Father a village magistrate, wished son to be educated for the priesthood. Received a good education, attending schools at Basel, Berne, and Vienna. In 1506 became parish priest at Glarus. While at Einsedelen developed remarkable gifts as a preacher. On thirty-sixth birthday, Jan. 1, 1519, became chief pastor in the Great Minster Church in Zurich, where he expounded the Scriptures. Sermons were fearless, scriptural, and evangelical. Attacked the celibacy of the clergy, the worship of the image of Mary, the selling of indulgences, and other abuses of the church. Erasmus Greek New Testament had greatly influenced his thinking and quickened his convictions. He was still a Bible Humanist and a son of Rome. The real turning point came later, 1519, when the plague broke out in Zurich and swept away one third of the population. His experience in being stricken and brought near to death led him to dedicate his life anew to the will of God. During the next three years became acquainted with and deeply interested in the writings of Luther. During these years the Bible Humanist matured into a Reformer. His open break with Rome came in 1523 when in his *Sixty Seven Articles* he rejected the Catholic co-ordination of Scripture and tradition; when he maintained that the Bible is the only infallible authority which a Christian can accept. The cleavage between the Swiss Reformers and Rome became definite and complete when in 1525 he replaced the Catholic mass by the first Reformed communion service in the Great Minster Church. The following years were busy years for him and fellow-reformers. In 1522 he had secretly married, but the marriage was not made public until 1524. In 1525 published principal literary works, *Commentary on True and False Religions* and in 1531 *An Exposition of the Faith.* During these years he came into conflict with the Anabaptists over baptism and also came into controversy over doctrinal matters with the Lutherans. In 1529 after the Marburg Colloquy, the Zwinglians and the Lutherns definitely parted company, Zwingli holding the Lord's Supper to be a memorial of Christ's death. The Catholic faith remained firm in the five Forest Cantons and leagued against the Protestants. A temporary settlement was reached in the Peace of Kappel in 1529, favorable to the Protestants. In 1531 the Catholics rebelled and defeated the Protestants. Zwingli was killed on the battle field. Oecolampadius, the logical successor of Zwingli, died later the same year. Zwingli's mantle then fell on Heinrich Bullinger, a warm friend of John Calvin.